THE JAPANESE CINEMA BOOK

THE JAPANESE CINEMA BOOK

EDITED BY
HIDEAKI FUJIKI AND ALASTAIR PHILLIPS

THE BRITISH FILM INSTITUTE
Bloomsbury Publishing Plc
50 Bedford Square, London, WC1B 3DP, UK
1385 Broadway, New York, NY 10018, USA

BLOOMSBURY is a trademark of Bloomsbury Publishing Plc

First published in Great Britain 2020 by Bloomsbury
Reprinted 2020
on behalf of the
British Film Institute
21 Stephen Street, London W1T 1LN
www.bfi.org.uk

The BFI is the lead organisation for film in the UK and the distributor of Lottery funds for film. Our mission is to ensure that film is central to our cultural life, in particular by supporting and nurturing the next generation of filmmakers and audiences. We serve a public role which covers the cultural, creative and economic aspects of film in the UK.

Copyright © Hideaki Fujiki, Alastair Phillips and contributors, 2020

Hideaki Fujiki and Alastair Phillips have asserted their right under the Copyright, Designs and Patents Act, 1988, to be identified as editors of this work.

For legal purposes the Acknowledgements on p. xx constitute an extension of this copyright page.

Cover design by Louise Dugdale
Cover image: Film, *Our Little Sister*, 2015 © Atlaspix/Alamy Stock Photo

All rights reserved. No part of this publication may be reproduced or transmitted in any form or by any means, electronic or mechanical, including photocopying, recording, or any information storage or retrieval system, without prior permission in writing from the publishers.

Bloomsbury Publishing Plc does not have any control over, or responsibility for, any third-party websites referred to or in this book. All internet addresses given in this book were correct at the time of going to press. The author and publisher regret any inconvenience caused if addresses have changed or sites have ceased to exist, but can accept no responsibility for any such changes.

A catalogue record for this book is available from the British Library.

A catalog record for this book is available from the Library of Congress.

ISBN: HB: 978-1-8445-7679-1
        PB: 978-1-8445-7678-4
        ePDF: 978-1-8387-1913-5
        eBook: 978-1-8445-7681-4

Typeset by Integra Software Services Pvt. Ltd.
Printed and bound in India

To find out more about our authors and books visit www.bloomsbury.com and sign up for our newsletters.

CONTENTS

List of Illustrations ... ix
Notes on Contributors ... xiv
Acknowledgements ... xx

Introduction
Japanese cinema and its multiple perspectives *Hideaki Fujiki and Alastair Phillips* ... 1

PART 1 THEORIES AND APPROACHES

1 Early cinema
Difference, definition and Japanese film studies *Aaron Gerow* ... 25

2 Authorship
Author, *sakka*, *auteur* *Alexander Jacoby* ... 38

3 Spectatorship
The spectator as subject and agent *Hideaki Fujiki* ... 53

4 Film criticism
Soviet montage theory and Japanese film criticism *Naoki Yamamoto* ... 68

5 Narrative
Multi-viewpoint narrative: From *Rashomon* (1950) to *Confessions* (2010) *Kosuke Kinoshita* ... 81

6 Gender and sexuality
Feminist film scholarships: Dialogue and diversification *Hikari Hori* ... 94

PART 2 INSTITUTIONS AND INDUSTRY

7 The studio system
The Japanese studio system revisited *Hiroyuki Kitaura* ... 109

8 Exhibition
Screening spaces: A history of Japanese film exhibition *Manabu Ueda* ... 126

9 Censorship
Censorship as education: Film violence and ideology *Rachael Hutchinson* ... 138

10	**Technology** Sound and intermediality in 1930s Japanese cinema *Johan Nordström*	151
11	**Film festivals** *Eigasai* inside out: Japanese cinema and film festival programming *Ran Ma*	164
12	**Stardom** Queer resonance: The stardom of Miwa Akihiro *Yuka Kanno*	179
13	**Experimental film** Forms, spaces and networks: A history of Japanese experimental film *Julian Ross*	192
14	**Transmedial relations** Manga at the movies: Adaptation and intertextuality *Rayna Denison*	203
15	**The archive** Screening locality: Japanese home movies and the politics of place *Oliver Dew*	214

PART 3 FILM STYLE

16	**Cinematography** The trans-Pacific work of Japanese cinematographers *Daisuke Miyao*	231
17	**Acting** Spectral bodies: Matsui Sumako and Tanaka Kinuyo in *The Love of Sumako the Actress* (1947) *Chika Kinoshita*	243
18	**Set design** Colour and excess in *Undercurrent* (1956) *Fumiaki Itakura*	259
19	**Music** When the music exits the screen: Sound and image in Japanese sword-fight films *Yuna Tasaka*	269

PART 4 GENRE

20	***Jidaigeki*** The duplicitous topos of *jidaigeki* *Philip Kaffen*	285
21	**Horror** The ghosts of *kaiki eiga* *Michael Crandol*	298
22	**Anime** Compositing and switching: An intermedial history of Japanese anime *Thomas Lamarre*	310
23	**Melodrama** Melodrama, modernity and displacement: *That Night's Wife* (1930) *Ryoko Misono* (with Hideaki Fujiki and Alastair Phillips)	325
24	**The musical** *Heibon* and the popular song film *Michael Raine*	335

25 The yakuza film
The yakuza film: A genre 'endorsed by the people' *Jennifer Coates* — 348

26 Documentary
'Filling our empty hands': Ogawa Productions and the politics of subjectivity *Ayumi Hata* — 361

PART 5 TIME AND SPACES OF REPRESENTATION

27 Ecology
Toxic interdependencies: 3/11 cinema *Rachel DiNitto* — 379

28 Rural landscape
The cinematic countryside in Japanese wartime film-making *Sharon Hayashi* — 394

29 The home
Separations and connections: The cinematic homes of the Shōwa 30s *Woojeong Joo* — 407

30 The city
Tokyo 1958 *Alastair Phillips* — 419

PART 6 SOCIAL CONTEXTS

31 Empire
Cinematic dualities: Shanghai film-making in the era of the Japanese Occupation *Ni Yan* — 439

32 The Occupation
Pedagogies of modernity: CIE and USIS films about the United Nations *Yuka Tsuchiya* — 453

33 Social protest
Japanese student movement cinema: A dialogic approach *Masato Dogase* — 466

34 Minority cultures
Whose song is it? Korean and women's voice in Ōshima Nagisa's *Sing a Song of Sex* (1967) *Mika Ko* — 479

35 Globalisation
Japanese cultural globalisation at the margins *Cobus van Staden* — 489

PART 7 FLOWS AND INTERACTIONS

36 Japanese cinema and its postcolonial histories
Technologies of coproduction: Japan in Asia and the Cold War production of regional place *Stephanie DeBoer* — 505

37 Japanese cinema and Hollywood
Frontiers of nostalgia: The Japanese Western and the postwar era *Hiroshi Kitamura* — 518

38 Peripheries
Japan and Okinawa and the politics of exchange *Andrew Dorman* — 530

39 Japanese cinema and Europe
    A constellation of gazes: Europe and the Japanese film industry *Yoshiharu Tezuka* 541

40 Transnational remakes and adaptations
    Casablanca karaoke: The program picture as marginal art in 1960s Japan *Ryan Cook* 556

Select Bibliography 567
Index 573

ILLUSTRATIONS

0.1	*Merry Christmas Mr. Lawrence/Senjō no Merry Christmas* (Ōshima Nagisa, 1983, Recorded Picture Company and Ōshima Productions). Is this really an example of 'Japanese cinema'?	2
0.2	A collage image of Tachibana Teijirō as an *onnagata* in *Katsudō gahō* (January 1917), reprinted in Makino Mamoru (ed.), *Nihon eiga shoki shiryō shūsei*, vol. 6 (Tokyo: San'ichi shobō, 1991)	3
0.3	*There was A Father/Chichiariki* (Ozu Yasujirō, 1942, Shōchiku)	4
0.4	*War at Sea from Hawaii to Malaya/Hawaii Malay oki kaisen* (Yamamoto Kajirō, 1942, Tōhō)	5
0.5	*Fallen Blossoms/Hanachirinu* (Ishida Tamizō, 1938, Tōhō). Noël Burch celebrated the unknown director Ishida Tamizō as an important auteur	6
0.6	The cover of Hasumi Shigehiko's *Eiga no kioku sōchi* (Tokyo: Film art-sha, 1997). The first edition of the book was published by Film art-sha in 1985	6
0.7	The cover of Hasumi Shigehiko's *Kantoku Ozu Yasujirō* (Tokyo: Chikuma gakugei bunko, 2016). The first edition of the book was published by Chikuma shobō in 1983	7
0.8	The cover of Yomota Inuhiko and Saitō Ayako (eds), *Otokotachi no kizuna, Asia eiga: Homosocial na yokubō* (Tokyo: Heibonsha, 2004)	8
0.9	*No Regrets for Our Youth/Waga seishun ni kui wa nashi* (Kurosawa Akira, 1946, Tōhō). Kyoko Hirano discusses the film in the context of the US Occupation of Japan (1945–52)	9
0.10	*Five Scouts/Gonin no sekkohei* (Tasaka Tomotaka, 1938, Nikkatsu). Peter B. High discusses this as a landmark film during the fifteen years of war in Japan	9
0.11	The cover of Aaron Gerow and Abé Mark Nornes (eds), *In Praise of Film Studies: Essays in Honor of Makno Mamoru* (Bloomington, IN: Trafford Publishing, 2007)	10
1.1	*Zigomar* (Victorin-Hippolyte Jasset, 1911, Éclair) and cinema as a threat	29
1.2	*A Page of Madness* (Kinugasa Teinosuke, 1926, Shin kankakuha eiga renmei and Kinugasa eiga renmei) and the problem of the pure film	33
2.1	*Eros Plus Massacre/Eros plus gyakusatsu* (Yoshida Kijū, 1970, Gendai eigasha)	45
2.2	*Still Walking/Aruitemo aruitemo* (Kore-eda Hirokazu, 2008, Cine Quanon)	49
3.1	*The Last Emperor* (Bernardo Bertolucci, 1987, Hemdale Film Corporation and Recorded Picture Company). An example of Rey Chow's notion of 'ethnic spectatorship'	58
3.2	An image that visualises the attempt to integrate the Japanese film industry into the Greater East Asian Co-Prosperity Sphere, published in *Eiga hyōron* (January 1942). The caption reads: 'the Greater East Asian War and the advancement of Japanese films overseas'	62
4.1	An example of shooting-in-depth in *Humanity and Paper Balloons/Ninjō kami fūsen* (Yamanaka Sadao, 1937, Tōhō)	76
5.1	*Rashomon/Rashōmon* (Kurosawa Akira, 1950, Daiei)	84
5.2	Watanabe walks up the stairs in *Confessions/Kokuhaku* (Nakashima Tetsuya, 2010, Tōhō)	89

5.3	The petrified woodcutter is shown from the dead samurai's point of view in *Rashomon/Rashōmon* (Kurosawa Akira, 1950, Daiei)	90
6.1	Hara Setsuko, far left, as Noriko in *Early Summer/Bakushū* (Ozu Yasujirō, 1951, Shōchiku)	99
6.2	Sakane Tazuko playing with a pet dog owned by Mizoguchi Kenji, date unknown. Private collection	100
6.3	The cover of Mizoguchi Akiko's *Theorizing BL As a Transformative Genre: Boys' Love Moves the World Forward/BL Shinkaron: Boy's Love ga shakai o ugokasu* (Tokyo: Ōta shuppan, 2015)	102
7.1	The evolution of Japanese film studios	110
7.2	*The Neighbour's Wife and Mine/Madame to nyōbō* (Gosho Heinosuke, 1931, Shōchiku)	113
7.3	*Death by Hanging/Kōshikei* (Ōshima Nagisa, 1968, Sōzōsha, ATG)	120
8.1	*Ugetsu/Ugetsu monogatari* (Mizoguchi Kenji, 1953, Daiei)	130
8.2	'The ground and second floor plan of the Denkikan', in *Kenchiku shinchō* vol. 6 no. 1 (1925), p. 17	133
8.3	'The ground floor plan of the Nihon gekijō', in *Kokusai eiga jigyō sōran Shōwa gonen ban* (Tokyo: Kokusai eiga tsūshinsha, 1930)	134
9.1	*Yojimbo/Yōjinbō* (Kurosawa Akira, 1961, Tōhō)	144
9.2	*Battle Royale* (Fukasaku Kinji, 2000, Battle Royale Production Committee)	147
10.1	The cover of *Viktor Harmonica Music Sheet* no. 61 featuring *Hometown/Fujiwara Yoshie no Furusato* (Mizoguchi Kenji, 1930, Nikkatsu). Fujiwara Yoshie is the tenor featured in the photograph	157
10.2	*Three Sisters with Maiden Hearts/Otome gokoro sannin shimai* (Naruse Mikio, 1935, P.C.L.)	157
11.1	*Rashomon/Rashōmon* (Kurosawa Akira, 1950, Daiei)	166
11.2	Poster of Nihon International Film Festival 1970. Courtesy of Kobe Planet Film Archive	171
11.3	Photograph of the 1989 Yamagata International Documentary Film Festival	172
12.1	*Black Lizard/Kurotokage* (Fukasaku Kinji, 1968, Shōchiku)	183
12.2	*Black Rose Mansion/Kurobara no yakata* (Fukasaku Kinji, 1969, Shōchiku)	184
12.3	*Black Rose Mansion/Kurobara no yakata* (Fukasaku Kinji, 1969, Shōchiku)	185
13.1	*Another Day of a Housewife* (Mako Idemitsu, 1977). Courtesy of Studio Idemitsu	196
13.2	*Dutchman's Photograph/Orandajin no shashin* (Isao Kōta, 1974). Courtesy of Image Forum and Isao Kōta	196
14.1	Chart of manga film adaptations 2004–12. *Source:* Eiren (Motion Pictures Producers Association of Japan) and the Japanese Movie Database	204
14.2	*Air Doll/Kūki ningyō* (Kore-eda Hirokazu, 2009, Kūki ningyō Production Committee)	204
14.3	*Sakuran* (Ninagawa Mika, 2007, Fella Pictures)	207
15.1	Another meaning of the term 'home movie' (*hōmu mūbii*). These small-gauge digest versions of theatrical releases were on display at the 2012 Ōizumi Home Movie Day held at the Tōei Film Studios in Nerima, Tokyo. Author's own photograph	218
15.2	Poster for the Adachi 8mm Film Archive, with a still from a 1955 home movie showing the Senjū Thermal Power Station	224
16.1	*Horse/Uma* (Yamamoto Kajirō, 1941, Tōhō)	237
16.2	*Taboo/Gohatto* (Ōshima Nagisa, 1999, Ōshima Productions)	239
17.1	Tanaka Kinuyo as Matsui Sumako (left) in *The Love of Sumako the Actress/Joyū Sumako no koi* (Mizoguchi Kenji, 1947, Shōchiku), publicity still	244
17.2	Katyusha (Matsui Sumako/Tanaka Kinuyo) sings in *Resurrection* in *The Love of Sumako the Actress/Joyū Sumako no koi* (Mizoguchi Kenji, 1947, Shōchiku)	247

17.3	Carmen (Matsui Sumako/Tanaka Kinuyo) lies dead on the floor in *The Love of the Actress Sumako/Joyū Sumako no koi* (Mizoguchi Kenji, 1947, Shōchiku)	255
18.1	*Undercurrent* (aka *River of the Night*)/*Yoru no kawa* (Yoshimura Kōzaburō, 1956, Daiei). The young artisan is dyeing yellow cloth. The colours yellow and blue are defined as opposite colours in colour theory, so the colours the two people are dyeing also represent the conflict between them	264
18.2	*Undercurrent* (aka *River of the Night*)/*Yoru no kawa* (Yoshimura Kōzaburō, 1956, Daiei). The young artisan is dyeing yellow cloth and Kiwa's father is dyeing blue cloth. The colours yellow and blue are defined as opposite colours in colour theory, so the colours the two people are dyeing also represent the conflict between them	264
18.3	*Undercurrent* (aka *River of the Night*)/*Yoru no kawa* (Yoshimura Kōzaburō, 1956, Daiei). The first shot of the hotel room provides a close-up of an *andon* (an oil lamp stand with a paper shade) hung on the veranda, lit in a burgundy colour	265
18.4	*Undercurrent* (aka *River of the Night*)/*Yoru no kawa* (Yoshimura Kōzaburō, 1956, Daiei). The camera tracks right to show Kiwa and Takemura. The red light of the *andon* helps to emphasise the erotic atmosphere	265
18.5	The burgundy light from the *andon* fills the frame in a similar fashion to a tinted image from the silent era	266
18.6	When Kiwa and Takemura begin to embrace and kiss, the camera starts to track from a close-up of their upper bodies to their legs and toes	266
18.7	At the end of the final shot of this scene, Kiwa's toes unfold and there is a fade-out	266
18.8	The action of rubbing blue dye from her cheek can be interpreted as Kiwa wiping away her depression and deciding to continue with her life	266
18.9	When Kiwa goes upstairs to watch the parade of workers for International Workers' Day, we see three sets of clothes in three different colours – red, white and blue – hanging out to dry, showing the three colours of the French flag	266
19.1	*The Million Ryo Pot/Tange sazen yowa: Hyakuman ryō no tsubo* (Yamanaka Sadao, 1935, Nikkatsu)	270
19.2	A sheet of music from *The Million Ryo Pot/Tange sazen yowa: Hyakuman ryō no tsubo* (Yamanaka Sadao, 1935, Nikkatsu)	271
19.3	*13 Assassins/Jūsannin no shikaku* (Kudō Eiichi, 1963, Tōei)	275
19.4	A sheet of music from *13 Assassins/Jūsannin no shikaku* (Kudō Eiichi, 1963, Tōei)	276
19.5	*13 Assassins/Jūsannin no shikaku* (Miike Takashi, 2010, Sedic International and Recorded Picture Company). A high-angle shot of the dead samurai from Miike's version. The dagger and his right hand, both soaked in blood, are evident	277
19.6	*13 Assassins/Jūsannin no shikaku* (Kudō Eiichi, 1963, Tōei). The same shot from Kudō's original version. While in Miike's film the head is turned to the left, here his head is facing screen right, and the dagger is hidden	277
19.7	A sheet of music from *13 Assassins/Jūsannin no shikaku* (Miike Takashi, 2010, Sedic International and Recorded Picture Company)	278
20.1	*A Diary of Chuji's Travels/Chūji tabi nikki* (Itō Daisuke, 1927, Nikkatsu)	289
20.2	*Capricious Young Man/Akanishi Kikita* (Itami Mansaku, 1936, Kataoka Chiezō Productions)	290
21.1	Japan's first monster-movie star, Suzuki Sumiko, in *bakeneko* ('ghost-cat') form and fighting a host of human adversaries in *The Cat of Arima/Arima neko* (Mokudō Shigeru, 1937, Shinkō Kinema)	302

21.2	Nakagawa Nobuo's *Mansion of the Ghost Cat/Bōrei kaibyō yashiki* (1958, Shintōhō)	304
21.3	A monster from the past invades the present in *Mansion of the Ghost Cat/Bōrei kaibyō yashiki* (Nakagawa Nobuo, 1958, Shintōhō)	305
22.1	Ōfuji Noburō working with celluloid sheets to single-handedly produce the animated short *Princess Katsura/Katsura hime* (1937). The film combined cel animation and cut-paper animation. Image taken from the 'making of film' in *Until The Colour Film Was Made/Shikisai manga no dekiru made* (Ogina Pictures)	314
22.2	*Momotaro's Divine Sea Warriors/Momotarō umi to shinpei* (Seo Mitsuyo, 1945, Shōchiku)	315
22.3	*Momotaro's Divine Sea Warriors/Momotarō umi to shinpei* (Seo Mitsuyo, 1945, Shōchiku)	315
22.4	The trailer for Tōei studios' first feature-length animated film, *The Tale of the White Serpent/Hakujaden* (Yabushita Taiji, 1958), proudly displays the large-scale organisation of labour and technology needed to produce such a film	316
23.1	*That Night's Wife/Sono yono tsuma* (Ozu Yasujirō, 1930, Shōchiku)	327
23.2	*That Night's Wife/Sono yono tsuma* (Ozu Yasujirō, 1930, Shōchiku)	329
24.1A–D	*Janken Girls/Janken musume* (Sugie Toshio, 1955, Tōhō)	341
24.2	Yukimura Izumi hand towel. 40 yen each, 10 yen for postage in *Heibon* (April 1956)	344
25.1	*Red Peony Gambler/Hibotan bakuto* (Yamashita Kōsaku, 1968, Tōei)	349
25.2	*Abashiri Prison/Abashiri bangaichi* (Ishii Teruo, 1965, Tōei)	351
26.1	*Magino Village Story – Raising Silkworms/Magino monogatari – Yōsanhen* (Ogawa Shinsuke, 1977, Ogawa Productions). Courtesy of Athénée Français Cultural Center	369
26.2	The script of *Magino Village Story – Raising Silkworms/Magino monogatari – Yōsanhen* (Ogawa Shinsuke, 1977, Ogawa Productions) and *Ogawa Pro News* no. 10 (1 July 1977)	370
26.3	Kimura Satoko and Shiraishi Yōko checking the quality of the cocoons in *Magino Village Story – Raising Silkworms*. Courtesy of Athénée Français Cultural Center	372
27.1	*Minamata: The Victims and Their World/Minamata: Kanjasan to sono sekai* (Tsuchimoto Noriaki, 1971, Higashi Productions)	382
27.2	*No Man Without Zone* (Fujiwara Toshi, 2011)	386
27.3	*311* (Mori Tatsuya, Matsubayashi Yojyū, Watai Takeharu, Yasuoka Takaharu and Yasuoka Takuji, 2012)	387
27.4	*Homeland/Ieji* (Kubota Nao, 2014)	388
28.1	*Earth/Tsuchi* (Uchida Tomu, 1939, Nikkatsu)	396
28.2	*Earth/Tsuchi* (Uchida Tomu, 1939, Nikkatsu)	398
29.1	*Good Morning/Ohayō* (Ozu Yasujirō, 1959, Shōchiku). The Ōkubos' kitchen in the background as seen from the Haraguchis' home	410
29.2	*Being Two Isn't Easy/Watashi wa nisai* (Ichikawa Kon, 1962, Daiei). A thread of yarn connects the two rooms. Depth of field and the fact the sliding doors of the adjacent rooms are all open unites the inner space of the house	415
30.1	The nocturnal world of the city captured on a studio set in *Equinox Flower/Higanbana* (Ozu Yasujirō, 1958, Shōchiku)	425
30.2	The nocturnal world of the city captured in a photographic montage in *Nishi Ginza Station/Nishi Ginza ekimae* (Imamura Shōhei, 1958, Nikkatsu)	427
30.3	Faces of the city in *Tokyo 1958* (Teshigahara Hiroshi et al., 1958, Cinema 58)	431
31.1	An advertisement for *Mulan Joins the Army/Mulan cong jun/Mokuren jūgun* (Bu Wancang, 1939, Zhonghua Shanghai Huacheng dianying zhizuo) in *Eiga hyōron* (October 1941)	441

31.2	An article about *Toward Eternity/Wanshi liufang* (Bu Wancang, Zhang Shankung et al., 1943, Zhonglian) in *Shin eiga* (January 1941)	446
31.3	*Toward Eternity/Wanshi liufang* (Bu Wancang, Zhang Shankung et al., 1943, Zhonglian)	448
31.4	*Toward Eternity/Wanshi liufang* (Bu Wancang, Zhang Shankung et al., 1943, Zhonglian)	449
32.1A–H	Brochure pages for *The United Nations and Japan/Kokuren to nihon* (UN Association of Japan, 1956)	459–460
33.1A–F	*Children of the Classroom/Kyōshitsu no kodomotachi* (Hani Susumu, 1954, Iwanami eiga)	468–469
33.2	A young male surrounded by student leaders in *Forest of Oppression – A Record of Struggle at Takasaki City University of Economics/Assatsu no mori –Takasaki keizai daigaku tōsō no kiroku* (Ogawa Shinsuke, 1967, Ogawa Productions). Courtesy of the Athénée Français Cultural Center	474
34.1	A beautiful young girl in *chima chogori* embodies an idealised image of the Korean motherland in *Pacchigi!* (Izutsu Kazuyuki, 2005, Cine Quanon)	481
34.2	*Sing a Song of Sex/Nihon shunka-kō* (Ōshima Nagisa, 1967, Sōzōsha)	482
34.3	The boys follow Kaneda like scolded children while she sings 'Mantetsu Kouta' in *Sing a Song of Sex/Nihon shunka-kō* (Ōshima Nagisa, 1967, Sōzōsha)	484
34.4	Kaneda's figure remains in the frame and tellingly identifies those depriving her of her voice in *Sing a Song of Sex/Nihon shunka-kō* (Ōshima Nagisa, 1967, Sōzōsha)	487
34.5	Kaneda's figure remains in the frame and tellingly identifies those depriving her of her voice in *Sing a Song of Sex/Nihon shunka-kō* (Ōshima Nagisa, 1967, Sōzōsha)	487
35.1	*Mighty Morphin' Power Rangers/Super Sentai* (TV Asahi, 1975–)	493
35.2	*Heidi, A Girl of the Alps/Alps no shōjo Haiji* (Zuiyō, 1974)	495
36.1	*Madame White Snake/Byaku fujin no yōren/Bai she chuan* (Toyoda Shirō, 1956, Tōhō and Shaw Brothers)	507
36.2	*Princess Yang Kwei-fei/Yōhiki/Yang Guifei* (Mizoguchi Kenji, 1955, Daiei and Shaw Brothers)	508
36.3	*The Great Wall/Shin shikōtei/Qinshi Huangdi* (Tanaka Shigeo, 1962, Daiei and Taiwan's Central Motion Picture Company)	510
37.1	*The Wandering Guitarist/Guitar o motta wataridori* (Saitō Buichi, 1959, Nikkatsu)	522
37.2	*Tampopo* (Itami Jūzō, 1985, Itami Productions)	524
38.1	*Profound Desires of the Gods/Kamigami no fukaki yokubō* (Imamura Shōhei, 1968, Imamura Productions)	535
38.2	*Dear Summer Sister/Natsu no imōto* (Ōshima Nagisa, 1972, Sōzōsha and ATG)	537
39.1	*Gate of Hell/Jigoku Mon* (Kinugasa Teinosuke, 1953, Daiei)	544
39.2	*Madam Butterfly* (Camine Gallone, 1954, Produzione Gallone Rizzoli Film). Kawakita's long-cherished desire was to produce *Madam Butterfly* with a genuine Japanese actress and to show 'real Japanese costumes and a real Japanese woman'	546
39.3	*The Written Face* (Daniel Schmid, 1995, T&C Film and Euro Space). The kabuki actor Bandō Tamasaburō and the art of men performing as women	550
40.1	*A Warm Misty Night/Yogiri yo kon'ya mo arigatō* (Ezaki Mio, 1967, Nikkatsu). Yūjirō in a mood	561
40.2	*A Warm Misty Night/Yogiri yo kon'ya mo arigatō* (Ezaki Mio, 1967, Nikkatsu). The world mapped on the wall in Yūjirō's night club	563

CONTRIBUTORS

THE EDITORS

Hideaki Fujiki is Professor of Cinema Studies in the Cinema Studies Unit and the Centre for Transregional Culture and Society at Nagoya University, Japan. His books include *Making Personas: Transnational Film Stardom in Modern Japan* (2014) and *Who is the Cinema Audience? A History of the Subject in the Media and Society, 1910–* [in Japanese] (2019). He is currently completing a monograph provisionally titled *Radioactive Documentaries: Ecology from Fukushima to the Globe*.

Alastair Phillips is Professor of Film Studies in the Department of Film and Television Studies at the University of Warwick, UK. His books include *City of Darkness, City of Light: Émigré Filmmakers in Paris 1929–1939* (2003); *Journeys of Desire: European Actors in Hollywood* (co-edited with Ginette Vincendeau, 2006); *Japanese Cinema: Texts and Contexts* (co-edited with Julian Stringer, 2007); *100 Film Noirs* (co-authored with Jim Hillier, 2009); *Rififi: A French Film Guide* (2009); *A Companion to Jean Renoir* (co-edited with Ginette Vincendeau, 2013); *Paris in the Cinema: Beyond the Flâneur* (co-edited with Ginette Vincendeau, 2018) and *Tokyo Story* (2021). He is an editor of *Screen*.

THE AUTHORS

Jennifer Coates is Senior Lecturer in Japanese Studies at the School of East Asian Studies, University of Sheffield, UK. She is the author of *Making Icons: Repetition and the Female Image in Japanese Cinema, 1945–1964* (2016). Her current ethnographic research focuses on early postwar film audiences in Japan.

Ryan Cook is Assistant Professor of Film and Media Studies, and an affiliated faculty member in the East Asian Studies programme at Emory University, USA. His research focuses on Japanese and East Asian film history. He has published on film criticism and theory and the work of individual film-makers. He is currently writing a book on 1960s Japanese film culture at the intersection of art, popular culture and discourses of national identity.

Michael Crandol is a Lecturer in Japanese Studies at Leiden University, the Netherlands. He is the author of articles on the films of Nakagawa Nobuo, the horror actress Suzuki Sumiko, and has contributed entries to *The Encyclopedia of Japanese Horror Films* (2016). He is currently writing a book on the early history of the horror film genre in Japan.

Stephanie DeBoer is Associate Professor of Cinema and Media Arts/Studies in the Media School at Indiana University, USA. She is the author of *Coproducing Asia: Locating Japanese-Chinese Regional Film and Media* (2014) and her articles on coproduction and collaboration have appeared in *Screen* and *Culture, Theory & Critique*. Her work on media and video arts and the co-constitution of media locations has appeared in *Framing the Global: Entry Points for Research* (2014) and *The Asian Cinema Handbook* (2018).

Rayna Denison is Senior Lecturer in Film, Television and Media Studies at the University of East Anglia, UK. She is the author of *Anime: A Critical Introduction* (2015) and the editor of *Princess Mononoke: Understanding Studio Ghibli's Monster Princess* (2018). She is the co-editor of the Eisner Award nominated collection *Superheroes on World Screens* (2015) and has also co-edited special issues of the *East Asian Journal of Popular Culture*, the *Journal of Japanese and Korean Cinema* and *Intensities*. Her articles on contemporary popular Japanese media have appeared in *Cinema Journal, The Velvet Light Trap, Animation: An Interdisciplinary Journal* and *Japan Forum*.

Oliver Dew received his PhD from Birkbeck College, University of London, UK, in 2012. He is the author of *Zainichi Cinema: Korean-in-Japan Film Culture* (2016).

Rachel DiNitto is Associate Professor of Japanese literature at the University of Oregon, USA. In addition to her books, *Fukushima Fiction: The Literary Landscape of Japan's Triple Disaster* (2019) and *Uchida Hyakken: A Critique of Modernity and Militarism in Prewar Japan* (2008), she has published translations of wartime and contemporary fiction as well as articles on Japan's 2011 triple disaster, author Kanehara Hitomi and manga artist Maruo Suehiro. Her work on film includes articles on Suzuki Seijun, and the disaster cinema of Fujiwara Toshi, Sono Sion and Uchida Nobuteru.

Masato Dogase is a post-doctoral fellow in the Graduate School of Humanities at Nagoya University, Japan, and received his PhD from this institution. He is also a lecturer at Chūbu University, Aichi Shukutoku University and Waseda University where he teaches Japanese cinema and animation culture. His essay on the postwar, modernism and Ozu has appeared in Tsuboi Hideto and Fujiki Hideaki (eds), *Postwar Japan as Image* [in Japanese] (2010). He is currently engaged in a research project on Japanese documentaries of the 1960s subsidised by a JSPS KAKENHI Grant.

Andrew Dorman has taught Film Studies at the University of St Andrews and the University of Edinburgh, Scotland, UK. He is the author of *Paradoxical Japaneseness: Cultural Representation in 21st Century Japanese Cinema* (2016). His articles include 'A Return to Japan? Restaging the Cinematic Past in Takashi Miike's *13 Assassins*' in *Frames Cinema Journal* (2014) and 'Kazuo Hara: Exposing the Fringes of Japan' in John Berra (ed.) *Directory of World Cinema: Japan 3* (2015).

Aaron Gerow is Professor of East Asian Cinema and Culture at Yale University, USA. His books include *Kitano Takeshi* (2007), *A Page of Madness: Cinema and Modernity in 1920s Japan* (2008), *Research Guide to Japanese Film Studies* (co-authored with Markus Nornes, 2009; Japanese version 2016) and *Visions of Japanese Modernity: Articulations of Cinema, Nation, and Spectatorship, 1895–1925* (2010).

Ayumi Hata is programme coordinator at the Yamagata International Documentary Film Festival. She has been educated in the UK and Japan in the field of documentary culture and theory, with particular interests in Japanese film history. Her articles include 'Rethinking *Forest of Oppression*: Body, Speech and Realism in Japanese Documentary Films of the Late 1960s' in *JunCture 01* (2010) and 'Beyond Media Activism: Japanese Independent Documentary Films and Social Movements around 1970' in Fujiki Hideaki (ed.), *Approaches to Cinema Audiences* (2011) [both in Japanese].

Sharon Hayashi is Associate Professor of Cinema and Media Studies in the Department of Cinema and Media Arts at York University, Toronto, Canada. Her current project, *Eco-tour: Currency, Community and Sustainability*, uses digital mapping and games to document and encourage rural revitalisation in post-growth Japan. Ongoing research projects include the historical digital mapping websites *Mapping Protest Tokyo* and *Tokyo Olympics 2.0: The Politics of Demolition and Displacement*. She has published essays on the travel films of Shimizu Hiroshi, the intersection of art and politics in Pink Films, and the resurgence of artistic and political collectives in urban Japan.

Hikari Hori is Associate Professor in the Faculty of Letters at Toyo University, Japan. Her books include *Promiscuous Media: Film and Visual Culture in Imperial Japan, 1926–45* (2018) and *Censorship, Media, and Literary Culture in Japan* (co-edited with Toeda Hirokazu et al., 2012). She has published articles and book chapters in *Japanese Studies, Mechademia* and Ōtsuka Eiji (ed.), *The Media-mix of Mobilization* [in Japanese] (2017).

Rachael Hutchinson is Associate Professor of Japanese Studies at the University of Delaware, USA. Her research focuses on censorship, national identity and postcolonial frameworks in Japanese literature, manga, film and video games. She has published widely on the films of Kurosawa Akira, Kitano Takeshi and Fukasaku Kinji. Her books include *Japanese Culture through Videogames* (2019), *The Routledge Handbook of Modern Japanese Literature* (co-edited with Leith Morton, 2016), *Negotiating Censorship in Modern Japan* (ed. Kitano Takeshi 2013) and *Nagai Kafu's Occidentalism: Defining the Japanese Self* (2011).

Fumiaki Itakura is Associate Professor at the Graduate School of Intercultural Studies, Kobe University, Japan. He specialises in film studies and the history of Japanese cinema. He worked as curator of the National Film Center at the National Museum of Modern Art, Tokyo from 2005 to 2012. His recent publications include *Cinema and Immigrants: Film Reception and the Identities of Japanese Immigrants in the US* (2016) and a chapter on amateur film culture during the war in Ōtsuka Eiji (ed.), *The Media-mix of Mobilization* (2017) [both in Japanese].

Alexander Jacoby lectures on the arts and culture of Japan at Oxford Brookes University, UK. He has curated film programmes at the British Film Institute and the Museum of Modern Art, New York, and is a frequent writer for *Sight and Sound*. His scholarly essays have appeared in Alastair Phillips and Julian Stringer (eds), *Japanese Cinema: Texts and Contexts* and Michael Smith and Irene González-López (eds), *Tanaka Kinuyo: Nation, Stardom, and Female Subjectivity* (2018). He is the author of *A Critical Handbook of Japanese Film Directors* (2008) and a forthcoming monograph on Kore-eda Hirokazu.

Woojeong Joo is Assistant Professor at the Graduate School of Humanities, Nagoya University, Japan. He is the author of *The Cinema of Ozu Yasujiro: Histories of the Everyday* (2017), which re-examines Ozu Yasujirō's films in terms of a socio-historical analysis of modern everyday life in Japan. His current research investigates the early discursive history of sound and visual media in East Asia with an emphasis on the development of the talkie film in Japan and colonial Korea in relation to technology, culture and politics.

Philip Kaffen is Assistant Professor in the Department of Languages and Culture Studies at the University of North Carolina, Charlotte, USA. He teaches courses on Japanese film and media, translation and cultural studies and has published on cinema and urban space, digital technology and disaster, image romanticism, and philosophy and film theory. His current research revolves around the relationships between technical images and sovereignty in Japan.

Yuka Kanno is Associate Professor in Queer Studies and Visual Culture at the Graduate School of Global Studies, Doshisha University, Japan. Her publications include 'Panpan Girls, Lesbians and Postwar Women's Communities: *Girls of Dark* (1961) as Women's Cinema' in Michael Smith and Irene González-López (eds), *Tanaka Kinuyo: Nation, Stardom, and Female Subjectivity* (2018), 'On LGBTQ Film Festivals' in *Gendai Shisō* vol. 43 no. 16 [in Japanese] (2015), and 'Love and Friendship: The Queer Imagination of Japan's Early Girls' Culture' in Mary C. Kearney (ed.), *Mediated Girlhoods: New Explorations of Girls' Media Culture* (2011).

Chika Kinoshita is Associate Professor of Film Studies in the Graduate School of Human and Environmental Studies at Kyoto University, Japan. She is the author of *The Cinema of Mizoguchi Kenji: The Aesthetics and Politics of the Film Medium* (2016) [in Japanese].

Kosuke Kinoshita is Associate Professor of Film Studies in the Faculty of Literature, Gunma Prefectural Women's University, Japan. His essays include 'The Caretaker Doesn't Care: Narrative Film Genre and Spectator's Identification' in *The Bulletin of Gunma Prefectural Women's University* no. 32 (2010), 'Virtual Worlds on Screen: From *Tron* to *Avatar*' in *JunCture* no. 3 (2012) 'FPS, GoPro, and Found Footage Films: Rethinking the Use of First-person Image in New Media' in *The Gunma Prefectural Women's University Bulletin*, no. 35 (2015) and 'Another Genealogy of Narrative Film and the Theoretical Limits of Focalization: Christopher Nolan's Puzzle Film, *Memento*' in *The Gunma Prefectural Women's University Bulletin*, no. 38 (2017) [all in Japanese]. His research focuses on spectatorial character construction during the reception process of narrative cinema.

Hiroshi Kitamura is Associate Professor of History at the College of William and Mary, USA. He is the author of *Screening Enlightenment: Hollywood and the Cultural Reconstruction of Defeated Japan* (2010; Japanese version 2014). He is currently working on two projects: a study of film critic Yodogawa Nagaharu and a monograph about postwar Japanese cinema in relation to economic high growth.

Hiroyuki Kitaura is Research Fellow in Humanities at Kyoto University, Japan. He is also a lecturer at Kansai University where he teaches film history. He is the author of *Japanese Movies during Television's Age of Growth: Dramatic Media Interactions* [in Japanese] (2018) and has written extensively in the area of Japanese film and television history.

Mika Ko is Associate Professor at the Faculty of Social Sciences of Hosei University, Japan. Her research mainly focuses on the cinematic representation of minority groups in Japan and the way these representations are related to their socio-historical contexts concerning production and reception. Her publications include *Japanese Cinema and Otherness: Nationalism, Multiculturalism and the Problem of Japaneseness* (2010) and an article entitled 'Neo-documentarism in *Funeral Parade of Roses*: The New Realism of Matsumoto Toshio' published in *Screen* vol. 52 no. 3 (2011).

Thomas Lamarre is Professor of East Asian Studies and Communications Studies at McGill University, Canada. He is the author of numerous publications on the history of Japanese media, thought and material culture, with projects ranging from the communication networks of ninth-century Japan (*Uncovering Heian Japan: An Archaeology of Sensation and Inscription*, 2000), to silent cinema and the global imaginary (*Shadows on the Screen: Tanizaki Jun'ichirō on Cinema and Oriental Aesthetics*, 2005), animation technologies (*The Anime Machine: A Media Theory of Animation*, 2009), and television and new media (*The Anime Ecology: A Genealogy of Television, Animation, and Game Media*, 2018).

Ran Ma is Associate Professor on the Global-30 'Japan-in-Asia' Cultural Studies and Cinema Studies programmes at Nagoya University, Japan. Her research interests include Asian independent cinema and film festival studies and she has published several journal articles and book chapters on these topics. She has recently contributed to *Chinese Film Festivals: Sites of Translation* (2017) and *Taiwan Cinema: International Reception and Social Change* (2017). She is currently completing a book tentatively titled *Independent Filmmaking across Borders in Contemporary Asia*.

The late **Ryoko Misono** (1975–2015) was Associate Professor in Japanese Studies and Cinema Studies at Tsukuba University, Japan, from 2013 to 2015. Her books include *Cinema and the Nation-State: Shōchiku Melodrama Films in the 1930s* (2012) and *Voices of the Cinema: On Postwar Japanese Cinema* (2016) [both in Japanese]. Her articles include 'Critical Media Imagination: Nancy Seki's TV Criticism and the Media Space of the 1980s and 1990s' in

Marc Steinberg and Alexander Zahlten (eds), *Media Theory in Japan* (2017) and 'Fallen Women at the Edge of the Empire: Shimizu Hiroshi's Yokohama Films and the Image of Imperial Japan in the 1930s' in *Journal of Japanese and Korean Cinema* vol. 5 nos. 1–2 (2014).

Daisuke Miyao is Professor and the Hajime Mori Chair in Japanese Language and Literature at the University of California, San Diego, USA. He is the author of *Cinema Is a Cat: A Cat Lover's Introduction to Cinema Studies* (2019); *The Aesthetics of Shadow: Lighting and Japanese Cinema* (2013) and *Sessue Hayakawa: Silent Cinema and Transnational Stardom* (2007). He is also the editor of *The Oxford Handbook of Japanese Cinema* (2014) and *Transnational Cinematography Studies* (co-edited with Lindsay Coleman and Roberto Schaefer, 2017). He is currently working on a book called *Japonisme and the Birth of Cinema*.

Johan Nordström is Lecturer in Film Studies at Tsuru University, Japan. He received his PhD from Waseda University in 2014 and is currently completing two projects: a book on the Tokyo-based early sound film studio P.C.L./Tōhō and an anthology (co-edited with Michael Raine) on Japanese cinema's transition from silent to sound. In addition to his academic work, he has co-curated several programmes on Japanese cinema for international film festivals.

Michael Raine is Assistant Professor of Film Studies at Western University, Canada. He is editing, with Johan Nordström, an anthology *The Culture of the Sound Image in Prewar Japan* and is writing up a book project titled *The Cinema of High Economic Growth: New Japanese Cinemas, 1955–1964*. He has published widely on Japanese cinema and media, including articles and book chapters in *The Oxford Handbook of Japanese Cinema* (2014), *New Vistas: Japanese Studies for the Next Generation* (2016), *Reorienting Ozu: A Master and His Influence* (2018) and *Film History* vol. 30 no. 2 (2018). He is co-editor of the *Journal of Japanese and Korean Cinema*.

Julian Ross is Assistant Professor at Leiden University Centre for the Arts in Society, the Netherlands. He has contributed book chapters to *A Companion to Experimental Film* (2019), *Japanese Expanded Cinema Revisited* (2017), *Preservation, Radicalism and the Avant-Garde Canon* (2016), *Slow Cinema* (2015) and *Impure Cinema: Intermedial and Intercultural Approaches to Film* (2014). He is a programmer at the Rotterdam International Film Festival.

Cobus van Staden is a senior researcher at the South African Institute of International Affairs, with a focus on China–Africa relations. He is also affiliated to the Department of Media Studies at the University of the Witwatersrand, South Africa. He writes on non-Western cultural globalisation and the uses of media in public diplomacy. He has published in several edited collections and journals, including the *Journal of African Cultural Studies* and *The Journal of Consumption, Markets and Culture*.

Yuna Tasaka received her PhD in Film Studies from Birkbeck College, the University of London, UK. Her thesis examined common themes in the films of Sergei Eisenstein and Kurosawa Akira and analysed the evolution of the two film-makers' ideas on art and cultural identity. Her recent research focuses on film music and the interrelation of sound and image in animation. Her publications include 'Innovation and Imitation: An Analysis of the Soundscape of Akira Kurosawa's *chambara* Westerns' in Kathryn Kalinak (ed.), *Music in the Western: A Routledge Handbook on Music and Screen Media* (2012).

Yoshiharu Tezuka is Professor of Media & Cultural Studies at Komazawa University, Tokyo, Japan. He was trained as a cinematographer and documentary film-maker at the National Film and Television School (NFTS). As the managing director of Chimera Films & Communications, he has coordinated and produced numerous film, television and advertising projects in Japan and the UK. His publications include *Japanese Cinema Goes Global:*

Filmworkers Journeys (2012) and 'Dynamics of the Cultures of Discontent: How is Globalization Transforming the Training of Filmmakers in Japan?' in Mette Hjort (ed.), *The Education of the Filmmaker* (2013).

Yuka Tsuchiya is Professor of American Studies in the Graduate School of Human and Environmental Studies at Kyoto University, Japan. Her publications include *Constructing a Pro-US Japan: US Information and Education Policy and the Occupation of Japan* (2009); *Occupying Eyes, Occupying Voices: CIE/USIS Films and VOA Radio in Asia during the Cold War* (co-edited with Yoshimi Shun'ya, 2012) and *De-Centering the Cultural Cold War: The US and Asia* (co-edited with Kishi Toshihiko, 2009) [all in Japanese]. She is now working on two book-length projects: one about the cultural Cold War and nuclear technology and the other about thermonuclear tests and tuna fishing.

Manabu Ueda is Associate Professor in Film Studies at Kobe Gakuin University, Japan. His books include *The Nikkatsu Mukōjima and Shinpa Film Era Exhibition Catalogue* (2011); *Exhibition and Audience in Early Japanese Cinema: Tokyo and Kyoto* (2012); The *Handbook of Asakusa Literary Arts* [in Japanese] (co-authored with Kanai Kanai, Kurumizawa Ken, Noji Katsunori, Tsukui Takashi and Hiroka Yuū, 2016). His articles include 'Child Spectators and the Modern City in the Early 1910s: An Analysis of *Kisha katsudō shashinkan*', ICONICS no. 9 (2008).

Naoki Yamamoto is Assistant Professor of Film and Media Studies at the University of California, Santa Barbara, USA. He has published on topics including the global dissemination of machine aesthetics in the 1920s, German–Japanese wartime film coproductions, and the Japanese reception of early Hollywood cinema and the British Documentary Film Movement. He is currently completing two books: *Dialectics without Synthesis: Realism, Film Theory, and Japanese Cinema* and *Mediology in the Era of Transition* [in Japanese], a co-edited volume of essays on media theory and practice in postwar Japan.

Ni Yan is Adjunct Professor at the Japan Institute of the Moving Image School of Film Studies. Her field of interest is the comparative history of Sino-Japanese film and cultural studies with an emphasis on symbolism. She is the author of *A History of Wartime Filmic Negotiations between Japan and China* (2010, recipient of the 2011 Minister of Education, Culture, Sports, Science and Technology's Art Encouragement Prize) and the co-editor of *Post-Manchurian Cinema: Exchange in Japanese and Chinese Cinemas* (2010). Her articles have appeared in *The Male Bond; Asian Cinema: Homosexual Desire* (2004); *Cinema and the 'Greater East Asian Co-Prosperity Sphere'* (2004); *Cinema and the Body/Sexuality* (2006); *The Actress Yamaguchi Momoe* (2006) and *Does Cinema Abandon Literature?* (2017) [all in Japanese].

THE TRANSLATORS

Thomas Kabara is a PhD candidate in the Department of Japanese Cultural Studies at Nagoya University, Japan, where he is researching Japanese film subtitling practices and their reception. He has been translating for the past nine years and is contributing a chapter on Japanese media translation to Nana Sato-Rossberg and Akiko Uchiyama (eds), *Diverse Voices in East Asian Translation Studies* (forthcoming). He currently teaches at Aichi Shukutoku University, Nagoya, Japan.

Satoko Kakihara is Assistant Professor of Japanese in the Department of Modern Languages and Literatures at California State University, Fullerton, USA. Her research focuses on studies of gender, migration and imperialism in modern and contemporary Japan. She has published on the topics of Japanese migration to the Americas in the twentieth century, the activities of women writers during and after colonialism in East Asia, and Japan–US relations since the Pacific War. She teaches courses on Japanese language, literature, film and popular culture.

ACKNOWLEDGEMENTS

We are enormously grateful to the many people who have assisted in the long gestation of this monumental project. Our warmest thanks go to Rebecca Barden who initially showed interest in the idea and helped steer the course of the book during its early stages. We are delighted that she has come back on board to see it through along with Rebecca Richards and Ken Bruce at Bloomsbury. We are very grateful for the expert assistance of Rebecca Willford and Linda Fisher at Integra and all the efforts of our copyeditor, Katherine Bosiacki. We especially owe a professional debt of thanks to every single one of the book's authors who have responded carefully, patiently and creatively at each step of the way. We also wish to express our special thanks to the translating team of Thomas Kabara and Satoko Kakihara. The book would not look the way it does were it not for the enthusiastic picture research and logistical support provided by Sophie Contento. We are also grateful to various colleagues and friends in the field that have helped us. These include Michael Baskett, David Bordwell, Marcos Centeno, Darell William Davis, Masato Dogase, Yuriko Furuhata, Ginoza Naomi, Woojeong Joo, Iwamoto Kenji, Vera Mackie, Nakane Wakae, Markus Nornes, Ayako Saito, Sasagawa Keiko, Isolde Standish, Marc Steinberg, Julian Stringer, Tomita Mika, Tsuchida Tamaki, Mitsuyo Wada-Marciano and Emilie Yueh-yu. At Nagoya University, special thanks go to Iida Yūko, Shota T. Ogawa and Nagayama Chikako for their generous collaborative support. At the University of Warwick, Richard Perkins remains, as always, a film library samurai. Catherine Constable, Tiago de Luca, Rachel Moseley and Karl Schoonover all offered exemplary collegial assistance. Finally, we have been incalculably helped by the dynamic presence of all our students in cinema studies at Nagoya University and the Department of Film and Television Studies at the University of Warwick. This book is dedicated to them.

INTRODUCTION
Japanese cinema and its multiple perspectives

Hideaki Fujiki and Alastair Phillips

Ranging from the work of renowned directors such as Ozu Yasujirō, Kurosawa Akira, Miyazaki Hayao and Kore-eda Hirokazu to samurai and horror films, the Godzilla series and anime, Japanese cinema has long been an enduring source of fascination and pleasure for critics, students, fans and scholars from around the world. It is both a prominent component of international film festivals and a key element of various global visual cultures. The question of the identity of 'Japanese cinema' and how it may be best construed remains, however, a live and contentious issue. Whilst distinguished auteurs and unique genres may continue to have an enormous following, they by no means represent the totality of Japanese cinema. At the same time, the categories of 'Japanese' and 'cinema' are neither necessarily self-evident nor self-contained.

To give just one significant example, is *Merry Christmas Mr. Lawrence*/*Senjō no Merry Christmas* (1983), directed by the Japanese director Ōshima Nagisa and coproduced by companies in Japan, the UK, Australia and New Zealand, really an example of Japanese cinema? (Fig. 0.1). When we watch it on television or tablet computer, can we even still call it 'cinema'? Is the film simply the product of a celebrated director's creativity dependent on the sense of a unique and stable Japanese culture largely isolated from any wider global historical context? These questions alone suggest that neither term – 'Japanese' or 'cinema' – might necessarily be pre-given, monolithic, self-sufficient or stable. The national boundary of 'Japanese' and the media boundary of 'cinema' remain instead fluid and contested on a number of levels. These include the production, distribution and exhibition of films, the use of technology, the circulation of advertising and promotional material, the response of audiences and fans, not to mention critical and popular discourse about film and various institutional practices involving the film industry, censorship, public and private associations, festivals, schools and even museums. This far more complex and multiple model of Japanese cinema has, furthermore, always been inextricably linked with a larger set of social, economic, political and ecological contexts that are themselves located within a number of intertwined local, national, regional and global histories.

The Japanese Cinema Book aims to acknowledge this complexity and offer the broadest possible perspective on the topic of Japanese cinema. In so doing, it will introduce a number of innovative approaches to the field. By examining Japanese cinema from a multiplicity of angles and contextualising these in relation to global history and international film theory, as well as key contemporary trends in international film and cultural studies, we hope this book will not only make a contribution to Japanese film studies per se but also numerous academic and non-academic film cultures with an ongoing investment in this wide-ranging topic.

HISTORICISING JAPANESE CINEMA STUDIES

Japanese cinema has been actively discussed in Japan since the 1910s and within Anglophone criticism since the 1940s.[1] Just as films and their related images have always circulated beyond geographical and linguistic borders, film-makers and critics too have travelled

Fig. 0.1 *Merry Christmas Mr. Lawrence/Senjō no Merry Christmas* (Ōshima Nagisa, 1983, Recorded Picture Company and Ōshima Productions). Is this really an example of 'Japanese cinema'?

regularly on a transnational basis. Having said this, although important English books and articles have often been translated into Japanese and have therefore influenced Japanese critics and scholars, the critical and academic cultures in the two different languages have in fact largely developed independently from each other. This pattern began to change over the last two decades and a more diverse range of interactions and collaborations between the two locations has now emerged. This book is, in itself, an important example of this welcome trend.[2]

As Arif Dirlik notes, the concept of global modernity allows us to not simply see non-Western countries and people as the victims of a Eurocentric model of modernisation, but as agents of a modernity that has unfolded unevenly on a global scale.[3] The cultural imaginary of Japanese cinema emerged in the 1910s and was thus, from the offset, interwoven with a global modernity structured by Eurocentric power relations.

Edison's Kinetograph and Kinetoscope, as well as the Lumières' Cinématographe, were imported in Japan by 1887 and the earliest work filmed by Japanese people appeared by 1899.[4] As Hiroyuki Kitaura's chapter on the studio system and Manabu Ueda's chapter on film exhibition show in more detail, the foundation in 1912 of Japan's first major film production company, Nikkatsu, and the growing number of moving picture theatres in major cities during the early 1910s, were both events that marked the emergence of the Japanese film industry. However, as Aaron Gerow's chapter 'Early cinema' also makes clear, the matter of what facilitated films as exemplars of Japanese cinema was less a matter of production and exhibition practice per se, than the introduction of the critical discourse advanced by the so-called 'Pure Film Movement' (*Jun'eiga geki undō*), which emerged with the publication of one of the earliest film journals, *Kinema Record* (1913–17). Under the terms of the same global conditions by which Euro-American colonialism and imperialism had dominated – advances in technology, the propagation of modern cultural values, and the use of economic and political force – critics used European and American films as the model for their evaluation criteria. In so doing, they castigated the supposed immaturity of existing Japanese film practices such as the fixed and extended long shot, the *benshi*, the *onnagata* (male performers playing female roles), and early stars such as, most notably, Onoe Matsunosuke (Fig. 0.2).[5] Despite the fact that different forms of film practice were not only taking place in Tokyo but also in Kyoto and several other cities, these forms thus began to be re-imagined within the single national framework of a 'Japanese cinema' that existed constantly in comparison to European and American film-making.

Fig. 0.2 A collage image of Tachibana Teijirō as an *onnagata* in *Katsudō gahō* (January 1917), reprinted in Makino Mamoru (ed.), *Nihon eiga shoki shiryō shūsei*, vol. 6 (Tokyo: San'ichi shobō, 1991).

In short, the construction of 'Japanese cinema' as an idea has never been a neutral project; from the outset, it has involved certain predilections conditioned by the global historical contexts of the time.

From here on in, the notion of 'Japanese cinema' became a powerful cognitive framework amongst film practitioners, bureaucrats, critics and fans in a number of ways. This was especially so during the interwar and wartime era (1914–45) during which the film industry developed in conjunction with the rise of modern capitalism. On the one hand, the importation of American and European films, as well as other forms of cultural products, served to generate a cosmopolitan consumer culture within which a range of domestic and foreign tastes, values and voluntary behaviours both coexisted and became contested in relation to each other. This happened to the extent that any single national framework was, in fact, exceeded.[6] At the same time, the position of cinema within the wider media ecology also changed gradually from being a more or less exhibition-based medium associated with popular amusements, such as vaudeville in small theatres, to a more fully reproduction-based medium associated with print media, advertising, records and radio. In this sense, the film industry did not therefore simply develop as an autonomous phenomenon but rather as a transmedial one within which different media platforms continuously shared fragments of images and/or narratives, which in the process became intricately connected with each other.[7]

On the other hand, the same interwar era also witnessed the inception of 'total war', which endeavoured to not only mobilise soldiers but also all nationals in the participation of any war which the Japanese emperor-centred state or the Japanese empire potentially committed itself to. Despite being more or less in conflict with each other, various organs of the Japanese government attempted to utilise cinema as a form of propaganda, hidden in consumer culture, that could both regulate people and tacitly lead them to voluntarily dedicate themselves to the war efforts of the state and empire. This climate reached its zenith after the National Spiritual Mobilization Movement was launched in 1937, the Film Law was implemented in 1939, and the Information Bureau introduced the notion of *kokumin eiga* (national cinema) through two prize competitions held in 1941 (Figs. 0.3, 0.4). Alongside the term *kokumin*, this went hand in hand with the trend by which bureaucrats such as Fuwa Suketoshi, entrepreneurs such as Kido Shirō and critics such as Gonda Yasunosuke, Imamura Taihei and Hasegawa Nyozekan, to name but a few, began to discuss 'Japanese cinema' in terms of a distinctive 'national cinema'.[8] This idealisation of the 'national' in terms of an egalitarian and unified community actually entailed, but also simultaneously concealed, numerous inequalities, contradictions and conflicts in terms of gender, class, locality and ethnicity within the expanding empire of the East Asian Co-Prosperity Sphere; something Ni Yan's and Hideaki Fujiki's chapters in this book discuss in relation to both the situation in Shanghai and spectatorship.[9] It should also be noted that during the wartime period the American anthropologist Ruth Benedict analysed Japanese films and other material in terms of the enemy's cultural production and, by doing so, designated various Japanese behavioural patterns as signs of a homogeneous and ahistorical group identity. This wartime report eventually resulted in the immediate postwar publication of *The Chrysanthemum and the Sword: Patterns of Japanese Culture* in 1946.[10]

From the mid-1940s to the early 1970s, during which time Japan emerged as both a de-militarised nation and a rising economic giant following the American-led Occupation (1945–52), Japanese cinema was increasingly seen as a closed and fixed phenomenon. This tendency can be seen in the two remarkable chronological histories of Japanese cinema published during this period: Joseph L. Anderson and Donald Richie's *The Japanese Film: Art and Industry* (1959) and Tanaka Jun'ichirō's three-volume *A History of the Developments of Japanese Film/Nihon eiga hattatsu shi* (1957).[11] Although they remain indispensable reference books to researchers today, both more or less reply on a linear model of historiography centred on film production and the achievement of individual auteurs.[12] Significantly, Anderson and Richie's book

Fig. 0.3 *There was A Father/Chichiariki* (Ozu Yasujirō, 1942, Shōchiku).

Fig. 0.4 *War at Sea from Hawaii to Malaya/Hawaii Malay oki kaisen* (Yamamoto Kajirō, 1942, Tōhō).

almost entirely neglects the history of film practices in Korea, Taiwan, Manchuria and other places under the aegis of the Japanese empire, thus echoing the postwar and Cold War process whereby, under the protection of the US, Japan was permitted to forget its responsibility for the past invasion of, and domination over, these areas. Moreover, this book and Richie's other books on Kurosawa Akira (1965) and Ozu Yasujirō (1977), as well as Paul Schrader's work on Ozu (1972), were all representative of a trend in Anglophone work at the time that can now be seen as Orientalist insofar as it understood Japanese cinema to 'reflect' the uniqueness of a Japanese aesthetic system different to the 'Western' conception of art.[13]

Tanaka's book does, on the other hand, albeit briefly, include a history of film practices within the Japanese empire, but despite its empiricist aspirations in terms of historiography, it largely resonates with so-called modernisation theory, a dominant intellectual view of the time that perceived history as a process of progression from an immature foundation to an advanced stage represented by American democracy and a materially affluent culture.[14] Two other noteworthy trends in Japanese criticism may be added to Tanaka's magnum opus: 'mass culture theory' (*taishū bunka ron*) – led by Tsurumi Shunsuke, Satō Tadao and Minami Hiroshi, amongst others – and Marxist criticism – developed by Yamada Kazuo and Tokizane Shōhei, amongst others.[15] Although their views were at times opposed to each other, these critics commonly discussed and evaluated Japanese cinema in terms of how it purported to represent democratic ideals. Both groupings did so while explaining, or implying resistance to, the systemic power of government and capitalism they saw being produced within the historical circumstances relating to the memory of total war and the American Occupation, the experience of rapid economic growth, and a transformational media ecology driven by the diffusion of television.

English- and Japanese-language Japanese cinema studies gradually entered the academy between the mid-1970s and the mid-1980s. Drawing on predominant theoretical approaches of the time in the humanities such as post-structuralism, semiotics and formalism, Anglophone film studies analysed Japanese films in terms of positioning them as an exceptional set of cultural texts forming an alternative to 'classical Hollywood cinema' or 'Western' bourgeois art. Heavily influenced by Roland Barthes's *Empire of Signs*,[16] Noël Burch's *To the Distant Observer: Form and Meaning in the Japanese Cinema* was a groundbreaking example of this direction (Fig. 0.5).[17] The book introduces a new mode of historiography in that it describes Japanese cinema not in terms of linear development or a process of modernisation, but a history of how Japanese films and their related practices such as the *benshi* or *onnagata* had anti-illusionist qualities from the very beginning. According to Burch, Japanese cinema inherited these practices from premodern Japanese traditional cultural forms such as Noh, kabuki, *bunraku*, *haiku*, picture scrolls, *ukiyo-e* and Japanese gardens and, as such, it had already peaked in the 1930s and the 1940s, before the so-called golden age of Japanese film history in the postwar period. Burch argued that Japanese film and traditional arts operate at the level of 'presentationalism', which provides a sense by which both the space of the screen and the space in the auditorium may be located in a single continuum, something clearly in contradistinction with the Western bourgeois mode of 'representationalism', which displays a more self-contained and naturalistic illusion of the world on screen. As Kosuke Kinoshita notes in his chapter, in the late 1970s and early 1980s, whilst David Bordwell, Kristin Thompson, Edward Branigan and Stephen Heath attempted to revise Burch's view by conducting rigorous formalist or post-structuralist analyses, they all similarly prioritised the formal dimensions of Ozu's or Ōshima's films as alternatives to those of classical Hollywood cinema.[18] It should come as no surprise to see these scholars comparing Japanese cinema with American and European films because they were already the authors of several distinguished books and articles on the latter whilst, at the same time, being neither Japanese speakers nor scholars of Japanese studies.[19]

The influence of post-structuralist and semiotic theories also became visible within Japanese-language film criticism when Hasumi Shigehiko came to prominence in the 1970s. Unlike existing film critics engaged in 'mass culture theory' and Marxism who claimed their place on the side of the masses, Hasumi, who received a PhD from the University of Paris, had no hesitation in expressing himself as a highbrow academic critic and as a master of state-of-the-art

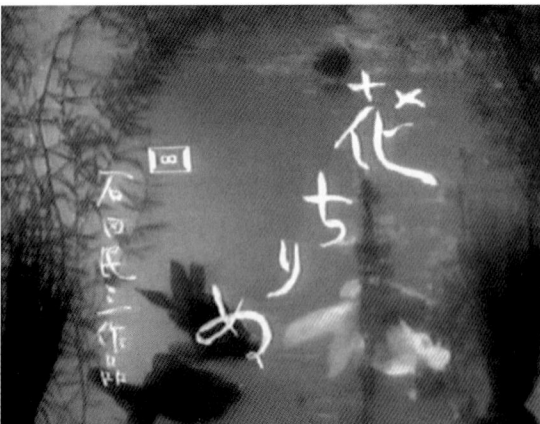

Fig. 0.5 *Fallen Blossoms/Hanachirinu* (Ishida Tamizō, 1938, Tōhō). Noël Burch celebrated the unknown director Ishida Tamizō as an important auteur.

Fig. 0.6 The cover of Hasumi Shigehiko's *Eiga no kioku sōchi* (Tokyo: Film art-sha, 1997). The first edition of the book was published by Film art-sha in 1985.

French intellectual thought, something apparent in his monograph *Foucault, Deleuze and Derrida* as well as his translation of Jean-Luc Godard's collected essays (Fig. 0.6).[20] As Alexander Jacoby and Ryan Cook's chapters partly show, Hasumi has mainly engaged with cinema as a critic rather than a scholar insofar as the numerous influential books that he has written in his signature writing style and the critical journals that he has edited have all been works of film criticism.[21] Despite this aspect, Hasumi taught cinema at the University of Tokyo and Rikkyō University in Tokyo, founded the University of Tokyo's Studies of Culture and Representation (*hyōshōbunka-ron*) programme in 1987, and later became the president of this university between 1991 and 2001 (Fig. 0.7).

The extensive introduction of film, media and cultural studies programmes at Anglophone universities and the more modest expansion of the field within Japanese universities led to a reconsideration of previous research and critical writing based around the text and the auteur from the late 1980s onwards. Mitsuhiro Yoshimoto and Rey Chow, amongst others, have both subjected Japanese film studies or Asian film studies, as well as film studies in general, to postcolonial critique. In his 1991 essay, 'The Difficulty of Being Radical: The Discipline of Film Studies and the Postcolonial World Order', Yoshimoto, for instance, problematised the tendency by which Burch and other modernist scholars scrutinised Japanese films as an 'Other for the West' and hence decontextualised these films from the 'specificities of Japanese cinema history and [its] social formation'.[22] In fact, around 1990, a number of scholars began to turn towards the historicisation of Japanese cinema in an attempt to avoid the Orientalist tendencies of Anderson, Richie and Burch. David Bordwell's *Ozu and the Poetics of Cinema* (1988), David Desser's *Eros Plus Massacre: An Introduction to the Japanese New Wave Cinema* (1988/2003), Donald Kirihara's *Patterns of Time: Mizoguchi and the 1930s* (1992), Arthur Nolletti Jr. and David Desser's edited volume, *Reframing Japanese Cinema* (1992), and Hiroshi Komatsu's work on early cinema, amongst others, all initiated this direction, although most of them, except Komatsu, still relied on English-language sources and secondary literature from Japanese studies and were largely centred on the production of auteur films and the textual analysis of this work.[23]

The following two decades saw the publication of an increasing number of books that balanced textual analysis with primary research related to Japanese-language discourse. Whilst auteur films have been critically revisited,[24] Japanese cinema has also been examined from a variety of other angles that include the study of early cinema, wartime propaganda, Japaneseness and ethnicity, gender and sexuality, genre (including documentary and anime), film style, stardom, modernity, Japan–US relations, the (post-) Japanese empire, the avant-garde, and questions of transmediality and intermediality.[25] And yet, as Yoshimoto and Chow have further pointed out, it is ironic that the increasingly rigorous and empirical historical study of Japanese cinema has also tended

Fig. 0.7 The cover of Hasumi Shigehiko's *Kantoku Ozu Yasujirō* (Tokyo: Chikuma gakugei bunko, 2016). The first edition of the book was published by Chikuma shobō in 1983.

to be seen as being marginalised within the field of film studies to the extent that this has re-enforced the division of labour between theory in the West versus culture in the rest (i.e. Japan).[26]

The development of Japanese-language Japanese cinema studies became more visible towards the end of the 1990s despite the lack of much debate between the parties involved. The distinguished non-academic critic Satō Tadao published his four volumes of *Japanese Cinema History/Nihon eiga shi* in 1995 but, retrospectively, this now appears to be the high watermark of a time when film researchers had no need of any legitimate academic background.[27] Scholars such as Iwamoto Kenji associated with Waseda University and/or Nihon University College of Art – both of which had actually begun to offer film studies programmes as early as the late 1940s – actively promoted academic research on film, especially from the 1980s onwards.[28] Yomota Inuhiko and Katō Mikirō also became prominent in the 1990s and published numerous books on Japanese cinema in ways that extended Hasumi's film criticism while, at the same time, differentiating themselves from it by bringing a more scholarly approach to research and writing (Fig. 0.8).[29] Critics of popular culture, especially anime, 'media-mix' and gaming, such as Ōtsuka Eiji, Azuma Hiroki and Ueno Toshiya, have since continued to update Japanese criticism in ways that do not simply see it in terms of journalistic practice but, like Hasumi, allow their work to be influenced by, and have an influence over, academic discourse.[30] Meanwhile, scholars with various academic backgrounds including sociology and cultural studies, media history, art history and literature, as well as film studies, have all published several important, empirically researched books and articles on Japanese cinema. These topics, mostly ones not covered in English-language scholarship on Japanese cinema, include Japan's wartime film industry and negotiations between the Japanese empire and Chinese, Taiwanese, Korean and/or Manchurian film-makers and critics; gender and sexuality; early cinema and pre-cinema; sound; the relationship between auteur cinema and its historical contexts; the global distribution of cinema; and the subject of audiences.[31] But, at the same time, as a growing number of Japanese-language scholars are educated at graduate schools within the Anglophone academy, the publication of dual-language editions – initiated by Kyoto Hirano's *Mr. Smith Goes to Tokyo: Japanese Cinema under the American Occupation, 1945–1952* (1992/1998) and Peter B. High's *The Imperial Screen: Japanese Film Culture in the Fifteen Years' War, 1931–1945* (2003/1995) – has become more and more common (Figs. 0.9, 0.10).[32]

It is interesting to see this transformation reflected in the production of four significant multivolume anthologies: the four parts plus one special volume of *A Lecture Series on Cinema/Eiga ron kōza* (1977); the eight volumes of *A Lecture Series on Japanese Cinema/Kōza nihon eiga* (1985–8); the fifteen volumes of *An Anthology of Japanese Cinema History/Nihon eigashi sōsho* (2004–11) and the eight volumes of *Japanese Cinema Is Still Alive/Nihon eiga wa ikiteiru* (2010–11). One obvious trait is the editors and authors. The 1977 volumes had the aforementioned Marxist critic, Yamada Kazuo, as the chief editor and

Fig. 0.8 The cover of Yomota Inuhiko and Saitō Ayako (eds), *Otokotachi no kizuna, Asia eiga: Homosocial na yokubō* (Tokyo: Heibonsha, 2004).

Introduction | 9

Fig. 0.9 *No Regrets for Our Youth/Waga seishun ni kuiwa nashi* (Kurosawa Akira, 1946, Tōhō). Kyoko Hirano discusses the film in the context of the US Occupation of Japan (1945–52).

many leftist and some non-leftist film-makers and critics such as Imamura Taihei, Yamamoto Satsuo, Yodogawa Nagaharu, Iwasaki Akira and Imai Tadashi as authors.[33] The late 1980s volumes had as their editors the 'mass culture theory' critics Satō Tadao and Tsurumi Shunsuke, as well as such film-makers as Imamura Shōhei and Yamada Yōji.[34] The 2004–11 series was supervised by Iwamoto Kenji and some of the volumes were not only edited by Waseda graduates like Murayama Kyōichirō but other scholars such as Ayako Saito.[35] The 2010–11 volumes had as their credited editors Yomota Inuhiko and Yoshimi Shun'ya (a prominent scholar in sociology, media and cultural studies) as well as such film-makers as Kurosawa Kiyoshi and Lee Bong-Ou, together with Ishizaka Kenji, Ueno Toshiya, Katō Mikirō, Komatsu Hiroshi and Aaron Gerow as associate editors.[36] It should also be noted that the final two series of the 2000s and 2010s have accommodated a diverse range of topics by writers who are scholars rather than critics and a considerable number of authors – such as Markus Nornes, Thomas Lamarre and Marc Steinberg – hail from primary bases not inside Japan. Equally important, as seen in these

Fig. 0.10 *Five Scouts/Gonin no sekkōhei* (Tasaka Tomotaka, 1938, Nikkatsu). Peter B. High discusses this as a landmark film during the fifteen years of war in Japan.

recent series as well as other publications, unlike the case prior to the 1980s, it has not become unusual for scholars to actively conduct archival research on primary filmic and non-filmic materials. These have not only been collected and preserved by film archives such as the National Film Archive of Japan (the former National Film Center) and the Kawakita Memorial Film Institute, but also by independent scholars such as Makino Mamoru whose enormous personal collection is now housed at Columbia University in New York (Fig. 0.11).[37]

In parallel with the larger social context of accelerating globalisation, the level of transnational interaction in Japanese cinema studies has become increasingly vital. Academic conferences such as the Society for Cinema and Media Studies (SCMS), the Association for Asian Studies (AAS), the Inter-Asia Cultural Studies Society (IACS), Kinema Club and

Fig. 0.11 The cover of Aaron Gerow and Abé Mark Nornes (eds), *In the Praise of Film Studies: Essays in Honor of Makno Mamoru* (Bloomington, IN: Trafford Publishing, 2007).

Mechademia have all provided lively platforms in which scholars and critics from different countries can get together and have discussions. While relatively old Japanese academic associations such as the Japan Society for Studies in Journalism and Mass Communication (since 1951) and the Japan Society of Image Arts and Sciences (since 1974) have especially offered sites for Japanese-speaking early-career scholars to deliver papers, newly established ones such as the Association for Cultural Typhoon (since 2003) and the Association for Studies of Culture and Representation (since 2006) have presented venues for both Japanese and English presentations. Other public fields have also played an important role in helping to mediate the work of scholars, critics, curators, film programmers and film practitioners from various countries in the gathering and exchange of information and ideas. These include film festivals (most notably the biannual Yamagata International Documentary Film Festival), as discussed by Ran Ma in her chapter, and various social networks (most notably the KineJapan mailing list) as well as various governmental, semi-governmental and non-governmental organisations such as the British Film Institute and the Japan Foundation. Moreover, numerous universities in both English-speaking countries and Japan have led to the publication of several important theses on Japanese cinema and the organisation of numerous lectures, symposia and workshops. Anglophone and Japanese universities have even begun to launch collaborative degree programmes with each other related to cinema and screen studies.[38]

Nonetheless, these growing transnational interactions have not necessarily been balanced or sufficient. The problem raised by Yoshimoto and Chow – the fact that the emergence of a more rigorous and empirical Japanese cinema studies has also simultaneously resulted in a degree of marginalisation from the larger field of cinema and media studies – remains a pressing one. It is still necessary to move beyond language barriers and boost collaboration between Japanese cinema studies and non-Japanese cinema and media studies. This is also the case with the relationship between Japanese cinema studies and other East Asian cinema studies. Whilst the Asian Cinema

Studies Society as well as the above-mentioned AAS and IACS, amongst others, have all provided potential opportunities for interaction, Japanese cinema is still predominantly not being taught and studied within cinema or media studies, but in area studies instead. *The Japanese Cinema Book* therefore aims to provide a set of varied conceptual principles to help regenerate both fields.

UPDATING JAPANESE CINEMA STUDIES

One of the key arguments of this book is that since the categories of 'Japan' and 'cinema' are neither pre-given and monolithic nor self-sufficient and stable, this therefore means that Japanese cinema cannot be isolated from its numerous global historical, social and ecological contexts. Rather, the idea of 'Japan' must always be seen as contingent on a process of historical construction: a process that not only involves established administrative frameworks and the idea of cultural heritage, but also certain forms of diversity, instability and contradiction. This might involve determinants such as the particular geopolitical territory of the country as well as various material conditions, institutional structures and forms of everyday experience, but we must also consider the flows and interactions of people, money, products, information and images in ways that extend beyond local, regional and national borders.[39] We argue that the idea of 'cinema' must similarly be seen as something historically shaped on multiple levels in terms of technologies such as the camera, the film projector, celluloid film footage and digital media; institutional practices involving production, distribution, promotion, exhibition and representation; site-specific screening venues and media platforms; and the sensory experience of audience bodies. It also becomes enacted via numerous intermedial and transmedial relations with other cultural forms including theatre, the magic lantern, photography, printed books and magazines, records, advertising, radio, television, the internet and social media. Film viewing not only takes place in cinemas and at film festivals – venues and facilities set up specifically for film – but also on different media platforms such as the television set, personal computer and smartphone/tablet as well as screens in public venues such as aeroplanes and schools.

The Japanese Cinema Book is organised into seven parts, but it has also been convened under the rubric of three interlocking themes that arise from our initial assumptions about the subject of Japanese cinema and how it may be fruitfully discussed: multiplicity, history and cross-boundary relations.

The intention behind the notion of multiplicity was our wish to examine Japanese cinema as a complex phenomenon capable of accommodating various issues and methodologies such as those discussed in Parts 1 to 4 involving film theory and criticism, film institutions and industry, film style and genre. At the same time we also wanted to extend this idea into the social realm in Parts 5 to 7 and consider such topics as ecology, social and cultural geography, geopolitics and transnational relations. As we have already seen, both Yoshimoto and Chow have pointed to a certain division of labour within film studies between theory in the West and culture in the rest of the world. Even if Japanese cinema has not necessarily taken a central position, it is certainly true that the topic has served as an integral reference point to many Western film scholars such as the case of Burch's deconstruction of Western bourgeois art forms, Bordwell's systematic account of cinematic formalism, Gilles Deleuze's idea of the time-image in film, Miriam Hansen's notion of vernacular modernism and Lúcia Nagib's discussion of new realism.[40] Nonetheless, even within these various theoretical constellations, Japanese cinema has tended mainly to be discussed in auteur-based terms. It is sometimes forgotten that Japanese cinema scholarship has also referred to, or tested, numerous theoretical issues or historical methods shared with film studies in general. These include topics such as early cinema, authorship, spectatorship, narrative and the representation of gender and sexuality as well as a wide range of subjects such as the idea of a studio system, film exhibition, censorship, technology, film festivals, genre, stardom, experimental cinema and the archive.

The Japanese Cinema Book has therefore been designed to encourage readers to see the abundant ways that Japanese cinema may be considered in ways that overlap with the study of other national, transnational and global cinemas. Two fields of study illustrate this approach: questions related to the figure of the body and issues concerning the matter of place and topography.

In her chapter – 'Gender and sexuality' – for instance, Hikari Hori discusses the dialogue between Anglophone and Japanese-language forms of feminist scholarship and argues that both fields of enquiry have generated significant degrees of overlapping concern despite their different temporal and spatial locations. Importantly, Hori introduces two further perspectives regarding the study of gender and sexuality in Japanese cinema: the impetus towards interdisciplinary contextualisation and the importance of building transnational narratives of film history that might specifically illuminate Japanese cinema's connection with other local or global film cultures. Yuka Kanno's chapter – 'Stardom' – on the queer stardom of Miwa Akihiro similarly draws upon queer and feminist film theory and existing work on Japanese stardom in order to not only contextualise her case study within a wider history of Japanese star culture but to also consider what the term 'queer' may mean in the context of Japanese film history as a whole. In her chapter – 'Acting' – on the representation of the figure of the stage actress Matsui Sumako in Mizoguchi Kenji's *The Love of Sumako the Actress/Joyū Sumako no koi* (1947), Chika Kinoshita takes an historically informed intermedial approach to the different ways in which the film enacts the multiple genealogies of screen acting in Japanese cinema, including debts to Western modes of performance. Jennifer Coates's chapter – 'The yakuza film' – pays particular attention to the realm of the female body in yakuza films such as *The Red Peony Gambler/Hibotan bakuto* series (1968–72) and argues that a more gender-balanced approach may uncover a broader range of emotional cues normally derived from other forms of film genre. In her chapter – 'Minority cultures' – Mika Ko unpicks the popular myth of Japanese cultural homogeneity to argue instead that Japan is a heterogeneous country consisting of various minority groups; each group possessing not only a Japanese identity but a culture, history and political agenda that relates uniquely to them. Her specific focus on female *zainichi* Koreans draws upon wider frameworks in cultural studies and film studies to convey a sense of how Korean women in Japan represent a double minority since being ethnically non-Japanese and female means marginalisation by dominant Japanese and Korean 'male' voices.

The Japanese Cinema Book takes a deliberately plural approach to the discussion of place and location with several chapters discussing questions of topography and geography at both the level of representation and exhibition. Rachel DiNitto's chapter – 'Ecology' – on Japanese films that discuss the toxic environmental legacy following the devastation of the nuclear reactor at Fukushima prioritises the notion of ecological interdependency in order to think through how Japanese cinema has sought to visualise the contaminated landscape. In her chapter – 'Rural landscape' – on the representation of the Japanese landscape in three films made between 1939 and 1941, Uchida Tomu's *Earth/Tsuchi* (1939), Miki Shigeru's *Living in the Earth/Tsuchi ni ikiru* (1941) and Kamei Fumio's *Notes on the Shinano Climate: Kobayashi Issa/Shinano fudoki: Kobayashi Issa* (1941), Sharon Hayashi considers the convergence of several social, political and aesthetic issues in relation to the Japanese countryside as an important site of meaning during wartime. Woojeong Joo's chapter – 'The home' – on the Japanese home, especially during the years of the so-called Shōwa 30s, draws upon various studies of domestic space to argue that the home, as visualised in two films from the period, *Good Morning/Ohayō* (Ozu Yasujirō, 1959) and *Being Two Isn't Easy/Watashi wa nisai* (Ichikawa Kon, 1962), became the key site of a much wider contemporary renegotiation between the public and the private sphere. Phillips's chapter – 'The city' – also considers the same era in a study of three films from 1958 in terms of their representation of Tokyo. Despite his synchronic focus on a single year in one location, Phillips argues that the cinematic city of Tokyo that year, like its real-world counterpart, was in fact a profoundly layered space that simultaneously looked backwards and forwards in time to mark a profound sense of contested transition within the everyday life of the present. In his chapter – 'Peripheries' – on the representation of Okinawa in Japanese cinema, particularly in *Profound Desires of the Gods/Kamigami no fukaki yokubō* (Imamura Shōhei, 1968) and *Dear Summer Sister/Natsu no imōto* (Ōshima Nagisa, 1972), Andrew Dorman refers to various ways in which scholars have sought to define the dialectical relationship between core and periphery within Japan, especially in terms of unpacking the similar kind of mythical national homogeneity discussed by Ko. Manabu Ueda's chapter – 'Exhibition' – offers an informative survey of Japanese film exhibition practice that not only considers the site of the cinema auditorium per se but also positions this location within a wider sphere of regional circulation and difference. Both Julian Ross's chapter – 'Experimental film' – on the history of Japanese experimental cinema and Oliver Dew's chapter – 'The archive' – considering the local impact of screening practices related to the home movie point to the significance of particular localities in understanding the event of film projection as a spatial phenomenon. These debates are extended further in Ran Ma's chapter – 'Film festivals' – examining various film festival practices such as the Tokyo International Film Festival and the Yamagata International Documentary Film Festival. Ma draws upon the work of the anthropologist Anna Tsing to argue for a worldly sense of friction between the global and the local that gets played out in terms of different degrees of scale at each event and in each location.

The Japanese Cinema Book has particularly sought to define the existing ways in which the topic of Japanese cinema has been organised historically and explore new ways in which Japanese film history may be opened up to alternative forms of critical scrutiny. As previously mentioned, the Anglophone history of Japanese cinema up until the 1980s largely tended to be described on the basis of the films made by a rota of key directors, whether this account was framed in terms of a single linear narrative model or not. Even when this work referred to various social contexts, this was only done to the extent that these contexts were connected to an overarching pattern of auteur production. Since then, however, we have seen a number of significant historical studies that have dealt with a far broader understanding of the multiple dimensions of Japanese cinema and the possible ways it may be contextualised historically. This work has revealed that Japanese cinema is not an ahistorical entity relying on an unproblematic inheritance from the culture of the Heian era (794–1185), pace Burch's culturalist view, but that it is instead a multifaceted and contested phenomenon in the constant process of reconstruction and recontextualisation. This book seeks to build on the accomplishments of this body of work and provide a means of mapping several of these divergent historical paths.

A number of contributions to the book thus seek to historicise what may initially seem to be a neutral and objective term. Alexander Jacoby's chapter on 'Authorship', for instance, charts the different ways in which the figure of the author has been deployed to the extent that not only does a richer sense of the term emerge but broader questions about the nature of the medium, the workings of the industry and the place of a national cinema in an evolving international context also come into view. Hiroyuki Kitaura's chapter – 'The studio system' – updates Anderson and Richie's auteur and studio-centred account of the Japanese film industry by offering an extended chronology of the so-called 'production committee formula' by which commercial films are produced via joint investment from several companies. He then positions this within a broader perspective of other related institutional practices that range from production to distribution and exhibition. Naoki Yamamoto's chapter – 'Film criticism' – on Japanese film theory, especially in the context of the notion of montage, highlights the spatial and geopolitical workings of film history. It argues that an historicised study of Japanese film criticism may in fact present an excellent vantage point from which to critically reflect on the very foundation of Japanese cinema, thus revealing a more hybrid understanding of what we normally consider 'Japanese' to be when it comes to the discussion of what he calls 'local film practice'. Rachael Hutchinson's chapter – 'Censorship' – on the topic of film censorship, especially in the context of the screen representation of violence in post-Occupation Japan, makes the point that enduring questions of ideology and politics have always been more important than the topic of violence itself when it comes to public access to the screen image. Her discussion traces this back to the 1920s when cinema became a component of policy formation regarding education and the control of public behaviour within the modern public sphere. Finally, Fujiki's chapter 'Spectatorship', suggests that the term is neither a universal nor a homogeneous concept. Rather, it possesses an ever-changing, contested and multivalent degree of subjectivity and agency that can only be made sense of in relation to a particular historical context.[41]

The matter of film style has been a significant aspect of the ways in which Japanese cinema has especially been discussed within English-language scholarship. We have sought to develop a more historicised understanding of this by presenting a set of chapters on key aspects of film form and meaning. Daisuke Miyao's contribution – 'Cinematography' – makes the point that not only have the technologies and production processes of cinematography been contested historically within Japan, but that the history of cinematography in Japanese cinema has also always been part of a wider account of international and/ or transnational conflicts concerning the medium of cinema as a whole. Chika Kinoshita's previously mentioned chapter re-contextualises the history of Japanese film acting traditions, whilst Fumiaki Itakura in his chapter – 'Set design' – provides a broad historical account of Japanese production design before honing in on a specific case study concerning Yoshimura Kōzaburō's *Undercurrent/Yoru no kawa* (1956) within the context of the late studio era and particular shifts concerning colour technology and screen censorship. In her chapter – 'Music' – Yuna Tasaka makes the point that music and sound remain one of the least well-explored topics concerning the aesthetics of Japanese cinema. In order to help readdress this issue, she presents three historical case studies in which the relationship between non-diegetic film music and diegetic sound became reconfigured within the traditional sword-fight genre or *chanbara*. In a related chapter – 'Technology' – Johan Nordström discusses the question of sound in connection with the wider historical context of the introduction of sound technologies within Japanese cinema during the 1930s. Central to Nordström's argument is the point that any history of Japanese screen sound must be written in relation to patterns of convergence and intermediality with other audio media forms such as broadcast radio and the record industry.

Of course, one of the most common ways in which Japanese cinema has conventionally been considered is through the prism of film genre and *The Japanese Cinema Book* seeks to advance this discussion in a number of ways that are related to both local and global patterns of film production. In his chapter – '*Jidaigeki*' – Philip Kaffen returns to the topic of the period film, or *jidaigeki*, to argue that in one sense the problem of the *jidaigeki* in Japanese cinema is no different from the broader question of how to understand Japanese film within the dynamic flow of world cinema as a whole. According to Kaffen, it 'is a question of culture and representation – of location'. What he calls the '*topos* of *jidaigeki*' in his words, is something that 'moves restlessly along the unstable boundary between cinema and life, guided as much by technology as history'. The term *jidaigeki* literally means 'play with historical time' and, as such, it should not just be understood in terms of a historical break with the past as in the advent of the Meiji Restoration in 1868, but also in relation to the break in history foregrounded by the aesthetic, technological and economic consequences of the invention of the moving image. In his chapter 'Anime', Thomas Lamarre points out that although it may be considered to be something generated especially in Japan, there are different and possibly incompatible ways in which anime's relation to the nation and the notion of 'Japaneseness' may be configured because of the multiple ways that it circulates within the world in terms of both production and reception. Lamarre's analysis arises from the development of four, loosely chronological, paradigms relating to art history, cinema, television and the advent of 'new media'. In the third case study related to generic forms conventionally presumed to be specifically Japanese, Jennifer Coates's previously mentioned chapter on the yakuza film reorientates discussion of its apparently masculine appeal towards a more diverse reading in terms of its appeal at the levels of representation and reception.

We have also sought to re-contextualise the history of Japanese cinema in relation to a number of broader generic forms such as the horror film, melodrama, the musical and documentary. Michael Crandol's chapter – 'Horror' – notes, for example, that the term *kaiki eiga* predates the emergence of the term 'horror film' in Japanese discourse by a number of years and argues for a more textured reading of both *kaiki* cinema and *horā* film that encompasses issues such as narrative style, critical reception and affect. While Ryoko Misono's chapter – 'Melodrama' – explores the relationship between forms of melodrama and modernity in Ozu Yasujirō's *That Night's Wife/Sonoyo no tsuma* (1930), Michael Raine's chapter – 'The musical' – investigates the Japanese musical, and supplements a brief history of the genre in Japanese cinema, with a more detailed discussion of the self-reflexive phenomenon of the popular song film in the context of the high-volume, low-budget production system of the 1950s. In particular, Raine analyses how the burgeoning media culture of the time worked to interweave the subjects of female stardom and female fandom with the fertile filmic and publicity structures of the musical form. Finally, Ayumi Hata's chapter – 'Documentary' – provides a study of the documentary film productions of Ogawa Productions, which builds on the groundbreaking work of Markus Nornes to examine three films from the late 1960s to the 1970s, *Forest of Oppression - A Record of Struggle at Takasaki City University of Economics/Assatsu no mori - Takasaki keizai daigaku tōsō no kiroku* (1967), *Sanrizuka – Heta Village/Sanrizuka – Heta buraku* (1973) and *The Magino Village Story – Raising Silkworms/Magino monogatari – Yōsanhen* (1977), that focus not just on the question of the subjectivity of those represented on screen but also the matter of authorial subjectivity and the implications that this had for the representation of socio-historical reality. In a related chapter – 'Social protest' – Masato Dogase considers the history of social protest cinema in the context of postwar trends in Japanese documentary practice. Dogase's discussion also includes the work of Ogawa Shinsuke, but his emphasis on the notion of what he terms dialogic film practice – a form of film-making that facilitates a dialogue between the film-maker, the people on screen and the screen audience – encompasses related films by Kawabe Kazuo and Fujita Shigeya, amongst others.

Perhaps the most significant way of signalling the critical intentions of *The Japanese Cinema Book* is through the question of cross-boundary relations. We have already repeatedly argued that Japanese cinema is not a single fixed or closed entity and that it may be best understood instead as a plural and multidimensional phenomenon. One way of conceptualising this is to think of Japanese cinema as a highly distinctive nodal point with a material and imagined framework that has been historically transformed through both the mediation of the image and various flows of information, finance and personnel. These processes have always existed, and continue to exist, across a diverse range of cultural, regional and geopolitical boundaries. It follows that these flows have involved certain degrees of negotiation and conflict. As we have previously noted, the Japanese distribution of European and US films and their related images in the 1910s motivated local film critics to imagine domestic film-making as 'Japanese cinema', but only within the orbit of a Euro-American structure of power relations. Between the 1920s and the mid-1940s, film-makers, critics, bureaucrats and entrepreneurs subsequently struggled to establish the idea of a national cinema that could incorporate some of the same technological and financial principles of modern film-making and film regulation that local film practices wished to share with their American and European counterparts. At the same time, especially in the late 1930s and the early 1940s, these personnel attempted to support and promote the Japanese empire that had now partly expanded to other East and South East Asian areas through the medium of cinema. Numerous Japanese film-makers, as well as significant amounts of resource, equipment and knowledge, travelled beyond the confines of the nation and interacted with local people in Keijō (Seoul), Taipei, Hsinking, Shanghai, Manila, Jakarta and elsewhere; often in profoundly unequal ways when it came to the unidirectional direction of travel between Japan and other territories within the region.[42] Following defeat at the end of World War II, however, many Japanese people came to think of Japan on a much smaller scale confined to the Japanese archipelago, even if this imaginary remained ambiguously defined due to the position of Okinawa and other islands; the latter (as Andrew Dorman discusses in his chapter on peripheries) was only officially 'returned' to Japan in 1972. At the same time, given the imperative to take the side of the West within the geopolitical structure of the Cold War, the majority of Japan's citizens simultaneously tended to forget until recently the fact that the Japanese empire dominated other Asian territories.[43]

These prewar and wartime contexts, not to mention the uneven transition in the postwar period in terms of remembering and forgetting the legacy of empire, all constitute a significant part of the ways in which Japanese cinema has been positioned and scaled in relation to the rest of the world, especially from the mid-1940s onwards. A number of chapters in the book especially focus on how this has played out in relation to American cinema and US governmental policy. Yuka Tsuchiya, in her chapter 'The Occupation', for example, considers the phenomenon of the circulation of Civil Information Education Section (CIE) or US Information Service (USIS) films about the United Nations during the American Occupation in order to argue that these supposedly 'neutral' informational films were in fact an aspect of a wider grassroots struggle to restore Japan's status of respectability within postwar international society. Hiroshi Kitamura, in his chapter 'Japanese cinema and Hollywood', examines one instance of how Japanese cinema appropriated the representational characteristics of American cinema in the case of the Japanese Western. As Kitamura suggests, this transnational creative phenomenon paradoxically articulated a specifically 'national' nostalgia for the untainted rural and provincial spaces of Japan in an era of accelerated modernisation. In his chapter – 'Transnational remakes and adaptations' – on the popular 'program picture' that presents Ezaki Mio's 1967 'remake' of *Casablanca* (1942), *A Warm Misty Night/Yogiri yo kon'ya mo arigatō*, as a case study, Ryan Cook posits the idea that if one thing distinguishes the coherence of Japanese film history it is the ways in which its various models of film-making have specifically negotiated the question of cultural influence.

And yet, as various other chapters show, the transnational flows of Japanese cinema have not only taken place between Japan and the US. Rather, the place of Japanese cinema has often been to complicate wider international circuits related to the model of a Eurocentric art cinema culture; something that Ran Ma points out in her previously mentioned chapter on film festivals. In his wide-ranging chapter – 'Japanese cinema and Europe' – on the history of Japanese cinema's interactions with Europe, Yoshiharu Tezuka similarly traces a constellation of different gazes by which Japan has engaged with Europe and Europe has engaged with Japan. *The Japanese Cinema Book* has also sought to extend these important geopolitical perspectives by offering discussion of other territories and regions. Cobus van Staden, in his chapter 'Globalisation', considers the South African reception of popular Japanese culture and in so doing offers a new and valuable geopolitical perspective on the processes of globalisation. Ni Yan, in her chapter 'Empire', discusses the complex history of Shanghai film-making during the era of the Japanese Occupation. Both Mika Ko, in the above-mentioned chapter, and Stephanie DeBoer, in her chapter 'Japanese cinema and its postcolonial histories', offer different perspectives on the legacy of Japan's empire within East Asia. In Ko's case, as we have seen, her interest lies in the representation of female *zainichi* Koreans, especially in Ōshima Nagisa's film, *Sing a Song of Sex/Nihon shunka-kō* (1967). In DeBoer's, she turns to the relatively under-examined phenomenon of the regional coproduction to argue that films such as *The Great Wall/Shin shikōtei/Qinshi huangdi* (Tanaka Shige, 1962) provide an exemplary instance of the ways in which certain Japanese film studios aspired to develop an 'internationalist' perspective on the region in the context of the consolidation of global film trade and the imperatives of the Cold War. DeBoer's argument rests on the removal of a simplistic model regarding the reiteration of colonial ties in favour of an approach that sees the various international film collaborations between Japan and Hong Kong or Taiwan from the mid-1950s to the early 1960s as instances of what she calls 'an uneven regional geography', something which can ultimately be read in terms of the Japanese film industry's emergence from earlier models of development dating back to the immediate postwar period.

Our coverage of cross-boundary relations also encompasses the important question of media boundaries in relation to the presence of Japanese cinema. This field has already begun to be shaped by a number of writers. Marc Steinberg's work on the notion of 'media-mix' argues that the presence of the dynamic figure of Astro Boy via different media platforms, initiated by the animated television series *Astro Boy/Tetsuwan atom* (1951–68), simultaneously enabled a specific connection between these different outlets through a transmedial sharing of the image.[44] Hideaki Fujiki dates this phenomenon back to developments in the Japanese film industry and the rising consumer culture of the late 1920s when it became commonplace for a figural image and/or narrative motif to be shared across different media platforms such as print media (including periodicals and posters), radio, audio recordings and theatrical plays.[45] A common thread across this work, including a number of contributions to the book, is the fact that whilst the appearance of new media forms such as television in the late 1950s; DVD players, personal computers and the internet in the 1990s; and social media in the 2000s may appear to have decentralised the popularity of Japanese cinema on one level, Japanese films themselves remain more visible than ever via the television monitor, the desktop, laptop and tablet computer and the smartphone.

Thomas Lamarre's chapter on anime therefore presents a broad historical survey of anime's interaction with different media technologies. Yuka Kanno and Michael Raine's chapters both discuss the production of film stardom in relation to the diversity of media forms whilst Masato Dogase specifically links developments in Japanese film documentary practice to emergent practices in the television industry. Kosuke Kinoshita's chapter 'Narrative' provides an analysis of the multi-viewpoint film and suggests that this lies at the point of intersection between a genealogical mode of Japanese narrative and a set of more cosmopolitan developments in storytelling that might be said to transcend cinema itself. Finally, Rayna Denison's chapter 'Transmedial relations' discusses the increasing popularity of the manga adaptation, argues that this requires us to rethink the boundaries of film-making in Japan and positions Japanese cinema instead as part of a larger set of intertextual networks that circulate across Japanese popular culture as a whole.

Needless to say, *The Japanese Cinema Book* by no means provides a comprehensive or definitive account of its subject. Rather, what we hope we have achieved is to display both the wealth of Japanese cinema itself and the diverse richness of the means by which it may be discussed and appreciated. We want *The Japanese Cinema Book* to provoke stimulating debate and discussion within the numerous academic and cultural contexts around the world where the subjects of Japan and cinema continue to arise. We certainly hope you will find many new and productive ways of thinking about this fascinating topic within the book and that you might even now feel challenged to take part in developing these debates for the future.

A NOTE ON JAPANESE LANGUAGE CONVENTIONS

We have kept to Japanese word order conventions for all names except for chapter authors and authors with Japanese names who have published widely in English (e.g. Kurosawa Akira, but Mitsuhiro Yoshimoto).

We have used the Japanese-language macron throughout, including capital letters. This rule has also been applied to the names of people (e.g. Ozu Yasujirō, not Ozu Yasujiro), the titles of publications (e.g. *Kinema junpō*, not *Kinema junpo*), the titles of films (e.g. *Sanshō dayū*, not *Sansho dayu*) and the names of companies and the major film studios (e.g. Shōchiku, not Shochiku). Prominent place names have been the only exceptions (e.g. Tokyo, not Tōkyō and Kyushu, not Kyūshū), along with words in quotations when the macron has also been omitted in the original text.

In general, we have used relevant translated English words/phrases first and then provided the original Japanese word on first mention in brackets. We have used our discretion as to whether the English-language translation or the Japanese-language term has been used in repeated mentions.

In the case of transliterated titles that contain European or North American words, the original word has usually been retained and not a romanised form of *katakana*. In cases where the distinction between the *katakana* and the non-Japanese language word is important to the author's argument, the *katakana* has been transliterated. In the case of terms that do not have a precise English equivalent, the translated term has usually been placed first in inverted commas and then the original Japanese term in brackets.

We have devised a few important exceptions to this rule:

1 It was deemed acceptable to use the Japanese language first when the author's argument rested on the formation of specific terms in the Japanese language for example in relation to:
   - a discussion of the specific cultural codes and genealogy of a type of film-making practice
   - commentary on particular social behaviours and conventions in Japan that require reference to a distinctive Japanese-language term
   - a discussion of the various types of dramatic figures or narrative tropes related to the evolution of a particular genre

2 In the case of public institutions, venues, events, conferences, government ministries, cultural organisations, formal agreements and items of legislation, we have given the unitalicised Japanese term first followed by the English translation (if deemed necessary) for example the Zen'ei eiga kanshōkai (the Avant-Garde Film Cine-Club).

3 In the case of Japanese film journals, we have generally not provided an English translation of the title for example *Eiga hyōron*, not *Eiga hyōron (Film Criticism)*.

Longer direct quotations from Japanese-language material have been translated into English with no Japanese transliteration.

Notes

1 Japanese cinema has, of course, been widely discussed in numerous other languages such as French, Chinese, Spanish, Korean and Portuguese.

2 See also Daisuke Miyao (ed.), *The Oxford Handbook of Japanese Cinema* (Oxford: Oxford University Press, 2014) and Joanne Bernardi and Shōta T. Ogawa (eds), *Routledge Handbook of Japanese Cinema* (Abingdon: Routledge, forthcoming).

3 Arif Dirlik, *Global Modernity: Modernity in the Age of Global Capitalism* (Abingdon: Routledge, 2007), pp. 1–9.

4 See Tsukada Yoshinobu, *Nihon eigashi no kenkyū: Katsudō shashin torai zengo no jijō* (Tokyo: Gendai shokan, 1980).

5 It is interesting to note that one of the earliest book-length accounts of cinema in the Japanese language, Gonda Yasunosuke's *Katsudō shashin no genri oyobi ōyō* (Tokyo: Uchida rōkakuho, 1914), barely mentions the idea of 'Japanese cinema'; instead, it highlights the medial differences between cinema and theatre. By contrast, in his *Katsudō shashin geki no sōsaku to satsueihō* (Tokyo: Seikyūsha, 1917), Kaeriyama Norimasa, one of the leading critics of the Pure Film Movement, emphasises the deficiency of Japanese films in contrast to American and European films. See pp. 9–12 of the expanded edition of this book, published by the same publisher in 1924. For more details, see Joanne Bernardi, *Writing in Light: The Silent Scenario and the Japanese Pure Film Movement* (Detroit, MI: Wayne State University Press, 2001); Aaron Gerow, *Visions of Japanese Modernity: Articulations of Cinema, Nation, and Spectatorship, 1895–1925* (Berkeley: University of California Press, 2010); Hideaki Fujiki, *Making Personas: Transnational Film Stardom in Modern Japan* (Cambridge, MA: Harvard University Asia Center, 2013).

6 See, for instance, William O. Gardner, *Advertising Tower: Japanese Modernity and Modernity in the 1920s* (Cambridge, MA: Harvard University Asia Center, 2006); Jordan Sand, *House and Home in Modern Japan: Architecture, Domestic Space and Bourgeois Culture, 1880–1930* (Cambridge, MA: Harvard University Asia Center, 2003); Fujiki, *Making Personas*.

7 See Hideaki Fujiki, *Kankyaku towa nanimonoka: Media to shakaishutai no kingendaishi* (Nagoya: University of Nagoya Press, 2019), chapter 2.

8 For more on the context of 'total war', see Katō Atsuko, *Sōdōin taisei to eiga* (Tokyo: Shinyōsha, 2003) and Fujiki, *Kankyaku towa nanimonoka*, chapters 2 and 3.

9 For cinema in the Japanese empire, see, for instance, Michael Baskett, *The Attractive Empire: Transnational Film Culture in Imperial Japan* (Honolulu: University of Hawai'i Press, 2008); Takashi Fujitani, *Race for Empire: Koreans as Japanese and Japanese as*

Americans during World War II (Berkeley: University of California Press, 2013); Kate Taylor-Jones, *Divine Work: Japanese Colonial Cinema and Its Legacy* (London: Bloomsbury Academic, 2017); Fujiki, *Kankyaku towa nanimonoka*, chapter 4.

10 Ruth Benedict, *The Chrysanthemum and the Sword: Patterns of Japanese Culture* (Boston, MA: Houghton Mifflin, 1946). Also see Fukui Nakao, 'Ruth Benedict, Jeffrey Gorer, Helen Mears no nihonjinron, nihonbunkaron o sōkatsu suru', *Kansei daigaku gaikokugogakubu kiyō* no. 7 (October 2012), pp. 81–9.

11 Joseph L. Anderson and Donald Richie, *The Japanese Film: Art and Industry* (Clarendon, VT: Charles E. Tuttle, 1959) and Tanaka Jun'ichirō, *Nihon eiga hattatsushi*, 3 vols. (Tokyo: Chūōkōron-sha, 1957). An expanded edition of Anderson and Richie's book was published by Princeton University Press in 1982. The fourth volume of Tanaka's book was published in 1968 and a fifth volume in 1980.

12 Eric Cazdyn discusses this point in *The Flash of Capital: Film and Geopolitics in Japan* (Durham, NC: Duke University Press, 2002), pp. 65–75.

13 Donald Richie, *The Films of Akira Kurosawa* (Berkeley: University of California Press, 1965); Donald Richie, *Ozu: His Life and Films* (Berkeley: University of California Press, 1977); Paul Schrader, *Transcendental Style in Film: Ozu, Bresson, Dryer* (Berkeley: University of California Press, 1972).

14 For more on modernisation theory, see, for instance, Harry D. Harootunian, 'American's Japan/Japan's Japan', in Masao Miyoshi and Harry D. Harootunian (eds), *Japan in the World* (Durham, NC: Duke University Press, 1993), pp. 196–221.

15 See Fujiki, *Kankyaku towa nanimonoka*, chapters 5 and 6. Discussions of mass culture differed from, but also partly overlapped with, discussions of mass society and mass communication, both of which constituted key trends in Japanese intellectual thought during the 1950s and 1960s.

16 Roland Barthes, *Empire of Signs*, trans. Richard Howard (New York: Hill and Wang, 1983). Originally published in French in 1970.

17 Noël Burch, *To the Distant Observer: Form and Meaning in the Japanese Cinema* (London: Scolar Press; Berkeley: University of California Press, 1979). Harry Harootunian points out that Burch's 'reliance on Barthesian semiology and its thematic inventory turned his admirable detour to the East into a journey away from history'. He also argues that 'it was important for Burch's agenda to account for the text of the Japanese film in such a way as to satisfy the Barthesian model to de-center prevailing certainties founded on the presumption of the sovereign, centered subject of Western philosophy'. See Harootunian, '"Detour to the East": Noël Burch and the Task of Japanese Film', in Noël Burch, *To the Distant Observer: Form and Meaning in the Japanese Cinema* (1979; reprinted electronically by the Center for Japanese Studies, University of Michigan, 2004), <https://quod.lib.umich.edu/c/cjfs/aaq5060>.

18 Edward Branigan, 'The Space of Equinox Flower', *Screen* vol. 17 no. 2 (1976), pp. 74–105; Kristin Thompson and David Bordwell, 'Space and Narrative in the Films of Ozu', *Screen* vol. 17 no. 2 (1976), pp. 41–73; Stephen Heath, 'Narrative Space', *Screen* vol. 17 no. 3 (1976), pp. 68–112.

19 It should be noted that we don't mean Japanese speakers are necessarily Japanese nationals.

20 Hasumi Shigehiko, *Foucault, Deleuze, Derrida* (Tokyo: Asahi shuppansha, 1978). Jean-Luc Godard, *Gordard zenshū/Oeuvres complètes de Jean-Luc Godard*, trans. Hasumi Shigehiko and Shibata Hayao (Tokyo: Takeuchi shoten, 1970–1).

21 Hasumi Shigehiko was a chief editor of the two influential Japanese journals of film criticism: *Lumière* (1985–8) and *Représentation* (1991–3).

22 Mitsuhiro Yoshimoto, 'The Difficulty of Being Radical: The Discipline of Film Studies and the Postcolonial World Order', *Boundary 2* vol. 18 no. 3 (1991), pp. 242–57.

23 David Bordwell, *Ozu and the Poetics of Cinema* (London: British Film Institute; Princeton, NJ: Princeton University Press, 1988)/*Ozu Yasujirō: Eiga no shigaku*, trans. Sugiyama Akio (Tokyo: Seidosha, 2003); David Desser's *Eros Plus Massacre: An Introduction to the Japanese New Wave Cinema* (Bloomington: Indiana University Press, 1988); Donald Kirihara, *Patterns of Time: Mizoguchi and the 1930s* (Madison: University of Wisconsin Press, 1992); Arthur Nolletti Jr., and David Desser (eds), *Reframing Japanese Cinema* (Bloomington: Indiana University Press, 1992); Hiroshi Komatsu, 'The Fundamental Change: Japanese Cinema before and after the Earthquake of 1923', *Griffithiana* nos. 38/39 (1990), pp. 186–96. The following year, Komatsu published the Japanese-language book, *Kigen no eiga*/*The Cinema in the Origins of Film History* (Tokyo: Seidosha, 1991).

24 See, for instance, Mitsuhiro Yoshimoto, *Kurosawa: Film Studies and Japanese Cinema* (Durham, NC: Duke University Press, 2000); Alastair Phillips and Julian Stringer (eds), *Japanese Cinema: Texts and Contexts* (London: Routledge, 2007); Aaron Gerow, *Kitano Takeshi* (London: British Film Institute, 2007); Abé Mark Nornes, *Forest of Pressure: Ogawa Shinsuke and Postwar Japanese Documentary* (Minneapolis: University of Minnesota Press, 2007); Catherine Russell, *The Cinema of Naruse Mikio: Women and Japanese Modernity* (Durham, NC: Duke University Press, 2008); Woojeong Joo, *The Cinema of Ozu Yasujiro: Histories of the Everyday* (Edinburgh: Edinburgh University Press, 2016); Jinhee Choi (ed.), *Reorienting Ozu: A Master and His Influence* (Oxford: Oxford University Press, 2018).

25 See, for instance, Gerow, *Visions of Japanese Modernity*; Darrell William Davis, *Picturing Japaneseness: Monumental Style, National Identity, Japanese Film* (New York: Columbia University Press, 1995); Abé Mark Nornes, *Japanese Documentary Film: The Meiji Era through Hiroshima* (Minneapolis: University of Minnesota Press, 2003); Daisuke Miyao, *Sessue Hayakawa* (Durham, NC: Duke University Press, 2007); Mitsuyo Wada-Marciano, *Nippon Modern: Japanese Cinema of the 1920s and 1930s* (Honolulu: University of Hawai'i Press, 2008)/*Nippon modan: Nihon eiga 1920–30 nendai* (Nagoya: University of Nagoya Press, 2009); Baskett, *The Attractive Empire*; Thomas Lamarre, *The Anime Machine: A Media Theory of Animation* (Minneapolis: University of Minnesota Press, 2009)/*Anime machine: Global media toshiteno nihon anime* (Nagoya: University of Nagoya Press, 2013; Hiroshi Kitamura, *Screening Enlightenment: Hollywood and the Cultural Reconstruction of Defeated Japan* (Ithaca, NY: Cornell University Press, 2010)/*Senryō nihon no bunka saiken* (Nagoya: University of Nagoya Press, 2014); Mika Ko, *Japanese Cinema and Otherness: Nationalism, Multiculturalism and the Problem of Japaneseness* (London: Routledge, 2011); Isolde Standish, *Politics, Porn and Protest: Japanese Avant-Garde Cinema in the 1960s and 1970s* (London: Continuum, 2011); Marc Steinberg, *Anime's Media Mix: Franchising Toys and Characters in Japan* (Minneapolis: University of Minnesota Press, 2012); Yoshiharu Tezuka, *Japanese Cinema Goes Global: Filmworkers' Journeys* (Hong Kong: Hong Kong University Press 2012); Daisuke Miyao, *The Aesthetics of Shadow: Lighting and Japanese Cinema* (Durham, NC: Duke University Press, 2013); Fujiki, *Making Personas*; Yuriko Furuhata, *Cinema of Actuality: Japanese Avant-Garde Filmmaking in the Season of Image Politics* (Durham, NC: Duke University Press, 2013); Stephanie DeBoer, *Coproducing Asia: Locating Japanese-Chinese Regional Film and Media* (Minneapolis: University of Minnesota Press, 2014); Oliver Dew, *Zainichi Cinema: Korean-in-Japanese Culture* (London: Palgrave Macmillan, 2016); Jennifer Coates, *Making Icons: Repetition and the Female Image in Japanese Cinema, 1945–1964* (Hong Kong: University of Hong Kong Press, 2016); Alexander Zahlten, *The End of Japanese Cinema* (Durham, NC: Duke University Press, 2017).

26 Mitsuhiro Yoshimoto, 'National/International/Transnational: The Concept of Trans-Asian Cinema and the Cultural Politics of Film Criticism', in Valentina Vitali and Paul Willemen (eds), *Theorising National Cinema* (London: British Film Institute, 2006), pp. 254–61; Rey Chow, *Sentimental Fabulations, Contemporary Chinese Films: Attachment in the Age of Global Visibility* (New York: Columbia University Press, 2007).

27 Satō Tadao, *Nihon eigashi*, 4 vols. (Tokyo: Iwanami shoten, 1995). An expanded edition was published in 2006.

28 Renowned critics such as Iijima Tadashi and Iwasaki Akira also engaged with these institutions up to the 1970s.

29 Iwamoto Kenji's books include *Roshia avant-garde no eiga to engeki*/*The Film and Theatre of the Russian Avant-garde* (Tokyo: Suiseisha, 1998) and *'Jidai eiga' no tanjō: Kōdan, shōsetsu, kengeki kara jidaigeki e*/*The Birth of the 'Period Film': From Kōdan, Novels and Swordplay to Period Drama* (Tokyo: Yoshikawa kōbunkan, 2016). Katō Mikirō's books include *Genre ron: Hollywood teki kairaku no sutairu*/*Essay on Genre: Hollywood Styles of Pleasure* (Tokyo: Heibonsha, 1996); *Nihon eiga ron, 1933–2007: Tekusuto to kontekusuto*/*Essays on Japanese Cinema, 1933–2007: Texts and Contexts* (Tokyo: Iwanami shoten, 2011). Yomota Inuhiko's books include *Ajia eiga no taishūteki sōzōryoku*/*The Popular Imagination of Asian Cinema* (Tokyo: Seidosha, 2003); *Nihon eiga to sengo no shinwa*/*Japanese Cinema and Postwar Mythologies*

(Tokyo: Iwanami shoten, 2007). Yomota has published more than one hundred books on film, literature, manga and other subjects.

30 See, for instance, Ōtsuka Eiji, *Teihon monogatari shōhiron/An Essay on Narrative Consumption* (Tokyo: Kadokawa shoten, 2001); Azuma Hiroki, *Otaku: Japan's Database Animals*, trans. Jonathan E. Abel and Shion Kono (Minneapolis: University of Minnesota Press, 2009), the translation of the original Japanese book published in 2001; Ueno Toshiya, *Kōya no ōkami: Oshii Mamoru ron/Wolf in the Wilderness: An Essay on Oshii Mamoru* (Tokyo: Seikyūsha, 2015). Examples of this new type of film critic include Miura Tetsuya, Hirose Jun, Ishioka Yoshiharu and Watanabe Daisuke.

31 See, for instance, Katō, *Sōdōin taisei to eiga/The General Mobilisation System and Cinema*; Yan Ni, *Senji nicchū kōshōshi/A Wartime History of Cinema in Sino-Japan Negotiations* (Tokyo: Iwanami shoten, 2010); Misawa Mamie, *'Teikoku' to 'sokoku' no hazama: Shokuminchiki Taiwan eigajin no kōshō to ekkyō/Between 'Empire' and 'Homeland': Negotiations and Border-crossing of Taiwanese Filmmakers in the Colonial Period* (Tokyo: Iwanami shoten, 2010); Ueda Manabu, *Nihon eiga sōsō ki no kōgyō to kankyaku: Tokyo to Kyoto o chūshini/Exhibition and Audiences in the Early Era of Japanese Cinema: Tokyo and Kyoto* (Tokyo: Waseda University Press, 2012); Misonō Ryōko, *Eiga to kokuminkokka: 1930 nendai Shōchiku melodrama eiga/Cinema and the Nation State: Shōchiku Melodrama in the 1930s* (Tokyo: University of Tokyo Press, 2012); Yi Young Jae, *Teikoku Nihon no Chōsen eiga: Shokuminchi melancholia to kyōryoku/Korean Cinema in the Japanese Empire: Colonial Melancholia and Cooperation* (Tokyo: Sangensha, 2013); Nagato Yōhei, *Eiga onkyō ron: Mizoguchi Kenji eiga o kiku/Examining Film Sound: Listening to Mizoguchi Kenji's Films* (Tokyo: Misuzu shobō, 2014); Ōkubo Ryō, *Eizō no archaeology: Shikakurironn, kōgaku media, eizō bunka/An Archaeology of the Image: Visual Theory, Optical Media, Image Culture* (Tokyo: Seikyūsha, 2015); Kinoshita Chika, *Mizoguchi Kenji ron: Eiga no bigaku to seijigaku/The Cinema of Mizoguchi Kenji: The Aesthetics and Politics of the Film Medium* (Tokyo: Hosei University Press, 2016); Kitaura Hiroyuki, *Terebi seichōki no nihon eiga: Media kan kōshō no nakano drama/Japanese Cinema in the Period of Early Television: Drama in the Negotiations between the Media* (Nagoya: University of Nagoya Press, 2018); Sasagawa Keiko, *Kindai Asia no eiga sangyō/Modern Asian Film Industries* (Tokyo: Seikyūsha, 2018); Fujiki, *Kankyaku towa nanimonoka*.

32 Kyoko Hirano, *Mr. Smith Goes to Tokyo: Japanese Cinema under the American Occupation, 1945–1952* (Washington, DC: Smithsonian Institute Press, 1992)/*Tennō to seppun: Amerika senryō kano nihon kenetsu* (Tokyo: Sōshisha, 1998); Peter B. High, *15 nen sensō to nihon eiga* (Nagoya: University of Nagoya Press, 1995)/*The Imperial Screen: Japanese Film Culture in the Fifteen Years' War 1931–1945* (Madison: University of Wisconsin Press, 2003). This is also the case with Bordwell, *Ozu and the Poetics of Cinema*; Wada-Marciano, *Nippon Modern*; Mitsuyo Wada-Marciano, *Dejitaru jidai no nihon eiga* (Nagoya: University of Nagoya Press, 2010)/*Japanese Cinema in the Digital Age* (Honolulu: University of Hawai'i Press, 2012); Lamarre, *Anime Machine*; Fujiki, *Making Personas/Zōshoku suru persona: Eiga stardom no seisei to nihon kindai* (Nagoya: University of Nagoya Press, 2008); Abé Mark Nornes and Aaron Gerow, *Research Guide to Japanese Film Studies* (Ann Arbor: University of Michigan Center for Japanese Studies, 2009)/*Nihon eiga kenkyū eno gaidobukku*, trans. Dōgase Masato (Tokyo: Yumani shobō, 2014); Kitamura, *Screening Enlightenment*; Inuhiko Yomota, *What is Japanese Cinema?*, trans. Philip Kaffen (New York: Columbia University Press, 2019)/*Nihon eiga 100 nenshi* (Tokyo: Shūeisha, 2000, expanded edn, 2014); Miyao, *Aesthetics of Shadow*; *Kage no bigaku: Nihon eiga to shōmei*, trans. Sasagawa Keiko and Mzoguchi Kumiko (Nagoya: University of Nagoya Press, 2019).

33 Yamada Kazuo (ed.), *Eiga ron kōza*, 4 vols. (Tokyo: Gōdō shuppan, 1977). This series also has an encyclopaedia as an additional volume: *Eiga no jitten* (Tokyo: Gōdō shuppan, 1978).

34 Imamura Shōhei, Satō Tadao, Tsurumi Shunsuke and Yamada Yōji (eds), *Kōza nihon eiga*, 8 vols. (Tokyo: Iwanami shoten, 1985–8).

35 The 15 volumes of the *Anthology of Japanese Cinema History* series, supervised by Iwamoto Kenji, include Murayama Kyōichirō (ed.), *Eiga wa sekai o kirokusuru: Documentary saikō/Cinema Records the World: Documentary Revisited* (Tokyo: Shinwasha, 2006); Ayako Saitō (ed.), *Eiga to shintai(sei)/Cinema and the Body (Sexuality)* (Tokyo: Shinwasha, 2006).

36 Kurosawa Kiyoshi, Lee Bong-Ou, Yomota Inuhiko and Yoshimi Shun'ya (eds), *Nihon eiga wa ikiteiru/Japanese Cinema Is Still Alive* (Tokyo: Iwanami shoten, 2010).

37 See Nornes and Gerow, *Research Guide to Japanese Film Studies*. For Makino, see Aaron Gerow and Abé Mark Nornes (eds), *In Praise of Film Studies: Essays in Honor of Makino Mamoru* (Ann Arbor, MI: Kinema Club, 2001). Makino supervised and edited numerous reprinted editions of articles and books from the prewar and wartime period. His efforts have enabled researchers to conduct an unprecedentedly wide range of empirical research on Japanese cinema of the time.

38 For instance, the University of Warwick and Nagoya University founded a collaborative PhD programme in Global Screen Studies in 2019.

39 This view builds on previous theoretical arguments related to the study of national cinema or national media cultures. See Mette Hjort and Scott Mackenzie (eds), *Cinema and Nation* (London: Routledge, 2000); Chris Berry and Mary Farquhar, *China on Screen: Cinema and Nation* (New York: Columbia University Press, 2006); Valentina Vitali and Paul Willemen (eds), *Theorising National Cinema*; Marc Steinberg and Alexander Zahlten (eds), *Media Theory in Japan* (Durham, NC: Duke University Press, 2017).

40 Burch, *To the Distant Observer*; David Bordwell, *Narration in the Fiction Film* (Madison: University of Wisconsin Press, 1985; London: Routledge, 1987); Gilles Deleuze, *Cinema 2: The Time-Image*, trans. Hugh Tomlinson (Minneapolis: University of Minnesota Press, 1989); Miriam Bratu Hansen, 'Vernacular Modernism: Tracking Cinema on a Global Scale', in Nataša Ďurovičová and Kathleen Newman (eds), *World Cinemas, Transnational Perspectives* (New York: Routledge, 2010), pp. 287–314; Lúcia Nagib, *World Cinema and the Ethics of Realism* (London: Continuum, 2011).

41 Whilst this chapter focuses on the situation in the early 1940s, his *Kankyaku towa nanimonoka* deals with a significant part of the history of Japanese spectatorship from the 1910s up to the 2010s.

42 See High, *The Imperial Screen*; Baskett, *The Attractive Empire*; Fujiki, *Kankyaku towa nanimonoka*.

43 See, for instance, Lisa Yoneyama, *Hiroshima Traces: Time, Space, and the Dialectics of Memory* (Berkeley: University of California Press, 1999); Sakai Naoki, *Nihon/eizō/Beikoku: Kyōkan no kyōdōtai to teikokuteki kokuminshugi* (Tokyo: Seidosha, 2007).

44 Steinberg, *Anime's Media Mix*.

45 Fujiki, *Kankyaku towa nanimonoka*, chapter 2. Of course, even before the 1920s, there were certain kinds of transmedial and intermedial phenomena such as the French film *Zigomar* (1911) and its related Japanese imitation film and novelisation in the case of the former and the chain drama (*rensageki*) in the case of the latter.

PART 1
THEORIES AND APPROACHES

1

EARLY CINEMA
Difference, definition and Japanese film studies

Aaron Gerow

Research on the early cinema of Japan has played a core, but often complicated, role in defining Japanese film studies, especially in terms of the nature of its object and its relation to the classical Hollywood mode. If the value of Japanese film, both domestically and abroad, has often been claimed in terms of its difference from other cinemas, the assertion that the first Japanese films were even more different has served as further evidence of that unique value. The extent and the nature of that difference, however, has been a long-standing topic of debate, one that has made research on early film a privileged space for negotiating and complicating the notion of difference in Japanese film studies, particularly as it relates to issues of nation, identity and the position of the scholar. This chapter will review the history of, and major debates within, studies of early Japanese cinema, focusing in particular on how the field has confronted the problem of difference.

THE DIFFERENCE OF EARLY CINEMA

For many years, the difference of early cinema was itself seen as a problem, so defined because the first works did not fit supposedly universal narratives of cinematic or cultural development. Early films in the 1910s that were described as mere long-take recordings of kabuki or *shinpa* plays,[1] lacking cinematic forms of narration and incomprehensible to anyone who did not previously know the play or had a *benshi* narrator on hand to explain the text, would conceivably be the most 'different' and 'Japanese', but as such they were not acclaimed by historians. Donald Richie and Joseph Anderson's groundbreaking history of Japanese film in English, *The Japanese Film: Art and Industry*, for instance, less celebrated than criticised these films for being 'simple illustrations for the *benshi*'.[2] Even Japanese authors such as Iijima Tadashi or Satō Tadao provide a tale of cinematic evolution that describes early films as backward and premodern.[3] Japanese cinema could be different only after it had moved beyond primitive forms of cinema, evolving to a filmic mode of narration seen as universal – but often defined by classical Hollywood cinema. As Mitsuhiro Yoshimoto has argued, the celebration of difference in the first histories of Japanese cinema were always framed within a universalist discourse of humanism that valorised 'national character' as that 'through which the humanistic ideals of universal significance are said to be represented concretely'.[4]

As such, many initial histories of Japanese film denigrated early films as theatrical, deviating too much from the core of cinema. They criticised the *benshi* for hampering the development of cinematic forms by eliminating the incentive for film-makers to find visual means to solve narrative problems. Histories thus focused on the transformations of the late 1910s and early 1920s, loosely termed the Pure Film Movement, which were begun by young reformers such as Kaeriyama Norimasa, Thomas Kurihara and Henry Kotani. Reformers and critics – led, in part, by Kaeriyama – expounded on such transformations in print, arguing that reform was necessary to make Japanese production more cinematic. Beyond arguing for the elimination of such theatrical trappings as the *onnagata* (men playing women's roles) and proscenium staging, they called for the use of screenplays to shift the origin of cinematic meaning from the theatre to the studio; or of editing to make the film itself speak, not the *benshi*. Most subsequent histories of Japanese cinema in effect adopted the critical perspective of the Pure Film Movement towards early film.

Film historiography in Europe and North America shared a similar objection to early cinema in the West until a crucial shift occurred in the late 1970s. Instead of picturing them as a primitive form of film, less important because they were only a preliminary stage in an evolution towards a more cinematic cinema, early films came to be seen as simply a different cinema, one that embodied different sociopolitical or cultural values. The shift towards the classical Hollywood style was then not the result of the inevitable evolution of the medium but rather a deeply historical process, where contingent factors both internal and external to the film world promoted some forms of cinema while suppressing others. Within media archaeology, the historical factors behind these selections become as important as the content of the change in cinematic practice, because they could indicate the cultural or ideological valences of those practices.

In the American and European contexts, this shift in early cinema research fostered explorations of the differences of the first films, from Charles Musser's research on the role of exhibitors in constructing cinematic meaning to Ben Singer's re-evaluation of such seemingly obvious terms as melodrama.[5] André Gaudreault and Tom Gunning explored the difference of early film narration, with Gaudreault seeing a form of 'monstration' (of showing) over narration (of telling), and Gunning famously describing a 'cinema of attractions', in which the shocks of tricks and new sights took precedence over narrative.[6] These sparked debates, but the results expanded the field of cinema studies into considerations that took on the history of perception (painting, magic, optics), pre-cinematic apparatuses (the magic lantern), theatre (phantasmagoria), geography (entertainment districts, amusement parks), transportation, commerce, capitalism, media, urbanism, gender, race and modernity in general, in order to understand cinema through a larger cultural history. Gunning was not alone in arguing that discovering these different forms was not an antiquarian endeavour, but helped reveal the parallels between the cinema of attractions and later experimental or modernist cinema. One could argue that the rise in early cinema studies was in part prompted by the decline of the classical mode and the need to understand the forms that were appearing as an alternative, from MTV to digital media.

Much of early cinema studies was shaped by politically informed theoretical models, from Marxism to feminism, from Frankfurt School cultural theory to semiotics. Early cinema became attractive in part because it offered an historical alternative to hegemonic forms of culture formed later in the twentieth century. Noël Burch's Marxist argument was a prominent example, as he saw 'Primitive Cinema' as embodying turn-of-the-century urban working-class culture, and the shift to the 'Institutional Mode of Production' as the 'embourgeoisement' of cinema, where the medium developed new forms of narration in an effort to reflect the values of the capitalist middle class.[7] Not all scholars agreed with this approach, but it was an example of how early cinema was being understood in terms of broader concepts of class, economy and power.

Burch helped make Japanese film central to this debate. For a time in the 1970s and 1980s, Japanese cinema was one of the primary fields of interest for North American and European film studies. Major figures in the field, from Stephen Heath to David Bordwell, pursued analyses of Japanese film, in part as a means to further the critique and understanding of the classical Hollywood mode and its alternatives. Burch's book *To the Distant Observer*, published in 1979, was a provocative yet problematic work that argued for the difference of Japanese cinema precisely by portraying its early cinema in a positive light. While identifying some stylistic elements shared between the early cinemas of Japan and the West, Burch wrote extensively on the Japanese example because of its unique characteristics: firstly, it lasted significantly longer than in the West, possibly up until World War II; secondly, it remained radically different from the classical mode even after being exposed to it; and thirdly, it was backed by a cultural tradition that accepted forms of signification and textuality on a mass level that in the West would be appreciated only by the avant-garde few. Burch was particularly intrigued by directors such as Ozu Yasujirō and Mizoguchi Kenji whom he saw clearly mastering the classical mode, yet still consciously opting for cinematic forms rooted in early cinema that deviated from Hollywood methods. He could cite a wide variety of stylistic differences, from the lack of close-ups or analytical narrative editing in Mizoguchi, to Ozu's breaking of the 180-degree rule, to the chaotic discontinuity of Itō Daisuke's camera movements, and ultimately tie them to attitudes towards the sign that he considered largely unchanged since the Heian era (794–1185).

Burch argued that Japanese cultural production features a unique intertextuality in which all film texts purposively refer to and rely on other texts to be understood, thus foregrounding their textuality. While modern Western texts hid their intertextuality in myths of originality and the individual author, presenting the text as a transparent window onto a world, Japanese culture, Burch claimed, made the intertexts a visible aspect of both signification and reader/viewer pleasure. Japanese cinema was supposedly like kabuki: more presentational than representational, more intertextual than diegetic. The *benshi* became emblematic to Burch of Japanese cinema's resistance to the colonisation of Japanese film by Western definitions of the cinematic. He felt the *benshi* split the fictional source of enunciation by assuming the role of narration; the film, or, more specifically, the illusory world viewed in the text, no longer spoke for itself but rather it was spoken for by an external figure. Not only was the system of representation fragmented, the signs that made up the text ceased to transparently transmit a seemingly pre-existing world. They were now read by the *benshi* as independently existing signs that must compete with the words the *benshi* produced. Spectators were unable to enter the world of the diegesis because they remained aware of the film as only a text. Burch contends Japanese prewar filmgoers did not succumb to the fictional effect of the film but instead treated spectatorship as the simultaneous viewing of the spectacle of the text and the reading of the film.[8]

Burch and the trends he represented were influential, even in the critiques they generated. Such shifts in perspectives on the *benshi*, in part sustained by revivals of *benshi* performances in Japan, led even established scholars such as Satō Tadao to write more positive histories of these narrators.[9] J.L. Anderson's work emphasising *benshi* narration (to him, the *katsuben*) as a continuation of the tradition of 'commingled media' in the Japanese arts, echoed Burch's arguments in claiming that,

> To most audiences, the film was an open text and one element in a complex, multi-media, live entertainment …. Indeed, the presence of the *katsuben* attacked the ontological status of the film. Was truth in the photographic images or in what the *katsuben* said?[10]

Jeffrey Dym's book on the *benshi* celebrated their art of 'explanation' (*setsumei*), even if he did not pursue the theoretical implications Burch or Anderson did.[11] Other scholars, such as Iwamoto Kenji, echoed some of Burch's claims about the deviations between prewar Japanese film style – for Iwamoto, the paucity of close-ups – and classical Hollywood cinema.[12] One could argue that Burch's work even helped inspire research on *benshi*-like figures in other cinemas, such as the *bonimenteur* in Quebec.[13]

Burch's argument, however, met with much criticism, even among those who sided with his efforts to re-evaluate Japanese early cinema. He was influenced by Roland Barthes's post-structuralist evaluation of Japan, *The Empire of Signs*,[14] so *To the Distant Observer* might also be seen as a similarly powerful intellectual exercise, imagining at a time when film studies was critiquing the Hollywood mode, a form of cinema that could be both critical of that mode and popular. Burch's celebration of a cinema based on an unchanging cultural tradition, however, was not only insufficiently Marxist but aligned with Orientalist visions of Japan.[15] His formalist analyses of films could often be insightful, but not all agreed with them. Scholars such as David Bordwell, for instance, countered his claims about the formal differences between prewar Japanese film and Hollywood cinema by arguing that Japanese cinema from the late 1920s onwards generally followed the classical mode.[16] Researchers such as myself and Joanne Bernardi have argued that the Pure Film Movement, which Burch largely dismissed as an example of the failure of Western cinematic modes to take root in Japan, was more complex and successful than that.[17] What Burch takes to be unquestioned cultural attitudes were often subject to conflict and division as Japan itself was riven by struggles between different classes, localities (city versus country), and vectors of modernity. Removing the ability of Japanese to question – to engage in theory, which Burch actually locates in the West, not Japan[18] – was an example of how Burch's Japan was sometimes a fictionalised unity, a projection serving the needs more of his 'distant observer' than those in Japan.

HISTORICISING EARLY CINEMA

Much subsequent research has focused on historicising many of the issues Burch did not. My research, for instance, has attempted to understand the historical valences behind the debates over Japanese cinema in the 1910s and early 1920s, in ways that does not simply reduce them to a battle between Westernised modernism and traditional Japan. Basic concepts such as cinema, textuality, signification, Japan, the West, the image, tradition, modernity or locality were not given but shaped by concrete practices, both discursive and practical, in often conflicted historical contexts that extended beyond just the film world. The question is less how early Japanese film embodied certain traditional modes, than how the interaction of, and struggle between, various practices in the 1910s and 1920s, both cinematic and non-cinematic, shaped not just the idea that cinema exists (or not) as a distinct mode and what makes it distinct, but also what 'Japan' or 'tradition' itself are.[19] Other scholars have historicised some of the other basic terms associated with cinema, with Hideaki Fujiki, for instance, questioning the claim that Onoe Matsunosuke was Japan's first movie 'star' by examining how the concept itself was shaped over time and competed with other movie-related stars, such as *benshi*.[20] Daisuke Miyao has looked at the transnational valences of the formation of early stars, especially Sessue Hayakawa and Aoki Tsuruko, who were popular, in complex ways, both in Japan and the US.[21] Masato Dōgase has similarly considered how the concept of the director emerged historically.[22]

Differing approaches to historicisation have, at the same time, foregrounded a number of issues central to early cinema research revolving around resources, periodisation, methodologies and theory, many of which have challenged and defined the field. A significant issue is the availability of resources, which first and foremost, means the lack of extant films. By some estimates, only 0.2 per cent of films from the 1910s exist and only 3.8 per cent from the 1920s.[23] This has made it difficult to make broad conclusions on the basis of textual analysis, even though Hiroshi Komatsu, the leading scholar of early cinema in Japan, has made significant inroads in this area of research. Some scholars have had to supplement textual analysis with descriptions of films available in contemporary publications,[24] but the problem has also pushed researchers to explore other approaches to or facets of early film culture. My work, for instance, influenced by Michel Foucault but resonating with the work of Lee Grieveson, Sabine Hake and others on European and American cinema, seeks to understand how the ways cinema was defined, seen and even made were shaped by how it written about, from film criticism to film regulations. Such an approach overlaps with other research in the history of film theory and criticism,[25] of film censorship,[26] and of spectatorship and reception.[27] The latter has been a particularly fruitful area of research as scholars have moved away from text- or apparatus-centred accounts of the film experience, to explore how historically embodied spectators, within concrete exhibition practices, are as important as stylistic analysis in comprehending how films were understood and how films functioned culturally.[28]

This variety of approaches has presented different definitions of what constitutes 'early cinema', which depend in part on methodology and theoretical stance. Recent research has questioned the narrative offered by teleological history, which has a clear beginning (usually the arrival of machines such as Lumières's Cinématographe in 1897[29]) and end (often the present, representing the culmination of cinematic development). Instead, it has pushed the history back before 1897, expanded its range beyond cinema proper, and questioned a single teleology. Iwamoto Kenji and Ōkubo Ryō have thus, for instance, looked at *gentō* and *utsushie* (forms of the magic lantern) as pre-cinematic practices.[30] Ōkubo and Manabu Ueda have also begun to illuminate how early cinema was not always 'cinema', given how forms such as *kineorama* (mixing film and the diorama) and the *shinematekku* (mixing cinema and panorama) evince the fundamentally hybrid nature of film exhibition in the first decade.[31] I have found that for many Japanese, from intellectuals to legal authorities, cinema was not itself an independently existing concept but rather another form of *misemono*, or fairground entertainment, until at least the years leading up to much-publicised banning of the French film *Zigomar* (Victorin-Hippolyte Jasset, 1911) in 1912 (Fig. 1.1).[32] It was when cinema began to be viewed as a threat that it began to take on the status of a unique object. At the same time, Ueda has argued that one can see a shift beginning around 1908 in the way films are exhibited and viewed, symbolised by the first boom in film-specific theatre production, one which he attributes not to the success of Russo-Japanese War films in 1904–5, but to broader transformations in urban modernity.[33]

Certainly the years before the formation of a more solidified object 'cinema' is itself a rich era of research, but disagreements also exist over how to characterise cinema afterwards and how long that period lasts. Hiroshi Komatsu has posited four stages in the development of Japanese film until 1923: the period of sporadic production from 1897 to 1908; the emergence of stable companies from 1908 to 1912; the formation of Nikkatsu in 1912 and the subsequent solidifying of Japanese film tradition; and the waves of Westernisation from the late 1910s that led to mixture of Japanese and Western forms. He has long argued that the majority of Japanese films from at least 1912 until about 1923, which he calls 'traditional', were defined by a strict

Fig. 1.1 *Zigomar* (Victorin-Hippolyte Jasset, 1911, Éclair) and cinema as a threat.

code that made it difficult for other forms of cinematic practice, such as those introduced by foreign movies, to enter into film-making.[34] This came after a period in which Japanese films emulated foreign chase films or hits such as *Zigomar*. Komatsu's account of mid-1910s film style resembles that of Burch and Anderson:

> The traditional formula of Japanese cinema did not aspire to such a film being told simply through the images. The linguistic aspect of the image was carried by the dialogue of the *benshis*. The image itself was the illustration of a storyline that existed independently.[35]

Komatsu refrains from the grand claims about early cinema's continuity with Heian aesthetics Burch makes, but he does conceive of 1910s cinema in opposition to Western film, albeit in a non-political fashion.

Disagreements remain over how rigid this film style was, although the paucity of extant films makes it difficult to resolve the debate.[36] Within his formalist analysis, Komatsu's use of the term 'traditional' for genres of cinema he has called 'kabuki cinema' adds to the impression of rigidity.[37] Other methodologies, however, can offer different perspectives. A cultural studies approach, for instance, could locate these texts in a new urban geography marked by burgeoning social inequalities and modern transformations in space, exemplified by places such as Asakusa, Tokyo's movie theatre district in this era. There, such 'kabuki' films would, for instance, be played in cinemas with garishly ornate Western exteriors. Such social or cultural hybridity could be aligned with other forms of textual hybridity, as the 1910s experienced not only the popularity of *rensageki* (chain drama), mixing film and theatre, but also a typical movie bill that combined foreign and Japanese films with *benshi*, musical interludes and occasional live acts. In her work on Taishō and early Shōwa culture, Miriam Silverberg has defined this culture through terms such as montage and code-switching, while I have called it a 'culture of combination'.[38] The possible question for researchers is how texts that seem stylistically standardised were read by spectators in this hybrid environment. Cinema's relation to pre-cinematic practices such as kabuki is extremely important, but one concern with labelling those practices or any early film style 'traditional' is that it not only obscures the processes by which tradition was formed and shaped at the contemporary moment (what Eric Hobsbawm has called the 'invention of tradition'[39]), but it also creates a division between tradition and modern that makes it difficult to see the porousness of their boundaries or their unequal relation. The challenge may be how to see Onoe Matsunosuke or *shinpa* film as not just traditional but also modern – albeit a different modern from that presumed by the pure film reformers. As I have argued, the opposition may then be less of tradition versus modern than of different possibilities for the modern enmeshed in the global/local nexus, with reformers pushing a top-down version of rationalised modernity against a bottom-up modernity of hybridity and mixture.

A discursive approach, which considers how what was said about cinema shaped its existence, would emphasise that even if some spectators could experience Japanese films as a closed, coded world, their practices and those of film producers were themselves described at the time by film reformers and political and cultural authorities as illogically mixing media, culture and industrial practices. The Pure Film Movement is in part called that because it perceived Japanese film at the time as impure, as pursuing forms of signification and spectatorship that were contradictory. While such discourses were certainly in conflict with others in moulding spectator practices, they did have real-world effects, and not simply in inspiring attempts at pure film. For instance, as Hase Masato and I have argued, police film regulations echoed the goals of film reformers and attempted to suppress the experience of cinema as a live, local event where meaning is constructed in the theatre and thus helped to establish cinema as a fixed text produced in the space of the studio.[40] A discursive analysis could complicate the notion of a traditional textual code by showing how even the possibility of a text with a code was partially the result of distinctly modern operations of discursive regulation and state power.

Approaches involving issues of nation, class and power could provoke still other questions. Komatsu uses the term 'national cinema' when describing how *shinpa* films between 1913 and 1918 rejected the 'internationalism' the genre had previously pursued (when it emulated aspects of foreign film style) and instead 'developed the uniqueness of customs, morals, and religion [of Japan] within the visual framework of cinema'.[41] This is one definition of national cinema, emphasising how the unique form and content of a country's motion pictures helped distinguish them from those of other nations. More recent scholarship, however, has followed the critiques of the nation developed by Benedict Anderson and Eric Hobsbawm, and considered less how film style and content may reflect unique national characteristics, than how cinema helps construct modern 'imagined communities' and their unique and invented traditions. This approach would shift the focus from the fact of nationality to the why, considering the local and global shifts in power, class, economy and modernity that contributed not only to the assertion of national identity but its form. Divisions between national and international styles would become more porous. In fact, as I have argued, those who critiqued the 'national cinema' Komatsu identifies were both internationalist and nationalist themselves in that they complained 'traditional' Japanese cinema was vulgar and a national disgrace, and argued for a modern nation defined through hierarchies within the world system and at home.[42] In this case, a scholar would ask how ideas of national cinema in the early years included and excluded certain texts, producers and audiences; who gained or lost power through such exclusions; and what conceptual divisions the notion of the nation produced and depended upon.

Such questions are important because Japan in the 1910s was in the process of becoming a modern imperial power. Constructions of the nation in or through cinema at the time both aided and hid that process, so researchers must take care not to naturalise those constructions by imposing borders. Scholars of 1910s cinema can consider not just the formation of dominant 'national' genres such as *shinpa* and *kyūha* (the 'old school' or kabuki-inspired period films) but also how Korean, Taiwanese, Okinawan or even rural Japanese approached these works; how the support for and criticism of these genres aided the construction of class, the modern 'masses', gender, 'Japaneseness'

and the empire;[43] and what caused other genres such as animation (begun around 1917) and actualities/documentaries to become marginal to the national cinema.[44] One of the exciting recent trends has been in local film histories, for instance Sasagawa Keiko's work on Osaka, Kobayashi Sadahiro's research on Nagoya, or Tomita Mika and Ueda Manabu's work on Kyoto,[45] which all complicates the picture of a uniform national cinema.

THE PURE FILM MOVEMENT

Debates continue on the nature of the cinema called early cinema, especially centred on the period of the 1910s. Depending on one's definition of that cinema, as well as of what followed it, one's conception of when it ends may change too. The first histories of Japanese film, written especially under the influence of pure film reformers, concluded the period of early cinema with the appearance of the Pure Film Movement. Burch is in some ways an extreme rejection of this, arguing that the Pure Film Movement failed and thus that many of the essential aspects of early cinema continued well into the wartime, even with the appearance of filmmakers who clearly knew the classical mode but opted not to use it. To him, it was the Occupation and the imposition of American culture and its cinema that marked the end of the difference of Japanese cinema in the majority of works.

Most subsequent research falls in between these two extremes. Few would disagree that by the late 1920s, many significant aspects of Japanese film production and culture had changed. *Onnagata* disappeared. *Benshi* still existed – at least up until the coming of sound – but certain forms of narration, such as *kowairo* (imitation of voices), which had been criticised by reformers, had given way to other forms. Even if one disagrees with Bordwell's argument that the norm by the late 1920s was the classical mode, the major studios did study the Hollywood studio system and develop forms of a hierarchical division of labour. The film text did begin to take on more of a role in narration, with the adoption of elements of analytical editing and explanatory and dialogue intertitles. With actresses, the female body took on a new role and styles of acting changed. The question remains, however, how much changed, when and why.

The answers are again determined in part by decisions about the object of research and methodology. Joanne Bernardi focuses on screenwriting and notes significant transformations in not only the form of screenplays but also the importance given to composing scripts, because of the writings of Kaeriyama and other reformers.[46] Many, however, note how even Shōchiku and Taikatsu, two studios begun in 1920 with declarations of strong support for the reformist cause, either went under or compromised on many of their goals. Daisuke Miyao, when researching cinematography, for instance, describes the ambitions of Kotani Henry at Shōchiku returning from Hollywood but underlines how he failed to produce changes in a style of lighting that differed little from that of kabuki.[47] His research echoes those who can cite the fact that major reformers such as Kaeriyama, Kurihara or Tanaka Eizō did not last long as directors, as a reason for doubting the completeness of film reform.

Komatsu sees the years between 1920 and 1923 as a transitional period, but has described the difference between the cinema that came before and after the Great Kantō Earthquake of September 1923 as similar to that of the biblical flood, exhibiting a complete break and rebirth.[48] The experience of mass urban destruction had an influence on cultural production, especially on modernists such as Murayama Tomoyoshi or the literary 'New Impressionists' (Shinkankakuha), but any argument about the quake's effect on film style requires a precise accounting of what was already underway, while also avoiding the tendency to reduce Japanese film history to that of Tokyo.

Focusing primarily on personnel and film style produces a mixed history at best. My research on discursive formations argues that over the 1910s and early 1920s, a particular set of conceptions about cinema as being inherently visual, as bearing an essence, about film texts possessing a universal or national meaning produced in the space of production, and about the geopolitical and cultural significance of cinema, became dominant in way that became interlaced with structures of class and power and struggles over the possibilities of modernity in Taishō Japan. Such discourses became so prevalent that they would not only effect the way many people spoke about cinema in Japan well into the postwar but create assumptions about what film 'naturally' was that forgot this contingent history. Certainly there is room for debate over how much a discursive history is sufficient to narrate early film history – though with the lack of film texts, that is often the only history available – but discourses did clearly intersect with actions on the ground. I end my book around 1925 in part because it is in that year that film censorship became national, when state authorities essentially declared cinema to be no longer a phenomenon defined by local conditions or the space of exhibition (e.g. the *benshi*). This was one milestone – one of many milestones – in the longer relation between film and state power in the prewar era.

That relation that was not free of contradictions, however. As I stress in the conclusion of my book, much pure film discourse suffered inherent contradictions over the relationships between text and critic, image and word, the masses and the intelligentsia, subject and nation, imperialism and capitalism, and Japan and the West. These would hamper subsequent discourses on cinema and complicate any claim that the Pure Film Movement was a success. It is therefore important not to see the Pure Film Movement as monolithic. In fact, the concept itself is a post facto construct since there was no set term 'jun'eigageki undō' at the time. In my work, I saw the Pure Film Movement 'less as a specific set of historical events than as the formation of a field of discourse, a group of "natural" assumptions both tacit and explicit about the cinema'.[49] It was then more an overdetermined constellation of forces than an organised group with a manifesto, but one aligned with transformations in capital and power in early twentieth-century Japan.

The discourses could come into conflict with each other and change over time. Ogawa Sawako, for instance, has noted shifts in the positions of pure film critics as the films they watched changed,[50] Naoki Yamamoto has noted the complex valences behind reforms' support for Bluebird films,[51] and Thomas

Lamarre has singled out the novelist Tanizaki Jun'ichirō as at least one reformer with a significantly different approach to the problem of cinematic essence.[52] My research on Kinugasa Teinosuke's *A Page of Madness/Kurutta ichipēji* (1926) shows how critics became divided after the mid-1920s over the concept of 'pure film', working off of different visions of modernity and modernism to support either a pure experimental cinema or the clear language of classical cinema (Fig. 1.2).[53] Komatsu has also noted how reformers did not monopolise the pages of all film publications, as fans of *onnagata* such as Tachibana Teijirō, did speak out in their defence.[54] Whether this could be said to constitute 'resistance' to the increasingly powerful forces of modernisation, perhaps as a form of class-consciousness, requires further investigation into the social and cultural dynamics of such discourses. Reformers definitely did treat the Japanese cinema of the time as inhabiting a realm that was not only cinematically but also socially and culturally other to what they considered the norms of the emerging Japanese nation. Thinkers such as Gonda Yasunosuke from the early 1910s or Iwasaki Akira in the late 1920s deviated from such class-based elitism and praised the relationship of film to the masses, but even Gonda's celebration of a cinema constructed by the masses was ambivalent towards Japanese film.[55] More research is needed to see if and how 'public spheres', in Miriam Hansen's sense of the term, operated in the era of early cinema in Japan.[56]

CONCLUSION

With the work of Noël Burch and others, research on early cinema in Japan was for a time at the forefront of not only efforts to delineate the difference of Japanese cinema but also research on alternatives to the classical Hollywood mode. In recent years, most research has retreated from making these grand claims, in part due to thorough historicisation that complicates overarching oppositions between East and West or Hollywood and oppositional cinema. Japanese early cinema is now important less because it serves scholars' need for a viable alternative to the dominant classical mode, than for the interesting issues it poses

Fig 1.2 *A Page of Madness* (Kinugasa Teinosuke, 1926, Shin kankakuha eiga renmei and Kinugasa eiga renmei) and the problem of the pure film.

with regard to cinema, signification, reception, class, gender, nation and globalism.

Early cinema research, however, has also become less prominent in the fields of film or Japanese studies, especially outside Japan. Given current interests in colonialism, globalism and political modernism, coupled with the difficulties associated with researching this era, recent research on Japanese film has focused more on the wartime era and the 1960s. There has been a new generation of Japanese scholars producing valuable work on early cinema in the last decade, but their work has been hampered by the lack of publishing venues and the general paucity of institutional support in Japan for film studies.

One more reason that research in Japanese early cinema has lost its previous prominence, however, is that it has ceased to play a leading role in the major conceptual or theoretical debates in film studies and related disciplines. For all his misconceptions, Burch still posed questions that energised scholars beyond disciplinary boundaries. My fear is that too much research on Japanese early cinema inside and outside Japan has become ghettoised by overly focusing on empirical issues, withdrawing from engagement in major conceptual debates and refraining from critical interactions with other disciplines. This is ironic because not only were theoretical pursuits crucial to the shaping of film culture in the 1910s and 1920s, but from the beginning, figures from that period as varied as Gonda Yasunosuke and Inagaki Taruho use their own theorisations of modernism to legitimise early cinema.[57] Rigorous archival research has been a fount for the field and has helped counter the overtheorising Burch and some others pursued, but the interpretation of the archive must still involve methodologies that interact with major conceptual issues. If it does not, Japanese early cinema research is in danger of itself, perhaps ironically, not making a difference, either for itself or for the field.

That would be a shame because work on early cinema in Japan holds the potential of doubly interrogating the field of cinema studies just at the point it is questioning itself. With the appearance of new digital media and the feared death of celluloid, film studies has turned back on itself to rethink what 'film' is, both to the discipline and to the culture as a whole. This has prominently included a return to early cinema, the years when film was the 'new media', with thinkers such as Lev Manovich finding parallels between the first digital media and the first films.[58] Researching Japanese early film holds great potential not only of joining this project, rethinking for instance what it means to talk about 'new media' in Japan, but also of rethinking the processes through which categories such as 'film' or 'film theory' came to be defined so Eurocentrically in world film culture and film studies. Claims about the newness of new media can be relativised not by reinscribing them in an earlier Euro-American film history but by reorienting them through parallels and differences with the early cinema of the non-West. Research of Japanese early cinema itself would become different, not by laying claim to Japan as the Other but by othering film studies and new media itself.

Notes

1 *Shinpa* (literally 'new school') was an early attempt at modernising Japanese theatre through the introduction of contemporary narratives. These often melodramatic stories, penned by such writers as Tokutomi Roka and Ozaki Kōyō, were frequently adapted to film, making *shinpa* one of the two main genres of the 1910s, as distinct from *kyūha*, the kabuki-influenced precursor to *jidaigeki*.

2 Joseph L. Anderson and Donald Richie, *The Japanese Film: Art and Industry*, rev. edn (Princeton, NJ: Princeton University Press, 1982), p. 35.

3 See Iijima Tadashi, *Nihon eigashi* (Tokyo: Hakusuisha, 1955); or the history Satō Tadao serialised in Satō Tadao, Tsurumi Shunsuke, Imamura Shōhei and Yamada Yōji (eds), *Kōza Nihon eiga* (Tokyo: Iwanami shoten, 1985–8).

4 Mitsuhiro Yoshimoto, *Kurosawa: Film Studies and Japanese Cinema* (Durham, NC: Duke University Press, 2000), p. 10.

5 Charles Musser, *High-class Moving Pictures: Lyman H. Howe and the Forgotten Era of Traveling Exhibition, 1880–1920* (Princeton, NJ: Princeton University

Press, 1991); Ben Singer, *Melodrama and Modernity: Early Sensational Cinema and Its Contexts* (New York: Columbia University Press, 2001).
6   André Gaudreault, *From Plato to Lumière: Narration and Monstration in Literature and Cinema* (Toronto: University of Toronto Press); Tom Gunning, 'The Cinema of Attractions: Early Film, Its Spectator and the Avant-Garde', *Wide Angle* vol. 8 nos. 3–4 (Fall 1986), pp. 63–70.
7   Noël Burch, *Life to Those Shadows* (Berkeley: University of California Press, 1990).
8   Noël Burch, *To the Distant Observer: Form and Meaning in the Japanese Cinema* (Berkeley: University of California Press, 1979), pp. 77–80.
9   See Satō Tadao's four-volume history, *Nihon eigashi* (Tokyo: Iwanami shoten, 2006).
10 Joseph L. Anderson, 'Spoken Silents in the Japanese Cinema; or, Talking to Pictures: Essaying the Katsuben, Contextualizing the Texts', in Arthur Nolletti Jr. and David Desser (eds), *Reframing Japanese Cinema* (Bloomington: Indiana University Press, 1992), pp. 286–7. Anderson prefers to use one of the many available terms for the *benshi*, *katsuben*, to refer to the institution since it is cinema specific, whereas *benshi* can equally refer to a regular orator.
11 Jeffrey Dym, *Benshi, Japanese Silent Film Narrators, and Their Forgotten Narrative Art of Setsumei: A History of Japanese Silent Film Narration* (Lewiston, NY: Edwin Mellen Press, 2003).
12 Iwamoto Kenji, 'Japanese Cinema until 1930: A Consideration of Its Formal Aspects', *Iris* no. 16 (1993), pp. 9–22.
13 See, for instance, Germain Lacasse, *Le bonimenteur de vues animées* (Quebec: Éditions Nota bene, 2000).
14 Roland Barthes, *The Empire of Signs* (New York: Hill and Wang, 1983).
15 See, for instance, Scott L. Malcomson, 'The Pure Land beyond the Seas', *Screen* vol. 26 nos. 3–4 (May–August 1985), pp. 23–33; or Harry Harootunian's preface to the electronic reprinting of Burch's book: '"Detour to the East": Noël Burch and the Task of Japanese Film', <https://quod.lib.umich.edu/c/cjs/graphics/filmburch.pdf>.
16 David Bordwell, 'Visual Style in Japanese Cinema, 1925–1945', *Film History* vol. 7 no. 1 (Spring 1995), pp. 5–31.
17 Aaron Gerow, *Visions of Japanese Modernity: Articulations of Cinema, Nation, and Spectatorship, 1895–1925* (Berkeley: University of California Press, 2010); Joanne Bernardi, *Writing in Light: The Silent Scenario and the Japanese Pure Film Movement* (Detroit, MI: Wayne State University Press, 2001).
18 Burch, *To the Distant Observer*, p. 13.
19 Gerow, *Visions of Japanese Modernity*.
20 Hideaki Fujiki, *Making Personas: Transnational Film Stardom in Modern Japan* (Cambridge, MA: Harvard University Asia Center, 2013).
21 Daisuke Miyao, *Sessue Hayakawa* (Durham, NC: Duke University Press, 2007); Daisuke Miyao, 'Nationalizing Madame Butterfly: The Formation of Female Stars in Japanese Cinema', in Daisuke Miyao (ed.), *The Oxford Handbook of Japanese Cinema* (Oxford: Oxford University Press, 2014), pp. 152–71.
22 Dōgase Masato, 'Kindai Nihon ni arawareta "kantokusha"', *Eizōgaku* no. 82 (2009), pp. 5–23.
23 These are figures calculated by the Museum of Modern Art, Tokyo, National Film Center based on their research on what was produced versus what is preserved in their collection. 'Eiga hozon to firumu ākaibu katsudō no genjō ni kan suru Q&A', National Film Center, <http://www.momat.go.jp/fc/aboutnfc/filmbunka/#eigahozon>.
24 For example, Yamamoto Kikuo, *Nihon eiga ni okeru gaikoku eiga no eikyō: Hikaku eigashi kenkyū* (Tokyo: Waseda daigaku shuppanbu, 1983).
25 See, for instance, Iwamoto Kenji, 'Film Criticism and the Study of Cinema in Japan', *Iconics* no. 1 (1987), pp. 129–46; or Aaron Gerow, 'The Process of Theory: Reading Gonda Yasunosuke and Early Film Theory', *Review of Japanese Culture and Society* vol. 22 (December 2010), pp. 37–43; Aaron Gerow, 'Critical Receptions: Historical Conceptions of Japanese Film Criticism', in Daisuke Miyao (ed.), *The Oxford Handbook of Japanese Cinema* (Oxford University Press, 2014), pp. 61–78.
26 Makino Mamoru, *Nihon eiga ken'etsushi* (Tokyo: Pandora, 2003); Hase Masato, 'The Origins of Censorship: Police and Motion Pictures in the Taishō Period', *Review of Japanese Culture and Society* vol. 10 (December 1998), pp. 14–23.
27 Fujiki Hideaki (ed.), *Kankyaku e no approach* (Tokyo: Shinwasha, 2011); Ueda Manabu, *Nihon eiga sōsōki no kōgyō to kankyaku* (Tokyo: Waseda daigaku shuppanbu, 2012); or Katō Mikirō, *Eigakan to*

28. For examples of recent research on exhibition, see the essays by Irie Yoshirō, Usui Michiko, Ueda Manabu, Watanabe Daisuke and Tajima Ryōichi in Iwamoto Kenji (ed.), *Nihon eiga no tanjō* (Tokyo: Shinwasha, 2011). The same collection sports essays on the *benshi* by Narita Yūta and Kobayashi Sadahiro, and on sound in the theatre by Daibō Masaki.

29. For a detailed history of the first year after the Cinématographe and the Vitagraph arrived, see Tsukada Yoshinobu, *Nihon eigashi no kenkyū* (Tokyo: Gendai shokan, 1980).

30. Iwamoto Kenji, *Gentō no seiki* (Tokyo: Shinwasha, 2002); Ōkubo Ryō, 'Utsushie kara eiga e', in Iwamoto Kenji (ed.), *Nihon eiga no tanjō* (Tokyo: Shinwasha, 2011), pp. 63–94.

31. Ōkubo Ryō, 'Kinodrama and Kineorama: Modernity and the Montage of Stage and Screen in Early Twentieth-Century Japan', *Iconics* 10 (2010), pp. 75–95; Ueda, *Nihon eiga sōsōki*.

32. Gerow, *Visions of Japanese Modernity*, pp. 40–65.

33. Ueda, *Nihon eiga sōsōki*.

34. Komatsu Hiroshi, 'The Fundamental Change: Japanese Cinema before and after the Earthquake of 1923', *Griffithiana* vol. 13 nos. 38/39 (October 1990), pp. 186–93; Komatsu Hiroshi, 'From Natural Colour to the Pure Motion Picture Drama: The Meaning of Tenkatsu Company in the 1910s of Japanese Film History', *Film History* vol. 7 no. 1 (Spring 1995), pp. 69–86; Komatsu Hiroshi, 'Shinpa eiga no keitaigaku', in Kurosawa Kiyoshi, Yoshimi Shun'ya, Lee Bong-Ou and Yomota Inuhiko (eds), *Eigashi o yominaosu* (Tokyo: Iwanami shoten, 2010), pp. 43–83.

35. Komatsu, 'From Natural Colour', p. 84.

36. See, for instance, my analysis of *Gorō Masamune kōshiden* (1915), in *Visions of Japanese Modernity*, pp. 102–3.

37. Komatsu Hiroshi, 'Some Characteristics of Japanese Cinema before World War I', in Arthur Nolletti Jr. and David Desser (eds), *Reframing Japanese Cinema* (Bloomington: Indiana University Press, 1992), pp. 229–58.

38. Miriam Silverberg, *Erotic Grotesque Nonsense: The Mass Culture of Japanese Modern Times* (Berkeley: University of California Press, 2006); Aaron Gerow, 'One Print in the Age of Mechanical Reproduction', *Screening the Past* no. 11 (2000), <http://tlweb.latrobe.edu.au/humanities/screeningthepast/firstrelease/fr1100/agfr11e.htm>.

39. For a consideration of invented traditions in Japan, see Stephen Vlastos (ed.), *Mirror of Modernity* (Berkeley: University of California Press, 1998).

40. Hase, 'The Origins of Censorship'; Gerow, *Visions of Japanese Modernity*, pp. 174–221.

41. Komatsu, 'Shinpa eiga no keitaigaku', p. 47.

42. See Aaron Gerow, 'Narrating the Nation-ality of a Cinema: The Case of Japanese Prewar Film', in Alan Tansman (ed.), *The Culture of Japanese Fascism* (Durham, NC: Duke University Press, 2009), pp. 185–211.

43. For an example of early cinema in the context of colonial Korea, see Pok Huan-mo, 'Kankoku Kōtaishi to Itō Hirobumi', in Iwamoto Kenji (ed.), *Eiga no naka no tennō* (Tokyo: Shinwasha, 2007), pp. 39–62.

44. For studies of early documentary and animation, see Abé Mark Nornes, *Japanese Documentary Film: The Meiji Era through Hiroshima* (Minneapolis: University of Minnesota Press, 2003); Daisuke Miyao, 'Before Anime: Animation and The Pure Film Movement in Prewar Japan', *Japan Forum* vol. 14 no. 2 (2002), pp. 191–209; and Tsugata Nobuyuki, *Nihon hatsu no animēshon sakka Kitayama Seitarō* (Kyoto: Rinsei shoten, 2007).

45. See Sasagawa Keiko, *Meiji Taishō Osaka eiga bunka no tanjō* (Suita: Kansai daigaku Osaka toshi isan kenkyū sentā, 2012).; Kobayashi Sadahiro, *Shinbun ni miru shoki Nihon eigashi* (Tokyo: Gakujutsu shuppankai, 2013); Tomita Mika, 'Koto kara eiga toshi sōsei no topology', in Kurosawa Kiyoshi, Yoshimi Shun'ya, Lee Bong-Ou and Yomota Inuhiko (eds), *Miru hito, tsukuru hito, kakeru hito* (Tokyo: Iwanami shoten, 2010), pp. 121–44; Ueda, *Nihon eiga sōsōki*.

46. Bernardi, *Writing in Light*.

47. Daisuke Miyao, *The Aesthetics of Shadow: Lighting and Japanese Cinema* (Durham, NC: Duke University Press, 2013).

48. Komatsu Hiroshi, 'Eigashi no aratana chihei', in Kurosawa Kiyoshi, Yoshimi Shun'ya, Lee Bong-Ou and Yomota Inuhiko (eds), *Eigashi o yominaosu* (Tokyo: Iwanami shoten, 2010), p. 10.

49. Gerow, *Visions of Japanese Modernity*, p. 107.

50. Ogawa Sadako, 'Gaikoku eiga to no taiji', in Kurosawa Kiyoshi, Yoshimi Shun'ya, Lee Bong-Ou and Yomota Inuhiko (eds), *Eigashi o yominaosu* (Tokyo: Iwanami shoten, 2010), pp. 85–115.

51 Naoki Yamamoto, 'Where Did the *Bluebird* of Happiness Fly?', *Iconics* vol. 10 (2010), pp. 143–66.
52 Thomas Lamarre, *Shadows on the Screen: Tanizaki Jun'ichirō on Cinema and 'Oriental' Aesthetics* (Ann Arbor: Center for Japanese Studies, University of Michigan, 2005).
53 Aaron Gerow, *Page of Madness: Cinema and Modernity in 1920s Japan* (Ann Arbor: Center for Japanese Studies, University of Michigan, 2008).
54 Komatsu, 'The Fundamental Change', p. 188.
55 See Gerow, *Visions of Japanese Modernity*, pp. 86–93.
56 Miriam Hansen, *Babel and Babylon: Spectatorship in American Silent Film* (Cambridge, MA: Harvard University Press, 1991).
57 See Gerow, 'The Process of Theory', and Ryan Cook, 'A Feeling for Endings: Inagaki Taruho's *Miroku* as a Memoir of Cinephilia', in Francesco Casetti, Jane Gaines and Valentina Re (eds), *Dall'inizio, alla fine. Theorie del cinema in prospettiva* (Udine: Forum, 2010), pp. 561–70.
58 Lev Manovich, *The Language of New Media* (Cambridge, MA: MIT Press, 2002).

2

AUTHORSHIP

Author, *sakka*, *auteur*

Alexander Jacoby

When, in 1959, Joseph Anderson and Donald Richie published the first English-language book-length history of Japanese cinema, it opened with a dedication to 'that little band of men who have tried to make the Japanese film industry what every film industry should be: a director's cinema'.[1] Unsurprisingly given their seminal role, the values represented by Anderson and Richie's book were to be mirrored in much early English-language writing on Japanese cinema, from Richie's own auteurist studies of canonical directors Kurosawa Akira and Ozu Yasujirō to Audie Bock's commentary on ten selected Japanese film directors.[2] While acknowledging that films are produced on a collaborative basis and in industrial conditions, these books nevertheless celebrated their chosen directors as artists displaying coherent thematic concerns and stylistic practices.

As in other areas of film studies, English-language scholarship of Japanese cinema from the 1980s onwards has broadened its focus to explore questions of genre, the conditions of production and socio-historical context. Such projects have sometimes been offered in deliberate opposition to an auteurist approach. Thus, recently surveying the field of academic scholarship on Japanese film in the West, Isolde Standish has challenged the traditional focus of Western critics on 'a clique of "art" or "high culture" film-makers around whom a critical *ortha doxa* has formed'.[3] In the past few decades, moreover, even some director-based studies have challenged traditional auteurist principles. Thus, Freda Freiberg's brief monograph, *Women in Mizoguchi's Films*, seeks 'to avoid discussing Mizoguchi's films as works of art created by a great artist' and points instead to film's status as a collaborative art created 'within a production system … which', due to a mixture of state censorship and commercial obligations, 'severely limits the powers of the individual artist to freely express his personal views'.[4] David Bordwell's canonical book on Ozu suggests that in the commentary of traditional critics, 'stylistic elements are yanked out of their formal systems and reified as typical Ozuian, or even typically Japanese'; instead, he insists on the need to situate that director's work in the context of wider film-making practices in Japan as a whole, arguing that 'only by comparison with prevailing standards and practices can we specify the particular workings of one film or a body of films'.[5] More recently, Catherine Russell's study of the films of Naruse Mikio contains a declaration that 'Unlike conventional auteurist studies, I cannot really testify to the distinctiveness of Naruse's cinema, the degree to which it departs from the industry norms of his career, or the degree to which it is representative and typical of other studio products'.[6] Nevertheless, Russell's project is an auteurist one in so far as it continues to trace a unified subject, that of 'vernacular modernism', through the output of a single director. Moreover, twenty-first-century scholarship on Japanese cinema still includes such firmly traditional auteurist studies such as Arthur Nolletti Jr.'s book on Gosho Heinosuke, which discusses the director's *oeuvre* in terms of 'a distinct style and set of themes that give unity and coherence to his career as a whole'.[7] Japanese cinema thus continues to be viewed in part through an auteurist lens.

In his influential reader on film authorship, John Caughie economically sums up the basic assumptions of the auteur theory in words that are suggestively echoed by Nolletti's on Gosho. The theory asserts that,

> A film, though produced collectively, is most likely to be valuable when it is essentially the product of its director …, that in the presence of a director who is genuinely an artist (an *auteur*) a film is more than likely to be the expression of his individual personality; and that this personality can be traced in a thematic and/or stylistic consistency over all (or almost all) the director's films.[8]

Caughie, like most Western scholars, traces these ideas to the French film journal, *Cahiers du cinéma*. But just as, in fact, earlier Western critics such as Paul Rotha had already insisted on the primacy of the director, so too questions of film authorship had long been a subject for critical debate in Japan.[9] In 1935, the Japanese critic Shimizu Chiyota opened an essay in *Eiga nenkan* with the question 'Who is the person who creates a film?', and acknowledged that 'as far as today's film-loving intellectuals are concerned, probably nine out of ten would say that the director is the creator of the film'.[10] While Shimizu went on to discuss the rival claims of the producer, his acknowledgment of an apparently broad acceptance of directorial authorship on the part of Japanese cinéphiles speaks for a long tradition in Japanese film criticism that anticipates the comparable assertions of the *Cahiers du cinéma* critics by some decades.

This chapter seeks to explore the way in which criticism both in the West and Japan has addressed the theme of directorial authorship in Japanese cinema. In the first place, I shall explore how Japanese critics debated and frequently championed the director's status as a film's primary author (*sakka*) during the prewar era. While to a degree this took place in an international context, as critics drew comparisons between Japanese and Western directors, a more profound international cross-fertilisation occurred in the postwar years with the popularisation of theories of directorial authorship via *Cahiers*. Elite Japanese film-makers became key auteurs in the analyses of Western writers, while the discourses advanced in *Cahiers* influenced a new generation of Japanese critics. While a critic such as Yamada Kōichi (who himself wrote for *Cahiers*) closely echoed the French line, influential figures such as Hasumi Shigehiko and Yoshida Kijū went on to challenge or undermine some of the values and assumptions of traditional auteurism, a process mirrored in a Western context by the seminal work of Noël Burch. Finally, I shall examine how recent academic criticism, notably that of Aaron Gerow, has proposed a modified auteurism in the context of the work of modern Japanese film directors who have courted the status of auteur with a postmodern self-consciousness. In charting these perspectives over time, I hope to show how questions surrounding the status of the director have not only addressed the specific question of film authorship but also helped to illuminate broader questions about the nature of the medium, the workings of the industry and the place of a national cinema in an evolving international context.

Commenting on the critical values espoused in the 1910s and early 1920s by the so-called 'Pure Film Movement', which sought to modernise Japanese cinema, Aaron Gerow observes that 'a version of auteurism was prevalent in film criticism from its first decades', albeit 'one first centered in the screenplay'.[11] As Gerow notes elsewhere, it was 'pure film directors like Kaeriyama [Norimasa who] were the first to be accredited, in journals, with authorial status', and 'by 1922, *Kinema junpō* was running a series of feature articles on the new pure film directors'.[12] This coincided with developments in the industry: 'with studios like Shōchiku soon organizing the studio structure into teams led by directors, the groundwork was laid for the Japanese director system'.[13]

By the late 1920s, what Komatsu Hiroshi refers to as 'the auteurist view of the cinema', centred on the director, was becoming established in periodicals such as *Eiga hyōron*. As Komatsu notes:

> Monographic studies were devoted not only to European and American directors, but also to some Japanese directors. In 1927 the monthly film magazine *Eiga hyōron* published special issues on Minoru Murata and Kiyohiko Ushihara (March and December respectively), along with monographic studies of Charles Chaplin, Jacques Feyder, Ernst Lubitsch and F.W. Murnau.[14]

Through the prewar era *Eiga hyōron* regularly dedicated specific issues to noted directors, including both domestic and foreign talents. Other journals and books essayed a comparable auteurist focus. The Japanese term *sakka*, analogous to 'author' or 'auteur', was already widely used in these publications to describe the director, and prewar Japanese-language analyses of directors described their work in terms of consistent stylistic traits and thematic concerns.

In 1936, *Eiga hyōron* devoted a special issue to Japanese film directors, with separate essays focusing on major film-makers of the prewar era including Mizoguchi Kenji, Ozu Yasujirō, Yamanaka Sadao, Uchida Tomu, Shimizu Hiroshi and Itami Mansaku. Throughout the text, the terms *sakka* and *eiga sakka* ('film author') are used to refer to the chosen directors, and at least one critic explicitly considered the claims of the director to be regarded as author of a film whose authorship might readily be contested. In an article under the somewhat polemical heading 'The Author of *Older Brother, Younger Sister* is Kimura Sotoji', Itō Akio discusses the authorship of *Older Brother, Younger Sister/Ani imōto* (1936), an adaptation by director Kimura of a respected short story by Murō Saisei, which had won the Bungei Konwakai Award, a prize established by the Home Ministry, on publication in 1934. Acknowledging the film's fidelity to its source text, Itō also observes that the screenwriter, Eguchi Matakichi, bears some authorial responsibility but goes on to discuss the film's relationship to Kimura's other works as director, and eventually concludes that 'the author of *Older Brother, Younger Sister* is, after all, Kimura Sotoji'.[15]

Likewise, in 1939 Tsumura Hideo structured his book *Film and Critique* primarily around directors, with individual chapters devoted to key Western and Japanese film-makers (along with such actors as Marlene Dietrich and Jean Gabin). Within Japan, Tsumura addresses directors such as Mizoguchi, Yamanaka, Kinugasa Teinosuke and Toyoda Shirō. His essay on Mizoguchi directly compares the director with various contemporaries, seeking to outline the dominant thematic concerns of each: thus, Naruse Mikio is presented as the maker of films about the private lives of artists, Gosho Heinosuke specialises in films about women and couples in the *shitamachi*, and Mizoguchi himself is the chronicler of the private lives of Gion's geisha.[16] Later in the essay, Tsumura, in terms strikingly anticipatory of Western postwar auteurist discourse, speaks of 'the director's vision', using the English-derived *katakana* word *bijon*.[17]

As Gerow notes, a stress on authorship was early associated with the project to modernise Japanese cinema and, in particular, with the desire to establish a stable text and authorial subject in contrast to the various and shifting texts created by the *benshi* commentary, which overlaid the visual discourse of Japanese silent films.[18] This project of modernisation was to some extent a project to align Japanese cinema with Western norms, and the deliberate evocation of Hollywood and European films in the works of prewar directors such as Ozu and Shimazu Yasujirō relates suggestively to their wider interest in the styles and techniques of Western film. This cosmopolitanism is reflected in some prewar Japanese auteurist criticism, so that, for instance, Tōdō Satoshi, writing in *Eiga shūdan* in 1936, suggests that 'it is indeed as if Itō Daisuke's footprints lead us instantly onto Sternberg's path' while one may 'catch the scent of René Clair' in the work of Itami Mansaku.[19] Already, then, in the prewar era, questions of authorship were being discussed in Japan in a transnational context. In the postwar years, this context was to be deepened as Japanese cinema itself became a transnational object. The discovery of Japanese cinema in the West opened it up as a subject of European and North American auteurist discourse, while, in turn, Western notions of film authorship began to exert an influence both on film criticism and film production in Japan.

POSTWAR JAPANESE CINEMA, THE AUTEUR THEORY AND THE *NŪBERU BĀGU*

In 1958, Marxist critic Iwasaki Akira wrote a study of Japan's *eiga sakka* with individual chapters dedicated to twelve established directors (Imai Tadashi, Yoshimura Kōzaburō, Toyoda Shirō, Naruse Mikio, Mizoguchi Kenji, Ichikawa Kon, Kurosawa Akira, Kinoshita Keisuke, Shibuya Minoru, Ozu Yasujirō, Gosho Heinosuke and Uchida Tomu – all, except Mizoguchi, then still living) plus an account of a number of emerging talents such as Kobayashi Masaki and Nomura Yoshitarō. Iwasaki had been critical of the concept of directorial authorship in the prewar era, and despite this ostensibly auteurist organisation, he explicitly acknowledges the complexities of film authorship:

> Discussing the author of a film is always a complex problem. At times, he is really a film artisan producing work at the company's behest, but at other times, pressing his own ideas on the company, he realises his own ambitions. Moreover, in either case, since he writes the scenario or directs, he is expected to stamp his personality everywhere, but for the many film personnel who do not naturally display a very strong individuality, the usual state of things is that this too is not conspicuous. With the exception of such people as Kurosawa Akira, Ozu Yasujirō, Shimizu Hiroshi and Yagi Yasutarō, who obviously are authors maintaining a characteristic personality, the discussion of the film author always encounters this kind of difficulty.[20]

Acknowledging that film authorship is a contested matter, Iwasaki includes not only directors such as Kurosawa in his list of 'obvious authors' but also a screenwriter, Yagi Yasutarō. Writing in the context of a director noted for his literary adaptations, Toyoda Shirō, he goes on to explore how the issue of authorship might be further complicated by the fact of his films' derivation from a pre-existing literary source.[21] Iwasaki opens his book by commenting on the increasing fame of Japanese directors in Europe, including not only Kurosawa Akira but also the less widely distributed Imai Tadashi. He notes the attention paid to Imai by French film historian Georges Sadoul, as well as reporting that French film star Gérard Phillipe, visiting Japan, had expressed the wish to meet him.[22] In a suggestive coincidence, the year 1951, which saw Kurosawa's *Rashomon/Rashōmon* (1950) scoop the Golden Lion at Venice, had also seen the first issue appear of *Cahiers du cinéma*, which, as we have seen, championed a model of film appreciation focused on the creativity and artistic personality of the director.

Although the polemical arguments about directorial authorship made in Europe and North America during the 1950s and 1960s occurred primarily in the context of Hollywood cinema, Japanese film nevertheless occupied an important position for the *Cahiers* critics. Their attention focused particularly on Mizoguchi, who was not only critically celebrated but would also prove a crucial influence on the later filmmaking practice of *Cahiers* writers such as Jean-Luc Godard and, especially, Jacques Rivette. Mizoguchi was also a favourite of the critics associated with the British magazine *Movie*, which championed an auteurist approach from its foundation in 1962; its editor, Ian Cameron, was to describe Mizoguchi as 'arguably the greatest of directors'.[23]

In both Anglophone and Francophone circles, claims for Mizoguchi's status as auteur were intense and highly felt. Having dismissed a considerable number of other Japanese directors as mere *metteurs en scène*, Rivette wrote that: 'Mizoguchi alone imposes the sense of a specific language and world, answerable only to him.'[24] Rivette's commentary suggested an awareness that the Japanese cinema, like that of Hollywood, emerged from a studio system in which creative freedom was not absolute. Thus, he dismissed a number of other Japanese film-makers by aligning them with French directors associated with the so-called *cinéma du papa*: Kurosawa with Claude Autant-Lara, Imai with André Cayatte, Kinugasa with Christian-Jacque.[25]

Three years after Mizoguchi's death, Eric Rohmer (writing not in *Cahiers* but in *Arts*) eulogised *Ugetsu/Ugetsu monogatari* (1953) in classic humanist terms: 'Like all great works, *Ugetsu* shatters the boundaries between genres and the frontiers between nations …. You will perceive clearly the common source of our humanity, the crucible from which emerged both the *Odyssey* and the Round Table cycle, works with which *Ugetsu* has troubling analogies.'[26] Jean-Luc Godard likewise drew comparisons with acknowledged masterpieces of Western literature: *Ugetsu*, he claimed, 'is *Don Quixote*, *The Odyssey* and *Jude the Obscure* rolled into one'.[27]

The *Cahiers* critics' admiration for Mizoguchi was shared not only by the *Movie* critics but by Anglo-Saxon writers associated with more conventional journals, and the tactic of championing Mizoguchi by reference to canonical literature can be found in

English-language sources as well as French ones. Eric Rhode's *Sight and Sound* review of *Ugetsu* (released commercially in the UK in 1962, just after taking fourth place in the *Sight and Sound* critics' poll) claims that Mizoguchi is 'generally recognised as one of the masters of the cinema' and compares the director successively with Jacobean drama, Hokusai, Malory (and Tolkien), Ibsen, Ancient Greek theatre and Shakespeare.[28] This tactic was followed also by early writers on Ozu, whose films were achieving notice in the West by the time of his death in 1963. Tom Milne, writing a few months earlier, compares the consistency of the director's work with 'those endless Picasso variations on the dove', and approvingly cites Alan Lovell's comparison of Ozu with Jane Austen as artists who 'usually [keep] to [their] little bit of ivory'.[29]

In addition to evoking figures of the highest stature within (primarily) the Western tradition, these comparisons constitute a powerful assertion of authorship on the part of Mizoguchi and Ozu, since the authorship of a painting or a literary text was, at the time (Roland Barthes was not to publish *The Death of the Author* until 1967), a relatively uncontroversial matter. By comparing Mizoguchi with Hokusai, Ibsen and Shakespeare, Rhode presents him not only as an artist of outstanding mastery but as indisputably the author of the films bearing his name. Indeed, as a statement of authorial consistency Austen's 'bit of ivory' (a figure of speech devised to contrast her own style with the 'strong, manly, spirited sketches' of her nephew Edward) is very close in spirit to Ozu's own description of himself as a restaurateur with a restricted menu: 'I only know how to make tofu …. Cutlets and other fancy stuff, that's for other directors.'[30]

These claims for directorial authorship on the part of specific, respected film-makers were more broadly reflected in Joseph Anderson and Donald Richie's book-length history of Japanese cinema. A chapter on directors singled out nine key film-makers either still or recently active (Mizoguchi Kenji had died in 1956; the others were all still living) and discussed the work of each in a medium-length profile. All nine directors eventually enjoyed retrospectives of their work in the West, and although these in some cases took place decades later, Anderson and Richie's role in canon formation for pre-1960 Japanese cinema cannot be overestimated.

Anderson and Richie's history was published in the year that witnessed the international emergence of the French New Wave, a movement that would decisively foreground the notion of directorial authorship. François Truffaut's *Les Quatre cents coups*, screened to great acclaim at Cannes in 1959, and Jean-Luc Godard's *À bout de souffle* were both released in Japan in March 1960.[31] Both film-makers saw their early film-making practice in part as an extension of the claims they had made in *Cahiers* for directorial authorship. Thus, Anderson and Richie's championship of the director was part of a broader trend in international film criticism and film-making, and although their book predated the general popularisation of auteur theory that emerged in the wake of the *nouvelle vague*, their vocabulary in relation to Japanese cinema was very similar. 'Obviously, as in any film industry, the really outstanding movie is the exception rather than the rule, and – just as obviously – it is usually the responsibility, if not the entire conception of a single man. It is these single men, all over the world, who have created the art of film.'[32]

For Eric Cazdyn, Anderson and Richie's perspective typifies a liberal individualist vision of authorship, a 'great man theory', which asserts that 'an individual can rise up and produce greatness within – if not transcend – any structure'.[33] Yet the claims for authorship made by Anderson and Richie on behalf of the Japanese director were grounded in the specific conditions of production in Japan. For the *Cahiers* critics, authorship was perceived primarily through patterns discerned in the films themselves – the 'thematic and/or stylistic consistency' of which Caughie speaks – rather than through the expressed aims of film-makers, or the empirical situation of directors working within a commercial system. The assumptions underlying Anderson's and Richie's argument derived from a more precise industrial context. Japan's studios, they claimed, operated according to a so-called 'director system' rather than a 'producer system' as in the West:

> The Japanese film director, as far as having the final say goes, is among the strongest in the world …. The

director is responsible for everything in a film ....
His duties and responsibilities are greater than those of his foreign counterpart for he must assume some of the duties which elsewhere would be handled by a producer.[34]

'The top-line directors,' they asserted, 'are generally given a free hand in producing what they want.' Audiences too, they claimed, understood the importance of the director: 'Directors in Japan often have a box-office appeal which in the West is usually exercised only by the stars.'[35]

These claims must be approached with one or two clear caveats. In the first place, 'the Japanese film director' as defined by Anderson and Richie is specifically a 'top-line' director, and they make no explicit claim for directorial authorship on the part of less prestigious film-makers. Moreover, they overlook different production policies at different studios: the 'director system' was associated primarily with Shōchiku, while Tōhō tended to operate according to a 'producer's system' more analogous to the Hollywood model. Moreover, as Hasumi Shigehiko has noted, one facet of the Japanese studio system, in contrast to Hollywood, was that directors 'consistently used the same staff',[36] so that the apparent coherence of a director's output may in part be attributed to the collaborative work of a team of personnel. Nevertheless, Anderson and Richie deserve credit for attempting to show how, in Japan, an auteurist discourse could plausibly emerge from conditions of production and reception. The perception of recurrent patterns and motifs in a director's cinema was explained in the light of the actual degree of responsibility exercised by the director in the creation of films, and the claims of importance being advanced for the director were justified by reference to their prominence in the marketing of films and their ability to secure audiences.

From the vantage point of 1959, this argument was advanced in the context of a commercial studio system at a time when independent production in Japan was minimal. But that year also marked a significant development in studio-based film production within Japan, and in particular at Shōchiku, where Kido Shirō, the influential head of production, broke with the norms of the traditional apprenticeship system, in a decision that, Maureen Turim suggests, was influenced by Italian neo-realism and the appearance in 1957–8 of early films by directors later associated with the *nouvelle vague*.[37] Like the French film-makers, Ōshima was an active film critic, who had harshly attacked the conventions of commercial film-making at Shōchiku's Ōfuna studios. Kido, Mark Downing Roberts claims, sought 'to promote intellectuals to the position of director, breaking with the old system of apprenticeship'.[38] This break was not, however, decisive, since conventionally trained directors, including those of an older generation, continued to work at Shōchiku; and, indeed, Ōshima and his colleagues had themselves served a traditional apprenticeship as assistant directors at Shōchiku even if they received promotion more rapidly than was the norm. In fact, as Roland Domenig writes: 'The Japanese Nouvelle Vague was essentially a product of the studios ... whereas the French Nouvelle Vague like many other innovative movements in Europe established itself outside the studio system.'[39]

Despite this vital distinction, the young directors operating at Shōchiku, who, alongside Ōshima, included Shinoda Masahiro and Yoshida Kijū (aka Yoshishige), quickly earned explicit comparison with their French contemporaries. As early as December 1959, *Eiga hyōron* had published a special edition entitled 'Japanese Cinema's New Wave', and by 1960, another Japanese publication, the *Shūkan yomiuri*, was using the phrase *nūberu bāgu* in conscious homage to the French term and thus in implicit endorsement of an auteurist perspective.[40] Finding their creative freedom inhibited by studio priorities, the *nūberu bāgu* directors were eventually to leave Shōchiku and work independently. Nevertheless, Shōchiku continued to distribute the films Ōshima made for his own production company, Sōzōsha, while the leading sponsor of art film in late 1960s and 1970s Japan, the Art Theatre Guild, received funding from one of Shōchiku's major competitors, Tōhō.

If the emergence of the *nūberu bāgu* directors suggests the growing international influence of their French compatriots on the level of film production, the 1960s was also marked by growing connections between

Japanese and French film criticism. Although the work of the *Cahiers* critics did not begin to be translated into Japanese until the late 1960s, it nevertheless exerted an influence on some of the leading Japanese critics of the era, a number of whom were Francophiles and French speakers.

By 1965, *Cahiers* had itself acquired a Japanese contributor. Yamada Kōichi, who had been François Truffaut's interpreter during his visit to Japan in 1963, wrote regularly for the magazine while on a government scholarship in Paris, focusing largely but not exclusively on Japanese cinema, conducting interviews and authoring film reviews and analyses of the work of directors such as Ichikawa Kon and Imamura Shōhei. Yamada's writings in *Cahiers* followed the auteurist line and shared some of the specific mannerisms of early Western auteurist analysis of Japanese cinema. Thus, he evokes canonical Western literature, comparing Kurosawa's *Living/Ikiru* (1952) to Tolstoy, and dismisses 'mere' *metteurs en scène* as opposed to genuine auteurs, so that Ichikawa's cinema is damned with faint praise as possessing 'a perfection which defines itself by the absence of flaws or remarkable qualities', and the director is condemned for accepting subject matter assigned to him by a company 'for which he is nothing but a salaried worker'.[41] At the same time, an early piece on Imamura offered precisely the *difficulty* of generalising about the director's style as evidence that his cinema was 'a powerful and effective means of approaching, studying and analysing reality', in which 'each subject can impose its own style'.[42] If this acknowledgment hints at a possible incompatibility between the *politique des auteurs* and the neo-realist aesthetic championed by André Bazin, Yamada nevertheless sees Imamura's commitment to realism precisely as the consistent authorial trait of his cinema.

After Yamada's return to Japan, he was to subtitle Truffaut's films and translate his writings. He also continued to author film criticism, with a focus on 'cinematic pleasure' and 'that which is beautiful'.[43] He addressed both Western and Japanese film and his focus on the latter spanned canonical auteurs such as Ozu, Mizoguchi and Kurosawa and popular genre film-makers such as Makino Masahiro and Mori Kazuo. The acceptance of such figures may represent a more generous evaluation of the talented *metteur en scène* than was implied by Yamada's dismissal of Ichikawa in *Cahiers*. Indeed, in a generally admiring 1977 essay on Makino, Yamada specifically denies the director's status as an auteur in the traditional sense, while nevertheless celebrating the diversity and craftsmanship of his films. After enumerating the huge variety of films in which he worked, from ninja film to melodrama to operetta and musical comedy, Yamada comments:

> Rather than calling him a film author, one might say that he would do anything as far as film was concerned; he was a film-obsessed artisan director. Of course he was not a perfectionist who, in order to persist with one theme and one style, would never compromise, but he would manage admirably with whatever subject and under whatever conditions he picked up his camera. He was an expert at being good enough, a master of snapshots.[44]

While this argument, in its willingness to celebrate the skilled artisan, moves generously beyond the relatively restrictive criteria of traditional auteurism, Yamada's focus remains largely on the celebration of individual films and film-makers. Two other critics of his generation, both strongly influenced by the French line, essayed a modified auteurism that challenged some of the assumptions behind notions of directorial authorship and attempted to develop a more extensive theoretical context. These were critic and scholar Hasumi Shigehiko and New Wave film-maker Yoshida Kijū.

Commenting on his own films in 1969, at the end of his first, most productive decade as a director and shortly after completing his representative work, *Eros Plus Massacre/Eros purasu gyakusatsu* (1970), Yoshida seems explicitly to assert his identity as an auteur in the classic sense of a director whose *oeuvre* displays a thematic consistency: 'When I look back on the past ten years and reflect on the many films I have tried to make as eloquently as possible, I realize that, in the end, I have persistently repeated just one single thing' (Fig. 2.1).[45] Yet Yoshida challenged a number of the ideological assumptions underlying an auteurist discourse. Under the telling heading, 'A Logic of Self-Negation', he argues against the author's

Fig 2.1 *Eros Plus Massacre/Eros plus gyakusatsu* (Yoshida Kijū, 1970, Gendai eigasha).

authority to define meaning, proposing an ideal of active, collaborative interpretation and understanding on the part of film-maker and audience. Yoshida critically associates the value traditionally placed on personal authorship with the particular conditions of the studio system; in this context of 'pre-fabricated' films, he asserts, 'what earns the greatest respect is the individuality of the filmmaker and a refined directing technique. The director then expects temperate, sensible, and appreciative behaviour from the audience.'[46]

In contrast to this, Yoshida offers an ideal of self-transcendence that opens up a space for creative interaction on the spectator's part. A new, egalitarian relationship is proposed in which the audience is as much the auteur as the director:

> Making a film is an act that transcends me ....
> The audience that receives this film also transcends the 'film they are made to watch,' insofar as they themselves create it. Within this new relationship ... the creator and the viewer enter into a free dialogue with one another.[47]

In the light of such comments, it is interesting to reflect on Yoshida's own in-depth analysis of Ozu, who became the subject of a book-length study by the younger film-maker. Written some three decades after the essay cited above, it both qualifies and sustains the premises advanced by Yoshida's early work on authorship. Calling Ozu 'a lone rebel',[48] Yoshida seems to align himself with traditional discourses of directorial individualism but, nevertheless, reads Ozu in the light of his own film theory and, in particular, of his belief that cinema should enable a free dialogue between director and audience. Yoshida's Ozu seems to anticipate Yoshida's own desire to avoid imposing meaning on the spectator and to allow an active, imaginative response. Criticising the ending of *A Hen in the Wind/Kaze no naka no mendori* (1948) for its excessive clarity of meaning, Yoshida writes:

> Ozu-san did not find it pleasurable when his images sent specific meanings to his viewers. He found it sterile. He was afraid that moving images ... would prevent his viewers from using their unlimited imaginations. He ... was afraid that what his film's images defined would disturb and distort the real state of the world. This means that he deeply loved cinema, but, at the same time he held strong doubts about it.[49]

The last sentence in particular suggests the influence of Yoshida's contemporary, Hasumi Shigehiko, also the author of a book on Ozu. A contradictory figure, Hasumi was explicitly indebted to the *Cahiers* critics and a close friend of Truffaut, whose films he championed in Japan. At times, Hasumi's work seems more or less traditionally auteurist, striving to identify recurrent motifs and themes in a director's *oeuvre*. For instance, an essay on John Ford demonstrates the persistence of the motif of throwing in the director's work and identifies it as 'a *theme* which, through its repetition, articulates the narrative structure of the films, whatever their genre …. It is a unifying element, making analogous moments from different films correspond.'[50] Yet Hasumi was also a critic who, like Yoshida's Ozu, 'held strong doubts' about cinema, and these doubts were expressed in a criticism that endeavoured to emphasise the limitations of the film medium. Ryan Cook contrasts this approach with traditional auteurist assumptions: 'Hasumi would not celebrate … authorial genius or the perfection of works as objects. What he has valued in directors are the peculiarities, perversions, failings, or handicaps that make films confess their own absurdity.'[51] Cook cites a famous essay on Howard Hawks – significantly, a totemic figure in Anglo-French auteurist discourse – in which Hasumi:

> Moves through the oeuvre and finds in film after film an insistent 'back and forth movement' …. Something displaced is preposterously put back …. The unique gesture becomes adequate to the general 'absurdity' of cinema … in relation to which form becomes empty and abstract …. The eye that thus encounters a Hawks film … sees past the dualism of thought that pits the classicism of the studio system against the avant-garde: the two are similar as abstractions that, far from denying cinematic absurdity, reflect it in their form.[52]

Thus, an auteurist analysis is used to undermine auteurism: the perception of recurrent motifs across the body of Hawks's cinema is developed into a claim about the medium as a whole that serves to erase distinctions between the *oeuvres* of different film directors and, indeed, between different production systems. Far from championing the artistic achievement a single director, Hasumi's iconoclastic appropriation of a key *Cahiers* auteur ironically questions the value of cinema as a whole.

Hasumi's book-length study of Ozu, published in Japan in 1983, offers a related perspective. While Hasumi accepts Ozu's individuality as a film-maker, his primary concern is to use Ozu as a case study to reveal general principles of cinema:

> It does not matter whether or not Ozu was an exceptional genius; the problem is not to evaluate his greatness in the history of cinema. The essential thing is … to discern, even in the moment of the 'filmic experience', what cinema is and what it is not.[53]

Again, Hasumi uses aspects of traditional auteurist analysis to challenge the premises of auteurism. Like an orthodox auteur study, the book is structured around the discussion of recurrent motifs in Ozu's work, several of which form chapter headings; and Hasumi does not deny that a director's attitudes and worldview may be expressed through his films. But he insists that this kind of 'personal vision' or worldview is less valuable than the degree to which a film-maker's practice may expose the workings of the medium itself:

> It is certain that like other filmmakers, Ozu wanted to express his own ideas, his conception of humanity. But just like the act of expressing oneself in words, the act of filming is possible only if one accepts constraints. An idea that one could communicate without highlighting the limits of film language will not have a positive value. Ozu's cinema is the attempt to express these limits.[54]

Hasumi's approach suggests a paradoxical response to auteur theory. Ozu's individuality as a director resides in the way in which his films highlight general properties of the film medium, which (Hasumi implies) are left unacknowledged by other film-makers. Ozu's ideas are valued not for themselves but in so far as they make these properties explicit.

One might compare the project of Noël Burch's classic English-language book, *To the Distant Observer*, which likewise enacts a subversive variant on auteurism in the context of Japanese cinema. Burch too retains a focus on individual directors: indeed, several chapters consist of the detailed formal analysis of the work of particular film-makers, and, as in a traditional auteurist study, Burch seeks to evaluate individual films, dividing them into masterpieces and minor works and locating them within the development of individual directorial careers. Burch's criteria for excellence, however, differ from those of traditional auteurists in that he aims not to champion the individuality of specific directors, but to demonstrate how they participate in a collective approach to cinema associated with long-standing Japanese aesthetic traditions and presented in specific contrast to the stylistic and structural norms of Western cinema. Writing as a self-confessed 'distant observer', Burch champions Japanese cinema as an oppositional mode to the Hollywood and European cinema he repudiates. It follows that he values particular Japanese films not primarily because they express a personal voice but because they conform to a national artistic tradition. Accordingly, Burch claims that like the work of 'the great [Japanese] poets, painters or sculptors of the past … Ozu's *oeuvre* is not merely an individual achievement but, more significantly, that of a historical and national collectivity'.[55] Likewise, Shimizu Hiroshi is acclaimed as 'an admirably representative figure, precisely because of the manner in which he remained so faithful and for so long to what we may regard as a combination of basic Japanese traits' – a statement immediately qualified by Burch's insistence that these traits 'seem to appear in a very large number of Japanese films indeed'.[56] Thus, while Hasumi seeks to appropriate concepts of directorial authorship to shed light on the principles of cinema as a whole, Burch does so to shed light on the principles of *Japanese* cinema in particular and to highlight its essential difference from that of the West. In doing so, he arguably paved the way for scholars such as Freiberg and Bordwell who, as previously mentioned, continued to focus on specific directors while challenging traditional auteurist principles.

AUTHORSHIP IN MODERN CINEMA

In 1991, a version of *Cahiers du cinéma* commenced publication in Japan. As its name suggested, *Cahiers du Cinéma Japon* incorporated not only translations from the French publication but also original writings in Japanese.[57] Although the French *Cahiers* was long past its auteurist heyday, the Japanese magazine was edited by a convinced auteurist, Umemoto Yōichi, and it numbered among its writers several men who had been students of Hasumi Shigehiko at Rikkyō University including aspiring directors such as Kurosawa Kiyoshi, Aoyama Shinji and Shinozaki Makoto.

The Japanese film industry that these young men entered in the latter years of the twentieth century had witnessed a drastic transformation in the conditions of production. The major studios had declined, alongside the 'director's system' that operated within them, yet the emergence of smaller or independent production companies has arguably opened up new spaces for authorial individuality. Satō Tadao writes that 'Japanese cinema has lost the strong support of investment capital, but it has gained more freedom in its production.'[58] Certainly, the return of Japanese cinema to broad international awareness in the past thirty years has been premised to a substantial degree on the identification and celebration of auteur directors. Even the growing appreciation of Japanese genre cinema such as so-called 'J-horror' has seen directors such as Kurosawa Kiyoshi, Nakata Hideo, Tsukamoto Shinya and Miike Takashi singled out for discussion. The importance ascribed to directors such as Kurosawa is premised mainly on their ability to bring a personal inflection to generic structures: Kurosawa's own comment that he works in genres 'in order to better distance myself from them', is paradigmatic.[59] Meanwhile, film-makers such as Kore-eda Hirokazu and Kitano Takeshi have been embraced as international auteurs, their work securing screenings at prestigious film festivals, commercial releases in Western countries and DVD releases. While classical Japanese directors such as Mizoguchi in the last years of his career and Kurosawa Akira after *Rashomon* worked in the knowledge that their films would probably be seen in the West as well as in Japan, modern Japanese directors such as Kore-eda and Kitano operate in a context where the status of auteur is an internationally marketable commodity, and potentially one to be self-consciously courted.

Aaron Gerow's book on Kitano proposes a novel version of directorial authorship that reflects suggestively on the situation of modern Japanese film-makers. Discussing a director who is primarily associated with a specific genre, the gangster film, but whose work has also incorporated period drama (*jidaigeki*), low comedy, drama and such generically unclassifiable works as *Dolls* (2002) and *Takeshis'* (2005), Gerow judges his work to be both a challenge to traditional auteurist assumptions and a model of a new, specifically Japanese brand of authorship. 'Kitano's works', he argues, 'may indeed constitute a single text, not one modelled on the bourgeois novel, as in auteur theory, but on the *manzai* act with its dialogic conflicts.'[60] For Gerow, Kitano is 'both an auteur and someone who self-consciously critiques auteurism, who pursues his unique worldview and escapes any who would define it'.[61] This latter statement helps to clarify the nature of Kitano's departure from auteurist norms. Mere diversity within the *oeuvre* of a director is no novelty; one might relate the generic variety of Kitano's output to the 'systematic series of oppositions' that Peter Wollen identified several decades ago in the contrast between adventure film and comedy in the work of Howard Hawks, or the 'shifting variations' he found in John Ford.[62] What sets Kitano apart is not his diversity but his self-consciousness – a quality that marks him out as an archetypal postmodern auteur.

This self-consciousness, and the complexity of Kitano's authorial personality, is expressed in part through the relationship between his various public faces. Kitano, like Charlie Chaplin, Woody Allen or Clint Eastwood in the West, is an auteur whose status as such is defined in part by his presence *in front of the camera* in most of the films he has directed. In modern Japanese cinema, similar assertions of authorship through acting can be seen in a film such as *A Snake of June/Rokugatsu no hebi* (2002), where director Tsukamoto Shin'ya plays the key role of the blackmailer, a character who functions within the narrative as a surrogate 'director'. Equipped with a camera he has used to take incriminating photographs of the heroine, he blackmails her into a series of sexually suggestive actions, contacting her by mobile phone to supply instructions. In these scenes, the off-screen, yet controlling presence of the blackmailer seems to symbolise the control exercised by the film-maker over his actors, who follow his instructions to create a performance observed and recorded by his camera. Tsukamoto's on-screen presence in this role seems a visible assertion of authorship on his part.

Kitano, however, complicates this by insisting on the distinction between his directorial and actorly personae, designating them with separate names: thus, the credits of his films list the star as 'Beat' Takeshi, while crediting 'Kitano Takeshi' as director. Gerow notes that *Getting Any?/Minna yatteru ka* (1995), which marked a move into slapstick and scatological comedy, was billed in advertisements as the 'début film of Beat Takeshi', and was 'implicitly a critique of auteurist discourses themselves'.[63] Even the title of a film such as *Takeshis'* highlights Kitano's challenge to auteurism: not merely 'a Takeshi Kitano film', the film is an explicit commentary on the duality of the actor–director's public persona. Through such tactics, the notion of authorial consistency is self-consciously problematised.

If Kitano complicates notions of authorship through the presentation of multiple on-screen and off-screen personae, Kore-eda does so through homage and allusion. From the beginning of his career in feature film-making, Kore-eda attracted immediate comparisons with the canonical directors of Japanese film and in particular with Ozu: as David Desser writes, 'there have been almost universal invocations of Ozu in reviews of *Maborosi/Maboroshi no hikari* (1995)',[64] and such comparisons have subsequently been repeated in the context especially of *Nobody Knows/Dare mo shiranai* (2004), *Still Walking/Aruitemo aruitemo* (2008) and *I Wish/Kiseki* (2011). Kore-eda's cinema frequently makes direct reference to Ozu, such as the shots of industrial chimneys belching smoke in *Nobody Knows* or the static 'pillow shot' of a vase at night and group shots of family members seated around a low table in *Still Walking* (Fig. 2.2). Although Kore-eda seems in many respects the most traditional of modern Japanese directors, his self-conscious redeployment of instantly recognisable motifs from a canonical film-maker again suggest a postmodern approach.

Discussing these elements of homage, Mitsuyo Wada-Marciano argues that Kore-eda situates himself not only into the context of Japanese film but also in that of the canon of international art cinema:

> What Kore-eda's film embodies through these acts of cinematic mimicry taps into the popular memory which is not limited to Japan but rather expanded

Fig 2.2 *Still Walking/Aruitemo aruitemo* (Kore-eda Hirokazu, 2008, Cine Quanon).

in the global market as 'Japanese cinema'. Those diversified and mixed 'memories' are displayed throughout the film's diegetic space as if they belong to 'Japan' or 'Japanese cinema'. The ingenuity of Kore-eda's films lies in how they shuffle those 'Japanese' memories with something else, such as the recurring images of hands … in *Still Walking*, which let us recall other similarly poetic images of hands in cinema, such as the one in Robert Bresson's *A Man Escaped* …. Those intertextualized images/memories are displayed in the memory-architecture that Kore-eda carefully builds on the already structured knowledge of film history in Japan or elsewhere, and he expresses it as a reproduction of 'home drama,' the popular family melodrama, which was itself made out of the postwar cultural imaginary.[65]

An authorial signature, Wada-Marciano argues, is created through allusion, and the distinctiveness of Kore-eda's cinema is ironically defined through recurrent patterns of intertextuality, of gestures that link his work to that of other cinematic auteurs, both Japanese and foreign, and to a generic classification that emerged from a shared postwar Japanese experience. While the auteur theory proclaimed a doctrine of directorial individuality, a Japanese auteur now ironically identifies himself as such through imitation.

Arguably, these practices are in keeping with long-standing Japanese traditions of the reiteration of motifs and techniques within vernacular art forms and the appropriation of imported motifs. Just as painters of *Nihonga* sustained, while subtly modifying, the styles of classical Japanese painting in the twentieth and twenty-first centuries, so too Kore-eda borrows motifs and images from classical Japanese cinema in a fashion characterised by critical awareness but without the irony that generally characterises the postmodern. And just as historical Japanese architects subtly transformed Chinese architectural styles into vernacular ones, so too Kore-eda integrates motifs from international art cinema into a Japanese narrative context.

James Udden has proposed that Taiwanese, South Korean and Japanese film-makers have in recent years jointly developed a pan-Asian film style characterised by long takes and a largely static camera.[66] Kore-eda's *Maborosi* is offered as the Japanese exemplar of this style. The internationalism of this style has been suggested by the fact that Taiwanese director Hou Hsiao-hsien has travelled to Japan to direct a homage to Ozu, *Café Lumière/Kōhī jikō* (2003), but such gestures in fact have operated in both directions and have expanded beyond an Asian context as Japanese directors have begun to work in the West.

In the late twentieth century, the opportunity to direct in the West was restricted to a very limited number of prestige directors, such as Kurosawa Akira and Ōshima Nagisa; indeed, even Kurosawa's attempts to direct in Hollywood proved abortive, despite his international fame, although he did later work in the Soviet Union and subsequently secured partial backing from American interests for projects made in Japan. But by the turn of the millennium, Kitano had made *Brother* (2000) in Los Angeles, while Nakata Hideo directed the US sequel to the remake of his Japanese horror film, *Ring/Ringu* (1999). If this was explicable in terms of his status as originator of the franchise, a few years later, the employment of Kitamura Ryūhei as director of the American Clive Barker adaptation, *The Midnight Meat Train* (2008) was premised on his recognised facility with horror and fantasy genres, but the material had no direct connection to his Japanese films. Likewise, in 2005, Suwa Nobuhiro (who with *H Story* [2001] had self-consciously reworked a classic French film on Japanese themes, *Hiroshima mon Amour*) made *Un couple parfait* in Paris and in French, with a French cast and crew. His subsequent *Yuki et Nina/Yuki to Nina* (2009), shot in both French and Japanese with scenes set in both France and Japan, was made under the acknowledged influence of André Bazin, founder of *Cahiers du cinéma*.[67] And in *Le lion est mort ce soir* (2017), in an obvious act of homage, Suwa cast Jean-Pierre Léaud, an actor famously associated with Truffaut and Godard, in the lead role.

These instances testify to a globalised cinema in which national boundaries have begun to dissolve. Presenting himself as a Japanese auteur in the twenty-first century, Kore-eda stands self-consciously in relation not only to a local but also to a worldwide cinematic tradition. As this chapter has argued, throughout film history concepts of cinematic authorship in Japan have developed in an international context. Today, perhaps, to be a Japanese *eiga sakka* is also, increasingly, to be an international auteur.

Notes

1. Joseph L. Anderson and Donald Richie, *The Japanese Film: Art and Industry*, rev. ed. (Princeton, NJ: Princeton University Press, 1982), p. 5.
2. See Donald Richie, *The Films of Akira Kurosawa* (Berkeley: University of California Press, 1998) and *Ozu: His Life and Films* (Berkeley: University of California Press, 1992), and Audie Bock, *Japanese Film Directors* (Tokyo: Kōdansha International, 1985). The original editions were published in 1965, 1974 and 1978 respectively.
3. Isolde Standish, *Myth and Masculinity in the Japanese Cinema: Towards a Political Reading of the 'Tragic Hero'* (Richmond, VA: Curzon, 2000), p. 8.
4. Freda Freiberg, *Women in Mizoguchi's Films* (Melbourne: Japanese Studies Centre, Monash University, 1981), p. 1.
5. David Bordwell, *Ozu and the Poetics of Cinema* (London: British Film Institute; Princeton, NJ: Princeton University Press, 1988), p. 1.
6. Catherine Russell, *The Cinema of Naruse Mikio: Women and Japanese Modernity* (Durham, NC: Duke University Press, 2008), p. xiii.
7. Arthur Nolletti Jr., *The Cinema of Gosho Heinosuke: Laughter through Tears* (Bloomington: Indiana University Press, 2005), p. 7.
8. John Caughie (ed.), *Theories of Authorship* (London: Routledge, 2001), p. 9.
9. Rotha, writing in the 1940s, states that 'although I respect highly the task of the screenwriter … I would suggest the only the director can be the main creative mind that really gives life and breath and emotion and meaning to the writer's ideas'. See Paul Rotha, *The Film Till Now: A Survey of World Cinema* (London: Spring Books, 1967), p. 49.
10. Shimizu Chiyota, 'Sekai eigakai no dōkō', in Iwamoto Kenji and Makino Mamoru (eds), *Eiga nenkan: Shōwa hen 1*, vol. 6 (Tokyo: Nihon Tosho Centre, 1994), p. 37.
11. Aaron Gerow, 'Critical Reception: Historical Conceptions of Japanese Film Criticism', in Daisuke Miyao (ed.), *The Oxford Handbook of Japanese Cinema* (Oxford: Oxford University Press, 2014), p. 63.
12. Aaron Gerow, *Visions of Japanese Modernity: Articulations of Cinema, Nation, and Spectatorship, 1895–1925* (Berkeley: University of California Press, 2010), p. 162.
13. Ibid.
14. Hiroshi Komatsu, 'The Foundation of Modernism: Japanese Cinema in the Year 1927', *Film History* vol. 17, nos. 2/3 (2005), p. 364.
15. Itō Akio, '*Ani imōto* no sakka ga Kimura Sotoji de aru', *Eiga hyōron* no. 129 (December 1936), p. 59.

16. Tsumura Hideo, *Eiga to hihyō* (Tokyo: Ōyama shoten, 1938), p. 159.
17. Ibid., p. 162.
18. Gerow, 'Critical Reception', p. 63.
19. Tōdō Satoshi, 'Itami Mansaku ron', in Makino Mamoru (ed.), *Senzen eizō riron zasshi shūsei* (Tokyo: Yumani shobō, 1989), p. 24.
20. Iwasaki Akira, *Nihon eiga sakka ron* (Tokyo: Chūōkōron-sha, 1958), p. 47.
21. Ibid., pp. 47–8.
22. Ibid., pp. 6–7.
23. Ian Cameron, 'Shin Heike Monogatari', *Movie* 5 (December 1962), p. 36.
24. Jacques Rivette, 'Mizoguchi Viewed from Here', trans. Liz Heron, in Jim Hillier (ed.), *Cahiers du Cinéma, the 1950s: Neo-realism, Hollywood, New Wave* (Cambridge, MA: Harvard University Press, 1985), p. 265.
25. Ibid., pp. 264–5.
26. Eric Rohmer, quoted in Keiko McDonald (ed.), *Ugetsu* (New Brunswick, NJ: Rutgers University Press, 1993), p. 123.
27. Jean-Luc Godard, quoted in Freiberg, *Women in Mizoguchi's Films*, p. 6.
28. Eric Rhode, 'Ugetsu Monogatari', *Sight and Sound* vol. 31 no. 2 (Spring 1962), p. 97.
29. Tom Milne, 'Flavour of Green Tea over Rice', *Sight and Sound* vol. 32 no. 4 (Autumn 1963), p. 186.
30. Ozu Yasujirō, quoted in Mark Schilling, 'Re-examining Yasujiro Ozu on Film', *Japan Times*, 7 December 2013.
31. See Nozaki Kan, 'Truffaut in the Mirror of Japan', in Dudley Andrew and Anne Gillain (eds), *A Companion to François Truffaut* (Hoboken, NJ: Wiley-Blackwell, 2013), p. 389.
32. Anderson and Richie, *The Japanese Film*, p. 350.
33. Eric Cazdyn, *The Flash of Capital: Film and Geopolitics in Japan* (Durham, NC: Duke University Press, 2002), p. 73.
34. Anderson and Richie, *The Japanese Film*, pp. 346–37.
35. Ibid., pp. 347–8.
36. Hasumi Shigehiko, 'On the Everydayness of a Miracle: Ozu Yasujiro and Atsuta Yuharu', <http://www.um.u-tokyo.ac.jp/publish_db/1999ozu/english/02.html>.
37. Maureen Turim, *The Films of Oshima Nagisa: Images of a Japanese Iconoclast* (Berkeley: University of California Press, 1998), p. 13.
38. Mark Downing Roberts, 'Masumura Yasuzo and the Cinema of Social Consciousness' (PhD thesis, University of California Berkeley, 2007), p. xxvi.
39. Roland Domenig, 'The Anticipation of Freedom: Art Theatre Guild and Japanese Independent Cinema', *Midnight Eye* <http://www.midnighteye.com/features/the-anticipation-of-freedom-art-theatre-guild-and-japanese-independent-cinema/>.
40. See Nozaki Kan, 'Japanese Readings: The Textual Thread', in Dudley Andrew and Hervé Joubert (eds), *Opening Bazin: Postwar Film Theory and its Afterlife* (Oxford: Oxford University Press, 2011), p. 324, and Roberts, 'Masumura Yasuzo'.
41. Yamada Kōichi, 'Notes sur Ichikawa Kon', *Cahiers du cinéma* no. 187 (February 1967), p. 10.
42. Yamada Kōichi, 'Les Cochons et les dieux: Imamura Shohei', *Cahiers du Cinéma* nos. 166–7 (May–June 1965), p. 25.
43. Yamada Kōichi, quoted in Kan, 'Japanese Readings', p. 392.
44. Yamada Kōichi, *Yamada Kōichi no Nihon eigashi* (Tokyo: Waizu shuppan, 1997), pp. 189–90.
45. Yoshida Kijū, 'My Theory of Film: A Logic of Self-Negation', trans. Patrick Noonan, *Review of Japanese Culture and Society* no. 22 (December 2010), p. 104.
46. Ibid., p. 109.
47. Ibid., p. 107.
48. Yoshida Kijū, *Ozu's Anti-Cinema*, trans. Daisuke Miyao and Kyoko Hirano (Ann Arbor: Center for Japanese Studies, University of Michigan, 2003), p. 53.
49. Ibid., p. 58.
50. Hasumi Shigehiko, 'John Ford, or the Eloquence of Gesture', trans. Adrian Martin, <http://www.rouge.com.au/7/ford.html>.
51. Ryan Cook, 'An Impaired Eye: Hasumi Shigehiko on Cinema and Stupidity', *Review of Japanese Culture and Society* no. 22 (December 2010), p. 141.
52. Ibid., p. 143.
53. Hasumi Shiguéhiko, *Yasujirō Ozu*, trans. Nakamura Ryoji and René de Ceccatty (Paris: Éditions de l'Étoile, 1998), p. 24.
54. Ibid., p. 151.
55. Noël Burch, *To the Distant Observer: Form and Meaning in Japanese Cinema* (London: Scolar Press; Berkeley: University of California Press, 1979), p. 185.
56. Ibid., pp. 256–7.
57. See Kan, 'Japanese Readings', pp. 326–7.
58. Satō Tadao, quoted in Mitsuyo Wada-Marciano, *Japanese Cinema in the Digital Age* (Honolulu: University of Hawai'i Press, 2012), p. 51.

59 Kurosawa Kiyoshi, quoted in Tom Mes and Jasper Sharp, *The Midnight Eye Guide to New Japanese Film* (Albany, CA: Stone Bridge Press, 2005), p. 97.
60 Aaron Gerow, *Kitano Takeshi* (London: British Film Institute, 2007), p. 220.
61 Ibid.
62 Peter Wollen, *Signs and Meaning in the Cinema* (Bloomington: Indiana University Press, 1972), pp. 93–4.
63 Gerow, *Kitano Takeshi*, p. 117.
64 David Desser, 'The Imagination of the Transcendent: Kore-eda Hirokazu's *Maboroshi*', in Alastair Phillips and Julian Stringer (eds), *Japanese Cinema: Texts and Contexts* (London: Routledge, 2007), p. 273.
65 Mitsuyo Wada-Marciano, 'A Dialogue through Memories: Still Walking', *Film Criticism* vol. 35 nos. 2–3 (Winter/Spring 2011), p. 118.
66 James Udden, 'The Future of a Luminescent Cloud: Recent Developments in a Pan-Asian Film Style', *Synoptique* no. 10, <www.synoptique.ca/core/en/articles/udden>.
67 See Kan, 'Japanese Readings', p. 328.

3

SPECTATORSHIP
The spectator as subject and agent

Hideaki Fujiki

The term 'spectator' is both elusive and convenient. Etymologically, while the word 'audience' derives from the Latin 'audire' or 'hear', the notion of the 'spectator' stems from 'spectare' or 'gaze at'. As many scholars have discussed following on from the dominance of gaze theory in the 1970s,[1] spectatorship may be conceptualised not only in visual terms but also in relation to auditory and other broader forms of sensory experience. In this sense, the term 'spectator' does not only rigidly pertain to the visual experience of film. On another level, while the idea of 'the audience' tends to suggest the concrete, flesh and blood or sociality of the person, or persons, actually experiencing a screened image, the 'spectator' remains an abstract, disembodied body that a film text or other cultural discourse only implicates as the person directly perceiving the film.[2] Moreover, even though we use the word 'spectator' as a general term to designate a film-perceiving person on both these levels, as I do in this chapter,[3] this may be an individual or collective, fixed or moving, and homogeneous or heterogeneous phenomenon. A further issue is that this book requires us to consider the spectator and spectatorship not simply in general terms but in the specific context of Japanese cinema. Despite all of these complications, however, the term 'spectator' remains a highly convenient one for us to use. Indeed, most critics usually use the term without showing who and what the spectator is, where and when s/he is, and how and why this idea can be said to work in practice.

How then can we approach this elusive, complex and paradoxical term? More essentially, what significance can we find in especially considering the spectator in the context of Japanese cinema? In this chapter, I argue that by taking the spectator into account, we may go beyond the conventional view that sees a film as the reflection, representation or mediation of history and society (especially here, Japanese history and society), and also take into account a film's dynamic relations with diverse social and ecological dimensions that may include politics, economics, aesthetics, education, ethics, psychology, technology and even the material existence of the object itself. It is, of course, impossible for one single study to cover all of these aspects and their relations in detail. While numerous attempts have been made to discuss the spectator in academic, economic, political and other sectors from the early stages of film history onwards, they remain necessarily partial and tendentious.

That said, we can observe a contestation between two predominant types of approaches within the variety of discourses on the spectator: the spectator as subject and as agent. Although the notion of the 'subject' and that of the 'agent' have long been debated inconclusively among philosophers, sociologists and scholars in other disciplines, I roughly define the former here as the ways in which one may see the spectator as a social identity and category that results from the effect of a filmic text and/or non-filmic discourses, and the latter as the ways in which one may see the spectator as an actor who acts voluntarily and autonomously, often exceeding an identity or category imposed by other forces such as the state.[4] Needless to say, these two terms are not clear-cut classifications but relative and, at times, they can overlap. It is equally important to note, however, the underlying assumption that while the subject may also appear to act on her/his will as the agent does, the term always implies that s/he be actually *subjected* to something; say, the nation state.

In what follows, I will firstly place Japanese cinema scholarship within the context of film studies in general and how it has attended to the spectator as subject and agent. From this theoretical perspective, I will then illuminate the historically specific instance when critical, journalistic, academic, industrial and bureaucratic discourses within the wartime Japanese empire during the early 1940s actively discussed ways the construction of the 'East Asian Race' (*Tōa minzoku*) might be facilitated through boosting cinemagoing. This case study enables us to see how dynamic relations between the idealisation of the spectator as the subject of the empire and the notion of spectators and non-spectators as agents did not precisely follow expectations in this particular historical context. By closely examining various discourses, I will reveal the complex structure by which the idea of constructing the 'East Asian Race' through cinemagoing involved an idealisation of the spectator that simultaneously disavowed any sense of contradiction concerning the agents situated under various discursive and institutional pressures.

THE SPECTATOR AS THE SUBJECT

In many countries and states, including the UK, the US and Japan, cinema audiences drew attention as early as the 1900s and early 1910s when cinema began to be recognised as a social problem amongst journalists and educators.[5] Theoretical books discussing the spectator also appeared in the 1910s, as did Hugo Münsterberg's *The Photoplay: A Psychological Study* (1916) and Gonda Yasunosuke's *Principles and Application of the Motion Picture* (1914).[6] Since then, many critics, scholars and practitioners including Rudolf Arnheim, Béla Balázs, Sergei Eisenstein, Siegfried Kracauer, Walter Benjamin and André Bazin, as well as Iijima Tadashi, Imamura Taihei and Minami Hiroshi, have incorporated issues of the spectator into their arguments. Since the 1970s, the point when film studies and cultural studies began to be fully founded as academic disciplines, theoretical and empirical research into the film spectator and film audience has diversified and it now deploys various positions such as psychoanalysis, postcolonial studies, cognitive theory, phenomenology, Deleuzian affect theory, modernity theory, fan studies and reception studies. In many cases, these have arisen from, and been folded into, one another.

The spectator-as-the-subject approach has become dominant in contemporary film studies scholarship. There are several strands to this. The study of Japanese film spectatorship cannot be understood by being separated from these debates. Most film studies scholars would consent that Jean-Louis Baudry, Christian Metz, Laura Mulvey, Stephen Heath and other authors in the British journal *Screen* of the 1970s are the founders of this tradition. Influenced by Louis Althusser's theory of the 'ideological state apparatuses' and Lacanian psychoanalysis, their thesis has been called 'apparatus theory', 'Screen theory', 'gaze theory' and 'subject-positioning theory'. Whatever it is called, as part of what David Rodowick terms 'political modernism',[7] this work shares the same political concern of disclosing how cinema functions as an illusory ideological apparatus through which the spectator is positioned, or interpellated, as the subject of dominant ideology – for example a bourgeois-centred, male-centred or Euro-American-centred perspective – and reproduces this ideology so as to perpetuate the status quo.

And yet, for our purpose, we should note one crucial divergence between Baudry and Metz and other scholars. I call this the distinction between a medium-based model and a form-based model. While the former, says Baudry, tends to link the film medium per se as an ideological apparatus with the spectator's identity being tied to the Western, bourgeois and anthropocentric subject,[8] the latter divides film into two opposing forms – a dominant form of cinema functioning as an ideological apparatus and an alternative form of cinema – and associates these forms with conflicts in the spectator's identity with regards to class, gender, ethnicity or other cultural background. Noël Burch's *Theory of Film Practice* (1969 in French and 1973 in English), for instance, classifies cinema into two contrasting forms – the illusionist form or what he later calls the institutional mode of representation (IMR) and its alternative form – suggesting that they assume different types of spectators: bourgeois citizens and lower-class people.[9] In her famous essay 'Visual Pleasure and Narrative Cinema' (1973) Laura Mulvey applies a similar dichotomy between the dominant entertainment film and the avant-garde film to the opposition between the phallocentric film (which positions the spectator as the subject of a male-centred ideology) and the feminist film (which complicates this ideological positioning).[10] Later, in their 1983 essay, Robert Stam and Louise Spence note an equivalent contrast between the colonialist film and anti-colonialist film.[11] All these writers assume that film form and the spectator's sociocultural identity correspond with one other. In this sense, the form-based model can also be said to be a culture-based model.

This form-based and culture-based model sheds light on differences both in film form and spectatorial identity. In so doing, it counters the monolithic assumption of the spectator in the medium-based model. Still, the form-based model is premised on a binary opposition between the dominant and the alternative. Furthermore, this model always assumes a uniform and fixed spectator as the ideological subject, whether it be bourgeois, male or Caucasian. In opposition to this, two different kinds of revisionist models become salient. One is the formalist or 'neo-formalist' model that incorporates cognitive studies into its arguments. In his book, *Narration in the Fiction Film* (1985), the representative scholar of this model, David Bordwell, developed Burch's views by considering four different types of filmic 'narration': classical, art-cinema, historical-material and parametric. He discusses the spectator as a cognitive 'agent' who actively constructs the story or *fabula* moment by moment by inferring cues provided by the plot or *syuzhet* on the basis of her/his prior knowledge and experience of other arts and everyday life. This dynamic model of spectatorship, nevertheless, assumes that the spectator's ideal cognitive activity is primarily defined by the expected narrational effect of each type of film and thus can been still be seen as bound by the notion of the 'subject'.[12] Bordwell's *Making Meaning* (1989) further illustrates the conventional schema many critics have tended to count on in order to interpret films. Bordwell does so while demonstrating an alternative critical analytical model or what he calls 'historical poetics', by which an ideal, trained spectator can understand the systematic formal quality inherent in each type of film through consideration of its historical context.[13]

The other model that attempts to revise the form-based model is what I call the history-based model. Whereas Bordwell's 'historical poetics' chiefly concerns the relation between a film's form and the time in which it is produced, the history-based model emphasises a historical shift from an early stage to a later stage, particularly in terms of the shift from early cinema to classical cinema.[14] A crucial point in this model is that this history is not fully grounded on empiricism. Rather, the more vital goal of this model is to challenge a teleological historiography that presupposes cinema has aesthetically developed from the immature to the mature. Moreover, sharing the same political concerns as the form-based model, the history-model tends to celebrate early cinema as an alternative to classical cinema, which is regarded as a dominant, bourgeois-oriented illusionist form. Indeed, Burch's *Life to Those Shadows* (1990) explicitly criticises the shift in the imaginary placing of the spectator, from a position of exteriority to the film image in the 'Primitive Mode of Representation' to being a subject that is immersed in an illusory 'motionless voyage' within the IMR.[15] Miriam Hansen's *Babel and Babylon* (1991) makes a more nuanced argument in that the shift, she suggests, occurred not simply in the textual positioning of the spectator but in what she calls 'the public sphere', which comprised contestations not only in textual conventions but also in exhibition practices, industrial institutions and people's (especially, immigrants') experiences. That said, echoing the basis of Burch's critique, the core of her argument is based on the shift whereby the process from a heterogeneous, locally specific public sphere to a dominant form of industrial institutionalisation promoted the spectator as a unified categorical subject between 1909 and 1919.[16]

It is within this context of contemporary film studies scholarship that the topic of the film spectator within Japanese film studies may best be understood. Several scholars in Japanese film studies have debated issues under the influence of these form-based and history-based models. Here again, Burch initiated things with his groundbreaking book, *To the Distant Observer* (1979), which demonstrated his usual binary opposition between illusionist forms and their alternatives. For Burch, many Japanese films, which he believes inherited traditional Japanese arts such as kabuki, the picture scroll (*emaki*), *bunraku*, *haiku* and older forms of Japanese architecture, counter and de-construct the illusory 'mode of *representation*' that dominates Western films. They do so while enacting a 'mode of *presentation*' that provides a sense that 'the actor, the audience, and the performance exist within the same psychologically undifferentiated world'.[17] As many scholars have pointed out, whilst this claim intervenes in the naïve teleological account that portrays Japanese film history in terms of the progress from the primitive to the advanced, it nonetheless provides a typical Orientalist view that homogenises, exoticises and idealises Japan, Japanese arts and Japanese people as ahistorical, 'pure' entities and subjects. Thus, although at first glance Burch may appear to highlight the audience of Japanese arts or films as agents who consciously participate in a *presented* work, they are in fact seen merely as spectators relating to what he alone imagines as the mode of presentation, unable to act autonomously beyond the prison of this predetermined construct.

Inextricably linked with film studies scholarship in general, Burch's form-based and culture-based model underlines the dichotomy between the West and Japan defied by the formalist-model and the history-based model. In his *Ozu and the Poetics of Cinema* (1988), Bordwell attempted to revise Burch's argument concerning the spectator in two ways. In the first place, rather than unifying all Japanese arts, including Ozu's films, as one single cultural entity, Bordwell historicises them in terms of the film industry, the filmic forms of Japanese cinema and the cultural elements selected in the process of an encounter between Japanese tradition and imported Western cultural factors. In this context, he places Ozu and other Japanese film-makers as the spectators of Hollywood films who selectively appropriated the narrative and stylistic characteristics of foreign films in their own film-making. On another level, Bordwell also reinforces the project of *Making Meaning* by setting up an idealised viewer who should observe the ways in which Ozu's films enact unique artistic and 'parametric' forms whilst also appropriating classical Hollywood cinema in a number of particular historical contexts. Here, the spectator is conceptualised as an ahistorical, transcendental subject expected to analyse films in a proper fashion.[18]

In opposition to this argument, as well as Burch's more Orientalist dichotomy, the history-based model endeavours to contextualise both Japanese cinema and the Japanese spectator in relation to the nation building of modern Japan. Mitsuyo Wada-Marciano's *Nippon Modern* (2008) thus refers to Miriam Hansen's influential concept of 'vernacular modernism', which, as I shall discuss in a more detail, complicates views of the reception of American films in countries and areas outside the US. Throughout the book, however, Wada-Marciano's primary interest rests in applying apparatus theory to her historically minded analysis so as to reveal how Japanese genre films of the 1920s and 1930s likely functioned to position the Japanese spectator of the time as the subject of modern national ideology.[19] While Wada-Marciano's analysis is centred on film texts, Aaron Gerow's *Visions of Japanese Modernity* (2010) pays attention to non-filmic discourses such as published criticism and reviews and matters related to exhibition and censorship. In so doing, he argues that in around 1917 when the Motion Picture Exhibition Regulations were enforced in Tokyo, these discourses constructed a new model of the film spectator as a self-disciplinary subject who internalised regulations so that the modern Japanese state could effectively manage them. Gerow largely follows Hansen's thesis regarding the public sphere in that he emphasises a shift in the dominant imaginary that pictures the spectator moving from being a heterogeneous character flocking to crowded sites of public film exhibition to a member of a homogeneous group controlled by an increasingly centralised film industry and governmental regulation.[20]

THE SPECTATOR AS AGENT

Meanwhile, in contrast to the spectator-as-the-subject approach, the spectator-as-the-agent approach has also flourished, both in film studies and cultural studies in general and within Japanese film studies. This approach sees the spectator as an agent because it places more importance on the spectator's autonomy than her/his apparent subjection to cinema as a medium in general or each film text and/or non-filmic discourse in particular. And yet, the 'agent' I refer to in this chapter is not completely identical with the flesh and blood 'audience' insofar as some theoretical models consider the agent to also be a socially and culturally constructed person. Again, in order to understand Japanese film studies' work on the spectator within a global framework of debate, it is necessary to briefly map out cultural studies, reception studies, fan studies, queer studies, postcolonialism and 'vernacular modernism' as major strands of the spectator-as-the-agent approach.

Many scholars agree that the seminal model is Stuart Hall's 'Encoding/Decoding' (1973), now a foundational essay within cultural studies. Primarily focusing on television (rather than film) and countering a unilateral 'mass-communication model', which assumes the receiver only receives the message sent by the sender, Hall proposes an alternative model whereby the 'viewer' can decode the programme encoded by the hegemonic industry not only in the way that the latter prefers but also in ways by which the former negotiates with, or even opposes, the latter. Here, in contrast to 'Screen theory', the decoder is seen as an autonomous agent rather than the subject positioned by the media text. Having said this, we should also not overlook the fact that Hall's model shares at least two points with 'Screen theory' or a culture-based model. For one thing, in its use of the phrase 'politics of signification', Hall's model remains centred around the dichotomy between dominant ideology and power on the one hand and its alternative on the other, even though it emphasises the decoder's autonomy rather than the subject-positioning of the spectator. Additionally, since encoding and decoding are always preconditioned by 'frames of knowledge', 'relations of production' and 'technical infrastructure', the audience as the decoder is not given, but socially and culturally constructed.[21] Following this essay, other cultural studies and film studies scholars such David Morley, John Fiske, Ien Ang and Jackie Stacey have taken more empirical, particularly ethnographic, approaches to their research. At the same time, they have more or less remained faithful to Hall's theoretical model, and highlighted the audience's conflicts with, and resistance to, dominant forms of signification while assuming the audience is one whose identity and category are already, and always will be, socially constructed in terms of class, gender and/or ethnicity.[22]

This initial cultural studies model has been both assimilated and challenged by subsequent studies of the spectator as agent approach. Issues that have been debated include the dichotomy between the idea of dominance and resistance, the construction of conventional social categories such as class, gender and ethnicity, a more contemporaneity-centred approach to screen–spectator relations and the single-medium relation between a film and a spectator. Judith Mayne's *Cinema and Spectatorship* (1993), for instance, questions the scheme of 'dominant and oppositional readings' in Hall's model, and instead proposes the idea that 'all readings as negotiated'.[23] Janet Staiger's *Interpreting Films* (1992) and other books place more emphasis on a model of reception undetermined by the film text and examine various elements that not only include identity formation, but the spectator's interpretive strategies, her/his emotional and cognitive behaviours, and the material conditions of exhibition – beyond conventional social categories such as class, gender, sexual orientation and ethnicity.[24] Matt Hills's *Fan Cultures* (2002) further pushes forward observing 'unexpected consumption practices' and their inherent contradictions without either reducing them to a moral dualism between good and bad, or a conventional logic by which the critic constructs a sustainable opposition between fan and consumer.[25] Barbara Klinger's 1997 essay, on the other hand, points out that previous studies have largely relied on the notion of 'synchronic' film viewing in which a film is produced and received within the same period, and opens up, instead, the importance of 'diachronic' viewing by which a film is received in other periods than the time in which it was originally produced.[26]

These models centred on screen–spectator relations, be they synchronic or diachronic, have also been reconsidered in a number of ways. Robert Allen, Mark Jancovich and Lucy Faire, among many others, have paid attention to the environments of exhibition such as architecture (in terms of both cinema interiors and exteriors), geographical conditions and the audience's various cinemagoing activities.[27] Fan studies have also revealed that fans' practices are not limited to their relationships with media texts but also their engagement in fan communities and other everyday activities are equally important.[28] Moreover, media scholars, most notably Henry Jenkins, have gone beyond focusing on the relation between a single medium and its spectator in order to explore the transmedial migration of audiences across different media platforms such as printed materials, television, radio, DVD/Blu-rays, the internet and mobile phones.[29]

While these reception studies, fan studies and media studies have complicated and diversified the assumptions of the initial cultural studies model as such, postcolonial studies, queer studies and 'vernacular modernism' have all elaborated on the original model of a power structure that Hall introduced. This aspiration can be seen in studies by Jacqueline Bobo, bell hooks, Stam and Shohat, Homi Bhabha, Rey Chow and Richard Dyer, to name just a few.[30] These scholars have made significant contributions to highlighting socially or globally marginalised people's actual and/or potential, alternative yet nuanced responses to socially dominant screened images. Chow, for instance, attempts to theorise what she calls 'ethnic spectatorship' so as to observe the tensions between the spectator as agent on the one hand and subject on the other; the latter being 'ethnicised' and 'othered' by visual manipulation within globally dominant visual media (such as Hollywood films, for example *The Last Emperor* [1987]) and Euro-American-centred modern historical conditions (Fig. 3.1).[31]

The significance of Hansen's concept of 'vernacular modernism' can be seen in this vein, not least because it concerns the uneven relationships between Hollywood

Fig. 3.1 *The Last Emperor* (Bernardo Bertolucci, 1987, Hemdale Film Corporation and Recorded Picture Company). An example of Rey Chow's notion of 'ethnic spectatorship'.

films and their reception outside the US. According to Hansen's argument, 'vernacular modernism' permits the 'ability to provide, to mass audiences at home and abroad, a sensory-reflexive horizon for the experience of modernization and modernity'.[32] While Hansen's empirical analysis concentrates on films (particularly, Chinese and Japanese films) with little direct mention of local non-filmic discourses and practices, she theorises the reception of Hollywood cinema outside the US in terms of agency. Unlike the case with the theorisation of cultural imperialism, which argues that the hegemonic power and 'universal narrative templates'[33] of American products have led to their popular acceptance outside the US, Hansen emphasises that the reason for the global prevalence of Americanism lies in a form of 'locally specific' heterogeneous reception in which the 'liberating impulses and pathologies of modernity were reflected, rejected or disavowed, transmuted and negotiated'.[34] In other words, where she tries to account for the mechanism of the global hegemony of Hollywood cinema, she foregrounds its reception outside the US in terms of the agent or the spectator who has various flexible 'sensory-reflexive' experiences – which may include both a form of discursively expressed inspiration and an immediate sensory response. In recent years, similar kinds of this dynamic model of global-local relations have also been claimed by many other scholars such as Michael Curtin interested in the transnational circulation of cinema and television.[35]

Japanese film studies has generally corresponded with and responded to these various strands of the spectator-as-the-agent approach in film studies, cultural studies and media studies. It has certainly rarely partaken in philosophical and ontological theoretical models of the spectator such as those based on phenomenology, Deleuzian affect theory, ethics and cognitivism. These models may question the very boundary between the idea of the spectator as subject and agent in that they explore ways cinema preconditions the spectator's being, becoming and 'pre-subjectivity'. They also tend to bracket off the cases by which the spectator may act autonomously as an agent from the effects of cinema in general or a film in particular.[36] In any case, although some Japanese films may serve as illustrations, Japanese cinema is not the main focus in these theoretical arguments. Specialists in Japanese film studies have resisted analysing the spectator in relation to these ontological models, though some such as Markus Nornes have examined the impact of Japanese films (particularly Ogawa Shinsuke's documentary films) on their audiences in terms of affect.[37] This situation reminds us of what Rey Chow suggests is an imbalanced tendency that sees Western film scholarship as the producer of theory and non-Western film scholarship as being something merely restricted to locally specific contexts.[38] Indeed, one of Mitsuhiro Yoshimoto's most significant projects in relation to this tendentious genealogy has been to specifically locate Anglophone critics and scholars of Japanese films themselves as spectators. His metacritique points out that Western scholars have tended to assume themselves as the subject and Japanese films as the object while simultaneously masking the specific power relations between them. In this sense, according to Yoshimoto, Western scholars' views have reproduced the broader 'epistemological colonization of the non-West' within film studies.[39] Several attempts to historicise the spectator and spectatorship have emerged within the context of this growing aspiration to overcome Orientalist discourse. While Gerow and Wada-Marciano's books are typical examples, other scholarly works have, to a lesser or greater degree, highlighted the spectator as both an historical and contemporary agent. Referring to Hansen's 'vernacular modernism' as well as Naoki Sakai's concepts of the 'epistemic subject' and the 'practical agent', Catherine Russell's *The Cinema of Naruse Mikio* (2008) tries to conceptualise the spectatorship of Naruse's films as the intersection of that produced by 'original historical spectators' (or the 'epistemic subject') who were positioned in the conditions of modern Japan, including the contemporary reception of Hollywood films, and that produced by the author herself as spectator (or 'practical agent') who analyses the films within the framework of current feminist concerns. In so doing, Russell attempts to disclose the articulation of the Japanese female subjectivity of the time in Naruse's films from the vantage point of a 'transnational feminism'.[40] As Hikari Hori's chapter in this book – 'Gender and sexuality' – discusses in more detail, Yuka Kanno's 2011 essay also reveals the queer spectatorship of Hara Setsuko and her character Noriko in *Early Summer/Bakushū* (1951) within both the transnational and 'diachronic' conjunctions between Hara and Katharine Hepburn, and between the spectator implicated in the film text and the one existing in the present.[41]

While these two works centre mainly around the spectator implicated in film texts, Hiroshi Kitamura's *Screening Enlightenment* (2010), my own *Making Personas* (2013) and Sandra Annett's *Anime Fan Communities* (2014) analyse not only films and television anime, but also a variety of non-filmic and non-televisual discourses and practices in order to show the relationships between the transnational circulation of media texts and national audience or transnational audience networks. Kitamura and I discuss respectively how audiences acted when faced with the circulation of American films and their related visual images such as posters, photogravures and advertisements. Kitamura illustrates how Japanese critics and fans actively embraced Hollywood cinema and, by extension, American culture, democracy and Cold War ideology in the context of the US Occupation managed by the General Headquarters, Supreme Commander for the Allied Power (GHQ/SCAP) after World War II.[42] My book illuminates the tension between Japanese fans' fanatical support and appropriation of Clara Bow's image and the reactionary criticism of this in the context of late 1920s' modernity in which nationalism and cosmopolitanism were contested and both forces conspired against each other.[43] On the other hand, drawing on the anthropologist Anna Lowenhaupt Tsing's concept of 'friction', defined as 'the awkward, unequal, unstable, and creative qualities of interconnection across difference',[44] Annett shows how anime fans 'from many national, gendered, and other personal backgrounds find a sense of connection across difference, engaging with each other through a shared interest while negotiating the frictions that result from their social and historical contexts'.[45] Particularly important here is how Annett's analysis highlights connections and negotiations among a number of multiple and fluid identities that are irreducible into one simple dichotomy between the dominant and the other.

Other Japanese scholars have taken the spectator-as-the-agent approach to examine more local historical contexts. Manabu Ueda's Japanese-language book *Exhibition and Audiences in Early Japanese History* (2012), which is partly summarised in his chapter for this volume, 'Exhibition', demonstrates empirically that the Sixth Arrondissement of Asakusa arose as the centre of cinema exhibition in Tokyo during the late 1900s not because the Russo-Japanese War of 1904 led to a dramatic increase in the popularity of cinema, as previous scholarship has explained, but because of the expanding population of lower-class people in urban areas due to the remarkable flow of people from regional districts. It was also because of the fact that audiences who had previously favoured small theatrical playhouses began to habitually go to cinemas that offered narrative films with cheaper admission, accompanied by traditional popular Japanese music (such as *gidayū*), which audiences were already familiar with.[46] Likewise, Yoshimi Shun'ya and Fumiaki Itakura, among others, have also conducted empirical research on printed materials from the period to investigate issues concerning audiences. Yoshimi highlights the transformation in the geographical distribution of cinema buildings according to their targeted audiences' class and habitus in postwar Tokyo, while Itakura discusses changes in audiences' behaviours and attitudes between the 1910s and 1960s in relation to changes in film form and the architecture of cinema buildings.[47]

Issues concerning fandom and transmediality have also drawn growing attention in Japanese film studies and beyond. Among many important works, Thomas Lamarre's project on the *otaku* is exceptionally noteworthy. The *otaku* may be seen as nothing but a unique type of fan who is obsessed with anime and manga, but Lamarre links the figure to larger issues such as the scholarship on fandom in cultural studies as well as the relations between economic political power and 'human capital'. Because *otaku* both consume and create anime and manga, he argues, they problematise the theoretical model that understands fans on the basis of the distinction between consumption and production. Moreover, by scrutinising Japanese critical, governmental and industrial discourses on *otaku*, Lamarre unveils the *otaku*'s ambivalent status: they have been exploited as 'human capital' in the market of popular culture as 'precariat' labourers while the *otaku* and the precariat have the potential of co-resistance to the technology of power.[48] In recent years, this issue has been vigorously discussed across different fields including cultural studies, anthropology and film studies. At the same time, the figure of the *otaku* inevitably relates to another vital aspect of the spectator-as-the-agent approach: that of transmediality, or 'media mix' in Japanese. Marc Steinberg has traced the history of 'media mix' that, according to him, began with the *Astro Boy/Tetsuwan Atom* television series (1963–6) and has since been developed as a sophisticated business strategy, particularly by Kadokawa[49] from 1978 onwards. Discussing 'media mix' as a congruence of different media platforms on the basis of a single anime character, in contrast to Jenkins's transmedial approach based on storytelling, Steinberg's argument suggests that the spectators or the users of an anime character should be no less seen as agents than as subjects.[50] While they have been positioned primarily as actual or potential consumers by a business strategy, their active and unexpected practices may freely migrate across different media platforms and have been a major source of the development of the phenomenon.

It is not my intention to mark a clear division between approaching the spectator as subject and as agent. Rather, while I have delineated the differences between the two tendencies emphasised in contemporary scholarship on the spectator, it is also important for us to consider the complex relations between them. The spectator may at once be conditioned as a subject by political, economic and social forces and act as an agent that does not perfectly follow them. As I will show in the next section, this conjunction of tension and cooperation can best be observed through an analysis of specific discourses concerning actual and potential film spectators and their practices.

THE SPECTATOR AS THE 'EAST ASIAN RACE'

Japanese-language discourse began to note the film spectator or film audience around 1911, when a Japanese newspaper wrote about the malicious influence of the French serial *Zigomar* (1911) over children, hence defining the film as a social problem.[51] Since then, numerous journalists, critics, scholars and general readers of magazines have referred to the notion of the film spectator, and they more often than not discuss this figure as the central topic. At the same time, the film spectator has been a weighty subject in critical, governmental and industrial discourses, although the degree and scale of this has changed over time. Analysing such a variety of discourses on film spectators – what I shall call spectator-discourse(s) – may reveal how spectators have functioned both as subjects and agents in complex ways with relation to their particular social, cultural, political, economic, ecological and historical contexts. To provide one example of this approach, I shall now briefly discuss a case study of the connection and conflation between the spectator and the idea of the 'East Asian Race' during World War II.[52]

The discourses by which film spectators were linked with the idea of the 'East Asian Race' emerged in the process whereby the slogan of the Japanese empire developed from 'Eight Corners of the World under One Roof' (*Hakkō ichiu*) to 'the Greater East Asian Co-Prosperity Sphere' (*Daitōa kyōei ken*). The former, whose source was the ancient canonised book *The Chronicles of Japan/Nihonshoki* (720), began to be justified and promoted as the chief principle of national policy in the movement for the General Mobilization of the National Spirit, which was launched in July 1937 when the Sino-Japanese War broke out. In July 1940, when the second Konoe Fumimaro cabinet approved the 'basic outline of national policy', they reformulated the 'Eight Corners of the World under One Roof' into the 'New Order of East Asia' and then established the plan of 'the Greater East Asian Co-Prosperity Sphere' so as to acquire British, French and Dutch colonies in East and South East Asia.[53] Meanwhile, the terms, 'subjects of the imperial nation' (*kōkoku shinmin*) and 'imperial subjects' (*kōmin*), gained wide currency in Korea (colonised by Japan in 1910) and Taiwan (colonised in 1895) in 1937.[54] In around 1941, overlapping with these two terms as well as the notion of 'the national' (*kokumin*), the new term of the 'East Asian Race' began to circulate in these and other colonised and controlled areas as well as Japan proper. What is crucial here is that while the notion of the 'East Asian Race' implied a cultural unity, it also concealed political and economic inequality among people, especially between the Japanese and the other. That is, despite the promotion of cultural assimilation, people from areas outside Japan proper were not allowed to obtain Japanese nationality.[55] Nor did they and all women in Japan proper have suffrage for the Imperial Diet (at least until men in Korea and Taiwan obtained it in April 1945).[56]

In this context, supposing that cinema functioned as an implicit form of propaganda, bureaucrats and critics argued that cinemagoing, or becoming a film spectator, was a vital step in an individual becoming a member of the 'East Asian Race'. This kind of idea had at least partly already been germinated around 1920 when the Education Ministry and the Home Ministry began respectively to commission research on film audiences because they had become concerned about the increasingly visible social influence of cinema. From then onwards, the former endeavoured to establish a system for the use of cinema as a tool of social education, while the latter devoted itself to establishing and maintaining various forms of censorship.[57] The Film Law, which was implemented in October 1939 and revised four times between December 1940 and June 1941, integrated these separate sectors into one and hence rose to the top of the governmental film policy agenda. Yet, from a legal level, as this film policy only targeted Japan proper and hence aimed to enlighten its residents on the 'national' (rather than the 'East Asian Race'), other film policies and measures in the Japanese empire were conducted separately in all colonised and controlled areas. For instance, the Korean Film Ordinance, which was enforced in August 1940, was very similar to the Film Law in Japan proper in terms of content, but it operated in a manner specific to Korea. The distribution of films across Japan proper and other areas in the empire was also highly imbalanced in terms of number and popularity. This situation suggests a fundamental contradiction meaning that while the idea of the 'East Asian Race' was to promote cultural unity among the residents of the empire, film infrastructure itself was unequal and out of kilter. But at the same time, both in Japan proper and the broader Japanese empire, film policy conceptualised film spectatorship as a significant stage in the process whereby residents voluntarily subjected themselves to the emperor-centred state.

There were three noteworthy characteristics in the discourses that prompted people to become film spectators and, in so doing, imagine themselves as the subjects of the Greater East Asian Co-Prosperity Sphere, that is, the 'East Asian Race' (Fig. 3.2). Firstly, discourse emphasised the commonality and sameness of the 'East Asian Race'. This attempt was fundamentally contradictory in that it demanded the creation of the 'East Asian Race' while also speaking as if it was a fait accompli. In his 1941 book *The Creation and Construction of Asian Cinema*, Ichikawa Sai insists that 'we have to form the base and culture firmly shared by the race in order to fully establish East Asian Sphere', while pointing out that the Sino-Japanese War of 1937 urged people to be aware that they are one 'East Asian Race'. He then advocated the construction of 'Asian culture' by sharing 'the common sensibility of the East Asian Race' through cinema.[58] As this argument suggests, the general idea of the commonality of the 'East Asian Race' that spectator-discourses mentioned was largely based on an as-it-were tacit consensus with no substantial evidence; hence it was, in fact, a signifier without any signified.

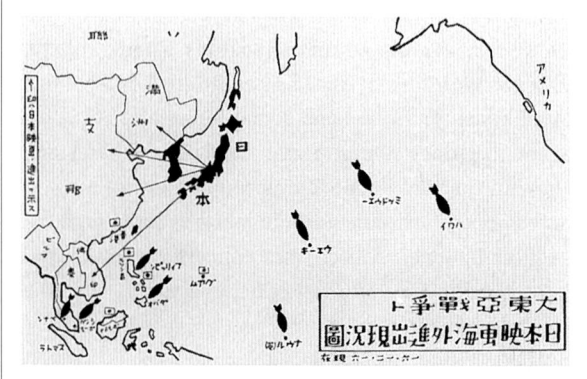

Fig. 3.2 An image that visualises the attempt to integrate the Japanese film industry into the Greater East Asian Co-Prosperity Sphere, published in *Eiga hyōron* (January 1942). The caption reads: 'the Greater East Asian War and the advancement of Japanese films overseas'.

Another characteristic of the discourses was to covertly set up or assume the centrality and privilege of Japan proper within its empire. There were three kinds of logic that attempted to sustain this status: culturalism, modernism and paternalism. These were, again, contradictory to each other, but they nevertheless appeared to coherently coexist because no one openly problematised the contradiction at the time. This is especially obvious between culturalism and modernism. The idea of culturalism was to place the highest value on the unchanging uniqueness of traditional Japanese culture. Modernism, on the other hand, did not mean the aesthetics of de-familiarisation but the assumption of an absolute standard of temporal progress from the immature to the advanced and thus the subsequent assessment of a race and culture by these means. This was inextricably linked with a way of understanding geographical space from the centre to its periphery. An influential critic of the time, Tsumura Hideo, used these two logics in a remarkably opportunistic way. He associated materialism with American culture represented by Hollywood cinema and harshly criticised it in a symposium,[59] but elsewhere he claimed that Japanese films should inspire South East Asian people by demonstrating how Japan was a materially advanced country.[60] Indeed, many critics and journalists pointed out that the icons of Japanese culture, such as the landscape of farms, Mt Fuji and kimono were not admired outside Japan proper; rather they would be misunderstood as the signs of an inferior culture.[61]

On the other hand, this modernistic view was also tied with paternalism. Paternalism meant positioning oneself in a superior way while supposing others to be inferior, but in so doing, it attempted to protect others by seeing them as immature and dependent. But because this attitude may have appeared to be superficially benevolent, its deceptiveness was often not recognised and acknowledged. This was epitomised by the influential social researcher Gonda Yasunosuke's statement that the nation of Japan proper assumed the status of being the leader of the one billion people within the East Asian Sphere.[62] This was inextricably linked to a notion by which the people from outside Japan proper were seen to have an inferior culture and should hence be enlightened.

These discourses failed to touch on the violence and contradictions in the Japanese empire and so they also functioned to uphold a structure of discrimination. The historian Misawa Mamie, for instance, suggests that Taiwanese audiences who watched the Korean Film *Volunteer/Shiganhei* (1941) had a sense of rivalry with Korean people in terms of becoming successful 'imperial subjects'.[63]

Finally, in addition to the ideas of commonality and sameness and tacit centrality, these spectator-discourses provided a sort of affect theory insofar as they aimed at infiltrating the ideology of the 'East Asian Race' into the entire physical bodies of Japanese empire residents, ranging from the level of the 'interior' or psyche to that of the somatic senses in general. The critic Iijima Tadashi explicitly stated that wartime cinema 'aiming at the construction of the Greater East Asia Co-Prosperity Sphere' should be accepted by the audience's 'stomach' (*hara*) and not just simply understood by their brains.[64] On the one hand, this idea was consonant with the term 'spirit' in the Deployment Plan of General Mobilization of the National Spirit approved by the Japanese cabinet in August 1937 in that both indicated people's physical and emotional investment and will without any further reflection and thought. This was exemplified by the bureaucrat Fuwa Suketoshi's famous assertion about the 'ideal' state: 'once we push the button, all people will immediately move into the state of cultural mobilization'.[65] On the other hand, this seemingly irrational mobilisation was based on a degree of intellectual thought that appeared to be scientifically rational. As the Deployment Plan of General Mobilization of the National Spirit associated the 'spirit' with the ideas of 'thought war' and 'propaganda war', it had theoretical support from social scientists such as Koyama Eizō and Yoneyama Keizō, conducting 'rigid' scientific studies into the propaganda of thought or ideology. Film critics such as Tsumura and Ichikawa were evidently under this influence, hence the promotion of affect theory.

But, of course, this is not to say that the government successfully mobilised residents in the Japanese empire into the 'East Asian Race'. Rather, the spectator-discourses suggested that in many cases people did not align themselves as Japanese bureaucrats and critics intended. After all, the idea of the 'East Asian Race' contained a fundamental contradiction. Its legitimate rationale was to form a Greater East Asian Co-Prosperity Sphere that existed beyond any differences in education, area and class, but, in so doing, it disavowed the fact that 'the Japanese' and others had been, and would always continue to be, unequal in terms of political rights. Thus, it always involved a degree of incongruence and conflict between the film spectator as an idealised subject and as an actual agent.

The history of the spectator as part of the 'East Asian Race' is but one case study in the history of Japanese film spectatorship. Throughout history, while the film spectator can be theoretically conceived in individual terms, it has also been associated with certain social groups in terms of not only class, gender and ethnicity (such as the 'East Asian Race') but also 'people' (*minshū*), the masses, 'the national', consumers and citizens, amongst others.[66] Although it is extremely difficult to study the figure of the spectator due to its essentially elusive and complicated nature, we can nonetheless still analyse discourses and practices on and by film spectators so as to explore the historically specific, and theoretically interesting, dynamic relations between the notion of the spectator as a socially constructed subject and agent that acts on their own. For instance, elsewhere I have discussed ways by which through the organisation of and participation in film screening events, citizens have been working as active agents in order to create nexuses within multilayered networks of media, knowledge, shared concern, action and citizenship, especially in relation to non-human ecological factors such as radiation.[67] This case indicates another set of historically unique dynamic relations between the spectator as agent and the spectator as subject pertaining to both economic and political power and the radioactively contaminated environment. In this way, paying attention to the spectator enables us to open up a milliard of aesthetic, social and ecological roles and potentials of cinema beyond what simply focusing on a film text may enable. The figure of the spectator in both its Japanese and global contexts still demands numerous further explorations from a variety of different angles.

Notes

1. For the gaze theory, see Linda Williams, 'Introduction', Linda Williams (ed.), *Ways of Seeing: Ways of Seeing Film* (New Brunswick, NJ: Rutgers University Press, 1994), pp. 1–20.
2. See, for instance, Annette Kuhn, 'Women's Genres', in Graeme Turner (ed.), *The Film Cultures Reader* (London: Routledge, 2002), pp. 22–5.
3. On the other hand, throughout this chapter I will use the term 'audience' to suggest an actual flesh and blood, or social person who is experiencing a film, although the distinction between this and the 'spectator' is only relative and not absolutely rigid.
4. For the concept of the agent, see Bruno Latour, *Reassembling the Social: An Introduction to Actor-Network Theory* (Oxford: Oxford University Press, 2005).
5. For cases relating to the US and the UK, see Josetein Gripsrud and Erlend Lavik, 'Film Audiences', in James Donald and Michael Renov (eds), *The SAGE Handbook of Film Studies* (London: Sage, 2008), pp. 455–6. In the Japanese case, see Aaron Gerow, *Visions of Japanese Modernity: Articulations of Cinema, Nation, and Spectatorship, 1895–1925* (Berkeley: University of California Press, 2010), pp. 52–65.
6. Hugo Münsterberg, *Hugo Münsterberg on Film: The Photoplay: A Psychological Study and Other Writings*, ed. Allan Langdale (London: Routledge, 2013); Gonda Yasunosuke, *Katsudō shashin no genri oyobi ōyō* (Tokyo: Uchida rōkakuho, 1914).
7. D.N. Rodowick, *The Crisis of Political Modernism: Criticism and Ideology in Contemporary Film Criticism* (Berkeley: University of California Press, 1995).
8. Jean-Louis Baudry, 'Ideological Effects of the Basic Cinematographic Apparatus', trans. Alan Williams, in Philip Rosen (ed.), *A Film Reader: Narrative, Apparatus, Ideology* (Bloomington: Indiana University Press), 1981, pp. 286–98. Its French original version was published in 1970.
9. Noël Burch, *Theory of Film Practice*, trans. Helen R. Lane (New York: Praeger, 1973). For IMR, see his *Life to Those Shadows*, trans. and ed. Ben Brewster (Berkeley: University of California Press, 1990).
10. Laura Mulvey, *Visual and Other Pleasures* (Bloomington: Indiana University Press, 1989), pp. 14–26.
11. Robert Stam and Louise Spence, 'Colonialism, Racism, and Representation', *Screen* vol. 24 no. 2 (1983), pp. 12–17.

12 David Bordwell, *Narration in the Fiction Film* (Madison: University of Wisconsin Press, 1985), pp. 29–62.
13 David Bordwell, *Making Meaning: Interference and Rhetoric in the Interpretation of Cinema* (Cambridge, MA: Harvard University Press, 1989).
14 Anne Friedberg's *Window Shopping: Cinema and the Postmodern* (Berkeley: University of California Press, 1994) serves as a representative work in this vein, although it emphasises more a continuation from the modern to the postmodern than a shift.
15 Burch, *Life to Those Shadows*.
16 Miriam Hansen, *Babel and Babylon: Spectatorship in American Silent Film* (Cambridge, MA: Harvard University Press, 1991), pp. 1–125.
17 Noël Burch, *To the Distant Observer: Form and Meaning in the Japanese Cinema* (Berkeley: University of California Press, 1979), p. 70. [Editors' note: see also Chapter 1 by Aaron Gerow and Chapter 5 by Kosuke Kinoshita in this volume.]
18 David Bordwell, *Ozu and the Poetics of Cinema* (London: British Film Institute; Princeton, NJ: Princeton University Press, 1988), pp. 17–30, 173–9.
19 Mitsuyo Wada-Marciano, *Nippon Modern: Japanese Cinema of the 1920s and 1930s* (Honolulu: University of Hawai'i Press, 2008).
20 Gerow, *Visions of Japanese Modernity*, pp. 174–221.
21 Stuart Hall, 'Encoding/Decoding', in Stuart Hall, Dorothy Hobson and Andrew Lowe (eds), *Culture, Media, Language* (London: Routledge, 1980), pp. 234–44. It was originally published in Centre for Contemporary Cultural Studies (ed.), *Culture, Media, Language: Working Papers in Cultural Studies, 1972–79* (London: Hutchinson, 1973).
22 John Fiske, *Television Culture* (London: Routledge, 1988); Ian Ang, *Desperately Seeking the Audience* (London: Routledge, 1991); David Morley, *Television, Audiences and Cultural Studies* (London: Routledge, 1992); Jackie Stacey, *Star Gazing: Hollywood Cinema and Female Spectatorship* (London: Routledge, 1993).
23 Judith Mayne, *Cinema and Spectatorship* (London: Routledge, 1993), p. 93.
24 Janet Staiger, *Interpreting Films: Studies in the Historical Reception of American Cinema* (Princeton, NJ: Princeton University Press, 1992); Janet Staiger, *Perverse Spectators: The Practices of Film Reception* (New York: New York University Press, 2000); Janet Staiger, *Media Reception Studies* (New York: New York University Press, 2005).
25 Matt Hills, *Fan Cultures* (London: Routledge, 2002).
26 Barbara Klinger, 'Film History Terminable and Interminable: Recovering the Past in Reception Studies', *Screen* vol. 38 no. 2 (1997), pp. 107–28.
27 Robert Allen, 'From Exhibition to Reception: Reflections on the Audience in Film History', *Screen* vol. 31 no. 4 (1990), pp. 347–56; Mark Jancovich and Lucy Faire, *The Place of the Audience: Cultural Geographies of Film Consumption* (London: British Film Institute, 2003).
28 See Jonathan Gray, Cornel Sandvoss and C. Lee Harrrington, 'Introduction: Why Study Fans?', in Jonathan Gray, Cornel Sandvoss and C. Lee Harrington (eds), *Fandom: Identities and Communities in a Mediated World* (New York: New York University Press, 2007), pp. 1–16.
29 Henry Jenkins, *Convergence Culture: Where Old and New Media Collide* (New York: New York University Press, 2006).
30 Jacqueline Bobo, 'The Color Purple: Black Women as Cultural Readers', in E. Deirdre Pribram (ed.), *Female Spectators: Looking at Film and Television* (London: Verso, 1988); bell hooks, *Black Looks: Race and Representation* (Toronto: Between the Lines and South End Press, 1992); Rey Chow, *Woman and Chinese Modernity: The Politics of Reading between West and East* (Minneapolis: University of Minnesota Press, 1991); Homi Bhabha, *The Location of Culture* (London: Routledge, 1994); Richard Dyer, *Heavenly Bodies* (New York: St. Martin's Press, 1987); Robert Stam and Ella Habiba Shohat, 'Film Theory and Spectatorship in the Age of the "Posts"', in Christine Gledhill and Linda Williams (eds), *Reinventing Film Studies* (London: Arnold, 2000), pp. 381–401; Michele Aaron, *Spectatorship: The Power of Looking On* (London: Wallflower, 2007).
31 Chow, *Woman and Chinese Modernity*, pp. 3–33.
32 Miriam Hansen, 'Fallen Women, Rising Stars, New Horizons: Shanghai Silent Film as Vernacular Modernism', *Film Quarterly* vol. 54 no. 1 (2000), p. 10.
33 Ibid., p. 12.
34 Ibid.
35 Michael Curtin, *Playing to the World's Biggest Audience: The Globalization of Chinese Film and TV* (Berkeley: University of California Press, 2007).
36 See, for instance, Vivian Sobchack, *Carnal Thoughts: Embodiment and Moving Image Culture* (Berkeley: University of California Press, 2004); Steven Shaviro, *The Cinematic Body* (Minneapolis: University of

Minnesota, 1993); Jinhee Choi and Mattias Frey (eds), *Cine-Ethics: Ethical Dimensions of Film Theory, Practice, and Spectatorship* (London: Routledge, 2013); Carl Plantinga, *Moving Viewers: American Film and the Spectator's Experience* (Berkeley: University of California Press, 2009).

37. Abé Mark Nornes, *Forest of Pressure: Ogawa Shinsuke and Postwar Japanese Documentary* (Minneapolis: University of Minnesota Press, 2007), pp. 144–63.

38. Rey Chow, *Sentimental Fabulations, Contemporary Chinese Films* (New York: Columbia University Press, 2007), p. x.

39. Mitsuhiro Yoshimoto, 'The Difficulty of Being: The Discipline of Film Studies and the Postcolonial World Order', in Masao Miyoshi and Harry D. Harootunian (eds), *Japan in the World* (Durham, NC: Duke University Press, 1993), pp. 338–53.

40. Catherine Russell, *The Cinema of Naruse Mikio: Women and Japanese Modernity* (Durham, NC: Duke University Press, 2008), pp. 19–38.

41. Yuka Kanno, 'Implicational Spectatorship: Hara Setsuko and the Queer Joke', *Mechademia* vol. 6 (2011), pp. 287–303.

42. Hiroshi Kitamura, *Screening Enlightenment: Hollywood and the Cultural Reconstruction of Defeated Japan* (Ithaca, NY: Cornell University Press, 2010).

43. Hideaki Fujiki, *Making Personas: Transnational Film Stardom in Modern Japan* (Cambridge, MA: Harvard University Asia Center, 2013).

44. Anna Lowenhaupt Tsing, *Friction: An Ethnography of Global Connection* (Princeton, NJ: Princeton University Press, 2005), p. 4.

45. Sandra Annett, *Anime Fan Communities: Transcultural Flows and Frictions* (New York: Palgrave Macmillan, 2014), p. 6.

46. Ueda Manabu, *Nihon sōsōki no kōgyō to kankyaku* (Tokyo: Waseda daigaku shuppanbu, 2012), pp. 117–44.

47. Yoshimi Shun'ya, 'Eigakan toiu sengo: Hen'yō suru Tokyo no sakariba no nakade', in Yoshimi Shun'ya, Kurosawa Kiyoshi, Lee Bong-Ou and Yomota Inuhiko (eds), *Nihon eiga wa ikiteiru vol. 3: Miruhito, tsukuruhito, kakeruhito* (Tokyo: Iwanami shoten, 2010), pp. 91–119; Itakura Fumiaki, 'Eigakan niokeru kankyaku no sahō: Rekishiteki na juyō kenkyū no tameno joron', in Yomota Inuhiko, Kurosawa Kiyoshi, Lee Bong-Ou and Yoshimi Shun'ya (eds), *Nihon eiga wa ikiteiru vol. 1: Nihon eiga wa ikiteiru* (Tokyo: Iwanami shoten, 2010), pp. 227–49.

48. Thomas Lamarre, 'Shōhi to seisan no aida: Otaku bunka to jinteki shihon', trans. Ōsaki Harumi, in Fujiki Hideaki (ed.), *Kankyaku eno approach* (Tokyo: Shinwasha, 2010), pp. 255–94.

49. Kadowkawa was founded as a publishing company in 1954 and now it can be seen as a media conglomerate.

50. Marc Steinberg, *Anime's Media Mix: Franchising Toys and Characters in Japan* (Minneapolis: University of Minnesota Press, 2012).

51. See Gerow, *Visions of Modernity*, pp. 52–65.

52. I discuss this in greater detail in my recent Japanese book, *Kankyaku towa nanimono ka: Media to shakaishutai no kingendaishi* (Nagoya: University of Nagoya Press, 2019), chapter 4.

53. Hasegawa Ryōichi, '*Kōkoku shikan*' *toiu mondai: Jūgo nen sensōki ni okeru monbushō no shūshi jigyō to shisō tōsei seisaku* (Tokyo: Hakutakusha, 2008), pp. 95–115.

54. Wan-yao Chou, 'The Kōminka Movement in Taiwan and Korea: Comparisons and Interpretations', in Peter Duus, Ramon H. Myers and Mark R. Peattie (eds), *The Japanese Wartime Empire, 1931–1945* (Princeton, NJ: Princeton University Press, 2010), pp. 41–67.

55. Endō Masataka, *Kindai nihon no shokuminchi tōchi niokeru kokuseki to koseki* (Tokyo: Akashi shoten, 2010), pp. 186–7.

56. Takashi Fujitani, *Race for Empire: Koreans as Japanese and Japanese as Americans during World War II* (Berkeley: University of California Press, 2013), p. 66.

57. See my 'Creating the Audience: Cinema as Popular Recreation and Social Education in Modern Japan', in Daisuke Miyao (ed.), *The Oxford Handbook of Japanese Cinema* (Oxford: Oxford University Press, 2014), pp. 77–99. A revised, developed version of this essay appears in my *Kankyaku towa nanimonoka*, chapter 1.

58. Ichikawa Sai, *Asia eiga no sōzō oyobi kensetsu* (Tokyo: Kokusai tsūshinsha, 1941), p. 2.

59. Tsumura Hideo, 'Nanio yaburubekika', in Nishitani Keiji, Moroi Saburō, Suzuki Naritaka, Kikuchi Masahi, Simomura Toratarō, Yoshimitsu Yoshihiko, Kobayashi Hideo, Kamei Katsuichirō, Hayashi Fusao, Miyoshi Tatsuji, Tsumura Hideo, Nakamura Mitsuo, Kawakami Tetsutarō and Takeuchi Yoshimi (eds), *Kindai no chōkoku* (Tokyo: Toyamashobō, 1979), p. 24. It was originally

published in the journal *Bungakukai* (September and October 1942).
60 Roundtable, 'Monbushō daijin to monbushō suisen eiga', *Eiga junpō*, 1 October 1943, p. 10.
61 Roundtable, 'Kessenki eigakai no shinro', *Eiga junpō*, 21 March 1943, p. 14.
62 Gonda Yasunosuke, *Goraku kyōiku no kenkyū* (Tokyo: Shōgakukan, 1943), pp. 1–2.
63 Misawa Mamie, '"Kōminka" o mokugeki suru: Eiga Tainanshū kokumin dōjō nikansuru shiron', *Gengo shakai* no. 7 (2013), pp. 109–10.
64 Iijima Tadashi, 'Daitōa kensetsusen notameno eiga' (1942), reprinted in *Shinbun kirinuki*, p. 8; *Senjiki tōseika eiga shiryōshū* vol. 11 (Tokyo: Yumani shobō, 2014).
65 Fuwa Suketoshi, *Eigahō kaisetsu* (Tokyo: Dainippon eigakyōkai, 1941), p. 124.
66 For detailed discussion, see my *Kankyaku towa nanimono ka*.
67 Hideaki Fujiki, 'Networking Citizens through Film Screenings: Cinema and Media in the Post-3.11 Social Movement', in Jason G. Karlin and Patrick Galbraith (eds), *Media Convergence in Modern Japan* (Ann Arbor, MI: Kinema Club, 2016), pp. 60–87. A revised, developed version of this essay appears in my *Kankyaku towa nanimono ka*, chapters 7 and 8.

4
FILM CRITICISM
Soviet montage theory and Japanese film criticism

Naoki Yamamoto

DENATIONALISING JAPANESE FILM CRITICISM

One of the remarkable features of English-language studies of Japanese cinema published in the last fifteen years has been the effort to make use of primary written or visual materials drawn from extensive archival research.[1] On a broader level, this increasing interest in an empirical approach has been inseparable from the major shift in film studies from the 1990s, in which both postcolonial scholars and cognitive scientists made numerous attacks on the one-sided, and often ahistorical, application of 'Grand Theory' to individual film texts and our own viewing experience. At the same time, however, this particular move towards more accurate historiographies also emerged as a collective response to David Bordwell's much earlier call for the reform of the study of Japanese cinema. In an essay written in 1979, almost ten years earlier than the publication of his book on Ozu Yasujirō,[2] Bordwell took issue squarely with a fantasy shared by film scholars of the time, one that allowed them to either celebrate or exploit Japanese cinema as a promising alternative to – or even an ideal 'Other' for – the institutionalised norms of Western film practice. To dispense with such Orientalist tendencies, Bordwell demanded a more rigorous historical examination of this national cinema, stressing the urgent necessity of using 'primary print materials' to investigate 'the complex interaction of economic and cultural factors that define cinema as a social practice'.[3] While Bordwell himself was incapable of putting this task into practice, it was taken up two decades later by a number of younger scholars who appeared on the scene with strong area studies and Japanese-language backgrounds.

Despite this ongoing methodological shift, one central question still remains unsolved: how can we critically address the existence of Japanese film criticism in its own right? Needless to say, scholars today frequently look into back issues of Japanese newspapers, film magazines and trade journals in an attempt to retrieve a more compelling, if not authoritative, picture of the objects or topics they study. But what seems to be missing in their relentless search for historical evidence is the question of how to situate the actual body of Japanese critical writings on film within the broader context of twentieth-century cultural production. One possible solution for this challenge is to deal with Japanese film criticism as a historical narrative. Aaron Gerow points out that film criticism in Japan has a long history since the emergence of local film journalism in the 1910s and argues that it constitutes a core part of the discursive operations at work in the very foundation and subsequent transformations of Japanese film practice over time. It is therefore imperative to examine 'the historical trends in film criticism and how critics have conceived their own roles', as it can provide us with 'a window onto how spectatorship and film production have been framed and debated within Japan'.[4] Addressed in this way, the history of Japanese film criticism stops being a handy archive of how certain film texts were seen and discussed by the local audience and instead transforms itself into a vital site of struggle over the shifting definitions of the cinematic experience.

Another way of liberating a corpus of Japanese film criticism from its current dormant status is to refrain from treating it as a self-contained discourse of the Other, deemed to be worthwhile only when we deal with issues related to local film practice. In other words, where Gerow traces the internal, chronological development of Japanese film criticism, I want to foreground its spatial, geopolitical dimension by situating it in the global history of film theory. Indeed, film criticism in Japan has been genuinely international from its inception, with successive generations of critics diligently writing about the latest artistic and discursive trends imported from abroad. Consequently, the general readership of this critical tradition not only became familiar with the names and achievements of foreign stars and directors, but also actively participated in the international debates on what one would call 'classical film theory', as nearly all major texts by Hugo Münsterberg, Béla Balázs, Jean Epstein, Rudolf Arnheim and members of the Soviet montage school became available to them through translation.[5] In this respect, too, a study of Japanese film criticism offers us a good vantage point from which to critically reflect on the very foundation of Japanese cinema, effectively revealing the hybrid nature of what we consider to be 'Japanese' in our discussion of local film practice.

This chapter examines the critical reception of Soviet montage theory in Japan from the late 1920s to the 1940s in the hope of illuminating such a hybrid – and ontologically impure – nature of Japanese film culture. As in other countries, critics in Japan welcomed this revolutionary discourse on film with great excitement, but their critical response became more complicated and prolonged than others precisely because Japan and its cultural traditions – ideograms, *haiku*, woodblock prints, drawing text books and kabuki – played a central role in Sergei Eisenstein's theorisation of dialectical montage.[6] As if to disavow Eisenstein's provocative statement that the idea of montage permeated everywhere in Japanese culture except film, film-makers and critics, especially those with leftist leanings, made collective efforts to achieve mastery of this theory through numerous translations and annotations that continued to be published well into the early 1940s. However, equally significant in this respect is that quite a few Japanese critics of the time also attempted to alter, challenge and even deny the alleged potency of montage as a sole principle of film-making through their own articulation of film and its shifting modes of expression. In this chapter, I will track this virtual, but highly insightful and informed, dialogue between Soviet and Japanese theorists; in so doing, I will also cast a new light on the historical constitution of Japanese film criticism from a truly transnational perspective.[7]

THE ARRIVAL OF MONTAGE THEORY

Most accounts of the Japanese reception of Soviet montage theory begin with Iwasaki Akira's second-hand translation (from German) of Semyon Timoshenko's *The Art of the Cinema: The Montage of Films* (1926), which appeared in the pages of the prestigious film magazine *Kinema junpō* from March to December 1928.[8] As Chika Kinoshita points out, while the first attempts to introduce Soviet films can be traced back to the Berlin-based businessman/essayist Hata Toyokichi's review of *Battleship Potemkin* (1925) in August 1926 or to the Moscow-based Marxist literary critic Kurahara Korehito's two-part report 'The Recent Soviet Film World' published in March and April 1927, Iwasaki's translation had a greater impact because it first introduced the term 'montage' to the Japanese readers.[9] Iwasaki's innovation lay in his decision not to translate this term into Japanese equivalents such as *kumitate* (the Japanese translation of the French verb *monter*) or *henshū* (editing) but decided to use its Japanese transliteration *montāju*. Thanks to this decision, the term 'montage/montāju' came to signify far more than a single technical method in film-making, in effect inspiring various – and sometimes conflicting – interpretations among its local practitioners.

Not surprisingly, the years that followed saw the dramatic upsurge of interest in this new theory. The major texts translated into Japanese in the late 1920s and 1930s include Vsevolod Pudovkin's 'The Film Director and Film Material' (1926), *Film Technique* (1933) and *Film Acting* (1935); Eisenstein's 'The Fourth Dimension in Cinema' (1929), 'Beyond the Shot' (1929) and 'The Dramaturgy of Film Form' (1929);

Dziga Vertov's 'From Kino-eye to Radio-eye' (1929); and Lev Kuleshov's 'Art of the Cinema' (1929) and *The Practice of Film Direction* (1935).[10] In addition, Iijima Tadashi's 1930 translation of Léon Moussinac's *Le Cinéma soviétique* (1928) was also widely read as a handy introduction to major Soviet films – including Eisenstein's *Battleship Potemkin* and Pudovkin's *Mother* (1926) – that remained unavailable to Japanese viewers of the time due to censorship.[11] It should be noted that these Japanese texts were often retranslated from English or German and inevitably contained some grammatical errors and misinterpretations of key concepts.[12] But as we will see shortly, this very inaccuracy had its own critical potential, as it helped transform the Japanese reception of Soviet montage theory from a passive form of assimilation to a more creative act of adaptation.[13]

The increasing critical attention paid to Soviet montage theory was inseparable from the rise of the Japanese proletarian film movement. Among active participants of this movement were members of the Proletarian Film League of Japan, known as Prokino for short. Founded in 1929 as the film unit of NAPF (Nippona Artista Proleta Federacio, or All Japan Federation of Proletarian Arts), Prokino not only produced agitprop films for and about striking and demonstrating workers, but also actively introduced the theory of revolutionary film-making in the Soviet Union through its own journals such as *Shinkō eiga* and *Purokino*.[14] Another notable current in the Japanese proletarian film movement was the rise of a genre called the *keikō eiga* (tendency film) that, although produced by major studios, depicted the plight of the lower-class and socially marginalised people. Given their palpable sympathy with leftist concerns, it is no surprise that directors of this genre also became ardent supporters of Soviet montage theory. Suzuki Shigeyoshi, whose 1930 film *What Made Her Do It?/Nani ga kanojo o sō sasetaka* became the biggest hit in this genre, publicly expressed his fascination with Pudovkin and even developed a new concept called *henshū eiga* (edited or montage cinema) after watching the director's *oeuvres* during his one-year trip to Europe.[15]

In the meantime, one can also understand Japanese enthusiasm for Soviet montage theory within the context of local theoretical debates on the properties of the film medium, especially those concerned to demonstrate the potential of this medium as a distinct art. As the film historian Satō Tadao has observed, on this level of reception the significance of montage theory rested less in its ideological implications than in its methodological privileging of editing; a process that 'increased the confidence of film critics who up until then had easily felt a sense of inferiority toward literature, theatre and other arts' by bestowing film directors a practical means of subjective expression.[16] In the general history of film theory, the effort to evince film's artistic potential through the negation of this medium's ability to mechanically duplicate the visual impression of physical reality is best represented in Rudolf Arnheim's *Film als Kunst* (1932). However, a similar concern had already been discussed among Japanese critics well before the Japanese translation of the same book came out in 1933. For this reason, they never failed to embrace montage as the most elaborated method of proving the plasticity of filmic composition, just like Arnheim did in his own writings. Shimizu Hikaru, one of the most dedicated advocates of Soviet montage theory in this period, wrote in 1930:

> It has already been proved [by Soviet film-makers] that film does not come into existence through a mechanical arrangement of photographic images, but it rather presupposes the intervention of an artist who creates a world in his own way by making use of those images as raw materials. So even if the photographic aspect of film is mechanistic, montage theory guarantees us the freedom of the artist, the realm of pure and spiritual creations.[17]

Despite its historical significance, Shimizu's statement here tells us little more than Kuleshov and Pudovkin's famous dictum: montage is the essence of cinema. Moreover, although Shimizu and his peers such as Sasaki Norio and Mitsui Tōru did refer to other key concepts such as Vertov's 'kino-eye' and Eisenstein's 'montage of attractions', in most cases their pedantic reading of Soviet montage theory revolved only around the metaphor of montage as a new visual language of filmic enunciation.[18] In this formula, as one critic put it, 'A shot in film corresponds to a word in literature [...]. Just as a literary work generates its meaning by arranging individual words, a film achieves its meaning only through montage.'[19] The problem with this comparison of cinema and literature was not limited to its ignorance of dialectic aspects of montage; it also highlighted a regressive tendency to apply a traditional, human-centred definition of art to film rather than exploring how the very notion of art had radically transformed itself in light of this medium's own properties.

As ideas of Soviet montage theory were disseminated though local discourse, a handful of Japanese directors set out to make films drawing on this new principle of film-making. In this respect, Kinugasa Teinosuke's tendency film *Before Dawn/Reimei izen* (1931) has served as a primary example. Although the film itself is not extant today, *Before Dawn* is said to have featured a montage of the ceremonial procession of a feudal lord and rituals practised at the Buddhist temple in reference to a similar montage of the religious procession of peasants and rituals practised at the Orthodox Church in Eisenstein's *Old and New* (1929).[20] But what actually made this film remarkable was Kinugasa's personal commitment to the globalisation of montage aesthetics: from 1928 to 1930, Kinugasa travelled around Europe via the Soviet Union and became acquainted with Pudovkin and Eisenstein; then, upon his return to Japan, he released *Before Dawn* as the first film to showcase what he learned abroad.[21] The public expectation about this first montage film in Japan was so high that the movie theatre was filled with a sense of awe when someone in the audience shouted, 'Montage! That's montage!' in recognising the scene described above.[22]

Perhaps one could further trace this sort of narrative of influence by examining the work of other major Japanese film-makers such as Mizoguchi Kenji, Ozu Yasujirō, Itō Daisuke, Yamanaka Sadao and Kamei Fumio.[23] But this is not what I intend to pursue here for a number of reasons. Firstly, the ways in which Japanese film-makers and critics employed the term 'montage' were so elusive – for some, it meant a powerful codification of film editing and its possible effects, but for others, it emerged as an allegorical method for overcoming the modern experience of fragmentation and alienation – that it remains difficult to detect actual usages and effects of montage in film unless the director clearly declared her/his indebtedness to it. Secondly, and more importantly, tracking both direct and indirect traces of montage theory in Japanese films would inevitably end up reaffirming the hegemonic relationship between the original (the Soviet Union) and its copy (Japan), a problem that is still prevalent in our conventional assessment of non-Western cultural production in the twentieth century. In other words, searching for such a unilateral influence is not reflexive enough to avoid reproducing the ideology of so-called modernisation theory, which tends to reduce diverse instances of modernity in the non-Western contexts into a single and teleological narrative always leading up to the supremacy of the West/original. To avoid this common pitfall, I will redirect my attention first to another group of Japanese critics who deliberately offered more inventive readings of montage theory, and second to the rise of anti-montage discourse in Japan from the late-1930s to the early 1940s.

OUTSIDER CRITICISM AND LOCALISATION OF MONTAGE

The impact of Soviet montage theory in Japan around the turn of the 1930s was not confined solely to the realm of film practice. For instance, it served as a major creative force behind the work of modernist writers associated with a new literary group called Shinkō geijutsuha (New Art School). In his short story entitled 'Pavement Snap', the New Art writer Ryūtanji Yū described his sensory experience of growing urban culture and spaces in Tokyo with the rhythmic repetition of brief sentences ending with specific nouns – Ginza, Chevrolet's advertising tower, blue sparks from the trolley, a department store, echoes from a jazz record, etc. – in an attempt to create a certain montage effect in the reader's mind.[24] This being but one of such examples, it would even be possible to treat montage as an overarching metaphor penetrating the formation and development of Japanese mass culture during the 1920s and 1930s, as Miriam Silverberg did in her book *Erotic Grotesque Nonsense*.[25] Not surprisingly, this overwhelmingly broad impact also left its mark on the field of cultural criticism, inviting a group of *kyokugai hihyōka* (outsider critics) to disclose their original interpretations of montage theory.

The most famous example in this category of 'outsider criticism' is the acclaimed physicist Terada Torahiko, who wrote numerous essays on literature, poetry and film under the pseudonym Yoshimura Fuyuhiko. Terada often criticised his contemporary film critics for their tendency to treat films within the framework of contemporary art alone. He thus devoted a good amount of his writings to the exploration of the structural affinity between *haiku* and Soviet montage theory, in response to Eisenstein's remark on Japanese traditional culture.[26] Being a *haiku* poet himself, Terada's stance towards montage remained less theoretical than impressionistic, assuming it to be a compositional technique of contrasting or associating two or more different elements in the world. Still, his interpretation was innovative enough in its own right, as he went so far as to suggest a more innovative application of montage to various media and cultural products ranging from radio drama to food layout.[27]

Terada's call for expanding the application of montage theory beyond the realm of film-making inspired the participation of many other outsider critics in the debate. Among those critics was the economist Ōkuma Nobuyuki who also wrote extensively about film and literature drawing upon his academic training in classical economics. Ōkuma took up Timoshenko's argument that montage's conceptual progressiveness lies in its ability to render film 'the most economic art' through its systematic control of the viewer's attention. According to Ōkuma, what Timoshenko meant by the term 'economic' had less to do with the capitalist logic of market economy than with its more vernacular usage found in a phrase such as 'the economy of thought'. Underlying this particular usage were ideas of rationality and purposiveness, as it necessarily aimed for the most efficient, cost-effective relationship between the ends and means of intellectual labour.[28]

This search for efficiency, adds Ōkuma, had previously been conceptualised in the form of utilitarianism and thus determined the direction of modern human activities since the days of Jeremy Bentham and John Stuart Mill. However, in post-revolutionary Russia, it was not only crystallised as the working principle of film-making but also began to serve as a new doctrine in refurbishing all sectors of commerce and communication beyond the exploitative (and thus still inefficient) nature of capitalism. Witnessing this ongoing historical shift, Ōkuma concludes that Soviet montage theory materialises what he calls 'the practical principle of the general technique', a paradigm that informs the dialectical relationship between art and industry prevalent in countless instances of twentieth-century cultural production.[29] Given Ōkuma's specific terminology, one would recognise a certain similarity between him and members of the Frankfurt School. Interestingly, this seemingly intuitive comparison can be justified on its bibliographical association, for Ōkuma himself referred to Georg Simmel's *On Social Differentiation* as one of the main inspirational sources for his socio-economic reading of montage theory.[30]

While most Japanese commentators on Soviet montage theory remained as annotators of the Russian original texts, the aesthetician Nakai Masakazu distinguished himself from others by developing his own concept of montage. As a graduate of the philosophy department at Kyoto University, where he studied with renowned Japanese philosophers such as Nishida Kitarō and Tanabe Hajime, and Kuki Shūzō, Nakai's academic background was in neo-Kantian aesthetics and continental philosophy. While Nakai is remembered today for his effort to introduce ideas of the Popular Front movement to Japan through his magazine *Sekai bunka* and weekly newspaper *Doyōbi* (Saturday, named after the French anti-fascist magazine *Vendredi*), Nakai's intellectual activities equally consisted of theoretical speculations on the rise of mass media and its decisive impacts on the shifting modalities of the modern subject and society. Beyond a simple criticism of the industrialisation of art, Nakai's writings on film addressed how radically this new medium of his times changed the forms and meanings of communication through its genuinely collective, participatory modes of production and consumption.

Nakai's take on montage theory is remarkable for his keen and unusual interest in Dziga Vertov. Unlike Kuleshov, Pudovkin and Eisenstein, the presence of Vertov in the Japanese reception of Soviet montage theory turned out to be a troubled one, always imbued with the lack of information and misinterpretations of his ideas. Certainly, Vertov was famous among the Japanese as the leading advocate of 'kino-eye' through a translation of his essay 'From Kino-eye to Radio-eye' and the belated release of *Man with a Movie Camera* in 1932. Nevertheless, relatively little effort was made to introduce this director's writing in its entirety, leaving his concept of 'interval' and other related ideas on montage completely unknown. As a result, Japanese critics of the time came to speculate on what they considered to be a 'Vertovian' montage through reading secondary literature on his work such as Moussinac's *Le Cinéma soviétique* and Fukuro Ippei's *A Voyage to Soviet/Russian Cinema*.[31] In these accounts, Vertov was introduced not only as a pioneer of documentary film-making but also as a pure formalist experimenting with what Eisenstein later categorised as 'metric montage', whose primary aim was said to be the mathematical calculation and arrangement of the length of the shots corresponding to expected emotional effects. However insufficient or misleading, it was this particular assessment of Vertov that informed Nakai's own conceptualisation of montage.

Nakai's fascination with Vertov was most clearly represented in his 1931 essay 'Continuity of *In Spring*'. Having yet to watch films by Vertov, Nakai in this essay decided to examine the recently released Soviet film *In Spring* (1929), which was indeed directed by Vertov's younger brother Mikhail Kaufman. However, more atypical than his non-restrictive choice of the film was the very method he applied in his analysis: to understand the film's distinct composition, he measured and jotted down the length and content of every single shot in the film with his friend sitting next to him holding a stopwatch. The result was something akin to a mathematical table filled with numbers and letters, one that effectively visualises the film's skilful orchestration of the shot lengths accentuated with the extensive use of fast cuttings. This revelation, on the one hand, led Nakai to celebrate *In Spring* as exemplary of 'the musicalization of associative thoughts', as was the case in previous commentators on Vertov. On the other hand, Nakai's real innovation lay in his discovery that the film's attractions derived from its promotion of what he termed a 'new construction of the senses', which taught him a new way of seeing, listening to and speaking about the world through the mediation of the cinematic apparatus.[32] Accordingly, in Nakai's view, the concept of montage took on a greater significance when it began to serve as a particular method of facilitating the mastery of this new sensory experience on the side of the spectator.

Nakai moved on to provide a more detailed account of his notion of montage in his review of the Universum-Film Aktiengesellschaft's (UFA) culture film titled *The Power of Plants* (1934). Here Nakai's emphasis is on how the film succeeded in combining 'plant time' and 'human time' through its innovative use of time-lapse photography, a technique that made it possible to capture the sprouting of buds in motion by dropping frames over a long period of time. In using this particular technique, he argued, filmic representation liberates itself from the constraints of human time perception, as it gradually 'penetrates into the plant's own temporality through the flexibility of the lens and film'.[33] As such, the sprouting of buds – a representation of plant time – is too slow for the human eye to perceive it as a continuous movement and is thus only visible to the camera's mechanical gaze. But it can still be perceptible to us when the director/editor carefully reassembles fragmented images captured on the filmstrip by adjusting the projection speed. It is in this synthesis – or even collaboration – of the human and non-human sensory apparatuses in the creation and reception of the moving image that Nakai locates the most important function of montage. He writes:

> *Montieren* [the German term meaning 'to create a montage'] by no means restricts itself to an operation based on acetone and a pair of scissors. It must designate the process through with both the logic of natural phenomena and the logic of human phenomena combine, imitate, penetrate, and reconcile themselves under the guidance of physical objectivity …. The purpose of true film art must be the realization of *Montage/montāju* in this specific sense.[34]

Undoubtedly, this is a powerful articulation of montage theory with a unique emphasis on its empowering effects on the human perception. It is thus no surprise that Nakai's writings not only influenced his contemporary film theorists such as Imamura Taihei and Nagae Michitarō, but in recent years have also provoked renewed interest among other media scholars.[35] That being said, Nakai's theorisation of film as a medium of a dialectical collaboration between human and non-human agencies was not without a problem as it paid little attention to actual formal changes that took place in both film-making and viewing with the advent of sound film. Nakai later presented a famous argument that structurally, film always lacks the copula – a verb or a verb-like word that connects the subject of a sentence to its predicate – in its enunciation, and that this semantic gap between the shots is only fulfilled by the desire of the masses to create meanings on their own.[36] But this attractive observation could easily be denied not only by means of basic techniques for continuity editing such as match on action and eye-line match, but also by sound film's increasing respect for the continuity of dramatic space and temporal duration guided by dialogue and diegetic sound. This would explain why Nakai's innovative interpretation of montage theory had less impact on the actual development of Japanese film practice; by the time Nakai published his writings on film in the mid-to-late 1930s, Japanese enthusiasm for Soviet montage theory had already lost its impetus, and the majority of film-makers and critics now began to develop a different set of discourses more suited to the production and reception of sound film.

SOUND FILM AND ANTI-MONTAGE DISCOURSE

One of the earliest critiques of Soviet montage theory in Japan appeared around 1936, when the film critics Kitagawa Fuyuhiko and Iijima Tadashi launched the Shinario bungaku undō (Scenario Literature Movement) in conjunction with the growing popularity of literary adaptation in sound film.[37] Above all, this movement sought to reinvent the notion of the film auteur by promoting written scripts as the primary means of a film-maker's subjective expression. And it is according to this line of inquiry that Sawamura Tsutomu, another major figure of the movement, disputed the premise of montage as a principle of film-making. Sawamura rightly observed that the goal of Soviet montage theory was to establish a distinct cinematic language that was said to be able to express abstract ideas and emotions without the help of verbal language. But born in 1915 and having witnessed the irreversible influx of spoken words in film, Sawamura couldn't but help dismiss this project as a pipe dream. 'When', he wrote in 1937, 'will montage be able to reach the same level of detailed concreteness as letters? If it took three thousand years before letters achieved their current expressive ability, it must require several times longer in the case of montage on the screen.'[38]

Despite the clarity of his polemic, Sawamura was not so different from previous supporters of Soviet montage theory. Indeed, Sawamura criticised montage for its degree of imperfection as 'a means for the direct depiction of thoughts' and in turn celebrated the superiority of written or spoken words over image in facilitating the creative intervention of human artistry within film-making.[39] Thus the question was again how to come to terms with the alterity of mechanically reproduced photographic images; in order to overcome this familiar problem, Sawamura and his peers in the Scenario Literature Movement suggested a more systematic use of language-based communication by refurbishing written scripts as a point of encounter between film-makers and viewers.

Around the same time, the film-maker Itami Mansaku also took issue with the common understanding of montage theory as the essence of film-making. As a professional cynic specialising in the production of sarcastic *jidaigeki* (period drama) films, Itami always condemned his compatriots' blind acceptance of 'theories of Western authorities' and in turn preached the necessity of developing a more practical theory based on the director's first-hand experience.[40] The target of Itami's criticism was the scriptwriter Kurata Fumindo, who in his 1940 book *A Theory of Screenwriting* argued that all scenes in a film should be arranged in conflict with one another following Eisenstein's famous theorisation of dialectical montage.[41] As might be expected, Itami did not buy into this argument because it was completely at odds with what he had learned from his own working experience. 'In principle', he said, 'cutting in film should avoid any conflicts' for the sake of the economy of film narration. Therefore, he continued:

> Insofar as it is represented by its theory of collision […] the true nature of theoretical debates on film montage is not far from a mere speculation. As a result, I have somehow come to form the impression that it [Soviet montage theory] was an illegitimate child in film theory who tried to take over the orthodox lineage of composition by taking its methodological tricks to the extreme.[42]

Itami admitted that his counterargument was no more than a repetition of the basic principles of classical film editing. But he nonetheless believed that 'a theory can never have the power to convince people unless it grasps a truth applicable to most cases', and for this reason Itami went so far as to reject calling Soviet montage theory a 'theory' in its strict sense.[43]

If Sawamura and Itami spoke mainly from the position of film-makers, the poet and film critic Sugiyama Heiichi opened a new perspective by foregrounding the issue of reception. Given his dual interest in film and poetry, it seems natural that Sugiyama started his career in the mid-1930s by joining the ongoing debates about literary adaptation within the Scenario Literature Movement. However, Sugiyama was highly critical of those who blindly celebrated the integration of film and literature in sound cinema because they were completely ignorant of different modes of receptive activities involved with these two distinct forms of expression. The specificity of reading a novel, he said, lay in the fact that it one-sidedly delivers ideas or stories that the author has already conceived in advance, inevitably imposing a certain kind of patience on the side of the reader. In watching a film, however, the spectator is given more freedom in interpreting the situation being unveiled on the screen precisely because the meanings of the images captured by the camera's gaze are far richer and more complex than those depicted by written words.[44] Sugiyama did not abandon the use of a written script in film-making, but he still maintained that once the shooting process began, film directors had to respect and negotiate with the existence of physical reality as it always spoke back to them within their composition of the film's fictional world.

Sugiyama's criticism of Soviet montage theory stemmed from his desire to reformulate the camera's ability to generate 'mechanically accurate reflections of reality' as a new principle of film art. In his 1941 book *Essays on Film*, Sugiyama turned down Pudovkin's famous experiments with montage by squarely attacking the director's overconfidence in the manipulability of the film image and the viewer's emotions:

> That Pudovkin was unable to achieve satisfactory results by simply filming the explosion of dynamite is not a definitive phenomenon applicable to all instances. The foundation [of film-making] should be grounded in one's intention to record an actual explosion. It is better if one can simply film a real huge explosion, and there is no reason to escape from it and rely instead on creation by montage. Because it was impossible to film a real scene of a man being killed in a car accident, Pudovkin created an editing technique based on rapid cutting. In any case, this is nothing but an escapist tactic called in to fulfil a need.[45]

It is obvious that Sugiyama was condemning Pudovkin's underestimation of the existence of the actual world reflected in individual shots, the property on which his notion of film practice – comprising both film-making (expression) and viewing (perception) – was founded. To remedy this problem, he proceeded to highlight two newly emergent techniques that he thought provided promising alternatives to montage.

The first was the long take. As I have argued elsewhere, it became a dominant technique among Japanese sound films from the late 1930s onwards and refined aesthetically by directors such as Mizoguchi Kenji and Uchida Tomu.[46] Anticipating postwar theorists such as Christian Metz, Sugiyama explained the potential of this technique by rephrasing the linguistic metaphor used in Soviet montage theory:

The Kuleshov School's idea of using a shot as a word has already been proven false by the fact that a shot in today's film obtains the contents that are far richer than a word and comparable with a short story.[47]

The second is what Sugiyama called *oku yuki no aru gamen*, a technique usually known as 'the shot-in-depth' or 'deep focus'. Although this particular technique is often associated with Orson Welles's *Citizen Kane* (1941) and its chief cameraman Gregg Toland, Sugiyama did not follow this view since the film was not officially released in Japan until the 1960s due to Japan's attack on Pearl Harbor in December of the same year. Nevertheless, Sugiyama was still able to detect earlier use of this technique in the work of Jean Renoir and Yamanaka Sadao and stressed how it helped fulfil the viewer's increasing desire to see 'as many things as possible' within a single shot.[48]

Sugiyama argued that the combination of these two new techniques would be more appropriate than montage in generating more fruitful effects on the reception of sound film. Rather than one-sidedly controlling the viewer's attention, these techniques aimed to stimulate the viewer's active participation in the creation and discovery of meaning in and of a film by showing two or more events simultaneously taking place within the continuous flow of time. In so doing, they succeeded in bringing back wonder and contingency to the experience of the filmed world, an element that had once been excluded by Soviet montage theory in its relentless pursuit of the distinctively unique visual language for filmic enunciation. Given such an astute observation of 'the evolution of the language of cinema', one might be tempted to celebrate Sugiyama as a precursor to André Bazin. But the fact that Sugiyama preceded Bazin by a decade in his call for the prohibition of montage does not simply attest to the originality of this Japanese critic. Rather, it is more productive for us to look at his argument in the light of the global circulation of classical film theory and practice. In this respect, Sugiyama's appraisal of Yamanaka as a pioneer of the shot-in-depth technique offers an intriguing point of reference. Sugiyama cited Hiroshige's nineteenth-century landscape woodblock prints as a possible inspirational

Fig. 4.1 An example of shooting-in-depth in *Humanity and Paper Balloons/Nijō kami fūsen* (Yamanaka Sadao, 1937, Tōhō).

source for Yamanaka's innovation, but this overtly ethnocentric reading remains mere speculation. A more plausible account is that in making his last film *Humanity and Paper Balloons/Ninjō kamifūsen* (1937), Yamanaka collaborated with the cameraman 'Harry' Mimura Akira, who, prior to his return to Japan in 1934, had worked in Hollywood for five years under the tutelage of acclaimed cinematographers such as George Burns, Alvin Wyckoff and, most importantly, Gregg Toland (Fig. 4.1).[49] This transnational web of collaboration, again, tellingly reveals the hybrid nature of Japanese film practice where what is rendered 'Japanese' has always developed in constant dialogue with ideas, concepts and techniques from abroad.

CONCLUSION

Soviet montage theory did not disappear from Japanese film criticism with the rise of the anti-montage discourse in the early 1940s. Indeed, it reappeared in the late 1950s with regard to the discursive formation of a film movement later known as the Japanese New Wave. While the film-maker Hani Susumu and the film theorist Okada Susumu called for a new approach to montage by suggesting the integration of 'the montage of sequences' and 'the montage within a shot' with the prevalent use of the long take in postwar cinema,[50] the literary critic Hanada Kiyoteru and the film-maker

Matsumoto Toshio revisited Eisenstein's concept of 'the montage of attractions' as a revolutionary method of breaking with the idea of descriptive causality and other narrative conventions still dominant in commercial film-making.[51] In the meantime, the period following the late 1950s was also a time when a handful of film critics began to historicise the Japanese reception of Soviet montage theory. Most of these accounts, however, were trapped in the logic of polarisation: whereas leftist critics such as Iwasaki Akira and Imamura Taihei argued that the influence of Soviet montage theory was so profound that it remained continuously visible in the work of Japanese film-makers,[52] Satō Tadao totally disagreed with this view by stating, 'despite the flamboyant popularity of montage theory, it did not have much actual influence on the development of Japanese film'.[53]

In this chapter, I have tried to illuminate what has been left untold between these two opposing assessments by tracking how Japanese film-makers and critics in the transitional period from silent to sound film adopted, altered and rejected (and revisited) the concepts of montage through their own articulation of cinema's shifting modes of expression and perception. Studying the history of Japanese film criticism, I argue, not only helps us foreground the complex association of word and image in the historical constitution of Japanese film practice; it also enables us to resituate Japanese-language film writing as an active participant in the global influx of classical film theory and practice beyond a simple, hegemonic narrative of influence from the Western centre to the non-Western periphery. Perhaps few concepts are more relevant than montage for this less Eurocentric, multidirectional mode of cultural exchange. If, in principle, the term 'montage' designates the creation of a new meaning through the generative, sometimes strikingly irruptive collision between two or more different elements, it also urges us to formulate a new configuration of the history of film theory and criticism in general. In other words, it requires by nature an approach that deepens and renews our understanding of cinema and its historical significance by dialectically integrating previously neglected voices from Japan and other non-Western countries.

Notes

1. See Joanne Bernardi, *Writing in Light: The Silent Scenario and the Japanese Pure Film Movement* (Detroit, MI: Wayne State University Press, 2001); Abé Mark Nornes, *Japanese Documentary Film: The Meiji Era through Hiroshima* (Minneapolis: University of Minnesota Press, 2003); Peter B. High, *The Imperial Screen: Japanese Film Culture in the Fifteen Years' War, 1931–1945* (Madison: University of Wisconsin Press, 2003); Jeffrey Dym, *Benshi, Japanese Silent Film Narrators, and Their Forgotten Narrative Art of Setsumei: A History of Japanese Silent Film Narration* (Lewiston, NY: Edwin Mellen Press, 2003); Thomas Lamarre, *Shadows on the Screen: Tanizaki Jun'ichirō and 'Oriental' Aesthetics* (Ann Arbor: Center for Japanese Studies, University of Michigan, 2005); Michael Baskett, *The Attractive Empire: Transnational Film Culture in Imperial Japan* (Honolulu: University of Hawai'i Press, 2008); Mitsuyo Wada-Marciano, *Nippon Modern: Japanese Cinema of the 1920s and the 1930* (Honolulu: University of Hawai'i Press, 2008); Aaron Gerow, *Visions of Japanese Modernity: Articulations of Cinema, Nation, and Spectatorship, 1895–1925* (Berkeley: University of California Press, 2010); Hiroshi Kitamura, *Screening Enlightenment: Hollywood and the Cultural Reconstruction of Defeated Japan* (Ithaca, NY: Cornell University Press, 2010); Harald Salomon, *Views of the Dark Valley: Japanese Cinema and the Culture of Nationalism, 1937–1945* (Wiesbaden: Harrassowitz Verlag, 2011); Hideaki Fujiki, *Making Personas: Transnational Film Stardom in Modern Japan* (Cambridge, MA: Harvard University Asia Center, 2013); Yuriko Furuhata, *Cinema of Actuality: Japanese Avant-Garde Filmmaking and in the Season of Image Politics* (Durham, NC: Duke University Press, 2013); and Daisuke Miyao, *The Aesthetic of Shadow: Lighting and Japanese Cinema* (Durham, NC: Duke University Press, 2013).
2. David Bordwell, *Ozu and the Poetics of Cinema* (London: British Film Institute; Princeton, NJ: Princeton University Press, 1988).
3. David Bordwell, 'Our Dream Cinema: Western Historiography of the Japanese Film', *Film Reader* no. 4 (1979), pp. 57–8.
4. Aaron Gerow, 'Critical Reception: Historical Conceptions of Japanese Film Criticism', in Daisuke Miyao (ed.), *The Oxford Handbook of Japanese Cinema* (Oxford: Oxford University Press, 2014), p. 62.

5   See Hugo Münsterberg, *Eigageki: Sono shinrigaku to bigaku* [The Photoplay: A Psychological Study], trans. Kuze Kōtarō (Tokyo: Ōmura shoten, 1924); Jean Epstein, 'Eiganōteki yōso' ['L'Elément photogénique'], trans. Okada Shinkichi, *Eiga ōrai* no. 24 (December 1926), pp. 34–7; Béla Balázs, *Eiga bigaku to eiga shakaigaku* [*Der Geist des Films*], trans. Sasaki Norio (Tokyo: Ōraisha, 1932); Rudolf Arnheim, *Geijutsu to shite no eiga* [*Film als Kunst*], trans. Sasaki Norio (Tokyo: Ōraisha, 1933). For Japanese translations of Soviet montage theory, see endnote 10.

6   Sergei Eisenstein, 'Beyond the Shot', in Richard Taylor (ed.), *Sergei Eisenstein: Selected Works*, vol. 1, *Writings, 1922–34* (London: I.B.Tauris, 2010), pp. 138–50.

7   For the Chinese reception and adoption of Soviet montage theory, see Jessica Ka Yee Chan, 'Translating "Montage": The Discreet Attractions of Soviet Montage for Chinese Revolutionary Cinema,' *Journal of Chinese Cinemas*, vol. 5 no. 3 (2011), pp. 197–218.

8   S. Timoshenko, 'Eiga geijutsu to kattingu 1', trans. Iwasaki Akira, *Eiga ōrai* (March 1928); 'Eiga kantoku to kattingu 2–12', trans. Iwasaki Akira, *Kinema junpō*, 11 July 1928–11 December 1928, repr. in Iwasaki Akira, *Eiga geijutsushi* (Tokyo: Geibun shoin, 1930), pp. 189–248.

9   According to Kinoshita, Hata's review appeared in the literary magazine *Bungei shunjū* and Kurahara's piece in *Kinema junpō*. See Chika Kinoshita, 'The Edge of Montage: A Case of Modernism/*Modanizumu* in Japanese Cinema', in Miyao, *The Oxford Handbook*, pp. 138–41. Analysing the discourse surrounding Mizoguchi Kenji's 1929 film *Tokyo March*/*Tokyo kōshinkyoku*, this essay offers an intriguing account of montage as a catalyst for articulating the cultural and historical conditions of Japanese modernity.

10 V.I. Pudovkin, *Eiga kantoku to eiga kyakuhonron* [retranslated from its German translation, *Film regie und Filmmanuskript*, 1928], trans. Sasaki Norio (Tokyo: Ōraisha, 1930); *Eiga haiyūron*, trans. Magami Gitarō (Tokyo: Naukasha, 1935); V.I. Pudovkin, *Eiga sōsakuron* [retranslated from its English translation, *Film Technique*, exp. edn, 1933], trans. Sasaki Norio (Tokyo: Eiga hyōronsha, 1936); Dziga Vertov, 'Verutofu no eigaron' [re-translated from its German translation published on *Die Forms*], trans. Itagaki Takao, *Shinkō geijutsu*, November 1929, repr. in Itagaki's *Kikai to geijutsu to no kōryū* (Tokyo: Iwanami shoten, 1929), pp. 153–69; Sergei Eisenstein, 'Yojigen no eiga', trans. Fukuro Ippei, *Kinema junpō*, 1 October 1929; 'Nihon bunka to montāju', trans. Fukuro Ippei, *Kinema junpō*, 11 January 1930–21 February 1930, repr. in Fukuro Ippei (ed. and trans.), *Eizenshutain eigaron* (Kyoto: Daiichi geibunsha, 1940), pp. 46–61, 9–45; *Eiga no benshōhō*, trans. Sasaki Norio (Tokyo: Ōraisha, 1932); Lev Kuleshov, 'Kureshofu eiga geijutsuron', trans. Magami Gitarō, *Eigageijutsu kenkyū* nos. 2–9 (June 1933–July 1934); *Eiga kantokuron*, trans. Magami Gitarō (Tokyo: Eiga hyōronsha, 1937).

11 Léon Moussinac, *Soviet Russia no eiga, cinema no tanjō, eiga geijutsu no mirai* [this translation also contains the first half of *Naissance du cinéma* by the same author], trans. Iijima Tadashi (Tokyo: Ōraisha, 1930). Soviet films officially released in prewar Japan include *Storm over Asia* (Vsevolod Pudovkin, 1928), *In Spring* (Mikhail Kaufman, 1929), *Old and New* (aka, *The General Line*, Sergei Eisenstein, 1929), *Turksib* (Victor A. Turin, 1929) and *Man with a Movie Camera* (Dziga Vertov, 1929).

12 For this reason, the Russian-speaking translators Fukuro Ippei and Magami Gitarō tried to reduce these errors by publishing essays and books directly translated from the Russian original.

13 Michael Raine also sheds light on the creative potential of adaptation in his recent article on Ozu Yasujirō. See his 'Adaptation as "Transcultural Mimesis" in Japanese Cinema', in Miyao, *The Oxford Handbook*, pp. 101–23.

14 For a detailed account of Prokino, see Nornes, *Japanese Documentary Film*, pp. 19–47.

15 Suzuki Shigeyoshi, '*Sangatsu tōka, Kono issen, Mamore ōzora*: Henshū eiga no koto', *Film Center* no. 11 (January 1973), pp. 10–11, 42.

16 Satō Tadao, 'Does Theory Exist in Japan?' trans. Joanne Bernardi, *Review of Japanese Culture and Society* 22 (December 2010), p. 19.

17 Shimizu Hikaru, 'Eiga to kikai', in Itagaki Takao (ed.), *Kikai geijutsuron* (Tokyo: Tenjinsha, 1930), p. 67.

18 See Sasaki Norio, 'Geijutsu to montāju', *Kinema junpō*, 21 February 1930, p. 50; and Mitsui Tōru, *Montājuron to yūon eiga riron* (Tokyo: Ōraisha, 1933).

19 Hirabayashi Hatsunosuke, 'Geijutsu no keishiki to shite no shōsetsu to eiga', in Hirabayashi Komako (ed.), *Hirabayashi Hatsunosuke ikōshū* (Tokyo: Heibonsha, 1932), p. 121.

20 Iwamoto Kenji, 'Nihon ni okeru montage riron no shōkai', *Hikaku bungaku nenshi* no. 10 (1974), p. 80.

21 For his trip to the Soviet Union, see Kinugasa Teinosuke, *Waga eiga no seishun: Nihon eigashi no ichi sokumen* (Tokyo: Chūōkōron-sha, 1977), pp. 101–34.
22 This episode is cited in Tsuji Hisakazu, 'Kaisō no Pudofukin', *Eiga hyōron* no. 146 (April 1938), p. 81.
23 Yamamoto Kikuo provides a prime example of this approach. See his 'Montāju to museiki no Nihon eiga', in *Nihon eiga ni okeru gaikoku eiga no eikyō: Hikaku eigashi kenkyū* (Tokyo: Waseda daigaku shuppanbu, 1983), pp. 177–98.
24 Ryūtanji Yū, 'Peevumento snnapu: Yonaka kara asa made', repr. in Unno Hiroshi (ed.), *Modan Tokyo annai* (Tokyo: Heibonsha, 1989), pp. 172–3.
25 Miriam Silverberg, *Erotic Grotesque Nonsense: The Mass Culture of Japanese Modern Times* (Berkeley: University of California Press, 2006).
26 Terada Torahiko, 'Renku zassō', *Shibugaki*, March–December 1931, repr. in *Terada Torahiko zuihitsushū*, vol. 3 (Tokyo: Iwanami shoten, 1948), pp. 45–99.
27 Terada Torahiko, 'Seiji no montāju', *Zatsumi*, December 1931, repr. in *Terada Torahiko zuihitsushū*, vol. 3, pp. 105–6.
28 Ōkuma Nobuyuki, 'Keizaigaku to eiga geijutsugaku: Keizaigaku ni okeru "ippan gijutsugaku" no taidō', in *Bungei no Nihon-teki keitai* (Tokyo: Sanseidō, 1937), repr. in *Geijutsu keizaigaku* (Tokyo: Ushio shuppan, 1974), pp. 359–61.
29 Ibid., pp. 361–2.
30 Ibid., p. 366.
31 Moussinac, *Sovieto Roshiya no eiga*; Fukuro Ippei, *Sovēto Roshiya eiga no tabi* (Tokyo: Ōraisha, 1931).
32 Nakai Masakazu, 'Haru no kontinuitī', *Bi-hihyō*, March 1931, repr. in *Gendai bijutsu no kūkan*, vol. 3 of Kuno Osamu (ed.), *Nakai Masakazu zenshū* (Tokyo: Bijutsu shuppansha, 1964), pp. 145, 149.
33 Nakai Masakazu, 'Kontinuitī no ronrisei', *Gakusei hyōron*, June 1936, repr. in *Nakai Masakazu zenshū*, vol. 3, p. 170.
34 Ibid., p. 171.
35 See, for instance, Gotō Yoshihiro, *Nakai Masakazu no media ron* (Tokyo: Gakubunsha, 2005); and Kitada Akihiro, 'An Assault on "Meaning": On Nakai Masakazu's Concept of "Mediation"', trans. Alex Zahlten, *Review of Japanese Culture and Society* no. 22 (December 2010), pp. 88–103.
36 Nakai Masakazu, 'Gendai bigaku no kiki to eiga riron', *Eiga bunka*, May 1950, repr. in *Nakai Masakazu zenshū*, vol. 3, pp. 192–3.
37 The late 1930s saw a series of publication on scenario literature. See, for instance, Iijima Tadashi, Uchida Kisao, Kishi Matsuo and Hazumi Tsuneo (eds), *Scenario bungaku zenshū*, 6 vols. (Tokyo: Kawade shobō, 1936–7); and Kitagawa Fuyuhiko, *Scenario bungakuron* (Tokyo: Sakuhinsha, 1938).
38 Sawamura Tsutomu, 'Eiga no hyōgen', in *Eiga no hyōgen* (Tokyo: Suga shoten, 1942), pp. 231–2. According to Sawamura, this essay was originally written in 1937 but remained unpublished until 1942.
39 Ibid., p. 226.
40 Itami Mansaku, 'Tenpo to iu koto ni tsuite', *Eiga hyōron*, February 1933, repr. in *Itami Mansaku zenshū*, vol. 2 (Tokyo: Chikuma shobō, 1961), p. 8.
41 Kurata Fumindo, *Scenario ron* (Kyoto: Daiichi geibunsha, 1940).
42 Itami Mansaku, '*Scenario ron* no naka no shomondai', *Kikan eiga kenkyū*, July 1941, repr. in *Itami Mansaku zenshū*, vol. 2, p. 79.
43 Ibid.
44 Sugiyama Heiichi, 'Camera no soshitsu to shite no shajitsu', *Eiga hyōron* no. 124 (July 1936), pp. 70–2.
45 Sugiyama Heiichi, *Eiga hyōronshū* (Kyoto: Daiichi geibunsha, 1941), pp. 9–10.
46 See my 'Talkie realism e no michi', in Yomota Inuhiko, Yoshimi Shun'ya, Kurosawa Kiyoshi and Lee Bong-Ou (eds), *Eigashi o yomi naosu* (Tokyo: Iwanami shoten, 2010), p. 230. As I pointed out, the average length of a shot in the first few scenes in Uchida's 1939 film *Earth/Tsuchi* is 32 seconds, with the longest being 88 seconds.
47 Sugiyama, *Eiga hyōronshū*, p. 9.
48 Ibid., p. 17.
49 For the relationship between Mimura and Toland, see Miyao, *The Aesthetic of Shadow,* pp. 230–54.
50 Hani Susumu, 'Atarashii montāju no kakuritsu o mezashite 4: Genjitsu ni ataeru shin-chitsujo', *Shinema* 58 no. 12 (1958), pp. 11–12; and Okada Susumu, 'Pōrando eiga no wakai sedai', *Eiga hyōron* (January 1959), p. 72.
51 Hanada Kiyoteru, 'Eiga kantokuron', in Noma Hiroshi, Sasaki Kiichi, Hanada Kiyoteru, Abe Kōbō, Haniya Yutaka and Shīna Rinzō (eds), *Bungakuteki eigaron* (Tokyo: Chūōkōron-sha, 1957); and Matsumoto Toshio, 'Zen'ei kiroku eigaron', in *Eizō no hakken: Avant-garde to documentary* (Tokyo: San'ichi shobō, 1963), pp. 47–56.

52 See Iwasaki Akira, *Eiga no riron* (Tokyo: Iwanami shoten, 1956), pp. 7–8; and Imamura Taihei, 'Soviet eiga no eikyō: Senzen no kaisō', in Iwabuchi Masayoshi (ed.), *Bessatsu sekai eiga shiryō: Soviet eiga no yonjū-nen* (Tokyo: Sekai eiga shiryōsha, 1959), pp. 42–4.

53 Satō Tadao, 'Nihon ni eiga riron wa attaka' (1977), translated as 'Does Film Theory Exist in Japan?', trans. Joanne Bernardi, *Review of Japanese Culture and Society* no. 22 (December 2010), p. 17.

5

NARRATIVE
Multi-viewpoint narrative: From *Rashomon* (1950) to *Confessions* (2010)

Kosuke Kinoshita

Nakashima Tetsuya's thriller *Confessions/Kokuhaku* (2010) problematises the critical status of Kurosawa Akira's most renowned film *Rashomon/Rashōmon* (1950) in international film history. Many scholars have noted *Rashomon* as a prototype of modernist film or an alternative to mainstream popular cinema precisely because it constitutes a multi-viewpoint narrative structure in which the same diegetic event is told several times, from the multiple viewpoints of several characters involved.[1] Indeed, while *Rashomon* was celebrated at international film festivals, we cannot say that the film had any critical and commercial success within Japan before it gained its global reputation.[2] *Confessions*, however, despite apparently being similar to *Rashomon* in terms of its multi-viewpoint narrative, did become commercially successful and critically prominent in Japan. While the film was not widely distributed in mainstream or art cinemas and festivals outside Japan, it won four prizes including the Picture of the Year at the 34th Japan Academy Awards, and earned 3.85 billion yen (approx. £20.12 million) at the domestic box-office, where it was placed seventh in 2010.

Whilst *Confessions* has never been seen as a modernist film, its multi-viewpoint narrative is actually even more complex than that of *Rashomon*. The film repeatedly, but with certain variations, narrates several events surrounding the murder of a 4-year-old girl, the female schoolteacher Moriguchi's daughter, from the viewpoints of five different characters: Moriguchi, Watanabe, Shimomura, Mizuki and Shimomura's mother. While the murder has apparently taken place at a junior high school, the incident is audiovisually narrated three times, firstly as the direct experience of Moriguchi who finds her daughter already dead in the swimming pool, next as told in confessions by Watanabe and Shimomura, two male students who commit the murder, and then again as a confession from Shimomura that is located much later in the film. The first two recollections can be seen in contradistinction to the last one; this discloses the crucial information that radically alters the story about the murder told by the first two. In addition, Moriguchi's initial confession of her act of vengeance on the two guilty students also turns out to be a lie when later retold by Moriguchi. Such deliberate structuring of evidence and counter-evidence gradually constitutes a mosaic-like façade of a narrative that complicates the notion of which piece of tile precisely reflects true diegetic reality. Even in its ending, the film provides one more confession that overturns the story that has only just appeared to be coherently concluded.

In reminding us of *Rashomon*, the complex narrative of *Confessions* raises a crucial question. How can we place such a multi-viewpoint narrative within a wider history of Japanese cinema? The remarkable popularity of *Confessions* no longer allows us to see this type of narrative structure as a unique or modernist experiment in the way that many scholars have characterised *Rashomon* as an alternative to mainstream popular film-making. In truth, it should be noted that the multi-viewpoint narrative of *Rashomon* and other films of this type might in fact derive less from modernist aspirations than from the original stories they adapted. *Rashomon*, for example, was an adaptation of Akutagawa Ryūnosuke's two novels *Rashomon* (1915) and *In a Grove/Yabu no naka* (1921), and *Confessions* is an adaptation of Minato Kanae's 2008 bestselling book of the same title. On the other hand, although it has never been a specifically dominant form, one may still identify a considerable number of Japanese film titles endowed with a more or less multi-viewpoint narrative. These include *Souls on the Road/Rojō no reikon* (1921), *Ghost of Yotsuya/Shinshaku Yotsuya Kaidan* (1949), *Living/Ikiru* (1952), *The Burmese Harp/Biruma no tategoto* (1956), *The Incident/Jiken* (1978), *A Stranger of Mine/Unmei ja nai hito* (2005), *The Foreign Duck, Native Duck, and God in a Coin Locker/Ahiru to kamo no coin locker* (2007), *The Kirishima Thing/Kirishima, bukatsu yameruttey0* (2012) and *The Snow White Murder Case/Shirayukihime satsujin jiken* (2014). As such, the form certainly merits further critical attention.

In this chapter I will thus explore multi-viewpoint narrative in Japanese cinema in terms of the narratological concept of 'focalisation' and closely examine *Confessions* as a case study from this standpoint. The term 'focalisation', originally proposed by Gérard Genette, has been theorised as a term to describe the way in which a narrative constructs multi-tiered structures of information in terms of character knowledge.[3] As I will elaborate further, the term helps us to analyse *Confessions*, as well as *Rashomon*, in an unprecedented way. While previous scholarship has dealt with *Rashomon*, Ozu Yasujirō's films and many other Japanese films in terms of modernist art cinema or as alternatives to mainstream Western cinema, particularly so-called classical Hollywood cinema,[4] few attempts have been made to disclose the specific nature and variations of a multi-viewpoint narrative cinema that has constituted a remarkable strand in both the contexts of world cinema and Japanese cinema. *Rashomon*, *Confessions* and many other Japanese films have all been produced within an intricate web of media in which they each explicitly, or implicitly, refer to the films, literature and other media work that have hitherto appeared in regions not necessarily limited to the nation. By considering the complex referential contexts of multi-viewpoint Japanese narrative films, rather than simply exoticising them as an alternative to the Western canon, we may therefore see how they each cultivate the idea of multiple focalisation as a distinctive filmic narrative strategy.

Like *Rashomon*, *Confessions* constitutes a narrative in which multiple characters' viewpoints are placed in conflict with each other in order to question an objective truth within its diegetic space. Yet unlike *Rashomon*, which foregrounds the relativity of the truth to characters' viewpoints as its main theme and hence maintains the credibility of each to some degree, *Confessions* problematises the credibility of all its characters' focalisations. Although the film presents the multiple viewpoints that each character performs, these subjective focalisations end up being a set of individual experiences, memories and recollections that remain incompatible with each other.

While there are few studies focusing on the question of narrative in Japanese cinema within Japanese-language scholarship, several Anglophone film scholars – most notably, Noël Burch, Stephen Heath, Edward Branigan, Kristin Thompson and David Bordwell – demonstrated narrative analyses of Japanese cinema from the late 1970s through to the 1980s. Despite this formative work, narratological studies have become relatively inactive since the 1990s as historical scholarship, as well as more theoretical work informed by Gilles Deleuze have both begun to become more dominant in the field. I will thus elaborate on the concept of focalisation as a tool for analysing filmic narrative by reconsidering the concepts that Genette, Mieke Bal, Seymour Chatman, Edward Branigan, Peter Verstraten and Jan-Noël Thon, among others, have theorised. By drawing on this work, I will provide a closer examination of the multi-viewpoint narrative of *Confessions* by comparing it with *Rashomon*. My argument as such will, I hope, contribute to the revitalisation of critical interest in the question of narrative and Japanese cinema.

JAPANESE NARRATIVE CINEMA REVISITED

We may identify two predominant trends in the diversity of research into Japanese film narrative.

These take an Orientalist and a modernist approach respectively. As I will argue, the multi-viewpoint narrative of *Rashomon* has been discussed within the intersection of these two approaches.

The Orientalist approach essentialises Japanese cinema as something historically unchanged and, in so doing, underscores the idea of Japanese uniqueness in distinction to the Western tradition. As seen typically in the work of Donald Richie, Stephen Prince and Paul Schrader,[5] the approach often associates itself with auteurism as it tends to discuss Japanese films on the basis of key directors such as Ozu Yasujirō, Kurosawa Akira and Naruse Mikio. Moreover, it emphasises two aspects of the film text: its thematic content and particular filmic style. The writers essentially treat Japanese cinema as the embodiment of a distinctive philosophical notion that underlines the essence of Japanese culture as a universal truth. Schrader notes, for example, that 'the concept of transcendental experience is so intrinsic to Japanese (and Oriental) culture, that Ozu was able both to develop the transcendental style and to stay within the popular conventions of Japanese Art'.[6] For Richie, this universal quality is endowed with 'the relationship between man and his surroundings' and therefore it can be acknowledged as 'the continual theme of the Japanese film, one which quite accurately reflects the oneness with nature that is both the triumph and the escape of the Japanese people'.[7] In a similar vein, Prince recognises in Kurosawa's films 'a cultural attitude [...] as dedication to the "human nexus"' and asserts that 'though it may be a basic moral requirement in all peoples, [this attitude] occupies a dominant position in Japanese social life'.[8]

Countering these thematic analyses, Noël Burch highlights the stylistic elements of Japanese films. Still, his analysis does not reach beyond the trend of Orientalism. In *To the Distant Observer*, he insists that the film styles of Ozu, Kurosawa, Mizoguchi and other directors take over the structural principles of traditional Japanese arts such as *haiku*, *ukiyo-e*, *kabuki* and *bunraku*, principles which all privilege surface over depth, presentation over representation, nonlinearity over linearity, and so on. For Burch, these principles provide an alternative to the norms of Western art, which integrates its formal components in order to achieve illusory representation. For instance, in discussing Ozu's films, Burch asserts that while narrative events are mostly progressed by dialogue, 'the relative autonomy of the imagery',[9] serves to develop its own graphic style. This autonomy of style is crucial because it stands up to the mode of Western classical cinema, which *represents* visual components in an illusory way rather than *presenting* them in a visible way.[10]

Significantly, Burch's Orientalist approach can also simultaneously be seen as part of the other trend in the narrative study of Japanese cinema, that is, the modernist approach. Both Orientalist and modernist approaches illuminate the uniqueness of Japanese cinema as an alternative to the Western canon, but while the former emphasises the continuity between traditional Japanese arts and Japanese cinema, the latter perceives the invigorating quality of Japanese cinema vis-à-vis the norms of classical Hollywood cinema. Whilst also based on auteurism, the modernist approach highlights the unconventional style of Japanese cinema as a set of devices that de-familiarise conventional forms of classical cinema by means of their anti-illusionistic, self-referential and experimental aspects. Kristin Thompson, David Bordwell and Edward Branigan are representative scholars who have taken this approach in their separate studies of Ozu.[11] Thompson and Bordwell, for instance, point to the system of spatial construction such as '360-degree shooting space'[12] in Ozu's films as being radically different from the paradigm of classical Hollywood cinema represented by the 180-degree principle. In classical cinema, they argue, constructed space is subordinated to the causal chain of narrative, but 'Ozu's films open a gap between narrative and various spatial structures' with their use of transitional shots ('pillow shots') or 360-degree shooting style. 'Within this gap we can glimpse the work of a cinema which (like Eisenstein's and Tati's) permits space to contest the primacy of the cause-effect chain.'[13]

Later, in his book on Ozu, Bordwell further discusses the Japanese auteur's films in terms of 'art cinema' and 'parametric cinema' while also contextualising Ozu's films within a wider social and industrial history of Japanese cinema.[14] For Bordwell, Ozu's films are 'art cinema' because they present 'ellipses', 'opaque characters' and 'overt narrational gestures', and they are 'parametric' because they emphasise the patterning of visual formal elements that cannot be reduced to the narrative structure of the films. Likewise, Branigan takes a modernist approach in proposing a geometrical analysis of the graphical composition and symmetrical editing of Ozu's work. For Branigan, as well as Thompson and Bordwell, Ozu's films consistently de-familiarise the narrative-centred conventions of classical cinema, and hence they are modernist films.[15]

While criticising these scholars for treating Ozu simply as a modernist film-maker, Stephen Heath posits Ōshima Nagisa as a more representative modernist or alternative film-maker who challenges classical Hollywood cinema.[16] For Heath, while Bordwell, Thompson and Branigan may illuminate Ozu's systematic construction of autonomous space over narrative causality, this does not merit the term 'modernism' because it only establishes a coherent system at the non-narrative level. Heath argues that what is also required is the disruption of narrative space so as to prompt the spectator to question and revise their way of thinking. It is Ōshima's 1968 film *Death by Hanging/Kōshikei* that most brilliantly epitomises this strategy, Heath contends. In this film, the past story of the Korean-resident protagonist named 'R' is arbitrarily constructed through the narration of other characters surrounding him, so that this 'excessively' coherent narrative actually prevents the spectator's smooth understanding of the main character. Moreover, the director's voiceover address to the audience in the concluding shot, as well as the realistically implausible camera-placement in the form of a reverse shot,[17] successfully functions to generate an anti-illusionist narrative space. This, Heath insists, is in sharp contrast with classical Hollywood cinema, whose coherent narrative space directly involves the spectator within it, thereby precluding their own thinking.[18] At this point, however, despite his critique of Bordwell and the others, Heath's argument rests on the same territory as theirs in terms of conducting a modernist-type of analysis.

These critical and scholarly contexts shed light on the multi-viewpoint of *Rashomon* (Fig. 5.1). Set in

Fig. 5.1 *Rashomon/Rashōmon* (Kurosawa Akira, 1950, Daiei).

twelfth-century Japan, the story of the film is centred on four characters – a woodcutter, a priest, a commoner and a bandit named Tajōmaru – who provide contradictory testimonies about the murder of a samurai in a forest. The testimonies take place one after another in a court with each voiceover account being accompanied by a visual track offering an ongoing flashback vision that corresponds to the individual's recollections. Paying attention to this multi-viewpoint narrative structure, Parker Tyler celebrates the film chiefly because it depicts an 'universal humanist' theme that shows that there is no absolute truth and that we depend, instead, on people's individual subjectivities. This representation, he contends, becomes possible through the unconventional, anti-realistic, multifaceted way of storytelling, which is akin to the art of the early modernist painters such as Picasso and Chagall. Bordwell also foregrounds *Rashomon* as an example of art cinema although, in some ways, he also shows hesitation in noting this film as modernist.[19] Bordwell sees the multi-viewpoint narrative of *Rashomon* is an alternative mode to that of classical Hollywood cinema in that it, 'like modernist fiction, holds a relativistic notion of truth' and hence counters 'the syuzhet of classical narration', which 'tends to move toward absolute certainty'.[20]

It should be also noted that while the narrative structure of *Rashomon* has drawn certain critical attention from Orientalist and modernist approaches such as Tyler's and Bordwell's, it has not done so from any other approach. Keiko I. McDonald's *From Book to Screen*, for instance, is a rare book devoted completely to exploring the relationship between modern Japanese literary works and their Japanese film adaptations. Nonetheless, it does not aim to propose an elaborate theoretical model for analysing the structural differences of narratives between literary texts and films.[21] Mitsuhiro Yoshimoto's monograph on Kurosawa criticises both Orientalist and modernist approaches while advocating a new perspective by which to situate Kurosawa's films within their sociocultural and institutional contexts, thereby not treating their narrative structure as the central subject of his study.[22]

In this way, only modernist and, to a lesser extent, Orientalist approaches have discussed the multi-viewpoint narrative structure of *Rashomon*. Equally importantly, as we have seen, *Rashomon* is treated as an exceptional film. However, as I have already noted, *Rashomon* is not necessarily a special film in the history of Japanese cinema; rather, it is a film that should be placed in the historical strand of multi-viewpoint films including *Confessions*. It remains essential for us to analyse the multi-viewpoint film not as an alternative to the Western norm, but simply as an interesting narrative strategy, which we should assume has developed within the confluence of domestic and international films.

THEORISING FOCALISATION IN NARRATIVE FILM

'Focalisation' has been one of the most actively debated subjects in literary and cinematic narratological studies. Since Gérard Genette introduced the term in 1972, scholars such as Mieke Bal, Seymour Chatman, Edward Branigan, Brian Henderson, François Jost and Peter Verstraten have attempted to revise and develop the term as a conceptual framework for theorising narrative. *Rashomon* has often been referred to as a prominent example of cinematic 'multiple focalisation' within these debates. Indeed, Genette cites *Rashomon* as the most accessible example of his own concept of 'multiple internal focalisation'.[23] While Henderson follows Genette's argument regarding Kurosawa's film,[24] Jost objects, pointing out that the film presents characters' appearances and their actions 'externally' rather than 'internally'.[25] This discrepancy between the external and the internal further inspired Verstraten to account for *Rashomon* as a film that combines 'internal narration' (in which the character in the diegesis narrates) with 'external focalisation' (which does not involve the character's psychology and only shows the character's actions).[26]

Despite these efforts, however, none of these theoretical models is sufficient enough to analyse the complex narrative structure of such a multi-viewpoint film as *Rashomon* or *Confessions*, for they do not take the credibility or incredibility of each character-narrator into consideration. Thus, below I will reconsider the concept of focalisation to accommodate the possible use of an unreliable narrator so that we can analyse a multi-viewpoint film in a more pertinent way.

The issue of the credibility or incredibility of the information seemingly provided through each character has tended to be overlooked primarily because Genette's original definition of focalisation is manifold and hence ambiguous. Genette describes narrative information, including focalisation, in two ways: its terms of its quantity and in terms of its quality, or what he terms 'the law of spirit'. This, in fact, involves two significant problems. One relates to which framework we can use to assess the quantity of narrative information. As Burkhard Niederhoff notes, Genette accounts for focalisation 'as a selection or restriction of narrative information in relation to the experience and knowledge of the narrator, the characters or other, more hypothetical entities in the storyworld'.[27] According to Genette, if a narrative segment is supposed to provide the same amount of information that the character is also supposed to have, this segment is 'focalised through' the character or named 'internal focalisation'. In contrast, the information 'which the hero performs in front of us without our ever being allowed to know his thoughts or feelings' is called 'external focalisation'. But this division between 'internal focalisation' and 'external focalisation' is necessarily arbitrary as it does not clarify which focalisation describes an idea that a character may conceal but visually suggest via their face over a certain period. Moreover, the idea that a character may provide the same amount of information the character actually possesses is fundamentally inappropriate because any character is first and foremost fictionalised. In either case, the categorical definition of 'internal' and 'external' remains a central issue, while the credibility of the information per se is hardly questioned.

The other issue with Genette's focalisation concerns the fact that he often deals with 'internal focalisation' as tantamount to the vision seemingly provided through the character. For 'internal focalisation', he states, 'the very principle of this narrative mode implies in all strictness that the focal character never be described or even referred to from the outside, and that his thoughts or perceptions never be analysed objectively by the narrator'.[28] On the other hand, however, his example of 'internal focalisation' from a novel does not offer the character's psychological thoughts; rather it presents 'what its hero sees'; for instance, in front of a dead body: 'A bullet, entering on one side of the nose, had gone out at the opposite temple, and disfigured the corpse in a hideous fashion. It lay with one eye still open.'[29] Genette's concept of 'internal focalisation' thus oscillates between the character's internal psychology and external viewpoint.

In effect, this double standard has inspired other scholars to re-conceptualise Genette's notion of 'internal focalisation'. However, they have tended to discuss 'internal focalisation' exclusively as the matter of the character's viewpoint while downplaying the matter of the character's psychology. This is probably because they stuck to the spatial metaphors – such as 'internal' and 'external' – that Genette originally introduced to theorise focalisation. This division was based on Genette's notion of 'a law of spirit', by which the narrator or source of narration could exist inside or outside a character's interiority, but could not do so simultaneously. Indeed, he could have explored different ways of describing focalisation, like 'psychological focalisation', without relying on a spatial metaphor, but he chose not to. Subsequent scholars have continued to concentrate on the matter of which space the character's viewpoint is located. Bal, for instance, re-formulises focalisation exclusively in terms of what the character perceives or not among the fragments of ongoing narrative information that the film provides, moment by moment.[30] Other theorists such as Jost and Verstraten, on the other hand, have introduced terminologies such as 'ocularisation' (which is specific to the character's viewpoint, differentiated from visualisation)[31] or 'internal narration' (which is the character's narration as noted above)[32] in order to conceptualise focalisation in relation to a character's viewpoint which should be distinguished from a viewpoint unspecifically related to any character as the source of narrative information.

In any case, they unquestionably presuppose the credibility of the information provided through any viewpoint, or the state in which a character is trusted to offer objective information. We can call this notion 'character-as-filter', borrowing a term proposed by Chatman.[33] The idea of 'character-as-filter' points to the assumption that a character always provides neutral and objective information with no distortion, fabrication or partial oblivion as if they were merely a transparent filter. On this point, Genette's concept of 'multiple internal focalisation' is not pertinent to *Rashomon* precisely because it is premised on the notion of 'character-as-filter'. *Rashomon* and *Confessions* both appear to adopt a character as an unreliable narrator, whose act of telling involves oblivion, distortion and fabrication of the diegetic events. In particular, the fabricated information should be regarded not as 'filtered through' but as totally or partially generated by a character's mental activities. Genette's concept of 'multiple focalisation' cannot account for this complexity.

How then can we conceptualise focalisation in order to effectively analyse multi-viewpoint films such as *Rashomon* and *Confessions*? In the first place, we can see this type of film problematises the very notion of 'character-as-filter' by utilising the focalisation of an unreliable character. Moreover, this focalisation of an unreliable character-narrator, as well as that of a reliable character-narrator, conveys narrational information not limited to the character's own optical vision. Based on this, Jan-Noël Thon's triplet system of narrative information is of excellent use in clarifying which characters share information at a particular narrative moment: 'subjective' (all the information is possessed by a single character), 'intersubjective' (more than two characters share the same information) and 'objective' (no character has the information included in the segment). To this triplet system, I would like to add the division between 'factual' (representing the diegetic truth) and 'imaginative' (in which all, or some, of the information is fabricated by a character). This remodelled system can be illustrated as a table, see Table 5.1.

This table helps us to recognise a characteristic of focalisation in each film. For example, the famous 'pillow shots' in Ozu's films – shots of a characterless landscape or setting preceding a narrative scene – can be classified in category III, factual/objective narration, because most 'pillow shots' can be interpreted as the presentation of non-human or equivalent agency in diegetic space, from a viewpoint that is not uniquely related to any mental activity of a character. The diagram also allows us to see how *Rashomon* employs imaginative/subjective focalisation. Although it is possible to assume that one of the main characters in the film tells the truth, the film does not give any hint at who this is. It should be noted here that although more complex cases exist, the table enables us to understand the very complexity of focalisation. For example, as Chatman points out, in a voiceover sequence in *Badlands* (1979), 'the voice of the heroine, Holly, tells a romanticized account of the escapade with the murderer Kit which is totally belied by the sordid action as we see it with our own eyes'.[34] In this sequence the voiceover can be seen as an example of imaginative/subjective focalisation, while the image track is an instance of factual/objective focalisation.

Indeed, this is what *Confessions* employs throughout its narrative. In some scenes, the visual track communicates the factual/objective focalisation of the diegetic space, while the soundtrack provides a voiceover narration based on the character's subjective account of the diegetic past. In the next section, I will analyse how *Confessions* intricately structures focalisation on its separate, yet also interrelated, audio-visual tracks, by comparing it to the relatively simple structure of focalisation in *Rashomon*.

CONFESSIONS

Rashomon may present the relativity of truth through its characters' focalisations but, paradoxically, it also preserves a certain degree of credibility in terms of the conditions by which one character and another compete to prove which of their testimonies is true. *Confessions*, on the other hand, problematises the credibility of *all* the focalisations involving its main characters. Here, the characters *perform* their own multiple viewpoints insofar as these subjective focalisations proceed as nothing but individual experiences, memories and recollections that can never be integrated into a coherent whole. This characteristic largely draws on three distinctive narrative strategies: (1) the provision of discordant narrative configurations of time and space through an incongruent set of image and audio tracks; (2) the abrupt overturn of the credibility of the narrative information in the middle of a character's ongoing confession; and (3) the presentation of the performative nature of the character's confession,

Table 5.1 The remodelled system of focalisation

I. factual/subjective focalisation	II. factual/intersubjective focalisation	III. factual/objective narration (=non-focalisation)
IV. imaginative/subjective focalisation	V. imaginative/intersubjective focalisation	

which plays with the facts of the murder rather than the telling of the truth.

Confessions brings about discordant spatio-temporal narrative configurations through discrepancies between the audio track and the image track. In other words, the audio track may hint at the spatio-temporal point at which a character's voiceover takes place, but this is not necessarily bound to the image track. For example, near the climax of the film, the final confession by Watanabe, one of the seemingly guilty students, is presented on the audio track in the form of a video file on his website. The word 'tomorrow' in his monologue suggests that what he is telling has already taken place. On the other hand, the image track of the same scene shows various elements in a random way without being restrained by the spatio-temporal position in which the subject of the voiceover is supposed to exist. In another case, during the first recollection, when Moriguchi is giving a farewell speech in her classroom, the camera leaves the location to show us some students playing on the rooftop of the school building, suggesting that her speech is unbearable for them. In yet another sequence, in which Mizuki is typing up her restaurant conversation with Moriguchi on a laptop, the image track presents a flashforward showing Mizuki being killed by Watanabe. In some cases, the visual track even presents non-focalised, seemingly objective, shots in the midst of a character's recollection. In Mizuki's recollection, the image track shows Moriguchi's intense cry and laughter while walking down a street, which takes place after she has learnt Watanabe's real motive for the murder (to gain attention from his beloved mother, who left home during his childhood). Moriguchi's action here, however, appears not to be witnessed by any other main characters, including Mizuki, because they have already parted from each other. All of these sequences indicate that there is a discrepancy between what is seen and what is heard within the film's narrative configuration of time and space.

Another narrative strategy undermining the credibility of the characters' focalisations is to make a character's ongoing narration suddenly become unreliable in the middle of its course. This is most evident in Watanabe's confession. Early in the aforementioned sequence, the image and audio tracks appear to be compatible and provide Watanabe's subjective narration of the murder through his focalisation. He speaks in the form of a video file on his website about his intention to kill both himself and his classmates through a handmade bomb. According to this confession, a bomb will explode during an assembly at the school gymnasium killing everyone once he presses a button on his mobile phone by remote control. In fact, the bomb does not explode. Instead, an abrupt phone call from Mizoguchi unintentionally catches him after he has pushed the button, and he is told that the bomb has already been secretly removed by Moriguchi. Moriguchi then admonishes Watanabe for his cowardly speculation that his mother abandoned him due to her remarriage stating that this is the true reason why Watanabe ran out of the lab in despair, despite his claim that he voluntarily stopped meeting his mother. During this time, Moriguchi's articulation of her interpretation on the image track appears to present faithfully what she is describing on the audio track. In this sense, the spectator is encouraged to believe that the *facts* of the matter are being presented through her focalisation.

However, at the moment when the image track begins to show what Watanabe seems to imagine while listening to Moriguchi's explanation, the spectator realises that what the image track has presented so far may not be factual but a fiction instead. Watanabe's imagining appears to begin right after Moriguchi reveals that she secretly moved the bomb from the gymnasium to his mother's workplace with the image track operating simultaneously as a flashback to show the conduct she describes. The image track then switches to show Watanabe shout loudly in the centre of the gymnasium, suggesting that the explosion of his bomb may have killed his mother rather than himself and his classmates. The image track then begins to show a more obviously fictional version through his focalisation or what he seems to imagine. Here, he appears to be helplessly climbing up the stairs of the campus building that has seemingly collapsed due to the bomb. In the middle of this, a number of consecutive shots suggest he begins to recall the counter-clockwise clock he invented years ago at the time when he was considered a boy genius. These are followed by shots that show him yearning to return to the past with a clock in his hand. His surrounding environment then appears to go back in time leaving only him in the present. Debris from the building is restored to its original position while the flames and smoke from the explosion are reversed. Amidst this reversal of time, Watanabe continues to walk up the stairs. Eventually, he reaches his mother's office and sees her smiling at him the moment before the bomb explodes. Yet, did the explosion really happen? Although Moriguchi's initial focalisation might appear to be true, it loses credibility precisely because the unreliable character Watanabe takes over with his own subjective focalisation. In the process, the spectator may suspect that Moriguchi has also told a lie for there is no guarantee she has told the truth (Fig. 5.2).

Furthermore, because any character's narration may not be reliable in the end, we might consider each recollection to be performative rather than descriptive. This is the third narrative strategy the film employs. One obvious example is Moriguchi's first 'confession' on the audio track, in which she tells her students in the classroom that she has injected HIV-positive blood into the milk the seemingly guilty students have already drunk (this is accompanied by inserted close-up shots of a syringe filled with blood, an injection needle puncturing a milk carton, and blood dissolving into milk). As she suggests later, the point of the statement is not to tell the truth but to toy with the students and get the class to bully the guilty students. A more pressing example is the previously discussed climactic sequence

Fig. 5.2 Watanabe walks up the stairs in *Confessions/Kokuhaku* (Nakashima Tetsuya, 2010, Tōhō).

in which Watanabe's audiovisual focalisation takes over Moriguchi's. These two characters' focalisations do not try to vindicate each of their arguments; rather, Moriguchi just aims to avenge her daughter by utilising Watanabe's mother complex and Watanabe aims to turn his desperate thoughts on his mother. Here, what matters is not what is true but how they each perform their own audiovisual focalisation in relation to the narrative context.

A comparison with *Rashomon* can help further clarify these three unique narrative strategies. Firstly, whereas *Confessions* often provides an incongruent combination of image with audio track in terms of time and space, *Rashomon* gives little sense of any spatio-temporal gap between the two. Individual testimonies usually start in the court and the voice continues as a voiceover in the present while the image track switches back to the wood in the past. Overall, the voice is perceived to describe what the image track shows. Secondly, unlike *Confessions*, which confuses the spectator by abruptly shifting the reliability of the character's focalisation, *Rashomon* makes every single character's focalisation coherent and independent from each other. To be sure, the film makes the spectator realise that each character's account of the murder is subjective, but it does so only by foregrounding the contradictions among the four characters' accounts and not by making one intervene with the another, as in *Confessions*.

Finally, the performativity of the character's focalisation in *Rashomon* is limited. On the one hand, the film has been celebrated as modernist because it explicitly presents each character's account as being something subjective, thereby challenging the conventional flashback or 'character-as-filter' based on the premise of showing a character tell the truth about a past event with no doubts raised. However, no matter what subjective account each character provides, the principle throughout *Rashomon* is that focalisation consistently concerns the matter of what the truth is. This is why the film makes us wonder who is telling the truth and poses the philosophical question whether absolute truth exists and, if so, how this is possible. By contrast, *Confessions* brings to the fore how each character narrates, rather than whether they are telling the truth while, at the same time, betraying or trifling with whatever desire for the truth the spectator may have. At this point, the film's ending is symbolic in that Moriguchi's remark, 'just kidding', overturns the truth about the murder that the film has just appeared to give a moment ago.

The structural differences between the two films can also be seen in terms of their relationships to their source novels. Whereas *Rashomon* largely retains the narrative structure of its source novels with the selection of its scenes, *Confessions* not only selects scenes but also radically changes the narrative structure of its source novel. This reflects the difference between the possibility of the truth being maintained in the former and the reliability or unreliability of the truth being performed in the latter. In Kurosawa's *Rashomon*, one of Akutagawa's stories simply functions as the framework for the other in which the three characters articulate contradictory testimonies. The film appears on the surface to accommodate most of the narrative information from *In a Grove* while, of course, it is also mediated through cinematic expression encompassing *mise en scène*, cinematography, editing and sound.

And yet, close examination reveals that the film selects the elements enhancing the credibility of each character's testimony and, at times, even adds information for this purpose, while also disregarding other elements. This is evident, for example, in the woodcutter's testimony. In *In a Grove* he says that:

> The body was lying flat on its back dressed in a bluish silk kimono and a wrinkled head-dress of the Kyoto style. A single sword-stroke had pierced the breast. The fallen bamboo-blades around it were stained with bloody blossoms. No, the blood was no longer running. The wound had dried up, I believe. And also, a gad-fly was stuck fast there, hardly noticing my footsteps.[35]

Here, the woodcutter provides detailed visual information about the corpse, corresponding to the inquest by the judicial chief. However, the film does not deploy this description at all. Instead, it only shows the stretched out, yet withered, upper arms and hands that seemingly belong to the dying man in the foreground and the petrified woodcutter looking on from the grove in the background. In another example, several shots in the film diverge from the way the focalisation of a character's testimony is consistently maintained in the novel, as is the case with the bandit's testimony in which a point-of-view shot of the killed samurai's wife suggests she is being raped. What both these examples have in common is that the addition of another character's point of view within a character's focalisation is completely absent within the novel. This suggests that this complex visual structure is exclusively integral to the film of *Rashomon*. Moreover, the subject of the testimony is seen and hence confirmed from another character's point of view, even within the focalisation of the testimony, as from the dying man's in the former and from the wife's in the latter. This more cinematic approach serves to enhance a sense of the credibility of each character's narration even though the content of the narration does not necessarily turn out to be true when one is compared with another (Fig. 5.3).

Confessions, on the other hand, reduces the credibility of each character's focalisation in a way that is, to a large degree, upheld throughout its source novel. While the original novel consists of six chapters, each of which is completely written in the first-person

Fig. 5.3 The petrified woodcutter is shown from the dead samurai's point of view in *Rashomon/Rashōmon* (Kurosawa Akira, 1950, Daiei).

voice of the main characters, the visual track of the film multiplies the agency of the narration and hence complicates the narrative we see unfurl. At the same time, it also foregrounds the performativity of each narration. The novel does not present Watanabe's mendacious motive for killing himself and his classmates in the gymnasium, expressed by himself in the video file on his website. Nor does it describe time rewinding around him while he alone remains in the present. The novel also lacks Moriguchi's final remark, 'just kidding'. All these differences between the film and its source novel make it clear that throughout its plot the film plays with the 'truth' rather than seeks it. It does this by re-narrativising some of the motifs of the source novel, most notably the idea of the characters' contradictory explanations, and exploring its own unique complex structure of characters' performative focalisations. While *Confessions* can therefore be placed within a genealogy of multi-viewpoint narrative cinema that includes *Rashomon*, it may also be seen as a vital film for the expansion of the potential of this type of filmic narrative, especially in terms of complicating the relationship between image and audio tracks, overturning the credibility of the character's focalisation and presenting its performativity.

CONCLUSION

Confessions is an interesting case in the history of the multi-viewpoint narrative film in Japanese cinema. It explores a narrative in which throughout the film's plot different characters' focalisations are placed in conflict with each other rather than being integrated into a coherent whole. This complex narrative structure is grounded in the subjective nature of personal experience, memory and recollection as well as the potential unreliability of a person's outward expression. At the same time, the film accomplishes this complex combination of multiple and performative focalisations in its exploration of audiovisual technique.

As I have discussed, we should not regard this type of multi-viewpoint narrative film as an essentially unique aspect of Japanese cinema as more Orientalist approaches have done. Nor should we see it uniquely as a modernist film. Rather, we need to further examine this narrative mode by placing it within the historical context of global cinema. Indeed, it is not difficult to identify similar types of films in, say, Hollywood cinema. A good example is the contemporary genre cycle called the 'mind-game film'[36] or 'puzzle film', which displays a 'fragmented spatio-temporal reality, time loops, a blurring of the boundaries between different levels of reality, unstable characters with split identities or memory loss, and multiple, labyrinthine plots, unreliable narrators, and overt coincidences'.[37] Films such as *The Usual Suspects* (1995), *Memento* (2000), *Secret Window* (2004), *The Machinist* (2004) and *Vantage Point* (2008) can all be classified into this category. Interestingly, almost all of these films eventually provide the sense of a factual, intersubjective or objective view of the story event, thereby reaffirming the authority of filmic storytelling as the guarantor of truth. Even if they appear to be similar, *Confessions* and other multi-viewpoint films challenge this type of narrative structure and instead mix up factual and imaginative focalisations.

Japanese multi-viewpoint narrative cinema has evolved by accommodating cosmopolitan interactions. The novels and films I have analysed have also been created within a complex historically shaping complex web of Japanese and foreign narrative works. As literary scholars have pointed out, Akutagawa's *In a Grove*, for instance, can be seen to have utilised ideas from Ambrose Bierce's *The Moonlit Road* (1907) and Robert Browning's *The Ring and the Book* (1868–9) as well as *Das Cabinet des Dr. Caligari* (1920).[38] Likewise, Kurosawa reportedly applied the technique of French silent cinema in the 1920s to the 'silent sequence' in *Rashomon* depicting the woodcutter's 'opening journey into the woods'.[39] *Confessions* would also not have been produced without the pre-existence of the global cycle of the 'puzzle film'.

In this way, the Japanese multi-viewpoint film can be seen as lying at the intersection between a genealogical mode of Japanese narrative and a set of more cosmopolitan developments in storytelling. Although a reflexive aspiration to challenge the conventional act of storytelling may drive this narrative mode, it does not account for everything, especially in the cases of *Rashomon* and *Confessions*. Multi-viewpoint filmic narrative deserve to be further explored and scrutinised within the broad perspective I have suggested in this chapter.

Notes

1. The term 'multi-viewpoint cinema' is, for example, used in the review of a 2008 political action thriller, *Vantage Point* by Tim Robey. See Tim Robey, 'Film Reviews: Vantage Point, Four Minutes, Diary of the Dead and More', *The Telegraph*, 7 March 2008, <http://www.telegraph.co.uk/culture/film/filmreviews/3671653/Film-reviews-Vantage-Point-Four-Minutes-Diary-of-the-Dead-and-more.html>. For the scholarship on *Rashomon*, see Avrom Fleishman, *The Narrated Films: Storytelling Situations in Cinema History* (Baltimore, MD: Johns Hopkins University Press, 2004); Gérard Genette, *Narrative Discourse: Essay in Mind*, trans. Jane E. Lewin (Ithaca, NY: Cornell University Press, 1983); James Goodwin, *Akira Kurosawa and Intertextual Cinema* (Baltimore, MD: Johns Hopkins University Press, 1994); Donald Richie (ed.), *Focus on Rashomon* (Englewood Cliffs, NJ: Prentice Hall, 1972); Donald Richie, *The Films of Akira Kurosawa*, 2nd ed. (Berkeley: University of California Press, 1984); Donald Richie (ed.), *Rashomon: Akira Kurosawa the Director* (New Bunswick, NJ: Rutgers University Prss, 1987); Peter Verstraten, *Film Narratology*, trans. Stefan van der Lecq (Toronto: University of Toronto Press, 2009) and Dolores Martinez, *Remaking Kurosawa: Translations and Permutations in Global Cinema* (Basingstoke: Palgrave Macmillan, 2009).
2. Japanese critics of the time typically praised the splendid cinematography by Miyagawa Kazuo and noted the hyperbolic acting style as an outstanding filmic element. Nevertheless, they did not appreciate the complex narrative structure of *Rashomon* when the film was first released. See, for example, Shigeno Tatsuhiko, review of *Rashomon*, *Kinema jumpō*, 1 October 1950, pp. 78–9. As for cinema attendance, Kobayashi Nobuhiko, a writer who saw the film at the time of its release at the age of eighteen, retrospectively notes in his diary his memory of an almost empty cinema at the end of August 1950. See his *Kurosawa Akira to iu jidai* (Tokyo: Bungei shunjusha, 2009), p. 84. [Editors' note: for more on the historical contexts of *Rashomon*, see also Chapter 9 by Rachael Hutchinson, Chapter 11 by Ran Ma and Chapter 39 by Yoshiharu Tezuka in this volume.]
3. Genette, *Narrative Discourse*, pp. 189–94.
4. For more on *Rashomon*, see David Bordwell, *Narration in the Fiction Film* (Madison: University of Wisconsin Press, 1985), pp. 208–9; Parker Tyler, 'Rashomon as Modern Art', in Richie, *Rashomon*, pp. 149–58. For Ozu, see Edward Branigan, 'The Space of Equinox Flower', *Screen* vol. 17 no. 2 (1976), pp. 74–105; Noël Burch, *To the Distant Observer: Form and Meaning in the Japanese Cinema* (Berkeley: University of California Press, 1979); Kristin Thompson and David Bordwell, 'Space and Narrative in the Films of Ozu', *Screen* vol. 17 no. 2 (1976), pp. 41–73. For Ōshima Nagisa, see Stephen Heath, *Questions of Cinema* (Bloomington: Indiana University Press, 1981), pp. 145–64.
5. Paul Schrader, *Transcendental Style in Film: Ozu, Bresson, and Dreyer* (New York: Da Capo Press, 1972).
6. Ibid., p. 17.
7. Donald Richie, *Japanese Cinema: Film Style and National Character* (New York: Doubleday, 1971), p. xix.
8. Stephen Prince, *The Warrior's Camera: The Cinema of Akira Kurosawa* (Princeton, NJ: Princeton University Press, 1999), p. 117.
9. Burch, *To the Distant Observer*, p. 175.
10. Ibid., p. 175. [Editors' note: see also Chapter 1 by Aaron Gerow and Chapter 3 by Hideaki Fujiki in this volume.]
11. See Branigan, 'The Space of Equinox Flower'; Thompson and Bordwell, 'Space and Narrative in the Films of Ozu'; David Bordwell, *Ozu and the Poetics of Cinema* (London: British Film Institute; Princeton, NJ: Princeton University Press, 1988).
12. Thompson and Bordwell, 'Space and Narrative in the Films of Ozu', pp. 55–69.
13. Ibid., p. 73.
14. See Bordwell, *Ozu and the Poetics of Cinema*.
15. See Branigan, 'The Space of Equinox Flower'.
16. Heath, *Questions of Cinema*, pp. 60–2.
17. In a riverside scene, the film's protagonist R finds a cat and talks to it. The exchange between the cat and R is depicted in terms of a set of shot/reverse shots. However, the camera position of one shot in the sequence – an over-the-shoulder shot of the cat – is diegetically illogical, since the previous shot shows a huge breakwater block behind the cat, i.e. from the position of the camera.
18. Ibid., pp. 64–9.
19. Bordwell, *Narration in the Fiction Film*, p. 310.

20. Ibid., p. 212.
21. See Keiko I. McDonald, *From Book to Screen: Modern Japanese Literature in Film* (New York: M.E. Sharpe, 1999).
22. See Mitsuhiro Yoshimoto, *Kurosawa: Film Studies and Japanese Cinema* (Durham, NC: Duke University Press, 2000).
23. Genette, *Narrative Discourse*, p. 190.
24. Brian Henderson, 'Tense, Mood, and Voice in Film: (Notes after Genette)', *Film Quarterly*, vol. 36 no. 4 (1983), pp. 4–17.
25. François Jost, 'The Look: From Film to Novel: An Essay in Comparative Narratology', in Robert Stam and Aressandra Raengo (eds), *A Companion to Literature and Film* (Oxford: Wiley-Blackwell, 2004), pp. 71–80.
26. Verstraten, *Film Narratology*, p. 135.
27. Shigehiko Hasumi, 'Everydayness of a "Miracle": Ozu Yasujiro and Atsuta Yuharu', <http://umdb.um.u-tokyo.ac.jp/DPastExh/Publish_db/1999ozu/english/02.html>.
28. Genette, *Narrative Discourse*, p. 192.
29. Ibid., pp. 192–3.
30. Mieke Bal, *Narratology: Introduction to the Theory of Narrative* (Toronto: University of Toronto Press, 1985), p. 142.
31. Jost, 'The Look: From Film to Novel', p. 74.
32. Verstraten, *Film Narratology*, p. 138.
33. Seymour Chatman, *Story and Discourse: Narrative Structure in Fiction and Film* (Ithaca, NY: Cornell University Press, 1978), pp. 143–4.
34. Ibid., p. 136.
35. Ryūnosuke Akutagawa, *Rashomon and Other Stories*, trans. Takashi Kojima (New York: Liveright Publishers, 1952), quoted in Richie, *Rashomon*, p. 103.
36. See Thomas Elsaesser, 'The Mind-game Film', in Warren Buckland (ed.) *Puzzle Films: Complex Storytelling in Contemporary Cinema* (Oxford: Wiley-Blackwell, 2009), pp. 13–41.
37. Warren Buckland (ed.), *Hollywood Puzzle Films* (London: Routledge, 2014), p. 5.
38. See Andō Kumi, *Akutagawa Ryūnosuke: Kaiga, kaika, toshi, eiga* (Tokyo: Kanrin Shobō, 2006).
39. Roger Ebert, 'Rashomon Movie Review and Film Summary', <http://www.rogerebert.com/reviews/great-movie-rashomon-1950>.

6

GENDER AND SEXUALITY
Feminist film scholarships: Dialogue and diversification

Hikari Hori

The field of feminist film studies has engaged critically with processes of knowledge production by re-examining the forms, themes and aesthetics of existing film-making practices, and by interrogating both the discipline of film studies and actual gender inequality in society. Numerous feminist film scholars have examined the stereotypical presentation of gender and sexuality, rediscovered forgotten minority film-making practices, elaborated on the notion of auteurism, and discussed ethnic and national identity as essential permutations of gender constructions.[1] It is from these various perspectives that this chapter aims to introduce the state of research on representations of gender and sexuality in the field of Japanese film studies.

I begin by noting the different development of feminist film studies in the Anglophone and Japanese-language scholarly communities. While films themselves travel across national boundaries, and do so faster than ever these days, theories of film and research on film are formed within various unique linguistic, socio-historical and geopolitical contexts. Nonetheless, I argue that the dialogue between Anglophone and Japanese-language feminist *scholarships*, and not just those focused specifically on Japanese cinema, should be highlighted throughout the chapter. This dialogue has not always involved direct communication and frequently there is no relationship of influence, in either direction. Yet both scholarships have articulated urgent concerns that resonate with each other despite their different temporal and spatial locations. Common questions that have been raised include: How does one understand the representation of women on screen? How should we theorise and historicise female spectatorship beyond dismissive stereotypes of women as emotional, masochistic viewers? Are works by female directors inherently feminist? How should issues of sexuality be theorised and contextualised socially and historically?

Along these lines of inquiry, I will organise important contributions to the field according to four analytical categories: representation, the category of women's film and women's cinema (*josei eiga*), spectatorship and authorship. These are also key concepts shared across existing Anglophone feminist film studies scholarship devoted to other national cinemas. This chapter aims to problematise discursively constructed identities of gender and sexuality and to question hierarchies of gender, sexuality and culture. Regrettably, due to space limitations, the scholarly contributions I have presented are therefore not comprehensive but restricted to representative works. They are important because they advance the examination of gender and sexuality to question even the notion of such identities. In doing so, they provide invaluable perspectives on both the social and historical specificity of Japanese film culture and its persistent construction of gender and sexual norms.

FEMINIST FILM STUDIES WITHIN THE JAPANESE ACADEMY

Feminist film studies only gained disciplinary visibility in the Japanese academy around the turn of the twenty-first century, while the Anglophone counterpart field was introduced to that academy, earlier on, in the 1970s. In addition, it was not until the 2000s that a rich body of scholarly publications on Japanese cinema, informed by studies of gender and sexuality, emerged in both the English and Japanese language.[2]

Though there was an interest in the representational politics of film amongst prewar feminists, documented in their writings and publications, it was the work of film scholar Ayako Saitō, including her 1992 translation of Laura Mulvey's 'Visual Pleasure and Narrative Cinema', that specifically promoted the importance of the discipline within the Japanese academy during the 1990s and 2000s.[3] Before the 2000s, the Japanese venues for thought and debate about gender and sexuality were largely located outside the academy and connected with the women's movement of the 1970s, in a similar way to Europe and the US; the Tokyo International Women's Film Festival (1985–2012), and the Tokyo International Lesbian and Gay Film Festival (1992–).[4] These film festivals were essential venues for the rediscovery, promotion and examination of female and queer authorship that created a physical space for critical engagement with, and enjoyment of, film texts.

Japanese feminist film criticism in Japan faced two representational problems: one related to discriminatory discourses on gender within the existing, domestic sphere of film criticism inside Japan and the other connected to the paternalistic view of Japanese (and Asian) women as submissive, sexualised and oppressed (something frequently seen in Western discourse). An index of this double predicament is provided by a comment from Takano Etsuko (1929–2013), the prominent film exhibitor and director of the Tokyo International Women's Film Festival, who was once herself an aspiring film director. When the festival was first launched in the mid-1980s, Takano was dismayed to find that not only were stereotypes of Japanese women as submissive widespread among female film-makers outside Japan, but that the idea of female directorship was also ridiculed by Japanese male critics.[5] Thanks to the efforts of Takano and other women, women's film-making was promoted by the screening of a variety of films directed by women, the establishment of a set of global networks of female film professionals, and the re-envisioning of Japanese film history through the introduction of various pioneer women film-makers that included Sakane Tazuko (1904–75), Tanaka Kinuyo (1909–77), Tokieda Toshie (1929–2012) and Haneda Sumiko (1926–).[6]

REPRESENTATION: IMAGES, SYMPTOMS AND VOLATILE IDENTIFICATION

One of the earliest and most urgent issues in the study of gender and sexuality in film studies was to underline the problematic stereotypes of women and gender relations. The pioneering monograph on this issue in Japanese cinema was *The Waves at Genji's Door* (1976) by the film critic Joan Mellen.[7] Her emphasis on the lives and social roles of women distinguished her book from other work on Japanese cinema, in both English and Japanese, up to then, and it still serves as a distinctively gendered guide to Japanese auteur directors for Western audiences.

It must be noted, however, that Mellen's conflation of textual strategies for the representation of gender identities and family relations with the actual lives and experiences of Japanese women is questionable, especially when combined with assumptions about authorial intention. For example, in an examination of Mizoguchi's films, she concludes that Mizoguchi was 'protesting against the oppression of the Japanese woman' because he so relentlessly describes women's suffering, misery and struggles.[8] This is not the place to discuss whether or not Mizoguchi was conscious of a feminist agenda, but it is important to point out that women's subjection, self-sacrifice and 'fall' is a cross-culturally deployed fictional currency. It invokes not only compassion in spectators but also voyeuristic and spectacular pleasure, which potentially implicates them in a deficient vision of gender disparity in society.[9]

Despite such problems, Mellen's work remains valuable. First and foremost, her work was one of the earliest pieces of Japanese film criticism that *problematised* gender norms. She pointed to women's obligation to labour for others, their limited choices in work and life, and changing gender roles in society, when many other critics were quite oblivious to the gendered construction of film texts. Another important point is that Mellen did not succumb to exoticising Japanese culture whereas some of her male contemporaries did.

Instead of, for instance, essentialising the culture as an eternally Buddhist society or one whose women lack agency, and in place of dismissing Japanese cinema as an imitator of or alien to Hollywood, she attempted to observe Japanese films in relation with, but not simply influenced by, Western cinema.[10]

Catherine Russell is not necessarily a direct descendant of Mellen, but she too has departed from existing paradigms that have emphasised the 'Japaneseness' of Japanese cinema, or promoted Orientalist discourses of alterity, by seeking the gendered articulations of Japanese modernity.[11] Inspired by the film theorist Miriam Hansen and the historians Harry Harootunian and Miriam Silverberg, Russell argues, in particular, that the auteur director Naruse Mikio's representation of women is a compelling site to locate vernacular modernism in Japanese film. In her examination of Naruse's representation of modern women's struggle to survive historical change, the relentless forward motion and speed of the time period, and gendered social conditions, Russell emphasises a Japanese version of women's experience of modernity that is encapsulated by unevenness, an ever-increasing speed of information circulation, consumerist cultures and the mediation of local film-making practices as responses to Hollywood classical cinema.[12] Such discussion of locally specific, diverse experiences of modernity is important since the notion of modernity has been often conceived as a lack, which non-Western nations must absorb from the West.

Mitsuyo Wada-Marciano also discusses Japanese modernity and reads representations of the modern girl, or *moga*, as an embodiment of vernacular modernism.[13] While a Caucasian flapper in Hollywood was threatening to docile, bourgeois femininity due to her excessive sexuality, aggressive self-definition and independent mind, the *moga* embodied Japanese modernity in a way that included the ethnic and national differences of Japanese vis-à-vis the West. Briefly, the *moga* was a media discourse about sexually deviant women that referred to those who embraced materialism and consumerism in the 1920s and was epitomised by the fictional female figure of Naomi in Tanizaki Jun'ichirō's novel *Naomi/Chijin no ai* (1925). *Moga* were understood as 'Westernised' and threatening to otherness, not only due to their fashion but also their attitudes, which were felt to be, at once, appealing and unacceptable for Japanese men. Wada-Marciano states that the cinematic *moga* was 'an imagined female subjectivity [that existed] as a visible reenactment of Japanese anxiety over the transformative aspect of modernity'.[14] In other words, this representation of a Westernised female body was mobilised to consolidate the national identity of Japanese masculinity.

Ginoza Naomi further advances these preceding arguments about modernity, pointing to the complicit relations between modernity/modernism, capitalism and imperialism.[15] She argues that people's everyday desires for a better, modernised life (*modan raifu*) were articulated especially by female characters through the orchestration of icons of consumer culture and leisure, as well as the textually manipulated interplay between the purported accessibility, and the denial of, such a life. Through examination of popular entertainment films with female protagonists from the 1930s, ranging from hits by the major studio Shōchiku to dramas by a minor small studio, she makes the excellent point that many entertainment films in the 1930s seem 'peaceful' and bright despite the rising death tolls of the ongoing wars of Japan with China and the gruesome colonial advancement of the Japanese state. Ginoza concludes that the overwhelming desire to be modern and prosperous led to minimised reference to the realities of warfare on screen, suggesting viewers' endorsement of the state's promise that colonialist war would bring them wealth if they endured it.[16]

Having introduced three recent works on women's representation in prewar and wartime films, I now turn to one particularly notable intervention into the analysis of gender and sexuality in postwar cinema. Though there are several important publications on postwar Japanese cinema, I want to focus on the queer visual culture theorist Mizoguchi Akiko's discussion of *Woman in the Dunes/Suna no onna* (Teshigahara Hiroshi,1964) since it remains one of the most heavily assigned films in Japanese cinema courses outside Japan.[17]

Notably, there is nothing lesbian about this film in terms of neither the director (a male auteur), the sexual identities of the characters or the targeted audience. Yet, Mizoguchi asserts, the film enables and encourages lesbian readings since, firstly, differences among characters, including gender identities, are visually confused and erased, and, secondly, the female protagonist's sexual pleasure is foregrounded with little reference to conventional heterosexist film languages of masculinised penetration. To elaborate, as soon as the cinematography establishes a dichotomy, including female/male, life form/non-organic form, human/non-human, part/whole and individual/collective, such boundaries are quickly erased and refuted by editing devices, including alternation of extreme close-ups with medium shots and various sound effects. For example, when the half-naked female protagonist touches a male nude body in a bathing scene, the deconstructive mode of editing de-emphasises the act as heterosexual contact. Instead, the visuals even confuse the distinction between the touching body and touched one, while the deployment of extreme close-ups stresses the sensuousness and sensuality arising from bodily contact. Mizoguchi argues that the film text erases the gender differences between its female and male characters, thus facilitating lesbian agency to identify with it, but she goes further to contend the film actually questions any categorical identities, including that of 'lesbian'.[18]

JOSEI EIGA: THE WOMAN'S FILM AND WOMEN'S CINEMA

Besides the problems of representation, another debated area within Anglophone feminist film studies has been 'the woman's film', which specifically refers to a Hollywood genre targeted at female viewers and often referred to as 'the weepie', especially in the 1930s and 1940s. There have been vigorous attempts to theorise a genre that scholars either argue was a sexist patriarchal construct or, in contrast, a complicated site for the enactment of agency on the part of female viewers. On the other hand, alternative film-making by female directors has been referred to as 'women's cinema'. These terms are thus polarised: while 'the woman's film' refers to a genre marketed by Hollywood studios to cater to women (the debate on female spectatorship), 'women's cinema' points to films directed by women in a conscious attempt to articulate a vision departing from the conventional scopic regime (the debate on women's film-making).[19]

A key point to bear in mind here is that, in Japanese, the term *josei eiga* corresponds to *both* 'the woman's film' and 'women's cinema' in English. Since there have been no prominent attempts to discuss the meaning of the term, it has been deployed in confusing ways within both English and Japanese language scholarship on Japanese cinema to the extent that it has ended up with different and unrelated meanings among different writers. For example, *josei eiga* has referred to a genre strongly associated with Shōchiku studio's marketing strategies aimed at women; any films that promote impressive female protagonists (but mostly in the films of male auteur directors), films that attract female cinemagoers, and films specifically directed by women. It is within this confusion that the queer film historian Yuka Kanno has proposed a theoretical reorganisation of the notion.[20] In doing so, Kanno draws attention to the film theorist Judith Mayne's re-conceptualisation of the key terms. Briefly, Mayne proposed to render ambiguous the distinction between 'women's film' and 'women's cinema' by pointing to both viewers' conflicting and multilayered responses to film texts and the presence of various female professionals within the film industry, including screenplay writers, continuity persons or editors. She problematises a simplified understanding of the viewing experience and dichotomised relation between production and reception and elaborates on the notion of 'women's cinema' in order to emphasise the continuity of experience between female authorship (not limited to directorship) and women's readings of film texts.[21]

Inspired by Mayne, Kanno thus defines *josei eiga* in terms of the depiction of the women's community that emerges in *Only Women at Night/Onna bakari no yoru* (1961). The story portrays women in a correction institution for prostitutes. Interestingly, *Only Women at Night* was directed by the prominent screen actress Tanaka Kinuyo and the script was written by a woman, whilst being based on a novel written by yet another woman. While acknowledging women's considerable involvement in the production process, however, Kanno also emphasises that the film does not have to be understood as presenting a resisting message from women (novelist, scriptwriter and director) directed to women (the audience). The film does not necessarily have to be regarded as a 'woman's film' (a film that addresses female spectators) simply because it features female protagonists and their stories. Instead, Kanno stresses the emerging, heterogeneous women's community that the film articulates by departing from the genre convention of the so-called *panpan eiga*.

The genre of the *panpan eiga* depicts prostitutes in the early postwar era, in which women are highly sexualised and presented to the voyeuristic gaze of viewers. The existing reiterated narrative patterns of the genre place women in firm polarities between chastity or sexual excess, security or predicament, and as part of the sacred domain or as objects of violation. Contrary to this genre convention, according to Kanno, the cinematic text of *Only Women at Night* firmly registers a women's community, not as a stable utopia but something in oscillation between the inclusion and exclusion of its members, including a lesbian character. Importantly, it is a community of volatility and fluidity instead of the conventional fixed division that secures the patriarchal fantasy of the possession of both docile and fallen femininities. This community is also constituted of women of different classes, social backgrounds and sexualities. It is a heterogeneous and intimate space. Kanno argues that the film is an example of 'women's cinema', in the sense of Mayne's re-conceptualisation. She locates parallels between the oscillation of the women's community in the cinematic text and female spectators' embrace and rejection of narrative. The film's particular presentation of female community thus critiques the 'scopic and narratological regime' of existing genre films.

QUEERING SPECTATORS AND FEMALE PERFORMERS

Though I fully agree with Mayne and Kanno who argue for a narrative that emphasises the continuous sphere of consumption and production, I wish to tentatively preserve spectatorship and authorship as separate analytical categories in order to illustrate recent developments in film theory and archival research.

Though feminist literary theory has illustrated female readers' heterogeneous negotiation with texts in ways that involve identification, endorsement, rejection or oppositional reading, female spectatorship has rarely been discussed as a subject of scholarly research within Japanese film studies. In this regard, recent developments have been both welcome and noteworthy.

The film historian Shimura Miyoko's 2007 study of the 1920s genre of the *Kikuchi mono* merits attention, for example.[22] The *Kikuchi mono* was a generic group of film adaptations of popular novels written by the novelist, Kikuchi Kan. According to Shimura, due to the popularity of the original novels among women, these films were initially targeted at female audiences by the commercial studios, but it turned out that the film adaptations failed to attract women as viewers. This fact shows that female spectators were as unpredictable as many of their male counterparts were, and they had their own way of choosing films despite the dismissive understanding of women by male film critics as an easily manipulated social group.[23]

To elaborate on viewers' negotiation with cinematic texts from a different approach, we may turn to the notion of 'implicational spectatorship', coined by Yuka Kanno. Kanno's term is illuminating as it shows an undiscriminating, yet politicising, attempt to examine the relationships between star and audience, star persona and gender norms, and the past and the present.[24]

In particular, Kanno examines the stardom of the actress Hara Setsuko, whose character Noriko in *Early Summer/Bakushū* (1951), directed by Ozu Yasujirō, is jokingly referred to as a pervert (*hentai*) by her male boss (Fig. 6.1). Noriko is shown to be an ardent admirer of Katharine Hepburn, then a Hollywood gay icon, while the actress Hara herself has been called an 'eternal virgin', desirable but inaccessible, a pure and innocent woman framed in, and described by, the typical heterosexual discourse of Japanese film history. The term 'virgin' points to a masculinist desire for conquest, but it also emphasises the inaccessibility of her body, which refuses such desires and contamination. Kanno argues that the body of Hara Setsuko/Noriko is situated within the liminal dualities of heterosexuality/

Fig. 6.1 Hara Setsuko, far left, as Noriko in *Early Summer/Bakushū* (Ozu Yasujirō, 1951, Shōchiku).

homosexuality, star/fan and performer/spectator when it comes to her overall relation to the globally circulated and sexually ambiguous icon of Hepburn. It is in this volatile space of identities that the off-screen spectator is 'implicated' in the text with a 'queer feeling'.[25]

In connection with the theme of liminal positionality and implied and precarious identities, Mizoguchi Akiko presents another illuminating case study that considers the contemporary female *benshi*, Sawato Midori.[26] The figure of the *benshi* provided an accompanying narration to silent films, complete with voice acting and plot explanation. It has been conventionally discussed in existing scholarship specifically within the context of 1920s film exhibition and film-making practices such as the Pure Film Movement. Mizoguchi, however, discusses a present-day female star *benshi* who is one of several currently reviving the art and considers her work in terms of the roles of the female spectator and queer performer.

Sawato, who closely studies film texts to write her own scripts for narration and voice acting, explains that she attempts to preserve the exaggerated gender differences, social norms and emotions presented by the films even when she herself is critical of them. Mizoguchi points out that Sawato is a unique female spectator whose re-reading of the film text is physically materialised in the form of her gender-bending performance. Her use of her own voice to animate multiple identities lies in contrast to existing discussion of female spectatorship in film studies that rests mostly in the domain of psychology. Mizoguchi further provides a compelling discussion of Sawato's performance as transgender, but if I might add to this analysis, it is also transnational and transmedia, as she constantly performs not only both female and male roles, but also actors of various ethnicities, ranging from a Japanese male samurai character to an innocent maiden, and from a Caucasian male such as Buster Keaton to a 'neutral' film narrator's voice, which is evocative of the performance style of traditional oral storytelling. The female *benshi*'s acting, as illustrated by Mizoguchi, resonates with Judith Butler's arguments about the performativity of gender, in which Butler contends that queer identity is the reiteration of a copy without an original, thus refuting the conventional copy/original relationship.[27]

In summary, through their examination of various specific, localised examples within Japanese cinema, both Kanno and Mizoguchi open up the theoretical articulation of gendered and queer spectatorship in relation to performers. Whereas the Japanese cinéphile idol Hara Setsuko can be conflated with the transnational lesbian icon Katharine Hepburn in order to create 'queer feeling' for 'implicational' spectators, the female *benshi* is at once both a female spectator and female performer who views, re-creates and re-narrates cinematic narratives and film history itself.[28]

AUTHORSHIP: ARCHIVAL RESEARCH AND HISTORICISATION

Along with the topics of representation and spectatorship, authorship has been one of the key critical concepts in the re-examination of Japanese film history.[29] A key role of women's and queer film festivals has been to introduce both historical and contemporary female and queer film-makers to the public.[30] For scholars, too, it is imperative to recover marginalised film-makers and re-read film history accordingly. This task of envisioning alternative authorships is a double one. Not only must it deconstruct existing male-centred narratives of auteurism but also it inevitably questions the broader existing narrative frames of film studies as a whole. As previously argued by the film theorists Teresa de Lauretis and Judith Mayne, the task is not to essentialise a feminine creative sensitivity, but to explore moments and techniques of subversion and to look into the various actors and historical conditions that are implicated in female directors' films.[31]

The film historian Ikegawa Reiko's work on 'the first Japanese woman director' Sakane Tazuko (1904–75) is an important example (Fig. 6.2).[32] Her remarkable archival research attempts to locate Sakane's filmmaking practices despite the scarcity of documents and films, as is often the case with many female pioneers regardless of their nationalities. It is also an essential, critical intervention that re-examines the concept of

Fig. 6.2 Sakane Tazuko playing with a pet dog owned by Mizoguchi Kenji, date unknown. Private collection.

feminism, its relation with Japanese imperialist history, Japanese women's ethnicised positions in 1940s Manchuria as colonisers and gender discrimination within the Japanese film industry.

After serving as an assistant director to the auteur director Mizoguchi Kenji, Sakane directed a feature-length drama film, released in 1936. After it flopped, she moved into documentary film-making. As an under-represented genre that involves much less capital investment and smaller film crews than drama feature film production, the world of documentary production is relatively tolerant of women entering the field.[33] Sakane eventually accepted a position as documentary director for the Manchurian Film Association, a Japanese studio founded in Changchun, China, in order to 'enlighten' and 'educate' the country's colonised citizens. This position was also, in part, made possible because of the 'total war' society of the late 1930s and early 1940s Japan, when demand for documentary production increased and the number of independent documentary film studios multiplied.[34] Employment opportunities did not, however, expand much for women in the postwar Japanese film industry. After the war ended in 1945 and her return to Japan, the studios denied her any directing role. She continued to work in the industry as a continuity woman until her retirement around 1970.

One of the most crucial points Ikegawa raises is that of Sakane's complicated social positionality as a wartime female director. On the one hand, her position as a director was gendered. Her professional ambition was circumscribed by the gender imparity of the Japanese film industry; her creativity was expected to be feminine and therefore second rate. On the other hand, her position was not only gendered, but also ethnicised and nationalised. Being a film director in the Manchurian Film Association in fact provided her with very limited career opportunities as a woman since she was especially assigned to produce propaganda targeted at both Japanese and Chinese women. Situated in the context of coloniser/colonised relations, her role in the Manchurian Film Association as a loyal imperial Japanese citizen-film-maker was to cooperate with, and promote, state colonial efforts. One of her films, *Brides of the Frontier/Kaitaku no hanayome* (1943), for example, was a recruitment film aimed at encouraging Japanese women to emigrate to Manchuria as 'settlers' brides. Coming from the most impoverished farming areas in Japan, these women were promised better opportunities and lives in China, instead of starvation. Their frontier lands had, however, been confiscated from local Chinese residents. Analysing this multilayered exploitation of class, gender and ethnicity, Ikegawa cleverly defines Sakane as a 'feminist imperialist', a term that points to both her predicament as a woman frustrated with Japan's gender inequalities and her endorsement of colonialism through her response to the call of the state.[35] I believe that this term also serves as an important call for further examination of the relations between middle-class feminism and imperialism in Japan, and elsewhere.

Something that is hinted at, but not fully explored, in Ikegawa's work is that many sources touch on Sakane's ambiguous sexuality. She was regarded as a cross-dresser, and some documents suggest Sakane had intimate relationships with women. It is not necessary to determine whether or not she was a lesbian, but it is important to note that despite these recorded ambiguities, her sexuality, and even her creativity, have consistently been conceptualised in terms of heterosexism. This is most obviously revealed in the title of her biography: *The Woman Who Loved Mizoguchi Kenji/Mizoguchi Kenji o aishita onna*.[36] This exemplifies the forceful discourse of heteronormativity that constantly erases other sexual identities, as well as the overwhelming tendency to see women's creativity as second rate and subjugated to male talent.[37]

INTERDISCIPLINARITY AND TRANSNATIONALITY

So far, I have concentrated on showing important scholarship on gender and sexuality and Japanese cinema and organised this to highlight common concerns shared with Anglophone feminist film studies that has principally addressed European and American cinemas. In lieu of a conclusion, I will briefly suggest two additional perspectives of great importance for the study of gender and sexuality in Japanese film. The first is the interdisciplinary contextualisation of film texts, something that has already been deployed by feminist scholars in many studies of other national cinemas but could be encouraged in Japanese film studies as well.[38] This is not to neglect analysis of the medium-specific aspects of film, but I argue that a film text must inevitably be situated in relation to recursive and prescriptive images both within and beyond film culture that are bounded by historical time and space and that circulate across all media in society.

The second perspective is the construction of transnational narratives of film history that do not place Japanese cinema in isolation, but instead they refute cultural essentialism and clarify Japanese cinema's connection with other local or global film cultures. As already alluded to above, such a project may be informed by the work of Miriam Hansen. Instead of reinforcing, or constructing, hierarchies between 'the West and the Rest', Hansen focuses on relationality among national cinemas. In particular, she notes that encounters between hegemonic Hollywood and local film cultures have also changed the nature of Hollywood films themselves.³⁹ This reinforces the film historian Andrew Higson's re-conceptualisation of the notion of national cinema, in which he argues that, instead of confining the study of national cinema to films produced by, and within, a particular nation-state, 'the range of films in circulation within a nation-state – including American and other foreign films' can also be examined as national cinema within the context of their local reception.⁴⁰

Representations of gender and sexuality serve in Hansen's work as an important point of analysis of specific social norms and local film languages as well as local film cultures' negotiation with hegemonic film cultures. Hansen demonstrates this in her examination of the configurations of femininities in 1930s Chinese and Japanese films by placing them in dialogue with each other, despite the division of these countries by war. This is a welcome approach that departs from the strong inclination of film studies to focus on the 'peculiarity' of non-Western national cinemas. It also does not contradict the aforementioned importance of the exploration of vernacular, localised specificities, such as the issue of Japanese modernity addressed by Russell, Wada-Marciano and Ginoza. It is crucial to highlight how the dynamics of cultural production are situated both in particular historical and social conditions and as part of the circulation of various film cultures.

One of the most compelling and revealing models of interdisciplinarity and transnationality is Mizoguchi Akiko's analysis of the 'gay film boom' in 1980s Japan.⁴¹ The 'gay film boom' refers to the persistent consumption of European films about male-male homosexuality, such as *Maurice* (James Ivory, 1988), by transgenerational Japanese female audiences during the decade.⁴² As a backdrop for the boom, Mizoguchi reminds us of the longer tradition of Japanese women's subculture and consumption of narratives of male homosexual relationships that exists in novels (for example by Mori Mari [1903–87]), Western films, *shōjo manga* (girls' comics), television dramas and the manga genre called *bōizu rabu* (Japanese transliteration of 'Boys' Love'), or *BL* (Fig. 6.3).⁴³

Specifically, Mizoguchi illustrates the connection between the gay film boom and *BL* consumption by

Fig. 6.3 The cover of Mizoguchi Akiko's *Theorizing BL As a Transformative Genre: Boys' Love Moves the World Forward/BL Shinkaron: Boy's Love ga shakai o ugokasu* (Tokyo: Ōta shuppan, 2015).

women and argues for the enactment of women's sexual fantasies and the exchange of such fantasies among women, regardless of their sexual identities, through their identification with sexualised male bodies and depictions of male-male sexual intercourse. Indeed, 'the gay film boom' among Japanese women serves an intriguing site of gender- and sexuality-bending. While the camp reading of actresses by male gay audiences has been one of the crucial contributions of Anglophone queer film studies, Japanese female spectatorship of 'the gay film boom' is a reversed, or even deviant, example. The orientalising gaze directed at non-Western women is inverted, and female viewers identify with male homosociality as well as male homosexuality. Departing from the discursive framework of Japanese screen femininity in terms of suffering and hypersexualisation, 'the gay film boom' uncovers a women's economy of sexualisation, objectification and appropriation of Western male bodies. Mizoguchi thus presents an intriguing case study of the re-examination and overturning of the hierarchy of the gaze between First World and Third World/non-Western cinema, and between female and male spectatorship.

It goes without saying that the study of gender and sexuality in Japanese film remains a promising and dynamic field and there is a variety of themes and topics that could be further explored, in addition to those discussed above. Work by newly emerging film-makers needs to be examined and more research is required, for example on postwar Japanese cinema and further transnational narratives between Japanese and other Asian cinemas. On the other hand, the 2010s has also been a decade that has proven especially challenging for scholars and activists as state censorship and hate speech have dramatically increased in Japan. During the era of the women's liberation movement in the 1970s and the 1980s, feminists hoped for the raised visibility of women and sexual minorities within public sphere, increased media literacy, and greater self-representation in the future. Over the past four decades in Japan, the participation of women in the labour force and politics, as well as consciousness of LGBT issues, have all improved to a certain degree. Access to world cinema continues to increase. Despite this, border disputes propel the distribution of illogical stereotypes of ethnic or national 'others', and the increasingly unequal distribution of wealth has also reinforced social stratification. In sum, the creation of transnational narratives of relationality, the demystification of monolithic value systems of cultural production, and the examination of the unevenness and anxiety of modernity are more necessary than ever for contemporary feminist film studies.

Notes

1 Briefly, by national cinema I mean a categorical framework in which film texts are considered to reflect national traits and the cultural essence of their country of origin. Auterism is the study of individual directors' *oeuvre* and style, which feeds the narrative mode of film history as a genealogical lineage of talented, genius individual (male) directors. Both are key concepts that have recently been problematised in film studies.

2 My division relies on the language of the publications regardless of the nationalities of the authors, because this indicates differently targeted readers.

3 Important anthologies edited by Saitō include, *Otokotachi no kizuna, ajia eiga, homosōsharu na yokubō*, co-edited with Yomota Inuhiko (Tokyo: Heibonsha, 2004); *Eiga joyū Wakao Ayako*, co-edited with Yomota Inuhiko, new edn (Tokyo: Misuzu shobō, 2016).

4 Examples include Matsumoto Yumiko, *Eiga o tsukutta josei tachi* (Tokyo: Cinema house, 1996); Ishihara Ikuko, *Sumireiro no eigasai* (Tokyo: Film art-sha 1996); Inoue Teruko, Nishiyama Chieko, Hosoya Minoru, Kimura Sakae and Fukushima Mizuho (eds), *Video de joseigaku* (Tokyo: Yūhikaku, 1999).

5 Takano Etsuko, Kotōda Eiko, Haneda Sumiko and Ōtake Yōko (eds), *Eiga ni ikiru joseitachi: Tokyo kokusai josei eigasai 20-kai no kiroku, 1985–2007* (Tokyo: Pado women's office, 2007), p. 17.

6 Some autobiographies and biographical accounts of these directors are available in English, including 'Tokieda Toshie', interview by Ayako Imaizumi, *Documentarists of Japan* no. 19, Yamagata International Documentary Film Festival website, <http://www.yidff.jp/docbox/21/box21-1-1-e.html>. Among other directors, female porn director Hamano Sachi's works, career and representation of female sexual desire in the Japanese porn industry deserve attention. See Hikari Hori, 'Aging, Gender and Sexuality in Japanese Popular Culture: Female Pornographer Sachi Hamano and Her Rebellious Film "Lily Festival" (*Yurisai*)', in Yoshiko Matsumoto (ed.), *Faces of Aging: The Lived Experience of the Elderly in Japan* (Stanford, CA: Stanford University Press, 2011), pp. 109–34; Miryam Sas, 'Pink Feminism?: The Program Pictures of Hamano Sachi', in Abé Markus Nornes (ed.), *The Pink Book: The Japanese Eroduction and its Contexts* (Ann Arbor, MI: Kinema Club, 2014), pp. 295–329.

7 Joan Mellen, *The Waves at Genji's Door: Japan through Its Cinema* (New York: Pantheon Books, 1976). Mellen was also a pioneer in writing about women in Anglophone scholarship, for example, *Women and Their Sexuality in the New Film* (New York: Dell, 1974).

8   Mellen, *The Waves at Genji's Door*, p. 252.
9   Freda Freiberg has questioned Mellen's methodology in her analysis of Mizoguchi's women. Departing from auteurism, Freiberg argues we need to understand the historical context of film production. In her examination of *Sisters of the Gion* (1936) by Mizoguchi Kenji, Freiberg argues that the depiction of female protagonists was deviant and unconventional, not because that was the specific authorial intention but because the film refused to aestheticise the institution of the *geisha*. See Freda Freiberg, *Women in Mizoguchi Films* (Melbourne: Japanese Studies Centre, Monash University, 1981).
10 For example, she compares the representation of working women of the 1940s in Kurosawa Akira's *Most Beautiful* (1944) and the roles of Katharine Hepburn and Bettie Davis as working women to argue for the similar gender construction of two societies. Mellen, *The Waves at Genji's Door,* pp. 42–3.
11 Catherine Russell (ed.), 'New Women of the Silent Screen: China, Japan, Hollywood', special issue of *Camera Obscura* vol. 60 (2005); Catherine Russell, 'Naruse Mikio's Silent Films: Gender and the Discourses of Everyday Life in Interwar Japan', *Camera Obscura* vol. 20 no. 3 (60) (2005), pp. 57–89; Catherine Russell, *The Cinema of Naruse Mikio: Women and Japanese Modernity* (Durham, NC: Duke University Press, 2008).
12 Miriam Hansen, 'Fallen Women, Rising Stars, New Horizons: Shanghai Silent Film as Vernacular', *Film Quarterly* vol. 54 no. 1 (2000), pp. 10–22; Miriam Hansen, 'Vernacular Modernism: Tracking Cinema on a Global Scale', in Nataša Ďurovičová and Kathleen Newman (eds), *World Cinemas, Transnational Perspective* (New York: Routledge, 2010), pp. 287–314; Harry Harootunian, *History's Disquiet: Modernity, Cultural Practice, and the Question of Everyday Life* (New York: Columbia University Press, 2000); Miriam Silverberg, *Erotic Grotesque Nonsense: The Mass Culture of Japanese Modern Times* (Berkeley: University of California Press, 2006). Though the term 'vernacular' invokes the dichotomised relation between the centre and the subjugated region, that is, Hollywood and Japan, for instance, Hansen also stresses the interactions between vernacular film cultures: between China and Japan, or between European countries and Japan. [Editors' note: see also Chapter 3 by Hideaki Fujiki in this volume.]
13 Mitsuyo Wada-Marciano, *Nippon Modern: Japanese Cinema of the 1920s and 1930s* (Honolulu: University of Hawai'i Press, 2008).
14 Wada-Marciano, *Nippon Modern,* p. 14, and also see chapter 4, pp. 76–110.
15 Ginoza Naomi, *Modern Life to sensō* (Tokyo: Yoshikawa kōbunkan, 2013).
16 In connection with the representation of gender and imperialism in the entertainment film, a pioneering work on Japanese colonial(ist) film and its representation of gender is Freda Freiberg's 1992 examination of the intersection of gender and ethnicity in *China Night*, which starred Ri Kōran (a bilingual Japanese star actress whose nationality was believed to be Chinese by the general public). Freiberg's argument that a gendered hierarchy is implicated in the relationship of the coloniser and colonised remains important. See Freda Freiberg, 'Genre and Gender in World War II Japanese Feature Film: *China Night* (1940)', *Historical Journal of Film, Radio and Television* vol. 12 no. 3 (1992), pp. 245–52.
17 Mizoguchi Akiko, '*Suna no onna* saidoku: Lesbian Reading no aratana kanōsei', Nishijima Norio (ed.), *Eizō hyōgen no alternative* (Tokyo: Shinwasha, 2005), pp. 245–74. There are two important works on the representation of male gender. One is Isolde Standish's analysis of constructed masculinities and male-male homoeroticism, though not necessarily homosexuality. It is noteworthy that she considers the yakuza (gangster) film genre of the 1960s and the 1970s, which is a refreshing departure from the conventional approach to gender representation in auteur films. See Isolde Standish, *Myth and Masculinity in the Japanese Cinema: Towards a Political Reading of the 'Tragic Hero'* (Richmond, VA: Curzon, 2000). The second is Ayako Saito's work on Kinoshita Keisuke and the reconfiguration of masculinities as castrated and injured during the Japanese Occupation (1945–52). See Ayako Saito, 'Occupation and Memory: The Representation of the Woman's Body in Post War Japanese Cinema', in Daisuke Miyao (ed.), *The Oxford Handbook of Japanese Cinema* (Oxford: Oxford University Press, 2014), pp. 327–62.
18 [Editors' note: for more on queer representation and Japanese cinema, see also Chapter 12 by Yuka Kanno in this volume.]
19 A series of rigorous debates was initiated within Anglophone feminist scholarship by Claire Johnston

and carried on by Teresa de Lauretis, Mary Ann Doane, Judith Mayne and others. See Claire Johnston, 'Women's Cinema as Counter Cinema' (originally published in 1973), in E. Ann Kaplan (ed.), *Feminism and Film* (London: Oxford University Press, 2000), pp. 22–33; Teresa de Lauretis, 'Aesthetic and Feminist Theory: Rethinking Women's Cinema', *New German Critique* no. 34 (1985), pp. 154–75; Mary Ann Doane, *The Desire to Desire: The Woman's Film of the 1940s* (Bloomington: Indiana University Press, 1987).

20 Kanno Yuka, 'Pan pan, lesbian, on'na no kyōdōtai', in Koyama Shizuko, Akaeda Kanako and Imada Erika (eds), *Sexuality no sengoshi* (Kyoto: Kyoto daigaku shuppankai, 2014), pp. 153–71.

21 Judith Mayne, *The Woman at the Keyhole: Feminism and Women's Cinema* (Bloomington: Indiana University Press, 1990), pp. 1–10.

22 Shimura Miyoko, 'Kikuchi Kan no tsūzoku shōsetsu to ren'ai eiga no henyō: Josei kankyaku to eigakai', in Iwamoto Kenji (ed.), *Kazoku no shōzō: Home drama to melodrama* (Tokyo: Shinwasha, 2007), pp. 75–102.

23 [Editors' note: for more on spectatorship and Japanese cinema, see also Chapter 3 by Hideaki Fujiki in this volume.]

24 Yuka Kanno, 'Implicational Spectatorship: Hara Setsuko and the Queer Joke', *Mechademia* vol. 6 (2011), pp. 287–303.

25 Kanno explains her queer reading of films through the concept of implication (*renrui*), originally coined by Tessa Morris-Suzuki as a means of evoking the responsibility of those who 'have not stolen land of others, but who live on stolen land'. The intention is not to recreate 'the unified, closed, past world of the text and the spectator of the time' but rather to respond to past texts and reconstitute their queerness in the present. Kanno, 'Implicational Spectatorship', p. 288.

26 Akiko Mizoguchi, 'Gender and the Art of Benshi: In Dialogue with Midori Sawato', *Camera Obscura* vol. 26 no. 3 (78) (2011), pp. 155–65.

27 Judith Butler, 'Imitation and Gender Insubordination', in Diana Fuss (ed.), *Inside/out: Lesbian Theories, Gay Theories* (New York: Routledge, 1991).

28 In this respect, Michael Raine's work on male stardom provides an illuminating case study of masculinity in Japanese cinema. Through an examination of the popular male actor Ishihara Yūjirō in the late 1950s, Raine defines his stardom as the construction of a semantic body, which is constituted through publicity hype, magazine photographs and articles, and other media and discourse around and beyond cinema. Michael Raine, 'Ishihara Yūjirō: Youth, Celebrity, and the Male Body in late-1950s Japan', in Dennis Washburn and Carole Cavanaugh (eds), *Word and Image in Japanese Cinema* (Cambridge: Cambridge University Press, 2001), pp. 202–25.

29 [Editors' note: for more on authorship and Japanese cinema, see also Chapter 2 by Alexander Jacoby in this volume.]

30 In addition to the aforementioned female directors, we may also note the following film-makers: Yamagami Chieko, whose debut work was on the first openly lesbian performance artist Itō Tari (*Dear Tari,* 2001); Lim Desiree, who was born in Malaysia, educated in Japan and makes transnational films; Hashiguchi Ryōsuke who has produced entertainment films; Oki Hiroyuki whose experimental works have been exhibited in art museums and invited to international film festivals; and Imaizumi Kōichi, who has appeared as an actor in porn films and directed films, including gay porn.

31 de Lauretis, 'Aesthetic and Feminist Theory'; Judith Mayne, 'The Woman at the Keyhole: Women's Cinema and Feminist Criticism', in Mary Ann Doane, Patricia Mellencamp and Linda Williams (eds), *Re-vision: Essays in Feminist Film Criticism* (Frederick, MD: University Publications of America, 1984), pp. 49–66, esp. 59–60.

32 Ikegawa Reiko, '*Teikoku' no iega kantoku Sakane Tazuko: 'Kaitaku no hanayome', 1943 nen, Man'ei* (Tokyo: Yoshikawa kōbunkan, 2011).

33 As Patricia White points out, documentary is the mode of film-making in which women's intervention has been most extensive and influential, and which remains most accessible to emerging minority artists. Patricia White, 'Feminism and Film', in John Hill and Pamela Church Gibso (eds), *Film Studies: Critical Approaches* (Oxford: Oxford University Press, 2000), p. 125.

34 The activities of Atsugi Taka (1907–98) are also noteworthy: she was a critic, screenplay writer, translator of British documentary film theory and co-director of a documentary film. For Atsugi, see Hikari Hori, *Promiscuous Media: Film and Visual Culture in Imperial Japan, 1926–45* (Ithica, NY: Cornell University Press, 2018), chapter 2.

Additionally, a number of female animators were recruited and trained in the early 1940s to replace male animators who had been drafted. See Yukimura Mayumi, 'Sensō to animation: Shokugyō toshiteno animator no tanjō process nitsuiteno kōsatsu kara', *Sociology* vol. 52 no. 1 (2007), pp. 87–102.

35 Reiko Ikegawa, 'The Female Japanese Director Sakane Tazuko, and Archival Materials Related to Japanese Colonial Films, the Manchurian Film Association', paper presented at the Makino Symposium, Columbia University, November 2011.

36 Ōnishi Etsuko, *Mizoguchi Kenji o aishita onna: Joryū kantoku daiichigō Sakane Tazuko no shōgai* (Tokyo: San'ichi shobō, 1993).

37 For the Occupation era, see Joanne Izbicki, 'The Shape of Freedom: The Female Body in Post-Surrender Japanese Cinema', *U.S.-Japan Women's Journal. English Supplement* no. 12 (1997), pp. 109–53. In addition, see Nakane Wakae's reading of the primary female character of a documentary as the 'director': Nakane Wakae, 'Sakusha to shite no shutsuen josei: Documentary eiga *Kyokushiteki eros: Renka 1974*', *JunCture: Chōikiteki nihon bunka kenkyū* vol. 7 (2016), pp. 138–51.

38 For example, Patrice Petro, *Joyless Streets: Women and Melodramatic Representation in Weimar Germany* (Princeton, NJ: Princeton University Press, 1989) and Antonia Lant, *Blackout: Reinventing Women for Wartime British Cinema* (Princeton, NJ: Princeton University Press, 1991).

39 Miriam Bratu Hansen, 'The Mass Production of the Senses: Classical Cinema as Vernacular Modernism', *Modernism/Modernity* vol. 6 no. 2 (1999), pp. 59–77, esp. 68–9.

40 Andrew Higson, 'The Concept of National Cinema' (originally published in 1989), in Alan Williams (ed.), *Film and Nationalism* (New Brunswick, NJ: Rutgers University Press, 2002), pp. 52–67.

41 Mizoguchi Akiko, 'Lesbian & gay eiga sai wa dare no mono?'. *Chūō hyōron* no. 246 (2003), pp. 79–82. On the gay boom, see Jonathan Mark Hall, 'Japan's Progressive Sex: Male Homosexuality, National Competition, and the Cinema', in Andrew Grossman (ed.), *Queer Asian Cinema* (Binghamton, NY: Harrington Park Press, 2000), pp. 31–82; Mizoguchi Akiko, *BL shinkaron: Boy's love ga shakai o ugokasu* (Tokyo: Ōta Shuppan, 2015), pp. 279–328.

42 Other films include *Querelle* (Rainer Werner Fassbinder, 1982), *Another Country* (Marek Kanievska, 1984) and *Caravaggio* (Derek Jarman, 1986).

43 The *BL* genre concerns male homosexual romance and relationships between men. Emerging in the 1990s, it is predominantly produced by female manga artists and female editors and aimed at female readers, regardless of their sexual identity.

PART 2
INSTITUTIONS AND INDUSTRY

7

THE STUDIO SYSTEM
The Japanese studio system revisited

Hiroyuki Kitaura
Translated by Thomas Kabara

The first film studio in Japan was built in 1908 by the Yoshizawa Company. Yoshizawa had already had major success importing, distributing and exhibiting films, but in that year, it erected the Glass Stage Building – an imitation of Edison's Black Maria Studio – in the Meguro district of Tokyo and began officially producing films. Two years later, another company, the Yokota Company, built a studio in Kyoto, to keep pace with its rival, Yoshizawa. Then, two more companies, M. Pathe and Fukuhōdō, built studios and began making films in Tokyo in 1909 and 1910 respectively. The Japanese film industry blossomed like this until 1912, when the above four companies merged and formed Nikkatsu, thus taking a major step towards cementing the industry.

Motion picture houses, which started appearing as cinema audiences began emerging, were behind this wave of film studio creation in those early years. The first cinema specialising in film exhibition was built in the Asakusa district of Tokyo in 1903. In 1907, a flood of cinemas started opening in Tokyo, and by 1910, there were reportedly as many as forty houses.[1] In Kyoto, the first cinema opened in 1908, but from then on the total number grew at a brisk rate.[2] This proliferation of cinemas reflected the growing demand for films and this in turn led to a wave of film studios being created.

This chapter will trace the genealogy of Japanese film companies, as shown in Fig. 7.1.[3] As can be seen from the way the film industry grew in its earliest days, it is impossible to discuss this genealogy without mentioning the factors of distribution and exhibition.[4] Like the Paramount Decision of 1948 in the US, which forbade the creation of monopolies via block booking (the practice where a production or distribution company would secure a market for their own films by making package-deal agreements with exhibitors for their titles),[5] in postwar Japan the major film companies were prohibited from controlling exhibition. By 1955, the Japan Fair Trade Commission had already cited four violations, including retrials, under such laws as the Anti-Monopoly Act and the Excessive Economic Power Deconcentration Law. The film companies promised to improve the situation. In the end, however, the companies failed to uphold their promise, and, having faced no legal repercussions, they intensified their market control through the practice of block booking.[6] Japanese studios supported themselves for a long time by exploiting this distribution system. Nevertheless, it was in the 1970s that this pattern of distribution began to unravel and the Japanese studio system headed towards collapse.

Joseph L. Anderson and Donald Richie's *The Japanese Film: Art and Industry* offers an important historical overview of Japanese film companies and studios in English.[7] Works in Japanese on the subject include *The History of the Developments of Japanese Film* by Tanaka Jun'ichirō, *Japanese Film History* by Satō Tadao, and *One Hundred and Ten Years of Japanese Film History* by Yomota Inuhiko.[8] While these volumes are useful for gaining a basic overview of Japanese film history, their historical accounts of the studios tend to focus primarily on the individuals involved, especially film directors. By contrast, this chapter will look at the way in which Japanese film studios operated

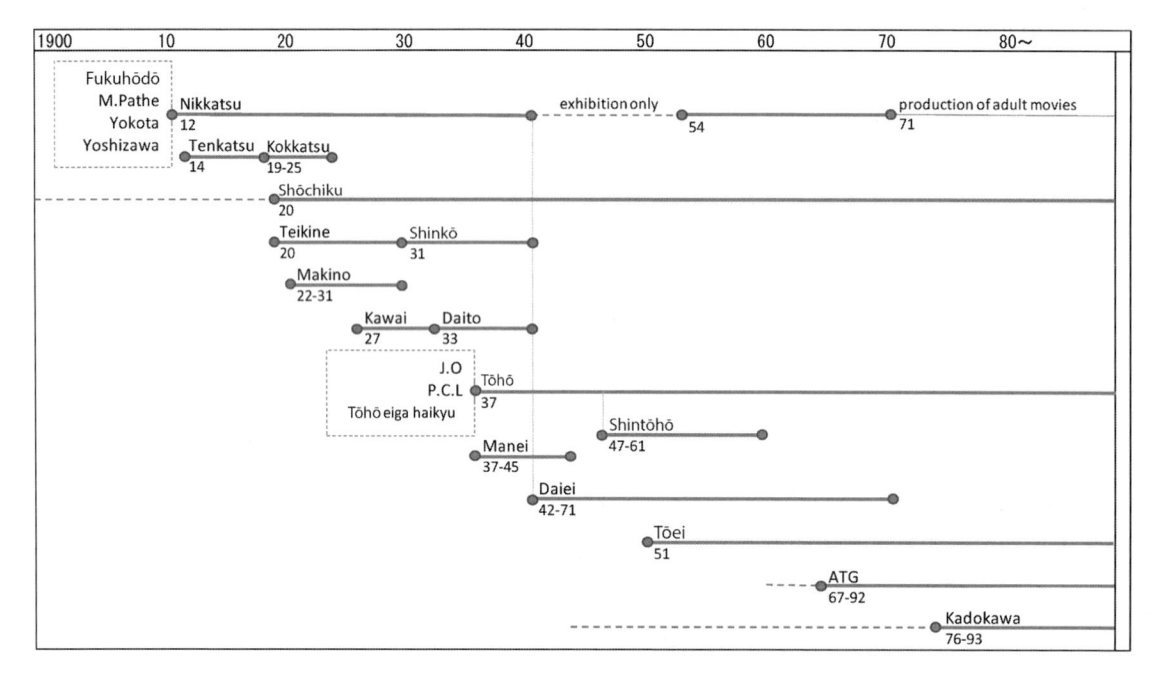

Fig. 7.1 The evolution of Japanese film studios.

more holistically in terms of institutional practice. Accordingly, it will re-examine the studios as places of production while also simultaneously directing attention to the different phases of distribution and exhibition that played a pivotal role in establishing the Japanese film industry and which the operations of Japanese film companies depended on over their long history. The central point of this chapter is thus to investigate the studios' relationship to the film industry as a whole as well as their specific histories after their collapse.

THE RISE OF THE FILM INDUSTRY (THE 1910S)

In the late 1900s, with the number of cinemas on the rise in Japan, four companies, Yoshizawa, Yokota, M. Pathe and Fukuhōdō, opened a stream of new film studios. With their sights set on monopolising the market, these four companies merged in 1912 and formed Japan's first major film company: Nikkatsu. This new company opened its first studio in Kyoto – as a successor to an old Yokota Shokai studio – and the following year, it completed construction on a new studio in the Mukōjima area of Tokyo. At the time, Japanese films were divided into two major genres: old dramas, or *kyūgeki* (films influenced by kabuki theatre), and modern dramas, or *shinpa* (films influenced by the new school of theatre that emerged during the Meiji period). *Kyūgeki* were made in Kyoto and *shinpa* were made in Tokyo. In other words, the fact that Nikkatsu had built these two studios destined the two genres to be separated according to the different studio locations. This system of specialisation that tied genre to a geographic location was largely passed down to future operations.

A unique feature of Nikkatsu's production system in the 1910s was what Hideaki Fujiki has called the 'troupe-based business model'.[9] At Nikkatsu's Kyoto studio, for example, nearly all film production centred around two figures: Makino Shōzō and Onoe Matsunosuke. Before joining Nikkatsu, Makino managed the Senbonza repertory theatre and also made films starring Onoe, a low-ranking kabuki actor at the time. These film productions were commissioned by Yokota. After Nikkatsu was formed, it continued

Yokota's arrangement with the theatre troupe, commissioning them to produce films. This sort of arrangement differed from the film business in the US, where the central producer system was established by 1914. In that system, directors, actors and staff handled film production based on predetermined budgets while working under the exclusive control of a central producer.[10] In contrast to the Hollywood system, Nikkatsu studios relied heavily on the existing conventions of repertory theatre.

Significantly, these conventions were closely tied to the system of film exhibition. At that time, film programmes were changed on a weekly basis, and each programme consisted of a combination of five or six long and short films. The Makino troupe met this considerable demand by producing as many as seven or eight films a month during peak times.[11] To that end, the troupe relied on existing tales from kabuki or traditional oral storytelling forms rather than creating brand new stories for their films; and it did most of its filming without rehearsals. The majority of films in Japan were silent until the early 1930s, so when these films were screened, they were regularly accompanied by a *benshi* (voice performer) who stood at the side of the screen explaining the plot and delivering the actors' dialogue. Thus, at least until the 1910s, producers paid little attention to making stories coherent, leaving it up to the *benshi* instead.[12]

In 1914, Tenkatsu was created as a competitor to Nikkatsu.[13] In the 1910s, these two companies almost totally monopolised the Japanese film market. Nikkatsu, in particular, had established what was essentially a block-booking system by turning half the cinemas in the country into Nikkatsu-affiliated cinemas by 1917.[14] Nevertheless, as Aaron Gerow points out, in the Japanese film market up to that point, it was the exhibitors who had seized authority in the industry. Even when they had distribution contracts with a particular film company, cinema owners could easily switch to another company; they were also able to charge production companies for the cost of cinema equipment; and they were fairly free to select the films they showed.[15] During this period, Makino-Onoe films and Nikkatsu-Mukōjima *shinpa* films, starring popular *onnagata* (male actors performing female roles) such as Tachibana Teijirō, were in high demand from exhibitors. To meet this demand, these films tended to be in constant mass production.

THE ESTABLISHMENT OF THE STUDIO SYSTEM (THE 1920S)

The year 1920 saw major changes in the way Japanese films were being produced and a steady stream of new film companies emerged, including Shōchiku, Teikine and Taikatsu. Film companies were also being restructured – as in the way the Kokkatsu had been formed by absorbing Tenkatsu the previous year. Additionally, while production companies generally used *onnagata* in their films until the 1910s, in this era of change, a couple of newcomers, Shōchiku and Tenkatsu, helped normalise the use of actresses instead; and by 1923, Nikkatsu had followed suit. This sort of innovation was prompted by the so-called 'Pure Film Movement', a trend in film criticism that started in the late 1910s and argued Japanese films were overly theatrical, outdated and in need of reform. In the 1920s, film companies were putting these reforms into practice. Shōchiku, which originated as a kabuki performance company, was especially interested in revolutionising film production in Japan. The company brought in new faces such as the former Hollywood cinematographer Henry Kotani as well as Osanai Kaoru, a theatre director from the *shingeki* style of theatre (which featured Japanese retellings of Western realist theatre), while the company president himself, Shirai Shintarō, brought his staff over to Hollywood to observe film-making there and then enthusiastically tried to introduce its production system into Japan.[16]

But what specific reforms took place during this period? This section will offer a brief look at the specifics while comparing the film studios of the 1910s with Shōchiku's studio in the Kamata neighbourhood of Tokyo. In the 1910s, studios functioned relying on a single specific production unit, as was the case with Makino and Onoe at the Nikkatsu studio in Kyoto. The Tokyo-Mukōjima studio similarly banked on the films of Tachibana Teijirō.[17] Shōchiku's Kamata studio took a different approach in the 1920s. First of all, actors were given individual contracts with the company, and they were then ranked as either star actors or non-star actors and cast accordingly.[18] Additionally, the company set up a system where each studio was organised into several production units, with the studio head taking on a producer-like role while supervising the whole operation, and with one of the company's many directors taking command of and representing a given unit. At Shōchiku, this producer/director division of labour became particularly clear-cut in 1924 when, future company president, Kido Shirō took over as head of the studios.

In the aftermath of the major earthquake that ravaged the Kantō region in 1923, the film companies closed their studios in Tokyo and moved their production units to the Kansai region. Shōchiku built a studio in Kyoto after the disaster and temporarily moved its entire production staff there. But after only two years, the company sent its modern drama department back to the Kamata studio in Tokyo, while keeping only its period drama production department in Kyoto. By contrast, Nikkatsu's modern drama production department did not return to Tokyo until 1934. In Kansai, Makino's independence inspired period drama stars, who had become popular under him, to start up a steady stream of new companies, thus popularising independent production there. In Tokyo, Shōchiku saw the opportunity to produce a flurry of new-style modern dramas that portrayed the everyday problems of average white-collar workers and students living in Tokyo – Japan's cultural centre – with a mixture of humour and irony. As Mitsuyo Wada-Marciano points out, they incorporated elements taken from Hollywood films, including 'Hollywood's vision of modern life in the optimism of its hard-luck protagonists, the happy ending and a thoroughly film-trained stable of actors'.[19] This genre, called the 'petit bourgeois film' (*shōshimin eiga*), grew in popularity and distinguished itself from the traditional *shinpa*.

As the case of Shōchiku illustrates, when the studio system was established in the 1920s, Japanese film became consolidated into a single industry. In the early part of the decade, Shōchiku and Nikkatsu both reduced funding for foreign film distribution, while simultaneously expanding investment in their own films. By 1924, the number of domestic films released in Japan exceeded that of foreign films.[20] In fact, the *Japanese Film Yearbook* marks 1925 as the heyday of Japanese film and concludes that, from that year on, film companies discarded their traditional showmanship approach and began making films under a more rational production system.[21] By establishing this studio system, the producers seized greater control of film production from exhibitors, and while it is hard to call this a total vertical integration – production companies controlling production, distribution and exhibition – it was nevertheless quite solid. Moreover, unlike in many other countries, this system was not eroded away by Hollywood movies. Indeed, the development of a robust domestic film market may be considered a major part of what made the Japanese film industry distinct.

THE TALKIES AND THE TŌHŌ BLOCK BLITZ (THE 1930S)

In 1931, Shōchiku produced Japan's first full talkie, *The Neighbour's Wife and Mine/Madame to nyōbō* (directed by Gosho Heinosuke), and with that, the Japanese film industry finally joined the sound film era (Fig. 7.2). This was not such a positive development for the independent production companies that had emerged in the 1920s. These companies were unable to keep up with investment in this technological innovation, and one by one they were absorbed by Nikkatsu and Shōchiku. However, there was one company that seized on the development of sound motion pictures to make a breakthrough into the market, a company that would go on to handle the films of Kurosawa Akira and in special effects movies, such as the Godzilla series. The company was Tōhō.

Tōhō began as the Tokyo Takarazuka Theatre Company, a business created in 1932 for the purpose of putting on stage theatre and showing motion pictures. In 1936, Tokyo Takarazuka merged with Photo Chemical Laboratory (P.C.L.) and J.O. Studios to form the Tōhō Film Distribution Company, which then became the Tōhō Film Corporation in 1937 (renamed Tōhō Co., Ltd. in 1943). One of the first incarnations of this company, P.C.L., was founded in 1929 and was originally on hire for on-site sound

Fig. 7.2 *The Neighbour's Wife and Mine/Madame to nyōbō* (Gosho Heinosuke, 1931, Shōchiku).

recording after having developed its own talkie sound system. But when Nikkatsu commissioned P.C.L. to join in a coproduction, this prompted the company to enter the film production business. Eventually, P.C.L.'s partnership with Nikkatsu fell apart, but since P.C.L. had already built a twin stage studio in the Kinutamura neighbourhood of Tokyo, the company decided to start producing films on its own in 1933. The place was reputed to have what was thought of at the time as state-of-the-art equipment. The fact that the origins of the company lay in powerful industrial conglomerates (*zaibatsu*) and blue-chip businesses permitted it to build this kind of production facility. P.C.L. advocated the introduction of modern rationalism into company management and thus put what was called 'the producer system' into practice. This system continued even after P.C.L. morphed into Tōhō in 1937.

So, in what specific ways did Tōhō's producer system differ from other companies? At Shōchiku, studio heads such as Kido Shirō took on a producer role and oversaw production; but at Tōhō, a person known as the production department manager assumed these responsibilities with associate producers working under them. Executive officers at Tōhō determined the production policy for the new fiscal year based on the previous year's business results, requests from cinemas and the situation of performers and directors. They also decided on the number of films to be produced and the total budget for the year or half year. Film production was then carried out based on these decisions. Associate producers (there were eight when the company was first launched) did not function as mere assistants; rather they acted as independent producers: each one submitted his own project ideas to the production department manager and took on the task of completing any projects that had been approved.[22] At other companies, it became customary in the 1920s for screenwriters to consult with directors to deliver project ideas,[23] but at Tōhō, producers had absolute authority and film productions originated with them. These producers would routinely stick their nose into scripts and even made decisions about casting and staff. Unlike at other companies, there were no production assistants on the job site; rather it was the people in producer positions that handled administrative work and kept things moving.[24]

Mimura Shintarō – famous for writing *Humanity and Paper Balloons/Ninjō kami fūsen* (1937) and other films directed by Yamanaka Sado – declared that at Tōhō the true leaders were the producers.[25]

Tōhō also differed from other companies in how it developed its exhibition assets. Despite falling behind Shōchiku and Nikkatsu in terms of the total number of cinemas under contract (Shōchiku had the most), Tōhō had managed to gain direct control over its cinemas, and by 1938 it had the greatest number of directly controlled cinemas in the world, using them to screen nothing but its own films. This was largely due to support during the P.C.L. era from Kobayashi Ichizō, the manager of a railway company and Tokyo Takarazuka Theatre (he later became the president of Tōhō). In 1938, Tōhō had direct control of twenty-two cinemas, Shōchiku had control of seventeen and Nikkatsu had only two.[26] Moreover, many of the cinemas Tōhō directly controlled were in major cities and each had large auditoria that could seat more than 1,500 to 2,000 people.[27] Threatened by this incursion from Tōhō, in April 1937, four companies (Shōchiku, Nikkatsu, Shinkō Kinema and Daito Films) demanded cinemas around Japan stop screening any films from the Tōhō Block (the distribution network formed by P.C.L., J.O. Studios and Tokyo Takarazuka prior to the establishment of Tōhō Films) and served notice that if the cinemas failed to comply, they would refuse to distribute their films to them in the future.[28] Naturally, Tōhō would not sit still for this, and a battle for control over cinemas unfolded between the businesses. At the time, the belief that permeated the film world was that power relations between film companies would be decided by the ability to control exhibition,[29] and in order for any company to grow, it was necessary to produce quality films whose success could lead to the acquisition of cinemas under contract.

THE WARTIME REGIME (THE LATE 1930S TO THE EARLY 1940S)

Ironically, it was wartime film regulations that quelled the clash between Tōhō and the other four companies. A string of circumstances – stretching from the Sino-Japanese War initiated by the July 1937 Marco Polo Bridge Incident to the Pacific War brought on by the December 1941 attack on Pearl Harbor – led the Japanese government to require motion pictures be used as tools to educate and guide citizens; and in 1939, it enacted the Film Law. This law subjected screenplays to pre-censorship and imposed a licensing system on production and distribution employees. As the war progressed, domestic film stock became counted as a military supply, overproduction was discouraged, and there was a call for more 'high quality' films that would contribute to the wartime regime.[30] In order to create competition for the production of a handful of top-calibre films under these conditions,[31] it was decided that the various film companies were to be consolidated. Two existing companies, Shōchiku or Tōhō, absorbed small and mid-sized production companies, while a third newcomer, Daiei was formed by merging the production departments of Shinkō, Daito and Nikkatsu. As of January 1942, just three companies were handling production of theatrical films: Shōchiku, Tōhō and Daiei.

Additionally, the human resources and organisational framework of companies with distribution departments were integrated, and in April 1942, a distribution company called Eihai was created in order to centralise administrative control over distribution. All 2,400 cinemas in Japan were divided into two groups – red and white – and the distribution rankings of cinemas (number one houses, number two houses, etc.) were restructured. Ehai distributed films to cinemas that had disentangled themselves from production companies, and it allotted exhibition revenues to film companies based on an established ratio of expenses to revenues.[32] This meant that the system of the vertical integration of production, distribution and exhibition that had established a rock-solid studio system for major film companies was being cut off at the point of distribution. Thus, production companies, which had dominated power relations in the film industry, no longer wielded influence over exhibition. Competition among film companies came to be determined more by the box-office performance of individual films.

The performance of each company for the 1942 fiscal year is reported in *The Film Yearbook*: Tōhō was the most prosperous, followed by Daiei, which was also in good shape, while Shōchiku was the only one in a slump.[33] Katō Atsuko has used these results to analyse the various production trends of each company.[34] Tōhō found success working on numerous military films after being given the opportunity to produce *The Burning Sky/Moyuru ōzora* (Abe Yutaka, 1940) as a project of the Army Aviation Film Production Committee and its creation of the Aviation Training Materials Production Company. The company made use of special effects to depict the spectacle of war in its major hit film of 1942, *The War at Sea in Hawaii and Malaya/Hawaii Malay okikaisen* (Yamamoto Kajirō). Tōhō's confident deployment of film technology was based on the long-held traditions of the P.C.L. era. It was thus able to effectively weather the storm of this difficult period by building a close relationship with the military, while incorporating current affairs even into their entertainment-oriented literary films and receiving a pass from censors.

Although Daiei was originally created to contribute to national policy, and while it did make films of this sort, it also improved its box-office performance by mass-producing popular entertainment films. Having a full line-up of Nikkatsu's accomplished swordsman stars, including Bandō Tsumasaburō, Arashi Kanjurō and Kataoka Chiezō, as well as Shinkō's Ichikawa Utaemon, was a major strength that brought confidence to their production of period dramas (*jidaigeki*). But since the staff of Nikkatsu's modern drama department was not taking part in production, and modern dramas were not Daiei's strength, rather than making straight modern dramas, Daiei produced early Meiji period genre films that sat somewhere between modern and period dramas.

In contrast to the success of the above two companies, Shōchiku performed poorly at the box office and drew criticism from government agencies and film critics for their petit bourgeois films and female-centred melodramas, which were seen as out of step with current affairs. Shōchiku took this into account and began making home-front dramas that still made use of the company's unique voice. However, these films lacked the graphic depictions of battle Tōhō's war films featured and thus failed to attract large enough audiences. The company also suffered from having too few performers with an image rugged and sturdy enough to fit the times.

During this period, a film production and distribution network designed to contribute to Japan's national policy was further set up in Japan's imperial colonies (Korea, Taiwan) and in regions under Japanese control (including Manchuria, Beijing, Shanghai and South East Asia).[35] Among them, many people involved in film-making headed to Man'ei, the Manchukuo film company Japan built in current Northeast China. Created in 1937, Man'ei was 'publicized as the studio with the largest lot in the orient, but after the war it was known as "the shame of Japanese film history"'.[36] Makino Mitsuo and Negishi Kan'ichi – who had once been in charge of Nikkatsu's studios and who eventually went on to construct the foundation of Tōei, the film company that pulled the Japanese film industry into the postwar era – moved there. Man'ei was essentially the only film company in Manchukuo. And while Man'ei was run independently owing to the fact that mainland Japan was too far away to effectively interfere, it functioned in an environment in which it was easy to control and easy to produce films that followed Japan's national policy. Moreover, Man'ei had a monopoly over distribution in the region, and it was through this company that Japanese films were also shown in Manchuria. Man'ei produced a total of 108 theatrical films in the eight years before the war ended in 1945,[37] promoting its star, Li Koran or Li Xianglan, whose original Japanese identity as Yamaguchi Yoshiko was intentionally concealed by the film company. But most of the films performed poorly at the box office. An additional attempt to expand the Man'ei distribution network throughout China was also unsuccessful. Nevertheless, since it had exclusive rights to distribution revenues in Manchukuo, Man'ei was able to use that revenue to continue making films.

THE OCCUPATION ERA (THE LATTER HALF OF THE 1940S)

In August 1945, the war came to an end, and in September, the General Headquarters, Supreme Commander for the Allied Powers (GHQ/SCAP) took over governance of Japan. Under SCAP, the Civil Information and Education department (CIE) was formed and placed in charge of the film industry where it enforced strict rules of censorship. The CIE manager David Conde blocked any films that might inspire militarism while welcoming movies with themes of freedom and democracy. As part of these restrictions, films 'portraying feudal loyalty or contempt of life as desirable and honourable' were banned, making it difficult to produce the period dramas that were so closely tied to those themes.[38] These CIE reforms roused film workers into action, prompting the formation of labour unions at all the film companies and stimulating the spread of democratic activities in the industry. Massive strikes occurred at Tōhō in particular. This caused a schism at Tōhō and ultimately the company split apart. In March 1947, a separate company was launched (although it was formally established in April 1948).[39] This new company was called Shintōhō.

From the beginning, Tōhō, which had been paralysed by its role as a producer, commissioned this new company to circulate films in Tōhō affiliated cinemas. The new company did well at the box office thanks to the performances of major stars brought over from Tōhō, including Ōkōchi Denjirō, Hasegawa Kazuo, Yamada Isuzu and Hara Setsuko. Eventually Shintōhō broke away from Tōhō, but when it began independent distribution in March 1950, almost all of those stars left, causing the company to lose its centripetal force. Moreover, even with this independent distribution, a lack of stars, and thus a lack of distinctive voice, made it difficult for Shintōhō to break into a market controlled by the cinemas already affiliated with the major film companies. While Shintōhō tried to sell its films to other company's affiliated cinemas one at a time through free booking, this plan did not go well. And even when the company did try to establish a system of affiliated cinemas, it failed because it lacked a unified business plan to properly distinguish itself in the market.[40]

Immediately after the war, Daiei made a similar push for free booking, a system where films were handled by the unit, as opposed to block booking where cinemas were tied to long-term exclusive contracts. Eihai, which presided over distribution during the war, was dissolved in October 1945, restoring independent distribution to the industry, and with this Shōchiku and Tōhō both declared they would distribute only their own films to their respective affiliated cinemas. This left Daiei the only company out of the loop. Since Daiei was created under wartime film regulations, it had never acquired any affiliated cinemas, so it decided that trying to adopt a block-booking system similar to the other companies would have been pointless; rather, it was wiser to try to compete with free booking.[41] Nevertheless, with cinema owners preferring the convenience and stability of the continuous programming block booking provided, Daiei was compelled to try to obtain its own affiliated cinemas. But unlike Shintōhō, Daiei actually succeeded in cultivating affiliated cinemas when its 'mother' films featuring Mimasu Aiko – i.e. 'maternal love melodramas' along the lines of *Stella Dallas* (King Vidor, 1937) – were well received in rural areas from the late 1940s to the mid-1950s.[42] But, at the same time, Daiei developed a production-centred management style under company president Nagata Masaichi, producing Japan's first 70mm film, *Buddha*/*Shaka* (Misumi Kenji, 1961), and pressing ahead with single-feature epic films after misreading market demand. Indeed, the company went ahead with the production of *Buddha* despite the fact that its affiliated cinemas did not even have 70mm projectors, and although roadshows at large cinemas did well, the film was met by a backlash from its affiliated cinemas and went largely ignored.[43]

When Ōkura Mitsugi took over as president of Shintōhō in 1955, the company implemented budgeting rules where films were made for 10 million yen or less.[44] While company management took a turn for the better by mass-producing erotic-grotesque films (a movement centred on the deviant and the bizarre), Shintōhō still ended up bankrupt in 1961. Similarly, Daiei found success in the 1960s with period dramas such as the *Zatōichi* and *The Sleepy Eyes of Death*/*Nemuri Kyōshirō* series but was also forced into bankruptcy in 1971. Both companies suffered from weak distribution and exhibition departments, and neither company could make up for this in the end.

THE TŌEI SURGE AND THE ERA OF NEW-RELEASE DOUBLE FEATURES (THE 1950S)

Tōei was founded in 1951, the same year the Treaty of San Francisco was concluded, marking Japan's independence and the launch of its postwar reconstruction. To Japanese people of the time, it was becoming obvious that Japanese film was flourishing on the international stage: Japanese film-makers won a string of awards, starting with Kurosawa Akira's *Rashomon/Rashōmon* (1950), which received the Golden Lion at the 1951 Venice Film Festival, and followed by Mizoguchi Kenji's successive prizes at Venice with *The Life of Oharu/Saikaku ichidai onna* (1952), *Ugetsu/Ugetsu monogatari* (1953) and *Sansho the Bailiff/Sanshō dayū* (1954). At the same time, domestic film audiences were increasing year on year. Calculations show that a Japanese person would visit the cinema once a month on average during this 'golden age', a fact that reveals how deeply movies had penetrated into people's lives.[45] The company that led the boom in filmgoing was Tōei.

Tōei originated with a company called Tōyoko Films, which had used capital from its railway company (Tōyoko Railway) in the Shibuya district of Tokyo to finance film exhibition before the war. After the war, Tōyoko's box-office returns were robust and business was brisk; and in 1947, the company borrowed Daiei's Kyoto studio – a former Shinkō Kinema studio – and went into film production. Tōyoko commissioned Daiei to distribute its films, but it was unable to collect on distribution revenues from Daiei as was planned and, as a result, Tōyoko went into considerable debt a mere year after starting production. Tōyoko Films determined that its debt would only worsen if it continued depending on other companies for distribution and concluded there was no other way but to distribute films for itself. Thus, Tōyoko, along with Ōizumi Films, a company that had precisely the same problem, decided to work together to force its way into a film exhibition sector dominated by the major players.[46] The two had acquired enough production capability to compete against the major production companies, and in order to conduct their own distribution and exhibition, they merged, incorporating a distribution company (Tokyo Eiga Haikyū) and relaunching as Tōei.

The new company began by pushing for the reform of existing distribution arrangements, as these were detrimental to newcomers such as Tōei. At the time, a typical cinema would have contracts with several film companies and would mix and match their films to premiere them as double features. However, when cinemas combined the films of latecomer Tōei with those from established companies such as Shōchiku and Tōhō, industry power relations dictated that Tōei's share from the distribution would be smaller, regardless of how popular its films were. To fight against this, Tōei began mass-producing films so it could pack these double-feature programmes entirely with its own titles, thus obviating the need to pair its titles with those of other companies. In January 1954, Tōei started combining its conventional feature-length theatrical films with mid-length period dramas. This practice of 'Tōei entertainment editions' (*goraku-ban*) also worked out well for cinemas since it was cheaper to sign contracts with a single company such as Tōei than with two separate companies. The *goraku-ban* films Tōei released included box-office hits such as the *Sorcerer's Orb/Satomi hakkenden* (1954) and the *Crimson Peacock/Shinshokoku monogatari benikujaku* (1954–5) five-film series.

While the production of period dramas had been discouraged during the Occupation, companies were now free to make these kinds of films and Tōei, having retained several major period drama stars as well as up-and-coming actors, successfully popularised the genre. With the positive reception for its double features, coupled with the popularity of its period dramas, the number of venues exclusively contracted to Tōei grew rapidly. At the end of December 1953, there were only forty-two Tōei-exclusive cinemas, but once the double features started playing, it took little more than half a year for that number to quadruple, and by the end of August 1954, Tōei had 155 venues to itself.[47] Moreover, Tōei was also expanding the market by driving the construction of cinemas over which it could then maintain direct control. Tōei was doing more than any other company to fully prepare cinemas (i.e. its point-of-sale) for selling mass-produced films. Thus, the same company that had originally suffered from a block-booking wall erected by the majors during its Tōyoko era, managed to build its own, even thicker, wall. And in doing so, it amassed considerable profits. Indeed, Tōei had completely paid off its debts from its early years and even ascended to number one in annual distribution revenue by 1956, just five short years after being first established.[48]

Naturally, the other major film companies were not going to sit by and silently watch this ambush. In January 1956, four of them began to increase their scale of production, Shōchiku, Daiei, Tōhō and Nikkatsu – which had just restarted production in 1954 – but not Shintōhō, which had no production capacity at the time.[49] Depending on the week, these companies might put out a single new title or show a film for a continuous two-week run, but generally each company premiered two titles every week with their eye solely on obtaining exclusive house runs. Nevertheless, no matter how prosperous the film industry was, the problem with using the mass production of films as a way to acquire exclusive runs was that it raised production costs, thus ultimately making it an unprofitable strategy. Shōchiku's president, Kido Shirō, claimed that 'forcing out double features' was 'tantamount to suicide', and with the watchwords 'quality over quantity', Shōchiku reverted to single-feature production,[50] with the other companies following suit. Tōei was the single exception. By 1957, Tōei had expanded its total number of exclusive houses to 837, surpassing the sum total of the other companies combined.[51] In order to stop Tōei from moving too far ahead of the pack, in the end, the other companies had no choice but to join the competition of 'quantity over quality'. Thus, in September 1958, a renewed competition over new-release double features emerged among the six major companies, including Shintōhō this time.

Tōei made sure its Kyoto studio was equipped with cutting-edge technical facilities to provide the finest working environment at the time. Nevertheless, Tōei's success remained grounded in a model of 'quantity over quality' film-making, and this ended up driving Japanese film in a dangerous direction. While the 1950s were certainly a successful time for Japanese films, television, which began broadcasting in 1953, was steadily infiltrating homes as an entertainment rival. In order to differentiate itself from television, in 1957, the Japanese film industry copied Europe and North America and began pushing the production of colour and widescreen films that expanded the conventional scale and composition of the film image. While these were certainly necessary technical innovations, they inevitably incurred a rise in production costs. More importantly, and somewhat ironically, by relying on the mass production of films to remain competitive, these companies may very well have been tying the nooses around their own necks.

At this point, it is useful to look at how the production departments of the film companies that had been consolidated during the war were absorbed by Daiei, and how Nikkatsu, which had become a distribution company, restarted production in 1954. When preparing to restart production, Nikkatsu had to gather talent from other companies so that it could have a ready supply of performers and staff; however, Shōchiku, Tōhō, Daiei, Shintōhō and Tōei all feared Nikkatsu would syphon away their talent, and so in 1953, the five companies signed a pact forbidding the hiring away of any director or actor under an exclusive contract. This was called the Five Company Agreement. The true purpose of this pact was to prevent the outflow of talent to Nikkatsu, but the result was that film-makers and performers could no longer move freely between companies. To them, the pact was an impediment that placed severe restrictions on their work and created an assortment of contractual problems. But at the same time, this agreement may have helped solidify the staff at these companies, which in turn helped give each studio its own distinctive voice.

While, as Wada-Marciano points out, certain Japanese film genres had been closely tied to certain film companies or studios before the war, this tendency was actually reinforced more strongly after the war.[52] Namely, Nikkatsu specialised in action movies; Tōhō made comedies and special effects pictures (especially monster movies); Tōei was famous for *jidaigeki* and yakuza films; Shōchiku continued to make traditional melodramas; and Daiei brought maternal films into fashion soon after the war and distinguished itself with *jidaigeki* in the 1960s. Even the short-lived Shintōhō brings to mind the erotic-grotesque films mentioned previously. Thus, while on the one hand the heated postwar race to acquire affiliated cinemas may in itself have forced companies to find a distinctive voice for their films, it may also have brought on the solidification of company staff and contributed to the further development of individualised genre film production at each company.

THE RAPID RISE OF TELEVISION AND THE SCALING DOWN OF THE STUDIOS (THE 1960S)

The 1960s were a period of dramatically high economic growth for Japan. Under the Ikeda administration's Income Doubling Plan, Japan's economic base strengthened and the income of a single person increased roughly 2.5 times in ten years, going from, for example, a hypothetical value of 100 in 1960 to 148.3 in 1965, and 245 by 1970.[53] This growth in income helped the mass consumption of leisure activities to blossom. The number of people travelling, engaging in different sports and attending various types of public entertainment events increased rapidly.[54] Among these new activities, the biggest rival to the film business was the fast developing television industry. In fact, the television set along with the washing machine and the refrigerator came to be known as the 'Three Sacred Treasures' – a symbol of contemporary consumer society.

In 1959, sales of television sets more than doubled, increasing sharply from about 1.5 million in the previous year to 3.5 million. It has been suggested that people's desire to watch the wedding parade of then Crown Prince Akihito and Princess Michiko on television accounts for television's rapid growth that year. Conversely, the size of feature film audiences went from its peak of 1.12 billion in 1958 to less than half that five years later with 510 million in 1963. The rapid decline of the film industry in the 1960s has often been tied to the sudden rise of the television

industry using this sort of statistical comparison. Indeed, many of the more conspicuous actions taken by the film companies in this period displayed an awareness of television's presence. The film industry's moratorium against releasing movies for television broadcast exemplifies the type of retaliatory measures the industry took. In October 1956, five of the major companies (Tōei, Shōchiku, Tōhō, Daiei and Shintōhō) discontinued issuing their films to television stations. Nikkatsu joined them in 1958. As a result, films from the majors were no longer broadcast on television – at least until Shintōhō's films leaked out due to its collapse in 1961. In the end, this measure continued until September 1964. It ended when box-office revenues for films were surpassed by revenues from television broadcasters, thus reversing the power relations between the two sides.[55]

Interestingly, while the film companies presented firm stances such as the one above, they were also developing policies specifically designed to make use of television. Four of the companies (Tōei, Shōchiku, Tōhō and Daiei) invested in private television stations and they all began producing 16mm films for television broadcast. In other words, while it is true the film companies exhibited a confrontational stance towards television, they also realised that they could exploit the new medium to their own advantage; and once they were thoroughly convinced the other side had the same ideas, they decided to work on a compromise with the television industry.

The companies had to face the harsh reality that with audiences no longer going to cinemas, they had to greatly decrease the number of films they distributed. Tōei, for example, was releasing more than 100 films a year during the 1950s but decreased its output to below 100 in 1961, and then took this down to fifty odd films by 1965. Similarly, the other companies decreased the number of films they released to around fifty each (Nikkatsu being the one exception, managing to put out sixty-five films that year), and the custom of new-release double features completely vanished.[56] At that point, some studios were no longer making films, and cutbacks were inevitable.

Shōchiku closed its studios in Kyoto in 1965 and put redundant staff on leave. Daiei took similar steps, reducing its staff out of necessity. For those without work at the time, Nikkatsu began producing its own television movies on film. Prior to this, Nikkatsu had been dispatching actors and directors to subcontractors to produce television films, but then it designated Stage One of its studios for television use and converted to independent production.[57] These sorts of measure were taken at each company under the pretext of 'streamlining'. Thus, their practice of blindly mass-producing films during the economic boom of the 1950s had come back to haunt them.

Streamlining was promoted not only in the production phase but in the stages of distribution and exhibition as well. As audiences decreased, the number of cinemas plummeted. Nevertheless, Tōei president Ōkawa Hiroshi stated in the basic management policy for 1965 that he wanted 'to be sure to have cinemas under the direct management of Tōei in any city with a population over 100,000', revealing an approach in which the company intended to enhance box-office control by accumulating dominating cinemas in major cities.[58] As a result, Tōei did in fact raise its total distribution revenue by 80 per cent in cities with populations over 100,000.[59]

But in addition to the problem of where to sell films, the question of how to sell films became of even greater concern. In the early 1960s, a number of film companies, such as Tōhō and Tōei, introduced 'advertising producers' whose job it was to integrate promotional activities for all phases (production, distribution and exhibition) to strengthen advertising. Film companies were no longer simply responsible for the mass production of films and their distribution to cinemas as they had in the past; now they were putting careful consideration into where and how they were going to sell their products.

While on the one hand, production departments at the major companies had been weakened; on the other hand, an opportunity had emerged to promote the development of independent film production. The Japan Art Theatre Guild (ATG), to give one example, started releasing art films to small-scale cinemas in large cities, but it quickly came to be known for granting directors with artistic ambitions the opportunity to make fully experimental films with budgets of 10 million yen. Films produced by ATG include Ōshima Nagisa's *Death by Hanging/Kōshikei* (1968) and Matsumoto Toshio's *Funeral Parade of Roses/Bara no sōretsu* (1969) (Fig. 7.3).

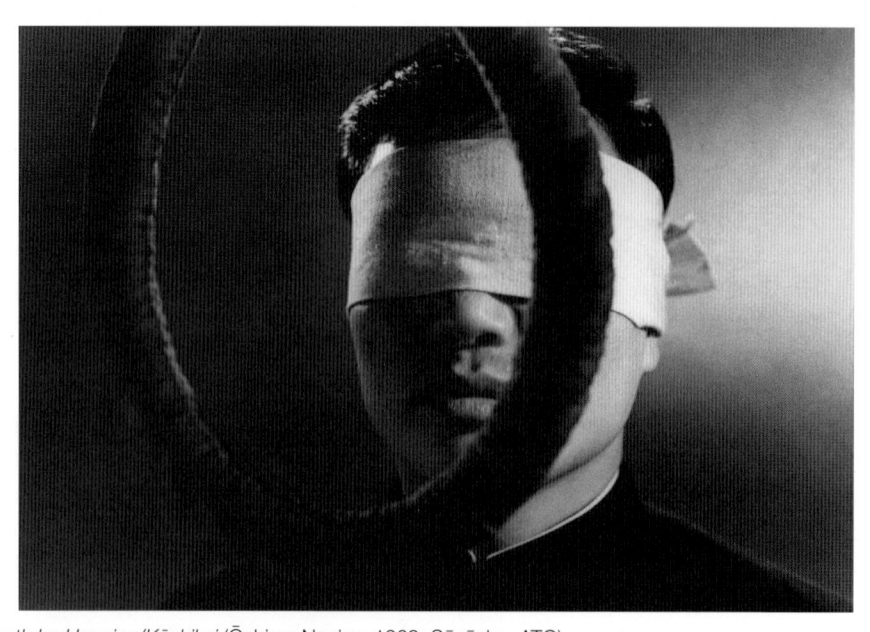

Fig. 7.3 *Death by Hanging/Kōshikei* (Ōshima Nagisa, 1968, Sōzōsha, ATG).

Additionally, the mid-1960s saw a deluge of production companies making low-budget independent adult movies called 'pink films'. These companies were segregated from regular production companies and looked down upon for their so-called 'eroductions' (erotic productions). Nevertheless, in 1965 nearly 40 per cent of movies produced in Japan were 'pink films',[60] and by 1970, approximately half were pink.[61] 'Pink films' were in particular demand at small cinemas that were losing customers. This represented the rise of independent producers in Japan, and it shook the studio system where the major film companies had control over production, distribution and exhibition.

THE COLLAPSE OF THE STUDIO SYSTEM AND FILM PRODUCTION IN THE AFTERMATH (THE 1970S TO THE PRESENT)

At the beginning of the 1970s, the quality of the management at the once dominant major film companies was deteriorating and the structure of the industry underwent a lasting major transformation. In 1971, Nikkatsu, the oldest of the film companies, stopped producing theatrical films for general audiences and, based on its success with 'pink films' from the 1960s, was reborn as a production company specialising in adult films. Indeed, its line of Nikkatsu Roman Porno, adult films with larger budgets than traditional 'pink films', proved popular and helped the company survive. With its distribution network weakened, Daiei, which had fought for free booking at every opportunity, went bankrupt in 1971. But unlike Nikkatsu, Daiei was unable to make a comeback.

The other major companies, Tōei, Tōhō and Shōchiku, continue to exist today, but in the 1970s, they shifted from production to specialising in distribution and exhibition in order to pick up momentum after the disappointing 1960s. In 1971, the same year Nikkatsu and Daiei went bankrupt, Tōhō, which had distanced itself from producing its own films from the beginning, split up its production department, and in 1973, it set up a 'film adjustment department' to select films to be brought in from outside.[62] This is plainly evident in a breakdown of Tōhō Distribution's titles in 1973. Namely, Tōhō was contracted for a total of forty-eight films, and only eight of those were produced by Tōhō, while the rest were made by subsidiaries or other companies.[63]

In this way, the film companies greatly reduced the number of in-house productions and switched to buying up films from independent producers and distributing those instead. It is at this point that a company called Kadokawa Shoten came along and saw an opening to exploit. Kadokawa, a publishing company, entered the film market in 1976 looking to use motion pictures as a way to increase book sales. In the 1970s and 1980s, it became an unmistakable leader in the film industry. The amount of money it was investing far exceeded anything the independent producers of the 1960s had spent; and it shook things up with its innovative 'media mix' strategies. The company was implementing methods that had been unthinkable in the traditional film industry: it was spending more money on advertising than production and was using television as a medium for advertising, a strategy that had been avoided until then. By that time, the Japanese film industry had already lost its ability to sustain a system of affiliated cinemas and with Kadokawa and other companies distributing a line-up of epic films (the dominant genre of the time) using a system of a free booking, cinemas operating under a book-blocking system began to weaken.[64] In short, Kadokawa Shoten's impact on the industry spurred the shift from block-booking practices to free booking.

The decline of block booking meant the decisive collapse of the studio system. It became difficult for film companies to distribute their films to cinemas with any stability. The studios that had stopped making films were no longer signing actors or directors to exclusive contracts. As a result, each of the companies lost their signature characteristics. Additionally, there were fewer opportunities for new artists in the industry to receive guidance from veteran producers: studios were no longer functioning as a place for cultivating human resources. At one time, one had to first undergo training as an assistant director in order to become a full director, but even this common practice was disintegrating. Director Ōbayashi Nobuhiko, a typical case at Kadokawa Shoten, had no actual experience as an assistant director at a studio; rather, his background was originally in directing commercials. In this sense, the emergence of Kadokawa Shoten can be seen as a landmark event that announced the opening of the post-studio era.

Ironically, the only company able to sustain a system of mass production within the studio system framework – albeit just barely – was Nikkatsu, even though it was supposed to have withdrawn from standard theatrical films. And while this allowed it to attract many young workers, in the long run, the spread of home video coupled with the sudden rise of adult video in the 1980s meant that even Nikkatsu had to cease production by 1988. As mass production ended, so did the era of film-makers learning the trade at well-respected studios. Film-makers were now cultivating skills at a variety of different venues instead. Television stars such as Kitano Takeshi were becoming directors, while aspiring film-makers, who had gained experience making amateur films in university film clubs, made their directorial debuts via independent film productions. Currently, experienced and accomplished directors and production staff members have taken up teaching at universities or vocational schools. This has drawn many aspiring artists to study film-making under them as a way to break into the industry.

Additionally, ever since the emergence of Kadokawa, television stations such as Fuji Television or the Tokyo Broadcasting System (TBS) have become an important part of film production and the movie industry has begun relying on media strategies that use up enormous amounts of capital. The 1990s saw the establishment of what is called the 'production committee formula', where films are produced via joint investment from several companies. This is still the dominant formula today. Several companies take part in these production committees, making it easier to amass funding and allowing companies to distribute risk in case a film fails at the box office. Furthermore, companies can expect larger profits from the sale of ancillary products, such as DVDs, manga tie-ins and books (novelisations, etc.), than from just box-office receipts. Now, in addition to erstwhile major film companies now functioning as distributors, such as Tōhō and Shōchiku, many television stations, internet companies, advertisers, newspapers, publishers and other media-related businesses take part in these production committees and develop multilateral advertising through the various media they own.

A single company no longer oversees all phases of a film from production to distribution and exhibition as was the case during the studio system. The once major film companies have come to function only partly as producers, placing chief importance on distribution activities and embarking on exhibition as well. But the days of distributing exclusively to affiliated cinemas are over. Entertainment films no longer open at some specified cinemas only; rather, wide-releases at a variety of cinemas have become the norm.

CONCLUSION

This chapter has taken a historical look at the unique features of the Japanese film industry, focusing on the modes and practices of the studios. From the very outset, the studios were run with a great importance placed on the ability to influence exhibition – a fact symbolised by their very origins in which studios were being built as a result of the rapid growth in cinemas in the late 1900s. Although the film companies of Japan managed to escape anti-monopoly laws and thus maintain a studio system for a time after World War II, they were overly fixated on fighting competitors for affiliated cinemas, a battle that had been ongoing since before the war, and therefore neglected the changing conditions that surrounded the film industry. Through this neglect, they precipitated their own demise. The fundamental question as to why film companies in Japan were able to evade anti-monopoly laws in the first place has not been sufficiently dealt with, but the answer to that question may very well reveal what makes the Japanese film industry unique. Perhaps the historical look at the Japan's studio system presented in this chapter may provide clues to the answer to the issue above as well as many others that have still not yet been fully addressed.

Notes

1. Ueda Manabu, *Nihon eiga sōsōki no kōgyō to kankyaku: Tokyo to Kyoto o chūshin ni* (Tokyo: Waseda daigaku shuppanbu, 2012), pp. 5–6.
2. Ibid., p. 146.
3. The film companies shown in Figure 7.1 are limited to those mentioned in this chapter. The other smaller-scale film companies founded throughout the history as well as the film companies established under the Japanese empire are omitted.
4. [Editors' note: for more on Japanese film exhibition see also Chapter 8 by Manabu Ueda in this volume.]
5. Douglas Gomery and Clara Pafort-Overduin, *Movie History: A Survey*, 2nd edn (New York: Routledge, 2011), p. 162.
6. Katō Atusko, 'Eiga kaisha no shijō ninshiki to kankyaku: 1930–1960 nendai o chūshin ni', in Fujiki Hideaki (ed.), *Kankyaku e no approach* (Tokyo: Shinwasha, 2011), p. 102.
7. Joseph L. Anderson and Donald Richie, *The Japanese Film: Art and Industry*, rev. edn (Princeton, NJ: Princeton University Press, 1982).
8. Tanaka Jun'ichirō, *Nihon eiga hattatsu shi*, 5 vols. (Tokyo: Chūōkōron-sha, 1957–68); Satō Tadao, *Nihon eiga shi*, 4 vols. (Tokyo: Iwanami shoten, 1995); Yomota Inuhiko, *Nihon eiga shi hyakujū nen* (Tokyo: Shūeisha, 2014), the English edition of which is *What Is Japanese Cinema: A History*, trans. Philip Kaffen (New York: Columbia University Press, 2019).
9. Hideaki Fujiki, *Making Personas: Transnational Film Stardom in Modern Japan* (Cambridge, MA: Harvard University Asia Center, 2013), pp. 69–74.
10. David Bordwell, Janet Staiger and Kristin Thompson, *The Classical Hollywood Cinema: Film Style and Mode of Production to 1960* (New York: Columbia University Press, 1985), p. 136.
11. Fujiki, *Making Personas*, p. 72. Programmes might also combine *kyūgeki*, *shinpa* and films imported from overseas.
12. Hiroshi Komatsu and Charles Musser, 'Benshi Search', *Wide Angle* vol. 9 no. 2 (1987), pp. 72–90.
13. Hiroshi Komatsu, 'From Natural Colour to the Pure Motion Picture Drama: The Meaning of Tenkatsu Company in the 1910s of Japanese Film History', *Film History* vol. 7 no. 1 (1995), pp. 69–86.
14. Aaron Gerow, *Visions of Japanese Modernity: Articulations of Cinema, Nation, and Spectatorship, 1895–1925* (Berkeley: University of California Press, 2010), pp. 165–6.
15. Ibid., p. 167.
16. See Joanne Bernardi, *Writing in Light: The Silent Scenario and the Japanese Pure Film Movement* (Detroit, MI: Wayne State University Press, 2001), 188; Fujiki, *Making Personas*, pp. 161–73. Although Shōchiku was aiming to make Hollywood-style films, Daisuke Miyao points out the conflict in making a complete shift when taking into consideration that audiences had become accustomed to traditional Japanese films. See his *The Aesthetics of Shadow: Lighting and Japanese Cinema* (Durham, NC: Duke University Press, 2013), pp. 15–66.
17. Komatsu Hiroshi, 'Shinpa eiga no keitai gaku: Shinsai mae no nihon eiga ga kataru mono', in Kurosawa Kiyoshi, Yoshimi Shun'ya, Kurosawa Kiyoshi and Lee Bong-Ou (eds), *Nihon eiga wa ikite iru, dai ni kan: Eiga shi o yomi naosu* (Tokyo: Iwanami shoten, 2010), p. 52.
18. Fujiki, *Making Personas*, pp. 167–70.
19. Mitsuyo Wada-Marciano, *Nippon Modern: Japanese Cinema of the 1920s and 1930s* (Honolulu: University of Hawai'i Press, 2008), p. 114. However, as Miyao points out, an emphasis on the contrast between light and dark can also be found in some Shōchiku films (e.g. the so-called 'street films'). See Miyao, *The Aesthetics of Shadow*, chapter 3.
20. Ishimaki Yoshio, 'Honpō eiga kōgyō gaikan', in *Nihon eiga jigyō sōran Taishō jūgo nen ban* (Tokyo: Kokusai eiga tsūshin sha, 1926), p. 52.
21. 'Taishō jūgo nen no eiga oyobi nihon eiga kai', in *Nihon eiga nenkan Taishō jūgo nen Shōwa ni nen ban* (Tokyo: Asahi shinbunsha, 1927), p. 12.
22. 'Dare ga eiga o tsukuru ka, Dai ichi wa', *Tōhō eiga*, 1 April 1938, p. 10.
23. 'Dare ga eiga o tsukuru ka, Dai ni wa', *Tōhō eiga*, 15 April 1938, p. 27.
24. 'Dare ga eiga o tsukuru ka, Dai san wa', *Tōhō eiga*, 1 May 1938, p. 28.
25. 'Dare ga eiga o tsukuru ka, Dai ni wa', *Tōhō eiga*, 15 April 1938, p. 27.
26. Yoshioka Jūzaburō, *Eiga* (Tokyo: Diamondsha, 1938), p. 207.
27. Tōhō gojū nen shi hensan iin kai (ed.), *Tōhō gojū nen shi* (Tokyo: Tōhō kabushiki gaisha, 1982), p. 164.
28. Ibid., p. 170.

29 'Gaika wa tsui ni Tōhō eiga e', *Tōhō eiga* vol. 1 no. 2 (October 1938), p. 5.
30 Peter B. High, *The Imperial Screen: Japanese Film Culture in the Fifteen Years' War, 1931–1945* (Madison: University of Wisconsin Press, 2003); Katō Atsuko, *Sōdōin taisei to eiga* (Tokyo: Shin'yōsha, 2003).
31 Ibid., p. 106.
32 For a specific example of Eihai's distribution methods see ibid., p. 117.
33 'Eiga gaisha gyōseki', in *Eiga nenkan Shōwa jūhachi nen ban* (Tokyo: Nippon eiga zasshi kyōkai, 1943), p. 37.
34 Kato, *Sōdōin taisei to eiga*, pp. 119–24.
35 See, for instance, High, *The Imperial Screen*; Kato, *Sōdōin taisei to eiga*; Michael Baskett, *The Attractive Empire: Transnational Film Culture in Imperial Japan* (Honolulu: University of Hawai'i Press, 2008); Yan Ni, *Senji nicchū eiga kōshōshi* (Tokyo: Iwanami shoten, 2010).
36 Yomota, *Nihon eiga shi hyaku nen*, p. 117. [Editors' note: see also Chapter 31 by Ni Yan in this volume.]
37 Hu Chang and Gu Guan, *Man'ei: Kokusaku eiga no shōshi*, trans. Yokochi Takeshi and Aida Fusako (Tokyo: Pandora, 1999), p. 233.
38 Kyoko Hirano, *Mr. Smith Goes to Tokyo: Japanese Cinema under the American Occupation, 1945–1952* (Washington, DC: Smithsonian Institute Press, 1992); Hiroshi Kitamura, *Screening Enlightenment: Hollywood and the Cultural Reconstruction of Defeated Japan* (Ithaca, NY: Cornell University Press, 2010).
39 Hirano, *Mr. Smith Goes to Tokyo*, chapter 6.
40 Shibata Ryūhō, *Eiga kai o kiru* (Tokyo: Seibunkan shoten, 1979), pp. 40–1.
41 Suzuki Akinari, *Rappa to yobareta otoko: Eiga Producer Nagata Masaichi* (Tokyo: Kinema junpōsha, 1990), p. 180.
42 Itakura Fumiaki, 'Daei "haha mono" no genre seisei to studio system', in Iwamoto Kenji (ed.), *Kazoku no shōzō: Home drama to melodrama* (Tokyo: Shinwasha, 2007), pp. 121–2.
43 Shibata, *Eiga kai o kiru*, p. 61.
44 'Akaji o kokufuku shita Shintōhō', *Kinema junpō*, 15 July 1958, p. 45.
45 Dividing the Motion Picture Producers Association of Japan attendance figures by the total population of 90 million, reveals that from 1957 to 1959 an average person would attend a movie twelve times or more in one year (Motion Picture Producers Association of Japan, Inc., 'Statistics of Film Industry in Japan', <http://www.eiren.org/statistics_e/index.html> [in English]).
46 The parent company of Tōkyū received a 40 million yen loan from Daiei and tried to resolve the situation; however, it was unable to earn enough from distribution to cover production costs, and it decided to start its own distribution. For details, see Tōei jū nen shi hensan iin kai (ed.), *Tōei jū nen shi* (Tokyo: Tōei kabushiki gaisha, 1962), p. 35.
47 'Nihondate kyōsō to nihon eiga no sin'yō', *Kinema junpō*, 1 November 1958, p. 65.
48 Tōei jū nen shi hensan iin kai, *Tōei jū nen shi*, p. 129.
49 Although maintaining the double-feature system was challenging and all companies had decreased their output, in 1958, they nevertheless began producing new-release double features once again.
50 'Gyōkai dōkō', in *Eiga nenkan 1959 nen ban* (Tokyo: Jiji tsūshinsha, 1959), p. 124.
51 Ōkawa Hiroshi, 'Toei goraku eiga ron', *Kinema junpō*, 15 November 1957, p. 61.
52 Wada-Marciano, *Nippon Modern*, p. 46.
53 Matsuda Nobukazu, *Kōdo keizai seichōka no kokumin seikatsu: Kōdo keizai seichōka ni okeru kokumin seikatsu no henka* (Nagoya: Chūbu nihon kyōiku bunkakai, 1983), p. 1.
54 Tsūshōsangyōshō kigyōkyoku shomuka (ed.), *Wagakuni eiga sangyō no genjō to kadai: Eiga sangyō hakusho Shōwa sanjū nana nen ban* (Tokyo: Shōbundō, 1963), pp. 92–4.
55 Furuta Hisateru offers another reason why they resumed supplying theatrical films. See his '*Tetsuwan atomu*' *no jidai: Eizō sangyō no kōbō* (Kyoto: Sekai shisōsha, 2009), p. 123. Due to the liberalisation of foreign film imports in July 1964, a large number of television and theatrical films were expected to be brought in from overseas. This engendered a sense of unease among the film companies and prompted the investment in private television stations by the major film companies discussed later in this chapter.
56 *Eiga nenkan 1967 nen ban* (Tokyo: Jiji tsūshinsha, 1967), p. 49.
57 Ibid., pp. 126–7.

58 'Tōei no takaku keiei no keikaku naru', *Eiga jihō*, May 1965, p. 29.
59 'Senmonkan no hokorobi o tsukurō', *Eiga journal*, June 1965, p. 53.
60 Satō Tadao, *Nihon eiga shi, Dai san kan* (Tokyo: Iwanami shoten, 1995), p. 75.
61 Yomota, *Nihon eiga shi hyakujū nen*, p. 180.
62 Tōhō gojū nen shi hensan iin kai, *Tōhō gojū nen shi*, p. 496.
63 Tanaka Jun'ichirō, *Nihon eiga hattatsu shi, Dai go kan* (Tokyo: Chūōkōron-sha, 1976), p. 268.
64 Misonō Ryōko, 'Shōjo, nazo, machine gan: "Kadokawa eiga" no sai hyōka', in Sugino Kentarō (ed.), *Kōsaku suru eiga: Anime eiga bungaku* (Kyoto: Mineruva shobō, 2013), p. 305.

8

EXHIBITION
Screening spaces: A history of Japanese film exhibition

Manabu Ueda

From the public premiere of the Cinématographe at the Grand Café in Paris in 1895 and the Japanese premiere of the same technology in Osaka's South District Theatre (Nanchi-enbujō) in 1897, through to the present, the matter of exhibition remains an important aspect of international film history. Film exhibition is enacted out of a number of complicated, relational elements. In terms of its practice, it mediates both films and their audiences since a film produced by its makers is only fully materialised by the reception of its spectators. When seen as a context, exhibition becomes a concept that involves a number of factors that might variously include the space provided by the location and architecture of the cinema; the way in which screenings are conducted (in conjunction with the *benshi* [silent film narrator], for example); various projection techniques; political issues related to production, distribution, censorship and control; and the technology and equipment used by various screen media.

Previous studies of Japanese film exhibition have focused on a diverse range of issues that includes regionality,[1] the narration of silent films,[2] colonialism[3] and the transition to sound.[4] There has, however, been little holistic historical research or analysis concerning the topic. This chapter will begin by presenting an outline of several problems that must be addressed (with an analysis of concrete examples) in order to understand the overall history of Japanese film exhibition. Firstly, I will clarify the ways in which an overall argument about exhibition may relate to the various elements included. Then, I will explore the meaning of the term 'exhibition' in the context of Japanese film by focusing in particular on a number of case studies that showcase the transition from silent films to 'talkies'. I will conclude by proving that the change from silent films to films with soundtracks affected not only sound technology, but also the expansion of space within the culture of Japanese film exhibition.

AN OVERVIEW OF THE HISTORY OF JAPANESE FILM EXHIBITION

In this section, I present an overview of the history of Japan film exhibition that is divided into several eras ranging from the end of the nineteenth century, when Japan imported films, through to the present day. Although I will focus on the characteristic problems of each era in order to fully assess the complexity of exhibition, each problem has also been diachronically present throughout the interwoven history of Japanese cinema.

The organisation of film programmes: 1897–1910

Exhibitors during this era had an absolute right to determine the organisation of film programmes. As Charles Musser has pointed out, American exhibitors in the 1900s volunteered to organise the early US film programmes, discounting the wishes of producers and proactively creating an overarching story for the whole exhibition.[5] The same approach was simultaneously adopted in Japan.

Together with production and distribution, film exhibition currently constitutes one of the three main areas of responsibility of the Japanese film industry. The production, distribution and exhibition of films are generally handled by different companies at each stage. In the late nineteenth century, however, the production, distribution and exhibition of films were not handled separately but managed by the same enterprise. The first Japanese film, *The Dance of Geisha/Geisha no teodori* (1899), for example, was produced by the advertising company Hiromeya. The film was not duplicated for distribution; exhibition was managed instead by Komada Kōyō, a clerk at Hiromeya, who undertook provincial screening tours around the country as the film's narrator.

Immediately after the start of the Russo-Japanese War in 1904, newsreels showing the battlefields gained in popularity. Duplicated reels were sold by Japanese production companies to exhibitors and various foreign-made films were imported. Exhibitors conducted provincial tours all over Japan showing purchased Japanese film reels in theatres and schools. The spread of inexpensive domestic projectors, which had already appeared in opposition to the expensive imported projectors of Edison, Pathé, Gaumont and Urban,[6] contributed to an overall increase in film exhibition. This led to a permanent division between the production and exhibition of film.

Because exhibitors purchased these duplicated reels independently, not tied to any specific contract with a production company, they were able to organise film programmes in any way they wished. Different organisational practices produced different meanings: newsreels of the Russo-Japanese War could be combined with *The Funeral of Commander Hirose, Admiral Itō and Other Visitors/Hirose chūsa no sōgi Itō taishō ika kaisō* (1904) to remember a deceased officer or combined with Lucien Nonguet's *L'assassinat du grand-duc Serge* (1905) to allude to the instability of the Russian political climate. These organisational montage practices were further strengthened by the art of narration within the exhibition space.

The first moving picture theatre, Denkikan (literally meaning 'the electrical hall'), appeared in Tokyo in 1903. This theatre was little more than a facility to screen worn touring film reels. By 1910, however, other cinemas began to appear in major cities of Japan such as Tokyo, Osaka, Nagoya, Kyoto, Yokohama and Kobe, and they soon became the mainstream venue for film exhibition. The appearance of cinemas established the convention of print distribution in agreement with specific production companies and the organisation of programming subsequently became dependent on this arrangement. In this way, the distinction between film production, distribution and exhibition became widely accepted in the Japanese film industry and the independent role in organising film programmes on the part of exhibitors diminished.

Geographical conditions: The late 1900s to the 1910s

Tokyo and Kyoto have always been home to most Japanese film studios as well as the locations where the majority of Japanese films have been shot. In this period, Japanese film production came to be coloured by regional differences; Tokyo became the centre of the *gendaigeki*, or contemporary film drama, whereas Kyoto became associated with the *jidaigeki*, or period drama film. In order to understand the geographical conditions from which these regional characteristics arose, this section will explore the regional differences among the moving picture theatres that emerged in the two cities.

Asakusa, Tokyo, and Shin-Kyōgoku, Kyoto, were both established as entertainment districts in the late nineteenth century. There were significant regional differences, however, in terms of the relationship between playhouses and moving picture theatres in both locations. In Tokyo, all the large, renowned playhouses, such as Kabukiza, were in central downtown areas such as Ginza. On the other hand, most of the moving picture theatres were constructed in Asakusa on the outskirts of the city.[7] The playhouses were thus in a separate urban space from the moving picture theatres with only one small playhouse, Tokiwaza, located in Asakusa. In contrast, in Kyoto, playhouses, both major and minor, as well as several variety theatres, all coexisted, and with the construction of a large number of moving picture theatres around 1910, the city saw the close proximity of large playhouses and moving picture theatres in some districts that included Shin-Kyōgoku.

The connection between urban space and the entertainment districts in Kyoto where large playhouses and moving picture theatres were closely situated had a significant impact on film-making trends. Makino Shōzō, who directed the early period film, *The Battle of the Honnoji Temple/Honnōji Kassen* (1908), was, for instance, the head of Senbonza, a playhouse in Kyoto. This suggests that the audience for kabuki was not so different from the audience for movies in the city. In Tokyo, however, where kabuki plays and film-making were clearly distinguished from one another, the geographical separation of moving picture theatres from large playhouses in the city centre was also reflected in the nature of film-making practice. In 1911, for example, the Tokyo Theatre Association made the decision to ban kabuki actors from appearing in movies altogether.[8]

Nevertheless, in the case of *shinpa* (contemporary plays of the Meiji era), several eminent actors such as Ii Yōhō and Fujisawa Asajirō did also appear in a number of contemporary drama films.[9] This may be related to the fact that the Kanda area was clustered with both moving picture theatres such as Kinkikan and Hongōza, a stronghold of *shinpa* at the time.

This distinction between the entertainment districts of Tokyo and Kyoto meant that the cities' different types of audience thus also offered the chance to produce different types of films and stars. As film-making gained momentum in Japan in the late 1900s, it served in Tokyo to deepen the antagonism in the entertainment industry between the playhouse and the moving picture theatre; in contrast, the regional characteristics of the entertainment districts in Kyoto, together with the presence of an audience who linked kabuki with period drama films, was instrumental in encouraging the development of a different film-making culture.

Politics: From the 1920s to the 1930s

The primary factor in changes to Japanese film exhibition was the transition from silent films to sound films (or 'talkies'). Before discussing this later on, I want to turn to the relationship between exhibition and politics, especially the nature of film exhibition in imperial Japan and within colonial or semi-colonial territories such as Taiwan, Korea, Manchuria and South East Asia. The films produced and exhibited in these areas cannot simply be distinguished from Japanese film in terms of national cinema. Film exhibition functioned as propaganda in order to justify the politics of domination enacted under Japan's colonial authority.

A consideration of Japanese film exhibition in Manchuria and its subsequent influence on film-making is revealing. Japanese film screenings targeted at immigrants from Japan in Japanese leased territory in Dalian and along the South Manchuria Railway (Mantetsu) were already taking place before the Japanese puppet state of 'Manchukuo' was established in 1932. In 1926, for example, there were four cinemas located in Dalian that screened Japanese films, as well as one close to Port Arthur; these films included productions by Nikkatsu, Shōchiku and Teikine.[10]

Japanese film exhibition in Manchuria was widespread. The difficulty of booking stage actors and vaudeville artists in Manchuria, compared with that in Japanese regional cities, meant that film exhibition in Dalian occupied an important position within the entertainment hierarchy. Koizumi Gorō, a Japanese exhibitor whose brother managed a cinema in Dalian, noted, for example, that Japanese entertainers avoided going to Manchuria and if they did go, it required a long-term contract of more than a month that also included a 50 per cent premium on the regular performance fee.[11] Such circumstances necessarily fuelled demand for screen entertainment amongst Japanese immigrants.

Mobile film exhibition also functioned as an important method of screening films in Manchuria. Screenings were held by various organisations on both a commercial and non-commercial basis. The Okayama Orphanage, for example, managed travelling film exhibition in Taiwan, Korea and Manchuria, in addition to Japan, and collected operating expenses in order to support orphans.[12] After the founding of Manchukuo, Kyōwakai, a fascist organisation in

Manchuria, as well as government offices such as the Ministry of Education and the Ministry of Civil Affairs, all held mobile screenings.[13] Another organisation was the film department of Mantetsu. Mantetsu, established in Dalian in 1906, created its own film section in 1923. Prior to this, it had screened films in various wayside concession areas. There were opportunities to show phonographs and magic lanterns, mainly to Mantetsu staff and the Japanese army; Japanese films were added in 1917. In 1922, Mantetsu began regular film screenings, three times a year, in wayside areas; they also initiated film screenings for elementary school students.[14] Su Chongmin has pointed out that these events took the forms of a 'cultural invasion' in order to promote the colonisation of areas along the railway, thus reflecting the intentions of Gotō Shinpei, the first president of Mantetsu and a renowned government official of colonial management.[15]

The Manchuria Film Association (referred to as Man'ei) took over the travelling film exhibition policy of Mantetsu's film section in 1937. Man'ei monopolised the distribution of Japanese and Chinese films,[16] and actively managed mobile film exhibition in areas without cinemas. Akagawa Kōichi stated, for example, that this should be organised 'into four touring companies and traverse three thousand two hundred kilometres, in total, over two hundred forty days'; a surprisingly long distance and period of time.[17] The touring screening programme at this point included *The Burning of a Brave Warrior*/*Sōshi shokuten* (1937), the first feature film produced by Man'ei; *A Rush for the Patriotism*/*Hōkoku bakushin* (1937), produced by Nikkatsu; and newsreels filmed by Man'ei and the Asahi Film Company as well as various documentary and animated films.[18]

Man'ei's growing control of film exhibition in Manchuria affected the nature of the films produced by the Mantetsu film section. In 1928, they invited Akutagawa Kōzō, a film critic working in Dalian, to start film production. The Mantetsu films produced by Akutagawa strongly reflected the politics of Mantetsu, justifying colonial rule. For example, just as *The Lytton Investigation Team in Manchuria*/*Manshū ni okeru Lytton chōsadan* (1932) included intertitles in French and English, and *Spring of the Founding*/*Kenkoku no haru* (1932) intertitles in English and Chinese, Mantetsu's own documentary films of the time also included foreign-language intertitles. The production of these Mantetsu films, intended for exhibition among Western and Chinese audiences, justified the establishment of Manchukuo.

The production of documentary films as a form of propaganda to justify Manchukuo began to shift from 1936 onwards. This seems to have been a result of Man'ei's expanded control of film exhibition within Manchuria. Man'ei and Mantetsu both increasingly specialised in film production and exhibition; Man'ei through both the production of propaganda documentary films distributed to cinemas in Manchuria and the organisation of travelling exhibition, and Mantetsu through the production of documentary films intended for exhibition in Japan through the distribution network of the Towa Trading Company, a leading Japanese import film company.[19] In 1936, the 'Draft Establishment of a Manchuria Film Company and Policy' (*Manshū koku eiga taisaku juritsu an*) was drawn up to found Man'ei, and the film section of Mantetsu was reorganised into the Mantetsu Film Studio. Mantetsu's film production thus became cut off from Man'ei's monopolised practice of film exhibition.

Most Mantetsu films after 1936, such as *Unexplored Region, Rehe*/*Hikyō nekka* (1936) and *The Barga Prairie*/*Sōgen Barga* (1936), both directed by Akutagawa, were documentary films that romanticised the landscape of Manchuria for Japanese people. In the background of these Mantetsu films, produced to discharge blatant propaganda, Man'ei completely managed Manchurian film exhibition. Many have suggested that these political changes regarding the nature of film exhibition in Manchuria directly influenced film-making practices as well.

The expansion of the film market: From the 1940s to the 1950s

Japanese film exhibition reached its golden age after World War II. The number of cinemas grew from 1,729, immediately after the war, to the figure of 2,205 in 1949, thus almost restoring things to prewar levels.[20] By the time Japan's high economic growth began in

1954, this figure had reached 4,291, with a total of four million audience admissions.[21] The expansion of regional exhibition markets played an important role in this growth. Prior to the war, particularly during the silent film period, cinemas were concentrated in Japan's major metropolitan areas such as Tokyo and Osaka. In 1953, however, the number of cinemas in Hokkaido was 366, greater than Tokyo's total of 339, Osaka's total of 224 and Aichi's (including Nagoya's) total of 194.[22] The number of locally based film exhibitors also increased significantly during this time. The exhibition trade magazine *Rengō tsūshin* was launched in 1946 with regional offices in Nagoya and Fukuoka, in addition to Tokyo.

The extension of the market to the provinces can also be associated with the breakthrough made by Tōei in the production of Japanese film. Only six years after being founded in 1951, Tōei grew to become Japan's highest-revenue film company in 1957. Unlike the case with Shōchiku and Tōhō, whose traditions had been established before World War II, Tōei did not directly manage its own fleet of flagship cinemas in the central districts of urban areas. To compensate for this disadvantage, Tōei actively promoted the direct management of cinemas in rural areas instead, despite the resulting trouble with already-established film exhibitors.[23] Though previous studies have attributed Tōei's breakthrough to the ratio of period films it produced,[24] this should also be considered in light of an increase in the number of rural cinemas and the overall expansion of the Japanese film exhibition market.

Japan's major film exhibition market had remained primarily domestic in the prewar era due to various linguistic and thematic constraints. Though Japanese films were exhibited in colonial and semi-colonial areas, as mentioned previously, this remained a specialist market, mainly targeting immigrants from Japan. Though some films were exported by individuals (*The Passion of a Woman Teacher/Kyōren no onna shishō* [1926], *Shadows of the Yoshiwara/Jūjiro* [1928]) or produced in collaboration with Germany (*Die Tochter des Samurai/Atarashiki tsuchi* [1937]) or China (*Road for the East Peace/Tōyō heiwa no michi* [1938]), the matter of Japanese film exports did not become a central issue in the Japanese film industry until the 1950s. The film industry promotion council, led by Nagata Masaichi, was founded in 1950 and in cooperation with the Ministry of International

Fig. 8.1 *Ugetsu/Ugetsu monogatari* (Mizoguchi Kenji, 1953, Daiei).

Trade and Industry, it began to promote the export of Japanese films in earnest as a method of foreign currency acquisition.[25]

The distribution of these exported films differed from patterns of prewar film exhibition in colonial areas in that the films were aimed primarily at Western audiences rather than Japanese immigrants. A number of Japanese films produced by Daiei under its president Nagata Masaichi (such as *Rashomon/Rashōmon* [1950], *Ugetsu/Ugetsu monogatari* [1953], *Gate of Hell/Jigoku mon* [1953] and *Sansho the Bailiff/Sanshō dayū* [1954]) all received awards at international film festivals in Europe and North America thus further promoting the export of Japanese films (Fig. 8.1).[26]

Alternative exhibition: From the 1960s to the present day

Box-office numbers in Japan reached 1.127 billion admissions in 1958; by 1960, the number of cinemas peaked at 7,457. The scale of film exhibition began to diminish thereafter coinciding with a decline in the volume of film production. Faced with these circumstances, alternative forms of exhibition began to appear outside the established system by which major film companies had developed the vertical integration of production, distribution and exhibition.

Typical examples include the adult film theatre and the midnight screening. Adult cinemas showing soft-core pornography, or so-called 'pink films', increased in popularity as a result of the rise in independent film production during the 1960s. In many cases, existing cinemas began to shift exhibition practice towards these adult films. In the 1960s and 1970s, for example, many cinemas in the Nishijin area of Kyoto's traditional theatre district, suffering from a stark decrease in audience numbers, rebranded themselves as adult cinemas simply in order to survive. The only remaining cinema in the area, Senbon Nikkatsu, became an adult film theatre in 1971 after Nikkatsu started its profitable Roman Porn film line.[27]

Midnight screenings, on the other hand, extended screening times in order to win over new types of audience. Prompted by excessive competition between cinemas, given the decline in audience numbers and cinema numbers, these forms of exhibition became increasingly popular into the 1970s with cinemas holding midnight screenings more than once a month accounting for about 70 per cent of total film exhibition in 1976.[28]

Japan's Art Theatre Guild (ATG) merits particular attention for the way it challenged the distribution system previously established by the major companies. The ATG was set up in 1962 by an alliance of ten cinemas explicitly with the purpose of screening non-commercial films. It came under the auspices of the Association of Japan's Art Theatre Movement (Nihon art theatre undō no kai), in which Kawakita Kashiko and others were active; the group, formed in 1957 through the expansion of 'Cinema 57', was organised by Teshigahara Hiroshi, Hani Susumu, Matsuyama Zenzō, Kawatō Yoshio and Ogi Masahiro.[29] ATG's exhibition centre, the Shinjuku Bunka Cinema, was a great success thanks to the popularity in the Shinjuku area of the form of underground drama called *angura*, also linked to ATG's production of independent films such as *Death by Hanging/Kōshikei* (1958).

Film exhibition in Japan has continued to evolve; a major contributing factor being the decrease in the number of cinemas called 'mini-theatres' screening noted or independent films. Iwanami Hall, which opened in 1968, was the first instance of a 'mini-theatre' and became well established in the city's film exhibition sector during the 1980s. When Tōhō, Kadokawa Shoten and other major film companies began to manage and expand their own multiplexes in the mid-2000s, these kinds of 'mini theatres' were forced into decline.[30]

In response to this, young, independent documentary film-makers have begun to exhibit their films on the web, taking advantage of video distribution services such as YouTube. A relatively clumsy film about the tsunami following the Great East Japan Earthquake of 2011 gained, and influenced, several million viewers.[31] Conversely, independent film-makers have also tried to adapt the documentary film genre, previously screened in the 'mini-theatre', to multiplex exhibition by appealing to a broader audience through the introduction of easy-to-understand editing and theme songs; examples of this trend include *Ending*

Note (2007) and *Director Disqualification/Kantoku shikkaku* (2007).³²

SCREENING METHODS AND SPACES: CHANGE IN FILM SOUND TECHNOLOGY

The factors informing film exhibition that I have previously described, including programme organisation, geographical conditions, politics, market expansion and alternative forms of exhibition, have all significantly influenced screening methods, technologies and spaces. In this particular case study, I will now consider the context of film exhibition within the space of cinemas during the era of the transition to sound.³³

During the silent era, the *benshi* played an important role in the space of the cinema with the figure being integral in the composition of Japanese film narrative. Similarly, the architectural style of cinemas allowed for the spaces to be adapted to the *benshi's* wording in which the Japanese film vernacular was promoted. The architectural spaces of cinemas across Japan changed with the spread of sound film. Once sound film exhibition became a practical reality, the volume of exhibition space increased in two ways: firstly, there was a growth in the size of urban cinemas and secondly, the number of cinemas in the rural provinces increased.

Sites of exhibition in the silent era

Though *benshi* played a highly significant role in the exhibition of silent film, they also had an impact on film production. In discussing the *benshi's* influence on film style, Tanaka Jun'ichirō, for example, stated that they had enough authority to demand the retake of shots they considered to be too short or a change in the editing, including flash cuts, if it became too difficult to marry the clever wording of the *benshi* with the style of the film.³⁴

The *kowairo*, a form of *benshi* narrator who imitated the voices of film characters or mimicked public figures, was the main form of *benshi* at the point that narrators had their strongest influence. Yoshiyama Kyokkō, one of the first film critics in Japan, stated that the *kowairo* became a mainstream standard from 1908, in conjunction with the increasing number of Japanese film screenings, and that this popularity continued until approximately 1925.³⁵ The figure of the *kowairo* dominated Japanese film narration styles during the 1910s and only became obsolete when Japanese film began to become more strongly influenced by the conventions of continuity editing in classical Hollywood cinema (something that began to develop around 1920 onwards). One such *kowairo* narrator was Tsuchiya Shōtō. An example of his popularity being that in the 1919 Grand Ranking of National Moving-Picture Benshi (*Zenkoku katsudō shashin benshi dai banzuke*), he was deemed the 'elder statesman' of *benshi*.³⁶ His great skill was his ability to 'use different voices for various persons', regardless of gender, and it was said that 'although a film may [normally] require five or six ordinary narrators, he narrates it alone'.³⁷

Fleeting Life/Ukiyo (1916), screened at a cinema called the Operakan in which Tsuchiya served as the chief narrator, serves as a good example of this phenomenon. *Fleeting Life* is the only film produced by Nikkatsu Mukōjima in the 1910s that still exists in an almost complete form. It hence provides valuable information about the nature of Japanese film during this decade, especially in terms of the influence of the *kowairo* who found it easier to narrate long-take films. The 35mm print of *Fleeting Life* is constituted of fifty-nine shots and is a total of 68 minutes long at a twelve fps screening. Excluding the opening credits and the twenty-one shots in the interlude, the average length of each shot is 1 minute and 47 seconds. Although there are three shots of less than 20 seconds, such as insert shots and chase-scene shots, and there are five shots of less than 1 minute, the majority are long-take shots of over 1 minute and the longest shot is 5 minutes and 11 seconds long.

Furthermore, the editing style of long-take shots indicates another aspect. As previously mentioned, the figure of the *kowairo* began to emerge as a substitute for live kabuki performance in the early modern period. As Katō Hidetoshi has shown, the *kowairo* provided a cheaper alternative means of live entertainment for the masses that were unable to view kabuki plays for economic reasons.³⁸ The use of long-take shots in films such as *Fleeting Life* can thus be considered to be a form of imitation of scenes in live theatre.

The notion that Japanese film exhibition provided an alternative to the theatre may also apply to the physical space of the cinema in the 1910s. Cinema buildings during this decade differed considerably from the basic show tent used during the early film era. These cinemas had features that imitated the theatres in which kabuki and *shinpa* plays were performed. Exhibitors began to devise Renaissance or Secession styles of decoration as a result of inexpensive construction methods. An example of this was the 'Kawasaki iron net' method, which involved cladding wooden architecture with concrete and thus afforded the means of creating various cement decorations. This trend towards Western-style architecture echoed what was happening in Japanese theatres during the same period. Even the original form of the Kabukiza, Tokyo's principal theatre, completed in 1889, was based on Western architectural forms and did not use traditional Japanese architectural construction methods.

The way that cinema buildings imitated theatres can be more characteristically confirmed by considering their interiors. The Denkikan in Asakusa, for example, was enlarged during this period and imitated kabuki theatres in terms of the inclusion of a space on the screen's periphery devoted to *gidayū* (traditional theatre music) reciters and musical accompanists in addition to the inclusion of theatre-style balcony seats on an enlarged second floor (Fig. 8.2).³⁹ In terms of screen visibility, the cinemas imitating these theatres were often unable to provide adequate viewpoints from the balcony seats on the upper floor. For example, balcony seats on the second floor of some cinemas were thus arranged in a curve in opera-house style.⁴⁰ Nonetheless, this still provided a poor sight line from the back row of seats.

The transition to the talkies

The style of Japanese cinema architecture in the 1910s was certainly not popular with intellectuals. Kaeriyama Norimasa, one of the most famous critics of the 1910s, for instance, criticised the imitative style

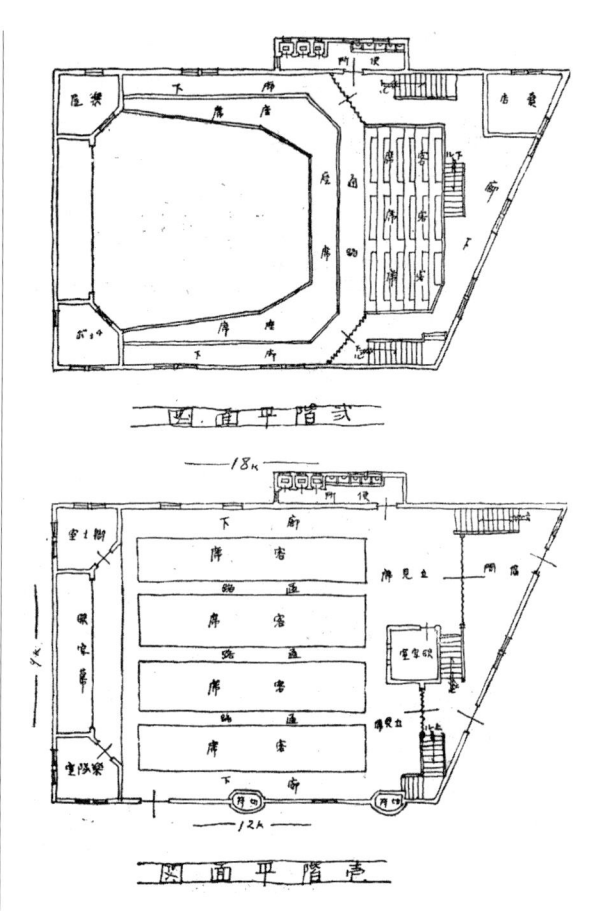

Fig. 8.2 'The ground and second floor plan of the Denkikan', in *Kenchiku shinchō* vol. 6 no. 1 (1925), p. 17.

of movie theatre architecture, writing: 'broad and shallow buildings with three floors are no good'.⁴¹ He also noted that: 'the new style of purpose-built cinemas in the West had a single floor and were oriented around a long axis'.

The end of Japanese and foreign feature films being screened in separate cinemas affected both the design of cinema buildings and also led to mainstream audiences attributing greater importance to the nature of the representations on screen. Japanese film-makers, especially the Shōchiku Kinema Company founded in 1920, concurrently began to explore the presentational style of international cinemas that incorporated the style of classical Hollywood cinema. The Musashinokan, equipped with seats with good sightlines, was built in 1920 and became a movie theatre representative of Shinjuku, Tokyo's new theatre district in the 1920s.

Katō Shū, who designed the cinema, said the reason he avoided theatre imitations was because Japanese and foreign films were shown there together.[42]

Film exhibition practice began to change from something featuring the attraction of live narrational performance to one that encouraged immersion in the world of the film's representation. In other words, changes to the sites of exhibition lay the groundwork for the appearance of the 'talkie'. It is revealing that the head *benshi* in the Musashinokan was Tokugawa Musei, a figure who avoided the traditionally excessive performance style of the *kowairo*.

The arrival of the 'talkie' influenced film exhibition in Japan in various ways. It inevitably hastened the unemployment of the *benshi* and band players, with variety shows becoming more popular between film screenings. Opinions regretting the disappearance of the silent moments in films were also expressed.[43] We should recognise that such silent moments may have existed in Japanese cinemas; however, we are likely to imagine them as noisy spaces featuring narration and a fusion of Japanese and Western music.[44]

The spread of the 'talkie' meant that not only were the oral arts of narration by live performers replaced by the voice of the speaker system in exhibition venues, but the sense of distance between the actual sound and the image source was extinguished thus creating a more homogeneous aural space. This shift might well have been linked to a parallel change to uniform seat pricing in movie theatres. After the Hibiya eiga gekijō was opened in 1934 by Tōhō, boasting a capacity of approximately 1,500 people, the cinema launched the unusual policy of having all seats priced the same at fifty *sen* (cents). Other cinemas soon followed.[45]

The homogenisation of sound in exhibition venues caused by the installation of speakers promoted an increase in the size and occupancy of cinema buildings. The Nihon gekijō, capable of accommodating approximately 4,000 people, was completed in 1933 (Fig. 8.3). Given that the Osaka shōchikuza, completed in 1923 and then a representative silent-era picture-palace in Japan, had a seating capacity of only approximately 1,000, the scale of the Nihon gekijō was therefore revolutionary. The Nihon gekijō was acquired by Tōhō in 1935 as the chain's flagship theatre and located in the centre of Yūrakuchō, a new theatre district that emerged in Tokyo in the 1930s.[46]

The spread of the talkie system also influenced the geographical expansion of film exhibition involving a substantial growth in the number of provincial cinema venues. The disparity in skills between *benshi* in the cities and the provinces had previously prevented the expansion of non-metropolitan film exhibition, but the talkie eradicated any such problems. We can specifically see this tendency in the change in the number of movie theatres between 1930 and 1934. The rate of increase in cinemas from 1930 to 1934 was 14 per cent for the Keihin area (Tokyo and Kanagawa Prefectures), 16 per cent for the Keihanshin area (Osaka, Kyoto and Hyogo Prefectures), –10 per cent for the Hokkaido area, 26 per cent for the Tohoku area, 26 per cent for

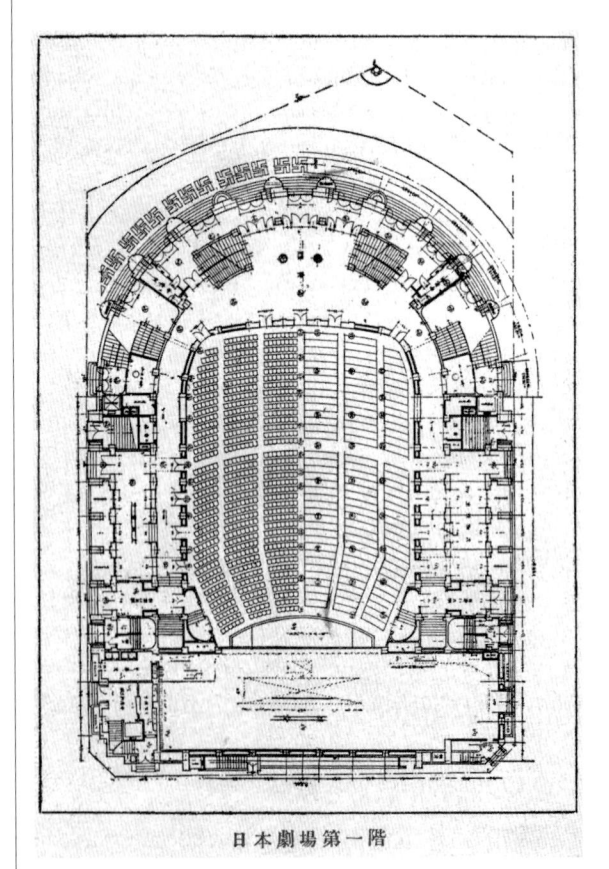

Fig. 8.3 'The ground floor plan of the Nihon gekijō', in *Kokusai eiga jigyō sōran Shōwa gonen ban* (Tokyo: Kokusai eiga tsūshin sha, 1930).

the Kanto area (Keihin excluded), 134 per cent for the Hokuriku area, 124 per cent for the Chubu area, 128 per cent for the Kinki area (Keihanshin excluded), 116 per cent for the Chugoku area, 129 per cent for the Shikoku area and 120 per cent for the Kyushu area as a whole.[47] The rate of increase in the number of movie theatres in the Tohoku, the Kanto, the Hokuriku, the Chubu, the Kinki, the Shikoku and the Kyushu regions exceeded that of the metropolitan areas of Keihin and Keihanshin, including Tokyo and Osaka.

CONCLUSION

Whilst it is almost impossible to completely reproduce and experience the nature of the exhibition spaces of silent films, it nonetheless remains possible to understand the various conditions that informed these spaces. This is not only a question of gathering historical knowledge, but also the necessary consequence of the act of analysing the nature of Japanese films and their representations. The evaluation of specific films cannot exist in ignorance of the original context of screen exhibition.

I have established that the contexts surrounding film exhibition may be best established within a complex grid of problems involving such things as the organisation of film programmes, geographical conditions, politics, and the expansion of the film market and its alternatives that I discussed in the first half of this chapter. Moreover, the nature of these problems continuously changes in terms of both the physical space in which films are seen and the advent of certain technologies, as discussed in the latter half of this chapter.

In the future, it will become increasingly necessary to discuss the exhibition of the text itself. In 2002, the National Film Center (the current National Film Archive of Japan), Tokyo, opened a permanent exhibition room for non-film materials, including matter related to film exhibition such as flyers, posters and projectors. In recent years, similar attempts have been made in the Japanese regions such as the opening of the Matsunaga Collection in 2009, which features film exhibition materials from the city of Moji in Kyushu. The increasing archiving of non-film materials will create a foundation for the analysis of texts involved in Japanese film exhibition. Historical research on the exhibition of Japanese film is in its infancy, however, it is certain that an elaboration of the full nature of screen exhibition remains essential in order to fully understand the complexities of Japanese film history.

Notes

1   For more information on Kyoto, see Tomita Mika, 'Koto kara eiga toshi sōsei no topology: Tsukuru hito, miru hito, kakeru hito no sōkan', in Yoshimi Shun'ya, Yomota Inuhiko, Kurosawa Kiyoshi and Lee Bong-Ou (eds), *Nihon eiga wa ikiteiru 3: Miruhito, tsukuruhito, kakeruhito* (Tokyo: Iwanami shoten, 2010), pp. 121–44. For more information on Osaka, see Sasagawa Keiko, *Meiji Taishō Osaka eiga bunka no tanjō: 'Local' na eigashi no chihei ni mukete* (Osaka: Research Center for Cityscape and Cultural Heritage of Osaka at Kansai University, 2012). For more information on Nagoya, see Kobayashi Sadahiro, *Shinbun ni miru shoki nihon eigashi: Nagoya to iu chiikisei o megutte* (Tokyo: Gakujutsu shuppankai, 2013).

2   Recent studies include the following: Aaron Gerow, 'Benshi ni tsuite: Juyō kisei to eigateki shutai', trans. Tsunoda Takuya, in Komatsu Hiroshi, Yoshimi Shun'ya, Yomota Inuhiko, Kurosawa Kiyoshi and Lee Bong-Ou (eds), *Nihon eiga wa ikiteiru 2: Eigashi o yominaosu* (Tokyo: Iwanami shoten, 2010), pp. 117–59; Hideaki Fujiki, *Making Personas: Transnational Film Stardom in Modern Japan* (Cambridge, MA: Harvard University Asia Center, 2013); Jeffrey Dym, *Benshi, Japanese Silent Film Narrators, and Their Forgotten Narrative Art of Setsumei: A History of Japanese Silent Film Narration* (Lewiston, NY: Edwin Mellen Press, 2003).

3   For more information on Korea, see Dong-Hoon Kim, 'Segregated Cinemas, Intertwined Histories: The Ethnically Segregated Film Cultures in 1920s Korea Under Japanese Colonial Rule', *Journal of Japanese and Korean Cinema* vol. 1 no. 1 (2009), pp. 7–26. For more information on Taiwan, see Misawa Mamie, '*Teikoku*' *to* '*sokoku*' *no hazama: Shokuminchi ki Taiwan eigajin no kōshō to ekkyō* (Tokyo: Iwanami shoten, 2010).

4   See Fujioka Atsuhiro, 'Nihon eiga kōgyō shi kenkyū: 1930 nendai ni okeru gijutsu kakushin oyobi kindaika to film presentation', *CineMagaziNet!*, no. 6 (2002), <http://www.cmn.hs.h.kyoto-u.ac.jp/cmn6/>.

5 Charles Musser, 'The Travel Genre in 1903–1904: Moving towards Fictional Narrative', in Thomas Elsaesser (ed.), *Early Cinema: Space, Frame, Narrative* (London: British Film Institute, 1990), p. 123.
6 Irie Yoshirō, 'Saiko no kokusan eishaki ni tsuite', *Eiga terebi gijutsu*, no. 612 (August 2003), pp. 48–57.
7 Shibata Masaru, 'Tokyo no katudo shashin (eiga) jōsetsukan no hensen' 1–10, *Eiga shiryō* no. 8–17 (1963–9).
8 'Katsudō shashin o utsushita haiyū wa yatowazu', *Yomiuri shinbun*, 14 November 1911.
9 *Katsudō shashin kikai dō film (renzoku shashin) teika hyō* (Tokyo: Yoshizawa shoten, 1910), pp. 1–9.
10 *Kokusai eiga jigyō sōran: Shōwa 2 nendo ban* (Tokyo: Kokusai eiga shinbun, 1926), p. 697.
11 Koizumi Gorō, 'Waga dairen waga seishun hōrō: Naichi geinōjin "yobiya" no kaisō', in *Bessatu ichioku nin no Shōwa shi: Nihon shokuminchi 4, zoku Manshū* (Tokyo: Mainichi shinbun sha, 1980), p. 102.
12 Ōno Kenjirō, *Okayama kojiin* (Okayama: Okayama kojiin, 1908), p. 73.
13 Yamaguchi Takeshi, *Aishū no Manshū eiga* (Tokyo: Santen shobō, 2000), p. 227.
14 Ishii Teruo, 'Manshū koku ni okeru junkai eisha', *Eiga junpō*, no. 55 (1942), p. 53.
15 Su Chongmin, *Mantetsu shi*, trans. Yamashita Mutsuo, Wada Masahiro and Wang Yong (Fukuoka: Ashishobō, 1999), p. 275.
16 Tsuboi Atae, 'Manshū eiga kyōkai no kaisō', *Eigashi kenkyū*, no. 19 (1984), p. 3.
17 Akagawa Kōichi, 'Junkai eisha zenki', *Senbu geppō* vol. 4 no. 7 (1939), p. 228. Akagawa Kōichi is the father of Akagawa Jirō, a popular Japanese novelist.
18 Man'ei Haikyūbu Kaihatsuka, 'Dai ikkai ensen junkai eisha hōkoku', *Senbu geppō*, vol. 4 no. 7 (1939), p. 234.
19 Tanaka Jun'ichirō, *Nihon kyōiku hattatsu shi* (Tokyo: Katatsumuri sha, 1979), p. 118.
20 *Eiga nenkan: 1950 nen ban* (Tokyo: Jiji tsūshin sha, 1949), p. 60.
21 *Eiga nenkan: 1955 nen ban* (Tokyo: Jiji tsūshin sha, 1954), p. 457.
22 An attached table in *Eiga nenkan: 1954 nen ban* (Tokyo: Jiji tsūshin sha, 1953).
23 Kitaura Hiroyuki, 'Kōgyōsha tachi no chōsen: 1950 nendai kara 1960 nendai no nihon no eiga sangyō', in Yoshimi Shun'ya, Yomota Inuhiko, Kurosawa Kiyoshi and Lee Bong-Ou (eds) *Nihon eiga wa ikiteiru 3: Miruhito, Tsukuruhito, Kakeruhito*, pp. 46–8.
24 Tanaka Jun'ichirō, *Nihon eiga hattatsu shi 4* (Tokyo: Chūōkōronsha, 1976), p. 144.
25 Tanaka Jun'ichirō, *Nihon eiga hattatsu shi 3* (Tokyo: Chūōkōronsha, 1976), p. 414.
26 [Editors' note: for more on Japanese cinema and film festivals, see also Chapter 11 by Ran Ma in this volume.]
27 Tanaka Yasuhiko, 'Nishijin no eigakan: Shibaigoya, yose', in *Nishijin no shiseki: Omoide no nishijin eigakan* (Kyoto: Kyō o kataru kai, 1990), p. 10.
28 Kitaura, 'Kōgyōsha tachi no chōsen', p. 58.
29 Satō Tadao, *ATG eiga o yomu* (Tokyo: Film art-sha, 1991), pp. 388–9.
30 Eiga geijutsu henshūbu, *Eigakan no tsukurikata* (Tokyo: AC Books, 2010), p. 11.
31 Yasuoka Takaharu, 'Film kara net dōga e: Gijutsu kakushin ga motarashita mono', in Ogino Ryō and the editorial staff (eds), *Social documentary: Gendai nihon wo kirokusuru eizō tachi* (Tokyo: Film art-sha, 2012), p. 6.
32 Ōsawa Kazuo, 'Documentary no "shōgyōsei" o toinaosu', in Ogino Ryō and the editorial staff, *Social documentary*, p. 105.
33 [Editors' note: for more on the introduction of sound in Japanese cinema, see also Chapter 10 by Johan Nordström in this volume.]
34 Tanaka Jun'ichirō, *Nihon eiga hattatsu shi 1* (Tokyo: Chūōkōronsha, 1975), p. 225.
35 Yoshiyama Kyokkō, *Nihon eiga kai jibutsu kigen* (Tokyo: Cinema to engei sha, 1933), p. 85.
36 Ueda Manabu (ed.), *Kikakuten zuroku: Nikkatsu Mukōjima to shinpa eiga no jidai ten* (Tokyo: Tsubouchi Memorial Theatre Museum at Waseda University, 2011), p. 38.
37 Kase Sohoku, *Gendai no jinbutsu kan buenryo ni mōshiage sōrō* (Tokyo: Nishodo shoten, 1917), p. 349.
38 Katō Hidetoshi, *Misemono kara terebi e* (Tokyo: Iwanami shoten, 1965), p. 182.
39 Katō Shū, 'Waga kuni ni okeru katsudō shashin kan no kenchiku enkaku', *Kenchiku shinchō* vol. 6 no. 1 (1925), p. 17.
40 Katō Shū, 'Waga kuni ni okeru katsudō shashin kan no kenchiku enkaku (4)', *Kenchiku shinchō* vol. 6 no. 4 (1925), p. 122.
41 Kaeriyama Norimasa, 'Jōsetsukan no kenchiku mata setsubi', *Kinema record* no. 28 (1915), p. 17.
42 Katō Shū, 'Waga kuni ni okeru katsudō shashin kan no kenchiku enkaku (7)', *Kenchiku shinchō* vol. 6 no. 9 (1925), p. 74.

43 Katō Shū, '"Tōkī" no shutsugen to eigakan kenchiku', *Kokusai eiga shinbun* no. 41 (1930), p. 24.

44 Rick Altman has discussed the possibility that silence was present in the screening of silent films: 'silent films were in fact sometimes silent, it seemed, and what's more, it did not appear to bother audiences a bit'. Rick Altman, 'The Silence of the Silents', *The Musical Quarterly* vol. 80 no. 4 (Winter 1996), p. 649.

45 Tanaka Jun'ichirō, *Nihon eiga hattatsu shi 2* (Tokyo: Chūōkōronsha, 1975), p. 243.

46 As is commonly known, Tōhō was originally founded as an exhibition company in 1932 under the name Tokyo Takarazuka Theatre Corporation Ltd. In 1935, it gained control of two small sound production studios, PCL (Photo Chemical Laboratories) and J.O. (Jenkins Osawa) Studio, and in 1937 it entered film production for the first time. Tanaka, *Nihon eiga hattatsu shi 2*, p. 255. See also Stuart Galbraith *The Toho Studios Story: A History and Complete Filmography* (Lanham, MD: Scarecrow Press, 2008).

47 *Nihon eiga jigyō sōran: Shōwa 5 nen ban* (Tokyo: Naigai eiga jigyō chōsa kenkyūjo, 1931), pp. 646–97; *Kokusai eiga nenkan: Shōwa 9 nendo ban* (Tokyo: Kokusai eiga tsūshin sha, 1934), pp. 106–8.

9

CENSORSHIP
Censorship as education: Film violence and ideology

Rachael Hutchinson

Japanese film censorship has consistently involved on the one hand thought guidance – teaching people how to think properly – and on the other thought control – shielding the public from dangerous ideas. Using films to disseminate ideology was a strategic endeavour of both the Imperial and Occupation administrative systems, whether for nationalistic military propaganda or democratic ideals. From 1949 the regulatory body Eiga rinri kitei kanri iinkai (Motion Picture Code of Ethics Committee), or Eirin, fulfilled a similar role – promoting 'good' values with ratings to encourage accessibility, while discouraging 'bad' values with restrictive ratings. This chapter analyses film violence and censorship, particularly in post-Occupation Japan, arguing that ideology and political context are more significant than violence itself when coming to a decision about public access to any individual film. I will also argue that the censors' fixation on sexual content had a lasting connection with the treatment of violence when applying censorship regulations to specific films.

The two directors who made the most innovative strides in representing violence on screen were Kurosawa Akira (1910–98) and Fukasaku Kinji (1930–2003), through their bold depiction of death and injury, original use of camera and sound, and constant striving to explore serious human issues through dynamic physical action. Their films provide good opportunities to examine the relationship between violence, censorship and ideology in post-Occupation Japan. As case studies, Kurosawa's *Yojimbo/Yōjimbō* (1961) and *Sanjuro/Tsubaki Sanjurō* (1962), as well as Fukasaku's *Battle Royale/Battle rowaiaru* (2000), will be placed in historical context to understand the directors' representations of violence and the reaction from the audience, censors and critics.

This chapter builds on the scholarship of Japanese film censorship by focusing closely on the issue of violence on the screen, through the twentieth century. Most works on film censorship in Japan focus more intensely on one period of time (Hideaki Fujiki on the interwar years, Peter High on the imperial wartime screen, Kyoko Hirano on the Occupation) or on one specific issue (Kirsten Cather on obscenity rulings or Monica Braw on atomic bomb imagery).[1] I therefore hope to address a gap in the literature and show how violence has faded in and out of censorship consciousness over time.

CENSORSHIP IN HISTORICAL PERSPECTIVE

Films made in the Meiji period (1868–1912) inherited much from kabuki drama, a medium with didactic aims: great care was taken to protect the audience from harmful ideas and to promote educational goals such as Confucian ethics or productive citizenship. Like kabuki plays, early films followed a structure of *kanzen-chōaku* (rewarding virtue, punishing vice), where all sorts of deranged and violent acts were possible as long as the villain was ultimately punished. Home Ministry censors, responsible for removing or modifying objectionable material, were concerned that scenes of a criminal or sexual nature would mislead vulnerable members of the audience – namely women, children and the lower classes.[2] The 1917 Tokyo Moving Picture Regulations, while not specifying exactly what content should be prohibited, required the classification of films into those suitable for children (under 15) and those suitable for adults.[3] It was thought that children under 15 years old could only perceive a narrative in terms of episodes and not as a whole, so they would enjoy the spectacle of crime without appreciating the punishment at the end.[4] The spectacle and display of the cinema as a visual medium thus undercut the narrative structure of *kanzen-chōaku*, requiring cinema to be treated differently to other art forms.[5] Regulations stipulated that *benshi* narrators acquire licences and be trained to interpret the film 'correctly' for the audience, while parents and teachers were encouraged to attend films together with children, ensuring the didactic significance of the narrative was maintained.[6]

Violence on screen was thus a non-issue in the 1917 regulations. Donald Richie emphasises the 'stagey artificiality' of early films, seen in the stylised, choreographed sword-fights known as *chanbara*.[7] Censors of the time were not dealing with realistic scenes of injury or death. The 1920s, however, saw an increase in realism on screen, as well as a sharper censorship focus on film content. The 1925 Motion Picture Film Inspection Regulations required state inspection of all films prior to public screening and distribution. Films could be banned or cut on the basis of offending public peace, manners and morals, and for the first time a list of offensive content was determined.[8] The rubric of 'manners and morals' covered religion, cruelty/ugliness, sex, work ethic, education, family and other.[9] Films censored for sex-related issues far outweighed those cut for any other reason, a trend that became more noticeable over time. In 1927, for example, 682 Japanese films were cut for sexual content and 583 for 'cruelty and ugliness'. The following year had 764 sex-related cuts compared to 473 for cruelty, and by 1932, sex-related cuts outweighed cruelty-related cuts by a ratio of 6 to 1.[10] The censorship standard 'cruelty and ugliness' covered both 'items related to brutality', such as blood and gore, as well as 'items giving rise to offensive feelings', such as depictions of people deformed by disease.[11] Taking this into account, scenes of physical violence involving injury and brutality incurred far fewer cuts than scenes of a sexual nature.

These regulations came in the context of the 1925 Peace Preservation Law, with a focus on ideology and restricting leftist thought. Most period dramas (*jidaigeki*) were unaffected – set in the past and featuring heroic samurai, they were perfectly suited to government ideals of respecting the emperor, upholding Confucian bonds and sacrificing all for honour. However, leftist and proletarian directors found that tales of downtrodden rebels such as masterless samurai (*rōnin*), yakuza outlaws and gamblers were also popular with audiences. These anti-heroes doubted feudal codes of honour and loyalty. While violent swordplay did not cause a problem with the censors, such outsider ideology was often cut or banned.[12] Directors of *gendaigeki* – contemporary social films aiming for a realistic picture of life in the capital – had even more trouble with new restrictions and 'moral codes'. Studios also found it difficult to tread the precarious line between the liberal values of 'Taishō democracy' and proletarian ideology.[13]

From the 1920s, cinema was incorporated into national policies to attain educational goals in wider society.[14] Film was seen as the ideal medium for education due to its popularity, its influence on the viewer in terms of intellect, bodily sensations and emotions, and its close relation to modern life.[15] Richard Mitchell, Gregory Kasza and Barak Kushner have provided much evidence to demonstrate the persuasive power of cinema in the 'thought war' of Imperial Japan.[16] From the 1930s, authorities took an increasingly utilitarian view of film, exploiting it more for propaganda purposes than for entertainment. The Home Ministry, and from 1934 the Film Control Committee, encouraged films with militaristic or nationalist themes, including sacrifice for the nation, love of the emperor and stoic women on the home front.[17] The 1939 Film Law codified this 'encouragement' into regulations specifying how many feet of film should be dedicated to educational nonfiction, and how often 'culture films' serving the state ideology should be screened in theatres. All films were subject to pre-production screening and censorship, while cuts were made according to the same censorship standards as the 1925 regulations.[18]

Violence was not frowned upon if it promoted the right kind of ideals, and war narratives as well as samurai films were popular. Swordplay, however, was formulaic, and war movies did not emphasise blood or violence done to the bodies of enemy soldiers. This also applied to foreign films – *All Quiet on the Western Front* (1930) was heavily cut. As Richie explains, 'Anything showing war as it was had to go. This included scenes of those dead in battle, scenes where men were killed, and the climactic sequence where Lew Ayres bayonets a French solider and is stunned at what he has done.'[19] While the glory of war could be expressed and idealised, the reality of men fighting and killing each other did not appear on screen.[20] Propaganda films sought to stimulate action, galvanising the audience for success in war.[21] In this climate, war films showing true brutality would fail in their aim. Further, wartime rationing meant that film stock was scarce, and only scenarios that passed inspection could ever make the transition onto celluloid. With production and distribution so tightly constrained, experiments in realism and human expression were almost impossible.[22] Unlike the film industries of the US or Europe, Japan was unable to develop a war genre that spoke to the human toll of war or the bloodshed and horror that soldiers experienced on the battlefield.

OCCUPATION POLICIES ON FILM VIOLENCE

Film censorship during the Allied Occupation (1945–52) was a two-pronged endeavour, with SCAP's Civil Information and Education section (CIE) promoting 'good' values like democracy and individualism, and the Civil Censorship Detachment (CCD) limiting 'bad' content and punishing offenders.[23] Much has been written on the practicalities of Occupation film censorship and the complexity of the Press Code, which caused headaches for film-makers and censors alike.[24] Most scholarship examines film from the perspective of ideology, or how specific directors worked within the strict regulations to express some kind of critique.[25] There is much debate over the degree to which directors complied with CIE directives and how much freedom directors could exercise in their work.[26] However, there is little scholarship on the representation of violence in this period and its treatment by censors. Examining the Press Code, we see a great deal written about objects not to appear on screen, most of them ideological in nature.[27] The long list of regulations does not mention violence, apart from one directive to avoid 'incitement to violence or unrest'. Materials cut or banned under this directive were often marked with the words 'disturbs public tranquility'.[28] This violence was thus the ideological kind – dangerous thoughts leading to social uprising rather than the representation of fighting or other violent acts.

Fighting in *jidaigeki* was still stylised in the 1940s, so the main concern of the Allied censors examining this genre was militaristic ideology, the glorification of feudal ideals or 'divine descent' nationalistic propaganda. Staple *jidaigeki* themes of honour, duty, military glory and revenge were all now taboo, so it became difficult to produce new films about samurai or set in the feudal period. Retroactive censorship also meant that many films of Imperial Japan were now banned and confiscated, particularly *jidaigeki* and war narratives. Kurosawa Akira's four wartime films – *Sanshiro Sugata/Sugata Sanshirō I* and *II* (1943), *The Most Beautiful/Ichiban utsukushiku* (1944) and *The Men Who Tread on the Tiger's Tail/Tora no o o fumu otokotachi* (1945) – were destroyed under these regulations. It was also difficult to make yakuza films, because the Press Code forbade any depiction of black market activities, starvation, economic hardship, or 'incitement to violence or unrest'. Gang violence and financial opportunism in the black markets came under these rubrics, and Robin Hood-style narratives would not work in a setting without poverty-stricken citizens requiring aid from the gangster cartels. Criticism of Occupation forces was also forbidden, so contemporary anti-authoritarian films would not survive the censorship process. Since films featuring the stock violent characters – samurai and yakuza – were both out of bounds, Occupation-era films tended to critique violence or avoid it altogether.

The film censorship office of the CCD was officially dismantled in June 1949 and Eirin was established to continue the monitoring of film content.[29] Eirin was envisioned as a self-regulatory body for the film industry, accordingly made up of representatives of the major film studios, although Adachi Kan describes the influence of CIE in the early days as 'tremendous'.[30] The initial regulations covered eight main categories: nation and society, law, religion, education, manners and morals, sex, and cruelty/ugliness. The last category focused on the director's responsibility to avoid arousing 'cruel or dirty feelings in spectators by sensationally treating the topics of capital punishment, torture, lynching, cruelty to women, children or animals, human trafficking of women or children, surgical operations (including abortion), and disabled people or sick and injured people'.[31] The use of weapons is not mentioned, nor is war. Bodily violence seems to have been seen in terms of 'normal' violence such as fistfights or swordplay between men, and 'abnormal' violence involving women, children or the disabled. This authorised manly violence as normative, opening the way for innovative representations of bodily violence in the 1950s.

PROBLEMATISING VIOLENCE: KUROSAWA'S JIDAIGEKI

The lifting of official CCD censorship regulations in 1949 gave film directors a new outlook on freedom of expression. Kurosawa Akira's *Rashomon/Rashōmon* (1950) challenged dominant conventions in the *jidaigeki* genre. Unlike anything that came before it, the film featured desperate, realistic swordplay, murder and rape in the depths of the forest. Films of 1950 were subject to a threefold check by the CCD, CIE and Eirin, but Kurosawa's reputation as a humanistic, 'democratic' director meant he was accepted as part of mainstream discourse and therefore not expected to be a troublemaker.[32] In his critical representation of *jidaigeki* violence, Kurosawa changed the genre and won the Golden Lion Award at the Venice Film Festival in 1951.

Although *Rashomon* is made in the *jidaigeki* mode, it does not valorise the military ideals of honour, glory and sacrifice in death. Rather, the ethos of *bushidō* is laid open to doubt. Because the tale is told from three different perspectives and changes each time in the telling, the samurai's tale is just as suspect as that of the woman and even the bandit. The samurai ethic of truth, courage and steadfastness is demolished by narrative uncertainty. Kurosawa also casts doubt on the *jidaigeki* genre by challenging the privileged tradition of the great set piece, *chanbara* swordplay. The pivotal fight between the samurai and bandit is shown twice – first in the fantasy narrative of the bandit and second in the realistic assessment of the woodcutter. The first fight is grand and heroic, while the second is frantic and cowardly, with both men gasping for breath and scrambling through leaves on the forest floor, falling and backing away more than striking or parrying. The second fight shatters the image of the first, and the *bushidō* ethic is undercut.[33] The bandit's look of triumph, mixed with the realisation he has actually killed his opponent, is not readily forgotten. Kurosawa problematises violence by foregrounding the brutality of the moment.

The Allied censors welcomed thoughtful treatments of human struggle in film. Realistic assessments of war, death, the impact of fighting and the consequences of violence were seen as evidence that the Japanese were adapting to new circumstances and coming to a new understanding of the meaning of violence and war. 'Problematization films', as they were called by the SCAP administration, allowed Japanese people to make sense of the aftermath of war and look forward to a new future.[34] Eirin also prized films that treated human struggle in a realistic and thoughtful manner. Kurosawa was one of the first Japanese directors to show violent death realistically on screen, in a critical appraisal of the impact of killing on the human soul. The triumphant look on the bandit's face in *Rashomon* contrasts with a scene in *The Seven Samurai/Shichinin no samurai* (1954), when the villager Yohei spears one of the invading bandits and kills him. Yohei's face is often troubled, but the contorted, open-mouthed stare of shock and dismay in this scene is extreme. While *The Seven Samurai* is more violent than *Rashomon*, with samurai duels and pitched battles between the bandits, samurai and villagers, the thrilling fight scenes are offset by quiet meditations on death, with Kikuchiyo's body lying face down in the pelting rain and the graves of the fallen dominating the hillside in the final scene. With these two films, Kurosawa was able to express what Japanese war films could not – the terrible guilt at taking another person's life, the futility of war and the unsupportable nature of feudal values. Kurosawa's realism allowed the Japanese audience to confront death, and the emotional outcome of perpetrating violence upon another human being.

SEX OVER VIOLENCE: PROTECTING CHILDREN FROM THE 'SUN TRIBE'

Film scandals in the mid-1950s prompted Eirin to establish the Committee on Children's Film Viewing in May 1955. The public was increasingly concerned about the effect of film on impressionable youth, particularly the 'Sun Tribe' films of 1956 – adaptations of Ishihara Shintarō's novels featuring rebellious youths indulging in sex, violence and antisocial behaviour. Furukawa Takumi's *Season of the Sun/Taiyō no kisetsu* (1956) is about a boxer who gets his girlfriend pregnant, while Ichikawa Kon's *Punishment Room/Shokei no heya* (1956) featured a college student drugging a woman with sleeping pills in order to rape her. The beating and stabbing he suffers at the hands of the girl and her male friends at the end of the film was justified by his heinous crime, in typical *kanzen-chōaku* ('reward virtue, punish vice') style. The *Asahi* newspaper, however, called for censorship, fearful of copycat crimes using readily available sleeping pills.[35] Nakahira Kō's *Crazed Fruit/Kurutta kajitsu* (1956) was the most controversial, with sex scenes between the heroine and two young brothers sparking public outrage. Local government bodies enacted ratings of 18+ for Sun Tribe films.[36] Eirin was criticised heavily, and the Ministry of Education announced it would establish laws to 'purge delinquent films'.[37] Faced with government intervention and possible disbandment, Eirin restructured in 1957 to include representatives from outside the film industry. Regulations on sexual depiction were now 'much more detailed and strict', and the Committee on Children's Film Viewing was upgraded to a council.[38]

A new ratings system was also introduced to indicate 'films geared towards adults' (*seijin muki eiga*) and 'films recommended for youths' (*seishōnen suisen eiga*). The cut-off point was 18 years of age. Distributors included the 'adult' mark on advertising materials, and theatres displayed signs asking patrons to comply with restrictions. 'Adult' films comprised five main categories: those inspiring anti-democratic thoughts and actions; incitement to violations of public order and morals; approving or glorifying violence; impeding the normal progression of sexual maturation; or any stimulation that would interfere with the nurturing of healthy human beings.[39] Here for the first time, the idea of 'approving or glorifying violence' (*bōryoku no yōnin mata wa sanbi*) came under direct scrutiny. Eirin official Kobayashi Masaru describes the regulations as somewhat vague, and much discussion was needed to decide ratings for specific films. In his memoirs and in Eirin questionnaires to the public, narrative justification for sex and violence was given much weight. Kobayashi lists six main themes as 'adult' in nature:

1 Works depicting gangs or other violent groups, the depiction of violent acts in modern life which may be considered as an incentive for youths;

2 Works including complicated social issues or the seamy side of society, which would be misunderstood by or cause anxiety in youths;

3 Works which focus on a taste for beauty (*enbi-shumi*) which are inappropriate for youths;

4 Works set in the licensed quarters which depict the complications of sexual desire, which would cause youths to have inappropriate thoughts;

5 Works that depict the mode of life of today's youth, or wild and incorrigible acts, which are excessively provocative for youths;

6 Works that depict such things as the yakuza trade, gambling dens, fights and so forth in narratives of gambler gangs, which may be considered as an incentive for youths.[40]

Three of these themes are concerned with violence, particularly gang or yakuza violence, and three with sex. Kobayashi's thematic understanding of 'adult films' suggests an equal concern with sex and violence. Both sex and violence involve human bodies coming into close contact with one another, generating a physical sense of subjectivity in the audience. Sex and violence impact upon us as we place ourselves in the position of the actors on screen. However, this impact is not treated equally in the Japanese film regulations that sought to avoid 'dangerous effects on youth'. Kirsten Cather demonstrates that film censorship trials from the 1950s through the 1970s focused primarily on the notion of obscenity (*waisetsu*) rather than violence. Concern for the well-being of the audience was foremost in the trial discussions, with women and children seen as needing specific protection from lewd ideas and images.[41] Obscenity was placed in binary opposition to 'social values'. However, the connection between these values and violence was more rarely discussed.

Looking more closely at *Season of the Sun*, the boxers are trained in physical endurance and fight to show their strength and prowess. Rambunctious bar brawls show club members acting wildly in an atmosphere of heady liberation. This kind of brawl could be seen in American Westerns and did not show serious injury. The physical blows themselves were not new to the screen. However, the context of youthful rebellion against the establishment was very new, illustrated in a single punch early in the film. The hero's father, proud of his fine physique, dares his son to punch him one morning. The son's cold gaze as he punches his father hard in the stomach is met with a look of disbelief and pain from the father. In this instant, we see the ideology of violence in the film – the freedom to act without restraint, without consideration for others or age-old traditions of respect and filial piety. The son is admonished by his mother for hitting with *honki*, 'real feeling'. The film as a whole may be seen as expressing the 'real feeling' of the younger generation, unleashed to the delight of younger audiences and the dismay of parents and educators. There is some critique of violence in the film – the hero's first boxing match drags on interminably, far past the point of comfortable viewing. But any critique was lost on the audience, since it is the boxer's sweaty, naked chest as he hits a punching bag that attracts the heroine and leads to the first sex scene. The physical representation of violence itself was not extreme in the Sun Tribe films. It was the connections made between violence and free expression, and between violence and sexuality, that were problematic.

CATHARTIC VIOLENCE AND DIDACTIC NARRATIVE

In 1959, Eirin revised its classification system to reflect growing concerns with obscenity in films. Regulations on sex and morals were expanded, but the category 'Cruelty/Ugliness' was eliminated.[42] This meant that physical violence was no longer covered by any particular category. It was in this climate that Kurosawa Akira re-imagined the depiction of violence on screen, in two films that set new industry standards in Japan and overseas. In *Yojimbo* (1961) and *Sanjuro* (1962), Kurosawa built on the realism of his previous films, but focused more closely on realism of the body (Fig. 9.1). *Yojimbo* opens with a dog trotting down the street with a severed human hand in its mouth, accompanied by discordant music to symbolise the upheaval of the town torn apart by gang rivalry. The end of the film sees Unosuke, the villain, lying in a pool of his own blood. *Sanjuro* took the bodily violence even further, with a geyser of blood gushing from the villain's chest and fountaining into the air. The graphic violence heralded a degeneration of *jidaigeki* in the popular 'cruel films' (*zankoku eiga*) from Tōei and Tōhō in the following year.[43] Despite the extreme violence, neither *Yojimbo* nor *Sanjuro* attracted an 'adult' rating from Eirin, and unlike the Sun Tribe films, Kurosawa's works did not cause uproar in the media or a new revision of the Eirin classification system. Why was Kurosawa able to be so violent in these films?

One reason was the combined star power of Kurosawa and Mifune, who had enacted realistic violence before in *Rashomon* and *The Seven Samurai*. Another reason was the high quality of *Yojimbo* in terms of artistic experimentation. Mifune Toshiro astounded audiences with his explosive fight sequences, partly a function of Kurosawa's use of the anamorphic frame, giving a feeling of extremely rapid movement to the action.[44] Another innovation was realistic sound effects for swords and weapons hitting human flesh. Stuart Galbraith sees the experimentation as a 'direct response to the mindless *chanbara* Tōei, Daiei, and Nikkatsu were churning out', while Mitsuhiro Yoshimoto names *Yojimbo* as the 'fatal blow' to Tōei studios, whose

Fig. 9.1 *Yojimbo/Yōjinbō* (Kurosawa Akira, 1961, Tōhō).

jidaigeki were still relying on tired old formulas.[45] The film also featured an original and exciting soundtrack. This was clearly a very entertaining film; a crowd-pleaser with many elements of which violence was only one part.

Yoshimoto also argues that humour set *Yojimbo* apart from other violent films of the time.[46] *Yojimbo* is a remarkably funny film, with many wisecracks that were duplicated in Sergio Leone's remake *A Fistful of Dollars* (1964).[47] This humour diffuses the emotional impact of the bodily violence, making it acceptable for the audience to laugh at the infliction of pain, injury and death on the characters. At one point Mifune's anti-hero is beaten to within an inch of his life, crawling under floorboards and hiding in a barrel to escape the town. When he rises from the barrel covered in blood, his co-conspirator gasps – 'You … you don't look human!', whereupon Sanjuro summons a deathly grin. 'It's worse when you smile!' the friend complains, eliciting laughter. This laughter makes the audience complicit in the violence, but it also acts to dispel, or at least disrupt, the spectator's discomfort. Nishimura Yūichirō emphasises the feeling of catharsis for the audience in viewing Mifune's violent and dynamic action, stressing the emotional power of violence experienced in the cinema.[48] Laughter then combines with the powerful catharsis of the bodily impact of violence on screen, to create an invigorating viewing experience.

Apart from the extreme violence, both *Yojimbo* and *Sanjuro* contain many thematic and visual elements that warranted an 'adult' rating from Eirin. *Yojimbo* combined the yakuza genre with the *jidaigeki* in a violent tale of warring gamblers, but gang violence, gambling narratives and yakuza trades were all seen by Eirin as dangerous incentives for youth.[49] Characters in *Yojimbo* also draw attention to their tattoos in an attempt to intimidate the hero, but tattoos were a visual taboo. Kobayashi devotes an entire chapter of his memoirs to the problem of tattoos in films, framing his account in terms of the 'righteousness' of the tattooed character. Narrative justification for visual elements and violent acts weighed heavily in the committee's decision-making process.[50] Although Mifune's character is morally ambiguous at best, he is still the hero, cleaning up the town and ridding it of the tattooed gangsters. The lack of an adult rating for *Yojimbo* and *Sanjuro* speaks to the enduring strength of *kanzen-chōaku* narrative structures in the modern period.

The combination of cathartic violence and *kanzen-chōaku* structures in *Yojimbo* and *Sanjuro* paved the way for the success of genre films in the 1960s, particularly the 'chivalry films' (*ninkyō eiga*) at Tōei. These usually featured a gangster in the lead role, striving to uphold the honour code of the yakuza just as samurai strove to uphold the values of *bushidō*. Genre films were not expected to carry a 'serious' critique or ideological message. Violence was taken as catharsis, while narratives adhered to convention. Isolde Standish argues that yakuza and samurai dramas projected a nationalistic vision of Japan, upholding a masculine ideology with violence that remained unthreatening to society.[51] While some yakuza films earned an 'adult' rating to protect youth from gambling narratives, the violence itself was unproblematic. The extremes of masculine anxiety were explored in 'pinky violence' films, where sexual violence was the norm. 'Pinky violence' and horror genres had much in common with late Tokugawa erotic novels – as long as the villain was appropriately punished at the end, he could commit all kinds of crimes, from bank robbery and gang violence to rape and cold-blooded murder.[52] While many 'pinky violence' films earned an adult rating at the cinema, only a few were banned from distribution. By the late 1960s, however, genre films had stalled. Tōei found a brief respite with the exciting *Red Peony Gambler/ Hibotan bakuto* series (1968–72) starring Fuji Junko, but her retirement signalled the end of Tōei's heyday. Fukasaku Kinji brought new life to both Tōei and the yakuza genre with his hyper-realistic films of the 1970s.

FUKASAKU KINJI AND 'HYPERREALISTIC' VIOLENCE

Unlike Kurosawa, universally accepted as a brilliant director who also incorporated violence into his work in interesting ways, Fukasaku Kinji seems to be either valorised or pilloried by his many critical reviewers.[53] Those who see his work positively argue that it offers a strong critique of social values in postwar Japan, with a bleak nihilism that points to the failure of Japanese authorities to take the country into a bright future. Fukasaku's critique here stemmed from his own wartime experiences in a munitions factory, which left him firmly anti-authoritarian in his outlook.[54] Critics who see Fukasaku in a negative light argue that he revels in violent images for their own sake, exploiting war narratives and the atomic blasts of Hiroshima and Nagasaki as convenient backdrops for on-screen thuggery.[55] The polarised nature of this critical literature seems to hang on Fukasaku's own morals in making his films. Where Tezuka Osamu's description of working in a munitions factory is taken at face value for his focus on war, death and the preciousness of human life in his manga, Fukasaku's almost identical story is seen as exploitative and base.[56]

There are a number of reasons for this. First, Fukasaku worked almost entirely within the yakuza genre, seen as a kind of 'pulp fiction' for the screen rather than a vehicle for serious social critique. Second, yakuza as persons are themselves morally questionable. Fukasaku Kinji created a more nuanced vision of the yakuza, which was more sympathetic to them as real, flawed human beings than the idealised vision of the chivalry films.[57] A director seen as sympathetic with this subject matter would naturally come under moral scrutiny. Third, the *jitsuroku* or 'authentic account' method of film-making mixed documentary-style handheld camera techniques with events based on reality, making the director seem less of an artist than an opportunist. Fourth, where Tezuka Osamu's works are also extremely violent and nihilistic, they remain on the page. Cinema is more immediate in its representation, with sound and moving images creating a direct and lasting impact on the audience. Lastly, Fukasaku's films were anti-American in outlook, which has the potential to divide American critics.

Taking Fukasaku's story at face value, it provides a strong reason for his interest in anti-war, anti-authoritarian narratives. It also explains the recurring photographic and filmic flashbacks to the war and the atomic bomb in particular. The much-discussed opening to *Battles without Honour or Humanity/Jingi naki tatakai* (1973) includes the ominous mushroom cloud, still photographs of taboo subjects from the 1945 Press Code, and American soldiers chasing a Japanese woman through the black market in order to rape her. Richard Torrance argues that Fukasaku's critique targets the American military, the Japanese police and the yakuza themselves, exposing the superficial moral justifications they give for their own violence.[58] Fukasaku's refusal to see violence as 'moral' in any way set his work apart from the previous chivalry films. While enacting extreme violence on the screen, the films are thematically critical of violence and the class system that perpetuates violence in the slums and black market of postwar Japan. In this, Fukasaku's 'postwar' has much in common with Kurosawa's 'problematization' films. Fukasaku enjoyed a long and profitable career making violent yakuza films, which were censored neither for violence, nor their anti-American or anti-authoritarian stance. However, this directorial freedom came to an end in 2000 with the controversial *Battle Royale*.

FUKASAKU'S BATTLE

The 1990s saw an escalation in youth violence in Japan, with a number of high-profile cases of juvenile crime involving horrific murders of children. This came in a context of increased school refusal and bullying, shut-ins (*hikikomori*), and a broader breakdown of family structures in a society reeling from economic turmoil, natural disasters and terrorist attacks. Aaron Gerow notes that Eirin revised its regulations and film classification system in 1998 in response to media concerns about the link between on-screen violence and youth crime.[59] The current Eirin website lists the three aims of the current film classification system as: 'to secure freedom of expression, to respect human rights and to protect children from early exposure to potentially harmful subjects and expressions'. Four categories dating from 1998 are G (unrestricted, for general audience), PG12 (unrestricted, recommending parental guidance for those under age 12), R15+ (restricted, for persons aged 15 and above) and R18+ (restricted, for persons aged 18 and above). According to the website:

> Films are classified according to the treatment and impact of the eight main classifiable elements of public concern, specifically theme, language, sex, nudity, violence & cruelty, horror & menace, drug use, and criminal behavior. Classification also depends on the context. It is illegal to show indecent images of minors under the age of 18, and to show a work that is obscene. Real explicit sex and detailed exposure of sexual organs are not allowed, nor is pornography.[60]

It is notable that 'sex and nudity' comes before 'violence and cruelty', and that illegality is still dictated by obscenity. 'Theme' is privileged as the first term, consistent with Kobayashi's thematic interpretation of the 1957 regulations. The fact that 'violence and cruelty' is so closely followed by 'horror and menace' here demonstrates the strength of J-horror and the increased cruelty in films by Miike Takashi and others by the 1990s. Coming right after the reclassification of Eirin ratings, during a tumultuous discussion between the Ministry of Education and the Diet about violence in films, it is little wonder that *Battle Royale* exploded into controversy (Fig. 9.2). Tōei executives were surprised by Fukasaku's choice of material, asking why he would film such a 'dangerous' idea.[61] The film's release coincided with a bill on juvenile crime under consideration by the Diet, and Fukasaku's vision cut too close to contemporary problems with youth violence.

The film follows middle school basketball star Nanahara Shūya and his classmates, sent to an island and forced to kill one another in a gruesome game organised by the government as a deterrent to juvenile delinquency. Each student is given weapons ranging from automatic machine guns and swords through to kitchen knives and pot lids, and a metal collar, which explodes if they enter forbidden areas. The one surviving student wins the game. Many took the film as an allegory for cut-throat high school competition, and the backstories of the students gave many different motivations for killing their classmates. Some students committed suicide rather than participate, while others fought against the system by hacking into government computers. Nanahara escapes the island, but not before killing one classmate by accident and unwittingly sparking off a massacre in the island's lighthouse, where five girls die from gunfire and poisoning. This

Fig. 9.2 *Battle Royale* (Fukasaku Kinji, 2000, Battle Royale Production Committee).

scene is considered one of the bloodiest of an already bloody film. Seeing the carnage, Nanahara runs to the top of the lighthouse and screams into the wind, 'I don't understand! It doesn't make sense!', tears flowing freely as he collapses from his own injuries.[62]

Takami Kōshun's original book, published in 1999, had a strong political and ideological focus, fantasising an alternate history where Japan heads a greater East Asia sphere under a dictator. In adapting the novel, Fukasaku changed the focus of the narrative from a political critique to a social one, establishing a stronger structure of binary opposition between youth and adults. The film addresses social issues such as school absenteeism, students attacking teachers, parental suicide, sexual abuse and child prostitution. These were all pressing issues of the time and all were previously addressed in films, literature, television, anime and manga.

But Fukasaku's coupling of the Japanese education system with the military arm of government, and the sadistic portrayal of the class teacher by Kitano Takeshi, make it seem like the entire institution of the 'Japanese Education System' is under attack in the film. Caren Pagel demonstrates that it was not the violent scenes themselves that determined the controversial reception of the film but the narrative insistence on the government, and all agents of the government, as 'bad', with the students portrayed as 'good' victims (no matter how outrageous their actions).[63] By 2000, Eirin officials included representatives from the Ministry of Education and university professors. That the film featured clear criticism of the Japanese school system did not help Fukasaku's case, let alone the fact that the murderous middle school students of the plot were played by actual middle school child actors.[64]

Fukasaku's choice of casting here speaks to his own teenage experience of the war. It is also consistent with the *jitsuroku* method in a bid for authenticity and a greater impact on the audience. The young faces of the actors spattered with blood gave a striking and unique visual impact that older actors could not have achieved. The film was truly shocking at the time and became a cult hit overseas.[65] After much discussion of the film's classification (which reached the Japanese Diet), Eirin determined an R15+ rating, meaning that middle school students could not view the film.[66] Fukasaku's message to Japanese youth was thus lost on the middle school audience. The final injunction to 'run!' – outwit the system and live your life – would have had a great impact on those students poised to undertake the gruelling high school entrance exams. In many ways, Fukasaku's film has a stronger ideological message about education than Takami Koushun's novel. However, Fukasaku's ideology was at odds with that of the Ministry of Education and the Diet, who wanted middle school children to continue their education rather than 'run' and disappear into the workforce, sports or the music industry. In the midst of parliamentary furore, and given its avowed dedication to the protection of youths from dangerous ideas, Eirin had little choice but to opt for a strong rating. However, I believe the choice of R15+ rather than R18+ shows consideration for the serious tone of Fukasaku's film. The overriding theme of the need to live one's own life and find an authentic existence in opposition to a corrupt government was perhaps seen as a useful idea for the older, high school audience.

CONCLUSION

An overview of censorship regulations and practice in regards to film violence suggests that violent physical imagery alone has not historically been a case for film censorship in Japan. What seems to matter most is the ideology accompanying the violence, and whether it upholds or threatens the political and social status quo. The threat of harmful ideas, a bad model of antisocial behaviour, or the possibility of real-life imitation of violence, carry more weight than mere blood on the screen. From the 1950s to the 1970s, Kurosawa Akira and Fukasaku Kinji were able to push the limits of representing violence, both stylistically and thematically, without being censored. Notably, neither director used young actors during this period. In contrast, the less violent narratives of the Sun Tribe films created uproar in the media, as the violence was linked to sex and a rebellious attitude that overtly challenged the establishment. *Battle Royale* raised a similar challenge to the status quo, highlighting the tense relationship between violence and ideology in Japanese cinema. The film can thus be best understood as a site of convergence between the worlds of censorship and education, where 'what is best for youth' remains a pressing concern.

Notes

1. See Hideaki Fujiki, 'Creating the Audience: Cinema as Popular Recreation and Social Education in Modern Japan', in Daisuke Miyao (ed.), *The Oxford Handbook of Japanese Cinema* (Oxford: Oxford University Press, 2014), pp. 79–97; Peter B. High, *The Imperial Screen: Japanese Film Culture in the Fifteen Years' War, 1931–1945* (Madison: University of Wisconsin Press, 2003); Kyoko Hirano, *Mr. Smith Goes to Tokyo: Japanese Cinema under the American Occupation, 1945–1952* (Washington, DC: Smithsonian Institution Press, 1992); Monica Braw, *The Atomic Bomb Suppressed: American Censorship in Occupied Japan* (Armonk, NY: M.E. Sharpe, 1991); Kirsten Cather, *The Art of Censorship in Postwar Japan* (Honolulu: University of Hawai'i Press, 2012) and 'Policing the Pinks', in Abé Mark Nornes (ed.), *The Pink Book: The Japanese Eroduction and its Contexts* (Ann Arbor, MI: Kinema Club, 2014), pp. 93–147. These works are indebted to the groundwork laid by scholars who included film regulations in their histories of censorship in different media: Richard Mitchell, *Thought Control in Prewar Japan* (Ithaca, NY: Cornell University Press, 1976) and *Censorship in Imperial Japan* (Princeton, NJ: Princeton University Press, 1983); Gregory Kasza, *The State and Mass Media in Japan, 1918–1945* (Berkeley: University of California Press, 1998).
2. Aaron Gerow, *Visions of Japanese Modernity: Articulations of Cinema, Nation, and Spectatorship,*

1895–1925 (Berkeley: University of California Press, 2010), pp. 197–207.
3. For details of the 1917 regulations see Gerow, *Visions of Japanese Modernity*, pp. 184–8.
4. Ibid., p. 198.
5. See Gregory Kasza on the implications of treating film as 'entertainment' rather than a speech act: *State and Mass Media in Japan*, pp. 56–7.
6. Gerow, *Visions of Japanese Modernity*, pp. 207–18.
7. Donald Richie, *A Hundred Years of Japanese Film* (Tokyo: Kōdansha, 2005), p. 26.
8. See Kasza, *State and Mass Media in Japan*, pp. 54–71.
9. See table, ibid., pp. 62–3.
10. Ibid.
11. Ibid., p. 68.
12. Richie, *Hundred Years of Japanese Film*, pp. 65–7.
13. Ibid., pp. 46, 90.
14. Fujiki, 'Creating the Audience'.
15. Ibid., pp. 86–7.
16. See Kasza, *State and Mass Media in Japan*; Barak Kushner, *The Thought War: Japanese Imperial Propaganda* (Honolulu: University of Hawai'i Press, 2006); Mitchell, *Thought Control in Prewar Japan* and *Censorship in Imperial Japan*.
17. On the establishment of the Film Control Committee (*Eiga tōsei iinkai*) and its role in developing the 1939 Film Law, see Kasza, *State and Mass Media in Japan*, pp. 149–53.
18. Kasza details the 1939 regulations, *State and Mass Media in Japan*, pp. 234–48. As before, sex-related cuts were by far the most numerous in the period 1937–42.
19. Richie, *Hundred Years of Japanese Film*, p. 93.
20. A striking exception is a 1944 film about Guadalcanal, which showed bodies of Japanese soldiers to stoke the flames of anti-American hatred. See Katō Atsuko, *Sōdōin taisei to eiga* (Tokyo: Shin'yōsha 2003), pp. 258–9.
21. Kushner, *Thought War*, p. 4.
22. Peter High's *The Imperial Screen* provides a detailed analysis of film-making and its constraints in the war years.
23. [Editors' note: for more on the political goals of the Occupation, see Chapter 32 by Yuka Tsuchiya in this volume.]
24. See Rachael Hutchinson, 'Kurosawa Akira's *One Wonderful Sunday*: Context, Censorship and Counter-discursive film', in Rachael Hutchinson (ed.), *Negotiating Censorship in Modern Japan* (London: Routledge, 2013), pp. 133–4, 145–6; also John Dower, *Embracing Defeat: Japan in the Wake of World War II* (New York: W.W. Norton, 1999), pp. 406–8.
25. See Edward Fowler, 'Piss and Run: Or How Ozu Does a Number on SCAP', in Dennis Washburn and Carole Cavanaugh (eds), *Word and Image in Japanese Cinema* (Cambridge: Cambridge University Press, 2001), pp. 273–92.
26. An interesting case study is Kurosawa's *No Regrets for Our Youth/Waga seishun ni kuinashi* (1946). See Hutchinson, '*One Wonderful Sunday*', pp. 135–9.
27. On the prohibitions and enforcement of the Press Code regarding film, see Dower, *Embracing Defeat*, pp. 410–15.
28. Ibid., p. 411.
29. On Eirin's establishment, see Cather, *Art of Censorship*, pp. 79–80, and 'Policing the Pinks' pp. 98–9; also Adachi Kan (ed.), *Eirin: 50-nen no ayumi* (Tokyo: Eirin kanri iinkai, 2006), pp. 38–44.
30. Cather's translation of Adachi: see 'Policing the Pinks', p. 98.
31. Ibid., p. 99. For original regulations see Adachi, *Eirin*, pp. 185–6; Kobayashi, *Kinjirareta film* (Tokyo: Shunyōdō, 1956), pp. 170–1.
32. Hutchinson, '*One Wonderful Sunday*', pp. 146–7.
33. Rachael Hutchinson, 'Orientalism or Occidentalism? Dynamics of Appropriation in Akira Kurosawa', in Stephanie Dennison and Song Hwee Lim (eds), *Remapping World Cinema: Identity, Culture and Politics in Film* (London: Wallflower, 2006), p. 176.
34. Hutchinson, '*One Wonderful Sunday*', p. 144.
35. Joseph Anderson and Donald Richie, *The Japanese Film: Art and Industry*, rev. edn (Princeton, NJ: Princeton University Press, 1982), pp. 264–5.
36. Ibid., p. 265.
37. Cather, *Art of Censorship*, p. 83.
38. Ibid., pp. 83–4.
39. Cather, 'Policing the Pinks', pp. 109–10; Kobayashi, *Kinjirareta film*, pp. 172–3.
40. Kobayashi, *Kinjirareta film*, frontispiece ff.
41. Cather, *Art of Censorship*.
42. Cather, 'Policing the Pinks', pp. 114–15.
43. Kurosawa later admitted his regret about this development. Nishimura, *Kurosawa Akira o motomete* (Tokyo: Kinema Junpōsha, 2000), pp. 117–18; Mitsuhiro Yoshimoto, *Kurosawa: Film Studies and Japanese Cinema* (Durham, NC: Duke University Press, 2000), pp. 290–1.

44 Rachael Hutchinson, 'A Fistful of *Yojimbo*: Appropriation and Dialogue in Japanese Cinema', in Paul Cooke (ed.), *World Cinema's 'Dialogues' with Hollywood* (New York: Palgrave Macmillan, 2007), pp. 176–8.
45 Stuart Galbraith, *The Emperor and the Wolf: The Lives and Films of Akira Kurosawa and Toshiro Mifune* (New York: Faber & Faber, 2001), p. 301; Yoshimoto, *Kurosawa*, p. 289.
46 Yoshimoto, *Kurosawa*, pp. 290–1.
47 The hero demanding 'three coffins' from the coffin-maker before he enters a fight is a notable example. On the remake see Hutchinson, 'Fistful of Yojimbo'.
48 Nishimura, *Kurosawa Akira o motomete*, p. 116.
49 Kobayashi, *Kinjirareta film*, frontispiece ff. [Editors' note: for more on the yakuza genre and the *jidaigeki*, see also Chapter 25 by Jennifer Coates and Chapter 20 by Philip Kaffen in this volume.]
50 Kobayashi, *Kinjirareta film*, pp. 56–9.
51 Isolde Standish, *Politics, Porn and Protest: Japanese Avant-Garde Cinema in the 1960s and 1970s* (New York: Continuum, 2011), pp. 84, 103.
52 [Editors' note: for more on the horror genre, see also Chapter 21 by Michael Crandol in this volume.]
53 Mark Schilling gives a good overview of the attitudes: *The Yakuza Movie Book: A Guide to Japanese Gangster Films* (Albany, CA: Stone Bridge Press, 2003), p. 43. [Editors' note: for more on Fukasaku Kinji, see also Chapter 12 by Yuka Kanno in this volume.]
54 Fukasaku describes the bombings and being forced to carry corpses from the factory ruins: Yamane Sadao, *Eiga kantoku Fukasaku Kinji* (Tokyo: Waizu shuppan, 2003), pp. 17–18.
55 For example, see Alexander Jacoby, *A Critical Handbook of Japanese Film Directors* (Albany, CA: Stone Bridge Press, 2008), p. 17.
56 Tezuka Osamu, *Boku wa mangaka* (Tokyo: Nihon tosho centre, 1999), pp. 42–3.
57 Richard Torrance, 'The Nature of Violence in Fukasaku Kinji's *Jingi naki tatakai* (War without a code of honor)', *Japan Forum* vol. 17 no. 3 (November 2005), pp. 389–406.
58 Ibid., p. 403.
59 Aaron Gerow, 'Censorship and Film', in Sandra Buckley (ed.), *Encyclopedia of Contemporary Japanese Culture* (New York: Routledge, 2002), pp. 61–2.
60 Eirin (Film Classification and Rating Organization), <http://www.eirin.jp/english/008.html>.
61 Yamane, *Eiga kantoku*, p. 493.
62 Fujiwara Tatsuya won 'Newcomer of the Year' at the 2001 Japanese Academy Awards. The film won Best Editing and Most Popular Film, and was nominated for Best Screenplay, Best Music Score, Best Sound and Best Film. Fujiwara was nominated for Best Actor and Fukasaku Kinji for Best Director.
63 Caren Pagel, 'Fearing the Youth: Economic Turmoil, Adult Anxiety and the Japanese *Battle Royale* Controversy' (unpublished MA thesis, Florida Atlantic University, 2011).
64 On the audition process see Yamane, *Eiga kantoku*, pp. 495–8.
65 Theatrical release in the US was denied, coming so soon after the Columbine high school massacre. Tom Mes and Jasper Sharp interpret the film as a return to Fukasaku's 15-year-old self, emphasising his message to the younger generation: *The Midnight Eye Guide to New Japanese Film* (Berkeley, CA: Stone Bridge Press, 2005), p. 51.
66 Pagel describes the pre-release discussions in detail; see 'Fearing the Youth', pp. 25–8.

10

TECHNOLOGY
Sound and intermediality in 1930s Japanese cinema

Johan Nordström

Between the end of the 1920s and the early 1930s, Japanese cinema began to undergo a prolonged transition to sound that was facilitated by, but also coexistent with, a number of imported technologies. This transition constituted both a rupture and a gradual process that gave birth to a broad range of indigenous technological solutions. The existing rigid infrastructure and business models of the established film studios offered numerous opportunities for new investment and, consequently, the corporate structure and power balance of the Japanese film industry was changed decisively. A cinema that, thanks to the *benshi*, had never really been silent, thus found a new electric voice in an era widely permeated by an increasingly mechanical sound culture. Much in the same way that the coming of electrical sound had brought about questions of medium specificity in Western classical film theory, Japanese critics, too, shared a concern with defining the supposed essence and unique legitimate artistic uses of sound film. In addition to charting a desirable course for its development, they also paid close attention to its specific technological requirements and industrial preconditions. In this sense, the views of both active industrial practitioners and critics and theoreticians informed the gradual process by which Japanese sound film was theorised.

This chapter will examine these contemporary discourses while situating them in the wider historical context of the technological changes and developments then taking place within the Japanese film industry. These changes would lead to a period of intense technological rivalry while simultaneously stimulating forms of media convergence and intermediality between radio, cinema and the record industry. Seen in the broader context of the worldwide transition to sound, these developments serve to further emphasise that despite Japan's relatively protracted transition, the industry retained what Michael Raine has called its 'global simultaneity and cultural permeability'.[1]

Technological change inevitably increases the visibility of the cinematic apparatus as technology, and its intricate networks of connections between human agents, technologies and objects. When technology is used, we are reminded that 'representational devices, however familiar, are neither static nor self-defining'. As James Lastra has argued in his succinct study of American cinema and sound technology, 'Instead we should understand devices as constitutively situated in networks of assumptions, habits, practices and modes of representation that extend well beyond instrument centred definitions of technology'.[2] The shift to a view of cinema as situated in complex interdependent networks of technology, industry, aesthetic and social norms and customs seems worthwhile. In his examination of national differences in sound-image recording practices between the French and American cinema, Charles O'Brien, for example, remains sensitive to the specifcs of such industry and locality based practices, while demonstrating the aesthetic consequences of fundamental national differences in how sound technologies were understood and used. This can be seen in the French preference for *son direct*, O'Brien argues, as such differences can be located in basic aesthetic and technical norms.[3]

An examination of Japanese cinema's turn to sound invites reflection on these networks, their industrial and technological underpinning, and the interrelation of the human and mechanical. They also invite a consideration of the artistic inflections, which simultaneously both shape and are shaped by the continuing evolution of these interconnected networks.

Although a full examination of the technological, structural and industrial changes that the Japanese cinema underwent in this transitional period lies outside the scope of this chapter, certain key motifs emerge in an examination of the transitional context within which contemporary reception and theoretical writing may be placed. These motifs point to what Bruce Bennett, Marc Furstenau and Adrian Mackenzie have aptly signalled as a 'complex field of engagement and interaction, where the meaning and value of technology emerges as the effect of its use rather than as the result of its inherent properties'.[4] In sum, this indicates the value of an approach that leaves behind the technical determinism of apparatus theory and narrow instrument-centred definitions of technology. Instead, it argues for a concept of technology that can maximise specificity yet maintain openness to ongoing revision and alteration so as to 'account for the rapid appearances and disappearances of cinema *as* technology and for the manifold relations and intersections of cinema *and* technology'.[5]

By examining the way that Japanese cinema's transitional phase was conceptualised in contemporary writing, this chapter examines how various networks of intermedial remediation and industry practice surfaced within broader debates around the evolving conceptualisation of both technological change and cinema as art and industry.

TRANSITIONAL MOVEMENTS: TECHNOLOGY, INDUSTRY AND EXHIBITION

The spread and popularisation of early sound film in Japan, although still very much an urban phenomenon, saw the proliferation of cinemas wired with some kind of sound film technology increase substantially from 23 in 1929, and 27 in 1930, to 92 in 1931.[6] That number more than tripled the following year to 339 at the end of 1932.[7] By 1934, more than half of Japan's cinemas had been wired for sound, and 1935 saw the number increase substantially from 806 to 1,207, or 78 per cent of Japan's total number of cinemas.[8] As Chika Kinoshita has pointed out, 'while wired theaters had steadily increased, the leap from 60 percent to 80 percent in a single year significantly altered the landscape of exhibition nationwide'.[9]

Although Japan released its first so-called talkie film (*tōkī eiga*) in 1927 with Osanai Kaoru's avant-garde expressionist film *Dawn/Reimei*, utilising Lee De Forest's Phonofilm sound-on-film technology, it wasn't until 1935 that sound became a majority means of film production, if we also include the so-called 'sound-version' (*saundoban*), i.e. silent films with a recorded music and/or special effects soundtrack, but without any synchronised dialogue.[10]

Although cultural reasons such as the power of the *benshi* as a vested interest within the Japanese film industry have often been used to explain Japan's prolonged transition to sound,[11] in actuality the reasons for delay were primarily economical and structural in nature. Hiroshi Komatsu has argued that the delay in introducing sound film in Japan can be understood as a result of the fragility in the economic foundations of the Japanese film companies with financial constraints thus delaying investment in the necessary technology.[12] Indeed, the transition to sound certainly occurred in the midst of economic severity, which culminated in the stock market crash of 1929 and the ensuing Great Depression. Severe market devaluation followed Japan's departure from the gold standard in December 1931, and the resulting sharp increase in the cost of foreign imports naturally had a negative impact on the film industry's ability to invest. As Kinoshita has also observed, the Japanese film industry was structured on an economic model geared to the quick production of cheaply made products designed for rapid dissemination, instead of the more expensive, high-end products that sound films, said to cost three times that of a silent film, constituted at that date.[13] As the transition to sound required wiring theatres as well as equipping studios – although the largest urban theatres were equipped with sound systems by late 1932 – the limited sphere of exhibition extended the timescale of the industry's transition. As Raine argues, another reason for the slow increase in the production of sound films at the major studios was the lack of sound stages.[14] For instance, Shōchiku, were reluctant to commit to full sound film production until they had finished their new studio at Ōfuna in 1936.

Even though the technical aspects of sound film production were improving throughout the 1930s, hesitation on the part of the major studios to fully commit to sound film was a reality acutely felt by those working in the industry. The director, Gosho Heinosuke, working at Shōchiku, argued in 1934 that the artistic development of the Japanese talkie was held back in part to the fact that staff and directors working at most studios had to divide their attention between talkies and silent films, which hampered the development of a distinctive 'sound film sensibility'.[15] Another reason, Gosho argued, was that sound films' production costs were inherently high and were only subsequently recapitulated by the film studios through a lowering in the level of films' intellectual sophistication so as to appeal to as wide an audience as possible. This, de facto, limited the Japanese talkie, at least those produced at Shōchiku, to the genre of melodrama.[16]

Regardless of the state of Japan's film industry, the steadily growing presence of foreign sound cinema in the early 1930s became a major reason for the initial proliferation of sound technology; it also spurred fierce competition amongst rival talkie technologies. As Tochigi Akira has acknowledged, the varieties of different sound film systems and sound recording systems in the late 1920s to the early 1930s were so numerous that 'at present it is difficult to determine all of the sound recording formats which appeared'.[17] This was reflected in the way contemporary industry journals were full of adverts for rival sound systems and sound film technology articles.

In the September 1932 *Kinema junpō* article 'Today's Problem for the Movie Theatres: Which Sound Machine is Good?',[18] Oka Sanmin lists sixteen different sound systems available to theatre owners wanting to make the switch to sound. All but three are Japanese, although many were undoubtedly based on reverse engineered Western technology.[19] In discussing the cost performance of the different technologies, Oka suggests that the reason Japanese sound systems only dealt with one aspect of sound film, i.e. either sound recording or playback, was that they usually originated in independent labs and research centres. The economic fragility of the Japanese film companies resulted in the initial dominance of a market model in which an established film conglomerate, often on a film to film basis, worked with an independent sound film specialist that would rent out equipment and facilities for a specific production. This symbiotic model saved the film conglomerates from being forced to make large economic investments in film infrastructure, and ensured that an independent enterprise could find exhibition outlets for their products in theatres that were controlled by the studios and otherwise mostly closed to them.

In general, the talkies around this time were classified according to both the extent of sound utilisation, i.e. part talkie or all talkie, 'sound film' (*saundo-ban* or *saundo eiga*) etc., and their playback technology, i.e. sound-on-film (*firumu tōkī*) or sound-on-disc (*disuku tōkī*). As in the US, where Fox Movietone, Western Electric and RCA used the former system, and Vitaphone represented the latter, a similar struggle for market dominance emerged in Japan. The two Japanese systems that most came to exemplify this format struggle were that of the Japanese sound film pioneer Minagawa Yoshizō's film production company Shōwa Kinema Co., Ltd., which released movies under the name 'Mina Talkie', and that of the sound-on-disc based Eastphone system, invented by the former Shōwa Kinema employee Tōjō Masaki and developed by the Nippon Talkie Co., Ltd., that was established in October 1928.

After Minagawa's first screening of imported Phonofilms in 1925, he created the company Shōwa Kinema and in 1927, he arranged for the screenings of several Japanese sound films, including *Dawn*. Although the films received some press attention, the screenings failed to make any artistic impact or turn a profit. Minagawa later restructured his company under the new name of Mina Talkie and this time, having secured a distribution deal with Nikkatsu, he supplied six machines for playback and started releasing films in 1929.[20]

Looking at the reception of the first Mina Talkie film *The Captain's Daughter/Taii no musume* (1929), it becomes evident that at the time of its release, Japanese talkies released by Minagawa's main competitor Makino Film Productions (Makino eiga seisakujo) utilising the Eastphone sound-on-disc technology were not perceived as 'real talkies'; a failing for which they were severely criticised. This is due to the fact that despite being marketed as full talkies, they utilised intertitles and were shot silent, the sound recorded on disc at a later stage. Furthermore, the sound quality of the Makino/Eastphone films was very poor, often to the point where voice distortion and unsynchronised sound made the films hard to engage with.

This can be compared to the reception of Mina Talkie's first release when Iijima Tadashi stated that the film's greatest achievement was its novelty and the quality of its sound; in particular, the fact that the actor's voices could be heard clearly, even over the noise of the projector.[21] Iijima, however, deemed it without value as a work of cinema due to the film's theatrical acting style and lack of camera movement and variation of camera angles. The limitations of the microphone technology, which constrained camera movement and encouraged the return to a more static style of shooting, meant that the Japanese critique of the stage-like film style of the early talkies was similar to that in the West, where the 'new' aesthetics of sound cinema were felt to stand in stark contrast to the more 'poetic' film style associated with many of the canonical works of the silent era.

The constant discussion of sound film, foreign and domestic, as well as the actual arrival of several foreign sound films, had created an awareness for Japanese audiences about what a sound film ought to look and feel like. At the time of the release of *Dawn*, audiences and reviewers had no reference point when judging a sound film except that of silent cinema. By the time of *The Captain's Daughter*, however, this had changed, which can clearly be seen in the more comparative way that the film was received by the contemporary press.

The Captain's Daughter and Mina Talkie's second film *A Romance of Kanaya-Koume/Kanaya Koume* (1929) set a new standard against which early talkies were initially judged. These films were full talkies, unlike the part talkies that had been released in Japan before, most notably those by Makino/Eastphone. Although they are now lost, judging from their reception, their sound quality was deemed higher than what had previously been achieved. The critique levelled at Mina Talkie for their lack of a cinematic sensibility seems, however, to have extended to their later work. In his review of Mina Talkie's fourth film, *Seven Miles to Nakayama/Nakayama Shichiri* (1930),[22] billed as Japan's first all talkie *jidaigeki*, Yamamoto Rokuba dismissed it as 'incorrigibly uncinematic', criticising both the direction and the acting, and describing the cinematography of film industry veteran Henry Kotani as 'a shadow of its former self'.[23]

Even though sound-on-film based technology came out as the winner in the format wars in Japan, as in the West, it was clear, by the early 1930s, that Minagawa's Phonofilm based Mina Talkie would not carry the Japanese film industry forward. It was the Western Electric system that instead came to be perceived as the benchmark of sound quality, followed by Shōchiku's Tsuchihashi system and, after 1933, the sound system of Japan's first successful all sound film studio, the Tokyo-based Photo Chemical Laboratory Co. Ltd. (Kabushiki kaisha shashin kagaku kenkyūjo) or P.C.L., which later merged to form Tōhō in 1938.

THE JAPANESE INDUSTRY AND MEDIA SYNERGY

The history of Japanese cinema must not be confined to simple binaries between silent and sound films, or screen and stage. As Thomas Elsaesser has argued, instead of looking at film history as an isolated object, we should relate film history to other media and remain sensitive to the various forms of cross-pollination and synergetic media interference that in many ways were instrumental in shaping the contours of the culture within which cinema existed.[24]

The cultural and corporate landscape out of which sound cinema emerged in the early 1930s was one pervaded by a newfound electric audio 'media synergy', in which a single story, character, song or other product was made available to consumers in multiple media forms and formats. Sound cinema thus became situated within and integrated into a paradigm shift of mechanical audiovisual modernity that permeated Japanese society. In other words, the direction that cinema took was one distinguished by both electric synchronised sound in itself *and* corporate cooperative interaction in the form of commodified intermediality.

The emergence of sound cinema in the Japanese film industry should be seen as something originating out of, and entering into, an intermedial landscape that constituted an intrinsic component of Japan's cultural modernity; a modernity that was characterised by what Elsaesser calls '"media-interference" from radio and the co-presence, or competition, of the gramophone industry'.[25] The multifaceted nature of Japan's sound culture in the first half of the 1930s, and indeed Japanese cinema's multiplicity of form and content, as well as its intermedial nature, was not contingent or accidental. Rather, it was structural – a condition that permeates the period as a whole, shaping film style and content as well as the conditions of merchandising and production.

Emerging technologies often temporarily destabilise the relations among existing media, resulting in a complicated process of media convergence, where form and purpose of old and new technologies are recast, and the rigid infrastructure of established corporate systems become increasingly fluid. The introduction and later refinement of various electrical sound technologies during the 1920s and 1930s is one such instance; much like digital technology, in its various forms, is in the process of changing the production, consumption and aesthetics of cinema today. Steve Wurtzler has argued in the context of the American cinema that 'the innovation of electrical sound technology prompted a restructuring and consolidation of corporate mass media interests, shifts in both representational conventions and patterns of media consumption, and a renegotiation of the social functions assigned to mass media forms'.[26] Similarly, in the context of Japanese cinema's transition to sound, one aspect of this process was the formation of Japanese cinema's cultural and economic links to the record industry.

Relations between the film industry and record companies differed between the US and Japan. Whilst corporate links between the record and film industry only initially solidified with the introduction of sound film in the US (even though the production and marketing of sheet music overtly linked to films was common throughout the 1920s), synergistic connections existed in Japan as early as the late 1910s or early 1920s,[27] despite being formed more out of mutual exploitation than any strategic collaboration. The success in 1919, for instance, of the popular song 'Konjiki yasha no uta', based on Ozaki Kōyō's novel *The Golden Demon/Konjiki Yasha* serialised in the *Yomiuri shinbun* between 1897 and 1902, was arguably due to the popularity of the Nikkatsu film of the same name, released the previous year. The song, however, was written, produced and released without the direct involvement of the film company, indicating that the use of popular songs as an active advertisement strategy had not yet commenced.[28]

As the 1920s progressed, the symbiotic relationship between record companies and film companies solidified, especially in conjunction with the *kouta eiga*, or 'ballad films', i.e. silent films screened with live or recorded songs, which became immensely popular around the time of the phenomenal success of Teikoku Kinema's *The Caged Bird/Kago no tori* (1924).

Up until recently, modern historians have largely dismissed the *kouta eiga*,[29] looking down on it, for essentialist notions of medium specificity, as merely a transitional form or crude commercial fad.[30] Likewise, even though the *kouta eiga* enjoyed immense popularity as a genre and was given much attention in the pages of contemporary journals, as was the case with *Ongaku to eiga*, most discussions and reviews of *kouta eiga* in film journals such as *Kinema junpō* saw its intermedial nature as a vulgar inflection of cinematic art. Nonetheless, as Thorburn, Jenkins and Seawell have argued, in order to understand the aesthetics of transition and the development of cinemas expressive devices 'we must resist notions of media purity, recognizing that each medium is touched by and in turn touches its neighbors and rivals'.[31] The *kouta eiga* constituted an apt example of this kind of intermedial cross-pollination, in that its form and content were closely tied to developments in sound technology and the introduction of new sound media, such as radio and records.

Tracing its history and intermedial networks, Sasagawa Keiko situates the *kouta eiga* within the mixed media film tradition of the *rensageki*, in which stage drama and film were utilised alternately on the same stage.[32] Sasagawa convincingly shows how the introduction of radio and proliferation of phonographic records, together with the further development of the record companies' 'business model', changed previously established patterns of song consumption, pushing the cinema and sound media industry towards closer collaboration with the *kouta eiga* eventually giving way to the artistic inflections of 'theme song films' (*shudaika eiga*) and 'popular song films' (*kayō eiga*).[33]

Towards the latter half of the 1920s, the dynamic intermedial connections of the Japanese media landscape thus resulted in a series of media 'synergy' products, in which a single story or song was made available to consumers in multiple media forms and formats. The enormous success of *Tokyo March/Tokyo kōshinkyoku* (1929) constitutes one of the clearest example of this kind of intermedial networks,[34] while also highlighting the technological difficulties inherent in the production of talkies at this time. Originally a novel by Kikuchi Kan that ran from June 1928 to October 1929 in the popular magazine *Kingu*, *Tokyo March* was later commodified into a radio drama, song record, sheet music and film. *Tokyo March* serves as but one example of the kind of integration between cinema and radio common throughout the late 1920s and 1930s. Radio versions of Japanese films, called 'film dramas' (*eigageki*), as well as radio versions of foreign films, called 'film stories' (*eiga monogatari*), enjoyed immense popularity on Japanese radio. The former were usually directed and performed by the cast of the original film, whereas the latter were performed by a *benshi*, with the help of music accompaniment and special effects.

Although *Tokyo March* was originally intended as a sound-on-disc talkie, after Nikkatsu failed to achieve properly synchronised sound, the film was released as a *kouta eiga*, and marked the onset of a second *kouta eiga* craze, *The Caged Bird* marking the first. Furthermore, *Tokyo March* constitutes one of the clearest early examples of the kind of synergistic collaboration between the record and film industry that was to become the market standard during the 1930s.

Whilst films based on popular songs were nothing new, what set *Tokyo March* apart was both the simultaneous development of the film and song and its integrated marketing. The song was released one month before the film, at which point it sold poorly. However, as has often been pointed out,[35] after an aggressive sales campaign by both record and film companies in the run-up to the film's release, it become a runaway hit, eventually selling 150,000 copies (3,000 records would represent a normal level of success) thus catapulting its singer Satō Chiyako into stardom and effectively becoming Japan's first 'movie theme song'.

This kind of joint effort in the marketing of theme song records, as well as tie-in films, where the record and movie companies, together with cinemas, often collaborated in disseminating information or advertisements for their respective products, became the norm during the 1930s. Posters advertised the records, as well as the films, and their images were re-used for record advertisement handouts with record stores sometimes offering discounted tickets or free passes to the movies with record purchases. The record companies created advertising records containing the theme song and dialogue from the film, which played at the cinemas during the intermission. And when the actual film was screened, its theme song was often played so that it could be heard in the street in front of the cinema (Fig. 10.1).[36]

In 1933, for instance, Paramount and Viktor employed various promotional strategies for the release of Josef von Sternberg's *The Blue Angel/Der Blaue Engel* (1930) such as inserting the advertisement leaflet for the record into the weekly cinema programme handed out at the cinema and attaching an advertisement for the film to the record in all Viktor record stores around Tokyo.[37] These record and film company tie-up collaborations quickly came to carry such importance that they were discussed and handled by film companies in the same way as the choice of the right source material, scriptwriter and director during pre-production. In the

Fig. 10.1 The cover of *Viktor Harmonica Music Sheet* no. 61 featuring *Hometown/Fujiwara Yoshie no Furusato* (Mizoguchi Kenji, 1930, Nikkatsu). Fujiwara Yoshie is the tenor featured in the photograph.

Fig. 10.2 *Three Sisters with Maiden Hearts/Otome gokoro sannin shimai* (Naruse Mikio, 1935, P.C.L.).

case of P.C.L., for instance, records reveal that whereas its tie-ups with the beer company Dai nihon bīru or the chocolate manufacturer Meiji seika kaisha were designated as such, most often using the Japanese words '*tai appu*' or '*teikei*', record company collaboration was seen as an integral part of the film's production process. Furthermore, the immense importance the studio placed on these collaborations can be seen in the way that the song and record label were often chosen before the actual director.[38]

On some occasions, collaborations between film and record companies also resulted in a visually embedded presence. For instance, in the case of Naruse Mikio's film *Three Sisters with Maiden Hearts/Otome gokoro sannin shimai* (1935), for which Polydor supplied the theme song 'The Song of the City'/'Machi no uta', P.C.L. also included shots of large Polydor neon signs as advertisements for the record company (Fig. 10.2).

INDUSTRY, TECHNOLOGY AND CULTURE: EARLY WRITINGS

Throughout this transitional period technological developments, as well as novel aesthetic inflections, were accompanied by a diverse abundance of theoretical and critical discourses in the pages of film magazines such as *Kinema junpō*, *Kokusai eiga shinbun*, *Eiga hyōron* and *Eiga geijutsu kenkyū* as well as more musically oriented magazines such as *Tōkī ongaku*, *Eiga to ongaku* and *Ongaku sekai*. Central to these early discourses on the expressive devices and medium specificity of cinema and the newly emergent sound cinema were well-known film scholars and theorists such as Iijima Tadashi and the Marxist film critic Iwasaki Akira; pioneering film-maker, theoretician and prolific writer Kaeriyama Norimasa, who entered the Japanese film industry in the 1910s and became one of its foremost early modernisers and a leading spokesman of the Pure Film Movement that, during the 1910s and early 1920s, advocated for the use of what were considered more modern and cinematic modes of film-making; scholar and musician Nakane Hiroshi, who became one of the foremost contemporary writers on sound cinema; Kakeshita Keikichi, head of the music division at P.C.L., one of the most prolific writers on sound cinema and talkie music in the 1930s, spearheading the journal *Talkie ongaku*; and the producer and theorist Mori Iwao, arguably one of the most important and influential figures in the history of the Japanese talkie.

Questions regarding the sound cinema and talkie music's intermedial relations were articulated, generally to advance the argument that the talkie should continue towards a completely artistically independent form, not reliant on established modes of theatre, film or music. Kakeshita argued, for instance, that just as the combination of poetry and music had given rise to 'popular songs' (*kayō kyoku*), dance and music to ballet music, and theatre and music to opera, the combination of film and music had now given rise to the new art of talkie music.[39]

In 1930, Nakane Hiroshi argued for the equal importance of sound and picture in relation to the soundtrack as a whole. He suggested that neither should become dominant and in exploring the combination of melody and harmony, stated that 'we have the talkie because we have the sound and picture, therefore … they must be joined on an equal setting and harmoniously combined'. Nakane's idea was that if music was the sum of melody and harmony, then melody was the picture, and harmony was the sound and he gave Von Sternberg's *Morocco* (1930) as an example of a film able to achieve this kind of organic merger.

In order to realise a 'pure' talkie, free from the historical norms of theatre and silent cinema, Nakane saw the need for artists involved to realise that the talkie represented a new art form, one where film, music and sound were organically joined together. Because of its mechanical nature, he argued that talkie music was more suitable for cinema than live orchestra arrangements, due to the difficulty of synchronisation.[40] Nakane viewed the talkie as a part of a new form of mechanised mass culture, and as such he argued that 'in the end … it is in vain for human directors and orchestras to accompany film that is driven by machine power'.[41]

The increasingly mechanical nature of cinema that Nakane alludes to was a common discourse among contemporary writers. In the 1928 article 'Regarding the Global Popularity of the Sound Film',[42] Mori Iwao discussed current sound film trends within an international context and conveyed an evolutionist reading of cinematic art that almost anticipates André Bazin[43] in his argument that cinema was, in essence, a scientific product and that further scientific development, like sound and colour, would represent not the destruction of cinema, but a natural step in the process of fulfilling its realist potential.[44] With regards to the actual technology of sound cinema Mori advocated avidly for the use of sound-on-film technology systems so as to facilitate the synchronisation of picture and sound. However, Mori tempered his view with the concern that Japan's current lack of equipment, and the cost of sound film productions, might make Japanese sound films unprofitable and decrease their chances of being made.[45]

It is partly for this very reason that earlier the same year Kaeriyama Norimasa, in contrast to Mori's support of sound-on-film technology, argued for the use of the sound-on-disc technology.[46] Kaeriyama penned a number of articles for *Kinema junpō* on sound cinema technology in 1928 and 1929. He anchored his arguments in the reality of contemporary exhibition practices, arguing that due to Japanese film prints being played more often, and on lower-quality machines than their American counterparts, sound-on-disc technology was preferable to that of sound-on-film in order to minimise wear and tear on the soundtrack. He advocated the creation and mass production of domestic equipment as a cheap alternative to the more costly Western systems such as Viktor's Vitaphone.[47] Even more interestingly, Kaeriyama argued that sound-on-disc technology would increase the cost efficiency of exhibition practices by enabling the replacement of the musicians' and *benshis*' live performance with that of their sound recording. These, he argued, could be jointly recorded on a disc, synchronised with the film, and played back in cinemas.[48] Kaeriyama can thus be said to have foreseen the turn the industry would take in the following years of utilising recorded discs as musical accompaniment, a development which, it has already been pointed out, would lead to the creation of the intermedial aesthetics of the *saundoban* and the intermediality of early sound film exhibition practices.[49] Chika Kinoshita has commented that:

Kaeriyama's conceptualization of the bricolage sound-on-disc system, as it were, embodied the epistemological configuration of the late 1920s Japanese soundscape. In this configuration, some of those boundaries we now tend to take for granted were blurred, such as the one between production and exhibition and that between the mechanically reproduced-homogeneous-global mass media and the live-heterogeneous-local performance.[50]

However, this intermedial aesthetic was generally looked down upon by contemporary critics who, arguing from the standpoint of medium purity, saw it as a crutch for Japanese film producers hesitant to fully commit to sound film.

As we have seen, another reason for the slow artistic development of the talkies was their inherently high production cost; something, according to Gosho, subsequently recapitulated by the film studios by lowering the level of intellectual sophistication of the films. Interestingly, Gosho's argument stems from a deep dissatisfaction with the Japanese film industry, much like the sound film critique advanced by many of those who were against converting to sound on the basis that the current Japanese film industry was not suited to sound film production.[51]

In contrast, the intermedial origin of 'talkie music', or sound film music, was celebrated by some as part of its very essence. Nakane, for instance, emphasised the technological and capitalist foundations behind the creation of sound film music. Regarding sound cinema's intermedial origins within electrical corporations, Nakane stated that 'We must be aware of the fact that the talkie's technological and artistic development towards completion is from start to finish completely dependent on the tempo of the electrical science's progress'[52] and advanced a technologically determinist reading of talkie music's development from classical to jazz. He sees the use of symphonic orchestras and classical music in early talkies as a remnant of the silent era for when the technological prerequisites materialised, the talkie cast classical music aside to embrace the more modern sound of jazz. Once more, Nakane saw the reason for this in the technological apparatus of the talkie itself, stating that it was 'Less for the reason that jazz is the favourite of the world, but more for the reason that the jazz instruments suit the microphone more than anything else.'[53] As for why jazz better suited electrical remediation, he does not explain; however, one can speculate that as the popularisation of jazz music went hand in hand with that of the wider spread of the gramophone and radio, jazz was, for many, associated with electrically reproduced sound to a greater extent than classical music.

Similar arguments regarding the talkie music's technological nature were common in other contemporary writing. Kakeshita Keikichi argued that unlike the case with classical music, the talkie had originated from technical innovation, commercialism and the quest for profit. Kakeshita argued against the view that the talkie music was therefore without artistic value by suggesting that these traits merely constituted some of its artistic characteristics or preconditions that the modern composer must contemplate:

The scientific production of talkie music is one of the very characteristics of 'modern' musical art, and for the contemporary composer it becomes an important task to explore electrical music and the composition of musical instruments in ways that are suitable for the microphone. It is likely that there is no 'modern' composer who writes music without taking microphone music into account be this records, radio, the talkie and, in the future, television.[54]

The improved quality of the phonograph players led several leading cinemas to switch from live music to recorded accompaniment for their screenings. In 1929, Paramount's Hōgakuza and the Asakusa denkikan installed Viktor's sound-on-disc system Electrola, as did Makino who mirrored this move in his theatres in the Kansai region. While leading urban screens were equipped with modern, often foreign, sound systems, many theatres utilised systems with poor sound performance.

Mori implicitly recognised the influence of technological kinship, the idea that sound fidelity equated not to real experience but other media, and located the reason for audiences' apparent acceptance of cinemas' often poor sound quality in familiarity with other forms of audio technologies, such as the radio and phonograph, which he argued exerted a negative influence on standards of acceptance.

For Mori, the elimination of cinema's live musical accompaniment and the introduction of new technologies to assist with the merging of picture and sound, were signs of how film production and screening practices were becoming increasingly mechanical and artificial. Mori saw the mechanisation of cinema in the wider context of a society on the cusp of modernity, stating that 'the Japanese cinema's shift to talkies simultaneously means that the Japanese cinema has stepped into a mechanical civilization, […] reminiscent of the industrial revolution'.[55] Although Mori expressed sympathy for cinema musicians, the ones he pitied most were the *benshi*, for whom he saw no future, stating that although 'it is unavoidable that the *setsumeisha* will lose their jobs and this is necessary from the viewpoint of mechanical civilization, as [victims of] a tragedy in the history of Japanese cinema history, they are worthy of our deep sympathy'.[56]

The *benshi*, however, did not leave the cinema quietly. Instead, through strikes, disruption of the physical exhibition spaces, and prolific coverage in the contemporary press and cinema journals, they became one of the most violently visible indicators of how cinema exhibition was changing in the early 1930s. Their struggle to negotiate cinema's technological identity increased cinemas visibility *as* technology. Raine has shown how the *benshi* struggle, as reported in the newspapers, configured anxieties about the precarious relation between human and machine culture, and, drawing on Lastra, how 'automatic speech produce[d] anxieties about the capacities of the human in the face of the machine'.[57] In essence, for a brief moment, the *benshi* became a tragic symbol of the human pitted against the process of mechanical modernisation.

As the *benshi* became dispossessed, another narrative formed within the broader film culture as well as the thriving left-wing film movement of the late 1920s and the early 1930s; one that recognised technology as an object of social and political negotiation and that engaged in critique of the talkies' content as well as discussions of its potential for politically subversive activity. In his aptly titled article 'What Should We Give Voice To?',[58] written in 1929, Kanbara Tai, an artist, art critic and key figure in the Japanese Futurism movement, argued for the progressive potential of the talkie film and music. According to Kanbara, the sound film held a greater subversive or propaganda potential than the silent film due to the strong effect of music which, when utilised with short catchphrases and suggestive visual cues, could facilitate greater audience acceptance of a film's message. Kanbara saw the talkie as a potentially powerful political weapon, with almost endless possibilities, and argued for its strong dialectical potential when sound was used in *counterpoint* to the image.[59] Kanbara argued, for instance, that if those against militarism used films depicting war while simultaneously speaking out against it, this would create a strong anti-war effect in the minds of the audience. Likewise, the use of recorded scenes of a failed strike, combined with the singing of the Internationale, would have the potential to create a powerful message.

The prominent left-wing Japanese film critic and historian Iwasaki Akira wrote extensively on the subject of the new media's revolutionary potential in his 1930 article 'The Talkie and the Proletariat'.[60] Iwasaki argued that even though the talkie was currently in the hands of the bourgeois, the working class must not see the talkie in itself as the enemy. Instead, Iwasaki argued that the talkie, in utilising both hearing and sight, could become a powerful tool for the cause of the proletariat and that they should appropriate and utilise the talkie for themselves.

CONCLUSION

Through examining the conceptualisation of Japanese cinema during its transition to sound, this chapter has argued for the significance of technical, intermedial and industrial underpinnings to the representational strategies employed by films and film exhibition. These representational strategies were the result of, as well as contributing factors in, a set of complex interdependent networks of technology, industry, human agency, aesthetic and social norms and customs.

The burgeoning talkie became the site for theoretical discussions about the nature of the cinematic apparatus, its social and political implications, and artistic potential. As Japan's cinematic soundscape became reconfigured, new forms of intermedial networks and artistic expressions appeared. Some solidified through processes of commodification whilst others disappeared or became transformed into yet other forms of mechanically reproducible mass culture. As Japanese cinema's visibility as a form of technology increased and as its identity became renegotiated, a multitude of critical voices made itself heard over its newly acquired electrical voice.

These debates, that raged in the pages of newspapers, books and journals, illustrate the complex relation between sound and image that existed during the Japanese cinema's conversion to sound, and the renegotiation of their epistemological boundaries. Bringing to mind Martin Heidegger's statement that 'the essence of technology is nothing technological',[61] these discourses on cinema's relation between sound and image are not only indicative of a highly literate and self-reflective industry, they also illustrate how technology, through the appropriation of sound and voice, brings to the fore issues of identity and the limits of the human in the context of mechanical modernity. They remind us that technology is never merely instrumental, nor does it function in a politically or culturally neutral context. Rather, it is a human activity and as such always exists within that 'complex field of engagement and interaction, where the meaning and value of technology emerges as the effect of its use, not as the result of its inherent properties'.[62]

Notes

1. Michael Raine, 'No Interpreter, Full Volume: The Benshi and the Sound Image in Early 1930s Japan', paper presented at Society of Cinema and Media Studies conference, March 2012.
2. James Lastra, *Sound Technology and the American Cinema: Perception, Representation, Modernity* (New York: Columbia University Press, 2000), pp. 61–2.
3. Charles O'Brien, *Cinema's Conversion to Sound: Technology and Film Style in France and the US* (Bloomington: Indiana University Press, 2005).
4. Bruce Bennett, Marc Furstenau and Adrian Mackenzie, *Cinema and Technology: Cultures, Theories, Practices* (London: Palgrave Macmillan, 2008), p. 5.
5. Ibid., p. 16.
6. Fujioka Atsuhiro, 'Nihon eiga kōgyōshi kenkyū: 1930 nendai ni okeru gijutsu kakushin oyobi kindaika to presentation', *CineMagaziNet!* no. 6 (2002), <http://www.cmn.hs.h.kyoto-uac.jp/CMN6/fujioka.html>.
7. Ibid.
8. Ibid. These numbers were also graphically presented by Raine, 'No Interpreter, Full Volume' and Chika Kinoshita, 'The Benshi Track: Mizoguchi Kenji's the Downfall of Osen and the Sound Transition', *Cinema Journal* vol. 50 no. 3 (Spring 2011), pp. 1–25.
9. Ibid., p. 6. [Editors' note: for more on the history of Japanese film exhibition, see also Chapter 8 by Manabu Ueda in this volume.]
10. Ibid.
11. See Joseph L. Anderson and Donald Richie, *The Japanese Film: Art and Industry*, rev. edn (Princeton, NJ: Princeton University Press, 1982), pp. 72–89; Freda Freiberg, 'The Transition to Sound in Japanese Cinema', in Tom O'Regan and Brian Shoesmith (eds), *History on/ and/ in Film: Selected Papers from the 3rd Australian History and Film Conference* (Perth: History and Film Association of Australia, 1985), pp. 76–80.
12. Hiroshi Komatsu, 'The Foundation of Modernism: Japanese Cinema in the Year 1927', *Film History* vol. 17, nos. 2/3 (2005), p. 365.
13. Kinoshita, 'The Benshi Track', p. 6.
14. Raine, 'No Interpreter, Full Volume'.
15. Gosho Heinosuke, 'Nihon talkie no danpenteki jōhō', *Ongaku sekai* vol. 6 no. 6 (1934), pp. 57–62.
16. See, for instance, Shōchiku's executive director Tsutsumi Tomojirō's 'Boku no talkie hantai ron', *Kinema shūhō*, 16 May 1930, p. 14, and the head of the Motion Picture Department of the Osaka Mainichi Newspaper, Mizuno Shinkō's 'Watashi wa talkie ni hantai suru', *Kokusai eiga shinbun*, April 2005, p. 521.
17. Akira Tochigi, 'Archiving of Early Japanese "Talkie" Films', in *Conservation and Restoration of Audio-Visual Recording Media: National Research Institute for Cultural Properties* (Tokyo: Reimei, 2013), p. 53.
18. Oka Sanmin, 'Tokushu eigakan kyō no mondai: Donna hasseiki ga yoika', *Kinema junpō*, 1 September 1932, pp. 61–6.
19. The sound systems enumerated are: Western Electric shiki (produced by Tōyō W.E), RCA Otophon shiki

(sold by Nihon Victor), Klangfilm Tobis shiki (sold by Siemens shukerto), Shinefon shiki and Pesento shiki, Shinpurekusu talkie projector (Osaka Acme Trading Company), Horumasu hassei eiga ki (sold by Osawa Trading Company), Jakki steroru hassei eiga ki (Noto Trading Company), Deburai hassei eiga ki (Okamoto yōkōyunyū), Shinta shiki, Nomura shiki intanashonaru, Rolla shiki, Niputon, Matsuda shiki orimupiya shiki, Ishibashi shiki, Eion system, Oka shiki moshofon.

20. 'Mina talkie "Taii no musume" nikkatsu fūgiri to kettei', *Kokusai eiga shinbun*, 10 November 1929, p. 7.
21. Iijima Tadashi, 'Taii no musume', *Kinema junpō*, 21 November 1929, p. 103–4.
22. A two-reel (42-minute) fragment of this film survives, in the holdings of the National Film Archive of Japan, and constitutes the only surviving material of Mina Talkie's own production output. Judging from the fragment, the sound is clear and intelligible, the cinematography consists of mostly static camera shots, and the acting can best be described as theatrical.
23. Yamamoto Rokuba, 'Nakayama shichiri', *Kinema junpō*, 1 January 1931, p. 208. [Editors' note: For more on Henry Kotani, see also Chapter 16 by Daisuke Miyao in this volume.]
24. Thomas Elsaesser, 'The New Film History as Media Archeology', *Cinemas: Journal of Film Studies* vol. 14 nos. 2–3 (2004), p. 88.
25. Ibid.
26. Steve J. Wurtzler, *Electric Sounds: Technological Change and the Rise of Corporate Mass Media* (New York: Columbia University Press, 2008), p. 2.
27. Ibid., pp. 20–1.
28. Kazuya Mori, 'Ginmaku no uta kaisōfu: Eiga kouta kara shudaika made', in *Nihon eiga shudaikashū 1 senzenhen* (Tokyo: Nihon Columbia, 1995), p. 4.
29. Recent historical research by such scholars as Tomita Mika, Sasagawa Keiko and Diane Wei Lewis constitutes a much needed re-evaluation of the genre of the *kouta eiga*. See Diane Wei Lewis, 'Media Fantasies: Women, Mobility, and Silent-Era Japanese Ballad Films', *Cinema Journal* vol. 52 no. 3 (2013), pp. 99–119; Sasagawa Keiko, 'Kouta eiga ni kansuru kiso chōsa: Meiji makki kara shōwa shoki o chūshin ni', *Engeki kenkyū centre kiyō* no. 1 (2003), pp. 175–96; Tomita Mika, 'Ba e no kaiki: Misasa kouta to iu sōchi', *Art research kiyō* no. 2 (2002), pp 105–14.
30. See, for instance, Tanaka Jun'ichirō, *Nihon eiga hattatsu shi*, vol. 2 (Tokyo: Chūōkōron-sha 1980), pp. 20–1; Iwasaki Akira, *Eiga shi* (Tokyo : Toyo Keizai shinpōsha, 1961), pp. 41–3; Iijima Tadashi, *Nihon eiga shi* (Tokyo, Hakusuisha, 1955), pp. 57–67.
31. David Thorburn, Henry Jenkins and Brad Seawell, *Rethinking Media Change: The Aesthetics of Transition* (Cambridge, MA: MIT Press, 2003), p. 11.
32. Sasagawa, 'Kouta eiga ni kan suru kiso chōsa'.
33. Raine, 'No Interpreter, Full Volume'; Keiko Sasagawa, 'Silent Films with Popular Music: The Intermediality of *Kouta* Films, 1896–1929', paper presented at Society of Cinema and Media Studies conference, March 2013.
34. For further analysis of *Tokyo March* and its intermedial networks, see Kinoshita, 'The Benshi Track', pp. 128–45; Nagahara Hiromu, *Unpopular Music: The Politics of Mass Culture in Modern Japan* (Cambridge, MA: Harvard University, 2011), pp. 33–54.
35. For instance, Kurata Yoshihiro, *Nihon record bunka shi* (Tokyo: Tokyo shoseki, 1979), pp. 331–3; Kinoshita, 'The Benshi Track'; Raine, 'No Interpreter, Full Volume'; Sasagawa, 'Kouta eiga ni kan suru kiso chōsa'.
36. Ōnishi Hidenori, 'Eiga shudaika "Gion kouta" kō', *Art research kiyō* no. 3 (2003), p. 158.
37. Minami Masatoshi, 'Record kaisha to no tie-up senden "Nagaki no tenshi" Tokyo fūkiri no mae', *Kinema junpō*, June 1931, pp. 21–2.
38. See the corporate journals by Eguchi, held in the Makino Archive at the Starr East Asian Library, Columbia University.
39. Kakeshita Keikichi, 'Talkie ongaku no konponteki mondai', in *Eiga to ongaku* (Tokyo: Shinkō ongaku shuppansha, 1943), p. 134.
40. Nakane Hiroshi, 'Talkie ongaku no tanjō to sono hattenkatei', *Ongaku sekai* vol. 6 no. 6 (1934), p. 18.
41. Ibid.
42. Mori Iwao, 'Hassei eiga no sekaiteki ryūkō ni tsuite', *Yomiuri shinbun*, 29 July 1928, p. 4.
43. André Bazin, 'The Ontology of the Photographic Image', trans. Hugh Gray, *Film Quarterly* vol. 13 no. 4 (1960), pp. 4–9.
44. Mori, 'Hassei eiga no sekaiteki ryūkō ni tsuite', p 4.
45. Ibid.
46. Kaeriyama Norimasa, 'Eiga no setsumei to ongaku o chikuonki ni yotte daiyō no kanōsei ni tsuite', *Kinema junpō*, 11 May 1928, pp. 31–2.
47. Kaeriyama Norimasa, 'Hassei eiga no jitsuyōteki sōchi to seisakuhō ni tsuite', *Kinema junpō*, 1 September 1928, p. 124.

48 Ibid.
49 Kinoshita, 'The Benshi Track'; Raine, 'No Interpreter, Full Volume'.
50 Kinoshita, 'The Benshi Track', p. 152; Gosho Heinosuke, 'Nihon tōkī no danpenteki jōhō', *Ongaku sekai* vol. 6 no. 6 (1934), pp. 57–62.
51 See, for instance, Tsutsumi, 'Boku no talkie hantai ron'; Mizuno, 'Watashi wa tōkī ni hantai suru'.
52 Nakane, 'Talkie ongaku no tanjō to sono hattenkatei', pp. 16–22.
53 Nakane, 'Talkie ongaku no tanjō to sono hattenkatei', *Ongaku sekai* vol. 6 no. 6 (1934), p. 19.
54 Kakeshita, 'Talkie ongaku no konponteki mondai', pp. 135–6.
55 Mori Iwao, 'Honkakuteki nihon talkie wa itsu kara hajimaru', *Yomiuri shinbun*, 20 May 1930 (page unknown).
56 Ibid.
57 Raine, 'No Interpreter, Full Volume'. See, also, Michael Raine, 'No Interpreter, Full Volume: The Benshi and the Sound Image in 1930s Japan', in Michael Raine and Johan Nordström (eds), *The Culture of the Sound Image in Prewar Japan* (Amsterdam: Amsterdam University Press, forthcoming).
58 Kanbara Tai, 'Wareware wa nani o hassei subeki ka', *Eiga ōrai* vol. 55 no. 5 (August 1929), pp. 18–21.
59 Ibid.
60 Iwasaki Akira, 'Talkie to musankaikyū', in Mori Iwao (ed.), *Talkie ron* (Tokyo: Tenjinsha, 1930), pp. 95–116.
61 Martin Heidegger, 'The Question Concerning Technology', in David Farrell Krell (ed.) *Martin Heidegger: Basic Writings* (New York: Harper, 1977), pp. 283–317.
62 Bennett, Furstenau and Mackenzie, *Cinema and Technology*, p. 5.

11

FILM FESTIVALS
Eigasai inside out: Japanese cinema and film festival programming

Ran Ma

The Nagoya Cinematheque, a local mini-theatre founded in 1982 with a single screen and a seating capacity of forty, has run its annual 'jishu seisaku eiga festival' since 1986. The term *jishu (seisaku) eiga* literally means 'autonomously made' or 'Do-It-Yourself films' and is understood here to mean the Japanese equivalent of independent cinema.[1] The success of this micro-scale 'film festival' showcasing Japanese independent films prompts consideration of the broader relationship between Japan's wider film festival culture and the variously scaled networks that currently circulate and exhibit Japanese cinema both within and beyond the country's borders.

As such, this chapter will investigate Japanese film festival culture 'inside out' from a two-pronged perspective. It will firstly chronicle the screening of Japanese films at European-American film festivals and situate the history of 'screening Japan' in the conjuncture of contemporary cinema and festival programming practice, both of which have been transformed from the early postwar period to the present day. Then, based on a preliminary survey mapping out the evolution of Japanese film festival culture in the postwar era, it will also examine a number of contemporary festivals within Japan and look at how they engage with the circulation and exhibition of Japanese films today.

EIGASAI AS FILM FESTIVAL(S): AN OVERVIEW

This chapter will tackle two conceptual layers that intersect within both the fields of film festival studies and Japanese film studies. One layer concerns the epistemological articulation of the term 'film festival' in relation to the Japanese context. Sometimes substituted by the katakana spelling of 'film festival', the notion of *eigasai* appears to be interchangeable with that of 'film festival', while it may also connote a certain localised conceptualisation and operational format – a topic I shall turn to later.[2] Akasaki Yōko points out in her brief, yet illuminating, historical exploration of Japan's *eigasai* that although similar forms of film exhibition may be traced back to events such as the Katsudō shashin tenrankai (The Exhibition of Moving Pictures) in the 1920s, the term *eigasai* itself was applied for the first time to the Tōnan Asia Eigasai (the South East Asian Film Festival, AFF), a peripatetic festival launched in Tokyo in 1954.[3] This festival was masterminded by the then president of Daiei, Nagata Masaichi, and developed under the auspices of another Nagata-led initiative, the Federation of Southeast Asian Film Producers that was established the previous year. The AFF set up a contingent interface for Asian film moguls to engage in collaborations via coproduction and technology transfer. It also played a significant role in Japan's cultural diplomacy in this region during the Cold War.[4] Despite the fact that more than fifty *eigasai* have been established in Japan since the turn of the new millennium and that there are over a hundred events self-labelled as *eigasai* held across the nation every year,[5] there has still not been any adequate form of academic inquiry, in either Japanese or English, into what forms these contemporary film festivals have taken, and what roles they have played, after the collapse of the Cold War world system and during the emergence of an environment of cultural-economic neoliberalism.

The second layer considers the notion and practice of festival programming, which essentially interlocks with the leitmotif of cultural translation between the model of the international film festival and the more vernacular, localised discursive articulation and practice of *eigasai*. Marijke de Valck has distinguished between festival *programming* and film *scheduling* at cinemas and multiplexes by reinforcing the former's cultural significance and emphasising a festival's curatorial commitment to handle 'cinema as [a form of] cultural expression and an evaluation of films as artistic accomplishments'.[6] Historically speaking, the institution of the European film festival evolved into 'the age of programmers' during the late 1960s against the backdrop of widespread anti-establishment social movements.[7] As de Valck reminds us, 'classical tropes' crucial to modern programming practice such as national cinema, auteur cinema and art cinema have been gradually broadened to accommodate more variety and possibility in terms of curatorial style.[8] Whereas we come to frame festival programming as an authored, creative practice that may distinguishes one film festival from another, the authorial, versatile role of the festival director and/or programmer has also been amplified, if not mythologised.[9]

This chapter sheds light on what de Valck has described as the third phase of film festivals, from the 1980s to the present, during which time they have become global phenomena while also undergoing an intricate process of institutionalisation and standardisation. What I have referred to as 'the international film festival model' underscores a sense of interconnectedness between festivals. It emphasises a trend that has seen an intensified level of networking in the global festival sphere that has necessitated and facilitated the development of various compatible, even shared, operational models and standards. These have allowed festivals to become temporally, spatially and even conceptually interlocked events within the global cultural economy. To fully grasp the scale of this 'international model' we may, for instance, refer to the criteria for international film festival accreditation stipulated by the Fédération Internationale des Associations de Producteurs de Films (FIAPF, established in 1931).[10]

While I agree that the historical formation of the world film festival system that emerged in Europe in the early 1930s is inherently hierarchical and has been inconsistently developed across certain geopolitical contours, I do not intend to subject my consideration of Japanese film festivals to a grid rigidly structured upon the dichotomies between the West and Asia, foreign and Japanese, or the centre and the periphery. Here, the anthropologist Anna Tsing's ethnographical work offers a valuable insight into the nature of global connections in that it locates 'worldly encounters' between the universal and the local in terms of 'frictions' – the contradictions and tensions produced when the universal interacts with, and circulates across, difference in various contingent, yet creative, ways.[11] Tsing illustrates how a specific sociocultural project of universalism, or cosmopolitanism, necessarily engages in a process of 'scale-making' to make itself relevant, namely through a set of articulations and practices that generate and delineate scale in order to signify 'the spatial dimensionality necessary for a particular kind of view'.[12]

By placing Tsing's insights alongside the sociologist Bruno Latour's notion of 'Actor-Network-Theory',[13] we may perceive the film festival as an assemblage of multiple, intersecting scale-making projects that articulate and produce various linkages and mechanisms that facilitate the festival's commitment to various local, regional, and even global, sociocultural and economic spheres, despite the fact that these endeavours might not be often neatly addressed or materialised on equal terms. I thus understand film festival programming as a dynamic, contingent and networked process that is choreographed and mediated by a wide range of festival stakeholders and actors such as film-makers, festival professionals (e.g. programmers, consultants, producers and distributors) and audiences as well as various related initiatives and entities at both an official and unofficial level. To put it more specifically, under the economic imperative of neoliberalism, programming may demonstrate a particular festival's changing sociopolitical agenda by situating itself in relation to differently scaled film networks of circulation and exhibition.

This chapter will particularly frame Japanese cinema and film culture in terms of the 'post-studio era' from the 1990s to the present, during which 'the whole film industry has gradually become financially dysfunctional'.[14] Instead of highlighting domestic *eigasai* as entities that structurally and conceptually deviate from, or contradict, the international festival model, I shall, instead, approach their differences as points of connection. In doing so, we may thus see the ways in which individual festivals have framed and developed local, regional and global networks of contemporary Japanese cinema through their particular forms of programming and exhibition practice.

SCREENING JAPAN OVERSEAS: AN INCOMPLETE HISTORY SINCE *RASHOMON*

In this section, I will single out three crucial moments not only to characterise the programming of Japanese entries at overseas film festival but also to foreground the sociopolitical discourses and cultural significance that have underlined these curatorial gestures. The intention here is to offer a set of meaningful comparative and referential frameworks that reconsider the relationship between this traffic and the domestic *eigasai*. The interconnections between Japanese *eigasai* and their international counterparts will also be placed in their historical context.

Screening *Rashomon*

According to Iwamoto Kenji, the Japanese film world first discussed potential international markets for films 'made in Japan' (*nihonsei eiga*) as early as the late Meiji era in the early 1910s.[15] Current studies that highlight the overseas expansion of Japanese cinema through international film festivals, however, almost never fail to highlight the 'origin' story of the aforementioned legendary figure of Nagata Masaichi from Daiei and his visionary festival enterprises during the height of the Cold War.[16] These accounts of how the cream of

Fig. 11.1 *Rashomon/Rashōmon* (Kurosawa Akira, 1950, Daiei).

Japanese films from the early 1950s were awarded top prize at the main European film festivals usually take Kurosawa Akira's 1951 Golden Lion winner *Rashomon/Rashōmon* (1950) as their opening chapter (Fig. 11.1).

Critical writing regarding the circulation and exhibition of Japanese cinema at European festivals often revolves around the discursive interplay between the 'Western gaze' and the notion of 'Japaneseness'.[17] *Rashomon*'s victory thus had a double significance. For the Japanese film industry, recognition from leading European festivals such as the Venice International Film Festival (established in 1932) and the Cannes International Film Festival (established in 1946) further elevated the Japanese entries to their 'stage of completion' by literally placing them in comparison and competition with other national cinemas in front of an assemblage of international juries and audiences that epitomised the Western gaze *par excellence*.[18] Yet, at the same time, it was also hard to disregard the nationalistic ethos and essentialised ideas of cultural identity that these festival triumphs invoked and eulogised.

The success of *Rashomon* inspired Nagata to launch 'various campaigns promoting the internationalization of Japanese cinema'.[19] Along with active strategies that facilitated the transfer of technology (often from Hollywood to Japan) and the launch of a variety of film coproduction projects, Japanese film companies, especially the more outward-looking Daiei, also developed epic period films such as *Gate of Hell/Jigokumon* (1953) and *Ugetsu/Ugetsu monogatari* (1953). These titles catered to the apparent promise of the international market with their reception at prestigious festivals being crucial to the parameters of industrial kudos. Yet, as Michael Baskett points out, it was partially because Nagata became dissatisfied with the way that the success of Japanese films at major Western festivals became fundamentally exploited in the 1950s, that he proposed the pan-Asian South East Asian Film Festival in order to 'sell Japan' and tap into 'more accessible markets' for Japanese cinema.[20] Daiei/Nagata's marketing outreach initiatives have been emulated by later generations of film producers seeking to actively explore opportunities for 'overseas expansion' at different keynote moments for the Japanese film industry.

Some scholars argue that Daiei's move into overseas expansion was a self-Orientalising stunt in which an exoticised and spectacular Japanese Other was constructed cinematically for a homogeneous West. Consequently, there has been an approach to the programming of Japanese films at (Western) film festivals (usually drawing on the 1950s' award winners as examples) that broadly reinforces how the festivals' selection of world cinema and recognition of cultural differences were subjected to the internal power structure of the festival system.[21] Despite their useful critique of the cultural politics underlying the festival institution itself, these insights have allowed less space for the contestation of the general essentialistic reading of Japanese cinema showcased at international festivals. Here, instead of deploying a similar framework to interrogate the superficial reception of Japanese cinema, I am thus more interested in testing other analytical approaches to festival programming and actually viewing the film festival as a site for the intricate processes of cultural translation.

Programming the New Waves

A review of the award-winning Japanese films at Cannes, Venice and other trend-setting film festivals in the post-*Rashomon* era suggests how these festivals have responded self-reflexively to the diversification, if not fragmentation, of Japanese cinema, no matter how limiting their scope and criteria of selection originally were. For instance, as indicated earlier, during the 1960s and 1970s, many top European festivals transitioned from a mode of working closely with national film industry associations such as Eiren (the Motion Picture Producers Association of Japan) to receive recommendations and scout for Japanese entries, to a more programmer-centric system. Many of these festivals shone light on the Japanese New Wave movement of the late 1950s to early 1970s by endorsing maverick film-makers such as Shindō Kaneto, Ōshima Nagisa, Hani Susumu, Teshigahara Hiroshi and Imamura Shōhei. While most *enfants terribles* of the New Wave started their career with studios such as Shōchiku, they later opted to produce films outside the studio system by starting their own independent production companies, which were closely connected to the distribution and production activities of initiatives such as the Art Theatre Guild (ATG, established in 1961). By juxtaposing these younger Japanese auteurs with established figures such as Mizoguchi Kenji and Kurosawa, international festivals were also reinforcing their edge in curating film histories and making visible, for example, the elements of continuity and rupture between Japanese studio production and independent experimentation.

Probably one of the best illustrations of European festivals' shift in focus was the so-called 'scandal' triggered in 1965 by the Berlinale's inclusion of Wakamatsu Kōji's *Secrets behind the Wall/Kabe no naka no himegoto* (1965), an independently produced soft-core porn film (*pink eiga*), in its competition section. This 'inappropriate' pink film was directly submitted to the festival through a Berlin-based agency, without going through the approval of Eiren. Its selection resulted in protests from Japan's Ministry of Foreign Affairs and the situation ended up with the collective resignation of the Berlinale's pre-selection committee.[22] To reduce the regeneration of Western festivals' programming agendas to a static assumption about the supposed pursuit of Orientalism thus risks a disavowal of the diversity and potential of Japanese cinema and an ellipsis in the discussion of critical issues that cannot be easily contained within the framework of national cinema.

To look at things from the other side of the coin, Japanese cinema has been struggling with its own decline since the 1960s, with one of the earliest major contributing factors being the 'increasing encroachment of television'.[23] There was further discouraging news throughout the 1960s and 1970s: cinema attendance fell, theatres were closed and film production plummeted. Veteran film-makers such as Kurosawa and Ōshima sought funding and production opportunities overseas. By the 1980s, leading European-American film festivals were thrilling to encounters with cinematic 'new waves' from the 'other Asias', such as those that emerged from Hong Kong (1978), South Korea (1980), Taiwan (1983) and the People's Republic of China (1984).[24] Nonetheless, Tony Rayns initiated an interest in 'new Japanese independent films' by programming the '25 Years of Japanese Cinema' strand at the Edinburgh International Film Festival in 1984.[25]

JAPANESE CINEMA: STILL ALIVE

Despite its sporadic embrace of specific Japanese titles and auteurs, the world festival circuit did not begin to celebrate Japanese emerging talent again until the 1990s, by which time Japanese cinema had entered the post-studio era. According to Mitsuyo Wada-Marciano, independent film-making 'has become the norm' since the 1990s with independent film-makers turned into 'major players',[26] an important context that I shall consider later. In other words, the three major Japanese studios, Shōchiku, Tōhō and Tōei, burdened with creative inertia and a decreasing volume of film production, now need to compete and/or collaborate with an increasingly heterogeneous independent film sector. Wada-Marciano's discussion of the 'post-studio' environment not only situates contemporary Japanese cinema within the interaction between the different sectors of the Japanese media and audio-visual industries, it also draws attention to the domestic film industry's 'impulses' towards overseas expansion. In this 'post' stage, outreach initiatives such as the coproduction and promotional deals managed at film festivals may be re-examined and tested against the new sociocultural and economic imperatives of neoliberalism and globalisation.

The year 1997 was nonetheless celebrated as a 'turning point' for the Japanese film industry.[27] Not only did Studio Ghibli's *Princess Mononoke/Mononoke hime* (1997) break domestic box-office records, there were two festival triumphs by film-makers not trained in the studio system: Kitano Takeshi walked away with the top award at Venice with his seventh feature *Hana-Bi* (1997), and the debutante film-maker Kawase Naomi's *Suzaku/Moe no suzaku* (1997) won the Caméra d'or prize at Cannes. Journalists began to speculate about the arrival of a third golden age for Japanese cinema – with the first and second golden ages being the 1930s and 1950s.[28] It is interesting to observe that despite an encouraging increase in domestic box-office returns, popular rhetoric still drew on the critical acclaim secured from the top (Western) film festivals as part of an indispensable external gaze that measured Japanese cinema's successful comeback.[29]

In his introduction to a 2011 anthology intriguingly titled 'Where Japanese Cinema is Heading', Yomota Inuhiko affirms his belief that Japanese cinema is still 'alive' against all the odds.[30] The fact that *certain* Japanese films and *certain* Japanese auteurs are programmed and endorsed by international festivals overseas today suggests as much an index of a 'living' Japanese cinema as an index of a transitioning model of the international film festival model. Contemporary festival programming has now outgrown its classical evaluative tropes, and it is telling that Japanese festival darlings such as Kurosawa Kiyoshi and Kitano Takeshi (based at his own agency, Office Kitano) have worked creatively with generic formulas to not only demonstrate an auteurist vision but also proffer innovative directions for Japanese cinema to reinvent itself. The goal here has been to better engage the domestic film market and also even inspire regional film-making in order to generate so-called pan-Asian genres such as the J-horror cycle. Kitano's debut experiment with period drama, *Zatoichi/Zatōichi* (2003), which won a Silver Lion at Venice and also became his highest grossing film, serves as an appropriate example.

International film festivals can no longer be merely idealised as Olympian arenas showcasing cultural products emblematic of an essentialised national identity. There is a need for more studies of how Japanese film professionals such as festival programmers, film-makers, distributors and producers, especially those from the independent sector, are currently working with the layered networks of contemporary film festivals as a central component of their expansion strategy. An instance epitomising Japanese independent cinema's links with the world film festival circuit in the 1990s, is the producer Sentō Takenori's *J Movie Wars* (1993–7): a *jishu eiga* series that consists of over thirty shorts and features developed and financed under Japan's first satellite television channel, WOWOW. The three-season production cycle of *J Movie Wars* concluded in 1997, the symbolic comeback year for Japanese cinema. By jumping on the *jishu eiga* bandwagon in collaboration with numerous talented film-makers from hybrid backgrounds, Sentō was also highly aware that major film festivals could potentially open up an overseas market for independent work, or at the very least the critical reputation won by the series could justify his production strategy. He thus utilised film festivals as a site of knowledge transfer to navigate his own role in connecting Japanese independent film to the global festival network.[31] Within a few years, he was able to successfully help emerging film-makers such as Aoyama Shinji and Kawase Naomi launch their auteur careers on the international film festival circuit.

REALIGNING *EIGASAI*

How do Japanese film festivals engage with the 'living organism' called 'Japanese cinema' through curatorial discourses and practices today?[32] Here, I will mainly turn to case studies of contemporary film festivals such as the Pia Film Festival and the film festivals at Yufuin, Tokyo and Yamagata. An understanding of the domestic *eigasai*'s programming practices hinges on a contextual study of their layered, dynamic interconnections with the Japanese film industry, a cinéphile-oriented film culture, and various national cultural and urban policies. Importantly, I will explore how these *eigasai* have developed as various scale-making projects connected to a set of local, regional and global film networks.

Jishu jōei: A different genealogy

Against the backdrop of Cold War tensions during the 1950s and 1960s, several national-level themed film festivals were launched by the Japanese state on top of the peripatetic AFF. These highlighted the cultural-pedagogical function of cinema under the umbrella policy of 'audio-visual education' (*shichōkaku kyōiku*) and included the Educational Film Festival (*kyōiku eigasai*), established in 1954, and the Science and Technology Film/Video Festival, launched in 1960.[33]

A crucial cultural phenomenon during this period was the diverse *jishu jōei* – independent film screenings that provided a form of grassroots-level film exhibition outside the conventional theatre system and network of commercial film exhibition and distribution. With a rich history dating back to the prewar era, and characterised by a wide spectrum of practices and agendas, the *jishu jōei* can often be conceptualised as an organic part of the *jishu eiga* movement. This commingled, independent film screening culture arguably planted the seeds for several future film festival initiatives across the country.

I want to propose two major models as a foundational framework to map out a different genealogy of Japanese *eigasai*, especially in terms of the festivals' structural layouts and programming visions. Leftist film organisations such as the Rōdōkumiai eiga kyōgikai (Labour Union Film Association) were set up in the immediate postwar period. The then flourishing democratic film movement, underscored by struggles such as the Tōhō labour dispute in 1948, sought new approaches to engage the public through the choreography of politically charged film-making with screenings aimed at social mobilisation. The establishment of the Zenkoku eiga circle kyōgikai (National Cinema Circle Association) in 1949 inspired, and laid the template for, the foundation of similar film organisations into the 1950s and 1960s. Joining forces with 'self-governing' student bodies nationwide, these activist groups also formed their own independent screening network. This highly politicised 'activist model' of the *jishu jōei* existed in parallel with a more cosmopolitan and cinéphilic model of exhibition practice spearheaded by cine-clubs and specific art spaces such as the Tokyo-based Sōgetsu Cinematheque and the ATG.[34] The Sōgetsu Art Centre (1958–71) functioned as a hub for the international exchanges of contemporary art. Its Cinematheque (1961–70) carefully curated a broad spectrum of film programmes made up of both Japanese and foreign titles; it also collaborated with foreign embassies and international film/cultural agencies to scout for suitable films. After launching the Sekai zen'ei eigasai (World Avant-garde Cinema Festival) in 1966 and the 'Underground Film Festival' in 1967, the Cinematheque initiated the first and only Sōgetsu Jikken eigaisai (Sōgetsu Experimental Film Festival) in 1967, which featured competitions, juries and awards.[35]

Both *jishu jōei* models must be understood in terms of the backdrop of the collapsing Japanese film industry.[36] Characterised by a high degree of autonomy in terms of programming and organisation, these two models differed in terms of their emphasis on social intervention and political engagement. They approached and choreographed networking between film professionals, films and spectators in a different manner – the legacies of which could still be observed in the subsequent development of public film exhibition and Japanese cinéphile culture such as the boom in mini-theatres during the 1980s. Both models noticeably played a crucial part in circulating a wide range of independent films (including fictional features, documentaries and experimental films) at a local level in response to both the rise of independent film-making and the emergence of 'amateur' film-makers who had been trying their hand at super-8 movies since the 1960s.[37] Rooted in a diverse array of art and cultural undercurrents, these two strands of *jishu* screenings would overlap, merge and generate new agendas. Some *jishu jōei* became regularly held and therefore institutionalised. Besides drafting manifestos and publishing screening-related documents, they would also routinely incorporate pedagogical sections such as talks with film-makers, film critics and scholars as side events.[38] The programming of some events became highly self-referential regarding their positioning within the nationwide networking of *jishu jōei* activities; an exhibition could inspire and cross-pollinate similar programmes, which might lay the basis for a future *eigasai*. As an example of this, a festival dedicated to experimental cinema, the Image Forum Film Festival (established in 1987) developed out of the annual Underground eiga shinsakuten (Exhibition of New Works of Underground Cinema) (1973–6) and the Experimental eigasai (Experimental Film Festival) (1981–5).[39]

The Pia Film Festival (PFF) enabled another noteworthy direction for the transition and diversification of the *jishu jōei* movement in the late 1970s. According to its current director Araki Keiko, when the PFF was founded in 1977 by the monthly listings magazine *Pia*, under the title of the Jishu seisaku eigaten (Independently produced Film Exhibition), the *jishu eiga* movement was in full swing with screenings taking place all over the country.[40] The PFF was established to showcase and discover rising (independent) film talents and innovative *jishu eiga* works that, according to Satō Tadao, also nurtured new hope for Japanese cinema at a time when professional training at film studios and so forth had become insufficient and difficult.[41] Since its inauguration, the festival has relied on submissions to its 'Call for Entries' in order to schedule its core section of 'Public Applications'. This was developed into a competition category called the PFF Award in 1988 when Tsukamoto Shin'ya became the first Grand Prix recipient for *The Adventure of Denchu-Kozo/Denchū kozō no bōken*. The PFF Award currently works in parallel with two other major sections, the 'Special Programme' and 'Screenings of Invited Works', to showcase both foreign and Japanese works. The process of generating PFF Award finalists is now undertaken by 'selection members' from various culture-related backgrounds such as the festival director (Araki herself), film-makers, journalists, writers, critics and cinema staff;

something which allows us to distinguish a specific mode of 'selection as programming'.[42]

YUFUIN, TOKYO AND YAMAGATA

Akasaki points out that the duo of trend-setting festivals originating in the 1970s, the PFF and the Yufuin Film Festival, exemplify two disparate paradigms for the programming of Japanese cinema: one is targeted at endorsing emerging *jishu eiga* work while the other is committed to themed showings of older titles.[43] These differences may also be grasped by looking at their connections to their host cities. The PFF usually kicks off by showing the PFF Award finalists in Tokyo and it then tours various programmes of selected work at major cities such as Nagoya, Kobe and Fukuoka, where local audiences also vote for the regional Audience Award. In contrast, the inaugural Yufuin festival resembled most A-list film festivals in attempting to stage the festival as an event that could brand the festival city's resources for tourism and regenerate local culture. During the 1970s and 1980s, riding high on the tide of economic growth and urban expansion, many regional city governments, as well as councils in rural towns and villages, collaborated with citizens and businesses to launch cultural events as part of a 'hometown building' (*furusatozukuri*) programme that would 'develop', or even 'invent', the unique attractions of a local place.[44]

The Yufuin Film Festival, reputed to be the country's longest-running festival, was established in Ōita, West Japan, in 1976; the host town of Yufuin is itself a famous hot-spring resort with no cinemas. The festival started as a collaboration between Yufuin's *machizukuri* or citizen-initiated, community-building group and a local cinéphile organisation, which sought to use the event to help brand and add cultural capital to the town. The festival was, however, more than the product of mere marketing fanfare. From early on, Yufuin identified itself as a platform that brought the fans of Japanese cinema and its creators together; screenings were often framed by intensive Q&A sessions and cinéphile-oriented symposia.[45] A closer look at Yufuin's screening history throughout the decades indicates that although it has conventionally highlighted studio productions, themed variously by genres, stars and directors, it hasn't turned a blind eye to innovative work and independent mavericks despite its small-sized programme.

Both film festivals in Tokyo and Yamagata were originally associated with their respective city governments' sociocultural development agendas, but the Tokyo International Film Festival (TIFF), hailed as Japan's first 'international' film festival, can also be placed in the same lineage as the preceding AFF and the one-off Japan International Film Festival of 1970, all of which attested to the major studios' and central government's shared ambition of showcasing Japan's cultural prowess on an international level (Fig. 11.2).[46] In a broader context, in the 1980s, under then-Prime Minister Nakasone Yasuhiro, Japan launched its official policy of 'internationalisation' (*kokusaika*), which was 'designed to make Japan a more internationalized country that

Fig. 11.2 Poster of Nihon International Film Festival 1970. Courtesy of Kobe Planet Film Archive.

contributes to the international community'.[47] As a satellite-event of the Expo Tsukuba 1985, the first TIFF was therefore supported by governmental bodies such as the Ministry of Foreign Affairs, the Agency for Cultural Affairs and the Ministry of International Trade and Industry (later reorganised as the Ministry of Economy, Trade and Industry, METI), a structure that has hardly changed to this day and that has literally circumscribed the festival as a state project with a vision potentially couched in nationalistic terms.

The TIFF swiftly and strategically applied for FIAPF accreditation, which lays out a set of international standards for the TIFF to grapple with, and the festival has now been firmly embedded within the hierarchy of the global festival system.[48] By its second edition in 1987, the festival had already installed an 'International Competition' category in parallel with the already existing 'Young Cinema Competition' section; both were buttressed by a generous sum of prize money. These high-profile competitions, together with the requirements for premieres, have constituted the main points of connection between the TIFF and the FIAPF's universal model. With its award incentives, the festival immediately played a pioneering role, especially in Asia, in terms of endorsing emerging international film-makers and potentially sustaining their future work on a financial basis.[49] Meanwhile, the act of joining the FIAPF has subjected Tokyo to the disadvantage of having to compete with other A-list counterparts such as Cannes, Berlin and Venice for new works by both veteran film-makers and promising talents. In addition, although the TIFF has increasingly given more curatorial attention to Asian cinemas as a way of engaging with this region, it has also been gradually outpaced by other latecomer Asian festivals which epitomise various national projects of 'being international' at Shanghai, Beijing, Busan and Taipei.

The emergence of the Yamagata International Documentary Film Festival (YIDFF) in 1989 may also be understood in the light of the *kokusaika* policy, although towards the end of 1980s Japan also started to realign its cultural exchanges with other Asian countries (Fig. 11.3).[50] The YIDFF arguably originated in the 'activist model' of *jishu jōei*, which was specifically embedded in the documentary-centred independent film movement integral to various other social movements in the late 1960s.[51] Ogawa Productions (1966–94), an independent documentary film collective revolving around the documentarist Ogawa Shinsuke, was one of the key organisations that not only produced films to engage in social struggles of the time, but also organised itinerant screenings and travelled to regional cities and towns in order to mobilise the public. In 1972, they decided to move to Magino Village, Yamagata Prefecture in Tohoku, Northeast Japan, to live together with the peasants; during their sixteen-year stay there they made seven documentaries. When the capital city of the prefecture, Yamagata, called for plans to celebrate its centennial anniversary in 1989, Ogawa proposed the idea of an international film festival of documentaries – a vision shared by a 'local media magnate', Tanaka Satoshi, who mediated between Ogawa and the local government.[52]

Today, the Yamagata festival necessarily situates itself within its nexus between the local government and citizen groups. Although the festival registered as an independently run non-profit organisation (NPO) in 2009, it still relies considerably on financial support from Yamagata city. In recent years, as the city has jumped on the 'creative city' bandwagon and utilised the film festival's prestige to brand its own cultural and tourism resources, the YIDFF has also started to assemble programmes that explore and curate Yamagata-related visual archives; these include films

Fig. 11.3 Photograph of the 1989 Yamagata International Documentary Film Festival.

that used the city as a shooting location. These themed collections have been presented in the 'Films about Yamagata' sidebar, launched in 2007. To keep the festival running, the organisers have at the same time had to generate a series of *machizukuri* agendas to mobilise local citizens and NPO groups' participation in, and support for, the festival. On the other hand, as I have indicated elsewhere, the YIDFF has also had to place itself tactically within a new festival ecology whereby other international (documentary) festivals have had to reinvent their roles as a marketplace for both completed films and projects in the pitching stage.[53] The YIDFF has followed its own course and tends to shun market initiatives and other upgrading strategies. In persistently underscoring the central role of exhibition and other cinéphile-centred events, Yamagata has, instead, developed a more localised model of the 'audience festival'.[54]

PROGRAMMING JAPANESE INDEPENDENT CINEMA IN THE POST-STUDIO ERA

As Watanabe Daisuke has suggested, Japan began to widely embrace a 'culture of entering international film festivals' (*kokusai eigasai ni dasu bunka*) in the early 2000s.[55] More specifically, independent film-makers and producers nowadays increasingly value the international festival circuit as an important interface for the development of distribution and exhibition networks. This trend may be partially framed within Japan's shifting cultural policies. In 2001, the Agency of Cultural Affairs issued the Bunka geijutsu shinkō kihonhō (Basic Act for the Promotion of Art and Culture), which, once and for all, defined film as art. This policy has laid the basis for several government-led initiatives to promote Japanese cinema with the Agency. These include setting up various subsidy programmes to encourage film (co)production; Japanese cinema's participation in overseas film festivals; the organisation of film exhibition events in Asian countries; and the cultivation of young film-makers and other film professionals (e.g. the 'New Directions in Japanese Cinema' programme).[56] These efforts have dovetailed with METI's aggressive measures since 2003 to promote the Japanese content industry and central government's ambitious manoeuvring to build Japan's 'soft power'.

Watanabe has insightfully suggested that while Yoshiharu Tezuka may believe the trend towards *kokusaika* in the post-studio era has generated new opportunities for independent film-makers and producers to engage with international markets, the paradox remains that, at the same time, this work is also undergoing a process of internalisation/localisation clearly orientated towards the domestic market and local audiences, no matter how limiting and self-sustaining these spheres of consumption might actually be. In resisting any binary division between the local and global, Watanabe suggests instead that Japanese independent films may be set in motion through a constant and dynamic set of connections and transformations between these two scales.[57] We can also locate such circulatory dynamics for independent cinema 'inside out' by looking at the scale-making strategies of Japan's own film festivals. Through their own internal programming, each *eigasai* has also leveraged a different assemblage of film networks to engage Japanese cinema, particularly when it comes to its independent sector.

The paradox for the TIFF is that it is exactly because of the fact that an international competition lies at the core of its A-list programming that the question of how to position Japanese cinema at this state-backed festival becomes most challenging. Tokyo has experimented with setting up various programmes to accommodate its Japanese entries, including the term 'classical cinema', the very inconsistency of which conveys the festival's own disorientation or inability to utilise a national cinema framework to curate 'Japan'.[58] The new millennium saw both 'Japanese Eyes' and 'Japanese Cinema Splash' being installed to accommodate and endorse independent Japanese films. With reference to Japan's new international auteurs such as Kitano, Kurosawa (Kiyoshi) and Kawase, it is telling that TIFF's A-list status still cannot guarantee a competitive edge in obtaining premieres for independent titles as such; nor can it serve as the launching pad for a younger, rising, generation of Japanese auteurs.

Although the PFF welcomes submissions regardless of the film-makers' nationalities, genres, formats or lengths, and therefore claims to be 'the most open among all the competitions in the world',[59] the festival essentially engages a pool of domestic talents (occasionally including ethnic/foreign film-makers residing in Japan) and audiences. The PFF is part of a network of connections between the forefront of Japanese independent cinema and a wide range of film festivals, at home and abroad, that share its programming orientation towards independent work and emerging film talents. Tellingly, the 2016 Berlinale Forum presented a special programme titled 'Hachimiri Madness: Japanese Indies from the Punk Years', which literally paid tribute to PFF's own exhibition history: it showcased a collection of 8mm movies produced during 1977 and 1990 by ten *jishu eiga* film-makers, many of whom debuted at Pia and have now become established international art cinema auteurs.[60] Moreover, the festival also actively participates in the production of independent films. Supported by its 'PFF partners', Pia set up a 'PFF Scholarship' as early as 1984 to annually select one film-maker from its finalists and offer her/him the financial and technical support to complete a feature film. This scholarship not only provides novice film-makers with an opportunity to enter the domestic industrial film-making milieu, it also leverages PFF's existing networking to efficiently connect young auteurs and their work to both the domestic and international film market. As evidence of Watanabe's observations on indie cinema's interest in the domestic market, after having had her debut film acclaimed at several international festivals, Tsuruoka Keiko, the recipient of the 23rd PFF Scholarship, released her sophomore feature *Lingering Memories/ Suguruhino yamaneko* (2014) mainly via a number of locally based mini-theatres.

Although the YIDFF may be short of a marketplace that directly funds and trades documentary projects, the festival has nonetheless provided a rare and indispensable platform for Japanese independent documentaries to engage their audiences, given the fact that there are actually very few exhibition channels for documentary cinema within Japan.[61] Crucially, through its own 'Perspective Japan' programme and other special strands, the YIDFF has managed a new and multilayered history of Japanese documentary cinema. Yamagata's programming also seeks to contest any essentialised reading of Japanese national cinema. By repeatedly returning to the events, people and locales that are cautiously discussed, or intentionally repressed, in contemporary Japanese society, such as World War II and imperialism, the Okinawan issue, the Zainichi Koreans and the aftermath of Fukushima's triple disasters, the festival performs its own kind of cinematic ritual to conjure the spectre of Japanese modern history and problematise any nationalistic rhetoric that sanitises and totalises the articulation of history and nation. Finally, we should also locate the YIDFF within a network of other emerging domestic documentary festivals such as Tokyo's Za-Koenji Documentary Film Festival (established 2010) and the Kobe Documentary Film Festival (established 2009) as well as other Asian festivals that aggressively programme digitally produced documentaries such as South Korea's DMZ International Documentary Film Festival (established 2009); the Cinema Digital Seoul Film Festival (Seoul, 2007–12); the Taiwan International Documentary Film Festival (Taipei, established 1998); the Yunnan Multicultural Visual Festival (or Yunfest, Kunming, PRC, established 2003); and the China Documentary Film Festival (Beijing, established 2003, merged into the Beijing Independent Film Festival in 2012). Not only have the programming ideals and practices of these festivals been greatly inspired by the YIDFF, they also constitute various nodes and surfaces through which Asian (independent) documentaries can travel transnationally in this region, as the nexus between the YIDFF and Yunfest has testified.[62]

EPILOGUE

In 2008, the national alliance of non-industrial film exhibition bodies, the Japan Community Cinema Center (established 2003; hereafter JCCC), paid particular attention to Japan's festival phenomenon and sought to archive and classify domestic film festivals in terms of their history, levels of internationalisation, geographical scope and overall purpose.[63] The JCCC has now drawn a clear distinction between the international (*kokusai*) and the local (*chiiki*) film festival. Such categorisation aims to frame film festivals within certain quantitative indexes so that the latter can secure policy and financial support from various levels of government and other local bodies.

Despite these issues, this chapter has also endeavoured to rethink discourses that variously reduce any sense of the dynamic links between the local and global, rely on oversimplified statistics and specifications, and pay no attention to the complexity and contingency of scale-making at domestic festivals. Through the perspective of film programming, this study has situated itself at the juncture of two strands of movement. One strand concerns the circulatory dynamics of contemporary Japanese cinema, specifically those of independent films. Another foregrounds Japanese *eigasai* as 'sites of friction' where a local exhibition culture engages with the seemingly universal festival ideals and practices laid down in the FIAPF accreditation criteria and applies the influential models set up at prestigious European film festivals in a number of inconsistent ways. One instance of this may be that although the aforementioned Nagoya mini-theatre 'film festival' is out of sync with any international festival template, its own programming agenda has grown out of this particular mini-theatre's historical affiliation with the national cine-club boom in the 1970s, rather than of any empty aspiration to simply copy international trends. While I do not intend to flatten the epistemological specificity of the term 'film festival' and argue that any self-labelled festival should be studied as such, I have shed light on how Japan's vernacular articulations and practices regarding *eigasai* have meaningfully enriched, redefined and even contested the international film festival model.

More specifically, in referring to Tsing's suggestion that scale 'must be brought into being' and even 'claimed and contested in cultural and political projects',[64] I have also emphasised how various case studies have devised programming that articulates and generates several different dimensions in the circulation and exhibition of Japanese cinema. It is through the exhibition mechanisms and channels of a film festival, a mini-theatre or even *jishu jōei* that Japanese independent film projects have travelled and thus established connections with other film networks on a local, national, regional (Asian or East Asian) and global scale.

These scale-making efforts are embedded within a wide range of converging, and sometimes competing, projects concerning localism, nationalism, regionalism and even globalism. This all underscores the fact that these festivals function as significant sociopolitical, economical and cultural undertakings. Here we might wish to review the claim to various scales that I have referred to throughout my case studies. I have understood localism as a fundamental cultural, and thus ideological, commitment to a local area (such as Tohoku) and a city or town (such as Yamagata, or Yufuin). Localism connects with the local polity, its economic and social affiliations, and also multiple communities and interest groups such as citizens' *machizukuri* groups. Despite its indirect link with nationalistic ideas, the term 'nationalism' here mainly underlies how festivals accommodate a series of projects intersecting with the shifting state of cultural policies and the development of a national film industry and film culture that somehow revolves around the leitmotif of the revitalisation of Japanese cinema. The notion of regionalism is associated with claims made to the region of Asia. As far as Japanese film festivals are concerned, they are often tied up with local and/or national policies that seek to redefine Japan's position in relation to its East Asian and South East Asian neighbours. Nevertheless, through mechanisms such as programming, funding and pedagogical initiatives, Japanese festivals have also channelled their inter-Asia connections with film-makers, films and film cultures in ways that can not be simply framed by state diplomatic agendas.

Finally, however crucial a part it currently plays in the global film festival system, the film festival/*eigasai* is necessarily place-based and local-specific. No matter how locally oriented or marginally positioned it is, no festival can be isolated from the flow of films or the encounter with globally travelling concepts and practices regarding the operation and curation of festivals. The claims to the global that an *eigasai* makes are never singular. We need to challenge any facile supposition about a commitment to facilitating the flow of films, capital, technologies and discourses. In turn, we should further interrogate the direction, velocity and intensity of such movement at various geopolitical levels. If neoliberalism has become the globalist project *par excellence* for film festivals worldwide to grapple with today, we still need to look at how this vision is articulated and located at a specific festival in close relation to the particular cultural economies and politics of the city and region. I have given two examples. As an instance of the Japanese government's eagerness to place itself within the regional/global terrain of the cultural and content industries, the TIFF has now 'significantly morphed into a contents market' since the early 2000s in 'constructing the nation for foreign consumption'.[65] On the other hand, in not readily associating itself with film markets and funding schemes, which increasingly characterise major international (documentary) festivals, the YIDFF has tried to resist the allure of a festival model that merely seeks to justify and emphasise a festival's economic value. With this said, a neoliberal logic still arguably underlines Yamagata's recent strategy to promote and address the city's urban regeneration plans and Tohoku's cultural identity. Whether this is a good idea or not, remains to be seen.

ACKNOWLEDGMENT

The research for this chapter has been supported by JSPS KAKENHI Grant Number 15K16665.

Notes

1. In the tradition of *jishu eiga*, individual film-makers often rely on resources and alternative networks outside the studio system (namely the majors) to finance, produce, exhibit and circulate their own works. See Jasper Sharp, 'JISHU EIGA', in Jasper Sharp (ed.), *Historical Dictionary of Japanese Cinema* (Lanham, MD: Scarecrow Press, 2011), pp. 111–13.
2. The Japanese term *eigasai* literally integrates both *eiga* (cinema) and *sai* (or *matsuri*, as both festival and celebration).
3. Akasaki Yōko, 'Eigasai towa nanka', in Community cinema shien center (ed.), *Eigasai to community cinema nikansuru chōsa* (Tokyo: Community cinema shien center, 2008), pp. 54–67. According to Kenji Iwamoto, whereas the *katsudō shashin tenrankai* only took place once in 1921, he gives examples of several cinema and cinema culture-related one-off exhibitions (*tenrankai*) that were organised by the state government between the 1930s and 1950s. See Iwamoto Kenji, 'Eiga tenrankai no kiseki to eiga hakubutsukan e no yume', in Kawasakishi Shimin Museum (ed.), *Eiga seitan hyakunen hakurankai: Cinema no seiki* (Kawasaki: Kawasakishi shimin museum, 1995), pp 8–13.
4. See Sangjoon Lee, 'The Emergence of the Asian Film Festival: Cold War Asia and Japan's Reentrance to the Regional Film Industry in the 1950s', in Daisuke Miyao (ed.), *The Oxford Handbook of Japanese Cinema* (Oxford: Oxford University Press: 2014), pp. 226–44. Michael Baskett, 'Japan's Film Festival Diplomacy in Cold War Asia', *The Velvet Light Trap* no. 73 (Spring 2014), pp. 4–18. AFF became what is now known as the Asia-Pacific Film Festival.
5. See Akasaki, 'Eigasai towa nanika', pp. 54–67. An updated list of *eigasai* compiled by the Nihon Eiga Broadcasting Corp could be traced at <http://cinemaga.nihon-eiga.com/filmfestivals-2015/list/>.
6. Marijke de Valck, 'Finding Audiences for Films: Programming in Historical Perspective', in Jeffrey Ruoff (ed.), *Coming Soon to a Festival near You: Programming Film Festivals* (St. Andrews: St. Andrew Film Studies, 2012), p. 26.
7. Marijke de Valck, *Film Festivals: From European Geopolitics to Global Cinephilia* (Amsterdam: University of Amsterdam Press, 2007), p. 167.
8. Valck, 'Finding Audiences', pp. 34–7.
9. See Jeffrey Ruoff, 'Introduction', in Ruoff, *Coming Soon to a Festival near You*, pp. 1–21.
10. Altogether, there have been fifteen festivals accredited to FIAPF's A-list film festival category, currently known under the term, 'Competitive Feature Film Festivals'. For accreditation, the organisation has established sets of requirements regarding a festival's organisational structure (e.g. the inclusion of an international competition with an international jury) and premieres.
11. Anna Lowenhaupt Tsing, *Friction: An Ethnography of Global Connection* (Princeton, NJ: Princeton University Press, 2005).
12. Ibid., p. 57.
13. ANT has been developed in the social sciences and emphasises the agency of both human and non-human actors within the network, something that in turn defines and offers substance to the actors. In film festival studies, scholars such as Thomas Elsaesser and Marijke de Valck have deployed ANT in tandem

with other social theories on flows and systems to construct the theoretical model of a film festival 'network', which is used to address the complexity of the festival system. In the network, 'film professionals, films, and accreditation systems equally have agency'. See Skadi Loist, 'The Film Festival Circuit: Network, Hierarchies, and Circulation', in Marijke de Valck, Brendan Kredell and Skadi Loist (eds), *Film Festivals: History, Theory, Method, Practice* (London: Routledge 2016), p. 50.
14. Mitsuyo Wada-Marciano, *Japanese Cinema in the Digital Age* (Honolulu: University of Hawai'i Press, 2012), p. 51.
15. Iwamoto Kenji, 'Nihon eiga no kaigai shinshutsu ganbō to jittai', in Iwamoto Kenji (ed.), *Nihon eiga no kaigai shinshutsu: Bunka senryaku no rekishi* (Tokyo: Shinwasha, 2015), pp. 13–38.
16. See, for example, Yoshiharu Tezuka, *Japanese Cinema Goes Global: Filmworkers' Journeys* (Hong Kong: Hong Kong University Press, 2012); Lee, 'The Emergence of the Asian Film Festival'; Koga Futoshi, 'Rashōmon no jushō to sonogo: Stramigioli Giuliana o chūshin ni', in Iwamoto, *Nihon eiga no kaigai shinshutsu*, pp. 273–304.
17. See Aaron Gerow, 'Narrating the Nation-ality of a Cinema', in Alan Tansman (ed.), *The Culture of Japanese Fascism* (Durham, NC: Duke University Press, 2009), p. 189; Aaron Gerow, 'Retrospective Irony: Film Festivals and Japanese Cinema History', in Alex Marlow-Mann (ed.), *Archival Film Festivals* (St. Andrews: St. Andrews Film Studies, 2013), pp. 189–99.
18. Gerow, 'Narrating the Nation-ality of a Cinema', pp. 185–211.
19. Tezuka, *Japanese Cinema Goes Global*, p. 42. [Editors' note: for more on film festivals and Nagata Masaichi, see also Chapter 36 by Stephanie DeBoer and Chapter 39 by Yoshiharu Tezuka in this volume.]
20. Baskett, 'Japan's Film Festival Diplomacy in Cold War Asia', pp. 7–8.
21. See Tezuka, *Japanese Cinema Goes Global*, pp. 52–3.
22. Kusabe Kyūshirō, *Sekai no eigasai o yuku* (Tokyo: Mainichi shinbunsha, 1999), pp. 19–21.
23. David Desser, *Eros Plus Massacre: An Introduction to the Japanese New Wave Cinema* (Bloomington: Indiana University Press, 1988), p. 8.
24. Inuhiko Yomota, 'Stranger than Tokyo: Space and Race in Postnational Japanese Cinema', in Jenny Kwok Wah Lau (ed.), *Multiple Modernities: Cinemas and Popular Media in Transcultural East Asia* (Philadelphia, PA: Temple University Press, 2002), p. 78. Symbolically, Yomota is singling out years when early significant 'New Wave' films were produced in Hong Kong, South Korea, Taiwan and the People's Republic of China (e.g. Chen Kaige's *Yellow Earth* [1984]).
25. Tezuka, *Japanese Cinema Goes Global*, pp. 106–7.
26. Wada-Marciano, *Japanese Cinema in the Digital Age*, p. 14. Box-office revenues for the major companies still outperformed those by the independents.
27. Wada-Marciano, *Japanese Cinema in the Digital Age*, p. 12. Also see Yomota Inuhiko, *Nihon Eigashi 110-nen* (Tokyo: Shūeisha, 2014), pp. 224–5.
28. Yomota, 'Stranger than Tokyo', p. 77.
29. See Wada-Marciano, *Japanese Cinema in the Digital Age*, pp. 12–13.
30. See Yomota Inuhiko, 'Futatabi iu, eiga wa ikimonono kiroku dearu', in Kurosawa Kiyoshi, Yoshimi Shun'ya, Yomota Inuhiko and Lee Bong-Ou (eds), *Nihon eiga wa ikiteiru*, vol. 8, *Nihon eiga wa dokomade ikuka* (Tokyo: Iwanami shoten, 2011), pp. 1–3.
31. Sentō Takenori, *Movie Wars: Zero karahajimeta producer kokutōki* (Tokyo: Nikkei business jin bunko, 1998), pp. 118–19, 130–6.
32. Yomota, 'Futatabi iu', pp. 1–3.
33. Murayama Kyōichirō, 'Hi-shōgyō jōei no rekishi: Sengo no keimō undō kara community cinema made', *Eiga jōei katsudō nenkan 2004* (Tokyo: UNIJAPAN, 2005), pp. 14–15.
34. Ibid., p. 17.
35. The repercussions of the events of May 1968 that interrupted Cannes resonated at Tokyo in 1969. A group of protesters and activists boycotted and successfully forced the cancellation of the Sōgetsu-based Film Art Festival, a festival that tried to synchronise the development of Japanese film culture and individual film-making with European-American trends.
36. Murayama, 'Hi-shōgyō jōei no rekishi', p. 18.
37. See Satō Tadao, *Nihon eigashi*, vol. 3 (Tokyo: Iwanami shoten, 1995).
38. Murayama, 'Hi-shōgyō jōei no rekishi', p. 17.
39. See Image Forum website, <http://imageforumfestival.com/bosyu2016/>.
40. Minagawa Chika, 'Special Interview: PFF (Pia Film Festival) Director Araki Keiko', *Kinema junpō* no. 1567 (2010), pp. 162–4.
41. Satō, *Nihon eigashi*, vol. 3, p. 312.
42. Taking the 37th PFF in 2015 as an example, sixteen 'selection members' worked to shortlist 44 films from 577 submissions in the first round. These were then

entered in a second round, at which point every selector would view all the entries for the first time. The second round this year agreed a line-up of twenty films. Apart from the audience awards, a different group of juries decided the final recipients of a variety of prizes, including the Grand Prix.

43 Akasaki, 'Eigasai towa nanka', pp. 61–2.
44 Schnell Scott, *The Rousing Drum: Ritual Practice in a Japanese Community* (Honolulu: University of Hawai'i Press, 1999), p. 271.
45 Ha Sena, Horie Mariko and Mori Takehiro, 'A Study on Social Innovations of Film Festivals: Comparative Studies of Yufuin Cinema Festival, Pusan International Film Festival and Tokyo International Film Festival', *Waseda daigaku daigakuin shakai kagaku kenkyūka toshi kyojū kankyō ron* (January 2011), pp. 1–17.
46 Morioka Michio, 'Eiga sai no jūchin ga kataru, real na eiga saishi!: Nihon kokusai eigasai kara Tokyo kokusai eigasai e', <http://2014.tiff-jp.net/news/ja/?p=17859>. Akasaki has regarded the one-off 1970 Osaka International Film Festival (Japan International Film Festival), launched as a side event of the 1970 Osaka World Expo, as a precedent in founding an 'authentic' (*honkakuteki*) *eigasai* in Japan. See Akasaki, 'Eigasai towa nanka'.
47 Kadosh Otmazgin Nissim, 'Geopolitics and Soft Power: Japan's Cultural Policy and Cultural Diplomacy in Asia', *Asia-Pacific Review* vol. 19 no. 1 (2012), p. 49.
48 See Note 10.
49 See Murakawa Hide, *Kokusai eigasai e no shōtai* (Tokyo: Maruzen books, 1999), pp. 198–9; Morioka, 'Eigasai no jūchin ga kataru'.
50 Nissim, 'Geopolitics and Soft Power', p. 50.
51 Hata Ayumi, 'Undō no media o koete: 1970 zengo no shakai undō to jishu kiroku eiga', in Fujiki Hideaki (ed.), *Kankyaku eno approach* (Tokyo: Shinwasha, 2011), pp. 385–411.
52 Abé Mark Nornes, 'Yamagata-Asia-Europe: The International Film Festival Short-Circuit', in Daisuke Miyao (ed.), *The Oxford Handbook of Japanese Cinema* (Oxford: Oxford University Press, 2014), pp. 245–62. [Editors' note: see also Chapter 26 by Ayumi Hata in this volume.]
53 Ma Ran, 'Mapping Asian Documentary Film Festivals since 1989: Small Histories and Splendid Connections', *Senses of Cinema* no. 76 (September 2015), <http://sensesofcinema.com/2015/documentary-in-asia/asian-documentary-film-festivals/>.
54 See Fujioka Asako, 'Sekai kara mita Yamagata: Toma san to Wang san no kasōdanwa', in Tohoku bunka kenkyū center (eds), *Tohokugaku*, vol. 2, *Nichijō o toru!: Yamagata kokusai documentary eigasai* (Yamagata: Tohoku geijutsu kōka daigaku Tohoku bunka kenkyū center, 2013), pp. 93–8; Nornes, 'The International Film Festival Short-Circuit'.
55 Watanabe Daisuke, 'Global ka jidai no naka no independent eiga: Sono "kokusaisei" towa nanika', in Iwamoto, *Nihon eiga no kaigai shinshutsu*, p. 367.
56 See the official site of the Agency, <http://www.bunka.go.jp/seisaku/geijutsubunka/eiga/>. Currently, it is Japan Arts Council's Japan Arts Fund that annually funds a selective number of domestic film festivals. In 2017, major revisions were made to the 2001 Act under the new framework of the Basic Act for the Culture and the Arts (*bunka geijutsu suishin kihon keikaku*), see <http://www.bunka.go.jp/english/policy/foundations/basic_act.html>.
57 Watanabe, 'Global ka jidai no naka', pp. 371–2.
58 Throughout its twenty-eight editions up to 2015, the TIFF has tried, through various programmes, to stay tuned to the latest developments of Japanese cinema. Since 1995, the 'Nippon Cinema Classics' sidebar has been inconsistently deployed to showcase Japanese classics from the studio production era.
59 Refer to the PFF website, <http://pff.jp/english/about/>.
60 Refer to the Berlinale 2016 online festival brochure, <https://www.berlinale.de/media/pdf_word/service_7/66_ifb/programmbroschueren/Forum_2016.pdf>.
61 Asako Fujioka, 'Some Notes on Independent Documentaries in Japan', in Jan H.C. Yu and Asian Documentary Network (eds), *Asian Documentary Today* (Busan: Busan International Film Festival, 2012), pp. 153–67.
62 See Ma Ran, 'Asian Documentary Connections, Scale-Making, and the Yamagata International Documentary Film Festival (YIDFF)', *Transnational Cinemas* vol. 9 no. 2 (2017), pp. 1–17.
63 See Akasaki, 'Eigasai towa nanka', pp. 63–7.
64 Tsing, *Friction*, p. 57.
65 Gerow, 'Retrospective Irony', p. 193.

12

STARDOM
Queer resonance: The stardom of Miwa Akihiro

Yuka Kanno

Miwa Akihiro is omnipresent in the Japanese media landscape. From popular magazines to television shows, radio programmes and theatre, his integration within Japan's everyday culture is impeccable enough to make his gender look almost irrelevant. And yet, many also remember Maruyama Akihiro, his name before he changed it to Miwa Akihiro in 1971, as an outlandish young boy singing at the French-inspired chanson club 'Gin-pari' in the early 1950s. While his extraordinary beauty and voice became legendary, making Miwa the object of admiration among the club's clientele of intellectuals, writers and artists, including Edogawa Ranpo and Mishima Yukio, his reputation soon moved rapidly beyond metropolitan cultural circles to nationwide fame with the success of 'Meke meke (méqué méqué)', a 1957 cover of the French song written by Charles Aznavour.

Miwa's voice, however, was not the only reason for his extreme popularity. Wearing frills, tight pants and lipstick on stage, his visual style clearly deviated from the gender norms of the time.[1] One can glimpse the visual register of this ambiguous gender crossing in films such as *The Betrothed/Nagasugita haru* (1957), *Warm Current/Danryū* (1957), *To Be a Woman/Onna dearu koto* (1958) and *Black Lizard/Kurotokage* (1968). All of these features presented Miwa as a singer with an alluringly feminine image. And yet, in a rejection of the female impersonator label, Miwa himself used to refer to his fashion sense as 'neutral'. In terms of both image and voice, Miwa's gender performance challenges the dichotomous logic of being either 'female' or 'male'.

Pascal-Alex Vincent's documentary film, *Miwa: A Japanese Icon* (2011), marked the performer's return to the international stage via the gay and lesbian film festival circuit nearly thirty years after his initial introduction to the US. The film places the inconsistency of Miwa's gender, sex and sexuality at the heart of the seductive image of this 'Japanese icon'.[2] Today, Miwa still retains this camp profile with an international image that mainly, but not exclusively, circulates through global LGBT film culture.

This gap between Miwa's international reception as a camp film star and his national reputation as a queerly ungendered figure is telling. Miwa Akihiro is a star who can neither be contained within the notions of camp and gay, nor within a more nationally specific cultural tradition of female impersonation such as the kabuki tradition of the *onnagata*. Rather, it is within this consistent refusal of compulsory categorisation, informed by heteronormative orders and rules, that we should locate his queerness more precisely.

In this chapter, I will discuss the stardom of Miwa Akihiro and, in turn, demonstrate how star studies as a field still operates on a dual-gender system thus making it difficult to fully consider the complex intersections of gender performance, sexual identification and desires embodied by his own star persona. By exploring Miwa's fame in the specific historical and cultural context of the 1950s through to the early 1970s, I hope to interrogate the ways in which his queer persona was shaped in relation to the dominant mode of heterosexual masculinity of the period.

In particular, I want to emphasise the critical role played by the Tokyo district of Shinjuku during the 1960s in the formation of Miwa's queer stardom. The conjuncture of culture and politics over this period can best be grasped by the notion of 'resonance'; a term I deploy to refer to the ways in which heterogeneous media, genres and styles may reverberate off one another in order to create intersectional dynamics across culture and politics. Miryam Sas likewise explains the artistic impulses surrounding Shinjuku in the same period by using the terms 'senses' and 'waves', both of which point to the 'numerous overlaps and personal connections between individuals involved in post-*shingeki* theatre, dance, cinema' and 'the intersection and deliberate combination of artistic productivity in multiple media'.[3] By exploring the notion of resonance in Miwa's stardom, I seek to expand this idea of 'interlocking networks of collaborators' beyond just the realm of art practice.

By deploying queer and feminist theory, while drawing simultaneously on the work of film historians on the Japanese star system, this chapter will thus attempt to read the queer meanings of Miwa Akihiro within the broader context of the history of Japanese film stardom. In particular, my reading critically rethinks the gender binary as a persistently dominant mode of analysis and consider what the term 'queer' can mean in the context of Japanese film history as a whole.

ONNAGATA AND THE BIRTH OF THE ACTRESS

Star studies remains one of the most vital areas of debate in film studies for, as the term 'star vehicle' suggests, stars have been one of the most consistent driving pleasures of film viewing. Conversely, films occupy a privileged place in the formation of a star's image, among other forms of related media. Edgar Morin's influential 1957 book, *Les Stars*, included a number of concepts and viewpoints of critical relevance to contemporary star studies. As Martin Shingler points out, topics such as the religious nature of star worship, the importance of publicity and merchandising, the mechanism of identification, and the relations between stars and characters and stars and audiences have all remained fundamental questions in the field.[4] Drawing on, yet departing from, previous discourses by Francesco Alberoni, Barry King, Edgar Morin and Richard Schickel, among others, Richard Dyer combined sociological and semiotic approaches to examine stars as both a social phenomenon and a set of images and signs. Dyer's *Stars* (1979) and *Heavenly Bodies* (1986) paved the field of star studies as we know it today. Building on Dyer's concern with star image and the idea of the star as text, subsequent developments have emphasised the historical and cultural contexts in which star images may be received and used. Such a dynamic, yet accurate, approach to the relations between sexuality, stardom and society has inspired my own thinking about how the complex intersection between gender and sexuality in Miwa's stardom was shaped in relation to the specific historical and cultural conditions of Shinjuku in the 1960s.

Japanese cinema, in its nascent stage, was under the strong influence of the theatre, whose convention of the *onnagata* (the male performer playing female roles) was also adapted to the screen. The shift in the 1920s from the *onnagata* to *joyū* (female actress playing female roles) marked a turning point in the domestic star system with the supposed desire for a 'real' female body often being used to explain this transition.[5] As Mishima Yukio and Fukasaku Kinji claim, Miwa Akihiro's stardom can thus be seen in this context as a ghostly return to, or modernisation of, an earlier theatrical tradition.

From the 1920s onwards, discourse on film stars in Japan historically involved a broad range of perspectives from various sexologists, film directors, critics and scholars.[6] It is not surprising that so many writers embraced film stardom as their object of analysis if we consider the ways in which the creation of stars was inseparable from the nation's modernisation. Stars as a social phenomenon thus simultaneously shaped, and were shaped by, the experience of modernity however unevenly experienced, and at the core of such experience lay the issue of gender and sexuality. Japan went through a variety of 'modern' experiences in the early twentieth century: aggressive imperialism, World War I, massive industrialisation, urbanisation in the 1910s, and the formation of mass culture, a new middle class and the trend of *ero guro nansensu* in the 1920s; all profoundly tied to contradictory movements.[7] On the one hand, gender and sexual divisions and normalisation were promoted as critical to the formation of Japan as a colonial power and advanced nation. On the other hand, this was also the era of the 'feminisation' of men and the 'masculinisation' of women – what Ronald Roden calls 'gender ambivalence'.[8]

The shift from the *onnagata* to the actress took place within this social milieu in accordance with the power of the American film industry and the cultural hegemony of which the US model of a star system was part. In *Making Personas*, for example, Hideaki Fujiki provides a comprehensive historical analysis of the formation of Japanese film stardom in the 1910s through to the 1930s by showing how it was deeply embedded within the American representational system.[9] Fujiki locates the replacement of the *onnagata* with actresses in Japanese cinema as a major incentive in the reconfiguration of the domestic star system.

The *onnagata*, or male actor in a female role in kabuki theatre, originated in the seventeenth century and became conceived as an ideal form of femininity not as expressed by the biologically sexed body but by bodily performance in terms of gesture, costume and behaviour. In *Acting Like a Woman in Modern Japan*, Ayako Kano describes how the definition of being a woman and what constituted an ideal feminine beauty shifted in the modern period from performance to the physical body:

> In the 1910s, the popularization of cinema … contributed to a shift in focus: cinematic close-ups of *onnagata* drew attention to body parts hitherto concealed through movement and distance, such as a prominent Adam's apple and bony hands. The visibility of the *onnagata*'s body contributed to the *onnagata*'s downfall: no longer disguised through clothing, movement, and distance, he lost the ability to achieve an ideal feminine beauty and was replaced by the actress, whose body now became the privileged sign of womanhood.[10]

The use of *onnagata* continued into the 1920s, but the desire for 'real' women and their bodies eventually drove it away. It is true to say that the *onnagata* and Miwa have both shared an enthusiastic female fan base, but what could be the pleasure for women to watch femininity being performed as merely a type, idea or technique? Miwa's rise to prominence poses this unsettling question. Today, Miwa's public persona has changed to being that of a maternal figure whose predominantly female followers eagerly await her advice. Although this may not be the same as the 'mutual imitation' between *onnagata* and female fans, discussed by Maki Morinaga, such an intimate relationship between Miwa and her female audience certainly merits attention.[11]

As mentioned earlier, Miwa's screen performance has largely been described in terms of 'drag' and 'camp' on the LGBT film festival circuit as well as by American film critics; something that can probably be attributed to Miwa's out homosexuality.[12] In her seminal work, *Mother Camp*, Esther Newton describes drag and camp as expressive performing roles that specialise in 'transformation' in the context of the 'gay world'.[13] Newton distinguishes drag and camp by describing the former as being concerned with 'masculine-feminine transformation' and the latter with 'a philosophy of transformation and incongruity'. In contrast to the notion of drag being seen in terms of a homosexual male who dresses in female attire, something relatively easily defined by the author, Newton seems to have much more difficulty in explaining what exactly camp is, and thus tries to pin it down as a type of strategy, ethos, style or taste. Although incongruity, theatricality and humour, the three key features of camp elaborated upon by Newton, certainly define Miwa's star performances, I find it more accurate to refer to the notion of 'camp-as-critique', as conceptualised by Moe Mayer.[14] According to Mayer, Camp gains its political validity through an ontological critique, and it functions to produce 'queer social visibility'.[15] Not merely a style or sensibility, as detailed in previous writing by Susan Sontag, Andrew Ross and Richard Dyer, among many others, Mayer insists on both the political and critical potential of camp, whose performative practices and strategies directly enact a queer social visibility.[16] Miwa's performance is not simply a matter of style or sensitivity, it provides, as I hope to show, a fundamental critique of the trinity of the sexed body, gender and sexuality. In this sense, Miwa's indeterminate queerness scrutinises the 'either or' logic underlying the rigid sex-gender system in Japan and the US.

MALE STARDOM OF THE 1950S AND 1960S

Miwa's rise to stardom as a singer coincided with the dominance of male stars in Japanese cinema from the late 1950s onwards, the peak and subsequent decline of the Japanese film industry, and the gradual disappearance of film actresses from the silver screen.

Often referred to as 'the second golden age', the 1950s is known as the heyday of Japanese cinema. Kurosawa Akira and Mizoguchi Kenji both gained recognition beyond the domestic audience from various prestigious international film festivals. The conjunction of international and critical acclaim and the popularity of more domestically marketed films, saw the Japanese film industry enjoying its highest ever box office in 1958. It was also the time that Nikkatsu started producing the 'Sun Tribe' (*taiyōzoku*) films, with Ishihara Yūjirō representing a new type of male film star in postwar Japan. Starring in *Season of the Sun/Taiyō no kisetsu* (1956) and *Crazed Fruit/Kurutta kajitsu* (1956), Yūjirō, with his tall and strong physicality, marked a clear difference from the docile corporeality of his predecessors.

Given the historical specificity of Japan's postwar situation, film historians have pointed out the crucial role played by Yūjirō's body in the rebuilding of Japanese masculinity as part of the recovery from the 'defeat' of the war and subsequent US occupation. Isolde Standish, for instance, argues that the Sun Tribe films depicted gender boundaries and their transgressions as the central motivation for conflict.[17] During the 1950s, the explosive young and athletic body of Yūjirō represented a hetero-masculinity, a type of masculinity that both appropriated and violated the female body and subjectivity. Following Yūjirō was Takakura Ken, the biggest yakuza star of the 1960s and 1970s. Yakuza films produced by the Tōei Studios remained the most popular and profitable domestic genre throughout the 1970s. Various writers have discussed the contradictions inherent in the popularity of such reactionary and quasi-feudalist narratives among those engaged in the leftist and student movements of the time. Along with such narrative lure, these films attracted an ardent body of male spectators; at the core of such spectatorial pleasure Takakura's body embraced what Ayako Saitō has described as 'an erotic dynamism inscribed in the about-to-explode body'.[18] Takakura's narrative positioning and visual construction as 'a man among men' worked, in fact, to endow a certain kind of homoerotic pleasure for spectators. Such desire and identification as part of the extreme popularity of Tōei yakuza films in the 1960s and 1970s suggests the idea that a supposedly hetero-male form of spectatorship may not always be straight.[19]

So, where were the female stars in this era of male stardom? With the decline of the Japanese film industry, their roles gradually began to diminish and many were pushed into television. The film historian Satō Tadao has noted that the main roles sought by the Japanese film industry in the 1960s were 'the mistress of the gangster for the action film, the docile yakuza's wife or his fierce female counterpart, or the shameless hussy who matched the men in rough male-dominated dramas'.[20] One could also add two more types: the woman who ended up abandoned or dead after being trifled with or raped, and the 'pure' woman, who acted as a foil to Satō's tough woman. With the disappearance of the film starlet and a mass exodus of women to the small screen, what followed, in the 1970s, was a transformation of film stars into television idols.

The yakuza genre nevertheless produced a female counterpart, the most well known being the *Red Peony Gambler* series (1968–72) staring Fuji Junko. Its precursor, however, was the *Woman Gambler* series (1966–71) starring the ice queen Enami Kyōko and female gambler films subsequently experienced a boom in the 1970s. In one of the series, *The Woman Gambler's Challenges/Onna tobakushi tsubokurabe* (1970), Miwa Akihiro co-starred with Enami as a female gambler, and the film contrasts Enami's vengeful determination with Miwa's merciful maturity, especially in the competition scene, which is the high point of the drama. In addition to Miwa's previous femme fatale characters in *Black Lizard/Kuro tokage* (1968) and *Black Rose Mansion/Kurobara no yakata* (1969), *The Woman Gambler's Challenges* added the figure of a compassionate woman, an image that remains a crucial aspect of the appeal of Miwa's star persona today.

These series of female yakuza films also had a number of elements that disturbed the gender order. On both a narrative and visual level, female gamblers engaged in the same violent and vengeful acts hitherto considered by the coding of the genre to be highly masculine. The series also catapulted their actresses into an unprecedented level of female stardom within the orbit of Tōei's male star factory.[21] Fuji Junko and Enami Kyōko proved that they were capable of things supposedly only 'a man among men' could do. Within this specific historical juncture, Miwa thus existed as a doubly perverse figure capable of overturning audience expectations of what constituted a gendered performance. At a time in which the very idea of the traditional film actress was on the wane, Miwa's presence provided a transgressive shimmer, flickering in and out of the fading light of Japanese female film stardom as a whole.

BLACK LIZARD AND BLACK ROSE MANSION

Black Lizard and *Black Rose Mansion* were the two films that came to define Miwa's film stardom. In both, his earlier personas as singer and stage actor coalesced into one inimitable cinematic presence.

Black Lizard, directed by Fukasaku Kinji, was based on Mishima Yukio's stage adaptation of a novel by Edogawa Ranpo (Fig. 12.1). The film is literally a star vehicle for Miwa Akihiro, around whom the central narrative and visual pleasures are organised. Miwa plays the character of Black Lizard, a notorious female jewel thief who tries to kidnap the daughter of a rich jeweller in order to obtain a precious diamond. Black Lizard loves collecting beautiful things and indulges herself in luxurious stones and the beautiful young men and women she turns into 'human dolls'. Throughout the film, Black Lizard and Akechi, the detective hired by a jeweller, work to outwit each other, and in so doing, develop a kind of mutual understanding and even intimacy.

The film opens with Miwa appearing as a mysterious woman at a secret club. Here again, Miwa's

Fig. 12.1 *Black Lizard/Kurotokage* (Fukasaku Kinji, 1968, Shōchiku).

striking display of femininity is immediately followed by his voice whose trembling and dramatic quality carries an emotional gravity. As is the case with *Black Rose Mansion* as well, visuality and vocality always supplement each other in Miwa's performances, thus disturbing the perception of any rigid gender binary.

Black Lizard elicits a multilayered queer intimacy. In the first encounter with Sanae, the daughter of the jeweller, Black Lizard/Miwa fixes her eyes on Sanae and breathes out: 'a beautiful, nicely proportionate body […] I can see the splendid curves of your breasts through your dress', 'you are beautiful […] your face and body'. Although implicit, this seduction marks one of the most erotically charged moments in the film and suggests lesbianism on a narrative level. At the end of the film, on the verge of murdering the girl, Black Lizard is confronted by Akechi and poisons herself. 'So you were alive,' murmurs the dying Miwa with a slight smile on her face. Unlike Ranpo's original novel in which the character kills herself out of despair of being captured by the police, Miwa's cinematic incarnation sacrifices herself out of fear of consummating her love with Akechi. This final scene registers Miwa's signature dramatic performance style, conveying the complexity of Black Lizard's psychic dilemma in the realm of emotional excess.

It is not too farfetched here to read a theme of narrative resistance to the fulfilment of heterosexual romance, for the ending clearly refuses the heterosexual, monogamous and reproductive love expected, at the time, to provide a backbone to national growth and development. As for the heterosexualisation of the story, Takeuchi Kayo points out that Mishima's adaptation diminished the eroticism and transgenderism imbued in the original Black Lizard character.[22] By turning her into a more 'feminine' figure, Takeuchi argues, their romance comes closer to a 'pure love' in line with the postwar ideology of 'romantic love' consisting of the trinity of sexuality-love-marriage.[23] This would certainly be the case if we read the film 'purely' on the narrative level. And yet, spectatorial knowledge inevitably calls the heterosexual nature of their relationship into question.[24] Since the late 1950s, Miwa's 'biological sex' was not a secret. In other words, spectators at the time would have known that it was not a woman playing the female jewel thief and this knowledge of the inconsistency in gender performance and the sexed body ultimately renders the narrative of 'pure (heterosexual) love' a fiction.

Through Miwa/Black Lizard, the film also suggests another queer instance; that of an alternative mode of family. The hunchbacked Matsukichi, Hina the old maid and other characters who have no one to depend on, are all effectively tied to Miwa's persona as a mother figure; a role he similarly plays today for his younger fans. This is a family that lacks either a father figure or any blood relations, and is juxtaposed with the romance between Black Lizard and Akechi. The queerness of the film thus not only lies in the star performance of Miwa Akihiro but also the ways in which his performance is fused completely with the concerns – from lesbianism to the alternative family – of the diegetic world.

Following the success of Black Lizard, Shōchiku requested a second Miwa film from Fukasaku Kinji.

Fukasaku and his crew conceived this as another star vehicle for and about Miwa Akihiro. The title of Black Rose Mansion resonates with the colour symbolism of the previous film (Fig. 12.2). It refers to a house that holds a secret salon and is entirely organised around an impossibly beautiful woman who mysteriously shows up and disappears from the salon. Little is known about this woman other than her name, Ryūko, and the rumour that she once was a singer in a club in Yokohama. Two men fall in love with her: Satake, the owner of the mansion, and his recently returned prodigal son, Wataru. Ryūko's presence only further deepens the rupture in an already broken family. Satake has another son who married a woman once in love with Wataru, and Satake's wife, the film alludes, tried in vain to elope with her lover, something that resulted in her confinement to bed. Her repeated complaints about her husband's 'niceness' underscore the oppression of family members under the veneer of the patriarch's kindness and generosity. Ryūko's existence scratches underneath the surface of the wealthy middle-class family to make this hidden oppression more visible and palpable. *Black Rose Mansion* presents a narrative solution by which the love of a father towards his son is seen to exceed the heterosexual love between Satake and Ryūko. This father–son relationship is a potential case of what Luce Irigaray calls a 'homosexual monopoly', which allows 'the transmission of patriarchal power, its laws, its discourse, and its social structures'.[25] Each of the men claims a possessive relationship with Ryūko and tells their own story about her in a way that constructs her image differently through separate flashbacks. This manner of constructing the image of

Fig. 12.2 *Black Rose Mansion/Kurobara no yakata* (Fukasaku Kinji, 1969, Shōchiku).

a woman ironically helps undo any fixed relationship between femininity and biological femaleness.

Unlike the previous film, Fukasaku and his crew wrote the script for *Black Rose Mansion* from scratch, except the idea of Miwa Akihiro as a lead. In a sense, the film was a result of a fortunate overlap between a business decision, authorial ambition and Miwa's unique star quality. In the face of the failing Japanese studio system and Shōchiku's particular hardship, the studio tried to revive the company through a reliance on a stock genre loyal to the studio's theatrical origins: a melodrama that incorporated elements of kabuki, particularly the *onnagata*. Also noteworthy is Fukasaku's relationship with Shōchiku for, with this film, he abandoned his exclusive contract with Tōei and made *Black Rose Mansion* as a freelance director (Fig. 12.3).

The tone and style of the film, with its mingled air of Gothic melodrama, action and noir, arose from these multilayered reasons, but one more factor also needs to be taken into account in relation to Miwa's film stardom during the 1960s. As I mentioned briefly, the 'men's film' and male stars dominated the screen over the decade with Nikkatsu studios still retaining Ishihara Yūjirō, the biggest film star of the previous decade, despite the fact that he could no longer guarantee a successful return at the box-office. Tōei's yakuza films with Tsuruta Kōji and Takakura Ken similarly enjoyed overwhelming popularity. It was within this predominately male film culture that the 'hyper masculine' Fukasaku intervened with a 'female' star, Miwa Akihiro, who possessed a 'femaleness' without any identifiable origin within a biologically sexed body. Both *Black Lizard* and *Black Rose Mansion* present Miwa's characters as mysterious women whose pasts and presents are untraceable. By refusing to anchor Black Lizard and Ryūko in time and place, these films made it absolutely impossible to fix their identities. This unknowability constituted the very riddle of the films, while an inconsistency of sex, gender and sexuality served as the lure of Miwa's star persona. Such mirroring relationships were precisely what made Miwa Akihiro a star at the time if, as Edgar Morin claims, a composite creature called 'the star' is born from the union of performer and character.[26]

THE VOICE OF A STAR

Another crucial factor in considering Miwa's performance style is the profoundly emotional as well as dense and richly textured quality of his voice that has continued to sustain his profile on stage and screen. Miwa played the role of a singer in *The Betrothed*, *Warm Current* and *To Be a Woman* and has repeatedly performed the role of Edith Piaf in live theatre. The deep and sonorous tonality of his vocal expression consistently allows his film characters to speak and sing with great feeling. In *Black Lizard* and *Black Rose Mansion*, for instance, Miwa's voice renders both of his characters convincingly enigmatic and erotic with part of this vocal allure arising from the matter of gender ambiguity. The manner, tone and modulation of his singing and speaking voice suspend any fixed notion of gender. Miwa's warm and sticky vocal expression sometimes invokes an almost excessive feminine quality whereas, at other times, his curt, menacing and low-pitched way of speaking achieves a more masculine effect.

As such, Miwa's vocality challenges existing theoretical concerns and conceptual frameworks regarding the voice in film; all of which tend to rely heavily on a gender binary. In his 1982 book, *The Voice in Cinema*, Michel Chion addresses the question of space in film in terms of the relationship between the voice and the body: 'speech, shouts, sighs or whispers, the voice hierarchizes everything around it'.[27] In order to play a hierarchical role, the voice itself has to be gendered. In discussing John Carpenter's *The Fog* (1980), for example, Chion argues that 'the voice of the woman seems to possess ubiquity by nature' and

Fig. 12.3 *Black Rose Mansion/Kurobara no yakata* (Fukasaku Kinji, 1969, Shōchiku).

that 'only a woman's voice can invade and transcend the space' in the film. Here, Chion presupposes that there are only two different kinds of voices: a woman's voice and that of a man.[28] From a psychoanalytical perspective, the feminist film theorist Kaja Silverman has partly critiqued, but also largely supplemented, Chion's argument that 'Hollywood requires the female voice to assume similar responsibilities to those it confers upon the female body.'[29] According to Silverman, the female voice functions as a fetish within dominant cinema, 'filling in for and covering over what is unspeakable within male subjectivity'.[30] Although her point may be well taken, in doing so, she too easily equates the female voice with the female body as if there is nothing outside the gender-based body-voice system. In claiming that 'listening to the voice inaugurates the relation to the Other' Roland Barthes makes the point that the voice does not have to be directly related to the body itself.[31] Barthes insists that we recognise others, their way of being and their psychological conditions, by the voice. And yet, for Barthes, the voice is not directly and essentially related to the body of a person, but rather to 'an image of their body'. As 'the privileged site of difference', it lies at the point of articulation between 'body and discourse'.[32]

Recent scholarship has emphasised the ways in which the voice is technologically mediated and the fact that this technological intervention denaturalises any organic link between the voice and body. And yet, a persistent underlying assumption in this work is that the gender of the voice is a given. In other words, the voice is either male or female, and critics rarely examine the very process by which the voice becomes gendered. Miwa's vocal stardom troubles such a mode of theorising based on strict gender dichotomies and asks what makes someone's voice inherently female or male?

Here, I don't mean to deny the seductive power of the voice in invoking the source of its production, be it the body or otherwise. Nevertheless, when the voice becomes a marker of sexual difference, this difference constantly ends up being referred to the body, male or female, along with the fantasy of the unified body. Given that Miwa's already ambiguous vocality calls upon a likewise corporeal ambiguity, there is no certainty of a female voice that guarantees a male body, or a male voice the male body. This voice is not only an 'interspace' between the body and discourse, but an interspace of gender and sexed bodies that further demonstrates a phantasmatic wholeness. In this sense, is Chion's related interest in sex-inversion (a woman with a male voice and a man with a female voice) in comedy-fantasy films, also suggestive of the possibility of a new set of relationships between the voice and body?[33]

Several films deploy Miwa's unanchored vocal qualities by casting him as a voice actor. In the animation film, *Armageddon: The Great Battle with Genma/Genma taisen* (1983), Miwa plays Floy, the energy of cosmic consciousness. As an invisible and formless being, Floy communicates with human beings via telepathy. Miwa's voice well conveys Floy's 'supernaturalness', which cannot be localised in any visuality. In *Princess Mononoke/Mononokehime* (1997) by the celebrated animator Miyazaki Hayao, Miwa performs the voice of Moro, the three-hundred-year-old wolf god/dess who adopts and raises a human girl. Moro is a supernatural being whose diegetically ambiguous position suspends and negotiates the opposition of human and non-human, female and male, nature and culture. Taking the form of a giant wolf, his supernatural character is not represented visually but vocally, for it speaks a human language.

In the follow-up to *Princess Mononoke*, *Howl's Moving Castle/Howl no ugoku shiro* (2004), Miwa's voices the 'Witch of the Waste', who turns into a witch after making a pact with the Devil. When the spell is broken, she returns to her human form, but is physically and mentally now a fragile old woman. Here again, Miwa's voice is crucial in breathing life into this otherworldly character as she walks the line between the human and the supernatural.

ZONE OF RESONANCE: SHINJUKU CULTURE IN THE 1960S

As noted previously, Miwa's star persona emerged out of the specific historical contexts and social conditions of Tokyo in the 1960s. These included the protests against Anpo (the US–Japan Security Treaty), high economic growth and various avant-garde movements that connected underground experiments in art, theatre and film. For many, the late 1960s, with its symbolic year of 1968, still live on in the mind as a significant turning point for Japanese politics, culture and society.[34]

Cinema played a critical role in the political and cultural dynamics that made Shinjuku a distinctive zone of resonance with films such as Ōshima Nagisa's *Death by Hanging/Kōshukei* (1968) and Matsumoto Toshio's *Funeral Parade of Roses/Bara no sōretsu* (1969). Art, theatre and *butoh* intersected with cinema, one inspiring the other and leading to the creative circulation of materials, people and ideas. Ōshima's *Diary of a Shinjuku Thief/Shinjuku dorobō nikki* (1968) provides one such testimony in the way that it showcases prominent cultural icons with perhaps the real protagonist of the film being Shinjuku itself.[35] Ōshima affectionately called Shinjuku 'my place', a place where 'new art emerges in the form of *fūzoku*, or mode of life'. For Ōshima, 'new art' meant the process by which 'the unreal becomes the real, and vice versa', and *Diary of a Shinjuku Thief* was an attempt 'to capture the dynamics of a changing real world and people'.[36]

Many artists and performers, including Miwa himself, were involved in the creative impulses articulated by Ōshima. The art performance collective Zero Dimension, Situation Theatre lead by Kara Jūrō and Terayama Shūji's Tenjō Sajiki both made a provocative break from existing conventions and institutional protocols, experimenting with new forms and styles through audience involvement. Pivotal to this was the Art Theatre Shinjuku Bunka as well as its underground theatre, Theatre Scorpio/Sasori-za, named by Mishima after his favourite film, *Scorpio Rising* by Kenneth Anger. While the Shinjuku Bunka provided a venue for films outside the studio system, the Sasori-za offered related opportunities for underground theatre and experimental films.[37]

Miwa Akihiro emerged directly out of this cultural milieu. Rediscovered as a stage actor by Terayama, Miwa first performed the role of an 'ugly old maid' in his play, *The Hunchback of Aomori/Aomori-ken no semushi otoko*, before appearing as a cross-dressing male prostitute in *Marie La Vison/Kegawa no Mari* in 1967. Terayama, who had already made his name as a poet in his early twenties, founded the theatre troupe Tenjō Sajiki in 1967 to great acclaim. The Shinjuku Bunka was the biggest sponsor of Terayama's troupe, producing his plays and films, and Shinjuku was his home ground. *Marie La Vison* was first performed at the Shinjuku Bunka, and Mishima, obsessed enough with the play to attend every day during its one-week performance, decided to have Miwa star in his own play, *Black Lizard*.[38] Fukasaku also claimed an enthusiasm equal to Mishima's as his motivation for hiring Miwa in his film.[39]

Funeral Parade of Roses offers further evidence of Shinjuku as a resonant zone, especially in terms of male homosexuality. The film tells a story of Eddie, a gay boy working in Shinjuku and frames the story of Eddie and his lover (who turns out to be his father) within the Freudian concept of the negative Oedipus complex. In a radically complex exploration of cinematic form and temporality, this film counters the logic of linear progress, essential to the narrative of Japan's high economic growth and development and production and reproduction, by offering an alternative view via Shinjuku's gay underworld. Different from Ōshima's Shinjuku, Matsumoto offers a vision of a space in which non-normative temporal and sexual practices both take place.

A number of writers have noted the increasing presence of gay, lesbian and cross-dressers in Shinjuku in the 1960s. In his *Shinkuku Modernologio/Shinjuku kōgengaku*, an ethnographic study of the city's urban landscape and practices around 1968, Fukasaku Mitsusada counted more than 120 gay bars as well as 3 or 4 lesbian bars and wrote: 'what is surprisingly spreading among the youth in Shinjuku is same-sex love'.[40] In *Shinjuku Story/Shinjuku*, a reportage depicting modes of life in Shinjuku, Itō Seiko characterises the city by its strong relation to homosexual and bisexual men.[41] In her survey of the historical and geographical development of gay areas in Shinjuku, the social historian Mitsuhashi Junko traces the increasing centralisation of gay bars and other commercial facilities back to 1958, when the Anti-prostitution Law came into force.[42] As a result of gay bars moving into the previously state-sanctioned *akasen* (red-line) prostitution areas, the 1960s brought about a high concentration of gay bars hitherto scattered in Asakusa, Ginza and Shinbashi to Shinjuku.⁴³

Miwa's public and private lives were both deeply implicated in the spaces of Shinjuku. He performed at the Shinjuku Bunka, lived in front of the Hanazono shrine and ran his own club where he spent time with his friends. As the films, underground theatre and street performances of the time demonstrate, sexuality constituted a critical part of this culture. Despite differences in genres, styles and thematic concerns, artists expressed political sentiments (if not explicit meanings) in sexual terms. Homosexual culture, in particular, thus became a meeting point between anti-establishment and leftist political movements and transmedia experimentation. Although Ginza might have been the place where Miwa's career began, his real stardom rose out of this vibrant landscape.

Certainly, this association is nothing new as the immediate postwar situation of Japan's defeat has always been perceived and represented as a very sexual defeat. And yet, we need to ask: who identified the national defeat as sexual? Who narrated and celebrated the liberation of the body and sexuality as the core of political freedom? From the 'literature of the flesh' to the Sun Tribe films of the 1950s and the underground theatre and films of the 1960s onwards, representations of violence and the abuse of women became too many to count. The revenge of injured heterosexual masculinity was justified, or even glorified as the symptomatic restoration of national pride and recovery from defeat. In fact, many of the so-called 'political films' produced in the 1960s only addressed the political in terms of the exploitation of the female body and sexuality, hence subjectivity.

As if in opposition to this, Miwa has practised different modes of presenting gender, either coded as masculine or feminine, by forcefully problematising the dominant model of hetero-masculinity prevalent in the postwar cultural landscape. He has not simply 'crossed' gender but resisted its very order and rules in his queer visual and vocal incarnations as 'sister boy', femme fatale, 'ugly' old woman, ageing cross-dressing male prostitute, kimonoed female gambler, heterosexual company man and, finally, an invisible form of cosmic energy and supernatural wolf god/dess.

To conclude, his sexual identity and practice are telling of both the historical gaps between the 1950s and the present and the insufficiency of a retrospective construction of his sexuality as either 'homosexual' or 'gay' from the vantage point of today's knowledge and language. During the 1950s through the 1960s, homosexuality, let alone gayness, was something that could not be clearly articulated or distinguished as such, and to call Miwa Japan's first 'gay' activist remains perplexing at best. Nevertheless, the effect of Miwa's star persona on both the queer community (particularly for gay men and cross-dressers) and the mainstream media is undeniably palpable. As a star, he has never offered a proto-image of a gay man, be it in positive or negative terms. Instead, his queerness can be found in his continuingly aggressive and sharp-tongued fight against homophobia, a resistance to a deep-seated gender-sexuality system, and perverted trespassing of the terms feminine and the masculine, female and male, homosexual and heterosexual on screen, television, stage and air. In resonating queerly with his past and diverse performances, the stardom of Miwa Akihiro therefore continually emerges anew.

Notes

1. Although Miwa's style was considered to be far too feminine, Mitsuhashi Junko, for instance, claims that Miwa can be seen as 'cross dressing' at best, not 'cross-gender dressing'. See Mitsuhashi Junko, 'Miwa Akihiro to josō', in *Miwa Akihiro toiu ikikata* (Tokyo: Seikyūsha, 2000), p. 210.
2. In 2010, Vincent's film premiered at Frameline, the pretentious LGBT film festival in San Francisco, as part of the festival's 'transgender film focus'. The programme described Miwa as 'a pioneer of gay activism' adding that Miwa was 'a legendary entertainer' and 'social critic' in Japan.
3. Miryam Sas, *Experimental Arts in Postwar Japan: Moments of Encounter, Engagement, and Imagined Return* (Cambridge, MA: Harvard University Asia Center, 2011), p. 132.
4. Martin Shingler, *Star Studies: A Critical Guide* (London: Palgrave Macmillan, 2012), p. 16.

5   [Editors' note: for more on Japanese film acting, see also Chapter 17 by Chika Kinoshita in this volume.]
6   To name but a few, the sexologist Habuto Eiji published *Kinema star no sugao to hyōjō*/The *Expressions and Faces of Cinema Stars* in 1928 and Tanaka Eizō, a director, screenwriter and actor himself, wrote on the subject in his *Eiga haiyū ron*/*On the Film Actor* in 1935. The noted leftist film critic Iwasaki Akira also wrote *Eiga star shōshi*/*A Short History of Film Stars* in 1951.
7   *Ero guro nansensu* is a shortened term for 'erotic, grotesque, nonsense', which refers to the decadent cultural trend that favoured sexual deviancy, bizarreness and absurdity during the 1920s. See Miriam Silverberg, *Erotic Grotesque Nonsense: The Mass Culture of Japanese Modern Times* (Berkeley: University of California Press, 2006).
8   Ronald Roden, 'Taisho Culture and the Problem of Gender Ambivalence', in Thomas Rimer (ed.), *Culture and Identity* (Princeton, NJ: Princeton University Press, 1990), pp. 37–55.
9   Hideaki Fujiki, *Making Personas: Transnational Film Stardom in Modern Japan* (Cambridge, MA: Harvard University Asia Center, 2013).
10 Ayako Kano, *Acting Like a Woman: Theater, Gender, and Nationalism* (New York: Palgrave, 2001), p. 31.
11 Maki Morinaga, 'The Gender of Onnagata As the Imitation Imitated: Its Historicity, Performativity, and Involvement in the Circulation of Femininity', *positions* vol. 10 no. 2 (2002), pp. 245–84.
12 For instance, Hal Hinson describes *Black Lizard* as 'an exercise in extravagant high camp', and Vincent Canby 'spectacular drag'. Stephen Hunter titles his film review 'Japanese Film "Black Lizard" Takes Camp to the Limit', while Kevin Thomas calls Miwa's 1969 film *Black Rose Mansion* a 'high-camp cult classic'. See Hal Hinson, 'Black Lizard', *Washington Post*, 23 November 1991; Vincent Canby, 'In Tokyo, A Queen of Crime in Drag', *New York Times*, 18 September 1991; Stephen Hunter, 'Japanese Film "Black Lizard" Takes Camp to the Limit', *Baltimore Sun*, 10 January 1992; Kevin Thomas, 'Two by Fukasaku', *Los Angeles Times*, 15 May 2003.
13 Ester Newton, *Mother Camp: Female Impersonators in America* (Chicago: University of Chicago Press, 1979), p. 104.
14 Moe Mayer, 'Reclaiming the Discourse of Camp', in Harry Benshoff and Sean Griffin (eds), *Queer Cinema, The Film Reader* (New York: Routledge, 2004), pp. 137–50.
15 Ibid., p. 139.
16 Susan Sontag, 'Notes on Camp', in *A Susan Sontag Reader* (New York: Vintage Books, 1983), pp. 105–19; Andrew Ross, 'Uses of Camp', in *No Respect: Intellectuals and Popular Culture* (London: Routledge, 1989), pp. 135–70; Richard Dyer, 'It's Being So Camp as Keeps Us Going', in *The Culture of Queers* (London: Routledge, 2002), pp. 49–62.
17 Standish astutely summarises the ethos of the Sun Tribe films; 'Under the terms of woman's newfound political/legal autonomy, a woman's place within the phallocentric economy of the Sun Tribe (*taiyōzoku*) films is reduced to that of a fetish to be exchanged between men, her active status thus rendered harmless.' Isolde Standish, *A New History of Japanese Cinema: A Century of Narrative Film* (New York: Continuum, 2005), p. 228. See also Michael Raine, 'Ishihara Yūjiro: Youth, Celebrity, and the Male Body in late 1950s Japan', in Dennis Washburn and Carole Cavanaugh (eds), *Word and Image in Japanese Cinema* (Cambridge: Cambridge University Press, 2001), pp. 202–25.
18 Saitō Ayako, 'Takaura Ken no aimai na nikutai,' in Saitō Ayako and Yomota Inuhiko (eds), *Otokotachi no kizuna: Asia eiga homosexuality na yokubō* (Tokyo: Heibonsha, 2004), p. 100.
19 [Editors' note: for more on the yakuza film genre, see also Chapter 25 by Jennifer Coates in this volume.]
20 Satō Tadao, *Nihon ēga joyūshi* (Tokyo, Hagashobō, 1975), p. 144.
21 Ueno Kōshi, *Ēga, han-ēyūtachi no yume* (Tokyo: Hanashi no tokushū, 1983), p. 117.
22 See, for instance, Takeuchi Kayo, 'Demo kore ga koi datoshitara: Akechi ni koishiteiru watashi wa dono watashi nano?: Mishima Yukio, "Kurotokage" ni kōsa suru sengo shihonshugi to heterosexualism', *Bunka hyōshō o yomu: Gender kenkyū no genzai* (Tokyo: F-GENS, 2008), p. 65.
23 Ibid., p. 67.
24 I use the term 'spectator' by following the concept elaborated by Judith Mayne. According to Mayne, the spectator is a site of negotiation between the viewer ('the real' person who watches a film) and the subject (the person assigned to the viewer by the institutions of cinema). See Judith Mayne, *Cinema and Spectatorship* (London: Routledge, 1993), p. 36.

25. Luce Irigaray, *This Sex Which Is Not One*, trans. Catherine Porter (Ithaca, NY: Cornell University Press, 1985), p. 193.
26. Edgar Morin writes: 'the actor does not engulf his role. The role does not engulf the actor. Once the film is over, the actor becomes an actor again, the character remains a character, but from their union is born a composite creature who participates in both, envelops them both: the star.' Edgar Morin, *The Stars*, trans. Richard Howard (Minneapolis: University of Minnesota Press, 2005), p. 29.
27. Michel Chion, *The Voice in Cinema*, trans. Claudia Gorbman (New York: Columbia University Press, 1999).
28. Ibid., p. 119.
29. Kaja Silverman, *The Acoustic Mirror: The Female Voice in Psychoanalysis and Cinema* (Bloomington: Indiana University Press, 1988), pp. 38–9.
30. Ibid.
31. Roland Barthes, *The Responsibilities of the Form: Critical Essay on Music, Art, and Representation*, trans. Richard Howard (Berkeley: University of California Press, 1991), p. 255.
32. Ibid., pp. 279, 255. In his essay 'The Romantic Song', Barthes points out that the revolutionary significance of the romantic lieder, particularly by Schubert, lies in the abolition of the men's and the women's voices. Barthes's discussion is critical in thinking about Miwa's voice here, for he not only suggests that the voice does not always refer to the sexed body but also emphasises the importance of the listener's role. Then the voice is not something that can be heard 'naturally' as such, but the very construct where the one who voices and the other who listens meet and negotiate. See Roland Barthes, 'The Romantic Song', in Barthes, *The Responsibilities of the Form*, pp. 286–92.
33. Chion, *The Voice in Cinema*, p. 171.
34. Immanuel Wallerstein argues, for instance, that 1968 was a revolution 'in and of the world-system', and 'its origin, consequences, and lessons cannot be analysed collectively by appealing to the particular circumstances of the local manifestations of this global phenomenon, however much of the local factors conditioned the details of the political and social struggles in each locality'. Although I agree that Japan's 1968 was not an isolated case but part of a global phenomenon, I am more interested here in 'the local factors' and 'the details of the political and social struggles' as well as the cultural manifestations that took place in the specific locality of Shinjuku, Tokyo, Japan. See Immanuel Wallerstein, '1968, Revolution in the World-System: Theses and Queries', *Theory and Society* vol. 18 no. 4 (1989), pp. 431–49.
35. The film casts artists such as Kara Jūrō and Yokoo Tadanori, Tanabe Moich, an essayist and founder of the Kinokuniya bookstore, and Takahashi Tetsu, a sexologist, among many others.
36. Ōshima Nagisa, *Kaitai to funshutsu* (Tokyo, Hagashoten, 1970), pp. 150–1.
37. The crucial role the Shinjuku Bunka played in Japanese film culture is worth stressing. It was the basis of the Art Theatre Guild (ATG), an influential distributor of foreign art films and the producer of Japanese independent and experimental films, including those by Ōshima Nagisa, Yoshida Kijū, Shinoda Masahiro, Imamura Shōhei, Shindō Kaneto, Hani Sususmu, Teshigahara Hiroshi, Matsumoto Toshio, Kuroki Kazuo, Higashi Yōichi and Terayama Shūji, just to name a few. See also Yuriko Furuhata, *Cinema of Actuality, Japanese Avant-Garde Filmmaking in the Season of Image Politics* (Durham, NC: Duke University Press, 2013), and Taro Nettleton, 'Shinjuku as Site: Funeral Parade of Roses and a Diary of a Shinjuku Thief', *Screen* vol. 55 no. 1 (2014), pp. 5–21. [Editors' note: see also Chapter 13 by Julian Ross in this volume.]
38. The play completely filled seats for twenty-four days at the Tōyoko gekijō in Shibuya, providing Mishima with fame as a playwright since, with the exception of *Rokumeikan*, his previous works had not had commercial success. See Toyoda Masayoshi, *Aura no sugao Miwa Akihiro no ikikata* (Tokyo: Kōdansha, 2009), pp. 229–32.
39. Fukasaku Kinji and Yamane Sadao, *Eiga kantotoku Fukasaku Kinji* (Tokyo: Waizu shuppan, 2003), p. 168. [Editors' note: for more on Fukasaku Kinji, see also Chapter 9 by Rachael Hutchinson in this volume.]
40. Fukasaku Mitsusada, *Shinjuku kōgengaku* (Tokyo: Kadokawa shoten, 1968), pp. 159–68.
41. She writes that 'Shinjuku has the air of a kind of a toy factory making toys for adults such as films and the theatre. A converging proto-energy, the city flows with film directors, cameramen, editors, actors, writers,

and homosexual and *okama* culture as a mode of life reaching its maturation'. Itō Seiko, *Shinjuku monogatari* (Tokyo: San'ichi shobō, 1982), p. 89. [Editors note: *okama* is a slang term for homosexual men.]

42 Mitsuhashi Junko, 'Sengo Tokyo niokeru "Danshoku bunka" no rekishi chiriteki hensen', *Gendai fūzokugaku kenkyū* no. 12 (2006), pp. 1–15.

43 A number of writers testified to the ways in which gay areas were expanding in Shinjuku around the 1960s. See Ōtsuka Takashi, *Nichōme kara uroko: Shinjuku gei sutorīto zakki chō* (Tokyo: Hieisha, 1995), p. 17. Mitsuhashi Junko, 'Gei boy, shisutā boy, burū boy', Inoue Shōichi and Kansai seiyoku kenkyū kai(eds), *Sei no yōgoshū* (Tokyo: Kōdansha, 2004), pp. 314–15.

13

EXPERIMENTAL FILM
Forms, spaces and networks: A history of Japanese experimental film

Julian Ross

The independent film collective [+] has voiced an aversion to being associated with the term 'experimental film' (*jikken eiga*) in Japan. While *jikken eiga* is most commonly used to designate such film-making practices, [+] member and historian Sakamoto Hirofumi has suggested that some film-makers feel the term sequesters their work and encourages a false presumption that it is separated from cinema at large.[1] This chapter proposes that the contribution to wider film culture made by such peripheral activities can nonetheless be best illuminated by loosely grouping them together and assessing certain shared tendencies in their practice. Tracing Japan's history of experimental film is to draw together a network of disparate creative voices each with their own unique history and distinct approach to film-making. Ranging from formal challenges to the limits of the medium to alternative explorations of identity, space and thinking, what these dispersed activities all have in common is their anti-institutional stance where personal expression is pursued unbound by the commercial incentives of industry.

Despite its extensive history in comparison to other Asian countries, experimental film-making has been mostly overlooked within historical accounts of Japanese cinema. The fact that the Japanese experimental film sector has stronger ties with the international film community than Japan's mainstream film industry may have accounted for this occlusion. On the other hand, international chronicles of experimental film have also painted a fragmented picture of Japanese contributions due to the paucity of available resources in other languages. In Japan, and elsewhere, experimental film challenges the medium specificity of film and often crosses over into the realm of the other arts; something that has also played a role in the situation.

Although preserving the idea of experimental film as a flexible form of classification has allowed for it to remain prevalent amidst developments in technology, industry and the changing status of art, this inclusivity has also proved problematic for both the purposes of definition and its critical development in Japan. Japanese experimental film was first described as avant-garde (*zen'ei*) in the late 1920s – the political connotations of the word often being one reason for confusion. In marked contrast to studio film-making, the use of narrow-gauge film led to such practices being categorised as 'small-form film' (*kogata eiga*), 'small film' (*shō eiga*) and, in the postwar re-emergence of amateur film-making, 'personal films' (*kojin eiga*). The rise of television and the increasing ubiquity of the screen in the 1950s also caused a renegotiation of terminology from movie (*eiga*) to image (*eizō*), a term that encompassed broader currents in moving image production.[2] As a means of showing allegiance with American experimental cinema, films came to be described as experimental (*jikken eiga*) and the notion of underground film, transliterated and shortened to *angura*, not only described cinema but also a whole culture of peripheral art and lifestyle in the 1960s. As artists increasingly began incorporating film, video and computer graphics into their practice, the term 'media art' became commonplace from the 1970s to describe artistic output related to, and beyond, moving images. Nonetheless, this chapter will still retain the use of the term 'experimental film' in order to interconnect these practices in Japan with a broader history and a wider global network.

While there have been several monographs devoted to American, British and Austrian experimental film cultures, there is still no complete history of Japanese experimental film in English. This chapter will therefore take the form of a survey in order to map out films, film-makers and activities that have shaped Japan's experimental film culture. While considering many key concerns in experimental film more broadly, the chapter will also dwell on local specificities in terminology, activity and development in order to shift the dominance of Western narratives of experimental film and encourage the internationalisation of the field of study. The chapter seeks to be a reference point not only for readers of Japanese cinema but also for those interested in broadening the conversation on localised experimental film cultures.

At least three concerns have continued to play a key role in shaping the development of experimental film in Japan and the chapter is structured around these in order to thoroughly address its peaks and pillars. Firstly, experimental film has a direct relationship with the medium – perhaps more than any other type of film-making due to the film-makers' intimate involvement with the film material and apparatus from production through to exhibition. While media continue to change along with developments in technology, experimental film-makers are often one of the first to not only try out new technologies but also identify what makes each medium unique from its predecessors. As such, the chapter's initial section, 'Medium', will outline in what ways the advent of technology and the availability of new cameras – from narrow-gauge to digital apparatuses – have influenced shifts in experimental film practice. Secondly, being positioned on the peripheries of the industry has led to experimental film-makers struggling to secure any permanent and dedicated space for their works. Finding accommodation in a diverse range of alternative spaces has, however, encouraged experimental film-makers to encounter new audiences and establish a sense of collectivity with one another. The second section, 'Screening spaces', will profile a number of such key spaces and explore their importance through a selection of significant events. Lastly, experimental film-makers have often built relationships with individuals working in other forms of artistic practice to achieve new joint approaches to cinematic expression. The final section, 'Networks', will highlight a number of case studies where intermedial collaborations, both domestic and international, have led to new challenges for the definition of cinema. Through an exploration of these three key concerns – medium specificity, screening spaces and networks – this chapter will thus offer a comprehensive overview of the multiple sites, histories and faces of experimental film in Japan.

MEDIUM

The first wave of experimental films to come out of Japan was instigated by the newly available apparatus of small-gauge film cameras in the domestic market and a burgeoning culture of avant-garde arts imported from Europe. The arrival of 9.5mm and 16mm cameras, and the newfound mobility they offered, encouraged non-industrialised film-making and led to a number of individuals taking up the production of what came to be known as 'amateur films'. Although most of what was produced resulted in sketches, travelogues and home movies, the Pathé Baby 9.5mm format and Kodak 16mm film, both introduced to Japan in 1923 for domestic use, offered opportunities to explore film-making unrelated to the codes of narrative, genre and drama developed by the major studios. The founding of amateur film societies, specialist magazines and film contests marked the emergence of an amateur film movement in the mid-to-late 1920s, the most notable being the Tokyo Pathé Kinema Club, who began organising a film contest in the same year it was founded, 1925. Ogino Shigeji, who started film-making in 1928, became a leading figure with his prolific and diverse approach to narrow-gauge film-making that involved experiments in abstraction, as seen in works such as *River* (1933) and *Rhythm* (1934).[3]

Although the films presented at such contests displayed a diversity of personal visions, the rise of amateur film coincided with the arrival of imported European avant-garde titles and this came to shape the direction films took. Walter Ruttmann's *Berlin: Symphony of a Great City/Berlin: Die Sinfonie der Großstadt* (1927), considered to be the first avant-garde film shown in Japan, and Dziga Vertov's *Man with a Movie Camera* (1929) both had an indelible impact as a surge of amateur film-makers began to shoot their own portraits of city life.[4] Despite the low number of imported films, translations and reports were published in film magazines where debates ensued about titles not yet been screened in the country. Higo Hiroshi, a manager of what was probably Japan's first art-house cinema, Cinema Palace, visited Chateau de la Sarraz, Switzerland, in September 1929 for the International Congress of Independent Film where European film-makers Alberto Cavalcanti, Hans Richter, Sergei Eisenstein and the Japanese critic Tsuchiya Moichiō were among the participants. Higo subsequently founded the Zen'ei eigasha (Avant-Garde Film Company) and Zen'ei eiga kanshōkai (Avant-Garde Film Cine-Club) on his return to Japan. When the programme was shown at the Hibiya Public Hall on 9 February 1930, with accompanying lectures, police interrupted the screening believing it to be a political gathering due to the use of the term 'avant-garde' in its promotion. Despite being censored by the state, French avant-garde films such as Man Ray's *The Starfish/L'Étoile de mer* (1928) and Germaine Dulac's *The Seashell and the Clergyman/La Coquille et le clergyman* (1928) were attacked for their neglect of social issues, in favour of questions of form, by leftist critics writing during the Shōwa depression.[5] The 9.5mm format was also preferred by Prokino as a tool to document protest events and address the public thus launching a debate on the role of narrow-gauge film in the film-making community.[6] This conjunction between art and politics set a precedent for the ways in which experimental film was to proceed with both remaining at its axis.

After World War II and the end of the US Occupation in 1952, the coincidence of developments in technology and shifts in social conditions once again laid the ground for the re-emergence of experimental film. Although the double-8 format had been available in Japan since 1932, 8mm film rose in popularity among amateur film-makers in the mid-1950s when 16mm film became more expensive as television stations used it to shoot their programmes. Takabayashi Yōichi's unique blend of documentary, travelogue and film poetry, such as *Ishikkoro* (1961), began to feature at amateur film screenings in the late 1950s and the director was the recipient of various prizes at international amateur film festivals in Italy. Ōbayashi Nobuhiko and Iimura Takahiko, both snubbed by amateur film contests, joined Takabayashi and the three started to screen their works together. After shooting 8mm films in Ohio as a teenager, the American film-maker and writer, Donald Richie, also made a number of short experimental films in Japan, where he lived from 1953. Richie introduced overseas experimental film to a younger generation of film-makers and joined these three and a number of others in submitting films to the film festival EXPRMNTL 3 in Knokke-le-Zoute, Belgium, where they received a group award in 1963. Despite impediments including its small image and increasing lack of availability, the 8mm film format continues to be incorporated into artistic practice for its particular aesthetic and mobility. In the 1980s and 1990s, personal dramas by Obitani Yuri, eerie animations of Kurosaka Keita, abstract textures in the *Ecosystem* series by Koike Teruo, and film poems by Yamada Isao, mostly shot on Super-8, have all testified to the perseverance of the 8mm format in the video and digital era.

The emergence of video similarly instigated another new phase in the history of Japanese experimental film. With its technological capacity for live transmission, video offered opportunities for film-makers and artists to present an image at the same time it was recorded. As such, live performance was utilised early on in the development of the format. The first presentation of video art in Japan is considered to be the performance that took place at the 'EX POSE '68: Nanika Ittekure Ima Sagasu' (Say Something Now, I'm Looking for Something to Say) event held in May 1968, where the art critic Tōno Yoshiaki sat cross-dressed in a separate room and spoke to the camera with the image fed live onto an onstage monitor. Japanese video art experienced a slow beginning before the collective Video Hiroba was founded in 1972. This is despite the introduction of the Sony Portapak in the domestic market in 1967 and the technician Abe Shūya, in collaboration with the Korean artist Nam June Paik, developing what is widely considered to be the first video synthesiser in 1969, the Paik-Abe Video Synthesizer. Video Hiroba's first event, 'Video Communication Do-It Yourself Kit', held at the Sony Building, Tokyo, in February 1972, became a landmark with presentations of local and international video art through the support of Canadian video artist Michael Goldberg. The show included *Eat* (1972), a performance by the artists Yamaguchi Katsuhirō and Kobayashi Hakudō, where the two sat across a table from one another and took turns recording each other eating while having this fed live onto a monitor. The particularities of the live feed in the video format continue to be utilised by younger artists to this day. In *Video Feedback Live Performance* (2011–), a performance by Hamasaki Ryōta and Kawai Masayuki (co-founder of Video Center Tokyo), flickering video signals from analogue video are manipulated to create synchronised audio beats and streams of colour.

As the television monitor became increasingly prevalent in domestic spaces across the country, it also became the subject of critique by Japanese video artists who explored its form as an object in performances and installations. The film-maker Matsumoto Toshio performed *Magnetic Scramble* (1968) at the Shinjuku discotheque L.S.D. where he distorted the transmitted image by placing magnetic coil against a monitor, an experiment that was later incorporated into a scene in his feature film, *Funeral Parade of Roses/Bara no sōretsu* (1969). Kawaguchi Tatsuo, Uematsu Keiji and Muraoka Saburō's performance for television broadcast, *Image of Image-Seeing/Eizō no eizō – mirukoto* (1973), showcased a destructive tendency in the artistic use of television monitors, which were taped over, smashed and thrown into a river.[7] In April-May 1969, at the Electromagica '69 exhibition held at the Sony Building, the artist Yamaguchi Katsuhirō presented *Image Modulator* (1969), where glass plates were placed in front of three colour television monitors to fragment and distort the images in a video art appropriation of his own *Vitrine* series of light sculptures developed during his time as a young artist in the 1950s.

As many of the early video artists in Japan had previously worked in film, the differences between film and video were emphasised in experiments with the latter. Beyond aesthetic concerns, the ability for video to instantly transmit information was also taken up to address social issues. Women artists, in particular, began incorporating the video format into their artistic practice. In collaboration with the artist Kobayashi Hakudō, Nakaya Fujiko completed her first video piece *Friends of Minamata Victims – Video Diary/Minamata o kokuhatsu suru kai – Tent mura Video nikki* (1972), where she documented a demonstration held at the headquarters of Chisso Corporation, the company whose mercury pollution caused the infamous Minamata disease. Nakaya placed a video monitor at the scene to produce a closed circuit where protesters were able to see themselves in action, thus utilising the format's capacity for communication and self-reflection. Nakaya was a founding member of Video Hiroba and began distributing works by video artists in 1979 through Processart Inc. She opened Video Gallery SCAN in 1980, started the Japan International Video Television Festival in 1987 and has remained a consistent advocate for the video medium. Feminist concerns in Japanese society are explicitly addressed in Idemitsu Mako's works, including *Another Day of a Housewife* (1977), which features a television monitor showing a close-up of Idemitsu's own eye staring at her as she takes on a series of house chores (Fig. 13.1). Since its introduction to the art scene in 1960s Japan, video has continued to remain relevant in the arts with support particularly from Tamura Gallery, Tokyo, and the Fukui International Video Biennale (1985–99).

Despite the increasing accessibility of video and digital equipment, some artists in Japan have continued to use film materials in ways that assert the uniqueness of the format through emphasis on its textual qualities and the existence of individual frames. Coinciding with the emergence of video, experimental film in the 1970s became increasingly artisanal in its approach. Matsumoto Toshio's *Atman* (1975) uses infrared film to shoot 480 still images of a man sat down wearing a Noh theatre mask from multiple angles. The director

Fig. 13.1 *Another Day of a Housewife* (Mako Idemitsu, 1977). Courtesy of Studio Idemitsu.

Fig. 13.2 *Dutchman's Photograph/Orandajin no shashin* (Isao Kōta, 1974). Courtesy of Image Forum and Isao Kōta.

activates a sense of spinning motion through still animation techniques that draw attention to film projection as the quick succession of photographic frames. This highly coordinated technique was hugely influential on various Japanese film-makers; it was honed to dynamic perfection in *Spacy* (1981) by Ito Takashi and its impact can still be seen in Sonoda Eriko's *Garden/ing* (2007) and Saitō Nasuka's *A Labyrinth of Residence/Kyojyū meikyū* (2008). The idea of film as a succession of still photographs was also accentuated with the visibility of the photographic frame in Isao Kōta's *The Dutchman's Photographs/Orandajin no shashin* (1976) and Kawanaka Nobuhiro's *Switchback* (1976), a tendency which the critic Darly Chin has identified as having echoes of Western 'structuralist film' – experimental film-making in the 1960s to 1970s that drew attention to the material conditions of film – albeit with the distinct principle of gratification and irony (Fig. 13.2).[8] The lack of accessible film laboratory equipment could perhaps explain the preference shown by Japanese artists for the re-photographing technique, often used in stop-motion animation, in their experimental films. Unlike the case with British counterparts such as the London Film-Makers' Co-operative, for example, artist-run film labs were not as prevalent in Japan since film laboratories were used to offering their services at a relatively low cost.

Another tendency that emerged in the use of film in the video and digital age was a reflection on, and artistic appropriation of, film history. In an early example of such film-making in Japan, Okuyama Jun'ichi's *Le Cinéma/Le Cinéma Eiga* (1975) utilised one second from a close-up shot of a woman in a Hollywood film and redesigned it into a short film by fragmenting the second by multiplying it and rearranging the order of the frames. Sueoka Ichirō similarly took a song sequence from *The Wizard of Oz* (1939) and subverted it through seemingly unending repetition in *The Rainbow of Odds/Fuwa no niji* (1998). Found footage from television also became subject to appropriation; it was, for example, violently painted over in *Work/Sakuhin* (1958) by Shimamoto Shōzō, a member of the Gutai Art Association, a leading postwar avant-garde art group based in the Kansai region. A younger member of Gutai, Imai Norio, also presented *Severed Film/Setsudan sareta film* (1972), an installation that involved abandoned film stock from a television production that was cut up to fit into a 35mm slide holder with the rest discarded on the floor of the exhibition space. For his series *Plate/Han* (1999–), Itō Ryūsuke created a collage out of found footage from various formats and processed it through direct contact printing onto the film, including its optical soundtrack, where the material became the image itself in what he called 'an image print'. More recently, the Montreal-based Japanese artist Daïchi Saïto has taken a fragment from a Kung Fu film for a double-projection piece, *Never a Foot Too Far, Even* (2012), where he presents two projections of a figure in a forest, one on top of another. Although the same image is shown, one of the reels includes an additional frame thus expanding its length and creating a sense of dissonance in the projection until both versions eventually become synchronised. Saïto has described the filmstrip as embodying a structural similarity to the Japanese writing pad and many Japanese contemporary film-makers who focus on individual frames, such as New York-based Nishikawa Tomonari and Sapporo-based Ōshima Keitarō, share his artisanal dedication to the film format.[9]

SCREENING SPACES

Existing on the peripheries of the film industry, experimental film in Japan has struggled to find a dedicated space for exhibition throughout its existence. Although sparse and often short-lived, spaces that can accommodate film-makers and artists have provided valuable opportunities for experiments and discussions to take place. As cinemas are mostly owned by, or contracted with, major film studios, films have often been presented together as one-off programmes in rented spaces. This is a screening practice that continues to this day. As small-gauge film projection doesn't require the cumbersome set-up of the 35mm format, projections are mobile and relatively easy to prepare. Due to their close relationship with the other arts, experimental films have also often been screened on the walls of small gallery spaces. The struggle for space is not only limited to Japan, it has also been a perennial concern for experimental film around the world. Nevertheless, close analysis of just a few spaces can reveal the particularities of Japan's situation.

After being ignored by the amateur film contests, Iimura Takahiko presented his debut screening at the Naiqua Gallery in August 1963, thus inaugurating the Naiqua Cinematheque film series, where he projected his 8mm films onto all walls with the audience sat on the floor. Previously a dental clinic, this unique space in Shinbashi, Tokyo, became a home to performance artists and visual artists such as Yoko Ono, Shinohara Ushio and the collectives Zero Jigen and Hi Red Centre. This established various interactions between film-makers and artists as seen in the presence of members of the Hi Red Centre in the panel discussion presented after Iimura's screening. Lunami Gallery in Ginza, Tokyo, similarly began a series of screenings in the form of the 'Lunami Film Gallery'.

The first space in Japan to present experimental film programmes in the form of a theatrical run was the Theatre Scorpio in Shinjuku – the refurbished basement of the Art Theatre Shinjuku Bunka, one of the nationwide chains of cinemas that showed films distributed and produced by the Art Theatre Guild (ATG) of Japan. Starting in 1962, the ATG was an initiative launched by Kawakita Kashiko to tackle the dearth of cinemas in Japan showing foreign art-house and local independent titles; later, in 1967, it also became a coproducer of local independent films. Managed by Kuzui Kinshirō, Shinjuku Bunka not only showed ATG titles but also staged productions by underground theatre troupes, such as Terayama Shūji's Tenjō Sajiki, and showed local experimental film-makers' works. The small-gauge films made by some of these artists were deemed unsuitable for the enormous screen in the space, thus encouraging Kuzui to convert the basement into a small underground art space. Named by the novelist Mishima Yukio after Kenneth Anger's *Scorpio Rising* (1963), the space opened with what is considered the first Japanese experimental feature-length film, Adachi Masao's *Galaxy/Gingakei* (1967), and quickly came to represent the pinnacle of experimental film culture until its closure in 1974.

Another pivotal art space was the Sōgetsu Art Centre (SAC) in Akasaka, Tokyo, that went on to become the epicentre of experimental arts in postwar Japan. Set up in 1959 by the film-maker Teshigahara Hiroshi, the SAC was located in the basement of Sōgetsu, a unique flower arrangement school ran by the film-maker's father. Under the auspices of Teshigahara, the space became a place where improvised music, modern dance, underground theatre and symposia on the arts were held regularly. The founding ethos of the space was to create a meeting point between different kinds of practice. In the early years, the organisers of the SAC invested considerable energy in the marriage of modern jazz and other art forms with events organised by the Association of Etcetera and Jazz in 1960 involving simultaneous presentations, some of which entailed projections of film, with participants including Terayama Shūji, the composer Takemitsu Tōru and the animator Manabe

Hiroshi. When Manabe founded the Animation Sannin no Kai (Three-Person Animation Circle) with Yanagihara Ryōhei and Kuri Yōji, they carried out similar experiments by reconfiguring the conventions of screening animation; Manabe's *Animation for the Stage/Butai no tameno animation* (1960), for example, involved his animation *Marine Snow* (1960) presented together with modern dance and live readings of dramatic poetry. The success of these events was such that in 1964 they organised the first animation festival in Japan at the SAC and encouraged graphic designers and illustrators, such as Yokoo Tadanori, Uno Akira and Tanaami Keiichi, to try out animation. The SAC was also the place where the first experimental film festival in Japan, the Sōgetsu Experimental Film Festival,[10] was held in 1967. Running for three editions, the festival presented a mixture of international titles and as many as 105 local films therefore revealing a strong contingent of experimental film-makers in Japan. The final edition of the festival was forced to cancel on the opening day by the 'Joint-Struggle to Destroy the Festival' (Festival funsai kyōto kaigi), a group of protesters who rejected the hierarchy imposed within the competition structure. The action effectively split the experimental film community, some members of which were involved in the protests, and instigated a debate on the importance of space (*ba*) for the presentation of films to cultivate new talents and audiences.

Other sectors of the film community affected by the cancellation were the Japan Film-makers' Co-operative, founded in March 1968 by the film critic Satō Shigechika (a.k.a. Jūshin) in order to establish a distribution network for experimental film, and the Japan Underground Centre (JUC), a screening initiative ran by Kawanaka Nobuhiro. Despite a strong relationship with members of the Joint-Struggle to Destroy the Festival, both Satō and Kawanaka refused the call for support they received on the grounds of ideological difference and subsequently converted the JUC into a distribution and exhibition unit. After temporarily organising screenings at a table tennis hall and in an apartment room, the JUC, changing their name to the Underground Centre, found a regular base in the basement of the Tenjō Sajiki theatre. When Tenjō Sajiki shut its doors in 1977, the Underground Centre renamed itself Image Forum, first relocating to Shinjuku and eventually Shibuya in 2000. Image Forum is now considered the centre for experimental film in Japan and in addition to editing the magazine *Monthly Image Forum* (1980–95), now distributes local film-makers' work internationally and organises its own annual experimental film festival, the Image Forum Festival (1987–).

Although Image Forum remains significant to this day, it is by no means the only platform for Japanese experimental film. Other key institutions and film festivals that have a strong representation of experimental film include the Yebisu International Festival of Art and Alternative Visions at the Tokyo Photographic Art Museum, the Yamagata International Documentary Film Festival and the Art Film Festival in Aichi Art Centre.[11] Clubs and music venues, such as Uplink in Shibuya, Shinsekai and SuperDeluxe, both in Roppongi, continue to facilitate film-makers that seek to incorporate aspects of live performance into their screening practice and create opportunities for interactions between new audiences and experimental film. Despite the continuing difficulties in securing a dedicated space for screening experimental films, other forms of exhibition have also begun to take place on virtual platforms, such as the streaming websites U-stream and Dommune, where film-makers present their works online and engage in discussions through social media.

NETWORKS

Due to the lack of studio support in Japan, experimental film-makers have been encouraged to proactively forge networks with one another in order to seek assistance with both production and exhibition. These relationships have not just been important for mutual support but also creativity, as film-makers influence and inspire one another. One of the first groups to emerge out of such conditions was the Film Independents, founded in 1964 in Tokyo, whose membership included Iimura Takahiko, Ōbayashi Nobuhiko, Donald Richie, Adachi Masao and Kanesaka Kenji. In December 1964, the group encouraged artists working in other fields to make a 2-minute film for an event they organised at the Kinokuniya Hall. The programme 'A Commercial for Myself' included submissions by the performance artist Kazakura Shō, artist Akasegawa Genpei and musician Tone Yasunao. The group's name itself was a reference to the vital annual exhibition series Yomiuri Independent (1949–63), where dissident artists found a platform for their practice with all works submitted being exhibited, demonstrating the collapsing boundaries between film and other arts.

Another space that enabled such interaction was the VAN Film Science Research Centre. An apartment converted into a film processing lab and communal living space, VAN was set up by students of the Nichidai Eiken (Nihon University Film Studies Club), a film discussion and production unit established in 1957 that made films under a collective name in defiance against the existing hierarchy of film production. With Adachi and Jōnouchi Motoharu as residents, VAN became a meeting point for a range of artists and film-makers, including Akasegawa, Tone, Kazakura, Iimura, the musician Kosugi Takehisa and Yoko Ono. VAN's first collective project was *Document 6.15* (1961), a project commissioned by the All-Japan Federation of Self-Governing Students (*Zengakuren*) for an event to mourn the death of a student protester, Kanba Michiko, during demonstrations against the Anpo US–Japan Security Treaty. *Document 6.15* became a multi-projection screening at the Kudan kaikan that involved projections of slides and film with involvement by Adachi, Jōnouchi and Iimura. In a follow-up to the event the following year, Tone arranged live music and a performance by the performance artists Kosugi, Kazakura and Ono, who the film-makers got to know at VAN.[12] Such interpretations of what a film screening could entail inspired film-makers, such as Jōnouchi and Iimura, to consider multiple versions of a single film and introduce live action into the event of film projection in a form that came to be known as expanded cinema. In 1963, for example, Iimura presented *Screen Play* at the SAC by projecting his film *Colour/Iro* (1962–3) on the back of the artist Takamatsu Jirō. Jōnouchi accompanied projections of his film *Shelter Plan* (1964) with live action that varied on each occasion, at times whipping the screen and at other times giving poetry recitals while his film was projected onto his body.

A term introduced in 1966 from the US, expanded cinema provided a way to group such film presentations that sought alternatives to the single screen format. Founded upon networks between film and other arts, expanded cinema intersected with the arrival of 'intermedia' as a concept to describe work that linked conventionally separated artistic forms. While the historian Miryam Sas has emphasised the relations between 1960s intermedia and 'total work of art' (*sōgō geijutsu*) theorised and practised in the 1950s,[13] my own research has called attention to the dance critic Ichikawa Miyabi's reading of intermedia as a 'scattered totality' (*bara-bara zentaisei*), where individual forms of artistic expressions retain their own identity.[14] Rather than *sōgō* that related to a sense of unification, a shift in terminological usage to the term 'mixedness' (*kongō*) took place for works more closely related to performances of the international art network Fluxus, from which the term intermedia originated.

In practice, expanded cinema in Japan incorporated both approaches. The notion of 'intermedia' was launched at the Lunami Gallery in May 1967 at a five-day series of event called 'Intermedia', which brought together painting, sculpture, performance and film, including Kanesaka Kenji's own Fluxus-inspired interruption of his film *The Easily Burning Ears/ Moeyasui mimi* (1967). A network was established, particularly between New York and Tokyo, and many Japanese artists who later participated in 'intermedia' events subsequently became associated with Fluxus. As expanded cinema rose to prominence, film-makers began incorporating multi-projection into their practice, something showcased at events such as the Intermedia Art Festival (1969) and Cross Talk Intermedia (1969). The film historian Yuriko Furuhata has pointed out the correlation between multi-projection formats and the surveillance control rooms of Expo '70, thus drawing attention to the influence of both the state and the industry.[15]

In Kyoto and Osaka, a group of young artists who had previously worked in the sculptural arts began producing experimental films under the name of the Art Film Association, a loose network that included Matsumoto Shōji, Imai Norio and Kawaguchi Tatsuo. Due to their background in the plastic arts, the group's approach to film also incorporated a strong focus on the presentation of their work thus leading to the advent of the film and video installation. Indicative of this shift was the Gendai no zōkei (Exhibition of Contemporary Plastic Arts), an annual series of exhibitions organised by members that began in 1968 as an outdoor sculptural exhibition, switched to film screenings in 1970, before being followed by a group exhibition of film installations in 1972, which integrated their sculptural beginnings into the presentation of film.[16] Film and video in the gallery or museum space increasingly shifted from singular events to looped installations with less focus on sequence in order to account for the particular visitor experience of such spaces. As video became more accessible, the Art Film Association artists moved into the fields of video art, video performance and video installation, and the Exhibition of Contemporary Plastic Arts became a key showcase for video work until it was discontinued in 1977.

Expanded cinema became commonplace in the 1960s, but there are earlier examples that explored alternative modes of projection and intermedial collaboration. Although it was peripheral to their work, the young artists' collective Jikken Kōbō Experimental Workshop experimented with film and the use of autoslide projection in their modern ballet productions and music concerts throughout the 1950s. One of their members, Yamaguchi Katsuhiro, made *Mobiles and Vitrines* (1954), about two *obuje* (*objet d'art*)[17] with the photographer Kitadai Shōzō. The film was projected together with slides at their collaboration with a strip show, *7 Peeping Toms from Heaven*, regularly staged between October and December 1954 at the Nichigeki Music Hall.[18] The Sanka zōkei bijutsu kyōkai, a theatre group inspired by the European avant-garde, presented their live performance, *Button*, at the Tsukiji Little Theatre in May 1925 along with several Dada films. Murayama Tomoyoshi, one of Sanka's members, formed the avant-garde group MAVO (1924–5) who staged theatre productions along with multiple projection and interaction between the performance and the on-screen image, in a manner inspired by the early cinema productions of *rensageki* (chain drama).[19] Kinugasa Teinosuke, the director of the landmark independent silent film *A Page of Madness/Kurutta Ichipeiji* (1926),

similarly collaborated with Senda Korenari to present *Kino Drama* (1937), a theatre production that involved screens on both sides of the stage and projections onto the set.

Various international networks have been crucial to the development of experimental Japanese film. As previously noted, early film-makers and critics became deeply invested in the activities of the avant-garde and, in many cases, work was discussed without access to the films themselves with people relying on reports, essays, stills and limited postal exchange. The movement to New York by artists in the 1950s and 1960s, in particular, therefore had an indelible impact on the Japanese art and experimental film scene as information exchange and the visibility of works strengthened. As well as screenings organised by Donald Richie in the US in the 1960s, Iimura Takahiko's six-month European tour in 1969, armed with reels of work by the Film Independents, also helped Japanese experimental film reach a wider audience. The migration of film-makers and artists out of Japan led to transnational collaborations that encouraged new developments in artistic practice. Ōe Masanori flew to New York in 1966 and spent four years in the US during which time he stayed at Third World Studios and Studio M2, where he shot activist documentaries of demonstrations, co-directed by Marvin Fishman, as part of the Newsreel collective. Some Japanese film-makers and artists found residence in overseas countries, including Daïchi Saïto who relocated to Montreal and founded the Double Negative film collective with other local film-makers. The long-standing activities of these film-makers who no longer call Japan their only home allows us to question the validity of national cinema as a framework in describing their work. We may also note that the intimate scale of experimental film production can allow a level of international mobility that is comparatively difficult to attain for directors restricted to mainstream narrative film-making.

Despite the internationalisation of experimental film, local networks have remained relevant by maintaining a sense of community between artists and film-makers that has enabled them to share information, attitudes and audiences. The screening collective Hairo, established in Shibuya in 1970, have continued to project 8mm and 16mm films in the same venue for over forty years. Ōnishi Keiji, who made a highly personal and confrontational experimental documentary about his father's death, *A Burning Star/ Gyōsei* (1999), ran the Cinema Train distributing local film-makers' work and showing experimental films from overseas. The collective [+], including the film-makers Makino Takashi, Hayama Rei, Tamaki Shinkan and the researcher Sakamoto Hirofumi, are the most vital force in the current circle of experimental film-making in Japan. Regularly presenting their own work in Europe and South East Asia, the collective also curate works by international film-makers that its members have discovered in their travels. In particular, Makino's abstract work that superimposes layers of images to immersive effect sees him collaborating with foreign musicians, including Lawrence English (Australia) and Jim O'Rourke (US/Japan) as well as film-makers such as the Dutch media art group Telcosystems (e.g. *Deorbit* [2013]). His unique merging of film and digital working processes is pulling Japanese experimental film in exciting directions and onto an international platform.

While retaining a position at the periphery of the industry, Japanese experimental film has continued to position itself at the forefront of cinematic expression. By taking three central themes into consideration – medium specificity, screening spaces and networks – this chapter has highlighted the peaks of creativity and significant activities that have contributed to the shaping of experimental film in Japan. As a call to internationalise the field of study and reconsider the Western hegemony in the current historicisation of experimental film, this chapter has offered a broad survey of experimental film that has contributed to the development of alternative film-making in Japan. What an overview of such work finally reveals is that the continuing evolution of Japanese experimental film is due, more than anything else, to the impetus of its film-makers to question every possible preconceived framework of cinema itself.

Notes

1. See Sakamoto Hirofumi, 'Jikken eiga e no gigi, sono rekishi-teki zentei', in Plus Publishing (ed.), *Plus Documents 2009–2013* (Tokyo: Engine Books, 2014), p. 9.
2. Yuriko Furuhata has provided astute analysis on this shift in the conception of the image. See her *Cinema of Actuality: Japanese Avant-garde Filmmaking in the Season of Image Politics* (Durham, NC: Duke University Press, 2013), p. 40.
3. The National Film Archive of Japan is currently undergoing an extensive preservation project of many Japanese pre-World War II amateur film titles, including works by Ogino Shigeji and Kansai-based Mori Kurenai. [Editors' note: For more on Ogino Shigeji, see also Chapter 15 by Oliver Dew in this volume.]
4. *Man with a Movie Camera* was released theatrically in Japan as *Korega Russia da!* (This is Russia!) in 1932 by the Yamani Yoko distribution company. *Berlin: Symphony of a Great City* received a theatrical release in 1928.
5. The Shōwa depression was a financial crisis in Japan that took place in 1927. While the post-World War I years saw an economic boom, Japan faced a downturn soon after in the 1920s with the economy slowing down and the Great Kantō Earthquake in 1923. For a comprehensive account of Japan's pre-World War II amateur films, see Nishimura Tomohiro, 'Nihon jikken eizōshi', *Aida* nos. 87–123 (2004–6), which also offers a comprehensive historical account of Japanese experimental film up until the 1970s.
6. Prokino is short for the Proletarian Film League of Japan (Nihon puroretaria eiga dōmei) who documented protests and workers' activities and organised screenings of their own work. For more on Prokino, see Abé Mark Nornes, *Japanese Documentary Film: The Meiji Era through Hiroshima* (Minnesota: University of Minnesota Press, 2003); and Chapter 4 by Naoki Yamamoto in this volume.
7. Throwing the television monitor into a river was probably a homage to Wolf Vostell's *Television Décollage* (1963) performed by Tone Yasunao and Akiyama Kuniharu at the artist Ay-O's Fluxus event 'Happening for Sightseeing Bus Trip in Tokyo' on 18 December 1966.
8. See Daryl Chin, 'The Future of an Illusion(ism): Notes on the New Japanese Avant-Garde Film', *Millennium Film Journal* no. 2 (Spring/Summer, 1978), p. 87.
9. See Daïchi Saïto, *Moving the Sleeping Images of Things towards the Light* (Montreal: Les éditions Le Laps, 2013).
10. The festival was renamed Film Art Festival Tokyo for its second and final editions, in 1968 and 1969 respectively.
11. Other committed journals and magazines that discussed experimental film titles include *Kiroku eiga*, *Eizō geijutsu*, *Eiga hyōron*, *Eiga hihyō*, *Kikan*

film, *Geijutsu club*, *Underground Cinematheque* and *NeoNeo*. Many of these journals were born out of discussion groups that brought together a multidisciplinary network of artists and critics that shared and discussed works, translated critical essays from overseas and organised events.

12 See Adachi Masao, 'Subetewa VAN eiga kagaku kenkyūjo kara hajimatta: Eiga undō ni kanshiteno danshō', in Hirasawa Gō (ed.), *Underground Film Archives* (Tokyo: Kawade Shobō Shinsha, 2002), pp. 96–99; and Hirasawa Gō, 'Politics, the Street, and the Expansion into Everyday Life', in Tasaka Hiroko (ed.), *Japanese Expanded Cinema Revisited* (Tokyo: Tokyo Photographic Art Museum, 2017), pp. 138–47.

13 See Miryam Sas, 'Intermedia 1955–1970', in Diana C. Stoll (ed.), *Tokyo 1955–1970: A New Avant-Garde* (New York: Museum of Modern Art, 2012), p. 143. Ken Yoshida also proposes a relation between Hanada Kiyoteru's understanding of *sōgō geijutsu* and 1960s intermedia in Japan. See his 'The Undulating Contours of Sōgō Geijutsu (Total Work of Art), or Hanada Kiyoteru's Thoughts on Transmedia in Postwar Japan', *Inter-Asia Cultural Studies* vol. 13 no. 1 (2012), pp. 36–54.

14 See Ichikawa Miyabi, 'Jizoku suru jikan to fukusū no basho', *SD* vol. 79 (April 1971), p. 123. For more on intermedia and expanded cinema, see Julian Ross, 'Beyond the Frame: Intermedia and Expanded Cinema in 1960–70s Japan' (PhD thesis, University of Leeds, 2015).

15 See Yuriko Furuhata, 'Multimedia Environments and Security Operations: Expo '70 as a Laboratory of Governance', *Grey Room* no. 54 (Winter 2014), pp. 56–79.

16 The exhibition itself was restaged at the Museum of Modern Art, Tokyo, in the exhibition Re: play 1972/2015 - Restaging 'Expression in Film '72', 6 October–13 December 2015, curated by Miwa Kenjin.

17 *Obuje*, the Japanese translation for *objet d'art* (the art object), was often used in postwar Japanese art circles to signify small items placed in an artistic context.

18 Other film experiments related to Jikken Kōbō include *Kine-Calligraphy* (1955) by Graphic Shūdan (Graphics Group), a direct animation inspired by Norman McLaren, and Matsumoto Toshio's first film *Silver Wheel/Ginrin* (1956) that involved contributions from its members.

19 *Rensageki* combined film and theatre in a mixed format presentation that saw short-lived success in the mid-1910s. See Diane Wei Lewis, 'Shinkō geijutsu undō to rensageki: Murayama Tomoyoshi o megutte', *Bandarai* vol. 12 (2013), pp. 195–205.

14

TRANSMEDIAL RELATIONS
Manga at the movies: Adaptation and intertextuality

Rayna Denison

When scholars think about adaptation, there is a long-standing tendency to think about the novel-to-film format and focus on the classical over the popular. Today's Japanese cinema is, however, now driven by a different kind of adaptation process, one that moves from manga to the moving image. Many of these manga adaptations fall into the category of Japanese cinema still least attended to within academic work. 'Japan's popular cinema, the often unexported movies seen by millions of ordinary Japanese citizens', remains, in Susan J. Napier's words of more than a decade ago, 'ignored or bemoaned by critics in the West, who … [continue to see] the rise of mass produced and mass marketed films as a link to a perceived decline in the quality of Japanese cinema overall.'[1] While the analyses of popular Japanese cinema represented by studies of anime, horror and famous directors are welcome, there is still much missing in terms of a more comprehensive consideration of the field. This chapter aims to expand these discussions of adaptation by examining two variants on the manga-to-film adaptation: firstly, direct adaptation and, secondly, the complex form of intertextuality that spans across Asian media production and that begins in Japanese manga and returns home as live action film (Fig. 14.1).

As this choice implies, manga adaptations come in diverse forms, marked by shifting descriptions such as live action manga films (*manga jissha eiga*); theatrical versions (*gekijōban*) of anime and live action television drama; and film versions of manga (*manga no eigaban*). They can be found at every level of Japanese film production: from the art cinema of Kore-eda Hirokazu (whose *Air Doll/Kūki ningyō* [2009] was based on a manga of the same name by Gōda Yoshie), to massive franchise productions that have produced film series spanning the last decade (for example, the *Umizaru* films and television drama, about Japan's sea search and rescue force, directed by Hasumi Eiichirō and based on a manga by Satō Shūhō) (Fig. 14.2). Manga adaptations are becoming increasingly ubiquitous, and they fit snugly within the diversity of genres that characterise Japanese cinema from art cinema to more commercial productions. In the case of popular Japanese cinema, manga adaptations are doubly commercial since they are adapted from one highly exploited popular medium (manga) into another (film), often by way of dispersed, transmedia franchises. In this respect, manga adaptations offer a new theoretical challenge, requiring us to rethink the boundaries of film-making in Japan and to see Japanese cinema as part of a set of larger intertextual networks that run throughout Japanese popular culture as a whole.[2]

Part of this challenge centres on how to accord value and meaning to manga adaptations, while another lies in how to study the complex diachronic networks of texts that such manga adaptations become bound up in. Here, the concept of the popular provides the kernel of an approach: by focusing on manga adaptations that have proven profitable for their makers, the political economy of such film texts within Japan's media industries provides a window onto Japan's contemporary film culture. As Janet Wasko argues, the

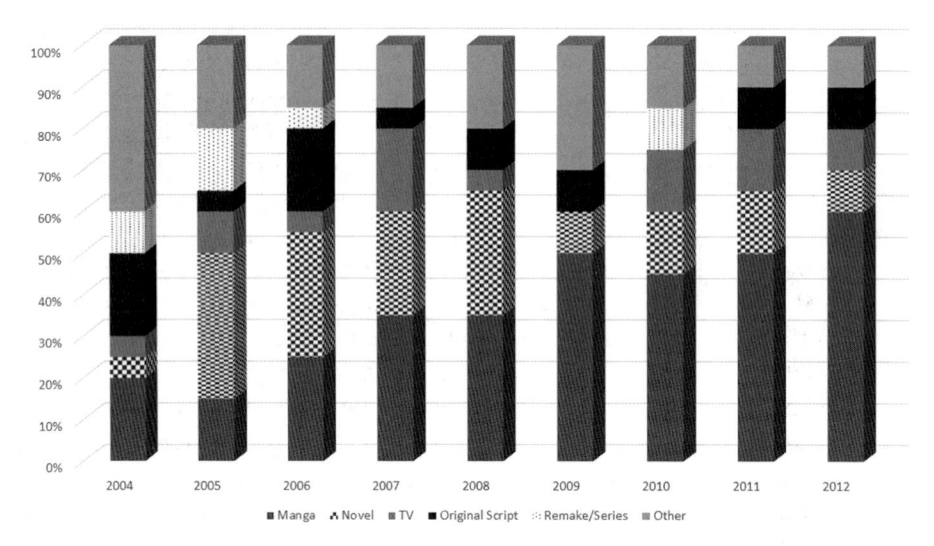

Fig. 14.1 Chart of manga film adaptations 2004–12. *Source:* Eiren (Motion Pictures Producers Association of Japan) and the Japanese Movie Database.

Fig. 14.2 *Air Doll/Kūki ningyō* (Kore-eda Hirokazu, 2009, Kūki ningyō Production Committee).

essence of political economy resides in 'research that examines the relationships of power that are involved in the production, distribution and consumption of media and communication resources within a wider social context'.[3] By making the relationships between manga and films the focus here – by seeking to explain the prevalence and popularity of manga as a source material for wide swathes of Japanese film production – the power and ideologies of these popular films become discernible.

FROM *KONTENTSU* (CONTENT) TO FRANCHISING: MEDIA MIX AND MANGA AS SOURCE TEXTS

Intertextuality, within franchising and adaptation, is normally discussed in Japan with reference to the content industry (*kontentsu gyōkai*) – reportedly worth over 12 trillion yen in 2011 – which divides media production between music, images (*eizō*) and text (or publishing).[4] Success in these debates is derived from the ability of producers to spread their *kontentsu* (a combination of texts and intellectual property) across a wide range of media platforms.[5] For manga, this means adaptation. The Institute for the Association of Japanese Animations cites three types of significant manga adaptation, while cautioning that:

> Once, manga adaptations [*manga no eizōka*] (into anime, television drama series [*dorama*], and film) were an effective way of bringing increased sales. However, in recent years, original manga have not sold after the broadcasting of adapted works has finished meaning the effect [of the strategy] has become far less significant.[6]

Despite the weakening of adaptation benefits for the manga industry, manga adaptations themselves are becoming bigger hits than in the past. For example, Figure 14.1 illustrates the growing significance of manga film adaptations since the mid-2000s. This trend is all the more significant because, since 2006, Japanese domestic films have retaken a majority share of their home market from overseas imports.[7] However, the coincidence between the rising success of Japanese films and the rising numbers of manga adaptations disguises a series of complex industrial systems enabling both.

The success of manga adaptations comes from the popularisation of specific industrial systems within Japanese film production cultures – namely, an increase in both production committees (*seisaku iinkai*), and a renewed emphasis on 'media mix'. In the first case, the use of production committees is an intensification of long-standing practices traceable back to the rise of postwar media conglomeration in Japan. The most studied and well-known example of this media conglomeration is Kadokawa shoten's development from a publishing house to a transmedia franchising conglomerate.[8] However, even where Japanese companies have bought up subsidiaries and created corporate partnerships to enable horizontally and vertically integrated conglomeration, they still tend to create texts through production committee arrangements.

A good example is offered by Fuji Television, which has been producing films since the late 1960s, and which is part of the larger Fuji Media Holdings group, which has over twenty different companies under its umbrella.[9] These companies work synergistically on media productions, adapting texts across formats (from manga to television to film in many cases) and also across media platforms (from broadcast and exhibition through to home entertainment). Having said this, even such conglomerated companies still enter into production committee arrangements. For instance, Fuji Television often works with Tōhō, one of Japan's major film studios and a major shareholder in Fuji Media Holdings, in order to ensure that Fuji TV's films have access to Tōhō's prestigious cinema chains in Japan.[10] In this way, Japanese media production often becomes a collaborative process, despite these cooperative arrangements taking place in a highly crowded, and competitive, media marketplace.

Production committees tend to be, 'formed for each project, and own all the copyrights to a film. Profits are divided among the companies that have invested in the film, in proportion to the level of each company's investment.'[11] Indeed, production committees are now the dominant production system for film and anime, bringing together copyright holders with media partners able to adapt, promote and distribute intellectual properties across a range of formats. Production committee membership is therefore carefully orchestrated around the planned exploitation of an intellectual property, ensuring that only one company represents each stage of the process.[12] Consequently, competition and power relations in Japanese franchise production take unusual forms, with individual companies often working in multiple competing production committees simultaneously. Competition, therefore, takes place between production committees rather than between individual content producers or distributors. Furthermore, despite such ostensibly short-term arrangements, intended to last for the duration of a production project, production committees are often extended when texts become successful, creating collective oligopolies around hit multimedia franchises that mimic conglomeration in other parts of the world. As a result, Japan now enjoys a relatively stable multimedia franchising system that has been helping to manufacture larger and larger film hits.

The success of this system is, in part, directly thanks to the 'media mix' strategies used by production committees. Marc Steinberg defines media mix in relation to Henry Jenkins's concept of media convergence: 'Japanese media convergence has its own name: the *media mix*. A popular, widely used term for the cross-media serialization and circulation of entertainment franchises.'[13] Jenkins, quoting Mizuko Ito, goes further claiming that US blockbusters such as *The Matrix* (The Wachowski Brothers, 1999) were fuelled by these same media mix strategies. He states that the Wachowskis'

Entire interest in transmedia storytelling can be traced to this fascination with what anthropologist Mimi Ito has described as Japan's 'media mix' culture. On the one hand, the media mix strategy disperses content across broadcast media, portable technologies such as game boys or cell phones, collectibles, and location-based entertainment centers from amusement parks to game arcades. On the other, these franchises depend on hypersociability, that is, they encourage various forms of participation and social interactions between consumers.[14]

For Jenkins, therefore, the creation of multi-platform story worlds in US cinema is a direct product of observations made by that industry about Japan's multimedia, multi-platform story adaptations. While Jenkins seeks to look at the way these cross-media production strategies are utilised to create holistic story worlds, the use of media mix in Japan is actually more complex than this, with media mix strategies used to produce a range of different kinds of franchising practice, not just the creation of distinctive narrative worlds.

There is variance in the definitions of media mix within academic studies of manga and anime franchising. Steinberg rightly asserts that these transmedia practices are nothing new, noting that Japanese media convergence emerged out of postwar connections between manga, anime and character merchandising industries.[15] Thomas Lamarre concurs, writing that, in media mix, 'Character merchandising, character licensing, and character franchises have long been important in generating and sustaining connections across media', but he terms these 'image alliances'.[16] Mizuko Ito also explains media mix in slightly different terms, arguing that in media mix, 'multiple media forms *concurrently* manifest an evolving but shared virtual referent'.[17] Whether read as a cross-industrial production system, as character-centred intertexts or as pre-planned media franchising with simultaneous release strategies, it is clear that the notion of media mix is coming to dominate Japan's media landscapes. Moreover, it is clear that the term describes a range of franchising strategies and practices. In fact, as will be shown hereafter, media mix usefully incorporates all of these varied definitions, describing a whole set of processes and their resultant intertexts.

As this suggests, the most relevant parallel between English language concepts and media mix is the notion of franchising. Franchising, like media mix, describes both a process and its results. Derek Johnson has claimed that 'the franchise must be understood not just as a function of textuality, but as an industrially and socially contextual dynamic constituted by historical processes and discourses' following Jason Mittell, who views genres as discursively constituted categories.[18] Examining the connections between media mix and franchising in Japan thereby offers a way into debates about the relative positioning of manga and film within an intertext. Doing so demands that the relationships between Japanese films and their urtexts be examined for what they reveal about the relative power and status of texts within a wider intertextual network.[19] In the sections that now follow, I therefore seek to examine the processes involved in the creation of two different kinds of manga adaptation in order to assess the differing strategies at work in Japan's media mix system.

MANGA ADAPTATION AS POPULAR 'ART' CINEMA

At one end of the Japanese market for manga adaptations, commercial practices are used to ensure the profitability of films even as they demand attention as art. The production of Ninagawa Mika's debut directorial feature, *Sakuran* (2006), offers a useful case study in this regard. Industrial discourse around the film continually highlighted both collaboration and competition between the creators of the urtext and film text (Fig. 14.3). *Sakuran*'s promotional campaign is also significant because it offers a particularly stark example of how such discourse can be tied to issues of industry and gender. For an example of the former issue, Matsutani Sōichirō paraphrases *Sakuran*'s associate producer, Tanishima Masayuki, regarding the relationship between publisher Kōdansha and his film's promotion:

Fig. 14.3 *Sakuran* (Ninagawa Mika, 2007, Fella Pictures).

Kōdansha was not in the production committee [*seisaku iinkai*] initially, but they played a key role in the publicity: their women's magazine *With* had a serial about [making] *Sakuran* for a year, and two books on the film were published by another magazine, *Tokyo isshūkan*. The publisher saw the reception of the magazine serial and the books, and then joined the production committee once the filming was finished.[20]

Kōdansha's tentative steps into committee membership are a useful indicator of the flexibility of the production committee system but also of the perceived risk involved in adapting *Sakuran* from manga to film. The long promotional campaign, containing cross-promotional making of manga texts and books, some published more than a year before the live action film's release, also reveals the construction of a transmedia audience in preparation for the live action film text.

Sakuran, a period film about the often competitive lives and loves of courtesans in the Yoshiwara pleasure district, was also carefully tied into contemporary Japanese women's cultures through this preparatory promotion. Furthermore, the association between gender and *Sakuran* was reinforced throughout the film's promotional campaign. *Sakuran*'s core advertising leaflet – a glossy, fold-out mini-brochure – highlighted the central role of female cast and crew members, announcing that, 'Now, the coolest of women are competing in this film!' alongside a list of female production staff that begins with director Ninagawa Mika, followed by the original manga author, Anno Moyoco, before listing the screenwriter, composer and star, all of whom are women.

This tactic was later repeated in *Sakuran*'s exhibition pamphlet sold in cinemas. After providing the same tag line and list of personnel, the brochure expands on the female-centred promotion, proclaiming:

> Creative women from all walks of life, each pouring their total energies into it, are showing they can deftly jump over the framework of Japanese films. The film *Sakuran* is vivid and filled with strength and was made as a film that deeply pierces the hearts of those of us living now.[21]

In these examples the 'competition' between the personnel is made to mimic *Sakuran*'s narrative content, which follows Edo period prostitutes vying for the status of *oiran*. The alignment is then given a contemporary twist, by the suggestion that women's presence in Japanese film-making is still unusual, that hurdles remain for women to overcome, and that it is the combined skills and energies of these women that allows them to do so. In these ways, the competitive-yet-collaborative collective authorship of *Sakuran* is used to offset the relative risk in Asmik Ace employing first-time director Ninagawa.

Nor does this artistic palimpsest stop at the realms of cast and crew members. Throughout the interviews and promotional articles for *Sakuran*, Anno Moyoco's reputation as a manga artist is used to authenticate the adaptation of her manga into film. In a shared interview, for example, Anno and Ninagawa discuss the idea of 'trust' at length, with Anno declaring, 'When a manga is adapted into another genre, I think I can only trust someone who treats the contents in the same way I do. From that point of view I was totally confident to trust Ninagawa.'[22] In another article, Ninagawa praises Anno and admits her trepidation about adapting *Sakuran*, saying, 'I wanted to avoid my favourite work by a woman whom I respect, but we received the rights smoothly. There was no going back anymore.'[23] In these examples, Anno's popular manga text is held up as an ideal, and her stamp of authorial approval is used to authenticate the adaptation of *Sakuran* from manga into a live action film. Likewise,

Anno's inclusion as an authorial presence within the promotion helps to create a feedback loop between the film and its precursor text, with the early marketing campaign also being used to generate reciprocal interest in both franchise texts. The accord between the two authorial voices is thereby used to assert a meeting of artistic visions in which the live action version of *Sakuran* complements rather than competes with the original manga, despite the competitive set-up in the film's publicity campaign.

Ninagawa's presence as an established artist outside film-making was also simultaneously emphasised throughout *Sakuran*'s promotional campaign. Ninagawa is one of Japan's foremost contemporary photographers and well known for her work in both still life and portraiture. She is also renowned for shifting between high art and commercial entertainment, with gallery exhibitions vying for attention alongside her high-profile spreads in Japanese fashion magazines such as *Vogue*.[24] Given her solid artistic reputation as a photographer, one who had already crossed between other types of production, the decision to invite Ninagawa to direct *Sakuran* was demonstrably less risky than it might first appear. In fact, her brand as a photographer was heavily used to sell *Sakuran* with dozens of her photographic images included in both promotional articles and interviews and in more direct forms of advertising such as the film's cinema pamphlet.

Many of these images directly echo Ninagawa's earlier work; particularly her earlier photographs of goldfish and flowers.[25] The cinema pamphlet alone contains four large Ninagawa photographs as well as a cover whose background is a collage of Ninagawa's goldfish images.[26] Each of these photographs is marked by an English-language credit to Ninagawa as photographer, further cementing the associations between her still and moving images. Additionally, the connection between Ninagawa's photographic art and her first film was compounded in the ancillary goods created for *Sakuran*'s release, which included a photograph collection based on the film and another on its star, Tsuchiya Anna. There was also a production diary written by Ninagawa.[27] In this cross-promotional media mix exercise, Ninagawa the photographer is brought into contact with her directorial persona in order that the former may authenticate the work of the latter (her dominant photography brand obfuscating her untested status as a director).

However, Ninagawa's own attempts to assert and legitimate her authorial vision for *Sakuran* rested elsewhere. 'All the ideas are based on an examination of historically accurate [images]' she declared, also discussing how she 'looked at literature, *ukiyoe* and *shunga* that were actually created in the Edo period, recreating what I felt about them in my film'.[28] In this way, Ninagawa claims to be able to counter the masculine visions of the past found in the Japanese period film (*jidaigeki*).[29] Ninagawa revisits the promotional narrative of *Sakuran* as a women's film in these statements but gives that narrative greater purpose, re-imagining it as a challenge to a patriarchal period film genre dismissive of women's history.

In so doing, Ninagawa sets *Sakuran* apart from its roots in manga and from connections to her earlier photography, situating the film as a politically motivated version of Japan's history as seen through the eyes of women and declaring her vision as an 'authentic' ideological challenge to *Sakuran*'s *jidaigeki* film predecessors. Throughout the promotion for *Sakuran*, therefore, threads of gender discourse create an image that challenges women's marginal status within both the contemporary Japanese film industry and its representations of Japanese history. While many of these claims simply function as gendered marketing palimpsest, there is a deeper claim to authenticity based on women's perspectives that insists upon artistic status for *Sakuran* despite its underlying commercial discourse. Even while *Sakuran* was being developed as a women's film, therefore, it became ideologically inflected by its source materials and personnel and was pulled between the twin poles of commerciality and politically informed art. This pull is laid bare in *Sakuran*'s merchandising, where sponsor Wakaba's Juicy Jewel perfume was juxtaposed with Ninagawa's photographic records of her film-making in a marketing effort that explicitly linked art and consumerism.

PRODUCTION CYCLES AND THE TRANSMEDIA FRANCHISE: *HANA YORI DANGO/BOYS OVER FLOWERS*

While *Sakuran* presents an example of direct adaptation, with close links between urtext and film iteration, other contemporary Japanese live action manga adaptations can present far more complex, indirect forms of adaptation that reach across decades, nations and industries. In one of the widest dispersals of a manga property to date, *Boys Over Flowers* has traversed across the borders of multiple Asian nations becoming the source for material for multiple local television drama hits from Taiwan and South Korea to China and the Philippines. In all of its iterations, *Boys Over Flowers* is a variant on the 'Cinderella' fairy tale in which a poor, working-class teenage girl comes into contact with a rich group of teenage boys from powerful families who begin by making her life very difficult, only to become either romantic interests or older brother figures.

Koichi Iwabuchi is not alone in focusing on the transnational reach of this text, arguing in 2004 that, for *Boys Over Flowers*, 'there is no original Japanese drama based on the comic series, but Taiwan's television producers skilfully adapted it to a drama form on their own initiative'.[30] Somewhat inevitably, a two-season live action drama hit soon followed in Japan, beginning in 2005 (directed by Ishii Yasuharu). But, the more important point here is Iwabuchi's elision of the earlier Japanese live action *Boys Over Flowers* film (Kusada Yasuyuki, 1995), the anime television series (Yamauchi Shigeyasu, 1996–7) and its related anime film (Yamauchi Shigeyasu, 1997); all of which pre-date overseas adaptations of *Boys Over Flowers*.[31] As the example of *Boys Over Flowers* suggests, popular and academic memory around large intertexts has a tendency to falter, particularly in the face of highly successful and geographically dispersed franchise texts.

Japanese industry commentators compounded this erasure in their assessments of the *Boys Over Flowers* franchise. *Kinema junpō*'s special issue magazine *Joshi ni eiga* (Movies for Girls), for example, contained a section called '*Boys Over Flowers* Adapted Works at a Glance', which relates the existence of the 1995 live action Japanese film, the Taiwanese television series (both seasons) and both seasons of the live action Japanese television drama but elides their earlier anime cousins.[32] As Jennifer Forrest and Leonard R. Koos note, 'remakes often do not credit their sources', but the question here is why some cycles of production become significant while others drop away within franchise discourses.[33] Rather than simply being seen as manga adaptations, or manga-originated franchises, the media mix for *Boys Over Flowers* seems to have been slanted towards particular moments of textual creation; most forcefully towards live action over animation. In this way, it suggests that individual texts are less important than clusters of texts that have coherent, medium-specific identities.

Outside Japan, cycles of production are most commonly noted in the case of film genres,[34] but media mix logic has instantiated various long-running franchises that all borrow from a single *kontentsu* (or content, a close cousin of Intellectual Property in English) in serialised chains of cross-media texts. For *Boys Over Flowers*, it appears that the repetition of cast and crew from live action television drama (*dorama*) into a finale film text (*Hana yori dango final* [2008]) replicates this pattern. Producer Setoguchi Katsuaki, says of the *Boys Over Flowers* film:

> We had a lot of discussions saying, 'If we can do it, let's not just scale up [*sukēru appu*] from here', and for that reason we decided that making it in the world of film would be best, and not doing a [television] sequel or Part 3. Saying, well, what do we do?!, that's where we started from.[35]

Repetition, in this comment, is weighed against the need for variety in texts, with sequels and new television series passed over in favour of a film. Scale is also made significant here and is weighed against the norm of 'scaling up' between television and film productions, a common discourse in Japanese transmedia franchising. By thinking differently, the producer argues, the *Boys Over Flowers* film would represent a break from normal media mix practices.

Film, then, becomes a way to differentiate between similar live action franchise products that aggrandise manga-originated television properties in order to demonstrate their growing cultural status.

Another way to measure this success comes through discourse around actors. *Boys Over Flowers*'s manga author, Kamio Yōko, has proclaimed, for instance, that the lead actress, Inoue Mao, 'had a really hard time playing Tsukushi for so long. It is an extremely hard role, but now, I have the sense that "Tsukushi = Mao".'[36] Kamio equates the television drama's female star directly with her character and connects the actress's trials with those faced by Inoue's character, Makino Tsukushi, after Tsukushi herself encountered the Flower Four (F4) group of super-rich boys at her elite school. Other commentators, however, were far quicker to note the comparative levels of stardom at the beginning of the show, as well as the franchise's effect on actors:

> By the time of the *dorama*, Matsumoto [Jun] was already popular, Oguri Shun's popularity rose terrifically playing the prince character, and Matsuda Shota and Abe Tsuyoshi's popularity can also be said to have risen remarkably.[37]

Television is seen here as a more significant site of star-creation than film, thus giving it a more prominent role in the media mix. In this way, the promotional material surrounding *Boys Over Flowers* suggests that television is the engine for stardom and star-creation in Japan. This may help to explain why television became so dominant within the franchise discourse, because television acted not just as a launching platform for manga adaptations but also as one for new transmedia stars.

Matsumoto Jun, who plays villain-turned-protagonist Dōmyōji Tsukasa in Japan's version of *Boys Over Flowers*, provides a pivotal example. Already famous for his work in the boy band Arashi, Matsumoto's role as Tsukasa allowed a huge amount of cross-promotional branding to take place within the franchise. Matsumoto's star presence as a singer even intrudes into the television text as his voice can be heard in the opening theme song, 'Love So Sweet'. Matsumoto's heavy use in promotion and his cross-promotional musical television presence worked to blur his performances and his wider star persona. At the same time, each element of Matsumoto's own media mix acted as a dispersible element that could be used to promote other texts within the franchise, thus creating a feedback loop between Matsumoto's stardom and *Boys Over Flowers*. For these reasons, the powerful agencies supplying star talent to adaptations of manga in Japan can be seen as a driving force behind the scenes of media mix creation.

The fast turnaround in live action production cycles (the whole of the *Boys Over Flowers* franchise lasted between 2005 and 2008) can be at least partly explained by its reliance on busy, ageing stars. The rapid reiteration of *Boys Over Flowers*'s narrative across national borders has also aided the intellectual property's overall longevity. New versions in new countries repeat the *Boys Over Flowers* narrative over and over again with each successful text seemingly triggering new adaptations (recently the franchise appears to have been moving even further abroad, with the announcement of an Indian version). This has all had the effect of throwing attention back onto the manga origin point for what is now a highly dispersed transnational media intertext.

As the copyright holder, Kamio Yōko has remained a significant presence in the promotion transnationally and at home. For example, Kamio appears in the cinema pamphlet for *Boys Over Flowers Final/Hana yori dango final*, the film that capped off the Japanese production cycle in 2008 by featuring the marriage of Tsukasa and Tsukushi. The pamphlet contains a double-page spread, with one page devoted to images of Kamio's manga covers and a further page given over to a long interview focusing on her opinion of the Japanese live action incarnations of her text. She says:

> Throughout the trilogy [3 *bu saku*] there are scenes in which Mao does a fighting and jumping pose. This is not in the original [*gensaku*], but I thought that it represents the foundation of the Tsukushi character really well, because it is live action.[38]

In Kamio's comments the live action production cycle consisting of the two seasons of the television drama and the subsequent film adaptation are treated collectively. This is unusual, because the language used, of a trilogy (or more literally a three-part work), does not differentiate between the television and film elements of the production cycle. This holistic approach to *Boys Over Flowers*' live action Japanese production cycle signals the normalcy of media mix thinking in Japan, while also revealing a perceived lack of hierarchy between the cultural status of film and television texts. However, Kamio is also quick to note how her work is the original (*gensaku*) and that Mao's performance may be drawing from media intertexts beyond her manga. Consequently, differences and uniqueness within each medium are affirmed, while at the same time each part of the production cycle is shown to build directly upon its predecessors. The expansion from television into film merely provides a different stage upon which to continue telling the same story, all of which comes close to Henry Jenkins's version of media mix theory, transmedia storytelling.[39]

The continually expanding transnational *Boys Over Flowers* intertext is consequently unusual because it consists of a set of self-contained production cycles with their own adaptations of Kamio's manga text, remade in ever-more languages for ever-more cultures. All of this has meant that *Boys Over Flowers* texts have been in near-continuous production for almost two decades. These texts share a single manga as their origin point, but they feed off of one another too, with the pan-Asian circulation of each new remake spurring new interpretations and variations, usually with increasingly large budgets.

Manga, therefore, may be little more than narrative inspiration, with entirely new character names, locations and cultural mores adapted around it. However, in other cases, new adaptations can exceed the manga's story, requiring new narratives to be appended, as was the case with the original script used to create *Boys Over Flowers Final* (written by Satake Mikio). These textual relationships are complex, and the interactions between texts varies, but the intertext of *Boys Over Flowers*-inspired 'works' is rich with associated meanings that challenge us to think beyond the logic of linear adaptation to see the complex networks of meaning that are comprised within contemporary media ecologies. In this instance, the live action production cycle in Japan abuts the fields of Japanese music, stardom and a transnational remake intertext, all of which inform its content and promotional discourses.

CONCLUSIONS

The manga industry in Japan is no longer a discrete entity but one enmeshed in the industrial logics of media mix and the exploitation of intellectual property. It is the sales of rights to adapt and remake manga texts that keep manga authors' work in the public eye, even long after the 'original' text has been completed. However, even this undersells the levels of intra-intertext competition that can take place, as new adaptations are produced in an attempt to erase or reinvigorate older texts.

This is why the industrial logic of *kontentsu* is so useful in Japan: in its combination of texts and intellectual property rights, *kontentsu* can describe the complex of industrial collaborations, partnerships and competition that works to popularise particular manga-originated texts. Even popular live action films such as *Boys Over Flowers Final* operate in this way, with a production committee orchestrating its production and dissemination. In this instance, the main producer, Tokyo Broadcasting System (TBS), one of Japan's largest television-film producers, joined forces with copyright holder Shūeisha, distributor Tōhō, the J-Storm talent agency and others to manage the release of this pre-planned hit film release.

As yet, the collaboration between companies in such production committees has not resulted in the production of a single dominant type of manga adaptation, even though this system has led to the proliferation of the use of manga as source texts in various forms of Japanese transmedia franchising. These tactics complicate even the simplest form of direct adaptation with art cinema being brought into closer conjunction with more popular forms of media texts, along with the sponsorship and branding that orbits around more commercial intertextual networks. At the end of the production scale oriented towards pre-planned, large-scale hit film-making, the meeting of the artistic and commercial is even more contentious.

Serial film-making has long existed in Japan, and even these long chains of production are now often just small interstitial moments in multimedia franchises that span across all available media platforms and across extended tracts of contemporary Japanese media history.

Within this landscape, the status of manga as a source for adaptation is likewise variable. Manga are used for everything from direct templates to 'inspirational' texts upon which other kinds of media are based. This may be why manga authors are often brought in to authenticate new iterations of, and variations on, their stories. In such cases, manga authors often talk about the elements that are unique to the adaptation medium, highlighting what has been added to their manga concepts, whether it is colour imagery, movement or character tropes of the kinds mentioned by authors in the case studies chosen here or, as in other instances, the new stories, additional characters and new worlds that reinterpret the original manga. Manga's roles in adaptation are, even at a textual level, therefore deserving of a case-by-case analysis to see what kinds of adaptation inform the large numbers of media in Japan that use manga *gensaku*.

The value of manga at the movies, however, goes beyond source materials into the wider worlds of media mix and *kontentsu*. As a set of practices and processes, these Japanese systems and strategies inform the ability of producers to carve out space for new media texts within Japan's complex and highly commercialised media markets. Manga lies at the heart of these systems, with texts that can be extrapolated across production formats in the search for ever-greater levels of intellectual copyright exploitation and profit. The cycles of production and long serial chains of texts seem largely dependent on the kinds of manga being adapted and the media in which they find their greatest profitability. The variety in franchising practices noted in this study is a consequence of the flexibility of Japan's media mix and *kontentsu* industry systems, with successful texts spun out across as many media as possible, while unsuccessful, or more limited, texts stagnate. As intellectual properties mixed across Japan's media, manga are now a crucial and pivotal force in Japanese film production cultures; perhaps more so than the genres and auteur directors that have organised our understanding of Japanese cinema to date. It is therefore not so much that we see manga at the movies in Japan, it is more that manga have become the heart and soul of Japanese popular cinema as a whole.

ACKNOWLEDGMENTS

The author would like to thank Dr Hiroko Furukawa for her assistance with translations for parts of the chapter, and the UK Arts and Humanities Research Council for the generous funding that made the research possible.

Notes

1. Susan J. Napier, 'Panic Sites: The Japanese Imagination of Disaster from *Godzilla* to *Akira*', *Journal of Japanese Studies* vol. 19 no. 2 (1996), p. 327. There are, of course, exceptions, most notably Frenchy Lunning's edited journal collection, *Mechademia* (Minneapolis: University of Minnesota Press, 2006-).
2. Marsha Kinder, *Playing with Power in Movies, Television, and Video Games* (Berkeley: University of California Press, 1991), pp. 40–6.
3. Janet Wasko, 'Studying the Political Economy of Media and Information', *Comunicação e Sociedade* vol. 7 (2005), p. 44. See also Eileen Meehan, '"Holy Commodity Fetish, Batman!": The Political Economy of a Commercial Intertext', in Roberta E. Pearson and William Uricchio (eds), *The Many Lives of the Batman: Critical Approaches to a Superhero and His Media* (New York: Routledge, 1991), pp. 47–65.
4. Nakano Akira, *Saishin kontentsu gyōkai no dōkō to karakuri ga yoku wakaru* (Tokyo: Shuwa System, 2013), pp. 10–13.
5. Marc Steinberg, *Anime's Media Mix: Franchising Toys and Characters in Japan* (Minneapolis: University of Minnesota Press, 2012).
6. Masuda Hiromichi, Hikawa Ryūsuke, Fujitsu Ryōta, Rikukawa Kazuo, Hayashi Masahiro, Mori Yūji, Liu Wenbing, Guo Wenfang, Itō Tadashi, Akita Takahira, Mitsuru Sōda, Yamamura Takayoshi, Hagura Hiroyuki, Shichijō Naohiro, Onouchi Megumi and Ishikawa Naoki (eds), *Anime Industry Report 2011* (Tokyo: Institute of the Association of Japanese Animation Database Working Group, 2011), p. 76.
7. Eiren, 'Statistics of Film Industry in Japan', <http://www.eiren.org/toukei/data.html>.

8. Darrell William Davis and Emilie Yeuh-yu Yeh, *East Asian Screen Industries* (London: British Film Institute, 2008), pp. 65–7; Steinberg, *Anime's Media Mix*.
9. *Fuji Television Annual Report 2007*, <http://www.fujimediahd.co.jp/en/ir/pdf/ar/2007/all.pdf>.
10. *Fuji Media Investors Information*, <http://www.fujimediahd.co.jp/en/ir/pdf/2013renewal/20110623198447.pdf >.
11. Kakeo Yoshio, 'Production and Distribution System: Some Characteristics', in Wakai Makiko (ed.), *The Guide to Japanese Film Industry and Co-Production*, trans. Yasuda Takuo (Tokyo: UNIJAPAN, 2010), p. 46.
12. Woojeong Joo, Rayna Denison with Hiroko Furukawa, *Manga Movies Project Report 1: Transmedia Japanese Franchising*, <https://www.academia.edu/3693690/Manga_Movies_Project_Report_1_-_Transmedia_Japanese_Franchising >.
13. Henry Jenkins, *Convergence Culture: Where Old and New Media Collide* (New York: New York University Press, 2006); Steinberg, *Anime's Media Mix*, p. viii. Emphasis in original.
14. Jenkins, *Convergence Culture*, loc. 2306 of 8270.
15. Steinberg, *Anime's Media Mix*, p. ix.
16. Thomas Lamarre, *The Anime Machine: A Media Theory of Animation* (Minneapolis: University of Minnesota Press, 2009), p. 300.
17. Mizuko Ito, 'Technologies of the Childhood Imagination: Media Mixes, Hypersociality, and Recombinant Cultural Forms', *Items and Issues: Social Science Research Council* vol. 4 no. 4 (Fall/Winter 2003), p. 32.
18. Derek Johnson, *Media Franchising: Creative License and Collaboration in the Cultural Industries* (New York: New York University Press, 2013), p. 29; Jason Mittell, 'A Cultural Approach to Television Genre Theory', *Cinema Journal* vol. 40 no. 3 (Spring 2001), pp. 3–24.
19. Thomas Austin, *Hollywood, Hype and Audiences: Selling and Watching Popular Film in the 1990s* (Manchester: Manchester University Press, 2002), p. 126.
20. Matsutani Sōichirō, 'Where does Manga Go? Media Franchising of Manga and the Present Situation of the Production Committee', trans. Furukawa Hiroko, *Tsukuru* (May 2007), pp. 40–6.
21. Hirano Misa, Ogawa Mieko, Kanai Reiko, Sekiya Nami, Kawase Yōko, Watanabe Emi, Tanijimi Tadashi and Uda Mitsuru (eds), *Sakuran* (Tokyo: Asmik Ace, 2007), p. 3.
22. Nobunaga Minami, 'An Intimate Talk: Ninagawa Mika and Anno Moyoco', trans. Furukawa Hiroko, *Bungei bessatsu: Ninagawa Mika* (Tokyo: Kawade shobō shinsha, 2009) p. 106; Suzuki Takashi, 'Mika Ninagawa (Director)', *Kinema jumpō* no. 1478 (March 2007), p. 38.
23. Suzuki, 'Ninagawa mika', pp. 38–9.
24. Ninagawa Mika, Official Website, <http://www.ninamika.com/ja/>.
25. Ninagawa Mika, *Eien no Hana* (Tokyo: Shōgakukan, 2006); Ninagawa Mika, *Liquid Dreams* (Tokyo: Kawade shobō shinsha, 2003).
26. Hirano et al., *Sakuran*, pp. 1–5.
27. Ibid., p. 26.
28. Takashi, 'Ninagawa mika', pp. 40–1.
29. For more on the relationship between *Sakuran* and Ninagawa's historical research, see Noma Sawako (ed.), *Sakuran: Official Guidebook* (Tokyo: Kōdansha, 2007), pp. 84–99.
30. Koichi Iwabuchi, 'Introduction', in Koichi Iwabuchi (ed.), *Feeling Asian Modernities: Transnational Consumption of Japanese TV Dramas* (Hong Kong: Hong Kong University Press, 2004), p. 17. See also Yoshida Hitomi, 'The Localization of the *Hana yori dango* Text: Plural Modernities in East Asia', *New Voices* vol. 4 (January 2011), pp. 78–99, <http://pdf.jpf-sydney.org/newvoices/4/volume4.pdf#page=89>.
31. Anon., '*Hana yori dango*', *Anime News Network*, <http://www.animenewsnetwork.com/encyclopedia/anime.php?id=1136>.
32. Kumasaka Tae, 'Hana yori dango eizōka no process', *Joshi ni eiga* no. 1510 (June 2008), p. 33.
33. Jennifer Forrest and Leonard R. Koos, 'Reviewing Remakes: An Introduction', in Jennifer Forrest and Leonard R. Koos (eds), *Dead Ringers: The Remake in Theory and Practice* (New York: State University of New York Press, 2002), p. 5.
34. For example: Martin Harris, 'You Can't Kill the Bogeyman: *Halloween III* and the Modern Horror Franchise', *Journal of Popular Film and Television* vol. 32 no. 3 (2004), pp. 98–120.
35. Katsuaki Setoguchi in Tomaru Yūko, 'Discussion', in Fujiwara Masamichi (ed.), *Hana yori dango final* (Tokyo: Tōhō, 2008), p. 27.
36. Tomaru Yūko, 'Yoko Kamio', in Fujiwara, *Hana yori dango final*, p. 29.
37. Kumasaka, 'Hana yori dango eizōka no process', p. 32.
38. Tomaru, 'Yoko Kamio', pp. 29–30.
39. Jenkins, *Convergence Culture*.

15

THE ARCHIVE
Screening locality: Japanese home movies and the politics of place

Oliver Dew

In recent years, categories such as the 'orphan film' and the home movie have become emblematic of both the dramatic expansion of moving-image archiving activity beyond canonical notions of national cinema, and the questions posed by this expansion to the established models of film archiving practice, indeed to the very notion of the archive itself.[1] The home movie as a potential archival object has been the subject of much debate within the archival community, both internationally and in Japan.[2] For much of the twentieth century, film archiving practice placed an emphasis on collecting known, published works representing the 'national cinema', holding them in a centralised national archive, and preserving them via reproduction. The home movie, however, is usually not a published 'known work' and, in the case of unstructured, untitled footage, might not even qualify as 'a work' at all; in these cases at a collection level it might be best catalogued by provenance rather than by title and author.[3] Moreover, the great majority of home movies were shot on reversal film stock, placing them outside the inter-negative system at the heart of cinematic reproduction, and thereby complicating efforts to preserve them via photochemical duplication.[4] The home movie then has required a different archival approach owing to both its super-abundance (the total quantity of home movies that have been made is unknowable) and its scarcity (duplicate prints do not exist, and photochemical duplication is often prohibitively expensive and complex).

Perhaps it should not be surprising then that one of the most widespread recent international movements to survey historical home movies has not been an archive but a festival (albeit one founded by archivists), Home Movie Day. This was established by members of the Association of Moving Image Archivists (AMIA) in Los Angeles in 2002,[5] and made its debut in Japan the following year, initially in Aichi and Fukuoka. Home Movie Day in Japan has grown since, particularly in metropolitan areas (sixteen sites in the Tokyo area alone have registered as Home Movie Day hosts over the years since the first events were held). Home Movie Day is the most visible face of a number of other overlapping organisations and networks in Japan that incorporate home movies into their remit. One of the most significant is the Film Preservation Society, founded in 2001 by Ishihara Kae, an AMIA member and a graduate of the Selznick School of Film Preservation in Rochester New York. The Film Preservation Society organised the first Home Movie Day in Japan, has been an associate member of the Southeast Asia-Pacific Audiovisual Archive Association (SEAPAVAA) since 2006, and acts as an important hub for other archival projects throughout the country. Several of these other community archival projects, such as the 8mm Film Archive projects in the Sumida and Adachi wards of Tokyo, host Home Movie Days, using the event both as a means to attract donations of film to their projects and to bring together an audience for these films. For many of the new archive projects, the Home Move Day event is the only moment at which the archive is publicly accessible at a physical site. Outside of the festival, they are dematerialised, existing only as a network or as an online presence, but lacking the permanent storage facility that the word 'archive' has historically referred to.

In his theorisation of heterotopia, Michel Foucault placed the archive and the festival in diametric opposition; whereas the archive is intended to be 'a place of all times that is itself outside of time and inaccessible to its ravages', the festival is bounded by the period over which it is held.[6] In this chapter, however, I want to explore the question of whether and how the festival can be an archive. This is not the 'archive festival' in the sense of a retrospective programming of films stored in archives but rather the festival itself (and its associated networks), modifying and performing the functions of the archive. This would be to imagine the archive as the site of 'material which has not been read and researched',[7] rather than to imagine it as the storehouse for the canon. The first set of questions that this chapter addresses revolve around how archival functions of selection, exclusion, inspection, cataloguing, conservation, preservation and access are modified once we move beyond the terrain of the canonical feature film, and once the archive as a centralised vault is dematerialised and dispersed. How are we to define these new archiving projects and what is their scope? Does the term 'home movie' refer only to works shot on (small-gauge) film, or is video also included? Is it coterminous to or in tension with neighbouring categories such as the amateur film or the *kojin eiga* (private film)? To what extent is 'home movie' a strategic labelling for capturing diverse and divergent currents of film practice?

What the term 'home movie' does do is foreground the question of place and the ownership of place. From its earliest usage, to describe small-gauge digest versions of theatrical releases, the phrase 'home movie' has always referred to the bringing of a public space and set of practices, the cinema and cinemagoing, into the domestic space. This public/private space of the home movie has been theorised sociologically as a 'semi-public sphere'[8] and psychoanalytically as 'extimacy' – a desire to externalise and specularise intimacy.[9]

Although the subset of home movies that capture neighbourhoods, community rituals and local events of note are already local films before they are inducted into any local archive, the home movie's production of place is nevertheless further modulated when privately owned films, rarely seen outside the home, are screened to a local interpretative community at an event such as a Home Movie Day. The ambiguity that is opened up when home movies are repurposed in this fashion is reflected in several ways: in the reported reluctance of some custodians to permanently relinquish their film to an archive (hence some of the largest amateur collections, such as the Ogino Shigeji collection held by the National Film Archive of Japan, were donated posthumously); in the corresponding concern on the part of home movie day hosts not to infringe on the privacy of donors (for instance by recording metadata in a catalogue); and in the tension in terminology between 'home movie' and 'private film', the latter term leaving no doubt of where ownership of the reels lie. For some custodians of the 'private film', the formal 'public archive' does not represent the potential for a public sphere but rather connotes an official, state-sanctioned narrative.[10]

One of the more intriguing features of the Home Movie Day movement in Japan compared to other countries is the way that it has manifested itself at a sub-metropolitan level. Tokyo in particular has seen a proliferation of Home Movie Day sites in wards across the city, in marked contrast to Home Movie Days elsewhere, which tend to organise at a metropolitan level (e.g. London Home Movie Day). There is a certain irony to the fact that while the network-as-archive frequently does not have any concrete site, these archival projects at the same time lay claim to a locality and repurpose the home movies that they gather as local films. Why is the new archiving so determinedly localised within Tokyo? Can the festival-as-archive open a third space set aside from public/private, a film commons? To begin unpacking these questions, I shall now turn to the relationship of the new archiving to the broader film archival landscape.[11]

FILM ARCHIVES AND AMATEUR FILM IN JAPAN

The National Film Center (NFC, the current National Film Archive of Japan) was established in 1970 and became a full member of the International Federation of Film Archives (FIAF) in 1990. It began the large-scale collecting of small-gauge works with the acquisition in 1992 of over four hundred films made by the celebrated amateur film-maker Ogino Shigeji, following his death the previous year. Their amateur collection further expanded with the acquisition of more than two hundred reels shot by Iida Tōkichi, including his fifty-two reel *Film Diary/Eiga nikki* shot between 1929 and 1966.[12] In the Kansai region, Kobe Planet Film Archive has the largest collection of amateur films, while other public institutions with a mandate, funding, and the facilities to acquire and preserve film such as Fukuoka City Public Library Film Archive (an associate member of FIAF), the Museum of Kyoto and Kawasaki City Museum have smaller collections of local amateur and home footage.[13]

The moving image archive landscape has become increasingly diverse since the 1990s. In the US, when the Association of Moving Image Archivists was formed in 1991, it had a broader and more inclusive membership basis than the original moving image archiving association, the FIAF, founded in 1938. The FIAF operated on the basis of institutional membership of national public-sector film archives tasked with preserving the national cinema and historically had an explicit aim of centralising archival resources; until 2000 it only allowed one member-archive per nation to acquire full membership. By contrast, AMIA was founded on the basis of individual membership for archivists, librarians, scholars, those in the media reformatting industry and so on. This diverse membership base showed that 'moving image archiving', and cultural heritage more broadly, was no longer the exclusive purview of the archival pioneers but was by this point a ubiquitous concern.[14]

A variety of smaller and more localised archiving projects also began to emerge to join the established public museums and archives in Japan. The Film Preservation Society's website lists details for thirty such projects across the country, all focusing on amateur, small-gauge work shot locally.[15] Many are audiovisual learning centres (*shichōkaku centre*) based at municipal libraries or citizens halls, or public museums of local history or folklore (Ishinomaki, Sendai, Utsunomiya, Ueda, Fukui, Yamanashi, Ueda, Sasayama), or are programmes of events organised with municipal backing (Bunkyō, Taitō and Kita wards in Tokyo). The others have a variety of organisational foundations that include events connected to film festivals, both international (Yamagata International Documentary Film Festival) and neighbourhood (Odawara Film Festival); projects based in, or in collaboration with art, media or humanities departments of universities (Sapporo Ōtani University; Niigata University, which has established the Niigata Local Screen Archive;[16] and Tokyo University of the Arts, whose faculty members have been involved in events in Sumida and Adachi wards in Tokyo); film appreciation circles; and archival or media advocacy groups instituted as non-profit organisations (NPOs) (the Film Preservation Society in Tokyo, REMO in Osaka). While some of these projects are short term or are no longer active, the activities of others span many years. Acting as an unofficial node for this activity is the Film Preservation Society (FPS), which was founded under the name Sticky Films in 2001, and was recognised as an NPO by the Tokyo metropolitan government in 2006. Since 2007, it has been based in Bunkyō ward, in the North East of Tokyo's centre.

It was the FPS that organised the first Home Movie Day events in Japan in 2003, in Aichi and Fukuoka, just one year after the movement was founded in Los Angeles.[17] Home Movie Day is a series of screenings of home movies, held on the same day each year (initially in August, then moving to the third Saturday in October from 2008 onwards), at a growing number of sites around the world. Over the years, forty-four locations in Japan (sixteen of these in Tokyo) have officially registered with the Center for Home Movies to hold Home Movie Day events, with the number of official venues in Japan in a given year rising to nineteen locations in 2012, and eighteen in 2013,[18] with additional, unofficial events taking place that do not register with the LA office or that hold Home Movie Day events at different times of year. The success of the movement in Japan is testament to the historical popularity of small-gauge film-making, and particularly of the domestic 8mm ecosystems created by Fujifilm.

There is much overlap between the Home Movie Day venues in Japan and the local archives I have outlined in the preceding paragraphs. As we shall see, Home Movie Day performs and modifies many of the important functions of the archive. This local archival activity is also closely interlinked with the broader ecosystem of formally instituted archives and the media reformatting industry. There is considerable overlap in terms of personnel being employed in a professional capacity for an archive or restoration/reformatting company, and also working in the voluntary sector on a pro bono basis on projects that are parallel to their professional work. In this sense, although there is a division of labour between the large archives with the resources and mandate to tackle capital-intensive restoration projects, and the smaller community archives, this boundary is porous and frequently crossed. Moreover, the local archives use the same private sector restoration and digitisation/reformatting companies that television networks and the NFC at times outsource their work to, such as Tokyo Ko-on or Imagica. An important forum that facilitates exchanges such as these is the Film Restoration and Preservation Workshop,[19] which has held nine editions to date since its inauguration in 2003, using the Museum of Kyoto as a base but holding breakout workshops at archives and reformatting companies in Osaka, Kobe and Kyoto. Like membership of the AMIA, applications to attend the workshop are made on an individual not institutional basis, which means that the workshop has a very broad attendance base. Its keynote talks and lightning sessions feature speakers from across the archival and heritage landscape, from representatives of the Agency for Cultural Affairs and the NFC, to individual Home Movie Day venues.

HISTORY OF A MODE, MEDIUM OR FORMAT?

Defining what kinds of media the new archiving works with is no simple task. There are many rubrics that gather films outside the feature film, including those that have long histories and international recognition, such as amateur film, small-gauge film, home movie, science film or PR film (and indeed large swathes of documentary and nonfiction film); those that have acquired traction since the archival turn, such as orphan film, found film, non-theatrical film or local film; and an abundance of terms that are specific to Japan, or at least do not translate easily to the standards of Anglophone archival practice (although they might have analogues in other languages). Among these we might include 'little cinema' (*shō-eiga*) (see below) and the 'private film' (*kojin eiga*), neither of which quite align with amateur (*amachua*), or the various terms for independent (*dokuritsu*) or self (*jishu*) production. Each of these terms represents a framework, a different perspective through which archivists, scholars and the public can approach a body of film practice, and although the terms overlap, they are not contiguous.

Modes of media practice frequently adopt, metonymically, the name of their physical carrier.[20] In the case of amateur or home-mode practice, a form of labelling that is a good example of this process is small-/narrow-gauge film (*kogata eiga*), referring to gauges that are narrower than the theatrical standard of 35mm, literally 'sub-standard', particularly 16mm, 9.5mm and 8mm. At least three unconnected magazines aimed at amateur film-makers have taken the name *Kogata eiga* throughout the period in which small-gauge film was the dominant amateur medium (a prewar run; the sole state-sanctioned amateur film magazine from 1940 to 1943; and a postwar title from 1956 to 1982), so that 'small-gauge film' and 'amateur film' might seem synonymous.[21]

However, amateur film-makers occasionally shot on 35mm,[22] and small-gauge film, particularly 16mm, was of vital importance to documentary, television, education and science films, PR films and so on. There is a sense then, that when 'small-gauge' is being used as a synonym for 'amateur' or home movie-making, particularly in the postwar era, it refers to sub-16mm. However, even 8mm and 9.5mm films were not exclusively used for non-commercial activity, as they had an important role as a commercial home projection format, with digest versions of theatrical features, tourism films and so on, sold in 16mm, 9.5mm and 8mm versions for viewing at home. Indeed, this was the original use of the 9.5mm system, as the projectors were imported to Japan two years before the cameras were.²³ Viewing commercial small-gauge films in the home was the original meaning of 'home movie' (*hōmu mūbii*), and this meaning of the word coexisted with the usage referring to home movie-making (Fig. 15.1).²⁴ As National Film Center researcher (and Home Movie Day host) Gōda Mariko reports, the NFC holds 669 of these commercially sold 8mm/9.5mm films, amounting to 40 per cent of their holdings of 8mm and 9.5mm works.²⁵ It is these commercially distributed items that are arguably the focus of the NFC's small-gauge preservation and screening efforts, as twenty-nine of them have been duplicated to 35mm projection prints (including some films for which there is no extant 35mm version such as Ozu Yasujirō's 1929 film, *A Straightforward Boy/Tokkan kozō*), compared to fourteen amateur works that have received similar treatment.²⁶ Responding to these definitional quandaries, Nada Hisashi, a pioneering researcher of amateur film, revived the term *shō-eiga*, common in the 1920s and 1930s, which he translates as 'little cinema', to avoid terms such as small-gauge film, which collapse a mode of practice into the physical carrier that the practice is most associated with.²⁷

Nevertheless, by examining the material basis of the home movie, and its historical specificity as small-gauge film media, one can glean valuable insights into the home movie as a mode of practice. In order to preserve these films archives must pay close attention to the specificity of the carrier; in cases where little else is known about the film, the carrier might be the only context that the film has. There is then a growing literature that delves into prewar small-gauge film held in archives in Japan,²⁸ reflecting both the archives' carrier-consciousness, and their necessary prioritisation of films in the most danger of being lost.

Restricting the home movie to works shot on small-gauge film creates a history stretching from the early 1920s to the winding down of small-gauge film sales in the 2010s, a history that is sharply divided into two periods by the war and its aftermath. Pathé Baby 9.5mm projectors and films for home viewing were imported to Japan immediately following their introduction in France in 1922, while the sale of cameras and film stock began in earnest from 1924. The first amateur film clubs and contests appeared in 1926, and by the early 1930s there were over 50 clubs and 500 shops dealing with 9.5mm.²⁹ Eastman Kodak's 16mm system was introduced in Japan in 1926, with 8mm following in 1932³⁰ to complete the triumvirate of popular prewar amateur film gauges. Although only the richest could afford these cameras, there was a spectacular growth in film clubs, contests and magazines. Twenty-one magazines devoted to small-gauge film-making appeared between 1926 and 1934.³¹ In 1927 the Nihon Amateur Cinema League was founded as a branch of the Amateur Cinema League in New York³² and published translations of the League's bulletins.³³ The production of film equipment and stock was gradually domesticated in the 1930s.

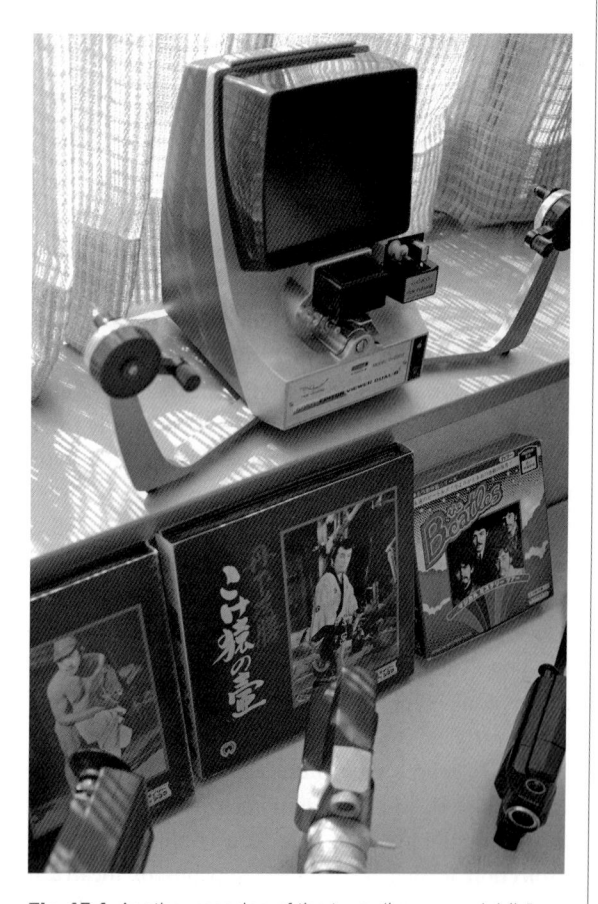

Fig. 15.1 Another meaning of the term, 'home movie' (*hōmu mūbii*). These small-gauge digest versions of theatrical releases were on display at the 2012 Ōizumi Home Movie Day held at the Tōei Film Studios in Nerima, Tokyo. Author's own photograph.

In 1934, Konishiroku (the present-day Konica) began selling semi-domestic 16mm film (their own emulsion applied to an imported acetate base) under their Sakura brand, adding Sakura 8mm Pancine Film in 1938[34] and eventually manufacturing their own diacetate based film stocks in 1940.[35]

This burgeoning amateur film scene was sharply curtailed by the increasing demands of war, and the government's expanding efforts to regulate film and print culture throughout the 1930s and 1940s. In 1937, the importation of film stock and materials was prohibited and the 1939 Film Law required potential amateur film-makers to pass an exam and obtain licences for screenings.[36] In 1941, the various journals of the amateur film scene were required by law to consolidate into one journal, *Kogata eiga*,[37] and the word *amachua* fell, officially at least, under the proscription of the 'language of the enemy' (*tekiseigo*).[38] The Film Law also mandated the screening of *bunka eiga* (culture or kultur films), largely shot on 16mm, at every theatrical film screening.[39] This deployment of 16mm film equipment and film-makers as an instrument of state education, a process that was paralleled in the US,[40] also created a large demand for 16mm documentaries. This use of 16mm for educational films and documentary accelerated during the Allied Occupation of Japan.

The second amateur film-making boom lasted from the mid-1950s until the early 1980s. This time the focus was on domestically produced 8mm systems. Initially this meant Regular/Double 8mm – the first domestically produced Regular 8mm film stock, Fuji's Neopan Reversal 8mm Film, went on sale in 1953,[41] with the first postwar domestically produced 8mm camera, the Cinemax 8A, going on sale the following year.[42] This was superseded in 1965 by Fujifilm's Single 8 system, which was launched alongside Eastman-Kodak's Super 8 system. Whereas Regular/Double 8 was actually a 16mm gauge in-camera, which registered an image down each half of the film-roll in turn (hence the name Double 8) and was only separated into two 8mm gauge strips during the developing process, Single 8 and Super 8 were 8mm gauge in-camera and reduced the size of the sprocket holes to increase the area of film registering the image, and both housed the film in a magazine to ease camera loading. The two formats were interoperable as projection formats, although not as shooting formats, owing to the different design of the magazines that held the film. Although they are at times in the Japanese literature grouped together as 'Single-Super 8' or 'SS8', the domestic Single 8 system was far more widespread, capturing 85 per cent of the market.[43] The miniaturisation made possible by the shooting format being a single 8mm film strip, the interoperability between the two formats and the falling prices of materials secured the dominance of the 8mm format for home movie-making in the postwar era.[44]

Sales of 8mm cameras and projectors peaked in 1975 but then went into a rapid freefall before bottoming out in 1982 when most manufacturers halted the manufacture of cameras and projectors. Sales of new cameras and projectors, however, tell us little about the life of these products, how they are used, maintained and sold on in second hand aftermarkets. That 8mm continued to be popular as an enthusiast format, if not as a mass home-mode medium, is indicated by the fact that Fujifilm continued to sell and process Single 8 film for a further thirty years after they stopped manufacturing the cameras. Fujifilm first announced the discontinuation of 8mm film sales in 2006. In response to a campaign organised by director Ōbayashi Nobuhiko, that decision was temporarily reversed in 2007.[45] The company finally halted Single 8 film sales in March 2012 and stopped processing the film the following year. In September 2012, it announced that all of their motion picture film stocks would be discontinued in 2013 apart from their Eterna film stocks, designed for producing colour separation archival intermediaries.[46] This discontinuation was labelled by some in the archival community as 'Fuji shock', in reference to earlier economic traumas such as the oil shocks of the 1970s.[47]

One publication offering a window into the enthusiast subculture of this three-decade 'twilight' period of 8mm film-making was *Eizō jikken-shi Fs: Experimental Image Movement*, published annually from 1992 to 2000. Although the magazine also covered developments in computer imaging and video, such as the appearance of digital video and PC-based non-linear editing (NLE) software in the mid-1990s, it was primarily a publication for small-gauge film enthusiasts and frequently made cover stars of 'vintage' small-gauge cameras. Each issue opened with an '8mm film manifesto' on such topics as 'private animation and 8mm' (1992); 'the rebirth of 8mm', covering telecining 8mm to video or blowing it up to 35mm (1993); and 'a guide to 8mm materials that can be acquired at present' (1994). It was also a centre for historical research into small-gauge film that included a special section on the Proletarian Film League (1996) and Nada Hisashi's nine-part series, 'A History of the Private Film in Japan, Pre-war Volume', which ran as a regular feature throughout the magazine's run.

In this period we again run into the question of the extent to which a medium's specificity is dependent on its material base (as opposed to its social and cultural use). Is home video an extension and reformatting of the home movie or a separate enough practice that it can be all but excluded from Home Movie Day and the like? The postwar run of the *Small-Gauge Film/Kogata eiga* magazine, perhaps unsurprisingly given its name, evidently found that its amateur cineaste readership did not crossover into videography. It published its final issue in October 1982, bewailing the outright collapse in 8mm camera and projector sales, and the subsequent exit from the market of the principal manufacturers, although its final issues did carry prominent full-page adverts for the latest video camera technology from Sony. Video presents a dilemma to the home movie archivist. On the one hand, archivists hosting Home Movie Day events in Japan are in the vanguard in terms of recognising the value and need for video archiving. Hence the fact that the various flyers, posters and online announcements that surround each Home Movie Day, inviting people to submit their home movies, do also call for video, and the Film Preservation Society in Tokyo does offer workshops and online guides, in video and text format, for the cleaning of various video tape formats.[48] In spite of this, hardly any video works have been screened at the Home Movie Days in Japan.[49] I do not wish to deny that video has its own specificity, both technological and social, and that excluding video from the remit of a project might be a necessary curatorial decision. Historical video formats have an even greater degree of non-interoperability than the various gauges of amateur film. This, combined with the abundance and disposability of video media, the ease with which hours of tape could be shot and erased, make it an even more problematic candidate for archival acquisition than small-gauge film. However, the danger of defining the home movie as an exclusively non-video practice is that the home movie becomes an historical, retro object rather than a practice that continuously reconfigures into the present.[50]

At certain points then, 'home movie' is a problematic term, in tension with parallel concepts and groupings. At Home Movie Day events that I have attended it has been clear that an enormous variety of genres and modes were being gathered under the banner of the home movie, and more than a couple of times I have heard the custodian of the film claim that a particular work was 'not really a home movie'. Home Movie Day is, in part, an act of strategic branding. In spite of these issues, I will use 'home movie' in this chapter in the same sense that recent archival discourse does: to describe a subset of amateur film, shot on domestically owned equipment, which was primarily intended for viewing in the home. 'Home movie' is a term that has continued to be used throughout the historical timeframe in question and has been successfully mobilised by the Home Movie Day movement.

THE HOME MOVIE FESTIVAL AS ARCHIVE

Film scholar Kubo Yutaka's account of his experience as a Home Movie Day host for Ichijōji in Kyoto in 2013 demonstrates how local cineastes and professional archivists are connected through the Home Move Day network, and how best practice is negotiated so that some archival practices are promoted, whilst others are modified or dropped.[51] His account includes eight points: (1) instead of outright acquisition and storage at a concrete site, Home Movie Day is a temporary gathering of materials at a series of decentred sites, restricted temporally to the months either side of the 'festival'; (2) Kubo, working with another Home Movie Day host who is a media reformatting professional, inspected the donated films for vinegar syndrome, shrinkage and damaged perforations, and assessed their ability to withstand a screening; (3) if necessary, simple repairs such as the replacement of the leader were carried out, acts one may characterise as conservation rather than preservation; (4) as well as these technical considerations, films were selected for screening and cataloguing based on archival criteria of provenance and the desire to present a coherent programme that maintained the integrity of the donated collections; (5) the hosts decided to catalogue in their entirety the two collections that dominated that year's donations, a total of 360 reels that took two months to document. Although cataloguing is currently ad hoc and local, discussions have been held at the Film Restoration and Preservation Workshop and on the Home Movie Day mailing list regarding the feasibility of creating a national database of submissions to each Home Movie Day in Japan; (6) a curated selection of these films was screened publicly, accompanied by discussions between the custodian(s) of the film, the event host and audience members; (7) the films were returned to the owners after the screenings (at some events, such as those organised by the Film Preservation Society, the reels are returned with literature on conservation techniques that can be carried out in the home); and (8) many Home Movie Day hosts write a report on their event, published on the FPS website.[52]

Like a film festival, Home Movie Day structures the film screening as a one-off event, a performance. This performativity does not just apply to the discussion, commentary or musical performances that accompany the films but also to the manner in which the venue, usually not a cinema, is transformed into one.[53] Given that many of these screenings are in extra-theatrical settings and require several non-standard projection formats, the various projectors, the cinematic apparatus itself, are placed in the midst of the audience rather than being sequestered in a sound-proof booth, and become part of the performance, the event of place. There is a focus on the materiality of the medium that is evident not just in the presence of the projectors and the frequent use of a set of gauges to define the purview of the event, but also as a result of showing the home movie outside the home. The films shown, with occasional exceptions, do not exhibit a high degree of narrative autonomy and at times would not best be characterised as narrative at all. This is the reason why context of place and performance – the presence of the film's custodian in a venue that lies within the neighbourhood on screen before an audience of people familiar with the location – becomes so important. Even though a custodian (the film-maker, a relative or someone who appears in the film) may authenticate and contextualise a film by their presence, they do not necessarily explicate or narrativise it, *benshi* style. Some of these films effectively become 'found films' for those audience members lacking any direct biographical relationship to the people and places on screen. Andrew Lampert, an archivist at Anthology Film Archives in New York City, has described a 'Perfect Film mind-state' in relation to the found film screenings he organises,[54] which is also evident at certain points in Home Movie Day.

These new local archival projects do not acquire films for long-term storage or apply the principle of preservation via photochemical duplication. Some of them do, however, make digital copies of selected small-gauge works for distribution via DVD or streaming via sites such as YouTube and Vimeo,[55] while other projects create original works that incorporate and contextualise the home movies that were submitted. Miyoshi Daisuke, a film-maker, Home Movie Day host and professor at Tokyo University of the Arts in Bunkyō ward, has to date made four films that remediate home movies, interspersing the home movie footage with interviews with the films' custodians. Two of these works, *8mm Memories/8mm no kioku* (2010) and *Memories of Adachi/Adachi no kioku* (2013), were created in conjunction with the Home Movie Days in the Sumida and Adachi wards of Tokyo respectively. These digital works mimic the interactive style of the events themselves. As well as showing us the digitised reels and the film's custodians discussing the pieces to camera, we also see families watching the digitised films, and their discussions continue on the soundtrack after the cut to the films themselves.

These works demonstrate the dilemmas facing a home movie discourse that is intensely invested in a cinephilic relationship with the materiality of small-gauge film, at a point when that carrier has already assumed 'heritage' status and is no longer readily available. At points the digitisation represents the analogue film strip in an excessive (and undeniably beautiful) way. This might include overscanning the frame or revealing elements that you could observe statically if you were handling the film strip itself, but which would be impossible to see if that strip were run through a projector: perforations and areas between perforations that have registered part of the image even though they lie outside the frame.

Sound is another critical part of the specificity of the small-gauge home movie. 8mm synchronised sound technology did not appear until 1975.[56] Although prior to this film-makers could record non-sync sound or dub sound on to their films after they had been shot (typically narration or music), the majority of small-gauge home movies are silent. This is what facilitates the discussion of the films during public screenings and allows remediating works to create a densely layered soundtrack. At certain points in Miyoshi's films, usually to establish the shift from the chronotope of the video interview in the present to the past tense of the small-gauge film, the sound of a projector is overdubbed, fading out after the shift has been established. Music is central to these re-presentations. *Memories of Adachi* was initiated and produced by its musical director, Nishioka Tatsuhiko, the associate dean of the music faculty at Tokyo University of the Arts, who arranged a full orchestral score for the film.

Digitisation is not without its ethical issues. Blowing up small-gauge films to 35mm, regarded as the best practical compromise by official national archives such as the NFC, is an act of translation that loses some of the specificity of the original carrier but gains the potential for decades of cost-effective conservation. For some, however, the duplication to digital, a complete transformation in the material base of the image, is a translation too far. The FPS report on the 2011 Home Movie Day acknowledges that digitisation can make it easier for people to access the work and that 'in the case of old and damaged film that can no longer be projected, digitisation is the only way to verify what the contents are'. However, critical clues from the film strip such as edge codes and splices are lost,[57] as is, the article avers, the inexpressible 'fascination and depth of the film projection'.[58] The English version of the report goes further, stating that digitisation 'just accelerates the disposal of the original home movies' (in other words, owners could be reformatting their old home movies precisely so that they can throw the original films away).[59] The implication of the report is that digitisation should be accompanied by the acquisition of the original film into a storage facility. There is not yet in Japan an archive that includes the systematic acquisition of home movies for long-term storage as part of its mission. As an alternative then, when FPS digitises films for the Bunkyō Ward Film Archive, the owners are provided with literature and training on how to conserve the film at home.

PLACE-MAKING AND POLICY

One unique feature of Home Movie Day in Tokyo, compared to other cities, is its persistent localism. As mentioned earlier, a total of sixteen venues in Tokyo have officially registered for Home Movie Day since 2004, and in some years there have been more than ten Home Movie Day events, both registered and unregistered, taking place in wards across the capital. Since 2010, a number of archive projects connected to these events have appeared in the city: the Archives for the Moving Image in Taitō; Bunkyō Ward Film Archive; the Frontier 21 project in Kita ward; Sumida 8mm film archive; Adachi 8mm film archive; and a sixth project in Koto ward is planned.

Rather than attribute this localism to an immutable characteristic of Tokyo,[60] we can locate the local archiving movement in a broader dialogue between community development, both grassroots and municipal government-based; individual connoisseurship of urban environments; and a discourse of heritage that cuts across government, voluntary sectors and the cultural industries. The archives that are not attached to and funded by municipal government have an ambiguous relationship with top-down initiatives. Although some of these such as FPS and REMO have taken advantage of the 1998 NPO Law to gain recognition of their non-profit status from metropolitan government, they have not been funded by the government. *Machi zukuri* or *machi okoshi* – highly elastic terms that can just as easily refer to top-down government policy as to grassroots activism, to demolition and 'regeneration' as much as to preservation projects – mark a point at which the relationship between policy and the grassroots is negotiated.[61] The most natural analogue for these terms in Anglophone civic discourse would be 'community development' or 'community building', but the somewhat over-literal translation of 'town-making' is also instructive in understanding the discourse of place-making that has animated much recent local archiving. The Frontier 21 home movie archiving project in Kita ward, Tokyo, is the most explicit in positioning its activities as *machi zukuri*. The project describes its archival activities as an act of cultural salvage and intergenerational cultural transmission that is pressing, urgent even, not because fragile film stock is decaying but because the population of the ward is falling,[62] showing that depopulation is a cause of anxiety amongst some policymakers even in a fairly central ward of a metropolis such as Tokyo.

The majority of archival projects avoid such instrumentalist conceptions of *machi zukuri* policy. We can conceive of their place-making activity occurring at several levels. In concrete terms these activities imaginatively transform local non-theatrical spaces into a place of performance and bring together a group of 'friends of interpretable objects' to participate in that performance. Secondly, in naming and structuring their events around a metropolitan neighbourhood, or *machi*, they contribute to the network of social meanings and affects that attach themselves to a physical space, thus turning it into a place. They are, in other words, imagining the neighbourhood and its community. Finally, this discourse does, at certain points, invoke metaphors of place, such as *hiroba* (plaza, public square or perhaps even commons), in order to imagine the model of civic participation they would like to realise. For example, a 2003 white paper from the Bunkachō (Agency for Cultural Affairs) titled 'On the Promotion of Japanese Cinema From This Point Onwards'/'Kore kara no nihon eiga no shinkō ni tsuite' called for the creation of public spaces for cinema outside commercial theatrical distribution, an *eiga hiroba*, or 'film plaza'.[63] The NPO Japan Community Cinema Center, a network of screening spaces independent from the major exhibition chains, including 'film festivals, film societies, cine clubs, art museums, public halls, local authorities, schools, libraries and art cinemas' was set up partly in response to the white paper in order to try to diversify screen culture.[64]

Although a neighbourhood is defined in part by the opportunity for face-to-face relations, it is still, particularly in the midst of a metropolis such as Tokyo, an 'imagined community'. That a relatively small area needs to be imagined is partly because in a city such as Tokyo that has undergone so many cataclysms and such rapid development, the landmarks that structure a neighbourhood may no longer be extant. Film offers one trace of these. The Adachi 8mm Film Archive, its associated Home Movie Day and the film it gave rise to, *Memories of Adachi*, all use an image of the iconic chimneys of the Senjū thermal power station, which was demolished in 1964, across the various posters and flyers used to promote the project and its events (Fig. 15.2). The image is a still taken from a 1955 home movie donated to the project. Although there is an act of curation, of selection occurring when a Home Movie Day is organised around a neighbourhood, the films selected were already local films before they were incorporated into the local film archive.

CONCLUSIONS

The home movie discourse that I have described in this chapter might appear sentimental or conservative. The films we see at events such as these certainly do not look how we expect a political cinema to look. Nevertheless, there *is* a politics in operation in these local archiving projects, one that resists the potential monumentalism of the term 'national cinema'. In place of the idea of the archive as a central, state-sanctioned storehouse and the model of culture as storage, these community projects see the archive as performance, network and event. Although this approach has partly been born out of necessity, out of the lack of the resources needed to mobilise a conventional, acquire-and-preserve approach to home/amateur movies, and out of the resistance of home-mode films to preservation-via-

Fig. 15.2 Poster for the Adachi 8mm Film Archive, with a still from a 1955 home movie showing the Senjū Thermal Power Station.

duplication, it is also one that is suited to the plural, decentred and private landscape of home movies. There is an anarchism to the idea of Home Movie Day, of holding multiple screenings simultaneously. In Tokyo, if you keep an eye on the train schedule, you might make it to two events in one day; but a panoptic overview is impossible.

These new local archives represent a very different conception of what constitutes an archive from the one mandated by FIAF (preserve the national cinema in a single state-sanctioned location; duplicate before screening). Nevertheless, as I argued above, events such as Home Movie Day do in some cases perform the archival functions of gathering (temporarily), inspecting, selecting, cataloguing (still at a formative stage), cleaning, repairs and conservation, public screening, digitisation (for certain works), training, advocacy and consciousness raising. They are a distributed archive that corresponds to what archivist Terry Cook describes as an emerging paradigm of community activist-archives,[65] or what Mike Featherstone has described as a decentred, network archive.[66] The focus is on encouraging owners to care for their own films, to 'raise ... the social recognition of home movies',[67] and, in turn, transform the status of the film object from, in some cases, something neglected and close to being trashed or orphaned to something being a prized heirloom or piece of folk art – an instance, in other words, of a significant domesticated historical practice or important strand of local micro history.

Notes

1. Caroline Frick, *Saving Cinema: The Politics of Preservation*, Kindle edn (Oxford: Oxford University Press, 2010), pp. 105–50; Patricia R. Zimmermann, 'The Home Movie Moment: Excavations, Artifacts, Minings', in Karen L. Ishizuka and Patricia R. Zimmermann (eds), *Mining the Home Movie: Excavations in Histories and Memories* (Berkeley: University of California Press, 2008), pp. 1–28; Patricia R. Zimmermann, 'Morphing History into Histories: From Amateur Film to the Archive of the Future', in Ishizuka and Zimmermann, *Mining the Home Movie*, pp. 275–88; Susan Aasman, 'Saving Private Reels: Archival Practices and Digital Memories (Formerly Known as Home Movies) in the Digital Age', in Laura Rascaroli, Gwenda Young and Barry Monahan (eds), *Amateur Filmmaking: The Home Movie, the Archive, the Web* (London: Bloomsbury, 2014), pp. 4567–806. On the 'orphanista' movement, see Dan Streible, 'The Role of Orphan Films in the 21st Century Archive', *Cinema Journal* vol. 46 no. 3 (2007), pp. 124–8; Dan Streible, 'Saving, Studying and Screening: A History of the Orphan Film Symposium', in Alex Marlow-Mann (ed.), *Film Festival Yearbook 5: Archival Film Festivals* (St Andrews: St Andrews Film Studies, 2013), pp. 163–76.

2. The first FIAF congress focusing on amateur film was held in Cartagena, Columbia, in 1997. See Jan-Christopher Horak, 'Out of the Attic: Archiving Amateur Film', *Journal of Film Preservation* no. 56 (June 1998), p. 50–3. For the chief curator of the National Film Center's report on this congress,

see Okajima Hisashi, 'FIAF no atarashii chōsen: Hozontaishō toshite amature eiga', *NFC Newsletter* vol. 3 no. 4 (July 1997), pp. 1–7.

3   Andrea Leigh, 'Context! Context! Context! Describing Moving Images at the Collection Level', *Moving Image* vol. 6 no. 1 (2006), pp. 33–65.

4   Ross Lipman, 'Problems of Independent Film Preservation', *Journal of Film Preservation* no. 53 (November 1996), pp. 49–58; Iola Baines and Gwenan Owen, 'The Massive Mess of Mass Memory', *Journal of Film Preservation* vol. 25 no. 52 (April 1996), pp. 7–14.

5   Zimmermann, 'The Home Movie Moment', pp. 12–15.

6   Michel Foucault, 'Of Other Spaces, Heterotopias', trans. Jay Miskowiec, *Architecture, Mouvement, Continuité* no. 5 (1984), pp. 46–9, <http://foucault.info/documents/heterotopia/foucault.heterotopia.en.html>.

7   Mike Featherstone, 'Archive', *Theory, Culture & Society* vol. 23 no. 2–3 (May 2006), p. 594.

8   Heather Norris Nicholson, *Amateur Film: Meaning and Practice, 1927–1977* (Manchester: Manchester University Press, 2012), p. 239.

9   Roger Odin, 'Reflections on the Family Home Movie as Document: A Semio-Pragmatic Approach', in Ishizuka and Zimmermann, *Mining the Home Movie*, pp. 255–71.

10 Tatsuro Hanada, 'The Japanese "Public Sphere": The Kugai', *Theory, Culture & Society* vol. 23 nos. 2–3 (May 2006), pp. 612–4; Kaori Hayashi, '"The Public" in Japan', *Theory, Culture & Society* vol. 23 nos. 2–3 (May 2006), pp. 615–6.

11 This chapter draws on my attendance at Home Movie Days at Nezu, Ōizumi and Sumida, and various conferences on archiving including the Film Restoration and Preservation Workshop (*eiga no fukugen to hozon ni kansuru workshop*) at the Museum of Kyoto; site visits including to the former National Film Center's (the National Film Archive of Japan's) archive at Sagamihara, Kobe Planet Film Archive, the Film Preservation Society, and the media restoration and formatting company Tokyo Ko-on; interviews I conducted with Miyoshi Daisuke (Adachi and Sumida 8mm Film Archives, Tokyo University of the Arts), Ishihara Kae (Film Preservation Society) and Yasui Yoshio (Kobe Planet Film Archive); and a roundtable discussion I chaired on 'Archiving Moving Image Practice' with archivists Tochigi Akira (National Film Centre), Uesaki Sen (Keiō University, Sōgetsu Art Centre Records) and Saitō Rie (Waseda University, Video Art Center Tokyo) at the *Japanese Cinema Revisited* conference at Meiji Gakuin University in February 2013. I was able to present the findings of this research at the *Nihon eiga workshop* at Meiji Gakuin University, and at *Film and Media 2014* in London. This research was made possible by a Postdoctoral Research Fellowship from the Japan Society for the Promotion of Science, held at Meiji Gakuin University in Tokyo. I would like to thank my host at Meiji Gakuin, Professor Ayako Saitō; the conference participants who responded to my presentation; my interviewees; and all of the archivists, scholars, Home Movie Day hosts and participants who shared their insights and passions with me over the course of this project. Any mistakes that remain are my own.

12 Gōda Mariko, 'Film Center shozō no kogata eiga korekushon: 9.5mm film chōsa no oboegaki', *Tokyo kokuritsu kindai bijutsukan kenkyū kiyō* no. 17 (2013), pp. 98–9. [Editors' note: For more on Ogino Shigeji, see also Chapter 13 by Julian Ross in this volume.]

13 For a guide to archival holdings in Japan and internationally, see Abé Mark Nornes and Aaron Gerow, *Research Guide to Japanese Film Studies* (Ann Arbor: Center for Japanese Studies, University of Michigan, 2009).

14 Frick, *Saving Cinema*, loc. 2509–15.

15 Film Preservation Society, 'Chiiki eizō archive link shū', November 2014, <http://filmpres.org/project/bfa/community/>.

16 Harada Ken'ichi and Ishii Hitoshi (eds), *Natsukashisa wa mirai to tomoni yattekuru: Chiiki eizō archive no riron to jissai* (Tokyo: Gakubunsha, 2013).

17 Amano Sonoko, 'Home movie ga kaettekita: "Home movie dei Tokyo 2004" o oete', *Eiga ronsō*, December 2004, pp. 104–7.

18 Film Preservation Society, 'Home movie no hi: kokunai kaisai kiroku', November 2014, <http://filmpres.org/project/hmd/hmd01/>.

19 I attended the 9th Film Restoration and Preservation Workshop (*Dai 9-kai eiga no fukugen to hozon ni kansuru workshop*), Museum of Kyoto, August 2014.

20 I use the moving image archivists' term 'carrier' interchangeably with 'format', to refer to the material basis of the medium, in other words the specific stock containing the image, for example 9.5mm reversal film.

21 Gōda, 'Film Center shozō no kogata eiga collection', p. 95.

22. For example, one of the Ogino Shigeji films held by the NFC was shot on 35mm. See Asari Hiroyuki, 'Ogino Shigeji kizō film mokuroku', *Tokyo kokuritsu kindai bijutsukan kenkyū kiyō* no. 18 (2014), p. 112.
23. Nada Hisashi, 'The Little Cinema Movement in the 1920s and the Introduction of Avant-Garde Cinema in Japan', *Iconics* no. 3 (1994), p. 40.
24. See, for instance, '16mm eiga jihō: Home movies library', *Eiga kyōiku* no. 55 (September 1932), pp. 32–5.
25. Gōda, 'Film Center shozō no kogata eiga collection', p. 98.
26. Ibid., pp. 100–1.
27. Nada, 'The Little Cinema Movement in the 1920s'.
28. Gōda, 'Film Center shozō no kogata eiga collection'; Film Preservation Society, *Senzen kogata eiga shiryōshū* (Tokyo: Film Preservation Society, 2010); Nada, 'The Little Cinema Movement in the 1920s'; Mika Tomita, 'Aspects of Small-Gauge Film in Interwar Japan: Another Face of the "Cinema City" Kyoto', trans. Takuya Tsunoda in Mika Tomita, Masaaki Kidachi, Ikuyo Matsumoto and Takao Sugihashi (eds), *Urban Images of Kyoto: Kyoto Culture and Its Cultural Resources* (Kyoto: Nakanishiya shuppan, 2012), pp. 223–39; Kubo Yutaka, 'An Analysis of the Significance of Japanese Home Movie through Consideration of the Relationship Between the Filmmakers and the Subjects' (Unpublished MA dissertation, Kyoto University, 2014); Yahiro Yoshiyuki, 'The History and Preservation of Japan's Small-Gauge Films Centered on 8mm Film', in National Film Center (ed.), *Searching the Traces: Archival Study of Short-Lived Film Formats, Records of the International Film Symposium*, trans. Jonathan M. Hall (Tokyo: Kokuritsu Bijutsukan, 2012), pp. 61–5.
29. Gōda, 'Film Center shozō no kogata eiga collection', p. 95.
30. Kubo, 'An Analysis of the Significance of Japanese Home Movie', pp. 21–3.
31. Film Preservation Society, *Senzen kogata eiga shiryōshū*, 17–19; see also Nada, 'The Little Cinema Movement in the 1920s', pp. 40–41.
32. Tomita, 'Aspects of Small-Gauge Film in Interwar Japan', p. 227; Kubo, 'An Analysis of the Significance of Japanese Home Movie', p. 22.
33. Arthur L. Gale and Kōmoto Masao, *Amateur eiga no seisaku: Riron to jissai* (Tokyo: Tokyo International Amateur Film Contest Organising Committee, 1933).
34. Film Preservation Society, *Senzen kogata eiga shiryōshū*, p. 12.
35. Hidenori Okada, 'Nitrate Film Production in Japan: A Historical Background of the Early Days', trans. Daisuke Miyao and Ayako Saitō, in Daisuke Miyao (ed.), *The Oxford Handbook of Japanese Cinema* (Oxford: Oxford University Press, 2014), p. 266.
36. Tomita, 'Aspects of Small-Gauge Film in Interwar Japan', p. 234.
37. Nada, 'The Little Cinema Movement in the 1920s', p. 41.
38. Tomita, 'Aspects of Small-Gauge Film in Interwar Japan', p. 227.
39. Yahiro, 'The History and Preservation of Japan's Small-Gauge Films', p. 63.
40. Patricia R. Zimmermann, *Reel Families: A Social History of Amateur Film* (Bloomington: Indiana University Press, 1995), pp. 96–111.
41. *Fuji film 50 nen no ayumi* (Tokyo: Fuji Film, 1984), p. 452.
42. *Natsukashi no home movie ten: Mukashi, boku no ie wa eigakan datta* (Tokyo: JCII Camera Museum, 1997), p. 14.
43. Kubo, 'An Analysis of the Significance of Japanese Home Movie', p. 25.
44. Yahiro, 'The History and Preservation of Japan's Small-Gauge Films', p. 63.
45. Ibid.
46. Fuji Film, 'Announcement on Motion Picture Film Business of Fujifilm', September 2012, <http://www.fujifilm.com/news/n120913.html>.
47. Okajima Hisashi, 'Film seisan shukushō jidai no eiga hozon: "Fuji shock" art no film archive', paper presented at *Japan Society of Image Arts and Sciences 39th Annual Conference*, Tokyo, 1 June 2013.
48. Film Preservation Society, 'First-Aid for Damaged Videotape', *Film Preservation Society*, July 2012, pp. 1–6.
49. According to 'The 6th Home Movie Day Japan Report' for example, 'We've been dealing with 8mm, 9.5mm and 16mm in past [Home Movie Days] but this year all films shown were 8mm.' Film Preservation Society, 'HMD Reports', December 2012, <http://www.homemovieday.jp/english/hmd-reports/>.
50. James Moran, *There's No Place Like Home Video* (Minneapolis: University of Minnesota Press, 2002), pp. 1–63.

51 Kubo, 'An Analysis of the Significance of Japanese Home Movie', pp. 73–92.
52 For example, <http://filmpres.org/project/hmd/hmd03/>.
53 If the venue is a cinema, it most likely will not have small-gauge projection equipment.
54 Joel Schlemowitz and Andrew Lampert, 'Unessential Cinema: An Interview with Andrew Lampert', *The Moving Image* vol. 12 no. 1 (2012), p. 111.
55 See, for instance, the Archives for the Moving Image in Taitō's YouTube playlist, <https://www.youtube.com/playlist?list=PL41EBC50367D7BC15>, and the Film Preservation Society's page on Vimeo, <https://vimeo.com/user28747137>.
56 The technical difficulties that came with the introduction of sound to 8mm film-making have been blamed in some accounts for the subsequent collapse in camera sales. See *Natsukashi no home movie ten*, p. 6.
57 For an example of how these clues from outside the frame can be used, see Gōda, 'Film Center shozō no kogata eiga korekushon', pp. 105–7.
58 Film Preservation Society, 'Dai 9 kai home movie no hi hōkoku', 2011, <http://filmpres.org/project/hmd/hmd06/>.
59 Film Preservation Society, 'HMD Reports'.
60 For example, 'Tokyo is actually in its construction more a collection of small towns, or neighbourhoods, than it is big, hard-core city'. Donald Richie, 'Attitudes Toward Tokyo on Film', *East-West Film Journal* vol. 3 no. 1 (December 1988), pp. 68–75.
61 Jordan Sand, *Tokyo Vernacular: Common Spaces, Local Histories, Found Objects* (Berkeley: University of California Press, 2013), pp. 54–87; Shun'ichi J. Watanabe, '*Toshi keikaku vs machizukuri*: Emerging Paradigm of Civil Society in Japan, 1950–1980', in André Sorensen and Carolin Funck (eds), *Living Cities in Japan: Citizens' Movements, Machizukuri and Local Environments* (London: Routledge, 2007), pp. 39–55.
62 Frontier 21, 'Kita-ku no jinkō genshō', 2013, <http://www.frontier21.jp.net/?page_id=167>.
63 Eiga shinkō ni kan suru kondankai, 'Kore kara no nihon eiga no shinkō ni tsuite', April 2003, <http://www.bunka.go.jp/1bungei/korekaranonihoneiga.html>.
64 See <http://jc3.jp/english/index.html>.
65 Terry Cook, 'Evidence, Memory, Identity, and Community: Four Shifting Archival Paradigms', *Archival Science* vol. 13 nos. 2–3 (2013), pp. 95–120.
66 Featherstone, 'Archive'.
67 Kubo, 'An Analysis of the Significance of Japanese Home Movie', p. 81.

PART 3
FILM STYLE

16

CINEMATOGRAPHY
The trans-Pacific work of Japanese cinematographers

Daisuke Miyao

The credits of Ōshima Nagisa's 1999 film *Taboo/Gohatto* read 'Satsuei kantoku Kurita Toyomichi', or 'Director of Photography Kurita Toyomichi'. Apparently, there is nothing extraordinary here. The credits clearly state that the cinematographer of this film is Kurita Toyomichi. However, in reality, Kurita had to go through an extraordinary set of negotiations in order to receive the title 'Satsuei kantoku'. To be more precise, it took extra effort for him to obtain the two Chinese characters, 'kantoku' after 'Satsuei' because just using the word 'Satsuei' is usually considered enough to indicate the caption 'cinematography by' in the credits of Japanese-produced films. The title of the director of photography is not regularly used. When I interviewed Kurita about his career, he confessed that he had a really difficult time during the production of *Taboo*; especially in the areas of production design and lighting. When Kurita has worked in Hollywood with such film-makers as Alan Rudolph, Robert Altman and Tyler Perry, he has not encountered these types of issues.

The hardships that Kurita experienced during the production of *Taboo* were a result of the tension-ridden process of how cinematographic technologies have developed and how discourses on cinematography have been constructed in the broader history of Japanese cinema. The historical analysis in this chapter also crosses national borders because the discussion of cinematography in Japan has almost always been connected to complicated international and/or transnational conflicts over technology, materials, funds and personnel. By taking this approach, I will illustrate that cinematographers have remained at the forefront of transnational cultural forms from the very beginning of film-making history. In other words, I will demonstrate that globalisation is nothing new in the history of cinema, particularly in the case of Japanese film-making and the context of contemporary cinema and the globalisation of audiovisual cultures through the transnational corporate dominance of media, Hollywood studio 'runaway productions' and multi-national coproductions, Hollywood remakes of Asian horror films or Hong Kong martial arts films, and the growing significance of international film festivals.

This chapter will pose the same questions that I have previously raised in relation to the technologies of lighting in Japanese film culture: what makes Japanese cinema and what roles should cinema play in Japanese society?[1] To be more specific, how has cinematography been conceptualised and practised in the history of Japanese film-making? Historically there has been an unequal geopolitical relationship, or an imbalance of power, between Japan and the US. There is no doubt that Hollywood has played a ubiquitous role in the development of lighting technology in Japan. Yet the relationship between Hollywood and Japanese cinema has not simply been marked by a binary opposition between the centres of production and distribution and the periphery, between cultural dominance and resistance, or between the global and the local. By bearing in mind the geopolitical tension between the transnational and the national, I will demonstrate how three prominent cinematographers in Japan, 'Henry' Kotani Sōichi, 'Harry' Mimura Akira and Kurita Toyomichi, have negotiated a path through the transnational networks of film culture. After defining the term, 'director of photography' in the context of Hollywood film history, I discuss the works of Kotani, Mimura and Kurita one by one in their relationships with the industrial practices of the Japanese film studios (and their aftermath), the conventional techniques of Japanese film-making, Japanese national identity politics and the Hollywood system. In the end, I will argue that their work serves as an example of the diversity of ways in which cinematographic technologies within hegemonic Hollywood cinema have been reconfigured within specific local contexts.

THE EMERGENCE OF THE DIRECTOR OF PHOTOGRAPHY IN HOLLYWOOD

It is not clear when exactly the title of the 'Director of Photography' was first used in the history of the motion picture. According to *American Cinematographer*, Roy Henry Klaffki, who worked with such film-makers as Erich von Stroheim and Lois Weber, 'held the title of Director of Photography at Metro Pictures in the early 1920s, shooting films as well as supervising the work of other Metro cinematographers and overseeing quality control in the lab'.[2] However, the title was rarely used in both the credits of films and articles published in *American Cinematographer* until the early to mid-1930s. Either the term 'cameraman' or 'cinematographer' was the most common means of describing the profession. It was arguably James Wong Howe who started defining his professional role as the director of photography in 1934. In an essay in which he explained his cinematographic strategy in *Viva Villa!* (Jack Conway, 1934), Howe emphasised the significance of 'co-operation' between two professions: 'the Art Director' and 'the Director of Photography' in order to build sets and to suit the camera treatment 'more efficiently'.[3] In his previous 1931 essay, 'Lighting', which appeared in the ASC's *Cinematographic Annual Volume Two*, he did not use the term 'director of photography' but only the phrase 'cinematographers'.[4]

What happened between 1931 and 1934? One possible factor behind the switch was technological. The advent of Supersensitive Panchromatic Type Two Motion Picture Negative Film by Eastman Kodak Company was announced on 5 February 1931. With emulsion reacting 'faster' to light – 75 per cent more speed to blue light, 200 per cent more to green light, and from 400 to 500 per cent more to red light – the Supersensitive Panchromatic Type Two extended latitude and enriched the gradation between black and white in order to render both much more diverse.[5] After the announcement, the relationship between lighting and film stock became a central topic of discussions amongst cinematographers. Hal Hall, the editor of the ASC's *Cinematographic Annual Volume Two*, wrote:

> Too many cinematographers confuse the improved speed with exaggerated contrast – a serious mistake. The aim of the cinematographer should be for natural tonal contrast with an artistic softness – and this softness cannot be attained with flat lighting. Soft lighting should be used – but it should be normally balanced, sacrificing none of the tonal and physical contrasts which the cameraman wishes to preserve.[6]

Thus, Hollywood cinematographers became more conscious about the fact that they were the ones who 'directed' lighting in order to make the best of the new sensitive film stocks.

The second possibility was financial and political. The emergence of the title of the director of photography was most likely related to the shifts in the Hollywood labour movement during the industry's recovery from the Great Depression. The International Alliance of Theatrical Stage Employees (IATSE), originally founded in 1893 when representatives of stagehands working in eleven cities met in New York and pledged to support each other's efforts to establish fair wages and working conditions for their members, had become one of Hollywood's most independent and comprehensive labour organisations by the 1920s. Cameramen working in the film industry in Los Angeles joined the IATSE in 1928 forming Local 659. As a consequence of the Great Depression, the studio bosses had insisted on across-the-board pay cuts of 50 per cent for anyone making more than 50 US dollars per week. While most other sectors of the industry accepted the cut, the IATSE did not. Instead, it threatened to send its people out on strike in 1933.[7] Cameramen or cinematographers needed a more suitable title for their business: the 'director' of photography.

By the 1950s, the term 'director of photography' had become the standardised title for cinematographers working in Hollywood and with it, a shared definition of the profession: the director of photography was the person who directs the lighting. In his March 1950 essay, 'The Men Who Light the Sets', Gordon Taylor clearly stated, 'The quality of the photography that results depends upon the light directed into the scene, how it is directed, its quantity and quality. That is the responsibility of one man – the director of photography.'[8] Taylor elaborates:

> The usual procedure is for the director of photography, after reading the script, to join with the director in a discussion of the photography of the picture. From this discussion, he usually develops the basic lighting pattern he expects to use […]. The gaffer is sometimes erroneously credited with lighting the sets. He and his crew do the physical work of handling and setting up the various lighting units, but placement of the lights is directed by the director of photography following his survey of the set and his decision as to its lighting equipment.[9]

In 1967, the veteran cinematographer Charles G. Clarke retrospectively defined the role of the director of photography in this way:

> Since the inception of the movies there have been cameramen. Then, as the peculiar technique of the cinema was developed, *the cameraman became the cinematographer*. As the industry progressed, cinematography took on specialized fields. The cinematographer now devoted more of his talents to composition and lighting and left the mechanics of the camera to members of his staff. Today he directs and supervises the efforts of a large crew of workers and is now known as the *Director of Photography*. He selects the composition[,] sets the exposure, conceives the lighting and designates the filters or other photographic controls to be employed.[10]

BEFORE THE EMERGENCE OF THE DIRECTOR OF PHOTOGRAPHY IN JAPAN: THE TRAVAILS OF 'HENRY' KOTANI SŌICHI

In contrast to Hollywood, it is very clear when the title of the 'Director of Photography' was first used in Japan – during the 1942 production of Yamamoto Kajirō's film, *The War at Sea from Hawaii to Malaya/ Hawaii Malay oki kaisen*. 'Harry' Mimura Akira, who had worked in Hollywood in the 1930s under the renowned cinematographer George Barnes (*Rebecca* [1940]) and with Gregg Toland (*Citizen Kane* [1940]) as a colleague, was appointed as the director of photography (*Satsuei kantoku*) of the film. It may be odd to have such a title imported directly from Hollywood in a film endorsed by the Japanese Navy to commemorate the first anniversary of the attack on Pearl Harbor. No matter, no such term existed before this date.

In Japan, cinematographers are usually called 'cameramen'. As the title indicates, this means they are normally only in charge of the cameras. Even though cameramen inform lighting technicians of their lighting plans, it is lighting technicians who decide which lights are used. Cinematographers and lighting technicians are still two separate positions with equal authority. From the 1920s onwards, lighting (*shōmei*) has been considered in terms of an autonomous studio department (the department of electricity, in many cases) that is separate from the department of cinematography.[11] Lighting technicians have their own conventions and standards for using equipment. In 1936, with the establishment of the Nihon Shōmei Kyōkai (Japanese Association of Film Lighting), the lighting technician system became officially recognised. Such separation might have made it difficult for cinematographers to realise their lighting ideas on the screen. Indeed, in 1929, the renowned cinematographer Isayama Saburō wrote, 'The most difficult thing is that the people of the lighting department cannot always be my good friends.'[12] And even after seventy years, Kurita Toyomichi pointed out a very similar issue in 1999. It was difficult for him to work on both the lighting and production design in *Taboo*.[13]

No document exists that clearly states why the department of electricity was set up separately from that of cinematography in the Japanese film studios. However, we may assume that this separation derived from Japanese theatrical tradition. Kabuki theatres already had electricity and lighting technicians. Motion picture cameras were new equipment and needed new people to be in charge, especially at such a company as Shōchiku that had entered the film business from the world of kabuki.

Shōchiku initially modelled itself on Hollywood when they established their own film studio in Kamata, Tokyo, in 1920. Shōchiku, aspiring to catch up with the standard of foreign films, made its own products exportable and became competitive with the Hollywood film industry, adopting an American-style capitalist-industrial modernity along with various Hollywood production process that included film-making techniques and technologies, distribution practices and the star system. The company invited various technicians from Hollywood to work for them, including the cinematographer 'Henry' Kotani Sōichi. After appearing in Japanese-subject films produced at the New York Motion Picture Company under Thomas H. Ince, Kotani worked as a cinematographer in Hollywood in the 1910s under the renowned film-maker Cecil B. DeMille. Between 1915 and 1916, DeMille 'sought to bring more dramatic and realistic lighting to the screen', and his cinematographer Alvin Wyckoff helped him achieve the effects DeMille desired – the so-called Rembrandt chiaroscuro.[14] What DeMille and Wyckoff visualised was called Lasky lighting, which the film historian Lea Jacobs defines as 'confined and shallow areas of illumination, sharp-edged shadows and a palpable sense of the directionality of light'.[15] Kotani was 'one of the best' assistants to Wyckoff.[16] In 1920, eagerly pursued by the representatives of Shōchiku and highly recommended by DeMille, Kotani returned to Japan. Despite the fact that the title of the director of photography had yet to emerge, even in Hollywood, Kotani was clearly aiming to become one based on his experiences with Wyckoff during the invention of the expressive photographic image via Lasky lighting. In his 1924 essay, 'How to Become a Mature Cinematographer', Kotani insisted that cinematographers would need to have an all-round knowledge of photographic images: '[Cinematographers] must be familiar with all the knowledge about tinting, developing, and exposing (…). With all of this knowledge,' a mature cinematographer 'is capable of freely capturing any scenes with his camera that any director wants.'[17] In Kotani's mind, cinematographers should certainly be considered as directors of photography.

However, it did not take long for Shōchiku to turn to their own kabuki-style conventions to produce their films, especially in terms of lighting practice. In kabuki, flat frontal lighting is used almost exclusively in order to flatly illuminate the entire stage, eliminate as much shadow as possible and render onstage acts more visible to the spectator. While Kotani introduced the expressive style of lighting from Hollywood, Shōchiku decided not to fully adopt it. Shōchiku did not want such expressivity because it cost much more to achieve it while general audiences did not seem to appreciate it. It was Shōchiku's choice based on its own industrial practice of rationalisation and its own attitude towards the modern mass audiences of their films.[18] Shōchiku thus did not simply reject their initial engagement with the Hollywood system and technology, but appropriated them for their own purposes.

Kotani left the Shōchiku Kamata studio as early as 1922, less than two years after his celebrated arrival. As a result, flat and bright lighting became the dominant mode in mainstream Japanese films, especially Shōchiku films, throughout the 1920s and 1930s. The goal of Shōchiku's film production was suggested in the company's slogan, 'bright and cheerful Shōchiku cinema' (*akaruku tanoshii Shōchiku eiga*). In addition to a bright and cheerful feeling, the idea of 'brightness' also referred to cinematography. In June 1922, after he had left Shōchiku's Kamata studio, Kotani claimed with disappointment, 'In general, the only things that a cinematographer [in Japan] is allowed to do are to use the best of the background, to make images cleanly visible […]. He should not go beyond this.'[19]

THE EMERGENCE OF THE DIRECTOR OF PHOTOGRAPHY IN JAPAN: THE CHALLENGE OF 'HARRY' MIMURA AKIRA

When the title of director of photography appeared for the first time during the production of *The War at Sea from Hawaii to Malaya*, the title was in name only. 'Harry' Mimura Akira, the 'Director of Photography', was just the head of a team of four cinematographers (Mimura himself, Miura Mitsuo, Suzuki Hiroshi and Hirano Yoshimi). Four cinematographers were required by the Japanese Navy to engage with the scale of the film's production, which necessitated photography in multiple locations over a short period of time. Instead of being called the 'head cameraman' or 'chief cameraman', the title of 'the director of photography' was adopted because it was the title commonly used in Hollywood, and it was suitable to give the title to Mimura because he had started his career in the US. Mimura was the first Japanese cinematographer to obtain membership of the cinematographers' union in Hollywood (IATSE Local 659). After studying at the New York Institute of Photography with Carl Gregory, D.W. Griffith's company man, Mimura began his career as an assistant to the acclaimed cinematographer George Barnes in the late 1920s. Gregg Toland, one of the most famous cinematographers of all time, was an assistant to Barnes at the same time as Mimura. One of Mimura's first projects with Barnes and Toland was *Trespasser* (Edmond Goulding, 1928), a star vehicle for Gloria Swanson.[20] Coincidentally, the camera operator was Alvin Wyckoff, Henry Kotani's mentor. After Barnes left the Goldwyn studio, Mimura worked for Toland until November 1933.

It certainly seems ironic that a Hollywood-trained cinematographer was assigned as the director of photography for this war propaganda film. One could put it down to Japanese film-making's dependency on the Hollywood style of production, but it might also have been down to a strategic choice to display Mimura's transformation from a Hollywood cinematographer to a Japanese one in order to emphasise the capacity of Japanese cinema to incorporate the Hollywood style and yet achieve its nationalist goals. In any case, it is clear that cinematography was at the threshold of a negotiation between the Japanese and the Hollywood-style models of film-making.

Mimura had experience of this negotiation before, working on *The War at Sea from Hawaii to Malaya*. Like Henry Kotani, Mimura was invited to Japan in 1934 to become the ace photographer of a new film company, Tōhō. Unlike Shōchiku, Tōhō was not a kabuki company. They did not follow the convention of bright and flat lighting and were willing to experiment with expressive lighting and cinematography thus leading to the emergence of 'two oppositional groups in film business'.[21] Tōhō challenged Shōchiku's dominance by resorting to Hollywood, even though Tōhō was not able to fully imitate Hollywood-style lighting, mainly because of the shortage of resources. As I have demonstrated in *The Aesthetics of Shadow: Lighting and Japanese Cinema*, there was an emerging discourse called the aesthetics of shadow that was closely tied into the rivalry between Tōhō and Shōchiku. Many Japanese cinematographers admired the form of low-key lighting practised in Hollywood cinema. They despaired at the limited material conditions in Japanese cinema compared to Hollywood's financial and technological means. When Japanese cinematographers realised that it would be difficult to achieve these results under the deplorable conditions of wartime Japan, they turned to one easily available aspect of Japanese art. The aesthetics of shadow did not stem from traditional Japanese aesthetics per se; it was instead a way of expanding the generic and compositional lighting codes from Hollywood. The advocates of the aesthetics of shadow justified their lighting scheme, which had originated in Hollywood, by resorting to the traditional appreciation of shadow and darkness in Japanese architecture.[22]

Mimura was aware of the limited material conditions in Japanese cinema and, at the same time, deeply concerned with the technological innovations in Hollywood. While he repeatedly showed his consciousness of realistic lighting in articles about Gregg Toland, his co-worker in Hollywood, Mimura had to try to achieve what Toland did in a different geopolitical location and an unfavourable technological situation. Even though it was written in 1948, after the war, Mimura's discussion of Toland's work in *Best Years of Our Lives* (William Wyler, 1946) illustrates his deep concern for documentary-style cinematography. Mimura noted,

> The most notable issue in the cinematography of this film is well-crafted lighting. Throughout the film, he [Toland] creates vivid and sharp images. Appropriate to its content, the tone of the film appears to be that of a documentary film.[23]

What was fortunate for Mimura, working in the Japanese film industry during a period of rising ultra-nationalism, was that Toland was not a typical representative of Hollywood cinematography but instead an exceptional figure who persistently explored 'the illusion of presence' on the screen.[24] Toland discussed with the director Orson Welles that in *Citizen Kane*, 'the picture should be brought to the screen in such a way that the audience would feel it was looking at reality, rather than merely at a movie'.[25] Toland and Welles tried to 'obtain the definition and depth' of the human eye in real life and not to require audiences to see things on the screen 'with a single point of perfect focus, and everything falling off with greater or less rapidity in front of and behind this particular point'.[26] To do so, Toland and Welles increased the level of illumination by adopting the hard light of arc broad lamps, which were generally used in Technicolor, in addition to using Super XX film 'with a super-speed emulsion'.[27] This was in contrast to the dominant 'modulating' style of Hollywood film at that time with its 'artful compromises', in which the lighting was adjusted from scene to scene and shot to shot as the emphasis changed from storytelling to realism and from pictorial quality to glamour.[28] Toland's fellow cinematographers even worried that his 'obsessive attention to one technique was bound to upset the delicate balance that a multifunctional style required'.[29]

In Japan, however, Toland's obsession with realism was shared by Mimura, accorded with the preferred documentary-style discourse of depicting the war and the lives of the Japanese soldiers in the battlefields. Critics praised how Mimura successfully managed the limited material conditions in Japan, especially in relation to his use of low-quality Fuji film stock, and how he effectively used lighting to depict Japanese spaces in a realistic manner. *Eiga gijutsu* journal praised Mimura's work for its 'well-prepared and careful lighting, which was perfectly appropriate for Fuji film stock'.[30] Most film production companies in Japan used Eastman Kodak film stock in the 1920s to early 1930s. It was only as late as January 1937 that Fuji first released its own Japanese film stock for sound films. In September of the same year, a law to control imports and exports was enacted and the amount of imported raw film was subsequently reduced. By 1939, only 6.5 per cent of film stock was imported, and this had fallen to zero by the end of 1941. As a result, Fuji became almost the sole provider of film stock for Japanese film production companies.[31]

The quality of Fuji's negative film was quite low. In 1942, the acclaimed cinematographer Sugiyama Kōhei noted that, 'in terms of the quality of Japanese made film, the contrast levels between dark and light elements were too strong thus leading to the viewers being distracted'.[32] In the same year, citing a report on the new negative by Tōhō laboratory, Nishikawa Etsuji, the head of film developing, pointed out that Fuji's newly introduced negative was even less sensitive to light than the previous version. It would therefore be necessary to 'sacrifice' the lighting of bright sections to depict details in the dark parts.[33]

Nishikawa noted Mimura's lighting scheme in *The Horse*/*Uma* (Yamamoto Kajirō, 1941), which incorporated the characteristics of the Fuji film negative with a sense of realism, something that was especially appropriate since the original idea of the film was to document the life of a horse-breeding family in the Tohoku area of Japan (Fig. 16.1). According to Yamamoto, what the director of *The Horse* had 'wanted to do for a long time' was 'semi-documentary', and this film was therefore the 'realization' of his dreams.[34] Nishikawa stated that 'Considering Mr. Mimura and Mr. Suzuki [Hiroshi]'s serious efforts to depict the local colour', he had 'tried to achieve the detail in the dark tones' when developing the film.[35] Nishikawa pointed out, 'We have to admit that the photographed film lacks medium

Fig. 16.1 *Horse/Uma* (Yamamoto Kajirō, 1941, Tōhō).

tones in its expression of darkness.'[36] Nishikawa first assumed that it was probably because the conditions of the set of the old country house made it structurally difficult to achieve sufficient gradation between light and dark. Nishikawa then noticed that, in some scenes, Mimura also used a sufficient amount of light to make a 1.4 density of brightness (high light) possible. Nishikawa thus concluded that the lack of medium tones was Mimura's strategic choice 'in order to depict the content of the drama in a realistic manner'.[37] As such, Mimura was playing the role of the director of the photographic images in *The Horse* in order to make the best of the Fuji film stock and to achieve the goal that the director of the film originally had.[38]

In *The War at Sea from Hawaii to Malaya*, Mimura did his best to play the role of a Hollywood-style director of photography in different geopolitical conditions. During pre-production, as when Hollywood directors of photography discuss lighting schemes with the directors and production designers, Mimura too gathered all the cinematographers, their assistants, and lighting technicians and clearly delivered his lighting plan for the film.[39] What Mimura emphasised throughout the production was 'severe realistic effects'.[40] As Markus Nornes points out, the fact that the special effects footage of this film has been presented as actual footage of the attack on Pearl Harbor in postwar documentary and news broadcasts is 'a testament to the documentary look of the wartime feature film'.[41] In particular, according to Mimura's production notes, he almost always spoke of realism in connection with the aesthetic of shadow. He abolished his usual make-up 'in order to emphatically depict the energetic look of the darkly tanned faces of the imperial navy' and, at the same time, 'banned reflectors from being used as much as possible on location in order to achieve documentary effects'.[42]

Nonetheless, Shimazaki Kiyohiko, who visited the set of the film as the head of the Association of Japanese Film Technology, argued that unlike in Hollywood, the director of photography of this film was not the one who should take 'responsibility in all photographic achievements' by planning all the visual schemes for the director and by managing the camera operators, gaffers and photo developers in the laboratory.[43] Instead, Shimazaki continued, Mimura only needed to be the one to 'formulate the goals and methods of cinematographic technologies for this film, to assign fellow cinematographers to appropriate scenes […] and to maintain control and consistency in technological manoeuvres along with the original goals'.[44] Shimazaki's distinction between the two systems – Hollywood and Japan – may seem quite ambiguous. The only difference in Shimazaki's definition is that in Hollywood the director of photography is the title of the profession and in Japan it is the name of the position for one film only – in this case, for the duration of the production of *The War at Sea from Hawaii to Malaya*. Even so, Shimazaki called the director of photography system that was adopted in an ad hoc manner in *The War at Sea from Hawaii to Malaya* 'a form unique to our country' and rather nationalistically claimed that the result of such a unique system would 'mark an unshakable cornerstone for the future' in order to achieve 'a new mission' … 'using locally made materials' and 'establishing a new and strong view of the nation and the world'.[45]

Such an ad hoc, case-by-case director of photography system that Shimazaki suggested may not be 'a form unique to' Japan, but it was certainly the one that Kurita Toyomichi continuously adopted when he worked in Japan. For the rest of this chapter, I will introduce Kurita's career and point out what kind of adjustments he has had to make when working as a cinematographer on the both sides of the Pacific.

KURITA TOYOMICHI: DIRECTOR OF PHOTOGRAPHY

When Kurita entered the film business in the 1970s, the studio system in Japan was on the brink of collapse. Both the number of Japanese-made films released and the number of cinemas had fallen to less than half their peak (236 titles in 1970 compared to 547 in 1960; 3,246 venues in 1970 compared to 7,457 in 1960). Audience numbers had also dropped to nearly one-quarter (254,799,000 in 1970 compared to 1,127,452,000 in 1958).[46] Daiei went bankrupt in 1971. Nikkatsu turned to making soft-core pornography the same year. Under such conditions, after making some experimental films under the influential cinematographer Suzuki Tatsuo, who started his own career at the documentary film company Iwanami Eiga Seisakujo, Kurita decided to go abroad in 1982 and study on the American Film Institute's (AFI) cinematography programme. It was the era when film schools flourished in the US after the disintegration of the Hollywood film studios. Instead of developing their practical skills in the studios, young and ambitious film-makers studied the theory and history of cinema and made their first films at school. As an institute aiming to train potential professionals for the Hollywood film industry, the AFI followed the Hollywood system. In other words, Kurita was trained as a future Hollywood director of photography, who 'designs lighting'.[47] While taking courses under such internationally famed cinematographers as Sven Nykvist and Vittorio Storaro, Kurita learned 'how to capture light and how to create certain tones by lighting in various works'.[48] Since then, Kurita's thoughts on the director of photography have not changed. In a December 2012 interview, Kurita claimed, 'I think lighting plays the most important role when creating images. In Japan, cinematography and lighting have traditionally been separated in film production. But I want to be in a position that can control light.'[49]

As such, Kurita has seemingly given up the systems of film-making in Japan. He has, however, been a rebel against the Hollywood system, too. Despite the fact that the position of being a director of photography in Hollywood allows him to control all the lighting schema, unlike in Japan, Kurita thinks that Hollywood's unions have created a different kind of segregation within the work of cinematography. Because of the regulations of the cinematographers' union, it is difficult for a director of photography to operate cameras in major Hollywood productions, for one thing. But Kurita does. According to him, as long as a camera operator is present on site, any person can operate a camera without violating the union rules! For Kurita, 'framing [i.e. camera operation] and lighting are inseparable in the act of cinematography', whether he is in Hollywood or in Japan.[50]

The ad hoc director of photography system that Shimazaki proposed back in 1942 thus still suits Kurita. Kurita 'formulate[s] the goals and methods of cinematographic technologies for' each film that he works on, case by case, and 'maintain[s] control and consistency in technological decision-making in line with the original goals of the director'.[51] The director of photography system that Kurita plays a role in is not 'a form unique to our country [Japan]' but something that is shared by Japan and Hollywood.

Kurita needed to deal with a number of problematic issues during the production of *Taboo* because of the nature of his own director of photography system (Fig. 16.2). *Taboo* was a period drama (*jidaigeki*), shot in Kyoto. Kyoto has been the second centre of film-making in Japan since the 1920s and has traditionally specialised in the production of period films. In particular, as I have discussed elsewhere, there have been very specific lighting conventions for films made in the city. Simply put, these are that the main focus of the lighting should be on the flash of the sword during sword fights and that interiors should be depicted in low-key light following the invented tradition of the aesthetics of shadow (naturalised by Daiei's renowned cinematographer Miyagawa Kazuo).[52]

Both Ōshima Nagisa and Kurita did not intend to make *Taboo* as a 'conventional' *jidaigeki*.[53] There are sword-fights in the film, but the focus is on setting an intimate mood between the two men and not the spectacular flash of the sword. Low-key lighting is adopted in some interior scenes but Kurita did not limit himself to candles and halogen lamps. Instead, he used fluorescent lamps to obtain a certain tone, something

Fig. 16.2 *Taboo/Gohatto* (Ōshima Nagisa, 1999, Ōshima Productions).

previously considered taboo for *jidaigeki*.⁵⁴ Moreover, there is a scene in which an episode of *Ugetsu/Ugetsu monogatari* is narrated by Okita Sōshi (Takeda Shinji) and shot in bright sunlight in extreme high key.

One of Ōshima and Kurita's goals was to achieve what they were supposed to do in their previous unrealised project. *Hollywood Zen* was a 1992 project about the relationship between Sessue Hayakawa (Sakamoto Ryūichi) and Rudolph Valentino (Antonio Banderas), two silent film stars. Only ten days before the production was supposed to start, the project was postponed indefinitely. The producer Jeremy Thomas failed to gather sufficient funds. Ōshima and Kurita were planning to recreate the style of the silent cinema of the 1910s and 1920s using equipment from the period, including not-super sensitive black-and-white film negatives and Klige lights.⁵⁵ According to Ōshima, they were targeting 'muted tones' that would not use vivid colours.⁵⁶ In other words, they were trying to make a film that was supposedly made when lighting effects seriously began to be taken into account in Hollywood and the director of photography system emerged accordingly. In the screenplay of *Hollywood Zen*, there is a scene at a movie theatre where *The Cheat* (Cecil B. DeMille, 1915) is screened. Ōshima and Kurita were planning to recreate films, including *The Cheat*, which is famous for its use of Rembrandt chiaroscuro (Lasky lighting) by DeMille and Alvin Wyckoff. But in order to achieve that in *Taboo* and make a Hollywood-style silent film in Kyoto, it was essential for them to have full cooperation from the lighting technicians.

CONCLUSION

Kurita Toyomichi has recently admitted that it is very difficult to fully make sense of current digital film-making conditions. 'Everything has been changing drastically over the last few years,' writes Kurita, 'and we are in an interesting time because of that.'⁵⁷ According to Kurita, the change from celluloid film to digital cinema is 'unprecedented in the history of cinema', so it is necessary to have 'a broader temporal and cultural perspective that goes beyond the speed of new developments in equipment and software'.⁵⁸

One of Kurita's recent films as the director of photography is *Brain Man/Nō otoko* (Takimoto Tomoyuki, 2013). While shooting entirely with a digital film camera, Kurita reiterates that 'The most important element in image making for this film was lighting.'[59] Kurita aimed for 'strong contrasts between light and shadow – like Daiei films in the past'.[60] In order to achieve a level of consistency between the lighting and colour grading, for the first time in the history of Japanese cinema, he used IS-100 – the latest image processing system developed by Fuji Film Company. Kurita directed all the digital image technicians (DIT) who were on the set for the purposes of managing the colour data. IS-100 is Fuji's attempt to adopt the Academy Colour Encoding System, the industry standard in Hollywood that the Academy of Motion Picture Arts and Sciences started to develop in 2004.[61] Kurita reports that IS-100 is extremely valuable because it enables the creation of large amounts of film in advance as well as the possibility of sharing this on every monitor or screen during the production and post-production process.[62] In other words, a consistency of tone is achieved much more easily to the extent that the equipment facilitates greater levels of communication between the director of cinematography and other staff. Nonetheless, according to Kurita, a significant problem did occur between the production and the distribution. When this independently produced film was delivered to Tōhō, one of the major distribution and exhibition companies, it was screened by a projector and on a screen that were compatible with 3D films, the standard of film-making in Hollywood now.[63] Three-dimensional films necessitate much brighter tones when they are exhibited. The projector and screen for 3D films inevitably make such a film as *Brain Man*, whose lighting is consistently low key, look annoyingly bright on the screen![64]

Just as Harry Mimura incorporated Fuji Film into his transnational goals for cinematography in the 1930s, so Kurita is trying to adopt the latest technology from Fuji and maintain a connection between Japanese and Hollywood film-making. As such, in this transitional period of film-making from analogue to digital, Kurita also represents the long history of cinematographers in Japan who have faced numerous challenges in the negotiations between national endeavour and transnational technology.

Notes

1. See Daisuke Miyao, *The Aesthetics of Shadow: Lighting and Japanese Cinema* (Durham, NC: Duke University Press, 2013), pp. 1–14. There are not many academic works on cinematography and lighting in Japanese cinema, especially in the English language. Beyond Japanese cinema, there are at least two important recent works: Frances Guerin, *A Culture of Light: Cinema and Technology in 1920s Germany* (Minneapolis: University of Minnesota Press, 2005) and Patrick Keating, *Hollywood Lighting from the Silent Era to Film Noir* (New York: Columbia University Press, 2010). The scope to 're-read' history of a national cinema from the trope of lighting technologies as well as from the transnational perspective makes *The Aesthetics of Shadow* different from these two books. In Japanese, most of the books on lighting and cinematography are memoirs/interviews of cinematographers while some of them incorporate contextual analyses. Such works include Watanabe Yutaka, *Eizō o horu: Kaiteiban satsuei kantoku Miyagawa Kazuo no sekai* (Tokyo: Pandora, 1997) and Miyajima Yoshio, *Tennō to yobareta otoko: Satsuei kantoku Miyajima Yoshio no Shōwa kaisō roku* (Tokyo: Aiikusha, 2002). The most extensive survey of the history of cinematography in Japan is Hirai Teruaki, 'Sokō Nihon eiga satsuei shi', a series published in *Eiga satsuei* from May 1969 to April 1991. Unfortunately the series did not go into the post-World War II period of film-making.
2. 'The Founding Fathers', *American Cinematographer* vol. 85 no. 8 (August 2004), <http://www.theasc.com/magazine/aug04/founding/page2.html>.
3. James Wong Howe, 'Upsetting Traditions with "Viva Villa"', *American Cinematographer* vol. 15 no. 2 (June 1934), pp. 64, 71–2.
4. James Wong Howe, 'Lighting', in Hal Hall (ed.), *Cinematographic Annual Volume Two 1931* (Hollywood, CA: American Society of Cinematographers, 1931), pp. 47–59.
5. Emery Huse and Gordon A. Chambers, 'Eastman Supersensitive Panchromatic Type Two Motion Picture Film', in Hall, *Cinematographic Annual Volume Two 1931*, pp. 103–8.
6. Hal Hall, 'Improvements in Motion Picture Film', in Hall, *Cinematographic Annual Volume Two 1931*, p. 95.

7. Local 600, the International Cinematographers Guild, 'Short History of the Guild', <https://www.cameraguild.com/aboutus/short-history-of-the-guild.aspx>.
8. Gordon Taylor, 'The Men Who Light the Sets', *American Cinematographer* vol. 31 no. 3 (March 1950), p. 85.
9. Ibid.
10. Italics in original. Charles G. Clarke, 'What Is a "Director of Photography"?', *American Cinematographer* vol. 48 no. 5 (May 1967), p. 352.
11. Watanabe Yutaka, *Eiga cameraman no sekai* (Tokyo: Iwanami shoten, 1992), p. 111.
12. Isayama Saburō, '"Cameraman" shikō kiroku', *Eiga Hyōron* vol. 6 no. 4 (April 1929), p. 339.
13. [Editors' note: for more on set design and colour, see also Chapter 18 by Fumiaki Itakura in this volume.]
14. Lee Jacobs, 'Belasco, DeMille, and the Development of Lasky Lighting', *Film History* vol. 5 no. 4 (1993), p. 408.
15. Peter Baxter, 'On the History and Ideology of Film Lighting', *Screen* vol. 16 no. 3 (Autumn 1975), p. 99; Jacobs, 'Belasco, DeMille, and the Development of Lasky Lighting', p. 408.
16. Kawaguchi Kazuo, 'Amerika eiga to Henri Kotani sensei', *Eiga terebi gijutsu* no. 238 (June 1972), p. 20.
17. Kotani Henry, 'Ichininmae no satsuei gishi ni naru made', *Katsudō club* vol. 7 no. 2 (February 1924), pp. 84–6.
18. See Miyao, *The Aesthetics of Shadow*, pp. 15–66.
19. Kotani Henry, 'Eiga ga dekiagaru made (1)', *Kinema junpō*, 11 June 1922, p. 5.
20. Kudō Miyoko, *Hollywood kara Hiroshima e: Eiga cameraman Harry Mimura no jinsei* (Tokyo: Shobunsha, 1985), p. 88.
21. 'Shōchiku block (4 sha) tai Tōhō no kōsō o ikani miraruruka?', *Kinema junpō*, 1 July 1937, p. 52.
22. See Miyao, *The Aesthetics of Shadow*, pp. 173–230.
23. Mimura Akira, 'Glegg Toland: Best iyāsu no satsuei ni tsuite', *Eiga geijutsu* vol. 3 no. 7 (August 1948), p. 13.
24. Keating, *Hollywood Lighting from the Silent Era to Film Noir*, p. 237.
25. Gregg Toland, 'Realism for "Citizen Kane"', *American Cinematographer* vol. 22 no. 2 (February 1941), p. 54.
26. Ibid., p. 55.
27. Ibid. See also Gregg Toland, 'Using Arcs for Lighting Monochrome', *American Cinematographer* vol. 22 no. 12 (December 1941), pp. 558–9, 588.
28. Keating, *Hollywood Lighting from the Silent Era to Film Noir*, p. 237.
29. Ibid.
30. '15 nendo Nihon eiga (geki) no satsuei gijutsu danmen', *Eiga gijutsu* vol. 1 no. 2 (February 1941), p. 86.
31. Okada Hidenori, 'Nihon no nitrate film seizō: Shoki no jijō (ge)', *NFC Newsletter* no. 31 (2000), pp. 12–15.
32. Sugiyama Kōhei, *Eiga to gijutsu*, January 1942, quoted in Hirai Teruaki, 'Sokō nihon eiga satsuei shi 56', *Eiga satsuei* no. 89 (July 1985), p. 73.
33. Nishikawa Etsuji, 'Eiga gijutsu no saishuppatsu: Shin taisei kakuritsu dai 1 nen o mukaete', *Eiga gijutsu* vol. 3 no. 1 (January 1942), pp. 42–3.
34. Hirai Teruaki, *Jitsuroku nihon eiga no tanjō* (Tokyo: Film art-sha, 1993), p. 269.
35. Nishikawa Etsuji, 'Uma no genzō: Rabo no kiroku o megutte', *Eiga gijutsu* vol. 1 no. 4 (April 1941), p. 253.
36. Ibid., p. 255.
37. Ibid.
38. For more detailed discussions on the cinematography of *The Horse*, see Miyao, *The Aesthetics of Shadow*, pp. 240–5.
39. 'Satsuei kantoku seido no kakuritsu o', *Kinema Junpō*, 1 July 1960, p. 90.
40. Mimura Akira, '*Hawaii Malay oki kaisen* no satsuei nisshi yori', *Eiga gijutsu* vol. 5 no. 1 (January 1943), p. 62.
41. Abé Mark Nornes, *Japanese Documentary Film: The Meiji Era through Hiroshima* (Minneapolis: University of Minnesota Press, 2003), p. 108.
42. Mimura, '*Hawaii Malay oki kaisen* no satsuei nisshi yori', p. 62.
43. Shimazaki Kiyohiko, 'Satsuei kantoku ni tsuite', *Eiga hyōron* vol. 2 no. 12 (December 1942), p. 75.
44. Ibid.
45. Ibid., pp. 75–6.
46. Motion Picture Producers Association of Japan, 'Nihon eiga sangyo tokei', <http://www.eiren.org/toukei/data.html>.
47. '29 sai de nyūgaku shita AFI no senpai ni wa Deviddo Rinchi ga ita', <http://www.webdice.jp/dice/detail/3731>.
48. Kurita Toyomichi, 'Dare mo mitakoto no nai "Bakumatsu"', *Eureka: Poetry and Criticism* vol. 32 no. 1 (January 2000), p. 98.
49. '29 sai de nyūgaku shita AFI no senpai ni wa Deviddo Rinchi ga ita'.
50. Kurita, 'Dare mo mitakoto no nai "Bakumatsu"', p. 101.

51. Ibid.
52. See Miyao, *The Aesthetics of Shadow*, chapter 2 and conclusion.
53. Kurita, 'Dare mo mitakoto no nai "Bakumatsu"', p. 106.
54. Ibid., p. 101.
55. The Klieg light is a carbon arc lamp used in film-making. It is named after its inventor John H. Kliegl and his brother Anton T. Kliegl.
56. New Yorker Films, *New Yorker Films Presents: Taboo: A Film by Nagisa Oshima*, Official Selection 2000: Cannes & Toronto Film Festivals, <http://www.kitanotakeshi.com/pdf/1104143782_taboo_pk.pdf>.
57. Email to Miyao from Kurita Toyomichi, 9 February 2015.
58. Ibid.
59. Previously accessed at <http://fujifilm.jp/business/broadcastcinema/mpfilm/exposure_news/008/>.
60. Previously accessed at <http://mantan-web.jp/2013/02/10/20130210dog00m200007000c.html>.
61. Oscars, 'What Is ACES?', <http://www.oscars.org/science-technology/council/projects/aces.html>.
62. Email to Miyao from Kurita Toyomichi, 9 February 2015.
63. Ironically, Tōhō did not distribute any 3D films in 2013.
64. Ibid.

17

ACTING
Spectral bodies: Matsui Sumako and Tanaka Kinuyo in *The Love of Sumako the Actress* (1947)

Chika Kinoshita

Mizoguchi Kenji's *The Love of Sumako the Actress/ Joyū Sumako no koi* (1947) centres on the romantic relationship between the pioneering actress Matsui Sumako (1886–1919) and her mentor and director Shimamura Hōgetsu, and dramatises the dawn of *shingeki* (New Theatre) and its practice of Western-style stage productions in Japan during the 1910s. Made under the Allied Occupation, this biopic poses a number of important questions about the wider subject of Japanese film acting. In particular, I shall begin this discussion by drawing attention to the glaring discrepancies that exist between the historical and contemporary reception of the acting in the film. In particular, Tanaka Kinuyo's performance as Sumako on stage within the film has been described as hyperbolic and offensive to the 'good taste' of the modern-day Japanese cinéphiles who admire Mizoguchi for extracting restrained performances from his actors.[1] In her performance as Carmen in a stage adaptation of Prosper Mérimée's novella, Sumako/Tanaka certainly screams loudly to her lover José, expresses her frustration with him by stretching her arms up in the air, has a tantrum lying on the table, and mocks him by thumbing her nose up at him. In addition, Tanaka does not even look like a Roma femme fatale with her wig, false eyelashes, big headset, jangling jewellery and a rose placed between her painted lips. In 1947, however, reviewers were nearly unanimously positive about Tanaka's acting and acclaimed her 'powerful performance' that was 'possibly ground-breaking for her career', even though they also criticised the film for lacking any depth when it came to both character psychology and historical consciousness.[2] No contemporary reviewer that I have read describes her performance as hyperbolic or overdone; she eventually received the 1947 Mainichi Film Award for Best Actress for this and two other films.[3] The wide gap between the historical and the modern reception of *The Love of Sumako the Actress* thus provides a reminder of the historicity of screen acting and, in turn, calls into question what 'good' screen acting actually is when it comes to Japanese cinema as a whole.

A careful look at the production history, publicity and critical reception for *The Love of Sumako the Actress* reveals a number of more complex issues than simply a change in aesthetic taste. In effect, thanks to both its subject matter and the extraordinary historical context in which it was made (i.e. the process of Westernisation and 'emancipation' under the semi-colonial environment of the Occupation), the film and its surrounding discourse serve to crystallise a history of performance in modern Japanese theatre and cinema. These circumstances largely explain contemporary audiences' discomfort with the film. Through a combination of historical research and textual analysis, this chapter will demonstrate that *The Love of Sumako the Actress* presented Matsui Sumako as an embodied New Woman in its theatre scenes and when it turned her into a spectral image on screen it thereby generated a new kind of cinematic body. In this intermedial and dialectical process, the film liberally capitalised on the heterogeneous genealogies of modern acting in Japan and the conventions of various film genres such as the backstage melodrama and the musical. In sum, this chapter thus sets out to map, demystify and re-contextualise Japanese film acting traditions and the various theories and assumptions that may inform them.

I will initially reconstruct the ways in which Occupation film policy and what John Dower calls 'the culture of defeat' both shaped the film's production and publicity.[4] I will then cast light on the theatre-historical context of the production of the plays within the film and position this within a general history of acting. Senda Koreya (1904–94), a celebrated *shingeki* director and actor, participated in *The Love of Sumako the Actress* together with his colleagues at the Haiyūza (Actors Theatre Company). He also directed its theatre scenes.[5] At the time that Senda participated in the film, he was deeply immersed in the ideas of Konstantin Stanislavsky. This section of the chapter will demonstrate that the film's stage scenes encapsulate how acting methods and styles in the West such as the Stanislavsky System were received through the conceptual and practical filters of Japanese acting traditions in the first half of the twentieth century.

Finally, I will return to questions of intermediality and the medium of film to examine how *The Love of Sumako the Actress* appropriated theatre in order to shape a new filmic discourse.

CONTEXTS

The story of *The Love of Sumako the Actress* begins around 1910 in Tokyo. Shimamura Hōgetsu (Yamamura Sō), a Waseda University professor, is a leading figure of literary and dramatic naturalism in Japan. He is an active member of Bungei kyōkai (Theatre Institute of the Literary Society), a *shingeki* organisation established by his mentor Tsubouchi Shōyō (Tōno Eijirō). Hōgetsu proposes to direct his dream project, Henrik Ibsen's *A Doll House* (1879) for Bungei kyōkai, but no actress seems capable of playing Nora. By chance, Hōgetsu witnesses Matsui Sumako (Tanaka Kinuyo), one of Bungei kyōkai's drama students, fiercely fighting with her ex-husband; he has found his Nora. With *A Doll House*'s historic triumph, Sumako becomes the first real

Fig. 17.1 Tanaka Kinuyo as Matsui Sumako (left) in *The Love of Sumako the Actress/Joyū Sumako no koi* (Mizoguchi Kenji, 1947, Shōchiku, a publicity still).

shingeki actress. Hōgetsu confesses his love to Sumako and they spend the night together. Their affair soon becomes a scandal. Hōgetsu eventually leaves his family as well as Shōyō, resigns from his positions at Waseda and Bungei kyōkai, and establishes Geijutsuza (Art Theatre), a new theatre group, together with Sumako and his friend Nakamura (Ozawa Eitarō). Geijutsuza suffers financial difficulties and has to go on the road. The artistic purists in the group leave yet Sumako's performances maintain popular appeal. In 1918, as Geijutsuza rehearses for a production at the prestigious Meijiza, Hōgetsu comes down with flu and unexpectedly dies (Fig. 17.1). During the course of a successful run of *Carmen*, Sumako hangs herself. It has been only two months since Hōgetsu's death.

Even though 'Hōgetsu-Sumako' had been a household name for three decades, a film that sympathetically depicted their extramarital relationship could not possibly have passed the Home Ministry's original censorship guidelines initiated in 1925 and more stringently developed in the late 1930s. After the end of the war, *Carmen Has Passed Away/Karumen ikinu*, a short story by Nagata Hideo, who worked with Hōgetsu and Sumako at Geijutsuza, appeared in the January 1947 edition of the prestigious literary magazine *Kuraku*.[6] While the story narrowly focuses on Sumako's death, its publication probably kindled the film industry's interest in the subject matter and this resulted in two competing projects: Mizoguchi's *The Love of Sumako the Actress* at Shōchiku's Kyoto studio and Kinugasa Teinosuke's *Actress/Joyū* (1947) starring Yamada Isuzu at Tōhō.

As a film made in 1947, *The Love of Sumako the Actress* had to claim it was making a contribution to the goals of the Occupation, and the commercial and artistic agendas of its production had to be negotiated with the film policy and censorship criteria of SCAP (Supreme Commander for the Allied Powers). As Kyoko Hirano, Tanikawa Takeshi and Hiroshi Kitamura have all shown, during the Occupation, precisely because SCAP highly valued the film medium's propagandistic power and mass appeal, two different entities conducted dual censorship of all the films shown in Japan.[7] CIE (the Civil Information and Education Section of SCAP) looked at every project's statement of purpose (*seisakuito*), synopsis, shooting script and final film, and at each stage of the process gave suggestions and advice in the light of the Occupation's goals regarding the demilitarisation and democratisation of Japan. CIE officials could demand film-makers to rethink, rewrite, reedit or, if necessary, reshoot a film. The CCD (Civil Censorship Detachment) was under the direct control of military intelligence and thus primarily answered its purpose.[8] The CCD screened the finished film and if it passed, with or without deletions, it was granted a Civil Censorship Identification Number;[9] the opening title of *The Love of Sumako the Actress* shows its CCD number being 1,303. Even though no records of the film's censorship process have yet been found in the CIE film censorship files, the copy of the script held at Shōchiku's Ōtani Library includes the film's *seisakuito*, a statement that attempts to justify the production in terms of its adaptation to the logic of the Occupation.[10]

This *seisakuito*, very likely written by the screenwriter Yoda Yoshikata, calls Sumako a 'New Woman' and aligns her actions with Hiratsuka Raichō's activism in the feminist journal *Seitō* and the English literature scholar Kuriyagawa Hakuson's eulogy of romantic love within the context of post-World War I democratisation. *Seisakuito*'s final paragraphs, pointing out gender inequality internalised by women, claim:

> We hope to raise a question about this problem and create an occasion for Japanese women to reflect upon their social status and gender relations. This is the reason for us to cast new light on the romance of 'Hōgetsu and Sumako' today.

Furthermore, *The Love of Sumako the Actress* was able to combine the topic of the emancipation of women with another subject the Japanese film industry was encouraged to work on: 'Dramatizing figures in Japanese history who stood for freedom and representative government.'[11] Since men exclusively performed major Japanese premodern theatrical forms such as Noh and kabuki, the very term 'actress' was considered both modern and Western in Sumako's lifetime. It signified either a pioneer or an anomaly, depending on where in the sociopolitical stratum the observer stood.[12]

Sumako's story was, however, an emancipation narrative that concerned love and sex as well as gender and career. Primarily because the CCD showed little interest in censoring Japanese print media for obscenity, popular publications called *kasutori* magazines, featuring an unparalleled degree of sexual explicitness for modern Japan, mushroomed in the early postwar years.[13] This, of course, immediately raises the question of whose desire was being emancipated.[14] In effect, *kasutori* culture meant a steep increase in the circulation of female nudity, both in print and in flesh, for heterosexual men's desire. Moreover, as recent feminist research in both English and Japanese has rightly demonstrated, this apparent sexual liberation only operated within a patriarchal structure that made those women placed outside the normative category of virgin/wife/mother provide US servicemen with sexual services.[15] Nevertheless, the flourishing discourse on sex did legitimise and celebrate women's sexual desire and pleasure under the rubric of marital life and romantic love based on gender equality. The affair between Hōgetsu and Sumako, one of the most sensationalised sex scandals of the liberal Taishō era (1912–26), was clearly reframed within this context.[16]

After Hōgetsu's untimely death, their sex scandal culminated in Sumako's suicide, which her contemporaries regarded as a form of *jōshi* (double suicide of passion). This well-known climax of the true story, however, sharply contradicted Occupation film policy that forbade any film from 'approving suicide either directly or indirectly'.[17] Seeing deep cultural links between the kamikaze suicide attacks in the Pacific theatre of World War II, the *bushidō* (Warrior's Way) code epitomised by *seppuku* and the sympathetic or romantic depiction of suicide on the Japanese screen, Occupation film policy tried to discourage or eliminate their representation by declaring them to be undemocratic and militarist. This policy influenced both the production and reception of the two Sumako films. In his published memoir, Yoda quotes Mizoguchi's written remark about an unidentified scene in a draft of the script that must have depicted Sumako's suicide: 'We have to omit this scene because GHQ has ordered us not to emphasize suicidal feelings (*jisatsukan*)'.[18] The result of this censorship was, from today's critical perspective, productive with Yoda and Mizoguchi creating a fascinating elliptical plot structure in which Sumako's performances of Carmen's death in the stage scenes replace her own suicide on screen.

INTERIORITY AND EXTERIORITY: SENDA KOREA DIRECTING TANAKA KINUYO PLAYING MATSUI SUMAKO

The stage scenes of *The Love of Sumako the Actress* spectacularly contradict the textbook understanding of *shingeki* as a bourgeois realist form. They look highly mannered, far removed from any kind of 'realism' we know today and occasionally outright ridiculous; and yet for all this they still remain powerful and involving. How, then, can we categorise these enactments and do justice to their fascination? This question must engage with a series of interrelated dichotomies that have shaped critical discussion on acting in Japanese theatre and cinema by distinguishing between the presentational and the representational, exteriority and interiority, and *kata* (patterns)-based acting and psychology-based acting.

According to Noël Burch, in presentational forms of theatre such as kabuki, neither the actor nor the audience take her/him to be a real person, and both acknowledge that he/she is acting on stage. In contrast, in the type of representational theatre that culminated in the emergence of bourgeois realism at the turn of the last century, 'the stage becomes an area of illusion', in which the actor pretends to be a real person separate from the space of the auditorium.[19] This 'illusion' is often produced and fortified by an approach to acting that valorises an actor's becoming/being the role from within through a form of interior identification. This approach, generally ascribed to the name of Stanislavsky, is opposite to that of those actors who construct or even 'become' the role by starting with elements of 'exteriority' such as facial expressions, gestures and bodily movements. In some cases, those exterior acting idioms are highly codified, as in kabuki's *kata*, thus providing a stark contrast with the bourgeois realist theatre where expressions and gestures must naturally emanate from the actor's identification with, or understanding of, the role's particular autonomous psychology. In line with Burch's celebration of both kabuki and Japanese cinema as presentational arts, these series of dichotomies have tended to be projected geographically onto the West and the East (or the rest). The stage scenes in *The Love of Sumako the Actress* are troubling precisely because they destabilise such dichotomies and projections.

In the famous seduction scene of the Japanese stage adaptation of Tolstoy's *Resurrection* Senda himself, as Takeda Masanori, plays Nekhlyudov. He and Katyusha Maslova (Matsui Sumako/Tanaka) spend Easter Eve together in his room. This incident results in Katyusha's unwanted pregnancy and fall into prostitution. As the scene fades in, an outside view signals the location as Teikoku Gekijō (Imperial Theatre), the most prestigious Western-style venue at the time in Japan. The sound of a bell continues from this external shot to the next shot on stage. The couple looks out the window, and during the following long shot, Nekhlyudov encourages Katyusha to sing so that her wish will come true. As he holds her hands, a cut occurs to offer a closer view of the couple. Katyusha sings the first verse of the famous 'Katyusha no uta'; Nekhlyudov listens screen right (Fig. 17.2). She ends her singing, receiving applause from the diegetic audience, and Nekhlyudov tells her that she should accept his kiss. As she recoils, the camera switches to a long shot that is closer than the previous proscenium shot even though it offers a full view of the stage. Nkelhlyudov forces a kiss on Katyusha and she frees herself to the right and pauses, confused. He catches her up and embraces her again; she initially says no, but her resistance weakens. The scene fades out.

Katyusha and Nkelhlyudov not only look as if they are in a fairy tale or on the Takarazuka (all-female revue) stage because of their costumes – Katyusha's gigantic headset, long blonde braids, beaded dress and childlike booties, and Nkelhlyudov's blond wig, shimmering silk shirt and riding pants – but also

Fig. 17.2 Katyusha (Matsui Sumako/Tanaka Kinuyo) sings in *Resurrection* in *The Love of Sumako the Actress/Joyū Sumako no koi* (Mizoguchi Kenji, 1947, Shōchiku).

because of the ways in which they hold themselves and deliver their lines. In particular, during Katyusha's song, she lightly joins her palms as if to pray (Fig. 17.2); Nkelhlyudov fixates on her, takes a deep breath, and shifts his weight, admiring her. As she sings, 'Shall I pray to God', she crosses herself, then joins her palms again and, taking a deep breath, ends her song.

Katyusha's attitude towards prayer in the film can be aligned with the question of 'realisation' – the re-enactment of an emblematic tableau or pose that formed a mode of representation that spread across various artistic genres during the course of nineteenth-century European culture.[20] This gesture of praying and/or beating time was widely circulated across different media forms in Japanese modernity and became synonymous with Matsui Sumako's performance in *Resurrection* as well as the wider rise of mass culture during the Taishō era. A lyricist, recalling attending one of Sumako's performances in Hiroshima as a teenager in 1915 stated: 'When she sang the song, she slightly angled her neck and made a gesture of beating time with her hands, like a child. I was so moved; it was heart-stopping.'[21] Nikkatsu's Mukōjima studio produced a film version of *Resurrection*, *Katyusha/Kachūsha*, shortly after its successful run on stage and in one of the remaining stills from the film, the legendary female impersonator Tachibana Teijirō, playing Katyusha, assumes exactly the same pose.

The origin of this attitude, in effect, dates back to the spring of 1903 when Hōgetsu saw Beerbohm Tree's rendering of *Resurrection* twice at His Majesty's Theatre in the West End of London.[22] In a report for a Japanese literary journal, as well as giving an account of the staging, Hōgetsu provided a detailed description of the facial expressions, postures and gestures of Lena Ashwell's Katyusha and Tree's Nkelhlyudov. His description of the song scene is vivid enough to convince theatre scholars that it must have inspired his own direction of the play. As for the posture, he noted:

> She sings a love song in a clear and deep tone, whose lyrics, as I recall them, went 'White snow melts in spring', lightly beating time with her hands in her seat. The man also lightly claps his hands. The orchestra accompanies her by playing a slight, thin line of melody. This is the most poetic, dream-like scene.[23]

In his history of acting techniques in modern Japan, Sasayama Keisuke points out how Hōgetsu's experience and recordkeeping of European theatre gravitated towards exteriority through facial expression and gesture:

> It is important to note that Hōgetsu did not simply describe each role's 'interiority' or 'feeling'; his description of an 'interiority' is always accompanied by its facial or gestural 'expression'. In other words, Hōgetsu saw the role's 'interiority' through the actor's 'expression'.[24]

Sasayama's emphasis on the 'exterior' nature of Hōgetsu's writing, as one of the founders of *shingeki*, is part of his revisionist corrective to the thesis of the 'discovery of interiority' in modern Japanese theatre. Karatani Kōjin, in his now classic work on modern Japanese literature, argues that while a kabuki actor's heavily made-up face presents a figure or concept for the audience's sensual appreciation, the emergence of Ichikawa Danjūrō IX's face, when the legendary actor appeared on stage without make-up, conveyed a meaning that exemplified the role's interiority.[25] According to Karatani,

> Interiority was not something that had always existed, but only appeared as the result of the inversion of a semantic constellation. No sooner had it appeared than it was seen as 'expressed' by the naked face. In the process of this transformation the meaning of dramatic performance was reversed.[26]

This thesis can be transferred to the link (or the lack thereof) between gesture and interiority. The *mie*, the grandiose posture a kabuki actor strikes, conveys, for instance, a 'concept' that the audience can only appreciate in the light of performance traditions and an intertextual network of literary and theatrical tropes; in contrast, a seemingly trivial gesture, such as putting on and taking off a glove, can be read as an expression of interiority, once this inversion has taken place.

Thrilling as it is, however, Karatani's narrative locating a rupture between the exterior-oriented acting of poses and tableaux and the interiority-based acting based on character psychology encounters a number of difficulties in the face of historical documents such as actors' memoirs, acting manuals and theatre reviews. For instance, as Sasayama demonstrates, Danjūrō IX, often considered to have introduced interiority-based acting and psychological realism to kabuki, in effect expressed a role's 'concept', such as heroic loyalty, not necessarily by psychology but through his body into which millions of *kata* had been inscribed through his lifelong training.[27] *Kata*, a central concept in traditional Japanese performing arts, refers to a specific set of *mise en scène* elements such as poses, attitudes, elocution, costumes and settings that belong to a specific actor, family, role or even acting tradition, which has been recognised as such and can be passed down to others. Furthermore, Sasayama draws attention to the rapid development of theatre lighting, the spread of photography and growing interest in physiognomy as a media environment that conditioned Danjūrō IX's appearance on stage with no or thin make-up and his concomitant emphasis on facial expressions.[28] Sasayama does not deny the emergence of interest in interiority at the turn of the nineteenth century in Japan; rather, he compellingly argues that in the case of both Danjūrō IX and Hōgetsu, keen attention to exteriority in Japanese theatre culture – the actor's body as a repository of *kata*, the increased visibility and circulation of actors' faces and the critics' fine-grained descriptions of minute details on the stage – all functioned as a matrix for the reception of interiority-based acting styles. Thus, Katyusha's prayerful attitude, seized by Hōgetsu's eyes in the West End, was circulated from stage to screen and mediated by such technologies of reproduction as photography, the phonograph and film as an emblem of *shingeki*'s – and perhaps Japanese modernity's – impure origins.[29]

This sort of nuanced approach to the dichotomy of interiority and exteriority in theatre history is in line with recent research on acting and performance in film studies. James Naremore, in his foundational work on film performance, makes a distinction between what he calls the mimetic, 'pantomime tradition', fortified in the late nineteenth century by François Delsarte's and his followers' acting manuals, and the 'quiet' naturalism of Stanislavsky that revolutionised acting between 1880 and 1920.[30] Roberta E. Pearson traces the ways in which the 'verisimilar code' emerged and distinguished itself from the pantomime tradition, which she calls the histrionic code, in D.W. Griffith's Biograph films (1908–12). The verisimilar code does not rely on formulated, ready-made attitudes and gestures; instead, actors who follow this code employ small gestures that evoke, or are based on, everyday life in a smooth, natural flow without showing them off.[31] This, however, differs significantly from Stanislavsky's interiority-based acting method as the term 'verisimilitude', which Tsvetan Todorov defines as 'the *mask* which is assumed by the laws of the text and which we are meant to take for a relation with reality', unmistakably indicates its status as an appearance.[32] Griffith often acted out a part's gestures and facial expressions himself, regardless of its age and gender, to show exactly what he wanted.[33] In other words, in order to achieve reality effects, the verisimilar code refers not to the prescribed semiotics of gesture but to everyday life; but actors do not necessarily have to 'live the parts' from within as they do in the Stanislavsky System.

In their thorough analysis of pictorialism, an acting style constituted by roughly the same set of characteristics and historical contexts as Naremore's pantomime tradition and Pearson's histrionic code, Ben Brewster and Lea Jacobs question the very validity of the dichotomy of interiority and exteriority, pointing out that throughout the nineteenth century, both performers and critics regarded gestures and attitudes as 'expressions' of inner emotions.[34] For Brewster and Jacobs, what differentiates Stanislavsky most starkly from pictorial acting is his denouncement of actors' self-consciousness regarding how they 'look' on stage; pictorialist actors, in contrast, seek to create poses that interest and convey dramatic meaning to the audience by often referring to paintings and sculptures.

In close dialogue with this line of historical research on film acting, Hideaki Fujiki has traced how leading figures in Japanese theatre and film received, introduced and discussed Western methods of performance in the first three decades of the twentieth century.[35] In brief, highly heterogeneous and often conflicting acting methods were introduced to Japan en masse. As we have seen, Hōgetsu's inspiration was Beerbohm Tree's pictorial acting and yet, he also translated and directed *A Doll House*, one of the milestones of theatrical naturalism. Between 1906 and 1907, the playwright Matsui Shōyō and kabuki actor Ichikawa Sadanji learned the Delsarte system at the Royal Academy of Dramatic Art established by Tree. Osanai Kaoru, arguably the most influential director and theorist of *shingeki*, saw Stanislavsky's *The Lower Depths* at the Moscow Art Theatre in 1912. Blown away, he attempted to re-create his production on the stage of the Tsukiji Little Theatre in 1925.[36] And yet, in 1920, at the Shōchiku Kinema School of which he was the director, Osanai had Matsui Shōyō lecture on the Delsarte system. In brief, performance theories and methods were taken out of their respective contexts and, as exemplars of the latest fad, grafted on the Japanese soil of *kata*-based acting traditions.

In view of such heterogeneous origins, it is intriguing to note how Senda, widely considered to embody mainstream *shingeki*, approached *Resurrection* and other stage productions in the 1947 production of *The Love of Sumako the Actress*. According to Senda's autobiography, his mother, a socialite, had seen Sumako's *A Doll House* and other early *shingeki* plays, but he learned to sing 'Katyusha no uta' through his brothers as a risqué hit song bourgeois young boys like them should not be heard humming.[37] There was a clear distance between Senda and Hōgetsu-Sumako. Having started his career at Tsukiji Little Theatre, Senda belonged to the *shingeki* orthodoxy originated by Osanai and Sadanji's Jiyū gekijō (1909–19), which ran parallel to, and in rivalry with, Tsubouchi Shōyō's Bungeki kyōkai and Hōgetsu's Geijutsuza.[38] Even though, or rather because, both the Shōyō-Hōgetsu and Osanai-Sadanji genealogies shared a basic understanding of *shingeki* as a modern, Western 'Theatre of Logos' characterised by a sense of the play as a sacred text, the director as the master/creator of the performance, and the actor as an interpretive slave or agent, Osanai harshly criticised Hōgetsu's use of song in *Resurrection* and derided Geijutsuza's run in the entertainment district of Asakusa for being a commercial compromise.[39]

Nonetheless, Osanai's disciple Senda's rendering of the stage scenes in Mizoguchi's film cannot simply be seen as a tongue-in-cheek mockery of *shingeki*'s embarrassing past. As the Occupation's cultural policy was generally enthusiastic about liberal, modern, anti-feudal, 'Western' theatrical forms, *shingeki* became reinvigorated and freed from the severe oppression of the wartime militarist government and a number of renowned *shingeki* figures were repatriated from foreign lands where they had been either stationed, detained or exiled. In this climate, Senda played a central role in building a sense of collaboration across troupes, genealogies and political sects, something emblematised by the all-*shingeki* joint production of *The Cherry Orchard* at the end of 1945.[40] Senda must have had a strong incentive to do a good job in reconstructing, and thereby celebrating, Hōgetsu-Sumako's legacy. In addition, he was acutely aware that working in the thriving film industry provided *shingeki* with an extraordinary chance to expand its clientele from the elite to the masses.

Shōchiku Weekly, reporting the start of the film's shooting, boasted of its strong connections with the world of *shingeki*, thus underscoring the historical authenticity of the theatre culture it was seeking to recreate.[41] Tanaka Kinuyo described the stage scenes being directed 'true to period flavour'.[42] Indeed, the *mise en scène* of *Resurrection*'s seduction scene, for instance, generally follows the photographs that the Mizoguchi team must have borrowed from the Tsubouchi Memorial Theatre Museum at Waseda University. At the same time, *The Love of Sumako the Actress* reflected Senda's current theory and practice. Since the mid-1930s when he wrote his *tenkō* (political 'conversion' from Marxism) statement and got out of jail, Senda had studied various acting methods and manuals, as well as books on psychology and physiology, in an effort to establish a practical textbook for actors. The first volume of his *Modern Acting Method/Kindai haiyūjutsu*, based on his 1947 to 1948 lectures at Haiyūza's drama school, was published in 1949.[43] Considering the timing, it is likely that the film's depiction of stage direction reflects at least the basic ideas of Senda's method rendered in *Kindai haiyūjutsu*.

Senda's understanding of the Stanislavsky System was solid. To be sure, it was mainly based on the Japanese translation of Stanislavsky's *An Actor Prepares*, the first volume of the severely compromised English version.[44] Yet, Senda's emphasis is on the actor's imaginative understanding of the role's social and psychological contexts. He stresses that an actor should start with the subjunctive clause 'if I were … this or that person' and imagine the world from that person's position. He then claims that it is this sort of creative imagination that 'enables us to imagine those "fabrications" on stage as real and thereby make the audience believe them'.[45] This closely corresponds to what Stanislavsky calls the 'magic if', a hypothetical circumstance that triggers the actor's imagination and enables her/him to 'live' the role.[46]

In effect, in contrast to Lee Strasberg's American interpretation that centres on the quasi-psychoanalytic and introspective process of working on the actor's 'affective memory', Senda's approach to Stanislavsky's System highlights its physiological and social facets. These characteristics of Senda's acting manual eventually drew criticism for their mechanical view of acting and naïve belief in science; it was seen to reduce acting to an exercise in types and situations.[47] In this light, the initial rehearsal sequence of *A Doll House* in Mizoguchi's film offers a fascinating glimpse into what Senda, his colleagues and the film-making community agreed to present as modern acting. Yoda and Mizoguchi both wrote the scene but Aoyama Sugisaku, who co-founded Haiyūza with Senda, played Helmer as Doi Shunshō and advised on its *shingeki* aspects.

In the scene, Hōgetsu (played by Yamamura Sō, who had a decade's work of *shingeki* under his belt) takes issue with Sumako's performance as she utters the line 'Getting out of costume' and he has her perform it eight times in eight different ways. At first, Sumako raises her right shoulder conspicuously. Hōgetsu tells her to act cold and ironic: 'She is extremely excited and boiling inside, but precisely because of that, she remains calm and cold on the surface.' In response, Sumako redoes the line, mockingly raising her shoulder with a sneering smile. In the following ninety seconds in a long take, Sumako unsuccessfully tries the same line six more times in different ways. Through these successive sessions, a pattern emerges: Hōgetsu gives advice, she carries it out in a deadly literal manner, he says no. Finally, he tells her:

> You are very good at bursting out with your feeling, but you have difficulties with suppressing it. You have to hold it inside tightly, and then let it go. You are stormy waves, which need a rock against which to crush in order to make the white crest. Try it like those waves.

As she listens, her expression lights up; it seems that she has finally got it. Nevertheless, she tries four more times with no approval coming. The scene fades out.

This presentation of modern acting showcases the multilayered historicity that *shingeki* was caught within. Hōgetsu's metaphorical yet also visual descriptions of the role's interiority seem modelled on the ways in which the historical Hōgetsu described performances in the West within his essays. Sumako mechanically tries the same line in various ways, which shows an affinity with the exercises in Senda's *Kindai haiyūjutsu*. To take one example, the acting manual encourages an exercise in 'surprise':

> Imagine you receive the following unexpected sensorial stimuli and practice your responses to them – a. Auditory: 1) an explosion nearby, then another faraway; 2) someone's shriek next door; 3) loud thunder; 4) your favourite music; 5) your friend's voice; 6) a stranger's calling your name; 7) an agitated crowd shouting outside and so on.[48]

The historical Hōgetsu's *kata*-based understanding of European theatre is being resurrected here in a version of the Stanislavsky System that gravitates more towards social contexts and physiological stimuli, thus creating a stark contrast with Actors' Studio that opened in New York in the same year, 1947.[49]

Moreover, the Occupation conditioned both Senda's acting manual and the stage scenes in *The Love of Sumako the Actress* in their shared emphasis on the emancipation of emotions from repression. As Sasayama points out, Senda's *Kindai haiyūjutsu* diverges most markedly from Stanislavsky's *An Actor Prepares* in its celebration of the 'emancipation of emotions'[50] and it is noteworthy how the above rehearsal scene centres on the means by which Sumako represents Nora's emotions. As I have shown, the Occupation admittedly emancipated many Japanese from an oppressive environment and the Occupation administration encouraged the simultaneous emancipation of sexual desire within the framework of marriage and romantic love. These freedoms were, however, closely interwoven with the issues of race and nationalism. *Shingeki*, as a Western-modelled art form based on physical immediacy, served to highlighted this in a salient fashion. Senda writes:

> Modern people, Japanese in particular, have been accustomed to repressing or disavowing emotions. Yet, repression and disavowal distort and spoil them. The movement of our facial muscles becomes constrained, or shows responses in a limited manner. As a result, we cannot honestly express our emotions. Furthermore, […] since emotions are inseparably connected to their expressions, if we do not express them candidly, our emotions themselves become distorted.[51]

For Senda, this difficulty in expressing 'our' emotions was closely connected to being Japanese. This assessment by someone occupied echoes the occupiers' valorisation of expressivity and the ethnocentric criticism of Japanese people for the lack thereof.

If *Sumako*'s stage scenes still look ridiculous, or unreal, it is precisely because Japanese actors such as Tanaka, Senda and Aoyama play Russians, Norwegians or Italians – in brief, Caucasians. To put it bluntly, *shingeki* was a form of racial drag. Senda's *Kindai haiyūjutsu* touches on this issue:

> Indeed, Takizawa Osamu has extraordinary techniques of disguise. In playing Ferdinand in *Intrigue and Love*, however, he was able to wear a blond wig suitable for a passionate German youth yet be unable to replace his black eyes for blue eyes.[52]

To be sure, Senda made this statement in a paragraph about the relationship between actors' physical features and their roles. Yet, the theatre theorist and critic Uchino Tadashi, quoting this passage, argues that it also reveals that *shingeki* materialised the Japanese desire to 'become Westerners'. *Kindai haiyūjutsu* was, in Uchino's reading, none other than a practical manual to fulfil this desire, enabling the actor to turn her or his own Japanese body into an invisible, transparent vehicle for the 'Theatre of Logos'.[53]

Kamiyama Akira has pointed out that as a form of realist theatre related to the notion of a 'Theatre of Logos', *shingeki* dissociated itself from the same fairground attraction roots shared with the traditional performing arts, despite the fact that in its very attempts to 'become Western' *shingeki* also turned itself into a form of *misemono* (attraction) called *akage-mono* (redhead genre).[54] Kamiyama, however, does not intend to censure *shingeki* for creating embarrassment. He recalls Tōno Eijirō's impressive *akage-mono* performance of King Lear not despite, but because of, its *misemono* character that involved various grotesque incongruities between Tōno's body and the role.[55] In the light of these remarks, and given that we finally have sufficient historical distance to celebrate both the inauthenticity and heterogeneity of *shingeki*, Tanaka's performance as Sumako now invites new forms of attention and critical approaches.

Tanaka's uncharacteristically expressive performance in the film's stage scenes was a function of the celebration of emancipation and expressivity under the Occupation. Yet, more importantly, her performance actually empowered and emancipated her as well. Tanaka devoted one chapter of her autobiography to *The Love of Sumako the Actress* and fondly remembers how the stage scenes with Senda and Aoyama provided her, as a film star, with the training and confidence to act on stage.[56] Her acting on stage in the film, no matter how highly stylised it may be, demonstrates her control and intensity in movement and poses. Katyusha moves gracefully and, at the same time, her controlled deep breathing conveys the fact she is actually singing, unlike the concert scene in the surviving part of the *Tree of Love* series, in which it is obvious that the voice on the soundtrack does not emanate from her body. On stage as Isabella, the mad Duchess who mourns her lover Giuliano's bloody death in Gabriele D'Annuzio's *The Dream of a Morning in Spring/Sogno d'un mattino di primavera*, she raises her body from the ground to a kneeling position, holds this for about twenty seconds, embraces her lover's imaginary body in her arms and then collapses again on the floor. Holding her body with a dancer's intensity, she delivers a passionate speech of mourning. In terms of the film's narrative, of course, this symbolist scene may also be read as a mirror of Sumako's own situation – she came to the theatre leaving her beloved Hōgetsu's corpse behind. But it is Tanaka's concentration, strength, physical suppleness and resilience that make this scene truly remarkable. This is, indeed, a theatrical body.

THE LOVE OF SUMAKO THE ACTRESS AS AN INTERMEDIAL EXPERIMENT

An auteurist examination of *The Love of Sumako the Actress* reveals its remarkable resemblance to some of Mizoguchi's wartime films such as *The Story of the Last Chrysanthemums*/*Zangiku monogatari* (1939) and *The Woman of Osaka*/*Naniwa onna* (1940, no extant print), in terms of their shared theatrical themes. In effect, this slips into being a genre study since these films, together with others such as Naruse Mikio's *Tsuruhachi and Tsurujiro*/*Tsuruhachi Tsurujirō* (1938), constitute something called the *geidō-mono* – a cycle of backstage melodramas set in the world of the traditional Japanese performing arts such as kabuki, *bunraku* (puppet theatre) and singing/storytelling arts such as *shinnai* (featured in *Tsuruhachi and Tsurujiro*). *The Love of Sumako the Actress* inherits three specific traits from the wartime *geidō-mono*: the foregrounding of woman's desire for romantic love, independence and autonomy; the formal exploration of medium specificity and cultural prestige through collaboration with, and differentiation from, older performing arts; and as an outcome of the convergence of these two traits, a narrative that is driven by the conflict between art and romantic love.

The Story of the Last Chrysanthemum was once considered a depiction of a woman's self-sacrifice for her kabuki actor lover, but more recently, critics have also noted her pride, strength, agency and far-sightedness: she is, in fact, the one who educates the actor.[57] *The Woman of Osaka*, starring Tanaka Kinuyo, centres on a talented, strong-willed woman who marries, educates and controls a *bunraku* musician. As I have argued elsewhere, the *geidō-mono* was established between 1938 and 1939 through the injection of a mixture of different genre ingredients into the world of the traditional Japanese performing arts that included the fast-talking dame from the screwball comedy, the egoistical male artist from the European and American biopic and the centrality of the number in the musical. It enacted a compromise between the film industry and the government that sought to mobilise both Japanese films and women for total war.[58] In this light, the matter of women's emancipation under the Occupation presents a surprising degree of continuity with wartime attempts to incorporate women as national subjects.

In effect, *The Love of Sumako the Actress* follows almost exactly the same plot structure as *The Story of the Last Chrysanthemums* in the first two-thirds of the film: a male artist, trapped in an oppressive environment, is deprived of the possibility of growth; he meets and falls in love with a woman, with whom he believes he can achieve both artistic success and happiness; his family and mentor strongly disapprove of their relationship; disowned, he begins a journey with the woman; the couple experience hardship as travelling actors; finally their work garners some recognition and this enables them to return to Tokyo. The most salient similarity between the two films lies in the ways in which the couple dies and thereby completes eternal union. *The Story of the Last Chrysanthemum* is based on a true story; while the film ends with the hero Kikunosuke's (Hanayagi Shōtarō) triumphant boat procession intercut with his wife Otoku's (Mori Kakuko) death, in real life, as well as in the short story on which the film is based, Kikunosuke also dies of tuberculosis a few years later.[59] As Nagato Yōhei has compellingly demonstrated, *The Story of the Last Chrysanthemum* is a spectral film. It starts with the backstage/stage sequence of *Ghost Story of Yotsuya*/*Tōkaidō Yotsuya kaidan* and, according to Nagato, after the film's diegetic time ends, Otoku's spectre eventually drags Kikunosuke to his death, as suggested by the final low-angle shot that simulates a ghostly gaze capturing him from beneath.[60] If the post-Otoku life of Kikunosuke had been dramatised, it might have looked like the last 20 minutes of *The Love of Sumako the Actress* in which the actress mourns her partner, acts out her feelings in the stage scenes and commits suicide off screen. It would have been spectral, necrophilic and self-destructive as in *The Love of Sumako the Actress*, and theatre scenes would have taken over life.[61]

The Love of Sumako the Actress does, however, reverse the gender dynamics of *The Story of the Last Chrysanthemum*. Certainly, it is Hōgetsu who leaves his job and family to embark on a journey yet, during their theatrical tours, the plot focuses not on Hōgetsu's artistic prowess but Sumako's. Interestingly, Mizoguchi's film does not particularly depict the legendary actress's growth as both a human being and artist, as in the case of the deadly serious Tōhō version. In effect, Sumako is a quintessential egoistic genius, a version of the familiar *male* protagonist of Hollywood biopics from *Bolero* (1934), a major influence on the *geidō-mono*, to *Citizen Kane* (1941). When Sumako appears in the film, she is already emancipated and fiercely driven. Hōgetsu is, as the film's dialogue repeatedly emphasises, a rock against which her waves can crush, someone who can channel her passion and energy into creativity. In a number of backstage scenes where Sumako publicly displays anger and frustration, Hōgetsu takes a more passive position, trying to calm her and acting as a mediator towards others. In a scene which recalls the brutally unsentimental long shot of the upstairs room in Osaka where Otoku dies in *The Story of the Last Chyrsanthemum*, when Sumako leaves her workplace and arrives at Hōgetsu's bedside, the doctor announces that he has already just died. In other words, Hōgetsu here assumes the background role more conventionally assigned to the figure of the 'wife' in the artist biopic.

Sumako is obsessed with death, but Occupation film policy did not allow the film-makers to depict her suicide as the act of passion that it is. Consequently, the film substitutes the onstage/backstage mourning and murder of *Sogno d'un mattino di primavera* and *Carmen* for the heroine's on-screen death. This tactic follows an important generic norm of the *geidō-mono*. Even though the *geidō-mono* has rarely been discussed in terms of its links to Hollywood musicals and their film-historical specificity as talkies, it does capitalise on the idea of the 'number', which in this case means extensive inserts of kabuki, *shinnai*, *shamisen* or *bunraku* scenes within the film. These numbers provide the audience with the sheer pleasure of music and performance; at the same time, they also function to underscore, or provide a substitute for, the film's dramatic content. In the Fred Astaire and Ginger Rogers series, the couple's elegant dance numbers provide a substitute for sex and/or conflict;[62] in *The Love of Sumako the Actress*, the passage from mourning to suicide on the part of the actress is completely displaced by the heroine's onstage actions, with all their expressivity and physicality.

Backstage, between acts, Sumako persistently has the young actor Nakai rehearse the scene of José's murder of Carmen, claiming that his form of attack is too weak and lacking in truth: 'You can't kill me like this!' Onstage in a long take, José, armed with his dagger, chases Carmen and eventually grabs her; Carmen, held tightly in his arms, turns her body to the camera and the diegetic audience. We learn that José has stabbed her through her short, intermittent and unearthly groans and the way her arms stretch out. José lays her on the floor; she is dead (Fig. 17.3). The diegetic music, based on George Bizet, begins and the scene cuts to a long proscenium shot in which a crowd of dancing people find Carmen's body. As the curtain promptly falls, the diegetic audience applaud then leave their seats, one after another. The scene fades out. Extra diegetic music then curiously starts up and fades out in the same shot leaving a beam of sunlight falling onto the empty auditorium. A bell rings, as if to notify the rise of the curtain. A sound bridge reveals that the bell is in fact a phone call from the Geijutsuza office that lets the theatre know of Sumako's suicide and the concomitant cancellation of the day's show.

As Linda Ehrlich has noted perceptively about this scene transition, it is typical of Mizoguchi's practice to ensure that 'the most violent scenes are presented obliquely'.[63] Yet, there is something more going on here. Sumako/Carmen dies onstage with a rare degree of rawness and brutality for late 1940s cinema. The change of lighting in the fixed shot of the auditorium miraculously represents the

Fig. 17.3 Carmen (Matsui Sumako/Tanaka Kinuyo) lies dead on the floor in *The Love of the Actress Sumako/Joyū Sumako no koi* (Mizoguchi Kenji, 1947, Shōchiku).

passage of several hours in twenty seconds as in similar scenes in Ozu Yasujirō's *The Only Son/Hitori musuko* (1936) and Mizoguchi's own *Ugetsu/Ugetsu monogatari* (1953). In the *geidō-mono*, extensive inserts of the performing arts paradoxically boast of film's medium specificity in its very impurity and the mechanical reproducibility of sound.[64] Mizoguchi's intermedial project in his film used the expressivity and raw physicality of the 1940s *shingeki* highly effectively and thereby conveyed the heroine's prohibited death in a doubly displaced manner. It is no coincidence that Mizoguchi relies on his signature high angle in capturing Carmen/Sumako's death (Fig. 17.3), unlike all the other stage scenes in the film that are shot from level camera positions. Life and theatre, reality and fantasy, the natural and the supernatural, all become finally blurred in this scene. Tanaka's theatrical body conveys Sumako's death at the very point where the two media, theatre and film, overlap with each other.

To conclude, *The Love of Sumako the Actress* capitalises on two historically specific contexts, the dawn of *shingeki* and the development of Occupation film policy, and in so doing, it offers a number of significant insights into the history of performance in modern Japan. The film's stage scenes may strike the sophisticated audience of today's Japan as hyperbolic and overdone, but they do highlight two fascinating aspects of *shingeki*. Firstly, they reveal how psychology-based acting in the West was introduced to Japan through the matrix of *kata* or exterior based acting traditions. Sumako/Tanaka's stylised moves and poses testify to this process of translation. Secondly, the film's representation of *shingeki* was largely determined by a celebratory 'emancipation of emotions' that carried racially charged overtones. These two aspects provided Tanaka Kinuyo with the opportunity to create a theatrical body in terms of her identity as a New Woman. Mizoguchi appropriated various elements of theatre – a mannered acting style, expressivity and Tanaka's theatrical body – into his film, thus transforming existing generic norms in order to generate a truly spectral, inorganic and awkward body of modern cinema.

Notes

1. Fujii Jinshi, 'Joyū Sumako no koi', in Hasumi Shigehiko and Yamane Sadao (eds), *Hajimete no Mizoguchi* (Tokyo: Asahi Shimbunsha, 2006), p. 36.
2. Kitagawa Fuyuhiko, 'Joyū Sumako no koi', *Kinema junpō*, 1 October 1947, p. 30; Tsumura Hideo, 'Joyū Sumako no koi o mite', *Kindai eiga*, November 1947, p. 5; Hata Ippei, 'Joyū Sumako no koi', *Screen & Stage* no. 19 (August 1947), p. 2.
3. 'Imahitotabi no', *Mainichi eiga concours*, <http://mainichi.jp/enta/cinema/mfa/etc/history/2.html>.
4. John Dower, *Embracing Defeat: Japan in the Wake of World War II* (New York: W.W. Norton, 2000), chapter 4.
5. Senda Koreya, *Mō hitotsu no shingeki-shi: Senda Koreya jiden* (Tokyo: Chikuma shobō, 1975). Senda is also known for introducing Bertolt Brecht's ideas to Japan.
6. Nagata Hideo, 'Karumen ikinu', *Kuraku*, January 1947, pp. 133–49; 'Sumako gensaku arasoi', *Screen & Stage*, 22 April 1947. [Editors note: *Screen & Stage* was published irregularly in both monthly and weekly editions.]
7. Kyoko Hirano, *Mr. Smith Goes to Tokyo: Japanese Cinema under the American Occupation, 1945–1952* (Washington DC: Smithsonian Institution Press, 1994), and her revised Japanese translation, Hirano Kyoko, *Tennō to seppun: America senryōka no Nihon eiga ken'etsu* (Tokyo: Shisosha, 1998), and Tanikawa Takeshi, *America eiga to senryō seisaku* (Kyoto: Kyoto daigaku shuppankai, 2002). Hiroshi Kitamura, *Screening Enlightenment: Hollywood and the Cultural Reconstruction of Defeated Japan* (Ithaca, NY: Cornell University Press, 2010). [Editors' note: for more on Japanese film censorship, see also Chapter 9 by Rachael Hutchinson in this volume.]
8. Hirano, *Mr. Smith Goes to Tokyo*, pp. 35–46.
9. Itakura Fumiaki, 'Senryō ki ni okeru GHQ film ken'etsu: Shōzō film kara yomitoku ninshō bangō no imi', *Tokyo kokuritsu kindai bijutsukan kenkyū kiyō* no. 16 (March 2012), pp. 54–60.
10. *Joyū Sumako no koi*, 1947, script collection, Shōchiku Ōtani Library. All the further citations of the script are to this version.
11. Hirano, *Mr. Smith Goes to Tokyo*, p. 38.
12. Ayako Kano, *Acting Like a Woman in Modern Japan: Theater, Gender, and Nationalism* (New York: Palgrave, 2001), esp. pp. 14–24.
13. Mark McLelland, *Love, Sex, and Democracy in Japan during the American Occupation*, Kindle edn (New York: Palgrave Macmillan, 2012), p. 60.
14. Joanne Izbicki, 'Scorched Cityscapes and Sliver Screens: Negotiating Defeat and Democracy through Cinema in Occupied Japan' (PhD thesis, Cornell University, 1999), pp. 300–18.
15. Yuki Tanaka, *Japan's Comfort Women: Sexual Slavery and Prostitution during World War II and the US Occupation* (London: Routledge, 2002), pp. 133–66; Mire Koikari, *Pedagogy of Democracy: Feminism and the Cold War in the U.S. Occupation of Japan* (Philadelphia, PA: Temple University Press, 2008); Hirai Kazuko, *Nihon senryō to gender: Beigun baibaishun to Nihon josei tachi* (Tokyo: Yūshisha, 2014).
16. For a discourse analysis of the cult of romantic love and sex in the Taishō era, see Kanno Satomi, *Shōhi sareru ren'airon: Taishō chishikijin to sei* (Tokyo: Seikyūsha, 2001).
17. Hirano, *Mr. Smith Goes to Tokyo*, pp. 44–5.
18. Yoda Yoshikata, *Mizoguchi Kenji no hito to geijutsu* (Tokyo: Tabata shoten, 1970), p. 149.
19. Noël Burch, *To the Distant Observer: Form and Meaning in the Japanese Cinema* (London: Scolar Press; Berkeley: University of California Press, 1979), p. 70.
20. Martin Meisel, *Realizations: Narrative, Pictorial, and Theatrical Arts in Nineteenth Century England* (Princeton, NJ: Princeton University Press, 1983).
21. Fujiura Koō, *Natsumero no hitobito* (Tokyo: Yomiuri shimbunsha, 1971), quoted in Kurata Yoshihiro, *Nihon record bunkashi* (Tokyo: Iwanami shoten, 2006), p. 89.
22. Iwasa Sōjirō, *Hōgetsu no beru epokku: Meiji bungakusha to shinseiki Europe* (Tokyo: Taishūkan shoten, 1998), pp. 77–82.
23. Shimamura Hōgetsu, 'Tsurī no resarekushon', in *Hōgetsu zenshū*, vol. 7 (Tokyo: Tenyusha, 1920), p. 43, originally published in *Shin seinen*, June 1903.
24. Sasayama Keisuke, *Engijutsu no Nihon kindai* (Tokyo: Shinwasha, 2012), p. 63.
25. Danjūrō IX (1838–1903) is one of the most celebrated actors of modern kabuki history, often credited with modernising kabuki acting.

26 Kōjin Karatani, *Origins of Modern Japanese Literature*, ed. and trans. Brett de Bary (Durham, NC: Duke University Press, 1993), p. 57.
27 Sasayama, *Engijutsu no Nihon kindai*, pp. 27–34.
28 Ibid., pp. 40–52.
29 In 1914, Sumako's 'Kachūsha no uta' was recorded on the phonograph and became the first mass-culturally mediated 'hit song' in the age of technological reproducibility in Japan. It made the actress a 'star'. Nagamine Shigetoshi, *Ryūkōka no tanjō: 'Katyusha no uta' to sono jidai* (Tokyo: Yoshikawa kōbunkan, 2010).
30 James Naremore, *Acting in the Cinema* (Berkeley: University of California Press, 1988), pp. 52–67.
31 Roberta E. Pearson, *Eloquent Gestures: The Transformation of Performance Style in the Griffith Biograph Films* (Berkeley: University of California Press, 1992), pp. 43–51.
32 Pearson, *Eloquent Gestures*, p. 28. Tsvetan Todorov, *The Poetics of Prose*, trans. Richard Howard (Ithaca, NY: Cornell University Press, 1977), p. 83, my emphasis.
33 Pearson, *Eloquent Gestures*, p. 89.
34 Ben Brewster and Lea Jacobs, *Theatre to Cinema* (New York: Oxford University Press, 1997), p. 89.
35 Hideaki Fujiki, *Making Personas: Transnational Film Stardom in Modern Japan* (Cambridge, MA: Harvard University Asia Center, 2013), pp. 173–6.
36 Sasayama, *Engijutsu no Nihon kindai*, pp. 130–8.
37 Senda, *Mōhitotsu no shingeki-shi*, pp. 16, 28.
38 Kamiyama Akira, *Kindai engeki no suimyaku: Kabuki to shingeki no aida* (Tokyo: Shinwasha, 2009), p. 8.
39 On *shingeki* as Theatre of Logos, see Kano, *Acting Like a Woman*, pp. 151–83.
40 Senda Koreya, 'Kaisetsuteki tsuisō', in *Senda Koreya engeki ronshū*, vol. 1, *1945–1949* (Tokyo: Miraisha, 1980), pp. 352–60. Ibaraki Tadashi, *Nihon shingeki shōshi* (Tokyo: Miraisha, 1966), pp. 109–12.
41 'Mondai no eiga! *Joyū Sumako no koi* satsuei kaishi', *Shōchiku Weekly* no. 26 (1947).
42 Tanaka, 'Watashi no rirekisho', in Nihon Keizai Shimbun (ed.), *Watashi no rirekisho: Joyū no unmei* (1975; Tokyo: Nihon Keizai Shimbunsha, 2006), p. 358.
43 Senda Koreya, *Kindai haiyūjutsu*, vol. 1 (Tokyo: Hayakawa shobō, 1949; 1951).
44 Yet, it is likely that Senda also had access to the 1940 German version, which was directly translated from the Russian manuscript. The Senda Koreya Collection, Senda's library donated by his family to Waseda University, includes *Das Geheimnis des schauspielerischen Erfolges* (Zurich: Scientia, 1940). For differences between the English version by Elizabeth Raynolds Hapgood and Stanislavsky's Russian manuscripts, their ramifications and the extraordinary copyright issues resulting from the translation processes, see Sharon Marie Carnicke, *Stanislavsky in Focus: An Acting Master for the Twenty-First Century*, 2nd edn, Kindle edn (New York: Routledge, 1998; 2009), part 2.
45 Senda, *Kindai haiyūjutsu*, vol. 1, p. 111.
46 Constantin Stanislavski, *An Actor Prepares*, Kindle edn (New York: Routledge, 1936), p. 65.
47 Watanabe Tamotsu, *Haiyū no unmei* (Tokyo: Kōdansha, 1981), pp. 171–87.
48 Senda, *Kindai haiyūjutsu*, vol. 1, p. 135.
49 For the differences between the System and the Method, see Carnicke, *Stanislavsky in Focus*, chapters 4 and 8; Cynthia Baron and Sharon Marie Carnicke, *Reframing Screen Performance* (Ann Arbor: University of Michigan Press, 2008), pp. 24–8.
50 Sasayama, *Engijutsu no Nihon kindai*, p. 262.
51 Senda, *Kindai haiyūjutsu*, vol. 1, p. 100.
52 Ibid., pp. 23–4.
53 Uchino Tadashi, 'Senda Koreya no *Kindai haiyūjutsu* o yomu', *PT* no. 11 (December 2000), pp. 42–6.
54 Kamiyama, *Kindai engeki no suimyaku*, p. 227.
55 Ibid., p. 228.
56 Tanaka, 'Watashi no rirekisho', pp. 342–70.
57 Satō Tadao, *Mizoguchi Kenji no sekai* (Tokyo: Chikuma shobō, 1982), pp. 145–6; Linda C. Ehrlich, 'The Artist's Desire: Eight Films of Mizoguchi Kenji' (unpublished PhD thesis, University of Hawai'i, 1989), p. 156; Hasumi Shigehiko, 'Kotoba no chikara: Mizoguchi Kenji kantoku *Zangiku monogatari* ron', in Hasumi Shigehiko and Yamae Sadao (eds), *Kokusai symposium Mizoguchi Kenji* (Tokyo: Asahi shinbunsha, 2006), pp. 228–49; Nagato Yōhei, *Eiga onkyōron: Mizoguchi Kenji eiga o kiku* (Tokyo: Misuzu shobō, 2014), pp. 148–56.
58 Kinoshita Chika, *Mizoguchi Kenji ron: Eiga no bigaku to seijigaku* (Tokyo: Hosei daigaku shuppankyoku, 2016), chapter 5.
59 Muramatsu Shōfū, *Zangiku monogatari* (Tokyo: Chūōkōron-sha, 1938), pp. 42–5.

60 Nagato, *Eiga onkyōron*, pp. 170–4.
61 One of the real-life Kikunosuke's acclaimed post-Otoku roles was *Kaidan botan dōrō*'s Shinsaburō, a *rōnin* who gets sexually involved with his lover's ghost and dies. Muramatsu, *Zangiku monogatari*, p. 43.
62 Rick Altman, *The American Film Musical* (Bloomington: Indiana University Press, 1987), pp. 160–71.
63 Ehrlich, *The Artist's Desire*, p. 192.
64 In the prewar and wartime era, the stage versions of *geidō-mono* did not show other performances from the performing arts.

18

SET DESIGN
Colour and excess in *Undercurrent* (1956)

Fumiaki Itakura

Production design involves a combined effort in the creation of aesthetic materials for cinema that includes set design, props, costumes and make-up. The production designer is the individual responsible for having a combined oversight of these aspects. It is well known that the profession of the production designer began to be officially recognised in the American film industry during the late 1930s.[1] As we shall see, the process was also underway in Japan at the same time.

The study of set design and production design began to gather pace in the 1990s with the first important work being Charles Affron and Mirella Jona Affron's *Sets in Motion* (1995).[2] This pioneering publication explored the function of sets in Hollywood cinema in both a concise and theoretical fashion. The authors argued that a set may be categorised in terms of five degrees of intensity regarding how it is foregrounded within a film: denotation, punctuation, embellishment, artifice and narrative. C.S. Tashiro's *Pretty Pictures* (1998)[3] followed up this work by criticising the Affrons' categorisation for the way that it restricted the impact of a set to its narrative function. Tashiro emphasised the fact that audiences 'receive' production design and he thus analysed set design in terms of a complex process of negotiation between various 'fiction effects' and 'reality effects'.[4] 'Fiction effects', according to Tashiro, relate to the artistic, aesthetic and stylistic creativity of sets while 'reality effects' relate to the process of location shooting and the authenticity of a particular historical background; the definition of the category of the 'real' may change depending on the contemporary period in question.

These studies are undoubtedly important, but they only cover part of the overall character of cinematic production design. We must recognise the fact that real production design is constructed through a process of negotiation involving a combination of different factors both inside and outside the film text itself. In other words, production design does not only have the function of inducing meaning in a particular narrative but, more broadly, it is also shaped in conjunction with the configuration of genres within the contemporary film industry; through the relationship between the director and production designer; the limits of contemporary film technology and the degree of agency that the production designer might have in the studio system, especially in terms of the power to secure the necessary budget to create a convincing diegetic world.

This chapter will examine how the production design of Yoshimura Kōzaburō's 1956 film, *Undercurrent/Yoru no kawa*, was configured by the interrelationship between narrative structure, *mise en scène*, generic codes, new colour technology and the censorship practices of the self-regulating Motion Picture Code of Ethics Committee (Eiga rinri kitei kanri iinkai), or Eirin.[5] My goal is thus to shed new light on the dynamic structure and historical contexts of film production design, neither of which the Affrons or Tashiro especially focus on.

Undercurrent was released during the heyday of the postwar Japanese film industry (film attendance went on to reach a record high in 1958). The six major film companies at the time – Shōchiku, Tōhō, Daiei, Shintōhō, Tōei and Nikkatsu – controlled the studio system. Daiei was therefore able to produce *Undercurrent* with a highly systematised staff and generous budget to the extent that Yoshimura Kōzaburō and his production designer Naitō Akira were able to deploy whatever production design features they wished.

The year 1956 was a turning point in terms of the dominance of colour in Japanese feature films. *Undercurrent* was the first film Yoshimura attempted in colour using Eastman Kodak film stock and, as we shall see, both he and Naitō used colour as a new element of the *mise en scène* in their production design. Generally, when a new technology is introduced in the film industry, there are a number of prominent films that make optimum use of the new technology during the early period of the technology's introduction. We can recognise this technological foregrounding when we reflect, for example, on the films of the early talkie period such as *The Neighbour's Wife and Mine/Madame to nyōbō* (Gosho Heinosuke, 1931) as well as the early colour films I shall be discussing in this chapter.[6]

More broadly, 1956 was also a year in which many factors around production design changed, overlapped and came into conflict with each other. If the most important reason for selecting *Undercurrent* as a case study for this chapter is that it clearly presents colour as an intrinsic element in the production design and *mise en scène*, we must also note the question of censorship that arose from the excessive depictions of sex and violence in such Japanese feature films of the same year as *Season of the Sun/Taiyō no kisetsu* and *Punishment Room/Shokei no heya*. These films had offended many social groups to the extent that the depiction of sexuality in *Undercurrent* was carefully controlled in order to avoid criticism from Eirin. The film thus permits the exploration of how production design may also act as a point of negotiation and allow one to trace the different social and cultural struggles that might be recognisable within the body of a single text.

A BRIEF HISTORY OF PRODUCTION DESIGN IN JAPAN

There are very few related studies in the English language that focus on the history of production design of Japanese cinema. Léon Barsacq's classic *Le Décor de film, 1895–1969* (1970) was the first comprehensive study on set design in French and was subsequently translated into English and Japanese.[7] Japanese set design accounts for just two pages of the work. There are multiple publications in Japanese in which well-known Japanese production designers are interviewed, but no detailed study exists on this theme.[8]

Set design in Japanese cinema followed the same process of development as in Western cinema; namely, the film set progressed from the theatrical set. In the late 1920s, production design work began to be systematised within the overall production process of the studio system. In 1928, the head of Shōchiku Kamata studio, Kido Shirō, came back from an inspection tour of Hollywood and decided to establish an official art department (*bijyutsu-bu*) in order to improve the aesthetic value of set design in the company. Before that, set construction was assigned to carpenters. Young and talented designers who studied art and design at art school were assigned to Shōchiku's new art department. Wakita Yoneichi and Kisu Takashi were amongst the first generation of Japanese production designers and heightened the atmosphere of Shōchiku's modern dramas such as *I Flunked, But … /Rakudai wa shitakeredo* (Ozu Yasujirō, 1930) and *Dragnet Girl/Hijōsen no onna* (Ozu Yasujirō, 1933) through their sophisticated deployment of set, props and costume design.

After the 1930s, the other major studios also established their own art departments. The work of production design in the Japanese studios was generally referred to as film art (*eiga bijyutsu*) and the professional responsible was known as the art director (*bijutsu kantoku*). Each art department in the Japanese film industry was subdivided into a design section, a stage carpenter section, a props section, a costume section and a hair and make-up section. The art section comprised a number of art directors and several assistant art directors.

By the mid-1930s, a number of ambitious production designers began to emerge who felt conscious of their responsibility for the entire aesthetic direction of the film. Such production designers worked in conjunction with the director and director of photography in the development of the film script, visited proposed locations to clarify the visual image of entire scenes, and managed the look of the costumes and props prior to shooting. The first genuine production designer in Japanese cinema who unified the entire image of film production was Mizutani Hiroshi (1906–71). Mizutani's name is relatively well known as he was responsible for the production design of many of Mizoguchi Kenji's films after 1933. In films such as *The Story of the Last Chrysanthemums/Zangiku monogatari* (1939) and *The 47 Ronin/Genroku Chūshingura* (1941–42), Mizutani achieved a particular depth of scale in his production design in harmony with Mizoguchi's unique form of *mise en scène* involving the long-take and tracking shot. In these films, Mizutani energetically researched the historical background for his costumes, make-up, props and many other minute elements of the *mise en scène*. In doing so, he contributed to the rise in profile of the production designer in the Japanese film industry.

Mizoguchi and Mizutani, for instance, researched the particular historical background of the late nineteenth century to create a unified production design for *The Story of the Last Chrysanthemums*. A remarkable moment in the design of the film occurs in the scene in which the two protagonists, Kikunosuke and Otoku, meet each other at midnight on a street near the riverbank. The scene is shot in an extended long take that lasts 4 minutes as the camera smoothly tracks the two protagonists walking rightwards. Mizutani especially created a long, horizontal riverbank set in order to facilitate the movement of the camera without cutting.

Another characteristic of Mizutani's production design lay in the skilful utilisation of depth of field in order to fit Mizoguchi's creative *mise en scène*. Following a 5-minute long take in the kitchen depicting the growing intimacy between Kikunosuke and Otoku, at just the moment when the two protagonists begin to approach each other, Kikunosuke's mother and her servants enter the room and stand between the two protagonists in the background of the frame, as if to separate them from each other. Mizoguchi's use of depth of field in the framing of this *mise en scène*

could only have been accomplished within the set designed by Mizutani. David Bordwell characterises Mizoguchi's staging in this brilliant scene in terms of 'blocking and disclosing', wherein actors both hide and reveal important elements within the background; the significance of Mizutani's production design, however, goes unmentioned.[9]

The studio system was pre-eminent in the Japanese film industry from the 1930s to the early 1960s. Many great directors were able to use a preferred production designer who was suited and responsive to the director's preference and intentions regarding *mise en scène*. Besides Mizoguchi and Mizutani, we can count several other famous director and production designer teams such as Kurosawa Akira and Matsuyama Takashi (and also Muraki Yoshirō after 1955), Ozu Yasujirō and Hamada Tatsuo, and Naruse Mikio and Chūko Satoshi. Yoshimura, on the other hand, did not pair with any one specific production designer because he worked with many different studios. Naitō, however, was well experienced as an assistant production designer under Mizutani's direction. As I will discuss later, he was very conscious of being a 'production designer' in sole control of the entire set of visual elements within the film.

A history of Japanese production design since the 1950s must also discuss the production design work of independent companies. Independent productions opened up new distribution networks in the 1950s and turned their budgetary and technological limitations into various creative opportunities for outstanding production design. The two most well-known production designers in this field during the 1950s and the 1960s were Marumo Takashi, who created many production designs for Kindai eiga kyōkai[10] in the 1950s, and Toda Jūsō, who created a number of impressive, abstract production designs for Ōshima Nagisa, Shinoda Masahiro and Kobayashi Masaki in the 1960s. Several independent production designers made good use of shooting on location in order to reduce production fees. *Naked Island/Hadaka no shima*, directed by Shindō Kaneto in 1960, depicts, for example, a married couple living self-sufficiently on a desert island. Small groups lived on the real isolated island for a month, shooting on location. This method of low-budget shooting used by independent productions influenced both the major films of the 1960s and the production of extreme low-budget films after 1962, such as the *pink eiga*.

Production design has been affected by the film formats and technologies that are dominant in each period. From 1956 onwards, for instance, the dominant aspect ratio gradually changed from 'standard' (1:1.33) to 'wide screen' (CinemaScope and VistaVision) and production designs consequently had to be expanded in combination with the change in the visible area within the frame. Some directors such as Ozu Yasujirō continued to shoot in standard aspect ratio whilst others such as Itō Daisuke willingly took advantage of the production design opportunities of the new widescreen frame in order to develop the staging of their *mise en scène*.[11] The main action scene in Itō's historical film *The Man Worth 10,000 Bushels/Kono kubi ichiman goku* (1963), for example, occurs in a set depicting the courtyard of a dyeing factory. Colourful clothes hang horizontally to emphasise the CinemaScope aspect ratio. In this strikingly oblong space, the protagonist warrior swings a very long spear horizontally to beat his enemies. A number of directors specifically used widescreen's planarity. The proscenium of a kabuki theatre resembles the CinemaScope frame and Itō Daisuke and Uchida Tomu both used this format to shoot in the key kabuki scenes in *The Gay Masquerade/Benten kozō* (1958) and *Love, Thy Name Be Sorrow/Koi ya koi nasuna koi* (1962).

After the turn of the millennium, computer-generated imagery (CGI) began to be used for many Japanese feature films, thus expanding the possibilities for effective production design. In the case of *jidaigeki* (historical films), production design budgets are generally higher than those for *gendaigeki* (contemporary dramas), with Shinoda Masahiro leading the way with the use of CGI in his production designs for *Owl's Castle/Fukurō no shiro* (1999). Recently, it has become almost impossible to produce historical films in Japan without CGI. As for contemporary dramas, *Always: Sunset on Third Street/Always: Sanchōme no Yūhi* (2005) has been highly praised for reproducing the lost appearance of 1958 Tokyo through the use of CGI.

THE PRODUCTION DESIGN OF *UNDERCURRENT*

Prior to directing *Undercurrent*, Yoshimura had long made good use of such elements of production design as sets, properties and costume within his *mise en scène*. Yoshimura entered Shōchiku Kamata studio in 1929 and was immediately assigned to the props division. He directed his first film in 1937. In a renowned film of his early directorial career, *Warm Current/Danryū* (1939), he practised a brilliant *mise en scène* that highlighted depth of field and used both the foreground and background spaces of sets to allow several characters' actions to proceed at the same time. *Warm Current* was shot on black-and-white film stock. It is the story of two women in conflict over their love for the same man. The conflict between the women is not only expressed through the film's dialogue but is also conveyed through the sets, costumes and props. In one scene, the women are seated across a table in a restaurant. There is a large window in the centre of the background. The wallpaper on the left side is white and that on the right is black. The woman on the left wears black cloth and has black hair. The woman on the right wears white cloth and has a white hat on her black hair. The colour of the teacups, the tablecloth and the flowers in the vase are also depicted in black on the left and in white on the right. Yoshimura recalled the intention of this scene in the following way: 'I tried to express the two opposite emotions of the characters by dividing the colour of each element between black and white such as black and white wallpaper, tablecloth, coffee cups and carnations on the table.'[12] Yoshimura also recalled how he had to meticulously plan the staging of the film and the location of all the props before shooting began.[13] From these comments, we can easily see how Yoshimura systematically prioritised sets and props as indispensable elements in the preparation of his *mise en scène*.

In his classic 1979 essay 'Minnelli and Melodrama', Geoffrey Nowell-Smith provides a 'symptomatic' reading of Hollywood melodrama of the 1950s by noting a parallel relation between the process of Freud's 'conversion hysteria' and the mode of 'excess' visible in the style of so many of these films.[14] He explains:

What is characteristic of the melodrama, both in its original sense and the modern one, is the way the excess is siphoned off. The undischarged emotion which cannot be accommodated within the action, subordinated as it is to the demands of family/lineage/inheritance, is traditionally expressed in the music and, in the case of film, in certain elements of the *mise-en-scène*. That is to say, music and *mise-en-scène* do not just heighten the emotionality of an element of the action; to some extent they substitute for it.[15]

Viewed in this light, Undercurrent displays similar characteristics to the work of Minnelli and Douglas Sirk, especially in terms of how the overflow of melodramatic 'excess' is rendered in the colours of the film's production design. How did the 'excess' of production design in Undercurrent emerge within the historical context of the Japanese film industry in 1956? Clearly, Undercurrent is a film in which all the production design elements (sets, costume and props) were affected by the new technology of colour film. In fact, the narrative set-up of Undercurrent clearly demonstrates a conscious effort to foreground the use of colour film stock by making the central female protagonist, Kiwa, a professional dyeing and weaving designer who, whilst visiting the famous Buddhist temple, Hōryū-ji, to receive inspiration for her new design project, meets Professor Takemura and falls in love with him. We soon learn, however, that Takemura has a dying wife and a teenage daughter. He tells Kiwa that his wife will pass away soon and that with a little patience, they will be able to marry. Kiwa does not wish for Takemura's wife to pass away and decides to end the relationship.

Before considering the function of colour in Undercurrent in detail, I will briefly summarise the history of colour film-making in Japan. Fujifilm company and Konishiroku film company were already working seriously on colour film stock during World War II, and by the late 1940s Japanese companies began to use national colour film stock for short documentaries or sections of feature films. Subsidised by the Japanese government to begin colour film production, Shōchiku produced the first Japanese colour feature film in 1951, *Carmen Comes Home/ Karumen kokyō ni kaeru*, on Fuji colour film stock. Film critics noted that the era of colour film had finally arrived in Japan. As Tomita Mika has argued, the development of a specifically Japanese colour film stock was one of the national projects engineered to embody the cultural and technological rehabilitation of postwar Japan.[16] The Japanese film industry also began to use Eastman colour film stock in 1953. The first Japanese film made in Eastman was *Gate of Hell/Jigoku mon* (1953); it won the Palme d'Or at the 1954 Cannes Film Festival and an Honorary Academy Award for Best Foreign Language Film and an Academy Award for Best Colour Costume Design in 1954.

It is important to recognise that black-and-white films were still predominant throughout the 1950s because the budget for colour film production was about 1.5 times higher than that of black-and-white productions. It was not until 1962 that the majority of Japanese feature films were made in colour.[17] We can nonetheless observe that there had been a significant rise in popularity of colour films by 1957 when the leading film magazine, *Kinema junpō*, published a special section on 'colour films in Japan' in their March issue.[18]

Undercurrent was the first film Yoshimura and Naitō made using colour film, in this case using Eastman stock.[19] Interestingly, Yoshimura himself was colour blind and unable to differentiate between green and red.[20] In order to compensate, he tried to control colour function from a more theoretical perspective by studying colour psychology extensively before shooting began.[21]

David Bordwell, amongst others, has argued that production design elements such as 'costume and setting can contribute to a film's overall narrative progression'.[22] A design system clearly informs the development of the story in Undercurrent. Yoshimura selected the base colour of each sequence in order to act harmoniously with the film's plot elements. He spoke of his colour planning in a production interview: at the beginning the colour tone would be yellowish-green, it would then pass to a purple-like register, shift to red when Kiwa and Takemura are in love with each other and return to black and white when Takemura's wife dies; the film would end on a blue note when Kiwa and Takemura finally separate.[23] In the sequence when Kiwa and Takemura first encounter each other at the temple in Nara, the key colour is set in green. When the two of them become intimate and fall in love with each other, the key colour changes to a warmer colour then shifts to burgundy. When the relationship becomes awkward, the colours of the production design move to colder blue or black-and-white tones.

Yoshimura and Naitō emphasised the principal colour points they wanted the audience to notice by rendering their background sets and props in grey. In the production design of the first scene set in the dyeing factory, for example, the colour field is uniformly grey apart from the costumes worn by the main characters. Other aspects of the film's production design include the expression of antipathy through the use of opposite colours, often described as complementary colours. The couple also worked on the effective selection of coloured properties.[24] In the film's first scene, for instance, Kiwa's father and a young artisan are discussing their working environment with feelings of hostility. The young artisan is dyeing yellow cloth and Kiwa's father is dyeing blue cloth (Figs. 18.1, 18.2). The colours yellow and blue are defined as opposite colours in colour theory, so the colours the two people are dyeing also represent the conflict between them.

We can also recognise the colour function of various film props such as the green necktie made by Kiwa and the clothes that are dyed in Kiwa's factory. The green necktie provides the role of a 'cue' for the scene transition from the kimono fabric shop in Kyotō to Hōryū-ji temple in Nara; it is also the cue for when Kiwa meets and leaves Takemura. After the final shot of the scene when the couple first meet, the next shot begins with a close-up of cloth being dyed red by Kiwa in her factory. Red is thus associated with Kiwa's love for Takemura. In the latter part of the film, when Kiwa receives news of the death of Takemura's wife, she is seen dyeing black cloth.

Kiwa and Takemura do not express their feelings and passions through explicit dialogue. On the contrary, the colour *mise en scène* displays this unspoken excess. This metaphorical expression of the characters' emotions through the use of colour must be seen in the context of the limitations presented by the climate of censorship in Japan at the time. The year prior to the release of *Undercurrent*, Eirin began using a rating system to prevent children from viewing films depicting excessive violence and sex. Yoshimura was forced to refrain from any excessive depiction of erotic themes and any explicit depiction of the central adulterous relationship between the female kimono designer and the male college professor with a wife and child. In addition, Eirin stipulated that the illicit relationship had to end before the film's conclusion.

Figs. 18.1 and 18.2 *Undercurrent* (aka *River of the Night*)/*Yoru no kawa* (Yoshimura Kōzaburō, 1956, Daiei). The young artisan is dyeing yellow cloth and Kiwa's father is dyeing blue cloth. The colours yellow and blue are defined as opposite colours in colour theory, so the colours the two people are dyeing also represent the conflict between them.

Set design | 265

We can see the outcome of these decisions more clearly by taking a detailed look at the interrelation between the production design of *Undercurrent* and the film's elements concerning melodrama, narrative, props and censorship. In the scene when Kiwa and Takemura make love for the first time, the climax of the narrative, we see Kiwa and Takemura walking along the street in Kyoto when it suddenly starts raining. They decide to take shelter in a room at a nearby hotel by the river. The first shot of the hotel room provides a close-up of an *andon* (an oil lampstand with a paper shade) hung on the veranda, lit in a burgundy colour (Fig. 18.3). The camera then tracks right to show Kiwa and Takemura. The red light of the *andon* helps to emphasise the erotic atmosphere. Initially, there is also an electric light in the room, but in the next shot a hotel employee (a close friend of Kiwa) sees a moth flying towards the light and turns it off just as we see the moth's silhouette pass across her face. The burgundy light from the *andon* fills the frame in a similar fashion to a tinted image from the silent era. Against the backdrop of this sensual lighting, Kiwa and Takemura's passions begin to escalate and the main musical theme of the film starts up.

The use of excessive colour not only provides a melodramatic substitute for the protagonists' ideological repression, as Nowell-Smith noted in the case of Minnelli, we also have to contextualise this in light of Eirin's representational restrictions on sex in the Japanese film industry at the time. In fact, when Kiwa and Takemura begin to embrace and kiss, the camera starts to track from a close-up of their upper bodies to their legs and toes. At the end of the final shot of this scene, Kiwa's toes unfold and there is a fade-out. *Undercurrent* thus applies the same tactics as those shown in Richard Maltby's analysis of the metaphorical depiction of sex in classical Hollywood cinema in his case study of *Casablanca* (1942). To deploy Maltby's terms, *Undercurrent* selects the metaphorical depiction of sex so that the 'sophisticated' adult audience could imagine an actual sex act but the 'pure' audience, i.e. children, would be left in the dark (Figs. 18.4, 18.5, 18.6, 18.7, 18.8, 18.9).[25]

In the film's final scene, Kiwa is shown gloomily dyeing clothes at her factory after she has parted from Takemura. She decides to start a new life and is seen giving a smile of relief. The change in her emotion is not expressed explicitly through verbal dialogue but by means of the production design. The sequence begins with a close-up of a tired-looking Kiwa dyeing blue cloth (in colour theory, blue is a 'cold colour'). She then stops and tries to wipe the perspiration from her face, taking a glance in the mirror to see that the blue dye has stained her cheek and forehead. She uses a handkerchief to rub the blue dye off and smiles

Fig. 18.3 *Undercurrent* (aka *River of the Night*)/*Yoru no kawa* (Yoshimura Kōzaburō, 1956, Daiei). The first shot of the hotel room provides a close-up of an *andon* (an oil lampstand with a paper shade) hung on the veranda, lit in a burgundy colour.

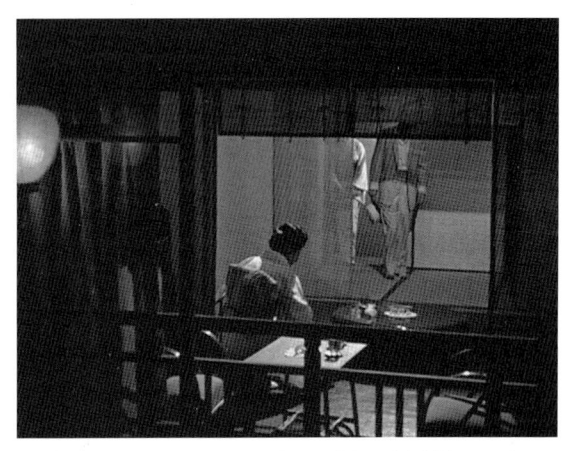

Fig. 18.4 *Undercurrent* (aka *River of the Night*)/*Yoru no kawa* (Yoshimura Kōzaburō, 1956, Daiei). Then camera tracks right to show Kiwa and Takemura. The red light of the *andon* helps to emphasise the erotic atmosphere.

Fig. 18.5 The burgundy light from the *andon* fills the frame in a similar fashion to a tinted image from the silent era.

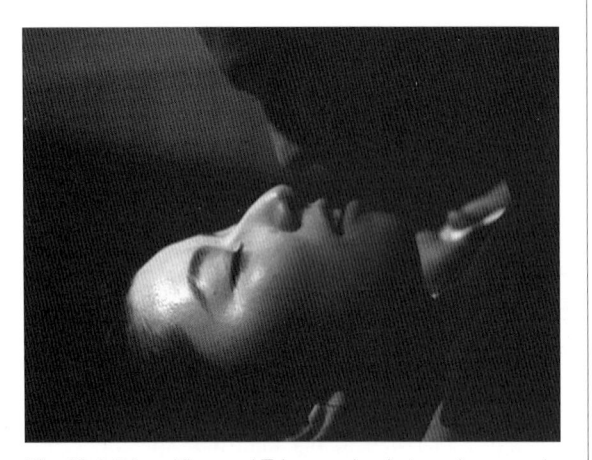

Fig. 18.6 When Kiwa and Takemura begin to embrace and kiss, the camera starts to track from a close-up of their upper bodies to their legs and toes.

Fig. 18.7 At the end of the final shot of this scene, Kiwa's toes unfold and there is a fade-out.

Fig. 18.8 The action of rubbing blue dye from her cheek can be interpreted as Kiwa wiping away her depression and deciding to continue with her life.

Fig. 18.9 When Kiwa goes upstairs to watch the parade of workers for International Workers' Day, we see three sets of clothes in three different colours – red, white and blue – hanging out to dry, showing the three colours of the French flag.

bitterly. Melodrama often manipulates the image of a mirror as an important prop to show both a character's situation and emotions.[26] The mirror in this shot also functions as a means to help Kiwa recognise that she has separated from Takemura. The action of rubbing blue dye from her cheek can be interpreted as Kiwa wiping away her depression and deciding to continue with her life. After this, a young worker runs up to Kiwa telling her to follow him upstairs to watch the parade of workers for International Workers' Day. As she reaches the upper stairs, we see three sets of clothes in three different colours – red, white and blue – hanging out to dry. Kiwa stands in front of them and looks, smiling, onto the parade. In the final shot, the camera tracks towards Kiwa and the words 'The End' appear on the screen. Yoshimura recalls:

> I tried to express liberty, brotherhood and equality by showing the three colours of the French flag. Through this combination of colour, I wanted to express that Kiwa was recovering from her broken heart and able to reconstruct her subjectivity through her everyday work.[27]

To conclude, the production design for *Undercurrent* emerged through a combination of different cultural contexts of the time. It is clear that we cannot solely recognise the interrelationship between production design, *mise en scène* and censorship in terms of a correspondence between narrative and script, as discussed by the Affrons, nor by solely analysing the antipathy between the 'fiction effect' and 'reality effect', as suggested by Tashiro. Yoshimura succeeded in organising the construction of his film's production design in terms of a specific focus on the new technology of colour and combining this with other elements of *mise en scène*, camera work and sound in order to depict his character's complex emotions. The approach I have taken in this chapter can be applied to countless other Japanese films of different periods and different genres. The history of Japanese production design, in all its complexity, has clearly still to be fully written.[28]

Notes

1 Jane Barnwell, *Production Design: Architects of the Screen* (London: Wall Flower, 2004), p. 13.
2 Charles Affron and Mirella Jona Affron, *Sets in Motion: Art Direction and Film Narrative* (New Brunswick, NJ: Rutgers University Press, 1995).
3 C.S. Tashiro, *Pretty Pictures: Production Design and the History Film* (Austin: University of Texas Press, 1998).
4 Ibid., p. 57.
5 [Editors' note: for more on film censorship, see also Chapter 9 by Rachael Hutchinson in this volume.]
6 Alexander Jacoby argues that the uniqueness of the use of colour in *Undercurrent* displays 'a marked self-referential quality' that 'repeatedly makes us aware that we are watching a film'. One of the reasons for Yoshimura's deliberate self-consciousness may well have been the recent introduction of new colour technology. See Alexander Jacoby, 'Kōzaburō Yoshimura and the Working Woman in the Old Capital', in David Desser (ed.), *A Handbook of Japanese Cinema* (Hoboken, NJ: Wiley-Blackwell, forthcoming).
7 The English translation was published in 1976 and the Japanese version was published in 1982. See Leon Barsacq, *Caligari's Cabinet and Other Grand Illusions: A History of Film Design* (New York: Graphic Society, 1976).
8 There are only a few prior studies of the history of Japanese production design: Japan Visual Art Council (ed.), *Eizō no ayumi episode I* (Tokyo: Japan Visual Art Council, 2010) and Iwamoto Kenji and Takamura Kuratarō (eds), *Sekai eiga daijiten* (Tokyo: Nihon tosho centre, 2008), pp. 143–5.
9 David Bordwell, *Figures Traced in Light: On Cinematic Staging* (Berkeley: University of California Press, 2005), pp. 119–23.
10 Kindai eiga kyōkai was an independent film company established in 1950 by Shindō Kaneto, Yoshimura Kōzaburō, Tonoyama Taiji and Itoya Toshio.
11 Kitaura Hiroyuki explores how the introduction of the widescreen aspect ratio in 1957 influenced the style of Japanese film directors. During the early widescreen period, technical depth of field limitations forced directors to stage actors in a horizontal line. See Kitaura Hiroyuki, 'Widescreen to nihon eiga no henbō', in Tsukada Yukihiro (ed.), *Eiga to technology* (Kyoto: Mineruva shobō, 2015), pp. 151–74.
12 Yoshimura Kōzaburō, *Eiga no gijyutsu to mikata* (Tokyo: Shibundō, 1952), p. 110.
13 Ibid., p. 178.
14 Geoffrey Nowell-Smith, 'Minnelli and Melodrama', in Christine Gledhill (ed.), *Home is Where the Heart Is: Studies in Melodrama and the Woman's Film* (London: British Film Institute, 1994), pp. 70–4.
15 Ibid., p. 73.
16 Tomita Mika, 'Sōtennenshoku no chōkoku: Eastman colour kara Daiē colour e no rikigaku', in Mitsuyo Wada-Marciano (ed.), *Sengo nihon eigaron* (Tokyo: Seikyūsha, 2012), pp. 306–31.
17 The following are the percentages of colour film titles for each year. 1954: 1 per cent (5 titles); 1955: 3 per cent (11 titles); 1956: 6 per cent (33 titles); 1957: 20

per cent (88 titles); 1958: 32 per cent (159 titles); 1959: 34 per cent (170 titles); 1960: 44 per cent (240 titles); 1961: 47 per cent (251 titles); and 1962: 53 per cent (200 titles). This data has been calculated by the author using *Eiga nenkan 1964* (Tokyo: Jiji tsūshinsha, 1965), p. 39.

18. 'Colour Films in Japan', in *Kinema junpō*, no. 171 (March 1957), pp. 36–50.

19. Eastman colour film stock had a very low degree of sensitivity at the time; colour became bluish in dark areas because of insufficient light. Production designers had to correct colour to compensate. See Barnwell, *Production Design*, p. 107.

20. Yoshimura Kōzaburō, *Kinema no jidai* (Tokyo: Kyōdō tsūshinsha, 1985), p. 348.

21. Yoshimura Kōzaburō recalls the most widely used reference book was the American psychologist Louis Cheskin's *Colour for Profit* (1951), the Japanese translation of which was published in 1954. See Yoshimura, '"Shikimō" kantoku no clour eiga ron', *Geijyutsu shinchō*, March 1959, p. 202.

22. David Bordwell and Kristin Thompson, *Film Art: An Introduction*, 6th edn (New York: McGraw-Hill, 2000), p. 187.

23. Katsura Yukiko, Togaeri Hajime and Yoshimura Kōzaburō, 'Yoru no kawa o megutte', *Kinema junpō* no. 156 (September 1956), p. 55.

24. During the production of *Undercurrent*, Yoshimura noted the 'hue circle' of the 'Muncel colour system', invented by Albert Muncel, in various reference books. See Yoshimura, *Eiga wa frame da: Yoshimura Kōzaburō hito to sakuhin* (Tokyo: Dōhōsha, 2001), p. 230.

25. See Itakura Fumiaki, '"Mukuna" kankyaku to "senren sareta" kankyaku', in Sugino Kentarō (ed.), *Eiga no naka no shakai/shakai no naka no eiga* (Kyoto: Minerva shobō, 2011), pp. 99–112; and Richard Maltby, 'A Brief Romantic Interlude: Dick and Jane go to 3 1/2 Seconds of the Classic Hollywood Cinema', in David Bordwell and Noël Carroll (eds), *Post-Theory* (Madison: University of Wisconsin Press, 1996), pp. 434–59.

26. John Mercer and Martin Shingler, *Melodrama: Genre, Style, Sensibility* (London: Wallflower Press, 2004), pp. 53–4.

27. Yoshimura, *Kinema no jidai*, p. 352. It is interesting to note here that Daiei's executives were reluctant to depict a parade of workers in the film's final scene because the major studios usually avoided this kind of leftist element. Yoshimura secretly shot the parade scene using red labour flags and succeeding in inserting them into the shot (pp. 351–2).

28. Among recent studies of colour films in Japan, Sarah Street explores the interrelationship between colour elements and narrative in *Gate of Hell* (1953) from the perspective of the global circulation of colour films in the 1950s. See Sarah Street, 'The Monopack Revolution, Global Cinema and *Jigokumon/Gate of Hell* (Kinugasa Teinosuke, 1953)', *Open Screens* vol. 1 no. 1 (2018), pp. 1–29, <http://doi.org/10.16995/os.2>. Although Street doesn't mention this, the painter Wada Sanzō (1883–1967) played an important role as the colour consultant on *Gate of Hell*. Wada studied Western colour theory from the late 1920s and collected colour samples from around the world in order to theorise the specific characteristics of Japanese colour combinations during the 1930s. As an expert on both Japanese and Western colour theory, Wada was therefore offered the role on the basis that he would understand the particular colour combinations Western audiences might like. See Wada Sanzō, *Haishoku jiten: Taishō Shōwa no shikisai jiten* (Kyoto: Seigensha, 2011).

19

MUSIC
When the music exits the screen: Sound and image in Japanese sword-fight films

Yuna Tasaka

Music remains one of the least explored areas in Japanese cinema studies in spite of its important role. Despite their strong effect on the spectator, the audio elements of a given film tend to remain elusive because of the obvious impossibility of freezing sound (unlike frame stills) and the difficulty of marking out the sound track for close scrutiny. In their groundbreaking textbook on the fundamentals of film analysis, David Bordwell and Kristin Thompson point out that 'sound is perhaps the hardest technique to study'.[1] On top of these practical issues, the implicit requirement to know (at least some) music theory or music history may also act as a substantial psychological barrier. Notable Japanese language publications on Japanese film music include: Akiyama Kuniharu's unfinished account of film music history; Ōmori Seitarō's exhaustive record of the reception of Western music in Japan; Kobayashi Atsushi's informative volumes on a number of Japanese film composers; Nagato Yōhei's extensive analysis of the sound effects in Mizoguchi Kenji's films and a series of insightful articles by film composers including Ifukube Akira, Hayasaka Fumio and Takemitsu Tōru.[2] Likewise, English-speaking researchers and musicians have published some illuminating research on film music, yet their valuable contributions cover only certain aspects of currently available Japanese films.[3]

This chapter aims to shed new light on the development of Japanese film music by exploring three key moments in cinema history in which the use of non-diegetic film music (i.e. original background music heard only by spectators and not by on-screen actors) was significantly reduced – developments that led to crucial reinvention in musical style. The chapter presents an accessible and practical way of analysing film music in order to provide a better understanding of the dynamic interrelation between the audio and the visual tracks of a film.[4] Some references suggest that the term 'film music' means only non-diegetic music or, in a narrower sense, the equivalent of a physical film score itself. In this chapter, however, I discuss not only such accompanying music but also music heard within the diegesis as well as other, more general sound effects. I mostly examine work in the traditional sword-fight genre (*chanbara*), because the long continuity of this genre allows one to clearly see how drastically Japanese film-makers have transformed their ideas about sound and music in order to accommodate changing patterns of spectatorship during periods of transition in the film industry. In the early sound film era, nondiegetic musical accompaniment deriving from the silent film tradition of live-on-stage accompaniment was initially suppressed by diegetic sounds (i.e. sounds heard by both spectators and on-screen characters).[5] The deployment of the pentatonic scale and use of a symphony orchestra nonetheless became clear hallmarks of the sword-fight genre film score as early as the mid-1930s. In the 1960s, Japanese film-makers again challenged the established function of non-diegetic music, which was to conspire with the visual image and provide continuity to the plot, delineate the characters' emotions and thereby guide the audience's response.[6] Film composers discarded the Western, symphonic music film score prevalent especially in popular Tōei period films (*jidaigeki*) in favour of new musical trends such as the use of authentic Japanese music and sounds.[7] In this section of my discussion, I will borrow from Miike Takashi the notion of 'sound regression', describing the simplification of the soundtrack and the limited use of music in his *13 Assassins/Jūsannin no shikaku* (2010), and suggest that Miike's film marks yet another phase in the history of Japanese film music, in which the controlled use of the audio track enhances the impact of graphic violence, attributing a notoriously disturbing character to the sound and the music in Miike's cinema.[8]

THE DEVELOPMENT OF FILM MUSIC IN JAPANESE CINEMA

The film music historian Akiyama Kuniharu has demonstrated that it was Yamada Kōsaku, one of the most well-established composers of Western-style music in the first half of the twentieth century, who composed the score of the first Japanese 'talkie' film, *The Dawn/Reimei* (1927).[9] Akiyama attempts to reconstruct what the film may have looked like, based on the film's screenplay and other existing references, but concludes that it is impossible to tell for which scene Yamada wrote music or, indeed, what kind of music it was. As an alternative view of the beginning of the talkie era, Daibō Masaki points out that the number of talkie (or partially talkie) films made between the late 1920s and the early 1930s was 'not negligible', and that these films used different recording systems developed simultaneously.[10]

In *The Neighbour's Wife and Mine/Madame to nyōbō* (Gosho Heinosuke, 1931), the first Japanese full talkie (Osanai Kaoru's *Dawn* being silent in parts), there is hardly any non-diegetic music.[11] This is consistent with K.J. Donnelly's discussion of the history of film music in Europe and Hollywood, in which he states that in 1931, films had almost no non-diegetic music.[12] *The Neighbour's Wife and Mine* is a comedy that portrays Shibano Shinsaku, a playwright who struggles to write a new script as he faces various obstacles including his nagging wife, who constantly urges her easy-going husband to get on with his work, and his noisy neighbour, who eventually turns out to be a popular jazz singer. Using a new sound-on-film system developed by the Dobashi brothers, the film shows – or, rather, lets the audience hear – different kinds of diegetic sounds, both on screen and off screen, such as the noise of mice running in the attic of Shibano's house, a crying baby, an alarm clock, a merchant's recitation to promote his goods, the sound of a treadle sewing machine, etc. The highlights of the film are two memorable jazz showpieces ('Speed Jidai' and 'Speed Hoy!') performed by the playwright's neighbour and her band, in quick tempi and in major keys. The two jazz songs' merry impression is further emphasised by the contrasting performance of Shibano's wife who sings in solitude a Japanese song (in a minor key) about a new bride who is in tears on the day of her wedding.

Especially because of the tradition of the *benshi*, silent film had a longer life in Japan compared to Europe or Hollywood, and it was only in the late 1930s that the talkie finally became the norm.[13] Akiyama Kuniharu asserts that it was P.C.L. (Photo Chemical Laboratories), originally a film company specialising in recording and developing talkies, that drastically changed the direction of film music in Japan.[14] P.C.L. hired Kami Kyōsuke, a leading jazz musician and conductor, to take charge of P.C.L.'s musicals and operettas. A series of musical films followed after the success of *Tipsy Life/Horoyoi jinsei* and *City of Purity/Junjō no miyako*, both directed by Kimura Sotoji in 1933. Kami also collaborated with director Yamamoto Kajirō to create, in 1934, the first

Fig. 19.1 *The Million Ryo Pot/Tange sazen yowa: Hyakuman ryō no tsubo* (Yamanaka Sadao, 1935, Nikkatsu).

instalment of a number of musical comedies casting Enoken as the main character, a series that soon gained huge commercial and popular success.

Yamanaka Sadao's *The Million Ryo Pot/Tange Sazen: Hyakumanryō no tsubo* (1935) shows a significant number of examples of how non-diegetic music evolved in the first few years of the sound era (Fig. 19.1). *Tange Sazen* was a popular *chanbara* series, starring the eponymous one-eyed and one-armed master swordsman. Compared with other preceding and subsequent Sazen films, Yamanaka's version shows few actual sword-fight scenes. The music was written by Nishi Gorō, one of among about a dozen composers who were working for various studios based in Kyoto (Nikkatsu, Shinkō, Daiichi Studios, for example).[15]

Below is an excerpt of the first tune that unfolds alongside the opening credits, heard after a series of minor chords with percussion (Fig. 19.2).

The beginning of this tune is in the G♯ minor scale. In the first four bars, the fourth note (C♯) and the seventh note (F♯) of the diatonic scale are missing. Missing the fourth (*yon*) and the seventh (*nana*) notes makes this melody a typical Japanese pentatonic tune, also known as the *yona nuki*, meaning 'without the fourth and the seventh'. *Yona nuki* melodies are often employed in lullabies and other folk songs, and the G♯ minor scale is often used in *enka* (a popular song genre).

The strings play the melancholic tune in unison, before moving on to the next phrase consisting of descending major thirds (G♯ and E). The tune is then played in the C♯ natural minor scale, again in *yona nuki* pentatonic, since F♯ and B are absent. This nostalgic phrase in the minor key continues two bars further, and then the melody is again transferred into another scale, this time in a major key. Nishi's film score serves as an important indicator that period film musical conventions – an orchestra with Western musical instruments playing pentatonic Japanese melodies – were already in place at the onset of the sound era. Another typical feature is that non-diegetic music consists of strings and percussions, while the piano is used less often. This opening score clearly sets the Japanese atmosphere of the film, even though later the music becomes more 'Westernized', i.e. in the style of a Hollywood classical score.

In one of the film's narrative highlights, Sazen, who had earlier witnessed a man being murdered by two thugs, is in an awkward situation in which he has to tell the news of the man's death to the victim's young son. Having learned that the child had no other family than his father, Sazen feels sorry for him and is at first unable to tell him the truth. Nishi, the composer, used the tune of a well-known folk song 'Tōryanse', juxtaposing it with the changing visuals, to render the different emotions of the characters. The tune enhances the

Fig. 19.2 A sheet of music from *The Million Ryo Pot/Tange sazen yowa: Hyakuman ryō no tsubo* (Yamanaka Sadao, 1935, Nikkatsu).

suspense when Sazen, sitting next to the boy, is about to reveal the news. The symphonic accompaniment stops when the boy tells Sazen that the only time he ever cried was when his mother died. Here, the music suddenly ceases. This abrupt interruption of music that was flowing steadily works as an equivalent to holding one's breath, inevitably focusing on the serious situation that lies ahead. This technique of letting the music flow in and out of the screen would be copied in Miike's *13 Assassins*.

The tune of 'Tōryanse' returns when Ōfuji asks Sazen whether he has succeeded in giving the boy the sad news. Intercut with a medium shot of the boy seated alone on the *engawa* (the strip of wooden flooring adjacent to the *tatami*-matted room), we see the couple sympathise with the boy's misfortune. Compared to the earlier head-on shot, the shot of the boy's back suggests his devastated and lonely state. Even though the tune is only instrumental, audiences familiar with the song would realise that the lyric here should be saying 'though you are scared, keep going': the unheard lyric describes the boy's current predicament precisely and at the same time it conveys an encouraging message that he should move on in spite of his loss.

Daibō Masaki argues that Yamada Kōsaku was one of the first Japanese composers to put in practice the theoretical writing of Soviet film-makers which asserted that sound should not merely be used as an addition to the image but also as an element in discord with the image.[16] He suggests that Sergei Eisenstein, Vsevolod Pudovkin and Grigori Alexandrov's 'Statement on Sound' – extremely influential among Japanese film-makers and critics in the early 1930s – may have served as the intellectual source of inspiration for Yamada when composing the music for *The Daughter of the Samurai/Atarashiki tsuchi* (Itami Jūzō/Arnold Fanck, 1937). It's useful here to note the fact that Eisenstein's sound films were long banned in Japan, and it was therefore left to film-makers' imaginations as to how to interpret the ways young Soviet film-makers put their theory into practice: *Ivan the Terrible Part One* (1944) was shown in Japan after the end of World War II, and *Alexander Nevsky* (1938) was only shown in 1962.[17]

In addition to such experienced composers as Yamada, some of the most influential film composers launched their careers during the 1930s, as P.C.L. was incorporated into Tōhō Studios along with another company in 1936.[18] Tōhō created a music department and hired Suzuki Seiichi and Itō Noboru as full-time composers. P.C.L./Tōhō's achievement was that it established a new system in which film composers worked as permanent staff, enabling younger composers to be trained by experienced ones. One of these was Hayasaka Fumio (1914–55), a self-taught composer from Hokkaido who became initially established in pure music (as opposed to film music). Hayasaka joined Tōhō in 1939 to work on Yamamoto Satsuo's *The Woman Who Knots the Ribbons/Ribon o musubu fujin*. Another composer who emerged in the 1930s was Ifukube Akira (1914–2006). Ifukube grew up in a small village deep in the Tokachi plain in Hokkaido, where he played with indigenous *Ainu* children while observing their traditional rituals in which dance, words and music were in an 'undifferentiated state'.[19] Ifukube's childhood experience of the *Ainu* had a lasting impact on him, as he continued to develop an interest in non-Western music throughout his musical life.[20]

The samurai film genre was in a process of constant change, and so was the music accompanying it. These experiments included attempts to present an historical setting using the conventions of traditional Japanese theatre, blending jazz with other contemporary music and borrowing musical idioms from foreign cinema. In *The Men Who Tread On a Tiger's Tail/Tora no o o fumu otoko tachi* (1945/52),[21] Kurosawa Akira's first period film, made for Tōhō, Kurosawa and the composer Hattori Tadashi focused on the similarity between the narrative music in Japanese theatre (*bunraku* puppet theatre, for example) and non-diegetic music in cinema.[22] In *Rashomon* (1950), Kurosawa's fifth collaboration with Hayasaka, the film-maker and the composer tested the possibilities of creating a sound film in which a combination of the visual and the music played a more vital role than the dialogue.[23] In Kurosawa's *The Seven Samurai/Shichinin no samurai* (1954), Hayasaka wrote individual musical motifs for each samurai, as well as using the plucking sound of archery bows for the opening music. The composer also took the radical step of integrating the *geza* music[24] of classical theatre with the non-diegetic music of *The Tale of Chikamatsu/Chikamatsu monogatari* (1954), thus combining Japanese traditional music and Western classical music.[25] Mizoguchi's *Street of Shame/Akasen chitai* (1956) was one of the earliest Japanese films (not a *chanbara*, though) to introduce contemporary music in order to subvert the conventional function of film music.[26] Nagato Yōhei has argued that Mayuzumi Toshirō employed atonal dodecaphony in some parts of the film's score, which, unlike tonal music that is effective in creating certain atmosphere as well as expressing particular psychological feel, instigates a sense of uneasiness among the audience, thus creating a certain gap between the audience and the screen. Mayuzumi also created a unique ensemble of jazz and American dance music juxtaposed with premodern Japanese settings in *Sun in the Last Days of the Shogunate/Bakumatsu taiyō den* (Kawashima Yūzō, 1957). Meanwhile, some period films such as Matsuda Sadatsugu's *Bored Hatamoto/Hatamoto taikutsu otoko* (1958) continued to follow the musical conventions established in the mid-1930s. The music accompanying the title credits and the Japanese drawings at the beginning of this film, written by Fukai Shirō, is symphonic music sprinkled with some Japanese-sounding themes. The piece begins with an outburst of percussion in which a series of elegant pentatonic scales are performed by the brass in unison, evoking the solemn and stylised life of elite samurai, making the score recognisably Japanese.

KUDŌ EIICHI'S *13 ASSASSINS* (1963) AND THE REJECTION OF THE TRADITIONAL ROLE OF FILM MUSIC

The 1960s mark a turning point in the history of film music.[27] Film directors in Europe participating in what Michel Chion calls the cinematic 'modernist' movement took drastic measures to diminish the use of music in their films or even to eliminate it entirely in order to subvert the narrative conventions and viewing habits derived from classic cinema. Another major change during this period was the introduction of the realistic depiction of violence and pain. *Yojimbo/Yōjinbō* (1961), Kurosawa Akira's classic *chanbara*, is considered to be the first Japanese film to have sound effects representing the severing of human limbs.[28] Clearly Kurosawa aspired to challenge the conventional notion of *chanbara*, a conservative genre saturated with audio and visual clichés – what Philip Kemp calls 'clean violence', i.e. no blood, no agony and certainly no severed limbs.[29] Borrowing the audio and visual grammar of the American Western, Kurosawa and the composer Satō Masaru created a new soundscape for the *chanbara* genre by using syncopated rhythm in the opening score, as well as the banjo, one of the Western's iconic instruments.[30]

Such innovative trends in diversifying film music in the 1960s were led further by Takemitsu Tōru (1930–96) who, for example, introduced authentic Japanese musical instruments to the non-diegetic music of period films. Kobayashi Atsushi has suggested that Takemitsu once said he wanted to oppose the current default trend for Western music in the non-diegetic music for *jidaigeki*.[31] In *Harakiri/Seppuku* (Kobayashi Masaki, 1962), for example, Takemitsu combined the *biwa* (Japanese lute) with prepared piano and other processed sounds of strings in order to design sound effects that connoted the transient existence and harsh fate of the samurai.[32] Another example from a major film from this period is the radical use of the drum and shouting in Shindō Kaneto's Noh theatre-inspired *Onibaba* (1964). Using real Noh masks, Shindō and composer Hayashi Hikaru transferred the demonic apparition of the traditional theatre from the artificial stage to a natural setting in the fourteenth century.[33] Takemitsu further explored the introduction of authentic Japanese sounds in non-diegetic music in Kobayashi Masaki's *Kwaidan* (1965) with the creation of a dream-like soundscape. Takemitsu created all the ambient sounds himself using real objects, recorded sound effects, prepared piano and electronic sound modification – a development of his earlier experiment with *musique concrète*. According to Kobayashi Atsushi, Takemitsu aspired to represent the 'unworldliness' of Lafcadio Hearn's ghost stories through sounds, including not only ominous sounds but also additional sound effects slightly out of sync with the image. These devices combine to produce a nightmarish atmosphere, as well as emphasise silence.[34]

Set in the *Bakumatsu* period,[35] Kudō Eiichi's *13 Assassins* brought drastic changes to both the audio and visual features of Tōei studio's all-star cast *chanbara*. The film pioneered a new type of movie called the multiple-hero sword-fight movie, or *shūdan kōsō jidaigeki*, in which several main characters collectively confront their enemies at the climax of the film. Unlike preceding Tōei *chanbara* movies, which exploited fantasised versions of famous ancient heroes, the scriptwriter of *13 Assassins* created original characters based on historical research. Ikegami Kaneo (later known as Ikemiya Shōichirō) initially built the film's plot upon a recorded anecdote about a tragic incident that took place during the return journey from Edo made by a *daimyō* and his retainers to their fiefdom.[36] Ikegami used this unusual historical event – an insane lord of a fiefdom brutally murders a child during the journey but is later assassinated by an unknown commoner – as the basis for a new story set in the 1840s, about twenty years before the end of the Edo period. The film's plot follows Shimada Shinzaemon, a samurai sent by a top bureaucrat of the Shogunate on a suicidal mission, with twelve accomplices, to assassinate Naritsugu, the current Shogun's brother known for his insane and cruel nature.

The first few seconds of the film's opening music immediately reveal Ifukube's desire to combine Western and Eastern music. The piece begins with a long sustained high note played by the Japanese flute; the low percussion sounds created by drums and low notes played on the piano then join in. We next hear the eerie, dissonant sounds of a keyboard instrument, probably the ondes Martenot, overlapping with the high tremolo sounds of a violin in the background.[37] The use of the ondes Martenot and the deployment of atonal and dissonant music both come from Ifukube's strong interest in contemporary French music and from his professional aspiration to study the works of his Western counterparts. In David Lean's *Lawrence of Arabia* (1962), for example, the composer Maurice Jarre used the ondes Martenot in a particular scene to evoke the heat of the desert.[38] Unlike Jarre's use of the instrument, however, there is no direct association between the sound of the ondes Martenot and the visuals in *13 Assassins*: the sound of the instrument neither represents nor delineates any particular visual feature; it also doesn't guide the spectator to empathise with the characters. Instead, it announces that the film is going to be an unexpected departure from Tōei's conventional *chanbara*. After this dramatic beginning, a male voice prompts the beginning of *wadaiko* drums, evocative of Noh theatre; a series of descending notes starts to be played simultaneously by an electric keyboard instrument (again, probably the ondes Martenot) and a Japanese *koto*. The main theme of the opening music then starts to unfold: the strings play a broad and dignified melody in a minor key, while the male voice and the *wadaiko* maintain their presence simultaneously with the melody. Through the rest of the film Ifukube used avant-garde, atonal music in a radical antithesis to the standard blend of tonal and pentatonic music. He also used the piano as the main musical instrument, contrary to the usual preference for strings and woodwinds. Kudō and Ifukube's endeavour to entertain their audiences with their novel soundscape in which contemporary classical music blends with traditional Japanese sounds resonates with Miike Takashi's later attempts to reconsider the role of sound and music in relation to the visuals in his own version of *13 Assassins*, which will be discussed in a later section of this chapter.

Notable developments also took place in European film music from the 1970s onwards when the collaboration with progressive rock musicians began.[39] Although popular and synthesised music became dominant in the 1970s, Kathryn Kalinak argues that the classical film score continued nonetheless to function as a basis of film music throughout the twentieth century, while simultaneously incorporating new trends and technical advances.[40] In the Japanese period film, the most remarkable use of the symphonic orchestra is found in Kurosawa Akira's *Ran* (1985). For the film's battle scene, Kurosawa requested Takemitsu Tōru to write a piece like a Mahler symphony. The composer had, however, only wanted to use cries and shouts during the battle scene.[41] Though Takemitsu conceded, he eventually modelled his work not only on Mahler's First Symphony, the piece Kurosawa requested he use as a template, but also Das Lied von der Erde,[42] a vocal piece with much greater narrative qualities, thereby allowing him to promote his own aesthetic model in defiance of Kurosawa's original request. Having previously contributed to the use of original Japanese music, Takemitsu's work once again set a new musical trend in the *jidaigeki*: the reintroduction of symphonic music.

SOUND REGRESSION: MIIKE TAKASHI'S *13 ASSASSINS* (2010)

Some half a century after Kudō and Ifukube's original film, Miike revived the much-acclaimed sword-fight classic, re-imagined with his idiosyncratic taste for visual excess (Fig. 19.3). Miike worked on several aspects to make his *13 Assassins* more historically accurate than previous sword-fight movies. To make the actors' wigs more authentic, for example, the costume department studied photos of samurai from the end of the Edo period and replaced the heavy, kabuki-like wigs used in traditional period dramas with new ones that left a wider part of the forehead bare.[43] Miike also took into account the darkness of the night in the Edo period before electric lighting. In the indoor scenes, Miike's camera crew attempted to capture the flickering of candlelight in order to represent realistic light and shadow conditions. 'If you think about how dark people's life must have been in those days,' Miike has said, 'it would make sense to use white paper on the *shoji* sliding doors: it was a way of allowing moonlight in while keeping the inside warm and private.'[44] In contrast, the costumes were made with a much lighter material than the normal kimono, thus allowing the actors to move more freely during the film's long battle scenes.

The film's score exhibits several distinctive traits. After a combination of low, sinister tremolos and a harmonic[45] note (E♭), a subdued cello melody accompanies the film's beginning (see Fig. 19.4). The phrase begins by following an ascending pentatonic scale (D♭, E♭, G♭ and A♭), all black notes on the keyboard, although it becomes a normal descending diatonic scale immediately afterwards. Oscillating between pentatonic and diatonic scales, the melody makes a smooth transition from one note to another. Another prominent feature of the score is that the

Fig. 19.3 *13 Assassins/Jūsannin no shikaku* (Kudō Eiichi, 1963, Tōei).

13 Assassins

Endo Koji

Fig. 19.4 A sheet of music from *13 Assassins/Jūsannin no shikaku* (Miike Takashi, 2010, Sedic International and Recorded Picture Company).

strings play without *vibrato*, accentuating the distance from symphonic music. The absence of vibrato gives a broad yet static feeling, and the chord discreetly played in the background, consisting of a perfect fourth (B♭ and E♭), is also evocative of *gagaku* (ancient court music), thus connoting the seemingly stable and unchanging rule of the samurai. The use of pentatonic melody is consistent with the period film's musical conventions, but the melody is fragmentary and fleeting, linking the initial written text describing the film's setting and the following frontal shot of a samurai. Seated on the ground, with a dagger in front of him, the samurai opens the upper part of his kimono in a determined manner. Although this long shot shows the samurai from a distant high angle, the sharp rustling sound of the silk kimono as he bares his chest seems strikingly close to the audience's ear. He is about to commit *seppuku* and, after a brief shot of the samurai touching his abdomen, a close-up shot of his upper body follows. Then the sound of the sword piercing his abdomen dominates the screen even though the image shows none of the actual incision; the camera captures only the samurai's face twisted in excruciating pain. The expression of the samurai's suffering is further enhanced by the sound of the dagger slowly cutting through his lower abdomen, then being lifted from the belly, only to make a new incision in the flesh in order this time to slice upwards. On completing this agonising process of disembowelment, the samurai finally collapses, and a high-angle shot shows the samurai's body in a sea of blood. A similar shot of a samurai who had just committed suicide was also present at the beginning of the original *13 Assassins* (Figs. 19.5, 19.6).

In Miike's opinion, music was redundant for the hara-kiri scene and it is the mere diegetic sound of the sword carving its way into human flesh, juxtaposed with the close-up shot of the samurai's face, that graphically conveys his physical and mental suffering to the spectator. By dramatising the actual process of disembowelment, not included in the original film, as the first scene of the film and without musical embellishment, Miike declares that his version will explore new limits in the representation of violence.

Miike's extremely close focus on the sound of the sword inflicting pain stands in sharp contrast to his treatment of the conversations of bureaucrats in the following scene. Their restrained voices are further muffled by the superimposed non-diegetic music. Intentionally undermining the significance of the dialogue in turn gives greater prominence to the diegetic sound Miike wishes to emphasise. Miike

Fig. 19.5 *13 Assassins/Jūsannin no shikaku* (Miike Takashi, 2010, Sedic International and Recorded Picture Company). A high-angle shot of the dead samurai from Miike's version. The dagger and his right hand, both soaked in blood, are evident.

Fig. 19.6 *13 Assassins/Jūsannin no shikaku* (Kudō Eiichi, 1963, Tōei). The same shot from Kudō's original version. While in Miike's film the head is turned to the left, here his head is facing screen right, and the dagger is hidden.

and his scriptwriter Tengan Daisuke also suppress superfluous dialogue and inner monologues that might make the main characters' feelings more explicit.

Furthermore, even though Endō Kōji, the composer of the film, pays tribute to conventional period film scores through the use of strings as the main instruments, his music remains a drastic departure from them in terms of its frequent use of harmonics. Harmonics represent madness, chiefly that of Naritsugu. They appear, for example, at the beginning of the film when the bureaucrats at a meeting mention his name, indicating that merely his name creates a sinister feeling among those who hear it.

Having gathered nine samurai, Shimada reveals the true objective of their mission: the assassination of Naritsugu. As the samurai hold their breath on hearing this, we hear the cello/viola playing long descending notes (E♭, D♭, C♭ and B♭), which symbolises that both this abrupt revelation and the men's subsequent realisation that their fate has now been sealed are slowly sinking into their minds. As they discuss their future plan, a motif with D♭ and C is presented. This combination of two adjacent notes constitutes one of the major themes of the score of *13 Assassins*. When a long shot shows Naritsugu's troupe leaving his residence and starting on their return journey to Akashi, for example, this scene is accompanied by a set of similar alternating notes but in two parallel sets: one part plays C and D♭, while another part plays F and G♭. Together the two parts comprise a perfect fourth (C and F, D♭ and G♭), the neutral and unaffected interval symbolising the irreconcilable distance between Naritsugu and his faithful retainers. The regular percussion sound in the score represents the sound of metal poles Naritsugu's men use in the procession. The accompanying music, in synch with the movement in the diegesis, thus crosses the line between the non-diegetic and the diegetic. The retainers progress in an orderly line wearing hats that cover their faces: the percussion sound, together with this train of anonymous people, creates a sinister atmosphere, as if this were a march of soulless people walking in their own funeral procession. Dissonances in the score indicate disputes among Naritsugu's subordinates. The string ensemble operates as a metaphorical linchpin to hold the unity of the collage of different scenes representing Naritsugu's journey and Shimada's preparation of the attack. Harmonics are used again when Shimada tells his men where they are to ambush Naritsugu. Nobody knows if their plan will really work as it depends on which route his opponents choose for their trip, but Shimada says he has decided to stake everything on one small village. After preparing for the battle with meticulous planning and hard training, Shimada makes the final crucial decision and likens it to a gamble, saying that in order to defeat a much more numerous enemy, they must 'have faith in luck'. The prevailing harmonic sound suggests that there is also an element of madness in Shimada's determination as well as in the team's assiduous endeavour, as if implying that, although Shimada and his men are all rational, what they are trying to accomplish is in fact a suicide mission with little chance of success.

In contrast to the fluid yet unsettling music accompanying the departure of Naritsugu's troupe, when Shimada's team leaves Edo, low strings play an up-tempo phrase in unison, connoting their solidarity and their staunch resolution to achieve their goal at any costs. The syncopated phrase, vigorously played by cellos, matches the image of the samurai on galloping horses, as well as signifying their dynamic and unpredictable movement in comparison with the smooth melody associated with Naritsugu's troupe (Fig. 19.7).

Superimposed upon the above passage, a melody begins with successive long notes, first played by cellos and then also by violas, in unison but an octave higher. It starts with a G♭ and then rises by a third and then descends to F (G♭, B♭, F). The next phrase is similar, starting again from G♭ to B♭, but instead of descending from there, it rises further to C♭, as if foreshadowing Shimada's team's perseverance and eventual success. The same combination of the persistent unison and the melody shown in Fig. 19.7 returns when Shimada and his men start their assault on Naritsugu's men, prompted by Shimada's shouting: 'we will slash, attack and massacre them all!' The score underlines Shimada's and his men's resolution to fight to their death in spite of their numerical disadvantage.

In the final battle sequence lasting nearly 45 minutes, music is used only sparingly. Miike in fact asked Endō to refrain from writing pieces of music that might influence audiences in the way they respond to certain scenes. In an interview, the director rejects determinedly the use of music as a tool to guide audiences:

> Our senses gradually become numb as we continue hearing [many different kinds of sound effects]. Usually that's when the music comes in so as to reinforce the impact of the film. That's exactly the kind of music I want to get rid of – music that underscores the actors' feelings or navigates audiences' interpretation. Instead, I want to let the audiences watch my film just hearing plain footsteps or simple sounds of the flesh being cut, for example. I don't want to manipulate their response [through music]. I don't tell them whether they should be feeling sad or otherwise: it's their job to decide how they should feel.[46]

Miike is critical of films embellished with non-diegetic music that influences the way an audience should respond to a certain scene, and believes that the absence of music allows for active and analytical viewing, thus exposing his film to multiple interpretations. Miike

Fig. 19.7 A sheet of music from *13 Assassins/Jūsannin no shikaku* (Miike Takashi, 2010, Sedic International and Recorded Picture Company).

called this tactical approach 'regression', a return to the ways films were made before advanced audiovisual technologies facilitated easy but uncritical viewing. Nevertheless, Miike uses this technique only sparingly, as seen in the above analysis in which the film score functions in the kind of the way he criticises.

The first recognisable point in which such regression occurs is when Hirayama, one of Shimada's master swordsmen, sets an opponent on fire and the fierce sound of burning extinguishes the non-diegetic music that was being heard until then. After the music stops, extremely amplified diegetic sounds are used, including footsteps and shouting of the samurais, as well as the sludgy dragging sound accompanying an image of a samurai's feet slowly moving forwards in mud. Miike also attributes exaggerated sounds to Koyata, the 'thirteenth samurai', seen and heard swinging his sling energetically, for example, and to other samurai wielding their swords with all their might. Gradually, these sounds grow heavier, suggesting the increasing tiredness and despair of the samurai. Other examples of magnified sounds include the disconcerting sound of metal being rubbed against Shimada's kimono while he wipes blood from his sword as well as the heavy thud of an arrow piercing the body of a small child. Focused sound effects create the illusion that the audience is physically closer to the scene, as though feeling the weight of the cold metal sword or the strong draft the catapult generates. This may be related to the fact that the ear not only transmits and amplifies sound, but it is also intimately involved with the inner functions of the body: maintaining balance, for example.[47]

Miike is convinced that the soundtrack is the key for augmenting the effect of on-screen violence upon the audience, even to a traumatic degree. Even though in some scenes he used music's undeniable power to underscore the psychology of the characters, in the main battle sequence Miike deliberately abandoned his search for appropriate music and exploited instead the power of diegetic sounds to affect the audience at a more primitive level. What Miike calls 'regression' is therefore not simply the rejection of music – rather, what he does is focus intently on selected diegetic sounds, disagreeable ones in particular. By emphasising unpleasant diegetic sounds that affect spectators physically through the ear, he intends the audience to actually feel the shock of the injury those lethal weapons produce as well as the resulting pain. Miike presents a unique soundscape that contributes to making film viewing a more tactile – and thus unforgettable – experience.

When Naritsugu tells his men that he feels so happy and excited about being in the middle of a battle that once he becomes a high official in the central government he will return the whole country to a state of civil war, all the sound disappears from the soundtrack and it is only Naritsugu's voice that we hear. This audio void speaks for Naritsugu's retainers' confused feelings: protecting their feudal lord in fact is morally questionable, since Naritsugu's survival would mean only the return of a world of chaos and atrocity. Despite his composed appearance and his calm way of speaking, Naritsugu's insane logic sounds so barbaric that it is as though he himself has created a kind of audio black hole that devours any loyal or rational words uttered around him. The retainers have, however, no time to stop and think about the profound consequences of their 'faithful' deeds nor reflect upon the fate that might befall the entire country as a result of Naritsugu's escape from his would-be assassins. The audio void here represents the absence of a sound critical mind – not only on Naritsugu's part but also of the people around him – a deficiency that paralysed the Tokugawa establishment and eventually brought an end to the rule of the samurai.

CONCLUSION

Although the classical orchestral score remains the dominant trend in the period film score today, film-makers have incessantly been seeking different ways of harmonising Western music with the screen image of the samurai. Experiments at such attempts include the introduction of Japanese pentatonic scales in non-diegetic music; the use of Japanese musical instruments and Western instruments together; and the playing of violins and other strings without *vibrato*. Focusing on three separate time frames and highlighting different approaches enables us to identify prominent musical styles in respective periods, which provides an alternative perspective for the broader study of audiovisual relationships in Japanese cinema. The drastic changes in the approach to sound and music at respective transitional periods discussed in this chapter played a crucial role in the reinvention of the sword-fight genre, generally considered an authentically Japanese domain, even though many other ways of portraying them were available from Hollywood and French cinema, for example.

The development of film music from the post-World War II period onwards coincided with the blossoming of avant-garde Japanese composers who recognised cinema's creative potential and advocated a view that film music was as artistically important as pure music. These composers include Hayasaka, Satō, Ifukube, Mayuzumi and Takemitsu, to name but a few. Their aspiration to innovate in the composition of film music manifested itself most distinctly in the *jidaigeki*, and they brought to Japanese cinema a new orientation that enabled film-makers to create rich and compelling soundscapes.

Composers in the 1960s further tested music's power by reducing and cutting its presence rather than by elaborating it. For the music accompanying the opening credits of Kudō's *13 Assassins*, Ifukube used avant-garde musical instruments alongside Japanese traditional instruments and forged a new musical idiom for this genre. Moreover, using piano, an 'unorthodox' musical instrument, as well as employing atonal music, Ifukube's music provided an important impulse for the reinvention of period cinema.

Juxtaposing the two versions of *13 Assassins* reveals that Miike strove to fill the audio and visual gap created by the unstated facts and the unshown scenes in Kudō's original version. Miike generates a soundscape that raises audiences' awareness, instead of merely wrapping them snugly in a seamless audiovisual harmony. The end result is a gruesome entertainment full of violence and pain. Whereas Kudō made his version at a time when cinemagoing in Japan was rapidly becoming an exclusive pastime of single mature men, Miike once said that in today's Japan one has to make a film that pleases young female audiences who now comprise the large majority of cinemagoers. Miike prefers, however, to be free of such domestic market pressures, since he believes that the concept of entertainment for everyone is non-existent. With *13 Assassins*, Miike certainly challenges his audience's aesthetic and critical capacities to their limit.

Notes

1. David Bordwell and Kristin Thompson, *Film Art: An Introduction*, 7th edn (New York: McGraw-Hill, 2004), p. 347.
2. See, for example, Akiyama Kuniharu, *Nihon no eiga ongaku shi 1* (Tokyo: Tabata shoten, 1974); Ōmori Seitarō, *Nihon no yōgaku*, vols. 1 and 2 (Tokyo: Shinmon shuppan, 1986/7); Kobayashi Atsushi, *Nihon eiga ongaku no kyosei tachi I: Hayasaka Fumio, Satō Masaru, Takemitsu Tōru, Koseki Yūji* (Tokyo: Waizu shuppan, 2001); Kobayashi, *Nihon eiga ongaku no kyosei tachi II: Ifukube Akira, Akutagawa Yasushi, Mayuzumi Toshirō* (Tokyo: Waizu shuppan, 2001); Nagato Yōhei, *Eiga onkyō ron: Mizoguchi Kenji eiga o kiku* (Tokyo: Misuzu shobō, 2014); Ifukube Akira, *Ifukube Akira tsuzuru – Ifukube Akira ronbun/zuihitsu shō*, edited by Kobayashi Atsushi (Tokyo: Waizu shuppan, 2013); Hayasaka Fumio, 'Composition Notes (Abstract)', 27 December 1941, published in the notes for *Piano Pieces for Chamber* [CD] (Tokyo: Camerata, 2004); Takemitsu Tōru, *Eizō kara oto o kezuru: Takemitsu Tōru eiga essay shū* (Tokyo: Seiryū shuppan, 2010).
3. Kathryn Kalinak, '"How … Were We Going to Make a Picture That's Better than This?" Crossing Borders from East to West in *Rashomon* and *The Outrage*', in Kathryn Kalinak (ed.) *Music in the Western: Notes From the Frontier* (London: Routledge, 2012), pp. 165–80; Miguel Mera, 'Takemitsu's Composed Space in Kurosawa's *Ran*', in Robynn Stilwell and Peter Franklin (eds), *Film Music Reader* (Cambridge: Cambridge University Press, forthcoming).
4. All the film scores cited in the chapter were transcribed by the author with the help of free software, thus showing the new possibilities of studying film sound now that the raw materials are available on DVD and in other formats that are convenient for repeated listening.
5. Nagato Yōhei proposes a new theoretical model for classifying sound in cinema, in which he divides diegetic sound in four subcategories. See Nagato, *Eiga onkyō ron*, p. 32. In my chapter, however, I stick to the two general categories of diegetic/non-diegetic that are most prevalent among English-speaking film scholars.

6. Claudia Gorbman, *Unheard Melodies: Narrative Film Music* (Bloomington: Indiana University Press, 1987), pp. 153–4, quoted in Kathleen M. Vernon and Cliff Eisen, 'Contemporary Spanish Film Music: Carlos Saura and Pedro Almodóvar', in Miguel Mera and David Burnand (eds), *European Film Music* (Aldershot: Ashgate, 2006), p. 45.
7. [Editors' note: for more on the *jidaigeki*, see also Chapter 20 by Philip Kaffen in this volume.]
8. Tom Mes and Jasper Sharp, 'Takashi Miike', in *The Midnight Eye Guide to New Japanese Cinema* (Albany, CA: Stone Bridge Press, 2005), p. 180.
9. Akiyama, *Nihon no eiga ongaku shi 1*, pp. 15–30.
10. Daibō Masaki, 'Todokanai melody: Nichi-doku gassaku eiga "Atarashiki tsuchi" no eiga ongaku ni miru Yamada Kōsaku no risō to genjitsu', in Sugino Kentarō (ed.), *Eiga to nation* (Kyoto: Minerva shobō, 2010), p. 9. [Editors' note: for more on the introduction of sound in Japanese cinema, see also Chapter 10 by Johan Nordström in this volume.]
11. Nagato devotes a whole chapter on Mizoguchi Kenji's *Furusato* (1930) to show that Mizoguchi's early talkie not only preceded *Madamu to nyōbō* but also that the way Mizoguchi used sound was more innovative than Gosho in his own first talkie. Nagato then proposes that the established view of assigning *Madamu to nyōbō* the prestige of being the first 'genuine' talkie should be re-examined. See Nagato, *Eiga onkyō ron*, pp. 73–109.
12. K.J. Donnelly, 'The Hidden Heritage of Film Music: History and Scholarship', in K.J. Donnelly (ed.), *Film Music: Critical Approaches* (Edinburgh: Edinburgh University Press, 2001), p. 8.
13. In the early sound era in Hollywood, the standard musical practice of non-diegetic film scores established itself as a prime component of classical cinema with the series of scores that Max Steiner wrote for such films as *Symphony of Six Million* (1932), *King Kong* (1933) and *The Informer* (1935). See ibid.
14. Akiyama, *Nihon no eiga ongaku shi* 1, pp. 33, 36.
15. Ōmori, *Nihon no yōgaku*, vol. 1, p. 239.
16. Daibō, 'Todokanai melody', pp. 12–4. [Editors' note: for more on Soviet montage theory and Japanese cinema, see also Chapter 4 by Naoki Yamamoto in this volume.]
17. Yamada Kazuo, *Eisnstein* (Tokyo: Kinokuniya shoten, 1994), pp. 3–4, originally published in 1963.
18. Akiyama, *Nihon no eiga ongaku shi 1*, p. 101.
19. Kobayashi, *Nihon eiga ongaku no kyosei tachi II*, p. 15.
20. Ibid., p. 19. For examples of Ifukube's writings, see Ifukube Akira, *Ifukube Akira tsuzuru: Ifukube Akira ronbun/zuihitsu shū*, edited by Kobayashi Atsushi (Tokyo: Waizu shuppan, 2013).
21. Kurosawa and his crew were in the process of production when Japan capitulated and World War II ended. The film, however, was only released in 1952 because of various problems Kurosawa had with the censors – both during and after the war. Yuna de Lannoy, 'The View from the Bridge: The Cinemas of Eisenstein and Kurosawa Between East and West' (unpublished PhD thesis, University of London, 2009), p. 143.
22. See ibid., pp. 143–8.
23. Ibid., pp. 203–6. See also Kathryn Kalinak's discussion in her chapter on *Rashomon*, in which she argues that the film's music anticipates 'Modernist' film scores of the 1960s. Kalinak, '"How … Were We Going to Make a Picture That's Better than This?"', pp. 169–73.
24. *Geza music is* the music performed by offstage musicians during the performance of a kabuki play.
25. Nagato discusses how critics, including Akiyama and Takemitsu, re-valued the film score of *Chikamatsu monogatari* in the early 1970s and observed such Japanese traits as the use of single sounds and silence. Nagato then argues that this critical reception was heavily influenced by John Cage's essentialising view of Japanese art. Moreover, he argues that the most significant feature of *Chikamatsu*'s score is the fact that the sound and the image comprise a 'monistic ensemble', originally Eisenstein's theoretical concept inspired by his viewing of kabuki theatre in Moscow in 1928. Nagato, *Eiga onkyō ron*, pp. 209–10.
26. Ibid., p. 245.
27. Michel Chion, 'Des classicismes au modernisme', in *La Musique au cinéma* (Paris: Fayard, 1995), pp. 146–149. See also Vernon and Eisen, 'Contemporary Spanish Film Music', p. 45.
28. Minawa Ichirō, who was in charge of sound effects, reminisced that this novel sound effect had to be used very discreetly at first as the use of sounds evoking violence was banned in Japan during the Allied postwar Occupation, and Japanese film-makers still had to be very careful about using such acoustic effects as late as the early 1960s. Minawa Ichirō, Interview in *Yōjinbō* [DVD] (Tōhō, 2002).
29. Philip Kemp, *Audio Commentary in* Yojimbo (London: British Film Institute, 2000).

30. See Yuna de Lannoy, 'Innovation and Imitation: An Analysis of the Soundscape of Akira Kurosawa's *Chambara* Westerns', in Kalinak, *Music in the Western*, pp. 117–30.
31. Kobayashi, *Nihon eiga ongaku no kyosei tachi*, vol. 1, p. 153. Kobayashi nonetheless gives neither the source nor the date of this account.
32. Ibid., p. 154.
33. Keiko I. McDonald, *Reading a Japanese Film* (Honolulu: University of Hawai'i Press, 2006), p. 116.
34. Kobayashi, *Nihon eiga ongaku no kyosei tachi*, vol. 1, pp. 163–6.
35. *Bakumatsu* refers to the end of the Tokugawa Shogunate era, roughly between the arrival of Commodore Matthew Perry's Black Ships in 1853 and the civil war of 1869.
36. See Yamamoto Hirofumi, *Sankin kōtai* (Tokyo: Kōdansha gendai shinsho, 1998), pp. 104–6.
37. Invented by Maurice Martenot in 1928, the instrument was frequently used by contemporary classical composers. I have been unable to access the original film score to verify the instrument used. Likewise, neither the Tōei Studio nor the composer's family were available to confirm this. A professional organist has, however, endorsed my view that the instrument used in the opening score *is* most likely to be the ondes Martenot. Special thanks to Asako Miyahara for her kind support.
38. Lochner, Jim, 'CD Review: Lawrence of Arabia', <http://filmscoreclicktrack.com/2010/09/cd-review-lawrence-of-arabia/>.
39. Donnelly, 'The Hidden Heritage of Film Music', pp. 118ff.
40. See Kathryn Kalinak, *Settling the Score: Music and the Classical Hollywood Film Score* (Madison: University of Wisconsin Press, 1992), pp. 188, 202.
41. Charlotte Zwerin, *Music for the Movies: Toru Takemitsu* [television movie] (Charlotte Zwerin, 1994, Alternate Current, Les Films d'ici, NHK, La Sept/Arte), quoted in Miguel Mera, 'Takemitsu's Composed Space in Kurosawa's *Ran*', in Robynn Stilwell and Peter Franklin (eds), *Film Music Reader* (Cambridge: Cambridge University Press, in press).
42. Mera, 'Takemitsu's Composed Space in Kurosawa's *Ran*'.
43. Miike Takashi in Kanazawa Makoto, 'Miike Takashi kantoku intabyū: Jidaigeki towa nanika, nihonjin towa nanika', *Kinema junpō* no. 1565 (September 2010), p. 31.
44. Ibid., p. 33.
45. Harmonics are higher pitched notes produced by lightly touching the string with a fingertip.
46. Miike, in an interview on the bonus track of *13 Assassins* [DVD] (Artificial Eye, 2011).
47. Yōrō Takeshi and Hisaishi Joe, *Mimi de kangaeru: Nō wa meikyoku o hossuru* (Tokyo: Kadokawa shoten, 2009), p. 37. In this engaging dialogue between Yōrō Takeshi, a well-known Japanese anatomist, and Hisaishi Joe, a composer who collaborated with several film directors including Miyazaki Hayao and Kitano Takeshi, the composer and the scientist exchange ideas about the relationship between hearing and the mind, and Hisaishi gives some revealing insights into the way he writes his film music.

PART 4
GENRE

20

JIDAIGEKI
The duplicitous topos of *jidaigeki*

Philip Kaffen

The term *jidaigeki* conventionally describes any Japanese film that is set in Japan prior to 1868. This is the date when the ruling order of the Tokugawa period – the Shogunate – finally gave way to a new, ostensibly democratic and modern order under the rule of the Emperor Meiji.[1] While this definition is clear, even today, many scholars, critics and fans struggle to identify what *jidaigeki* is.[2] This confusion stems from the difficulty of locating a proper place for it.

Most writing on Japanese cinema locates a large grouping of films based on the notion of a fixed national identity and then, within that, smaller groupings of films: *gendaigeki* (films set after 1868) and *jidaigeki*. This presumes we know what Japanese cinema is. Yet, as the director Ōshima Nagisa pointed out several decades ago, even the category 'Japanese cinema' no longer has any meaning and should be abandoned entirely.[3] It would seem that we find ourselves caught up in a constellation of terms that refer to each other without illuminating anything.

Ōshima's critique, written in the early 1990s, was aimed at the strange place Japanese cinema had found itself in after the collapse of the studio system, when there were no more studios to produce 'Japanese films'. While *jidaigeki* are frequently associated with that system, his critique should nonetheless give us pause in the twenty-first century when we look back and attempt to organise various genres, and modes of production. Moreover, his comments are also a form of provocation: to think of *jidaigeki* beyond Japanese cinema.

There are indeed many good reasons to do so. For even if we could point to a stable national cinema, we would still have to confront a similar conundrum of trying to understand a smaller subset of films within a larger subset, like nested dolls. It is this understanding that has given rise to various attempts to grasp *jidaigeki* as a genre, or mode, which might then be understood in relationship to analogous genres in Hollywood or elsewhere, such as the Western or Chinese martial arts film (*wuxiapian*). We may then try to identify the conventions of each – in terms of narrative patterns, ways of speaking, dress, gestures, locations and settings, and so on.

These conventions often involve 'cultural' generalisations. *Jidaigeki*, with their 'premodern' settings, seem exemplary in this regard. Do they not portray traditional values, such as the struggle of obligation versus personal desire (*giri* and *ninjō*)? Or draw on earlier art forms, such as kabuki or Noh? Or borrow from contemporary culture – mass literature or historical novels? Undeniably, they do. To study such films seems to require knowledge that could be used to decode their cultural conventions and avoid misunderstandings or Orientalist approaches.[4]

Yet, the problem is more complicated. In a major work on *jidaigeki* from the mid-1980s, Hashimoto Osamu begins by noting all the ways that the codes of *jidaigeki* are 'cinematic' first and foremost – in other words, fictional.[5] This forces us to ask what 'culture' means for cinema? How can films be representative of one traditional culture while also being embedded in the sprawling, global forces of capitalism and technology? At the same time, we cannot ignore their singularity, and leave them wallowing in generality, interchangeable with any other form. The problem of *jidaigeki* in Japanese cinema is no different from the problem of Japanese film in world cinema. It is a question of culture and representation – of location. In other words, the problem of *jidaigeki* may not be solely a question of 'when' but also 'where'. Is there thus a way to locate a new place for *jidaigeki*?

To develop this idea, I would like to draw on the philosopher Nakai Masakazu's notion of *topos*. Borrowing from classical Greek logic, Nakai identified *topos* not as a static place but rather as a site full of activity and movement (*keiki*) – a multidimensional site of struggle.[6] The *topos* of *jidaigeki* moves restlessly along the unstable boundary between cinema and life, guided as much by technology as history. Indeed, in his writings on cinema and aesthetics, Nakai saw the camera lens itself as an 'Archimedes lever', potentially overthrowing existing aesthetic understanding.[7] Cinema developed and extended the range of technical images that had spread from the middle of the nineteenth century, recasting the world through a modern lens – not just in the form of a representation but as a copy. Whereas photographs mainly presented contemporary life, cinema bled over into the past, creating and projecting endless duplicates. By absorbing the past into a world of moving images projected in the present, *jidaigeki* destabilised 1868 as any kind of definite break through which Japan became 'modern'.

A world of images that extends everywhere, in which even the past is not safe, imbues the narrative, visual and critical elements of *jidaigeki* with a consistent anxiety over *duplicity* – of living in a doubled and therefore potentially 'false' world. This duplicity may not simply refer to what is on screen but affect relations to history and the world more generally. Yet, *jidaigeki* speak equally to a desire to get beyond this image world, driving numerous impulses in film history and politics – the nihilism and radicalism of the 1920s; the period of realism and empire in the 1930s and 1940s; and reflections on responsibility and democracy after World War II. More broadly, this duplicity illuminates the particular *topos* of *jidaigeki*, insofar as it remains incommensurable with national/imperial history or any other sovereign order.

AGAINST THE IDEA OF THE LOST HOME

Japanese cinema (or what would become 'Japanese cinema') begins as a tale of two cities: Tokyo and Kyoto. This division is at once geographical, institutional and aesthetic. Conventionally, Tokyo is the home of *gendaigeki*, and Kyoto is the home of *jidaigeki*. Yet, even more fundamentally, as one scholar put it recently, Kyoto is the 'cradle' of Japanese cinema.[8] The first cinematograph screening took place there in 1897; the first studio was built there in 1910; Makino Shōzō, the 'father of Japanese cinema', along with the first Japanese film star, Onoe Matsunosuke, started producing ninja films (*kyūgeki*) there, one every three days.[9] With the proliferation of Onoe films in the 1910s, we might say that even before there was 'Japanese cinema' and even before there was 'cinema' in Japan at all,[10] the *mise en scène* that filled screens was entirely within the historical frame of *jidaigeki*. Japanese cinema and cinema as such – pure cinema – were not the frames within which *jidaigeki* appeared – just the opposite was the case.

Are *jidaigeki* then the home of cinema in Japan? The great cultural critic Kobayashi Hideo reflected on the uncanny attractions of *jidaigeki* in his search for Japan's 'lost home'. *Jidaigeki* resonated with the masses, but in this they shared an odd affinity with foreign films; one not of distance but proximity.[11] Kobayashi felt that their sense of style possessed an 'unimaginably powerful charm and fascination' that made distant worlds – and both the deserts of Morocco and the manners and mores of *jidaigeki* films qualify *equally* – feel more familiar than contemporary Ginza in the eyes of the masses.

The idea of *jidaigeki* as origin must also be complicated. Indeed, if earlier projected images did not quite constitute cinema then the Onoe films, while set prior to 1868, were not technically '*jidaigeki*'. According to many, *jidaigeki* truly began in 1923. The Great Kantō Earthquake in September of that year destroyed much of Tokyo, bringing down Nikkatsu's Mukōjima studio as well as Shōchiku's Kamata studio, and forcing directors such as Mizoguchi Kenji and Inagaki Hiroshi to move to Kyoto. Although Tokyo's studios and theatres recovered quickly by most accounts, Kyoto, the old capital, still known for its preponderance of temples and shrines, became the centre of film production. As film historian Tanaka Jun'ichirō writes, 'It was *jidaigeki* that unified the spirit of spectators in the wake of the earthquake.'[12]

In addition, 1923 marked the first use of the word *jidaigeki* in journalism (in reference to Itō Daisuke's no longer extant *The Pirate and the Woman/Kaizoku to onna*). Mitsuhiro Yoshimoto has argued that this new name indicates a significant shift. The theatrical terms that had been employed – *kyūgeki* and *kyūha*, or 'old dramas', and *shingeki* or *shimpa* (new dramas or plays) – gave way to the terms of *jidaigeki* and *gendaigeki*, which refer more explicitly to divisions in periodisation. This shift from dramatic to historical categories made the break of 1868 more explicit, allowing Japanese people, at a mass level, to understand that they were 'modern' by providing a clear depiction of a premodern world. In doing so, this transition was also largely responsible for the constitution of historical consciousness and a broken or belated modernity (insofar as the world outside the cinema was never as 'modern' as the contemporary world projected on screen). It was also even complicit in the project of empire building.[13]

This explanation also needs revision since the term *jidaigeki* was in fact not often used in journalism. Other terms – including *chanbara* (the term that comes closest to swashbuckling; it is an onomatopoeia for crossing swords), *matatabimono* (films about wandering gamblers, especially after 1929) and *kengeki* (action-oriented films that foreground sword-fighting) – were all used with more frequency. Having said this, not even all *jidaigeki* are *chanbara* or *kengeki* since there is nothing particular about *jidaigeki* that specifically requires sword-fighting.

Moreover, according to Japan's leading film journal, *Kinema junpō*, the categorisation of films remained unstable between 1924 and 1930, vacillating between foreign and domestic, art and entertainment, and silent and sound films.[14] How should we therefore understand this shift to historical categories alongside the shift to foreign/domestic or, to put it in terms of global cinema, silent and sound film? Was the division between theatrical/historical in film journalism more important than what was projected on screen? How does this historical break coincide with divisions in other arts such as literature and theatre?

One way to respond to such questions is to push towards a richer sense of what a media-focused study might offer that veers away from the break presented by a historical (imperial) reading. *Jidaigeki* – befitting the literal translation of the word as a 'play with historical time' – provides an optimum site for such a transformation in the study of the media and history. *Jidaigeki*'s re-framing of the past as a copy engendered by modern technology exposes a divided world – not exactly premodern versus modern, but rather, before and after *film*. The contemporary world is subject to exposure and capture by photochemical processes, with their concomitant economic and technological imperatives. More threatening though is the fact that cinema does not stay on the side of the modern but rather aestheticises a 'pre-cinematic' world. This doubled past proliferates, creating endless image worlds. In short, it thus becomes suspect or 'duplicitous'.

RADICALLY INTERESTING: *JIDAIGEKI* AMIDST NIHILISTIC TENDENCIES

The utopian desire to overcome the duplicity of this world of images – as well as the frustration of that desire – informs many radical works of the 1920s. While *jidaigeki*'s 'hometown' of Kyoto, as the 'old' capital, seems to fit hand in glove with the image of 'old' historical films, Kyoto was in fact the site of the earliest radical experiments in film-making and politics. Futagawa Buntarō's *The Serpent/Orochi* (1925), produced at the Makino Tōjiin studio by Bandō Tsumasaburō, who was also the star of the film, is a well-known example. Its screenwriter, Susukita Rokuhei, was a noted radical, associated with the strong trend towards nihilism that permeated many *jidaigeki* in the late 1920s.[15]

Now considered among the greatest of Japanese films, *The Serpent* was not necessarily praised by reviewers at the time. That said, the film's final sword-fighting sequence (*tate*), though borrowing from theatrical conventions, was recognised as something new.[16] It established a style of action combining wild but precise bodily movement and large-scale choreography with equally dexterous editing and camerawork. Ishino Seizō's camera darts in and out, shifting distances and perspectives – crane shots, rooftop shots, close-ups – at blistering speed, thus forging one of the most striking sequences in all of Japanese cinema.[17] Moreover, scenes in which we can see the sword touch the body, along with shifts in performance styles and bodily movement, all established the affective 'realism' of *jidaigeki*.[18]

This affective realism must be grasped in relation to the film's preoccupations with deception and justice. *The Serpent* begins with a written warning that not everyone is as they appear; some 'who appear benevolent wear masks that hide their treacherousness'. This problem, rather than any narrative in particular, is what drives the remainder of the film as its protagonist, the anti-hero Kuritomi Heizaburō (Bandō), tries to overcome this false image to reveal the truth: the violence of the powerful.

This sense of politics was no distant abstraction. The effects of legal and political pressure were pronounced within cinema and across other arts. The year the film was released, 1925, was also the year in which the Peace Preservation Law was passed – the law most responsible for the state's curbing of radicalism in its girding up for war. In addition, film censorship was centralised at the state level for the first time.[19]

As if to confront such pressures, *jidaigeki* gave birth to numerous independent production companies, beginning with Bandō's own company, Bantsuma Pro, which produced *The Serpent*.[20] Bandō's example inspired numerous *jidaigeki* stars including Kataoka Chiezō and Arashi Kanjurō to do the same. In a sense, this movement was among the earliest of new waves, comprising film artists committed to establishing independent spaces to pursue artistic and political freedom within the context of a major industry and against state power. Institutionally and socially, *jidaigeki* provided a kind of refuge amidst the tumult.[21] Yet, this refuge was never wholly secure. Indeed, while independently produced, *The Serpent* was also subject to heavy censorship. Censors demanded a title change (the initial title was *Outlaw/Buraiha*) and cut 1,400 feet of film.

Besieged with tensions over its subsumption by capital, policing and technology, cinema has never been an autonomous art. While this is true of all arts, this entanglement lies right on the surface of the medium. To be exposed on film necessarily requires this subsumption, which means that even the most radical *jidaigeki* has had to confront its own embeddedness – it could not simply critique from the outside, even as an 'independent production'.[22] The spectacular sword-fighting scenes that shape the look, feel and movement of *The Serpent*, and *jidaigeki* in its wake, can therefore be read as utopian efforts to break free of their very status as images – efforts that often remain frustrated or even ironic.

The sense of irony is part of cinema's own self-reflection. As *The Serpent*'s intertitles explicitly note: 'A righteous man with the image of an outlaw lives side by side with an outlaw who appears as a righteous man. The world truly is one of irony.' That this intertitle appears over the image of Heizaburō himself – rather than over the image of the corrupt official Heizaburō refers to – suggests that it may not always be easy to decide which is which. How does one break out of the false image from within it? This contradiction is central to *jidaigeki* in terms of confronting economic tumult and political corruption. Their tendency was thus to immerse themselves in the representation of history while holding open new spaces for movement and new ways of seeing and gathering. This is most evident in the close connections between *jidaigeki* and *keikō eiga* (tendency films) – conventionally defined as socialist-leaning films produced by the major studios.[23]

Seeking to rewrite Japanese film history during the 1970s, following the collapse of the student movement, the journalist Takenaka Rō returned to this earlier period of political radicalism, conducting numerous long interviews with forgotten figures of Japanese film. He begins with the director Itō Daisuke. Takenaka and Itō agreed that the term 'tendency films' referred not simply to a strand of loosely 'socialist' oriented films made by the major studios, but pointed instead to the political climate of cinema and politics more generally at the time – a tendency age – when radicalism was slipping from the Left to the Right within the global phenomenon of an unstable climate for interwar democracy.[24]

It was within this climate that Itō created such powerful works, especially the silent films he made with the actor Ōkōchi Denjirō and the great cinematographer Karasawa Hiromitsu. Though he started as a writer and director of *gendaigeki* for Nikkatsu, Itō came into his own when he switched to *jidaigeki* with the extraordinary work *An Unforgettable Grudge/Chōkon* (1926). While Itō's works in the 1920s such as *Man-Slashing, Horse-Piercing Sword/Zanjin zanbaken* (1929) helped elevate the visual image of radical politics, his film-making was either critical of some strands of radicalism or tried to reshape them. Long before Ozu Yasujirō began employing a system of discontinuity that, for some, disrupted the primary principles at work in the imperial system of Hollywood,[25] Itō was already employing off-centre framing and creating scenes into which figures wandered rather than tracking them.

We can see an example in a scene from *A Diary of Chūji's Travels/Chūji tabi nikki* 1927), a three-part film that follows a yakuza boss – Chūji of Kunisada (Ōkōchi) – as he tries to evade the law. On the run, Chūji disguises himself (strategic duplicity) by working for a sake brewer whose young daughter, Okume (Sawa Ranko), becomes infatuated with him. In an unexpected sequence, the two follow one another through a maze of enormous empty sake casks. Throughout, Itō plays with this space as one of visibility and invisibility, as well as female desire, as the casks tilt and jut out in different directions (Fig. 20.1). Arguably the first person to deserve the name auteur in Japan, Itō builds the *mise en scène* from the shapes, textures and lines of the casks. He was as adept at composing such 'interesting'[26] images as he was with developing the rhythms of on-screen action.[27] It is as if the confrontation with corrupt power not only entails the critical procedures of revelation but, equally, a sense of play, imagination and desire.

Fig. 20.1 *A Diary of Chuji's Travels/Chūji tabi nikki* (Itō Daisuke, 1927, Nikkatsu).

REALISM IN WARTIME

Under the pressures of war, this sense of play was subject to a demand for order through a different kind of realism. This realism aimed to combat cinema's conversion of the past into an image, one secretly harbouring the seductive force of Americanisation. Japanese history, for some, was in danger of becoming a product of Hollywood.

During the late 1930s, as Japan launched a full-scale invasion of the continent, the critic Tsumura Hideo wrote an open letter to the director Kinugasa Teinosuke that criticised him for his failure to depict the true past of Japan in his period films. He went on to castigate *jidaigeki* for their lack of 'realism'.[28] Tsumura argued that with its precise rendering of a world of infinite detail, cinema might serve as the perfect vessel to show what the past was really like, were it not compelled to contradict history itself in the name of frivolous entertainment, or what he called 'the present'.[29] He advocated replacing *jidaigeki* with the new category of *rekishi eiga* (historical films)[30] in order to overcome duplicity with the single truth of history that only film could carry. His writing sparked various debates on the question of realism in film,[31] whilst broader calls for a return to the realities of nation and history enveloped politics, philosophy and the arts.[32]

Tsumura's argument provides a sharp critique of the permeation of the global cultural imagination by the fantasies of Hollywood and Americanisation. While compelling, his argument presumes that *jidaigeki* were both intended and received as straightforward historical reconstructions that subsequently came to be distorted by foreign ideas. What his argument misses is the ways that *jidaigeki* were already entangled in issues of truth and duplicity – the fact that the 'reality' with which they engaged could already be considered suspect. As previously suggested, this sense of duplicity can be traced back to *The Serpent*. If this were an anomaly we might think little of the force of deception in the film. However, a preoccupation with deception – and more specifically the question of whether it is possible to live in a just world beyond images – is by no means limited to this one film, a particular meaning or even politics in general.[33] Nor is it solely a matter of *jidaigeki* wearing the 'mask' of the past in order to offer a disguised critique of the present. While it would be absurd to claim this affected all films, we cannot fail to note its odd prevalence – not simply as a plot device (as with noir, or a mystery) but also as part of the very découpage of the films that informs its *mise en scène*, its gestures, patterns of speech, plot machinations, costumes and morality.

Such a focus on duplicity exposes deeper currents beneath the surface that go well beyond Tsumura's critique: the frustrated desire to escape a world of images (nihilism), the struggle to overthrow false images masking power (ideology) as well as the call for a return to real history during a time of war (realism). *Jidaigeki* expose, and are shaped by, the contradictory affects at the heart of modernity itself: the impossible desire to locate some stable truth beyond the bombardment of new media images.

Not all felt this image flood as a source of anxiety. Itami Mansaku was one of the directors most guilty of indulging a duplicity that contradicted the true history of Japan. Itami extolled the virtues of 'nonsense' – the refusal of cinema to be limited to saying *one thing only*[34] – and claimed it should always be *duplicitous*. We can see this duplicity in *Capricious Young Man/ Akanishi Kakita* (1936), a work based on a Shiga Naoya's story about a notorious case of conspiracy in Sendai during the seventeenth century. One of the two films almost fully extant directed by Itami,[35] *Capricious Young Man* follows the titular samurai, Akanishi, a fictional character who works (in disguise) to uncover the conspiracy and attempt to seize power by the corrupt Harada Kai (an actual historical figure). Itami cast the same actor (Kataoka Chiezō) in both roles, with wholly different styles of speech, dress and performance. The narrative world is rife with duplicity: stolen documents, disguises, doubled figures, false leads, fake letters, suspicious characters and hidden threats.[36] Even duplicity itself is never one single thing (Fig. 20.2).

The film plays with class, identity and power around the famous historical disturbance, while also satirising the conventions of *jidaigeki*. The marvellous sequence in which Akanishi receives a response to a love letter he has sent to Sazanami (Mori Mineko) is exemplary. She appears as a kind of ghost that rises out of her

Fig. 20.2 *Capricious Young Man/Akanishi Kikita* (Itami Mansaku, 1936, Kataoka Chiezō Productions).

letter as he unfolds and reads it. She boldly but humbly expresses the unexpected welling up of love within her. His letter was, however, initially false and, under the assumption that a young, beautiful woman would want little to do with such a homely man, a way to distract attention so he could escape. The unexpected love of a woman – with full agency, in the face of class opposition (she is the daughter of merchants, not samurai) and in response to an act of duplicity – constitutes the path through which the conspiracy to violence is finally brought down.

THE RESPONSIBILITY OF DECEPTION

The tensions around realism and duplicity extend beyond the frame of *jidaigeki*, cinema or art. In the immediate postwar period, deception was one of the major issues confronting a shaken nation contending with occupation and the legacy of the firebombing, while also struggling with its responsibility for the violence that it had directed at its own colonies in the name of ethnic unity and anti-colonialism. Itami addressed this question of responsibility directly in a short essay, 'The Question of Who is Responsible for the War', among the most famous film essays in Japan.[37] While many protested that they were not responsible for the war because they were deceived by the authorities, Itami argued that being deceived did not absolve anyone of responsibility; on the contrary, it was precisely the matter of being deceived that made one responsible. Itami's reluctance to name war criminals not only suggested that no one was undeceived in Japan but also made the issue of deception central to the consideration of democracy more generally. Having said this, Itami's work also suggests that just because we cannot break out of a world of images does not mean we need to abdicate responsibility or yield to a world of cynicism. It is possible, and even necessary, for deception and responsibility to coexist. *Jidaigeki* provided a place for this mingling.

We may rethink the place of the world's most famous *jidaigeki*, Kurosawa Akira's *Rashomon/Rashōmon* (1950), from this perspective on duplicity and responsibility. As the film that put 'Japanese cinema on the map', its interrogation of the ways in which we deceive ourselves may owe something to Itami, especially since the scriptwriter, Hashimoto Shinobu, developed the initial ideas for the script following extensive consultation with him.[38] Subsequent *jidaigeki* may be less concerned with duplicity (individual films aside). However, given *Rashomon*'s key place in expanding the frame of world cinema, we might say that global film history is indebted to this history of *jidaigeki*, even if its lessons about deception and power have been lost in the fog like Mifune Toshiro's 'Macbeth' character Washizu in *Throne of Blood/Kumonosujō* (1957).

In some ways, it is extraordinary that *Rashomon* surfaced at all given that it was made during the Occupation of Japan by the US, which took place between August of 1945 and April of 1952. The CIE (Civil Information and Education Division), under directives from the Supreme Commander for the Allied Powers (SCAP), prohibited most *jidaigeki* as violent remnants of a feudal past, inappropriate to the new democratic orientation of peace and prosperity. *Jidaigeki* were equally suspect to the occupiers. Yet, not only did *Rashomon* become a landmark film but also a slew of artistically ambitious *jidaigeki* by Kurosawa, Mizoguchi Kenji, Kinugasa Teinosuke and Inagaki Hiroshi swept up film festival prizes in its wake and helped to usher in what would later be called 'global' (non-European) cinema. The 'golden age' of Japanese film was rooted in the artistic flowering of *jidaigeki*.

Having said this, there were two different kinds of *jidaigeki* that belonged to almost distinct film worlds. The former was not even largely considered as *jidaigeki*, but seen as auteurist or national cinema instead. The latter was considered a more local product, marked less by directorial genius than by a mood of lightness accompanying a rising economy, increasing distance from the war (despite the ongoing Korean War) and a new vitality in urban life. Such films often appeared not as lone masterpieces but as series, less amenable to circulation through film festivals or art-house cinemas. Studios churned out such works, about 150 per year, amounting to half of all film output at a time when the number of screens and viewers was at its peak.

We might picture this bifurcated golden age as a kind of iceberg with the peak represented by a small number of famous works and film-makers, while an extraordinary proliferation of idiosyncratic works spread voluminously beneath the surface. An example of the latter is the nine-part series, *Jirochō's Tale of Three Provinces/Jirochō sangokushi*, which was made at Tōhō studios between 1952 and 1954 and directed by Makino Masahiro.[39] Although he was 'adapting' Murakami Genzō's novel, serialised contemporaneously, Masahiro – who had previously made films based on the legendary nineteenth-century yakuza boss Jirochō of Shimizu – worked at such a feverish pace that the films surpassed the serialised fiction and became the 'original'.

The serial form of *Jirocho*'s picaresque narrative harks back to early cinema – such as the films of Louis Feuillade – while also anticipating the contemporary televisual mode on various cable and internet platforms. What emerges through this form is a different and more fluid sense of time, one accentuated by the film's light and playful tone; something that is evident in the opening of the first film in which Jirochō (Kobori Akio) fights two hoodlums at a pub. Though he believes he has murdered them (the act is elided on screen), the entire sequence – including the fighting – is marked by levity and humour. The ebullient tone and near musical sense of rhythm recalls Masahiro's own wartime *jidaigeki* – *Duel at Takadanobaba/Chikemuri takadanobaba* (1937) and *Singing Lovebirds/Oshidori utagassen* (1939). While some see in *Jirocho* an expression of the 'joy of cinema itself as pure entertainment',[40] others argue that the duplicitous tendencies of *jidaigeki* such as *Jirocho* – which portrayed violent gangsters as benevolent, paternal figures – reeked of lingering fascism. In the pages of the liberal journal *The Science of Thought*, for example, Jirochō was deemed a 'little Hitler'.[41]

By any measure, the golden age was short-lived. During the 1960s, production dropped to 10 per cent of its late 1950s peak, though numerous striking *jidaigeki* appeared. The 25-film *Zatōichi* series, beginning in 1962 just as major studio cinema began its slide, provided an entirely different kind of international recognition from that of the golden age. Produced mostly at Daiei, each film was centred on the star, Katsu Shintarō, who eventually helped it transition into a successful television series from 1974 until 1979 through his own production company, Katsu Pro.

While *Zatōichi* is a *jidaigeki*, the character of Ichi is not a samurai but a gambler, a lowly outcast. He was not above deception and cheating and thus hardly an untainted force of 'good' that could be appropriated by the state as an idealised role model. Ichi thus not only managed to evade charges of fascism but, as Yomota Inuhiko has also argued, his underdog duplicity – using his weaknesses, such as blindness, to take advantage of a corrupt elite – endeared him to mass audiences throughout South East Asia and beyond. For Yomota, *Zatōichi* is interesting precisely because for its many Asian fans – in contrast to the elite appreciation of Ozu by Western cinéphiles – it bears no traces of zen philosophy, Eastern exoticism or even rigorous decoupage.[42] As the titular character reminds us repeatedly, he is 'just Ichi' (*tada no Ichi*).

After 1973, *jidaigeki* were produced at an average rate of approximately five per year (about the same number as that produced during the Occupation), and they never recovered a spot in cinemas. Television is often accused of 'killing' Japanese cinema due to the inverse relationship between the rise of the medium and the collapse of studio output from the mid-1960s. However, this was not necessarily harmful to *jidaigeki*, which migrated into the home and came to occupy a privileged position within the 'golden hours' of prime-time television broadcasting. During the early 1990s, about three hundred *jidaigeki* were produced annually for television, doubling the numbers produced even at its peak during the 1950s in cinemas. Its numbers dropped again from the mid-1990s, however, and it has now fallen out of commercial favour.[43]

Many reasons exist for the collapse of *jidaigeki* according to Kasuga Taichi: an attachment to fixed patterns of performance, narrative and expression; the dilapidated state of studios and facilities in Kyoto; poorly trained actors, directors and producers; overly strong female characters; and a lack of dramatic focus. Fundamentally, Kasuga takes *jidaigeki* not as a representation of the past but as the presentation of a fantasy world that is relatable, inhabitable and, in that sense, 'real'. According to Kasuga, it is in abandoning the site of fantasy (by adapting 'naturalist' performance styles, for example), that *jidaigeki* have forfeited their distinction and their place.[44]

Kasuga's arguments about the 'fall' of *jidaigeki* seem to call for a restoration of the form. With some exceptions, however, *jidaigeki* have rarely had a rightful place; they are a rogue element of the cinematic world. *Jidaigeki* are not solely inhabitable fantasies and should not merely be seen as self-contained entertainment. This characterisation threatens to smooth out their agonistic and contradictory history, and their entanglements in terms of authority and the law. It also threatens to obscure the myriad ways that their sense of play with historical time has, at different points, placed them in conflict with almost every side of Japanese culture. In this sense, they may thus be more accurately characterised by the more ambiguous notion of duplicity.

This duplicity does not refer to a stable fictional ground opposed to real history. Rather, it stems from the *topos* of *jidaigeki* as a multidimensional site of struggle and movement, a splintering of chronological time rather than the permanent mark of a single event or date. It is the effort to contain this movement, to arrest time within the national space that has incited antagonism – whether this involves the upholding of the security of the imperial state, ensuring a more accurate history and better national self-image, or the location of responsibility and promotion of democracy. In the work of its most profound proponents – writers, directors, producers, critics and stars – duplicity, far from being a problem that must be stopped, actually appears heroic in terms of its creative restlessness.

FROM THE PAST TO THE FUTURE

I began this chapter by suggesting that the conventional definition of *jidaigeki* – any Japanese film set prior to 1868 – does not provide an adequate explanation of the term. The reliance on this temporal break in scholarship and criticism tends to limit our focus to a fixed space without ever calling that particular space into question. This emphasis also leads to equally misleading frames of genre or culture, both of which are equally inadequate. I have thus directed our attention to questions of place – *topos* – rather than time. I do not, however, want to suggest that time is unimportant. *Jidaigeki* hold contradictory senses of time together, moment by moment. Each of these moments is in itself moving and multidimensional and duplicates both itself and its world over and over again.

Such restless duplicity works to undermine the imperial break of national history and expose sovereignty as both a temporal and spatial concern. At the same time, however, *jidaigeki* do not exist simply for the purpose of upholding or destroying national space or time. One clear reason for moving away from the conventional framing of the form is that in defining a subcategory of a larger notion of national cinema, this framing also fails to consider what make *jidaigeki* exciting and creative in their own right.

A further important question is to ask what the *topos* of *jidaigeki* might be after 'Japanese cinema' itself is declared dead. I will conclude by pursuing two trajectories of *jidaigeki* today. The first comes from Yamada Yōji's *Twilight Samurai/Tasogare seibei* (2002). The film focuses on Seibei (Sanada Hiroyuki), a samurai who is treated with bewilderment or disdain by his peers because he forsakes the glory and benefits of his status in order to care for his daughters and senile mother. Seibei's refusal of glory is echoed in the *mise en scène* of the film, evident especially in the arduous final duel between Seibei and Zen'emon Yogo (Tanaka Min). Eschewing the typical sword-fight spectacle, it recalls Clausewitz's well-known distinction between war in theory and war in practice: while the former lacks friction, 'action in war is like movement in a resistant element'. We feel the weight of this resistance, the heaviness of the sword – literally and figuratively – in the wearying movements and inky, cramped space. Seibei is less a victor than a survivor, and even when this grimness gives way to bright sunshine in the final shots, the voiceover informs us that the hero would die shortly thereafter in the Boshin War, on the wrong side of modernisation.[45] This marks one trajectory of *jidaigeki* that subtly inverts its superficial nostalgia and hearkens back to its former glory to show that it was never glamorous in the first place.

In this, nonetheless, the film belongs to a tradition that goes back at least as far as Itami Mansaku and Yamanaka Sadao. Meanwhile, if *Twilight* serves as a kind of fighting elegy, Miike Takashi's *Izo* (2004) offers pure explosion. With restless surrealism and outlandish violence, *Izo* blithely transgresses the 1868 break and weaves newsreel wartime footage through its genre-hopping, time-travel narrative. Are we in the past, anxious about a coming war of devastation that still lurks ahead? Or are we like Klee's *Angelus Novus*, as immortalised by Walter Benjamin, in the future looking back at the damage that has already been wrought? Is it the past or the future that flashes up in a moment of danger? It is impossible to say. In some ways, *Izo* also hearkens back to the even earlier *jidaigeki* of the 1920s with their dark-hearted nihilism and contempt for conventions and propriety. It also points to the never-ending quagmire of war and the postwar, a wholly other temporality that demands a radical new kind of *jidaigeki*. If *Izo* offers any response, it is in transposing *jidaigeki*'s anxiety over the past into a question about its future. Is there room for a different kind of re-imagining? This may be the most important question for *jidaigeki* today.

Notes

1. The Meiji Restoration of 1868 is one of the most significant events of Japanese history. It brought an end to the Shogunate with its hierarchical system of ruling samurai; replaced castle-centred domains with prefectures; instituted the apparatuses of the modern state (the Diet, a reformed educational system, a constitution, etc.); ushered in a flood of new knowledge and technologies from the West; gave birth to new political struggles and ideologies such as the Freedom and People's Rights Movement; and otherwise permeated nearly every facet of culture, politics and everyday life. While some consider it the break between 'modernity' and 'premodernity', many scholars have contested this break and pointed to the Edo period (early modern) or even the medieval Muromachi period instead.
2. As late as the 1990s, an anthology was published in Japan with the title, *What is Jidaigeki?* The essays by a range of international scholars cover *jidaigeki* from different eras and in terms of various methodologies. The title of the collection directly suggests that it is not obvious what *jidaigeki* is, either for scholars within Japan or outside the country. See Tsutsui Kiyotada and Katō Mikirō (eds), *Jidaigeki to wa nanika* (Kyoto: Jinbun shoin, 1997).
3. Nagisa Ōshima, *Cinema, Censorship, and the State*, trans. Dawn Lawson, ed. Annette Michelson (Boston, MA: MIT Press, 1993). Ōshima's premise is that once the studios stopped producing films, they abandoned the ethical community of the nation and that the term 'national' cinema had therefore lost its meaning.
4. Indeed, this is the approach informing the only book-length work in English on the topic, Sybil Thornton's *The Japanese Period Film: A Critical Analysis* (Jefferson, NC: McFarland & Co., 2008). To ward off Orientalism, Thornton provides illuminating cultural knowledge of various codes for the foreign viewer: 'The narrative is comprehensible only when one understands the basic assumptions of how the world works upon which the narrative itself is premised. These basic assumptions are what make up the intangible mental culture of the Japanese. [...] As long as the view or perception of the world differs from community to community, from ethnic group to ethnic group, and from nation to nation, we may well speak of a national character in film' (p. 6). The question of a national character of cinema is a large debate but either way, the argument is misdirected as a critique of Orientalism, since Edward Said's famous argument concerned not ignorance but the ways that knowledge serves (and constructs) power.
5. Hashimoto begins with a humorous account of the ways that tooth-blackening moved from desirable (in the pre-cinematic) to grotesque (in the post-cinematic), necessitating a change in the image that had to accord with cinema and history rather than representing historical truth. *Kanpon chanbara jidaigeki kōza* (Tokyo: Tokuma shoten, 1986), pp. 1–28.
6. Nakai wrote that we must remain attentive to the fact that the concept of *topos* never merely indicates a flat place (*heimenteki na basho*) but rather implicates a 'multi-dimensional *moment* as a site of struggle' (*rittaiteki na tōsōteki keiki*). See 'Iinkai no ronri', in Kuno Osamu (ed.), *Nakai Masakazu zenshū*, vol. 1 (Tokyo: Bijutsu shuppansha, 1965), pp. 46–108.
7. See Nakai Masakazu, 'Film Theory and the Crisis of Contemporary Aesthetics', trans. Phil Kaffen, *Review of Japanese Culture and Society* vol. 22 (December 2010), pp. 1–8.
8. Kasuga Taichi, *Jidaigeki shinazu!* (Tokyo: Shūeisha, 2008), p. 9.

9 Onoe was not only popular with young boys but was arguably the first great imperial star – a favourite of the crown prince. See Tanaka Masasumi, 'Jidaigeki eigashiron no tame no yobiteki kōsatsu (senzen hen)', in Tsutsui and Katō, *Jidaigeki eiga to wa nani ka*, p. 22.

10 Aaron Gerow points out that it was not until the late 1910s that the word 'cinema' (*eiga*) came to replace 'moving pictures' (*katsudō shashin*) as a result of attempts by elite critics and reformers to purify cinema of its lingering backward theatrical elements. See *Visions of Japanese Modernity: Articulations of Cinema, Nation, and Spectatorship, 1895–1925* (Berkeley: University of California Press, 2010).

11 Kobayashi Hideo, 'Literature of the Lost Home', in *Literature of the Lost Home*, trans. Paul Anderer (Palo Alto, CA: Stanford University Press, 1995), pp. 46–54.

12 Film historian Tanaka Jun'ichirō writes, 'Within small capital production films, it was mostly *jidaigeki*, beginning with Makino […] that unified the spirit of spectators in the wake of the earthquake, the open demand for vigour and intensity'. *Nihon eiga hattatsushi*, vol. 2, *Musei kara talkie* (Tokyo: Chūōkōron-sha, 1968), p. 12.

13 See the chapter on 'Seven Samurai' in Mitsuhiro Yoshimoto, *Kurosawa: Film Studies and Japanese Cinema* (Durham, NC: Duke University Press, 2000), pp. 205–45. [Editors' note: for an argument building on Yoshimoto's insight, see also Chapter 23 by Ryoko Misono (with Hideaki Fujiki and Alastair Phillips) in this volume.]

14 The journal started awarding prizes in 1924, initially only for 'foreign' films though the films were not identified as 'foreign' but as either 'artistically superior films' or 'the best entertainment films'. Two years later, the categories of 'art' versus 'entertainment' were replaced by 'Japanese' and 'foreign' films. Although the cinema yearbook declared in 1930 that 'pictures based on modern life are steadily [*sic*] eclipsing the popularity of those concerned with the life of the old Samurai days', that year saw Japanese cinema divided between contemporary films (*gendai eiga*) and period films (*jidai eiga*), while foreign film was divided between sound and silent cinema. From the following year, such divisions disappear leaving only the categories of Japanese and foreign films. See 'An Outline of the Motion Picture Industry in Japan', *Nihon eiga nenkan*, (Tokyo: Asahi shibunsha, 1930), p. 4.

15 The Tokyo Imperial University Research Group (Teikoku daigaku kenkyūkai) wrote: 'From long ago, the nihilistic trend of *jidaigeki* represented by such people as Shinami Nishika, Yamagami Itarō, or even further back, Susukita Rokuhei, has spread, in the present moment, to cover almost the entirety of *jidaigeki* film.' 'Cinemateki nihirizmu no shoyōsō', *Eiga hyōron*, November 1929, p. 499.

16 Scholars have devoted entire books to the cultural history of *tate*, tracing its links to kabuki and earlier theatrical traditions. See Ogawa Naoko's *'Tate' to iu bunka: Chanbara jidaigeki eiga o saguru* (Tokyo: Sekai shisōsha, 2007).

17 David Bordwell offers an extended close reading of the final fight sequence. See his post, 'Bandō on the Run' on his blog, *Observations on Film Art*, 24 June 2007, <http://www.davidbordwell.net/blog/2007/06/24/bando-on-the-run/>.

18 Ogawa Naoko writes, 'In the Onoe Matsunosuke films, it was rare to see a sword directly touching the body of the opponent. To audiences accustomed [to this convention], *tachimawari* in which the sword struck the body of the opponent when he was cut, appeared shocking. Hence, we can surmise that this is what audiences deemed "real".' Ogawa, *Tate' to iu bunka*, p. 96.

19 See Makino Mamoru, *Nihon eiga ken'etsushi* (Tokyo: Pandora, 2003).

20 Bantsuma Pro moved from Shōchiku to Teikine to Shinkō kinema to Daiei and then to Tōyoko films in the postwar period, which then became Tōei and produced the most popular *jidaigeki* of the 1950s.

21 Kuno Osamu emphasises cinema as a gathering point for 'anti-academically oriented, intellectual youth fascinated by the attractions of cinema as a new collective art, the dregs of society who had a real love for films and threw themselves wholly into producing works'. Kuno Osamu, *Doyōbi fukkokuban* (Tokyo: San'ichi shobō, 1974), p. 4. The political philosopher Maruyama Masao also emphasised *jidaigeki* as a kind of shelter. He would tell his parents that he was going to see films approved by the Ministry of Education, but instead he would sneak into *jidaigeki*. Maruyama Masao, 'Eiga to watashi', in *Maruyama Masao zenshū*, vol. 11 (Tokyo: Iwanami, 1996), pp. 3–34.

22 *The Serpent* impressed Joseph von Sternberg (who watched it repeatedly) as well as Universal Film Studios, the first Hollywood studio in Japan. They set up a coproduction company with Bandō. A failed venture, it nonetheless resulted in the provision of important new equipment and technologies (including the Eyemo camera that Karasawa used).

23 The year 1929 was the peak of the tendency film. It was also the first time that a film journal devoted an entire issue to *jidaigeki*. *Kinema junpō*'s best films of that year are almost all *jidai eiga*.
24 Takenaka Rō, *Keikō eiga no jidai* (Tokyo: Shirakawa Shoin, 1974).
25 See Noël Burch's *To the Distant Observer: Form and Meaning in Japanese Cinema* (London: Scolar Press; Berkeley: University of California Press, 1979).
26 Murakami Tadahisa praises the 'interesting' quality (*omoshirosa*) of Itō Daisuke's works in his *Nihon eiga sakkaron* (Tokyo: Ōraisha, 1936), pp. 2–29. *Omoshirosa* would become one of the watchwords of postwar cinéphiles such as Hasumi Shigehiko, Yamane Sadao and Ueno Kōshi. I would like to thank William Carroll for alerting me to this reference.
27 Itō was praised for his skilful ability to maintain continuity in actions scenes of great intensity (thus, earning him the sobriquet, *Idō Daisuki* – crazy about movement). See Itakura Fumiaki, '"Itō wajutsu" to wa nanika – Itō Daisukeron josetsu', <http://www.cmn.hs.h.kyoto-u.ac.jp/CMN3/text7.html>. Itakura points to Itō's borrowing from the avant-garde in France (Marcel L'Herbier's *L'Inhumaine* [1924] and Abel Gance's *La Roue* [1923], especially). Itō himself cites G.W. Pabst, Josef von Sternberg, Robert Siodmak and René Clair, as inspirations but reserves the greatest respect for Soviet film-makers.
28 See Tsumura Hideo, 'Kinugasa Teinosukeshi e no tegami' as well as 'Rekishiki eiga ni tsuite', in *Eiga to hihyō* (Tokyo: Yumani shobō, 2004), pp. 115–57. The former was originally written in 1937, while the latter was originally written in 1938. Both appeared in book form in 1938, under the title *Eiga to hihyō*.
29 As the only film critic who participated in the 1942 conference dedicated to the idea of overcoming modernity, Tsumura made a distinction overlooked by all other participants: between the modern (*kindai*) and the present (*genzai*). Cinema belonged to the latter: it was already after the modern. See Tsumura Hideo, 'What is to be Destroyed?', in Richard F. Calichman (ed. and trans.), *Overcoming Modernity: Cultural Identity in Wartime Japan* (New York: Columbia University Press, 2008), pp. 115–27.
30 Tsumura Hideo, *Eiga no bi* (Tokyo: Kōfukan, 1947).
31 Bemoaning the fact that *jidaigeki* had no stable definition, the critic Hattori Shisō decried *jidaigeki*'s propensity for 'violence directed at past history'. 'Jidai eiga no shomondai', *Nippon eiga*, 1938. See the reprinted edition edited by Makino Mamoru (Tokyo: Yumani shobō, 2002), p. 2.
32 While Tsumura was sympathetic to the imperial project, even the Marxist film theorist, Imamura Taihei – who also noted the intimate relationship between Hollywood and *jidaigeki* – argued for *jidaigeki*'s return to realism. See his 'Jidaigeki eiga kō', in *Imamura Taihei eizō ronshū*, vol. 1, *Eiga geijutsu no keshiki* (Tokyo: Yumani Shobō, 1991), pp. 363–8. For a discussion of the emergence of historical films, see Yamada Kōichi, 'Rekishi eiga kō', in *Edison-teki kaiki* (Tokyo: Seidosha, 1997), pp 189–218. For an excellent discussion of the debates on realism, see Naoki Yamamoto, 'Realities That Matter: The Development of Realist Film Theory and Practice in Japan, 1895–1945' (unpublished PhD thesis, Yale University, 2012).
33 To name only the most well known and readily available, we could point to the following films: *Wanderlust*/*Hōrō Zanmai* (Inagaki Hiroshi, 1927), *Diary of Chuji's Travels*/*Chūji tabi nikki* (Itō Daisuke, 1927), *Jirokichi the Rat*/*Oatsurae Jirokichi kōshi* (Itō Daisuke, 1931), *Peerless Patriot*/*Kokushi musō* (Itami Mansaku, 1932), *An Actor's Revenge*/*Yukinojō Henge* (Kinugasa Teinosuke, 1935), *Tange Sazen and the Pot Worth a Million Ryo*/*Tange Sazen to hyakuman ryō no tsubo* (Yamanaka Sadao, 1935), *Miss Okichi*/*Ojō Okichi* (Takashima Tatsunosuke, 1935), *Kōchiyama Sōshun* (Yamanaka Sadao, 1936), *Akanishi Kakita* (Itami Mansaku, 1936), *Singing Lovebirds*/*Oshidori Utagassen* (Makino Masahiro, 1939), *The Man Who Disappeared Yesterday*/*Kinō kieta otoko* (Makino Masahiro, 1941).
34 See his essay, 'Thoughts with Regard to New Period Films', initially published in the periodical *Eiga kagaku kenkyū*, April 1931, reprinted in *Itami Mansaku Zenshū* (Tokyo: Chikuma shobō, 1982), pp. 5–16.
35 The other extant film is *Kyojinden* (1938), an adaptation of Victor Hugo's *Les Miserables*.
36 Tsumura draws explicitly on Mori Ōgai and the historical case also provided the basis for Mori Ōgai's 'historical fiction', *Suginohara Shina*. Ōgai's version dwells on facts and psychology and an archival confrontation with historical details that was emblematic of his argument about the importance of truth in fiction. See David Dilworth

and J. Thomas Rimer (eds and trans.), *The Historical Fiction of Mori Ogai* (Honolulu: University of Hawai'i Press, 1991).

37 See Itami Mansaku, 'Sensō sekinin no mondai', in *Eiga shunjū*, January 1946, pp. 32–37.

38 Though he does not state the precise details of what Itami taught him, Hashimoto devotes considerable space to his training under Itami in discussion of *Rashomon*. See Hashimoto Shinobu, *Compound Cinematics: Akira Kurosawa and I* (New York: Vertical, 2006). [Editors' note: for more on the narrative structure of the film, see also Chapter 5 by Kosuke Kinoshita in this volume.]

39 Masahiro's absence from scholarly writing on Japanese cinema in English is among the most egregious of many. While attention is paid to his father as the 'father of Japanese cinema' (albeit usually only in passing), it is Masahiro as director and his brother, Mitsuo, as producer, who provided the backbone of Japanese cinema throughout the studio era. See Makino Masahiro, *Eiga tosei: Ten no maki*, ed. Yamada Kōichi and Yamane Sadao (Tokyo: Heibonsha, 1977). Recently, Ritsumeikan University has established a Makino Project, which attempts a digital archive of research, <http://www.arc.ritsumei.ac.jp/archive01/makino/>.

40 See Yamada Kōichi, *Jirochō sangokushi: Makino Masahiro no sekai* (Tokyo: Waizu shuppan, 2002). Yamada compares Masahiro to Howards Hawks.

41 See Satō Tadao, 'Ninkyō ni tsuite', *Shisō no kagaku*, August 1954. Reprinted in Satō Tadao, *Kangeki ni umeru shisō: Taishūteki chisei no tankyū* (Tokyo: Yomiuri shinbunsha, 1971), pp. 187–97. This anxiety about the return of fascism was felt keenly so soon after the war. The first *Jirochō* film opened in December 1952, less than a year after the Occupation ended (in April 1952).

42 See Tsutsui and Katō, *Jidaigeki eiga to wa nani ka*, pp. 182–93.

43 In the twenty-first century, the only remaining television *jidaigeki* with any consistency was TBS's *Mito Kōmon*, which had the distinct aroma of being elderly friendly and was itself cancelled in 2011. See Kasuga Taichi, *Naze jidaigeki wa horobiru no ka* (Tokyo: Shinchōsha, 2014).

44 Ibid.

45 The Boshin War (1868–9) was a civil war overlapping with and sharing the concerns of the Meiji Restoration. The Shogun, Tokugawa Yoshinobu, in a last bid effort to preserve power, tried to seize the imperial court at Kyoto by military means but was defeated by forces loyal to the Emperor.

21

HORROR
The ghosts of *kaiki eiga*

Michael Crandol

Horror is one of the most enduring and easily identifiable film genres in the English-speaking world. Although film theorists occasionally debate its boundaries, any casual fan likely will tell you that *Dracula* (1931), *Psycho* (1960), *The Exorcist* (1973), *Friday the 13th Part VI* (1986) and *The Blair Witch Project* (1999) are – for all their vast differences in style and mode of production – unquestionably horror films. The not-unreasonable assumption that a film which features some horrific elements designed to elicit scares or a sense of dread from its audience is, in effect, a 'horror film' has led some scholars and critics to apply the same breadth of generic classification when writing in English about Japanese cinema. Essays collected in the 2005 volume *Japanese Horror Cinema*, for example, include art films such as *Ugetsu/Ugetsu monogatari* (1953) and *Onibaba* (1964) along with the ultra-violent *Battle Royale/Battle rowaiaru* and rape-revenge film *Freeze Me/Furīzu mī* (both 2000) all under the generic umbrella of horror.[1] However, as Mitsuyo Wada-Marciano has discussed, none of these pictures were conceived of as horror films in Japan, and such forms of labelling divorce them from the cultural-historical contexts of their production, marketing and reception in their home country.[2] Few, if any, Japanese film fans would imagine these pictures as belonging to the same generic category as *The Wolf Man* (1941) or *Night of the Living Dead* (1968).

Much of this confusion can be traced to the transnational popularity of the J-horror phenomenon at the turn of the millennium. 'J-horror' became part of global vernacular in the wake of the international success of director Nakata Hideo's *Ring/Ringu* (1998), which spawned numerous sequels, a big-budget Hollywood remake and countless imitations both in Japan and abroad. In the West, J-horror quickly became a catch-all label for any Japanese film featuring a ghost or some other motif associated with the horror genre, and English-language 'J-horror lists', which include everything from golden age art house cinema to direct-to-video pornography, still proliferate the internet.[3] In Japan, meanwhile, J-horror (or *J-horā*) is generally understood to have a more precise meaning, which Chika Kinoshita has summarised as referring to a cycle of low-budget films produced in the last twenty years by a closely knit group of film-makers, which emphasise atmospheric and psychological fear over graphic gore, and capitalise on urban legends proliferated through mass media and popular culture.[4] The seeds of the movement were laid in direct-to-video productions such as *Evil Spirit/Jaganrei* (1988) and *Scary True Stories/Hontō ni atta kowai hanashi* (1991), achieved worldwide fame with the release of *Ring*, and reached its zenith of popularity with the complimentary Japanese and American series of *The Grudge/Ju-on* films directed by Shimizu Takashi between 2000 and 2006. Accordingly, *J-horā* in fact only accounts for a comparatively small and rather brief moment in the history of Japanese cinema. What then to call the vast majority of Japanese films featuring ghosts, monsters and other horrific elements that do not fit this definition?

FROM *HORĀ* TO *KAIKI* AND BACK AGAIN: A GENERIC OVERVIEW OF JAPANESE HORROR FILM

Drop the 'J' from *J-horā* and one is left with the transliterated English word *horā*, which entered the Japanese language as a filmic term along with the arrival of the home video market and the new American subgenre of horror, the slasher film, in the early 1980s.[5] Today, the term carries the same breadth of meaning as its English equivalent, retroactively applied to classic black-and-white Daiei and Tōei films as much as it is to more recent pictures such as *Ring* and Miike Takashi's *Audition* (2000). Prior to the establishment of *horā* as a film genre category, however, *kaiki eiga* was the most common generic term for what we would call a 'horror film' in English. Literally meaning 'strange' or 'bizarre' film, *kaiki eiga* encompassed Western horror films such as *Dracula*, *Frankenstein* (1931) and almost anything starring Vincent Price as well as a healthy output of domestic titles, typified by adaptations of famous Edo Period (1603–1868) ghost stories such as *The Ghost Story of Yotsuya/Yotsuya kaidan* and innumerable *bakeneko* or 'ghost-cat' tales. In this chapter, I will reconsider the English-language concept of 'Japanese horror cinema' in the native context of *kaiki eiga* as well as one of the genre's central figures, director Nakagawa Nobuo, whose work represents both the pinnacle of *kaiki* filmmaking and the emergence of a more contemporary, *horā*-esque style.

Most domestic *kaiki eiga* were not lyrical art house features such as *Ugetsu* but 'B' films churned out by minor studios for matinee audiences. They enjoyed brisk box-office business and abysmally low critical reviews – features also typical of most Hollywood horror. Assuming a simple *kaiki*-equals-horror equation, however, greatly oversimplifies matters. For one thing, many successfully exported Japanese films such as *Godzilla/Gojira* (1954) that get associated with the horror label abroad seldom are considered as part of the *kaiki* genre in Japan.[6] For another, the use of *kaiki* as a category of film in Japanese predates the coinage of the phrase 'horror film' in English by at least several years.[7] And while horror has endured as an active film genre to the present day in the English-speaking world, by the mid-1970s the term *kaiki eiga* had fallen largely out of usage in Japan, soon to be replaced by *horā*. The difference between *kaiki* and *horā*, then, is in part a temporal one, with the antiquated term *kaiki* now reserved for vintage or 'classic' horror. But the fact that the old generic label needed to be retired and replaced by a new one also suggests that the difference between *kaiki* and *horā* runs deeper than mere age. The Japanese word for 'horror', *kyōfu*, has been used occasionally in the past in generic terms for certain pictures such as *Psycho* or *Les Diaboliques* (1955) that ultimately feature no fantastical source of fear or danger, but the onetime primacy of the categorical label *kaiki* for what we want to call 'horror films' in English suggests that, in Japan, the emotional affect of horror was not considered the defining aspect of the genre. When asked about the difference between *kaiki* and *horā*, J-horror director Kurosawa Kiyoshi has responded thus:

> *Kaiki*'s nuance might be termed 'gothic horror' in English. It's things like Hammer films and *The Ghost Story of Yotsuya*, period pieces in which ghosts or mysterious figures like Dracula appear, and the whole thing has a sense of taking place 'not now,' but 'long, long ago.' I suppose that's very similar to gothic horror. Those films aren't mainly about horror, the ones I want to call *kaiki*. They're atmospheric, moody. Even if they're provisionally set in the modern day, the action will take place in some old mansion, like in [Georges Franju's] *Eyes Without a Face* (*Les Yeux sans visage*, 1960). It's actually 'the present' yet it has a very old, period feel to it. […] I would say fear isn't even a necessary element of *kaiki eiga*.[8]

Advertising for *kaiki eiga* often promised the film would be 'thrillingly scary!' (*kowai ga tsūkai!*), and a common critical complaint was that domestically made *kaiki* pictures were not frightening, indicating that – for the cinemagoing public, at least – fear was an expected part of the *kaiki* package.[9] But Kurosawa is undoubtedly correct when he suggests an atmosphere of an Othered time and place distinguishes *kaiki* films from the rest of the *horā* genre. Many domestic *kaiki eiga* accomplish this simply by virtue of the fact they are *jidaigeki*, or 'period pictures', their worlds of samurai and geisha already Othered for a contemporary Japanese audience.[10] On a formal level, Kurosawa and others also point out that the stylised art direction and set work of classic *kaiki eiga* help to create the impression that the film's action takes place in a space physically and/or temporally removed from our own everyday, mundane existence.[11] The director Sasaki Hirohisa notes that even the exterior scenes of many *kaiki* films are shot on set, creating what he calls a sense of 'super-realism' (*sūpā riarizumu*).[12] Perhaps the most obvious example of this might be termed the 'spooky forest' sets that feature prominently in *kaiki* works both domestic and foreign, and can be seen in everything from *The Wolf Man* to *The Ghost Cat of Otama Pond/Kaibyō otama ga ike* (1960).

If *kaiki* is distinguished more so by an ambience of the strange and unusual, rather than the quantity of scares it delivers to its audience, this also helps explain some of the narrative differences between domestic *kaiki eiga* and Western horror cinema. In a great many Japanese *kaiki* pictures the 'scary' element frequently does not appear until comparatively late in the picture's runtime. This is in obvious contrast to most Western horror films, which tend to introduce their monsters early and make them the central focus of the plot. Yet the monsters do invariably turn up, although in most domestic *kaiki* pictures made until the late 1950s their function in the narrative is often strikingly similar to the samurai hero of more conventional *jidaigeki*.

GHOST CAT VERSUS SAMURAI: THE CLASSICAL *KAIKI*

Of the more than one hundred *kaiki eiga* made in Japan before 1945, less than a dozen are known to survive, most of them incomplete and in poor condition. Still haunted by the legacy of their poor critical standing, they remain a low priority for restoration efforts, with the limited funds available for such work going to more prestigious titles. Yet these precious few examples that survive, along with film reviews and promotional material for a great many pictures that do not, afford a glimpse of the prewar *kaiki* scene.

The earliest *kaiki* films were among the first examples of narrative cinema in Japan. Adaptations of the most popular kabuki ghost story plays, including *The Ghost Story of Yotsuya*, *The Dish Mansion at Banchō/Banchō sarayashiki* and variations on the popular *bakeneko* cat monster, were remade on a semi-annual basis from about 1910 onward. By the middle of the decade it was not unusual to see as many as a dozen such pictures released in a single year, with all of the major studios frequently producing competing versions of the same story. Unfortunately, in most cases all the information that survives regarding these early pictures is a title, the name of the studio and a release date. Several of Nikkatsu's first *kaiki* films were directed by Makino Shōzō and starred Onoe Matsunosuke, respectively the first great director and actor of Japanese cinema, and it is likely that their versions of *The Ghost Story of Yotsuya* (1912), *The Dish Mansion at Banchō* and *The Peony Lantern* (both 1914) were similar in style to the massive amount of period films the duo produced during this time,[13] which were characterised by a one-scene, one-take set-up in long shot, with the addition of Georges Méliès-style camera tricks to depict the ghosts and goblins. Méliès's legacy is clearly visible in the earliest surviving snippet of a *kaiki* film, which consists of 11 minutes of footage from an unidentified production of *The Dish Mansion* produced sometime before 1923.[14] In it, we see a samurai lord and his retainer sitting near a well. An audience familiar with the Dish Mansion legend would know the body of a murdered maid, Okiku, lies at the bottom of the well, and viewers would not be disappointed when Okiku's ghost rises from its depths to torment her murderer, the samurai lord. The effect is achieved with a simple double-exposure technique as Okiku's transparent form fades in atop the well, and her later appearance in the lord's bedchamber is marked by the use of stop-motion photography to illustrate her psychic manipulation of objects. Much like Méliès's own ghost-story film *The Haunted Castle/Le Manoir du diable* (1896), the intent appears to have been not to frighten the audience but to enthral them with the magic spectacle of early cinematic tricks.

By the late 1920s, such films had become an established fixture of Japanese popular cinema, with an emerging sense that they belonged to their own distinct genre of film-making conventions. 'Kaiki' – which does not appear to have become a standardised term until the 1920s – was not the only label used at the time for these pictures. Adaptations of the most famous Edo period ghost stories were typically identified as *kaidan* ('ghost story') films, though promotional materials and reviews from the 1920s show that the same works were sometimes called *obake eiga*, which literally means 'monster films' and would remain a synonymous term for *kaiki* films in Japan to the present day. But by the 1930s, *kaiki eiga* had become the all-encompassing generic umbrella for the subgenre of native *kaidan eiga* adapted from famous works such as *The Ghost Story of Yotsuya*, as well as original *obake eiga* stories and imported horror films such as the Universal *Dracula* and *Frankenstein* series.

The Shinkō Kinema studio – one of the smaller 'B' picture outfits based in Kyoto, ultimately became the premiere producer of *kaiki* pictures in the years leading up to World War II. A critical hostility towards the genre had built up by this time, with reviewers for the major film journals such as *Kinema junpō* and *Eiga hyōron* deriding *jidaigeki* in general and *kaiki* films in particular for their perceived backwardness in both style and content.[15] In truth, the small studios lacked the capital to compete artistically with major studios such as Shōchiku and Tōhō, instead catering to the not-insignificant demand for popular genre pictures. After scoring a hit with the *bakeneko* picture *Legend of the Ghost Cat of Saga/Saga kaibyō den* in early 1937, Shinkō touched off a *kaiki* boom among the minor studios, with over forty *kaiki* films being released over a subsequent three-and-a-half year period.

The three most substantial surviving *kaiki* films of the prewar era are all Shinkō efforts: 1937's *The Cat of Arima/Arima neko* and two pictures from 1938 – *The Ghost Story of the Mandarin Duck Curtain/Kaidan oshidori-chō* and *The Ghost Cat and the Mysterious Shamisen/Kaibyō nazo no shamisen*. All three feature the famous 'ghost-cat actress' Suzuki Sumiko, Japan's first horror star, who by the late 1930s was as synonymous with playing film monsters as Bela Lugosi and Boris Karloff. The first two pictures were both directed by Mokudō Shigeru, the most prolific *kaiki* film-maker of the prewar sound era, and the combination of Suzuki and Mokudō makes it fair to assume we have two rather typical surviving examples of the prewar *kaiki* genre to examine. *Mysterious Shamisen*, directed by the acclaimed former Shōchiku director Ushihara Kiyohiko, contains many stylistic flourishes and points of departure from the other two, and provides a useful counterpoint for considering the breadth of style and content the genre allowed for. It is therefore telling that all three films follow a rather conventional revenge narrative arc typical not only of most traditional *kaidan* ghost stories but many non-*kaiki jidaigeki* as well. The problem of the mere existence of the monster is not the crux around which the plot turns, as in a typical Universal horror film from the same era. Instead the monster is an avenging agent injected into the narrative to exact retribution upon the villains for the murder of the heroine, its monstrous status almost incidental to the main story. While it is the literal ghost of the main protagonist in *The Ghost Story of the Mandarin Duck Curtain*, the other two films utilise a *bakeneko* cat-spirit acting on the victim's behalf. In both *Mandarin Duck Curtain* and *Mysterious Shamisen*, the monster assumes a supporting function in the final act of revenge, which is ultimately achieved by the victim's still-living younger sister, further marginalising the monster from the centrality of the narrative. *The Cat of Arima* allows its monster to carry out the actual act of punishment itself, but of the three films it withholds its appearance the longest, only revealing the *bakeneko* in the final climatic moments and with virtually no prior foreshadowing that a *kaiki* conclusion is in store to what is otherwise a pretty mundane *jidaigeki* tale (Fig. 21.1).

On a formal level, the manner in which the monster is filmed is often little different than the way a human hero might appear in a non-*kaiki jidaigeki*. Gone is the emphasis on trick cinematography, which characterised the silent era *kaiki* films. The Shinkō pictures make sparing use of double exposure and reverse filming, the main focus of spectacle being transferred to the body of Suzuki Sumiko. Audiences delighted in seeing the sexiness of the onetime silent cinema vamp transformed into the grotesque half-woman, half-cat *bakeneko* spirit, and the films downplay special effects in favour of a more physical (and physically present) monster. While Ushihara employs some creative tricks such as a kaleidoscope effect to portray his *bakeneko* as a more ethereal presence in the film's diegesis,

Fig. 21.1 Japan's first monster-movie star, Suzuki Sumiko, in *bakeneko* ('ghost-cat') form and fighting a host of human adversaries in *The Cat of Arima/Arima neko* (Mokudō Shigeru, 1937, Shinkō Kinema).

Mokudō's monsters are most often shot engaging the villain and their henchmen in conventionally staged, choreographed fight scenes (*tachimawari*) that are largely interchangeable with any other *jidaigeki* swordplay picture of the day. Suzuki Sumiko's wire-assisted acrobatic leaps and concrete, physical engagement against her human opponents often bear little difference from the feats of the samurai action heroes with whom she shared the matinee bill.

Early postwar *kaiki* films continued largely in this vein. Government censorship under the 1939 Film Law had effectively shut down production of all 'frivolous' *kaiki* pictures, a policy continued under the American Occupation ban on 'feudalistic' elements of *jidaigeki*, which included the revenge vendettas typical of *kaiki* narratives.[16] With the end of the Occupation, beginning in 1953, Daiei studio head Nagata Masaichi immediately reinstated the annual production of *kaiki* pictures that had been a mainstay of Shinkō, Nagata's prewar studio and one of three companies merged to create Daiei in 1941. Several of these were direct remakes of the prewar Shinkō *bakeneko* pictures, and apart from replacing Suzuki Sumiko with Irie Takako, the second great *bakeneko* actress, they replicate the old familiar formal and thematic patterns of their earlier counterparts. Arai Ryōhei's 1953 version of *The Cat of Arima* features a *tachimawari* conclusion shot in nearly identical set-up to Mokudō's 1937 film. Kato Bin's *The Ghost Cat of the Okazaki Rebellion/Kaibyō okazaki sōdō* (1954) is at pains to open with a shot of Irie's monster-cat, perhaps catering to the demands of an audience desirous to see the monster frontloaded in the style of Hollywood horror films, but Kato achieves this only by starting his picture with a brief flash-forward sequence, subsequently banishing his monster from the screen until the 60-minute mark of a less than 90-minute picture.

Articles and reviews of the time from *Kinema junpō* suggest that there was a growing dissatisfaction with the established *kaiki* formula. The critics who were once dismissive of the genre altogether now seemed more willing to engage *kaiki* films on their own terms, yet they invariably complained that the Daiei pictures with their third-act monsters lacked enough genuine scares. *Junpō*'s review of Arai's *Cat of Arima* remake typifies the attitude of the day when it says, 'The film-makers didn't have a single truly creepy (*kai-i*) idea [...] before it would frighten the children in the audience, it would more naturally induce howls of laughter.'[17] Audiences too were more demanding that the pictures should focus more on the horrific potential latent in the strange and bizarre world of *kaiki*.[18] Partly in response to these desires, another B-studio, Shintōhō, would take the first steps towards the turn from *kaiki* to *horā*.

MARVELLOUSLY TERRIFYING: SHINTŌHŌ STUDIOS, NAKAGAWA NOBUO AND *KAIKI*'S UNCANNY TURN TO HORROR

Although both prewar and early postwar Japanese *kaiki* films occasionally employed conventions also found in Hollywood horror, such as thunder and lightning effects, expressionistic shadows and double-exposure, see-through ghosts, we have also seen how *kaiki* could by and large differ from horror via a comparatively marginal privileging of the monster in terms of plot and its *tachimawari* fight set pieces, thus giving the monster both thematic and formal similarity to the samurai heroes of *jidaigeki*. The *kaiki* pictures produced by the Shintōhō studio in the latter half of the 1950s, however, took the genre in some striking new directions. Despite the studio's reputation for lurid exploitation, its *kaiki* output was the most critically acclaimed in the history of the genre. The most significant of these films were directed by Nakagawa Nobuo under orders from studio boss Ōkura Mitsugi, who attempted to save the financially floundering studio by moving into the production of *kaiki* and other disreputable yet popular genres. Ōkura treated these pictures as A-list efforts, assigning the studio's top talent to work on what the other studios would dash off as programme pictures in between major projects, and several of Shintōhō's *kaiki* films were shot in widescreen and colour, an extravagance the struggling studio could only afford for a select few productions each year.[19] Along with the art director Kurosawa Haruyasu, Nakagawa brought the genre newfound critical respect and laid the groundwork for much of the style that would eventually inform the J-horror movement decades later.

The studio's first significant *kaiki* hit was Mōri Masaki's revival of *The Ghost Story of Yotsuya* (1956), which had been adapted for cinema more than twenty times before the war. Kinoshita Keisuke filmed a two-part production in 1949, but had virtually eliminated the *kaiki* elements. Shintōhō's version, meanwhile, amplified the lurid aspects of the original 1825 kabuki play and featured a degree of on-screen blood, violence and implied sexuality that was, for the time, considered rather shocking and transgressive. When the picture proved a box-office success, Ōkura implemented a policy of producing at least two new *kaiki* films each year in time for the summer *obon* season, and made sure at least one of them was made by Nakagawa, who by this time was the studio's most experienced director.[20] His first *kaiki* assignment for the studio was *The Ghost Story of Kasane's Swamp/Kaidan kasane ga fuchi* (1957), based on another classic period ghost story.[21] In some ways *Kasane's Swamp* is very much a traditional Japanese *kaiki* film. Like *Yotsuya*, the monster is the disfigured female ghost of a jilted wife, and as with the Shinkō and Daiei *kaiki* films, its appearance is withheld until late in the picture's runtime. Yet the script deliberately weaves ghostly, uncanny elements into the narrative at steady intervals, foreshadowing the eventual appearance of the monster and sustaining a sense of dread throughout, rather than suddenly unleashing the monstrous near the climax as in *The Cat of Arima*. Perhaps even more significant is the manner in which Nakagawa presents these *kaiki* moments. Like his Shinkō and Daiei counterparts, Nakagawa includes ample shots of his ghost engaging with the human characters in a direct, physical manner, but he also crafts scenes that create a subtler sense of horror by only implying the presence of the monster. Following the death of his wife, the male protagonist flees with his mistress to a tea house, taking a private room upstairs. Upon settling in they realise the maid has prepared three cups of tea, and when they enquire as to the reason, the maid tells them the third cup is for the woman who accompanied them upstairs. The horrified looks of the adulterous couple followed by a close-up of the third teacup are all Nakagawa requires to infuse the moment with an uncanny horror that exemplifies the 'less-is-more' aesthetic prized by many horror film-makers and aficionados.[22]

This turn from a Todorovian world of the Marvelous towards a greater emphasis on a more

Freudian sense of the uncanny represents a key innovation of the Shintōhō *kaiki* films. Prior to the Shintōhō pictures, most Japanese *kaiki* films were more firmly rooted in Tzvetan Todorov's 'Pure Marvelous', one of the literary genres he posits in his study of 'Fantastic' literature. These are narratives in which the existence of magic or the supernatural is understood from the outset to be part-and-parcel of the diegetic cosmology, and the presence of a ghost or monster provokes no sense of disbelief in the other characters.[23] The premodern *jidaigeki* worlds of the typical *kaiki* film fit this description perfectly, where the appearance of a ghost or a *bakeneko* may instil fear but not disbelief among the Edo period characters. This potentially dilutes the sense of horror for the modern-day audience, who approach the filmic text as representing a closed-off fantasy world dislocated from our own, and indeed excludes the majority of *kaiki* films entirely from some of the major theoretical conceptualisations of the horror genre, which depend on the figure of the monster as representing a rupture in the presumed cosmological make-up of the diegetic world.[24] *The Ghost Story of Kasane's Swamp* also fits the 'Pure Marvelous' mould, but moments such as the teahouse scene transcend the safe distance of the film's fantasy setting, creating a sense of horror via an invocation of the Freudian uncanny. Todorov limits his 'Uncanny' to a scenario in which seemingly supernatural occurrences receive a rational explanation at the conclusion of the story, but the uncanny as Freud conceptualises it is less concerned with narrative structures and more about the emotion of fear engendered by coincidences and repetitions across time and space, which suggest the existence of magical forces beyond explanation. These moments can exist independent of any narrative explanation and thus overcome the sense of aesthetic distance engendered by a 'Pure Marvellous' setting.[25]

Nakagawa's *kaiki* follow-up to *Kasane's Swamp*, the *bakeneko* picture *Mansion of the Ghost Cat/Bōrei kaibyō yashiki* (1958) best illustrates how this use of the uncanny was reshaping the genre along more horrific lines (Fig. 21.2). Spurred on by the critical and commercial success of *Kasane's Swamp*, *Mansion of the Ghost Cat* became the studio's first colour, widescreen *kaiki* production. The long middle section of the film presents an all-colour *jidaigeki* ghost-cat tale much like its black-and-white Daiei counterparts, but by bookending the period piece with a monochrome prologue and epilogue set in the modern day, Nakagawa's *bakeneko* film does something truly innovative with the old familiar

Fig. 21.2. Nakagawa Nobuo's *Mansion of the Ghost Cat/Bōrei kaibyō yashiki* (1958, Shintōhō).

kaiki formula. The picture begins with a doctor's wife being haunted by the mysterious spirit of an old woman who appears suddenly in the middle of the night, eventually causing the wife to fall into an unexplained illness. The doctor's visit to a nearby Buddhist temple reveals the old woman is the lingering spirit of a *bakeneko*, which had plagued his wife's ancestors. Rather like *The Wizard of Oz* (1939), the film then moves from a black-and-white everyday world to a full-colour fantasy, recounting the origins of the *bakeneko* curse in a marvellous Edo wonderland in which characters and audiences alike would expect to find a ghost-cat or two lurking in the shadows. But to see the traditional *kaiki* monster removed from its contained setting and deposited into the monochromatic, yet infinitely more relatable, present day creates an entirely different atmosphere. The uncanny rupture of the boundaries between the marvellous and the mundane worlds makes the *kaiki* presence truly disturbing.

Comparing the way in which the film alternately frames its monster in the present-day and period sequences demonstrates how the effect is achieved. The *jidaigeki* sequence does not shy away from showing its *bakeneko* in a direct fashion. She appears in close-up in high-key lighting, and can be seen leaping about the wicked samurai's palace with the same wire-assisted acrobatics that mark the Suzuki Sumiko and Irie Takako vehicles. On a narrative level this is the same monster that we see in the modern-day sequences, yet her presentation is strikingly different here as Nakagawa keeps his camera at a distance, rarely showing the monster's obscured face, and the conventional leaps and bounds of the ghost-cat are discarded for a slow, deliberate creeping action. When possible the camera avoids showing the monster altogether, implying its stalking presence via point-of-view shots from the monster's perspective that would become a hallmark of the slasher film in later decades. As reviews and audience polls indicate, the wholly marvellous worlds of more conventional *kaiki* films were found wanting for effective scares, but plucking the monstrous out of the marvellous and depositing it in the mundane meant that the fantasy bogies of the premodern past suddenly took on a genuinely horrific quality (Fig. 21.3).

Mansion of the Ghost Cat was another critical and commercial success for the studio and Shintōhō followed up the film with the similarly themed *Ghost Cat of Otama Pond* in 1960, the directorial debut of Nakagawa's assistant director, Ishikawa Yoshihiro, which also featured a contemporarily set prologue invaded by monsters from the premodern past. The studio would further continue the trend of setting *kaiki* pictures in the modern day with works such as

Fig. 21.3 A monster from the past invades the present in *Mansion of the Ghost Cat/Bōrei kaibyō yashiki* (Nakagawa Nobuo, 1958, Shintōhō).

Lady Vampire/*Onna kyūketsuki* and *Diving Girls in a Haunted House*/*Ama no obake yashiki* (both 1959), two films which also demonstrated a more obvious debt to Western horror film by adapting the European vampire and the Gothic haunted house mystery to a Japanese setting. Yet it is not the vampires in Bela Lugosi tuxedos and creaky Gothic mansions that make these *kaiki* more horrific so much as setting them in a modern, rational world where their mere existence proves an uncanny anomaly (even if the ghosts in *Diving Girls* are ultimately revealed, in Scooby-Doo fashion, to be criminals posing as ghosts to scare people off).

FORMALIST FEARS AND MONSTROUS MONTAGE

Most important of all, however, was the marshalling of cinematic techniques in the service of conveying a sense of dread on a formal level. The importance of Nakagawa's sophisticated film-making in creating genuinely horrific *kaiki* films can be seen even when entirely in the Pure Marvellous mode, as in what is widely held to be the director's masterpiece and the best of the many screen versions of *The Ghost Story of Yotsuya* (1959). Just three years after Mōri's version of the tale had inaugurated Shintōhō's run of *kaiki* pictures, Ōkura decided to revisit the grand dame of Japanese ghost stories in a full colour, widescreen production with Nakagawa as the film's director. The difference in the two films runs much deeper than the mere technological innovations. A comparative look at the pivotal moment in both Mōri's and Nakagawa's respective films, in which the viewer gets their first look at the ghastly, poison-disfigured face of the tale's heroine, Oiwa, demonstrates the superior horrific affect of the latter film. Mōri stages his reveal in a basic shot-reverse-shot set-up. After unwittingly drinking poison, Oiwa clutches her face, moans in pain and falls to the floor. The camera quickly cuts to a close-up of the startled, horrified reaction of the servant Takuetsu, then quickly cuts back to a high-angle reverse shot of the now disfigured Oiwa on the floor, her grotesque deformity plainly revealed by the high-key lighting. Nakagawa's film, conversely, delays the reveal of Oiwa's face to create an atmosphere of dread and suspense. As in Mōri's film, the horrified reaction of Takuetsu anticipates the reveal, but instead of a close-up, Nakagawa frames the moment in a wide shot that includes the figure of Oiwa laying on the floor in the foreground. Low-key lighting keeps her face hidden from the viewer, and there is no cut as Oiwa slowly, agonisingly crawls to her mirror. Finally the camera cuts to a point-of-view shot of the mirror itself, Oiwa's trembling hand slowly entering the frame to remove the mirror's cover, and the viewer's first glimpse of her hideous face is that of her own shocked, horrified reaction in the mirror. The intrusion of Oiwa's ghost on her unfaithful husband's wedding night is handled in a similar fashion. Mōri again gives us a simple shot-reverse-shot in high-key lighting, first of Oiwa's wicked husband Iemon gazing at his new bride Oume, then a cut to an over-the-shoulder shot in which Oiwa's ghost rises up into the frame from Oume's position. Nakagawa, meanwhile, stages the moment in a single take, having Oume demurely drop out of the frame as if lying on the nuptial bed, only to have the hideous Oiwa slowly rise back up into the frame from Oume's place to a menacing crescendo of *doro-doro* drums. Here Nakagawa demonstrates that by *not* cutting the camera, the effect of horror may be increased, contrary to the comparatively rapid cutting of Mōri's film.

The climax of Nakagawa's version, a delirious montage of images that depict Oiwa's final assault on Iemon, also stands in sharp contrast to the straightforward *tachimawari* fight with the monster that concluded most *kaiki* films prior to Shintōhō's innovations. Rather than have the monster physically engage its victim in a choreographed confrontation in the manner of Suzuki Sumiko and Irie Takako, Nakagawa barely even shows Oiwa and Iemon in the same frame. Instead, Oiwa's ephemeral, spectral presence is conveyed via a series of quick montage shots, suggesting she is at once everywhere and nowhere, making escape impossible for the increasingly unsettled Iemon. Simultaneously pursued by Oiwa's sister and brother-in-law, Iemon finally attempts to flee straight towards the camera, only to have Oiwa's ghost suddenly fly in to fill the frame in close-up. The sequence never resorts to the double-exposure technique of filming a see-through ghost, making Oiwa a physical, concrete and more threatening presence, yet her ghostly status is effectively conveyed via a montage assault of images rather than a physical assault on her victim.[26]

A year after the release of Nakagawa's *Ghost Story of Yotsuya*, Shintōhō would finally collapse, bringing its brief but influential run of *kaiki* films to a close, although the other studios would continue in the direction pioneered by Nakagawa and his crew. The 1960s proved to be the twilight of the *kaiki* genre, but it was a fertile twilight, as directors at Daiei and Tōei strove to follow Shintōhō's lead and portray their ghosts and monsters in a more experimental fashion that would utilise the cinematic medium to convey a sense of horror. Traditional *kaidan* adaptations continued to appear, but with an eye to emulating the montage and *mise en scène* of Nakagawa, while directors such as Satō Hajime made greater use of *kaiki* elements in modern-day settings to activate a sense of the uncanny in pictures such as *The Ghost Story of the Hunchback/Kaidan semushi otoko* (1965). Tōhō even tried to directly imitate the Hammer Dracula series with the so-called 'Bloodsucking Trilogy' (*Chi o sū no sannbusaku*, 1970–4). Although the genre finally faded away by the mid-1970s, this final decade of *kaiki* production, spearheaded by the achievements of Shintōhō and Nakagawa, left a profound impression on the young generation who would grow up to resurrect many of the motifs and techniques of latter-day *kaiki* in the form of J-horror.[27]

CONCLUSION: THE *KAIKI* LEGACY OF J-HORROR

The concurrent arrival of the home video market and the American slasher film in the early 1980s not only brought the word *horā* to Japanese shores but set the course for more than a decade of Japanese horror cinema that would stand diametrically opposed to *kaiki* conventions. Typified by the work of director Miike Takashi, the direct-to-video *horā* cinema of the 1980s and 1990s frequently exceeded its Western counterparts in depictions of explicit gore and acts of brutality. Trading the period settings and stylised sets of *kaiki eiga* for more economical urban location shooting, this trend in 'splatter' (*spurattā*) aesthetics reached its artistic apex in Miike's *Audition* in 2000. The film's international success briefly cemented the image abroad that Japanese horror cinema's distinguishing feature was a shocking excess of graphic violence. This proved a short-lived preconception, however, as the worldwide success of the J-horror pictures at the turn of the millennium – with their partial return to the atmospheric techniques of *kaiki eiga* – usurped the ultra-violent slasher film's place as the representative face of Japanese horror cinema.

As mentioned at the outset of this chapter, Japanese film scholars and aficionados make a clear distinction between *kaiki* and *J-horā*, marked not only by a film's age but its narrative and formal approach to portraying the monstrous. The Shintōhō pictures had made the first move towards a more *horā*-esque style, but both Nakagawa's films and the ones that immediately appeared in his wake retained ample *kaiki* elements as well, featuring period settings or else an explicitly Gothic ambience suggesting the action takes place in some Othered space. The J-horror pictures that first appeared in the 1990s, meanwhile, appear on the surface to be largely stripped of traditional *kaiki* trappings such as ghost-cats and large, creepy mansions. Several of the major creative players in the J-horror movement, however, admit to a strong *kaiki* influence in their work. While Western ghost films such as *The Innocents* (1961) and *The Haunting* (1963) are the most often cited sources of inspiration, figures such as the director Kurosawa Kiyoshi and the screenwriter of *Ring*, Takahashi Hiroshi, acknowledge that the central recurring motif of J-horror, the ubiquitous 'long-haired ghost girl', has her origins in the *kaiki* films of Nakagawa and his contemporaries.[28] The most iconic image of J-horror is the ghost, Sadako, emerging from the well at the climax of *Ring*, which deliberately recollects the legend of Okiku's ghost in *The Dish Mansion at Banchō*. The iconography of the female *onryō*, or vengeful ghost, can be traced back at least as far as Edo period woodblocks and painted scrolls, but it was in the *kaiki* films of the postwar years that she was given the concrete physicality that impressed future film-makers such as Kurosawa, who strove to replicate the effect of a ghost that was alternately ethereal and yet corporally present and threatening in films such as *Pulse/Kairo* (2001) and *Retribution/Sakebi* (2006). Beyond the formal level, the uncanny presence of a traditional monster such as the *onryō* in the high-tech, postmodern landscapes of J-horror evokes the same sense of the uncanny that *kaiki* pictures such as *Mansion of the Ghost Cat* and *The Ghost Cat of Otama Pond* achieved by displacing the monsters of the past into the present. J-horror, however, goes a step beyond the Shintōhō ghost-cat pictures by wholly removing its monsters from their *kaiki* landscapes. To encounter the uncanny *kaiki* in the contemporarily set Shintōhō pictures, the protagonists must first journey to some suitably *kaiki* locale, such as the old, dilapidated dwelling of the wife's ancestors in *Mansion of the Ghost Cat*. In *Ring*, the haunted well journeys to the protagonists, appearing in their very living rooms via a cursed videotape that brings the monster directly into the heart of everyday existence.

Sadako crawling out of her well seems a fitting place to end this discussion of Japanese *kaiki* and *horā* cinema, evoking as she does the uncanny on multiple levels. The long-haired ghost girls of J-horror represent the return of the repressed – the bogies of centuries-old *kaidan* legends no longer harmlessly contained in the marvellous past but quite literally reaching out through the screen to get us. But they are also the ghosts of *kaiki* cinema itself, harkening back to that precious bit of surviving silent-era footage of Okiku's spirit crawling out of her own well in a spectacular display of the uncanny miracle of cinema. What once thrilled early cinema audiences now also returns to chill new ones to the bone.

Notes

1. Jay McRoy (ed.), *Japanese Horror Cinema* (Edinburgh: Edinburgh University Press, 2005).
2. Mitsuyo Wada-Marciano, 'J-horror: New Media's Impact on Contemporary Japanese Horror Cinema', in Jinhee Choi and Mitsuyo Wada-Marciano (eds), *Horror to the Extreme: Changing Boundaries in Asian Cinema* (Hong Kong: Hong Kong University Press, 2009), p. 34.
3. For example, the website *Japanzine*'s list of 'Alternative J-Horror' includes *Ugetsu*, the musical black comedy *Happiness of the Katakuris/Katakuri ke no kōfuku* (2001), and S&M soft-core offerings *Guinea Pig 2: Flower of Flesh and Blood/Ginī piggu 2: Chiniku no hana* (1985) and *Flower and Snake/Hana to hebi* (2004). See 'J-horror: An Alternative Guide', <http://www.japanzine.jp/article/jz/955/jhorror-an-alternative-guide>.
4. Chika Kinoshita, 'The Mummy Complex: Kurosawa Kiyoshi's *Loft* and J-horror', in Choi and Wada-Marciano, *Horror to the Extreme*, p. 104.
5. Uchiyama Kazuki, 'Nihon eiga no kaiki to gensō', in Uchiyama Kazuki (ed.), *Kaiki to gensō e no kairo: Kaidan kara J-horā e* (Tokyo: Shinwasha, 2008), p. 26.
6. Godzilla and his ilk christened the genre of *kaijū* films, which means 'strange beast' but might be better rendered as 'giant monster', as *kaijū* are invariably as tall as skyscrapers. These pictures usually were seen as distinct from the *kaiki* genre. In a July 1957 article for *Kinema junpō*, Izawa Jun explains why *kaijū* films lack the relevance of true *kaiki* films ('Kaiki to wa?', *Kinema junpō*, 1 July 1957, p. 45), and the magazine's special edition from August 1969 devoted entirely to 'Kaiki to kyōfu' (or '*Kaiki and Horror*') omits all *kaijū* films from its pages.
7. As Robert Spadoni discusses in *Uncanny Bodies: The Coming of Sound Film and the Origins of the Horror Genre* (Berkeley: University of California Press, 2007), the term does not appear until the mid-1930s. Murakami Hisao's review of *Dracula* for the 21 October 1931 issue of *Kinema junpō*, meanwhile, opens by calling it 'a *kaiki eiga* about vampires'.
8. Author's interview with Kurosawa Kiyoshi, 3 June 2013.
9. Polling viewers as to their reasons for attending *kaiki eiga* in 1957, Yanagi Masako found the most common response was 'to see something scary' (*kowai mono mita sa*). See Yanagi Masako, 'Kaiki eiga to kankyaku', *Kinema junpō*, 1 July 1957, p. 51. Critical complaints that domestic *kaiki eiga* were not frightening can be found in the *Kinema junpō* reviews for *The Legend of the Saga Ghost Cat/Saga kaibyōden*, (1937), *The Ghost Cat of Arima Palace/Kaibyō Arima goten* (1953) and *The Ghost Cat and the Clockwork Ceiling/Kaibyō karakuri tenjō* (1958), among others.
10. [Editors' note: for a wider discussion of *jidaigeki*, see also Chapter 20 by Philip Kaffen in this volume.]
11. Kurosawa Kiyoshi and Shinozaki Makoto, *Kurosawa Kiyoshi no kyōfu no eigashi* (Tokyo: Seidosha, 2003), p. 40.

12 Q&A with Sasaki Hirohisa, 13 April 2013.
13 The term 'jidaigeki' was not in use when Makino was making his films.
14 Kamiya Masako estimates the film was made during the 1910s. See 'Nihon eiga no kaiki to trick', in Kazuki, *Kaiki to gensō e no kairo*, pp. 38–40.
15 Shimura Miyoko, 'Shinkō kinema no kaibyō eiga', *Eigagaku* no. 14 (2000), pp. 51–63.
16 Ibid.
17 Ogi Masahiro, 'Kaibyō Arima goten', *Kinema junpō*, 15 February 1954, p. 65.
18 Yanagi, 'Kaiki eiga to kankyaku'.
19 Shimura Miyoko, '"Misemono" kara "eiga" e: Shintōhō no kaibyō eiga', *Engeki eizō* no. 43 (2003), pp. 13–21.
20 Ōsawa Jō, 'Shintōhō no obake eiga to "Tōkaidō yotsuya kaidan": Genre no fukkatsu to kakushin', in Kazuki, *Kaiki to gensō e no kairo*, pp. 68–94.
21 Nakagawa's 1956 *jidaigeki*, *The Ceiling at Utsunomiya/Utsunomiya no tenjō*, is sometimes listed among the director's *kaiki* works, but the ghostly elements figure only in a brief subplot largely negligible to the main story.
22 According to Kawabe Juji, this moment was not included in the original shooting script and was improvised on set. See *B-kyū kyoshōron: Nakagawa Nobuo kenkyū* (Tokyo: Shizukado, 1983), pp. 122–4.
23 Tzvetan Todorov, *The Fantastic: A Structural Approach to a Literary Genre*, trans. Richard Howard (Ithaca, NY: Cornell University Press, 1975), pp. 41–5.
24 Noël Carroll considers this an absolutely essential element of the horror genre. See *The Philosophy of Horror* (New York: Routledge, 1990), p. 16. Izumi Toshiyuki also says the monster in a *kaiki* film must come 'from beyond the limits of human understanding' and 'represent a threat to rational human thought', which ironically can be understood to disqualify a great many films he goes on to discuss as *kaiki*. See Izumi Toshiyuki, *Ginmaku no hyakkai: Honchō kaiki eiga taigai* (Tokyo: Seidosha, 2000), p. 21.
25 Freud concludes his essay on the uncanny with the caveat 'The uncanny that we find in fiction – in creative writing, imaginative literature – actually deserves to be considered separately. […] The imaginative writer may have invented a world that, while less fantastic than that of the fairy tale, differs from the real world in that it involves supernatural entities such as demons or spirits of the dead. Within the limits set by the presuppositions of this literary reality, such figures forfeit any uncanny quality that might otherwise attach to them.' I would disagree with Freud here, for such moments as the teacup scene in *Kasane's Swamp* do have an uncanny affect for many viewers, perhaps suggesting that the Bazinian realism of the cinematic image can overcome the overtly marvellous nature of the fiction it portrays or (more likely) the viewer's ability to imagine a similarly uncanny experience in the real world may also lift the moment out of the marvellous narrative as a felt uncanny experience. See Sigmund Freud, *The Uncanny*, trans. David McLintock (New York: Penguin, 2003), pp. 155–6.
26 For a more detailed discussion of Nakagawa's use of montage, see Hirose Ai, 'Eiga "Yotsuya kaidan" kō: Nakagawa Nobuo no jikkenteki kaiki hyōgen', *Shōkei gakuin daigaku kiyōdai*, 2 September 2011, pp. 47–62.
27 As Kurosawa Kiyoshi explained to me, 'Nakagawa provided the model, but it wasn't just him that was producing this imagery. […] We (the J-Horror filmmakers) are influenced by the entirety of ghost imagery from that era.' Author's interview with Kurosawa Kiyoshi, 3 June 2013.
28 Takahashi confirmed Kurosawa's comments to this effect in an interview on 19 June 2013.

22

ANIME
Compositing and switching: An intermedial history of Japanese anime

Thomas Lamarre

The term anime (pronounced animé) is an abbreviation of the Japanese pronunciation of the word animation (*animēshon*). As such, the scope of the term may differ greatly in accordance with the context in which it is used. For North American fans, for instance, anime indicates animations made in Japan for a Japanese audience, and the term is largely synonymous with the neologism 'Japanimation'. Debates sometimes rage among anime fans, however, because there are animated series produced in Japan for non-Japanese audiences that nonetheless utilise the basic conventions associated with anime. Take, for instance, *Cybersix* (1999), adapted from an Argentine comic, produced and directed in Japan for a Canadian audience, and later released in Japan with a Japanese dub. Although it feels like anime, *Cybersix* is sometimes not deemed to be anime because it was not originally made for the Japanese market. Similarly, the heavy use of outsource studios in South Korea, China and the Philippines in producing anime tends to encourage a definition of anime less in terms of site of production and more in terms of the targeted audience. Fans, when they insist on a Japanese audience, tend to impart a Japanese cultural unity to the form.[1]

The increased visibility of the global fandom for anime since the 1990s has certainly affected the meanings of anime in Japan.[2] Government initiatives have emerged since the late 1990s to build on the global success of 'Japanese animation' with the aim of increasing the export potential and global market share of Japan's multimedia franchises under the rubric of the 'contents industry'.[3] Their take on anime differs from that of fans, however. Although government initiatives also stress the Japaneseness of anime and related products, they avoid defining anime as animation produced in Japan for a Japanese market. Their emphasis veers towards design or conceptualisation: anime is construed as something generated in Japan, whose production may be outsourced, provided it is made in accordance with Japanese design concepts (duly licensed), for local or global audiences, and ideally for both. In other words, even when anime is defined as Japanese animation, there are different, potentially incompatible ways of demarcating its relation to Japan, not to mention competing ways of demarcating Japan and Japaneseness.

In other contexts within Japan, such as rental and retail stores, the term anime may comprise animation in general, regardless of where it is made and for whom. In yet other contexts, particularly those in which different lineages of Japanese animation are acknowledged and contrasted, the term is commonly used to refer more specifically to television anime (*telebi anime*) in contrast to original animated films produced for theatrical release. The Studio Ghibli animation director Miyazaki Hayao, for instance, distinguishes his studio's animated films from anime, placing them in the prewar lineage of *manga eiga* or cartoon films, which continues into *dōga* or 'animated pictures' of the postwar era, particularly those of Tōei.[4]

In sum, on the contemporary scene, anime is clearly a baggy term, which ranges from designating animation in general, to singling out a distinctively Japanese style, concept or culture, to delineating a specific lineage of television animation within Japan (in contrast to *manga eiga* or to *dōga*, for instance). The protean nature of the term anime is a function of the vast and unruly variety of animations produced in, for or by Japan. Even in its most constrained usage, anime still comprises so many different forms, formats, genres, franchise strategies and markets that it is impossible to define it in any one simple way. Different takes on anime imply different sets of interests and divergent worldviews, and frequently they mobilise those interests or worldviews explicitly. As such, a simple neutral definition of what anime is, is impossible, as is a neutral account of the relationship between anime and cinema. Nonetheless, even if a simple neutral take remains out of reach, an exploration of the historical contours of different paradigms for situating or defining anime may contribute to a better understanding of the complexity of anime, and may afford a keener sense of what is at stake in 'doing anime', whether as a producer or user, a connoisseur or scholar.[5] To this end, four paradigms for anime may be proposed, in a loosely chronological fashion.

First, the art historical paradigm (up to 1930) typically comes to the fore in accounting for the art sources or origins of Japanese animation, usually pivoting on the pre-cinematic history of Japanese animation or on the early years of cinema, or both. Second, the cinematic paradigm (1930–60) becomes salient when the point of reference is theatrical release animations and thus the period when animation was predominantly experienced in movie theatres, as cinema. The third paradigm, centred on television (1960–90), comes to the fore with the popular success of animated television series in the early 1960s, which led to the rapid proliferation and diversification of animated series and patterns of serialisation, which was in turn intensified with the expansion of television media to include videocassette recorders and home video game consoles through the 1970s and 1980s. Finally, by the end of the 1980s, transformations in media infrastructures and platforms culminated in the proclamation of an era of 'new media' in Japan, which might also be called, to acknowledge the continued importance of broadcast television, the era of 'new television' (1990–2015). Each of these paradigms implies a transformation in the relation between anime and cinema. The exploration of 'what animation is' within these different paradigms thus provides a useful point of departure for evaluating 'what cinema is' or more precisely, 'what cinema and anime may be'.

ANIMATION ARTS (UP TO 1930)

Animation has traditionally relied on artwork, generally making the use of colour, line, texture, form, design and composition (to name a few concerns) into a major source of attraction. For much of its history, animation has depended on the sequential photography of handcrafted images or models, and animators have often come to animation with a background in art and with experience as artists. In fact, animation is sometimes distinguished from cinema due to its extensive usage of art to be photographed. Such a bias persists in the contemporary post-digital distinction between live action cinema and animation. Digital animation is sometimes purported to entail a manually produced reality in contrast to the photographed reality of cinema.[6] The history of trick photography and of special effects in cinema provides a reminder that such a distinction is, at best, a fluid one: so-called live-action cinema has wholeheartedly embraced manually produced realities throughout its history. Nonetheless, for all its continuity with cinema, animation does indeed tend to deploy artwork differently than cinema. Animation not only uses artwork more extensively than cinema does but also it uses artwork that is generally smaller in scale. This relatively small-scale art gravitates towards set-ups reminiscent of miniature theatre or small-scale dioramas, or illustrated books and hand scrolls, or today, the computer screen. This combination of factors explains why the analysis of animation has often focused on the parameters of artwork, and why the sources of animation have been sought in art, with a consequent emphasis on art historical parameters of line, colour, design, composition or some other formal feature. A propensity thus arises to situate the sources of animation in art forms prior to or outside cinema.

The artist Murakami Takashi made the boldest gesture in this direction with his conceptualisation of a superflat lineage of Japanese art in 2000.[7] Building on the art historian Tsuji Nobuo's account of an eccentric or idiosyncratic lineage in artworks of the Edo period (1603–1868),[8] Murakami singled out a style of composition based on flattening the sense of depth across the multiple planes or layers of the image.[9] As a result of this flattening of depth, the viewer's eye, unable to move into depth, moved erratically across the surface of the image, restlessly zigzagging, in a manner that anticipated contemporary ways of scanning for information. Murakami found the same operations at work in a range of contemporary Japanese artworks (and in some American ones as well), and especially in anime. The work of animator Kanada Yoshinori on animated television series such as *Galaxy Express 999/Ginga tetsudō 999* (1978–81) figured prominently in the genealogy of superflat, for instance. Perhaps not surprisingly, the superflat lineage largely ignores cinema as well as connections between cinema and anime. Anime is situated in what is, in effect, a Japanese lineage of new media or computational media, retroactively constructed around traditional art forms in a (successful) bid to move Japanese pop art into the forefront of the global art marketplace.

In contrast, the Studio Ghibli director Takahata Isao has proposed that, as early as the twelfth century, Japanese illustrated hand scrolls (*emakimono*) were already like cinema (*eiga-teki*) and like animation (*anime-teki*), both in terms of the movement implied in their sequential layout of images and in terms of the simple brushwork used to render characters in comic manner.[10] In his discussion, Takahata draws on the venerable lineage of 'Toba pictures' (*Toba-e*), a form largely consolidated in the eighteenth century, which drew inspiration from works attributed to Toba Sōjō such as the twelfth-century *Scrolls of Frolicking Animals and Humans/Chōjū jimbutsu giga emaki*. Takahata finds the origins of Japanese animation in this tradition. Yet, despite its extensive descriptions of features within *emakimono*, Takahata's account is intentionally prescriptive, even normative. He does not claim that all Japanese animation derives from or looks like *emakimono*. He wishes to single out and promote a tradition of artful animation with Japanese characteristics, comparable for instance with the work of French animator Paul Grimault.[11] As his emphasis both on 'cinema-like' and 'animation-like' features attests, Takahata's goal is an *animation cinema* with Japanese characteristics.

Takahata's gesture meshes with that of his Ghibli colleague Miyazaki Hayao, when Miyazaki styles his work as manga film in contrast with anime. Indeed, in 2004, a major exhibition toured Japan that proposed a lineage of manga films, beginning with the manga films of the 1920s and 1930s, spanning the Tōei animated films or *dōga* through the 1950s and 1960s, and culminating in the works of Studio Ghibli in the 1980s and 1990s.[12] The exhibition defined manga films as distinctively Japanese and as 'animated films for cinema release with high degrees of originality. They also must have a happy ending or else evoke strong optimism.'[13] In keeping with this overall initiative, Takahata's contribution was to piece together an art historical lineage that provides Japanese characteristics for Ghibli's manga films or animation cinema. Needless to say, as with the concept with superflat, the gesture is retroactive: Takahata begins with the perspective of animation cinema, seeking traditional Japanese arts that may be read cinematically, whose techniques may be incorporated into animation.[14] This conceptualisation of the relation between traditional arts and the modern art of animation cinema plays out in greater complexity across his movies, such as *Pom Poko/Heisei tanuki gassen ponpoko* (1994), *My Neighbours the Yamadas/Tonari no Yamada-kun* (1999) and *The Tale of Princess Kaguya/Kaguya-hime no monogatari* (2013).

In sum, in the 2000s, in response to the global success of Japanese animation, two powerful bids appeared to ground it within very different art historical paradigms. Murakami's lineage of superflat evokes a breezily postmodern remix of surfaces without depth, whose pop ebullience verges on a dissociative experience of Japanese history – the buoyant apocalypse of playfully militarised little boys surfing the shock waves of atomic blasts and global destruction. Ghibli's reprise of the idea of a cinema with Japanese characteristics adopts the stance of a beleaguered liberal humanism, the waning tides of national modernism with its historical dreams and moral optimism. Murakami's lineage grasps the art of anime from the perspective of multimedia franchises, while Ghibli's lineage strives to limit the art of animation to stand-alone theatrical release movies. The two stances are highly polarised on many levels, signalling a deeper schism within the contemporary context of Japanese animation.

Now, given that both stances are highly ambitious and idiosyncratic in their historical reach, it is fair to ask whether they afford any insight into the actual historical complexity of animation art in Japan or whether they ultimately suppress it to promote their overarching worldview of art. With all their faults, they do raise one basic question unambiguously: when is animation? In other words, when (and how) does animation emerge as a distinctive mode of existence, as a form not only distinguishable from a range of other arts but also expandable and capable of assimilating other arts, making other arts feel somehow animation-like?

Transformations in media today have made it feasible, and sometimes desirable, to give animation 'mediological' priority over cinema by calling on a number of optical devices used to produce moving images, prior to the invention of the movie camera and projector, that range from rotating discs to magic lanterns. Nonetheless, when it comes to animation as a distinctive art, it is clear that such an art emerged with cinema, alongside it. As Aaron Gerow and others have shown in detail in the Japanese context, cinema as such did not spontaneously emerge with the invention of the camera and projector, but occurred through the constellation of a number of relations, including critical reception and aesthetic discourse; forms of production; circuits of distribution; exhibition practices; regulatory measures; formal conventions and audience expectations and habits – what is often called an 'apparatus' or a 'social technology'.

The same is true of animation. Until the mid-to-late 1910s, motion pictures using animation techniques – such as the sequential photography of drawings – frequently appeared as one element within a larger performance, as did motion pictures in general. With the establishment of a movement to reform motion pictures in the late 1910s, that is, to differentiate cinema from other entertainments, journals devoted to cinema began occasionally to mention animation; yet, even if its techniques were distinctive, animation was still associated with motion picture entertainment and thus swept up into the general transformation of moving pictures and thus into the apparatus or social technology emerging around cinema. This does not mean that animation was simply subordinated to and subsumed by cinema. Even as the movement to reform motion pictures was trying to distinguish the art of cinema from the received forms of theatre and stage shows, animation was trying to find a place for art techniques within cinema, particularly techniques of drawing and sketching. Early animators drew on a range of materials and styles. But a consistent problem arose: how to transform the image without having to redraw the entire image? Using pencils and erasers seems an obvious solution, but pencilled lines did not produce a sufficiently sharp image for projection, and constant erasing made for smudging and tearing. Shimokawa Ōten claimed to have made his first animated film in 1917 by drawing images in white chalk on blackboard, and then erasing and adding new lines.[15] He then turned to using black ink on white paper, and then whiting out areas to be redrawn. Finally, still in 1917, for his fifth and final film, he tried printing numerous copies of the same background and then drawing the different stage of the moving figures upon them.[16] In other words, producing motion pictures using techniques of drawing and sketching resulted in working with a gap or interval between background and foreground, in an attempt to streamline the animating process. The appeal of cut-out animation – or cut-paper animation as it was developed in Japan – is easy to understand in such a context.

Kitayama Seitarō, who was employed at Nikkatsu Studies primarily to make artful intertitles for live-action films, is frequently styled as the father of Japanese animation due to his impressive series of short animated films made in his spare time in 1917 and 1918. Among them are a number of cut-paper animations, such as the often cited *Urashima Tarō* (1918) in which Kitayama moves cut-outs of characters (sometimes with moveable limbs and features) across backgrounds, frame to frame, and intermittently produces effects of depth by using three layers, a motionless foreground and background, with the figures moving in the middle layer. The use of cut-outs significantly reduced the amount of drawing and largely eliminated the process of erasing or over-painting and redrawing, and at the same time, allowed animators to work with a layered depth within images. While experiments with various art techniques continued throughout the 1920s, it is sometimes said that animation in Japan advanced under rather severe restraints.

In particular, the price of celluloid placed constraints on experimentation with cel animation, that is, animation in which images are drawn and painted upon transparent celluloid sheets. As such, animators tended to work instead with sheets of paper, with drawings and cut-out figures, compressed and held in place with glass plates. Ōfuji Noburō emerged as a master of such techniques, experimenting with traditional Japanese papers, and held to them long after the general transition to using celluloid (Fig. 22.1). His animated short *Whale/Kujira* (1927) received screenings in France and the Soviet Union.[17] In other words, despite limitations on cel techniques, Japanese animators were nonetheless working with the same basic parameters of animation, sometimes masterfully, and often innovating with them. Consequently, in the 1930s, when celluloid became cost effective and the animation stand gradually emerged as the dominant technical apparatus for (cel) animation, Japanese animators were already familiar with and indeed had long experience with its basic operations. The animation stand is a frame allowing animators to stack multiple layers of celluloid and to alter their relative position, while photographing down through the layers from above (rostrum camera). Cel animation and the animation stand would dominate animation production for nearly sixty years, albeit with major refinements.

The multiple planes of anime images that Murakami Takashi situates within his superflat lineage derive, in fact, from the animation stand, with its layers of celluloid sheets or 'cel books' as they came to be known in Japanese. While the multilayered image of anime may indeed show some affinity with the multiple layers of Edo *ukiyo-e*, its material arrangement and technical apparatus are quite different. Likewise, while it is possible to envision, as Takahata does, an affinity

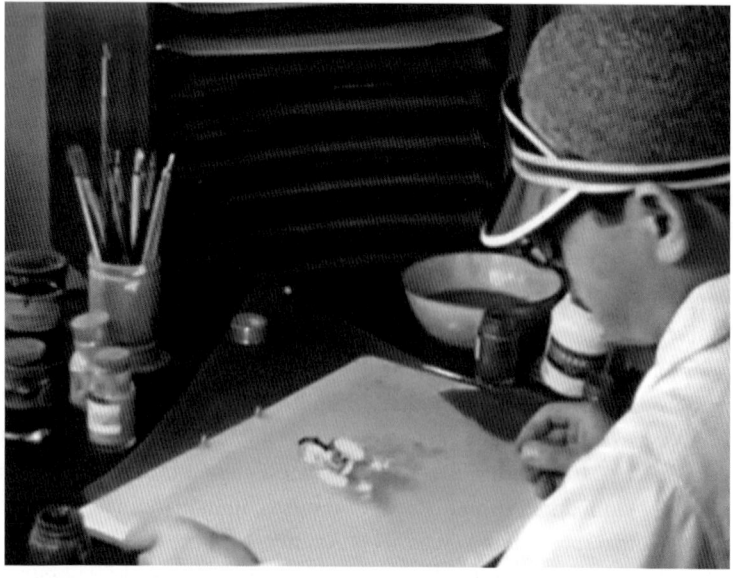

Fig. 22.1. Ōfuji Noburō working with celluloid sheets to single-handedly produce the animated short *Princess Katsura/Katsura hime* (1937). The film combined cel animation and cut-paper animation. Image taken from the 'making of film' in *Until The Colour Film Was Made/Shikisai manga no dekiru made* (Ogino Shigeji and Ōfuji Noburō, 1937, Ogina Picture).

between cartoon characters and the brushwork of Toba-e, two new techniques related to cinema utterly transformed the artwork: the process of redrawing figures or manipulating cut-outs to generate motion with pictures and the use of ink to make bold simple lines suitable for cinematic projection. Here the ink work of Otto Messmer, the Fleischer Brothers and Walt Disney was an important mediator, along with conventions developing in Japan for the use of drawings and cut-outs, not to mention a host of new manga styles stemming from the proliferation in the number and range of publication venues for comics throughout the 1910s and 1920s.

ANIMATION CINEMA (1930-60)

From the late 1910s through the 1920s, a number of other factors affected the relation between animation and cinema, as cinema was taking shape as a distinctive art and apparatus and gaining in popularity. As the career of Kitayama indicates, as does that of the other putative father of Japanese animation, Masaoka Kenzō, animators typically entered film production with an art background, to work on graphics for intertitles. Studios did not focus attention on animation, because markets for it were not particularly profitable. Animated films were, above all, shorts to be shown alongside the main feature. What is more, its ready use of pranks and tricks, in conjunction with the sense that it was addressed to young audiences, made animation a suspect object in a context of increasing concern about movies encouraging juvenile delinquency.[18] Animated shorts, then, occupied the margins of the emerging cinema formation, economically and culturally. Yet, by the late 1930s, the status of animation had dramatically changed, leading to longer and increasingly sophisticated works shown in movie theatres, and eventually culminating in a feature-length animated film in 1945, *Momotaro's Divine Sea Warriors/Momotarō umi to shinpei*, directed by Seo Mitsuyo with funding from the Naval Ministry (Figs. 22.2, 22.3).

What is more, by the late 1930s, animation had become an object of critical attention in its own right. The film critic Imamura Taihei began to publish essays on animation from the mid-1930s, which formed the basis for his publication in 1941 of the world's first book centred on animation, *On the Cartoon Film/Manga eiga ron*, whose impact extended well through the 1960s, with revisions and republications in 1948 and 1965.[19] As the rubric 'cartoon film' duly indicates, the emergence of animation as a distinctive art depended on the transformation of animation into a kind of cinema. Significantly, in Imamura's work, the cartoon film was not merely a genre or subset of cinema. Instead, together with documentary film, on which Imamura also published a monograph in 1940, the cartoon film became the key to cinema. This is the wave that Studio Ghibli still wishes to ride today. Indeed, when Studio Ghibli began to promote its animated

Fig. 22.2 *Momotaro's Divine Sea Warriors/Momotarō umi to shinpei* (Seo Mitsuyo, 1945, Shōchiku).

Fig. 22.3 *Momotaro's Divine Sea Warriors/Momotarō umi to shinpei* (Seo Mitsuyo, 1945, Shōchiku).

films as 'manga films' in contrast to anime, it backed a reissue of Imamura's *Manga eiga ron* (2005), and Takahata's account of an animated cinema with Japanese characteristics draws heavily on Imamura's book.

In sum, by the late 1930s, animation had emerged in its own right, as a kind of cinema, typically under the rubric of cartoon or manga films. What contributed to the transformation of struggling animation arts on the margins of cinema into a well-fledged cinema? It is tempting to dwell on the impact of Disney, whose cartoons were salient amidst the increasingly prevalent American popular culture in 1920s Japan, especially Hollywood movies. Indeed, Disney's animated films became almost synonymous with the transformation of animated shorts into feature-length movies. Although the Fleischer Brothers's cartoons also played a significant role in the 1930s, Disney cartoons eventually emerged as the major point of reference and as the standard of excellence, both in Imamura's treatises of cartoon films and in Sergei Eisenstein's essays from roughly the same period. It is as if a host of cartoon methods (kinds of character, backgrounds, movement, sound, music, for instance) were gradually folded into the Disney machine, to the point where putting Japanese animation on par with Disney animation would become a persistent cultural nationalist trope. Famously, in 1957, Ōkawa Hiroshi, the head of Tōei studio, announced that the ambition of the Tōei Dōga or Tōei Animation was to become the Disney of the East (Fig. 22.4).[20]

Rivalry with Disney – the dream of a Japanese rupture and reinscription of the Disney machine, so to speak – is an epiphenomenon, however, a ripple on the surface arising where various socio-historical currents related to government initiatives, commercial opportunities and media circuits set up crosscurrents. Kitayama's career is again instructive, for, as early as the late 1910s, he found commercial opportunities in producing animation for public service or promotional purposes, and relocated his 'studio' (not much more than a room with basic equipment) to Osaka. The result was a lineage of animation production located in western Japan (Kansai) with a growing expertise in work geared towards commercial and government messages.[21] Also in the 1920s, government initiatives

Fig. 22.4 The trailer for Tōei studios' first feature-length animated film, *The Tale of the White Serpent/Hakujaden* (Yabushita Taiji, 1958), proudly displays the large-scale organisation of labour and technology needed to produce such a film.

to promote animation in Japan encouraged the production of educational films, not for theatrical release.[22] In the context of movie theatres, mounting concern over juvenile delinquency reinforced a trend within animation towards parables, fables, folklore, legends, myths and other traditional forms.[23] Under such conditions, gag-like antics and manic slapstick, and the elastic and plastic (deforming) potentialities of animation, were coordinated with, and gradually subordinated to, what was deemed morally appropriate or edifying for children – even if the take-home message was not always so clear-cut. In sum, by the late 1920s, animation production had gradually become stretched across two different kinds of cinema, that is, narrative entertainments and promotional or educational materials, which implied different, almost contradictory modes of address, of exhibition and of funding.

In the 1930s, various strategies emerged that effectively drew on both tendencies in animation, combining or assembling them in the manga film. Significantly, the manga film was eventually associated with, and sometimes classified among, 'culture films' (*bunka eiga*); especially in the context of military funded cartoon films in the 1940s, such as Seo Mitsuyo's much hyped and highly popular *Momotaro's Sea Eagles/Momotarō no umiwashi* (1943). Culture films, inspired by the German *Kulturfilm*, were documentary or educational movies contributing to the cultural education or enculturation of film audiences on a variety of topics, often with an emphasis on science and nature.[24] The association of the manga film with the cultural film not only serves as a reminder of the powerful current of educational and promotional animation in Japan but also speaks to the historical assemblage of polarised tendencies within the manga film – polarised, that is, in terms of production, exhibition and consumption. Such assembling, of course, is never neutral. In the case of *Momotaro's Sea Eagles*, the comic, slapstick or gag-like potentiality of cartoons is included only to be disavowed, with cameos by American cartoon characters such as Bluto at the bombing of Pearl Harbor, where their 'cartoonish' behaviour appears as an innate liability. Seo Mitsuyo's two Momotarō films also entailed an increasingly sophisticated use of celluloid sheets due to refinements of the animation stand.

Other successful ways of assembling these polarised tendencies in animation appeared, such as the series of animated shorts based on Tagawa Suihō's manga series, *Norakuro*. The *Norakuro* comics centre on the happy-go-lucky misadventures of a stray black dog, Norakuro, somewhat reminiscent of Felix the Cat, who enters the Japanese army. As Norakuro bumbles his way through his military duties with an aura of innocent good nature, each of his mishaps unexpectedly turns into a windfall for the army on the battlefield, and the stray black dog is successively promoted in rank. The gesture towards aligning cartoonish high jinks with military success allowed Norakuro to duck military censorship, despite its lack of a clear educational or moral stance.

Norakuro discovered new possibilities for funding and distributing cartoons. *Norakuro* began serialisation in 1931 in *Shōnen club*, a monthly publication whose initial mission was to provide high-quality, morally appropriate, yet entertaining stories for boys. In light of the boom of comics across a variety of newspapers, magazines and journals throughout the 1920s, it is not surprising that *Shōnen club* would also start to include manga, which had become a major source of attraction for readers. More surprising, however, was the extension of the manga series into serialisation across media. Animated shorts based on the Norakuro manga appeared as early as 1931, amidst efforts to produce sound cinema. While the Norakuro shorts did not have integrated soundtracks, phonograph records of comic dialogue featuring Norakuro were released, in keeping with a fad for phonograph soundtracks to be played during screenings and the fad for 'radio manga'. Advertisements regularly appeared in *Shōnen club* not only for the next instalment in the comic series but also for the records and animated films suitable for home projectors. *Norakuro* turned into a multimedia series, including cinema, print and sound media – an ad hoc precursor to the Japanese strategies of multimedia franchising later dubbed 'media mix'.

These two examples of wartime (1931–45) configurations of the cartoon film – the techno-aesthetic refinement of cel animation in Seo's Momotarō films and the multimedia serialisation of the Norakuro series – signal the emergence of animation cinema not only as a distinctive art of cinema but also as an apparatus or social technology, which holds together polarised tendencies in production, exhibition and consumption. Accounts of Japanese animation generally avoid this genuinely historical dimension of animation, burying it in a linear, chronological succession of works and creators. Ōtsuka Eiji's account of wartime animation is a notable exception. Across a series of publications, Ōtsuka points to an overall polarisation in the visual structure of the manga film.[25] He detects, on the one hand, a plastic, elastic, death-defying capacity for deformation with vitalist connotations, which attains new power in Disney. On the other hand, he finds an operative drive towards mechanistic organisation of the visual field, evident in the detailed schematics of weaponry as well as in angular and planar constructions associated with montage and monumental cinema. For Ōtsuka, then, the polarised stances today announced in Murakami's superflat versus Ghibli's manga films are the evidence of a history, of a social apparatus of animation, which has not passed. In fact, the advent of television and new media would serve to exacerbate this polarisation within animation cinema, spurring vaster and more intimate strategies of assembling throughout the social field.

TELEVISION ANIMATION (1960-90)

With the advent of broadcast television in Japan, inaugurated with NHK and NTV in 1953 and quickly expanded to comprise four additional major broadcasters, animation began to appear on the small screen, in the form of television commercials, dubs of American series and some stand-alone features. As the first continuously serialised television animation produced in Japan, however, Tezuka Osamu's *Astro Boy*/*Tetsuwan Atom* (1963–6) has enjoyed pride of place in histories of anime. *Astro Boy* is largely seen in terms of a profound rupture with past forms of animation and the harbinger of a new era. An analogous bid in manga history to posit Tezuka Osamu as the god of Japanese comics has only reinforced the sense of a nearly miraculous origin for both manga and anime. This insistence on a historical rupture is in keeping with a broader socio-historical discourse intent on extricating postwar Japan from its imperial past or military defeat, or both – to wit, the sense of a creative miracle to match the economic miracle.

The idea of a quasi-miraculous creative break has been contested in the context of manga, to the point where manga studies are often predicated on such contestation.[26] In the context of animation, it is relatively easy to contest the miraculous break and to trace the continuity between the prewar manga film and Tezuka. After all, not only did Tezuka praise *Momotaro's Divine Warriors on the Sea* in his recollections but he also started his career as an animator working on feature-length animated films at Tōei Dōga. Tōei Dōga had acquired Nichidō, which Masaoka Kenzō had established in Kansai and gradually absorbed animators who had gained experience working on wartime manga films.[27] What is more, Tezuka frequently proclaimed his desire to produce animations like those of Disney and consistently shifted part of his energies into animation cinema. While insisting on continuity over and above discontinuity would be equally rash, it is clear that, if we wish to address the historical transformation in animation due to broadcast television, such continuity must be also borne in mind, to temper the proclamations of a radical break in the context of *Astro Boy*, which have been articulated in different registers.

Above all, *Astro Boy* is commonly said to break with animation cinema and to inaugurate a lineage of anime, that is, television animation. Not surprisingly in light of his investment in the manga film, Miyazaki Hayao, for instance, holds Tezuka responsible for the destruction of animation in Japan. With his keener sense of its history, Tsugata Nobuyuki writes persuasively of two 'axes' of animation in Japan in the wake of *Astro Boy*.[28] These two axes of animation may be considered in terms of a contrast between full animation and limited animation. Limited animation does not present a radical break with (or stand in opposition) to full animation but rather, as the term implies, works with a more limited number of drawings per second. Limited animation has often been characterised in terms of stillness or still images, in contrast with mobility or moving images, with an implicit devaluation of its art, as cheap, as limited in its creativity. In fact, however, limited animation placed greater emphasis on certain techniques for working with movement, many of which were already used within so-called full animation. In effect, then, limited animation works upon a fracture point within full animation, where there is a 'stop on movement' within the moving image. It is a matter of difference in degree (of limitedness), not in kind or nature (full versus limited). It is matter of a contrast, of two axes of animation, as Tsugata puts it, instead of an opposition between categories or genres.

Limited animation entails a transformation of classical cel animation cinema, that is, the manga film, at the level of its apparatus: the use of multiple layers or planes within the moving image. It finds that sliding the drawings imparts a sensation of movement, by pulling the layer with the figure of a bird sideways to make it fly, for instance, instead of drawing each flap of its wings. Moving the drawings (or pieces of them) begins to take precedence over drawing the movement. Reconfiguring elements of drawings takes precedence over drawing them anew. Finally, instead of continuous fluidity and continuity of motion, limited animation focuses on the stopping and starting of movement, which may simply be overlooked as an artefact of cheapness or may be prolonged into an artful manner of composition. Such procedures were widely deployed in prewar animation but, for the reasons discussed above, were regarded as obstacles to the cinematic conventions of artfulness (especially continuity in movement) that were the basis for feature-length animation cinema. In the context of television, however, such procedures found a fit.

Usually, the fit between television and limited animation procedures is explained entirely in economic terms, in terms of the need to produce more animation, and faster, due to the demands of weekly serialisation.[29] Economic determination is only half of the story, however. The fit of limited animation with television also came about because of an affinity with the televisual regime of 'switching'. Not only did television introduce breaks between episodes but also it introduced a regime of internal switching of codes. *Astro Boy*, for instance, not only broke for commercials between story segments but also divided the episode into differently coded segments, such the opening song and ending song.[30] There was also an 'external' switching due to breaks between episodes, and the steady increase in the number of channels and stations paved the way for switching in the familiar sense of switching channels as well. In other words, television mobilised a series of procedures of segmentation, within and across programmes, within and across channels. As such, television programming began to relentlessly stop on continuous movement, thus making switching into a general paradigm.

Because procedures of limited animation afforded new ways of composing with stops-in-movement, they meshed smoothly with switching functions of television programmes, such as the switching of codes from opening song to commercial and from commercial to story as well as from show to show. This is how television animation came to serve as the linchpin for strategies of multimedia franchising, which would eventually incorporate television animation and feature-length animated films as components within a larger 'media mix' comprising music, anime, manga, toys, novels, games and other products.

Discussions of media mix are divided on the question of what allows for composition across media forms: narrative or character. Ōtsuka Eiji has shown how each component within a media mix acts as a story fragment from a larger narrative world, and consumers are thus enjoined to make little stories and fit them into this broader world structure.[31] Building on Ōtsuka's account, Azuma Hiroki has argued that the notion of a 'grand narrative' vanishes from the Japanese scene in the 1990s, making for a more character-centred media mix, consisting only of characters and minor consumer-generated stories about them.[32] He also contends that a 'grand database', an underlying database structure, has replaced the totalising function of the grand narrative within a media mix. Consequently, in his view, the act of composing across media has largely turned into a self-enclosing combinatory system; a personalised response to information stimuli. Drawing on these somewhat polarised accounts (narrative totality versus media totality), Marc Steinberg has proposed that *Astro Boy* is the constitutive moment in the formation of a character-based media mix through the way that it invites consumers to construct little stories or personal worlds.[33] Instead of grand narrative or grand media, marketing supplies the totalising function in his account due to its drive towards a character-centred and affect-based synergy. According to Steinberg, limited animation serves these ends by stopping on, and thus isolating, the anime character and bottling up its affective charge for resale.

A consideration of the fit between limited animation and television adds a twist to these accounts of media mix, for it stresses the material or medial role of television in two registers. First, as Tsugata Nobuyuki has eloquently demonstrated, the advent of television initially spurred the production of animation for commercials, building on a legacy of educational and promotional production already established in the Kansai area.[34] Tōei Dōga, for instance, primarily envisioned producing animated commercials, rather than story or art animation, when it acquired Nichidō. As such, the educational and commercial modes of address that arose prior to and continued alongside the feature-length animated film took on new functions in the context of television. Instead of two fairly discrete kinds of animation (the feature-length film and the shorter educational or commercial attraction), television animation deployed them as different codes within an episode, switching readily between commercials and story, story and song, for instance. The increasing reliance of television animation on investment from multiple sources reinforced this trend. Second, with the subsequent expansion of television to include peripheral devices, television allowed animation to play an increasingly central role in 'media-switching'. Media-switching entailed an expansion and intensification of code-switching. Already in the 1930s, manga film music and dialogues were played on the radio and sold in phonograph form, and thus a code (or set of codes) within the animation became entangled with a media form entailing a different mode of distribution and circulation. The serialisation of *Norakuro* across media is a prime example. It was the expansion of the television set from its receiver function into a set of monitor functions in the course of the 1970s and 1980s, however, which truly consolidated and harnessed the energies of this phenomenon.

Both the videocassette recorder (VCR) and the home video game console appeared in the 1970s and became familiar, even standard, features by the end of the 1980s. Such plug-ins, often developed and manufactured in Japan, effectively suspended the broadcast receiver function and deployed the television set in a more interactive and computational fashion. The VCR affected the experience of anime in a number of ways. Because it allowed for repeated viewing and for stopping on the moving image, anime fans began to consider the construction of various series in detail, focusing more and more on information retrieval. By the mid-1980s, animated series could be recorded from broadcasts, rented, collected, shared, and even subtitled and distributed outside Japan. While the VCR experience differed greatly from the cinematic experience, it gave new life to cinema (or a borrowed life, some might say). Miyazaki's 1985 film *Castle in the Sky/Tenkū no shiro Rapyuta* is sometimes credited with saving the animation cinema industry, and yet its success depended as much (or more) on videocassette sales as the box office. Finally, the VCR gave birth to a new form of animation, the original video animation or OVA.

The promise of the OVA lay in its potential to produce animations of a higher quality than television animation that were also geared more towards adults. They allowed for stories of a (generally shorter) length than standard seasonal runs for television animation, which could also be made on a lower budget than animation cinema. An evaluation of the impact of the OVA hinges, then, on the extent to which it went beyond television animation. In his account of the first fifteen years of the OVA, Tokugi Yoshiharu argues that the emphasis on a higher quality animation than television gradually diminished in favour of the rapid and cheap production of 'what you can't do on TV', namely, sex and violence, as in Kawajiri Yoshiaki's *Wicked City/Yōjū toshi* (1987).[35] The OVA also allowed animators to experiment with mecha designs independently of toy manufacturers who dominated the television market, but this trend gradually shifted towards OVA featuring fan-targeted parodies of special effects films (*tokusatsu eiga*) or well-known anime such as Anno Hideaki's *Gunbuster/Top o nerae* (1988).[36] Ultimately, rather to the disappointment of Tokugi, sequels and alternative episodes for television series eventually came to dominate the OVA series. Put another way, for all its potential as a circuit breaker, the OVA came to function more as a 'media switch' in the expanding circuitry of television animation and media mix, rather than as an autonomous media form, which is not entirely surprising in light of the VCR's original 'peripheral' relation to the television set.

The home video game console further enlarged the paradigm of media-switching centred on animation. Although video games and television animation did not become thoroughly enmeshed until the mid-1990s, the two media forms were in constant dialogue during their development in Japan. In fact, Japanese companies played a key role in the development and production of both the game console and the games, and a new distinction took hold by the late 1980s, between hardware (game console or VCR) and software (games or video cassettes).[37] Games became 'game software' (*gēmu sofuto*), and animation on cassette, laser disc or DVD became 'video software' or 'anime software' (*anime sofuto*). On the one hand, then, animation was now primarily situated as one computer-ready medium circulating among others rather than as animation for cinemas or animation for broadcast. On the other hand, however, television animation was not just one medium among others but began to emerge as the multifunctional ground for this expanded and intensified paradigm of media-switching. In sum, by the end of 1980s, television animation had expanded and intensified the polarised tendencies of animation cinema to the point where animation became at once a ubiquitous media form and multifunctional media ground for the era of new digital media.

ANIMATION MEDIA (1990-)

In the late 1990s and early 2000s, sweeping claims were made for animation subsuming cinema, due to the expanded use of digital technologies in film production. In 2004, Oshii Mamoru provocatively declared, 'All cinema is becoming anime.'[38] Likewise, in 1999, in the context of new media studies, Lev Manovich announced a reversal: animation, once subsumed by cinema, was now subsuming it.[39] Such pronouncements situated animation (or anime) at the centre of a crisis, at a moment of historical overturning of 'old' media paradigms or topologies associated with cinema. Around the same time, film studies began to reconsider the historical scope of cinema, drawing connections between 'early cinema' and 'late cinema' (ranging across expanded cinema, digital cinema, new media).[40] Gradually, this sense of crisis around the 'death of cinema' has been shunted into an emphasis on the numerous historical transformations within the medium. Animation has thus come to afford a new perspective on cinema,[41] and maybe a renewal and enlargement of film studies, rather than presenting an all-out crisis in which animation subsumes cinema in the era of new computational or digital media.

Considering historical transformations of animation in Japan – from artwork, to cinema, to television, to new media – allows us to avoid positing a stark opposition between cinema and (new) media. Instead, we see how broadcast television and then 'expanded' television (with its peripherals) have historically operated between cinema and digital or computational media. Interesting enough, debates on new media in Japan arose in the 1980s in the context of expanded television; expanded in terms of infrastructure (cable and satellite), platform (peripherals) and the density of information (multiple tracks within the signal).[42] What is more, a genealogical view of anime reminds us that the forms or formal features of animation arise within a broader apparatus or social technology. Simply put, anime is not one thing, precisely because it has always historically been a site for assembling polarised tendencies related to production, distribution, consumption and exchange.

While it is possible to identify distinct formations or paradigms and to array them chronologically, the polarised stances of Murakami's superflat and Ghibli's manga film, which appeared in the 2000s, remind us that these distinct paradigms remain in play today and even continue to jockey for position. Murakami grasps television anime from the angle of its transformation into new media in the 1980s and 1990s, while Ghibli rejects anime and television to promote animation cinema as it arose between 1930 and 1960. Nonetheless, insofar as Ghibli films, especially Mizayaki's, have enjoyed unparalleled success at the box office in Japan and have met with critical and popular acclaim around the world, the history of the manga film has clearly not passed. In fact, animation films tend to dominate the Japanese box office and to outperform other kinds of cinema. For the most part, however, such films are extensions of a larger multimedia franchise that already includes animated television series and are targeted towards children and families, as with the *Doraemon* (1969–) and *Crayon Shin-chan/Crayon Shin-chan* (1990–) franchises, or towards the fan base, as with the *Naruto* (1997–) and *One Piece/One piece* (1997–) franchises. Generally, although called films, they feel more like television anime or game-like animation media than like cinema.

Nonetheless, within these confines, animators and directors have often produced dazzling visual, sonic and narrative experiments in animation, which have opened new opportunities to produce stand-alone animated films. Hara Keiichi's career is a great example. While his *Crayon Shin-chan* animated films owe nothing to the manga film, they intensify the conventions of television animation to the point where the 'franchise animation film' appears transformed into a distinctive media genre. Similarly, but from the other direction, cineastes such as Kurosawa Kiyoshi and Miike Takashi have risen to the challenge not only by incorporating animation into cinema but also, and more importantly, by treating cinema itself as a media genre. Such films reopen animation's history of assembling tendencies instead of making a bid to subsume cinema within animation or vice versa.

The sheer variety and quantity of animation produced via Japan today makes for a plethora of forms, formats, genres, franchises and markets. This situation makes it impossible to identify a unified form of anime, which is sometimes a source of consternation, particularly on the part of non-Japanese fans. Rumours of the current decline and demise of anime tend to dwell on the impact of digital animation (the loss of an anime style) and on the production of anime deliberately geared to international tastes (the loss of Japaneseness). From the historical perspective, however, such developments appear less as a break with prior paradigms and more of a transformation of them. Digital animation, for instance, seems to have amplified the paradigm of media-switching.

Digital animation first appeared in larger budget productions in the late 1990s, such as *Spriggan/Supurigan* (1998), and has gradually come to dominate the wider market in the course of the 2000s. A new kind of polarisation has thus entered anime – a sort of 2D to 3D polarisation.[43] On the one hand, some digital animation deliberately strove to prolong the look and feel of cel animation, such as the animated film *Blood: The Last Vampire* (2000). On the other hand, the late 1990s and early 2000s also saw the entrance of fully computer-generated imagery (CGI) or 3D digital animation films into the commercial market, with features as different as *Malice@Doll* (2001), the notorious *Final Fantasy: The Spirits Within* (2001), and *Galerians/Garerianzu* (2002). Even in these films, however, there are moments where 2D and 3D textures appear to be at odds with each other, as if deriving from different realities, different worlds.

This sense of a discrepancy between media realities is sometimes dismissed as an artefact, as a result of insufficient funds or skills to composite the textures digitally. Yet it may also be taken as an amplification of the use of layers in cel animation, combined with the tendency in television animation to allow for a great degree of relative movement between layers. The result is an open compositing of media layers, which resonates with the paradigm of media-switching. Recent animated series show a variety of ways of working between media textures. *Re-Kan!/Rēkan!* (2015) has 2D characters moving flatly upon 3D textured backgrounds. *Love Live!/Love live!* (2013) alternates between 2D and 3D textures across scenes to suggest different relations between anime characters and audience ('live' performances take on 3D textures). Both *Knights of Sidonia/Sidonia no kishi* (2014–15) and *Attack on Titan/Shingeki no kyojin* (2014–15) continually flatten volumetric textures into planar textures or unfold flattened planes into 3D textures, which heightens the sense of movement in scenes with very little character animation.

The question of whether such animations are still 'anime' or 'Japanese' surely remains an open one. But the history of animation in Japan suggests that they arise from transformations of an apparatus or social technology geared initially towards combining education and entertainment, and then later towards code-switching, and finally towards media-switching. The history that has led to the emphasis on the simultaneous use of techniques of compositing and switching makes the compatibility of anime with contemporary mobile media and social media less of a mystery. It also invites us to consider anime as an ongoing challenge to, and thus as a source of possibility for, contemporary cinema and television.

Notes

1. Ueno Toshiya first addressed the potential Orientalism of anime fans and offered the notion of the 'japanoid' as an intervention, in 'Japanimation and Techno-Orientalism', <http://www.t0.or.at/ueno/japan.htm>. See also Susan Napier, *From Impressionism to Anime: Japan as Fantasy and Fan Cult in the Mind of the West* (New York: Palgrave Macmillan, 2007).

2. Numerous publications have appeared in Japan to assess how anime affected Americans' impressions of Japan. See, for instance, Kusanagi Satoshi, *America de Nihon no anime wa, dō mirarete kita ka?* (Tokyo: Asahi shinbunsha, 2003). In contrast, in *'Japanimation' naze toreru ka* (Tokyo: Kadokawa shoten, 2005), Ōtsuka Eiji and Onuma Nobuaki consider how a history of relations with the US enabled Japanese animation to be promoted to Americans as Japanese.

3. See, for instance, Kukhee Choo, 'Nationalization "cool": Japan's Government's Global Policy towards the Content Industry', in Nissim Otmazgin and Eyal Ben-Ari (eds), *Popular Culture and the State in East and Southeast Asia* (London: Routledge, 2012), pp. 83–102. [Editors' note: see also Chapter 14 by Rayna Denison in this volume.]

4. See, for instance, Miyazaki Hayao, 'Animation to manga eiga', in *Shuppatsuten: 1979–1996* (Tokyo: Tokuma shoten, 1996), pp. 151–8.

5. Instead of a 'simple' neutral point of reference, I resort to these four paradigms across which a 'complex' neutral point may emerge, in the manner of the pluralism of radical empiricism.

6. Lev Manovich, 'What is Digital Cinema?', in *The Digital Dialectic: New Essays on New Media* (Cambridge, MA: MIT Press, 1999), pp. 173–267.

7. Murakami Takashi (ed.), *SUPER FLAT* (Tokyo: MADRA Publishing, 2000).

8. Tsuji Nobuo, *Kisō no keifu* (Tokyo: Chikuma shobō, 2004).

9. Murakami Takashi, 'Super Flat Nihon bijutsu ron' and 'A Theory of Super Flat Japanese Art', in Murakami, *SUPER FLAT*, pp. 8–25.

10. Takahata Isao, *Jūni seiki no animation: Kokuhō emakimono ni miru eigateki – animeteki naru mono* (Tokyo: Tokuma shoten, 1999).

11. Takahata Isao, *Animation no kokorozashi: 'Yabunirami no bōkun' to 'Ōto tori'* (Tokyo: Iwanami shoten, 2007).

12. Ōtsuka Yasuo (ed.), *Nihon manga eiga no zenbō: Sono tanjō kara 'Sen to Chiro no kamikakushi', soshite …* (Tokyo: Tokyo-to gendi bijutsukan, 2004). In addition to this catalogue based on the exhibition, a series of essays appeared elsewhere that strove to prove Miyazaki's works as *animēshon* in contract to anime, such as Hikawa Ryūsuke, 'Genjitsu no sokubaku o koeru: Miyazaki-shiki "animation" no chikara', in Kiridōshi Risaku (ed.), *Miyazaki Hayao no sekai* (Tokyo: Takeshobo, 2005), pp. 78–86.

13. See the opening statements in Ōtsuka, *Nihon manga eiga no zenbō*, pp. 12–15.

14. Ōtsuka Eiji makes precisely this point in 'An Unholy Alliance of Disney and Eisenstein: The Fascist Origins of Otaku Culture', in Frenchy Lunning (ed.), *Mechademia*, vol. 8, *Tezuka's Manga Life* (Minneapolis: University of Minnesota Press, 2013).

15. Yamaguchi Katsunori and Watanabe Yasushi, *Nihon animation eiga shi* (Osaka: Yubunsha, 1978), p. 9.

16. Jonathan Clements, *Anime: A History* (London: British Film Institute, 2013), p. 25.

17. Daisuke Miyao, 'Before Anime: Animation and the Pure Film Movement', *Japan Forum* vol. 14 no. 2 (2002), p. 200.

18. Clements highlights the importance of this issue in *Anime*, pp. 26–8; Aaron Gerow provides a fuller account of it in *Visions of Japanese Modernity: Articulations of Cinema, Nation, and Spectatorship, 1895–1925* (Berkeley: University of California Press, 2010).

19. Imamura Taihei, *Imamura Taihei eizō hyōron*, vol. 5, *Manga eiga ron* (Tokyo: Yumani shobō, 1991). In English, see Imamura Taihei, 'For the Sake of Japanese Cartoons', in Frenchy Lunning (ed.), *Mechademia*, vol. 9, *Origins* (Minneapolis: University of Minnesota Press, 2014), pp. 107–24.

20. Yamaguchi and Watanabe, *Nihon animation eiga shi*, p. 62.

21. Tsugata Nobuyuki carefully traces this lineage in *Terebi anime yoakemae: Shirarezaru Kansai-ken animation kōbōshi* (Kyoto: Nakanishiya shuppan, 2012), and Jonathan Clements builds on his account in *Anime*.

22. Miyao, 'Before Anime', p. 203.

23. Clements, *Anime*, p. 42.

24. The double focus in Imamura Taihei's film theory at the time, on documentary and on cartoons, presages this linkage of manga film and culture film.

25. Two essays by Ōtsuka give a good sense of his overall concerns: Ōtsuka, 'An Unholy Alliance of Disney and Eisenstein', and Ōtsuka Eiji, 'Disarming Atom: Tezuka Osamu's Manga at War and Peace', in Frenchy Lunning (ed.), *Mechademia*, vol. 3, *The Limits of the Human* (Minneapolis: University of Minnesota Press, 2008), pp. 111–25.

26. Natsume Fusanosuke makes this point clear in *Tezuka Osamu wa doko ni iru* (Tokyo: Chikuma shobō, 1995).

27. Ushio Sōji tends to emphasise a smooth transition from manga eiga to Nichidō to Tōei Dōga in *Tezuka Osamu to boku* (Tokyo: Sōshisha, 2007).

28. Tsugata Nobuyuki adopts this framework in *Nihon animation no chikara: Hachijūgo nen no rekishi o tsuranuku futatsu no jiku* (Tokyo: NTT shuppan, 2004).

29. While animation production always entails economic determination, when economic determination is treated in the first instance rather than the last instance, to adopt Althusser's terms, the result is simple determinism that tends to rule out the social.
30. Hatakeyama Chōko and Matsuyama Masako provide a structural analysis of the segmentation of three examples of television animation, among them *Tetsuwan Atomu*, in *Monogatari no hōsō keitairon: Shikakerareta animation bangumi* (Kyoto: Sekai shisōsha, 2006).
31. Ōtsuka Eiji, 'World and Variation: The Reproduction and Consumption of Narrative', in Frenchy Lunning (ed.), *Mechademia*, vol. 5, *Fanthropologies* (Minneapolis: University of Minnesota Press, 2010), pp. 99–116.
32. Azuma Hiroki, *Otaku: Japan's Database Animals*, trans. Jonathan E. Able and Shion Kono (Minneapolis: University of Minnesota Press, 2009).
33. Marc Steinberg, *Anime Media Mix: Franchising Toys and Characters in Japan* (Minneapolis: University of Minnesota Press, 2012).
34. Tsugata, *Terebi anime no yoake mae*.
35. Tokugi Yoshiharu, 'OVA no jūgo nen', in Misono Makoto (ed.), *Zusetsu terebi anime zensho* (Tokyo: Hara shobō, 1999), p. 311.
36. Ibid., pp. 310, 314.
37. Shiga Nobuo addresses the implications of the new media paradigm of hardware and software in *Shōwa Terebi hōsōshi*, vol. 3 (Hayakawa shobō, 1990), 316–7.
38. Oshii Mamoru, *Subete no eiga wa anime ni naru* (Tokyo: Tokuma shoten, 2004).
39. Manovich, 'What is Digital Cinema?'
40. See, for instance, Miriam Hansen, 'Early Cinema, Late Cinema: Transformations in the Public Sphere', in Linda Williams (ed.), *Viewing Positions: Ways of Seeing Film* (London: Routledge, 1997), pp. 134–52.
41. See, for instance, Tom Gunning, 'The Transformed Image: The Roots of Animation in Metamorphosis and Motion', in Suzanne Buchan (ed.), *Pervasive Animation* (London: Routledge, 2013), pp. 52–69.
42. See Shiga Nobuo, *Shōwa terebi hōsōshi*, vol. 3, pp. 316–21; Watanabe Midori, *Gendai terebi hōsōgaku: Genba kara no message* (Tokyo: Waseda daigaku shuppanbu, 1989), pp. 176–83; and Hidaka Ichirō, *Nihon no hōsō no ayumi* (Tokyo: Ningen no kagakusha, 1991), pp. 250–61.
43. See, too, Jasper Sharp, 'Between Dimensions: 3D Computer Generated Animation in Anime', in Martha-Christine Menzel (ed.), *Ga-Netchū: The Manga Anime Syndrome* (Frankfurt am Main: Deutsches Filminstitut, 2008), pp. 120–33.

23

MELODRAMA
Melodrama, modernity and displacement: *That Night's Wife* (1930)

Ryoko Misono (with Hideaki Fujiki and Alastair Phillips)

Melodrama is not a fixed universal category but instead a fluid and historically contingent mode of expression. In his seminal book on the subject, Peter Brooks points out that theatrical melodrama emerged in the turbulent years following the French Revolution of the late eighteenth century.[1] Likewise, Thomas Elsaesser's groundbreaking essay on film melodrama, first published in 1972, discusses the eighteenth-century sentimental novel as another important precursor of the genre.[2] These historical conditions were crucial for the emergence of melodrama precisely because for Brooks the era represented the collapse of ecclesiastical moral values and because for Elsaesser the period was also one of 'intense social and ideological crisis'.[3]

Subsequent scholarship on film melodrama has particularly addressed two aspects: the mutability and the ubiquity of the genre and the question of historical specificity. Rick Altman, for example, considers melodrama or the 'woman's film' in terms of a process of gentrification. His discussion of the ways in which the genre has changed examines practices that not only include the production of the films but also their subsequent distribution, exhibition, promotion and reception.[4] Linda Williams has gone further to argue that there is actually no need to consider melodrama as a genre in its own right. Instead, it may be best understood as a mode that functions across the spectrum of the different genres existing under the rubric of classical cinema. For Williams, melodramatic components such as the home, moral legibility, timing, the dialectic between pathos and action, spectacle, 'excess' and Manichaean conflict are not at odds with each other; rather, they are elements that work in combination with realist causal narrative or the conventional core attributes of classical film-making.[5] In terms of the historical specificity of melodrama, Ben Singer has focused on the 'sensational melodramas' of the 1900s and 1910s, instead of the famous 'family melodramas' of the 1950s, to discuss how these films cluster concepts such as pathos, overwrought emotion, moral polarisation, non-classical narrative strategy and sensationalism within the broader context of a modernity characterised by urbanisation and forms of hyper-stimulation and social atomisation driven by capitalism.[6]

Although valuable, much of this work has tended to be confined to the discussion of American and European cinema. How then can we approach the topic within the specific context of Japanese film? One possible method is to identify the unique characteristics of Japanese melodrama in comparison with American and European melodrama. Under the influence of the theatrical conventions of *shinpa* theatre, the early history of Japanese cinema had a genre known as *shinpa* or *shinpa-higeki*, which literally means 'new school' or the 'new school tragic play (or tragedy)'. While some historians have translated this genre as '*shinpa*-melodrama' rather than '*shinpa*-

[Editors' note: Ryoko Misono (1975–2015) was an accomplished scholar of Japanese film who very sadly died during the gestation of this book. We have made the decision to complete this chapter in honour of her memory.]

tragedy', one might argue that it is in fact a unique Japanese cultural form untranslatable in any other language or culture. This, however, runs the risk of separating Japanese melodrama from its wider global contexts and overlooking its relationship with foreign melodramatic forms, especially those relating to the Hollywood system of production and the forces of modernity thriving beyond national borders.

Against this background, contemporary scholars such as Mitsuyo Wada-Marciano and Catherine Russell have conveyed a more nuanced argument that places melodrama in its specific Japanese historical context at the same time as considering the confrontation between a historical model of Japanese film production and Hollywood cinema. In so doing, both have drawn on Miriam Hansen's influential concept of 'vernacular modernism'[7] and explored how 'classical Japanese cinema', including melodrama, transfigured and/or negotiated the conventions of Hollywood cinema so as to represent issues related to elements of modernity such as the formation of national identity and the sensory experience of the urbanising environment under the historical conditions of the 1930s and beyond.[8]

This chapter will build on these significant insights into the tension between the local and the global and further explore the complex relationship between melodrama and modernity in the historical context of Japanese cinema in two particular ways. Firstly, rather than trying to pin down such stable concepts as 'classical Japanese cinema' or 'Japanese melodrama', we will instead shed light on how Japanese film of the pre-1940s involved a degree of intricate interaction between the idea of melodrama as a genre and as a mode. In this sense, the melodramatic mode can be seen to reach across a number of different genres and be constituted not only in relation to a number of conventions, noted above, but also a more fluid, unstable and contested terrain. Secondly, we will briefly elucidate how one single melodramatic film mediated modernity in its specific historical context. Here, modernity should neither be seen as something confined to national circumstances nor as something solely determined by Euro-American phenomena; rather, it should be understood as a set of shared yet uneven processes that involved various sociocultural borders such as the ones related to class, gender, region, nation, and the public and private sphere. These borders were all conditioned by the growth of capitalism, urbanisation, consumer culture and the various geopolitical relationships between Euro-American powers, Japan's empire and the rest of Asia.[9]

To this extent, Ozu Yasujirō's 1930 film, *That Night's Wife/Sonoyo no tsuma* makes an exceptionally interesting case study since it is not only an established masterpiece by a key auteur, but also because it at once accommodates and resists the melodramatic mode. Through its negotiation with Hollywood melodramatic conventions, it both establishes and transgresses borders concerning class, gender, family, urban space, global geopolitics and even the categorisation of genre in terms of its levels of symbiosis and conflict with both melodrama and the gangster film. As such, *That Night's Wife* may be said to displace melodrama as a genre, thereby enabling us to see the contact zone between both the melodramatic mode and a multifaceted and historically located modernity (Fig. 23.1).

HISTORICISING GENRE AND MODE

In her book, *Global Melodrama: Nation, Body and History*, Carla Marcantonio emphasises melodrama as a 'mode that underpins both (genre and classical narrative) […] not [only] within the bounds of American cinema but in the context of global cinema as well'.[10] Here, the idea of a genre retains the sense of a more specific category, while a mode may be seen as something more ubiquitous that operates across different genres and national borders, even though both remain ever-changing concepts. At the same time, both the idea of a genre and a mode are constituted from an intricate set of relations conditioned by a variety of period specific factors. This is indeed the case in the history of Japanese cinema as a whole and Japanese melodramatic cinema in particular.

As previously noted, the *shinpa-higeki* has often been identified with melodrama as it has sometimes been translated as '*shinpa*-melodrama'. Most Japanese cinema historians would agree that pre-1920 Japanese

Fig. 23.1. *That Night's Wife/Sono yono tsuma* (Ozu Yasujirō, 1930, Shōchiku).

motion pictures could be classified into two large genres: the *shinpa* and the *kyūha* (or *kyūgeki*), which literally means 'old school' (or 'old play'). This formation of film genre corresponded to the existing theatrical genres of *shinpa* theatre and kabuki. As the term 'shin' or 'new' suggests, while kabuki emerged around 1600 and continued throughout the Edo era (1603–1868) and afterwards, *shinpa* theatre arose in the late nineteenth century or the Meiji era (1868–1912) and differentiated itself from kabuki, which it saw as being outmoded in terms of its representation of modern society. In other words, *shinpa* was an emerging theatrical form that corresponded to the new shape of Meiji society, which by the late 1860s had replaced the feudalism of the Tokugawa period. The *shinpa-higeki* was a dominant subgenre of *shinpa*, which also had the comedic play (*kigeki*) and the action play (*katsugeki*) as related subgenres. Just as the *kyūha* film mostly adopted its narrative themes, setting and acting styles from kabuki, so the *shinpa* film did from *shinpa* theatre. Although both *kyūha* film and *shinpa* film developed their own cinematic techniques to some extent,[11] the former was influenced by the ways that kabuki depicted, say, samurai fighting in a stylised form, while the latter was influenced by the ways that *shinpa* theatre portrayed conflicts within the family in a more realistic, but still stylised, manner. Nonetheless, the *shinpa* film also assimilated another newly emerging genre of the 1900s and 1910s, *shingeki* or New Theatre, which was based on the translation and adaptation of European and Russian plays. Furthermore, the major source of stories in *shinpa* theatre and film were works called *shinbun shōsetsu* (newspaper fiction) and *katei shōsetsu* (home fiction), both of which gained currency in the developing print media of newspapers and magazines of the early twentieth century.[12] This was in contrast to *kyūha*, whose narrative sources were kabuki and *kōdan* (oral narratives), which originated in their oral form in the Edo era but began to circulate in print form in the Meiji era.[13]

Despite these various distinctions, it is not difficult to see melodramatic elements such as the family problem and the Manichaean juxtaposition between good and evil as a common feature of both *kyūha* and *shinpa*. One of the few extant *kyūha* films, *Shibukawa Bangorō* (1922), which features the distinguished *kyūha* star Onoe Matsunosuke in the title role, for instance, showcases a melodramatic moment in which the daughter of the family comes into conflict with her elder brother over whether or not they should protect Shibukawa (Onoe Matsunosuke) from the government. While the opening scene shows the daughter and her father being rescued from the villain by Shibukawa, the middle sequence shows him being trapped by another evil character and consequently being treated as a criminal, even though they eventually escape from prison. Here, the family conflict occurs in the context of an overarching opposition between the essentially virtuous hero and his supporters on the one hand, and the villainous characters on the other. Variations of melodramatic narrative elements can also be seen in *shinpa* as well. Indeed, using the umbrella term of the melodramatic mode, the literary scholar Ken Ito has revealed the complexity of melodramatic elements in such representative home fiction stories as Ozaki Kōyō's *The Golden Demon/Konjiki yasha* (1897–1903), Tokutomi Roka's *The Cuckoo/Hototogisu* (1898–9) and Kikuchi Yūhō's *Raised as Sisters/Chikyōdai* (1903),[14] all of which were repeatedly adapted into *shinpa* plays and films. Likewise, in his analysis of the narratives of Nikkatsu Mukōjima studio *shinpa* films from the 1910s, the film historian Hiroshi Komatsu has highlighted coincidence, moral conflict and family discord as the dominant components of the genre.[15]

The melodramatic mode can also be observed after the early 1920s when genre configurations began to dramatically change. In parallel with the renaming of cinema from *katsudō shashin* (motion photography) to *eiga* (screened picture), the distinction between *kyūha* and *shinpa* was replaced by the terms *jidaigeki* (period drama) and *gendaigeki* (contemporary drama). And yet, this was not simply an act of renaming. Rather, as Mitsuhiro Yoshimoto has argued, it also suggests a stronger degree of historical consciousness in general. Whereas the *shinpa* and *kyūha* were both derived from theatrical genres, the *gendaigeki* and *jidaigeki* drew on a new sense of time by which the present had to be clearly distinguished from the past.[16] Having said this, while the 1920s saw a nascent boom in adaptations of new popular novels called *taishū shōsetsu* (most notably, those of Kikuchi Kan), *gendaigeki* films also continued to adapt the *katei shōsetsu* (home fiction) of authors such as Kikuchi Yūhō, Yanagi Shun'yō and Izumi Kyōka.[17] Despite this change of genre configuration, the *taishū shōsetsu* and the *katei shōsetsu* both shared a similar melodramatic mode since their narratives mainly centred on the family and were often driven by coincidence and an opposition between differing cultural values. The Shōchiku *gendaigeki* film, *Modern Woman/Gendai no josei* (1923), for example, unfolds on the basis of the contrast between a traditional woman and a new woman while not necessarily presenting any clear-cut distinction between the moral values of good and evil.[18]

In addition to the relationship between pre-1920 and post-1920 genre configurations, we should also not overlook the fact that the circulation of American and European films constituted part of Japanese film culture of the period. The film historian Yamamoto Kikuo has highlighted similarities between the well-known American melodrama *Stella Dallas* (1925, released in Japan in 1926) and several later Japanese films of the late 1920s and early 1930s. The climax of *Waitress/Jokyū* (Kitō Shigeru, 1930), for instance, shows the mother looking on at her daughter's wedding from a distance as in the last scene of *Stella Dallas*.[19] In effect, this transnational cultural milieu led to the term 'melodrama' being widely used by the early 1930s, often in the sense of a pejorative implication similar to that of *shinpa-higeki*.

In sum, despite the fact that the two terms, *shinpa-higeki* and 'melodrama', both have complex relationships to their respective historical contexts,[20] they may to some extent be seen as variations of the melodramatic mode. In this sense, the melodramatic mode remained a ubiquitous yet mutable entity that prevailed across different media platforms, different genres, different periods and different geographical frameworks. Having said this, it is still important to note that melodrama as a genre has often been exclusively associated with the idea of the modern and the contemporary and has therefore been aligned with the *shinpa* not the *kyūha*, and with the *gendaigeki* not the *jidaigeki*. Crucially, this fact suggests that melodrama has been typically expected, albeit allegorically, to confront contemporaneous sociocultural circumstances. Just as the popularity of film 'melodrama' in the 1950s and early 1960s may be seen as a response to the postwar Japanese historical situation,[21] each film within the melodramatic mode of the 1930s similarly mediated the multifaceted modernity of the time.[22] This idea of an historically contingent melodramatic mode will now be seen in a discussion of *That Night's Wife*.

THAT NIGHT'S WIFE AS A MELODRAMA

That Night's Wife was Ozu's sixteenth film and based on a short story by Oscar Schisgall, 'Nine to Nine', published in the 9 April 1927 issue of *Shinseinen*.[23] The film opens in the night-time setting of a large and anonymous modern city – a darkened space in which we initially see a police officer moving a homeless man on from living rough. The scale of the modern civic and commercial buildings and the framing of the shots picturing the interaction between the figures both convey an overwhelming sense of oppressive solidity. Next, we see a masked gunman, Hashizume (Okada Tokiko), robbing a bank and an extensive police hunt ensues through the nocturnal streets. The doctor attending Hashizume's desperately sick child Michiko (Ichimura Mitsuko) and wife Mayumi (Yagumo Emiko) tells the thief over the phone that he must come back immediately. Hashizume makes it with the help of someone he assumes to be a taxi driver, but when the driver shortly visits the family's apartment and reveals himself to be a police officer, Mayumi decides to take control over events and forces the policeman to stay put at gunpoint until the morning, by which time the daughter's crisis has been alleviated. The film ends with Hashizume returning to his family after an attempted escape in order to finally surrender to the force of the law.

In terms of its decision to contain the central proportion of its crime narrative within the congested and emotionally charged spatial confines of the family apartment, *That Night's Wife* clearly operates within Williams's definition of the melodramatic mode. The compression of the lit room and attention to an intensified register of feminine feeling articulated by the prevalence of the watchful shots of Mayumi's gaze

Fig. 23.2. *That Night's Wife/Sono yono tsuma* (Ozu Yasujirō, 1930, Shōchiku).

all operate in contradistinction to the darker, more fluid, masculine, grandiose and fragmented substance of the film's opening (Fig. 23.2).

The pathos at the heart of the four-way set of relations between the couple, the police officer and the child is articulated on both a spatial and a temporal level in order to strengthen the emotional weight of the melodrama and regulate an awareness of the moral and social implications of the plight the family face. A frontal long shot used regularly in the early part of the film, for example, displays the bed of the child in the right-hand third of the frame, a chair in the centre and a small table with kettle on the left. This arrangement allows the viewer to see both the degree of attentiveness on the part of the mother as she moves back and forwards between the two stations and the internalised cost of her ordeal when she occupies a more private zone of feeling away from her daughter. In one significant sequence of shots, for example, Ozu moves into close-up to reveal Mayumi's protective anxiety, but when she gazes off-screen right, we're also reminded about the second tier of her plight: the absent father who unbeknownst to her, but known to us, has just committed a significant crime. We see Mayumi cross back screen left and then the film cuts to a tightly framed external view of her at the nearby window looking out. A plant on the ledge flutters in a light breeze – an emblem of the excessive fragility of her child's predicament and an expression of the overall uncertainty of the situation. Finally, we cut to an empty point-of-view shot of the gates leading to the street beyond before returning to a medium shot of the sick child turning in her bed unable to move yet wishing both her parents to be present.

If the melodramatic potential of this brief moment is about a series of spatial exchanges and absences, it is also typical of the film's wider operations concerning the regulation of time in terms of its shift between the emotional intensity of the diegetic present, the much desired consequences of a wished for future and a melancholic awareness, at least on the part of the film spectator, that what has just occurred in the recent past is also going to have significant repercussions for both of these temporal frames. In short, it's now too late.

The typically melodramatic trope of being 'too late' is rendered omnipresent through the film's condensation of time since the entirety of its narration occurs across the duration of one single night. In this sense, the temporal claustrophobia of the narrative thus matches the spatial claustrophobia of the room. Two levels of anticipation operate within a significant part of this linear timeframe that also fulfil Linda Williams's typology: the question of whether the daughter will survive (the pathos of the drama) and the question of whether the father will get away with his crime (the moral action of the drama). What makes the film so interesting as an instance of the melodramatic mode is how it seeks to answer these questions in such an irregular and distinctly multifaceted fashion.

That Night's Wife negotiates a set of tensions between the accelerated intensification of space and time and an alternative dilation of these elements. In one of the most melodramatically laden sections of the crime narrative, Hashizume is seen sitting anxiously in the rear of the car being driven by the police officer. Ozu intercuts between him lighting a cigarette and the urgent and sensation laden flashing of the streetlamps passing by outside. The sense of anxiety that is represented by the figure's gestures and his glances is only deepened by a sense of geographical uncertainty and a mounting degree of contraction in the length of the shots as the vital moments tick by. In an operation typical of the film as a whole, we swiftly cut from an extreme close-up of Hashizume tying his shoelaces and tapping his feet to a longer shot of his daughter's toy figure lying prostrate at home. There's an intermediary shot of a child's notebook and crayons and then a similar shot of various adult shoes. The camera then begins to track left to reveal Mayumi's own feet and shoes as she lies fretting, half-asleep, on the edge of her daughter's bed. The rapid conjugation of elements shown here produces a sense of affective simultaneity that also registers a sense of profound displacement as it is still by no means clear if the father will make it back in time and whether indeed the child will even survive the night.

At the same time, this attention to the domestic and ordinary features of ordinary life also matters to another one of the film's methods, which involves instead the expansion of time to express both a sense of elongated duration and a tension filled feeling of apprehension and anticipation. During the latter stages of the night as Mayumi watches over the policeman, for instance, the film offers a highly detailed and extensive mobile survey of all the significant elements of the apartment including the furniture, washing, clothing, visual decoration and cookware before reaching a static medium close-up of the dozing figure of Mayumi who wakes to find herself now the bearer of the gaze of the policeman and the gun.

The film's ability to hold the sensibility and material reality of a domestic realist drama in conjunction with the intensified space and time of the melodrama and the crime film is especially prevalent when one considers the family apartment in terms of a series of portals. *That Night's Wife* is constructed around a series of entrances and departures into and away from the room, all of which are managed by the emphatic visualisation of the doorway. In the sequence detailing the arrival of the policeman, for example, the film intercuts between rapid tracking shots towards the door from the vantage point of inside, close-ups of the door from outside, and then tightly framed shots of the opening of the door and the initial fraught exchange between Mayumi and the police officer. The passageway between the private and the public spheres thus also becomes a point of transfer between two forms of genre practice: the heightened emotion of the family melodrama and the investigative morality of the crime or gangster film.

TRANSGRESSING MELODRAMA AND MODERNITY

Whilst it remains useful to consider *That Night's Wife* as a melodrama in textual terms, the emphasis on the notion of the portal within the structure of the film's *mise en scène* also invites reflection on a broader set of borders related to the wider question of modernity and social experience. In other words, we need to attend more closely to the subject of what the door of the apartment might serve as a gateway from and a gateway onto.

In his textured and original analysis of the film, Daisuke Miyao argues convincingly that the film only really properly makes sense within the context of the fluid economic and sociopolitical currents of Japan at the turn of the decade. As Miyao reminds us, 1930 was a moment of both anxiety and confidence.[24] On the one hand, the country was still experiencing the severe consequences of the banking crisis of 1927 and the Wall Street crash of 1929, hence the picturing of the insecure and nomadic existence of the homeless man at the beginning of the film. On the other hand, the city was also now almost completely reconstructed and in the midst of full-scale expansion following the devastation of the Great Kantō Earthquake of 1923, hence the impressive solidity and scale of the architectural features that accompany the scene.

This argument makes even greater sense when one begins to situate the representation of the space beyond the family apartment in the context of both the technological modernity represented by the presence of electric illumination on the street within the narration, and the mediation of the properties of light and darkness in the form of the impressive modern cinematographic properties of the film itself. The point of the presence of the police and the motif of detection, especially in the opening section that especially resists the boundaries of the melodramatic form, is that both develop the idea of social control at the very moment when questions of authority and state power were beginning to resume as Japan prepared for imperial expansion. For Miyao, instead of merely posing as a form of structural interval within the progression of the screen diegesis, the streetlamps within the *mise en scène* also 'symbolically embody the surveillance system of [a] technological modernity that reveals everything under bright light and leaves nothing to be hidden from [the act of] policing'.[25]

This emphasis on the cultural implications of the properties of illumination also makes sense in relation to the film's attention to the visualisation of the body and domestic sphere. Here, the doorway of the apartment thus serves as a conduit for a way of looking that arguably transgresses the original intimacies of the melodramatic form to focus equally instead on the moral legitimisation of the police officer who seeks to regulate the criminal behaviour of the film's main protagonists. In this sense, Mayumi becomes a split agent torn between the confines of her responsibility to her daughter, her commitment to her husband and her subservience, as a makeshift gangster herself, to the force of the legal authorities. In Miyao's discussion of the film's cinematographic properties, for example, he draws attention to the synergies between the technological and aesthetic accomplishments of German cinema of the period and the 'sustained interest and lively discussion among film critics and filmmakers in [Japanese] film journals that highly valued' this form of expression.[26] The mastery of hard lighting contrast, admired by the film's assistant cameraman Atsuta Yūharu, comes into its own in the way that the features of Mayumi's face and the objects of the world that around her are illuminated to show what the Japanese film critic Iwasaki Akira called 'inward expression' and 'tactile value'.[27] Mayumi's body and the room she occupies become a charged forcefield of meaning in which the conflicted expression of her feelings (and what she conceals as well as reveals) also become mapped onto the sharpened contours of the possessions that make up the material conditions of her existence. They speak of both a profound presence – this is all she has – and a profound sense of impending absence (ultimately, they matter little when it comes to the plight of both her daughter and husband who might soon depart).

The doorway of the apartment therefore does not only solely represent an expressive portal onto a stable, self-contained and feminine sphere of generic domestic representation. It also mediates an unstable class and moral dimension for, as the film makes clear, Hashizume has had to resort to this course of criminal action because he lacks the economic means to pay for his daughter's medication. In the sense of Miriam Hansen's notion of a contingent reflexivity typical of many Hollywood and commercial international films of the period,[28] he is thus pictured being as adrift in the wider world of the modernising city as the homeless figure seen at the beginning of the narrative.

Again, *That Night's Wife* conveys this sense of the unequal consequences of modernity in a distinctively plural fashion. As well as paying detailed attention to the objects and vessels of Japanese everyday life through the visual economy of an internationally recognisable form of cinematographic practice, the film also conveys a degree of transnational awareness in the very subject of its representation. As such, the local features of the couple's life inside the boundary of the apartment are also placed in counterpoint to a set of prominently placed visual signs in the form of popular posters and design elements that represent the wider Euro-American and Asian components of a more global modernity. The genesis of these arrangements that feature Hollywood film posters, a map of India and European avant-garde typography is never properly explained, except to suggest that Hashizume might be an impoverished visual artist. These elements do however suggest one further kind of gateway; one leading onto a wider social sphere that contains a modernity not just within and beyond the room in the city, but within and beyond the nation as a whole.

CONCLUSION

In conclusion, despite the intensified constraints of its organisation of space (one apartment) and time (one night), *That Night's Wife* clearly operates as a highly fluid genre film that tests the boundaries of the melodramatic form in terms of both its subject and its methods of representation. In numerous ways, sketched briefly here, it recognises several of the attributes of the melodramatic mode identified by Linda Williams and transposes them onto a set of conventional circuits of meaning more often associated with the realist social drama and the gangster film. At the heart of this multiple sense of interaction lies the figure of Mayumi who acts as suffering mother, dutiful wife and prospective criminal gangster. In his earlier writing on the context for the emergence of the literary melodrama, Thomas Elsaesser argues that the form sought to aestheticise 'a particular, historically and socially conditioned *mode of experience*'.[29] The same remains true in the case of Ozu's film in ways that it speaks of the unevenly distributed and divided process of Japan's modernisation in this important year of material and political transition. As such, the film ends not with a final moment of transgression or even reconciliation, but a carefully staged separation as we see the work of the window and the doorway operate one more time within the film's system of expressive *mise en scène*. Mayumi's final gaze is onto a moment of disappearance as her husband turns the corner out of view with the arresting police officer. The work of one genre – the criminal drama – is now complete, but the nature of the melodramatic form means that there is clearly no resolution and no degree of certainty for the female protagonist. Just as the figure of Mayumi has been suspended between two generic forms throughout the course of the film, she is now also suspended within the ongoing continuum of an unfinished modernity.

Notes

1. Peter Brooks, *The Melodramatic Imagination: Balzac, Henry James, Melodrama, and the Mode of Excess* (New Haven, CT: Yale University Press, 1976).
2. Thomas Elsaesser, 'Tales of Sound and Fury: Observations on the Family Melodrama', *Monogram* vol. 4 (1972), pp. 2–15. Reprinted in Christine Gledhill (ed.), *Home is Where the Heart Is: Studies in Melodrama and the Woman's Film* (London: British Film Institute, 1987), pp. 43–69.
3. Ibid., p. 45.
4. Rick Altman, 'Reusable Packaging: Generic Products and the Recycling Process', in Nick Browne (ed.), *Refiguring American Film Genres: History and Theory* (Berkeley: University of California Press, 1998), pp. 1–41.
5. Linda Williams, *Playing the Race Card: Melodrama of Black and White from Uncle Tom to O.J. Simpson* (Princeton, NJ: Princeton University Press, 2001). For more on the idea of classical Hollywood cinema, see David Bordwell, Kristin Thompson and Janet Staiger, *The Classical Hollywood Cinema: Film Style and Mode of Film Production to 1960* (New York: Columbia University Press, 1985).
6. Ben Singer, *Melodrama and Modernity: Early Sensational Cinema and Its Contexts* (New York: Columbia University Press, 2001).
7. See Miriam Hansen, 'The Mass Production of the Senses: Classical Cinema as Vernacular Modernism', in Christine Gledhill and Linda Williams (eds), *Reinventing Film Studies* (London: Arnold, 2000), pp. 332–350.
8. Mitsuyo Wada-Marciano, *Nippon Modern: Japanese Cinema of the 1920s and 1930s* (Honolulu: University of Hawai'i Press, 2008); Catherine Russell, *Naruse Mikio and Japanese Modernity* (Durham, NC: Duke University Press, 2009); Catherine Russell, *Classical Japanese Cinema Revisited* (London: Continuum, 2011). Other studies on Japanese film melodrama include Keiko McDonald, *From Book to Screen: Modern Japanese Literature in Film* (New York: M. E. Sharpe, 1999). For a more recent discussion of one seminal Japanese melodrama, see also Michael Sooriyakumaran, 'Movie-Made Japan: Japanese Modernity and Narrative Space in Naruse Mikio's *Wife! Be Like a Rose* and *Every-Night Dreams*', *Frames Cinema Journal*, <https://framescinemajournal.com/article/movie-made-japan-japanese-modernity-and-narrative-space-in-naruse-mikios-wife-be-like-a-rose-and-every-night-dreams/>.
9. For more on this conceptualisation of modernity in the Japanese context, see Harry Harootunian, *Overcome by Modernity: History, Culture, and Community in Interwar Japan* (Princeton, NJ: Princeton University Press, 2000). The scholarship of modernity in relation to Japanese cinema includes Wada-Marciano, *Nippon Modern*; Russell, *Naruse Mikio and Japanese Modernity*; Thomas Lamarre, *Shadows on the Screen: Tanizaki Jun'ichirō and 'Oriental' Aesthetics* (Ann Arbor: Center for Japanese Studies, University of Michigan, 2005); Aaron Gerow, *Visions of Modernity: Articulations of Cinema, Nation, and Spectatorship, 1895–1925* (Berkeley: University of California Press, 2010); and Hideaki Fujiki, *Making Personas: Transnational Film Stardom in Modern Japan* (Cambridge, MA: Harvard University Asia Center, 2013).
10. Carla Marcantonio, *Global Melodrama: Nation, Body, and History in Contemporary Film* (London: Palgrave Macmillan, 2015), p. 6. The parentheses are added.
11. See, for instance, Fujiki, *Making Personas*, chapter 2.
12. See Ken K. Ito, *An Age of Melodrama: Family, Gender, and Social Hierarchy in the Turn-of-the Century Japanese Novel* (Stanford, CA: Stanford University Press, 2008), pp. 16–21.
13. For more detailed description of the formation of the genre see, for instance, Joanne Bernardi, *Writing in Light: The Silent Scenario and the Japanese Pure Film*

Movement (Detroit, MI: Wayne University Press, 2001), pp. 38–44; Fujiki, *Making Personas*, pp. 5–6, 162–4, 288.

14. Ito, *An Age of Melodrama*, pp. 16–21.
15. Komatsu Hiroshi, 'Shinpa eiga no keitaigaku: Shinsaimae no nihon eiga ga katarumono', in Kurosawa Kiyoshi, Yoshimi Shun'ya, Lee Bong-Ou and Yomota Inuhiko (eds), *Nihon eiga wa ikiteiru 2: Eigashi o yominaosu* (Tokyo: Iwanami shoten, 2010), p. 68.
16. Mitsuhiro Yoshimoto, *Kurosawa: Film Studies and Japanese Cinema* (Durham, NC: Duke University Press, 2000), pp. 212–22. [Editors' note: for a critical view of this account, see Chapter 12 by Philip Kaffen in this volume.]
17. See Fujiki, *Making Personas*, p. 222.
18. Ibid., pp. 228–9.
19. Yamamoto Kikuo, *Nihon eiga ni okeru gaikoku eiga no eikyō: Hikaku eigashi kenkyū* (Tokyo: Waseda daigaku shuppanbu, 1983), p. 234.
20. Chika Kinoshita discusses the case in the late 1930s and early 1940s. See her 'Merodorama no saiki: Makino Masahiro *Hototogisu* (1942) to kankyaku no kanōsei', in Fujiki Hideaki (ed.), *Kankyaku eno approach* (Tokyo: Shinwasha, 2011), pp. 199–228.
21. For more on the postwar Japanese melodrama see Mitsuhiro Yoshimoto, 'Melodrama, Postmodernism and Japanese Cinema', in Wimal Disanayake (ed.), *Melodrama and Asian Cinema* (New York: Cambridge University Press, 1993), pp. 101–26.
22. Examples include *Namiko* (Tanaka Eizō, 1931), *Our Neighbour, Miss Yae/Tonari no Yae-chan* (Shimazu Yasujirō, 1934), *The Downfall of Osen/Orizuru Osen* (Mizoguchi Kenji, 1935), *Avalanche/Nadare* (Naruse Mikio, 1937) and *The Tree of Love/Aizen katsura* (Nomura Hiromasa, 1938), to name just a few.
23. For more on the adaptation, see Michael Kerpan, 'That Night's Wife', in *The Gangster Films* (DVD booklet, British Film Institute, 2013), pp. 14–19.
24. Daisuke Miyao, 'Bright Lights, Big City: Lighting, Technological Modernity, and Ozu Yasujirō's *Sono yo no tsuma* (*That Night's Wife*, 1930)', *positions: asia critique* vol. 22 no. 1 (Winter 2014), p. 164.
25. Ibid., p. 171.
26. Ibid., p. 183.
27. Iwasaki quoted in ibid., p. 184.
28. See Miriam Bratu Hansen, 'Vernacular Modernism: Tracking Cinema on a Global Scale', in Nataša Ďurovičová and Kathleen Newman (eds), *World Cinemas, Transnational Approaches* (New York: Routledge, 2010), pp. 287–314.
29. Elsaesser, 'Tales of Sound and Fury', p. 49.

24

THE MUSICAL
Heibon and the popular song film

Michael Raine

In a 1957 round-table discussing the shift towards more youthful audiences, Tōhō studio's head of production, Fujimoto Sanezumi, claimed that rather than aim for 'home run' blockbusters (such as the films he produced with Kurosawa Akira), he would keep hitting 'double and triples' with company worker comedies and 'youth melody' films made with young singing stars for young audiences. As it turned out, those types of films became the studio's biggest earners in the years after his pronouncement, thus solidifying Tōhō's hold over the young urban market and, in the case of the youth melody films, filling cinemas beyond capacity with a fandom linked by 'song and film entertainment magazines' (*uta to eiga no goraku zasshi*) such as *Heibon*.[1] Fujii Hidetada claims that 1950s musical films, in particular those starring postwar superstar Misora Hibari, were distinct from Hollywood musicals and formed the foundation of a local genre of 'popular song films' (*kayō eiga*). He describes these provisionally and somewhat mockingly as films in which 'singers appear and sing with reckless abandon in the gaps between the acting'.[2]

The popular song film's shameless exploitation of musical celebrity guaranteed an audience in a high-volume, low-budget production system: Japanese cinema in the 1950s 'golden age' dominated foreign film at the box office, but the studios still struggled with overproduction, putting out around five hundred feature films per year. In the US too, many musical films (for example, rock 'n' roll musicals) found any excuse for a song. The spectacular display associated with Hollywood's Broadway adaptations has inspired some of the most productive analyses of the relation between a film's structural principles and its subject matter, but recently scholars have sought a broader understanding of the role of the 'musical moment' in cinema.[3] Most of those analyses still interpret the irruption of musical performance in relation to the film's narrative. However, limit cases such as the popular song film raise questions about genre itself: how important are canonical structures to genre typology? What relation should musical moments have to narrative and what requirement do texts have to produce a coherent diegesis at all?

After a brief history of the development of the musical film in Japan, this chapter will focus on the boom in popular song films in the late 1950s. It will deal in most detail with a trilogy of films starring Misora Hibari along with two other popular singers, Eri Chiemi and Yukimura Izumi. It proposes that the films *Janken Girls*/*Janken musume* (1955), *Romance Girls*/*Romansu musume* (1956) and *On Wings of Love*/*Ōatari sanshoku musume* (1957) are semantically and syntactically distinct from the classical musicals analysed by Rick Altman, and that their coherence comes not from what he terms the far-flung and invisible 'constellated community' of filmgoers that regulates the genre by recognising it, but by an even more widely spread community of fans, coupled by fan magazines organised around an intimate relation to celebrities rather than films.

THE MUSICAL GENRE IN JAPAN

Song and dance were ubiquitous in the development of sound film in Japan, as was the reliance on Western technologies and genres. From the loose synchronisation of image and sound recorded on wax cylinders in the 1910s to the importation of Lee de Forest's sound-on-film Phonofilm system in the 1920s, these not particularly successful sound formats featured singers, orchestras and dance performances. The Japanese majors' first sound films also highlighted musical performance: Nikkatsu's *Hometown/Furusato* (Mizoguchi Kenji, 1930) was shot in part on Minagawa Yoshizō's Mina talkie (Phonofilm) system and starred the renowned operatic tenor Fujiwara Yoshie. Shōchiku's first sound film, *The Neighbor's Wife and Mine/Madame to nyōbō* (Gosho Heinosuke, 1931), used the in-house Tsuchihashi system. It featured on- and off-screen performances by the Miyata Harmonica Band and ended with the protagonists singing 'My Blue Heaven'. Those films were often shown in cinemas specialising in Western films that had installed their first Western Electric and RCA systems to play Hollywood talkies in 1929. The 'slow transition to sound in Japan' is too complex a topic to be discussed here, but even though most of the big studios' cinemas were wired for sound by 1932, their production arms were slow to follow up on these early experiments, despite the relative popularity of foreign musicals and the importance of recorded music to Japanese film exhibition.[4] In their place, the new Photo Chemical Laboratory (P.C.L.) studio (later to become part of Tōhō) supplied musical films strongly reminiscent of Western models at the same time that they incorporated the intermedial aesthetics of contemporary Japanese stage revues.[5]

The P.C.L. studio's first feature films, both directed by Kimura Sotoji in 1933, were the operetta *A Tipsy Life/Ongaku kigeki horoyoi jinsei* and the backstage musical *Junjō no miyako*. *A Tipsy Life* displayed the utopian optimism of *Love Me Tonight* (Reuben Mamoulian, 1932) while *Junjō no miyako*, which was shown as a double bill with the *42nd Street* knock-off *Moonlight and Pretzels* (Karl Freund, 1933), echoed the earlier, more melodramatic syntax of films such as *Applause* (Reuben Mamoulian, 1929). The link to Western cinema could also be more direct: the opening scene of P.C.L.'s *Enoken's Tale of Youth's Folly/Enoken no seishun suikoden* (Yamamoto Kajirō, 1934) is a citation, though on a smaller scale, of the Busby Berkeley-choreographed opening number of *The Kid From Spain* (Leo McCarey, 1932), which played in Japan in August 1933. The connections to America were personal as well as textual: the Hollywood sequence was shot by Gregg Toland and his assistant 'Harry' Mimura Akira, a Japanese cameraman who went to work for P.C.L. in 1934, while the music for all the early P.C.L. films was arranged by Japan's first real jazz musician Kami Kyōsuke, who spent two years studying at UCLA.

Were these Japanese films 'musicals'? Iwamoto Kenji points out that reviews of the early P.C.L. films described them with a transliteration of the phrase 'musical plays' even as they were found wanting by the standards of Hollywood film.[6] The films satisfy Iwamoto's minimum semantic requirement for the musical – 'a film in which multiple protagonists express their feelings in song and dance' – but the desultory dance sequences pale beside the Busby Berkeley-style choreography that Japanese critics identified as typical of the Hollywood musical after 1933.[7] Although there were musical stage revues in Japan – the Asakusa opera (more like comic operetta) and the Takarazuka all-female revue, along with the 'dancing teams' that Shōchiku and other studios developed for live stage shows during the sound period – there was no strong tradition of musical theatre or Broadway-style musical staging for Japanese films to draw on. As Aaron Gerow argues in an essay on the Japanese film musical, Japanese film-makers and critics were too aware of the differences between local films and Hollywood, the dominant foreign cinema, for the musical to be accepted as a Japanese genre. The films were instead given alternative labels, such as 'music films' (*ongaku eiga*), 'films that sing' (*utau eiga*) or, the group of films that I will focus on in the second half of this essay, the popular song film.[8]

In one of his earliest forays into genre theory, Rick Altman argued that genres are often identified by their semantic and syntactic properties – the elements that typify the genre and the way those elements are articulated by the narration.[9] In Altman's influential theory, semantics and syntax interact dynamically, sustaining genres over time while providing audiences with pleasures that could also be seen as ideological. For example, in his work on the American musical, Altman regards the typical 'dual focus' alternation between the male and female protagonists as a narrational syntax that signifies heterosexual romance to the audience, a 'cultural myth' that by uniting male and female characters also brings together desirable antinomies that cannot be resolved on a narrative level, such as the tension between wealth and beauty, or work and play in the world of the film. In this sense, the musical works as a 'cultural problem-solving device', to give the audience pleasure by reconciling conflicts that would otherwise disturb.[10]

Altman's theory was from the beginning a theory of reception: his analysis of the three major subgenres of fairy tale, folk and show musicals draws on the existence of 'interpretive communities' or 'symbolic spectators' to resolve felt tensions in their culture. For this reason, he thinks, the musical as he identifies it should be seen as a specifically American genre.[11] Even if we find a similar intersection of semantic and syntactic dimensions in Japan, the interpretive community is different; the curve will not cross the axis at the same points. While we can find examples of Japanese fairy tale and folk musicals, for example, it is not typically sex in the guise of heterosexual romance that governs the narrative resolution but the restoration of the family, torn apart by war and male philandering. However, the majority of the Japanese films that fit Altman's categories are focused on entertainment as commerce: the show musical and in particular its most rudimentary form, the revue.

Altman recognises the show musical as the most changeable in his typology, 'more closely tied to the recording industry' and more susceptible to semantic shifts caused by changing musical tastes.[12] In that sense, like the children's musical, it tests the limit of Altman's definition of the musical genre as a historically developing interaction of semantic units with syntactical forms. Like the 'music films' and 'films that sing' mentioned above, Japanese genres are primarily semantic, and short-lived. In particular, the intermedial tie-up of record and cinema in the popular song film often eschews even the 'putting on a show' syntax of the show musical. It is more like Altman's illustration of the limit case: 'When is a musical not a musical? When it has Elvis Presley in it.'[13] Altman expands on the semantic and syntactic approaches in later work by showing how genres are maintained extra-textually, by being affirmed by 'constellated communities' of film fans. But in the Japanese case that recognition came from fans of the performers themselves: their concern was not with the type of film but the persona of the star, and her/his characteristic pose. The rest of this chapter will argue that the Japanese musical film has always been characterised by the 'irruption' of music within existing genres rather than as a stable syntax of its own. It deviates from the idealised version of the classical Hollywood musical, but it also stands as an example of the semantic reach of popular music that has more recently been recognised in American film as well.

As Carrie McDonnell argues in her survey of musical genre theory, film studies in general has turned away from canonical 'integrated' musicals such as *Meet Me in St. Louis* (Vincente Minnelli, 1944) to consider the broader overlap of music and film, for example in the careers of multimedia stars such as Bing Crosby and Gene Autry, whose films have not usually been described as musicals.[14] Ian Conrich and Estella Tincknell also argue that the traditional musical genre is too constraining a frame through which to comprehend the 'moments' of musical performance on film 'within specific historical and cultural contexts'. For them, the 'musical moment' is both excessive and expressive: disruptive of diegetic coherence but also in some sense embodying a film's affective or thematic significance.[15] We might better understand musical films in Japan by adopting a similar approach to the musical moments of the popular song films aimed at youth audiences that reached their peak in the 1950s and 1960s. Even more than the films analysed in the Conrich and Tincknell anthology, popular song films in Japan foreground the moment, not the genre – the song performance itself, usually already available on record and audible on the radio, as well as mediated by entertainment magazines. The song is not so much expressive of the film's broader concerns as exemplary of the direct relation between fan and star: these songs by famous singers are inserted into narratives in which those singers double the audience as ordinary characters, who often either dream of or achieve musical fame.

MUSICAL MOMENTS IN JAPANESE FILM

Tie-ups between film and popular song in Japan preceded their synchronisation on the screen: 'ballad films' (*kouta eiga*) that played off the lyrics of popular songs were a feature of the late silent industry and many film releases were coordinated with a theme song (*shudaika*) even before the arrival of the talkie.[16] Later, musical films often comically juxtaposed song with existing genres, as in *Singing Lovebirds*/*Oshidori utagassen* (1939), a vehicle for jazz singer Dick Mine and period film star Kataoka Chiezō marketed with the tagline, 'a rare operetta in which jazz bursts into the period film'.[17] Even after the tide of militarism and Japan's invasion of East Asia rendered such montages of film and popular song suspect, song and film were promoted as part of a new national film policy. For example, after a public competition 'The Patriotic March'/'Aikoku kōshinkyoku' was released to promote Japanese nationalism in December 1937. A documentary film accompanied the song when it was first released and played before the main programme in cinemas throughout the war.[18] It was followed in 1938 by a biopic of the same title, based on the life of the composer Setoguchi Tōkichi, whose other famous tune, 'The Battleship March'/'Gunkan kōshinkyoku', was even more ubiquitous. The film was directed by Fushimizu Osamu, who went on to direct several of the Ri Kōran (also known as Yamaguchi Yoshiko) wartime musical vehicles and was rivalled only by Makino Masahiro in the creation of popular wartime musical films.[19] For all the protestations that the musical is alien to Japan, song was so commonplace in Japanese film that Hara Setsuko was known as the only star who did not sing – a reputation that Ozu Yasujirō tweaked when he had her hum the tune of 'Haru' off screen in *Late Spring*/*Banshun* (1949).[20]

Music also had a special place in the reformulation of Japanese cinema after World War II, providing the compensations of entertainment in straitened times and reconciling prewar popular music with the new forms of Western 'jazz' heard in the streets and on the radio. Some of the first films made by the postwar film industry were revues, simple musical presentations such as *Sing! Sun*/*Utae! taiyō* (Abe Yutaka, 1945) and *Grand Show 1946*/*Grand shō 1946-nen* (Makino Masahiro, 1946) that introduced and advertised new musical forms.[21] Jazz, shorthand for mainstream swing, pop music and novelty songs, as well as the harder bebop of aficionados, was one of the most pervasive aspects of occupation culture. It was broadcast by the Armed Forces Radio Service (AFRS), later the Far East Network (FEN), and was quickly learned by local musicians who made a living playing on Allied military bases and clubs. From avant-garde composer Mayuzumi Toshirō and staples of future musical films such as the comic jazz band the Crazy Cats, to musician-turned-talent agent Watanabe Shin, an entire generation made a living on American popular music. Kasagi Shizuko was the female face of this 'dregs culture' (*kasutori bunka*), singing outrageously suggestive boogie-woogie on the radio, in clubs and on film.[22]

Postwar jazz was not just a style but a symbol of the geopolitical power relation between Japan and the US. Musicians entertained occupation troops with covers of American popular music but they also adapted those songs, alternating lyrics in English and in Japanese (*eigo majiri*) in a practice seen now as the training ground for lyricists such as Ida Seiichi to create the one-*mora*-per-beat 'teenage pop made in Japan' (*wasei teenage pops*) that displaced American singers from the charts in the 1950s and 1960s.[23] This is the culture from which the stars of the 'youth melody' films would emerge.

THE STARS: MISORA HIBARI, ERI CHIEMI, YUKIMURA IZUMI

Later known for more traditional *enka* songs, Misora Hibari first came to prominence as a 'genius kid who sings adult songs better than adults can' on NHK radio's *Proud of My Voice*/*Nodo jiman* amateur singing show, where she sang a cover of 'The Apple Song'/'Ringo no uta' from the first postwar hit film *Gentle Breeze*/*Soyokaze* (1945).[24] After Misora's performance was featured in a knock-off film '*Proud of My Voice*'-*Crazy Age*/*Nodo jiman-kyō jidai* (1949), the majority of her songs were tie-ins with the films in which she appeared. Misora's first record, a comic 'Kappa boogie-woogie', was the theme song of the musical comedy *Dancing Dragon Palace Castle/Odoru ryūgūjō* (1949). Her imitation in that song of 'dregs culture' singer Kasagi Shizuko's imitation of American vocal and bodily performance drew on a tradition of mimicry (*mono-mane*) that boomed during the 1950s.[25] What made Misora truly famous was another popular song and film tie-up, *The Sad Whistle/Kanashiki kuchibue* (1949), a sad love song and a family reunification melodrama in which the song taught to a young girl by her older brother reunites them after they are separated during their repatriation at the end of the war. The song is integral to the narrative, the only means to link the spaces of Misora's rising celebrity in the beer hall and her brother's life of crime. Misora is reunited with Kenzō when he hears her song in the street and then is pressed in among the spectators as he watches her perform. Although the performance has a film intertext – Marlene Dietrich in *Morocco* (1930) – the song preceded the film, on radio and record, which converts the characters into an audience for a performance of the song. The film emphasises the intermediality of the musical moment: Kyōko hears Mitsuko (Misora) through the speakers in a beerhall, as if she is on the radio. In addition, *The Sad Whistle* was adapted from a story in *Heibon* magazine, which like the song went on sale a few weeks before the film was released.[26]

Along with Misora, two other *monomane* singers made up the backbone of the youth melody form of the popular song film that I am examining here: Eri Chiemi and Yukimura Izumi. Eri sang on American bases – her stage name derives from the nickname she was given by GIs – and her recording career began with covers of Doris Day, Peggy Lee and Theresa Brewer. She was often called the 'second Misora Hibari'; the same age, with a similarly big voice and dramatic interpretive singing style. Yukimura Izumi was also born in 1937 but started her career later. Nonetheless, her perfect imitation of Theresa Brewer's 'Till I Waltz Again With You', in a language she did not yet speak, launched her on a similar trajectory. After achieving success as popular singers, Misora, Eri and Yukimura appeared, alone or in combination, in dozens of musical films in the 1950s. The films usually played as the second half of double bills and were widely disparaged by critics, even as they recognised that the films had a built-in audience who were brought into the cinema by the popularity of the performer, as mediated by song recordings and the magazine *Heibon*.[27]

The stereotypical narratives of Eri and Yukimura's films sometimes feature them in a cameo, singing a recent hit song in quasi-direct address to fans. When they play the lead, it is usually as a young singer who finds fame after some travail. For example, *Cheers to the Jazz Girl/Jazu musume kanpai* (1955) ignores romance for the baroque tale of a stern vaudevillian who won't let his daughters become singers. When he is temporarily blinded they seize their chance. Unlike the nostalgia of 'putting on a show' Hollywood musicals such as *Babes in Arms* (1937), *Birth of the Jazz Girl* is forward-looking: the young people have part-time jobs at a film studio and their big break comes when the studio needs a quick musical filler (a description of the film as well as the film within the film). Eri Chiemi, the studio chief's granddaughter, helps out by jumping on the calypso bandwagon to sing a version of Eartha Kitt's 'Somebody Bad Stole De Wedding Bell' in mixed English and Japanese, while Yukimura Izumi plays one of three daughters who becomes a star, performing Eddie Fisher's 'Oh My Papa' and Dinah Shore's 'Blue Canary', also in English and Japanese. These popular song films were not classical musicals, but they were also distinct from the mere insertion of popular singers singing popular songs in genre films, such as Julie London in *Man of the West* (1958) or Ricky Nelson in *Rio Bravo* (1959). There are certainly similarities to the problematic Elvis vehicles discussed by Altman, but these films came earlier and are even more focused on the process of becoming or admiring a star, and even less concerned with creating a convincing diegetic world.

Misora Hibari was a superstar who appeared in a wider range of genres than the others, but her youth melody films are perhaps even more focused on fandom and celebrity. For example, in *Sing! Youth: Hard-Working Girl/Utae! seishun: Harikiri musume* (1955), one of five films Misora released in December 1955, she plays a bus conductor and Misora Hibari fan nicknamed 'Bibari', because she is the spitting image of the singer except for a mole on her nose (likened to the voicing mark that converts 'hi' to 'bi' in Japanese writing), and the fact that she cannot sing. To the audience, of course, she *is* Hibari: the film makes comedy out of the diegetic gap between the character and her pro-filmic identity by cutting to a gigantic poster of the singer on the front of the Nichigeki theatre, where Misora was appearing in concert, as Bibari distractedly announces the singer's name instead of the theatre name when the bus stops outside. She also watches a television broadcast of Hibari's Nichigeki show at the bus garage and, improbably, one of Bibari's conductor friends (most of them are played by popular Japanese singers) is also a friend of the real Hibari. The two girls end up sharing a split-screen dinner at the Tōhō studio. Hibari's encouragement is all Bibari needs to learn to sing, and the film ends with both singers on 'stage' at the bus garage, where Hibari presents her latest release. More than simply collapsing the diegesis into another direct-address performance, this final scene is constructed through a series of eye-line matches between Bibari and Hibari, so that we can admire in medium close-up both the charming shyness of the fan and the magnanimity of the star. The ostensible narrative, another family reunification melodrama, is lost under these layers of reflexivity. All the audience, and the characters, care about is Misora Hibari: even Bibari's brother comes home singing the theme song from *Janken Girls*, the first of the 'three girl' films that was released the previous month, also directed by Sugie Toshio.

THE THREE GIRL FILMS

Janken Girls, starring Misora Hibari, Eri Chiemi and Yukimura Izumi, has precursors that stretch back to the Deanna Durbin musical comedy *Three Smart Girls* (1936), but it is semantically, syntactically and discursively distinct from the canonical Hollywood genre. While it meets the minimum semantic standard of incorporating song into the film text, *Janken Girls'* account of femininity displaces the heterosexual romance seen as central to 85 per cent of Hollywood films in favour of a comic sorority in which female friendship predominates, producing a narrative syntax that avoids the 'dual focus' that, as we have seen, Rick Altman regards as characteristic of the American film musical.[28]

The 'three girl' films inflate to bursting point the popular song film conceit of singing stars who just happen to find themselves singing in genre films. *Janken Girls* was propelled by its youth audience to the biggest box office of modern-day films in 1955; the second film in the series, *Romance Girls*, was second only to Kurosawa's *Throne of Blood/Kumonosu jō* (1956) for Tōhō; and the third film, *On Wings of Love*, was the studio's top film in 1957.[29] As will become clear, narrative coherence was less important to these films than a direct relation between fan and star, which was developed not simply through identification with the image, nor direct address to the audience, but through extra-filmic paratexts such as photographic spreads, fan goods and signing events (*sain-kai*).

The narrative of *Janken Girls* can be laid out quite briefly: two high school girls Yumi (Eri) and Ruri (Misora) go on a class trip to Kyoto. They meet a rich young man, also on vacation, and 'Pyua-chan' (Yukimura), a poor apprentice geisha. Later, Pyua-chan arrives in Tokyo looking for a boy called Saitō, her last hope of escaping a bald company boss who wants to make her his mistress when she becomes a geisha. Meanwhile, Ruri's father is about to become the Japanese ambassador to France and, with the death of his only legitimate child, comes to reclaim Ruri from her mother, an ex-geisha who runs a teahouse. In a familiar melodramatic coincidence, it turns out that Saitō is indeed the same young man that Yumi and Ruri met by chance. When the girls find him, he refuses to marry Pyua-chan (he is in unrequited love with Yumi) but instead tricks his father into paying off her contract, so allowing her to re-enter society. The two girls go to support Ruri, who is performing in a traditional dance recital watched by her father. After some resistance, Ruri reconciles with her father and is absorbed into his legitimate family.

More important than this plot summary, *Janken Girls* puts improbable characters in improbable situations, such that they act out aspects of fandom and celebrity. They pose for photographs, get excited by location shoots, collaborate on a media production and search for the ideal man in *Heibon* magazine. Each performer is assigned a character ('cute', 'boyish' and 'working class' [*shitamachi*] respectively) that is not so much established through actions as reiterated in stereotyped poses and differentiated through colour-coded costuming associated with each character. The entire look of this, one of Tōhō's first colour films, is reminiscent of the colour scheme of *Heibon* or the fashion illustrations by Naito Rune in *Junior Soleil* magazine (Fig. 24.1a–d).[30]

The film constantly disrupts its own diegetic coherence by inviting audiences to recognise the extra-filmic existence of the performer. For example, when Yumi invents a ditty about an overbearing teacher, the lyric is to the tune of Eri Chiemi's 'Uska Dara' song, released in 1954 and itself a cover of Earth Kitt's version of the Turkish folk song. When the teacher goes to Ruri's house to complain, Eri's original song is playing on a radio that, to her embarrassment, the teacher cannot turn off.[31] That comic reflexivity reaches a pinnacle when the three girls, played by the three stars, go to see a stage show by the Tokyo Takarazuka company (a Tōhō subsidiary) but instead end up fantasising of themselves as stars – which they are, of course. As Yumi, says: 'Hey, hey, hey! It's no good just watching! If I really like a star it's as if she becomes me.' It is not that she identifies with or imagines she becomes the star: more aggressively, *the star becomes her*. Before each solo musical stage number, the character played by the corresponding star, sitting in the audience, closes her eyes. As she opens them we cut to the same performer on stage

Fig. 24.1a–d *Janken Girls/Janken musume* (Sugie Toshio, 1955, Tōhō).

as she starts her number, in a space quite distinct from the stage shown at the beginning and end of the scene. That is, the performance takes place in a private mental space constructed by each star-as-fan's eye-line match. Through this depiction of fandom the film acknowledges the determining power of fan culture – the films are defined less by their narrational coherence than by the ways they activate the fandom of their viewers. That active investment in fantasies of celebrity was central to the interest in postwar film stars who appeared on the screen as both character and performer.

As I have already tried to suggest, the coiled relation between fan and star extended far beyond the screen. The premiere of *Janken Girls* featured a mimicry contest, in which fans competed to imitate their favourite stars, who were themselves well known as mimic singers; in the film, they sing songs by Eartha Kitt, Edith Piaf and even Nat King Cole. Eri Chiemi also burlesques Marilyn Monroe in *There's No Business Like Show Business* (1954) for her performance on the stage within the film. As the Japanese film importer/exporter Kawakita Kashiko recognised, the *inauthenticity* of these films is precisely what made them representative of postwar Japanese popular culture. In a round-table discussion she claimed that she would love to show *Janken Girls* to foreigners as an example of contemporary Japanese film, but the melodies had been lifted from Western popular songs and 'clearing the rights would cost a fortune!'.[32] The popular song film is often disparaged – for instance Hasumi Shigehiko's critique of its 'constantly repeated cheap filmmaking patterns' – but the real subject matter of *Janken Girls* is not a self-enclosed fictional diegesis but the culture of celebrity itself.[33] The foregrounding of famous singers playing characters who imagine that they are themselves is not an unavoidable complication but the point of the film.

In the second film in the series, *Romance Girls*, the three girls play high school characters who again go to see themselves perform (as stars). They have been invited to the show by the captain of the school tennis team, but the film is less concerned to establish the romantic potential of this invitation than to joke with the audience about the appearance of the stars as ordinary girls; a fact that is underlined by a tilt down from a poster of the performers to the characters sitting in a similar arrangement. Their conversation in the sequence is overshadowed by a figure that interrupts our view as it passes, like a pendulum, back and forth in front of the camera. A reverse shot then reveals a middle-aged man looking between the poster of the stars and characters sitting beneath it, as if to remind us of the absurd collapse of the distinction between the diegetic and the pro-filmic in the film. Things only become more absurd once the show starts when it turns out that each character is a fan of one of the other stars, and does not even recognise her own resemblance to the celebrity that plays her.

Heibon

To understand why these films are so invested in the culture of celebrity we have to recognise their dependence on the song and movie entertainment magazines such as *Heibon* and, to a lesser extent and more in Western Japan, *Myōjō*. *Heibon*, which translates as 'ordinary' or 'everyday', was started in 1945 as a popular literary journal that rejected the grandiosity of wartime cultural nationalism. By the late 1950s it was a visual magazine that opened with an extensive photographic section. It tied into visual culture by publishing serialised stories that were often adapted into films, as well as publicity articles on singers and film stars, which were illustrated by photographs and line art. According to Etō Fumio, two-thirds of *Heibon's* readers were female and 80 per cent were between 13 and 18 years old, a teenage demographic that had come into existence with the magazine at the end of World War II. Selling over one million copies a month from 1953 until the late 1960s, it was one of the most widely read magazines in Japan, with readers distributed throughout the country and even among Japanese living abroad.[34]

In the 1950s, print media linked the industries of film and popular music with other media, such as radio and later television, to produce a kind of infrastructure for the development of a new youth culture around the youth melody film. Misora Hibari was the reigning celebrity of *Heibon*'s teenage demographic: she appeared on the cover of the monthly magazine thirteen times between 1953 and 1958, and featured in dozens of the front matter photospreads, often accompanied by Eri Chiemi and Yukimura Izumi. As Yukimura recalled, she would agree to any request from *Heibon* since the magazine was a star maker; once people saw you in it they knew you were a star.[35] In May 1956, six months after the appearance of *Janken Girls*, Misora topped the *Heibon* readers' popularity poll for the fifth time in a row. Eri came in second and Yukimura came in fourth.[36]

If we approach *Janken Girls* from the perspective of the fandom organised by *Heibon* then we must recognise that the film is not the primary text. *Heibon*, in concert with Tōhō, wove an intermedial network that allowed audiences to engage in multiple affective relations to these three celebrities, understood as characters with highly stylised personalities. The magazine commissioned a 'serialised novel' (*rensai shōsetsu*) of *Janken Girls* written by Nakano Minoru that is much longer and quite different from the film, and then planned the film production with Tōhō to commemorate the magazine's 10th anniversary. *Heibon* printed readers' responses after each episode of the serialised stories: Kondō-san from Gunma said that reading *Janken Girls* was like watching a film, while Endō-san from Tokyo imagined Misora Hibari playing the lead in a Shōchiku film. Only *Heibon* could bring these actresses together, albeit at the Tōhō studio. The subsequent two instalments in the film series were also first printed in *Heibon* magazine, with images of the film's performers decorating the page.[37]

Between the serialisation and the release of the film, the magazine issued a 'Heibon film novel' that reprinted all the magazine episodes. It also added a brief novelisation and a front section of publicity stills for the film as well as conversations with the stars.[38] The film's release was then further supported by stills from the film, reproduced in the *Heibon* photospread section. There was also a long round-table conversation between the three girls in the month that *Janken Girls* was released, which was broadcast in part on the magazine's radio show, *Heibon Hour*.[39] The round table mostly ignores the story of the film and instead discusses non-narrative features such as the colour coordination of the costumes and the distribution of songs, and gives us a script of their conversation so that readers can imagine the three girls' in-character interactions: Izumi is cute, Chiemi is 'masculine' and Hibari is the girl next door.

HEIBON SUPPLEMENTS: STARS AT YOUR FINGERTIPS

Postwar popular film fandom was physical, and stars were ubiquitous and close to the body. Unlike in the prewar period, stars were not seen as inaccessible, 'above the clouds' (*kumonoue*). *Heibon* often came with 'supplements' (*furoku*) or 'bonus items' (*omake*) such as bookmarks with star images that served to keep them within reach. In addition to these free objects, the magazine's 'service department' also sold 'fan goods' such as wallets in which you could carry your favourite miniature 'bean photograph' (*mame shashin*), or hand towels that figuratively brought your favourite stars even closer (Fig. 24.2).[40]

These goods depended on the postal system to bring fans closer to stars and to each other. Advertisements always included the cost of postage as well as the price. *Heibon* itself had a wide rural readership, which received the magazine by subscription as third-class mail as well as by picking it up at local bookstores.[41] The magazine even released envelopes and writing paper with a *Janken Girls* theme. Taken together, all these goods constituted their own medium of communication for the affective elements of celebrity intimacy among a widely distributed population of fans.

In his later work on film genre, Rick Altman recognises the 'lateral communication' among 'constellated communities' that discursively sustains genres as a form of fandom.[42] But at least in the case of the popular song film that discourse was organised around celebrity, not genre. If the smooth 'audio dissolve' between narrative and number is characteristic of the musical, then the popular song

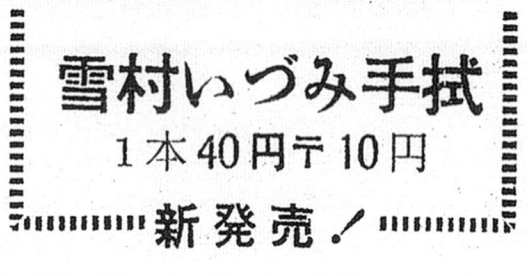

Fig. 24.2. Yukimura Izumi hand towel. 40 yen each, 10 yen for postage in *Heibon* (April 1956).

film's imbrication with records and the radio, through the mediation of fan magazines, foregrounds a form of 'audio cut' in which popular music obtrudes not simply into the narrative but through the surface of the film itself. Fans' engagement with the film, and with each other, was certainly intensified by their standing-room-only experiences of mass enthusiasm in the cinema, but it was also extended, and even replaced, by their consumption of the star persona across a multiple range of media.

CONCLUSION

In 1950s Japan, at the start of the era of high economic growth, a long history of intensely mediated popular celebrity became combined with a highly centralised cultural industry (radio, records, film and print) to create a 'media mix' of a form now almost ubiquitous. Marc Steinberg has already made that case for Japanese animation: Tezuka Osamu's turn to television animation in the early 1960s was based on a business model in which the programme itself was a loss-leader that promoted the spread of the Atom Boy character from manga through television to advertising endorsements, stickers and toys, as well as foreign sales. As Steinberg shows, that process is best understood through a close reading of the character as a set of dynamic poses that mobilised an image from the printed page through the (limited) animation screen to the advertisements and goods on which it appeared. Those goods extended beyond consumer objects to stickers that children bought and applied to their own possessions, and bodies, extending the domain of reception of the Atom Boy character from a weekly animation show and occasional print advertisements to a ubiquitous presence in everyday life.[43] Similarly, this essay has argued that Misora Hibari, Eri Chiemi and Yukimura Izumi played stereotyped, and therefore repeatable, 'characters' in the media mix sense rather than 'characters' in the classical sense – diegetic beings with an interiority fleshed out through action. When we study these films and their actors through the mass media that extended them in both time and space, it becomes clear that the repeatable image or 'pose' that attached to certain performers became the condition of their celebrity within the media network of the popular song film.[44]

Of course, the concept of the 'ordinary star' was a lie. The bulk of *Heibon* readers were working class: the disparity between the ordinariness of stars that promised fans could share in star experience, and the immiseration of the underprivileged Japanese who tried to pull them close, led one fan of Misora Hibari to throw acid on her at a concert just one year after *Janken Girls* was released. Hibari's happy-go-lucky working-class persona had nothing in common with the girl's life as a maid, brought to Tokyo from the provinces to work for a company director. Fortunately, Hibari was not badly hurt, but the incident speaks to the intensity of adulation and resentment, as well as to the material conditions of deprivation, in the real lives of the fans of these apparently ordinary figures.[45]

The shift in film studies from the analysis of musicals as a genre to the recognition of 'musical moments' in many films gives us a way to talk about popular song films in which narrative is subordinate to 'attractions', and character is 'reduced' to a media mix. *Janken Girls* had a larger budget than the B-movies that Fujimoto Sanezumi called 'youth melody' films, but it shared their template of reflexively figuring fans becoming stars by having stars perform fans, for audiences that actively consumed those stars as media mix characters in multiple forms: from film narratives and magazine articles to record sleeves and disembodied voices, still further to mini-photographs and hand towels and the discourse of the fans themselves. The three girl films were consequently followed by multiple 'three girl' film series as well as by 'three girl' singing trios on 1960s television shows that, as television replaced the cinema at the centre of Japanese mass culture, were sometimes adapted into films by Tōhō.

The popular song film was particularly important in mediating that transition: the films foreground fandom and celebrity, being a star or becoming one, and the direct appreciation of a performance and star persona developed outside the cinema. The music of those musical moments, even for originally Caribbean musical genres such as mambo, calypso and chachacha, arrived in Japan only after being channelled through the US. But the development of what Yamagishi Ichirō called 'teenage pop made in Japan' out of the 'mixed English' lyrics of cover songs and the promotion of Japanese celebrities brought into bodily proximity through the medium of fan goods was also the basis of a local popular culture. Unheralded at the time, and ever since, the extreme reflexivity and joyful commercial exploitation of the youth melody films give us an outline of the coming 'idol culture' of young musical celebrity and its intense transmedia fandom for which Japan is famous today.

NOTES

1 Fujimoto Masazumi's remark in the round-table discussion titled, 'Wareware wa zenryoku de yatte iru: Kakusha daihyō producer wa kataru', participated by Makino Mitsuo, Matsuyama Hideo, Ōtani Ryūzō, Watanabe Kunio, Fujimoto Masazumi, Itō Takerō and Yamazaki Tatsuo, published in *Kinema junpō*, 1 June 1957, p. 36. These genre categories made sense to his film journalist interlocutors but not necessarily to the public at large.
2 Fujii Hidetada, *Gosanke kayō eiga no ōgon jidai* (Tokyo: Heibonsha, 2001), p. 7
3 Rick Altman has done groundbreaking work on genre and the American film musical. Drawing on structuralist genre theory, he argued in *The American Film Musical* (Bloomington: Indiana University Press, 1988) that the interrelation of semantic and syntactic elements in the American film musical works to resolve major antinomies in the social lives of its audience. Other canonical analyses of the film musical also analyse the structural relation between narrative and number to understand the significance of the genre. See the contributions in Steven Cohan (ed.), *Hollywood Musicals: The Film Reader* (London: Routledge, 2002), for examples. In *Film/Genre* (London: British Film Institute, 1999) Altman supplemented his earlier theory with a sociolinguistic analysis of the importance of 'constellated communities' that link producers and consumers of genres through discourse. More recently, attention has shifted from textual analysis and genre studies to the links between musical films and other media industries, as in Peter Stanfield, *Horse Opera: The Strange History of the 1930s Singing Cowboy* (Champaign: University of Illinois Press, 2002), which highlights the importance of singing radio stars, or to the importance of 'musical moments' even in non-musical genres, as in the essays collected in Ian Conrich and Estella Tincknell (eds), *Film's Musical Moments* (Edinburgh: Edinburgh University Press, 2006). Amy Herzog argues that such musical moments can highlight dissonance or disjointedness in ways that test the canonical boundaries of the film musical. See Amy Herzog, *Dreams of Difference, Songs of the Same: The Musical Moment in Film* (Minneapolis: University of Minnesota Press, 2010).

4   For more on this transition see Michael Raine, 'No Interpreter, Full Volume: The benshi and the "sound version" in 1930s Japan', in Michael Raine and Johan Nordström (eds), *The Culture of the Sound Image in Prewar Japan* (Amsterdam: Amsterdam University Press, forthcoming).

5   [Editors' note: for more on the introduction of sound technology in Japanese cinema, see also Chapter 10 by Johan Nordström in this volume.]

6   Iwamoto Kenji, *Silent kara talkie e: Nihon eiga keiseiki no hito to bunka* (Tokyo: Shinwasha, 2007), p. 94

7   Ibid., p. 92.

8   Aaron Gerow, 'Japan', in Corey Creekmur and Linda Mokdad (eds), *The International Film Musical* (Edinburgh: Edinburgh University Press, 2012), p. 157–70. Gerow rightly claims that the 'failure' of Japanese musical films was also a form of success: incorporating aspects of the Hollywood musical constituted an ironic practice of genre re-reading that self-consciously mediated the fraught cultural relation between Japan and the US, acknowledging the 'incompleteness' of Japanese modernity while, at the same time, 'relishing its inadequacy' (p. 158).

9   Rick Altman, 'A Semantic/Syntactic Approach to Film Genre', *Cinema Journal* vol. 23 no. 3 (1984), pp. 6–18.

10 See Rick Altman, 'The American Film Musical as Dual Focus Narrative', in *The American Film Musical* (Bloomington: Indiana University Press, 1987), esp. p. 27.

11 Ibid., p. 340.

12 Ibid., p. 271.

13 Rick Altman, 'A Semantic/Syntactic Approach to Film Genre', *Cinema Journal* vol. 23 no. 3 (1984), p. 7.

14 Carrie McDonnell, 'Genre Theory and the Film Musical', in David Neumeyer (ed.), *The Oxford Handbook of Film Music Studies* (Oxford: Oxford University Press, 2013), pp. 245–69.

15 Ian Conrich and Estella Tincknell, 'Introduction', in Ian Conrich and Estella Tincknell (eds), *Film's Musical Moments* (Edinburgh: Edinburgh University Press, 2006), p. 6

16 For details see Sasagawa Keiko, 'Kouta eiga ni kansuru kiso chōsa: Meiji makki kara Shōwa shoki o chūshin ni', *Engeki kenkyū center kiyō* no. 1 (2003), pp. 175–96; and Diane Wei Lewis, 'Media Fantasies: Women, Mobility, and Silent-Era Japanese Ballad Films', *Cinema Journal* vol. 52 no. 3 (2013), pp. 99–119. Chika Kinoshita has traced the tie-up between the film and record version of *Tokyo March/Tokyo Kōshinkyoku* (Mizoguchi Kenji, 1929), one of many such examples from the period, in 'The Edge of Montage: A Case of Modernism/Modanizumu in Japanese Cinema', in Daisuke Miyao (ed.), *The Oxford Handbook of Japanese Cinema* (Oxford: Oxford University Press, 2014), pp. 124–51.

17 See the advertisement for the film in *Asahi shinbun*, 14 December 1939, p. 4, for the description of *Singing Lovebirds*.

18 See Kurata Yoshihirō, *Nihon record bunkashi* (Tokyo: Tokyo shoseki, 1992), p. 202, for an account of the creation of the song and Matsuura Kōzō, *Nihon eigashi taikan* (Tokyo: Bunka shuppankyoku, 1982), p. 125, for an account of its ubiquity in the cinemas.

19 The model for this kind of musical celebrity was Deanna Durbin, whose *100 Men and a Girl* (Henry Koster, 1937) started a classical music boom in Japan.

20 See Fujikake Ichirō, 'Hara Setsuko', in Negishi Hiroyuki (ed.), *Utaeba tengoku: Nippon kayō eiga deluxe: chi no maki* (Tokyo: Media Factory, 1999), p. 133, for this anecdote.

21 For a description of these films see Hirosawa Ei, *Nihon eiga no jidai* (Tokyo: Iwanami shoten, 2002), pp. 91–134.

22 See for example the nightclub scene in *Stray Dog/Nora inu* (1949). For more on Kasagi, see Michael Bourdaghs, *Sayonara America, Sayonara Nippon: A Geopolitical Prehistory of J-Pop* (New York: Columbia University Press, 2012), pp. 11–48. Kasutori referred to the rotgut distilled from the leftovers of sake production, the stereotypical drink of starving artists in early postwar Japan. The culture was described by John Dower in *Embracing Defeat: Japan in the Wake of World War II* (New York: W.W. Norton, 1999) as 'a commercial world dominated by sexually oriented entertainments and a veritable cascade of pulp literature' that nevertheless 'exhibited an ardor and vitality that conveyed a strong impression of liberation from authority and dogma' (p. 148).

23 Yamagishi Ichirō, 'Tōhō sannin musume a go go', in Negishi, *Utaeba tengoku*, p. 164.

24 Fujikake Ichirō, 'Misora Hibari', in Negishi, *Utaeba tengoku*, p. 148.

25 For the comparison with Kasagi Shizuko, see Honda Yasuharu, *Sengo Misora Hibari to sono jidai* (Tokyo: Kōdansha, 1987), pp. 77–89. The Japanese phenomenon

of *monomane* was quite a common practice and included lookalike photos, covers of foreign singers, as well as various other forms of imitation and parody on comedy shows and at public events.

26. See Sakamoto Hiroshi, *Heibon no jidai: 1950-nendai no taishū goraku zasshi to wakamono-tachi* (Tokyo: Shōwado, 2008), p. 106.

27. See for example the review of *Singing Phoenix/Utau fuyajo* (Mizuho Shunkai, 1957) in *Kinema junpō*, 11 February 1957, p. 73.

28. For the claim about romance and Hollywood cinema, see David Bordwell, Kristin Thompson and Janet Staiger, *Classical Hollywood Cinema: Film Style and Mode of Production to 1960* (New York: Columbia University Press, 1987), p. 16.

29. The figures are collected in the 'box office figures table' (*seiseikihyō*) section of *Kinema junpō* magazine for their respective week, and later in the *Film Yearbook* (*eiga nenkan*) for the corresponding year. See *Eiga nenkan 1957*, p. 92; *Eiga nenkan 1958*, p. 47; and *Eiga nenkan 1959*, p. 46, for details. *Janken Girls* was the first film in which the three stars appeared together. This 'three girl' series was succeeded by another, starring three different actresses, and then another: the format generated a series of series that continued throughout the 1970s in at least six different incarnations.

30. This last connection is noted in Yamagishi Ichirō, 'Tōhō Sannin musume a gō gō', in Negishi, *Utaeba tengoku*, p. 165.

31. The song was *also* released, with different lyrics, by Yukimura Izumi in 1954 but audiences would have been more familiar with Eri's version, which she sang on NHK's overwhelmingly popular year-end radio broadcast.

32. Kawakita Nagamasa and Kawakita Kashiko, interviewed by Tanaka Jun'ichirō. 'Europe eigakai kinkyō arekore', *Kinema junpō*, 1 February 1957, reprinted in *Best of Kinema junpō 1950–1966* (Tokyo: Kinema junpōsha, 1994), p. 555.

33. Hasumi is quoted in Negishi Hiroyuki, 'Kayō eiga e no michi: 1938–1958, 1934–1962', in Negishi, *Utaeba tengoku*, pp. 88–9.

34. See Etō Fumio, *Miru zasshi, suru zasshi: Heibon bunka no hakkensei to sōzōsei* (Tokyo: Heibon shuppan, 1966), unpaginated back matter for the circulation and regional distribution in 1965, and p. 78–88 for a discussion of 'visual magazines'. The claim that the 'teenager' only came into existence in Japan after World War II was made by Minami Hiroshi's Social Science Research Institute, quoted in Sakamoto, *Heibon no jidai*, p. 10.

35. See the long quotation from Izumi in Sakamoto, *Heibon no jidai*, pp. 69–72.

36. See 'Misora Hibari gokanen renzoku number one no eikan!: Mina-sama ga eranda 1956 nendo no daihakkai danjo kashu hanagata best ten happyō', *Heibon*, May 1956, p. 146. Misora won the contest every year from 1952 to 1965.

37. *On Wings of Love* began serialisation in *Heibon*, May 1956, and *Romance Girls* was a one-shot story in this issue.

38. Nakano Minoru, *Heibon eiga shōsetsu janken musume* (Tokyo: Heibon shuppan, 1955).

39. 'Kanpai janken musume', *Heibon*, November 1955, pp. 110–16.

40. See the advertisement in *Heibon*, April 1956, p. 291.

41. See Sakamoto, *Heibon no jidai*, p. 54, for the reference to third-class mail.

42. Rick Altman, *Film/Genre* (London: British Film Institute, 1999), pp. 162–3.

43. Marc Steinberg, *Anime's Media Mix: Franchising Toys and Characters in Japan* (Minneapolis: University of Minnesota Press, 2012).

44. This was not always accepted by even progressive critics at the time. See, for example, poet Hasegawa Ryūsei's criticism of Misora Hibari as a superstar whose fans want her to 'pose', not act, in 'Taishū eiga haiyūron nōto: Ushiro ni mo shō ga aru', *Eiga hihyō*, April 1958, pp. 20–4.

45. This notorious incident is described at length in Misora's autobiography, in which she reports that at later shows some would call out, 'Hey, Hibari, we're going to pour acid on you again.' See Misora Hibari, *Hibari jiden: Watashi to kage* (Tokyo: Sōshisha, 1971), p. 160.

25

THE YAKUZA FILM
The yakuza film: A genre 'endorsed by the people'

Jennifer Coates

Before collecting his Order of Culture Award in 2013, the veteran yakuza film actor Takakura Ken (1931–2014) told journalists 'If you want to understand why the yakuza films were endorsed by the people, you can't do it without thinking of the social situation at the time.'[1] Takakura's comment clearly links his high-profile award for services to Japanese culture with the yakuza genre's popular appeal; something apparent in box-office records, contemporary journalism, and in the high incidence of serials and remakes of yakuza tales. This chapter suggests that the genre's popularity and consequent impact on Japanese and global cinemas can be better understood by taking a wider approach to the genre than extant scholarship allows.

In particular, it will draw from Japanese-language film criticism of the 1960s and 1970s to make a case for the yakuza film as a wide-ranging genre encompassing diverse narratives and imagery previously coded in earlier film genres and cultural products. Like the wandering gambler characters (*matatabimono*) on which modern yakuza film protagonists are based, the yakuza genre has absorbed influence from its surroundings, picking up tropes from other film genres and art forms as well as real-life events. Takakura's reference to 'the social situation at the time' can be interpreted in terms of reference to real-life social change, which scholars such as Isolde Standish read in the narratives of 1960s and 1970s yakuza film.[2] However, the 'social situation' of this era must also be understood as something highly media-aware; as cinema attendance declined from a peak of over one billion viewers per year in 1958,[3] remaining audiences in the 1960s and 1970s were film-literate and highly attuned to influences and borrowings from other periods and genres in the yakuza film. Understanding the roots of the yakuza genre therefore also allows us to better understand its popular reception.

Existing scholarship has generally concerned itself with the 'pure' yakuza film; contemporary tales set in 1970s urban Japan or in prisons, focusing on young male protagonists and imagined to cater to a largely masculine audience.[4] Criticism published in popular film magazines of the period such as *Kinema junpō* and *Eiga geijutsu*, however, shows that a large number of yakuza films also featured female yakuza or gambler protagonists. My own interviews with viewers indicate the audience of the yakuza film included elite students of both genders and suburban, as well as urban, audiences. It is therefore a secondary project of this chapter to reinstate the gender balance of 1960s and 1970s film criticism and audiences into contemporary accounts of the yakuza genre, and place analysis of female yakuza characters and narratives alongside their male contemporaries.

Taking a wider approach to the yakuza film in terms of both gender and genre allows us to understand more about its popular appeal. While scholarship on the male yakuza hero notes the nostalgia of yakuza narratives and imagery, a more gender-balanced approach reveals a wider range of emotional cues at work in the yakuza genre, from desire to melodramatic affect. By considering the genre as a hybrid of pre-established tropes, we can therefore understand the emotion central to the yakuza film as something borrowed and repeated from earlier narratives. As these tropes

A BRIEF HISTORY OF THE YAKUZA FILM

Between 1960 and 1976, films featuring yakuza characters consistently ranked among the top ten box-office earners and gradually began to appear in critics' and viewers' lists of the best films of each year.[5] While the yakuza genre is now one of Japanese cinema's best known, its development as a stand-alone genre is relatively recent. Early films such as *Chūji's Travel Diary/Chūji tabi nikki* (Itō Daisuke, 1927–8, in three parts) told of the wandering gambler and swordsmen figures who would become contemporary yakuza, but these films were not widely recognised as a genre in their own right until the postwar period. The 'wandering gambler' figure had been a recurring subject of popular entertainment since the Edo period (1603–1887), when wandering samurai (*hatamono-yakko*) and townsmen gangs (*machi-yakko*) came together to gamble. A subcultural identity grew around these gamblers (*bakuto*) and peddlers (*tekiya*), forming the basis of the modern yakuza legend.[6] The *bakuto* gambler was referred to as a 'yakuza' on losing at cards – 'ya-ku-za' can be translated as 'eight, nine, three', which is a losing hand in the *hanafuda* card game similar to blackjack.[7] A loser at cards became a yakuza; a term subsequently applied to other fringe groups in the general sense of people who were considered 'good for nothing'.

In contrast to the culture depicted in 1970s yakuza film, Eiko Maruko Siniawer suggests that during the Edo period, yakuza culture was seen as 'neither extreme nor deviant'.[8] As the Tokugawa shogunate weakened however, the yakuza began to operate in a power vacuum, challenging local and national authorities.[9] Siniawer conflates the *bakuto* with the *shishi*, or 'men of spirit' who made up the 'violent arm of the modern state' under the Tokugawa shogunate; both used skills honed defending political and economic territories to attempt to overthrow the shogunate and negotiate a favourable position for themselves during the Bakumatsu period of civil unrest (1860–7).[10] While the *shishi* did not survive the Meiji Restoration (1868), the *bakuto* went on to form the organised crime 'families' we now recognise as modern yakuza.

The codes and rituals of contemporary yakuza film therefore draw from a wide range of historical influences; the vertical hierarchies of the yakuza 'family' stem from the Meiji reorganisation of groups of *bakuto* and ex-*shishi* (*shizoku*) into structured quasi-legal bodies, while the formal introductions performed by yakuza characters such as Fuji Junko's[11] Oryū in *The Red Peony Gambler/Hibotan bakuto* series (1968–72) are borrowed from the wandering peddlers and craftsmen of the *tekiya*, who performed similar petitions for lodgings during their travels

Fig. 25.1 *Red Peony Gambler/Hibotan bakuto* (Yamashita Kōsaku, 1968, Tōei).

(Fig. 25.1). The modern yakuza image also has antecedents in the legends of *kyōkaku*, or 'chivalrous commoners', Robin Hood-style townsmen who protected their local communities. These figures are frequently referenced in yakuza film titles such as the series *An Account of the Chivalrous Commoners of Japan/Nihon kyōkaku den* (1964–71) and its female equivalent, the '*Nihon jokyōden*' series including *Chivalrous Geisha/Nihon jokyōden: Kyōkaku geisha* (Yamashita Kōsaku, 1969) and *Bright Red Flower of Courage/Nihon jokyōden: Makkana dokyōbana* (Furuhata Yasuo, 1970).

The yakuza genre drew from popular myth as well as history; the Chūji character of *Chūji's Travel Diary* is based on the quasi-mythical *bakuto* hero Kunisada Chūji (1810–50) who epitomises many of the tropes still central to yakuza film.[12] Before his crucifixion by the Tokugawa authorities, Kunisada was a fencing student born into a farming family, similar in background to the *kyōkaku*, though somewhat less chivalrous. After murdering an opponent, he severed ties with his family and was removed from the village census, becoming a *mushuku*, or homeless wanderer. As Kunisada picked up followers around modern-day Gunma prefecture assisted by the *bakuto* bosses of the region, his fame grew, and the modern yakuza legend of exiled warrior turned gang leader was born. Kunisada's legend fuses aspects of several pre-yakuza identities, from the *kyōkaku* to the *matatabimono*, in much the same way as the yakuza genre film.

Drawing from such varied historical sources, it is easy to see why yakuza tales became popular in a variety of early mass media including woodblock prints (*ukiyo-e*), stage plays and novels. *Yakuza eiga* similarly work across genres to attract a diverse range of audience demographics; with the postwar development of the *gurentai* style of yakuza gang modelled on American gangsters, the *yakuza eiga* came to incorporate elements that appealed to fans of historical drama (*jidaigeki*), samurai tales, the youth genre known as the 'Sun Tribe' (*taiyōzoku*) and even the romance film in subplots centred around love interests resisted, left behind or encountered on the road. In the late 1950s, Misora Hibari popularised the *jidaigeki* yakuza musical, while stars such as Takakura Ken, Fuji Junko and Kaji Meiko drew on both film and musical audience demographics by recording *enka*-style hits of the title songs of their 1960s and 1970s yakuza films.[13] In the early 1960s even the non-conformist avant-garde directors who comprised the studios' '*nouvelle vague*' (*nūberu bāgu*) and would go on to spearhead the postwar independent film movement incorporated yakuza themes into films such as Imamura Shōhei's *Pigs and Battleships/Buta to gunkan* (1964). The yakuza genre thus had diverse appeal due to such numerous subsets and offshoots.

The wide-ranging popularity of yakuza motifs is often ignored in contemporary scholarship, which tends to focus on the peak popularity of the yakuza genre in the 1970s. This late peak owes much to historical circumstance; despite, or perhaps on account of, the great popular appeal of yakuza tales, authorities took a dim view of the genre throughout the twentieth century, delaying its distribution and development. *Chūji's Travel Diary* had been popularly received in the late 1920s; part two of the trilogy was voted the best film of 1927 by critics in *Kinema junpō*'s 'Top Ten', while part three was listed as the fourth best film of the same year.[14] As Japan embarked on the expansionist Fifteen Years' War in the Asia-Pacific region (1930–45) however, yakuza heroes were considered 'unfit for wartime'.[15] Though films featuring characters based on Kunisada were produced into the mid-1930s, wartime censorship significantly impeded the popular distribution of the yakuza film.

During the Allied Occupation following Japan's defeat (1945–52), occupying forces ran a similarly rigorous system of censorship. The offices of the Supreme Commander for the Allied Powers (SCAP) constructed a list of banned topics and a system for screening films for censorship violations both before and after production. *Jidaigeki* period dramas were banned on the grounds that their 'feudal' themes were reflective of the attitudes that had led Japan to war; as yakuza narratives focused on *bakuto*, *shishi* or *kyōkaku* were often set in the premodern era, yakuza films were banned along with period film during the Occupation, though modern yakuza characters feature in SCAP-approved 'humanist' films such as Kurosawa's *Drunken Angel/Yoidore tenshi* (1948).[16]

Yakuza motifs grew in popularity from the 1950s, though the studios were generally slow to begin production of the new genre. Within the postwar Japanese studio system, each of the 'big five' studios (Tōhō, Shōchiku, Tōei, Nikkatsu and Daiei) specialised in a particular genre or genres. Daiei and Tōhō produced *jidaigeki* films centred on samurai and wandering masterless samurai (*rōnin*) characters as well as the sword-fighting (*chanbara*) subgenre films, which would contribute tropes and audience demographics to the yakuza film. Shōchiku made melodramas and *shomin eiga* ('common people', or petit bourgeois, films), whereas Nikkatsu developed the Sun Tribe youth genre and Tōhō made monster and sci-fi films (*kaijū eiga*) as well as award-winning drama. While most studios eventually produced films that could be described as *yakuza eiga*, Tōei marketed itself as the home of the yakuza genre film from the 1960s (though Daiei was first to produce a popular female yakuza series, with the *Woman Gambler/Onna tobakushi* series [1967–71], which ran to twelve instalments). By the 1970s, the studios were producing almost a hundred yakuza films a year, comprising over a fifth of the total film production in Japan.[17]

The growth in the purchase of television sets coincided with mass social migration towards the *danchi* apartment blocks in the suburbs, far from city centre cinemas, meaning that the postwar housewife audience increasingly restricted itself to watching television in the home. Film production began to focus on student and working audiences, as studios attempted to 'increase their appeal for modern audiences by making more masculine films' (*otokoppoi eiga*)[18] in 'rapid-fire' succession.[19] Cinema managers are reported to have 'deplored the yakuza film, on the grounds that female and teenage fans were few',[20] however the *Red Peony Gambler* series opened up the genre to a wider audience from 1968 and became particularly popular with students of both genders.[21] The first instalment screened as a double bill with *Soldier Gokudo/Heitai Gokudō* (Saeki Kiyoshi, 1968) in Tokyo on 14 September 1968, selling an unprecedented 30,200 tickets in the first week and 70 per cent of that total in the following week, largely due to the popularity of stars Fuji Junko and Wakayama Tomisaburō.[22] While the *ninkyō* or 'chivalrous' yakuza film, which presented tales of self-sacrifice and adherence to *giri* (duty) over *ninjō* (personal feeling), was originally marketed to a salaryman audience demographic, with its reflection of the hierarchal and anti-individualist structure of the Japanese company, the *ninkyō* yakuza film did not exclude female audiences. Standish suggests that Fuji's films 'opened up the genre to a female viewing position by specifically addressing issues of patriarchal loyalty as they applied to women', resulting in a female audience base which also attended the *ninkyō* yakuza films focused more closely on male characters, such as the *Abashiri Prison/Abashiri bangaichi* series (1965–8) (Fig. 25.2).[23]

Fig. 25.2 *Abashiri Prison/Abashiri bangaichi* (Ishii Teruo, 1965, Tōei).

In an effort to appeal to younger audiences, the studios began to produce an anti-authoritarian subgenre of yakuza film based on memoirs and news events known as the 'true record' (*jitsuroku*) film. At the same time, many studios fused the yakuza genre with the soft-core pornographic 'pink film' (*roman porno*) popularised by Nikkatsu, to develop the 'pinky violence' films exemplified by the 'girl boss' (*sukeban*) subgenre.[24] These films were generally quick and cheap to make thus minimising the risk to the studios, which had begun to suffer from the vertically integrated nature of Japanese film production as popular interest in the cinema declined. Like the *jitsuroku* subgenre, the low-budget handheld shooting style of the 'pinky violence' film gave a sense of immediacy and intimacy popular with soft-porn audiences. The *sukeban* film was likewise easily adapted to long-running series and spin-off media such as pin-up posters that increased revenue.

As many cinemas closed due to low attendance, 'art house' yakuza films such as those of Kitano Takeshi began to appear at film festivals around the globe, lauded for their powerful imagery, intricate codes and high-impact recurring tropes. Kitano's yakuza films were also popular and critical hits at home; *Sonatine* (Kitano Takeshi, 1993) was voted the fourth best film of 1993 by *Kinema junpō* critics and rated fifth by readers.[25] At the same time, long-running series such as *Gangster Women/Gokudō no onnatachi* (1986–95), based on the bestselling *Gangster Wives/Gokudō no tsumatachi* books written by Ieda Shōko, suggest the continuing popularity of the yakuza genre on video and television as well as in film.

WHAT MAKES A YAKUZA FILM? THE CASE FOR EXTENDING GENRE DEFINITIONS

Given the many mythic and historical motifs and conventions on which the yakuza genre draws, and the wide global and historical impact of yakuza tropes, it is difficult to determine exactly what constitutes a yakuza film. From the genre's roots in *jidaigeki* to the adoption of key yakuza motifs and imagery by other genres and other cinemas, such as the indie hit *Memories of Matsuko/Kiraware Matsuko no isshō* (Nakashima Tetsuya, 2006) or the transnational *Kill Bill I* (Quentin Tarantino, 2003), it is impossible to differentiate a yakuza film from a film featuring yakuza characters, ideology, imagery or themes. Paul Schrader argues that the first 'authentic' yakuza film dates from 1964, with the release of *Gambler/Bakuto* (Ozawa Shigehiro),[26] however the critic Akiyama Kiyoshi refers in 1968 to both 'prewar' yakuza film (*senzen no yakuza eiga*) and yakuza films as a phenomenon that has mainly been popular over the last twenty years.[27] Defining the yakuza genre by time period alone is therefore problematic.

Schrader does not specify why he considers *Gambler* more 'authentic' than its predecessors; given the arrangement of his article, the 'authenticity' of *Gambler* appears to be defined in contrast to earlier films of the 1950s and 1960s, which fused yakuza and *jidaigeki* conventions. If we are to make this kind of distinction, we must discount films that include elements of other genres from the 'canon' of yakuza film, including those that stray into 'pink' territory. However, these hybrid yakuza films are often those that have had the greatest impact on the wider history of Japanese and global cinema, producing the most popular, recognisable and frequently imitated characters, narrative tropes and imagery. For example, *Lady Snowblood/Shirayuki hime* (Fujita Toshiya, 1973) while not a yakuza film by Schrader's definition, inspired the yakuza character O-Ren of *Kill Bill I*. On the other hand, yakuza genre films such as *Yakuza Graveyard/Yakuza no hakaba: Kuchinashi no hana* (Fukasaku Kinji, 1976), voted fifth best film of 1976 by *Kinema junpō* readers and eighth best by critics, often take as protagonists undercover police rather than yakuza, and focus on parallel issues such as police and government corruption. Observing a trend in 1970 that combined 'cruel scenes of killing with mannerisms from classical theatre', the film critic Hōjō Nobuhiko argued for a kind of 'ultra yakuza film' (*chōyakuza eiga*), which incorporated 'everyday content' relevant to 'aesthetics, society, politics and erotics'.[28] The wide range of influences, including other film genres, incorporated in the yakuza genre was apparent to Japanese film critics as early as 1970; it therefore seems unwise to delimit the definition of yakuza film to those films featuring only yakuza characters, narratives, themes and stars.

Schrader himself struggles to make his argument for 'pure' yakuza film cohere, as he splits the developmental period of the genre's production into two parts, 1964–1967 and 1968–1972. These periods are distinguished by an initial low-budget, 'B movie' approach to making yakuza film pursued by Tōei alone from 1964 to 1967, as opposed to a better-funded, 'classier' approach to production from 1968 to 1972, which incited other studios to 'get in on the act'.[29] Reducing the yakuza genre to this limited period risks underplaying the impact of the yakuza film on later productions, and discounts the influence of earlier 'B' movies on the yakuza genre. For example, 'B' movie star Mihara Yōko repeatedly played American-styled *chinpira*, or 'punk' gangsters' molls, and female gang bosses in the 'Queen Bee' series,[30] before taking kimono-clad supporting roles in the *Red Peony Gambler* films and moving into the *sukeban* soft-porn subgenre in the 1970s. Mihara's roles in the new 'pink' yakuza genre fused motifs from her 1950s and 1960s careers, and were predicated to a great extent on her star persona, honed in previous performances and genres. Examples such as Mihara suggest that we must take a longer historical view of the yakuza film than the eight years highlighted by Schrader in order to fully understand the development of key themes, star personas and characterisations. We cannot consider the yakuza films of Schrader's narrowly defined peak period free from influences and borrowings from other genres and time periods. In this sense, a 'pure' yakuza film seems impossible.

APPROACHES TO STUDYING YAKUZA FILM

Much of the extant literature on yakuza film follows Schrader's 'top down' model, focusing on studios, directors and actors. Chris Desjardins's *Outlaw Masters of Japanese Film* provides access to directors' and stars' opinions on the yakuza genre through long-form interviews that define yakuza film according to the working histories of participants.[31] Mark Schilling's *The Yakuza Movie Book* combines a history of the yakuza film with interviews with top-billing stars and directors of the genre, while Aaron Gerow's *Kitano Takeshi* considers the director's art-house yakuza films in the context of his wider body of work.[32] Keiko McDonald has provided an overview of the yakuza film beginning from the 1950s when, she argues, a 'more positive yakuza protagonist' appeared due to 'a popular appetite for cultural continuity' with the past.[33] However, her claim that *The Red Peony Gambler* series introduced the first yakuza heroine discounts earlier yakuza musicals starring Misora Hibari, Daiei's *Female Gambler* series and yakuza themes in other genres.[34] Higuchi Naofumi comes closest to a broad taxonomy of the yakuza genre, juxtaposing two subgenres of 1970s yakuza film to demonstrate how major themes and series shade into other popular genres.[35] Meanwhile, Yomota Inuhiko and Washitani Hana include the female yakuza heroine in a broader study on female representation in action film, isolating female performances by narrative theme rather than genre from the 1920s to the present day.[36] At the more populist end of the spectrum of *yakuza eiga* literature, Sugisaku J-tarō and Takeshi Uechi intersperse directors' interviews with picture galleries visually illustrating the development of the yakuza heroine from Fuji Junko's Oryū to Ike Reiko's girl boss characters.[37] However, none of this literature specifically interrogates the yakuza genre's popular appeal mentioned by Takakura Ken when he received his 2013 award. By contrast, Isolde Standish does approach yakuza film in the terms suggested by Takakura, thinking of 'the social situation at the time' to 'understand why the yakuza films were endorsed by the people'. Her consideration of selected films and series within the sociopolitical history of their production gives a detailed and informative sense of yakuza film's relevance and appeal for audiences.

As genre is a cyclical phenomenon in which the success, failure or subcultural popularity of a film has an impact on the reception of future films marketed as belonging to the same genre, the production history of a genre, a lateral view of production across genres and the sociopolitical historical background of a genre's production are all important elements in understanding a genre's appeal and success. Desjardins's and Schilling's interviews clearly demonstrate that directors and stars engaged with the history of the yakuza film preceding their own contributions and thought carefully about how to push the genre in new directions. Lateral studies such as Yomota and Washitani's, Higuchi's and Gerow's work demonstrate that this innovation does not occur in a vacuum; Gerow situates Kitano's yakuza creations in the context of his work in other genres while Yomota, Washitani and Higuchi consider selected images and themes across a number of genres. Standish's sociopolitical approach to understanding the historical background of 1960s and 1970s yakuza genre film may be extrapolated in this context to give a longer historical assessment of the yakuza film that also considers influences from other genres.

POPULAR ENDORSEMENT AND THE 'SOCIAL SITUATION': FUJI JUNKO AS THE *RED PEONY GAMBLER*

Having outlined the case for taking a wider approach to the yakuza film in terms of genre and gender, this chapter will now consider the appeal of the yakuza film by taking *The Red Peony Gambler* series as a case study. Connecting the popular 'endorsement' of yakuza film to 'the social situation of the time', as Takakura Ken suggests, requires a brief theorisation of the question: how does the sociopolitical context of a film impact on its reception? Miriam Hansen has suggested that viewers use cinema to make sense of their social situations, particularly in periods of rapid or unnerving social change; film may thus be seen as a 'cultural horizon' on which social and historical change is 'reflected, rejected or disavowed, transmuted or negotiated'.[38] Mitsuyo Wada-Marciano makes a similar claim for interwar Japanese cinema, arguing for 'film-makers' works and popular films as the cultural "translation" of ordinary people's desires, needs and hopes' in the 1920s and 1930s.[39] I suggest that popular engagement with the yakuza film worked in a very similar way and that Takakura's connection of the popular endorsement of the genre to the social situation around its development indicates that the yakuza film's reflection, rejection, disavowal, transmutation or negotiation of the social situation of 1960s and 1970s Japan had a particular appeal for viewers, who could read their own diverse 'desires, needs and hopes' into the yakuza genre's narratives, tropes and imagery.

Isolde Standish has linked developments in the yakuza genre to major changes in Japanese history and society; the cinema both referenced the social situation in which films were made and offered escape from aspects of postwar life many found difficult. Standish suggests that the *Abashiri Prison* series appealed to men struggling with the pressures and boredom of their secure 'salaryman' jobs; the 'powerful masculinity' represented by the inmate characters of the series provided both a means of aspiration and release in terms of their performance of a type of male identity 'predicated on physical strength and stoicism'.[40] In such a nuanced relation between yakuza film and the social situation, we can see Hansen's hypothesis at work as viewers would have recognised elements of their own experience in screen narratives, but also found space to reject or renegotiate difficult or unpleasant aspects of their lives and identities. Standish has argued that the main character of the *Abashiri* series, actually played by Takakura Ken, 'closes the gap between the ideological image of masculinity and social experience, thus offering a vicarious solution to the eternal consequences lived by most men'.[41]

Cinema does not only express and rework the social situations experienced by viewers, but can also impact on the meanings made of social situations at a wider level. Standish suggests that 1960s yakuza films 'can be analysed as sites where academic *nihonjinron* discourses are fictionalised in popular form'.[42] In this way, cinema not only makes sense of the social, it can actively *make* the social; a new sense of 'being Japanese' may be born out of film representations that express and renegotiate particular social circumstances. Hōjō argued in 1970 that yakuza film not only reflected sincere human observations on living a proper life but that people often looked to such fictions for a sense of stability.[43]

Yakuza film actively mediated and renegotiated what it meant to occupy a certain gendered, national or generational position in relation to others during periods of rapid social change. By analysing popular female-led yakuza series such as *The Red Peony Gambler*, we can also see yakuza tropes used to 'close the gap' between the ideological image of femininity and social experience in the aftermath of an occupation that had placed strong emphasis on encouraging gender-equal attitudes in a neo-Confucian patriarchal society. Characters such as Fuji Junko's 'Red Peony' Oryū, Misora Hibari's cross-dressing musical yakuza characters and Enami Kyōko's female gambler negotiated the changing status of women in postwar Japanese society in a manner consistent with the yakuza genre's wide appeal. The female yakuza characters who fought alongside men and were thus accorded equal status can be interpreted as literal manifestations of Article 24 of the 1947 Constitution, which stated that 'laws shall be enacted from the standpoint of individual dignity and the essential equality of the sexes'. However, many Japanese citizens reported that gender roles and relations remained relatively unchanged, even decades after the Constitution was ratified.[44] Female yakuza film referenced the social experience of being female in a man's world by isolating female yakuza characters within largely male-dominated narratives. The appeal of these characterisations and narratives is broad with an element of catharsis or problem solving in the closure of the gap between ideology and experience. While strong female characterisations may have had an aspirational appeal for younger and female viewers, traditional or conservative narrative tropes and settings simultaneously appealed to those nostalgic for an imagined 'traditional' Japan.

The female-led yakuza film charmed critics with its depiction of 'smart women standing shoulder to shoulder with men'[45] while positive comparisons of Oryū's swordsmanship with that of the legendary Zatōichi indicate that many female-led yakuza narratives were placed on a par with male-led films, as does a roughly equal amount of critical coverage devoted to male- and female-led yakuza films in the cinema press from 1968.[46] While female yakuza characters were a means of imagining the strong active female gender performances advocated during the postwar occupation of Japan, and discussed at length in popular media, their demonstration of a potential postwar female identity was also simultaneously bound by the 'traditional' norms of patriarchal social structures. Oryū is 'innocent and beautiful' rather than deadly, while her 'astonishing strength' is contrasted with her beauty in a way that led critics to interpret her characterisation as 'quite removed from real life'.[47] While some audiences may have appreciated the yakuza genre's nod to gender-equal ideals in the characterisation of female yakuza, it is also possible to read these characterisations according to pre-Occupation gender normative ideals and thus observe how they packaged the beauty and innocence associated with the more traditionally gender-normative 'daughter role' in a fantastical narrative of female empowerment, which many critics saw as an oddity or a form of 'lowbrow comedy'.[48]

This contradiction between strong female gender performances and familiar 'traditional' gender roles is epitomised in the characterisation of Oryū, who symbolically renounces her femininity in order to avenge her murdered father. Fuji Junko came to the 'masculine' role prepackaged in a way that did not challenge the patriarchal status quo; her father Shundō Kōji, the principle producer of *ninkyō* yakuza films at Tōei, was widely reported to have opposed her career as an actress until it became apparent that other studios would likely recruit his daughter. In this sense, the origin story of Fuji's star persona mirrored the narrative of the *Red Peony Gambler* series, in which Oryū becomes a yakuza out of necessity and against the wishes of her dead father.

The centrality of the father figure to Oryū's narrative and Fuji's star persona casts both figures as filial daughter characters. Fuji had played upright daughter roles in a number of yakuza and *jidaigeki* films before the *Red Peony Gambler – Three Yakuza/Matatabi sannin yakuza* (1965) and *13 Assassins/Jūsannin no shikaku* (1963), for example – and continued to intersperse the six-film series with roles as filial daughters avenging dead fathers in films such as *Bright Red Flower of Courage*. The *Red Peony Gambler* series, already at a 'fever pitch of popularity' even before its release in September 1968, emphasised these characteristics and critics noted that her star persona, predicated on 'beautiful daughter roles', was consistent with the role of Oryū.[49] Seen this way, the gender-progressive aspects of the narrative of *The Red Peony Gambler*, which repeatedly pits a female yakuza against male gangsters as an equal, are constrained by the more conservatively gendered characterisations of Oryū and Fuji herself. Balancing the narrative expression of new roles for women in postwar Japan with the attractions of more traditional modes of femininity allowed the series to appeal to gender-progressive and retrogressive or nostalgic audiences alike, and thus close the gap between ideological and experiential femininity in a cathartic manner.

Fuji's body is both sexualised and representative of a nostalgic appeal to chaste femininity. Critics regularly mention her 'red lips',[50] and the narrative tropes of Oryū's tattooed shoulder and repeated fight scenes necessitate regular disrobing throughout the series. Love interests are resisted or spurned, however, as Oryū also interprets her renunciation of female gender norms as the renunciation of heterosexual love. She bares her tattooed shoulder only for other female characters or while fighting alongside male yakuza 'brothers', and always as a form of proof that she is 'no longer a woman'. When Oryū displays her shoulder to a young woman who has been sold into prostitution in the first film, she compares her loss of femininity, symbolised by the tattoo, to the woman's situation, and after buying her freedom encourages the woman to resume her female-gendered way of life as, unlike Oryū herself, she is not physically marked as 'unfeminine'. While Oryū's sober kimonos and tight chignon are modest in comparison to the looser kimonos of supporting characters such as Mihara Yōko's in *The Red Peony Gambler: Oryū's Visit/Hibotan bakuto Oryū sanjō* (1970), her dress situates her at the ungendered mid-point between her hyper-feminine younger self, shown in flashbacks in the first film in bright pink flowered kimono with a 'split peach' hairstyle, and the ultra masculine Ōtaka, an elder female yakuza boss who serves as Oryū's mentor (*oyabun*) and who wears a man's kimono with her *obi* tied low across her hips. Masculine or non-normative gender performance is articulated as a point of shame for women; opposing yakuza bosses repeatedly refer to Oryū as unwomanly, or 'a sight', thus triggering violent outbursts from her supporters. Ryūko, Oryū's younger pre-yakuza incarnation, runs off in shame when her father's junior gang members (*kobun*) tease her for her proficient and 'unwomanly' swordsmanship during a flashback to her youth. Even among friends, Oryū is articulated as firmly outside the realm of female sexual availability, as her host families refer to her as 'Auntie' (*obachan*).

In Oryū's emotional relationships with resisted love interests, junior or suffering women, and small children, screen fantasies of female empowerment are further constrained within tropes borrowed from melodrama. Fuji explicitly connected both modest femininity and the female yakuza film to the melodrama genre in a 1968 interview with *Kinema junpō*, saying 'I want to become a melodrama actress, so I don't want to show nudity.'[51] In many ways Fuji's statement sums up the delicate balance with which the yakuza genre addressed the 'social situation' of gender roles and performance in postwar Japan; her chaste refusal to show nudity indicates a reliance on female-gendered tropes of innocence and beauty in female yakuza characterisation, while her career goals and the revelation that she demanded changes to the original *Red Peony Gambler* script suggest a star persona predicated as much on strength and ambition as beauty. In another interview, Fuji joked about her competitive attitude to Daiei's Enami Kyōko, star of the *Female Gambler* series: '"Enami Kyōko? I don't want to lose to her!" Fuji said, laughing.'[52] The core of strength and ambition in Fuji's star persona is wrapped up with references to her innocence, filial position and beauty; the sentimental 'feminine' tropes of melodrama cover the desirable and dangerous affect of the 'strong woman' trope. In this way, emotion is used to close the gap between the progressive gender ideologies implemented during the Occupation and the everyday experiences of Japanese citizens who found gender roles and expectations relatively unchanged.

SENTIMENT AND EMOTION IN THE YAKUZA FILM

From the homosocial relationships between the *nagare mono* wanderers of the *ninkyō eiga* to the fiery passions of the *sukeban*, the yakuza genre is suffused with emotion. Male gang members profess undying loyalty to their 'brothers', while female bosses lament their requisition of feminine gender norms that prohibit romance. Even the stoicism of Kitano Takeshi's arthouse yakuza is imbued with a sadness that sees Murakawa of *Sonatine* take his own life. Hōjō argues that 'emotion is indispensable' to the yakuza film, suggesting that the yakuza film viewer can feel a 'sense of community' in the 'camaraderie' of the ensemble cast and 'distraction' in the genre's 'silly humour'.[53] Fuji Junko and Takakura Ken were particularly popular as 'the perfect pair to depict a woman's sadness and a man's pain',[54] indicating that the emotional cues of the yakuza film ranged from humour and distraction to cathartic community feelings and outpourings of sadness.

The cyclical and repetitive nature of the yakuza genre is central to the production of emotion, as repetition can heighten the emotional impact of a motif. Deleuze and Guattari argue that a musical refrain may create and sustain a heightened level of affect, or emotional response, through repetition;[55] while this particular refrain is of the musical kind, I believe we can draw a parallel with any repetitive motif. The repetitive title songs recorded by yakuza actors and actresses and played at moments of heightened emotion, as well as over title sequences, are an aural example of an overall commitment to repetitive motifs that extends to the visual and the narrative levels of the yakuza genre. Plot devices such as lost love, murdered family members, and deep friendships or relations of loyalty formed in precarious or temporary situations are repeated with great frequency, as are visual motifs such as tattooing, traditional weaponry and kimono. In the *Red Peony Gambler* series, for example, Fuji's Oryū is repeatedly forced to prioritise revenge for her father and yakuza loyalties over potential love matches. In each instalment of the series, the title song plays again over repeated scenes of Oryū walking away from a would-be lover, heightening the pathos of her situation by reminding the viewer that she is doomed to repeat this hardship until she finally achieves vengeance for her father. The reuse of the title song here, as well as the repetitive lyrics of the song itself ('onna no, onna no') underscore the extreme sadness of renouncing love and Oryū's continued strength in doing so.

Yakuza film not only repeats tropes specific to the yakuza genre but also draws heavily from the tropes of other genres with which it shares settings, stars or narrative themes, including the *jidaigeki*, the melodrama, the horror film, the musical and the pornographic film, as discussed above. Linda Williams identifies melodrama, horror film and pornographic film as 'genres of excess'[56] in that they invite strong emotions from the viewer, who makes a physical connection with the film by emitting tears, flinching with horror or becoming aroused. I suggest that the yakuza genre draws its excesses of emotion from other 'genres of excess'; borrowing tears from the melodrama in tropes of frustrated romance, exile and the death of loved ones, suspense and terror from the horror film in scenes of fighting and ambush, and the qualities of the pornographic film in the 'pinky violence' subgenre. Among many examples of such borrowing, *Blind Woman's Curse*, also known as *Black Cat's Revenge/Kaidan nobori ryū* (1970), blends the unlucky black cat trope of the ghost story (*kaidan*) with the peer bonding motif of the prison film, the revenge plot of the yakuza film, the noble values of the *ninkyō eiga*, the nudity of soft porn and the vocal performances of the musical[57] in the early Meiji period setting of the *jidaigeki*. In this way, the yakuza genre draws on the affective devices used by other genres to encourage the viewer to invest emotion in yakuza characters and narratives. Rather than forging a new affective connection between the film and the viewer, the yakuza genre makes use of the well-trodden paths made by the melodrama, horror and pornographic genres of excess to access the viewers' emotions directly and predictably (an important issue for film-makers in this era of declining cinema attendance).

Excesses of emotion were thereby incorporated into the yakuza formula and repeated in various long-running series and spin-offs, thus enhancing their impact. While Williams acknowledges that genres of excess can often cause the viewer to feel manipulated by the film text, she argues that 'To dismiss them as bad excess whether of explicit sex, violence or emotion, or as bad perversion, whether of masochism or sadism, is not to address their function as cultural problem-solving.'[58] Affective identification with a film text can result in a kind of catharsis whereby excesses of emotion are spilled out in the safe or closed-off spaces of the cinema rather than in public. In this way, film can become an outlet for emotional responses considered inappropriate for public expression, as well as a space to practise or test out new attitudes or reactions. Takakura's suggestion that we look to the 'social situation' of popular yakuza film to understand why the genre was 'endorsed by the people' is consistent with the idea of the excess affect of the yakuza film as a form of 'cultural problem solving'. In 1968, Akiyama linked the yakuza film's reflection of contemporary circumstances to its emotional charge, arguing that 'yakuza films express today's consciousness',[59] using sentiment and cathartic emotion to 'somehow give comfort to the viewer's heart'.[60] This 'somehow' is more readily explainable when we take into account the long history of borrowing and repetition that has imbued the tropes of the yakuza film with such powerful emotional charge. The professional salarymen and politicised students who made up the yakuza film audience, as well as the female fans of Fuji Junko and Takakura Ken and the sex workers who visited the late night yakuza cinemas before or after work, may have found in the yakuza genre an outlet for emotions suppressed in their working lives and through this a form of comfort.

CONCLUSION: WANDERING ON

The selection of Takakura Ken as recipient of the high-profile Order of Culture Award clearly signals that the yakuza film has become a nostalgic emblem of national culture for many contemporary Japanese. As the famously taciturn star pointed out in a rare interview, the 'endorsement' of audiences has been central to the installation of the yakuza film into the canon of Japanese popular culture. In order to understand how this has occurred, we have to consider the position of yakuza film today in terms of the genre's long history. Just as the yakuza introduction places an importance on genealogy and family lineages, film scholars must also take account of the many historical cinematic influences on the yakuza genre. To do this, we must think across genres, much as the *matatabimono* wanders the countryside picking up information and influences along the way. Just as emotional attachments both motivate and sustain the yakuza hero or heroine's quest for justice or vengeance, so the emotional excess of the yakuza film sustains popular engagement with the genre. In conclusion, in order to fully understand the popular appeal of the yakuza genre, we must therefore take our own form of 'wandering' approach that considers the wider history, influences and emotional impacts of the yakuza film in a way that allows for a broader definition of the genre than the one that exists to date.

NOTES

1   Nathalie Kyoko Stuckey and Jake Adelstein, 'Yakuza Movie Icon Takakura Ken Talks to JSRC about Yakuza Movies', trans. Nathalie Kyoko Stuckey, *Japanese Subculture Research Center*, January 2014, <http://www.japansubculture.com/yakuza-movie-icon-takakura-ken-talks-to-jsrc-about-yakuza-movies-exclusive/>.

2   Isolde Standish, *Myth and Masculinity in the Japanese Cinema: Towards a Political Reading of the 'Tragic Hero'* (London: Curzon, 2000) and *A New History of Japanese Cinema: A Century of Narrative Film* (London: Continuum, 2005).

3   Satō Tadao, 'Humanism no jidai', in Imamura Shōhei, Shindō Kaneto, Yamada Yōji, Satō Tadao and Tsurumi Shunsuke (eds), *Kōza nihon eiga vol.5: Sengo eiga no tenkai* (Tokyo: Iwanami shoten, 1987), p. 3.

4   For example, Chris Desjardins's *Outlaw Masters of Japanese Film* (New York: Palgrave Macmillan, 2005) restricts its account of female-led yakuza film to an appendix, excepting a single interview with Kaji Meiko.

5   According to *Kinema junpō* records listing the top ten box-office earners, critical successes and popular hits each year, films featuring yakuza characters entered the box-office top ten in 1960 with *Road of Chivalry/Ninkyō nakasendō* (1960), a sequel in the *Jirochō* series featuring Kunisada Chūji. The film made 350,910,000 yen, the highest box-office taking that year. See *Kinema junpō best ten 85 kai zenshi 1924–2011* (Tokyo: Kinema junpōsha, 2012), p. 158. The plot follows gambling samurai and inter-gang warfare, with Chūji as a Robin Hood-type cameo star. While the *Kinema junpō* figures are rounded to the nearest 10,000 yen and fluctuate over time due to inflation and changes in the tax on ticket prices in 1973, it is evident that the top earning film each

year was the most popular and widely seen, at least until video rental. Yakuza films begin to appear in the *Kinema junpō* reader's choice of best ten films in 1972 with *Female Prisoner no. 701: Scorpion/Joshū 701 gō: Sasori* (1972) in seventh place, *Theatre of Life: Story of Youth, Passion and Spirit/Jinsei gekijō: Seishun, aiyoku, zankyō hen* (1972) in eighth place and *Modern Yakuza: Outlaw Killer/Gendai yakuza: Hito kiri yota* (1972) in tenth position. See *Kinema junpō best ten 85 kai zenshi 1924–2011*, p. 294. In 1973, readers voted *The Yakuza Papers vol. 1: Battles without Honour and Humanity/Jingi naki tataki* (1973) the best film of the year, *The Yakuza Papers vol. 2: Deadly Fight in Hiroshima/Jingi naki tatakai: Hiroshima shitō hen* (1973) fourth best and *Yakuza Tale/Nihon kyōka den* (1973) in ninth position. Critics voted *The Yakuza Papers vol. 1: Battles without Honour and Humanity* the second best film of 1973, with *The Yakuza Papers vol. 3: Proxy War/Jingi naki tatakai: Dairi sensō* (1973) as number eight. See *Kinema junpō best ten 85 kai zenshi 1924–2011*, p. 304. Yakuza films appeared in every box-office's, readers' and critics' top ten lists each year until 1976.

6   Mark Schilling, *The Yakuza Movie Book: A Guide to Japanese Gangster Films* (Albany, CA: Stonebridge Press, 2003), p. 20.

7   Eiko Maruko Siniawer, *Ruffians, Yakuza, Nationalists: The Violent Politics of Modern Japan 1860–1960* (Ithaca, NY: Cornell University Press, 2008), p. 194.

8   Ibid., p. 191.

9   Yasumaru Yoshio (ed.), '*Kangoku' no tanjō: Asahi hyakka rekishi o yominaosu*, vol. 22 (Tokyo: Asahi shinbunsha, 1995), p. 28.

10 Siniawer, *Ruffians, Yakuza, Nationalists*, p. 12.

11 Fuji Junko was the stage name used by Shundō Junko for the first part of her career. The actress starred as Fuji Junko in a series of *jidaigeki* and yakuza films in the 1960s, before retiring in 1972 on her marriage to kabuki theatre actor Onoe Kikugorō VII. She returned to television as Fuji Sumiko in 1974, before moving back into cinema, this time largely in melodrama and romance genres. She was awarded the Blue Ribbon Prize for best supporting actress in 1999 and 2006.

12 Following Yukitomo Rifu's play *Kunisada Chūji* (1919), characters similar to Kunisada or based on his life have appeared in many films including Makino Shōzō's *Kunisada Chūji* (1924), Kinugasa Teinosuke's *Young Chūji: Murder at Midagahara/Wakaki hi no Chūji: Midagahara no satsujin* (1925), Inagaki Hiroshi's trilogy (*Kunisada Chūji: Travel and Hometown/Kunisada Chūji: Tabi to kokyō no maki; Kunisada Chūji: Story of Constant Change/Kunisada Chūji: Rurō ruten no maki; Kunisada Cūji: Clear Skies over Akagi/Kunisada Chūji: Hareru hagi no maki*, all 1933), Yamanaka Sadao's *Kunisada Chūji* (1935) and Taniguchi Senkichi's *Kunisada Chūji* (1960). A ten-reel epic, made by actor Bandō Tsumasaburō's company, *Kunisada Chūji: Flight to Ōshū/Kunisada Chūji ochiyuki Ōshūji* was rumoured to have been made in 1926 but does not survive.

13 Like many yakuza motifs, *yakuza enka* have outlasted the peak popularity of the yakuza film; Kaji Meiko's *The Flower of Carnage/Shura no hana*, the title song of *Lady Snowblood/Shirayuki hime* (1973) was included in Quentin Tarantino's *Kill Bill I* (2003), while the theme songs of yakuza films starring Misora Hibari, Fuji Junko, Takakura Ken and others are readily available in the catalogues of karaoke emporiums such as the Shidax chain and on YouTube. Examples include Misora Hibari's title song for *Ishimatsu the One-Eyed Avenger/Hibari no mori no Ishimatsu* (1960) and male drag performance in *Daughter of Romance/Romansu musume* (1956) as well as her many televised appearances singing *yakuza enka* such as 'Hibari no wataridori da yo' and 'Edo no Yamitarō'. Fuji Junko's title song for the *Red Peony Gambler/Hibotan bakuto* series and Takakura Ken's title song for the *Abashiri Prison/Abashiri Bangaichi* (1965–1968) series also continue to prove popular today.

14 Cinema 1987, '1927 nen Kinema junpō best ten', <http://cinema1987.org/kinejun/kinejun1927.html>.

15 Schilling, *The Yakuza Movie Book*, p. 21.

16 [Editors' note: for more on the *jidaigeki*, see also Chapter 20 by Philip Kaffen in this volume.]

17 David E. Kaplan and Alex Dubrow, *Yakuza: Japan's Criminal Underworld* (Berkeley: University of California Press, 2012), p. 142.

18 Anon., 'Kōgyō kachi: Daiei yakuza no nagurikomi', *Kinema junpō*, 1 March 1969, p. 74.

19 Anon., 'Kōgyō kachi: Yakuza to kodomo shōbu', *Kinema junpō*, 15 March 1969, p. 72.

20 Anon., 'Kōgyōkai: Yakuza bangumi ni gaika', *Kinema junpō*, 11 November 1968, p. 83.

21 Iijima Tetsuo, 'Nihon eiga hihyō: Hibotan bakuto', *Kinema junpō*, 15 November 1969, p. 70.

22 Anon., 'Kōgyōkai', p. 83.

23. Isolde Standish, *A New History of Japanese Cinema: A Century of Narrative Film* (London: Continuum, 2005), p. 309.
24. The colloquial term 'pinky violence' was popularised by Sugisaku J-taro and Takeshi Uechi in their *Pinky Violence: Tōei's Bad Girl Films* (Tokyo: Tokuma shoten, 1999).
25. *Kinema junpō best ten 85 kai zenshi 1924–2011*, p. 516.
26. Paul Schrader, 'Yakuza: A Primer', *Film Comment*, January–February 1974, p. 10.
27. Akiyama Kiyoshi, 'Yakuza eiga wa sara ni manpukukan o ataeyo: Eiga shūkan to Narutaki izumu', *Eiga geijutsu*, 1 May 1968, p. 64.
28. Hōjō Nobuhiko, 'Yakuza eiga no kōryoku', *Kinema junpō*, 1 March 1970, p. 50.
29. Schrader, 'Yakuza: A Primer', p. 10.
30. The *Queen Bee* series at Shintōhō (*Queen Bee/Joōbachi* [Taguchi Satoshi, 1958]; *Queen Bee's Anger/Joōbachi no ikari* [Ishii Teruo, 1958], *Queen Bee and the School for Dragons/Joōbachi to daigaku no ryū* [Ishii Teruo, 1960]) was based on a remake of the Daiei film of the same name (*Queen Bee/Joōbachi* [Tanaka Shigeo, 1952]).
31. Chris Desjardins, *Outlaw Masters of Japanese Film* (New York: Palgrave Macmillan, 2005).
32. Mark Schilling, *The Yakuza Movie Book: A Guide to Japanese Gangster Films* (Albany, CA: Stone Bridge Press, 2003); Aaron Gerow, *Kitano Takeshi* (London: British Film Institute, 2007).
33. Keiko Iwai McDonald, 'The Yakuza Film: An Introduction', in Arthur Nolletti Jr. and David Desser (eds), *Reframing Japanese Cinema* (Bloomington: Indiana University Press, 1992), p. 173.
34. Ibid., p. 181. [Editors' note: for more on Misora Hibari, see also Chapter 24 by Michael Raine in this volume.]
35. Higuchi Naofumi, *Roman porno to jitsuroku yakuza eiga: Kinjirareta 70 nendai Nihon eiga* (Tokyo: Heibonsha, 2009).
36. Yomota Inuhiko and Washitani Hana (eds), *Tatakau onnatachi: Nihon no eiga no josei action* (Tokyo: Shohan, 2009).
37. Sugisaku and Takeshi, *Pinky Violence*.
38. Miriam Bratu Hansen, 'The Mass Production of the Senses: Classical Cinema as Vernacular Modernism', in Christine Gledhill and Linda Williams (eds), *Reinventing Film Studies* (London: Arnold, 2000), p. 341–2.
39. Mitsuyo Wada-Marciano, *Nippon Modern; Japanese Cinema of the 1920s and 1930s* (Honolulu: University of Hawai'i Press, 2008), p. 130.
40. Isolde Standish, *Myth and Masculinity in the Japanese Cinema: Towards a Political Reading of the 'Tragic Hero'* (London: Curzon, 2000), p. 160.
41. Ibid., p. 161.
42. Ibid., p. 167. *Nihonjinron* is a body of writing that refers to a 'theory of Japaneseness'. See Harumi Befu, *Hegemony of Homogeneity: An Anthropological Analysis of Nihonjinron* (Melbourne: Trans Pacific Press, 2001).
43. Hōjō, 'Yakuza eiga no kōryoku', p. 50.
44. Koyama Takeshi, *The Changing Social Position of Women in Japan* (Paris: UNESCO, 1961), p. 45.
45. Takasawa Eiichi, 'Nihon eiga hihyō; Nobori ryū yawarakada kaichō', *Kinema junpō*, 1 April 1969, p. 70.
46. Kosuge Shinsei, 'Nihon eiga hihyō: Hibotan bakuto', *Kinema junpō*, 20 September 1968, p. 63.
47. Ibid., p. 63.
48. Ibid.
49. Ibid.
50. Iijima Tetsuo, 'Nihon eiga hihyō: Nihon jokyōden: Makkana dokyōbana', *Kinema junpō*, 15 February 1970, p. 77.
51. Anon., 'Kōgyōkai', *Kinema junpō*, 1 November 1968, p. 83.
52. Anon., 'Kōgyō kachi: Daiei yakuza no nagurikomi', *Kinema Junpō*, 1 March 1969, p. 74.
53. Hōjō, 'Yakuza eiga no kōryoku', p. 50.
54. Iijima, 'Nihon eiga hihyō', p. 77.
55. Gilles Deleuze and Felix Guattari, *A Thousand Plateaus: Capitalism and Schizophrenia* (London: Continuum, 2003), p. 339.
56. Linda Williams, 'Film Bodies; Gender, Genre and Excess (1979)', in Leo Braudy and Marshall Cohen (eds), *Film Theory and Criticism: Introductory Readings* (Oxford: Oxford University Press, 1999), p. 701.
57. Star Kaji Meiko performs the title track 'Taking Care of Duty'/'Jingi komori uta', which was released as her first single.
58. Williams, 'Film Bodies', p. 714.
59. Akiyama, 'Yakuza eiga wa sara ni manpukukan o ataeyo', p. 65.
60. Ibid., p. 64.

26
DOCUMENTARY
'Filling our empty hands': Ogawa Productions and the politics of subjectivity

Ayumi Hata

POSTWAR DOCUMENTARY FILM HISTORY

In October 1989, the Yamagata International Documentary Film Festival (YIDFF) was launched in Yamagata, a city far north of Tokyo, as the first international documentary film festival in Asia. From the first through to the fifth editions of this biennial festival, YIDFF organisers presented a series of retrospectives tracing the history of Japanese documentary films: *The Dawn of Japanese Documentaries* (YIDFF 1989), *The Postwar Flourishing of Japanese Documentary* and *Media Wars: Then & Now* (YIDFF 1991), *Japanese Documentaries of the 1960s* (YIDFF 1993), *Japanese Documentaries of the 1970s* (YIDFF 1995), *The Pursuit of Japanese Documentary: The 1980s and Beyond* (YIDFF 1997) and *Imperial Japan at the Movies* (YIDFF 1997). This meticulously planned series, which extended over the best part of a decade, was fuelled by a strong passion on the part of the programmers to catalogue and show as many notable early documentaries as possible, including numerous hidden and underestimated independent films. The comprehensive line-up consisted of over 250 historical films in total ranging from prewar newsreels, leftist Prokino films, educational films, culture films (*bunka eiga*) and national propaganda films (*kokusaku eiga*) to postwar films such as avant-garde documentaries, experimental films, science films, PR films and political activist films.

Supplemented by subsequent special programmes featuring films from the geographical and social periphery of the nation, including programmes on Okinawa (YIDFF 2003) and ethnic minorities such as *zainichi* (YIDFF 2005), this ambitious long-term project encompassing the entirety of Japanese documentary history – and the very existence of the film festival itself – has indisputably been crucial for the development of documentary film studies in Japan. Documentary film had been regarded as a minor element of the domestic film industry until around the 1980s, and its historiographical study has received relatively less attention than that paid to fiction feature films. Furthermore, conventional accounts of Japanese documentary film history had previously centred on the ideas, methods and life stories of pioneer auteurs such as Kamei Fumio, the sole wartime film-maker to be imprisoned as a result of supposed anti-war sentiments in *Fighting Soldiers/Tatakau heitai* (1939), and the legendary independent postwar documentarists Tsuchimoto Noriaki and Ogawa Shinsuke. YIDFF programmes, and the substantial catalogues that accompanied each programme, demonstrated that many historical and theoretical aspects of this genre still remained untouched, thus inspiring researchers and critics to begin filling in the blank parts of this history.

Markus Nornes, the renowned expert in Japanese and Asian film history and a YIDFF special programme coordinator, stands out amongst other scholars for his series of important essays and books on Japanese documentary history. Nornes revisited prewar Japanese documentary film-making and discourse within the social and political context of the times in his influential book *Japanese Documentary Film: The Meiji Era through Hiroshima*.[1] Providing detailed analysis of the 'hard' style of wartime propaganda films and Kamei Fumio's negotiation with that style in particular, he articulated the importance of understanding the complicated relationship between film-making practices and state power as well as the conflict between public and hidden discourse inscribed in artistic expression. Nornes then moved on to a biographical study of Ogawa Shinsuke (1936–92) and his collective Ogawa Productions (or Ogawa Pro) in his next book *Forest of Pressure: Ogawa Shinsuke and Postwar Japanese Documentary*.[2] In this, he analysed the evolution of the philosophy and film-making style of Ogawa and his collective in relation to the postwar sociopolitical context they lived through. While the unique film-making and distribution styles of Ogawa Productions have long intrigued many film scholars in and outside Japan,[3] Nornes's thorough and in-depth research, supported by abundant primary sources, helped to delineate several significant turns in Ogawa's innovative film-making journey and to historicise the collective's achievements in compelling historical detail.

As these preceding studies note, the impact of Ogawa Pro's film-making and screening practices upon the development of Japanese documentary film was immense. One of their most significant contributions was an exploration of the film-maker's relationship with the *taishō*, a Japanese term referring to the subject of a film or the object to be filmed. From the *Forest of Oppression – A Record of Struggle at Takasaki City University of Economics/Assatsu no mori – Takasaki keizai daigaku tōsō no kiroku* (1967) to the seven-part Sanrizuka series (1968–77), Ogawa and his crew kept their cameras alongside protesters in the midst of their struggles and acted as an film squad (*eigahan*) for the benefit of struggling students or farmers. Their consistent and enduring devotion to these struggles impressed contemporary critics and film-makers,[4] while also encouraging young talents such as Hara Kazuo and the 'post-Ogawa' generation, which included the radical film-making collective Nippon Documentarist Union (NDU), to develop their own philosophies regarding the *shutaisei* (subjectivity) of the documentary film-maker and their relationship with the filmed object.

While the Japanese terms *shutai* (the subject) and *shutaisei* are complicated and problematic words to define, they have frequently been used in a variety of ideological contexts since the early twentieth century. They were particularly conspicuous in early postwar discourses of Japanese Marxists, sociologists and philosophers relating to political developments such as the ongoing process of democratisation by the Occupation forces and the resurrection of the Japanese Communist Party. As the historian J. Victor Koschman has noted, the intellectual class believed that the success of the bourgeois democratic revolution in postwar Japan depended upon modern individuals who could actively commit to sociopolitical activities as revolutionary subjects or in terms of their active historical 'agency'.[5] In this context, the words *shutai* or *shutaisei* were used to emphasise political activity as the characteristic of an ideal postwar subject.

Reflecting the legacy of this political implication, the issue of authorial subjectivity also occupied a central place in postwar film criticism. In the field of documentary film, an intense *shutaisei* debate played out in the journal *Kiroku eiga* from 1958 to 1964. The discussion was led by film-makers such as Matsumoto Toshio and Noda Shinkichi, who rejected the conventional naïve documentary realism of the older wartime generation and fiercely accused this generation of losing their subjectivity as creative artists. Matsumoto stressed the necessity of creating a documentary method based on a new concept of independent subjectivity, which film-makers could achieve through strict self-interrogation regarding their attitudes towards a pro-filmic reality. In addition, as Nornes has pointed out, unlike other radical film-makers such as Ōshima Nagisa who concentrated on the issue of the cinematic representation of a film-maker's subjectivity, Matsumoto's avant-garde documentary theory focused instead on the revelation of the existential force of an object or the actual people filmed through the process of subjective film-making. This perspective influenced the following generations of young film-makers, including Ogawa Shinsuke.

The aim of this chapter is to revisit the unique trajectory of Ogawa Productions' exploration of the subjectivity of their filmed objects and their pursuit of an ideal subjectivity in filming, with a particular focus on the period when the collective moved from Sanrizuka to Magino village in the late 1970s. In his influential book, Nornes analyses the transformations in Ogawa Pro's treatment of the subject/object relationship in each work. Many critics agree that *Sanrizuka – Heta Village/ Sanrizuka – Heta buraku* (1973) was a radical keystone in both Ogawa's early artistry and the development of Japanese postwar documentary history: the pinnacle of Ogawa's cinematic quest in Sanrizuka and a film that most effectively revealed the subjectivity of the filmed people and their sense of temporality by minimising the director's control over the pro-filmic reality. At the same time, the later Ogawa epic *The Sundial Carved with a Thousand Years of Notches - The Magino Village Story/ Sen'nen kizami no hidokei – Magino mura monogatari* (1986) may also be seen as the culmination of Ogawa Productions' work; a film in which all the techniques, philosophies and approaches to the filmed objects that the collective had until then developed were intricately interwoven into a united whole.

By largely concurring with this historical description of the works of Ogawa Productions, I will focus upon the approach Ogawa and his crew took towards developing their own authorial subjectivity. Throughout their film-making, they persistently took a decisive position by allying themselves with the people they filmed, while also undergoing a transformation in their film-making identity that accompanied the change experienced by their subjects. To illustrate the course of their efforts, I will refer to three films the collective itself suggested were 'crucial' to their film-making history in a statement they made in 1982 – *Forest of Oppression*, *Sanrizuka – Heta Village* and *The Magino Village Story – Raising Silkworms/Magino monogatari – Yōsanhen* (1977).[6] *Forest of Oppression* was Ogawa's earliest masterpiece, a film that first won him notice as a radical independent documentarist. As we will see in the next section, this critical acclaim can be attributed to the expression of the film-maker's 'subjective' attitude towards the struggle of the object that was achieved through a one-sided camera position and a series of repetitive close-up shots. This approach had its roots in the intense aforementioned debate on the postwar subjectivity of documentary film-makers that took place in the late 1950s, a debate that had a major effect on film-making practices of the 1960s. After *Forest of Oppression*, Ogawa turned his camera on the struggle of farmers opposed to the construction of the New Tokyo International Airport in Sanrizuka, Narita, making seven Sanrizuka films in all. Over the years, his collective developed a relationship with the protesting farmers and devoted itself to capturing the farmers' subjectivities on film as individual and active agents of social revolution. This positive representation of farmers was also interrelated with the rise of the 'people's history' (*minshūshi*) movement, a contemporaneous trend that emerged in the field of historical studies from the mid-1960s to the 1970s. By focusing on the collective's involvement with the *minshūshi* doctrine during and after the Sanrizuka period, we will see the process through which Ogawa developed the idea of a 'desirable' film-making subjectivity qualified to portray the intrinsic nature of farming and traditional rural villages in Japan.

Ogawa's own inclusion of *The Magino Village Story – Raising Silkworms* among his most notable works comes as a surprise when compared with the other two films, which are frequently cited as exemplary works in Ogawa's career by many critics and researchers. In contrast, *The Magino Village Story – Raising Silkworms* has largely been ignored in the past; it has often been described as a study film intended for the collective's young trainees, and a passing lapse into an outdated educational film mode that served as a beginner's introduction to the detailed process of traditional domestic sericulture. Although this is an apt description of the film, or perhaps for this very reason, this study film assumes greater significance in the Ogawa Pro filmography in the context of the collective's ongoing focus on subjective film-making. During the years they spent studying and filming farming in Magino, the collective members became convinced that they themselves had developed a new form of subjective existence within the village via a medium capable of communicating the essence of the village's indigenous wisdom, lifestyle and stories to the outside world. By retracing Ogawa Pro's film-making journey from the end of the 1960s to the 1970s, this chapter will thus address one of the most formidable tasks Japanese postwar documentary film-makers grappled with: namely, their effort to establish a democratic relationship between the film-maker and the filmed object through subjective film-making.

BEFORE MAGINO: POSTWAR SUBJECTIVITY AND DOCUMENTARY PRACTICE

The sensation caused by *Forest of Oppression* brought Ogawa's name into the spotlight as a promising new directing talent. Public screenings of the film at universities and public halls in large cities started from the end of 1967 and were supported by networks of New Left students and their university press associations. Not a few film critics viewed the film in university classrooms or auditoria and appraised its form of stark realism filled with the 'actual' faces and voices of student activists who had barricaded themselves inside the student hall of a university in Takasaki. The leftist critic Matsuda Masao described this work as an 'unquestionable masterpiece' because of its powerful expression of political agitation and the solidarity and urgent reality that the activist students had shared.[7] The avant-garde film-maker Matsumoto Toshio also praised Ogawa and his crew for their determination to share the generational agony painfully epitomised by the struggle of the students and for documenting the 'real voices' suffused with a pain that appealed directly to the emotions of viewers.[8]

This high acclaim and the attention paid to *Forest of Oppression* resulted not only from the positioning of the camera in the film alongside the students inside the barricade but also from the accumulation of extreme close-up shots of the debating students. In comparison with his earlier film about correspondence university students, *Sea of Youth – Four Correspondence Course Students/Seinen no umi – Yonin no tsūshin kyōikuseitachi* (1966), Ogawa and cinematographer Ōtsu Kōshirō visibly increased their use of close-ups in *Forest of Oppression*. In a press interview conducted in 1967, Ogawa explained this strategy as a means of utilising the specific ability of close-ups to uncover the 'true face' of the filmed subject and allow viewers to appreciate this reality more deeply.

We talked a lot about whether we could more graphically depict the state of isolation the students had been driven to by remaining in a room of the Student Hall. We wondered whether we could take close-ups of their faces, eliminating everything else, and use these close-ups to express the entirety of what was happening.[9]

Ogawa's statement clearly contains echoes of the debate on auteurist subjectivity that appeared in the documentary film journal *Kiroku eiga*, in particular the issue focusing on Matsumoto Toshio's avant-garde documentary film theories and his experimental film-making practices of the 1960s. Referring to Freudian and Marxist concepts, Matsumoto argued that film-makers do not accept the world as it appears but attempt to explore its invisible, hidden aspects as well as their own inner selves by questioning our habitual perceptions via their cameras. This theorisation of avant-garde documentary film-making, as Yuriko Furuhata argues, owes a great debt to the avant-garde documentary theories advocated in the 1950s by the Marxist critic Hanada Kiyoteru, whose concern regarding the artistic defamiliarisation of social reality was closely connected with contemporary trends of documentary journalism in the mass media, television and literature.[10] Strongly influenced by his tenets, avant-garde artists and film-makers of the day including Matsumoto, Ōshima Nagisa and the writer Abe Kōbō worked to establish their own brand of documentary film-making that shed conventional perceptions of reality. Ogawa and Ōtsu entered the late 1960s with a strong aspiration to counter the superficial press coverage of the heated student movement that was flooding the mass media. In *Forest of Oppression*, Ogawa chronologically documented the progress of the Takasaki student struggle on site from January to September 1967, while also undertaking subjective film-making by applying a contemporary avant-garde approach with extreme close-ups that revealed the true depths of the spiritual world of the young activists.

Ogawa continued with this film-making style in his next project documenting the Sanrizuka protests. In *The Battle Front for the Liberation of Japan – Summer in Sanrizuka/Nihon kaihō sensen – Sanrizuka no natsu*

(1968), the first of the seven Sanrizuka films, the camera is placed on the side of the protesting farmers, just as it is in *Forest of Oppression*. It captured both violent clashes with riot police in open fields and quiet indoor shots that documented discussions between the farmers and recorded monologues describing their desperate struggle against the authorities. However, after the second instalment of the Sanrizuka series, *Winter in Sanrizuka/Nihon kaihō sensen: Sanrizuka* (1970), Ogawa gradually shifted the central motif from the direct reportage of the Sanrizuka struggle to the history and daily lives of Sanrizuka villagers. In addition, although sequences of villager discussions and monologues had previously occupied only limited portions of *Winter in Sanrizuka*, they now became central elements in *Sanrizuka: Heta Village*. In *Sanrizuka: Heta Village*, the film starts with a narrative of the village history given by a resident called Grandpa Tonojita, then shows long village meetings in which residents discuss selling their graveyard or the arrests of their sons, scenes of New Year's rituals performed by women, and a monologue in which another resident known as Grandma Hanzemu talks about her personal history. As many critics have observed, Ogawa and his collective's folkloric interest in traditional customs and history specifically comes to the fore in their portrayal of the village community.

This gradual shift from the battlefront to the daily lives of villagers may be partially explained as a manifestation of the collective's long commitment to Heta village. It is natural that the growing friendship with Heta farmers motivated Ogawa to record the stories of farmers in this vanishing village for the sake of preservation. There was likely also a direct link with the sociopolitical climate of the day. By the time of the first oil crisis of 1973, the turmoil of the New Left movement had dramatically subsided, and the Sanrizuka protest movement was gradually abating after a bloody clash between farmers and riot police that followed a second forcible expropriation of land in 1971. The rapid pacification of such movements affected the work of the Ogawa Pro collective and they were searching for new subjects and styles that would appeal to their audience. What is even more interesting, however, is to link the advent of the *minshūshi* movement with the portrayal of farmers in Ogawa's film-making during this period.

INTERSECTION WITH THE *MINSHŪSHI* MOVEMENT

As the screening tour of the fourth Sanrizuka film, *Sanrizuka – Peasants of the Second Fortress/Sanrizuka – Daini toride no hitobito* (1971), gained in momentum, Ogawa met a variety of intellectuals at screenings nationwide and in Sanrizuka. These included the folklorist photographer Naitō Masatoshi, the artist Tatsumi Shirō, the historians Irokawa Daikichi, Yasumaru Yoshio, Hani Gorō, Hayashi Takeji and Ichii Saburō, the kabuki researcher Tomita Tetsunosuke, the Kyushu-based writers Ishimure Michiko and Ueno Eishin, and the farmer-poet Makabe Jin in Yamagata. All felt great sympathy for the oppressed farmers in Sanrizuka and supported the production process and screenings of the Ogawa Pro Sanrizuka films in various ways. In fact, Ogawa's close association with these academics, especially *minshūshi* historians such as Irokawa, provided him and his crew with many hints on understanding the history of traditional farming villages and culture. There are two key links between Ogawa Pro and the *minshūshi* movement: firstly, Ogawa's dedicated study of Tanaka Shōzō and the Ashio Copper Mine Pollution Incident of the late nineteenth century,[11] and secondly, his close friendship with Irokawa Daikichi.

After completing *Summer in Sanrizuka*, Ogawa struggled to find a different perspective from which his next film could reveal the reality of the ongoing Sanrizuka strikes. He had expected to release the second Sanrizuka film by October 1969, but found himself unable to do so. However, the decision to postpone the film's release gave Ogawa a whole year to intensively study the history of farmer rebellions in Japan. It was at this time that the young would-be director Fukuda Katsuhiko joined the Ogawa Pro collective after graduating from Waseda University, where he had studied history under the tutelage of historian Kano Masanao, an important *minshūshi* scholar who had just published the influential book *Social Order Consciousness in the Formative Period* of Capitalism/*Shihonshugi keiseiki no chitsujo ishiki* (1969). Kano suggested to Fukuda and Ogawa that an examination of the life of Tanaka Shōzō and the Ashio Pollution Incident might help them in their effort to portray the true nature of the protesting farmers in Sanrizuka. Ogawa devoted himself the study of Tanaka and the Yanaka villagers who had been forcibly relocated by the government, and this knowledge ushered in a new phase in his examination of farmers. Ogawa makes direct references to Tanaka and the Ashio Incident in the poster visuals for *Winter in Sanrizuka*, which borrow powerful slogans attributed to Tanaka. Ogawa also became acquainted with other specialists on the Ashio Incident including the philosopher Hayashi Takeji, author of *Tanaka Shōzō: Sono sei to tatakai no 'konpongi'* (1974), with whom he established a long friendship. Ogawa's assiduous study of the Ashio Incident and his interactions with these intellectuals provided him with a fundamental understanding of old Japanese farming villages and a broader historical perspective on the resistance of the non-elite to the authorities.[12]

Irokawa Daikichi and Naitō Masatoshi were probably the most dedicated intellectual supporters of Ogawa Pro and their films, and their knowledge and ideas influenced Ogawa Pro's approach to film-making in Sanrizuka and Magino village to a considerable degree.[13] In particular, Irokawa, a well-known historian and an influential founder of the *minshūshi* movement, fervently supported Ogawa Pro films over the course of several decades. Declaring himself the 'lead supporter' (*ōendanchō*) of Ogawa Productions, he generously provided Ogawa with both material and intellectual support for many years until Ogawa's death in 1992. As a historian researching the ideology of the non-elite, Irokawa was profoundly interested in the determined rebellion carried out by Sanrizuka farmers, for whom he felt a deep sympathy. Ogawa and Irokawa first became acquainted during the screening tour of *Summer in Sanrizuka* in 1968, and they developed a close friendship in the years that followed.

An early example of the animated exchange of ideas between Ogawa and Irokawa took place in August of 1970 after the completion of *Winter in Sanrizuka*, the second film in the series. Immediately following its first preview, Irokawa wrote a short review of the film for *Asahi Shimbun* entitled 'Farmers in the Meiji Era and the Present Day'/'Nōmin: Meiji to gendai'.[14] In this article, he wrote that it had been a question posed to him by Ogawa after the screening that had helped him to understand what constituted the 'core' of the protesting Sanrizuka farmer mentality: 'Of the several villages in Sanrizuka, why did the most democratic village fold so easily, while the most "feudalistic" village put up the strongest fight? Isn't that odd, and the opposite of what you'd expect?' Recognising the inability of conventional 'scientific' approaches or scholarly theories 'polluted' by modernism to offer an explanation for this critical situation, Irokawa contended that the film demonstrated the importance of the 'premodern' village community and popular morality; something which lay at the core of the Sanrizuka farmers' obstinate mind-set and kept them in opposition to the oppressive power of the nation state and hollow postwar democracy. In addition, he noted that the film's intense discussion scenes illustrated how these farmers, when faced with the restructuring of their communities and neighbourhoods, had already come to terms with the fact that the old blood-based family (*ie*) relationships of the past were no longer sufficient to sustain their social relationships. Instead, they were relying more on the pure sense of solidarity born between individuals during the strikes crucial to the formation of their new communities. Irokawa learned of this pivotal transformation of the modern farming village through Ogawa's Sanrizuka films. Around that time, Irokawa was involved in a research project working to unearth primary historical materials on the Chichibu Incident, a ten-day uprising by armed farmers that occurred in 1884 in Chichibu, Saitama. The similarities between the Sanrizuka incident and his own research prompted Irokawa to visit Sanrizuka and himself explore the reality of the struggling farmers there.

Intellectual interaction through film production and nationwide screening movements became increasingly common at the same time that increased attention was being paid to the non-elite people (*minshū*) in historical studies in Japan. As Takashi Fujitani notes,

The *minshūshi*, or 'people's history' project, was part of a larger intellectual movement of the 1960s and 1970s that sought to construct new representations of the *minshū*, or nonelite 'people' as political and historical agents, and overcome the view that they had been inert and passive objects of rule throughout history.[15]

The rise of *minshūshi* studies was ushered in by Irokawa's monumental book *Philosophical History in the Meiji Era/Meiji seishinshi* (1964), which vividly described the thoughts, inner conflicts and life histories of the sons of village leaders in the Santama area of suburban Tokyo who had participated in the Meiji era Freedom and People's Rights Movement (*jiyū minken undō*). Irokawa and two other historians galvanised by his work, Yasumaru Yoshio – the author of *Japan's Modernization and Popular Thought/Nihon no kindaika to minshū shisō* (1969) – and Kano Masanao, became central to the *minshūshi* project, which proposed that the delineation of non-elite individuals as active agents of history should be the new agenda for postwar historiography. The three figures turned their focus to uncovering the philosophical achievements and activities of these nameless people – farmers, workers and other oppressed groups – who they believed had become the motive force of modernisation in Japan.[16] In addition, many researchers of the history of the *minshūshi* movement have pointed to this project as a critique against the postwar historical studies, including Marxist historiography, modernism and modernisation theory, sustained by Cold War discourse.[17] Irokawa, Yasumaru, Kano and their followers attempted to present an alternative history from the viewpoint of the marginalised as a means of decentring conventional historical narratives framed by the works and philosophies of leading intellectuals.

The *minshūshi* project was also motivated by a broader social context. Its influence on Japanese historical scholarship was greatest from the mid-1960s to the early 1970s, when the nation's political and economic circumstances were undergoing dramatic change. The historian Narita Ryūichi suggested that the political agenda of recognising non-elite people as active agents for social change was clearly a response to the current socio-economic situation and a reflection of prevailing inclinations towards 'criticism of orthodox Marxism, the loss of reality in political terms such as "class distinction" and "social reform", an increased consideration of human sensibility, emotion and despair, and an awareness of the sense of alienation brought about by capitalism'.[18] The central issue of their project was to shed light on the mentality of individuals alienated from modern society and capitalism, which would hopefully lead to the realisation of a new democracy. Indeed, with the upsurge of a new social movement around 1968, the influence of *minshūshi* studies expanded and a great number of writers and researchers published books on the spiritual lives of alienated people living at the lower end of society. *Minshūshi* historians encountered Ogawa, Tsuchimoto and their documentaries in this very context; a natural result of their deep fascination with those who were doggedly raising their voices against the unjust violence brought about by modernity.

Apart from their intense commitment to the oppressed, Ogawa and the *minshūshi* scholars also shared a preference in methodology. As mentioned above, Ogawa showed a strong inclination towards showing people speaking and engaged in discussions in *Forest of Oppression* and the Sanrizuka series. It was 1971 when Ogawa Productions finally acquired the Éclair16 16mm synchronised camera; up until then they had to come to terms with imperfect lip-sync shots by inserting cutaways and close-ups during scenes of people speaking. The new system allowed them to capture the entirety of hours-long interviews and a new sense of space with sync sound, something that Ogawa had long desired throughout his filmography:

> We want to film as much as we can with sync sound, since this helps us capture everything, without losing any of the mood or atmosphere of the moment. When you film a person, you should try to film from their perspective, without trying anything fancy like taking a high position, and film the person as he or she is. We're making our documentary in the *kikigaki* style.[19]

Kikigaki (dictation, or interview-and-writing) was originally a technique used by folklorists to collect stories during their fieldwork, but this term has not only been used in the field of folklore scholarship but also in wider scholarly fields such as historical studies. Ogawa was partial to this method and even coined the original term *kikitori* (interview-and-filming) for his collective's interview technique. When producing *Sanrizuka – Heta Village*, the crew filmed a great number of interviews with farmers about the anti-airport struggle in addition to the history of the village, folk tales, rituals and family histories. The most conspicuous example of *kikitori* in this film is a long interview with Grandma Hanzemu captured in synchronous image and sound; a scene often later on referred to by the collective as the personal history (*jibunshi*) sequence. In fact, the farmers' lengthy, unsophisticated and unique narrations of their own life stories in front of the camera left a strong impression on Ogawa as well as Irokawa. Ogawa continued to utilise similar *jibunshi* interview sequences in his next project, *Dokkoi! Songs from the Bottom/Dokkoi! ningenbushi – Kotobukichō: Jiyūrōdōsha no machi* (1975), and subsequent Magino films, while Irokawa published a book recounting his own spiritual history and that of Hashimoto Yoshio as representative examples of the non-elite *minshū* titled *A History of the Showa Era: An Attempt to Document a Personal History/Aru shōwashi: Jibunshi no kokoromi* (1975). It became one of the year's best sellers.[20]

The gradual shift in subject matter from the spectacle of political struggle to village history and culture in the Sanrizuka series can clearly be attributed to this increasing interaction with the *minshūshi* movement. It should be noted here that while the Sanrizuka films consistently evoked a sense of admiration for the fortitude of farmers and the substantial quality of lives they spent working their land, Ogawa's attitude was far removed from nostalgia or a sentimental yearning for disappearing local culture and village communities, something for which the historian Carol Gluck has criticised *minshūshi* scholars.[21] Rather, as Kitakōji Takashi acutely points out, Ogawa recorded the ongoing transformation of the farmers' subjectivity that liberated them from the 'traditional' or 'premodern' position imposed upon them in the established structure of Japanese society.[22] Although Ogawa Pro shared the *minshūshi* project's fundamental objective of revealing the mentality of the oppressed non-elite, their films captured the more complex reality of a changing community and the shifting subjectivities of protesting farmers engaged in a struggle, which extended far beyond the expectations of academic theoretical frameworks.

The screening tour of *Sanrizuka – Heta Village* commenced in 1973. During the tour, Ogawa and his collective decided to move from Sanrizuka to Magino village, Yamagata. As many critics have pointed out, the collective had several reasons for moving to a quiet rural village in the Tohoku region in 1974, including financial issues and a need to restructure the collective. In addition, there was also a fundamental question they faced during this period concerning their subjectivity as a film-making collective. Despite their long commitment to the Sanrizuka community and their documentation of the residents' struggles and thoughts on farming, they realised that their films did not reveal the true essence of the village life and farm labour that the Sanrizuka farmers continued to carry out every day of their struggle. In a *Sanrizuka – Heta Village* screening in a rural city in eastern Japan, a farmer in the audience asked the film crew why they did not include actual farming scenes in the film, and Ogawa responded that he and his crew felt that they lacked the ability to capture the essential nature of farming culture at that point in time.[23] The collective members metaphorically described this feeling as a sensation of 'emptiness' in their hands and bodies. As Shiraishi Yōko, a former collective member and Ogawa's wife, recollected, this emptiness arose partially from a sense of powerlessness at their inability to change society or politics through the Sanrizuka protests or the New Left movement.[24] However, the incisive criticism he received from the farmers mattered even more to Ogawa, and the collective members decided to devote themselves to farming in Magino as a way of gaining the capacity to film the invisible essence of farming life. Although their subjectivity as film-makers in Sanrizuka had once been evident in their camera position, they now faced the difficult challenge of 'filling up' their 'empty' subjectivity and finding a reason to carry out film-making in Magino, a peaceful ancient village where nothing of special note ever happened.

THE MAGINO STORY – RAISING SILKWORMS: ACQUIRING A NEW SUBJECTIVITY

The Magino Story – Raising Silkworms (1977) was originally made as a study film by assistant cameraman Hara Tadashi with an 8mm camera (Fig. 26.1). Ogawa Pro moved to Magino village in Yamagata in 1974 and started growing rice at the same time that they were completing *Dokkoi! Songs from the Bottom* and *Interview at Clean Centre/Clean centre hōmonki* (1975). During the three-year period following their move to Magino, many staff members left the collective and Ogawa himself suffered from depression. In this period of stagnation, the core staff members devoted themselves to learning rice farming and silkworm rearing under the guidance of Magino villagers. They also took notes of the many things villagers told them, from farming advice and hints to family histories, village episodes and local old sayings, reporting these discoveries in their newsletters accompanied by data, illustrations and excerpts from production diaries. For many generations, silkworm cultivation had been the work of village women, and Shiraishi Yoko took on the sericulture work for the collective. Although Hara began filming the sericulture work process as 'visual notes' to practise his filming skills, Ogawa became interested in these shots, edited them into a completed feature production and blew them up into a 16mm film. Shiraishi played a central role in this project, not only on the screen, where she helped to explain the work processes and also acted as an interviewer, but also as a scriptwriter and publicist for the film. Issue No.10 of the newsletter *Ogawa Pro News*, published in July 1977, was a special edition edited by Shiraishi dedicated to the process of rearing silkworms. The newsletter featured Kimura Satoko, a village wife engaged in silkworm cultivation in the early autumn of 1976, with descriptions of each step of the process accompanied by stills, illustrations and explanations of techniques. This detailed report eventually became the scenario for the film (Fig. 26.2).

Interestingly, this undertaking became a sort of mixed media project. All the elements, namely the film, newsletters and film script, were equally usable

Fig. 26.1 *The Magino Village Story – Raising Silkworms/Magino monogatari – Yōsanhen* (Ogawa Shinsuke, 1977). Courtesy of Athénée Français Cultural Center.

Fig. 26.2 The script of *The Magino Village Story – Raising Silkworms/Magino monogatari – Yōsanhen* (Ogawa Shinsuke, 1977, Ogawa Productions) and *Ogawa Pro News* no. 10 (1 July 1977).

for the educational purpose of learning traditional sericulture to the extent that the film itself, *Raising Silkworms*, can be seen as a single part of a larger whole, with each medium supplementing the others. The film, for instance, mainly consists of depictions of the steps and techniques used to nurture silkworms, while also including *kikitori* interview sequences such as those conducted with a villager known as Grandma Min, who recounts folk tales and relates the history of the Kimura family and the village. The film script, on the other hand, not only provides dialogue, subtitles and stills extracted from the film but also includes additional explanations of places and things shown on the screen. Each of these media would be enough to give the viewer or reader a basic grasp of traditional sericulture, but the combined whole provides a much fuller understanding.

This 'textbook' project clearly stands out from Ogawa Productions' past film-making practices. Despite its simple appearance as a conventional educational film, the completion of *Raising Silkworms* changed somewhat the concept of cinema the collective had conceived until then. As Ogawa himself stated,

> Our attitude had changed in that we knew that our presence would have an effect on things, whether you called our presence a 'happening' or something else, and that the act of filming itself was a 'happening'. This is something we believed from the time of *Sanrizuka – Heta Village* to *Dokkoi! Songs from the Bottom*, but something changed around the time of *Raising Silkworms*. […] To try to explain this change in simple terms, if we ever find ourselves raising silkworms again, this is the film we will be watching. If we find that we have forgotten how to do something, we will use this film to remember. Our way of using a film has changed, at least to a small extent.[25]

Ogawa had clearly found a greater ethnographic significance for cinema as a means of documenting and preserving the indigenous traditional culture of the village in an audiovisual medium for future reference. In fact, as Nornes has pointed out, Ogawa was inspired by the works of naturalist and ethnographer Minakata Kumagusu (1867–1941), which encouraged the collective to actively gather data and mundane minutiae after their move to Magino.[26] The collective's penchant for portraying detailed work processes could be already seen in *Interview at Clean Centre* (1975); but *Raising Silkworms* illustrates an even more passionate attentiveness to detail in the documentation of the traditional sericulture that had long been carried out in Magino.

There are two key characteristics that seem to differentiate this film from previous Ogawa productions. Firstly, as mentioned above, the major emphasis in the comprehensive *Raising Silkworms* project was given to the detailed representation of the sericulture process through multiple media and audiovisual devices. In the film, Shiraishi and Kimura Satoko explain the various steps and techniques by means of word and gesture, while Shiraishi sometimes uses her narration to clarify Kimura's halting speech with its strong regional dialect, along with the feelings and thoughts related to silkworm raising that Kimura herself has trouble articulating. In Issue No.10 of *Ogawa Pro News*, the collective chronologically documents the Kimura family's working schedule and describes their strategies for nurturing silkworms and mulberry leaves with explanations, illustrations and stills. The newsletter and the film are also filled with Kimura's original terminology and ideas on sericulture, which had up to then only been shared in private conversation between family members. The most memorable example in the film is her humorous description of the silkworms' tendency to simultaneously lift up their heads resembling 'thousands of Tokyo Towers standing up!' An intertitle shot repeating this phrase immediately follows, amusingly emphasising its uniqueness. Shiraishi and the production staff painstakingly compiled these original words and phrases and explained their meanings. Their ambition to document everything about sericulture in Magino was remarkable and the successful realisation of their goal consequently gave Ogawa and his crew the confidence to proceed with the same method in their subsequent 1980s masterpieces, *A Japanese Village: Furuyashikimura* and *Magino Village: A Tale*.

The second factor is the fresh perspective this documentary project on sericulture provided the collective with regarding their film-maker subjectivity. Ogawa and his crew found themselves another potential object (*taishō*) for their films, namely the depiction of their own existence, filled with the practical experience and sensory knowledge of farming, as farming practitioners in the film. By learning about and practising traditional sericulture in Magino for three years, the crew steadily gained the relevant knowledge and skills, while also accumulating specific senses and memories in their bodies and minds. As described above, Shiraishi controlled the pro-filmic elements on sericulture during the filming, and her confidence as the central figure in this endeavour is reinforced not only by her accumulation of plain knowledge but also her thorough appreciation of the world of sericulture that had been carried out by generations of Kimura family members. This was the moment the Ogawa Pro members felt that their empty hands had finally been 'filled', in other words, that they had developed a new subjectivity that gave them the capacity to depict the farmers' unspoken rules and sentiments on farming with their cameras (Fig. 26.3).

It should be noted that this transformation of the film-makers' subjectivity did not mean that they stood on an equal footing with the indigenous farmers who had lived in Magino for generations. They never thought of assimilating themselves into the village community, but neither did they assume the role of outsider by keeping a certain distance from the people being filmed. Rather, they attempted to become something different in the village. In their newsletter, Shiraishi wrote that:

> I believe that 'work' is the accumulation of concentrated time – all the tradition, experience, skills and judgement that are expressed through the filter of a worker's individuality. How can we take the concentrated time that has gone into Kimura Satoko's lifetime of tending to silkworms and express it in cinematic time? That is something we'll have to work hard at.[27]

Fig. 26.3 Kimura Satoko and Shiraishi Yōko checking the quality of the cocoons in *The Magino Village Story – Raising Silkworms*. Courtesy of Athénée Français Cultural Center.

She clearly recognised the difficulty of expressing Kimura's 'concentrated time' on film and the challenge that Ogawa Pro faced as mediator in realising this transfer. Kimura's accumulation of experience and her individual character were inseparable from each other, and they were what most fundamentally characterised her sericulture business. For Ogawa Pro, the problem was how to capture such a unique and personal world on film. The collective believed that it would be impertinent for them to attempt to 'represent' the Kimura family, no matter how close their relationship with the family had become. Instead, they established an identity as a unique existence with a movie camera in the village: farming practitioners from a different region, who had settled in the village solely for the purpose of filming the science of farming, the land and its weather, and the village history and geography.[28] In this regard, *Raising Silkworms* was their first successful attempt to portray a world in the way that they managed to show the Kimura family's sericulture business, through their newly acquired senses and words via minutely detailed audiovisual explanations.

Thus, it was through the production of *Raising Silkworms* that Ogawa Pro's endeavour to capture the essence of farming in Magino achieved its first satisfactory result. Through this process, they took their quest to achieve an 'ideal' film-maker subjectivity to the next level: not only did they document their establishment of a relationship with the *taishō* of the film, but they also allowed the 'filled-up' subjectivity of the mediator to become an added element of the object. In their following epics, '*Nippon*': *Furuyashiki Village/Nippon koku Furuyashiki mura* (1982) and *The Sundial Carved with a Thousand Years of Notches – The Magino Village Story*, they took this ideal subjectivity even further with the idea of 'the human possessed by the rice plant' (*ine ningen*), an imagined, metaphorical entity that they strove for in order to capture the essence of rice cultivation.[29] Indeed, in both films their unique stance as enthusiastic practitioners of a subject, collecting detailed data and documenting their results and discoveries, is quite pronounced, thus distinguishing these films from similar documentaries of the day such as Himeda Tadayoshi's acclaimed folklore film *Echigo okumiomote: Yama ni ikasareta hibi* (1984), which documents life in a small mountain village fated for destruction due to the construction of a new dam, and Kamei Fumio's environmental film on the perpetuation of organic farming, *All Must Live: People, Insects and Birds/Minna ikinakereba naranai: Hito, mushi, tori, Nouji minzoku-kan* (1984).

CONCLUSION: OGAWA'S LEGACY

Ogawa Productions' long journey spent pursuing an 'ideal' subjectivity in film-making that began in the late 1960s peaked in the Magino series, showing the collective's determined efforts to understand the world of farming and the currents of time in old villages. The postwar subjectivity debate of the 1950s and various avant-garde documentary theories in art and literature underpinned Ogawa's sensational debut with *Forest of Oppression*, while the theoretical intersection with the *minshūshi* movement during and after the time of the Sanrizuka series provided the collective with a wider perspective, encompassing a socio-historical background that helped to foster the independent subjectivity of the protesting farmers. After moving to Magino, Ogawa and his collective did not merely document a traditional world of farming in an old village that was at risk of disappearing with the advent of modern industrialised society, they also attempted to take a more subjective approach to the filmed object by transforming themselves into another medium capable of conveying the essence of farming and village life to the audience. Interestingly, this process of transformation in the subjectivities of both the struggling farmers in Sanrizuka and the Ogawa Pro collective in Magino embodies what Koschman refers to as the 'dynamics of subjectivity', a post-structuralist perspective that argues human subjectivity is not a pre-existing quality but is instead formed situationally and contingently as an active agency opposed to other forces.[30] Ogawa Pro's long and painstaking effort to achieve an 'ideal' film-maker subjectivity assimilated philosophical and academic responses to the concurrent sociopolitical situation of the late 1960s and 1970s, and established a completely unique and subjective film-making style that has made its mark in documentary film history.

It is important to note, however, that the collective's films, especially those in Magino, also revealed their methodological limitations. Firstly, while Ogawa Pro deeply probed the lifestyle and farming culture of Magino, they never applied any critical perspective to the negative aspects of the closed village community or its farming business. For example, while *Raising Silkworms* delineates the details of the sericulture business as a respectable task carried out by the women of a family, Ogawa never went too far in exploring the real struggles of these village women in their conservative closed community, nor did he examine the possibility of their growing awareness of gender issues. In order to continue their communal life and filming within the village, the collective avoided criticising villagers and focused instead on learning and portraying the science of farming and the stories the villagers wanted to tell them. This attitude in Magino clearly entailed the risk of conforming to the romanticised, essentialist representation of the farmers that the *minshūshi* movement found itself trapped in. As Nornes points out, Ogawa's lack of perspective on the latest critical trends in the literature and the art of the day, including feminist theory, might well epitomise the decline of creative documentary practice in Japan since the 1970s.[31]

Secondly, the collective members gradually lost sight of the significance of their film-making as they carried out their farming life. The Ogawa Pro members, except for Ogawa himself, appeared in the Magino films as skilful practitioners and mediators of farming, but they never worked as film directors. Consequently, the staff there existed only for the sake of Ogawa's personal cinematic art, and not for the political solidarity that they had once shared – they were not allowed to establish identities as independent film-makers during Ogawa's lifetime. The contradiction in pursuing subjective film-making as a collective was clearly revealed in the Magino series and many would-be directors in the collective left Magino in despair. In fact, this difficult situation affected film-making practices of other contemporary documentarists in and after the late 1970s such as Hara Kazuo, who never chose to form a film-making collective and pursued, instead, a unique self-documentary method.

Nonetheless, Ogawa Pro's long-term and consistent devotion to establishing a subjective relationship with the people they filmed was undoubtedly the most radical venture in Japanese documentary history. Ogawa's films and uncompromising attitude towards film-making fostered young talents of the next decade such as Satō Makoto (1957–2007), the director of *Living on the River Agano/Aga ni ikiru* (1992). Both continue to have a great impact on directors in Japan and throughout the world up to the present day.[32] Recently, we can also hear the resonance of the Ogawa legacy in documentaries about the Great East Japan Earthquake of 2011. Many documentarists entered the affected areas and reported on the unprecedented disaster and its aftermath, and some of them have once again faced this old, but unavoidable, problem of film-maker subjectivity and the relationship with the filmed object – in this case, the affected people of the region.[33] It should be noted that some young film-makers and artists, including Sakai Kō, Komori Haruka and Seo Natsumi, have moved to the affected areas and continue to record the transformation of the daily lives of the people over the long term. We will see whether these devoted efforts remain within the paradigm of the late 1960s to 1970s or whether their work will lead to new directions and fresh perspectives for the future of documentary film-making in Japan.

Notes

1 Abé Mark Nornes, *Japanese Documentary Film: The Meiji Era through Hiroshima* (Minneapolis: University of Minnesota, 2003). [Editors' note: for more on prewar and wartime Japanese documentary film-making, see also Chapter 28 by Sharon Hayashi in this volume.]

2 Abé Mark Nornes, *Forest of Pressure: Ogawa Shinsuke and Postwar Japanese Documentary* (Minneapolis: University of Minnesota, 2007).

3 See, for instance, Joan Mellen, *The Waves of Genji's Door: Japan through its Cinema* (New York: Pantheon Books, 1976); Noël Burch, *To the Distant Observer: Form and Meaning in the Japanese Cinema* (London: Scolar Press; Berkeley: University of California Press, 1979); David Desser, *Eros plus Massacre: An Introduction to the Japanese New Wave Cinema* (Bloomington: Indiana University Press, 1988); Eric Cazdyn, *The Flash of Capital: Film and Geopolitics in Japan* (Durham, NC: Duke University Press, 2002); and Kitakōji Takashi, 'Hantōchaku no monogatari: Ethnography toshiteno Ogawa Pro eiga', in Hase Masato and Nakamura Hideyuki (eds), *Eiga no seijigaku* (Tokyo: Seikyūsha, 2003), pp. 303–51.

4 See Ōshima Nagisa's fervent admiration for Ogawa's long and deep engagement with the *taishō* in *Forest of Oppression* and early Sanrizuka films in his long essay 'Ogawa Shinsuke: Tōsō to datsuraku', in *Eiga hihyō*, December 1970, pp. 15–25. [Editors' note: for more on *Forest of Oppression*, see also Chapter 33 by Masato Dogase in this volume.]

5 J. Victor Koschman, *Revolution and Subjectivity in Postwar Japan* (Chicago: University of Chicago Press, 1996), pp. 1–7.

6 'Ogawa puro, sandaihyōsaku no jōeikai hiraku', *Yomiuri shimbun*, evening edition, 16 January 1982, p. 9. Ogawa chose these three films to be shown at a three-day screening event in Yotsuya kōkaidō Hall at the end of January 1982. The event was held as part of a fundraising campaign for Ogawa Pro's next film *'Nippon': Furuyashiki Village/Nippon koku Furuyashiki mura* (1982).

7 Matsuda Masao, 'Agitation no ne: Kirokueiga *Assatsu no mori*', *Eiga hyōron*, January 1968, pp. 81–3.

8 Matsumoto Toshio, 'Nihon ni okeru seiji eiga no kanōsei', *Kinema junpō*, late April 1968, pp. 63–5.

9 Ogawa Shinsuke and Ōtsu Kōshirō, 'Takakeidai o toraeru me: Interview *Assatsu no mori* seisaku undō kara', *Hitotsubashi shimbun*, 1 November 1967, p. 1. (All translations are mine, unless otherwise noted.)

10 Yuriko Furuhata, 'Refiguring Actuality: Japan's Film Theory and Avant-garde Documentary Movement, 1950s-1960s' (PhD thesis, Brown University, 2009). Also, see Yuriko Furuhata, *Cinema of Actuality: Japanese Avant-garde Filmmaking in the Season of Image Politics* (Durham, NC: Duke University Press, 2013).

11 The Ashio Copper Mine Pollution Incident was the first pollution incident in modern Japan. Suffering from repetitive floods caused by mining pollution, affected farmers in the Watarase basin started campaigns against the pollution led by the politician Tanaka Shōzō. When the authorities designated Yanaka village as a flood retarding basin in 1907, the villagers protested against the relocation but were forced to leave.

12 Author's interview with former Ogawa Pro member Iizuka Toshio, 15 January 2015.

13 Naitō met Ogawa after the completion of *Winter in Sanrizuka* and they subsequently formed a long and close friendship. Naitō was then a fledgling young photographer known for his beautiful photos of folkloric culture in the mountains of the Tohoku region. While he acted as a casual adviser for the post-production process of Ogawa films, he also made contributions as a still photographer for *Sanrizuka – Heta Village* and *Sundial Carved with a Thousand Years of Notches – The Magino Village Story*. His strong interest in traditional village communities and customs stimulated a similar interest in Ogawa and the collective members at discussions that took place in Ogawa Pro's Heta and Shinjuku production houses.

14 Irokawa Daikichi, 'Nōmin: Meiji to gendai', *Asahi shimbun*, 8 September 1970, p. 7.

15 Takashi Fujitani, '*Minshūshi* as Critique of Orientalist Knowledge', *positions* vol. 6 no. 2 (1998), pp. 303–22.

16 The term *minshū* was originally invented in the context of Enlightenment thought (*keimō shisō*) at the end of the Tokugawa era, indicating the advent of the newly enlightened masses. With the upsurge of 'Taishō Democracy', the idea of *minshū* reappeared both as a politically active form of agency and a means of evoking the masses who enjoyed access to popular culture. See Hirota Masaki, 'Pandora no hako: Minshūshisōshi kenkyū no kadai', in Sakai Naoki (ed.), *National history o manabisuteru* (Tokyo: University of Tokyo Press, 2006), pp. 3–45. On the positioning of the *minshū* by the social education policy of the government in the 1920s and its relationship with audiences in cinema, see Hideaki Fujiki, 'Creating the Audience: Cinema as Popular Recreation and Social Education in Modern Japan', in Daisuke Miyao (ed.), *The Oxford Handbook of Japanese Cinema* (Oxford: Oxford University Press, 2014), pp. 79–97.

17 On *mishūshi* history, in addition to Fujitani and Hirota's aforementioned articles, see Carol Gluck,

'The People in History: Recent Trends in Japanese Historiography', *Journal of Asian Studies* vol. 38 no. 1 (1978), pp. 25–50; Narita Ryūichi, *Rekishigaku no narrative: Minshūshi kenkyū to sono shūhen* (Tokyo: Azekura shobō, 2012), pp. 109–52.

18 Ibid., pp. 127–8.
19 Ogawa Shinsuke, 'Dōkisei ni kodawaru genbashugi', extract from a lecture held in the Athénée Français Cultural Center in April 1973 in Yamane Sadao (ed.), *Eiga o toru: Documentary no shifuku o motomete* (Tokyo: Ōta shuppan, 1993), pp. 109–10.
20 With his book's great popularity, Irokawa even started a *jibunshi* movement later on and urged ordinary people to write their own personal histories.
21 See Gluck, 'The People in History'.
22 See Kitakōji, 'Hantōchaku no monogatari', pp. 303–51.
23 Ogawa, 'Dōkisei ni kodawaru genbashugi', pp. 125–6.
24 Author's interview with Shiraishi Yōko, October 2012.
25 Ogawa Shinsuke, '1979 nen Magino no natsu: Ogawa Shinsuke "Inasakuhen" o kataru', in Suzuki Shirouyasu (ed.), *Documentary eiga no kaku: Ogawa production 14 nenkan no kiseki* (Tokyo: Image Forum, 1979).
26 Nornes, *Forest of Oppression*, p. 182.
27 Shiraishi Yōko, *Ogawa Pro News* no. 10 (1977), p. 3.
28 Author's interview with Shiraishi. Kitakōji Takashi also argued that Ogawa Pro's films after *Heta Village* showed a 'transformation' in terms of both the process of filming and the subjects filmed, something that was similar to a concurrent trend in fieldwork research in ethnography. See Kitakōji, 'Hantōchaku no monogatari', pp. 303–51.
29 Author's interview with Shiraishi.
30 Koschman, *Revolution and Subjectivity in Postwar Japan*, pp. 239–41.
31 Nornes, *Forest of Oppression*, pp. 137–45.
32 For instance, *Eiga o toru: Documentary no shifuku o motomete*, the collection of Ogawa's essays mentioned above, was translated into Chinese by the film-maker Feng Yan, who started film-making in 1994 strongly inspired by Ogawa Pro films and Ogawa's book. Ogawa's films and his dogma have now begun to spread in Chinese-speaking countries and have encouraged many would-be radical documentarists in those territories.
33 [Editors' note: see also Chapter 27 by Rachel DiNitto in this volume.]

PART 5

TIME AND SPACES OF REPRESENTATION

27
ECOLOGY
Toxic interdependencies: 3/11 cinema

Rachel DiNitto

In discussing the media coverage of Love Canal, the environmental disaster of a residential neighbourhood built atop an industrial waste site, Lawrence Buell highlights the significant disjuncture of normalcy and toxicity in images and narratives of contaminated communities.[1] As a visual medium, cinema can deploy powerful images to make this toxic damage visible. The three nuclear meltdowns at the Fukushima Daiichi Nuclear Power Plant in 2011 created an environmental crisis of unimaginable proportion, yet this 'accident' was only the latest in a series of nuclear and environmental disasters in Japan's postwar era. How has Japanese cinema deployed its powerful images to bring these disasters to the screen? Do such films constitute an ecological cinema?

As in Japanese literary studies, an ecocritical perspective has only recently begun to feature in Japanese cinema studies.[2] The 2011 nuclear disaster, also known as 3/11, has occasioned hundreds of filmic productions, but few have been concerned strictly with the environmental impact of the disaster.[3] In considering how to analyse these films, we can look back to a larger body of filmic work on humans and the toxic environment starting with *hibakusha* cinema, or the films produced about the atomic bombings of Hiroshima and Nagasaki.[4] The connection to Fukushima is apparent in the menace of the nuclear, a theme that extends to the works of documentary film-makers such as Kamanaka Hitomi and her films on nuclear power and reprocessing plants that precede and postdate the accident at the Fukushima Daiichi Nuclear Power Plant (NPP). However, equally as important is the documentary corpus of Tsuchimoto Noriaki, who dedicated almost forty years of his life to filming the victims of mercury poisoning around Japan's Shiranui Sea.

Before turning to an examination of a number of important 3/11 films, as well as an analysis of these predecessors, it is important to define how the term 'ecology' will be used in this chapter. The term 'ecological' implies a variety of critical positions. Some critics adhere to a deep ecological perspective that shifts focus from a human-centred to a nature-centred view.[5] Others seek to denaturalise or problematise the 'conflation of humanity and nature' specifically in 3/11 cinema.[6] Here, I look to Cheryll Glotfelty's emphasis on the relationship 'between human culture and the physical world', especially on 'interdependent communities, integrated systems, and strong connections among constituent parts'.[7] Glotfelty distinguishes her 'eco-' approach from an 'enviro-' one that, in her view, would imply a separation of humans from that which surrounds them. I focus on this interdependency as seen in cinematic images of the relationship of humans to their environment. This chapter will examine the damage that toxins, like mercury and radiation, have inflicted on that ecological relationship of a human–nature interdependency. But interdependency does not equal harmony; neither are residents in toxic areas allowed to live in harmony with the land, nor are those communities in agreement about the risks of the environmental contaminants – be they unsure or unaware of the risks or unwilling to admit to them because of loss of livelihood or social ostracisation. Interdependency is visible in images of both normalcy and toxicity, but the latter is especially difficult to render when dealing with invisible environmental toxins. In this chapter, the ecological concern of interdependency is examined primarily through the cinematic mechanisms for making toxic/contaminated landscapes visible.

AN ECOLOGY OF LANDSCAPE

Martin Lefebvre has expounded on the relationship between landscape and film, warning that cinema can harness natural settings, but the simple presence of one does not 'necessarily constitute a landscape'.[8] In my analysis I draw on two related arguments by Lefebvre. In his essay, 'Between Setting and Landscape in the Cinema', he distinguishes images of the natural world that are integral to the diegetic narrative flow of the film as setting, as opposed to those that can be contemplated outside the narrative as landscape. In the case of the latter, the 'autonomizing' gaze that 'makes possible the transition from setting to landscape' can be either an intentional effect of the film-making or something the spectator brings to the viewing experience that allows them to contemplate the landscape outside the narrative flow.[9]

In a later article 'On Landscape in Narrative Cinema', Lefebvre revisits these ideas and expands on an alternate view of landscape and its relation to narrative, namely that of landscape as 'lived and inhabited environment' that 'acquires its significance' by moving the viewer '*into* it' partly through narrative. In the former, argument about setting, narrative 'conceals' landscape while narrative 'serves' landscape when portrayed as lived space.[10] Both of these modes are at work in the films examined below. In my discussion, I will analyse the cinematic techniques used to create these different types of landscape. In some films, landscape as lived space enables the toxic/contaminated environments to become visible, while in other films the representation of the post-disaster world as an autonomous landscape is problematic specifically because it allows the viewer to disengage from the narrative of contamination.

Human–nature interdependency is addressed through images of the disaster landscape in 3/11 cinema. Several 3/11 films have however been criticised as voyeuristic for the way they cast a fetishistic gaze on these scenes of destruction.[11] Landscape plays an important role in the films discussed below as a means of capturing both the pre-disaster beauty and the post-disaster damage as well as the close relationship between the victims and their environment, since many films focus on subjects who live off the land and sea.

We can ask in these films whether the camera permits the viewer to contemplate the images on screen as an autonomous landscape, allowing for a suppression of narrative and the creation of distance, or whether it specifically places the viewer within that landscape as a lived space. What technical aspects of film-making enable this and what are the effects? Are these landscapes empty or peopled? If the latter, who occupies them? Christine Marran argues that Tsuchimoto Noriaki does not use landscape shots that are absent of humans, and other films such as Kamanaka Hitomi's *Rokkasho Rhapsody/Rokkashomura rapusodī* (2006) and *Ashes to Honey: Toward a Sustainable Future/Mitsubachi no haoto to chikyū no kaiten* (2011), Sono Sion's *Land of Hope/Kibō no kuni* (2012), and Kubota Nao's *Homeland/Ieji* (2014) are similarly occupied by farmers, ranchers and fishermen making their living.[12] On the other hand, there are also many empty landscapes in 3/11 cinema that verge on autonomous landscapes that can be contemplated separately from narratives of contamination.

In either case, whether the landscapes are peopled or empty, we need to ask when speaking of these invisible toxins, if they are bounded, zoned or marked in some way to indicate their toxicity. These are not necessarily disaster films, and the land is not always marked by debris, the ravages of nature or some visible damage, despite the fact that there are plenty of shots of debris fields in 3/11 cinema. Is there a way to know that these landscapes are contaminated? In some films, they are marked with the signage and warnings of officially designated disaster zones, but in others there is no such visible indication. Film-makers use different techniques to indicate this danger. The debris-strewn landscapes in Fujiwara Toshi's *No Man's Zone/Mujin chitai* (2012) serve as a visible counterpoint to empty, pristine, yet contaminated landscapes. In other films, the invisibility of radiation can only be seen in readings on Geiger counters, thyroid scans, other technical devices or in data visualisations. Part of the problem is that the violence wrought upon nature and humans by this toxicity is the type of slow and invisible violence that Rob Nixon discusses in his work on climate change, deforestation, oil spills and other environmental hazards.[13] Difficult to detect, this toxicity introduces an ambivalence into the human–nature relationship of interdependence – the desire to or necessity of living on and working the land competes with a knowledge or suspicion that it is contaminated. Nature is not a 'therapeutic sanctuary' that can offer refuge from environmental problems.[14] It is part of the problem.

Beyond the technical choice of how to film contaminated landscapes lies the larger question of what it means to represent a landscape as dangerous, as opposed to safe. In Japan, and in these films, this is a political act. Kristina Iwata-Weickgenannt speculates that the small number of fiction films about the Fukushima nuclear disaster is due to the silencing power of Japan's nuclear village.[15] Ian Thomas Ash chose not to distribute his film about families affected by radiation in order to protect his interviewees from public attacks.[16] Do these films reinforce a particular ideology or are the film-makers seeking to emphasise the relation between film and a 'knowable extra-filmic reality' in order to promote ecological agency?[17] Patrick Brereton argues that in certain Hollywood films 'evocations of eco-nature become self-consciously foregrounded and consequently help to promote an ecological meta-narrative, connecting humans with their environment'.[18] But many of the films examined below show how toxic contaminants in Japan sever that connection or makes it a dire choice between abandoning the natural environment or choosing to live in it at the cost of one's own life. Beyond identifying the contemplative mode of autonomous landscapes, Lefebvre seems unconcerned with its effects, meaning the potential disengagement of spectators with the narrative. However, for film-makers such as Kamanaka Hitomi, who see their films as a form of activism, engagement is vital.

TSUCHIMOTO NORIAKI: MINAMATA DISEASE AND THE POISON SEA

Any discussion of ecological issues in Japanese film would be incomplete without reference to the work of one of the giants of Japanese documentary cinema, Tsuchimoto Noriaki.[19] Between 1965 and 2004, Tsuchimoto made seventeen television and film documentaries about methylmercury poisoning in Minamata City and the surrounding areas caused by the Chisso chemical plant's dumping of effluent into the Shiranui Sea. As Justin Jesty argues, Tsuchimoto's body of filmic work constitutes 'one of the most detailed and long-running studies of environmental disaster on film'.[20] Below, I briefly discuss two of his films: *Minamata: The Victims and Their World*/*Minamata: Kanjasan to sono sekai* (1971) and *The Shiranui Sea*/*Shiranuikai* (1975) (Fig. 27.1). It is not just the subject of his camera but the style of Tsuchimoto's film-making that is ecological. Rather than view the film-maker as wielding complete authorial control, Tsuchimoto and his crew engaged in a 'symbiotic' practice that created meaning through the interaction of those on both sides of the camera.[21]

This symbiotic relationship makes for a level of intimacy in the interviews and testimonials from victims and relatives that forms the core of Tsuchimoto's films. These interviews are organic in nature: appearing in the order in which they were shot, Tsuchimoto allows his subjects to speak at length, with the conversation often seeming to veer off topic. The audience are not allowed to be passive viewers, but neither is Tsuchimoto a passive documentarian.[22] His sympathetic film-making does not strive for a distanced objectivity in order to avoid intervention. Rather, he came to know the community after joining the victims' movement in 1970, and he actively sought to positively change their situation through his films.[23] His activism is part of what makes his films ecological.

These testimonies fill the screen visually and audibly, but do not fetishise images of diseased bodies. These bodies are not presented as a type of landscape for voyeuristic contemplation. Rather, the victims and their families are filmed within their daily living and

Fig. 27.1 *Minamata: The Victims and Their World/Minamata: Kanjasan to sono sekai* (Tsuchimoto Noriaki, 1971, Higashi Productions).

working environments, tied to their occupation as fishermen in an interdependent relationship to a sea that is now irreparably damaged. Just as Minamata's victims are filmed within their local contexts of home, family, work and activism, Minamata's landscapes are also shot in context, as a 'lived and inhabited environment'.

Tsuchimoto achieves this through both shot selection and narrative. The establishing shot for *Minamata* focuses on fishermen, as the camera moves from long shots to close-ups of their bodies at work. In Tsuchimoto's *Shiranui Sea*, the first film to 'give sustained attention to the great natural beauty' of the larger ocean community affected by mercury, the landscape is a place of human activity rather than one where humans are relegated to the margins.[24] *Shiranui Sea* opens with an extreme long shot of a man by the ocean and the shores of Minamata Bay before moving to close-ups of fish and long shots taken from a boat of other fishing vessels at sea. Both the narrative and the shot selection allow for landscape to function this way, moving the spectator from the long shots of the ocean to focus in on the local residents who rely on it but have also been poisoned by it. The spectre of mercury poisoning is never eclipsed by these landscapes, nor is the viewer encouraged to 'extract' the landscape from the narrative flow.[25] His films document a way of life, and his ethnographic touch allows his films to represent the slow violence of mercury poisoning 'without resort to spectacle'.[26]

Tsuchimoto addresses the question of interdependency and harmony when he highlights a central tension in the livelihood of these fisherman: the community continues to fish even though Chisso continued to dump mercury into the sea until 1968. *Minamata* includes close-ups of sulphuric acid wastewater exiting the plant into the ocean, and *Shiranui Sea*, released in 1975, follows congenital victims. However, as victim after victim repeats, fishing is their only livelihood, and Tsuchimoto's films show the community inevitably returning to the sea.

The residents of Minamata started to suffer the effects of mercury poisoning in the mid-1950s, and Tsuchimoto documented this through multiple generations of victims. One clear purpose of his films is to *show*, or force the viewer to *see*, the somatic damage caused by this disease. He makes the toxic effects of mercury poisoning visible. He dedicates significant screen time to showing the victims as they try to walk, eat, communicate or rehabilitate their bodies. This documenting of their hindered movements, be they obvious or barely perceptible, is key to having those symptoms officially recognised as Minamata disease. Tsuchimoto's films helped make these victims and their disease visible. *Minamata* contains numerous intertitles with information about the disease, deaths and court cases. His films, which travelled around the world, brought medical recognition on a national and international level; locally they created a social visibility for these fishermen since as members of the lowest class, they were shunned and pressured, often by their own people, to forgo diagnosis lest they harm the community and way of life.

Many have observable symptoms and the somatic damage is there to *see* in a way it is not for more recent films about radioactive contamination. Victims of radiation and 3/11 cannot be documented in the same way as Minamata victims, because neither the damage nor the victims are so readily visible.[27] Kamanaka discussed this in a conversation with Tsuchimoto when talking about her film *Rokkasho Rhapsody* about a nuclear fuel reprocessing plant:

> What's hard about Rokkashomura [village] is that no one has gotten sick yet. While there's a build-up of radioactive materials, there aren't any patients. The damage will take a while to appear, and even then, if it takes the form of an illness that anyone can get such as cancer or leukemia, it will be hard to prove that it's caused by radiation.[28]

As discussed below, the problem for Kamanaka is not just visualising the damage but doing it in such a way as to spur anti-nuclear awareness and activism in her audience. In what follows, I will discuss her strategies for making visible the contaminated landscape and the threat it poses.

KAMANAKA HITOMI: TOXIC LANDSCAPES FROM THE LOCAL TO THE GLOBAL

Kamanaka Hitomi is the only film-maker in Japan who has dedicated herself to nuclear documentaries for over twenty years.[29] In many ways, her relationship with and treatment of her subjects is an extension of Tsuchimoto's ecological symbiosis. Like Tsuchimoto, she shows them working the land (fishermen, farmers, ranchers) and fighting government and industry exploitation. She takes the viewer into the homes and workplaces of her subjects. Her films are sympathetic, allowing the viewer to get close to those affected by the threat of radiation and see their struggles – from locals protesting against the building of nuclear power plants, to mothers trying to decide if they should remain in contaminated areas. Kamanaka also appears regularly in her films either on screen with her subjects, overheard in conversation with them, as the narrator for her documentaries, or on site. As a film-maker, she seeks to intervene.[30] Like Tsuchimoto, her aim is activism.

In Kamanaka's films landscape is an immersive, lived space. One of her primary techniques for making toxic landscapes visible as lived space is through narratives and images that provide a more global sense of resonance to the fragile interconnectedness of humans and their environment. Kamanaka connects the irradiated landscapes in Japan to those in Belarus, Iraq, the UK and the US. This is visible in a film such as *Radiation: A Slow Death/Hibakusha: Sekai no owari ni* (2005) in a series of establishing shots. The film opens with a trucking shot of a Baghdad street only to cut to the leukaemia ward of a paediatric hospital where children suffer from exposure to depleted uranium (DU) munitions. When Kamanaka shifts to Hiroshima, the camera moves from a shot of the sky to the Genbaku Dome, the building that symbolises the atomic bombing, but she keeps the spectator within the narrative by moving to an interview with a doctor who has been working with radiation patients since the two atomic bombs. Finally, Kamanaka takes the viewer to the US with a shot of trucks driving along an agricultural road, followed by a pan that moves from a set of farms to the river before stopping on the buildings of the Hanford Nuclear Reservation in the distance of eastern Washington State. She interviews farmers and experts about the effects of radioactive releases and seepage from this famous plutonium processing plant that made material for the bomb dropped on Nagasaki. These interviews prevent the viewer from seeing the Washington countryside as an autonomous landscape that can be extracted from the narratives about the Hanford Reservation or radiation's global effects. Kamanaka's opening intertitle also speaks to her global agenda: 'In Japanese, *hibakusha* refers to survivors of the atomic bomb. The film uses "hibakusha" to describe all victims of radiation.'[31]

Her shots in *Rokkasho Rhapsody* and *Ashes to Honey* centre on locals farming and fishing in Rokkasho and Iwaishima villages. The opening sequence in *Rokkasho Rhapsody* situates the locals, their livelihood and the reprocessing plant through a series of shots that show rice planting, farming and cows, before cutting to the chimneys and a pan of the reprocessing plant. The sequencing of shots emphasises the local economy and ecology, including a shot of wind turbines behind the village that is meant to show how the production of electricity can coexist with this rural life. This visual shorthand for peaceful coexistence precedes images of the plant in order to show the importance of life before nuclear power and the harm caused by the plant. There is a similar 8-minute sequence in the beginning of *Ashes to Honey*. The normalcy of country life is visually contrasted with symbols of toxicity, like the plant chimneys, to show that interdependence does not equal harmony. Later shots of nature in *Rokkasho Rhapsody* are similarly tied to the damage done by the plant. A close-up of grasses blowing in the wind is used to explain the downwind status of the farms. Shots of would-be picturesque, snowy northern landscapes are contrasted with chimneys of the plant to explain how the discharge of radioactive substances falls on the farm with precipitation. In *Ashes to Honey*, we learn of the unique biodiversity of the ocean creatures and plants as well as the importance of local farming – all threatened by the proposed nuclear power plant, as is the health of the residents.

For Kamanaka, radiation is an environmental problem. Her films look outward to places like Sweden for alternative energy solutions and to sites of radioactive contamination around the world. These global perspectives allow her to reveal the danger of, and alternatives to, Japan's spent fuel reprocessing plants and nuclear power plants, such as the one that melted down in Fukushima prefecture in spring 2011. She provides historical contexts and spatial continuity for the problem of nuclear contamination.[32] By taking her film-making outside Japan, she features specialists who can comment critically on Japan from the viewpoint of these global disasters, accidents and tragedies. Kamanaka skilfully employs the global to question the local pronuclear agenda and to make visible radiation's global ecological threat.

These strategies allow Kamanaka to make the invisible dangers of radiation visible and to show its impact on the interdependent relationship of humans and their local environments. Kamanaka's films are an act of 'political intervention', and she is concerned with finding filmic techniques that can relay the 'truth' in order to give rise to a new consciousness.[33] With the 2011 disaster, the reality of radiological contamination was writ large on northeastern Japan. Kamanaka admits her feelings of powerlessness and a sense that her previous cinematic work had failed.[34] Nonetheless, she has continued to document radiation's danger with films such as *Surviving Internal Exposure/ Naibu hibaku o ikinuku* (2012) and *Little Voices from Fukushima/Chiisaki koe no canon – Sentaku suru hitobito* (2014). Here, she shows the disaster landscapes of 3/11, but in voiceovers that narrate 'the difficulty of decontamination rather than the beauty of the nature'.[35] She also focuses on the victims, for whom there are no easy choices regarding daily activities such as finding safe food to feed their children. In this sense, her *oeuvre* stands as an important document of these local struggles that do not regularly feature in 3/11 cinema.

DISASTER LANDSCAPES AND THE ETHICS OF VIEWING: *NO MAN'S ZONE* AND *311*

The majority of 3/11 documentaries take a critical stance on the nuclear industry and government power.[36] But, that does not necessarily mean they focus on environmental concerns about radiological contamination. Many films are records of the disaster area meant to memorialise loss, and in the process they give screen time to the disaster landscape. This landscape dominates much of 3/11 cinema, but it is a space mostly empty of humans. The nuclear disaster was precipitated by a massive earthquake and tsunami that levelled and emptied many coastal towns, rendering northeastern Japan a landscape 'emancipated from the presence of human figures'.[37] Additionally, many areas were closed off because of dangerous radiation levels and citizens were evacuated, leaving behind their farms, ranches, fishing boats, homes and jobs. Unlike the contaminated ocean in Tsuchimoto's films that remains a source of livelihood and sustenance for the residents despite its toxicity, the irradiated land and sea of northeastern Japan have, in many cases, been off-limits for victims of the nuclear accident. This absence of human habitation, combined with the invisibility of radiation, presents additional challenges to making this ecological problem visible and to speaking of interdependency.

Films about the 3/11 disaster treat landscape in a variety of ways, not all of which are controversial or political. Fujiki argues that the pro-government *Living in Fukushima: A Story of Decontamination and Reconstruction/Fukushima ni ikiru: Josen to fukkō no monogatari* (2013) 'celebrates the natural environment', while Funahashi Atsushi's documentary *Nuclear Nation/Futaba kara tōku hanarete* (2012) 'sentimentalizes the ruined scenery'. Yet others such as Kamanaka show the landscape as 'contaminated land' in their 3/11 works, while Ian Thomas Ash's strategy in *A2-B-C* (2013) is to make landscape only 'minimally present' so as to focus his documentary on the impact of radiation on children's thyroids and general health.[38]

What kind of landscape shots have film-makers used in the disaster zone? Do these landscape shots comment on the ecological problem of radiation or make visible the severed relationship of the human–nature interdependence? Do the films present landscape as a 'world we are living *in*, or a scene we are looking *at*'?[39] How are shots of the natural world related to the narrative? In the case of the atomic bomb, film-makers used the pan to scan the landscape from a fixed point, as a means of depicting 'the incomprehensible magnitude of the disaster'.[40] In contrast, critics at the Yamagata International Documentary Film Festival in 2011 commented on the ubiquity of debris landscapes seen through the 'long, slow tracking sweep, usually filmed from the window of a slowly moving car'.[41] These 'truck' shots contrast with Fujiwara Toshi's insistence on using a tripod so he could pan the landscape or Ian Thomas Ash's rejection of the tripod because he was trying to capture 'pure human feelings'.[42] The director Jamie Morris has argued that 'Formally, these camera movements [trucking shots] are perfectly suited to the endless panorama of the tsunami's destructive path. Ethically, however, these shots reinforce the gross disjuncture between the perspectives of the out-of-town observer and the local victim.'[43] Do any of these films allow or encourage us to understand the impact of radiation damage beyond emptying the landscape and displacing the population? Are viewers ever allowed to cross this disjuncture between observer and victim, a move that would be vital to film-makers hoping to inspire activism.

Below, I examine two 3/11 films that use cinematic techniques to encourage the viewing of the landscape as an autonomous spectacle that in one case 'halts the progression of narrative',[44] while in the other is produced through a narrative that encourages this type of viewing. This landscape encourages not only contemplation but voyeurism or disaster tourism. The first film, Fujiwara Toshi's documentary *No Man's Zone* contains some of the most prominent use of landscape footage in 3/11 cinema. Although it is driven by a self-consciousness about the lure of disaster images, as expressed through a voiceover by Armenian-Canadian actress Arsinée Khanjian, it is simultaneously complicit in their consumption. Fujiwara filmed inside the 20-kilometre exclusion zone around the Fukushima NPP in April 2011 when the border was still permeable. He set out to record images of areas that would soon be off-limits to human habitation. Khanjian's voiceover chides the viewer for the voyeuristic spectatorship involved in viewing these images of disaster.

No Man's Zone opens with a 360-degree pan of a massive debris field that lasts for 3 minutes, and the only sound is the background noise of wind and waves (Fig. 27.2). Fujiwara intentionally assaults the viewer

Fig. 27.2 *No Man Without Zone* (Fujiwara Toshi, 2011).

with raw images of the disaster area pre-clean-up, and the filming style encourages the viewer to contemplate this landscape outside any narrative. The scene is one of both visible earthquake and tsunami damage and invisible radioactive contamination. The latter is only detectable for those who can recognise the chimneys of the nuclear power plant in background (although the voiceover informs the viewer of its presence after the segment ends). *No Man's Zone* investigates the roles played by image-makers and viewers in the consuming of disaster, and Fujiwara's autonomous landscapes facilitate such consumption.

One of the most controversial of the disaster documentaries, Mori Tatsuya's *311* (2011), exemplifies 'the gross disjuncture between the perspectives of the out-of-town observer and the local victim' (Fig. 27.3). The film follows the team of four film-makers as they attempt to enter the nuclear exclusion zone and end up traversing the earthquake and tsunami affected areas instead. The film features trucking shots of abandoned irradiated areas and earthquake/tsunami damage. Unlike Fujiwara's tripod shots that halt the narrative, these landscapes are part of a narrative, but one that specifically encourages the viewing of them as a series of autonomous landscapes that never move beyond disaster tourism to become lived spaces. The camera takes a perspective aligned with the viewpoint of the film-makers who actively play the part of voyeur. The soundtrack is filled with their exclamations of shock and nervous laughter, and the screen shows them donning slapdash hazmat gear. Ultimately *311* is all about watching the film-makers film themselves entering the disaster zone rather than about the effects of radiation (or the earthquake and tsunami) on the area or its populace. The interviews in *311* feel intrusive since the film-makers have no relationship with the victims, unlike the intimate interviews in Tsuchimoto's and Kamanaka's films. Rather than coming to know the victims and their circumstances – in other words seeing the landscape as a lived space – the camera focuses on the faces of the film-makers so the viewer can see *their* reactions to these impromptu interviews and scenes of destruction. We are not so much *in* the landscape as merely driving *through* it. We are not there to contemplate environmental damage as we are there to join their search for dead bodies.

Fujiwara also indulges in empty landscape shots and visits these two zones (nuclear and earthquake/

Fig. 27.3 *311* (Mori Tatsuya, Matsubayashi Yojyū, Watai Takeharu, Yasuoka Takaharu and Yasuoka Takuji, 2012).

tsunami), but he moves the scenes from landscape back into setting through the narrative power of voiceovers (Khanjian and local residents) and on-screen interviews with evacuees. He also contrasts his establishing shot, and other images of debris later in the film, with shots of beautiful and untouched, yet highly irradiated landscapes outside the 20-kilometre zone. As I have argued elsewhere, the contrast of these two landscapes of visible and invisible damage, combined with interviews of residents awaiting evacuation from areas more contaminated than those around the plant, works to make visible the damage of radiation.[45]

Fujiwara's focus is not on ecological issues. He is more interested in questioning our voyeurism and criticising the Japanese government for mishandling the disaster. However, he does include interviews with ranchers and long-time residents who cannot come to terms with the mandatory evacuations since there is no visible evidence of the radiological danger. He also interviews victims who worked for the nuclear power plant, highlighting the difficult choices made by residents of such company towns with few economic options.

This tension is also apparent in Kamanaka's *Ashes to Honey* when the locals are engaged in a showdown to prevent the nuclear power plant from being built. Plant officials try to discourage the protesters, saying that their only future is to take good jobs at the plant that will economically sustain them and their descendants. In *Little Voices from Fukushima*, Kamanaka interviews residents who decide to stay in the contaminated zone because of their jobs or family members. Although the obvious path would seem to be evacuation or relocation, such scenes depict the heart-wrenching choices facing residents of toxic areas. These films depict the way ecological decisions often conflict with personal and economic ones. Interdependency is a bargain that comes at a high price in towns with toxic facilities.

PASTORAL NOSTALGIA AND TOXIC AMNESIA: KUBOTA NAO'S *HOMELAND*

Kubota Nao's fictional *Homeland* uses images of the agrarian Japanese countryside less as extreme long shots for contemplation outside the narrative, and more as a series of shots (close-ups to long shots) that show the characters inhabiting and working the land. Kubota does not share in 3/11 cinema's fascination with disasterscapes. Rather, he emphasises the deep ties local residents have to the land. Although he shows this rural landscape as lived space where humans reside in harmony with nature, the presence of radiation makes his fictional space an impossibility. His narrative conceals the reality of life in a contaminated zone, ultimately rendering the danger invisible. This is ironic given that he had to request permission to film on location in restricted areas of Fukushima, where almost 99 per cent of the scenes were shot on contaminated land.[46]

Homeland is about a farming family displaced by a nuclear accident and living in temporary housing. Forcibly evacuated, the husband (Shōji) and stepmother are at a loss as to what to do with themselves. Meanwhile, Shōji's long-lost younger brother, Jirō, returns to the family home and starts farming in the irradiated area. In the end of the film, Jirō takes his mother back with him to the family farm, and Shōji resettles on a farm in a different part of Fukushima prefecture. Kubota makes the land a focal point for a reinstitution of the family through the evocation of a nostalgic, traditional way of life that ignores the dangers of radioactive contamination.

The first 8 minutes of the film show Jirō on the farm, including a long take of him burying a cow that was born in 2011. Through a series of long shots and close-ups, the audience watches Jirō dig; we hear his breathing and the sound of dirt being turned. The camera cuts away to shots of barriers and signs indicating restricted entry as well as to wild animals on the road. These shots are visual shorthand for radioactive contamination, but it is not clear to the viewer exactly where in the zone the farm lies. There is little to no other visual indication that the land is dangerous. Nobody wears protective gear, including the police who patrol the area and block the roads. The idea of the land as contaminated fades into the background and essentially becomes invisible as scenes of characters living on that land dominate. The camera in *Homeland* does not leave this rural farmland until over 8 minutes into the film, and it returns to the family farm in several key sequences examined below.

Unlike Fujiwara's pans, which allow the viewer a distance on the landscape, Kubota puts the viewer in close contact with the natural surroundings, restricting the view to traditional images of the human–nature relationship of interdependence. Kubota's camera lingers over the landscape moving from long pans of the farms and mountains to close-ups of Jiro rebuilding a dam near a small waterfall, drinking the water, and carrying some back to prepare rice in a traditional cooker. The close-ups and extreme close-ups of the rice – from seedlings to its fully cooked state – reinforce the portrayal of the land as a lived space that is safe. It is there for Jiro to work, and in return it sustains him. Unlike the residents of Minamata or Kamanaka's films who stay in contaminated landscapes because they have no choice, Jiro returns willingly, saying that nature called to him – the rice paddies, fields, cows and mountains. He chooses to ignore warnings from the police and a drifter – a temporary clean-up worker at the NPP – who stays briefly with Jiro and reminds him that he cannot live on the land.

Kubota uses the land as a site of reconciliation between family members. In one sequence, Shōji confronts Jirō who is preparing a field for planting. This is the first time Shōji has seen Jirō since the younger brother went missing in Tokyo. The two brothers end up fighting in the dirt, rolling in it as it covers their clothes and bodies. Although the viewer is told that the land is toxic – a neighbour commits suicide while driving a truckload of contaminated dirt towards the Diet building – and contaminated dirt has been the topic of discussion in the post-3/11 clean-up in Japan, this scene of the brothers contains no fear of contamination. The dirt that covers them is visible, but its toxins are not. This contrasts sharply with scenes in Kamanaka's *Little Voices* where residents attempt to decontaminate their living areas by removing topsoil. Neither Jirō nor Shōji worry that they are in contact with contaminated dirt, drinking contaminated water, eating contaminated rice or breathing contaminated air.

This evocation of the land as refuge and 'therapeutic sanctuary' culminates in the final sequence in which Jirō takes his mother – who is starting to suffer from dementia – to live out her days on the farm with him. *Homeland* ends with them planting rice seedlings as Kubota's camera closes in on the water flooding the field, frogs in the paddies, and the synchronised motions of mother and son stepping into the flooded paddies, bending down, planting the rice in neat rows (Fig. 27.4). This sequence slips from setting to autonomous landscape, as the shots evoke a timeless Japanese practice of sowing rice that exists outside a temporalised lived space, specifically the lived space of irradiated Japan. The sequence is so picturesque that even the police silently retreat, allowing Jirō and his mother to stay in the zone. Similarly, the viewer is encouraged to retreat from the controversial discussions of radiological contamination in Japan.

Fig. 27.4 *Homeland/Ieji* (Kubota Nao, 2014).

Kubota's rice planting sequence can be contrasted with one of the final sequences in Kamanaka's *Rokkasho Rhapsody* that features a local rice farmer. Kamanaka's camera similarly lingers over the natural beauty: close-ups of frogs in the rice paddy give way to medium and close-up shots of the rice fields, and extreme close-ups of the plants and spiders building their webs. But, the preceding sequence forces a different interpretation of nature than in *Homeland*. In the interview that directly precedes this, the farmer talks about how she realised that her long-held position of neutrality was in essence one of support for the reprocessing plant. She is an organic farmer, but it is becoming difficult for her to sell her rice because of fears of contamination. Kamanaka's documentary film-making creates a narrative that makes the contamination of the beautiful rural landscapes visible in a way that Kubota does not.

The harmonious relationship of humans to the land and the naturalness of human death on that land is evoked in the final sequence of *Homeland* when Jirō carries his mother on his back after the family has decided it is best for her to live out her life on the family farm. In an interview, Kubota has talked about his decision to have Jirō and the mother return to the contaminated farm. He wanted to show that life in the exclusion zone was better than the mother's purposeless life in temporary housing or Jirō's homelessness in Tokyo. Although his point about the bleakness of these other living conditions is well taken, he reinforces government campaigns that pressured residents to remain in or return to contaminated or so-called decontaminated areas.[47]

Ultimately, Kubota is not interested in a political argument. The characters voice the futility of this when Shōji and Jirō go to retrieve their dead neighbour's truck full of contaminated soil. They stop short of dumping it at the Diet building themselves, deciding that is a 'dead end'. The viewer can take this comment to mean political protest is futile. For the brothers, the only choice is to return to the land. Kubota made the film in order to depict the trials of dislocated families, but his evocations of the land fall short of 'critically-minded pastoralism'.[48] His narrative focus on the family conceals the real reason for their dissolution and displacement, radioactive contamination.

ASSESSING DANGER OUTSIDE THE ZONE: UCHIDA NOBUTERU'S *THE TRANQUIL EVERYDAY*

As discussed above, many of the 3/11 films that focus on traditional, agrarian landscapes and the human–nature relationship of interdependence do not specifically function as ecological films. Setting does not guarantee an ecological message. In this last section, I turn to Uchida Nobuteru's fiction film *The Tranquil Everyday/Odayaka na nichijō* (2012) and his depiction of characters attempting to protect themselves from radiological danger in an urban setting that is supposed to be at a safe remove from the threat of radiation.

Unlike the case with my discussion of previous films, I do not wish to examine *The Tranquil Everyday* for its images of landscape. The film's setting outside the disaster zone allows us to move beyond the 'rhetoric of pastoral betrayal'.[49] Uchida may not engage in landscape shots, but the film is deeply concerned with problems of visibility when it comes to radiological contamination. The film engages with the following ecological issues: the complications of assessing radiation outside officially designated zones; the way the government and industry shifted responsibility to personal choice as the danger was domesticated; and finally, the social mechanisms of containment that prevent individuals from expressing fears, and the concomitant labelling of such whistleblowers as paranoid in an attempt to reinforce and protect the message of safety.

The Tranquil Everyday begins with an earthquake and nuclear accident as the story follows the lives of two women: Yukako lives next door to Saeko, the mother of a young girl, Kiyomi. The two women struggle to understand the deluge of information about the nuclear disaster and to keep their families safe. This film is set exclusively in urban areas outside the official evacuation zones, but the dangers of contamination are seemingly ever present. Saeko and Yukako are left to make their own judgments about radiation, which neither visibly marks the landscape nor is visibly marked by the signage and warnings of the disaster zone, and hence is harder to identify. The spread of radiation beyond these visible markers/boundaries is a source of anxiety for these women. This anxiety, something that gets characterised as paranoia, is one narrative mechanism that Uchida uses to make the threat visible.[50]

In real life, the Japanese government and operators of the NPP have refused to take responsibility for the Fukushima meltdowns and disaster mismanagement. They have privatised risk and turned it into a dilemma for individuals to solve through personal decisions about whether to evacuate, where to live and what to eat.[51] In *The Tranquil Everyday*, those private choices become problematic when they mark a shared public space that is assumed to be safe. This public marking of radiation in non-disaster zones is a dangerous act that must be contained lest it compromise the shared public desire for a belief in safety. When the women in *The Tranquil Everyday* challenge this system of safety by voicing fear and doubt, the community perceives them as a threat. Saeko's public choices to protect her daughter – making her wear a mask and bring her own lunch to school – are met with resistance and rejection by the community of other mothers at the school. She and, to a lesser extent, Yukako are marked, and the threat they represent is contained through ostracisation, public pressure and medical discourse.

The film turns into a domestic drama of women becoming unhinged by their fears of radiation, fears that other characters in the film do not share (at least openly), because the systems of nuclear signification indicate that no danger is present. Visible markers of radiation – images of no-entry signs, barriers or even empty streets – are absent in *The Tranquil Everyday*. Surrounded by mothers who seek to maintain their belief that the lack of such markers indicates their safe remove from the radiation, Saeko is confronted by the narrative of 'nothing happened here'.[52] This narrative combines with the lack of official markers of danger to allow the mothers and school officials to maintain a status quo ignorant of the radiological dangers. This social pressure to conform is a dynamic that has been documented in the disaster area.[53] *The Tranquil Everyday* shows how that same dynamic is at work outside the zone as well.

CONCLUSION

The films examined in this chapter all engage to different degrees with the ecological concerns of 'interdependent communities' as many of them examine the fragile, and often broken, connection between humans and the natural world. That natural world is visualised through shots that function as either part of the setting or as autonomous landscapes for the viewer to contemplate. Films such as Tsuchimoto's and Kamanaka's portray the natural world as lived space and retain close narrative ties to the concerns of toxic contamination. In this way, they make visible the effects of that contamination on their subjects' lives.

The 3/11 films vary in their approach but often fall prey to the voyeuristic draw of the massive debris fields, which as autonomous landscapes can hinder an examination of the nuclear threat by allowing the viewer to contemplate them outside the narrative. Although Fujiwara Toshi tries to counter this with contrasting images of destruction and normalcy, the viewer is still engaged as a voyeur. Set outside the disaster zone, Uchida's *The Tranquil Everyday* removes the attraction (or distraction) of autonomous landscape shots in order to focus on individual choice.[54] Uchida looks beyond the nostalgia for a pastoral refuge to ask important and, in Japan, political questions about how we define landscapes or geographical regions as 'safe' or 'dangerous'. Those choices function as visible effects of living in toxic environments. Of all these films that attempt to make visible these invisible threats, the absence of activist options in Uchida's film makes it one of the bleakest portrayals of life in the contaminated zone.

Notes

1   Lawrence Buell, *Writing for an Endangered World: Literature, Culture, and Environment in the U. S. and Beyond* (Cambridge, MA: Harvard University Press, 2001), pp. 35–6.

2   Yuki Masami, 'Ecocriticism in Japan', in Greg Garrard (ed.), *The Oxford Handbook of Ecocriticism* (London: Oxford University Press, 2014), pp. 519–26.

3   These include fiction and documentary films by well-known directors and many documentaries by amateur or independent film-makers that never made it past domestic film festivals to larger distributors. See Hideaki Fujiki, 'Networking Citizens through Film Screenings: Cinema and Media in the Post-3.11 Social Movement', in Jason G. Karlin and Patrick W. Galbraith (eds), *Media Convergence in Japan* (Ann Arbor, MI: Kinema Club, 2016), pp. 60–87. For more on 3/11 films and environmental cinema see, Hideaki Fujiki, 'Problematizing Life: Documentary Films on the 3.11 Nuclear Catastrophe', in Barbara Geilhorn and Kristina Iwata-Weickgenannt (eds), *Fukushima and the Arts: Negotiating Nuclear Disaster* (London: Routledge, 2017), p. 95; Hideaki Fujiki, 'De-Naturalizing the Anthropocene: Landscape, Animals, and Place in Post-3.11 Nuclear Disaster Documentaries', in Scott Slovic, Winnie Yee and Kiu-wai Chu (eds), *Asian Ecocinema Studies* (Hong Kong: Hong Kong University Press, forthcoming).

4   See the essays in Mick Broderick (ed.), *Hibakusha Cinema: Hiroshima, Nagasaki and the Nuclear Image in Japanese Film* (London: , 1996). See Nornes's chapter, 'The Body at the Center- The Effects of the Atomic Bomb on Hiroshima and Nagasaki', for more on this science documentary about the aftermath, shot in 1945 and confiscated by the American government. See Nornes, p. 153 n. 34, for a list of films that use footage from this. The volume also discusses mainstream fiction films such as Kurosawa Akira's *Record of a Living Being/Ikimono no kiroku* (1955) and Imamura Shōhei's *Black Rain/Kuroi Ame* (1989).

5   Greg Garrard, *Ecocriticism*, 2nd edn (New York: Routledge, 2011), p. 24. Christine Marran seeks a new ecology of landscape that accounts for the agency of things 'beyond the human gaze'. Christine L. Marran, *Ecology without Culture: Aesthetics for a Toxic World* (Minneapolis: University of Minnesota Press, 2017), p. 56.

6   Fujiki, 'De-Naturalizing the Anthropocene'.

7   Cheryll Glotfelty, 'Literary Studies in an Age of Environmental Crisis', in Ken Hiltner (ed.), *Ecocriticism: The Essential Reader* (London: Routledge, 2015), p. 123.

8   Martin Lefebvre, 'On Landscape in Narrative Cinema', *Canadian Journal of Film Studies* vol. 20 no. 1 (Spring 2011), p. 62.

9   Martin Lefebvre, 'Between Setting and Landscape in the Cinema', in Martin Lefebvre (ed.), *Landscape and Film* (New York: Routledge, 2006), p. 29.

10 Lefebvre, 'On Landscape in Narrative Cinema', pp. 72, 74, 76.

11 See, for example, Sono Sion's fictional *Himizu* (2012) and *Land of Hope/Kibō no kuni* (2012) and the Mori Tatsuya team's documentary *311* (2011). Sono added scenes of the disaster landscape to the already written scenario of *Himizu*, which 'appeared almost gratuitous, reducing the catastrophe to the well-known image of the postapocalyptic world and a dystopian nation'. He was accused of 'irreverence' for scenes filmed in one of the disaster towns even before the debris had been cleared. See Christophe Thouny, 'Land of Hope: Planetary Cartographies of Fukushima, 2012', *Mechademia* vol. 10 (2015), p. 21; Kristina Iwata-Weickgenannt, 'Gendering "Fukushima": Resistance, Self-Responsibility, and Female Hysteria in Sono Sion's Land of Hope', in Geilhorn and Iwata-Weickgenannt, *Fukushima and the Arts*, p. 112.

12 Marran, *Ecology without Culture*, p. 57.

13 Rob Nixon, *Slow Violence and the Environmentalism of the Poor* (Cambridge, MA: Harvard University Press, 2013).

14 Patrick Brereton, *Hollywood Utopia: Ecology in Contemporary American Cinema* (Bristol: Intellect Books, 2005), p. 13.

15 Iwata-Weickgenannt, 'Gendering "Fukushima"', p. 111.

16 Fujiki, 'Problematizing Life', p. 107 n. 11.

17 David Ingram, 'Rethinking Eco-Film Studies', in Garrard, *The Oxford Handbook of Ecocriticism*, p. 468.

18 Brereton, *Hollywood Utopia*, p. 13.

19 [Editors' note: for more on Japanese documentary cinema, see also Chapter 26 by Ayumi Hata in this volume. For more on Tsuchimoto Noriaki's documentary, see also Chapter 33 by Masato Dogase in this volume.]

20 Justin Jesty, 'Making Mercury Visible: The Minamata Documentaries of Tsuchimoto Noriaki', in Sharon L. Zuber and Michael C. Newman (eds), *Mercury Pollution: A Transdisciplinary Treatment* (Boca Raton, FL: CRC Press, 2011), p. 140.

21 Ibid., p. 146.

22 Takuya Tsunoda, 'Toward Dialogical Cinema: Noriaki Tsuchimoto's Documentary', in *The Documentaries of*

Noriaki Tsuchimoto: The Shiranui Sea [DVD] (Hamden, CT: Zakka Films, 2013).
23. Jesty, 'Making Mercury Visible', p. 144.
24. Ibid., p. 154.
25. Lefebvre, 'On Landscape in Narrative Cinema', p. 69.
26. Marran, *Ecology without Culture*, p. 60.
27. Olga Kuchinskaya criticises depictions of wounded bodies in Chernobyl films such as *La Sacrifice* (2003) and *Chernobyl Heart* (2003) for being sensational. Olga Kuchinskaya, *The Politics of Invisibility: Public Knowledge about Radiation Health Effects after Chernobyl* (Cambridge, MA: MIT Press, 2014), pp. 85–93, 115–36.
28. Hitomi Kamanaka, Noriaki Tsuchimoto and Norma Field, 'Rokkasho, Minamata and Japan's Future: Capturing Humanity on Film', trans. Ann Saphir, *Asia-Pacific Journal: Japan Focus* vol. 5 no. 12 (1 December 2007), <https://apjjf.org/-Kamanaka-Hitomi/2614/article.html>.
29. Hitomi Kamanaka and Katsuya Hirano, 'Fukushima, Media, Democracy: The Promise of Documentary Film', trans. Margherita Long, *Asia-Pacific Journal: Japan Focus* vol. 16 no. 6.3 (7 August 2018), <https://apjjf.org/2018/16/Kamanaka.html>.
30. She is also present at the screenings of her films to get feedback from the audience. See Kamanaka's website for more on arranging a screening: <http://kamanaka.com/>.
31. Hitomi Kamanaka, *Radiation: A Slow Death A New Generation of Hibakusha* [DVD] (USA: Choices, Inc., 2005).
32. Kamanaka and Hirano, 'Fukushima, Media, Democracy'.
33. Ibid.
34. Ibid.
35. Fujiki, 'Problematizing Life', p. 100.
36. Ibid., pp. 92–3.
37. Lefebvre, 'On Landscape in Narrative Cinema', p. 62.
38. Fujiki, 'Problematizing Life', pp. 100, 103. For more on Ash's film, see Fujiki, 'Problematizing Life'.
39. The quotation is from Martin Lefebvre as cited in Marran, *Ecology without Culture*, p. 56.
40. Mark Downing Roberts, 'Observations on Japanese Cinema after 3/11', Culture360asef.org, 16 January 2012, <https://culture360.asef.org/magazine/observations-japanese-cinema-after-311>.
41. Jamie Morris, 'Facing the Earthquake: "Cinema with Us" at the YIDFF', Yamagata International Documentary Film Festival Film Critics', Workshop Day 3, 10 October 2011, <https://mubi.com/notebook/posts/yamagata-international-documentary-film-festival-filmcritics-workshop-day-3>. Morris talks about how Morimoto Shūichi goes to great lengths to get these shots, even switching from a car to a bicycle in *Lives after the Tsunami/Tsunami no ato ni* (2011) when roads become impassable.
42. Ian Thomas Ash, Timothy A. Mousseau and Lisa Onaga, 'Orbiting in the Field: A Taidan (Conversation) on Ecology and Filmmaking in Tohoku, Japan', *positions* 26, no. 2 (2018), p. 232. Nornes uses 'truck' for these 'lengthy shots photographed from moving vehicles'. Markus Nornes, 'Yamagata Halfway', *KineJapan*, 9 October 2011. Fujiwara commented on the tripod: 'One thing that differentiated us from the standard media footage, and especially from other film-makers and media journalists, is that they always used a handheld camera. I knew we had to bring a tripod. That way the camera would be more concentrated on the landscape, because that's one thing that was totally missing, a sense of landscape.' Toshi Fujiwara, 'A Conversation with Toshi Fujiwara about *No Man's Zone*', interview by Chris Fujiwara, 2012, <www.docandfilm.com/pdf_press/2012_02_InterviewToshiFujiwaraFullVersion.pdf>. Fujiwara also uses trucking shots.
43. Morris, 'Facing the Earthquake'.
44. Lefebvre, 'Between Setting and Landscape', p. 29.
45. Rachel DiNitto, 'Narrating the Cultural Trauma of 3.11: The Debris of Post-Fukushima Literature and Film', *Japan Forum* vol. 26 no. 3 (2014), pp. 340–60.
46. MOViE MOViE, *MOViE MOViE PEOPLE: Kubota Nao Homeland hōmon*, 2014, <https://www.youtube.com/watch?v=apgKBFcf_UM>; C2 yokoku & intabyū dōga, *'Ieji' Kubota Nao kantoku Interview*, 2014, <https://www.youtube.com/watch?v=RBSqHU0pjIc>.
47. The subtlety of Kubota's critique was lost on international audiences. See Maggie Lee, '"Homeland" Review: Nao Kubota's Ho-Hum Fukushima Drama', *Variety*, 17 February 2014, <https://variety.com/2014/film/asia/berlin-film-review-homeland-1201109899/>.
48. Ryan Holmberg talks about 'critically-minded pastoralism' in manga artist Katsumata Susumu's work. Ryan Holmberg, '"Fukushima Devil Fish": A Nuclear Pastoral', *New York Review of Books* [blog], 18 August 2018, <https://www.nybooks.com/daily/2018/08/18/fukushima-devil-fish-a-nuclear-pastoral/>.

49 Buell, *Writing for an Endangered World*, p. 39.
50 For more on the portrayal of these women as paranoid, see Rachel DiNitto, 'The Fukushima Fiction Film: Gender and the Discourse of Nuclear Containment', *Asia-Pacific Journal*, 1 January 2018, <https://apjjf.org/2018/01/DiNitto.html>.
51 Fujiki, 'Problematizing Life', p. 92. Also see Majia Holmer Nadesan, *Fukushima and the Privatization of Risk* (Basingstoke: Palgrave Macmillan, 2013).
52 Adriana Petryna, *Life Exposed : Biological Citizens after Chernobyl* (Princeton, NJ: Princeton University Press, 2002), p. xix.
53 David H. Slater, Rika Morioka and Haruka Danzuka, 'Micro-politics of Radiation: Young Mothers Looking for a Voice in Post–3.11 Fukushima', *Critical Asian Studies* vol. 46 no. 3 (3 July 2014), pp. 485–508, <https://doi.org/10.1080/14672715.2014.935138>.
54 Lefebvre talks about landscape as 'distracting' imagery that interrupts the 'forward drive and flow of narrative'. Lefebvre, 'On Landscape in Narrative Cinema', p. 65.

RURAL LANDSCAPE
The cinematic countryside in Japanese wartime film-making

Sharon Hayashi

'Landscape can never be cut off from the lives of the people who live there'.

— Kamei Fumio

With a few notable exceptions, Japanese film studies have largely concentrated on urban settings by analysing cinema as part of the lived, or imagined, experience of urban life.[1] While cinematic images of city life both reinforced and supplemented the experience of urban modernity in the early to mid-twentieth century,[2] cinema also played a central role in creating the rural geographic imaginary of Japan.

Cinematic landscapes developed in dialogue with earlier literary, poetic and aesthetic conventions of landscape even though the early theorisation of landscape in Japan was propelled most strongly by the political need to create a cultural identity distinct from other nations. Shiga Shigetaka's widely popular *Theory of Japanese Landscape*,[3] published during the first Sino-Japanese war in 1894, defined Japan's unique beauty through a combination of scientific analysis and Japanese poeticism. Shiga, dubbed 'the Japanese Ruskin', felt the elite and passive aesthetic appreciation of nature in *haiku* and *bonsai* was too limited, and sought to encourage a new way of interacting with the landscape through the promotion of an active enjoyment of the outdoors by all.[4] The building of a national awareness and solidarity through an appreciation of the unique aspects of the Japanese landscape contributed to the excessive patriotism that eventually led to Japan's imperial expansion in World War II.

Japanese cinema only began to really portray the country's rural landscape in the 1930s thanks to a series of technological developments. Location shooting outside urban areas was enabled by the advent of portable cameras and sound equipment along with the expansion of the nation's railway system. The countryside promoted by this newly minted cinematic mobility initially functioned as a form of pastoral playground for the urban middle-class characters of modernist comedies. As film-makers experimented with the possibilities of landscape as a new form of cultural expression, once bucolic portrayals of the cinematic countryside soon shifted to reflect the increasingly dire socio-economic conditions of depression era rural Japan.

The outbreak of the second Sino-Japanese War (1937–45) further altered representations of the rural landscape. The wartime expansion of the Japanese empire provided many film-makers with their first opportunity to travel to Asia and the chance to film the war in China on location. Realist depictions of the war in the swell of newsreels and documentaries of the front were initially celebrated but by the end of 1939, with no end to the war in sight, these were replaced by romantic and heroic dramas.[5] It was at this moment that documentary films, and films influenced by documentary realism, turned their focus inwards on the Japanese countryside. Rural landscape became increasingly equated with the farm village, both as a site of labour and as an axis of colonisation within the empire.[6] Representations of land and landscape became imbricated with power and territory. The theme of the farmer and the countryside was alternately used as social critique and justification for Japanese expansionism.

This chapter will examine the complex way that rural landscape was deployed in three films made during the tumultuous years of 1939 to 1941: Uchida Tomu's *Earth/Tsuchi* (1939), Miki Shigeru's *Living in the Earth/Tsuchi ni ikiru* (1941) and Kamei Fumio's *Notes on the Shinano Climate: Kobayashi Issa/Shinano fudoki: Kobayashi Issa* (1941). These three films lie at the convergence of the social, political and aesthetic movements that redefined the role of the countryside during wartime. Uchida Tomu's *Earth* showcased the convergence of documentary realism and fiction film-making that characterised the film world's representation of rural life after 1936. The foregrounding of documentary realism stemmed from an earlier project Uchida was slated to film – a documentary on rice production. For Uchida, the rural landscape was a place of labour and discrimination and he used a documentary-inflected dramatic style not only to portray the harshness of nature but also the underlying feudal systems that led to suffering in the countryside.

Notes on the Shinano Climate: Kobayashi Issa embodied an innovative way of representing the reality of rural inhabitants and, in turn, created a new cinematic rural ecology. Editor-director Kamei Fumio and cameraman Miki Shigeru had previously collaborated on the war documentaries *Shanghai/Shina jihen kōhō kiroku: Shanhai* (1938) and *Fighting Soldiers/Tatakau heitai* (1939). Unlike many war documentaries that refused to show the enemy, *Shanghai* portrayed the daily lives of Chinese inhabitants and a landscape marred by gravestones and the detritus of war. While working on these documentaries in China, Kamei developed a theory of montage that sympathetically portrayed the difficult life of impoverished farmers and soldiers in a way that superseded national boundaries. After returning to Japan, Kamei merged his theory of montage with environmentalism to create a new form of *haiku* montage in *Kobayashi Issa*. The materialist historical perspective of the film, combined with his exposure of the misery of the Shinano farmer, led in part to his arrest in 1941. Although lauded in the postwar period as an anti-war hero because of his incarceration, Kamei asserted that his intent during this period was not to make anti-war films, but his 'greatest concern was to thoroughly describe the pain of the land and the sadness of all people, including soldiers, farmers, and all living things like horses'.[7] With *Kobayashi Issa*, Kamei thus created a melancholic form of eco-Marxism.

Miki Shigeru shared Kamei's concern for the inhabitants of the rural landscape and sought to document both the work and the cultural rituals of farming communities in order to fully portray the life of farmers. In opposition to the increasingly rationalised image of the farmer and farming techniques that promoted rice productivity for the national cause, Miki emphasised both the agency and desires of rural inhabitants. *Living in the Earth* signalled a convergence between native studies and documentary film production. It also revealed a tension between the use of documentary film to preserve rural culture and the need to create films that were acceptable to rural audiences. For these three film-makers working contemporaneously, the rural landscape did not simply mean a contemplative view but a lived and inhabited environment. Through their depiction of the inhabitants of the rural landscape, these film-makers engaged creatively with the changing reality of the countryside in order to think through issues of land and labour, agency, cultural memory and ecology.

LANDSCAPE AND LABOUR: UCHIDA TOMU'S *EARTH*

To early twentieth-century utopian agricultural writers such as Miyazawa Kenji, Japan's mountains and villages were a place of new ideal communities empty of the oppression and dirt of daily farming life.[8] In this incarnation of the idyllic village, the intellectual travelled to the countryside in search of a space outside the ravages of capitalism. By the late 1930s, however, the dire conditions of farm villages called for a more active investigation of the countryside. In addition to this, following the start of the Sino-Japanese war in 1937, the youths of the nation were being sent off to the war front and farm villages were being burdened with extra rice production quotas in order to feed the soldiers. The farm village film recast the countryside as a place of subordination to the land, sketching the inequities of the landowning system in dramatic form (Fig. 28.1).

Uchida Tomu's *Earth* was chosen by *Kinema junpō* as the best film of 1939 and was awarded a prize by the Ministry of Education.[9] *Earth* was one of the first farm village films to be widely watched in Japan and was based on the naturalist novel of the same title by Nagatsuka Takashi, written in 1910.[10] The popularity of *Earth* stemmed not only from its designation as a masterpiece by the cultural authorities but because it took up the plight of the farmer at a time when the agricultural crisis was a growing concern. The film can be seen both as a reflection of a general societal concern about the farm village and as part of the popular revival of Nagatsuka's novel in particular. In 1937, Mizoguchi Kenji directed a radio drama based on Nagatsuka's novel that also inspired several theatrical and successive radio versions.[11] Capitalising on this trend, the Nikkatsu Tamagawa Film Production Company, which had a long tradition of producing films about the earth, dirt and mud, asked its director Uchida Tomu to direct *Earth*.

Although the novel *Earth* had been written during the Meiji period (1868–1912), its theme of suffering and hardship resonated with the literary and cinematic interest in the countryside in the late 1930s. Uchida's film portrays the farm village as an economically and emotionally harsh place empty of the communal warmth of the sentimental homeland melodramas that had populated screens a decade earlier. Here, the family drama is used to show conflicts that arise from a landowning system that subjects farmers to inescapable debt and poverty. Throughout the film, the farmer-protagonist Kanji labours ceaselessly in the rice fields in order to feed his family. Despite endless hours of toil, Kanji and his self-sacrificing daughter Otsugi remain trapped in a cycle of inescapable debt incurred by his family a generation earlier. Forced to turn over his rice harvest to his landlord, Kanji out of hunger and desperation, steals his neighbour's millet and becomes a fugitive and outcast in his own village.

By filming *Earth*, a story about the plight of farmers in the Meiji period instead of a more contemporary

Fig. 28.1 *Earth/Tsuchi* (Uchida Tomu, 1939, Nikkatsu).

scenario, Uchida was able to tackle the growing problem of farm village poverty through the lens of feudalism and its lasting structures. The turn to the past afforded Uchida the opportunity to describe discrimination in a way that was becoming increasingly difficult to do in contemporary dramas that were more likely to be censored. Uchida would continue to use the historical drama to highlight discrimination in society in his postwar career.

The suppression of political texts affected the literary and film worlds of the time. In the early to mid-1930s, both the proletarian literature and film movements faced mounting political repression that eventually led to their demise. A literary classic renaissance immediately followed in their wake. The process of filming a literary classic about farm life allowed Uchida to continue taking up the theme of labour after the disappearance of the genre of proletarian farm literature.

The Sino-Japanese War's impact on film-making cannot be understated. Although various documentary films movements had been active in Japan since the early 1930s, the flood of newsreel films documenting the Sino-Japanese war had a profound effect on dramatic films after 1937. The deepening influence of documentary film-making prompted a redefinition of realism in the world of dramatic film. Naturalism was cast as an enemy to be expelled. Film critics such as Imamura Taihei spearheaded this attack on naturalism, especially in articles such as 'Notes for A Film Aesthetics: Against Naturalism' and 'Japanese Film Naturalism'.[12] According to Imamura, the timing of Japan's adoption of naturalism coincided with the emergence of film, unlike the case in Europe where a re-evaluation of naturalism had already occurred before the advent of the medium. The lack of any thoughtful rejection of naturalism had led to an incorporation of literary naturalism into film that remained on the level of formalism without any sense of capturing its underlying intention. The realism that Uchida attempted to create in *Earth* was thus a remedy for the superficial surface description that naturalism had come to be associated with. The medium of film, in particular, was deemed the best suited for realist description, and thus *Earth* resurrected a naturalist text but at the same time gave it a new realist form.

Although it was originally considered to be a dramatic film, the screenwriter Wada Den accurately described *Earth* as, 'a documentary style film that vividly describes the four seasons of a farming village'.[13] A large section of the film is devoted to documenting the many different aspects of rice farming and foregrounding the labour of the protagonists against the unpredictable and uncooperative forces of nature (Fig. 28.2). Long shots of Otsugi and Kanji culling driftwood or harvesting rice emphasise the harsh but beautiful landscape. As the film tracks the production of rice from planting to harvesting through the seasons, Otsugi and Kanji strike dramatic poses or run dynamically, if exhaustedly, across the screen. In contrast to the static, interior shots of the farmhouses and temple, travelling shots and pans supplemented by quick cutting and dramatic drum music accompany these scenes of rice growing. Many shots are devoted entirely to the rice itself – scorched stems of rice are kept barely alive by small buckets of water carried great distances by the two protagonists. As the title suggests, the earth itself at times becomes the real protagonist of the film.

The cyclical nature of the farm village, dependent on the weather and seasons, is captured vividly in the outdoor scenes. Uchida himself called *Earth* a semi-documentary and the extended period of shooting gives the film a documentary-like quality as it spans the seasonal changes over a year. The time devoted to filming natural phenomena was an essential aspect of Uchida's portrayal of the life of the farmer. Uchida had originally planned to shoot for at least a year and a half but in the summer of 1938, he was told to stop as the film's portrayal of the apparent misery of farm life would not attract spectators. Uchida and his staff, feeling compelled to complete the seasonal portions of the film, continued to shoot using resources allocated for other films. Through the effective and selective use of documentary aesthetics, he turned a naturalist historical novel into a factual representation of man labouring in the landscape that has the feel of a documentary film shot in the past.

Fig. 28.2 *Earth/Tsuchi* (Uchida Tomu, 1939, Nikkatsu).

Uchida did not only respond to the turn to realism in visual terms. When making the film version of *Earth*, he went back to the original novel rather than using the recent radio drama as the basis for the film. The main characters of his film do not merely flavour their dialogue with colourful dialect endings against a backdrop of extras who, following custom, speak entirely in dialect, they speak themselves in an authentic Ibaragi dialect. Uchida strove to achieve a more consistent form of dialect throughout the duration of the film.

Earth was a representation of an individual's alienation from a farming community and a description of the farm village as an oppressive economic system. In positioning the farmer in relationship to the land through his labour, Uchida manages to very explicitly connect the landscape to issues of land ownership and labour. The representation of farm villages ignited several dynamic debates about subjectivity, community, labour and landscape. The question of how the reality of a farm village should be portrayed was to remain an issue that dramatic and documentary film-makers faced alike.

DOCUMENTING THE RURAL: MIKI SHIGERU'S *LIVING IN THE EARTH*

With the rise in documentary film-making in Japan, came calls to focus documentary practices on the representation of the countryside. This increasing attention to the rural echoed the native studies scholar Yanagita Kunio's interest in using film to document rural practices. Yanagita's native studies were an attempt to find an alternative to a perceived European and American dominance over urban culture. He looked to the nation's undeveloped pockets of countryside as the storehouse of Japanese customs and traditions and realised that film, when used properly, could be the best method for the preservation and transmission of knowledge about these rural customs. Yanagita's emphasis on the *chihō*, meaning village, local place or periphery, was taken up by the film world.[14]

Yanagita sought to transform the urban bias of Japanese cinema. He believed that most documentaries shown in the countryside were inappropriate for a rural audience, either because they focused strictly on the city or because they were filled with insulting portrayals of country folk. Yanagita was also convinced that merely informing the urban masses about the customs of the countryside was not sufficient. As someone who had travelled widely through the country, he realised that the people of Japanese villages only knew their own land and nothing about other places. He was intent on using film to allow farmers in different regions to share knowledge about deep customs and learn about each other. He advocated the 'education of the farmer beyond entertainment' and envisioned an exchange of knowledge that did not originate in the cities.[15] Film was the method that best allowed this form of comparison and that could best promote this interest.

Yanagita praised the successful use of the new technology of synchronous sound recording to capture dialects (*hōgen*).[16] Sound film provided a way to record and disseminate differences in regional dialects that were themselves being silenced. For Yanagita, dialects were an important part of the customs (*fūzoku*) of the farm village. His hope was that the recording of dialects would not be restricted to adding realism to film, but could be used to catalogue the variety of regional dialects slowly being destroyed by the spread of urban culture and the increasing imposition of standardised Japanese across the nation and the empire.[17]

Like earlier critics of literary naturalism, Yanagita was dissatisfied with shallow and deceptive description that failed to grasp its object of inquiry.[18] For Yanagita, sound film could overcome naturalism's inability to penetrate a visual appreciation of landscape and reach an interpretation of the meaning of village life.[19] Although critical of the uses of film and photography as mere reproduction, Yanagita believed in the potential of film, especially in its new incarnation as both a visual and audio recording device, to archive older customs as they were disappearing.

In 1940, as part of his renewed interest in the archival possibilities of film and photography, Yanagita served as the de facto adviser on a film shot and directed by the renowned cinematographer Miki Shigeru. A year later he again collaborated with Miki on a book detailing the lives of Tohoku farmers and featuring photographs of their dress, farming techniques, implements and festivals.

Yanagita published his writings in film journals and cultivated relationships with prominent members of the film community in order to ensure that his vision of the countryside would be realised. In a round-table discussion devoted to Yanagita and the relationship between native studies and documentary films held in March 1941 by the film magazine *Shin eiga*, Yanagita encouraged the influential head of documentary film production at Tōhō, Mura Haruo, to implement systematic and efficient changes in the production of documentary films about the countryside. His suggested topics for documentaries – a survey of different rice drying techniques and a record of various greetings from different regions throughout Japan – were incorporated into the studio's documentary productions.

As a former official of the Ministry of Agriculture and Commerce, it is no coincidence that Yanagita would develop strong ties with Tōhō studios.[20] Tōhō was a leader in documentary film production and actively and successfully cultivated ties with various government ministries. Tōhō distributed films to farm villages across the nation.[21] When Yanagita criticised the urban bias of films and their intoxicating and debilitating effects on the countryside, Mura admitted to having no appropriate culture films to bring to the countryside.[22] *Living in the Earth* (1941) was seen as a solution to this dilemma. Mura gave Miki the resources and time to shoot the film over the costly course of a year in part because of Yanagita's participation and authority.

Living in the Earth reflected the Ministry of Agriculture's campaign to increase rice production. As a documentary about a vanishing lifestyle, *Living in the Earth* recorded the changes that had taken place in line with state policy towards the countryside. If Uchida Tomu's film *Earth* had tried to portray the lasting traces of injustices of the feudal system by setting his film in the earlier Meiji period, Miki's documentary was about farmers in the present. Although landlords still possessed power in the countryside, by the late 1930s the new bureaucrats in the Ministry of Agriculture were turning their attention away from the landlords and rural elite and beginning to emphasise the role of farm operators. This served two purposes. Firstly, by dealing with those actively involved in cultivation, information about increasing production could be disseminated and put into practice more readily. Secondly, and perhaps more importantly, the focus on increasing yields and running farms smoothly took emphasis away from the issue of land ownership and tenancy disputes.[23] The increased production quotas placed on the countryside by an increasingly desperate government greatly burdened farmers and many felt that the colonies were being paid for by the blood of the countryside. Miki's film was an attempt to respond to the desire of farm villagers for spiritual nourishment in the face of being categorised solely as producers.[24]

The inclusion of festival scenes separates *Living in the Earth* from most documentary films of the time that focused exclusively on work for the good of the nation and the war effort. In contrast, Miki felt the need to portray both the process of rice production and the cultural life of villagers. In doing so Miki presents neither the joys nor the hardships of labour. The rhythmic motions of the farmers in Miki's documentary are as regular as the rice-polishing machines they manipulate. Sweat and tears have been abolished from the process. Although the film no longer exists in its entirety, the reels that remain suggest that Miki, in trying to describe the way villagers lived, was intent on showing the process of rice production in a systematic and rational way. The systematic portrayal of work in Miki's film was balanced by the detailed examination of the cultural activities of the village.

Armed with a letter of introduction from Yanagita, Miki spent over a year tracking the seasonal and related cultural activities of the people in a typical village in Akita in the Tohoku region.[25] He was less interested in the dying vestiges of traditional rituals than Yanagita and focused instead on the living practices of the farmers, as the title of the film *Living in the Earth* suggests. Like many documentary film-makers of the time, he was especially interested in how to photograph people within the space of the landscape and how to capture the activities of their lives on a visual level. Although they worked on the film together, Miki's emphasis on the agency of farmers differed significantly from Yanagita's vision of the folk as vessels of tradition.

According to Nara Kannosuke, another native studies scholar, literary descriptions of farming had up until this time only reflected the subjectivity of the author.[26] In emphasising either the sublime beauty or the intense suffering of farming life, neither trend had grasped the essence of this existence. In contrast, Miki's detailed research, combined with his restrained but innovative camerawork, was deemed to be 'objective'.[27] Miki attempted to show things exactly as they were.[28] It was not that Miki was unaware of the mediating effects of both his camerawork and the directing and editing processes. Miki, instead, staunchly believed that the camerawork needed to suit the subject. In a 1939 essay entitled 'On Culture Films: The Centrality of the Camera', Miki argued against the irresponsible emphasis on camera technique that had plagued the documentary film-making world.[29] According to Miki, the increasingly common phenomenon of allowing the camera to decide on shooting technique without any regard for content was due in part to the expanded role of nature and landscape in documentary films and had 'led to an overemphasis on and indulgence in the camera's vision'.[30]

The filming of human subjects in relationship to landscape became a particular concern for those working on documentary films. In his article, 'Realism, Landscape and People', the film critic Murao Kaoru suggests the camera must avoid being fixed like a painting, yet it must also be careful to remain centred on a person during pans of the landscape in order not to turn the image into a moving picture scroll.[31] Miki would try to surmount an overemphasis on aesthetic technique and landscape in *Living in the Earth* by focusing on the daily life of farmers in the landscape. Any shots of the landscape would either show the farmers themselves and their daily life, or in their absence, would suggest their presence in the traces of their work or by the inclusion of their work songs on the soundtrack.

In *Living in the Earth*, Miki sought to rethink the notion of productivity in documentary films. Miki's aim, in this film and others, was to recast the documentary film genre in order to provide a necessary antidote to the state's notion of farmers as producers and to address the state's failure to take into account the actual conditions and morale of the people working in the countryside. The film's inclusion of the spiritual and cultural aspects of village life did not contest the state's representation of the village as a harmonious community void of labour strife and land disputes, but it provided a better description of the reality of people's lives and human agency during a period when these areas were being increasingly controlled by the government.

HAIKU MONTAGE: KAMEI FUMIO'S KOBAYASHI ISSA

According to the film critic Iida Shinmi, there were basically two types of films about farm villages. In his article 'Documentary Film and the Farm Village', Iida suggested that the farm village film either took up the social problems of the village or portrayed the village in terms of climate, landscape and tradition.[32] Kamei Fumio's *Notes on a Shinano Climate: Kobayashi Issa* accomplishes both of these tasks by exploring the history and geography of the region.

Although the trilogy *Notes on the Shinano Climate* was made under the auspices of the Nagano Prefectural Department of Tourism, Kamei chose to use the regional term, Shinano, rather than the official name of Nagano Prefecture. Shinano had not officially been a province since 1871 when it was incorporated into Nagano Prefecture, and the belief that the Shinano people possessed a tenacity of character related to the harsh and mountainous climate continued to hold sway long after the name of the region had been officially changed.[33] The choice of Shinano for the title thus reflects Kamei's interest in describing the relationship of the people to their land.

The first part of the trilogy uses the poetry of Kobayashi Issa (1763–1827), the poet-representative of small birds, bugs and flowers, to convey the melancholy of the region.[34] The difficult life of Kobayashi Issa, the impoverished farmer-poet, was a natural choice for a director interested in describing the poverty of the farmer during the Edo period (1603–1868), in order to allude to the contemporary misery of the farmer during wartime.

Five years earlier in 1935 Kamei had written the script for *Hiking Song/Haikingu no uta*, a promotional film for the Office of Tourism of the Ministry of Railways. The film was part of the ministry's campaign to encourage the use of railroads and improve the health and welfare of the country's urban citizens by introducing them to the great outdoors.[35] The rural landscape of *Hiking Song* is presented as a space of rejuvenation and leisure for city dwellers. In stark contrast, *Notes on a Shinano Climate* is a critique of tourism. Rather than focusing on the beautiful scenery of the mountainous Shinano region, Kamei juxtaposed farmers who live and work on the land to tourists who simply come to enjoy the beautiful scenery. The landscape, which for hikers presents an enjoyable challenge, is for the farmer a difficult and unforgiving terrain to cultivate. The difficulty of farming had forced the people of the region to rely on tourism to survive. In order to contrast the different relationship to the land of farmers and tourists, the labour of farmers, whether cultivating the fields or weeding a golf course, is contrasted with shots of leisurely vacationers in the resort town of Karuizawa famed for its many summer homes. Tourism, Kamei suggests, is not just a consumer activity for the urban bourgeoisie but an unfortunate necessity for the farmers. Although the film was made as a tourist film to promote the region, it functions more like a deconstruction of tourism than a promotion of it.

In an essay describing his motivations for making the film, Kamei states, 'Landscape can never be cut off from the lives of the people who live there.' He was interested in how the lives of the people who inhabited the region were related to the landscape and climate. He examines the Buddhist beliefs of farmers as part of the local customs tied to the climate and connects the Buddhist prayers for the silkworm to the region's severe frost that endangers the mulberry leaves upon which the silkworm feeds. In contrast to Yanagita, Kamei's investigation of local custom does not lead to a mythic past but instead to an analysis of cultural transition. The film is a challenge to 'experience local customs and compare them to modern ways of life and discover historical change'.[36]

Earlier, Kamei had written the script for *Geology of Fuji/Fuji no chishitsu* (Akimoto Ken, 1943) based on Wakimizu Tetsugorō's 1939 *Notes on a Japanese Landscape*.[37] Wakimizu's book was itself inspired by Shiga Shigetaka's *Theory of Japanese Landscape*. Kamei, however, used geology to undercut rather than support the thesis of a unique and eternal Japanese beauty based on landscape. Instead of exalting the sanctity of Mt Fuji, for example, Kamei turned the film into a geological and environmental study of the mountain. The film describes the ecology of Mt Fuji and the local customs of the area such as mountain climbing by pilgrims. It is also an explanation of the mountain's formation and erosion. Instead of discussing the eternal nature of Mt Fuji, Kamei pointed to its inevitable transformation and decay. According to Peter B. High, this scientific analysis of an ageless symbol of the 'Eternal Land of the Gods' was deemed a sacrilege by the press and met with disapproval from the Home Ministry.[38]

Whereas history in Kamei's cinematic vocabulary signalled constant change, for many of his contemporaries it connoted the eternal. In 1938, the conservative writer Yasuda Yojūrō penned an article entitled 'The Beautiful Japanese View' for the film journal *Nippon eiga* in which he argued for the inseparability of Japanese literature from Japanese landscape.[39] By way of an almost inevitable conclusion, in 1942 Yasuda published *Landscape and History* that directly linked Japan's landscape to the emperor.[40]

Kamei's analysis of climate stands out against the cultural nationalism of the period. In contrast to Watsuji Tetsurō's philosophical treatise *A Climate*, which attributed the uniqueness of Japanese culture to its climate,[41] Kamei's understanding of climate as a historical and ecological system strove to create a 'bird's eye view' that moved beyond national boundaries and the nationalist use of landscape and climate. Expanding the conventional notion of the bird's eye view as an elevated vantage point of a bird in flight, Kamei sought to create a non-human-centred view of climate.

As the title of the trilogy suggests, *Notes on the Shinano Climate*, Kamei wasn't only interested in investigating the plight of farmers but the climate as a whole. The joy of spring after the harshness of winter is reflected in the playfulness of the children of the village, but the camera reserves its most celebratory moments and music for images of rivers overflowing with melting snow and trees blossoming throughout the valley. Kamei's depiction of the seasons captures the lives of plants, insects, birds and animals, among them man, whom he refuses to distinguish from his environment. For Kamei, landscape can never be viewed as separate from the lives of the people who live there and nor can humankind be privileged before the landscape.

Kamei used an eclectic mix of montage theory and environmentalism to express his ontological view of landscape. Kamei mistrusted simple empirical reality and believed that reality was too multidimensional for humankind to grasp, and that life exceeded humankind. He also rejected a naturalist methodology that he believed floated in superficial description. Instead, he employed a practice of montage that disturbed surface reality by cutting it up and rearranging it to arrive at truth. Paradoxically, in order to allude to the totality of reality, Kamei believed that reality must first be splintered before being reconstructed. In order to portray 'all living beings', Kamei relied on the mechanical eye of the camera and the mechanics of montage. Truth itself could not be filmed, but rather it had to be constructed by editing the phenomena captured by the camera. Inspired by the dynamic technique of Sergei Eisenstein's motivational montage, Kamei created a new form of essay film and location reportage which he called 'haiku montage'.[42]

Whereas *haiku* expressed landscape or nature in a contemplative way, Kamei used a mixture of overlapping music, narration, titles and images in a rhythmic ensemble to represent an ecological vision and historical portrait of Shinano that extended well beyond the poet Issa. Kamei fuses multiple layers of the image and audio tracks to compare the farmer to the frog. Over an image of a farmer overlooking his frost-ravaged crop of mulberry trees a narrator reads the poem:

Scrawny frog, fight on! Issa to the rescue.

For added emphasis, the poem is written on the screen and then projected in larger characters. Images do not illustrate the audio but overlap unevenly in a slightly staggered pattern to force the spectator to construct the film in his or her mind. Kamei believed that film was a process that only came together in the 'minds of the audience'. With overlapping audiovisual tracks, Kamei was able to create a visually complex and ideologically complicated poetic film that went beyond the parameters of *haiku*. In Kamei's estimation, the film did not go far enough in encouraging the audience to question their assumptions about the Shinano landscape. He registered his disappointment with the film by using an animal metaphor. 'I set out to sketch a tiger, but ended up with a cat,' he lamented. He realised that the film was, 'too indirect for an audience used to watching tourism films with the dulled eyes of domestic animals'.[43]

Although the scene portrays the difficulty of the farming in the region, the farmer in the frame is contrasted with the frog in the poem in order to give hope to the farmer. The next sequence shows farmers going back to work the land with a renewed sense of vigour after being 'rescued' by Issa's poem. While the difficulty of the situation creates sympathy for the farmer, the tragedy of the frost is also portrayed from a non-human perspective. Highlighted within the shots of farmers and mulberry leaves is a close-up of a silkworm inching up a mulberry branch. Despite the tragic nature of the sequence, it is not without humour. The scene ends on a poem suggesting a farmer's serene enjoyment of the landscape whilst we are shown a farmer urinating in the fields. To be sure, no other director of the time portrayed man's organic relationship to nature so clearly.

CONCLUSION: SHIFTING LANDSCAPES

Cinematic portrayals of the rural landscape changed dramatically from the early to the late 1930s, from bucolic pastoral playgrounds to documents of the agricultural crisis. By 1939, the countryside had become the focus of the documentary realism instigated by the Sino-Japanese War. In contrast to nationalist conceptions of landscape that foregrounded an eternal Japanese landscape of largely empty vistas and national monuments, the farm village films that I have discussed here all provided a social critique of the rural landscape that emphasised man's relationship to, and inhabitation of, the rural landscape.

Against increasingly shrill calls from conservative critics and intellectuals to equate landscape and climate to an eternal or unique Japaneseness, Kamei used the farm village film to undermine nationalist uses of landscape. *Notes on the Shinano Climate: Kobayashi Issa* is a melancholic Marxist analysis of the inhabitants of a difficult rural climate that develops a non-human-centred understanding of the landscape as a site in which all living beings are part of an integrated ecology. Sensing the urban bias of film-making during this time, Yanagita aimed to create a network of films about and for a rural audience. Although he wrote extensively about landscape, his cinematic interest lay in the soundscape of dialects that could capture the traces of a disappearing communal spirit and lead to a deeper analysis of the landscape than mere vision allowed. His collaborator Miki emphasised the agency of farmers in *Living in the Earth* and remained critical of an over-aestheticisation of landscape that determined the visual frame without regards to content. For Miki, humans and their work, represented in the image or on the audio track, were essential parts of the rural landscape. Alternating between drama and documentary, Uchida infused labour into the rural landscape in *Earth* in order to show the lasting inequities of the feudal landowning system. For Uchida, landscape was a vehicle to examine forms of discrimination embedded in the history of the land.[44]

Rural cinematic landscapes functioned in a new set of coordinates in the postwar period. While it would be impossible to do justice to the role of rural landscapes in new postwar configurations of regional formations and imaginaries, tracing select continuities of these three wartime films can help elucidate some general differences and suggest potential lines of future research.

An early postwar version of *Earth* by the director Imai Tadashi and entitled *Rice/Kome* (1957) extended Uchida's critique of discrimination against those marginalised by historical and economic forces into the 1950s. Imai made two fundamental changes that reflected both early postwar individual humanism and gendered demographic patterns. Employing a humanist framework to show the vestiges of unfairness that continued into postwar democratic society, he used sentimentality to describe the difficulties of impoverished fishing-farming families who are forced to rely on the paltry income from menial cottage industries for their survival. Acknowledging the dearth of men in the immediate postwar period, he also replaced *Earth*'s male head of the household with a struggling and heroic mother. The male protagonists and innocent maidens of the prewar period were frequently replaced by the figure of the mother in early postwar Japanese films.

Each postwar decade suggests a new rural cinematic geographical imaginary. High economic growth in the 1960s continued to depopulate the Japanese countryside as the working-age population migrated to urban areas. At the same time, a series of spectacular crimes including serial murders came to be associated with the cinematic countryside.[45] The rural landscape harbouring the fugitive was simultaneously seen as a refuge from capitalist overdevelopment and a utopian destination for those retreating from the failure of radical politics. *Magino Village: A Tale* (1987) is perhaps the most striking filmic-ethnographic return to the rural that echoes Miki's *Living in the Earth*. In the 1970s after spending nine years filming farmer opposition to the building of Narita International Airport, Ogawa Productions, a collective led by Ogawa Shinsuke, moved to Magino Village in the northeast mountains of Japan. Living collectively in a farmhouse while cultivating rice and making films for sixteen years, Ogawa Productions formed deep relationships with residents and painstakingly recorded the daily life of farming in the village.[46] The very tactile quality of the filming of rice production that immerses the spectator into the sensorium of Magino Village reflects Ogawa Productions' deep immersion in the life of the farm village and the collective's desire to not just capture life but form new social relations in the rural landscape. Miki's earlier study of the farm village had tried to capture the lives and agency of farmers.

Domestic space, however, remained noticeably absent from the film and revealed Miki's refusal to analyse the gendered division of labour and space in a rural setting. Ogawa Productions, like so many collectives in the 1960s that had striven to create new social relations, also failed in many ways to address gender dynamics.[47]

Tracing the return to the farm village film in the postwar period signals the importance of a gendered analysis that takes into account the agency of women. Kamei revisited the environmentalism and ecology of his wartime films in his last two films, *All Must Live: People, Insects, Birds/Minna ikinakerebanaranai: Hito, mushi, tori* (1984) and *All Living Things Are Friends: Lullabies of Birds, Insects and Fish/Ikimono minna tomodachi: Tori, mushi, sakana no komoriuta* (1987). In an accompanying essay, Kamei castigated the individualism of society and eulogised the communal body, calling for a return to the social formation of village life based around hunting.[48] In contrast to his wartime films, Kamei presented an ecological conception of rural landscape that reduces human life to mere reproduction and unquestioningly accepts the reproduction of the social formation of the village.[49] When emptied of social critique, the farm village film can thus lead to dangerous conceptions of the rural and remind us that questions of agency and gender must always remain an important component of any analysis of the rural landscape in Japanese cinema.

Notes

1   Although there continues to be a dearth of Japanese cinema studies that explicitly analyse rural cinema, a number of recent essays have addressed the intermingling of postwar rural and urban landscapes in a nuanced way including Yuriko Furuhata, 'Returning to Actuality: *fūkeiron* and the Landscape Film', in *Cinema of Actuality: Japanese Avantgarde Filmmaking in the Season of Image Politics* (Durham, NC: Duke University Press, 2013); Alastair Phillips, 'Fractured Landscapes: Detection, Location and History in Uchida Tomu's *Kiga kaikyo/A Fugitive from the Past*', *Screen* vol. 52 no. 2 (July 2011), pp. 215–32; and Julian Ross, 'Ethics of the Landscape Shot: *AKA Serial Killer* and James Benning's *Portraits of Criminals*', in Tiago de Luca and Nuno Barradas Jorge

1. (eds), *Slow Cinema* (Edinburgh: Edinburgh University Press, 2016), pp. 261–72.
2. [Editors' note: see also Chapter 30 by Alastair Phillips in this volume.]
3. Shiga Shigetaka, *Nihon fūkeiron* (Tokyo: Seikyūsha, 1894).
4. Masako Gavin, *Shiga Shigetaka 1863–1927: The Forgotten Enlightener* (London: Routledge, 2001), p. 33.
5. Jen Wei Ting, 'Shina in Wartime Japan: The Cinematic Portrayal of Japanese Relations in Early Wartime Japan (1937–1940)', <http://eigagogo.free.fr/en/shina-in-wartime-japan>.
6. It was around this time that the term earth (*tsuchi*) began to frequently appear in film titles. Japan's first European coproduction with Germany in 1936, entitled *New Earth/Atarashiki tsuchi*, represented a justification for Japan's invasion of, and emigration policy to, Manchuria that was argued through the perspective of a Japanese farmer. It was the incorrectly portrayed Japanese landscape that became a major point of contention between the German and Japanese directors that led Itami Mansaku to reshoot the film and eventually produce his own version.
7. *YIDFF Kamei Fumio Retrospective Catalogue* (Yamagata: Yamagata International Documentary Film Festival, 2001), p. 49.
8. Miyazawa Kenji captured local difference in short stories such as *Matasaburō of the Wind/Kaze no Matasaburō* (Tokyo: Hata shoten, 1939), and 'The Night of Taneyamagahara/Taneyamagahara no yoru', which was made in into an anime of the same title directed by Oga Kazuo and released by Studio Ghibli in 2006.
9. The film was released just before the restrictive Film Law of 1939 was established and played for three consecutive weeks.
10. Translated into English as Nagatsuka Takashi, *The Soil: A Portrait of Rural Life in Meiji Japan*, trans. Ann Waswo (Berkeley: University of California Press, 1994).
11. For a detailed discussion of Mizoguchi's radio drama and the '*Earth* revival' from 1937 to 1939 that it inspired, see Tanaka Masasumi, *Ozu Yasujirō no hō e: Modanisumu eigashi ron* (Tokyo: Misuzu shobō, 2002), p. 127.
12. 'Eigabigaku no tame no oboegaki: Shizenshugi ni hankō seyo', *Eiga shūdan*, June 1936, pp. 14–21 and 'Nihon eiga no naturalism', *Eiga shūdan*, July 1937, pp. 28–33.
13. '*Tsuchi*', *Nippon eiga*, May 1939, p. 41.
14. Yanagita wrote several essays specifically addressing the question of what might constitute appropriate entertainment for the countryside. See 'Chihō goraku o jishuteki ni', *Nippon eiga*, February 1941, p. 16.
15. Roundtable discussion, 'Yanagita Kunio-shi o kakonde: Bunka Eiga to minzokugaku', the moderator was Tsumura Hideo, and the participants were Yanagita Kunio, Miki Shigeru, Mura Haruo and Hashiura Yasuo, published in *Shin eiga*, March 1941, p. 62.
16. Review of the film *Snow Country/Yukiguni* (1938), *Kinema junpō*, 11 May 1939, np.
17. Yanagita's vision of the role of film as a catalogue of differences that could preserve the entire diversity of countryside customs conflicted with the official policy of reinforcing and exporting standardised Japanese. Yanagita's perspective from the periphery also contested the central government's strategy to economically revive the countryside by encouraging farmers to migrate to the colonies and rationalise rice production.
18. Harry Harootunian, *Overcome by Modernity: History, Culture, and Community in Interwar Japan* (Princeton, NJ: Princeton University Press, 2001), p. 314.
19. For an elaboration of Yanagita's notion of landscape see Satō Kenji, *Fūkei no seisan fūkei no kaihō: Media no arukeorojī* (Tokyo: Kōdansha, 1994).
20. Tōhō was officially established on 26 August 1937 in a merger of three film companies owned by Kobayashi Ichizō in order to compete with the Nikkatsu and Shōchiku studios. Lacking stars and a strong production system, Tōhō turned its efforts to making documentary films. See Makino Mamoru, 'Documentary Filmmaker: The Times in Which Kamei Fumio Lived', *YIDFF Kamei Fumio Retrospective Catalogue*, pp. 29–30.
21. An agreement between Tōhō studios and the Cultural Association of Farm, Mountain and Fishing Villages (*Nōsangyoson bunka kyōkai*) gave Tōhō the rights to distribute films in rural areas.
22. During the war documentaries were called culture films (*bunka eiga*) from the German *kulturfilm*.
23. Ann Waswo, 'The Transformation of Rural Society, 1900–1950', in Peter Duus (ed.), *Cambridge History of Japan*, vol. 6 (Cambridge: Cambridge University Press, 1989), pp. 539–605.

24 Miki recounts his encounters with farmers in roundtable discussion, 'Yanagita Kunio-shi o kakonde', p. 66.
25 Miki Shigeru, 'Kome to nōmin seikatsu ni kansuru eiga', *Miki Shigeru eigafu* (Tokyo: Yuni tsūshinsha, 1979), p. 22
26 Nara Kannosuke, 'Nōmin seikatsu to *Tsuchi ni ikiru*', *Bunka eiga*, September 1941, p. 46.
27 Ibid., pp. 46–9.
28 Yanagita Kunio and Miki Shigeru, *Yukiguni no minzoku* (Tokyo, Kōchō shorin, 1944), pp. 283–4.
29 Miki Shigeru, 'Bunka eiga ni tsuite: Camera o chūshin ni', *Nippon eiga*, August 1939, p. 45. Influenced by Paul Rotha's *Documentary Film* (translated by Atsugi Taka as *Bunka eiga ron* [Tokyo: Daiichi bungeisha, 1938]), Miki agreed with Rotha's position on the dangers of warping reality by the overuse of aesthetic techniques.
30 Ibid., p. 45.
31 Murao Kaoru, 'Jissha to fūkei to jimbutsu', *Kinema junpō*, 11 May 1939, p. 55.
32 Iida Shinmi, 'Kiroku eiga to nōson', *Bunka eiga*, April 1942, p. 50.
33 Karen Wigen, 'Constructing Shinano: The Invention of a Neo-Traditional Region', in Stephen Vlastos (ed.), *Mirror of Modernity: Traditions of Modern Japan* (Berkeley: University of California Press, 1998), p. 229.
34 Shinano was the famous setting of Shimazaki Tōson's novel *Before the Dawn/Hakai* (1906), a story about a teacher who slowly realises that he is part of the *burakumin* outcaste class.
35 For a history of the tourist industry during the 1930s and 1940s in Japan, see Takaoka Hiroyuki, 'Kankō, kōsei, ryokō: Fashizumuki no tsūrizumu', in Akazawa Shirō and Kitagawa Kenzō (eds), *Bunka to fascism* (Tokyo: Nihon keizai hyōronsha, 1993), pp. 9–52.
36 *YIDFF Kamei Fumio Retrospective Catalogue*, p. 75.
37 Wakimizu Tetsugorō, *Nihon fūkeishi* (Tokyo: Kawade shobō, 1939).
38 Peter B. High, *The Imperial Screen: Japanese Film Culture in the Fifteen Years' War, 1931–1945* (Madison: University of Wisconsin Press), pp. 129–30.
39 Yasuda Yojūrō, 'Nihon no bikan', *Nippon eiga*, December 1938, pp. 1–9.
40 Yasuda Yojūrō, *Fūkei to rekishi* (Tanba, Nara: Tenri jihō, 1942).
41 Watsuji Tetsurō, *Fūdo: Ningen teki kōsatsu* (Tokyo: Iwanami shoten, 1935), translated as *A Climate: A Philosophical Study* by Geoffrey Bownas (Tokyo: Ministry of Education, Japan, 1961). Watsuji had set out to describe how man, in both the social and individual sense, apprehends himself in climate. *A Climate* was a critique of Heidegger's failure to address issues of space and social existence in his treatment of the structure of human existence as one of time and individual consciousness.
42 *YIDFF Kamei Fumio Retrospective Catalogue*, p. 33.
43 Kamei Fumio, 'Shinano fūdoki seisaku no dōki', *Bunka eiga kenkyū*, November/December 1940, pp. 672–3.
44 In the postwar period, Uchida would continue to make dramatic films about the effects of discrimination such as *The Outsiders/Mori to mizuumi no matsuri* (1958) that deconstructs stereotypes of the Ainu in Hokkaido.
45 *AKA Serial Killer/Ryakushō renzoku shasatsuma* (1969) and Imamura Shōhei's *Vengeance is Mine/Fukushū suru wa ware ni ari* (1979) are two of many examples. For a discussion of Landscape Theory in *AKA Serial Killer*, see Furuhata, *Cinema of Actuality*, pp. 118–20.
46 Abé Mark Nornes, *Forest of Pressure: Ogawa Shinsuke and Postwar Japanese Documentary* (Minneapolis: University of Minnesota Press, 2007), p. 203. [Editors' note: see also Chapter 26 by Ayumi Hata in this volume.]
47 Barbara Hammer's documentary *Devotion* (2000) includes interviews with members of Ogawa Productions and expresses the difficulties women members of the collective faced.
48 Kamei Fumio, 'Shizen hakai ga jinrui no kiki o maneite iru koto o hayaku kizuite hoshī', *Cine front* no. 123 (1987), pp. 4–5.
49 The feminist critic Aoki Yayoi points out how this ecological approach using a women's body as a mere vessel for the reproduction of the species, denies the subjectivity of women in 'Kaihō no shisō toshite no ecology, *Shin nihon bungaku* no. 481 (1988), pp. 14–15. [Editors' note: for an ecocritical approach to the representation of Japanese landscape in post 3/11 film-making, see Chapter 27 by Rachel DiNitto in this volume.]

29

THE HOME
Separations and connections: The cinematic homes of the Shōwa 30s

Woojeong Joo

The period between the late 1950s and early 1960s, known as 'the Shōwa 30s' (1955–64), is generally considered a special time of change in Japan. Compared with the previous decade, when the nation struggled in destitution with the devastation that accompanied defeat in the Pacific War, the Shōwa 30s became the cornerstone of the accelerated period of growth that the nation would witness in the following years. At the same time, the Shōwa 30s also can be characterised as a final age of innocence, the point when older social bonds and the traditional values of family life began to significantly shift as the nation advanced further into becoming a highly developed industrial society. Since the late 1980s, this now lost time has been frequently summoned in Japanese popular culture and media with the retrospective title of 'Shōwa Nostalgia' – a term by which the Shōwa 30s is idealised as the era when a better future still seemed obtainable while warm relationships among members of society also still remained intact.[1] The epitome of such an imagined past can be found in the film trilogy *Always: Sunset on Third Street/Always: Sanchōme no yūhi* (2005, 2007 and 2012), the success of which made Shōwa Nostalgia a huge cultural phenomenon during the 2000s. Set in a small working-class neighbourhood in central Tokyo, the series creates a vision of an urban idyll in the Shōwa 30s; something functionally separated from the outside world but, at the same time, open wide in terms of the community inside, where the everyday life of neighbourhood people binds them closely together to form one family. The studio set of the neighbourhood is intentionally designed so that 'houses are not divided from each other, but rather the whole neighbourhood forms one big house', as the director Yamazaki Takashi acknowledges.[2]

The Shōwa boom suggests that certain values related to a communal way of life – such as closeness, openness and togetherness – constitute an important prototype in the cinematic representation of Japanese home and family; something previously introduced and reproduced in the works of Ozu Yasujirō, Naruse Mikio, Gosho Heinosuke, Kinoshita Keisuke and Yamada Yōji. The collective image of the neighbourhood in the *Always* series can be regarded as an extended variation of this long stylistic tradition in Japanese cinema. On the opposite side of this outward or community-oriented model, there exists another type of tendency based on the individual and separate spatial use of home, as seen in *High and Low/Tengoku to jigoku* (Kurosawa Akira, 1963), *The Family Game/Kazoku gēmu* (Morita Yoshimitsu, 1983) and *Nobody Knows/Dare mo shiranai* (Kore-eda Hirokazu, 2004). This represents the collapse of familial and communal relationships that Japanese society has increasingly faced since the onset of the high economic growth era.[3] Shōwa Nostalgia, after all, is a collective response to this historical flow that swept away the times when 'all members of society were recognised' and 'given a meaning of life' through the notion of community.[4]

The tension between an isolated versus an open domesticity is a fundamental issue in Japan's modern history, as well as Japanese society. The idea of home (*hōmu*) as 'a bounded space around the immediate family associated with private family life' was an output of the social reforms of the Meiji period (1868–1912), when reformers actively adopted and promoted the concept from the West.[5] Since they regarded themselves as middle class, the reformers' ideal of *hōmu* concerned 'a materialisation of the bourgeois investment in family privacy' in the form of an owner occupied suburban house, 'sequestered from the public sphere and the market'.[6] This modern domesticity also can be considered in relation to the traditional distinction between inside (*uchi*) and outside (*soto*), a 'deeply held [...] system of classification' for the Japanese to not only differentiate internal and external space for sanitary reasons, but also insiders from outsiders in order to define appropriate behaviour in various social circumstances.[7] Watsuji Tetsurō thus argues that the Japanese house closes nature off from the exterior through its boundary structure of the veranda (*engawa*) and garden; in contrast, the interior is open without any form of partition.[8]

Such a characterisation may, however, restrict the meaning of the Japanese home to terms implying a form of cultural essentialism, thereby missing historical evidence that broadens the concept of domesticity beyond private boundaries into an imbricated area that exists in time as well as in space. As Jordan Sand notes, *ie*, a modern family law system founded upon the notion of extended family and primogeniture, was a 'temporal concept' that emphasised the lineage between parents and children, thus appearing to be antithetic (yet not mutually exclusive) to the more spatially defined idea of *hōmu*.[9] With neither blood relations nor cohabitation being a requisite of being a member of an *ie*, the system remained permeable on a functional level, allowing the flow of members in and out of a family through either adoption or marriage.[10] The relation between *uchi* and *soto* is also relative as the concept of the former postulates the phased expansion towards the latter. Whether it be from an individual and family to local communities or interest groups, all may form various junctions of social contact.[11] This centrifugal relationship with society internalised in the structure of domestic life is exemplified by the central location of the reception room for guests in the traditional Japanese house, the form and function of which, again, shifts historically according to changes in lifestyle.

The primary issue regarding the home in Japanese cinema therefore arises not from an absolute perspective that contrasts aspects of spatial isolation and connection, but from an examination of the ways in which both coexist and may be related to the historical context of Japan's modernisation. This approach should not only be distinguished from the formal analysis of cinematic space, as seen in Edward Branigan's early study of Ozu, but also from a tendency to reduce the issue to a matter of genre history, such as the family drama or melodrama, that recognises cinematic representations of the home as part of a larger patterned narrative of familial relationships or their disruption.[12] Drawing from studies that actively evoke the temporal aspect of Japanese modernity,[13] the following discussion will examine how the spatiality of the Japanese home and its outer sphere may be compared from a perspective that emphasises historical specificity. The Shōwa 30s is one of the most productive sites to explore this relationship as it was the critical point when all the relevant issues – the rise of consumerism, a decrease of household size, the growth of large housing estates and a change in community relations – began to appear and develop. Neither of the two Shōwa 30s films that this chapter mainly analyses, *Good Morning/Ohayō* (Ozu Yasujirō, 1959) and *Being Two Isn't Easy/Watashi wa nisai* (Ichikawa Kon, 1962), present a home space that simply exists in isolation without any kind of social context. Instead, they both deal with the complexity of contemporary Japanese domesticity in an ironic tone, concentrating on the conflicts arising from the contact between the private and the public sphere. The emphasis of each film can, however, be differentiated: *Good Morning* focuses on the notion of connection in a neighbourhood that comprises several detached private houses whereas *Being Two Isn't Easy* articulates a sense of isolation experienced in a large public apartment complex.

CONNECTION (IN SEPARATION)

As mentioned previously, the intimate representation of community space had long been a tradition in

Japanese cinema going back to before World War II. The genre of *shitamachi ninjōgeki* (films dealing with the lives of shitamachi townspeople) is an example, typically involving the representation of active community life where the space and time of work and leisure intermingle in a seamless fashion. As an old commercial district established in the Edo period, *shitamachi* was packed with small shops of merchants and artisans with their tiny row-houses (*nagaya*) adjoining at the back and thus advocating a 'wide-open, no-secrets, communal life'.[14] Its spatial compactness and close human relationships has provided the prototype of many neighbourhood settings in Japanese cinema, most notably in Ozu Yasujirō's series of films known as *kihachimono* and Yamada Yōji's *It's Tough Being a Man/Otoko wa tsurai yo* series.[15] In *Passing Fancy/Dekigokoro* (1933), for instance, the first instalment of Ozu's *kihachimono*, the protagonist Kihachi lives in a typical *nagaya*, but the cramped space is extended towards the outside through a narrow alley at the front of the house. The hub of this external connection is a nearby restaurant where his family has everyday meals and spends their leisure time with a number of close acquaintances. The line between the domestic and the public areas is thus blurred, but this does not completely negate the distinction between *uchi* and *soto*, for Kihachi's neighbourhood still functions as the inside shielded from its outside, as in the case of *Always: Sunset on Third Street*.

The cinematic representation of *shitamachi*, however, was a constructed fantasy from the very beginning. Shitamachi in reality had already begun to disappear with the coming of Meiji modernisation in the nineteenth century, and more rapidly after the Great Kantō Earthquake that destroyed Tokyo in 1923. Many residents at that point moved into newly built suburban houses, of which the spatial nature was more individual than communal. In this sense, the extended home and community life depicted in Ozu's *kihachimono* should be considered more in terms of a retrospective idealism that attempted to apply the spatiality of *shitamachi* to the reality of industrial capitalism in the 1930s. It would thus be a natural process that the gap between nostalgia and reality

only deepened in postwar Japanese film. Ozu's last authentic *shitamachi* drama was *Record of a Tenement Gentleman/Nagaya shinshiroku* (1947), after which he moved the major setting of his films to the white-collar middle-class home.[16]

In the case of other representative directors of *shitamachi* films – Gosho Heinosuke and Naruse Mikio – a sense of community remained intact in the early 1950s, though it gradually became weaker as the Shōwa 30s proceeded. *Where Chimneys Are Seen/Entotsu no mieru basho* (1953), one of Gosho's most well-regarded works, retains many of the genre's typical sentiments. In the film, the sense of connection to the domestic neighbourhood is suggested in the form of an aural, as well as visual, invasion of privacy. The protagonists, a childless couple Mr and Mrs Ogata, not only live next to their landlady but also with two single individuals who sublet separate rooms upstairs. The Ogatas' living space downstairs is vulnerable to the presence of the two tenants passing by, and moreover it is constantly harassed by the noise from outside. This spatial proximity ensues as a problem again when the couple accidentally take up the responsibility of fostering an abandoned infant, whose cry is loud enough to annoy the neighbours. This infant, however, eventually helps revive the communal solidarity: outside noise is diminished for fear of disturbing the sick baby, and Kenzō, one of the tenants upstairs, makes an effort to look for the birth mother. Naruse's films during this period, such as *Mother/Okāsan* (1952), *Lightning/Inazuma* (1952), *Husband and Wife/Fūfu* (1953) and *Wife/Tsuma* (1953), also articulate the existence of community, something that is frequently suggested in both the street market scenes featuring itinerant musicians and the representation of cohabiting characters in the home. However, as both Arthur Nolletti Jr. and Catherine Russell point out in regard to Gosho and Naruse respectively, these are a representation of 'the prewar *shitamachi*' that would soon lose touch with reality as Japan rolled into the late 1950s and 1960s.[17]

In this regard, Ozu's *Good Morning* can be considered as the director's experiment in questioning and reinterpreting the meaning of communal life previously represented in *shitamachi* dramas, in the new context of the postwar privatised home. Although the setting is not a *shitamachi* town but a suburban Tokyo neighbourhood with detached houses for the middle classes, the narrative of *Good Morning* is driven by a sense of communal spatiality created by the neighbours in their everyday life. This sense of connectivity is suggested at two different (yet interrelated) levels: physical movement and verbal communication. The film features five households in the neighbourhood located next to or across from each other, and the neighbours (mostly housewives and children) frequently walk to visit the other houses, producing a complex web of choreographed movements outside their homes. The meeting points in this community space include alleyways where the walking neighbours come across one another and entrance areas (*genkan*) where a visitor has free access, through an unlocked door, to start conversation with the hostess.[18] Ozu's unique frontal *mise en scène* often captures neighbouring residences in the form of an overlapping perspective within the frame, something that is especially noticeable in his *shitamachi* films. In this way, the room or kitchen of a neighbouring house is visible behind the foreground space, thus emphasising the spatial connection among neighbours. In *Good Morning*, for instance, the side entrances of two houses that belong to the Ōkubos and the Haraguchis face each other across an alley and are always left open, through which the kitchens of both houses can be seen together (Fig. 29.1).

The close spatiality of the neighbourhood entails the transfer of objects: this is a world where small everyday goods such as a bottle of beer or a bus ticket are casually borrowed or paid for on behalf of a neighbour. The material connection, however, also accompanies various misunderstandings and conflicts, which in turn reveal the material desires that obsessed the middle-class homes of the Shōwa 30s. The first third of the film's narrative, for instance, is driven by an anecdote about the lost dues of the neighbourhood women's society, which are supposed to be collected and transferred to Ms Haraguchi (Sugimura Haruko), the head of the group, whose mother however fails to hand the money over to her. The ensuing misunderstandings and rumours among the neighbourhood housewives, unfolding

Fig. 29.1 *Good Morning/Ohayō* (Ozu Yasujirō, 1959, Shōchiku). The Ōkubos' kitchen in the background as seen from the Haraguchis' home.

and being resolved in the course of their successive visits to each other, all imply the negative side of close community life in the suburbs. An important point of the scandal is that Ms Haraguchi is suspected of having appropriated the money to purchase a washing machine, one of the so-called 'Three Sacred Treasures' (*sanshu no jingi*) – along with the television and the refrigerator – which were marketed as essential household goods and symbolised Japan's change into a mass consumerism society in the late 1950s. The rumour thus conceals the complex psychology of the housewives' envy and desire for 'homogenisation' (i.e. buying what others have), something Marilyn Ivy has noted as a characteristic of the newly privatised postwar Japanese middle class.[19]

For the children of the neighbourhood, it is television that plays the role of articulating both a connection with, and differentiation from, the community. Since only one young couple among the five households has a television set, the children gather at their place for viewing, crossing the alleys between the houses, just as their mothers do. Because of the television set, the young couple's home is the most public space in the neighbourhood; the couple not only open their living room to visiting viewers but also connect them to the contemporary mass-cultural scene as a sumo game being broadcast on television, for example, suggests. Public viewing (on the street as well as at home) was indeed a fad in Japan after NHK began broadcasting in 1953, until the television set became popularised in the late 1950s. The *Always: Sunset on Third Street* series also includes scenes of public-television viewing at home, alongside a communal party to celebrate the arrival of the new medium into the neighbourhood. Not coincidentally, what the neighbours watch together are sports (professional wrestling and volleyball), a genre that greatly encourages a viewer's identification with other participants.

Television's early history can thus be interpreted as an extension of collective cultures into the private sphere. Its representation in *Good Morning*, however, picks up a critical side of this permeation too, comparable to the episode about the housewives' rumour of the appropriation. As their mother prevents them from going over to the young couple's house to watch television, the Hayashi family's two children finally ask for a private set at their home, a tough demand for their salaryman father nearing his retirement age. But what eventually makes him decide to purchase one is less the children's persistence than his consideration of his relationship with a neighbour, Mr Ōkubo, who has recently retired from a company and managed to get a new job as an electronics salesman. Mr Hayashi (Ryū Chishū) feels he can hardly ignore Mr Ōkubo's mild (yet earnest) persuasion. This situation, made possible through the open spatiality between the private entrance and the public sphere, has already been anticipated in previous scenes by such anecdotes as the unannounced visit of a high-pressure salesman (*oshiuri*) and a drunken Mr Ōkubo who enters the Hayashis's home by mistake. The *uchi* is thus actually highly permeable in relation to the *soto*, and domestic concerns, such as consumption, are placed within a complex web of external relations. It is the uneasy tension arising from this interaction between the private and the public that distinguishes the homes of the Shōwa 30s from their re-representation in *Always: Sunset on Third Street*, where private life is identified more closely with a celebratory communal unity, as seen in the scene of the collective television viewing of sports games.

SEPARATION (IN CONNECTION)

Good Morning's detailed investigation of community life in relation to the private sphere is an exceptional approach in Ozu's works of this period. The more conspicuous image of the director's films in the Shōwa 30s is that of a stabilised middle-class nuclear family living detached from other neighbours around, as found repeatedly in *Equinox Flower/Higanbana* (1958), *Late Autumn/Akibiyori* (1960) and *An Autumn Afternoon/Sanma no aji* (1962). In these films, the connection with the outside is largely left to salaryman fathers who are often seen spending time in bars and restaurants with their old male friends. The tone has become comparably light and optimistic, though not without conflicts among family members, especially in relation to a daughter's marriage. Sakamoto Kazue categorises these films into the home drama (*hōmudorama*) genre, characterised by a narrative of the patterned, serene, everyday life of a white-collar family living in separation from the concerns of external society, such as unemployment.[20] Dealing with the theme of safe and self-contained family life, the home drama can be said to be the true dramatic incarnation of the postwar ethos of privatisation, enabled through the changes in Japanese society towards political democracy and economic equality.

The *chanoma* (living and dining room) was a characteristic space that epitomised the private home of the home drama. Originally situated to the rear of the middle-corridor style house (*nakarōka*), which was divided into two sections (the south-front and the north-back) by a long corridor, the *chanoma* gradually moved into the front, meaning that its function of facilitating private family life became more and more significant in terms of the spatial hierarchy of modern domesticity.[21] As Inge Daniels clarifies, the centre of this space was not so much a 'sofa' than a 'dining table', especially the low-height table called a *chabudai*, around which families could gather, eat and spend leisure time together on an equal basis.[22] One of the representative cultural symbols of the Shōwa 30s, the *chabudai* often appeared in the home drama to visualise the stable unity of a family. In Ozu's *Equinox Flower*, for instance, the *chabudai* typically occupies the central position of the frame, around which the protagonist Hirayama's family and visitors sit and converse as they pass the relaxed, unstructured time of ordinary daily life. The sight of the neighbouring house is blocked behind a bamboo wall, clearly distinguished from the more transparent perspective found in *Good Morning* and other *shitamachi* films. The tone of the space is also optimistic, with brightly coloured interior objects and the tinkling non-diegetic sound of the song 'Home, Sweet Home' suggesting the safe integrity of this home apart from any external intrusion. This is a vision of the ideal postwar white-collar nuclear family that evades the existence of its surrounding neighbourhood, a possibility that *Good Morning* denies in an ironic tone.

An extreme case of this isolation appears in Kurosawa Akira's *High and Low*, where the theme of class conflict is visualised through the spatial distance between the bourgeois home up on a hill and the shabby neighbourhood down below. In contrast, Ichikawa's *Being Two Isn't Easy* provides a more nuanced observation of the middle classes who are spatially and economically equalised, but nonetheless feel isolated from society. Set in the space of a *danchi*, a large-scale apartment complex mainly constructed on a housing estate in the suburban area of a metropolitan city, the film is one of the earliest examples of the *danchi* film along with *An Urban Affair/Kigeki: Ekimae danchi* (Hisamatsu Seiji, 1961), *Elegant Beast/Shitoyaka na kedamono* (Kawashima Yūzō, 1962) and *She and He/Kanojo to kare* (Hani Susumu, 1963). The rapid postwar development of *danchi* is closely related to the Japanese government's housing policy of implementing long-term public-housing construction plans with the establishment of the Japan Housing Corporation in 1955.[23] This 'interventionist' housing policy, as Richard Ronald argues, reflected the 'political imperatives [of the Japanese government] around [...] promoting standard nuclear families and a social mainstream middle class society'.[24]

As residential buildings, *danchi* apartments were unique in their functional use of small space, as represented by the term 'DK' (combined dining room and kitchen), an 'invention that revolutionised the layout of the postwar Japanese house' and moved the centre of family life into a new area.[25] Moreover, though compact in terms of space, the structure of the *danchi* apartment prioritised privacy in contrast to previously available public dwellings. Not only were parents' and children's sleeping rooms now separated, but *danchi* became the first mass-oriented residence equipped with an indoor family bathtub (*ofuro*) and a cylinder lock on the entrance door, something developed by the Japan Housing Corporation itself in order to secure the domestic safety of housewives and children during the day.[26] Based upon the segregation of gender roles as well as a separation between the private sphere and the public one in terms of its structure and function, the *danchi* apartment became the epitome of Japanese middle-class 'my-home-ism' (*maihōmu shugi*), a 'general concept regarding the sensitivity, consciousness and lifestyle of people oriented towards private life'.[27]

The *danchi* was also a highly unique place in sociological terms. The *danchi* tribe (*danchizoku*), the residents who had the good fortune of moving into a *danchi* through winning a competitive lottery, were not only a small number of people – about one million, that is, 1 per cent of the entire Japanese population in 1960 – but also the ones economically categorised as the 'new middle class' (i.e. highly educated white-collar families who could afford a very expensive rent).[28] The majority of them were young couples in their twenties and thirties with (or without) children, mostly comprising nuclear families of up to four people per household.[29] The restricted space meant that a *danchi* was not usually suitable for an extended family. This reflected a significant social change in the Shōwa 30s concerning the attitude of the younger generation, after they had grown up and married, towards sharing the same space with elderly family members.[30] With their purchasing power, the *danchi* tribe also played a leading role in accelerating commodity-consumption culture; new home appliances – the rice cooker, the vacuum cleaner and the electric/gas stove as well as the aforementioned Three Sacred Treasures – filled up their apartments faster than in other non-*danchi* homes in rural and urban areas.

The individualism and consumerism of the *danchi* tribe did not, however, mean that the *danchi* was devoid of social life. From the beginning, it was a major concern of the Japan Housing Corporation to provide *danchi* areas with various public facilities such as schools, playgrounds, markets, parks and assembly areas as well as a railway station for commuters.[31] In paying attention to *danchi* residents' strong concerns about this infrastructure and their collective activities to secure political support, Hara Takeshi argues that the *danchi* was a socialistic space, where 'pro-privacy ideology' coexisted with 'regional autonomy'.[32] In this regard, the *danchi* was a contradictory space, its collectivistic structure being founded upon individualistic concern. There is also, however, a more pessimistic view to be taken on the communal nature of the *danchi*: by comparing life in the *danchi* to a beehive, Nishiyama Uzō argues that the possibility of a community lifestyle was soundly negated by the *danchi* tribe's 'distorted my-home-ism', which, based upon heated competition for commodity consumption, justified family egoism and thus contributed to the maintenance of class difference in Japanese society.[33]

This dilemma between the private and the public reaches a schizophrenic level for the family of protagonists in *Being Two Isn't Easy*. The film deals with the everyday life of a young couple living in a small *danchi* apartment with their 2-year-old baby, Tarō. From the beginning, the film contrasts the mellow vision of home seen through the newborn baby's eyes in a brief prologue with a scene of intense tension where Tarō, now sufficiently grown to leave the safe boundary of the household, is found and saved by his mother (Yamamoto Fujiko) after he has climbed a steep staircase outside by himself. The space outside the home is filled with chaos and danger: strolling in the *danchi*, Tarō is bitten by a dog and a family picnic to a zoo ends up with him getting lost from the parents. There is also the possibility of Tarō picking up a disease, especially a contagious one such as measles, which amplifies the parents' fear of his contact with others. This aversion to the world apart from the home seems to exemplify the operation of *uchi* and *soto* in practice, as the former represents 'purity, cleanliness and safety', while the latter is related to being 'dirty, impure, dangerous and strange'.[34]

Ichikawa articulates this sense of hysteric obsession by showing the obstructed use of space inside the family's apartment. After Tarō's adventure on the outside staircase, his parents decide to place a safety gate not only around him in the room but also at the front door of the apartment to prevent his escape. In the scene where Tarō's father (Funakoshi Eiji) is making the gate, Ichikawa's camera produces a densely packed frame with both sides blocked by wall and door, leaving only a narrow strip in the middle for the appearance of the working father. This congested *mise en scène* is foregrounded in various other shots of the film where not only objects but also human faces and bodies occupy in close-up a large portion of the frame, thus pushing the main object of interest into a corner. This directorial style is seen in variation to Ichikawa's previous films such as *Odd Obsession/Kagi* (1959) and *Her Brother/Otōto* (1960), where mysterious domestic spaces such as a dark corridor fill the widescreen frame, suggesting the oppressed domestic atmosphere of an ailing family. The 1.37:1 format of *Being Two Isn't Easy* is even more effective in conveying the cramped feel of the *danchi* apartment space. The irony of the *danchi* therefore lies in the disparity between its claustrophobic spatiality and the comfort and safety it is supposed to provide for its residents. Tarō makes a playful effort to get out of that cage-like place (as implied by the bars on the safety gate imprisoning him), but an escape would mean a deadly threat to his anxious parents. The neurotic dilemma of the white-collar family reaches a climax when another baby in the *danchi* falls off a window ledge while playing with its bars, a visual replica of the safety gate installed in Tarō's own apartment. Though the baby is luckily saved by a passing milkman, the accident confirms the vulnerability of the psychological as well as physical barriers set by the *danchi* residents between the inside home and the outside world.

It is therefore impossible that Tarō's home can exist within the vacuum of social and communal relationships. Throughout the film, many neighbours and relatives of the family appear raising doubts about the absurdity of *danchi* life, although their visits to Tarō's apartment are fewer and more limited in comparison with the freer and more complex spatial movements in *Good Morning*. For instance, a neighbour (the mother of Atsushi, a friend of Tarō's) visits Tarō's apartment, but her attempt to enter the front door is instantly blocked by the very same safety gate installed to deter Tarō from going out. But on the other hand, the extrafamilial relationships in *Being Two Isn't Easy* are of a more altruistic kind than the rumours and misunderstandings in *Good Morning*. In addition to the passing milkman who saves the child's life, other neighbour characters play an essential role in helping Tarō's parents ease their obsessive tensions and present alternative options to the prescriptions of the *danchi* lifestyle. Atsushi's mother, for instance, is the character of conscience in the film. The reason for her sudden visit, mentioned above, is to inform Tarō's mother that Atsushi has contracted measles and to advise that Tarō must be vaccinated to avoid contagion. Sensitivity for the public good is also revealed in her plan to build a nursery inside the *danchi,* voluntarily operated by mothers, further supporting Hara Takeshi's positive interpretation of the self-governing activities of *danchi* residents.

The notion of the *danchi* as a public sphere is, however, never realised in the film. Tarō's parents instead choose to retreat to a more isolated suburban home in order to live with Tarō's grandmother who happens to be left alone; something which divides the film into two significant parts. The spatial nature of the single detached house is completely different from the previous apartment: wooden, open and spacious, with an *engawa* and flowering garden that both function as indiscrete 'liminal spaces' and 'meaningful zones of exchange with the world outside'. This is a proper Japanese dwelling, ideal for raising a child, as Tarō's mother herself acknowledges.[35] Interior shots of the house obtain a depth of field by showing unblocked, successive rooms and sliding doors, something impossible to achieve in the *danchi* scenes. Ichikawa deploys the spatial connectivity of the house to articulate a temporal connectivity that runs between the generations – that is, from the old grandmother through the parents to the baby Tarō. As Catherine Russell points out, such interfamilial connections suggest the functioning of *ie*, by which Tarō's parents take refuge from the modern family system operating in the *danchi* apartment.[36]

The relationship in this accidentally formed extended family begins with trouble because of the conflicts between Tarō's mother and the stubborn, old-fashioned grandmother. At the point they become reconciled over their common concern for Tarō, the grandmother suddenly dies of high blood pressure. Her invisible existence, however, makes a symbolic return to the house after her death. One night, while Tarō's father lies beside his sleeping son and looks at the face, reminiscing about the memorable moments over the past two years of the baby's life, a knitting ball rolls by itself into Tarō's room from the drawing room (*zashiki*) where the grandmother has died. The father picks up the ball, and the following long point-of-view shot shows an unwound thread of yarn coming from the drawing room through to the adjacent rooms. The deep perspective of the shot, a kind that should be differentiated from the inter-domestic connection exhibited in *Good Morning*, provides the spatial background for the temporal continuity that runs through the generations inside the family (Fig. 29.2). The father later confesses to his wife that, through living in the house and watching the relationship between the grandmother and Tarō, he has learned that 'human beings are supposed to be connected with each other'. In the end, the house and the family are not as completely isolated as they seem; the connection only exists more strongly in time than in space, more within the family than across the families.

Other Shōwa 30s films also deal with the subject matter of intergenerational conflict and the distribution of domestic space, but not all of them conclude with the same optimistic vision as the case of Tarō's family. In Naruse's *Daughters, Wives and a Mother/Musume tsuma haha* (1960), the second daughter of the protagonist family wants to live separately from her mother-in-law so she suggests to her husband that they move into an apartment, an alternative form of living that might guarantee privacy and comfort for the childless young couple. A crisis concerning breakup however comes to her own mother later when the eldest son, with whom the mother has lived, has to sell the family house and the siblings are forced to reluctantly face the responsibility of deciding who will take care of the mother from now on. A more radical form of disruption can be found in Nikkatsu's so-called 'Sun Tribe' (*taiyōzoku*) films such as *Season of the Sun/Taiyō no kisetsu* (1956), where home and family are almost left behind in the background of the reckless life of its delinquent youths. Even when the existence of a family is revealed in the youth films, it is often a dysfunctional one, typically suffering from the extramarital relationship of a father, as seen in *The Baby Carriage/Ubaguruma* (1956) and *A Slope in the Sun/Hi no ataru sakamichi* (1958). The Shōchiku 'Nouvelle Vague' films, which appeared a little later in the 1960s, have even been considered to be the 'first attempt for the Japanese to make a film that has nothing to do with family (*ie*) or village (*mura*)'.[37] At the opposite end of the spectrum, the sheltered domesticity of the

Fig. 29.2 *Being Two Isn't Easy/Watashi wa nisai* (Ichikawa Kon, 1962, Daiei). A thread of yarn connects the two rooms. Depth of field and the fact the sliding doors of the adjacent rooms are all open unites the inner space of the house.

home drama, which Shōchiku excelled in, was safely transferred into the medium of television where the genre's typical everydayness blossomed in a more extended format.

This diversity confirms the complex degree of negotiation between the individual and society or between the private and the public prevalent in the representation of the home in the Japanese cinema of the Shōwa 30s. As discussed, the main driving force behind this tension, which makes this era so distinctive in the history of Japan's modernisation, was the advancement of privatisation, supported by economic growth and technological innovation, which greatly transformed the spatial conditions of the home. It is essential to notice that both *Good Morning*'s suburban house and *Being Two Isn't Easy*'s *danchi* apartment are newly commodified spaces themselves, not to mention the fact that the consumer goods that fill the space inside define and facilitate the residents' private lifestyle. However, as I have also suggested, the private domestic sphere in the two films is still vulnerable to the concerns of external society, which, in reverse, define and regulate the process of privatisation. The irony inherent in the anecdotes of purchasing a television set from a neighbourhood seller and being advised to take a vaccine by an already-infected neighbour shows a contradictory relationship between the home and society that the two films handle, to a degree, with satire.

The merit of *Good Morning* and *Being Two Isn't Easy* therefore lies in their acknowledgment that *uchi* can never exist apart from the permeation of *soto*. According to Augustin Berque, an 'assimilation to environment' is a basic mechanism in the Japanese personality, something that is practised in gradations from the individual to wider levels of society.[38] This cultural tenet should not however annul the reality of privatisation as a central historical phenomenon of the Shōwa 30s onwards, and the conflict between the two articulates the quintessential dilemma that the Japanese home, as a private institution, has to carry forward in modern society. It is this dilemma, rather than the ideally 'assimilated' community imagined in *Always: Sunset on Third Street*, that is the real prototype of the Japanese home that is still constantly being referred to and reproduced in Japanese cinema today.

Notes

1. For a sample media survey of the Shōwa 30s, see 'Tokushū, Shōwa 30 nendai: Daremoga yume o motteita jidai', *Tōkyōjin*, August 2006, no. 230, pp. 12–79.
2. Yamazaki Takashi and Yashiro Tomonari, 'Shōwa 30 nendai o saigen shitemite: Eiga *Always: Sanchōme no yūhi* no Yamazaka Takashi kantoku ni kiku', *Sumairon* no. 81 (Winter 2007), p. 11.
3. The trend of individualisation in postwar Japanese society can be verified in the change in household structure. While the proportion of nuclear families remained stable throughout the postwar years, that of single person households greatly increased (3.4 per cent in 1955 to 29.5 per cent in 2005) in parallel with a decrease in non-nuclear extended family households (36.5 per cent to 12.1 per cent). See Naikakufu (ed.), *Kokumin seikatsu hakusho, Heisei 19 nen ban* (Tokyo: Jijigahōsha, 2007), p. 247.
4. Uno Tsunehiro, 'Shōwa nostalgia boom no shomondai: Rekishi to dō mukiauka', *SF Magazine* vol. 49 no. 4 (April 2008), p. 92.
5. Richard Ronald, 'Homes and Houses, Senses and Spaces', in Richard Ronald and Allison Alexy (eds), *Home and Family in Japan: Continuity and Transformation* (London: Routledge, 2011), p. 181.
6. Jordan Sand, *House and Home in Modern Japan: Architecture, Domestic Space, and Bourgeois Culture, 1880–1930* (Cambridge, MA: Harvard University Asian Center, 2003), pp. 10–13.
7. Joy Hendry, *Understanding Japanese Society*, 3rd edn (London: Routledge Curzon, 2003), pp. 47, 49–50.
8. Watsuji Tetsurō, *Fūdo*, quoted in Augustin Berque, *Vivre l'espace au Japon*, trans. Miyahara Makoto (Tokyo: Chikuma shobō, 1987), p. 154–6.
9. Sand, *House and Home in Modern Japan*, p. 22.
10. Ron P. Dore, *City Life in Japan* (London: Routledge Curzon, 1999), p. 103.
11. Nakano Takashi, 'Uchi to soto', in Sagara Tōru, Bitō Masahide and Akiyama Ken (eds), *Chitsujo* (Tokyo: Tokyo daigaku shuppankai, 1983), pp. 333–6.
12. Edward Branigan, 'The Space of *Equinox Flower*', *Screen* vol. 17 no. 2 (Summer 1976), pp. 74–105. On the generic study of the cinematic home, see Iwamoto Kenji (ed.), *Kazoku no shōzō: Home drama to melodrama* (Tokyo: Shinwasha, 2007); Sakamoto Kazue, *Kazoku image no tanjō: Nihon eiga ni miru home drama no keisei* (Tokyo: Shinyōsha, 1997).

13 Alastair Phillips, 'Pictures of the Past in the Present: Modernity, Femininity and Stardom in the Postwar Films of Ozu Yasujiro', *Screen* vol. 44 no. 2 (Summer 2003), pp. 154–66; Catherine Russell, *The Cinema of Naruse Mikio: Women and Japanese Modernity* (Durham, NC: Duke University Press, 2008).

14 Dore, *City Life in Japan*, p. 12.

15 The *kihachimono* or Kihachi films were a series of films, directed by Ozu, about the male protagonist, Kihachi, a poor working-class man, and his family and neighbourhood people. During the mid-1930s, Ozu made four Kihachi films: *Passing Fancy/Dekigokoro*(1933), *A Story of Floating Weeds/Ukigusa monogatari* (1934), *An Innocent Maid/Hakoiri musume* (1935) and *An Inn in Tokyo/Tokyo no yado* (1935).

16 As Ozu once revealed in an interview, the reason for this translocation was that the communal consciousness that had enabled the existence of *shitamachi* – both in reality and on screen – no longer existed in postwar Tokyo. Ozu Yasujirō, 'Eiga e no aijō ni ikite', in Tanaka Masasumi (ed.), *Ozu Yasujirō sengo goroku shūsei: 1946–1963* (Tokyo: Film art-sha, 1993), p. 107.

17 Russell, *The Cinema of Naruse Mikio*, p. 243; Arthur Nolleti Jr., *The Cinema of Gosho Heinosuke: Laughter through Tears* (Bloomington: Indiana University Press, 2005), p. 214.

18 In Japanese houses, the *genkan* functions as 'a liminal zone of transition between inside and outside' to facilitate the 'separation of, and movement between, two qualitatively different realms'. See Ronald, 'Homes and Houses, Senses and Spaces', p. 194.

19 Ivy argues that homogenisation, even though it fostered the equalisation of households, could also mean 'an elimination of differences as nuclear familial units constructed themselves as "micro-utopias" sealed off from external conflict', resulting in the 'dangerous shrinking of social networks and forms of association into the modular confines of "my home"'. See Marilyn Ivy, 'Formations of Mass Culture', in Andrew Gordon (ed.), *Postwar Japan as History* (Berkeley: University of California Press, 1993), p. 250.

20 Sakamoto, *Kazoku image no tanjō*, pp. 246–8.

21 Ronald, 'Homes and Houses, Senses and Spaces', p. 183.

22 Inge Daniels, *The Japanese House: Material Culture in the Modern Home* (Oxford: Berg, 2010), pp. 35–6. The practice of eating together 'shifted the focus from discipline and hierarchy engrained in the notion of filial piety to the creation of harmonious, interpersonal relationships'. Ibid., p. 36.

23 In 1955, the demand of new housing was estimated to be 2.7 million nationwide, and a three-year plan was devised to supply 420,000 houses, out of which 160,000 would be built by the government. See Nishiyama Uzō, *Sumai kōgengaku: Gendai nihon jūtakushi* (Tokyo: Shōkokusha, 1989), p. 344; Shimokawa Kōshi and Katei sōgō kenkyūkai (eds), *Shōwa Heisei kateishi nenpyō: 1926–2000* (Tokyo: Kawade shobō shinsha, 2001), p. 256.

24 Ronald, 'Homes and Houses, Senses and Spaces', p. 184.

25 Nishiyama, *Sumai kōgengaku*, pp. 345, 347. Since the kitchen was combined with the dining space, there arose a need to sanitise the old draining system, resolved by the adoption of the aluminium sink. The shiny bright image of the aluminium sink became both a symbol and sales point of the *danchi*. Ibid., pp. 348–9.

26 Ronald, 'Homes and Houses, Senses and Spaces', pp. 185–6; Shimokawa et al., *Shōwa Heisei kateishi nenpyō*, p. 271; Hara Takeshi, *Danchi no kūkan seijigaku* (Tokyo: NHK shuppan, 2012), p. 24.

27 Yamamoto Rina, *My-home shinwa no seisei to rinkai: Jyūtaku shakaigaku no kokoromi* (Tokyo: Iwanami shoten, 2014), p. 109.

28 Keizai kikaku chō (ed.), *Kokumin seikatsu hakusho: Shōwa 35 nen ban* (Tokyo: Nihon keizai shinbunsha, 1960), pp. 140–2. The average rent for a *danchi* (5,300 yen in 1958) was more than six times as expensive as an entire leased house in Tokyo (850 yen). Ibid., p. 142. In some cases, a high level of income was a prerequisite of applying for an apartment. See Hara, *Danchi no kūkan seijigaku*, p. 35.

29 Keizai kikaku chō (ed.), *Kokumin seikatsu hakusho* pp. 138–9.

30 In the postwar period, the proportion of newly married couples who co-resided with parents fell considerably from 64 per cent in 1955 to 23 per cent in 1998. Almost half of this decline occurred during the first ten years (i.e. the Shōwa 30s). See Naohiro Ogawa and Robert D. Retherford, 'Demographics of the Japanese Family: Entering Unchartered Territory', in Marcus Rebick and Ayumi Takenaka (eds), *The Changing Japanese Family* (London: Routledge, 2006), p. 28.

31 Nishiyama, *Sumai kōgengaku*, p. 345.

32 Hara, *Danchi no kūkan seijigaku*, p. 57.
33 Nishiyama, *Sumai kōgengaku*, p. 346.
34 Ronald, 'Homes and Houses, Senses and Spaces', p. 175; Hendry, *Understanding Japanese Society*, p. 49.
35 Ronald, 'Homes and Houses, Senses and Spaces', p. 180.
36 Catherine Russell, 'Being Two Isn't Easy: The Uneasiness of the family in 1960s Tokyo', in James Quandt (ed.), *Kon Ichikawa* (Toronto: Toronto International Film Festival Group, 2001), p. 263.
37 Irokawa Daikichi, 'Nihon eiga ni arawareta ie', in Imamura Shōhei, Shindō Kaneto, Yamada Yōji, Satō Tadao and Tsurumi Shunsuke (eds), *Kōza nihon eiga vol. 8: Nihon eiga no tenbō* (Tokyo: Iwanami shoten, 1988), p. 47.
38 Berque, *Vivre l'espace au Japon*, p. 246.

30

THE CITY
Tokyo 1958

Alastair Phillips

INTRODUCTION

Tokyo is a place that resists any sense of enduring stability. The French geographer and philosopher Augustin Berque defines it, for example, as 'an urban composition in which the very contingency of the arrangement of the [city's] – highly autonomous – parts, might be said to generate the cohesion of the whole'.[1] Berque's play between fragmentation and unity, or perceptual oscillation between the locality of a discrete neighbourhood and the idealised image of a finished map, is in many ways typical of much discussion of the Japanese capital in that it points to an ongoing problem of definition concerning the general scale and duration of the metropolis. But suggestively, in terms of emphasising the specific question of provisionality, Berque also hints at some aspects of Tokyo discourse that might in fact be generative in terms of thinking about Tokyo as a cinematic city – a topic that with a number of significant exceptions, which I shall address in this chapter, has been relatively under discussed within the wider literature on Japanese cinema.

The problem of cohesion is clearly both a spatial and a temporal one; something Donald Richie identifies in his book on Tokyo when he argues for the absence of any true centre in the heart of the Japanese capital, not least because the scale of the grounds of the Imperial Palace provide a kind of cartographic void. Furthermore, as Richie also points out, 'Tokyo seems always to be under construction. Indeed, it will never be finished.'[2] How best then to define the nature of a city that appears to resist any genuine kind of fixity? One way might be to pursue a geographical approach that respects the material coordinates of the city's topography. In his influential study of the Japanese capital, Jinnai Hidenobu suggests that despite the city's long history of conflagration and destruction – the most egregious examples in the twentieth century being the Great Kantō Earthquake of 1923 and the USAAF firebombing of 1944–5 – the spatial framework of the city has lasted in terms of a 'complex intersection of plateaux and valleys'.[3] This has not only had significant repercussions for the organisation of recurring navigational and architectural features, it has also determined the social composition of the city with the social elite, be they samurai, diplomats or senior officials and businessmen, located amongst 'the high city's hills and cliffs, winding roads, shrine groves' and the commoners, small businesses, craft workers and farmers placed amongst 'the low city's canals and bridges, alleyways and storefront planter pots, and crowded entertainment centers'.[4]

A second method, one taken by Henry D. Smith, would be to privilege a more historical or palimpsest-like approach that assumes an intersectional layering of discursive social experience. Many of these distinctions may be found in various cinematic iterations of Tokyo, be they through the prism of the *jidaigeki* or the contemporary drama. All cities assume some form of mediation with the pre-urban or the ongoing presence of the countryside to which they operate in contradistinction, and Smith initially argues that in the case of the Tokugawa era capital (1603–1868) this mattered from within in terms of the point of view of the samurai class that saw Tokyo as 'the city of power'[5] and from without in terms of an agrarian class that saw the city in terms of a value system based on 'corruption and change'.[6] For the indigenous *chōnin*, or commoner class, bound to particular forms of urban locality and social expression, the city, he suggests, was both a site of 'play' and of 'family'[7] – something that has continued to resonate in later, more mythical, screen representations of the capital.

Following the opening up of the city to the world during the Meiji period (1868–1912) and a widespread programme of civic renewal and infrastructural development, the post-earthquake city of the late Taishō (1912–26) and early Shōwa eras (1926–89) redefined itself in terms of the accelerated rhythms of modernity. The new patterns of middle-class consumption culture, or *bunka seikatsu*, especially in the expanded *sakariba* or bustling shopping and entertainment districts such as the Ginza, was discussed by some, such as the prominent journalist Ōya Sōichi, in terms of a directionless or even 'nihilistic escapism'. The interconnected notion of the contemporary city 'as trickster', Smith argues, referred to a sense that Tokyo was an untrustworthy place now existing 'wholly in the moment' and 'freely accepting of modern change'.[8] And in the midst of this, was the ongoing, shifting and flowing temporality of everyday 'ordinary life', something increasingly being documented in the films that mass audiences flocked to at cinemas located in these new centres of urban experience. All three of these modalities – escapism, deception and flow – will, to a greater or lesser degree, be taken up in relation to the case studies for this chapter.

A third, more integrated, approach to the question of understanding Tokyo would be to meld these topographical and socio-historical perspectives together and consider the city more as a modern text that may be read in both spatial and temporal terms. This method is certainly visible in the pioneering ethnographic work of Kon Wajirō and Gonda Yasunosuke who, writing in the 1920s, understood the modernising public sphere of the Japanese capital to be the quintessential site for what the historian Miriam Silverberg has called 'the construction of a historically grounded and historically conscious culture constituted by the practices of daily life'.[9] Kon and Gonda were cultural ethnographers – the latter especially fascinated by the exhibition of the moving image – who framed the city and its culture in differentiated experiential terms that were not just germane to a broader sociological understanding of the class and gender dimensions of modernity, but also the more precise ways in which the city became produced as a modern place that existed conterminously in both space and time. As Harry Harootunian has pointed out in his discussion of the work of the urban literary scholar Maeda Ai, itself heavily influenced by Kon, it is fascinating to observe how these acts of descriptive cultural definition were also determined simultaneously by a realisation of what was increasingly no longer there. To read the city cartographically, to see it in relation to a set of knowledge about the precise location of various streets and sites of commerce and entertainment, thus also means to acknowledge the historical disappearance of a 'claim to autonomy promised by the older division of labor between town and country'. As Harootunian puts it succinctly, 'Concern for the maintenance of the division between city and countryside appeared precisely at the [very same] moment [that] the new metropolitan cities [of Japan] embarked on their expansion and colonization of space' beyond their traditional boundaries.[10]

With these thoughts in mind, this chapter will begin by discussing previous critical writing about the subject of Tokyo as a cinematic city. It will then propose an unusually synchronic approach to the screen representation of the capital by looking at three films made within the single year of 1958: Ozu Yasujirō's *Equinox Flower/Higanbana*, Imamura Shōhei's *Nishi Ginza Station/Nishi Ginza ekimae* and the collectively made film, *Tokyo 1958*. 1958, as we shall later see in more detail, was a transitional year for both the Japanese film industry and the wider culture of the nation as a whole. It represented a high water tidemark for cinema admissions and a wider consolidation of the social and material consequences of Japan's postwar high growth economy. As such, it provides a useful vantage point from which to assess how Japanese cinema sought to mediate the complexities of contemporary urban experience at a time of accelerating rationalisation on the part of city authorities. These films, two commercial and one experimental, clearly address the subject of the Japanese capital in a number of strikingly different, but also similar, ways. The focus on one single year will, for example, enable a more close-up view of the provisional character of Tokyo that Berque identifies. It will demonstrate the ways in which the cinematic city of Tokyo might be said to continuously come into being within the specific conjugation of the space and time of everyday life and the distinctive spatio-temporal coordinates of the film frame. In particular, it will present a sense of how Tokyo's emergence at the time as the largest city in the world was both a matter of rigid planning *and* contingent experience. But more than this, it will also point to the value of identifying one particular temporal mark in the flow of Tokyo's history that allows one to simultaneously look back at the city's recent past, examine some of the more contested intricacies of the urban present, and anticipate some of the consequences of these facets that would only later become apparent in the future decade to come.

TOKYO AS A CINEMATIC CITY

The perceptual and conceptual links between the cinema, city and modernity have been well rehearsed within the general literature on the cinematic city through the formative scholarship of film scholars such as Ben Singer and Tom Gunning who have argued that not only was the cinema in itself one aspect of modernity, but that in terms of the spectatorial experience of film's rhythmic mobile framing and dynamic cutting, it was also analogous to the fragmentary spatio-temporal experience of the metropolitan environment that coexisted beyond the frame.[11] Alongside this work, Charlotte Brunsdon has also summarised a more European literary and cinematic 'city discourse' that notes 'the rhythms of the city' but does so in a way that often coexists with 'a kind of melancholic wandering related to the sensation of being alone in the crowd' and noticing the 'unexpected juxtaposition; [the] disregarded detail; [and a] fleeting glimpse of beauty'.[12] This mode of seeing, largely evoking the Baudelarian figure of the flâneur, has often found its home in more essayistic cinematic work, but its attention to random and transient urban notation is also relevant to the widely discussed city-symphony film and certain cinematic narratives that privilege the ambulatory sensations of walking the streets of the city.[13]

It's notable that neither of these approaches have been especially taken up in much of the existing literature on Tokyo as a cinematic city. Instead, authors have proposed a number of different tacks, several of which have been informed by my preceding discussion of Tokyo's status as a text located in both space and time. In an early survey discussion of the representation of Tokyo on film, for example, Donald Richie offers a typology of different places that in films such as Uchida Tomu's *The Naked Town/Hadaka no machi* (1937) and Chiba Yasuki's *Downtown/Shitamachi* (1957) demonstrate a sense of the contemporary Japanese capital being a site of struggle and disappointment, very often in counterpoint to the values of stability and security articulated by the idea of the *furosato*, or rural hometown.[14] Satō Tadao argues for a more consolidated sense of oppositional space within the capital itself that concentrates either on the bourgeois, upper-class values of uptown (*yamanote*) districts such as Aoyama (e.g. Tomotaka Tasaka's *A Sunny Hill Road/Hi no ataru sakamichi* [1958]) or the lower middle-class, working-class districts of downtown (*shitamachi*) (e.g. Ozu Yasujirō's *The Only Son/Hitori musuko* [1936]). Significantly, Satō also locates these concerns within the twin contexts of studio practice and Japan's star system, especially in the cinema of the 1930s and 1940s. Shōchiku's rosta of directors such as Gosho Heinosuke, Ozu Yasujirō and Shimazu Yasujirō, especially when still based in the south east of Tokyo at Kamata, developed what Satō calls 'the first interest in the lower middle class in film history' in conjunction with female stars such as Tanaka Kinuyo.[15] Likewise, the more sophisticated urban female persona of Hara Setsuko was promoted in films such as Shimizu Hiroshi's *Light and Shadow/Hikari to kage* (1940) during Hara's tenure at Tōhō studios, then located in Kinuta west of Setagaya.

Catherine Russell's work has been instrumental in terms of consolidating this congruence between urban geography, genre, authorship and stardom by arguing that 'Tokyo […] is always producing and reproducing itself as an imaginary place.'[16] Crucial to Russell's method, one which matters to the approach taken later in this chapter, is her argument that in order to fully understand the spatio-temporal rhythms of Tokyo on screen, one must not just take into account the singular textual distinctiveness of the urban tracking shots of Mizoguchi Kenji or the narrow architectural *mise en scène* of Naruse Mikio; one must also come to terms with the fact that the city will always resist representation in terms of one collective image. Instead, the idea of Tokyo as a cinematic city must be one that 'it is deeply implicated in the production of discursive space'.[17] This lack of fixity, as well as singularity, takes us back to the question of contingency and the possibility of also locating screen representations of Tokyo's distinctive urban geography of entertainment districts, homes, offices and railway networks to what Russell terms 'the spatial configuration of modern Japanese subjectivity'.[18]

Part of Russell's claim thus rests on a very material sense of instability in the sense that in order to coordinate a sense of experiential flux, numerous Tokyo screen narratives foreground the image of the train journey, usually by way of an indication of the routine experience of making the transition from the domesticated space of the urban suburb to various centres of professional or leisured metropolitan activity. But in another sense, one that has its antecedent in the pioneering work of Miriam Hansen,[19] Russell also argues for an understanding of popular Japanese cinema as *the* 'emblematic site where the tensions, contradictions, and possibilities of Japanese modernity were played out within the terms of popular culture, spectacle, and gender'.[20] In thinking of the cinematic city of Tokyo through the lens of vernacular modernism, in the sense of a form of mass cultural translation, or visualisation, of the contested subjectivities of urban modernity, we thus reach a sense of how Japanese cinema did not simply represent the city on screen in aesthetic terms but how it also displayed a politicised audiovisual language for thinking through the sociocultural realities of this intrinsically new sphere of human experience.

Hansen's work has influenced many scholars, including Russell, whose own work on Naruse Mikio films set in Tokyo such as *Late Chrysanthemums/Bangiku* (1954) and *Flowing/Nagareru* (1956) privileges the interlinked prisms of gender and genre in the context of the melodramatic representation of the urban Japanese home.[21] In her scrupulous analysis of the intermedial 'Tokyo March' phenomenon on the late 1920s that culminated in the Mizoguchi Kenji film of the same name in 1929, Chika Kinoshita, for example, specifically draws upon various forms of historical discourse to suggest how people at the time drew links between popular film and everyday urban modernity.[22] Mitsuyo Wada-Marciano's groundbreaking study of post-earthquake Japanese cinema of the 1920s and 1930s, redefines the *shōshimin eiga*, or social drama of lower middle-class life, in terms of an often intensified, self-reflexive awareness of the pressures of modern urban life.[23] In his longitudinal study of the films of Ozu Yasujirō in the context of their representation of the Japanese everyday, Woojeong Joo argues the director's genre films of the immediate postwar period navigated 'an acute sensitivity to distance' on both a spatial and temporal level to the extent that present-day Tokyo was seen as both a place in relation to what was now lost or what now could be regained, and a place in constant juxtaposition to other cities or towns such as Kyoto or Kamakura that acted as informing counterparts to the capital.[24] Importantly, just as in the case of Russell's writing on Naruse, Joo's take on Ozu's genre based conception of postwar urban lifestyle (*seikatsu*) focuses attention on the screen representation of the very women who comprised the films' imagined audience to the extent that the female everyday could 'provide an active revelation of the rigidity and oppressiveness of the male-driven history of [both the] war and the postwar'.[25] As we shall see, this particular topic provides the central focus of *Equinox Flower*.

TOKYO IN THE 1950S

Before turning to the substance of the films in question, what then of the general subject of the Japanese capital in the 1950s? The decade witnessed the intensification of the urbanisation of the country with approximately one million people a year leaving the countryside for cities such as Tokyo and Osaka.[26] This was accompanied by a significant infrastructure programme that not only entailed the reconstruction and development of industrial plants, but also private and public investment in urban road and rail transportation that signified this new potential for mobility. Japan's powerful construction industry accounted for 30 per cent of all national spending therefore enabling a fundamental shift in the material fabric of city life.[27] In 1956, the Japanese government famously declared in a white paper that 'the postwar' was now finally 'over' thus defining both the emergence of the new 'high growth' (*kōdo seichō*) economy and an increasing emphasis on letting go of the travails and negative associations of the past in favour of a bright modernity defined by collective national enrichment and personal material prosperity.[28]

It would, however, be a mistake to render a smooth and linear account of the lived experience of Tokyo's residents during this period of the kind represented by Kimura Shōhachi's *Tokyo hanjōki* (Report on the Prosperity of Tokyo), published in 1958.[29] William Kelly, for example, cautions against a governmental or corporate narrative modelled in terms of a 'rising middle-class homogenisation'.[30] Political economists, bureaucrats and urban planners may have emphasised the virtues of the 'ultimate "managed society" (*kanri shakai*)' but, as Kelly points out, what in fact distinguished 'the social order of middle and late Shōwa' was 'the *absence* of a strong center' based neither on 'elite coercion nor negotiated consensus'. The social sphere of 1950s Japan may well be 'better described as co-optive, complicit and contested'.[31] All urban modernities stay uneven, unfinished and display multiple tonalities within the everyday interaction and experience of ordinary city life. The neighbourhood Tokyo of traditional community neighbourhoods (*machi*), local shopkeepers and back lanes (*roji*) thus continued, for example, to coexist in a porous fashion; all of which remained visibly present in contemporaneous cinematic representations of the capital.[32]

The year 1958 nonetheless represented the condensation of a number of new and significant social trends in relation to leisure, consumption and sexuality – all elements key to much popular and experimental cinema of the subsequent decade. Firstly, the phenomenally successful introduction of instant ramen noodles served as a visible index of the general accelerated convenience and commodification of urban life.[33] Secondly, the opening of Tokyo's Sōgetsu Art Center under the directorship of Teshigahara Hiroshi in a building designed by Tange Kenzō, along with an important exhibition devoted to the Gutai Bijutsu Kyōkai (Gutai Art Association) at the Takashimaya department store in Osaka,[34] both clearly signified the increased prominence of the postwar avant-garde on Japan's urban cultural scene. And then thirdly, as Mitsuhashi Junko has especially argued, the coming into force of the anti-prostitution legislation passed the previous year was leading to the increased repurposing of Tokyo's Shinjuku ni-chōme neighbourhood in favour of a more prominent male gay clientele.[35]

Most notable of these social trends remains the greater visibility of a renewed, and at the same time emergent, middle-class consumer culture. This culture may not only be defined in terms of the acquisition of the so-called 'three S's', *senpūki*, *sentaku* and *suihanki* (electric fan, washing machine, electric rice cooker), for the urban home, it may also be considered in relation to the greater visibility of the capital as a symbol of progressive value.[36] The rising phenomenon of domestic tourism, especially to cities such as Tokyo, was for instance articulated by the figure of the female tour guide who specifically featured in films that year such as *Tokyo Bus Girl*/*Tokyo no bus girl* (Sunohara Masahisa) and Yamamoto Kajirō's Shirley Yamaguchi vehicle *Tokyo Holiday*/*Tokyo no kyūjitsu*.[37] The arrival of the jet age and more internationalised patterns of travel were also announced by both the staging of the Asian Games and the introduction of a new long-distance airline route to the US via Anchorage. Most noticeable of all though was the completion in October of Naitō Tachū's Tokyo Tower in Minato-ku that came to symbolise the modernity of the postwar capital on a public level and was soon incorporated into the *mise en scène* of films such as *Tokyo Tower at Twilight*/*Tasogare no Tokyo tower* (1959).[38]

Tokyo Tower was, of course, designed to service mass communication and it is important to note that 1958 also represented the high watermark of the commercial heyday of Japanese cinema. Japan's film industry had continued to prosper until relatively late and there were over a billion paid admissions that year with important successes including *Ballad of Narayama/Narayama bushikō* (Kinoshita Keisuke), *Giants and Toys/Kyojin to gangu* (Masumura Yasuzō), *Hidden Fortress/Kakushi toride no san akunin*, (Kurosawa Akira) and *Summer Clouds/Iwashigumo* (Naruse Mikio). In 1958, there were a total of 1 million television sets in people's houses. Just over ten years later, however, that figure had risen to 22 million and cinema admissions had fallen to just 300 million.[39] This tension between both looking back and looking forward in terms of popular cinematic practice informs the context for the first two films under discussion.

SPACE AND SEPARATION: *EQUINOX FLOWER*

Ozu Yasujirō's *Equinox Flower*, released in September 1958, is a light social comedy largely set in Tokyo. The plot of the film revolves around the various inconsistent interactions between the middle-class businessman and family patriarch Hirayama Wataru (Saburi Shin), and a number of younger women in his family, social and professional life when it comes to the pressing question of marriage. Of these predicaments, the most significant is that of his oldest daughter Setsuko (Arima Ineko), who has recently announced to her father and mother Kiyoko (played splendidly by Tanaka Kinuyo) that she intends to marry the young office worker Taniguchi (Sada Keiji) and move with him to the city of Hiroshima.

In previous critical scholarship on the film, *Equinox Flower* has largely been discussed in terms of its prominent formal qualities and these merit noting. *Equinox Flower* was Ozu's first colour film for Shōchiku, largely at the request of the studio in order to match its investment in one of the film's key female stars, Yamamoto Fujiko (Yukiko), then on loan from Daiei. Ozu made the critical decision to choose Agacolor over Kodak Eastmancolor or Fujifilm with its subsequent emphasis on the deep tonalities given to the reds that are prominently signalled in the film's *mise en scène*. These reds, recurring in numerous images in the form of domestic and commercial artefacts from the urban everyday, allude to the specific form of crimson amaryllis that gives the film its seasonally relevant title. As David Bordwell notes in his typically ingenious commentary on the film, the use of colour exudes a playful and at times potentially disruptive presence that when taken in conjunction with other formalistic aspects of the film's structure such as its elliptical narration conveys an 'overarching structural rigor' that potentially 'work[s] to minimize character psychology as a textual feature'.[40] In his now famous discussion of the handling of space in the film, Edward Branigan concurs with this question of diminished identification of character with cinematic space, but he relates this more specifically to the ways in which the film's use of empty transitional shots and temporal ellipses serve to 'create a tension of uncertainty through repetition and variation for we know that characters have travelled, may travel, actually travel, or sometimes travel through the space'.[41]

Whilst not wishing to deviate from the significance of this line of argumentation, I do want to argue that these qualities, and in fact other instances of the film's textual procedures, may also be taken as significant aspects of the film's wider discourse about the modern city as a site of indeterminacy and contingency. The question of social and generational transition is at the heart of *Equinox Flower*, and this is at least partly mediated through the film's spatial and temporal apprehension of the Japanese capital. It is thus significant that the film's first prominent word both seen on screen and heard on the soundtrack is 'Tokyo'. The fact that this occurs at the heart of the city on the platform at Tokyo station simultaneously announces both the specific matter of departure occurring within the diegesis and the wider sense of coming and going that makes up much of the rest of the film's organisational structure.

All this to-ing and fro-ing can be read in terms of the particular predicaments faced by both the older and younger members of the Hirayama family, especially when it comes to the various arrivals to and departures from the home on the part of the main daughter in question, Setsuko. But Ozu also laces this web of disenfranchisement and disappointment with a vivid sense of a much wider social sphere that is, for the most part, represented through the construction of the city achieved by Hamada Tatsuo's set design. Only a few relatively minor exterior still shots of Tokyo such as the station, the hospital and the street outside the family home intervene within the overall tightly controlled visual structure of the film. These spaces, which include the offices of Hirayama and his colleagues, the Luna and Wakamatsu bars as well as separate flats in the Ginza area and in Suginami (where Setsuko's fiancé lives), are all managed in a remarkably consistent fashion. In each case, they are repeatedly introduced via a set of horizontal and vertical axes that show both the length of a corridor or passageway in long shot and the activity of various personages moving from left to right or vice versa at the rear of the frame. In one sense, this is an economic means of communicating some of the density of social activity that comprises life in the modern capital, and it is certainly worth noticing the fidelity with which Ozu's film transcribes the visual details of ordinary city life within each image, but in another sense, and this also due to the film's organisation of plot duration as well, the overall effect is of repeated dispersal and fragmentation (Fig. 30.1).

The version of Tokyo that we receive in *Equinox Flower* is thus of a city in which no one person is placed in a position of cognitive authority regarding the spatial contours of the capital. Characters do repeatedly signal the socio-geographical relevance of a particular character – it's important to know, for example, that the scheming Mrs Sasaki's (Naniwa Chieko) latest candidate for her daughter Yukiko's hand in marriage comes from Tsukuji (a more working-class location than the rather well-to-do Hirayama family mansion on the hill in Azabu) – but the film generally makes much of the gaps in knowledge that characters have in terms of understanding where everybody is and what everybody does in the course of the film's narration. The city becomes the means not so much of defining an organic awareness of shared spatial knowledge but instead its opposite: a growing certitude that one of the consequences of postwar modernity has been the fragmentation of urban life into specifically gendered

Fig. 30.1 The nocturnal world of the city captured on a studio set in *Equinox Flower/Higanbana* (Ozu Yasujirō, 1958, Shōchiku).

and generational patterns in which people are in fact separated from each other in just the same way that the Hirayama family are never quite seen together within the same frame.

Equinox Flower extends this idea in two important senses: both through the managed use of off-screen space. The first of these occurs in the course of the family outing to Hakone where we see the parents seated separately from the two daughters who are enjoying a boat ride on the lake. The sequence initially introduces Mr and Mrs Harayama in extreme long shot as if to emphasise the scale of the location and the quiet isolation of the married couple. We cut to a closer seated two-shot, but Mrs Harayama rises immediately and moves to the border of the lake screen left. She waves and there is then a near point-of-view cut to an image of the two daughters on the water waving back. It's a moment of cross-generational female affiliation that re-establishes the wider film's wider system of female bonding and understanding at the general expense of men's misunderstandings and misgivings. In the course of the ensuing conversation between Kiyoko and Wataru, they discuss the fact that this may well be the last time they will spend time together. Kiyoko then turns to reminisce about the war and how she felt closer as a family when they shared the space of the air-raid shelters during the intensive bombings of the capital. It's a longing for an off-screen time and place in contrast to what we have already seen of the present-day city: a world of segregated routine, of anonymous architectural office features and rows of external windows linked to rows of male office workers inside, separated from the vicissitudes of the home by administrative routine. We then cut to a repetition of the two shots of Kiyoko rising then crossing to the fence by the lakeside. This time, Wataru repeats the gesture and we now see the couple wave and in a subsequent shot have their wave returned by the daughters in the long distance. Linked in cinematic space and time within the moment through off-screen space relations, they are also separated in terms of both a singular distant memory and a present spatial reality as there now exists an insuperable gulf in distance between the two sets of generational figures.

This conjunction of a shared and disconnected awareness of the city and its environs matters to the ways in which *Equinox Flower* also makes sense of the distinctiveness of the capital in relation to other regional cities. If the film begins with a train in Tokyo, it ends with a train journey taking Wataru from the old capital of Kyoto to the new postwar world of Hiroshima where his daughter and her husband now live. In fact, the comings and goings of almost all the main characters that are conveyed by a repeated *mise en scène* of doors closing and opening are also reiterated by a wider sense of movement that demonstrates both the gravitational pull of Tokyo as a metropolis and an apprehension that Japan's urban modernity has always been constructed in a relational sense. We learn, for instance, that Taniguchi used to work with Wataru's subordinate Kondo in the Kyushu city of Hakozaki. The film briefly shows the Kyoto inn that Mrs Sasaki manages and we're told in the course of an exchange about the virtues of another one of her daughter's suitors, a pharmacist from Osaka, that the city, Japan's second largest, 'is on its way up'. In sum, the Tokyo of *Equinox Flower* is a site of multifaceted fluidity and generational flux.

DISPLAY AND DECEPTION: *NISHI GINZA STATION*

Nishi Ginza Station was the second of three 'B' films that Imamura Shōhei made for Nikkatsu in 1958 at the beginning of his directorial career. As Tony Rayns points out, the studio largely saw it as a commercial property in order to capitalise on the success of the Hawaiian-Japanese singer Frank Nagai's song 'Let's Meet in Yurakucho'/'Yūrakuchō de aimashō' released the previous year. The title song, an invitation to both the protagonists and the audience to meet in front of the Nishi-Ginza subway station in Tokyo, signals an intention to link the two melodies as the latter was but one block away from the more down to earth Yūrakuchō district famous then, as now, for the popular drinking stands and eating places of Gādo-shita set underneath the railway tracks that take trains into the hub of nearby Tokyo station (Fig. 30.2).

Fig. 30.2 The nocturnal world of the city captured in photographic montage in *Nishi Ginza Station/Nishi Ginza ekimae* (Imamura Shōhei, 1958, Nikkatsu).

If Ozu's and Imamura's films both begin and end with images of the central station district of modern-day Tokyo, they could not be more different in terms of their textual operations and fields of social representation when it comes to their actual depiction of the city. In 1958, the world of the Ginza had recovered both its prewar level of commercial density and prosperity and role as a symbol of aspirational consumption and leisured urban modernity. Nishi Ginza Station on Tokyo's central upscale Marunouchi subway line had opened at the end of 1957 and was emblematic of this transition. Instead of the highly composed visual graphics of the studio-bound city at night in *Equinox Flower*, we thus see a denser and more freeform image of the nocturnal city that is shot mainly on location. Whereas Ozu's film may be read as an account of genteel female resistance to the threatened presumptions of patriarchal authority, Imamura's film represents an urban social sphere in which the male protagonist, Ōyama Jutarō (Yanagisawa Shin'ichi), is from the offset emasculated and henpecked by his assertive and humourless wife Riko (Yamaoka Hisano), who owns the underground station pharmacy in which he works. The rather ludicrous plot revolves around his escapades and daydreams over the course of his wife and children's brief absence on a trip away during which he is seen alternatively trying to seduce Yuriko (Hori Kyōko), who works in the watch shop nearby,

and reminisce about the female tropical islander he lusted after fifteen years previously when he was a soldier during the war.

Despite its profoundly regressive sexual politics concerning blame for the predicament of its male lead, the film nonetheless posits a number of issues that are not only relevant to Imamura's subsequent career in terms of his projection of the non-metropolitan spaces of Japan but also contemporaneous discourse about the modernisation of Tokyo. In his pioneering article on the director, for example, Donald Richie refers to a now often-quoted distinction between Imamura's rejection of the stifling corporate order of 'official' Japan in favour of the libidinous rural authenticity of 'real' Japan,[42] and to some extent this is certainly mediated in the form of Jutarō's idle daydreaming of escape from the confines of the city and its claustrophobic world of work in the shopping mall beneath the bustling streets above. But Imamura's film also makes it clear that any fulfilment of this desire is but a transparent illusion and in its final image, we thus see the reunited couple literally being swallowed up once more as they begin their routine descent down the steps off the street into the now Hades-like portal of the station. Far more interesting, therefore, is the way that the film, at least in part, also foregrounds the merging of the fantastic and the real in its visual construction of the city itself as if to also convey a more local set of tensions between surface and depth relevant to the social experience of Tokyo's modernity at this key moment of social transition.

A closer look at the role of Nagai and his titular musical number at the film's beginning is instructive. The opening shot provides a familiar skyline of modern Tokyo at night replete with commercial neon signage. The sound of a clock chiming signals the close of the working day and in the subsequent high-angle shot looking down on the street below we see a two-way stream of office workers, couples and shoppers signifying the everyday flow of life in the city. We then cut to a medium-long shot at street level showing a more multidirectional stream of people passing by that exacerbates the image of density and routine. The camera identifies a young woman as she moves in front and simultaneously tilts down and tracks forward to hold her in the centre of the frame. She passes in front of a standing figure and the camera then pauses and tilts up to reveal Nagai's medium profile, his eyes still gazing off-screen left as they track the woman's progress down the street. He then turns and addresses the camera saying 'The Ginza's the best. It's just so cool.' The complicity being staged here is developed when he asks us where we are from and says 'Oh from that way?' meaning he's assuming that the spectator is either not a local or from Tokyo at all. From now on, we must assume that he is supposed to have a certain degree of mastery over the image track as the film's storyteller, as well as authority about the subject of the Ginza, but what he actually goes on to reveal demonstrates instead a perhaps inadvertent level of oscillation between the credibility of what he tells us, the credulity of the protagonists and the ironic fact that the myth of the Ginza he initially proposes actually turns out to be nothing but a redundant trick.

The central way in which this process works is through the tropes of display and deception. When Nagai snaps his fingers and calls for music, we cut to a silhouetted Tokyo skyline across which the title of the film appears in flashing electric letters to the accompaniment of a jazz-based drum roll. Whilst this might simply be a method of announcing that the film is beginning properly, it is also tempting to conclude that in the light of what ensues, the film is also revealing the artificial nature of both its own construction and any consolidated idea at all of what modern-day Tokyo might actually consist of. Although the modernity of the urban backdrop and titling signifies the particular location of the Ginza, the song itself is sheer nonsense based around the sung letters 'A, B, C' and 'X, Y, Z' and various frenetic comic declarations from a drunk businessman, a gaggle of leaping teenagers and a man in a Hawaiian shirt being led in handcuffs up the stairs of the station by a policeman. In her groundbreaking work on another formative epoch in the development of Tokyo's mass culture, the 1920s and 1930s, the historian Miriam Silverberg has argued that 'the principle of montage was central to popular consciousness [… in that t]he cultural articulations of the Japanese consumer-subjects constantly juxtaposed distinct ideas […] because culture was seen as fragmented in time and space'. This related, according to Silverberg, to the then contemporaneous presentation of the 'active and often sophisticated process of moving between pieces chosen from various cultures within and outside Japan' that she sees as a particular form of 'code-switching'.[43] Whilst Silverberg perceives the time of 'erotic, grotesque, nonsense' (*ero guro nansensu*) as containing a form of liberatory potential for the expression of rebellious sensuality and freedom from political authority,[44] it is hard to retrieve any kind of progressive potential from the particular form of urban montage that we have here. Indeed, the two following images indicate merely an ironic nod to commodified pleasure and sexual libertarianism; the first of which taking the form of a close-up of a nodding model of the iconic Fujiya chocolate girl licking her lips (à la the ironic style of insertion shot found in Walter Ruttmann's *Berlin: Symphony of a Great City/Berlin: Die Sinfonie der Großstadt* [1927]).[45] This is then followed by a shot of a seated woman on the street having her shoes cleaned. As the camera tilts down, a kneeling man looks up at her and sings lasciviously 'doesn't it look enticing?' thus clearly aligning the figure of the real-life female office worker with the figure of a toy devised to sell confectionary.

We then cut to a shot on an underground train platform of a singing station officer who leads us to Nagai atop a ladder adjusting the clock to ten o'clock in the morning. This announcement of both a temporal ellipsis and a gear change in terms of Nagai's role in the film is undercut immediately as we are introduced to the character of Riko, who starts telling him that he has the wrong time and that it's one minute later than he thinks. Riko's bossy assertiveness is generally seen negatively in the film, but here the interaction also serves to pull the apparently dependable narrator down a peg or two at the same time; a point underscored moments later when Riko and Ōyama's children actually pull the ladder down from under Nagai's feet as they attempt to retrieve their beach toy. From here on in, the image track, like the clock itself, seems permanently slightly out of kilter with the absence of a reliable, ordered and convincing reality coexisting with the lack of any genuine authority on the parts of the narrator, the main protagonists (who all deceive each other), and even indeed the city itself, which increasingly seems disjointed and undesirable, despite the initially enticing promotional edifice of the title song.[46] Imamura's film, in this sense, reproduces the sense of a far more disordered urban modernity than the one initially suggested by the images of the gleaming frontage of the brand new city centre railway station.

TOKYO 1958: CONTINGENCY AND CARTOGRAPHY

Apart from their obvious shared interest in contemporary Tokyo, what initially seems to link Ozu and Imamura's two commercial feature films with the collectively made and independently funded nonfiction film *Tokyo 1958* is the prominence of the mobile world of the Ginza and the motif of the family wedding and the ensuing idea of generational transition. Both elements certainly feature significantly within its overall design, but *Tokyo 1958*'s joint fascination with the messy nature of the space and time of the modern-day Japanese capital also embraces a wider field of urban film-making that, in this case, reflects both on the subject and the manner of representation.

Tokyo 1958 was the work of Cinema 58, a nine-person experimental film-making group that comprised Teshigahara Hiroshi, Hani Susumu, Matsuyama Zenzō, Kusakabe Kyūshirō, Ogi Masahiro, Kawazu Yoshirō, Maruo Sadamu, Mushanokōji Kanzaburō and Sakisaka Ryuichirō. All members played a role in the screenwriting, directing and editing process and the film was entered in the World Experimental Film Competition held in Brussels. The project in many ways follows the 'city symphony' template of several avant-garde films of the 1920s that configures the temporal and spatial rhythms of a major metropolis within a structure that looks at a cross-section of the ordinary social and commercial activities of the city in relation to a loosely coordinated timeframe that shifts from day to night. In so doing, the film foregrounds the social and material progress of the postwar period through a combination of numerical statistical evidence about the ballooning scale of Tokyo's growth and extensive documentary footage of Tokyo's streets and architecture that provides a set of densely layered information about past, present and emerging forms of urban experience.

In addition to this, *Tokyo 1958* also represents the consolidation of an ongoing set of contemporaneous debates within the city's intellectual and artistic circles about the nature of the screen image and intersecting questions of documentation and the apprehension of present-day social change. As Yuriko Furuhata has demonstrated, the second half of the 1950s marked the development of several significant interventions within the field that included the founding of the Kiroku Geijutsu no Kai (Association of Documentary Arts) in May 1956 and the publication of the first issue of the journal *Kiroku eiga* in May 1958.[47] As both Takuya Tsunoda and Yuri Matson also point out, the rationale of this work was to extend a politically driven and experimental concern with the image into more popular forms of expression with the aim of melding the concrete realities of the external world with an intensified awareness of the inner fluidities of the subjective gaze.[48] As Matsumoto Toshio put it in his article 'On the Method of the Avant-Garde Documentary Film' in the inaugural issue of *Kiroku eiga*, 'Today, reality appears as an extremely surrealistic world in which the ordinary laws of causality as they apply to the surface of things have been stripped away … We liberate the word "document" from the shackles of naturalism. The word "document" has a new meaning today. It denotes the documentation of the actual material reality of fact as fact and, at the same time, the scrupulous documentation of the corresponding inner reality.'[49]

Tokyo 1958 might thus be fruitfully situated within a wider discourse of 'debate on the image' (*eizō ronsō*) that, as Furuhata discusses, began to proliferate in the year of the film's production and included significant contributions by the likes of the film scholar Okada Susumu and the documentary film-maker Hani Susumu.[50] In her commentary on the term *eizō*, Furuhata is careful to distinguish between a notion of the image in general and the specific act of visual mediation engendered by the mechanical apparatus of the film, television or still photography camera. What makes *Tokyo 1958* so fascinating is not just how it speaks directly about the nature of this relationship between the printed and recorded image, but when it comes to the representation of the Japanese capital that it still does so in a way that reanimates many of the social tensions we have already observed in the two previous films. In what follows, I want to briefly discuss these tensions in relation to three intersecting themes: the depiction of movement, the presentation of the face and the question of intermediality.

Tokyo 1958 begins with a set of shots of a young Donald Richie looking at a shop window containing a set of *ukiyo-e* prints. The sequence initially sets up a system of intercutting between the 'live' filmed pictures of his body on the street and the still woodblock pictures that are the object of his gaze. As we progress, however, this pattern becomes more complicated as the intermediary plane of the window glass presents not just an image of the framed prints beyond but a sense of the reflected frames of the modern urban office windows behind. This correlation between two fields of meaning – the past and the present, the individual and the corporate, the photographic and the printed – might initially seem to suggest a degree of continuity, but this is immediately vanquished when the film disrupts both Richie's and the spectator's field of vision by having the characters within the prints move and superimposing the eyes of the figures onto the face of the astonished onlooker. The unsettling impact of these shots is underscored by a series of canted framings and rapid shifts in shot scale as the film jolts between long shot and close-up. *Tokyo 1958* thus immediately becomes not so much a film about the progressive linearity of the city's history, as articulated by the completion of the landmark Tokyo Tower, but a more haphazard portrait of the capital that is questioning the cost of a centrally planned urban modernity on the individual subjectivities of its citizens. This animation of the stillness represented by the traditional woodblock print thus has two functions. It is firstly a playful method of intensifying one's awareness of the visuality of the film, but secondly, and far more importantly, through its recurrent and increasingly subversive presence it unfixes any sense of the stability of the 'high growth era' of the Japanese capital. In one street scene, for example, we see the modern flow of traffic being frozen as a procession of Edo period tradesmen move across the screen on a reverse axis of action. In another, a still wood block print of a man's head is superimposed over what is a live shot of a grey and dull looking Michiru Sekitome, chairman of a major construction company.

This juxtaposition between the two realms of image making is intensified when it comes to the film's representation of the face and in particular, the eyes. As in the case of *Nishi Ginza Station*, the object of this attention seems not simply to picture the virtues of Tokyo's prosperity and the novel brightness of urban material consumption. Not long after its opening, for example, the film shifts to a complex sequence about make-up and the application of facial treatments in a city department store. In his discussion of the film's gender politics, Marcos Centeno rightly makes the point that as a film partly made to be shown overseas, *Tokyo 1958* risks the re-assertion of a pattern of looking by which the West 'plays the masculine role and is the subject of the gaze, while Japan plays a feminine role and becomes an object of desire'.[51] He goes on to argue that a key instance of this is the way that the female body is, in turn, 'used throughout the documentary as a metonym for Japanese society'.[52] Part of the way this process is certainly enacted by linking the commodification of the female body to an urbanised consumption culture; something which is frequently the case in other city symphony films. The film, however, at least in part, resists validating this move by representing the application of beauty products in terms of a deliberately performative gesture that is signalled in counterpoint to other sets of facial close-ups representing the female face caught unawares on camera. The act of presenting and putting on a face to collude with the virtues of the accelerated consumer economy, is thus contrasted with a more mobile and more credible documentary gaze that continuously reasserts the vitality of the ordinary Tokyo citizen (Fig. 30.3).

This theme is developed in another sequence that visualises the phenomenon of the modern singing contest. The film observes a set of contestants re-enacting the vocal and performance style of popular American musicians, and the winning female singer is

Fig. 30.3 Faces of the city in *Tokyo 1958* (Teshigahara Hiroshi et al., 1958, Cinema 58).

naturally presented with a set of make-up as her prize. It also depicts the adoring and distracted gazes of various local Tokyo dwellers in the audience. However, instead of merely providing a direct transcription of this in terms of an audiovisual record of a live public event, the film also takes us back to the winning contestant's local neighbourhood. This is done in a manner that clearly reveals the uneven modernity of the city at the time.

The sequence shifts from the spaces of the stage and the auditorium to the interior space of the van journey, and then from the space of the working-class street to the interior of the family home. Initially, the structure of this sequence appears to be merely busy and celebratory, but the field of vision that subsequently opens up becomes more reminiscent of the work of socially conscious still photography documentarists of the time such as Kuwabara Kineo or perhaps the photographic reports of contemporary Tokyo that Hani Susumu made with the photographer Natori Yōnosuke for the collection *Iwanami Bunko* between 1952 and 1956.[53] In one particular long shot, we see a picture of various city residents in the centre of a street of worn wooden buildings. The overground electric cabling and the presence of a moving train in the distance indicate an emerging process of modernisation still at odds with the milieu that the contestant has just left. This message is reinforced by the arrival of other prize goods into the home including those symbolic attributes of the postwar economy, the washing machine, fridge and vacuum cleaner. On closer inspection though this shift from the impact of live documentary to the aesthetics of still photography is but one part of the film's wider process of intermedial performativity that began with the incorporation of the vivid contours of the *ukiyo-e* print. The re-assertion of ordinary Tokyo life is itself re-presented as a spectacle that signals the advent of a more televisual mode of looking. At the point the van arrives outside the family home, instead of taking us into the home with the girl, the film cuts to a long shot from within the house so that we watch her entrance through the open doorway from the vantage point of her parents. The whole event has therefore clearly been deceptively staged as if it is part of a modern-day reality television show being played out in front of our eyes. The illusory appeal of consumer gratification and commodity worship is aligned with a sense of the now pervasive mediatisation of urban reality to the extent that any true presence of the ongoing flow of 'the real', and thus Tokyo, is being directly questioned by the very operations of the film itself.

CONCLUSION

To conclude, all three case studies have to varying degrees demonstrated the different attributes of Tokyo discussed by Augustin Berque and others at the beginning of the chapter. They reveal the impossible task of achieving a holistic and completed sense of the capital on film. Having said this though, they do suggest a remarkable degree of consistency in terms of understanding the city in spatial terms that reiterates the value of adopting a more synchronic perspective to the subject. A closer look at one single year within the long screen history of the capital not only reveals a place with a strong awareness of its past and present, but also somewhere with a clear sense of uncertainty about a provisional future only just beginning to come into view. Despite the efforts of the Japanese government to regulate a sustained and linear sense of progressive urban modernity – something materialised by the construction of the Tokyo Tower – both popular and experimental Japanese cinema presented a more contested sense of the direction that the city was taking. Issues of separation, escape and dislocation permeate both the narrative and *mise en scène* of the three films in ways that visibly challenge the particular logic of completion and achievement that would culminate in the grand internationalising gesture of the Tokyo Olympics of 1964.

All three films recalibrate the notion of the singular flow of an officially sanctioned model of accelerated modernisation and instead posit the idea of a more multiple, fragmented and unfinished arrangement of time and space that existed both within and well beyond the metropolis. In some ways, this duality might be said to be a feature of all developing global cities, but as these films also show, there were distinctively local aspects to the process by which urban tradition, loss, displacement and adjustment were all felt and noticed. This might well be what most clearly distinguished Tokyo as a cinematic city at the time: the ability to mediate the holding on to the more contingent and layered heritage of the city's past in ways that explicitly denied or implicitly subverted the administratively planned repression of the present and the growth driven aspirations of the future.

The year 1958 was certainly a significant moment in the cinematic imaginary of the capital even if no one at the time could have imagined how the year would return decades later in the form of the Shōwa nostalgia boom of the early twenty-first century that re-presented the era to old and young audiences alike. In the highly textured *mise en scène* of such commercially successful films as *Always: Sunset on Third Street/Always: Sanchōme no yūhi* (Yamazaki Takashi, 2005)[54] we see a more consensual and embalmed sense of the time and space of the capital that acknowledges, perhaps subliminally, a longing for a different model of the city that once was, that had yet to come into being and that perhaps would never quite fully emerge.

The wider matter of how the subject of the city may be addressed within future work on Japanese cinema remains a fascinating one. One relatively unexplored direction might involve focusing instead on a particular spatial, rather than temporal, phenomenon; something Jennifer Coates has recently done in her compelling discussion of Tokyo's Yamanote Line.[55] Although there has been significant work published on districts such as Asakusa, Shinjuku and the Ginza,[56] there are numerous geographical and cultural aspects of the capital that certainly remain under discussed. Furthermore, as several chapters in this book also suggest, there are many other approaches to the topic that include questions related to exhibition, reception, production and the circulation of transnational screen cultures. Finally, there is still little work on the screen representation of Japan's regional cities such as Osaka and Kyoto that matches the level of aspiration conveyed by the cultural historian Louise Young in her study of the provincial modernism of the interwar years and the ways that it articulated a response to the social, cultural, economic and political changes of the time.[57] What is clear, as we have already seen in a number of ways, is that Tokyo itself has always existed in a relational sense to elsewhere in Japan. This particular line of thought might in itself contain hitherto unanticipated, but nonetheless revealing, directions of cinematic travel around not just the metropolis but the country as a whole.

Notes

1. Augustin Berque, *Japan: Cities and Social Bonds* (Yelfertoft: Pilkington Press, 1997), pp. 126–7.
2. Donald Richie, *Tokyo: A View of the City* (London: Reaktion Books, 1999), p. 51.
3. Hidenobu Jinnai, *Tokyo: A Spatial Anthropology* (Berkeley: University of California Press, 1995), p. 11. The book was originally published in Japanese. See *Tokyo no kūkan jinruigaku* (Tokyo: Chikuma shobō, 1992).
4. Ibid., p. 2. This delineation also informs the two volumes of Edward Seidensticker's history of Tokyo: *Low City, High City* (Rutland, VT: Charles E. Tuttle, 1984) and *Tokyo Rising: The City since the Great Earthquake* (Rutland, VT: Charles E. Tuttle, 1991). See also Ronald P. Dore, *City Life in Japan: Life in a Tokyo Ward* (London: Routledge and Kegan Paul, 1958), Theodore C. Bester, *Neighbourhood Tokyo* (Stanford, CA: Stanford University Press, 1989), Paul Waley, *Tokyo: City of Stories* (New York: Weatherhill, 1991).
5. Henry D. Smith, 'Tokyo as an Idea: An Exploration of Japanese Urban Thought until 1945', *Journal of Japanese Studies* vol. 4 no. 1 (Winter 1978), p. 49.
6. Ibid., p. 50.
7. Ibid., pp. 51–2.
8. Ibid., p. 71.
9. Miriam Silverberg, 'Constructing the Japanese Ethnography of Modernity', *Journal of Asian Studies* vol. 51 no. 1 (February 1992), p. 32.
10. Harry Harootunian, 'Foreword: A Walker in the City: Maeda Ai and the Mapping of Urban Space', in Maeda Ai, *Text and the City: Essays on Japanese Modernity* (Durham, NC: Duke University Press, 2004), p. xiii. For more on Tokyo and the topic of cultural memory and nostalgia, see also Gala Maria Follaco, *A Sense of the City: Modes of Urban Representation in the Works of Nagai Kafū (1879-1959)* (Leiden: Brill, 2017) and Evelyn Schultz, 'Mapping Environments of Memory, Nostalgia, and Emotions in "Tokyo Spatial (Auto) Biographies"', in Barbara E. Thornbury and Evelyn Schultz (eds), *Tokyo, Memory, Imagination and the City* (Lanham, MD: Rowman & Littlefield, 2018), pp. 69–96.
11. See Ben Singer, *Melodrama and Modernity: Early Sensational Cinema and Its Contexts* (New York: Columbia University Press, 2001) and Tom Gunning, 'The Whole Town's Gawking: Early Cinema and the Experience of Modernity', *Yale Journal of Criticism* vol. 7 no. 2 (Fall 1994), pp. 189–201.
12. Charlotte Brunsdon, 'The Attractions of the Cinematic City', *Screen* vol. 53 no. 3 (Autumn 2012), p. 222.
13. See, for example, Anke Gleber, *The Art of Taking a Walk: Flanerie, Literature and Film in Weimar Culture* (Princeton, NJ: Princeton University Press, 1998) and Steven Jacobs, Eva Hielscher and Anthony Kinik (eds), *The City Symphony Phenomenon: Cinema, Art and Urban Modernity between the Wars* (New York: Routledge, 2019). For more on walking and Tokyo culture, see Evelyn Schultz, 'Walking the City: Spatial and Temporal Configurations of the Urban Spectator in Writings on Tokyo', in Christoph Brumann and Evelyn Schultz (eds), *Urban Spaces in Japan: Cultural and Social Perspectives* (Abingdon: Routledge, 2012), pp. 184–202.
14. Donald Richie, 'Attitudes towards Tokyo on Film', *East-West Film Journal* vol. 3 no. 1 (December 1998), pp. 68–75.
15. Satō Tadao, 'Tokyo on Film', *East-West Film Journal* vol. 2 no. 2 (June 1998), pp. 1–12.
16. Catherine Russell, 'Tokyo, the Movie', *Japan Forum* vol. 14 no. 2 (2002), p. 215.
17. Ibid., p. 223.
18. Ibid., p. 222.
19. See Miriam Hansen, 'The Mass Production of the Senses: Classical Cinema as Vernacular Modernism', *Modernism/modernity* vol. 6 no. 2 (1999), pp. 59–77, and Miriam Hansen, 'Fallen Women, Rising Stars, New Horizons: Shanghai Silent Film as Vernacular Modernism', *Film Quarterly* vol. 54 no. 1 (Autumn 2000), pp. 10–22.
20. Catherine Russell, 'Too Close to Home – Mikio Naruse and Japanese Cinema of the 1950s', in Linda Krause and Patrice Petro (eds), *Global Cities: Cinema, Architecture and Urbanism in a Digital Age* (New Brunswick, NJ: Rutgers University Press), pp. 87–8.
21. See Catherine Russell, *The Cinema of Mikio Naruse: Women and Japanese Modernity* (Durham, NC: Duke University Press, 2008).
22. Chika Kinoshita, 'The Edge of Montage: A Case of Modernism/Modanizumu in Japanese Cinema', in Daisuke Miyao (ed.), *The Oxford Handbook of Japanese Cinema* (Oxford: Oxford University Press, 2014), pp. 124–51.
23. Mitsuyo Wada-Marciano, *Nippon Modern: Japanese Cinema of the 1920s and 1930s* (Honolulu: University of Hawai'i Press, 2008).
24. Woojeong Joo, *The Cinema of Yasujiro Ozu: Histories of the Everyday* (Edinburgh: Edinburgh University Press, 2017), p. 184.

25. Ibid.
26. Andrew Gordon, *A Modern History of Japan* (New York: Oxford University Press), p. 251. See also Donald Richie, 'Tokyo', *Sight & Sound*, October 2001, pp. 32–5.
27. Raffaele Pernice, 'The Transformation of Tokyo during the 1950s and Early 1960s: Projects between City Planning and Urban Utopia', *Journal of Asian Architecture and Building Engineering* vol. 5 no. 2 (2006), p. 254. Pernice discusses how in April 1958, the president of the Japan Housing Corporation, Kuro Kano, proposed filling in the land on the east side of Tokyo Bay in order to develop a new residential and industrial area.
28. Carol Gluck, 'The Past in the Present', in Andrew Gordon (ed.), *Postwar Japan as History* (Berkeley: University of California Press, pp. 65–72.
29. Schultz, 'Mapping Environments', p. 80.
30. William W. Kelly, 'Finding a Place in Metropolitan Japan: Ideologies, Institutions and Everyday Life', in Gordon, *Postwar Japan as History*, p. 189.
31. Ibid., p. 216.
32. Evelyn Schultz ('Mapping Environments') discusses the idea of porosity in relation to Walter Benjamin's writings on Naples.
33. Japan's first supermarket, Daiei, opened in 1957. Isao Nakauchi founded the chain in Osaka. See Taiga Uranaka, 'Daiei: From Rags to Riches Back to Rags', *Japan Times*, 20 October 2004, <https://www.japantimes.co.jp/news/2004/10/20/business/daiei-from-rags-to-riches-back-to-rags/#.XNVNIaZ7kXo>.
34. For more on the Gutai Art Association (1954–72), see Yoshihara Jirō, 'Gutai Art Manifesto (1956)', in Doryun Chong, Michio Hayashi, Fumihiko Sumitomo and Kenji Kajiya (eds), *From Postwar to Postmodern: Art in Japan, 1945–1989* (New York: Museum of Modern Art, 2012), pp. 89–91, and Ming Tiampo, *Gutai: Decentering Modernism* (Chicago: Chicago University Press, 2011).
35. [Editors' note: for more on Shinjuku as a zone of 'queer resonance', see also Chapter 12 by Yuka Kanno in this volume.]
36. See Simon Partner, *Assembled in Japan: Electrical Goods and the Making of the Japanese Consumer* (New York: Columbia University Press, 1999).
37. Alisa Freedman, 'Bus Guides Tour National Landscapes, Pop Culture and Youth Fantasies', in Alisa Freedman, Laura Miller and Christine R. Yano (eds), *Modern Girls on the Go: Gender, Mobility and Labor in Japan* (Redwood City, CA: Stanford University Press, 2013), pp. 107–30.
38. See Alexis Agliano Sanborn, 'Burn, Fade and Glow: The Cultures and Times of Tokyo Tower, 1958–1990', <http://www.academia.edu/2974839/Burn_Fade_and_Glow_The_Culture_and_Times_of_Tokyo_Tower_1958-1990>. [Editors' note: for more on Tokyo Tower as a site of memory, see also Chapter 29 by Woojeong Joo in this volume.]
39. See Richie 'Tokyo' and Marilyn Ivy, 'Formations of Mass Culture', in Gordon, *Postwar Japan as History*, pp. 239–58.
40. David Bordwell, *Ozu and the Poetics of Cinema* (London: British Film Institute, 1987), p. 70.
41. Edward Branigan, 'The Space of *Equinox Flower*', *Screen* vol. 17 no. 2 (Summer 1976), p. 76.
42. Donald Richie, 'Notes for a Study of Shōhei Imamura', in James Quandt (ed.), *Shohei Imamura* (Toronto: Toronto International Film Festival, 1999), p. 26.
43. Miriam Silverberg, *Erotic Grotesque Nonsense: The Mass Culture of Japanese Modern Times* (Berkeley: University of California Press, 2006), p. 4.
44. Ibid., p. xv.
45. According to Chika Kinoshita, the film was introduced into Japan by the film critic and historian Iwasaki Akira. See Kinoshita, 'The Edge of Montage', p. 134. See also Michael Cowan, *Walter Ruttmann and the Cinema of Multiplicity* (Amsterdam: Amsterdam University Press, 2014).
46. For discussion of the critical reception of the film, see Jennifer Coates, 'The Making of an Auteur: Shōhei Imamura's Early Films 1958-1959', in Lindsay Coleman and David Desser (eds), *Killers, Clients and Kindred Spirits: The Taboo Cinema of Shohei Imamura* (Edinburgh: Edinburgh University Press, 2019), pp. 21–40.
47. Yuriko Furuhata, *Cinema of Actuality: Japanese Avant-Garde Filmmaking in the Season of Image Politics* (Durham, NC: Duke University Press, 2013), pp. 37–52.
48. See Yuri Matson, 'The Word and the Image: Collaborations between Abe Kōbō and Teshigahara Hiroshi' (unpublished MA thesis, University of British Columbia, 2002), pp. 35–6, and Takuya Tsunoda, 'The Dawn of Cinematic Modernism: Iwanami Productions and Postwar Japanese Cinema' (unpublished PhD thesis, Yale University, 2015), pp. 439–40.

49 See Matsumoto Toshio, 'On the Method of Avant-Garde Documentary Film', in Chong et al., *From Postwar to Postmodern: Art in Japan, 1945–1989*, pp. 142–5.

50 See Furuhata, *Cinema of Actuality*, pp. 37–43, and Marcos P. Centeno Martín, 'Postwar Narratives and the Avant-Garde Documentary: *Tokyo 1958* and *Furyō Shōnen*', in Blai Guarné, Artur Lozanzo-Méndez and Dolores P. Martinez (eds), *Persistently Postwar: Media and the Politics of Memory in Japan* (New York: Berghahn Books, 2019), pp. 41–62. [Editors' note: for more on the relationship between television and documentary film practice in the 1950s, see also Chapter 33 by Masato Dogase in this volume.]

51 Centeno, 'Postwar Narratives', p. 47.

52 Ibid., p. 47.

53 Ibid., p. 48. The French photographer Marc Riboud also shot an important series of photographs in Tokyo in 1958.

54 See Katsuyuki Hidaka, 'Consuming the Past: Japanese Media at the Beginning of the Twenty-first Century' (unpublished PhD thesis, School of Oriental and African Studies, 2011).

55 Jennifer Coates, 'Circular Thinking: The Yamanote Line on Film', *Japan Forum* vol. 30 no. 2 (2018), pp. 224–39.

56 See Aaron Gerow, *Visions of Modernity: Articulations of Cinema, Nation and Spectatorship, 1895–1925* (Berkeley: University of California Press, 2010); Taro Nettleton, 'Shinjuku as Site: *Funeral Parade of Roses* and *Diary of a Shinjuku Thief*, *Screen* vol. 55 no. 1 (Spring 2014), pp. 5–28; Irene Hayter, 'Modernism, Gender and Consumer Spectacle in 1920s Tokyo', *Japan Forum* vol. 27 no. 4 (2015), pp. 454–75.

57 Louise Young, *Beyond the Metropolis: Second Cities and Modern Life in Interwar Japan* (Berkeley: University of California Press, 2013). See Alexander Jacoby, 'The Old Capital on Film: The Representation of Kyoto in Japanese Cinema 1945–1964' (unpublished PhD thesis, University of Warwick, 2010).

PART 6
SOCIAL CONTEXTS

31

EMPIRE
Cinematic dualities: Shanghai film-making in the era of the Japanese Occupation

Ni Yan

Translated Satoko Kakihara

In thinking about the emergence of Japanese imperialism, one has to look back as far as the First Sino-Japanese War (1894–5) and the Russo-Japanese War (1904–5). After the clash between Japan and Qing dynasty China over the concession of the Korean Peninsula, the area that later became Manchukuo and even the Yellow Sea, the First Sino-Japanese War was concluded with the signing of the Treaty of Shimonoseki in which the Qing dynasty ultimately accepted the cession of these territories to Japan. Roughly ten years later, however, Japan went to war against Russia over the control of the Korean Peninsula and southern Manchuria and gained victory. Through American mediation, Japan signed the Treaty of Portsmouth that disadvantaged Russia, once again experiencing victory over a large state. What encouraged Japan's ambition to expand its territory can be said to have been the pride of winning these two wars during the span of just twenty years and the fact that these victories also influenced the formation of Japan as a modern empire within Asia.

Although film, which developed at the end of the nineteenth century, was introduced to Japan and China at roughly the same time, the Japanese empire quickly established an inseparable relationship with the moving image. The newsreels reporting on the Russo-Japanese War, supported by commentary provided by *benshi*, encouraged audience members to see themselves collectively as the people of a victorious nation. Film thus began not only to function as a device recording the history of the Japanese empire but also to serve a significant propaganda function.

Following defeat in the Opium War, the Qing dynasty signed the Treaty of Nanking with the United Kingdom in 1842. Shanghai immediately became divided among various powers leading to the introduction of the British Concession, the Shanghai French Concession and the Shanghai International Settlement. This meant that areas that were no longer Chinese territory came to occupy the central parts of the city. The first Chinese screenings of Western films took place in Shanghai and Westerners also established the first film company there. Although *The Battle of Dingjunshan/Dingjunshan*, China's first live action film, was actually produced in Beijing in 1903, film production, importation and distribution during the pioneer days all began in Shanghai. Upscale cinemas that helped in early film distribution were built in the Concession and in the Hongkou District (the Japanese residential district within the International Settlement). Japanese proprietors built and operated two cinemas during the 1910s, both of which imported Japanese films that were mainly screened to Japanese audiences.

An understanding of such a complex historical context is essential to placing together film history and the wider geopolitical significance of the metropolis. In having to face the 'humiliating' reality of having areas that did not belong to its own country, while also enjoying the benefits of colonial modernity, Shanghai experienced both the light of superficial prosperity and the shadow that was far removed from the image of the 'mystical metropolis' held by foreigners. In recent years, extensive research has been conducted on the relationship between the Japanese empire and film that focuses on such historical circumstances. Needless to say, the Japanese empire should not only be conceived in terms of mainland China, including Manchuria, but also Taiwan, Korea, South East Asia, and Okinawa and Hokkaido/Sakhalin. In the context of focusing on Japan–China relations, Japanese critics and practitioners such as Satō Tadao, Tsuji Hisakazu and Shimizu Akira began in the 1980s and 1990s to examine the intertwining of films from Japan and China, particularly through Zhonghua Dianying Gufen Youxian Gongsi/Chūka Den'ei Funko Yūgen Kōshi (hereafter Zhonghua Dianying) that developed joint ventures between Japan and the puppet states established in Shanghai and Manchuria.[1] The Chinese language scholar Li Daoxin has also discussed Chinese film production under Japanese occupation in the Lunxian District focusing for the first time on the three Japanese-oriented film companies, Man'ei, Zhonghua Dianying and Huabei Dianying. Li's work presents a modest challenge to a previous taboo area within China-based film studies despite the continuing pressures imposed by the ideologies of the Chinese Communist Party.[2]

In contrast to this work, the US-based film scholar Poshek Fu has argued that, despite belonging to a propaganda film production company, Chinese film-makers clearly remained committed to a non-cooperative mind-set and the production of apolitical melodramas, right up to 1945.[3] Moreover, there have been various attempts to break out of a unilateral form of film studies and capture the film history of an empire that evolved across various national boundaries. They include works by Peter B. High, Katō Atsuko, Michael Baskett, Misawa Mamie, Yi Young Jae, Takashi Fujitani, Kate Taylor-Jones and Dong Hoon Kim as well as my own publication, *A History of Wartime Filmic Negotiations between Japan and China* (from which this chapter has been drawn).[4]

This chapter will focus on the organisational duality of both the national policy film company Zhonghua Dianying, established in Shanghai under Japanese imperial occupation, and the Zhonghua Lianhe Gufen Zhipian Gongsi/Chūka Den'ei Rengō Kōshi (hereafter the Zhonglian), which was centralised after the start of the Pacific War. It will examine two case studies concerning the process from production to reception of *Universal Brotherhood/Boai* (eleven directors including Zhang Shankung, Ma-Xu Weibang and Zhang Shichuan, 1942) and *Toward Eternity/Wanshi liufang* (Zhang Shankung, Bu Wancang, Yang Xiaozhong, Ma-Xu Weibang and Zhu Shilin, 1943). By refuting the conventional dichotomies of imperialism versus resistance, or cooperation versus resistance, this chapter will reveal how the process of filmic negotiation between Japan and China took place against the backdrop of a complex history of Shanghai that can be best described as a kind of a grey zone. Although *Universal Brotherhood* superficially follows the national policy trumpeted by Japan and the puppet regime, we can nonetheless detect a call to the audience to support the refugees who have fled to Shanghai after their homes have been destroyed by war. In *Toward Eternity*, while noting that the film skilfully incorporates the intention to resist foreign invasion, we can also detect a non-cooperative attitude under the guise of cooperation. At the same time, both films were interpreted entirely differently in Japan and China during the course of the war.

SHANGHAI: THE DUAL STRUCTURE OF ZHONGHUA DIANYING

Soon after the completion of the Sino-Japanese coproduction *The Road to Peace in the Orient/Tōyō heiwa no michi* (1938), the later renowned producer Kawakita Nagamasa arrived in Shanghai with a request from the military to establish Zhonghua Dianying. One year later, Chinese and Japanese collaboration shifted back to the city.

In 1937, the Battle of Shanghai had left many film studios completely or partially destroyed by gunfights and shelling, and the city's film industry subsequently fell into a state of paralysis. Not counting those who had migrated southward, the remaining individuals associated with the film industry had no choice but to escape to the Shanghai International Settlement – or the French Settlement and the UK and US Co-settlement – along with the rest of the city residents. In the first half of the following year, Xinhua Yingye Gongsi/Shinka Eigyō Kōshi (hereafter Xinhua) was the first company to recommence film production within the International Settlement under the direction of President Zhang Shankung. After producing several low-budget films, Xinhua filmed an epic historical drama *Diao Chan* (Bu Wancang, 1938), which became a box-office success in the International Settlement that in the meantime had become an 'orphan island', known as *gudao*, meaning an enclave unoccupied by Japan. This prompted a boom in historical drama production. Among these, the film that Xinhua produced after *Diao Chan*, *Mulan Joins the Army/Mulan cong jun/Mokuren jūgun* (Bu Wancang, 1939), set new box-office records and caused a major sensation inside the International Settlement (Fig. 31.1).[5]

At the time, in addition to major film production companies such as Yunhua Yingye Gongsi/Geika Eigyō Kōshi (hereafter Yunhua) and Guohua Yingye Gongsi/Kokka Eigyō Kōshi (hereafter Guohua), smaller companies such as Hua Xin, Guangming, Wuxing, Ming Hua, Xingguang and Tiansheng also began to recommence production. Regardless of the size of the companies, the films produced regenerated a Shanghai film market that had experienced a downturn immediately following the war. Xinhua produced the highest number of films by the end of 1941, with a total of forty releases. Yunhua reportedly produced fifteen, Guohua thirteen.[6] Production mainly seemed to focus on historical dramas. Films such as *Mulan Joins the Army*, *The Hate Remaining at the End of the Ming Dynasty/Ming mo yihen*

Fig. 31.1 An advertisement for *Mulan Joins the Army/Mulan cong jun/Mokuren jūgun* (Bu Wancang, 1939, Zhonghua Shanghai Huacheng dianying zhizuo) in *Eiga hyōron* (October 1941).

(Xinhua, Chen Yiqing, 1939) and *Yue Fei Serves the Country Loyally/Yue Fei jinzhong baoguo* (Xinhua, Wu Yonggang, 1940) deployed the notion of *jiegu fengjin* (the borrowing of past events as topics to satirise current events), while there were also several film adaptations of classical theatre pieces such as *Legend of the White Snake/Baishe chuan* (Xinhua, Yang Xiaozhong, 1939), *San xiao* (Yunhua, Yue Feng, 1940) and *Lady Meng Jiang/Meng jiang nü* (Guohua, Wu Cun, 1939). Although these titles took the form of adaptations, in reality they mixed escapism and *jiegu fengjin* to refract the anxiety and resistance found in the hearts of many working within the film industry.

Kawakita took over the helm at Zhonghua Dianying just as *Mulan Joins the Army* was taking the media by storm and historical dramas were entering their golden age. However, unlike Beijing's Huabei Dianying Gufen Youxian Gongsi/Kahoku Den'ei Kofun Yūgen Kōshi (hereafter Huabei Dianying), which had inherited the foundations of Shinminkai, a private organisation founded in 1937 by Kita Seiichi of Japan's secret military agency in conjunction with the Provisional Government of the Republic of China,[7] Zhonghua Dianying started with a clean slate. At the time of its foundation, for example, it faced the problem of negotiating a Chinese film production system that was already in place.

As was the case with Huabei Dianying, Zhonghua Dianying, which received investment from the puppet government known as the Reformed Government of the Republic of China,[8] remained a company that was jointly operated by Japan and China, at least in name. The puppet government was involved from the start and those who filled leadership posts were related to both states. If we consider the participation of Chinese individuals in the production of *The Road to Peace in the Orient* as still being a matter of personal choice, then to have the puppet government even nominally involved meant that the political system of the Sino-Japanese alliance had finally involved itself in film production in Shanghai.

With that said, relations were not necessarily equal between the Chinese and Japanese. In the case of Shanghai at least, unlike Beijing, which was then completely under Japanese Occupation, there was little intervention from Japan despite the fact that the city was under siege. Until the beginning of the Pacific War, a number of remaining non-occupied districts in the International Settlement allowed for a certain amount of freedom of expression. These geographical factors, as well as the city's complex political map, exerted a decisive influence on the establishment of Zhonghua Dianying.

It is clear that the singular approach taken by some of the previous research on Zhonghua Dianying cannot fully account for the nature of the company. Because it had two levels of organisational structure, we must verify the rhetoric from both the Japanese and Chinese sides while also paying attention to its dynamic internal structure. In the case of the differences in opinion or contradictions between the two unequal parties, we need to clarify how they surfaced and how such discrepancies in expectations operated in the film productions and the results they yielded.

Various discrepancies exist in the words of both the Japanese and Chinese leadership of Zhonghua Dianying at the time it was founded. For example, Kawakita described Zhonghua Dianying's ambitions thus:

> The goal, as much as possible, is to support diplomatic relations by restoring the operations and resources of the Chinese film industry destroyed by the Incident; to reconstruct and unify the joint Japanese and Chinese film market; and to form a joint venture between the two film industries. This is indeed one of our national missions as filmmakers […] and it may also be a step forward in the expansion of Japanese film overseas.[9]

Kawakita's piece ran on the same page as an article written by Xu Gongmei[10] of the puppet government's Ministry of Education, since editorial staff wished them to be read in conjunction with each other. In his piece, Xu used such headings as 'Mutual Aid Partnership Between Both Cultures', 'Resuscitating Western Pressure' and 'The Goal of Constructing a New Order in East Asia' to move his argument forward. Meanwhile, the Parliamentary Secretary of the Ministry of Education interpreted 'the importance of Sino-Japanese goodwill through cinema' by saying, 'The cultural construction of a new China must not only involve China, Japan should also cooperate significantly.'[11]

Setting aside Kawakita's attempt to bring Japanese films overseas, particularly into occupied areas, and the subtle nuances of the words of an officer in the Ministry of Education who saw the expansion of cultural projects involving China through the framework of the puppet government, we can see that Xu was euphemistically demanding financial and technical assistance from Japan for Chinese film. It is likely that this assistance referred to the rebuilding of the film production infrastructure destroyed in the war. The reason Kawakita continued to supply film stock to Chinese companies, even after such resources became limited in Japan, may have been because he was directly responding to Xu's request.[12]

Despite the fact that Chu Minyi,[13] who later served as Foreign Minister in Wang Jingwei's Reorganized National Government of the Republic of China, became Zhonghua Dianying's Chairman, the relationship of dependency and subordination between the puppet government and Japan was directly reflected in the organisation of the company. Chu's role was merely an honorary post with the real power being held by Kawakita, the vice-chairman.[14] It must have seemed contradictory for those occupied to seek assistance from the occupying forces to rebuild a Chinese film industry that had been destroyed by war, even if this support was seen as a last resort. In a sense, Zhonghua Dianying can be said to have functioned as an organisation that bound the complex intentions of each side of the arrangement together.

It is worth noting, however, that in discussing the ideals of Zhonghua Dianying Kawakita intentionally avoided phrases that positioned Japan at an advantage. Instead, he explained:

> Although this company is a national company, it is also a joint-stock company – and we therefore want to publicize our financial situation and business practices as much as possible and be thorough in doing so. In this way, we wish to develop the market in Mainland China and we see it as our duty to create an international film industry that is unique to East Asia.[15]

Furthermore, Kawakita mentioned that Western films still continued to dominate the Shanghai market but emphasised that they were 'based within a liberal system'. Mentioning this was akin to maintaining and permitting the distribution rights of the many branches of Western film companies based in Shanghai. Kawakita emphasised that Zhonghua Dianying should grow so that by developing its stakes in the Shanghai film market, it would be able to compete freely with Western film companies. This attitude may be compared to Xu Gongmei's parallel discourse of expelling Western film power, something he repeatedly stated in his piece published alongside Kawakita's. Kawakita's international outlook and emphasis on 'free competition with the West' developed a position of flexibility that prioritised the film business and later proved to be an essential element in prompting the conversion of Zhang Shankung, leader of the film world in the 'orphan island'.[16]

THE ZHONGLIAN: ESCAPE FROM REALITY

As mentioned previously, the majority of historical dramas from the 'orphan island' period deployed the method of *jiegu fengjin*, simultaneously providing a source of entertainment for the people and appealing to sentiments of resistance against the Japanese Occupation. The practice of *jiegu fengjin*, which spread to other genres such as literature and drama, also stimulated the cultural economy of the 'orphan island', and the historical drama boom following *Mulan Joins the Army* continued for some time. Zhonghua Dianying was established in the midst of this discursive space. Although many of the names of the puppet state's dignitaries were connected, at this point not only did Zhonghua Dianying have no connections with members of the established Chinese film industry fighting in the 'orphan island', it stood in the contradictory position of being both occupier and occupied. Each party seemed almost to confront the other from within the occupied and the non-occupied districts.

Being familiar with this confrontational relationship, Kawakita intentionally moved Zhonghua Dianying's main office to the International Settlement outside the occupied district in order to begin operations. In so doing, he was able to disrupt the relationship on a geographical level. Upon establishing this groundwork, Kawakita set his sights on an alignment with Zhang Shankung, who had produced anti-Japanese films in the past and was even then representative of the film-makers who continued their resistance through the method of *jiegu fengjin*. Assisted by Liu Naou, who was later assassinated,[17] Kawakita managed to meet with Zhang and held several secret conferences with him. Seeing that Zhang's wariness towards him was gradually dissolving due to his proficiency in Chinese, Kawakita brought up the issue of acquiring the distribution rights of films from the 'orphan island' and laid out the following concrete conditions:

> One, although we cannot avoid censorship by the Japanese military, we will absolutely not alter the content of work that has already been permitted. Two, we will put down an advance payment for the price of the films. Three, materials such as raw film stock whose importation has become difficult due to the International Settlement becoming an 'orphan island' will be acquired and provided by Japan.[18]

For the 'orphan island' film community that lacked film-making equipment and faced great poverty, the opportunity to improve the distribution of films within the occupied districts and not have films subjected to tampering must have represented an enormous advantage. It is said that Zhang accepted these conditions because they were approved by the Chongqing government, but there are no sources to prove this.

Advances in the war provided a decisive opportunity for the establishment of the Zhonglian. The whirlwind of changes in the political map of Shanghai such as the launch of the New Film System (September 1940–September 1941) and the Wartime Emergency Film System (September 1941–August 1945) in Japan,[19] as well as the occupation of the International Settlement by the Japanese military after the start of the war, all forced the Shanghai film world into an extreme situation. With the International Settlement suppressed by the Japanese military and having lost the ground that had previously guaranteed their safety, Chinese film-makers faced difficulties denying Japanese control, much less resisting it.

In the Sokai Shinchūki (Records of the Occupation of the International Settlement), Tsuji Hisaichi provides a detailed description of the day the Japanese military occupied the International Settlement. On the morning of 8 December 1941, Kawakita, Ishikawa Toshishige[20] and Tsuji went to Xinhua in order to:

> Meet producers with the intention of placing the leading Chinese filmmakers of the International Settlement under Japanese control through the most peaceful means, without destroying any of their operational mechanisms and simply replacing content and continuing their work as it has been carried out up to now.[21]

There was such an air of tension between the two parties that when they arrived at Xinhua, Tsuji had a pistol hidden in his coat pocket. As can be seen from this episode, from this day on, Zhang and the other film-makers who stayed on in Shanghai had no choice but to depend on Zhonghua Dianying. It is obvious that the loss of the 'orphan island' and the change in political force brought about by the Japanese military occupation were the most important factors in the conversion of those who had previously been clamouring for resistance against the Japanese forces. Of course, in the midst of the various intricate power relations amongst the Japanese military, Chongqing's KMT, the puppet government and communist forces, we cannot ignore Kawakita's personal knowledge of Chinese affairs and the efforts made by both himself and his colleagues.[22]

In April of 1942, led by the three major film companies of Xinhua, Yihua and Guohua, a total of twelve film companies (including Jinxing, Hezhong, Meicheng, Minhua, Guanghua, Fuhua, Huanian,

Huamei and Lianxing) were integrated to form the Zhonglian. Lin Baisheng, the head of the publicity department of Wang Jingwei's Reorganized National Government of the Republic of China,[23] became its chairman, and Zhang was appointed its general manager. Most members of the leadership were Chinese, as Kawakita, who was appointed vice-chairman, was the only Japanese to be trusted by the Chinese side to join the Zhonglian's leadership. While Kawakita had now achieved the aspirations that began with setting up an office in the 'orphan island', he also had the role of having to maintain a sense of trust based on personal relationships. The situation thus came one step closer to the second phase that he had initially envisioned.

In August 1942, *Eiga junpō* reported the following about the launch of the Zhonglian:

> Although these production companies were initially permitted to continue autonomous production thanks to courtesy on our part, they became subject to guidance by the military news department and the China Film Company following the outbreak of the Great East Asia War and the advancement of our military into the International Settlement on 8 December of last year. With our continuing victories disillusioning them of their British-U.S. dependence and forcing them to renounce the future of the Chongqing regime, the companies have decided to re-launch with a new face. As a result of a swift compromise, finally reached in April in full agreement with the China Film Company, we have recently witnessed the establishment of the Zhonghua Lianhe Zhipian Gufen Youxian Gongsi through the unification of all the Chinese production companies.[24]

The article confirms the fact that Chinese film companies that had previously operated independently within the International Settlement now had to submit to Zhonghua Dianying under the terms of the Japanese Occupation. It was therefore naturally the case that the anti-Japanese sentiments that had previously been expressed through the *jiegu fengjin* production tactic could no longer be deployed either. The Zhonglian soon shifted its direction from the production of historical dramas (*guzhuang pian*) to the production of contemporary dramas (*shizhuang pian*).

The first films produced by the Zhonglian were all contemporary romantic dramas, starting with *Madame Butterfly/Hudie furen* (Li Pingqian, 1942), a Beijing opera adaptation of *La Dame aux camélias*, and continuing with *The Return of the Swallow/Yan guilai* (Zhang Shichuan, 1942), *Under the Peony/Mudan hua xia* (Bu Wancang, 1942), *The Flower-Selling Girl/Mai hua nü* (Wen Yimin, 1942) and *The Scent of Quilts on a Warm Spring Day/Xiang qin chunnuan* (Yue Feng, 1942). Although Zhonghua Dianying still felt that the Zhonglian's production policy remained a far cry from national policy, it genuinely welcomed the operation and expressed relief that 'all in all, it is gradually distancing itself from the nightmare of yesteryear's anti-Japanese sentiments and heading towards a commercialism based on a star system'.[25]

THE AMBIVALENCE OF 'GREATER EAST ASIA FILM': *UNIVERSAL BROTHERHOOD* AND *TOWARD ETERNITY*

In May 1942, following the introduction of Japanese feature films in the International Settlement,[26] the Tōhō Dancing Team performed in both Shanghai and Nanjing.[27] The arrival in Shanghai of a Japanese film and dance culture that turned a blind eye to the harsh realities of occupation was influential. Fang Peilin incorporated a performance by the Tōhō Dancing Team in one of the episodes of *The Narcissus Fairy/Lingbo xianzi* (1943) and in his following film, *Myriad of Colours/Wanzi qianhong* (1943),[28] he used the troupe as the hinge for the comical depiction of a romance. The climax of the film consists of a sequence in which the heroine appears on stage with young children to sing a seemingly endless song about the subject of refugee aid. In the midst of the Pacific War, while 'Greater East Asia Films' were being produced one after the other in Japan, the Zhonglian in Shanghai was producing musical films that had nothing to do with war. This ambivalent phenomenon – of sabotaging Japan's cultural policy under occupation in this way, while also reacting sensitively to Japanese culture – began to appear in a number of the Zhonglian productions that staged the encounter between the modernism of Shanghai film and the glamour of Japanese popular culture.

Films said to be in line with national policy also began to appear, such as the epic *Universal Brotherhood*, which began filming in the second half of 1942, and *Toward Eternity* (Fig. 31.2).[29] Chinese and Japanese film historians have offered different critiques of these two films. While *Zhongguo dianying fazhan shi* (edited by Cheng Jihua) considers them 'traitorous' and deletes them completely from Chinese film history, Li Daoxin's *Zhongguo dianying shi 1937–1945* discusses them within the context of an era that considered them taboo at the time.[30] Li's detailed research seems unable to break out of the existing dualism between national policy films and entertainment films, and distinguishes between the series of films by the Manchukuo Film Association being 'direct national policy films' and *Universal Brotherhood* and *Toward Eternity* being 'indirect national policy films'. Rather than concentrate on questions of definition, my discussion will focus instead on the films themselves and their respective circumstances of their production. In particular, I will concentrate on the matter of national film policy and examine how the production of these films disrupted this policy while also appearing to display an attitude of adaptation towards it.

Universal Brotherhood was an omnibus film that took its title from the motto of the French Revolution – liberty, equality, fraternity – and comprised eleven

Fig. 31.2 An article about *Toward Eternity/Wanshi liufang* (Bu Wancang, Zhang Shankung, Ma-Xu Weibang and Zhu Shilin, 1943, Zhonglian) in *Shin eiga* (January 1941).

short films. It featured an all-star cast of celebrity actors, and the principal directors of the Zhonglian were each responsible for one. It is a work in which the various stories are connected by the theme of 'love' for a different object, such as 'love for a hometown' and 'love for children'.

Eiga junpō reported widely on the shooting of *Universal Brotherhood* and *Toward Eternity*[31] in their special column 'Shanghai Film World News Flash'[32] and recognised these two films as the highlight of the Konka tairiku eiga renmei kaigi (Summer Continental Film Federation Conference). Regarding the former, it commented that:

> The title *Universal Brotherhood* is a bit vague and even has a sense of modesty to it, but in essence, it certainly expresses the intention to serve as supportive propaganda for the principles of 'peaceful nation-building' and 'peace for all.'[33]

To what extent did the Zhonglian's *Universal Brotherhood* really serve as 'supportive propaganda'? A piece that ran in *Zhonglian yingxun* entitled 'We Must Fundamentally Solve the Refugee Problem' criticised the ruthlessness of some in Shanghai and argued that 'we must feel a larger community's spirit of universal brotherhood and put our efforts into assisting in the lives of the refugees and fight together in this era'.[34] Certainly, the surge of refugees into Shanghai escaping from the fighting in the surrounding areas of the city had become a very real social issue. Faced with such turbulent social circumstances, the Zhonglian was asking citizens not to be mere bystanders and act instead to help their compatriots. The message of *Universal Brotherhood* may thus be best seen as containing the element of moral indoctrination found in Chinese film tradition and, as such, proposing a model of virtuous enlightenment conceived to edify the people.

That said, despite the lack of anti-Japanese sentiment detectable in *Universal Brotherhood*, it should not be seen as supportive propaganda in comparison with the *jiegu fengjin* works of the 'orphan island' period. What we must not overlook is that, contrary to Japanese media reports that the film took a propaganda approach to the topic of general peace, we can also detect a sense of quiet militancy in sorrowfully phrased questions from the production side that asked, 'Who can ensure that it will be calm and peaceful forever?' Although the Zhonglian was finally beginning to display support for national policy, the production team itself were clearly seeking to make a film that expressed love for their fellow compatriots who had suffered the ravages of war. The agendas of the two sides of this work were far apart from each other.

After the start of the war, Japan's film magazine *Shin eiga* established a special column titled 'Kyōeiken eiga' (Co-Prosperity Sphere Film) that alternately ran introductions to, and reviews of, films by Man'ei, the Zhonglian and Huabei Dianying. Just as domestic continental films became incorporated into the framework of 'Greater East Asian film' after the start of the war, continental films produced in China's occupied districts also became folded into the cinema of the Co-Prosperity Sphere. It was therefore natural that the mass media discussed *Universal Brotherhood* within the wider discourse of Greater East Asian Co-Prosperity Sphere films.

The year 1942 represented the 100th anniversary of China's defeat in the Opium War and the signing of the Treaty of Nanking with the UK. While Shanghai citizens enjoyed the 'modern' values propagated from the West and based around the French Concession and the International Settlement, they could not forget the humiliation of a conflict that had forced the city into a state of semi-colonisation that lay the foundations for the expansion of imperialism within Asia. The Japanese Occupation directly evoked this memory. In this sense, when such doubly woven feelings regarding the matter of occupation were projected onto the screen, they naturally encapsulated a double set of implications. For the Zhonglian, which had inherited film-making staff from the 'orphan island', the inclusion of the heroine of *Mulan Joins the Army* in *Toward Eternity* might have been expected as a method of reviving *jiegu fengjin*.

Having said this, power relations among the nation-states in Asia had changed rapidly over the last one hundred years, and from this point of view Japan had begun to harbour vigilance against the West, while at the same time increasing its own imperialistic ambitions towards other Asian territories. The Manchurian Incident, the Second Sino-Japanese War and the Great

East Asia War all broke out in rapid succession against this background; for Japan, however, to have the 100th anniversary of the Opium War during the Pacific War was deeply significant since it clearly provided suitable material for expulsion of 'demonic Westerners' (the phrase *kichiku beiei* in Japanese) from Asia. The fact that Tōhō's *Opium War* (Makino Masahiro, 1943) was produced at roughly the same time as *Toward Eternity* speaks to the anticipated propaganda value of the subject for the wider Pacific War (Figs. 31.3, 31.4).

Unlike the case with the 'vague love' of *Universal Brotherhood*, *Toward Eternity* was praised uniformly within Japan. *Shin eiga* saw *Toward Eternity* as a 'pioneer of Greater East Asia cinema' and found in it the form of 'Greater East Asia film' that should exist.[35] Yet, was *Toward Eternity* really a film as good as that expected by the Japanese media? To discuss this, we cannot ignore the context of Japanese and Chinese film history leading up to this point. In other words, if we consider the films of the 'orphan island' period, the films by Man'ei, and the path of the production of continental films within Japan more comprehensively,

we might take away a completely different message from both the narrative and casting of *Toward Eternity* and the discourse that supported them.

When people recall the Opium War, they tend to think of Lin Zexu boldly setting fire to British opium, but although Lin Zexu appears in *Toward Eternity*, his actions on the front stage of history do not serve as the central axis of the film. Instead, the fictional character of Zhang Jingxian – who continues to think of Lin Zexu and later becomes the leader of the anti-British guerrillas – is the film's main protagonist, and it is her relationship with Lin Zexu and his wife, as well as the anti-smoking movement that she leads, that becomes the key element that carries the story along from beginning to end.

The role of the girl who sells confectionary in the opium den is also noteworthy. Despite being a supporting character, a two shot of both her and the film's heroine graced the pages of various newspapers and magazines since Li Xianglan (also known as Ri Kōran) played the role. Because of such events, *Toward Eternity* was prominently advertised as a

Fig. 31.3 *Toward Eternity/Wanshi liufang* (Bu Wancang, Zhang Shankung, Ma-Xu Weibang and Zhu Shilin, 1943, Zhonglian).

Empire | 449

Fig. 31.4 *Toward Eternity/Wanshi liufang* (Bu Wancang, Zhang Shankung, Ma-Xu Weibang and Zhu Shilin, 1943, Zhonglian).

joint production between Zhonghua Dianying, the Zhonglian and Man'ei, although it is said that the extent of Man'ei's involvement was restricted to Li Xianglan and her adviser Iwasaki Akira.[36] With that said, the casting of Li Xianglan had extremely significant implications. Despite the fact that she had previously been scorned by media and film specialists, her film *China Nights/Shina no yoru* (1943) had achieved significant Japanese box-office success. When screened in China, although it received various forms of criticisms on the one hand, it also surpassed other Japanese films in box-office sales, to the extent that even the theme song became a major hit. Li Xianglan thus became recognised by the public for *China Nights* and not for her work with Man'ei. As a result, she became the unintentional representative symbol of transnational continental film. Her casting in the Shanghai-based film epic *Toward Eternity* was seen as a major aspect of the mutual compromise between the continental film of *naichi* and *gaichi* and the work of Man'ei, Zhonghua Dianying and the Zhonglian.

Even more interestingly, the film's heroine was played by Chen Yunshang, an actress as well known in Japan and China as Li Xianglan. Chen Yunshang may have been chosen because of the producers' intention to make use of her popularity to increase audience attendance, but that may not have been the only reason. The Zhonglian magazine suggested that since she had previously played the part of the heroine who dressed as a man to fight a foreign enemy in *Mulan Joins the Army*, she was already therefore recognisable as a metaphor for the spirit of the 'orphan island'. The intention of the film's producers to proudly assert the 'orphan island's spirit of *jiegu fengjin* through the body of Chen Yunshang is certainly a daring form of expression.

Any work with the Opium War as its subject matter would surely make Lin Zexu its main protagonist. Furthermore, in terms of genre, *Toward Eternity* might initially be seen as a love story featuring two heterosexual couples with the conflict as a backdrop. Despite the existence of a male–female love triangle in the film, however, the two women both remain rational characters who do not compete with each other for Lin's love. In fact, while nursing romantic feelings for Lin Zexu, even after talk of their engagement is nullified due to his rude behaviour towards her father, Chen Yunshang runs away from home and devotes herself earnestly to opium eradication and the anti-British movement – an act that is respected, even by Lin's wife. Separately from this male–female relationship, another male–female relationship between the young sweet vendor Feng gu and her opium addict lover is incorporated in a multilayered manner. *Toward Eternity* presents a melodrama familiar to Shanghainese audiences at the time, skilfully intertwining these two male–female relationships and making Chen Yunshang – who actively participates in the opium eradication movement – and Li Xianglan its double heroines. Instead of making Lin Zexu its hero, the film ensures the two women leave the strongest impression on audience members. At the end of the film, the Lin family visit Chen's grave and sing the praises of the heroine Zhang Jingxian. This moment can be seen as an appeal to audience members to similarly remember the heroine of *Mulan Joins the Army*, also played by Chen Yunshan, and note that even with the Shanghai film world under the umbrella of the Zhonghua Dianying during Japanese Occupation, the notion of *jiegu fengjin* was still alive and well.

The Zhonglian's decision to have Chen Yunshang and Li Xianglan co-star in a film thus had clear implications. On the one hand, Chen Yunshang had been catapulted into being the darling of the 'orphan island' film as the heroine of *Mulan Joins the Army*. On the other hand, Li Xianglan typically played the role of a Chinese girl who had a romantic relationship with a Japanese boy, and she was praised as the personification of the pro-Japanese 'coexistence and co-prosperity' policies of the 'Sino-Japanese alliance'. If Li Xianglan had been given symbolic pro-Japanese roles up to this point, then Chen Yunshang was also unmistakably seen as an enduring advocate of the refusal to submit to foreign invasion.[37] Opposite Li Xianglan whose character bravely disguises herself as the diva Feng gu and sacrifices herself to secure the eradication of opium, Chen played the part of Jingxian, who grows to become the leader of the anti-British guerrilla movement and finally dies in battle. That the two actresses joined together to portray roles that fought against foreign invaders is meaningful. The Zhonglian magazine article mentioned previously noted that the Zhonglian had Li Xianglan play the role of Feng gu while projecting Mulan's image onto Chen Yunshang/Zhang Jingxian because it wanted to erase the conventional image of a young girl being conquered by the occupiers and reverse the previous metaphor that had soaked into Li Xianglan's star body. This is the reason that the heroine of *Toward Eternity* was Jingxian, something that can be confirmed by both the final scene of the film showing Jingxian's grave with the four characters of 'wanshi liufang' (of the film's title) engraved on it and the voiceover that states, 'Jingxian sacrificed herself, and the name of *wanshi liufang* will live on forever.'[38] Zhang Jingxian thus became the protagonist in place of the real-life Lin Zexu and, as if to take advantage of the fact of her fictional existence, the image of Mulan was superimposed on Zhang Jingxian through the body of Chen Yunshang.

CONCLUSION

The filmic negotiations between Japan and China that had continued for over a decade were suddenly put to an end with the collapse of Man'ei, Zhonghua Dianying and Huabei Dianying in 1945. In January 1946, under the terms of the American Occupation, more than twenty individuals, starting with Kawakita Nagamasa, involved directly in militarist cultural production through their key positions in the film industry from before the outbreak of the Pacific War, were expelled from their posts.[39]

In Shanghai, the film-makers who had been working in the service of the Zhonglian and Huaying had no time to taste the joy of being freed from Japanese Occupation after the return to Japan of the Japanese employees of the Zhonghua Dianying. Instead, they lived each day in fear. Seeing their former fellows who had travelled south be greeted by the people as triumphant war heroes, they began to feel anxious regarding their own film activities during the Occupation period. Before long, what they feared secretly in their hearts became a reality. Starting in the Autumn of 1946 in Shanghai, a movement began to pursue those who had collaborated with the Japanese during the Occupation and numerous film managers, directors and actors who were called *funi yingren* (film-makers who were complicit with the rebel KMT) were summoned, one after the other, to face trail.[40]

The end of the war thus saw a Japanese film industry that continued production under US Occupation and a Chinese film industry that remained based in Shanghai – a city that was, at the same time, embroiled in civil war between the KMT and the Communist Party. With the birth of a new political composition in East Asia, the Japanese and Chinese film industries, which had previously become so intimately entangled, were now forced to separate and shut down their policy of mutual negotiation. These new asymmetric relationships gradually became entangled in the realities of Japan's defeat in World War II, the Cold War, the loss of the KMT and the outbreak of the Korean War.

The relationship between imperialism and film did not, however, come to an end just because of the conclusion of the Asia-Pacific War. There are numerous examples that demonstrate the series of breaks and continuities that mark this complex history. These include the number of Japanese film critics who continued to actively write criticism about Chinese film as they had done before the war, or the Japanese technical staff from Man'ei that remained in Manchuria and became involved in the production of *Bridge/Qiao* (1949) and *The White Haired Girl/Baimao nü* – films seen as the models for New Chinese film. We might also consider figures such as Mochinaga Tadahito who moved from Manchuria to Shanghai and continued his activities as a pioneer of New Chinese animation. It therefore remains clear that East Asian film historians must continue to deepen their exploration of film within the empire and post-empire in ways that resist being forced into the restrictive framework of a cultural history of one single state.[41]

Notes

1   Satō Tadao, *Kinema to hōsei: Nicchū eiga zenshi* (Tokyo: Libroport, 1985); Tsuji Hisakazu, *Chūka den'ei shiwa: Ippeisotsu no Nicchū eiga kaisōki 1939–1945* (Tokyo: Gaifūsha, 1987); Shimizu Akira, *Shanghai sokai eiga shishi* (Tokyo: Shinchōsha, 1995).
2   Li Daoxin (ed.), *Zhongguo dianying shi 1937–1945* (Beijing: Shoudu Shifan Daxue chubanshe, 2000).
3   Poshek Fu, *Between Shanghai and Hong Kong: The Politics of Chinese Cinemas* (Stanford, CA: Stanford University Press, 2003).
4   Peter B. High, *The Imperial Screen: Japanese Film Culture in the Fifteen Years' War, 1931–1945* (Madison: University of Wisconsin Press, 2003); Katō Atsuko, *Sōdōin taisei to eiga* (Tokyo: Shin'yōsha, 2003); Michael Baskett, *The Attractive Empire: Transnational Film Culture in Imperial Japan* (Honolulu: University of Hawai'i Press, 2008); Misawa Mamie, *'Teikoku' to 'sokoku' no hazama: Shokuminchiki Taiwan eigajin no kōshō to ekkyō* (Tokyo: Iwanami shoten, 2010); Yi Young Jae, *Teikoku Nihon no Chōsen eiga: Shokuminchi melancholia to kyōryoku* (Tokyo: Sangensha, 2013); Takashi Fujitani, *Race for Empire: Koreans as Japanese and Japanese as Americans during World War II* (Berkeley: University of California Press, 2013); Kate Taylor-Jones, *Divine Work: Japanese Colonial Cinema and Its Legacy* (London: Bloomsbury Academic, 2017); Dong Hoon Kim, *Eclipsed Cinema: The Film Culture of Colonial Korea* (Edinburgh: Edinburgh University Press, 2017); Yan Ni, *Senji Nicchū eiga kōshōshi* (Tokyo: Iwanami shoten, 2010).
5   See Yan, *Senji nicchū eiga kōshōshi*, chapter 7.
6   The number of films produced is taken from Li, *Zhongguo dianying shi 1937–1945*.
7   For more details of Shinmin eiga kyōkai, see Zhang Xinmin, '"Shinmin eiga kyōkai no seiritsu" to sono katsudō jōkyō ni tsuite', *Chūgoku gakushi* no. 27 (December 2012), p. 10.
8   The Reformed Government of the Republic of China was a puppet government established by Japan during the Second Sino-Japanese War on 28 March 1938 in Nanjing.
9   Kawakita Nagamasa, 'Chūka eiga gaisha no shimei koko ni ari', *Kokusai eiga shinbun*, August 1939, jōjun-gō, p. 2. [Editors' note: for more on Kawakita Nagamasa, see also Chapter 39 by Yoshiharu Tezuka in this volume.]
10 Xu Gongmei was a playwright and critic who served as the acting director of the Department of Social Education, Ministry of Education, of the Reformed Government of the Republic of China.
11 Xu Gongmei, 'Shin Chūgoku no eiga seisaku', *Kokusai eiga shinbun*, August 1939, jōjun-gō, p. 7.
12 The shortage of exportable raw film stock from Japan to Manchuria and China was exacerbated because of the limited imports available from the Eastman Kodak Company to Japan as a result of the Wartime Emergency Film System (see endnote 22). See Katō, *Sōdōin taisei to eiga*, p. 101.
13 Chu Minyi, born Chu Mingyi, studied abroad in countries such as Japan and France and served as a member of the Tongmenghui. After returning to China in 1924, he was elected as a member of the KMT Central Committee Executive Committee. In 1946, he was executed for the crime of being a *hanjin*, a traitor to the Han Chinese nation.
14 See Tsuji Hisakazu, 'Chūgoku eigajin hyōden 2: Zhang Shankun', *Eiga junpō*, 1 November 1942, p. 26.
15 Kawakita, 'Chūka eiga gaisha no shimei koko ni ari', p. 4.
16 See Tsuji Kazuhisa 'Chūgoku eigajin hyōden: Zhang Shankun', *Eiga junpō*, 1 November 1942, p. 70.
17 Born Liu Canbo, Liu Naou studied French at Shanghai's Aurora University and established the Dayixian shudian in 1928. He became president of Wenhuibao in 1939; he was assassinated that same year. Yang Biyun and Chang Wei (eds), *Taiwan lishi cidian* (Taipei: Chan wei, 1997), p. 161.

18. See Tōhōtōwa Co., *Tōwa no hanseiki, 1928-1978* (Tokyo: Tōhōtōa, 1978), p. 286.
19. The New Film System can mainly be characterised by restrictions on film production and the obligatory exhibition of documentary film or 'culture film' under the terms of the Film Law (enforced in October 1939 and revised in September 1940). The Wartime Emergency Film System may be chiefly defined by the monopolisation of film distribution. See High, *The Imperial Screen*, chapter 8; Katō, *Sōdōin taisei to eiga*.
20. Ishikawa Toshishige served as general manager of Zhonghua dianying and then as vice president of Huaying.
21. Tsuji Hisakazu, 'Sokai shinchūki', *Shin eiga*, February 1942, p. 52.
22. To give one example, Kawakita quickly arranged for the special release of *Mulan Joins the Army* in Nanjing in July, the same month he began operations at the Zhonghua dianying. For an examination in detail, see Yan, *Senji Nicchū eiga kōshōshi*, chapter 7.
23. Lin Baisheng was executed after the war as a *hanjin* traitor. After being sentenced to death, he was imprisoned in the same cell as Zhou Zuoren. See Motoyama Hideo, *Zhou Zuoren 'Tainichi kyōryoku' no tenmatsu: Hochū* Pekin kujūanki *narabini gojitsuhen* (Tokyo: Iwanami shoten, 2004), p. 292.
24. 'Chūka rengō seihen kōshi no seiritsu to genkyō', *Eiga junpō*, 11 August 1942, p. 22.
25. See 'Banshi seikō', *Zhonglian yingxun*, 14 April 1943, p. 1.
26. Japanese feature films were released in the International Settlement from May 1942. For the advancement of Japanese feature films into the International Settlement, see Yan, *Senji Nicchū eiga kōshōshi*, chapter 6.
27. In the 24 March 1943 issue of *Zhonglian yingxun*, there is a report titled 'The Tōhō Dancing Team comes to Shanghai, Fang Pilin uses the opportunity to shoot a film'.
28. Because of the acclaim of his previous film *Lingbo xianzi*, Fang Peilin hoped for even higher box-office returns and thus decided to film *Myriad of Colours*. See 'Shanghai eiga tokuhō', *Zhonglian yingxun*, 14 April 1943.
29. There were five directors for *Toward Eternity*, but the one in charge of placing the final touches was Yang Xiaozhong. See '*Wanshi liufang* gongde yuanman, Yang Xiaozhong zong qi dacheng', *Zhonglian yingxun*, 27 January 1943, p. 2.
30. Cheng Jihua (ed.), *Zhongguo dianying fazhan shi* (Beijing: Zhongguo dianying chubanshe, 1963); Li, *Zhongguo dianying shi*.
31. The first title of *Toward Eternity* was *Opium War/Yapian zhi zhan*. See *Eiga junpō*, 11 October 1942, p. 18.
32. Xingian tekan, 'Shanghai eigakai tokuhō', *Eiga junpō*, 11 November 1942.
33. 'Chūren sakuhin hihyō: *Hakuai*', *Eiga junpō*, 11 December 1942, p. 44.
34. Xinpian tekan, '*Boai*', 'Tongshi tianya lunluoren', *Zhonglian yingxun*, 1942.
35. '*Bansei ryūhō* tokushū', *Shin eiga*, June 1944, p. 8.
36. According to Yamaguchi Yoshiko (Li Xianglan) and Fujiwara Sakuya, *Ri Kōran: Watashi no hansei* (Tokyo: Shinchōsha, 1986), the Japanese individuals who were involved with *Toward Eternity* were Li Xianglan and Iwasaki Akira, who was in charge of development on the Man'ei side as part of its support system.
37. I analyse the physicality of Chen Yunshang in more detail in *Senji Nicchū eiga kōshōshi*, chapter 7.
38. '*Wanshi liufang* benshi' '*Zhonglian yingxun* Xinpian tekan *Wanshi liufang*', 1943, China Film Archive, Beijing.
39. See High, *The Imperial Screen*, p. 468.
40. On the trials of '*funi yingren*', see, for example, the report 'Gaojian chu zuo chuan xun funi yingren' in the 5 November 1946 issue of *Wenhuibao*, or the report 'Funi xianyi nüxing Li Lihua Chen Yanyan zuo shoushen' in the 11 December 1946 issue of *Wenhuibao*.
41. See Yomota Inuhiko and Yan Ni (eds), *Post-Manshū eigaron: Nicchū eiga ōkan* (Kyoto: Jimbun shoin, 2010), Yan Ni, 'Nihon eiga to 1950-nendai no Chūgoku', in Yomota Inuhiko, Kurosawa Kiyoshi, Lee Bong-Ou and Yoshimi Shun'ya (eds), *Nihon eiga wa ikiteiru*, vol. 3, *Miru hito, tsukuru hito, kakeru hito* (Tokyo: Iwanami shoten, 2010), and Stephanie DeBoer, *Coproducing Asia: Locating Japanese-Chinese Regional Film and Media* (Minneapolis: University of Minnesota Press, 2014). [Editors' note: see also Chapter 36 by Stephanie DeBoer in this volume.]

THE OCCUPATION
Pedagogies of modernity: CIE and USIS films about the United Nations

Yuka Tsuchiya

In October 1956, an educational film titled *The United Nations and Japan/Kokuren to nihon* (1956), featuring Hara Setsuko, was released in Japan. The film was produced by a Japanese film-maker under the orders of the UN Association of Japan, and distributed by the US Information Service (USIS) – the US government's overseas information dissemination agency. Hara, one of the country's most famous film stars, best known for her performances in Kurosawa Akira's *No Regrets for Our Youth/Waga seishun ni kui nashi* (1946), and Ozu Yasujirō's *Late Spring/Banshun* (1949) and *Tokyo Story/Tokyo monogatari* (1953), played the role of Miss Aoki, a writer/editor for a Junior High School student magazine. In the film, Miss Aoki interviews the Director of the UN Association of Japan and the former Ambassador to the UN for a special issue commemorating the 'United Nations Day' of 24 October. On 18 December of the same year, Japan was unanimously accepted as the eightieth member of the UN.

The film is almost totally forgotten today and it might seem stunning to many people that such a well-known actress as Hara performed in an obscure educational film about the United Nations. This was, however, not her first role in a government-sponsored film. As an iconic starlet, she appeared in various wartime Japanese propaganda films such as *The New Earth/Atarashiki tsuchi* (1937) and *Toward the Decisive Battle in the Sky/Kessen no ōzora e* (1943).

The United Nations and Japan embodied the complicated web of US overseas information policy, Japanese national desire and Cold War ideology.

The year 1956 marked the beginning of Japan's re-emergence in the international community. It had been four years since the end of the US Occupation, Japan's conservative Liberal Democratic Party (LDP) had firmly established a stable pro-US regime and Japan's postwar 'economic miracle' had begun to take off. The world that Japan faced, however, was full of rapid, often violent change, such as the decolonisation of Third World countries and the Cold War realities symbolised by the brutal suppression of an anti-Soviet uprising in Hungary. Under the façade of East–West cultural exchange, the US and the Soviet Union were engaged in a severe propaganda battle to 'win the hearts and minds' of people in other countries. All these factors affected the films distributed by the USIS. The purpose of this chapter will thus be to reveal how 'educational' films about the UN reflected the multilayered meanings deeply embedded in postwar international relations.

The United Nations and Japan was but one of the forty-four films about the United Nations distributed by the USIS during and after the US Occupation. At the end of World War II, Japan was occupied by the Allied Powers. However, the Far Eastern Commission – the official Allied Occupation authorities consisting of eleven countries – did not function well because of veto powers held by the US and the Soviet Union. For this reason, the US army, which had made the greatest contribution and sacrifice in the Pacific theatre, was authorised to be in charge of the Occupation administration. The US Occupation Forces established the General Headquarters, Supreme Command for the Allied Powers (GHQ/SCAP), which included various civil affairs sections such as the Government Section (GS), the Economic and Scientific Section (ESS) and the Civil Information and Education Section (CIE).[1] The CIE showed some four hundred short CIE educational films to the Japanese. These were US government-sponsored films produced, or procured, by various departments and agencies of the US government. The GHQ/SCAP ordered the Japanese Ministry of Education to set up an audiovisual library in each Prefecture. The Prefectural libraries stored and loaned out the CIE films to Japanese educators, companies, and various private and public groups that organised CIE film shows.[2]

After the end of the Occupation, the CIE films were placed under the control of the USIS and were called USIS films. The USIS was a branch of the State Department's overseas information section and, later, of the US Information Agency (USIA), which was established in August 1953. USIS branches existed in about eighty countries around the world. The USIS in each country showed USIS films specially selected or produced for that county. Some of the USIS films were locally produced for the audiences of the given country. *The United Nations and Japan* was one such example. In post-Occupation Japan, the 'American Centres' showed USIS films, while Prefectural audiovisual libraries continued loaning out the films, too. Some USIS films were broadcast on television. As a result, although on a smaller scale than during the Occupation, Japanese people kept watching USIS films throughout the 1950s and 1960s.

Why did the US government distribute so many CIE or USIS films on the United Nations? Why were some of them produced in Japan? What messages did they convey to the audiences and how can these films be located within the broader history of Japanese cinema and that of Cold War international relations? To answer these questions, this chapter will analyse some of these films and examine them in the context of the domestic and international environment. Such an attempt will reveal the political implications of these seemingly neutral 'educational' and 'informational' films, and establish the USIS films as a window through which to reveal the struggle to restore Japan's status of respectability within postwar international society.

JAPANESE CINEMA DURING AND AFTER THE OCCUPATION

Japan's experience of such total and miserable defeat meant that feelings of exhaustion and despair overwhelmed many Japanese in the immediate postwar period. At the same time, defeat also brought a sense of liberation and opportunity after so many years of perseverance and government dictates. These were the reasons why the Japanese people did not resist the Occupation but instead 'embraced' the victor's gifts of material culture, freedom of expression and democratic reform. Numerous progressive reforms in the law, governance, economy and education emerged out of discussion and cooperation between American and Japanese experts, but they also occurred within the encouraging atmosphere created by the Occupation forces.[3] As the Cold War intensified and domestic ideological battles involving Communism flared up, however, Occupation policies increasingly assumed an anti-communist tone. Anti-communist propaganda became especially prevalent after the outbreak of the Korean War. Leftist Japanese who welcomed the initial democratic reforms bitterly labelled the shift in Occupation policies 'the reverse course'. The USIS films also reflected this transition. The early USIS films introduced American education, industry and technology and demonstrated how democracy functioned in the everyday life of ordinary Americans, while later on more overt anti-communist messages became increasingly visible.[4] One should remember, however, that the USIS films had political goals from the beginning, with or without anti-communism. They were not benign entertainment but government-sponsored films aimed at nurturing pro-American democracy in the target country.

The existing scholarship on Japanese cinema in the Occupation and post-Occupation periods can be divided into two categories: work on entertainment films including Hollywood features, and work on educational films including the CIE and USIS films. In the former category, Kyoko Hirano has explored how the Occupation forces tried to strengthen 'democratic' elements and eliminate militaristic or authoritarian expressions in Japanese entertainment cinema through censorship.⁵ Hiroshi Kitamura has covered such diverse groups as the American film distributor Central Motion Picture Exchange (CMPE), Japanese exhibitors and various 'cultural elites' including critics, journalists, scholars and cinemagoers in order to show the complicated dynamics by which Hollywood films became the icon of democracy and modernity within occupied Japan.⁶ Hirano and Kitamura's books vividly capture the cultural atmosphere of the Occupation period when both the Occupation authorities and the Japanese people explored ways of building a modern, peaceful and cultured nation. Hollywood films provided one model, as Kitamura demonstrates, and, as the following scholars have also shown, the CIE films provided another.

Tanikawa Takeshi has dealt with both the Hollywood films and the CIE films from the perspective of the US government's overseas film policy.⁷ He highlights the continuity between the wartime overseas information activities of the Office of War Information (OWI) and the postwar establishment of the Central Motion Picture Exchange (CMPE), the agency that imported Hollywood films to occupied areas. Tanikawa is probably the first scholar to discuss the relationship between film and US overseas information policy and calls the information officers who used film the 'salesmen of democracy'.⁸ Educational historians have also paid considerable attention to the CIE films and discussed the positive influence of the CIE films on the modernisation and democratisation of Japanese education. Abe Akira, for example, has discussed the contribution of the CIE films to the progress of Japanese audiovisual education.⁹ Shiba Shizuko has focused on the effective use of the CIE films in the development of Japan's postwar home economics education.¹⁰ The film historian Nakamura Hideyuki, in contrast, has situated the CIE films in the context of Japanese educational films and examined how educational film specialists have evaluated the CIE films.¹¹ Misaki Tomeko has analysed the image of the 'democratic family' portrayed in CIE films from a gender studies perspective and argued that such images promoted fixed gender norms.

Such a wide-ranging and interdisciplinary discussion reveals the confusingly 'multi-lateral' face of the CIE films. They were not only US government information films but also tools for educational reform, healthy entertainment for people in rural areas and a form of social control aimed at consolidating gender and other social norms. The complexity and multifaceted character of the CIE films has motivated the authors of an anthology to analyse the CIE films from various different perspectives such as the US government policy, Japanese reception, anti-communism, international comparison and film technology. This book also includes interviews with film-makers, actors and technicians involved in CIE film production.¹²

The CIE and USIS films were produced or procured by the US government with clearly set political goals then systematically distributed by the US and Japanese governments and shown free of charge. During the Occupation, the US Department of the Army's Reorientation Branch sent hundreds of documentary and educational films to occupied areas including Japan. In Japan, the CIE of the Occupation forces selected the most effective films, inserted Japanese subtitles or dubbing, had Japanese film-printing companies make dozens of prints and send them to the various Prefectural audiovisual libraries. It is estimated that each Japanese citizen watched between eight to ten CIE films in total.¹³ The films were screened in commercial theatres before feature films and in schools, town halls and department stores on the 16mm 'Natco' mobile projectors provided by the US Army. 'Natco' was an abbreviation for 'National Company', the Chicago based manufacturer of the projectors, but the term became so popular that the Japanese called the CIE films 'Natco films'. As the film shows were mostly managed by Japanese educators, film technicians and librarians, the audiences did not view the CIE films as an information tool of the US government.¹⁴

The CIE films covered a variety of themes from US culture, education, science, industry and the country's democratic political system, to international relations and information on other countries. Although some films conveyed an overt political message, such as *The Communist Conspiracy/Aka no inbō* (1952), which depicted the Japanese Communist Party in a negative light, most included only subtle messages embedded within their otherwise generally pleasant, entertaining and informative content. *New Neighbors/Atarashii rinjin* (1952), for example, introduced a Japanese American family living on Seabrook Farm in New Jersey, a modern, mechanised farm where residents formed an affluent, multi-ethnic, classless society. Mary Ting Yi Lui has pointed out the film's erasure of inconvenient facts such as the internment of Japanese Americans, racial injustice and class conflict. In a similar manner, *White Collar Worker/America no salaryman* (1951) celebrated the lifestyle of a fictional white, middle-class nuclear family, focusing on a male protagonist working for a large company. The film erased any seamier side to US society and gave the impression that the US capital was the home of happy families and a peaceful society.[15] Neither of these two films included any overt propaganda and both provided their information in conjunction with pleasant music and images. They nevertheless conveyed the subtle message that US society was free of class, racial and gender injustice thanks to the combination of advanced technology and benevolent capitalism.

Approximately fifty CIE films were produced in Japan, especially for the Japanese audiences. They dealt with issues such as democratic reform, the modernisation of everyday life and Japan's relations with the world. *For a Bright Home Life/Akarui katei seikatsu* (1950), for example, showed two high school girls carrying out 'home project' assignments to modernise their kitchens and dining rooms, while *Men Who Fish/Sunadoru hitobito* (1950) documented democratising reform within a small seaside village.[16] The former was produced by the Ōizumi Film Company (established in 1947 and merged with Tōei in 1951), and the latter was made by Shū Taguchi Productions with a young cameraman named Okazaki Kōzō, who would later become one of the most successful film-makers of Japan. Japanese film-makers were placed under strict government control during the war and forced to make propaganda movies by using government-allocated materials. When the war ended, they lost their jobs, and some of them made their living by making CIE films for the Occupation forces.[17]

It should also be noted that various famous documentary films were included amongst the CIE films such as *Louisiana Story* (1948) and *Nanook of the North* (1922), both directed by Robert J. Flaherty. These well-known films by established film-makers remained a small minority in comparison with the hundreds of CIE films produced by government-contracted companies and government-employed film-makers.

Japanese audiences greatly enjoyed the CIE films, both as a form of entertainment and as a means of accessing information on the wider world. Even though post-screening surveys conducted by the Occupation forces indicated that the majority of the audience did not view the films as propaganda, it is clear that the CIE films were effective in impressing the Japanese with the scale of US modernity. A Japanese man who watched *Modern Highway/Kindaiteki na dōro* (1950) was, for instance, so impressed with the 'wonderful, beautiful patterns of the American highways' that he wished Japan would someday have such a similar system. A group of dairy businessmen who watched *Blue Ribbon and Gold Cup: CIE Film Sketch No.8/Aoi ribbon to kinpai* (1949) and *American Stock Raising/America no bokuchiku* (1949) were struck by the 'greatness of the large-scale farm management' and the 'peaceful family life' of American farmers. They 'envied' the American lifestyle and felt that the film 'provided guidance for [their] future dairy business'. One organiser of the CIE film show wrote that the audience of *Vacation Sports: CIE Film Sketch No.17/Kyūka no supōtsu* (1949) were '100 percent engaged' and 'they just expressed admiration'. 'We cannot make such an awesome film in Japan,' the organiser continued, 'I just marvelled and felt that only Americans could do this.' A teacher of a girls' high school who watched *An American Women's College/Amerika no joshi daigaku* (1948) 'changed her mind' about American women. Although she had previously thought that 'American girls were flamboyant', it was a pleasant surprise to see the 'simple and down to earth' lifestyle of the female college students introduced in the film.[18]

In sum, the CIE films were one aspect of the US government's information and education programme to nurture pro-American democracy. It would be too simplistic, however, to call them 'propaganda' films. The CIE films had a variety of themes and some of them were produced by Japanese film-makers. Although they certainly had embedded political messages – and these often seem to have worked effectively – they also had multiple functions such as the dissemination of new knowledge and technology, the provision of entertainment in rural areas and the arousal of a general desire for modernity, affluence and the recovery of a sense of national pride.

CIE AND USIS FILMS ABOUT THE UNITED NATIONS

Although it is impossible to examine all the USIS films on the topic of the UN, this section will examine some of their content and discuss their general characteristics. Some initial explanation about the storage and availability of the CIE and USIS films and scripts is necessary. Many reel films and film scripts are stored at the US National Archives at College Park, Maryland. The scripts and brochures for *The United Nations and Japan* are, for example, stored there. Some CIE films have also been collected and stored at the National Film Archive of Japan, with the cooperation of the University of Tokyo, Shin nihon eiga Company and the International Research Center for Japanese Studies. Some of the USIS films on the UN are included in this collection.

Table 32.1 provides a list of USIS films about the UN, which I have been able to confirm from various sources. The most helpful source for this has been the Japanese USIS Film Catalogue published by the USIS Japan every few years during the 1950s and 1960s.[19] Overall, about forty-four films on the UN were released in Japan through the 1950s and 1960s, although some of them were retired and others were newly added during this period.

Table 32.1 A list of USIS films

USIS No.	Title (Japanese/English)	Released in Japan
42	Kokusai rengō kenshō/Charter of the United Nations	08/13/48
107	Kokurensai/United Nations' Week Festival: CIE Film Sketch #9	05/27/49
238	Shinryaku ni kotaeru kokuren/United Nations Answers Aggression	08/15/50
245	Kokuren to sekai no funsō/United Nations and World Disputes	09/22/50
246	UNESCO to watashitachi/UNESCO and Japan	02/01/52
247	Kokuren honbu no tanjō/United Nations Finds a Home	10/13/50
249	Umi wa waga kokyō/The Sea – My Native Land	10/18/50
262	Kokurenki no shitani/Under the United Nations Flag	10/20/50
264	Jiyū no tameno tatakai/Fight for Freedom	02/06/53
268	Kokuren screen magazine 1/UN Screen Magazine No. 1	01/26/51
303	Kyōsanshugi no ashiato/Communist Footprints	03/09/51
318	Kokuren screen magazine 3: Ecuador no jishin/UN Screen Magazine 3: Earthquake in Ecuador	06/15/51
319	Kokuren screen magazine 4: Sekai no daigaku/UN Screen Magazine 4: University of the World	07/27/51
342	Kokuren screen magazine 5/UN Screen Magazine No. 5	04/19/51
343	Kokuren screen magazine 6/UN Screen Magazine No. 6	12/14/51
353	Kokuren kinensai/UN Anniversary: CIE News Magazine No. 35	11/30/51
362	Eien no tatakai/Eternal Fight	10/19/51
369	Kokuren screen magazine 8/UN Screen Magazine No. 8	03/28/52
379	Nihon no UNESCO kanyū/Japan Joins UNESCO	12/21/52

USIS No.	Title (Japanese/English)	Released in Japan
386	Kokusai rengō no igi/The Meaning of the United Nations	02/08/52
387	ECOSOC no hanashi/ECOSOC and Its Sub-Agencies	03/14/52
390	Ningen no kenri/Human Rights	02/29/52
391	Sekai no tsudoi/Town Meeting of the World	05/07/52
397	Kokuren screen magazine 7/UN Screen Magazine No. 7	02/15/52
404	Inago/Locust: USIS News Magazine No. 36	11/07/52
510	Heiwa eno keikaku/Plan for Peace	03/13/53
518	Sampson fujin/Edith Sampson	05/08/53
523	Senko no noroi/Ancient Curse, The	11/14/52
548	Nobel heiwa shō/Workers for Peace	02/26/54
555	Genshiryoku o heiwa e/Atomic Power for Peace	02/12/54
563	Kiro/Men at Crossroads	01/10/55
569	CARE no jijo keikaku/CARE Self-help Program	02/20/56
5701	Kokuren screen magazine 9/UN Screen Magazine No. 9	07/16/56
5710	Kokuren to nihon/The United Nations and Japan	10/16/56
5711	Danny Kaye to Asia no kodomotachi/Assignment Children	10/16/56
5724	Our Times 4–25	02/17/57
5729	Kumon suru Hungary/Hungary in Agony	01/24/57
5735	Senkusha Wilson/Woodrow Wilson: Spokesman for Tomorrow	03/11/57
5736	Asuwa taijuni/Toward Tomorrow	05/31/57
5737	Kono wakaki sedai no ikari: Hungary no higeki/Tragedy of Hungary	03/20/57
5740	Our Times 9-31	06/04/57
5801	Kishi shushō no hōbei: nichibei kankei ni shinjidai o/Prime Minister Kishi's Visit to the US	07/22/57
5804	Jinrui no takara/The Greatest Treasure	12/20/57
5904	Watashitachi no UNICEF/Three of Our Children	11/12/58

Several of the UN films include the same form of subtle political messaging embedded in a pleasant, entertaining content that was typical of the USIS films in general. *The United Nations Finds a Home/Kokuren home no tanjō* (1950), for example, is a very well-made film featuring the attractive scenery and lively people of New York City. It takes the form of a dramatised story about the construction of the UN headquarters in New York City. The story unfolds as an architect working on the project stops by at a nearby café where a bunch of children come in to complain to the café's owner that their playgrounds will be lost because of the building work. The architect overhears the complaint and explains to the children that architects from all over the world are cooperating with each other to build the UN headquarters, as if the UN's ideal of international harmony is reflected in the actual construction process. When part of the project is completed, the children are invited to a tour of the headquarters. Learning that the UN is helping needy children all over the world, the children become impressed with the UN's goals and decide to give up their playgrounds in the name of a good cause. The close-ups of ethnically diverse workers and children are a reminder of the New Deal films of the 1930s celebrating egalitarian ideals. The racial diversity of New York is aligned with the UN's ideal of peaceful coexistence to the extent that American society is presented in the form of a miniature UN.[20]

By contrast, some films on the UN, especially those produced immediately after the outbreak of the Korean War, included overt anti-communist messages. *Town Meeting of the World/Sekai no tsudoi* (1952) is one example. The film was originally produced as part of the 'March of Time' documentary film series by Time Inc., presented by the US Army, and then procured as a USIS film. The film initially shows representatives of various countries arriving at the UN headquarters to attend the General Assembly; it then introduces various organisations within the UN. The voiceover explains that even non-UN member countries such as Japan participate in the activities of affiliate organisations such as UNESCO and UNICEF. The camera focuses on a Japanese-language sign reading 'Many Thanks to UNICEF' and we see Japanese children having lunch at a day care centre. The film then explains the history of the Korean War telling viewers how the Soviet Union obstructed the UN Security Council's efforts to drive away the North Korean 'aggressors' by international cooperation. The film goes on to explain how the Soviet Union blocked Japan's admission to the UN. The San Francisco Peace Treaty 'marked the beginning of the new era of independence' for Japan, and it opened up the opportunity to 'work together with the other free people of the earth'. For this reason, 'Japan was eager to participate in the UN' while 'Moscow opposed the freedom of Japan'.[21]

The United Nations Answers Aggression/Shinyraku ni kotaeru kokuren (1950), *The United Nations and World Disputes/Kokuren to sekai no funsō* (1950) and *Under the Flag of the United Nations/Kokurenki no shitani* (1950) all dealt with the Korean War and assumed a strong anti-communist tone.[22] Although these propagandistic films were frequently screened during the Korean War, they quickly lost their raison d'être after the 1954 armistice and by 1956 they had disappeared from the film list.

Some of the films produced in Japan also included anti-communist messages, but they were bound up with the Japanese desire to become a member of the UN. *The United Nations and Japan* was an example. Although the film was sponsored and distributed by the USIS, according to the film's opening title it was 'presented by the UN Association of Japan' – a non-profit organisation (NPO) established in 1947 to promote Japan's entry to the UN – with the 'assistance of the Ministry of Foreign Affairs and the Asia Association' and 'produced by the Japanese filmmaker Geiken KK'. In other words, the film was the hybrid product of US–Japan and governmental-private cooperation (Figs. 32.1a–h).

Two slightly different versions of the brochure and an English-language script are stored at the US National Archives. The front cover of each brochure carries a different photo of Hara Setsuko smiling beside a miniature model of the UN headquarters building.

460 | The Japanese Cinema Book

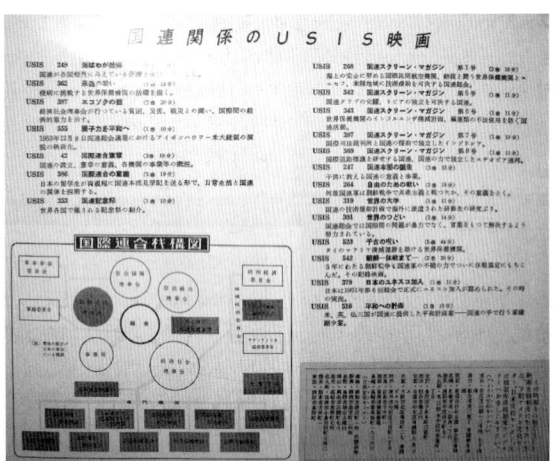

Figs. 32.1a–h Brochure pages for *The United Nations and Japan/Kokuren to nihon* (UN Association of Japan, 1956).

The brochures explain outright that although Japan 'has sincerely wished to gain UN membership and free countries, including the United States, have supported Japan' it 'has still not been able to gain membership because of the veto by the Soviet Union'. Nonetheless, Japan is 'already a member of various specialist organizations under the UN and has been playing a substantial role as an advanced country within Asia, especially in relation to technological aid'.[23]

The story unfolds as Miss Aoki (Hara), a youth magazine editor, plans to publish an issue commemorating UN Day.[24] To collect information, she interviews Satō Naotake, the director of the UN Association of Japan. Satō had been a diplomat and minister of foreign affairs in prewar Japan. In 1942, he was appointed ambassador to the Soviet Union and stayed in Moscow until the war's end. In 1947, he was elected to the House of Councillors and served until his retirement in 1965.[25] As an experienced diplomat and prominent politician, Satō was an influential figure in the promotion of Japan's entry to the UN. After a short sequence during which Satō explains the UN's history and goals, a voice narration introduces the organisational structure and functions of the UN. The narration refers to the 'power of veto' mentioning 'that [the fact that] Japan's admission to the UN was blocked by the Soviets' veto is still recent enough to be fresh in our minds'.[26]

Aoki also interviews the former ambassador to the UN, Sawada Renzō. Sawada was also a diplomat in the prewar era and served as the Emperor Hirohito's interpreter.[27] Although Sawada was temporarily purged during the Occupation, he made a swift comeback and was appointed to be the first Japanese ambassador to the UN in 1952. Sawada states that 'There is no reason to doubt that Japan is capable of carrying out the United Nations Charter and that she is a peace-loving nation.' He continues, however, to declare that 'Russia has used her veto power to prevent Japan's UN entry each time a vote has been called.' He also emphasises that Japan is not only receiving benefits from the UN but also providing benefits to other countries. 'No matter what you say, Japan is still the most advanced nation in Asia,' he says, explaining that Japanese technical assistance has been directed to many parts of the world. The film ends with Miss Aoki's monologue that 'Japan must join the United Nations as early as possible so that we can cooperate with the United Nations in achieving its objectives hand in hand with all nations. This, in the end, is the surest road to peace.' In sum, *the United Nations and Japan* was a hybrid: it was an educational film offering factual information about the UN, an anti-communist film denouncing the Soviet Union and a statement to the Japanese audiences appealing to their sense of nationalism in order to support Japan's membership of the UN.

Some of the Japanese-produced films assumed a more didactic tone by introducing commendable attitudes or desirable activities so that Japanese people could become enlightened citizens of an internationally acknowledged nation. *UNESCO and Japan/UNESCO to watashitachi* (1952), produced by the Riken Film Company, was one such example. The film combines dramatised dialogue, a voice narration and live filming of activities by members of Japanese UNESCO Associations. It opens with film of the chaotic urban scenes of postwar Japan showing street children, prostitutes and exhausted soldiers returning home from abroad. The camera then captures an elderly farmer grumbling 'Oh, I hate wars,' as he watches his family happily tending the farm. The camera switches to a young fisherman telling his fellows 'Most of my friends died in the war. It is miracle that I am still alive. Now I really wish to build a peaceful nation.' We then focus on a group of young men and women sitting idly in the ruined city. One young man says 'We should purge the politicians who led the war.' A young woman replies saying that 'We should elect politicians who would work for peace. I am fed up with militarists.' A second woman says 'We should write in the constitution that we will never fight a war again.' The first man then says, 'But first of all, everyone has to determine never to cause a war' because 'peace and war begin in the minds of men.' After this opening sequence, the film introduces the establishment of UNESCO and the Japanese UNESCO Associations, which sprang up in many cities even before Japan became a member of UNESCO in 1951.

The film shows the activities of the UNESCO Associations and UNESCO Clubs – youth groups affiliated with the UNESCO Associations. Two college students, who are members of a UNESCO Club visit a rural village, for example, and call for a town meeting on 'how to improve human relations'. A young woman speaks up and complains about the 'undemocratic and premodern' customs still remaining in her village. The two students leading the discussion urge the villagers to find solutions through group discussion. A voice narration says 'Cooperation with UNESCO, just as this example indicates, means the application of UNESCO's spirit of peace to familiar issues.' The film also introduces a UNESCO Women's Association activity involving the study of domestic life overseas through the use of English-language home magazines. We are informed that 'Impressed with the rational and scientific manner' of home life shown in the magazine, the group have decided to purchase an electric washing machine. 'This way', the voice narration says, 'the women's group learned the spirit of cooperation.' Moreover, to deploy the time they have saved by 'rationalising' their housekeeping chores, they have volunteered to fundraise for the 'reconstruction of Korea campaign'. The film then goes on to show the 'UNESCO Children's Exhibition' held in the 'UNESCO Village' – a kind of UNESCO theme park with miniature houses representing all sixty-four UNESCO member countries.[28]

The film thus interprets 'cooperation with UNESCO' as a modernisation project involving the eradication of 'undemocratic' and 'premodern' elements from rural villages, the introduction of home electronics to 'rationalise' home life and the creation of a modern version of childhood protected by a healthy and educational environment. UNESCO society members such as the students visiting rural villages and the women studying the 'domestic life of foreign countries' were the 'interpreters' of modernisation, who before the eyes of the villagers, as well as the screen audience, embodied the 'spirit' of UNESCO in a tangible form. In this sense, the UN or UNESCO assumed a similar status to Hollywood film in occupied Japan as 'fountains of culture' from which audiences could learn a modern and democratic way of life and thought. Just like the 'cultural elites' in occupied Japan who promoted an 'enlightenment campaign' using Hollywood films, students and housewives used UNESCO to promote their own modernising project.[29] One should remember, however, that *UNESCO and Japan* was a USIS film sponsored by the US government. For the US government, the UN and UNESCO remained a door through which to invite Japan to become part of the US-centred, postwar world order on a political, economic and cultural level.

These diverse examples of USIS films about the UN indicate that they did not convey one single, unified message. They also differed in terms of the overtness of their political message or the degree to which they included elements of entertainment. The films produced in Japan were especially hybrid in the way that they combined factual information, anti-communist propaganda, messages of enlightenment and modernisation, and an appeal to Japanese national pride to participate in the UN. Just like the CIE films, the USIS films about the United Nations were thus multifaceted entities. In sum, they were neither simple propaganda movies nor neutral and apolitical tools of education.

THE JAPANESE DESIRE FOR UN MEMBERSHIP

Although the USIS films about the UN reflected the US government's worldview that they wished the Japanese to understand and internalise, the films also reflected a desire on the part of the Japanese to become a legitimate member of international society. As soon as the San Francisco Peace Treaty became effective and Japan regained independence in April 1952, the Japanese government applied for UN membership. This wish did not however come true until 1956, mainly because of the Soviet Union's veto in the UN Security Council. It was only after the Soviet–Japanese Joint Declaration, signed on 19 October 1956, that the Soviet government finally agreed to support Japan's application. Since the Soviet Union had not signed the Treaty of Peace with Japan in 1951, this declaration officially restored diplomatic relations between the two countries for the first time since World War II.

There were roughly two strands of thought underlying Japan's aspiration to join the UN; one concerning the strategic needs of the government and the other concerning nationalistic sentiment at a grassroots level. Firstly, the US–Japan Security Treaty and the development of a stable relationship with Third World countries were the twin pillars of postwar Japanese diplomacy, and UN membership served both purposes. Since the new Japanese Constitution prohibited Japan from having armed forces, the Japanese government needed some form of legal basis to allow Japan's military alliance with the US, namely the US–Japan Security Treaty. The UN Charter that 'admits countries to have the right of collective self-defence' functioned as a useful excuse for the Japanese government to legitimatise the Security Treaty.[30] Likewise, UN membership helped to improve relationships with Third World countries. Many Asian countries remembered Japanese military expansionism during World War II and were suspicious of Japan's re-emergence on the international stage. To win support from Third World countries, the Japanese government undertook diplomatic efforts such as participating in the Bandung Conference (Asian-African Conference) held in April 1955. Out of the twenty-nine countries from Asia and Africa present at the conference, seventeen were already UN members. The conference adopted a resolution to promote UN membership of the non-member countries, including Japan. As soon as it successfully gained UN membership, Japan also entered the 'Asia Africa Group' of the organisation in order to seek stronger ties with Third World countries.[31]

The second line of thought came from the aspiration of Japan's citizens to become a legitimate member of the 'family of nations', although it is also important to understand that such an aspiration was boosted, and even exploited, by influential political and business leaders. As Hiroshi Kitamura has pointed out, Japanese people, tired of a long and gloomy war, maintained a sincere desire for a democratic, modern and cultured society.[32] The non-governmental 'UNESCO Movement' was founded in Sendai on 19 July 1947 with the goal of achieving UNESCO membership, and the movement soon spread rapidly across the nation. When Japan was admitted to UNESCO in 1951, five years before gaining UN membership, Maeda Tamon,[33] head of the UNESCO movement, stated that 'The spirit of UNESCO is the guiding principle for Japan, which is on the path of rebuilding itself as a peace-loving and democratic state.'[34] The UN Association of Japan was also organised in 1947. Soon after the San Francisco Peace Treaty was signed, the Association collected 300,000 signatures on a petition asking the UN to admit Japan's membership. Although this may sound like the representation of a genuine grassroots interest in the UN, in fact the signatures were systematically collected by local branches of the UN Association and submitted to the UN by three influential men: Uchiyama Iwatarō, director of the Kanagawa branch of the association; Odawara Daizō, executive director of the Kansai branch, and Nakanishi Binji, vice-director of the Tokyo branch. Uchiyama was a retired diplomat specialising in Spanish-speaking countries and had served in the Japanese embassies in Spain, Chile, Brazil and Argentina before the war. He played an important role in persuading the Philippines to support Japan's admission to the UN. The Philippines had badly suffered during the Japanese military invasion and therefore held strong resistance against Japan's UN membership. Odawara was president of Kubota Steel Company and was an important figure in the business community. Nakanishi was vice-chairman of the Tokyo Metropolitan Assembly. He was present at the General Assembly of 21 December 1952, when voting results allowed the UN membership of Japan – only to see that the vote was later vetoed by the Soviet Union in the UN Security Council.[35] These influential leaders backed the so-called 'grassroots' movement motivated by civic nationalism.

CONCLUSION

The CIE and the USIS films were both first and foremost an overseas information programme on the part of the US government. They aimed to disseminate favourable images of the US and win the hearts and minds of people in foreign countries. Many had subtle pro-US or anti-communist messages although a small number conveyed more overt forms of communication. The USIS films about the UN displayed the same tendencies. Many of them had entertaining elements, and subtle political messages were embedded in their stories. A small number, especially those films produced immediately after the Korean War, assumed an overt anti-communist tone.

Some of the CIE films produced in Japan dealt with the modernisation and democratisation of Japan. This was also true with the USIS films about the UN produced in Japan, but their narratives were more complicated. These films conflated Japan's participation in international organisations with the progress of Japanese society. The films educated Japanese people to strive for a modern, democratic and cultured nation and cooperate with the UN membership movement. If they made progress, the films implied, Japan would rediscover a decent place within international society. The films both boosted and exploited civic nationalism as they mobilised people for the UN movement by appealing to their genuine desire for a better society.

The Japanese initiative to acquire UN membership was both a top-down and bottom-up phenomenon. On the one hand, it came from the Japanese government's ambition for power and the US government's reliance on Japan as a prominent anti-communist ally. Nonetheless, active participation of Japanese citizens in various UNESCO and the UN Association activities also reveals a degree of bottom-up initiative on the part of the Japanese citizens themselves. Although the two associations were led by former diplomats and business leaders, and were therefore not purely spontaneous citizens' organisations, they were also supported by citizens' genuine hopes for a new, democratic Japan and a more modern and enlightened way of living.

As John W. Dower has argued, the US Occupation stirred up an 'efflorescence of popular sentiment and initiative' that involved 'the refashioning of the very meaning of "Japan"'. There was also a lot of 'grass-roots thinking about what embracing democracy might mean'.[36] The bottom-up initiative to promote UN membership also reflected a grassroots momentum to create a new, democratic and respectable national identity for Japan. At the same time, as the USIS films about the UN produced in the post-Occupation period such as *The United Nations and Japan* indicate, the bottom-up initiative was also fuelled by a form of popular nationalism stirred up by the end of foreign occupation and newly gained independence.

The USIS films about the United Nations thus formed a unique genre of educational and documentary films in postwar Japan. They were not neutral information tools; instead, they assumed a number of loaded meanings that vividly reflected both US and Japanese governmental and non-governmental desires and ambitions of the period.

Notes

1. There is a wide literature on the Japanese Occupation in both Japanese and English. English-language examples include John W. Dower, *Embracing Defeat: Japan in the Wake of World War II* (New York: W.W. Norton, 2000); Eiji Takemae, *Inside GHQ: The Allied Occupation of Japan and Its Legacy* (London: Continuum International Publishing Group, 2002).
2. The author's Japanese-language book (revised and translated from an English-language doctoral dissertation in 2004) focuses on the activities of the CIE including its film programme. See Tsuchiya Yuka, *Shinbei nihon no kōchiku: America no tainichi jōhō kyōiku seisaku to nihon senryō* (Tokyo: Akashi shoten, 2009).
3. Dower, *Embracing Defeat*, pp. 88–9, 121–2, 244–53.
4. For changes in the CIE films, see Tsuchiya, *Shinbei nihon no kōchiku*, pp. 146, 151.
5. Kyoko Hirano, *Mr. Smith Goes to Tokyo: Japanese Cinema under the American Occupation, 1945–1952* (Washington, DC: Smithsonian Institute, 1992). [Editors' note: for more on the question of censorship during the Occupation, see also Chapter 9 by Rachael Hutchinson in this volume.]
6. Hiroshi Kitamura, *Screening Enlightenment: Hollywood and the Cultural Reconstruction of Defeated Japan* (Ithaca, NY: Cornell University Press, 2010).
7. Tanikawa Takeshi, *Amerika eiga to senryō seisaku* (Kyoto: Kyoto University Press, 2002).
8. Ibid., p. 236.
9. Abe Akira, *Sengo chihō kyōiku seido seiritsu katei no kenkyū* (Tokyo: Kazama shobō, 1983).
10. Shiba Shizuko, *Sengo kateika kyōiku seiritsu kankei shiryō ni kansuru chōsa-kenkyū*, Report of the JSPS Kaken, 2001–2002 (2003).

11 Nakamura Hideyuki, 'Senryōka beikoku kyōiku eiga ni tsuiteno Oboegaki: *Eiga kyōshitsu* ni miru Natco (eishaki) to CIE eiga no juyō ni tsuite', *CineMagaziNet!* no. 6 (2002), <http://www.cmn.hs.h.kyoto-u.ac.jp/cmn6/nakamura.htm>.

12 Tsuchiya Yuka and Yoshimi Shun'ya (eds), *Senryō suru me, senryō suru koe: CIE/USIS eiga to VOA rajio* (Tokyo: University of Tokyo Press, 2012).

13 This figure is based on the statistical data collected by Occupation forces. The author's examination of records kept by one Prefectural audiovisual library confirms this to be approximately correct.

14 For details on the CIE films, see Tsuchiya, *Shinbei nihon no kōchiku*, pp. 128–55, and Tsuchiya and Yoshimi, *Senryō suru me, senryō suru koe*, pp. 3–6.

15 Mary Tin Yi Lui, 'Nōson seinen no California hōmon: America bunka gaikō no batoshite no kazoku nōjō', in Tsuchiya and Yoshimi, *Senryō suru me, senryō suru koe*, pp. 157–82; *New Neighbors/Atarashii rinjin* (1952), 9 mins; *The Communist Conspiracy/Aka no inbō* (1952), 21 mins; *White Collar Worker/America no sararīman* (1951), 21 mins. Courtesy of the University of Tokyo.

16 *For a Bright Home Life/Akarui katei seikatsu* (1950), 21 mins; *Men Who Fish/Sunadoru hitobito* (1950), 25 mins. Courtesy of the University of Tokyo.

17 Interview with Okazaki Kōzō, in Tsuchiya and Yoshimi, *Senryō suru me, senryō suru koe*, pp. 345–53.

18 The audience reactions were originally cited in Tsuchiya, *Shinbei nihon no kōchiku*, pp. 185–91. The original sources are stored at the US National Archives in College Park, Maryland, RG331, CI&E, box 5269.

19 *The USIS Film Catalogue* in Japan was published, at least, in 1953, 1959 and 1966.

20 *United Nations Finds a Home/Kokuren honbu no tanjō* (1950), 23 mins. Courtesy of the University of Tokyo.

21 *Town Meeting of the World/Sekai no tsudoi* (1952), 14 mins. Courtesy of the University of Tokyo.

22 *USIS Film Catalogue 1953*.

23 'Kokuren to nihon', brochure, RG306, Entry A1 1098, box 47, the National Archives at College Park.

24 On 24 October 1945, the UN Charter became effective as more than half of the signatories (fifty countries) have ratified it. Since then, that day has been celebrated as UN day. UN Information Center website, <http://www.unic.or.jp/info/un/>.

25 He was one of the Japanese delegates who marched out of the League of Nations General Assembly in 1933 when the League adopted the report of the Lytton Investigation Mission denying the legitimacy of Japanese-controlled Manchukuo. 'Kindai nihonjin no shōzō', Japanese National Diet Library website, <http://www.ndl.go.jp/portrait/datas/413.html?cat=11>.

26 *United Nations and Japan*, script, RG306, Entry A1 1098, box 47, National Archives at College Park.

27 Sawada was married to Miki, granddaughter of Iwasaki Yatarō, founder of the Mitsubishi Zaibatsu. Miki is the founder of the Elizabeth Sanders Home, an orphanage for children born between US soldiers and Japanese women. Tottori Prefectural Archives (ed.), *Sawada Renzō to Miki no jidai* (2010).

28 *UNESCO and Japan/UNESCO to watashitachi* (1952), 20 mins, Riken Film Company. Courtesy of the University of Tokyo.

29 Kitamura, *Screening Enlightenment*.

30 Kawabe Ichirō, 'Kokuren chūshin shugi', *Nihon to kokuren: Tagenteki shiten karano saikō: Kokuren Kenkyū* no. 13 (June 2012), pp. 56–9.

31 Nomura Akio, 'Nihon to kokuren: Reisen jidai no 30-nen', in Akashi Yasushi, Takasu Yukio, Nomura Akio, Ōshiba Ryō and Akiyama Nobumasa (eds), *Oral History: Nihon to kokuren no 50-nen* (Kyoto: Minerva shobō, 2008), pp. 1–3.

32 Kitamura, *Screening Enlightenment*.

33 Maeda Tamon was a prominent bureaucrat and politician throughout the prewar and postwar years. He served as minister of education in 1945 to 1946, but was purged by the US Occupation Forces because of his political career before and during the war. He was rehabilitated in 1950, and until his death in 1962, he engaged in various civic and international causes including UNESCO. Kōdansha, JapanKnowledge Lib, <https://japanknowledge.com/lib/display/?lid=10800ED003004>.

34 National Federation of UNESCO Associations in Japan (NFUAJ) website, <http://www.unesco.or.jp/unesco/role/>.

35 UN Association of Japan, *Kokuren kamei sokushin kokumin shisetsudan kikoku hōkokusho*, February 1953, pp. 1–8, 13–4, 19–22.

36 Dower, *Embracing Defeat*, pp. 121–2, 239–44.

33
SOCIAL PROTEST
Japanese student movement cinema: A dialogic approach

Masato Dogase

What approach can a film take to effectively engage people in social protest? Historically, many Japanese films have dealt with this theme going back to the emergence of the tendency film (*keikō eiga*) in the late 1920s and early 1930s, which, because of state censorship, only implicitly portrayed protest by impoverished peasants and Marxists. In the immediate post-World War II period, well-known films such as Kurosawa Akira's *No Regrets for Our Youth Life/Waga seishun ni kui nashi* (1946) and Yamamoto Satsuo's *Zone of Emptiness/Shinkū chitai* (1952) depicted various acts of social protest: the former celebrated prewar student protests at Kyoto University while the latter tried to support the postwar anti-war movement by revealing the concealed wartime violence committed by the Japanese army. The subsequent number of fiction films designed to represent social protest is vast. Some films have only allegorically depicted postwar Japanese social movements – such as those about the liberation of Japan's discriminated communities (*burakumin*), the miners' labour movement, the student protest movement and the anti-nuclear movement – by weaving these topics into a more general representation of the past and/or by adopting a commercial form of melodramatic expression. Other production companies have not necessarily made profit a priority. Independent production companies, most notably the Art Theatre Guild (ATG), subsidised film-makers – such as Ōshima Nagisa, Matsumoto Toshio, Yoshida Kijū and Terayama Shūji – who pursued film-making as an artistic practice rather than a commercial activity. Porn film (*pink eiga*) production also provided film-makers such as Wakamatsu Kōji, Adachi Masao and Takechi Tetsuji with the benefit of securing their freedom of expression, and allowing them to incorporate otherwise taboo pro-protest themes into their films.[1]

Documentary films have traditionally taken a more direct approach as film-makers have committed themselves to pro-filmic action in order to support different forms of social protest. Examples here include the work of *Prokino* (the Japanese Proletarian Film Alliance), which made films in order to promote the proletarian movement in the late 1920s and early 1930s;[2] Kamei Fumio's *Record of Blood: Sunagawa/Ryūketsu no kiroku: Sunagawa* (1956), which engaged in the protests against the construction of the US military base in Sunagawa, and Matsumoto Toshio's *Security Treaty/ANPO jōyaku* (1959), which explored a form of experimental film editing to represent the resistance to the planned amendment of the new Japan–US Security Treaty of 1960. Aside from different forms of filmic representation, film-makers have at times also directly committed themselves to protests such as the series of disputes at Tōhō studios in the later 1940s. Grassroots activists have also endeavoured to support the expansion of social protest through screenings of the above-mentioned films and others.[3] The 1950s and 1960s are a vital period in this context not only because social movements were thriving but also because no other period in Japanese film history has seen film-makers – especially documentary film-makers – so ardently engaged on both a personal and professional level.

Several film scholars have discussed the issue of how documentary film can boost social movements. In Jane Gaines's influential essay 'Political Mimesis', she explores how documentary film can mobilise an audience to commit themselves to social protest, especially through the visceral image of a body on screen.[4] Markus Nornes deploys this concept when he examines Ogawa Shinsuke's documentary *Summer in Sanrizuka/Nihon kaihō sensen: Sanrizuka no natsu* (1968), and contends that it succeeded in mobilising audiences to protest against the construction of Narita International Airport in Sanrizuka precisely because it generated a degree of political mimesis between the protester on screen and the audience off screen.[5] While this view is certainly persuasive in the way that the filmic image may affect the audience, it is still questionable whether political mimesis can actually drive people who are indifferent to a particular social movement to the point of protest. In fact, documentary film-makers of the 1950s and 1960s were pursuing a different approach from that of political mimesis. This is what I call, instead, the 'dialogic mode'. Even if the term itself did not exist at the time, I will use it to refer to the ways in which a documentary film may facilitate a form of dialogue between the film-maker, the people on screen and the audience.[6]

This chapter will discuss the dialogic mode as it was theorised by documentary film-makers of the 1950s and 1960s and presented in their work. Ogawa's *Summer in Sanrizuka* can, for example, be seen as a representative work that embodies not only the spirit of political mimesis but also the matter of dialogism. This is apparent when we compare it with Kamei's *Record of Blood: Sunagawa*. The latter represents farmers and students' protest against the government's confiscation of land for a US military base, and uses voiceover narration to provide a political commentary with the aim of soliciting the audience's participation in the protest. In contrast, the former repeatedly shows the arguments and voices of its on-screen characters without rendering their opinions in a one-sided fashion; instead, the film presents them debating in conflict with each other. Thus, while *Summer in Sanrizuka* makes it difficult for the audience to understand its dialogue due to the confusing variety of differing opinions, this very difficulty urges the spectator to think more precisely about what the protest and the characters' struggle mean.[7] This form of cinematic expression was deliberate and aimed to construct a dialogic relationship not only amongst the people on screen but also between these people, various types of audiences and the film-makers themselves.[8]

Ogawa was not alone in exploring this dialogic mode; the same was true for Tsuchimoto Noriaki, Hara Kazuo and the Nihon Documentarist Union,[9] thus making this a significant strand in Japanese documentary practice of the time. In what follows, I will firstly illustrate how this mode was conceptualised in documentary practice and theory during the 1950s, ranging from the Iwanami Film Company's film-making practice to the theories of Iwanami's leading figure Hani Susumu and the work of Yoshida Naoya, a pioneer of the emerging form of the Japanese television documentary. I will then move on to scrutinise two documentary films from the 1960s: *Forest of Oppression – A Record of Struggle at Takasaki City University of Economics/Assatsu no mori – Takasaki keizai daigaku tōsō no kiroku (1967)*, directed by Ogawa, and *Japan, Year Zero/Dokyumento kōsei: Nippon zero nen* (1969), directed by Kawabe Kazuo and Fujita Shigeya. By analysing these documentaries, both of which filmed the student protests of the late 1960s, I will show how they attempted to guide audiences with different personal concerns to engage themselves in protest through their relationship with dialogism.

As I will argue, the development of this style of documentary film-making was closely related to the intermedial situation of the 1950s and the 1960s in which the ways of making film, television and radio programmes both clashed and colluded with each other. This was also connected to the social conditions at the time. By the early 1970s, Japanese society was enjoying a period of economic high growth and had gradually come to favour stability while simultaneously rejecting the young people who carried forward the idea of 'revolution' through violent means. In other words, as well shall now see, the dialogic mode was a necessary means for documentary film-makers to confront the difficult conditions and isolation of young students without necessarily harming the social majority's general feelings about society.

A GENEALOGY OF DIALOGIC EXPRESSION IN POSTWAR JAPANESE DOCUMENTARY

A prototypical example of dialogism may be found in several 1950s' documentaries where the question of how to treat the diversity of people's voice and posture was pursued in order to promote postwar democratisation. A typical example appears in the conversation scenes of the films produced by the Iwanami Film Company, the outfit that dominated Japanese documentary at the time. A comparison between their work and the democratic propaganda films produced under the control of the Civil Information and Education Section (CIE) in the Occupation period (1945–52) reveals how they created this new form of expression. In the most famous of the CIE films, *Children's Council/ Kodomo gikai* (1947), for example, which designated a new means of child education through children's own arguments, the film's staging and editing appear to be fictitious since the script was obviously prepared for the children and there is a didactic voiceover for the purpose of democratic enlightenment.[10] In the representation of their discussions in particular, the children's dialogue proceeds impartially, on a one by one basis, with the camera almost always focusing specifically on the child who is talking. At the point a child finishes her/his speech, the image cuts to the next speaker. The simple editing technique of always matching the voice of the child with her/his speaking face may mean that the spectator is able to easily locate the child speaking on screen, but the debate also appears like a staged performance.

The Iwanami films work in contrast to this. *School for Village Women/Mura no fujin gakkyū* (1957), for example, shows women having a discussion in a classroom. The staging and editing are more based on reality, and we see people speaking without any form of a script. In the debate scene, for instance, a woman starts to make a number of remarks. Then, while her voice continues on the soundtrack, the image switches to the faces of other women listening to her words as she proceeds. This method immediately makes both the opinion of the speaker and the response of the people around her available through the combination of image and sound and, in turn, represents the discussion as a whole. Although Iwanami's films were often criticised for being conventional because of the way their themes aligned with the democratic enlightenment objectives of the CIE, they were also epoch making in terms of exploring how to express democracy on its own terms.[11]

Hani Susumu was the most important film-maker at Iwanami. His representative work, *Children of the Classroom/Kyōshitsu no kodomotati* (1954), is seen today as a historical masterpiece for the way that it reveals the lively figures of the children of the day through the same audiovisual methods mentioned above (Figs. 33.1a–f). Generally though, his work did not show the same sophisticated means of representation of other films that deployed the dialogic mode. Nornes, for example, sees Hani's films as little more than examples of the observational techniques of Direct Cinema.[12] It is nevertheless important to investigate Hani's ideas because the theory polished in his writings

Figs. 33.1a–f. *Children of the Classroom/Kyōshitsu no kodomotachi* (Hani Susumu, 1954, Iwanami eiga).

apparently anticipated this link. Hani's book, *Camera and Microphone/Camera to maiku: Gendai geijutsu no hōhō* (1960), an anthology of essays written at the end of the 1950s, reveals two things that motivated him in his search for a new mode of expression. The first was his desire to overcome the same classical forms of film style as the *nouvelle vague*. As Yuriko Furuhata argues, Hani and Matsumoto Toshio, along with the film critic Okada Susumu, all came under the influence of French film discourse in their attempt to disseminate the concept of *eizō* (image) as a counter mode of visual expression to the continuity editing methods of classical Hollywood cinema and the old techniques of Soviet montage.[13] Here, Hani was no mere follower; he created many unique concepts of his own derived from his personal film viewing, and it was these ideas that went on to inform his subsequent examination of dialogical expression. The second motivation was a shift in the overall media environment along with the emergence of television; something which Furuhata calls that era's 'remediation'. Here, Hani had to consider how documentary film expression would accommodate this new reality.

Through his appreciation of Italian and French cinema, Hani advocated an observational single long-take aesthetic that in not depending on editing techniques apparently aligned himself with Okada Susumu's ideas derived from French film discourse. But reading Hani carefully, it also becomes apparent that his writings embraced several unique differences from Okada. A typical example may be found in what he meant by the use of the word *gyōshi* (fixed view), which he used as the Japanese translation of the single shot aesthetic. What he was stressing with the word *gyōshi* was less the photogenic beauty of the image itself than the practice of the film-maker and audience in trying to grasp this reality from the pro-filmic world.[14] Arguing from his stance as a documentary maker, Hani did not see the seemingly observational image represented through the single shot and long take as an untamed event simply being presented to the spectator; rather, he imagined the film-maker as someone fixing their camera and reflecting on the targeted event in order to capture the image as though it was the apparent expression of their own will and practice.

The aim of his argument, in contrast to the observational mode, was to engrave the trace of the film-maker's thought on the pro-filmic event with a new audiovisual mode of expression that also included the observational image. This idea definitely appears in his theory of 'new montage' that he planned to combine with the *gyōshi* form of expression. The key is that he conceived this not only in terms of the relationship between the film-maker and the object image, but in terms of a relationship that included the view of the spectator. To put it more simply, it was an attempt to combine the long-take *gyōshi* aesthetic with montage, both of which were both antithetical to the observational form. Hani described this in Eisensteinian language, claiming that 'new montage' would mean both the *gyōshi* image's 'collision with, and resistance against, fragmented montage as well as the collision of various fragmented images with each other'.[15] For Hani, 'montage', like the *gyōshi*, was therefore not merely an effect of filmic representation but a manifestation of the film-maker's 'endeavour to think [about the event] through film. Unlike the case with Hollywood cinema's system of continuity editing, which concealed any trace of editing behind the smooth transmission of narrative, the combination of *gyōshi* and 'montage', both of which revealed the trace of that film-maker's thinking, formed a relationship by which both forms of expression were accentuated in the collision of potentially equivalent aspects. This produced a very strong form of expression where the trace of the film-maker's thinking was 'revealed in front of the spectator all the time'.[16]

On the other hand, this new form of editing meant that the spectator had to confront the traces of the film-maker's thoughts on the pro-filmic event revealed through the *gyōshi* and montage. Here, Hani claimed that spectators were not being confronted with a 'formalistic montage', intended to agitate them in a way akin to the expressive propaganda of Soviet socialism, but instead they were being given the chance to 'take part in the film-maker's thought processes about the event'.[17] 'New montage' was thus an imaginary site from where the film-maker and the spectator could think dialogically about the object event shown. Hani was acutely aware of spectatorial address with this mode of expression. He did not aspire to the smooth transmission of information 'filling in the holes or bridging the gaps between each documented fragment'; rather his goal was 'to reveal how deep the rifts are', to reveal contradictions, confusion and complexity, and 'to brace the spectators and inspire' them.[18]

The dialogic mode used in documentaries at the end of 1960s goes back to a methodological discourse at the end of 1950s that Nornes calls 'a turning point for documentary in Japan'.[19] Moreover, such methodology existed in tandem with the new media environment of the 1960s that Furuhata has suggested as the point at which 'the existing boundaries of media and artistic genres were finally dismantled'.[20] While Hani's ideas originally arose from French filmic discourse discussed by Okada Susumu in his writing, it was the specific emergence of television that prompted him to deepen his theory on different forms of cinematic expression. Television forced Hani and other film producers to reconsider the relationship between the film-maker and their audience. Here, interestingly, Hani not only focused his discussion on television but also radio programmes; something that remains relatively unexplored in the field of Japanese documentary studies. In fact, in his theory of 'new montage', Hani intended to find a means of 'collaboration utilizing the unique characteristics of the three media'.[21] Although radio was seen as an 'old medium' at the time, it had also been an important one after the war when the General Headquarters, Supreme Commander for the Allied Power (GHQ/SCAP) set about changing Japanese views by dramatising the atrocities of the

Imperial Japanese Army.[22] One of those programmes, *Street Recordings/Gaitō rokuon*, produced by collecting various uninhibited opinions from passers-by on the street, was very popular and eventually became a major element of the radio landscape in the postwar democratic era.[23] In addition, this kind of programme, later called acoustic recorded composition (*rokuon kōsei*), was put together by editing the raw audio recordings of citizens' statements along with narration from a radio announcer.[24] The radio's recording microphone, not limited by a frame the way the camera was, not only picked up the voices of interviewees on the street but also other voices and noises behind them. Furthermore, because the programmes were not organised around a continuity structure that dictated how they should be edited – as with the match cuts of visual media – such variegated audio sources were edited together in a way that was purely based on the whim of the producer. This generated a far more innovative form of radio programme. Hani stated that:

> It is a way of recording which exploits the context of their [the object of the recording's] own manner of talking as much as possible, and includes the contradictions and confusion buried in themselves, the social inevitability behind their seemingly selfish excuses, and a form of logic within their strange behaviour.[25]

Hani directly attempted to bring this new form of audio expression derived from the radio to the way his filmic method revealed the 'chaotic' factual complexity of his subjects. In this sense, he conceptualised a dialogic model of film theory whereby the film-maker faced the documented object. Rather than subjecting the object to her/his intention by merely observing it, his method also included the audience and their thoughts thus creating a dialogue between the film-maker, the documented object and the spectator.

At the time, many film producers and critics, including Matsumoto Toshio, actively sought new modes of media expression such as the one Furuhata discusses, and this led to a form of reciprocal interaction between film and television practice and theory. Among them was a pioneer in Japanese television documentary, the influential NHK television programme producer Yoshida Naoya. Yoshida was the leading producer of the famous programme *The True Face of Japan/Nihon no sugao* (1957–64), which opened the door to the television documentary boom at the end of 1950s. The programme's production staff members were originally radio producers with no knowledge of film-making so they applied production strategies used in radio and ended up producing numerous innovative documentaries. The eighth programme in the series, 'Japanese and Jirochō/Nihonjin to Jirochō' (1958), which focused on gambling patterns amongst actual yakuza, resonated with audiences as 'it was distinct from other yakuza movies' and 'impossible to see by any ordinary way'.[26] Hani was, in fact, conscious of forms of expression found in radio when developing his theory, and his ideas came from a sincere admiration for the art of the radio producer.[27] Yoshida was often criticised for proposing the idea of 'fairness and neutrality' (*kōsei chūritsu*) that afterwards became a symbol of the NHK's non-political stance in its programme making. He also fomented a dispute on documentary methodology with Hani in the famous journal *Chūōkōron*, which was a memorable event for many television producers.[28] Yoshida, however, shared some of Hani's ideas about documentary making such as the importance of renovating conventional cinematic methods or depicting the process of the film-maker's thinking in the documentary production.

The reconsideration of the relationship between voice and image that Hani and Yoshida both proposed at approximately the same time directly anticipated the dialogic mode. At a round-table discussion with Hani and others, Yoshida put forward the idea of a 'new way of using the *eizō*' in which, through phrases such as 'thinking mediated through words', 'thinking with the image' and 'thinking through sound only', he envisaged the separate functioning of human thought about the word, the image and sound. Yoshida imagined a mode of expression that swung between these elements 'like a pendulum', sometimes being dominated by the image and at other times overwhelmed by sound.[29] Hani immediately responded to this idea, discussing an unsynchronised form of audiovisual expression being a novelty for television. He argued that 'in film, sound is subordinate to image', which therefore calls for its synchronisation with the image, and noted that since in radio there is nothing but sound, it bears a heavier responsibility for providing explanation. However, according to Hani, in television 'sound has the power not to be inferior to the image', since it can be free from its 'expository function'.[30] In this way, the traditional hierarchical cinematic relationship between image and sound was being reconsidered in the form of a more 'televisual relationship' that emerged from discussions between the two men. Thereafter, as Nakamura Hideyuki argues in his essay on Tsuchimoto's *Minamata: The Victims and Their World* (1971), this eventually became a means of expression that stimulated the spectator's thought through an active discrepancy between the movement of the speaking patient's lips and the image and her/his audible voice on the soundtrack.[31]

Furthermore, Yoshida conceptualised a method of depicting the film-maker's process of thought as a 'working hypothesis' (*sagyō kasetsu*), and explained this by contrasting it to documentary films of the past. As a member of the younger generation, Yoshida originally had doubts about the ideologically biased portrayals in Iwanami's documentaries or Kamei's *Record of Blood: Sunagawa*, which prejudged good and evil in the clash between students and the riot police and tried to 'explain the justness' of the students to the spectator.[32] Yoshida thus formulated a method that 'hypothesised' the film-maker's view of the documented object, and composed the documentary film as a process of examination into whether the hypothesis was right or wrong. In this way, he argued, unlike the case with 'foregone documentaries' that relied on 'ideological notions', the film-maker could demonstrate 'a process of thinking' without 'concealing' anything that contradicted the original working hypothesis.[33]

Although sometimes associated with the idea of 'fairness and neutrality', Yoshida's own theory was never meant to produce apolitical films that silenced the film-makers' own stance or opinions; in fact, it did the opposite and stressed the film-maker's thoughts. The idea of 'fairness and neutrality' was a way for the film-maker to declare their political stance and criticise ideological bias. What might be criticised is the fact that Yoshida proposed his method as a scientific formula applicable to all documentary objects and to be used by everyone. Satō Tadao condemned this, claiming that in cases dealing with a straightforward issue such as Minamata disease, where it is obvious who the victims are, Yoshida's theory was likely to 'abandon from the beginning any chance of speaking from those victims standpoint'.[34] Furthermore, in his collaborative work on Japanese television, Yoshida had no claim to sole authorship for the programmes he worked on, and other colleagues, superficially following his idea of 'fairness and neutrality', gradually assimilated classical cinematic methods into their work. As a result, *The True Face of Japan* took an observational approach that rendered the film-makers and their thoughts invisible. Hani had already sharply criticised Yoshida for this at the end of 1950s, and it became the impetus for a dispute between the two men who otherwise shared similar ideas.[35] However, as Satō mentioned, ideas such as the working hypothesis were 'occurring so naturally everywhere in the television documentary world' that traces of it could also be found in the dialogic mode films discussed in the next section.[36]

A DIALOGUE BETWEEN THE INCOMPATIBLE: MODES OF EXPRESSION IN STUDENT PROTEST FILMS

How did successive documentarists take up this dialogic mode and the critical arguments raised by Hani and Yoshida? Independent documentaries by Tsuchimoto Noriaki and Ogawa Shinsuke provide clear characteristics of this form of expression. Tsuchimoto and Ogawa not only had ties to Iwanami Film, since they started their film careers there, they were also influenced by the growth of television documentaries, including various programmes directed by Yoshida, that overlapped with their adolescence – the time they set their sights on becoming film-makers. From a thematic perspective, much of this work appeared in films about the student protest movement. In this section, I will focus on two student protest films, Ogawa Productions' *Forest of Oppression* and the most 'dialogic' work of all, *Japan, Year Zero*, in order to explore how and why the student protest documentaries of the late 1960s relied on a dialogic style in their pursuit of young students with cameras and microphones. One possible factor was the gap in social status between the film-makers and the younger students who were the subject of the documentary. As Oguma Eiji has pointed out, while Japanese avant-garde cultures depicting students and young people were flourishing at that time, the actual producers of this culture were from an older generation and thus already taking a more active role in society than the subjects of their work.[37] Needless to say, Ogawa, Tsuchimoto and the producers of *Japan, Year Zero* were no exception and not the central actors of the student movement. They were essentially mere observers watching from the outside of youth culture. In order to recognise their status as outsiders, they thus actively confronted the young students on a dialogic basis in an attempt to transcend the limitations of an observational style of documentary film-making.

Tsuchimoto joined Iwanami in admiration of Hani's work and strove to pursue Hani's style. Apart from producing commercial PR films for Iwanami, which he did when he began working there, he was also impressed by the television documentaries produced for Yoshida's *True Face of Japan* that 'depicted not products, but humans'.[38] This became the motivation behind the production of one of his masterpieces, *An Engineer's Assistant/Aru kikan joshi* (1963). For his part, Ogawa often incorporated both the Hani-esque techniques he learned at Iwanami and Yoshida's more 'hypothetical' methods into his films. An example may be seen in *Report from Haneda/Gennin hōkokusho: Haneda tōsō no kiroku* (1967), a post-mortem of the Haneda incident when a student died after a clash with riot police. Using a free montage of testimonial photographs and audio recordings of the incident, Ogawa investigated the cause of the death based on his hypothesis that the police had killed him deliberately.

These documentarists sought to support the repressed minorities' social protests in the struggle against Minamata disease, the construction of Narita airport and in the student movement as a whole. However, looking at the work more thoroughly, it also appears that the documentaries do not uncritically espouse the justice of the protests; nor do they call for immediate solidarity from the audience. Rather, they reveal the different paradoxes of the social protests by capturing the various attitudes and voices connected to them, something that indeed follows the tenets of dialogic practice.[39] The most outstanding example of this appears in Ogawa's *Forest of Oppression* about the student movement at Takasaki City University of Economics. A production planning document left by the Jishu jōei soshiki no kai (Independent Screening Organization), or Jieiso for short, organised by Ogawa, stated that the project was 'built on the solidarity of the "subjects" (*shutai*), i.e. the students at Takasaki Economics University and the *shutai* of Jieiso',[40] suggesting a sense of unified film-making activity closely affiliated with the student protests. Nevertheless, the finished work itself does not manifest any apparent intention on the part of the film-makers and students to call for solidarity with the movement. At the beginning of the film, a calm male voiceover narration explains the threats that the student protesters have received from the university administrators and student athletes. In the scenes that follow, however, with the exception of brief explanations of the events shown on screen, the film devotes itself to avoiding explanation and captures the students and their enthusiastic voices so vividly that it does not have the chance to call on the audience's participation. As Oguma mentions, the immaturity of the young people prevents them from having the proper words to explain the complex suffering of modern society, meaning that the students can never clearly illustrate the reason they are fighting. Furthermore, the film does not help the students' attempt to explain their position; in fact, it seems to be attempting to confound an understanding of the students' spoken political ideology with its use of unsynchronised voices and mouths. While it flaunts the film-makers' critical attitude towards the school administrators in one scene where Ogawa himself argues with the students, it also displays an ambiguous stance towards the students that tends to call the justness of their position into question. Dissent among the students themselves is frequently on display. In one memorable scene at the beginning of the film, male student protesters cruelly converge on a female student. In another scene, they censure a person from the university's journalism society who does not cooperate with them and, in a later part of the film, they even force a student trying to escape in order to enjoy a summer vacation to return with them back to the protests (Fig. 33.2). In the midst of these scenes, Ogawa's camera and microphone continue to capture dissent between the protesters and the other neighbouring students without taking sides to the extent that an occasional sense of imperiousness is even uncovered amongst the protesters. Here, by depicting the students through neither an 'observational' nor a 'participatory' mode, but by means of a dialogic form of expression instead, the film reveals the fissures and contradictions amongst the students directly from inside the heart of the protest. Despite the use of the word 'oppression' in the title, which implies a form of public authority suppressing the students, the film depicts a situation in which the students' protests are isolated and corrupted because of their failure to gain their neighbours' understanding.

Unlike the case with the distribution of major film releases, *Forest of Oppression* was exhibited instead through the Jieiso's independent network and a number of small grassroots screenings in university circles. Nonetheless, it was highly praised in various quarters and helped Ogawa make his mark as a documentary film auteur. The accolades from critics and audiences centred not on the film's political ideology but rather its dialogic means of displaying the fissures and paradoxes within the documented object. The left-wing critic Matsuda Masao, for example, found an agitating force to the work and called it a masterpiece. But his evaluation was complicated. Focusing on the students' behaviour in terms of their 'mutual discussion', Matsuda completely denied the possibility of any solidarity amongst them. Instead, he was only engrossed by the dissent displayed by the film, calling it 'a drama of glibness, anger and quarrelling' that revealed 'a serious process from which an inexpressible sense of fissure comes' or 'a drama of non-discussion' in which 'any verbal communication fails'. Paradoxically, he judged that only this dissent could stimulate hostility to the power of authority on an emotional level.[41] By the same token, a viewer enthralled by the film said in one fan letter to a film magazine that in contrast to the people involved in the film's production who 'fanatically' stirred up anti-authority sentiments after the screening, 'the film's images might betray the film-makers because the 'matter-of-fact approach' to film-making that they took did not seem to be intended to stimulate agitation. He went on to say, 'one feels nothing but an almost frantic grimness' from the students and that he could but sympathise with the film's embodiment of a 'sense of isolation among modern people' that is the opposite of solidarity.[42] In this sense, instead of actually maintaining solidarity with the student's political ideology, the film's form of representation revealed the fractures or contradictions of its protagonist's position and evoked, in the form of a dialogic approach, the politically diverse audience's process of thought about the students.

A paradox thus arose in terms of how the film initially aimed at creating solidarity with the student protest. Although Nornes and Onozawa Toshihiko, a member of Jeiso, have both highlighted the film's solidarity with the protesters, particularly at screening activities, the matter of whether the film-makers were actually seeking solidarity in the first place remains open to debate.[43] The Ogawa Production cameraman Ōtsu Kōshirō (also the cameraman on *Japan, Year Zero*) has, for instance, said that both he and Ogawa avoided meeting up with the political groups in the production process and were 'thinking about film art

Fig. 33.2. A young male surrounded by student leaders in *Forest of Oppression – A Record of Struggle at Takasaki City University of Economics/Assatsu no mori – Takasaki keizai daigaku tōsō no kiroku* (Ogawa Shinsuke, 1967, Ogawa Productions). Courtesy of Athénée Français Cultural Center.

and its independence from politics'.[44] Ogawa has also mentioned in an interview that he declined a request to join their struggle from a student with a long wooden stick (*gebabō*) and swore that he would maintain his journalistic position 'with his camera as his weapon'.[45] It could thus be said that at least for these two leading makers of the film that the aim was not to 'participate' in the students' political protest.

The inclusion of the word composition (*kōsei*) in the title of the film, *A Documentary Composition: Japan, Year Zero/Document kōsei: Nippon zero nen*, consciously foregrounds its origins in radio and television's *rokuon kōsei* in a manner that intentionally utilises both Hani-esque and Yoshida-esque methodologies. As with *Forest of Oppression*, it is a record of the student movements of the day that features a male student participant, Ikegaya Hōmei, during the zenith of Tokyo University's struggles from the summer of 1968 to the Yasuda auditorium battle in January 1969. In a similar fashion to *Forest of Oppression*, the film does not aim at political solidarity with the students. By positioning the students within the whole of Japanese society, it explores how society confronts and interacts with them instead of displaying their isolation from it. So, while the film does focus on a single male student as the object of the documentary, it also turns its camera and microphone towards various other people, recording their interview responses and sometimes including the interviewee's questions. The documented objects, in these cases, include not only those close to Ikegawa, such as his lover (a theatre actress) and parents (both educators), but also his fellow youths who have no actual connection to him. These figures include a young woman (Sano Ryōko), called a '*fūten*', who has no regular job but makes a living in the city, and members of the Self-Defence Force who, at the time, were often portrayed in contrast to students within contemporary journalism.[46] In addition, the film critic Satō Tadao has an interview scene with Ikegaya and, in the latter part of the film, atomic bomb survivors argue with the students.

Nearly every image in this documentary shows individuals speaking, but these figures never develop any mutual understanding amongst each other. Rather, the dialogic mode reveals the rifts between them.

These rifts are divided into two main branches: one between the generations and the other within the young generation itself. In the first sequence, every opinion of the older generation collected from the streets expresses dislike for the students' protest; they say, for example, that they hate the idea of conflict 'amongst their fellow Japanese'. In the next scene we see the confusion that the older generation feels over the youth protests when Satō questions Ikegaya about whether they will continue their demonstrations after graduation and the film represents Ikegaya responding in a jumble through the desynchronisation of the sound of his words and the image of his mouth. After stressing these intergenerational rifts, the film then attempts to reveal a rift amongst the young themselves by turning their camera and microphone towards them. Ikegaya's lover 'S' sympathises with him more than anyone else in the film, but she also says she disagrees with the students over both their criticism of capitalism by way of an abrupt association with the Vietnam War and their failure to form any alliance with all students due to continuing internal discord.

While the rift between Ikegaya and 'S' appears in the direct representation of their actual discussions, the one between him and other youths is displayed through montage. The everyday activities of Sano as a *fūten* and the members of the Self-Defence Force are often inserted into pivotal episodes involving Ikegaya. Although the scenes involving these three agents are linked through parallel montage, they do not have any personal relationship with each other. On the one hand, the camera pursues Sano's activities in Shinjuku and captures her arguing about her way of life as a *fūten* with a few men at a bar and on the street. Having little interest in social and political issues, she simply indulges in wandering around town in search of her own identity. On the other hand, the scenes involving the Self-Defence Force comprise the film-maker pointing a microphone at the men and posing questions. In contrast to the interviews with the protesting students, the result is a collection of non-political voices. When asked about the reasons for their enrolment, some give personal reasons: rather than having any patriotic sentiments, they enrolled in order to earn a living or to have a worthwhile life. When asked about their awareness of the threat of war, one answers that he does not think war will happen anytime soon. Another young member gives his impression of the students, stating that, 'they are far removed from us,' symbolically showing that the Self-Defense Forces (SDF) members, the *fūten* and the students have no actual or political connections to each other. The juxtaposition of these scenes through parallel montage makes the fractures between them clear.

It might be said that *Japan, Year Zero* also uses the dialogic mode in order to depict the deep chasm surrounding the youth and their posture of isolation. However, it also seems that the film offers the glimpse of an advance beyond this. After revealing the rifts between the generations and between the youths, Ikegaya goes with 'S' to Hiroshima on the anniversary of the dropping of the atomic bomb since his mother was a survivor. There, the film-maker prepares a meeting with two bomb victims and they suddenly start an argument about the protest movement as if to expose the fact that the film-maker has staged the encounter. In contrast to Tsuchimoto's student protest film, *Prehistory of Partisans/Partisan zenshi* (1969), in which Nornes sees 'no serious links to other social movements', what this scene seeks to achieve is both a form of dialogue between the student protest movement and the protest movement against the atomic and hydrogen bomb (*gensuikin undō*), and a dialogue between the people who participate in social protest and those who do not. The one victim here is Emi, a woman working at an inn. After being forced to abort her unborn child due to radiation exposure, she embraces a hatred of the atomic bomb, but she disagrees with the boisterous *gensuikin undō* at the 6 August Memorial Day and simply wants to express her condolences to the victims silently without saying anything directly about their suffering. As for Ikegaya, although he partly sympathises as the son of a victim, he clashes with her over her unwillingness to take part in the protest. The other victim is a city employee named Takahashi Akihiro who has a major scar exposed on his arm as a result of the bomb. Takahashi's own wartime experience has prompted him to become involved in the *gensuikin undō* as an anti-war and anti-nuclear protester. He however criticises the students'

protests against the Vietnam War because he fears their ideological struggle will give rise to 'civil war' conditions. Although the *gensuikin undō* has ties to the Communist Party, causing ordinary citizens such as Emi to draw away from the movement, Takahashi thinks the movement must continue its anti-war and anti-nuclear demands without dwelling on ideology. Ikegaya agrees entirely with his opinion, and says that it is the manifestation of human anger towards war that is important and, at least on 6 August, he wants to call for a less politicised form of anti-war protest at Hiroshima. At the point this argument amongst the four, including 'S', concludes, Ikegaya immediately returns to the students' ideological struggle. Although all four struggle to find a way of reconciling their disparate political views, in the end their dialogue only serves to clarify the chasm between them. At this point, what matters more than any result is the 'process of thinking' about the student protests or social movement that has been expressed through the dialogic mode. Through a montage of the figures voicing their views, the film creates a more dialogic form of documentary that moves beyond the dichotomies between the agents and involves instead both the different patterns of thought of all the participants in the discussion and the original rationale of the film-makers who have helped to arrange the exchange. Because they were based on an ideological struggle, the student protests and the social movement it expressed were complicated and contentious issues for the majority of Japanese living in a capitalistic society of rapidly acquired wealth. Without providing any ideologically biased or simplistic answers, the film thus represents the complexity of this 'thinking' in its raw state through the negotiation of image, voice and actual argumentation.

To conclude, the dialogic form of expression in Japanese documentaries that started with the CIE film developed into a more specific mode involving the new production methods of both the postwar television and radio sectors in Japan. By the end of the 1960s, it had played an important role in the dialogic capture of the complexities of a society dramatically changed by a period of enormous economic growth.

In terms of the question of how a film may facilitate social protest, as Yoshida's argument reveals, this mode also contained the risk of hampering such a role. Dialogic expression overlapped with the method that Bill Nichols has called ethnographic 'participant-observation' in which the film-maker relates to the documented object but keeps an observational distance, thereby emphasising a disparity between the film-maker/spectator and the documented actors.[47] Certainly, as the film critic Kitakōji Takashi argues, *Summer of Sanrizuka* suggested a contrasting attitude to that of the ethnographic documentary that, he says, ignored the coevals between the film-maker from the colonising country and the documented colonised object that was based on the assumption of colonial superiority.[48] A film's dialogic approach may run a similar risk in that it still seeks to emphasise the social fissures and differences among its various agents.

After appearing in *Japan, Year Zero*, Satō called it a 'document for the discussion of the people'. This was an apt description since this method was not merely a means of exhibiting the views of film-makers and documented actors, it was also a way of displaying the film-maker's 'personality and social status in a critical manner'. It also served to inspire audiences to engage in discussion and make judgments for themselves as a way of facilitating democracy amongst what was, in fact, a non-homogeneous Japanese population.[49] In this way, the dialogic mode may best be considered as the manifestation of Japanese documentary film-makers' consciousness of postwar democracy and the significance of a diverse engagement with the social protests of the time.

ACKNOWLEDGMENT

This work was supported by JSPS KAKENHI Grant Number JP16K13182.

Notes

1. For discussion of protest on the part of Japanese film-makers, see Isolde Standish, *Politics, Porn and Protest: Japanese Avant-Garde Cinema in the 1960s and 1970s* (New York: Continuum, 2011).
2. Namiki Shinsaku, *Nihon proretaria eiga dōmei 'Prokino' zenshi* (Tokyo: Gōdō shuppan, 1986).
3. See Hideaki Fujiki, 'Cinema Citizens through Film Screenings: Cinema and Media in the Post-3.11 Social Movement', in Patrick W. Galbraith and Jason G. Karlin (eds), *Media Convergence in Japan* (Ann Arbor, MI: Kinema Club, 2016), pp. 60–87.
4. Jane M. Gaines, 'Political Mimesis', in Jane M. Gaines and Michael Renov (eds), *Collecting Visible Evidence* (Minneapolis: University of Minnesota Press, 1999), pp. 84–100.
5. Abé Mark Nornes, *Forest of Pressure: Ogawa Shinsuke and Postwar Japanese Documentary* (Minneapolis: University of Minnesota Press, 2007), pp. 98–103. [Editors' note: for more on Ogawa Productions, see also Chapter 26 by Ayumi Hata in this volume.]
6. The term is specific to the documentary film, but the idea can be traced back to Mikhail Bakhtin's *The Dialogic Imagination: Four Essays*, trans. Caryl Emerson and Michael Holquist (Austin: University of Texas Press, 1975).
7. Ayumi Hata suggests that the three critics, all with separate political views, were more attracted to the vivid presence of the young students than any sense of advocacy in their political arguments. See Hata Ayumi, 'Assatsu no mori saikō: 60 nendai ni okeru shintai to kotoba no sōkoku to realism', *JunCture* no. 1 (January 2010), p. 184.
8. Although this is applicable to the 'observational mode' or 'participatory mode' that Bill Nichols explains was a worldwide trend in documentary at the time, I also see it as a specific mode in Japanese documentary of the day that focuses on a manner that intentionally confuses the spectator and tries not to induce any easy understanding of the issues documented in the discussion. See Bill Nichols, *Introduction to Documentary* (Bloomington: Indiana University Press, 2010), pp. 172–94.
9. Yoshio Yasui and Noriko Tanaka (eds), *The Legendary Filmmaking Collective NDU and Nunokawa Tetsuro* (Kobe: Cinematrix and Kobe Documentary Film Festival Committee, 2012).
10. Nornes, *Forest of Pressure*, pp. 4–9. [Editors' note: for more on the CIE films, see also Chapter 32 by Yuka Tsuchiya in this volume.]
11. Toba Kōji, *1950 nendai: 'Kiroku' no jidai* (Tokyo: Kawade shobō shinsha, 2010), p. 82. On the significance of the Iwanami film's expression, see Nakamura Hideyuki, 'Akatsuki ni deau made: *Iwanami Eiga* no "me" no shakaiteki sōzō', in Niwa Yoshiyuki and Yoshimi Shun'ya (eds), *Kiroku eiga archive*, vol. 1, *Iwanami eiga no ichi oku film* (Tokyo: Tokyo daigaku shuppankai, 2012), pp. 39–57.

12. Abé Mark Nornes, 'Private Reality: Hara Kazuo's Films', in Ivone Margulies (ed.), *Rite of Realism: Essay on Corporal Cinema* (Durham, NC: Duke University Press, 2002), p. 150.
13. Yuriko Furuhata, *Cinema of Actuality: Japanese Avant-Garde Filmmaking in the Season of Image Politics* (Durham, NC: Duke University Press, 2013), pp. 43–4.
14. Hani Susumu, *Camera to maiku: Gendai geijutsu no hōhō* (Tokyo: Chūō kōronsha, 1960), p. 66.
15. Ibid., p. 68.
16. Ibid., p. 39.
17. Ibid., p. 40.
18. Ibid., p. 69.
19. Nornes, *Forest of Pressure*, p. 22.
20. Furuhata, *Cinema of Actuality*, p. 51.
21. Ibid., p. 60.
22. Handō Kazutoshi, *Shōwashi: Sengohen 1945–1989* (Tokyo: Heibonsha, 2009), pp. 98–9.
23. Nihon hōsō kyōkai (ed.), *20seiki hōsōshi jō* (Tokyo: Nihon hōsō shuppan kyōkai, 2001), pp. 221–4.
24. Niwa Yoshiyuki, 'Terebi documentary no seiritu: NHK "Nihon no sugao"', *Mass communication kenkyū* no. 59 (July 2001), p. 167. For further argument on this issue, see Miyata Akira, 'Rokuon kōsei no hassei: NHK documentary no genryu to shite', *NHK hōsō bunka kenkyūjo nenpō* vol. 60 (Tokyo: NHK shuppan, 2016), pp. 101–71.
25. Hani, *Camera to maiku*, p. 67.
26. Satō Tadao, *Nihon kiroku eizōshi* (Tokyo: Hyōronsha, 1977), pp. 185–6.
27. Hani, *Camera to maiku*, pp. 67–8, 82–3.
28. Ibid., p. 180; Niwa, 'Terebi documentary no seiritu', pp. 168–9; Yonekura Ritsu and Matsuyama Hideaki, 'Documentary ron: Nihon no sugao ronsō o chūshin ni', *Hōsō kenkyū to chōsa* vol. 63 no. 9 (September 2013), pp. 2–15.
29. Ushiyama Jun'ichi, Okamoto Yoshihiko, Yoshida Naoya and Hani Susumu, 'Warera wa terebi producer', *Chūōkōron* vol. 74 no. 6 (May 1959), p. 227.
30. Hani Susumu, 'Onsei to eizō', *Chūōkōron* vol. 74 no. 14 (October 1959), p. 248; Hani, *Camera to maiku*, p. 216.
31. Nakamura Hideyuki, 'Minamata no koe to kao: Tsuchimoto Noriaki *Minamata: Kanjasan to sono sekai* ni tsuite', in Kurosawa Kiyoshi, Yoshimi Shun'ya, Yomota Inuhiko and Li Bong-Ou (eds), *Nihon eiga wa ikiteiru*, vol. 7, *Fumikoeru documentary* (Tokyo: Iwanami shoten, 2010), pp. 13–35. [Editors' note: for more on Tsuchimoto's documentary, see also Chapter 27 by Rachel DiNitto in this volume.]
32. Yoshida Naoya, *Terebi, sono yohaku no shisō* (Tokyo: Bunsen, 1973), p. 30.
33. Ibid., pp. 32, 58.
34. Satō, *Nihon kiroku eizōshi*, pp. 181–3.
35. Hani Susumu, 'Terebi producer eno chōsenjō: Kagami ni natte shimatta mado', *Chūōkōron* vol. 74 no. 16 (November 1959), pp. 198–207; Yoshida Naoya, 'Hani shi no chōsen ni kotaeru', *Chūōkōron* vol. 74 no. 17 (December 1959), pp. 118–26.
36. Satō, *Nihon kiroku eizōshi*, p. 184.
37. Oguma Eiji, *1968: Wakamonotachi no hanran to sono haikei* (Tokyo: Shin'yōsha, 2009), p. 81.
38. Nornes, *Forest of Pressure*, p. 15.
39. For instance, Tsuchimoto's student movement documentary, *Prehistory of the Partisans/Partisan zenshi* (1969) focuses more on the divide between violent revolution and wealthy Japanese society than solidarity amongst the students. See Nornes, *Forest of Pressure*, p. 77.
40. Ibid., p 48.
41. Matsuda Masao, 'Agitation no ne: Kiroku eiga *Assatsu no mori*', *Eiga hyōron*, 1 January 1968, pp. 82–3.
42. Shūma Kaname, 'Angura o kangaeru: *Assatsu no mori* o mite', *Eiga hyōron*, 1 March 1968, p. 18.
43. Ibid., p. 44–5; Onozawa Toshihiko, '1968 nen no documentary eiga saizensen', in Yomota Inuhiko and Hirasawa Gō (eds), *1968 nen bunkaron* (Tokyo: Mainichi shinbunsha, 2010), pp. 162–89. Hata has also suggested such solidarity was formed in the screening events prevailed around that time where audiences' diverse responses arose. See Hata Ayumi, 'Undō no media o koete: 1970 nen zengo no shakai undō to jishu kiroku eiga', in Fujiki Hideaki (ed), *Kankyaku e no approach* (Tokyo: Shinwasha, 2011), pp. 385–411.
44. Suzuki Kazushi, Ogawa production, '*Sanrizuka no natsu*' o miru: Eiga kara yomitoku Narita tōsō (Tokyo: Ōta shuppan, 2012), pp. 16, 62.
45. Hasebe Hideo, 'Sanrizuka de tatakau Ogawa puro', *Eiga hyōron*, 1 September 1968, p. 26.
46. 'Fūten' is, in a sense, a Japanese translation of 'Hippie'. See Nanba Kōji, *Zoku no keifu gaku: Youth subculture no sengoshi*, (Tokyo: Seikyūsha, 2007), pp. 154–73.
47. Nichols, *Introduction to Documentary*, p. 181.
48. Kitakōji Takashi, 'Han tōchaku no monogatari: Ethnography to shite no Ogawa pro eiga', in Hase Masato and Nakamura Hideyuki (eds), *Eiga no seijigaku* (Tokyo: Seikyūsha, 2003), pp. 303–51.
49. Satō, *Nihon kiroku eizōshi*, p. 329.

34

MINORITY CULTURE
Whose song is it? Korean and women's voice in Ōshima Nagisa's *Sing a Song of Sex* (1967)

Mika Ko

Contrary to popular myth and the prevailing discourse of Japanese cultural homogeneity, Japan is a heterogeneous country that consists of various minority groups. These minority groups include, for instance, the *Ainu* (the indigenous population of Hokkaido) and *zainichi* Koreans (Korean residents in Japan). Moreover, a number of immigrant workers from various countries such as China, the Philippines, South Korea and Brazil, as well as various mixed-race people born out of an increasing number of international marriages, have all contributed to the ethnic and cultural diversity of Japanese society. Minority groups within Japan are not, of course, simply defined on the basis of their ethnicity or relationship to Japaneseness, but also include other socially and culturally marginalised groups such as sexual minorities and the disabled. While these groups may share similar problems such as discrimination, prejudice, and a marginalised and disadvantaged position in society, each minority group also possesses a culture, history and political agenda that are specific to them.

It is also important to note that while a person is a member of a minority group, s/he may also belong to a dominant group within a different sociocultural and historical context. A straight Korean man living in Japan, for instance, may be marginally positioned in relation to the dominant Japanese society while nonetheless occupying a position of power within the Korean community in terms of gender, sexuality and economic background. Similarly, it is also the case, as Kimberlé Williams Crenshaw has indicated in her notion of 'intersectionality',[1] that some people are subjected to multiple, and often intersected, forms of subordination. Williams Crenshaw originally raised the issue in the context of black feminism, and this 'intersectionality' is most evident in the position of women of minority groups who not only suffer multiple disadvantages but also may be left invisible in feminist and anti-racism campaigns. Similarly, in her famous essay 'Can the Subaltern Speak?', Gayatri Chakravorty Spivak raises another question concerning the position of women in so-called Third World countries and the conditions that conspire to silence their voices.[2] Spivak suggests that in both Western intellectual discourses that appear to speak 'for' them and in the representations of them 'within' the Third World, the voices of subaltern women are rendered absent by masculine ideology and agendas. In criticising traditional white middle-class feminism for its omission of the voices and experiences of minority women, black feminists such as Williams Crenshaw and bell hooks[3] go on to suggest the importance of understanding the way in which women's experiences are determined not by gender alone but by multiple and intersected factors, which not only include gender but also class and race.

By way of an investigation into the relationship between Japanese cinema and minority cultures, this chapter will examine the cinematic representation of *zainichi* Koreans in Japanese cinema. In particular, by referring to Ōshima Nagisa's *Sing a Song of Sex/Nihon shunka-kō* (1967) as a case study, the chapter will focus on gender politics and investigate the particular treatment (or absence) of the voices of Korean women in Japanese cinema. The critical perspectives offered by various radical feminists on the position of women in ethnic minority groups will provide an insightful framework through which to investigate the position of *zainichi* Korean women.

Zainichi Koreans, one of the largest ethnic minority groups in Japan, consist of 'permanent Korean residents in Japan' who (or whose descendants) came to Japan during the colonial period. As both ethnically non-Japanese and as women, Korean women in Japan represent a minority in a double sense in that their own voices have been marginalised by both dominant Japanese and Korean 'male' voices. As Jung Yeong-hae points out, identity politics and the political movement of *zainichi* Koreans faced a profound turning point in the mid-1980s as an increasing number of women and members of the younger generation started engaging in activism. As a result, the voices of women criticising gender inequality and sexism within the *zainichi* Korean family and community started to surface.[4] Moreover, since the 1990s, transnational feminist solidarity has developed in the wake of the issue of wartime 'comfort women' – women and girls forced into sexual slavery by the Imperial Japanese Army before and during World War II. Having said this, postwar *zainichi* political activism has largely been led by the first generation of *zainichi* male Koreans and their particular form of ethno-nationalism. In other words, it has developed as a male-centred movement aimed not only at criticising Japanese imperialism and institutionalised discrimination against *zainichi* Koreans, but also at recovering a form of masculinity and ethnic pride undermined by the experience of Japanese colonialism.

Such a male-centred tendency is also reflected in the way in which *zainichi* Koreans have been represented in Japanese cinema. Although *zainichi* Koreans have been featured in many Japanese films, representations have tended to focus on male characters and their ethnic minority status in Japanese society.[5] Female characters and their voices have thus often been overshadowed by male voices fighting against, or suffering as result of, the economic and political predicament of the 'ethnic minority group'. In other words, the theme of *zainichi* Koreans has been predominantly mobilised in the stories of men. In many cases, male *zainichi* characters have been represented as active subjects questioning and exploring their ethnic identity through which the discriminatory treatment of them in Japanese society is unveiled. Moreover, these films often display the masculinity of the Korean male characters by drawing upon fights and yakuza conflicts as the main narrative framework.

On the other hand, even when they take a central role in films, female characters often appear as more passive and marginalised subjects or as persons who serve, directly or indirectly, the male-centred narrative of 'resistance'. As Yang In-Sil points out, female *zainichi* characters appearing in films often wear *chima chogori* (traditional Korean clothing) that symbolises the homeland of Korea.[6] Yang also argues that while young male *zainichi* characters may struggle to confirm their national and ethnic identity, or sometimes claim their subjectivity beyond their Koreanness, the Korean identity of female characters is always 'given' and endorsed by their traditional Korean costume as a marker or symbol of their ethnicity.[7] As a form of imagined homeland, the women in *chima chogori*, in turn, serve as anchors to mediate and confirm male Korean identity. Indeed, beautiful young girls in *chima chogori* such as Yonja in *Pacchigi!/Pacchigi!* (Izutsu Kazuyuki, 2005), Yun in *Town of Yun/Yun no machi* (Kim Wo-seon, 1989) and a high school girl in *Go/Gō* (Yukisada Isao, 2001), all seem to represent the notion of a beautiful motherland idealised in the male imagination (Fig. 34.1). Their feminine beauty also flatters and emphasises the masculinity of the male *zainichi* characters. Moreover, since these girls are often desired by Japanese men, they not only create but also mediate conflict and reconciliation between the male Japanese and Korean characters in the film; something that facilitates the male bonding implicit in the male-centred narrative.

There are some strong and assertive female characters such as Soonohk in *The River of the Strangers/Ihōjin no kawa* (Lee Hak-in, 1975) and the woman who is addressed as *neisan* (sister) by the main character in *Death by Hanging/Kōshikei* (Ōshima Nagisa, 1968). While they are still young and beautiful, they are far more assertive than the male protagonists and eloquently and resolutely advocate Korean ethnic pride

Fig. 34.1. A beautiful young girl in *chima chogori* embodies an idealised image of the Korean motherland in *Pacchigi!* (Izutsu Kazuyuki, 2005, Cine Quanon).

as well as denouncing the discriminatory practices and structures of Japanese society. No matter how eloquent they are, however, they remain placed in the position of speaking for male-led *zainichi* Korean political activism and awakening the Korean identity of the male protagonists (that has not yet been fully developed). This does not, of course, mean that political discourse belongs only to the men. However, in speaking on behalf of male activists or of 'Koreans' preaching ethnic pride and criticising Japanese imperialism, these women are often denied a subject position to speak about female experience. In other words, although female characters physically appear and speak in the films, their voices are nonetheless absent.

In this respect, Ōshima's *Sing a Song of Sex* provides an intriguing example of a text that reveals the way in which the bodies and voices of *zainichi* women have been misappropriated in a number of ways. Through a particular song, 'Mantetsu kouta', sung by a young *zainichi* female character, *Sing a Song of Sex* betrays the dissonance between the 'female voice' and the 'male voice' in a specific ethnic minority context. Moreover, the song not only criticises male sexism but also directs a rather cynical view towards some aspects of the so-called progressive movements of the 1960s. By analysing various scenes in detail, I shall now explore the role of the female voice (or song) in the film, its critical power and the way in which it is eventually misappropriated.

Ōshima's *Sing a Song of Sex* drew inspiration from Soeda Tomomichi's book of the same title about Japanese bawdy songs and its thesis that erotic folk songs represent the oppressed voices of ordinary people.[8] Ōshima is known as a director who often dealt with the issues of *zainichi* Koreans in his films as part of his general critical interrogation of the Japanese state.[9] However, unlike *The Forgotten Army/Wasurerareta kōgun* (1963) and *Death by Hanging*, *Sing a Song of Sex* does not directly address the issues of the Korean minority in Japan. There is one character who is implied to be Korean but, despite her striking presence in the film, she plays only a supporting role.

The narrative of *Sing a Song of Sex* revolves around four apolitical high school students – Nakamura and his three male friends – who come to Tokyo for their university entrance examination. After becoming attracted to Mayako, a beautiful girl they see at the examination hall, the group start indulging themselves in the sexual fantasy of raping her. They find out where she lives and the four boys and their female classmate Kaneda, as well as the fiancée of their former teacher Ōtake, all visit Mayuko's home. They openly profess to Mayuko that they have raped her in their fantasies. At Mayuko's own suggestion, the boys attempt to re-enact their fantasy at the end of the film. While the plot may sound rather simple, as is the case with many of his other films, Ōshima abandons conventional realism and verisimilitude in favour of a complicated blend of fantasy, reality and dramatic 're-enactment'. As a result, the narrative structure is, in fact, extremely loose and the film becomes increasingly intricate towards its end (Fig. 34.2).

While *Sing a Song of Sex* draws on various types of songs ranging from wartime military songs to anti-Vietnam War folk songs, as the title of the film suggests, *shunka* (erotic folk songs) dominate the film. Following Soeda's original idea, the film clearly treats *shunka* as the oppressed voice of ordinary people. After learning about Soeda's thesis themselves, the four boys repeatedly sing cheerful but sexually explicit and masculine songs to both identify with 'oppressed' ordinary people and express their own 'repressed' sexual interests and desires. Although male songs dominate the film, there is one female *shunka* that is sung twice in the film by the Korean girl Kaneda.

Fig. 34.2. *Sing a Song of Sex/Nihon shunka-kō* (Ōshima Nagisa, 1967, Sōzōsha).

The setting for the first occasion of Kaneda's singing is the vicinity of Shinjuku station. While Nakamura and the three other boys sing an erotic folk song, their singing soon develops into an aggressive sexual fantasy involving Mayuko. While they entertain each other by revealing their individual fantasies, Kaneda suddenly appears and joins them. Prior to this scene, she has not had much of a presence and has simply been shown as one of the boys' female classmates. Kaneda cheerfully asks the boys if she can also sing a song. The boys welcome and encourage her. Because of her cheerful tone prior to singing, the male students, as well as the audience, expect an amusing or jolly song to be sung. Contrary to such assumptions, Kaneda sings a rather plaintive song – 'Mantetsu kouta'/'The Song of the Manchurian Railroad':

In the rainy evening
Peeping through the glass window is
You, a foolish man of the Manchurian Railroad
In a uniform with gold buttons
Fifty cents to touch but free to see
If you give me three yen and five cents
I will be yours till the rooster crows in the morning
Coming in or not, what are you gonna do?
Hurry up and make up your mind
Once you decide, take your shoes off and come in
Sir, paper is expensive these days
Out of regard for the pay desk
Please give us fifty cents as a tip
Then I will sleep holding you in my arms
With extra services
I will make love with you till the rooster crows.

'Mantetsu kouta' is an adaptation or 'filk' of the popular Japanese military song, 'Tōhiko', that came out in the 1930s. The original song was about the hard life of soldiers at the battlefront in China, and it was popular amongst both the military and civilians. While using the same melody, the lyrics have been completely changed in 'Mantetsu kouta' to express the life and sorrow of Korean prostitutes working in the brothels in Manchuria – the Japanese puppet state established in 1932 in China.[10] Although it is a Japanese song, the Korean accents in the lyrics emphasise the 'otherness' or 'Koreanness' of the song, while the word 'Mantetsu' anchors the song to the specific historical context of Japanese imperialism and colonialism. How then can we interpret the song that is rather abruptly sung in Ōshima's *Sing a Song of Sex* by a high school girl whose Korean ethnic background is implied by her family name? In order to examine the role and significance of 'Mantetsu kouta' in relation to the voice of women, I shall compare this scene with scenes from two Japanese yakuza films made in the 1970s in which the same song is sung instead by male characters.

In Yamashita Kōsaku's *Violent Islands Japan/Nihon bōryoku rettō* (1975), there are two scenes in which the main yakuza characters, Hanaki and Kanemitsu, both sing 'Mantetsu kouta'. Although it is never made explicit in the film, the conversation between the characters and the consumption of Korean drinks and foods both imply that they are ethnically Korean. In the development of the plot featuring a yakuza conflict, their Korean background or 'otherness' plays an important role in the male bonding between the two characters. Their singing of 'Mantetsu kouta' is also used to symbolically imply the ethnic roots that they cannot reveal. Kanemitsu sings 'Mantetsu kouta' earlier on in the film when he and other members of Hanaki's yakuza group celebrate Hanaki's release from prison. As Kanemitsu and Hanaki know that they share the same ethnic origin, Kanemitsu's singing may be heard as an expression of his Korean identity and bonding with Hanaki. Toward the end of the film, 'Mantetsu kouta' is sung again, this time by Hanaki after Kanemitsu's death. After the identification of Kanemitsu's dead body at a police station, Hanaki, alone in his dark office, starts to sing quietly. The scene includes several shots of Kanemitsu's dying moments (when Hanaki was not present). As such, 'Mantetsu kouta' not only marks their Korean ethnic background but also confirms the bonding between the two male Korean characters on a sentimental level.

'Mantetsu kouta' is also used in another yakuza film, *The Mamushi Brothers/Chōeki Taro: Mamushi no kyōdai* (Nakajima Sadao, 1971). In a scene towards the end of the film, the two main yakuza characters, Katsu and Masa, launch an assault against a large yakuza clan. On a night of heavy rain, they are driving a truck on a sneak raid. Along the way, Katsu starts playing 'Mantetsu kouta' on his harmonica. Masa asks, 'Hey brother, what song is that?' to which Katsu replies, 'don't know. I often heard this song when I was a small child.' He continues: 'I see a face of a woman whenever I hear this song.' After a few seconds silence, Katsu murmurs, 'Maybe, it's my mother.' When Masa repeats Katsu's word, 'mother', 'Mantetsu kouta' sung by a female vocal comes on as background music. As in *Violent Islands Japan*, the use of 'Mantetsu kouta' in this scene suggests that Katsu's mother, of whom he has little memory, may have been Korean.

In his psychoanalytical discussion of the relationship between 'music' and the 'maternal', Guy Rosolato suggests that 'the musical process' provides 'the means by which original plenitude and the lost maternal object are restored'.[11] He also argues that music responds to 'the subject's nostalgia for its original fusion with mother' and 'plays out the imaginary scenario of separation and reunion between subject and mother'.[12] Likewise, in the scene in *The Mamushi Brothers*, 'Mantetsu kouta' is used to evoke Katsu's nostalgia for his original fusion with the lost maternal object. This is clearly confirmed by Katsu's own remark referring to his mother. However, the 'mother' being evoked here may not only be referring to the biological mother but to the mother country of Korea. In *The Mamushi Brothers*, the female vocal that takes over Katsu's harmonica does not have any corporeal source in the film. While this may be heard as non-diegetic background music, it can also be understood as part of the diegesis insofar as it may be Katsu's recollection of a song sung by a woman whom, he believes, may be his mother. Nonetheless, the film does not specifically deploy a flashback to show the face of the woman whom Katsu imagines singing the song. In this way, the song, at least as used here, does not actually belong to his mother. Instead, it is only heard specifically in relation to the memory process of the male character. As Mary Ann Doane and Kaja Silverman both point out, the use of a disembodied voice in, for instance, documentary film is often linked to the representation of 'authority' or 'omnipotence'.[13] In *The Mamushi Brothers*, the absence of the actual figure of the mother is not linked with any sense of authority as such. Here, it functions to connect the voice (i.e. the song) not only to the actual mother but also symbolically to the motherland of Korea. Moreover, because of her 'absence', the mother becomes more of an abstract, nostalgic and idealised figure.

While 'Mantetsu kouta' is mobilised in both *The Mamushi Brothers* and *Violent Islands Japan* to confirm the Korean identity of the male characters in terms of a symbolic motherland, it also connects the marginalised status of both the Korean prostitutes in Manchuria, to whom the song originally belongs, and the male characters living as Korean yakuza in Japanese society. The identification of the marginality of the yakuza with that of female prostitutes, however, obscures the problem of the oppression of women through sexual exploitation that was immanent in the original song. It is also important to emphasise that in both films, the song is linked to the homosocial and narcissistic bonding of the male characters. As Caryl Flinn suggests, this kind of 'fantasmatic unity is offered to a specifically male subject',[14] and 'music works chiefly to abet and uphold the male subject'.[15] What is therefore at stake in these films is not so much the female subject, be this Katsu's mother or the prostitutes in Manchuria (the assumed original singers of the song), as the subjectivity of the male protagonists. In this sense, it is important to note the position of the Japanese audience in relation to the song. Both *Violent Islands Japan* and *The Mamushi Brothers* conform to the narrative and stylistic conventions of classical Hollywood cinema that encourage audiences to identify with the protagonist of the film. In other words, they invite the audience to share the sentimentality of the male Korean heroes and not confront, or reflect on, Japan's colonial past.

'Mantetsu kouta' is deployed in *Sing a Song of Sex* in a radically different way. Although Kaneda's singing confirms her Korean ethnic background, unlike the case with *The Mamushi Brothers* and *Violent Islands Japan*, it is not linked to any nostalgic longing for an idealised motherland. Rather, as Sekine Hiroshi points out, as the voice of an oppressed minority (or the formerly colonised), Kaneda's song vividly reminds its audience of Japan's imperialist past.[16] Likewise, as Satō Tadao argues, the main character, Nakamura, is shocked by Kaneda's song in this scene.[17] While his own singing is meant to demonstrate cynicism about the deceptions of postwar Japanese democracy, Nakamura does not expect someone of his own age to sing a bawdy song in such an emotional and assertive manner.[18] Kaneda's song not only surprises Nakamura and the other boys, but it also shocks the audience. The film has not previously offered the audience an opportunity to identify emotionally with Kaneda. In other words, unlike the case with the two yakuza films that encourage identification with the sentiments of the protagonist who sings the song, *Sing a Song of Sex* forces the audience to directly confront Japan's colonial past and its legacy, that is to say the presence of Koreans in Japan.

Nonetheless, it remains problematic to simply regard Kaneda as the representative of political opposition to Japan's colonial past. Although many critics have interpreted the song as the voice of formerly colonised subjects or the voice of the oppressed Korean minority in Japan, such a reading overlooks its highly important gender dimensions. When Nakamura asks her, 'What is that song?', Kaneda answers clearly 'it's a *woman's* song'. This remark thus suggests that Kaneda sings the song from two positions: one as a Korean and the other as a woman. In other words, by specifically bringing the gendered aspect into view, Kaneda seems to refuse an interpretation of the song as simply the voice of Koreans criticising Japan's imperial past and present inequality. Instead, she appears to emphasise that it is also the voice of women questioning male dominance over, and exploitation of, female sexuality. 'Women' here do not simply refer to Korean prostitutes in Manchuria, the assumed original singers of the song. If '*Mantetsu kouta*' may be heard as a song that evokes the experiences of women whose sexuality has been sold or exploited by their family or the state, the notion of women's voices should also include, for instance, those of Japanese prostitutes ('*Karayuki-san*') who were sold to East and South East Asia in the late nineteenth century as well as other Asian military comfort women and prostitutes mobilised during World War II. Moreover, the presence of the US in Japan implied in the scene through such things as a Coca-Cola sign also evokes the women who had to work in comfort stations set up for the Occupation army personnel after the end of World War II; something that points to the state's and men's continuing violence against, and sexual exploitation of, women. Similarly, Kaneda's remark 'it's a *woman's* song' may also be heard as criticism of Korean men (especially male activists) who often conflate violated women with a violated (colonised) nation within an ethno-nationalist discourse that criticises Japan without questioning their own responsibility for the oppression of women. Finally then, Kaneda's 'Mantetsu kouta' may also insinuate criticism against her male classmates who position themselves alongside the 'oppressed commoner' singing bawdy songs but find no problem in fantasising about rape. As a slow tracking shot reveals, the boys do nothing but walk like miserable scolded children behind Kaneda while she sings (Fig. 34.3).

We also need to pay attention to the 'politics of the look' in this scene. In response to Nakamura's question 'where did you learn the song?', Kaneda starts singing the second verse. The camera captures Kaneda gazing at Nakamura. A reverse shot then shows Nakamura looking at Kaneda, which is followed by a close-up of

Fig. 34.3 The boys follow Kaneda like scolded children while she sings 'Mantetsu Kouta' in *Sing a Song of Sex/Nihon shunka-kō* (Ōshima Nagisa, 1967, Sōzōsha).

Kaneda. Here, Kaneda's close-up does not present her as a passive object being subjected to the eroticised male gaze of either Nakamura or the audience. The song may involve a sexual invitation to men, but because of the Korean accents and colonial history implied in the lyrics, and because of her resolute facial expression, Kaneda's close-up provides neither Nakamura nor the audience with any form of 'visual pleasure'. Rather, it is Kaneda's gaze that is provocatively directed at Nakamura and forces him to look at her. Kaneda's eyes do not allow Nakamura, as a Japanese man, to avoid a confrontation with responsibilities concerning the violence of Japanese colonialism and that of men towards women.

The protest against the male sexual objectification of women that is mobilised by Kaneda's song nonetheless quickly disappears and becomes transformed into a form of motherly compassion instead. Upon listening to Kaneda's song, Nakamura confesses to Kaneda that he might have contributed to the death of Ōtake, their former teacher who died accidentally from gas poisoning the previous night. Kaneda reacts to Nakamura's admission as if she was his mother, making a phone call for him and advising him what he should do. As such, Kaneda's performance of the song in this scene assumes a number of ambivalent roles: she is at once a Korean criticising Japanese imperialism, a woman protesting against male sexual violence and the exploitation of female sexuality, and a maternal figure who tolerates and amends the mistake committed by her male friend.

After being encouraged by Kaneda, Nakamura attends Ōtake's wake where he confesses to Ōtake's fiancée, Takako, that he abandoned Ōtake to his fate after having noticed the gas leak. Meanwhile, Nakamura's three male friends and Kaneda visit Mayuko, the beautiful girl whom the boys saw at the examination hall the previous day. In the garden of her luxurious home, Mayuko is holding a folk song party to protest against the Vietnam War. There is a large pond in the garden at the centre of which there is a coffin covered by the American Stars and Stripes. While apparently affluent urban university students enjoy singing American folk songs, the three boys feel out of place. They start singing a bawdy song to which no one pays attention. While the boys are left feeling dispirited and isolated, Kaneda suddenly approaches a group of young men and women singing and snatches their microphone. After a brief silence, she starts singing 'Mantetsu kouta'.

Here, Kaneda seems to sing 'Mantetsu kouta' in order to criticise the young people involved in an apparently 'progressive' movement. Hasebe Hideo has pointed out that while the young people sing like school children without any genuine spirit of protest, Kaneda actually sings a real protest song.[19] Indeed, Kaneda's rendition of 'Mantetsu kouta' is clearly sung to challenge the university students who have gathered to condemn American violence in Vietnam but seem totally indifferent to Japan's own past imperialism. While all sound in this film was added during post-production, the lack of any sound perspective especially stands out in this sequence since it both underscores the way the folk songs are disconnected from their historical and original context, and emphasises the inherent superficiality and artificiality of the event and its participants. As Kaneda sings, the camera slowly pans from left to right and then right to left, capturing reflected images in the pond of the young participants and the various national flags hanging at the event. These reflected images also reinforce the self-indulgent narcissism and ignorance of the participants.

It is clear that the young people do not understand what Kaneda's 'Mantetsu kouta' is all about. When Kaneda finishes her song, a group of young men lead her away. Some young women approach the three boys and ask, 'Was it an African song?' and 'It's a Japanese folk song, isn't it?' The scene then cuts to Ōtake's wake, which Nakamura is attending. When the scene cuts back to the concert, Kaneda is standing by the pond looking at an image of herself lying on a raft. The blood spreading on the surface of the water implies that she must have been sexually violated. Both Kanedas – the one standing and the one lying on the raft – seem invisible to everyone except Mayuko as if to suggest that for the young people protesting against the Vietnam War, Kaneda's rape is not a recognisable act of violence but an expression of guilt-free 'sexual freedom'. They see no contradiction or discrepancy between their act of protest against American violence and their act of raping Kaneda.

Mayuko, the only person who has recognised the violence towards Kaneda, also leaves the scene, singing 'Goodnight Irene'. In the next shot, Kaneda appears in a garish, sexy dress that, along with the blood in the previous scene, signifies she has lost her virginity and innocence. The three boys, who have by then comfortably adapted themselves to the atmosphere, instantly realise what has happened. Soon Nakamura and Takako arrive. Takako talks to Kaneda about her own past experiences and tells her not to forget the pain; Kaneda shows no reaction and walks away. While Takako talks to Kaneda, the camera again captures the reflected images in the pond. This suggests that the narcissism and vanity of the young concert participants may also be found in the previous generation of activists that Takako represents and their patronising attitude towards an oppressed minority group. Moreover, Takako's words to Kaneda suggesting that as a woman she shares a similar pain make us question whether their sufferings are, in fact, identical. As Takako's remark suggests, the sexual violence against Kaneda may certainly be criticised in terms of gender politics or of 'male' violence towards 'women' in general. At the same time, however, it should not be seen simply as a matter concerning gender politics – it is also a matter of Japanese violence against Koreans. In some senses, the scene thus presages the trans-Asian feminist controversies of the 1990s over the issue of wartime 'comfort women'. While the prominent Japanese feminist sociologist Ueno Chizuko proposes the importance of a transnational feminist solidarity that transcends nationalist politics, the *zainichi* Korean feminist historian Kim Puja argues that feminist solidarity across Asia first requires that the women of the colonising nation (Japan) acknowledge their own complicity with their nation's imperialism of the past and present.[20] Takako's attitude in *Sing a Song of Sex* raises exactly the same question and reveals the difficulties inherent in creating a transnational women's solidarity that does not nullify questions of nationality, ethnicity and history.

The next shot shows a number of young people singing 'Mantetsu kouta' around Kaneda, who is now seen in Korean costume. Kaneda stands in silence with a totally emotionless face. In fact, she has remained silent since singing 'Mantetsu kouta' in an earlier scene and does not utter a single word for the rest of the film. It is tempting to interpret this allegorically in that having been raped and deprived of language, Kaneda and her situation may be seen as analogous to the position of Korea under Japanese colonial rule. However, Kaneda's silence is not simply a metaphor for colonial oppression, it also possesses a critical dimension. As Trinh T. Minh-ha suggests, silence is a 'voice, a mode of uttering, and a response in its own right'.[21] There is a difference between 'silence' and the 'absence of voices'. Indeed, silence can be very eloquent. In particular, here in *Sing a Song of Sex*, Kaneda's silence, when juxtaposed with people who try to speak on her behalf, tellingly identifies those who are depriving her of her voice. For instance, without recognising, let alone reflecting upon, their acts of violence, the young men who raped Kaneda appropriate 'Mantetsu kouta' as an anti-Vietnam war song. They also do not forget to set up Kaneda in a Korean costume as a symbolic heroine representing the oppressed. Mayuko, the organiser of the concert and the implied leader of the next generation of the New Left, also appropriates Kaneda as a metaphor of 'violated girl' into her speech that criticises the Japan–US security alliance, while tolerating her male fellows' sexual violence towards Kaneda. The characters in the film are ignorant of the contradiction in their acts: they supposedly support the weak and minority groups but, at the same time, they deprive them of their voices.

These contradictions are exposed in the film's textual operations, and therefore to the audience, in a number of scenes in which we see Kaneda's figure remaining in the frame, often in a corner or in the background of the image (Figs. 34.4, 34.5). Moreover, Kaneda's silence and emotionless look also prevent the spectator from sympathising or identifying with her, thereby refusing any kind of catharsis. The fact that Kaneda remains in the frame (albeit not necessarily as a dominant presence), and the fact that her emotional expression is completely restrained, assume great significance. If she were not present, both Kaneda and her 'silence' would become non-existent. If she expressed her

Figs 34.4–34.5 Kaneda's figure remains in the frame and tellingly identifies those depriving her of her voice in *Sing a Song of Sex/ Nihon shunka-kō* (Ōshima Nagisa, 1967, Sōzōsha).

anger and suffering as the oppressed ethnic minority or as a woman in an emotionally charged manner, the audience would be invited to emotionally identify or sympathise with her. Instead, Kaneda's silence and emotionless face determinedly refuse any provision of catharsis and dismiss a superficial and irresponsible sense of identification and solidarity. In other words, Kaneda's silence can be seen as an act of resistance against the ways in which the voices of minority groups may be exploited by inappropriate expressions of empathy and solidarity.

At the end of the film, Takako hysterically quotes her dead fiancé's thesis that Koreans and Japanese are of the same origin. As she shouts, 'The Japanese come from Korea,' Takako moves right and stands just in front of Kaneda, as if to assume Kaneda's position. She then proceeds towards the front while Kaneda is left alone exactly where she was. This scene vividly illustrates the way in which so-called progressive intellectuals and activists, while assuming to speak on behalf of minority groups, often use minority groups as an alibi to underwrite their political claims. In this respect, Kaneda's silence not only resists the misappropriation of the minority voice for the sake of superficial identification and solidarity, it also betrays the problems inherent in the Japanese New Left movement that was later criticised for having 'taken advantage of' the issues of minority groups for their own convenience in the name of an 'internationalism' that failed to question the history of Japan as the oppressor.[22] Ironically, this criticism may also, to some extent, be redirected at Ōshima himself, who often utilised Koreans in his films in order to radically interrogate and criticise Japanese state power and the Japanese who colluded with it.

By way of conclusion, *Sing a Song of Sex* clearly presents a number of the problems raised by black feminists in relation to the position of women from minority groups and the Third World. Radical feminists, such as Williams Crenshaw, hooks and Spivak, have all problematised the way in which the voices of such women have been repressed, ignored or exploited by white feminists, men of the same minority group and so-called progressive intellectuals. Ōshima's *Sing a Song of Sex* raises similar questions regarding the position of *zainichi* Korean women whose experience as women, members of an ethnic minority group and the formerly colonised all intersect in a complex manner when these women's voices remain so often ignored or exploited. *Sing a Song of Sex* does not allow Kaneda to fully recapture her 'voice' – either as a *zainichi* Korean or as a woman. Likewise, the film shows no interest in feminist politics as such. Nonetheless, through both Kaneda's song and her silence, the film, at least, begins to critically unveil the often-invisible and naturalised structures and processes whereby the voices of women and minority groups have been exploited and marginalised in Japanese culture as a whole.

Notes

1   Kimberlé Williams Crenshaw, 'Demarginalising the Intersection of Race and Sex: A Black Feminist Critique of Anti-discrimination Doctrine, Feminist Theory, and Anti-racist Politics', in Helma Lutz, Maria Teresa Herrera Vivar and Linda Spuik (eds), *Framing Intersectionality: Debates on a Multi-faceted Concept in Gender Studies* (Farnham: Ashgate, 2011), pp. 25–42.

2. Gayatri Chakravorty Spivak, 'Can the Subaltern Speak?', in Bill Ashcroft, Gareth Griffiths and Helen Tiffin (eds), *The Post-Colonial Studies Reader* (London: Routledge, 1995), pp. 24–8.
3. bell hooks, *Ain't I a Woman: Black Women and Feminism* (Boston, MA: South End Press, 1981).
4. Jung Yeong-hae, 'Identity o koete', in Inoue Shun, Ueno Chizuko, Osawa Masaichi and Yoshimi Shunya (eds), *Sabetsu to kyōsei no shakaigaku* (Tokyo: Iwanami shoten, 1999).
5. For a detailed discussion on representation of *zainich* Korean in Japanese cinema, please see, Oliver Dew, *Zainichi Cinema: Korean-in Japan Film Culture* (London: Palgrave Macmillan, 2016) and Mika Ko, *Japanese Cinema and Otherness: Nationalism, Multiculturalism and the Problem of Japaneseness* (London: Routledge, 2011).
6. Yang In-sil, 'Sengo nihon eiga ni okeru "zainichi" joseizō', *Ritsumeikan sangyō shakaironshū* vol. 39 no. 2 (September 2003), pp. 113–31.
7. Ibid.
8. Soeda Tomomichi, *Nihon shunka kō: Shomin no utaeru sei no yorokobi* (Tokyo: Kōbunsha, 1966).
9. For a critical discussion on Ōshima's work, please see Maureen Turim, *The Films of Oshima Nagisa: Images of a Japanese Iconoclast* (Berkeley: University of California Press, 1998). Some of Ōshima's own writings are translated into English in Nagisa Ōshima, *Cinema, Censorship, and the State: The Writings of Nagisa Oshima 1956–1978*, ed. Annette Michelson, trans. Dawn Lawson (Cambridge, MA: MIT Press, 1992).
10. 'Mantetsu kouta' is not included in the book by Soeda that inspired Ōshima to make the film. Indeed, there is little coherent information regarding the origin of the song in terms of its original context. Some have suggested Korean prostitutes started singing the song while others claim that the Japanese wrote and sang the song to insult Koreans and make fun of the Korean accent when speaking Japanese. Other sources suggest that it was still sung by Japanese men over drinks during the 1960s. While it is not possible to determine the song's definite origin, it is probably reasonable to assume that the song was originally sung by Korean prostitutes in Manchuria, then became known and sung by Japanese thus becoming gradually separated from its original context. See Takenaka Rō, *Geijutsu no ronri* (Tokyo: Kōyō shuppan, 1972); Nishi Haruka, *Koe ni dashite utaō nihon no shunka* (Tokyo: Takeuchi shoten shinsha, 2002) and Hiraoka Masaaki, *Nogeteki* (Tokyo: Kaihō shuppansha, 1979).
11. Guy Rosolato, quoted in Caryl Flinn, *Strains of Utopia: Gender, Nostalgia, and Hollywood Film Music* (Princeton, NJ: Princeton University Press, 1992), p. 54.
12. Ibid. p. 54.
13. Mary Ann Doane, 'The Voice in the Cinema: The Articulation of Body and Space', in Philip Rosen (ed.), *Narrative, Apparatus, Ideology: A Film Theory Reader* (New York: Columbia University Press, 1984), p. 341; Kaja Silverman, 'Dis-Embodying the Female Voice', in Patricia Erens (ed.), *Issues in Feminist Film Criticism* (Bloomington: Indiana University Press, 1990), p. 311.
14. Flinn, *Strains of Utopia*, p.55.
15. Ibid., p. 69.
16. Sekine Hiroshi, 'Kūsōka to bōryoku kakumei', *Eiga geijutsu*, May 1969, p. 39.
17. Satō Tadao, *Ōshima Nagisa no sekai* (Tokyo: Chikuma shobō, 1973), p. 217.
18. Ibid., p. 217.
19. Hasebe Hideo, 'Ōshima rorensu no "Nihon shunka-kō"', *Eiga geijutsu*, May 1967, p. 36.
20. Ulrike Wöhr, 'A Touchstone for Transnational Feminism: Discourses on the Comfort Women in 1990s Japan', in Andrea Germer and Andreas Moerke (eds), *Japanstudien 16: Grenzgänge – (De-) Konstruktion kollektiver Identitäten in Japan* (Munich: Iudicium Verlag, 2004), pp. 59–90.
21. Trinh T. Minh-ha, *Woman, Native, Other: Writing Postcoloniality and Feminism* (Bloomington: Indiana University Press, 1989), p. 82.
22. Suga Hidemi, *1968* (Tokyo: Chikuma shobō, 2006), p. 176.

35
GLOBALISATION
Japanese cultural globalisation at the margins
Cobus van Staden

The description of Japan as a cultural Galapagos has recently become a popular trope in domestic discussions of Japanese culture.[1] The implication is that Japan's isolation has led to the evolution of rare cultural forms not found in the rest of the world. At first glance, Japan has certainly evolved several cultural products unseen in other countries. Just like the iguanas and turtles of the Galapagos, cultural forms such as girlfriend games, maid and butler cafes, and *Power Rangers*-themed porn might exist in other countries, but Japan has specifically turned them into rare, mutated versions of themselves.

The Galapagos analogy breaks down, however, when one views Japan in the context of globalisation. After all, the Galapagos iguanas never left their island, while Japanese cultural products have found a myriad of fans all over the world. Yet, the mechanisms that made this possible deserve more attention. During the 1980s and 1990s, cultural globalisation was frequently characterised as emanating from a Western centre to a non-Western periphery. It was decried as the Western generic wiping out of the non-Western specific. Over time, this view of globalisation has been challenged by a more complex model that has become known as the 'flows and scapes' model that draws on the work of Arjun Appadurai.[2] The earlier model was arguably overly concerned with Western unipolar dominance, casting non-Western cultural industries as permanently folkish and on the verge of annihilation. The 'flows and scapes' model errs on the other side, imagining a world where information and culture flow freely, unhindered by state power. In fact, this model rests on an assumption that the state is becoming, in the words of Manuel Castells, 'just a node (however important) of a particular network, the political, institutional, and military network that overlaps with other significant networks in the construction of social practice'.[3]

Positioning the global circulation of Japanese cinema within, and as part of, the story of globalisation, gives us the chance to complicate both these narratives. Japan's role as a non-Western centre of media production disrupts the earlier narrative of globalisation as Western hegemony. But this circulation, albeit widespread, is not total. An investigation of the factors that impede the global spread of Japanese media may also begin to re-infuse the 'flows and scapes' model with an acknowledgment of how power imbalances continue to shape the global flow of culture.

An analysis of how Japanese culture has spread allows us to take the first step towards formulating new models of cultural globalisation based on the spread of non-Western culture. Japan provides a valuable starting point because the transmission of its culture has not been based on the same diaspora networks that have aided, for example, the spread of Indian and Nigerian popular cinema. Rather, Japanese cinema and pop culture have thrived through the creation of new forms of cosmopolitan self-definition open to anyone, irrespective of national or linguistic background. The fact that Japanese pop culture has managed to spread beyond the ethnoscape, while also not depending on the global geopolitical hegemonies that supported the spread of Hollywood and European (colonial) culture, makes it particularly valuable for thinking about the processes of cultural globalisation as a whole.

This chapter takes a tentative step towards thinking how the modes through which Japanese culture has spread globally can help us to build new models of globalisation. This step involves the creation of a new taxonomy of these modes and I thus aim to achieve two goals through this approach. Firstly, I hope to contribute to an analytical vocabulary that aids the discussion of how Japanese globalisation may help us to understand globalisation as a whole. Secondly, I hope to provide a glimpse of how this process of globalisation has sparked instances of cosmopolitanism at the margins. By this term, I mean that Japanese popular culture fandom has succeeded in creating small enclaves in societies as distant from East Asia as South Africa. In this case, shared fandom can be said to momentarily transcend the stark racial and gender boundaries that still structure South African society. Given the proviso that this phenomenon still only takes place within middle-class spaces, from which the vast majority of South Africans are excluded, the consumption of Japanese popular culture in South Africa can thus show us both the power and limitation of popular Japanese fan culture to shape non-elite forms of cosmopolitanism.

This chapter is divided into three sections. Firstly, I provide a theoretical foundation that focuses on how the concepts of globalisation and cosmopolitanism have evolved. Secondly, I provide a taxonomy of the different modes of Japanese cultural globalisation by identifying mechanisms through which Japanese media have spread to foreign markets at different moments in history. In the third section, I provide a set of South African case studies that focus briefly on the importation of Japanese anime during the apartheid era, the role of Japan in the popularity of martial arts film from the 1970s to the present day, and contemporary anime fandom. I show how the mechanisms I will identify in the second section almost always operate in tandem and how Japanese media have created small enclaves of proto-cosmopolitanism that undercut the hegemony of European and American culture in South Africa.[4]

FOUNDATIONS

Since emerging as a buzzword in the 1980s, the term globalisation has come to mean several different things. On the one hand, it has been conflated with the aggressive deregulation and market expansion that has come to be known as neoliberalism.[5] On the other, it has also come to be associated with the near instantaneous global flow of informational and economic currents, irrespective of national boundaries.

Scholars have also extended the term backwards into history, pointing out that far from suddenly erupting in the late 1970s, globalisation should be understood as a steadily accelerating process of global cultural exchange, interaction and conquest that includes such events as the Crusades and the rapid expansion of transnational imperialism and slavery from the 1500s.[6]

Many have come to define globalisation negatively as the expansion of industrialised power into erstwhile autonomous communities. This has been especially true during the 1990s after the fall of the Soviet Union and the rise of a unipolar world dominated by the US. Fears that the rapid expansion of media networks, together with the economic might of the US during the Clinton era, resulted in a flattening of cultural difference and the new global dominance of American power led to the conflation of cultural globalisation with cultural imperialism. This was related to controversy over the inclusion of film and television as commodities in WTO negotiations, with pressure being put on governments to let more Hollywood films into their markets.[7]

Some, nonetheless, have also raised doubts about the idea of monocultural domination. Media scholars, especially those associated with the Frankfurt School, have begun to question traditional models of consumption. Authors drawing on the traditions of Cultural Studies have emphasised the active role of the cultural consumer in using mass-produced culture to her/his own ends.[8] Others have questioned the neat overlap of Western hegemony and capitalism. Arif Dirlik, for example, has argued that the global expansion and interconnectedness of capitalism has broken the traditional link between capitalism and Western culture.[9] Against this background, Appadurai's more complex model of multidirectional flows has also gained support. This model has been strengthened by a growing awareness of the economic might of non-Western nodes of cultural production, including Japan, India, Hong Kong and Nigeria.[10]

This sense of the complexity of cultural consumption, as well as immigration flows and economic interconnectedness, has led to new articulations of globalisation, away from associations of direct imperialism and towards cosmopolitanism. Authors such as Michael Held have argued for the power of cosmopolitanism to transcend a narrow national identity and facilitate the solving of complex problems that face the world as a whole.[11] Critics have however pointed out that proponents of cosmopolitanism have also tended to bundle their conception of the cosmopolitan subject with a conception of the transcultural intellectual. This conception elides the development of transcultural skills from below.[12] This is particularly problematic in the context of the global south.

Current conceptions of cosmopolitanism, especially attempts to draw on the Stoics and Kant to reformulate the concept in the context of human rights, also tend to foreground the physical experience of crossing borders.[13] In contrast, I would echo Sheldon Pollock (et al.) in calling for a conception of cosmopolitanism based on 'how people have thought and acted across the local'.[14] Cosmopolitanism is useful in looking at how different media can enable viewers to imagine alternative lives. However, I want to temper this conception via Aihwa Ong: 'Seldom is there an attempt to analytically link actual institutions of state power, capitalism and transnational networks to such forms of cultural reproduction, inventiveness and possibilities.'[15]

Japan's prominence as a non-Western centre of globalisation allows us to question the conflation of globalisation with Western cultural imperialism. That said, Japan is still a part of the global north and the consumption of Japanese popular culture in South Africa therefore simultaneously provides a glimpse of the cultural cachet of the global north in the global south, while also showing the systemic biases resulting from colonial history that still frequently block the consumption of non-Western culture in a country so fundamentally shaped by Western colonialism and the neo-imperialist forces of the Cold War. Mapping the consumption of Japanese culture allows us to track the flows of non-Western culture while forcing us to question the idea of frictionless cultural flows. At the same time, it also allows us a glimpse into the potential and limits of popular culture consumption (and cultural reproduction via this consumption) that affect the structures listed by Ong.

MODES OF GLOBALISATION

This taxonomy of the modes of Japanese cultural globalisation is aimed at identifying mechanisms rather than historical phases. While not all mechanisms have been active at all moments, they have frequently acted concurrently and in tandem. For this reason, they should not be seen as distinct factors but rather as channels that sometimes bifurcate and sometimes reunite. My taxonomy is not aimed at creating isolated categories but to momentarily impose divisions for the sake of clarity.

Film festivals, art-house and elite DVD label distribution

Film festival screenings and art-house distribution have both played a crucial role in spreading Japanese film to the rest of the world.[16] The achievement of Kurosawa Akira's *Rashomon/Rashōmon* in winning the Golden Lion at the 1951 Venice Film Festival is frequently seen as a breakthrough moment in the international recognition of Japanese film. According to Donald Richie, this success also caused controversy within Japan because it undermined the division between films aimed at domestic audiences and films prepared for export.[17] Since then, film festivals and related distribution channels such as the elite Criterion Collection on DVD and online, have contributed to the global prominence of several generations of Japanese film-makers. Central to this form of distribution is the continued appeal of auteurism. Despite being questioned in academic film studies, auteurism remains a potent distribution strategy. Contemporary directors find themselves positioned and repositioned in relation to auteurs from the past who are also periodically revived (*Rashomon* itself received the Lion of Lions award at the 50th anniversary of the Venice Film Festival in 1982).[18] The succession of Japanese film directors gaining prominence through the machinery of high-profile film festivals, then being shown in art-house cinemas and finally receiving luxury DVD distribution, is frequently woven together as representing a kind of story of Japanese film itself with Mizoguchi Kenji, Kurosawa Akira and Ozu Yasujirō 'leading to' Ōshima Nagisa, Suzuki Seijun, later Kitano Takeshi, and finally Kore-eda Hirokazu and Kawase Naomi.[19] Film festivals retain a crucial role as a generator of publicity, but they also play a significant role in creating an imaginative construction of a country. In addition, they also remain spaces of cosmopolitanism, albeit of a particularly elite variety.[20]

Mainstream foreign distribution

In isolated cases, Japanese films and television have secured distribution by partnering with international distribution systems. While prominence gained at film festivals can lead to this kind of opportunity, the distinction between this and the former modes of distribution is that even if the work does achieve visibility by being showcased at film festivals, it also manages to break free of the relatively narrow circuit of art cinema distribution. A good example of this process is the work of Studio Ghibli. Ghibli films, such as *Spirited Away/Sen to chihiro no kamikakushi* (2001) have received considerable international attention by being dubbed into English and distributed by Disney.[21]

This category, however, covers any kind of Japanese cinema that has managed to gain international prominence by being transformed into a globalised commodity. A notable example is *Pokémon*, which became a global phenomenon through a hybridisation of narrative modes from Japanese video games and anime with the global distribution might of Hollywood and the logic of transnational capitalism.[22] This process has led to films and television programmes that are less narrowly defined in terms of national origin than art cinema. In fact, their success depends on making the signifiers of national origin operate in a new game of globally accessible identity formation. Rather than simply erasing Japaneseness, these works use signs signifying national origin in a way that allows non-citizens to insert this into their own identity formation. Franchises such as *Pokémon* and *Final Fantasy*, and in East Asia *Doraemon* and *Crayon Shin-chan*, are not completely scrubbed of Japaneseness. Rather, the signs of Japaneseness are rearranged to allow universal access in the same way that the signs of a specific kind of Britishness have functioned to make the *Harry Potter* franchise more of a global property. In addition, it is important to point out that as with *Harry Potter*, these are multi-platform franchises rather than individual works, where the active fandom (and its not-for-profit media production) accrued around the intellectual property is as significant as any individual official iteration across various media platforms, including feature film, television, manga, games and so on.

Intertextuality

The engagement between Japanese and other cinemas has frequently taken the form of conversations between different individual works and *oeuvres*. A classic example would be the global exchange of signifiers of masculinity that occurred between Kurosawa Akira and Western film-makers during the mid-twentieth century. A series of adaptations and remakes essentially constituted a dialogue on the nature of heroism and the role of on-screen violence. Notable moments in this process include the remake of Kurosawa's *The Seven Samurai/Shichinin no Samurai* (1954) as the Western *The Magnificent Seven* (1960), while Kurosawa either adapted, or was inspired by, Dashiell Hammett's noir novel *Red Harvest* in his making of *Yojimbo/Yōjinbō* (1961).[23] This film again provided the basis for Sergio Leone's *A Fistful of Dollars* (1964).[24] The process of remaking certain archetypes of masculinity in different period costumes set up a conversation between Japanese and other masculinities that extended to the influence of Kurosawa on such non-Western American classics as *Star Wars*.[25] In addition, this conversation extended into a homosocial collegiality that led to George Lucas, Francis Ford Coppola and Steven Spielberg producing Kurosawa's *Dreams* (1990).[26]

This conversation between masculinities has explicitly influenced films such as Miike Takashi's *Sukiyaki Western Django* (2007) and Guy Moshe's *Bunraku* (2014). This trope might be best summed up by a debate at the 2014 Fantastic Fest in Austin, Texas, which pitted participants against each other under the challenge: 'The samurai is infinitely more badass than the cowboy in cinema.' While the cowboy contingent unsurprisingly won this particular debate, the larger point is that Japanese and American films repeatedly redefine 'badass' in an intertextual conversation that has raised the prominence of Japanese cinema in the rest of the world.[27]

Marginal genres and audiences

Japanese cinema has entered various foreign markets obliquely through marginalised genres in order to sidestep the monopoly of Hollywood in mainstream markets. The two most dominant such genres during the mid-twentieth century were science fiction/creature films (most notably, the *Godzilla/Gojira* franchise) and children's television programming. The latter was a major engine of Japanese cultural globalisation from the postwar era until the early 1990s and became a regular presence on schedules during this era. It is may be the foremost example of what Koichi Iwabuchi

Fig. 35.1 *Mighty Morphin' Power Rangers/Super sentai* (TV Asahi, 1975–).

has described as the phenomenon of Japanese cultural commodities being scrubbed of 'Japaneseness'.[28]

In the case of the children's series *Mighty Morphin' Power Rangers* (1993–)/*Sūpā sentai* (1975–), for example, dialogue sections featuring Japanese actors were reshot with Western actors (Fig. 35.1). These sections were then cut into the original Japanese action sequences.[29] Children's programming, while a mainstay on television schedules, was also a relatively marginalised, low-budget sector of the industry. By offering children's animation and creature effects cheaply, Japanese companies found international distribution during a time when most other sections of the schedule were closed. Despite the commercial success of these properties, their limitation to children's programming functioned as a form of marginalisation from the cultural centre of power and taste. This shows that the marginalisation of audiences and genres essentially remains a single process, with the one feeding into the other. One could view film festival and art-house distribution as another iteration of this form of distribution. While film festivals occupy positions of high status, art-house distribution occupies a negligible sliver of the market. However, with the marginalisation of children's and creature genres also came the loss of the integrity of the work demanded by auteurism. While art-house audiences demanded correct aspect ratios and good subtitles, marginalised works were sliced and diced to fill up television space cheaply.

Global conversations about 'Asianism'

The logic of marginalised genres and art-house distribution came together with the targeting of niche audiences from the 1980s onwards. The era also saw the rise of the term 'Asian' as a distribution category. 'Asian cinema' essentially didn't exist as a category before this time. Instead, film vocabulary tended to rely on national origin in order to distinguish the different cinemas of Asia.[30] Mitsuhiro Yoshimoto has pointed to three factors that led to the rise of Asian cinema as a category within world distribution: the global economic rise of East Asia, the questioning of the concept of national cinema by film critics and the positioning of Asian cinemas against Hollywood by film festivals.[31] I would argue that the latter factor doesn't only relate to the prominence of film festivals but also the increasingly complex variety of film festivals on the global stage. The rise of niche or genre film festivals focusing on horror or fantasy film has led to the logic of auteurism also being applied to marginalised genres. The result has been not only the rise of 'Asian cinema' as a distribution category but also its coupling with extremity. This was particularly visible in the case of the London-based DVD label Tartan Asia Extreme.[32] Labels such as these created a space within which Asian auteurism was reformulated in terms of extremity, leading to the prominence of a new set of 'extreme' auteurs. In an article about the director Miike Takashi, Tony Williams set up a straw man: 'Takashi Miike's films contain excessive features of cinematic outrage similar to those found in the work of his contemporary Shinya Tsukamoto which often offend Western sensibilities.'[33] Of course, offending Western sensibilities was a crucial marketing strategy, and Miike and Tsukamoto consequently became known as auteurs of extremity, together with Park Chan-wook and Kim Ki-duk from South Korea, and the Pang brothers from Hong Kong.

The rise of 'Asian cinema' also reflects how the East Asian media industry is increasingly influenced by flows of capital, personnel and narrative tropes between different national industries.[34] The breadth and depth of this exchange demands a more fine-grained discussion than space permits here although I do return to it below.

Identity-based distribution

The internet has revolutionised the distribution of Japanese pop culture. Its effect has not only been restricted to the speed and ease of both legal and illegal distribution – a factor that affects all kinds of pop culture. The circulation of Japanese popular culture has especially been aided by the speed with which the internet has allowed the dissemination of new identities. The most vivid example of this process has been the evolution of the term *otaku* from a label for a particular Japanese subculture to a globalised identity that can be claimed by anyone. One of the powerful aspects of *otaku* as a form of self-identification has been that it sets up an identity that is simultaneously Japanese and transnational. Through adding a layer of self-identification to the simple consumption of Japanese pop culture, *otaku* identity has been the harbinger of wider trends of cultural consumption in the twenty-first century.

Otaku identity has received the widest attention, yet other examples of identity-based distribution have been noted by researchers focusing on the influence of Japanese popular culture in Asia. Shuling Huang has pointed out that the popularity of Japanese and Korean television drama in Taiwan has led to certain fans defining themselves via their consumption. One popular writer of books on Japanese pop culture described her level of fandom as 'Eating only Japanese food, watching only Japanese TV dramas, seeing only Japanese movies, listening only to Japanese songs and buying only made-in-Japan products.'[35] Pop culture fandom doesn't only segue into consumer behaviour; these consumption patterns also lead to identity formation (which of course informs future consumer choices). This aspect of Japanese pop culture dissemination has also become a central building block in Japanese cultural diplomacy with different ministries collaborating to expand the customer base for Japanese products in emerging markets, while also linking those products with ideas of Japanese values.[36]

These modes of dissemination should not be seen as operating discretely. How they overlap and reinforce each other will be explored in the case studies below.

COSMOPOLITANISM AT THE MARGINS: JAPANESE POP CULTURE IN SOUTH AFRICA

In this section I refer to three case studies in order to show how the modes of globalisation identified above have produced new forms of cosmopolitanism. It is important to remember that these cases are doubly marginal: South Africa is on the margins of globalisation, and film culture in South Africa has remained stubbornly narrow over the last century.

This is due to three main factors. Firstly, South Africa's circuits of film exhibition and distribution remain dominated by vertically integrated near monopolies. Secondly, these monopolies have been, and remain, closely aligned with Hollywood; at times due to direct investment from the US studios. Thirdly, until democratisation in 1994, successive South African governments used censorship to maintain the apartheid system, not only by cracking down on films deemed critical of the government but also by explicitly fostering segregated viewing patterns for segregated audiences. In particular, during much of the twentieth century, the state combined censorship and segregation to keep violent films from African audiences.[37] In addition, certain kinds of imported culture were manipulated to bolster the apartheid state's perceptions of itself.

The resultant narrowness of South African film culture has meant that Japanese film has also been marginalised *within* South Africa. These case studies will, however, show that the very marginal nature of Japanese film and media has also worked to subtly undercut the monopolies that have defined the consumption of popular culture in South Africa thus creating spaces of proto-cosmopolitanism.

Japanese children's anime during apartheid

Heidi, A Girl of the Alps/Alps no shōjo Haiji (1974) was a landmark work in Japanese television animation (Fig. 35.2).[38] The commercial success of this adaptation of Johanna Spyri's novel initiated a series of similar anime adaptations of Western children's novels, released under Nippon Animation's Sekai Meisaku Gekijō (World Masterpiece Theatre) name and circulated via television markets in Europe.[39] While this series enjoyed success within Japan, it was also aimed at foreign markets. *Sekai Meisaku Gekijō* never featured adaptations of Asian works – all the adaptations were of Western books, and it is not surprising that they soon found their way into children's television schedules all over the world. This means *Heidi* and other series such as *The Wonderful Adventures of Nils/Nils no fushigi na tabi* (1980) (broadcast in Afrikaans as *Nils Holgersson*) and *Dogtanian and the Three Muskehounds/Wanwan sanjūshi* (1981) (broadcast in Afrikaans as *Brakanjan*) should be seen as examples of dissemination via marginalised genres and audiences, in the sense that they were limited to children's schedules. All this anime was dubbed, which, together with their European settings, obscured their Japanese origin.

Heidi was acquired for the South African Broadcasting Corporation from television markets in Germany. Here, one can see how the circulation of Japanese content intended for marginalised audiences also took place via Western distribution mechanisms. In interviews, members of the dubbing team have told me that they acquired the series with a German soundtrack and used the German version as the basis for their Afrikaans translation. This was standard for the anime adaptations of European children's literature broadcast throughout the 1980s. In fact, in one instance when they had to work with the Japanese original, they simply made up dialogue to fit the animation; something that resulted in significantly altered storylines.[40]

The apartheid-era dubbing of Japanese anime adaptations of European novels into Afrikaans should be seen in the context of apartheid cultural politics – especially Afrikaner claims of representing a European heritage in Africa. In fact, the works were sometimes made more 'European'. For example, the Afrikaans version of *Heidi* replaced the original Japanese-language theme song, not with an Afrikaans version but with a different song in German (sung by an Afrikaans singer – complete with yodelling).[41]

Fig. 35.2 *Heidi, A Girl of the Alps/Alps no shōjo Haiji* (Zuiyō, 1974).

The effacement of the Japanese origin of these works, together with their distribution through the Western-dominated television market system, essentially allowed Afrikaners to symbolically insert themselves into a European ideoscape. In fact, some of Heidi's original dubbing team were even unaware that the series was originally Japanese.

In a more global sense, these works also facilitated the expansion of this European ideoscape through reinforcing ideas that European children's classics exemplified 'quality' entertainment for children – at a lower price. In interviews, South African television buyers emphasised this combination of 'quality' with cheapness repeatedly.

The *Sekai Meisaku Gekijo*-style of anime adaptations were not the only children's anime that reached South Africa during the 1980s. At least two science fiction series cobbled together by American studios from unrelated anime series were also broadcast. They were *Robotech* (1985) (edited together from *Super Dimension Fortress Macross/Chōjikū yōsai Macross* [1982], *Super Dimension Cavalry Southern Cross/ Chōjikū kidan southern cross* [1984] and *Genesis Climber MOSPEADA/Kikō sōseiki Mospeada* [1983]) and *Voltron, Defender of the Universe* (1984) (made up of *Beast King GoLion/Hyakujū-ō golion* [1981] and *Armored Fleet Dairugger XV/Kikō kantai dairugger fifteen* [1983]).[42]

How did these two kinds of anime affect South African cosmopolitanism? On the one hand, the anime's facilitation of Afrikaner claims on a European legacy can be seen as undercutting cosmopolitanism. However, it was also impossible to completely erase Japaneseness from these products because their animation styles were so distinct from the US animation broadcast on the same channels. As a child during the 1980s, for instance, I could not only detect differences in the visual design but also in the narrative. Arguably, the different modes of storytelling and visual design were subliminally disruptive of the Euro-American hegemony. This point can seem fantastic from a contemporary perspective. However, one must consider the stringency of censorship during apartheid. In a totalitarian system focused on policing and suppressing difference, and one simultaneously fixated on the trappings of Europe, the smallest visual differences functioned as traces of a larger world of difference erased by censorship. Anime adaptations of European classics managed to enter under the apartheid radar because they both performed 'Europeanness' and were for children. The former coded them as vaguely wholesome, and the latter as unworthy of further scrutiny because of the implicit assumption that children's programming is inherently cheap, repetitive entertainment. However, to this viewer, they provided glimpses of a different world, not provided by the Europe represented on screen but by the style of animation itself, which was markedly different from the American cartoons that populated apartheid television schedules. This was enabled by the marginalisation of children's animation as a genre.

Martial arts and African-Afrikaner cosmopolitanism

Martial arts film undercut apartheid hegemony much more explicitly than children's anime. In particular, it weakened apartheid's use of differential censorship to keep on-screen violence away from black audiences.

Martial arts film stepped into the gap created by shifts in apartheid. First, increased suburbanisation and white flight from the inner city led to the slight desegregation of inner city areas and with it the partial desegregation of inner city cinemas.[43] Second, the rise of VHS made partial censorship much more difficult to maintain and led to the proliferation of videocassette recorder (VCR) mini-cinemas in South African townships. These developments roughly coincided with the global popularity of martial arts film, in the wake of Bruce Lee.

The development of the martial arts film should be seen as one of the central examples of what I have called Japan's participation in transnational intertextual conversations about masculinity, as well as Japan's contribution to Asian cinema as a set of narratives and practices. While the Hong Kong martial arts film was influenced by Japanese *chanbara* and *judō* films, the global success of Bruce Lee also influenced the course of Japanese film. Direct Japanese adaptations of Hong Kong films were produced and action film narration and stardom shifted to reflect the influence of Hong Kong.[44]

One of the main figures of the Japanese post-Lee martial arts film was Shinichi (Sonny) Chiba. Chiba took part in the wider redefinition of Asian film that followed the global popularity of Lee and the coupling of Asia and extremity, long before the rise of Asia Extreme as a distribution category. *The Streetfighter/Gekitotsu! satsujin ken* (1974) starring Chiba was the first martial arts film to receive an X rating for violence.[45] The film was also banned in South Africa.

Asian martial arts film represented a perfect nexus of the different modes of globalisation I have outlined above. In addition to contributing to intertextual conversations about masculinity, and to the development of new Asian identities and their coupling with extremity, the martial arts film was also a marginalised genre sold to marginalised audiences in South Africa (and elsewhere). Mainstream (and therefore, white) cinemas maintained their focus on mainstream Hollywood film through the official channels that enabled overlapping state censorship and corporate control. Asian martial arts film was, however, not deemed worth distributing. The owners of the newly emerging video stores and partially desegregated inner city theatres needed inexpensive content and ordered these films directly or through informal agents. Martial arts film therefore stepped into a lacuna created by the weakening of differential censorship, which kept violent content away from African audiences. East Asian martial arts films provided working-class African audiences with their first chance of enjoying on-screen violence. These films remain popular to this day.

The martial arts boom clearly created spaces of cosmopolitanism at the margins. Interviews with movie distributors and video store owners indicate that martial arts films generated some of South Africa's first mixed audiences, especially working-class Africans and Afrikaners. In addition, by providing spaces for shared fandom, these video stores and cut-rate cinemas created some of South Africa's first spaces of cosmopolitan enjoyment, spaces that live on in the form of South Africa's satellite television channels dedicated to martial arts film.[46]

Martial arts film also creates a fantasy world of Asian cosmopolitanism on screen. *The Streetfighter*, for example, starts off in Tokyo and halfway through the action moves to Hong Kong. Both cities are depicted as sites of simultaneous modernism and tradition made manifest in different fighting styles. Martial arts film set up a fantasy cosmopolitanism of violence where national and cultural difference was manifested through styles of fighting. Cosmopolitanism in these films was created through reifying national difference, while simultaneously constructing pan-Asian ideas of loyalty, revenge and perseverance.

The centrality of Asia as the origin of shared meaning and the presence of Asians as central protagonists were revolutionary concepts in the context of apartheid. The Asian setting also arguably created safe spaces where South African working-class audiences could imaginatively try out cosmopolitanism.

What was the role of Japanese film in all of this? This question brings us to the limits of national cinema as a concept. While Chiba occupies a central position in the history of Japanese cinema, his role in developing a dialogue around both the constitution of Asian film and the transnational development of ideas of masculinity was, arguably, even greater. In other words, focusing on Japan's position within a dialogic relationship potentially brings more insight than an approach solely focused on national cinema. Marginalised genres such as the martial arts film are particularly suited to this kind of enquiry because they are produced outside the prestige economy of auteurs and film festivals that generally construct our understanding of national cinema. Chiba has worked in Japanese films influenced by, and responding to, Hong Kong and American action film as well as in actual Hong Kong and American productions. At the same time, his performances for Japanese directors such as Fukasaku Kinji have created archetypes that have influenced film-makers in several other countries. The consumption and production of East Asian martial arts film should therefore be seen as spaces of cosmopolitanism at the margins – a form of cinematic cosmopolitanism to which Japan has made a crucial contribution.

Anime and internet fandom in contemporary South Africa

Since 2004, the Japanese government has promoted anime as a part of its cultural 'soft' diplomacy. The budget to promote Japanese popular culture in foreign markets has ballooned.[47] Far from fostering the popularity of Japanese media in foreign markets, this official attempt has, however, been akin to running after a train that has already left the station. Japanese pop culture has managed to spread far beyond the markets actively targeted by the government. South Africa provides a case in point. While Japan's official relationship with Africa is still dominated by aid and the continent is still largely ignored by the promoters of Japanese pop culture, South Africa has a rapidly expanding fan community.

This expansion is almost completely dependent on the internet. While a small amount of anime comes to South Africa via DVDs from American distributers, all the anime fans I have interviewed say they either download it themselves or trade downloaded copies between friends. Online social networks for South African anime fans play a crucial part in this circulation. This goes beyond the simple circulation of anime. Identities are also constructed, expanded and shared through these networks. Members of the Cosplay SA Facebook group,[48] for example, frequently have conversations about anime plots, characters and creators, but they also use the network to exchange tips on making costumes, finding props and also build enthusiasm for large fan events.[49]

The expansion of such networks even in such a marginal anime market as South Africa has a number of implications for the future distribution of Japanese film and television. Firstly, conventional media have become increasingly irrelevant in the global circulation of Japanese pop culture. A satellite television channel and a magazine aimed at South African anime fans have both failed, while online networks continue to expand. My own interviews with South African anime fans have shown that many do not own televisions and have never watched anime on DVD.[50] Secondly, the borders of individual works are becoming increasingly diffuse. This is not only due to the effects of media convergence but also the importance of anime in the formation of identity. In earlier auteurist modes of distribution, and even the freely recut children's anime of the Cold War era, the borders of the work remained relatively intact. Contemporary identity-based distribution has radically decentred the film or television programme as a discrete entity. Instead, it makes more sense to think of it as a nucleus of meaning embedded in a wider cloud of related works, including video games and anime spin-offs, fan art, cosplay and so on. The way the work functions as a trigger for fans' self-definition therefore becomes crucial to its distribution, because they are essentially creating new pieces of this *Gesamtkunstwerk* through social media.

Japan has become a pioneer of this mode of distribution. While American studios tended to crack down on unauthorised reproductions, the Japanese *dōjinshi* system[51] and the industry's dependence on outsourced merchandise has normalised a process whereby an original work leads to a wide swathe of user-generated subworks, frequently representing strikingly different tones, genres and national vocabularies.[52] This openness to fan contributions has facilitated the international spread of Japanese anime because it has also encouraged social networking. It is striking that Japanese pop culture has not spread through diaspora-based ethnoscapes as in the case of Indian and Nigerian film. Rather, *otaku* identity has formed a kind of ideoscape, which anyone can join through the act of self-definition.

One aspect of this process of self-definition is the maintenance of distance from the mainstream. This means that online communities of *otaku* are per definition cosmopolitan – because they are made up of people who define themselves as minorities in relation to their own dominant cultures. While being cosmopolitan in make-up, these communities are thus also marginal enclaves.

This is also true for South African *otaku*. These communities are both racially and culturally more mixed than the still-segregated consumption communities in South Africa's mainstream. Yet, they remain marginal in terms of class. When reading online discussions on anime fan bulletin boards, one is struck by how most of this fandom is out of the reach of South Africans without either a sufficiently strong internet connection to stream or download anime or the money to pay for tickets to fan events.[53] This is also true for fans of Japanese games as well as the fans of 'extreme' Japanese cinema. Miike's *Ichi the Killer/Koroshiya Ichi* (2001) was, for example, banned in South Africa due to violence. A censored cut was then released by a South African distributor, but it was deemed a failure because most fans sidestepped the censorship by simply downloading the original version or ordering the DVD from UK labels specialising in 'extreme' Asian cinema.

While both anime and contemporary 'extreme' Asianism are potential sites of cosmopolitan fandom, this is limited by access to material resources – a fact that echoes criticism of cosmopolitanism as a political ideal. *Otaku*-powered distribution has certainly helped to pioneer the Möbius strip connection between cultural consumption and identity and the expansion of consumer identity to global ideoscapes, yet as this form of distribution becomes more important, the lack of access to these enclaves of cosmopolitanism becomes more problematic.

CONCLUSION

This chapter has made an attempt to describe the different modes of postwar Japanese film and television dissemination. Instead of dividing this topic up into discrete historical eras, I have tried to identify a number of common modes running across the period. The aim of this approach has been to hone in on the particularity of Japanese globalisation and how Japanese culture has managed to find international audiences despite the global hegemony of Western culture. At the same time, the approach also fits into a model of globalisation that describes a set of flows and counterflows within and across a number of 'scapes', or fields of cultural power and organisation. In other words, by looking at the wider conversation between Japanese and non-Japanese popular culture, as well as the sometimes partial or prohibited movement of individual Japanese popular culture products, we may gain a view of globalisation that refuses easy assumptions about monocultural domination. We may also see the impact of these products on niche markets far from the international or even national mainstream. Japan is a cultural powerhouse and yet it is also non-Western. This makes it a valuable case through which to question and rethink cultural globalisation as a whole. The spread of Japanese culture disproves the idea that globalisation is simply the erasure of regional cultures by Western mass culture. Yet, a frank look at the ways in which Japanese pop culture flows have been impeded, and how Japanese films and television series have been stripped of any cultural specificity in foreign markets, also makes clear that we need to focus more on how global power imbalances still structure and limit cultural globalisation. These power imbalances operate on a transnational level as well as within local communities. In fact, certain communities' lack of access to broadband internet remains a central problem.

Japanese pop culture has succeeded in creating numerous important spaces of transnational fandom. In some cases, these spaces have come into being thanks to the need of isolated fans to create a community of consumption. The growth of community around the kernel of individual consumption (rather than more traditional factors such as religion or nationality) has, to a certain extent, enabled some of these communities to overcome racial and gender barriers. Yet these forms of cosmopolitanism – from art cinema fans to contemporary cosplayers – still remain bounded by the economics of cultural consumption and therefore continue to be inherently organised around class lines. In a global south country such as South Africa, this means that the consumption of Japanese popular culture creates enclaves that are simultaneously relatively cosmopolitan and exclusive. While Japanese cultural fandom offers South Africans the opportunity to transcend momentarily some of the country's racial and gender barriers, as well as the global Euro-American hegemony that has structured South African society geopolitically, the economic realities undergirding this consumption nonetheless mean that it still excludes the vast majority of South Africans.

Notes

1. See, for example, Yoshikawa Naohiro, *Galápagos suru nihon* (Tokyo: Kōdansha, 2010); and Asahi shinbun, *Galápagos desu kedo, nanika?* (Tokyo: Asahi shinbunsha, 2014).
2. Arjun Appadurai, *Modernity at Large: Cultural Dimensions of Globalization* (Minneapolis: University of Minnesota Press, 1996), pp. 216–26.
3. Manuel Castells, *Communication Power* (Oxford: Oxford University Press, 2011), p. 19.
4. I have found it useful to conflate cinema and television in certain cases, while distinguishing them in others. This is because the networks of fandom that spread Japanese media frequently spread both forms (as well as other forms, such as manga) simultaneously. This is especially true for contemporary circulation based on consumption identity. However, when the cases of film and television are distinct, I make this clear.
5. David Harvey, *A Brief History of Neoliberalism* (Oxford: Oxford University Press, 2007).
6. Robbie Robertson, *Three Waves of Globalization: A History of a Developing Global Consciousness* (London: Zed Books, 2002).
7. See, for example, Edward S. Herman and Robert W. McChesney, *The Global Media: The New Missionaries of Corporate Capitalism* (London: Continuum, 1997); John Tomlinson, *Cultural Imperialism: A Critical Introduction* (London: Continuum, 2002).
8. See, for example, John Fiske and John Hartley, *Reading Television* (London: Routledge, 2004).
9. Arif Dirlik, *After the Revolution: Waking to Global Capitalism* (Hanover, NH: Wesleyan University Press, 1994).
10. Paul Hopper, *Understanding Cultural Globalization* (Cambridge: Polity, 2007).
11. David Held, 'From Executive to Cosmopolitan Multilateralism', in David Held and Mathias Koenig-Archibughi (eds), *Taming Globalization: Frontiers of Governance* (Cambridge: Polity, 2003).
12. See, for example, Aihwa Ong, *Flexible Citizenship: The Cultural Logics of Transnationality* (Durham, NC: Duke University Press, 1999); Robert J. Holton, *Cosmopolitanisms: New Thinking and New Directions* (London: Palgrave Macmillan, 2009).
13. See, for example, Jacques Derrida, *On Cosmopolitanism and Forgiveness* (London: Routledge, 2001).
14. Sheldon Pollock, Homi K. Bhabha, Carol A. Breckenridge and Dipesh Chakrabarty, *Cosmopolitanism* (Durham, NC: Duke University Press, 2002), p. 10.
15. Ong, *Flexible Citizenship*, p. 15.
16. [Editors' note: for more on film festivals and Japanese cinema, see also Chapter 11 by Ran Ma in this volume.]
17. Donald Richie, *Rashomon: Akira Kurosawa, Director* (New Brunswick, NJ: Rutgers University Press, 1987), p. 20.
18. Kenichi Kawano, 'A Phenomenological Inquiry of *Rashomon*', *Contributions to Phenomenology* vol. 69 (2014), pp. 295–309.
19. See, for example, 'A Short History of Japanese Cinema', Volta, <https://www.volta.ie/#!/page/651/a-short-history-of-japanese-cinema>.
20. Can-Seng Ooi and Jesper Strandgaard Pederson, 'City Branding and Film Festivals: Re-evaluating Stakeholder's Relations', *Place Branding and Public Diplomacy* vol. 6 no. 4 (2010), pp. 316–32. [Editors' note: for more on globalisation and Japanese cinema, see also Chapter 39 by Yoshiharu Tezuka in this volume.]
21. Rayna Denison, 'Star-Spangled Ghibli: Star Voices in the American Versions of Hayao Miyazaki's Films', *Animation: An Interdisciplinary Journal* vol. 3 no. 2 (2008), pp. 129–46.
22. Anne Allison, 'New-Age Fetishes, Monsters, and Friends: Pokémon Capitalism at the Millennium', in Tomiko Yoda and Harry Harootunian (eds), *Japan after Japan: Social and Cultural Life from the Recessionary 1990s to the Present* (Durham, NC: Duke University Press, 2006).
23. Joseph L. Anderson, 'When the Twain Meet: Hollywood's Remake of *The Seven Samurai*', *Film Quarterly* vol. 15 no. 3 (1962), pp. 55–8.
24. Geoffrey Nowell-Smith and Joseph Sullivan, 'Variations on a Theme: *Yojimbo*, *A Fistful of Dollars* and the "Servant of Two Masters"', *Journal of Romance Studies* vol. 4 no. 1 (2004), pp. 79–90.
25. This influence is now part of the canon of officially approved *Star Wars* fandom. See 'The Cinema behind Star Wars: The Seven Samurai', <https://www.starwars.com/news/the-cinema-behind-star-wars-seven-samurai>.
26. Noriko Reider, 'Akira Kurosawa's Dreams, as Seen through the Principles of Classical Japanese Literature and Performing Art', *Japan Forum* vol. 17 no. 2 (2005), pp. 257–72.

27 Matt Singer, 'Fantastic Fest: Bunraku Reviewed', Independent Film channel, <http://www.ifc.com/fix/2011/09/bunraku-review>.

28 Koichi Iwabuchi, *Recentering Globalization: Popular Culture and Japanese Transnationalism* (Durham, NC: Duke University Press, 2002).

29 Shu-Ling C. Everett, 'Mirage Multiculturalism: Unmasking the Mighty Morphin' Power Rangers', *Journal of Mass Media Ethics* vol. 11 no. 1 (1996), pp. 28–39.

30 Olivia Khoo, 'Bad Jokes, Bad English, Good Copy: Sukiyaki Western Django, or How the West was Won', *Asian Studies Review* vol. 37 no. 1 (2013), pp. 80–95.

31 Mitsuhiro Yoshimoto, 'National/international/transnational: The Concept of Trans-Asian Cinema and the Cultural Politics of Film Criticism', in Valentina Vitali and Paul Willemen (eds), *Theorizing National Cinema* (London: British Film Institute, 2006), pp. 254–61.

32 Oliver Dew, '"Asia Extreme": Japanese Cinema and British Hype', *New Cinemas: Journal of Contemporary Film* vol. 5 no. 1(2007), pp. 53–73.

33 Tony Williams, 'Takashi Miike's Cinema of Outrage', *CineAction* no. 64 (2004), p. 55.

34 See, for example, Stephen Teo, *The Asian Film Experience: Styles, Spaces, Theory* (London: Routledge, 2012).

35 Shuling Huang, 'Nation-branding and Transnational Consumption: Japan-mania and Korean Wave in Taiwan', *Media, Culture & Society* vol. 33 no. 3 (2011), p. 10.

36 Author's interview with Kishimori Hajime, head of the Public Diplomacy Division, Ministry of Foreign Affairs in Tokyo, July 2014. [Editors' note: for more detailed discussion of an intermedial approach to popular Japanese culture, see also Chapter 14 by Rayna Denison in this volume.]

37 Martin Botha, *South African Cinema 1896–2010* (Bristol: Intellect, 2012); Keyan Tomaselli *The Cinema of Apartheid: Race and Class in South African Film* (Sandton: Radix, 1989).

38 [Editors' note: for more on anime, see also Chapter 22 by Thomas Lamarre in this volume.]

39 Freddy Litten, 'Kinderleid un Kinderfreud: Nippon Animations "World Masterpiece Theatre"', in *FUNime: Magazin für Anime und Manga* no. 49 (2007), pp. 6–9.

40 Cobus van Staden, 'Moomin/Mūmin/Moemin: Apartheid-Era Dubbing and Japanese Anime', *Critical Arts* vol. 28 no. 1 (2014), pp. 1–18; Cobus van Staden, 'The Golden Glow of the Alps: Anime Reimagines Europe', in Felicia Chan, Angelina Karpovich and Xin Zhang (eds), *Genre in Asian Film and Television: New Approaches* (London: Palgrave Macmillan, 2011), pp. 178–93.

41 Van Staden, 'The Golden Glow of the Alps'.

42 Fred Patten, *Watching Anime, Reading Manga: 25 Years of Essays and Reviews* (Albany, CA: Stone Bridge Press, 2004).

43 Tomaselli, *The Cinema of Apartheid*.

44 Chris Desjardins, *Outlaw Masters of Japanese Film* (London: I.B.Tauris, 2005); Kinnia Shuk-ting Yau, 'Interactions between Japanese and Hong Kong Action Cinemas', in Meaghan Morris, Siu Leung Li and Stephen Chan Ching-kiu (eds), *Hong Kong Connections: Transnational Imagination in Action Cinema* (Durham, NC: Duke University Press, 2005), pp 35–48.

45 Bill Palmer, Karen Palmer and Ric Meyers, *The Encyclopedia of Martial Arts Movies* (New York: Rowman & Littlefield, 1995).

46 Author's interview with Nada Ghannam, Tony Karam and Rafich Mohamed, on 1 July 2014, in Johannesburg.

47 Author's interview with Kishimori Hajime, on 14 July 2014, at the Ministry of Foreign Affairs in Tokyo.

48 Cosplay is a form of fan practice characterised by fans reenacting scenes from anime series while dressed in elaborate (frequently homemade) costumes.

49 Cosplay SA Facebook Group, <https://www.facebook.com/groups/3415749605/?fref=nf>.

50 Catherine Duncan, 'Fan Practices in South African Global Popular Culture Fandoms' (unpublished PhD thesis, University of the Witwatersrand, 2018).

51 A system where aspirant manga artists gain experience and fame through self-published manga that frequently draw on existing properties of the medium.

52 Nicolle Lamerichs, 'The Cultural Dynamic of Doujinshi and Cosplay: Local Anime Fandom in Japan, USA and Europe', *Participations* vol. 10 no. 1 (2013), pp. 154–76.

53 Duncan, 'Fan Practices in South African Global Popular Culture Fandoms'.

PART 7
FLOWS AND INTERACTIONS

JAPANESE CINEMA AND ITS POSTCOLONIAL HISTORIES
Technologies of coproduction: Japan in Asia and the Cold War production of regional place

Stephanie DeBoer

Both domestic and international posters of the 1962 epic film *The Great Wall/Shin shikōtei/Qinshi huangdi*, directed by Tanaka Shigeo, featured an impressively wide anchoring backdrop of an imperial fortress wall. The imposing figure of the first emperor to consolidate all of China, played by the leading Japanese actor Katsu Shintarō, was featured above it alongside his colourfully costumed empress lording over a vast army – a distant formation of imperial soldiers played by extras solicited from the film's shooting location. Advertised solely as a production of Japan's Daiei studio, the landscapes, intrigue and massive battle scenes promised by these posters were enabled by a collaboration with Taiwan's Central Motion Picture Company, which had garnered Japanese studio access to the Taiwanese shooting locations and the numbers of soldiering extras and staff needed to produce the epic scenes that were the feature of this film. Yet, as the captions of these advertisements claimed prominently, these scenes were also produced through the latest in international film technologies. Made with Technicolor, the leading US colour motion picture process alongside which Japanese studios were then developing their own colour patents, *The Great Wall* was further hailed as Japan's second production of a 70mm film. The film's deployment of the latest developments in extreme widescreen and colour formats, proclaimed the Japanese press, would raise *The Great Wall* to a standard fit for 'world' audiences.[1]

These posters for *The Great Wall* illustrate one significant strategy for film coproduction and collaboration between Japan and Asia during the early Cold War. Particularly from the mid-1950s, Japanese film studios combined regional images and shooting locations with the latest in international colour and widescreen technologies. They did so with an aim to produce films appealing to the 'world' – largely meaning Euro-American markets. Japanese collaborations with Hong Kong and Taiwan were particularly marked in this context and thus offer a locus for examining the competing aspirations and practices, as well as problems, that made up Cold War film production and coproduction in the region. As I have argued elsewhere, film and media coproductions constitute a 'technology of production' assembling 'film and media imaginaries, promotion and production practices, and industry mandates and aspirations' to a variety of contingent ends.[2] Certainly, coproductions might be made with an eye towards a range of material aims including, as Barbara Selznick has put it, the 'pooling of financial resources, accessing subsidies and incentives, accessing partner's markets, accessing third country markets, learning from partners, reducing risks, and accessing resources […] and locations'.[3] Coproductions in this sense both mobilise and rely upon uneven geographic scales and dynamics – scales and dynamics that held to particular implications, practices, histories and imaginaries in early Cold War East and South East Asia. Japanese studios' intermittent use of regional, in particular Chinese, collaborations was indicative of a desire for Japan's place at the vanguard of a then emergent 'Asian' arena of cinematic output. *The Great Wall*'s promotion of a strategy of combining regional locations with a platform of the latest in international image production technologies proved a brief yet resonant formula. This formula combined, to deploy Yoshiharu Tezuka's phrasing from a different context, film image 'content' and technological 'form' to bring Japanese cinema – with other regional cinemas following – on par with the more 'developed' standards of Euro-American film festivals and markets.[4]

To address films such as *The Great Wall* within these collaborative contexts is to interrogate film coproduction's roles in the production of regional place and its construction, as cultural geographers such as Doreen Massey have long argued, through ever contingent geometries of practice and power.[5] Regional coproductions from the mid-1950s are also exemplary arenas for examining the particular film practices through which Japanese studios aspired to create an 'internationalist' sense of the region. Studios negotiated the Cold War interests and images of Japan, the West and 'Asia' (here the locations of Taiwan and Hong Kong) in order to enable its cinemas to travel to world markets. Certainly, as Kinnia Yau and others have argued, the making of film coproductions between Japan and Hong Kong as well as Taiwan was in part enabled by the industrial contacts and relationships that had been unevenly created in Japan's earlier imperial occupation and colonisation of locations throughout East and South East Asia.[6] Yet as our scholarship, criticism and curatorial practices increasingly pay attention to the interconnections among regional film industries over the past century and more, we must also better understand the particularities of exchange that have been formed and maintained from one moment to the next. This means attending to not only the continuities but also the discontinuities in temporality and practice, all in addition to the particular dynamics of power enabled by specifically located geopolitical regimes and geographic relations.[7]

Regional coproductions in the early Cold War, in this sense, were produced in the vastly different regional landscape and context of imperialisation – a distinct internationalist regime formed in the divides of development and underdevelopment, East and West, and 'free' capitalist and communist arenas.[8] No simple legacy of colonial ties (though certainly refracting them), the studios' pursuit of regional Asian coproductions in the mid-1950s to early 1960s was largely driven by a desire for Japanese cinema to move forward from its relative underdevelopment in the immediate postwar period to achieve more 'international' (read Euro-American) standards of film-making. Americanist Cold War terms for exchange were thus a central geographic frame and the grounds from which studios pursued international and regional film-making. As the epic films of this chapter suggest, China played a prominent role in the formation of these aspirations. This China, on the one hand, was expressed as a series of variously epic and exotic images of mythical China that arguably appealed to Euro-American markets and tastes.[9] Yet these images also stood upon a platform of location shooting – and film collaboration more generally – reliant upon a Cold War contemporary regional geography articulated in divides between capitalist and communist China, the perceived relative development of Japan, Hong Kong, Taiwan and their industries, and the wider regional and international markets to which they aspired.

It is within this negotiation of the Cold War region that this chapter examines the practices, technologies and locations of image production for large-budget films coproduced between Japan and Hong Kong as well as Taiwan in the mid-1950s to early 1960s. By the time of *The Great Wall*'s promotion in 1962, this strategy of combining 'Asian' locations and film images with the latest in technological advances had already been established in the other two coproductions addressed by this chapter. Mizoguchi Kenji's 1955 *Princess Yang Kwei-fei/Yōhiki/Yang Guifei* was a colour epic period drama produced with Hong Kong's Shaw Brothers studio and Japan's Daiei studio. Toyoda Shirō's 1956 *Madame White Snake/Byaku fujin no yōren/Bai she chuan* was similarly a colour epic produced between Japan's Tōhō studio and Shaw Brothers (Fig. 36.1). While these earlier films were successful in establishing precedents for this formula, as they garnered recognition and awards from European festivals, my aim is not to address the 'success' or 'failure' of such strategies in film collaboration. Rather, I aim to interrogate the negotiations of regional place and location that made up these coproductions, in terms of the aspirations and efforts – industrial, technological

Fig. 36.1 *Madame White Snake/Byaku fujin no yōren/Bai she chuan* (Toyoda Shirō, 1956, Tōhō and Shaw Brothers).

and image-based – produced within the uneven relations of Cold War internationalism that made up the region at this time. This chapter thus situates studio desires to sit at the vanguard of film technologies and image production within a region caught between the developmental ideals of the Cold War and the legacies of colonisation and imperialisation. In this regard, Japanese film studio efforts to capitalise upon the Cold War divides of development and underdevelopment, East and West, and free capitalist and communist arenas that made up the region of the 1950s and early 1960s, largely subsumed recognition of the colonial or imperial relations that had previously set the stage for regional film collaborations. While particular to the cinematic and regional geographies of this moment, such strategies and their concomitant negotiations also resonate with other efforts in the region. I thus end with a brief reflection on a number of Hong Kong films that utilised similar strategies for their own distinct studio contexts, local/regional dynamics and international aspirations.

FILM TECHNOLOGIES AND COLD WAR LOCATIONS

The Great Wall, announced the Japanese film magazine *Kinema junpō*, was one of a significant number of widescreen films produced by Japan in 1962. Films such as *Storm Over Kinmen Bay/Kinmontō ni kakeru hashi/Haiwan fengyun/Jinmen wan fengyun* (1962) and *Star of Hong Kong/Hong Kong no hoshi/Xianggang zhi xing* (1962) joined *The Great Wall* within a slate of films whose scale and potential impact were indicative of the ever 'widening' or 'expanding' scope of Japanese cinema. The year 1962, as the author indicated, had been the first year of market decline for the Japanese film industry, as box-office takings fell in relation to the sharp rise in television sets and leisure industries that had emerged from the late 1950s – a problem that such widescreen production was meant to address as well.[10] 'Widening' or 'expanding' thus held a dual meaning in this context. Such reports celebrated the increasingly spectacular span of the projected film screen that new developments in widescreen cinema production enabled; these widescreen image formats were at the same time deemed an important strategy in gaining expanded access to world markets. As promotional accounts for *The Great Wall* further indicated, the combined sensibilities of new colour technologies with new developments in widescreen cinema were considered equally important to bringing Japanese cinema to the more developed standards of world filmmaking, and thereby to the reach and acceptance of international audiences and markets.

For all the Japanese industry's international aspirations, the technologically enabled films that accompanied *The Great Wall* were at the same time notably predicated upon Asian shooting locations and image content. This list of coproduced films is thus a locus for considering the interdependence of regional production practices and international market aspirations – and, in particular, the geographic problems and possibilities that resulted from there in the early Cold War. In addition to *The Great Wall*, for example, *Storm Over Kinmen Bay* utilised locations in Taiwan's Kinmen Island and the straights between Taiwan and mainland China to support its narrative of Cold War intrigue. *Star of Hong Kong* travelled to Hong Kong and Macau to enable its stories of international romance. Many such coproduced films highlighted the contemporary aspirations of the Cold War region. These two particular films depicted the difficulties of international romance and regional networks against new possibilities in terms of fashion, international occupation and 'jet set' forms of transport. They further set their differentiated possibilities against the backdrop of an East and South East Asia rapidly developing at various rates in relation to incursions of Americanist capital and geopolitics. In the midst of this 1962 list of regionally produced films, however, *The Great Wall* maintained an imaginary earlier established in such coproduced films as *Princess Yang Kwei-fei* and *Madame White Snake* (Fig. 36.2). Here, spectacularly set widescreen costume genres featuring images and intrigue of an ancient, mythic China continued to be produced. While certainly also produced to compete with Euro-American and world markets, *The Great Wall*'s epic images remained nonetheless reliant upon

Fig. 36.2 *Princess Yang Kwei-fei/Yōhiki/Yang Guifei* (Mizoguchi Kenji, 1955, Daiei and Shaw Brothers).

the navigation of a contemporary Cold War regional geography, as its wide colour scenes were also made through the production practices of regional location shooting. Indeed, the 1962 coproduction is a reminder of the contradictions and collusions at play as new film images rendered for international circulation were dependent upon a Cold War regional geography.

A series of forums in the 1955 and 1956 editions of the weekly magazine *Sunday Mainichi* had earlier announced Japan's place within the contemporary 'co-production boom' of the film world, and set developments in coproduction at the centre of the potential advancement for the Japanese film industry.[11] For all its difficulties – film-makers' navigation of differences in language, culture and film practice were cited as persistent problems – international coproduction was here highlighted as a new 'capitalist' mode of film-making that would 'bring about [new] exchanges in culture' in its unprecedented reach across the world. Japan, as a contemporary 'mecca' for coproduction, was to stand at the centre of the new possibilities in capitalist film-making signalled by coproduction – whether it be in the sharing of finances, in the exchange of production staff or stars, or in a greater access to shooting locations and audiences. Japan had become what the article termed the 'new face on the block' for world film-making following the unexpected success of *Rashomon/Rashōmon* in the Venice film festival of 1951. Full participation in this platform for film production and circulation – and thereby in access to the dollars and yen that would enable the development of its industries – were dependent, for these writers, upon the staff, stars and new narratives that accompanied them.[12] Coproduction at this moment was also deemed a platform that would enable the development of the new film technologies that were simultaneously considered central to Japan's development into international standards of film-making. Indeed, it was the 'international success of *Rashomon*' that reportedly 'whetted Nagata's [the president of Daiei studio] appetite' for international collaborative efforts that were to enable the technological capabilities of Japanese cinema. Nagata Masaichi thus 'sent his filmmakers to learn about the latest filmmaking technologies in the US'.[13] Colour patents were particularly desired in this context, as advances in Technicolor, and from there local patents in Fujicolour, Daieicolour and so on, were to set Japanese film upon a trajectory of 'developed' film-making well received by world and festival circuits.[14]

In their links to regional geographies, these internationalist desires for advancement in film technology were contained and produced within Americanist models and ideals – models and ideals that remediated the imperial legacies of East and South East Asia. Following its postwar retreat from its occupied East and South East Asian territories, Japan looked to regain access to its formerly imperial markets. For example, as I have articulated elsewhere, Taiwan proved to be a particularly desired market for Japanese studios in the immediate postwar period. Japan had renewed its export of contemporary films to Taiwan in 1953 as part of a broader set of trade agreements that were linked to the renegotiation of ties between the former coloniser and colonised, as established in the 1952 Japan–Taiwan Peace treaty. From 1953 to 1954, Taiwanese quotas for Japanese films were consistently set at a maximum of twenty-four imports per year, dramatically lower, as Japan's studio representatives complained, than the industry's Hollywood or Hong Kong counterparts. Against these restrictions, Japan's studio focus on the potential of Taiwan as a central market in the region for Japanese film products continued throughout the decade. In 1957, studio annals projected that Taiwan held the largest potential for Japanese film exports in the region – a status that was the product of Japanese industry focus on regional markets with linguistic or cultural affinities in the first two decades following its colonial occupation of the island. Japanese industrialists of the 1950s into the 1960s thus aspired to the development of regional markets that promised, for Japanese film, a shared 'free capitalist' regional system as well as an 'Asian' cultural proximity in the context of a world market bifurcated between East and West, communism and capitalism. These aspirations were predicated, however, on perceptions of a Taiwanese audience already well cultivated by the colonial policies of assimilation into a Japanese empire that had supported the reception of Japanese and imperial films in Taiwan up to 1945.[15]

While this market hope was thwarted in the postwar period by Taiwan's continued refusal to remove quota restrictions on Japanese film imports, Hong Kong was increasingly the recipient of industry-wide focus. By the late 1950s to early 1960s, Japanese industry reports solidly highlighted Hong Kong as the more central location for film-making in the region. The negotiations that characterised this shift in market focus between Taiwan and Hong Kong underscore how developmentalist ideals and de-imperialising sentiments worked in tandem with each other in postwar industrial imaginings of Asia. Japanese studio concerns for East and South East Asia's promise of cultural affinity were predicated on a colonial backdrop. Hong Kong was already beginning to exemplify an aura of affinity between colonialism and internationalisation for world industries in terms of its particular status as simultaneously 'both'. Indeed, for Japanese studios, Hong Kong's potential lay not simply in its long-standing status as a gateway for the distribution of Japanese films into South East Asia; it resided just as well in the colony's increasingly large-scale studios and 'exotic' locations that inserted themselves well into the uneven international terms of film production at the time. In the face of this understanding, Taiwan was increasingly presented as simply a cog in these market transformations, as geopolitics linked to decolonisation, and the nationalisms that accompanied it, disrupted Japanese industry appeals for 'equitable' trade with its former colony. In mainstream Japanese film industry reports at the very least, Taiwan thus appears as a locus of anticipation and desire. As its affinities were naturalised within the capitalist marketplace, Japanese studios deferred the implications and thereby the recognition of their former colonial and imperial status against an overwhelming rhetoric of progress and market expansion. It was these very open-market multinational ideals that Hong Kong would increasingly exemplify for Japan in the 1950s and 1960s.[16]

It is here where the significance of the 1962 Taiwan–Japan coproduction *The Great Wall* lies, as the discourses that surrounded the film illustrate the continued tensions of development and decolonisation through which desires for technological development and international film coproduction were articulated in the early Cold War region (Fig. 36.3). Against the above market shifts, occasional collaborative activities continued between Taiwan and Japan, even into the early 1960s. A report in *Kinema junpō* featured a wide still photo of a battle scene from *The Great Wall*, its central Japanese star Katsu Shintarō set in warrior regalia in the foreground against a vastly populated battle scene in the background. The caption and article to follow emphasised the size and span of the film.[17] Its 70 mm widescreen size and production scale were, as the article indicated, exemplary of the kind of film-making that was to bring national-regional production of Japan 'up' to international standards and thereby world market appeal. Indeed, the impact of such efforts towards bridging national,

Fig. 36.3 *The Great Wall/Shin shikōtei/Qinshi Huangdi* (Tanaka Shigeo, 1962, Daiei and Taiwan's Central Motion Picture Company).

regional and international/world circuits were debated across other film-making efforts of the time, as well. The 10th annual Asian Film Festival, held in Tokyo in 1963, opened with the promotional logo of a three-dimensional globe encircled by the title of the festival printed repeatedly in large capital letters. This encompassing of the globe within the purview of the regional festival announced, as one critic in Tokyo declared, the particular 'international flavour' and aspirations of the gathering.[18] The festival had been established ten years earlier under the Federation of Motion Picture Producers in Asia (FPA) on the initiative of Nagata Masaichi, the president of Japan's Daiei studio, and under the vice-presidency of Run Run Shaw, who led studios in Singapore and Hong Kong. Encompassing a total of eight member state studios at that point, among them Taiwan, South Korea, Malaysia, Thailand, the Philippines and Indonesia, the collective sought to advance the film industries of the region towards higher technocultural standards.[19] Yet such efforts met with mixed reception. This same Tokyo-based critic, for example, called on the federation to cultivate 'more meaningful technological exchanges' and 'more meaningful co-productions'.[20] Only through such endeavours could Asian film dig itself out of the comparative underdevelopment it faced in relation to other parts of the globe. Critical debates within the Taiwanese popular press also questioned the efficacy of such coproduction practices. Citing a number of Taiwan-Japan coproductions, including *The Great Wall*, a 1963 *United Daily* critical review questioned the uneven benefits of international film collaboration for Taiwan. As coproductions from the US, Hong Kong and Japan utilised Taiwan as a location backdrop, this critic argued, Taiwanese film sat unequally within an uneven worldwide production geography.[21]

Promotions of *The Great Wall*, however, strongly praised the coproduction for its effective bridging of these regional landscapes, further underscoring their particular Cold War construction. The Taiwanese shooting locations of the film were to stand for mainland China. While *The Great Wall* featured China as a narrative site of conflict and then consolidation under its first emperor, contemporary mainland China was at the time largely inaccessible to 'free capitalist' production. Indeed, promotions strongly emphasised how the coproduction's access to its Chinese locations was the result of the Japanese studios' (here Daiei's) powerful brokering with the structures of the region, as negotiations with Chiang Kai Shek and the KMT/Nationalist government achieved access to not only Taiwanese shooting locations but also the vast number of staff and extras needed to populate the film's massive battle scenes.[22] At the heart of popular press promotion, then, was praise for the film's mobilisation of a Cold War regional production geography that was not only expressed in the aspirations of development and underdevelopment, but also the divides between 'free' capitalist and communist arenas. Speaking to wider contexts of production at the time, scholars such as Sangjoon Lee and Yoshiharu Tezuka have also argued for how the Asian Film Festival was formed to rekindle and transform regional imperial relations within the context of a new 'free capitalist' and Cold War Asia. As Tezuka points out:

> Unlike the discourse of pre-war *Asianism*, which articulated the spiritual commonality of Asian People and set it in opposition to the West as a whole, the Federation of Motion Picture Producers of Southeast Asia was specifically set up with the political goal of subsuming the Asian film industries within a Western sphere of influence, while simultaneously setting them against the perceived rising tide of communism.[23]

Indeed, promotional accounts of *The Great Wall* within the Japanese popular press were premised on an assumption of the Japanese studio's leadership role in bringing regional film into this sphere, thereby mirroring Japan's more general positioning at the forefront of the Americanist geopolitical structuring of the region. As the industry expertly navigated Cold War Americanist landscapes to produce films of the latest technological standards, promotional and studio accounts inflected a regional context in which the problems of 'development' and the relative perils of 'underdevelopment' were deeply felt and acted upon.

'ADVANCEMENTS' IN FORM, CONTENT AND REGIONAL PLACE

Beneath the linked desires for international coproduction and technological advancement, and thereby expansion into world markets, that largely motivated film collaborations between Japan and Hong Kong or Taiwan from the mid-1950s to early 1960s, lay an uneven regional geography. In other words, the then 'widening' scope of Japanese cinema was dependent upon regional Cold War relations that further remediated earlier imperialist legacies in Asia. Concerted inquiry into the contradictions of film production and its related discourses, as James Caldwell has also argued, can enable new understandings of the meanings of film and its content.[24] The promises and problems of regional location and place for these coproductions can thus be most significantly addressed within the production contexts of early Cold War East and South East Asia. The 1956 Japan–Hong Kong collaboration *Madame White Snake* was released with great fanfare for its featuring of the latest in 'photographic filmic effects'. The coproduction was advertised as a 'tie-in' between studios in Hong Kong and Japan. Yet these effects were more singularly lauded as evidence of Japanese film studios having reached 'Hollywood standards' as Tōhō led the production of lavishly shot scenes of a mythical and 'old Chinese legend of a white snake transformed into a lady'.[25] Advancements in film technologies were thus central to the rendering of regional place, further producing a sense of an East and South East Asia that explicitly revolved around Japan's regional leadership in the development of film technologies. Against the backdrop of concerns for the shooting of Chinese scenes and landscapes – both on location and in the studio – these coproductions underscored the relative contradictions of film technologies and film content deemed central to the formation of the contemporary region and its production landscape.

By the time of *Madame White Snake*'s release in 1956, depictions of regional 'Asian' and 'Japanese' place had already been established within Japanese cinema as a strategy for appealing to world markets through a complex relationship between film content and the technologies of production. Yoshiharu Tezuka has argued for seeing the 1953 Japanese film *Gate of Hell/Jigokumon* as a model for understanding how Japanese film content was produced in the early Cold War to appeal to international markets, and the perceived significance of film technologies produced in dialogue with the US to this process. For him, *Gate of Hell* was 'an early example of the conscious hybridization of local media "content" with global technological "forms"', which 'produced a[n aspirational] formula for other internationally successful Asian films in the coming years'. Extending Richard Wilk's notion of global 'structures of common difference', Tezuka argues that 'this film is a clear example of how, as Wilk suggests, "the global system of common differences" selects a particular kind of difference that is developed in dialogue with Western modernity'. Briefly explicating the film's narrative, he thus argues that:

> The international success of [*Gate of Hell*] had a lot to do with this combination of traditional Japanese content alongside the use of the latest Western technological form. The Japanese settings, the self-sacrificing virtue of the female protagonist, the costumes, the make-up and so forth made [*Gate of Hell*] different from the cinema of the West, while the use of Eastmancolor film stock gave [*Gate of Hell*] a distinctive feel of Western modernity.

Re-framing our understanding of how producers operated in relation to film technologies, Tezuka underscores how studio leaders such as Daiei's Nagata understood that 'the colour technology (form)' made its 'otherwise inaccessible foreign cultural content enjoyable for the wider Western audiences'. The success of *Gate of Hell* was thus a confirmation of Nagata's decision that this first colour film for Daiei would be on Eastman Kodak, as the studio 'developed the colour cinematography techniques used in [*Gate of Hell*] in dialogue with the latest American technology'.[26]

Beyond simple speculation concerning the success or failure of this formula in film-making, this interlinked regime of content and form provides a model for inquiring into the senses of regional place and location that were coproduced in the

China-centred films of this chapter. *Princess Yang Kwei-fei*, produced in 1955 between Hong Kong's Shaw Brothers and Japan's Daiei, was among the first concerted postwar collaborations between Japan and Hong Kong. *Madame White Snake*, coproduced between Shaw Brothers and Japan's Tōhō studio, followed suit in 1956. Promotional posters and stills for *Princess Yang Kwei-fei* displayed interior sets of court and courtship and the film's prominent Japanese stars Kyō Machiko and Mori Masayuki – all depicted in lavish colours and costume to foreground the Daiei colour format in which the film was being released. Promotions for *Madame White Snake* similarly featured its central female star, Yamaguchi Yoshiko, depicted in lavish costume and Eastmancolor, even as advertisements emphasised the appeal of the film's further photographic 'fantastic effects'.[27] In addition to the magnitude of their costumes, sets, colour and effects, and the prominent display of their leading female stars such as Yamaguchi and Kyō, both films garnered regional if not world acclaim. The prominent auteur status of the directors Mizoguchi Kenji and Toyoda Shirō also placed them in dialogue with other regional, here European, film efforts to further dialogue with Hollywood.

Peter Lev has outlined the predominant modes of the Euro-American art film from the postwar period. Lev argues that 'European made Hollywood spectacles circa 1960 (*Ben Hur*, *El Cid*, *Cleopatra*)' attempted 'a synthesis of the American entertainment film (large budget, good production values, internationally known stars) and the European art film (auteur director, artistic subject and/or style)' with the aim of reaching larger audiences. It was here 'typical to make spectacle films which took full advantage of the low cost of European labor, costume and sets', for example 'biblical epics […] adventure and war films of the distant past'.[28] In their efforts to produce a film on the scale of *Princess Yang Kwei-fei*, *Madame White Snake* or, later, *The Great Wall*, East Asian producers also took advantage of the relative benefits of coproduction. They did so within a more concertedly uneven regional context, in particular through dialogue with the technical advances deemed to be of Hollywood, and thus 'world', standard.

The uneven formation of the regional production geography of early Cold War East and South East Asia is underscored in the practices and promotions that surrounded the shooting – both on location and on set – of the films under discussion. For the popular press, the technologically enabled size and scale of *The Great Wall* was linked to its transformative access to Taiwanese shooting locations. Promotional material for the earlier *Madame White Snake*, on the other hand, focused on its reformulation of the studio set through its deployment of the latest film technology and thus consequent transformation of the 'Chinese' content and images of the film. Publicity advertising the 'fantastic story' of 'the desperately passionate affair of a lady who is really a white snake transformed' appeared in both Hong Kong and Singapore and hailed the 'highlight' of this Chinese story being 'Tōhō's special techniques [which were] given full play to produce [the] fantastic effects' of the film. Without these 'photoplay' effects, ventured the advertisements, 'these scenes would have come to nothing'. Accounts of the making of the film offered views into the back story of its intimate interior boudoir interludes and the acclaimed scenes in which Madame Pai uses her 'magical powers' to take 'her beloved husband Hsu Hsieh to a heavenly tour' as 'the couple floats and dances through the clouds'. The 'tremendous[ly scaled] scene' of the Flood of Chin Shan, however, attracted the most spectacular accounts. Photos of 'the 1,800 sq. feet island' that was 'built amidst a 18,000 sq. feet lot gigantic pool' featured captions documenting the 'thirty odd days, costs [of] 13 million Yuen and labour of 1,200 workers' in the production. Focusing on the 'actual scene of the filming of the flood', these accounts foregrounded the set location techniques through which the magnitude of this scene was produced, as lights and cameras atop a crane powerfully shot 'the rising waters surg[ing] toward the temple buildings on the back ground'.[29] Popular press accounts of film effects are notoriously inaccurate and vague and are often more interested in hiding trade secrets than revealing their details. What this publicity worked to reveal, however, was the modernity of the film and the industrial complex that produced it. This modernity was further produced within a particular regional formation of industrial and technological advancement. As studio-linked accounts boasted, *Madame White Snake* was poised to be the 'grandest production in the history of Japanese movies'. Yet its significance was further couched in its status as a 'glorious production [that] is the pride of the Eastern world', in the same way that Japan was poised to lead East and South East Asian film towards the technological standards of the 'world' market.[30]

To understand the dynamics of this production geography structured in the effects and location-driven 'technological modernity' of Japanese cinema, it is important to set Japanese industrialists and technicians' perceived leadership of East and South East Asian production within the sphere of larger regional negotiations. In this case, this also means interrogating the particular dynamics of the mythical 'Chinese' story and content of *Madame White Snake* as it was coproduced between the contemporary Japanese and Hong Kong industries. Kwai-cheung Lo has underscored how 'China usually symbolizes an archaic, unmodernized, and mysterious Asia in the modern Japanese consciousness.' Throughout the colonial, Cold War, as well as present-day, contexts of Japanese cultural and film production, argues Lo, the 'erasure' of modern China has been central to the 'formation of modern Japanese identity'.[31] To be sure, *Madame White Snake*'s depiction of a 'Japanese version of [this mythic] Chinese story' was front and centre in publicity of the film in Hong Kong and Singapore alike. To foreground the Japanese Yasumi Toshio as the film's famed scriptwriter was to underscore the particularly 'modern' rendition of this Chinese story, given Japan's positioning at the forefront of the Cold War development of the region, as well as its leadership in bringing 'Eastern' film into the fold of the world market. The 'erasure' involved in such representation is also underscored in the contexts of film production and coproduction. While Shaw Brothers paid 30 per cent of the production budget of *Princess Yang Kwei-fei*, the actual creative role that the Hong Kong partners played was very limited. As Tezuka has underscored,

> Princess Yang Kwei-fei was directed by [...] the Japanese director Kenji Mizoguchi, with an entirely Japanese crew and cast and shot in the Tokyo Daiei Studio, despite the fact that it was a Chinese period costume drama. In the original agreement, Shaw Brothers was supposed to supply five actresses, a hairdresser, a costume person, a historical adviser, a fight director, a set designer and so forth.[32] However, in the end, only three credits were given to the Chinese in the finished film – the producer, Run Run Shaw, the scriptwriter, Tao Qin and a historical adviser. In the case of *Madame White Snake*, the film carried no Chinese credits at all apart from Shaw Brothers as the co-production company.[33]

The aspirations towards world and Euro-American markets that were widely linked to such lavish colour and spectacularly shot coproduced films as *Madame White Snake* and *Princess Yang Kwei-fei* stood upon a starkly uneven, even non-reciprocal, regional production landscape. The sense of regional place engendered by these production discourses and practices remediate what Harry Harootunian has called 'the uneven development generated by capitalism as it enters societies at different moments and different rates of intensity' – something that has long constituted East Asian cultural production and experience.[34] Here, the entwined development of international coproductions and new film technologies reflected the spatio-temporal logics of early Cold War capitalism, which differentiated regional locations across relative scales and thereby proximities to the 'modern' development then being signalled by Japanese cinema. In this sense, the transformational promise of colour and later widescreen technologies brought to bear the wider underlying tensions of Japanese consumer products and technologies at this moment. Yoshimi Shun'ya has sharply delineated the bifurcated ways in which Japan came to mediate 'America', as both 'model' and 'ideal' within East and South East Asia during the Cold War of the 1950s and 1960s. In its mediation of the US as an ideal, Japan came to stand at the forefront of consumerist aspirations in the region, 'whether through material goods or media images'. Here Tokyo's technological advances gave way to 'American lifestyle[s] [...] presented as *ideals* to be emulated'. Tokyo's technological and infrastructural advances were thus to pave the way towards a new horizon of prosperity. The ideal US that Japan then mediated, as Yoshimi further demonstrates, also worked to distance itself from the coexisting 'model' of militarisation and anti-communist hegemony that simultaneously structured America's regional presence, as signalled by its military bases in Okinawa, South Korea, the Philippines and elsewhere.[35] To be sure, however, particular actors throughout the region positioned themselves, and thus navigated these ideals differently, depending on their own locational concerns.

Indeed, for regional film-making at large, location shooting remained a central practice and means of access to such ideals of technological advancement and thereby industry development, even if it was distinctly articulated here by the Japanese or Hong Kong industries. Throughout the 1950s, Hong Kong film studios such as Shaw Brothers and MP&GI produced a significant number of films that were shot on location in Japan. The widely promoted 1955 *Miss Kukiko/Juzi guniang*, for example, overtly signalled Japan as its 'modern' backdrop. Hong Kong studio accounts of *Miss Kukiko* focused on the central film star, Lin Dai, in a series of outdoor shooting locations throughout Japan. Photo ops set her next to her shooting crew in front of the massive Buddha in Nara, the famed imperial park in Tokyo, and alongside various everyday shopping streets.[36] These traditional, imperial and everyday landscapes indicated a proximity to the new possibilities of travel and tourism being signalled by the impending growth of leisure industries in Japan at the time. In terms of film production practice, such accounts simultaneously indicated Hong Kong studios' greater proximity to advanced technologies and processes of film-making, as partnerships were forged to gain access to shooting locations, set lots, technological training and, importantly, post-production equipment, since Japan occupied the only post-production film centre in the region at the time. Hong Kong studio and promotional materials alluded directly to such aspirations thus further indicating the complex regional geographies that the films negotiated. Popular accounts of the 1957 *Scarlet Doll* underscored how its Hong Kong film crew toiled under difficult conditions 'on location under Mt. Fuji'. Publicity featured scenes of a stark and barren landscape and explained 'the locale of this colossal picture in Eastman Colour' to be 'the plains of Northern China in wintry weather'.[37] As would later be the case for the 1962 *The Great Wall*, Hong Kong studios were unable to shoot in the actual locations of northern China, given the PRC's location outside the 'free capitalist' arena of the Cold War region; other regional locations were therefore made to stand in for it. Articulated as significant to both narrative and production contexts, such references to China underscore how 'the invocation of place is a highly unstable gesture' for moving image media.[38] The indexical reference for these scenes, ostensibly China, was at the same time as complex as the ideals and models of the US's Japan. 'Reports from Japan where *Scarlet Doll* is being filmed', publicity claimed, 'indicate this spectacular picture in Eastman Colour has all the possibilities of being the greatest moving picture ever made'. Utilising US colour patents in relation to Japanese production contexts worked, for the MP&GI studio, to 'raise the level of Chinese movies to the international standard'. Indeed, promotional material commented upon the ways in which, 'Japanese observers who were on the scene pointed out that the way MP&GI was shooting the picture was just as grandeur [*sic*] in scale and scope as any Hollywood production.'[39]

These promotional discourses and production practices suggest how the possibilities of regional place – and film-making's centrality to it – was variously produced (and at times contested) in relation to a model of Cold War internationalism, which aspired towards 'developed' and 'free capitalist' production methods when it came to the making of Eastern/Asian films for the wider world. In the early 1960s, Shaw Brothers studio shifted from strategies of locational transfer – whereby location shooting gained proximity to actual and discursive film technologies – to more direct modes of technological transfer through the recruitment of film workers and technicians from other film industries, most notably Japan, to their studios. The same year as the release of the Taiwan-Japan coproduction *The Great Wall*, Shaw Brothers released its own 1962 cinematic take on *Yang Kwei-fei*. The lavish colour epic won the Special Technical Award for colour cinematography at the Cannes Film Festival in 1962 – Shaw's first 'international' (read Euro-American) recognition. The film was produced 'in dialogue with Japanese and Hollywood technologies and standards'. The cameraman Nishimoto Tadashi had first been 'borrowed' by Shaw Brothers from his 'Japanese employer Shintoho in 1957 to improve the quality of colour cinematography' in its Hong Kong film studios.[40] The studio then invited Nishimoto back to Hong Kong more permanently when they were about to shoot *Yang Kwei-fei*. A Chinese epic based on the same story as the earlier coproduction with Daiei about 'a woman of matchless beauty who caused the collapse of a Chinese dynasty', this was, as many have noted, 'the first film of a series of similarly extravagant period films featuring legendary Chinese beauties including *The Empress Wu Ze Tian* (Li Han Hsiang, 1963), and *Beyond the Great Wall/ Wang Zhao Jun* (Li Han Hsiang, 1964)'.[41] Such films showcased Hong Kong cinema to world markets as another 'Asian' expression of the latest in colour and widescreen technologies. Indeed, these film practices have led scholars such as Tezuka to argue that we must recognise how such Hong Kong films, 'using the same global form' in film-making to which Japanese cinema had aspired, similarly 'submitted Chinese "content" to the selection process of the "global structures of common difference"'.[42]

What we might further recognise is the uneven regional and Cold War geographies that contributed to these film-making strategies. As far as this chapter's case studies were concerned, this did not simply mean a repetition of the film-making legacies of the prewar era, in which relationships of occupation and colonisation were the bedrock of collaborative film-making in the region. No less invested in Japan's position at the vanguard of film production for East and South East Asia, the model of regional coproduction advanced by Japanese studios in the 1950s and early 1960s may also be placed within a set of 'international' aspirations fully cognisant of the Cold War divides of development and underdevelopment, East and West, and free capitalist and communist arenas that then made up regional, if not global, film production and distribution. Interrogating the technologies of production through which these aspirations were materialised – whether or not they were successful in market terms – is central to understanding the modes of 'Asian' cinema in which these and other industries were invested. It is only from here that we can begin to unpack what regional film locations were used and thereby what kinds of regional sense of place were enabled (or not) in terms of particular production practices, discourses and imaginaries. However unstable and changing these sites were, they clearly always remained embedded within uneven relations and dynamics of power.

Notes

1 Iida Shinbi, '*Tai shikō tei to* 70 miri no iryoku', *Kinema junpō* no. 328 (1962), p. 80.
2 Stephanie DeBoer, *Coproducing Asia: Locating Japanese-Chinese Regional Film and Media* (Minneapolis: University of Minnesota Press, 2014), p. 5.
3 Barbara Selznick, *Global Television: Co-producing Culture* (Philadelphia: Temple University Press, 2008), pp. 17–18.
4 Yoshiharu Tezuka, *Japanese Cinema Goes Global: Filmworkers' Journeys* (Hong Kong: Hong Kong University Press, 2012), pp. 52–3.
5 Doreen Massey, *Space, Place, and Gender* (Minneapolis: University of Minnesota Press, 1994).
6 Kinnia Yau, *Japanese and Hong Kong Film Industries: Understanding the Origins of East Asian Film Networks* (London: Routledge, 2010).
7 My concern that we attend to the particularities of transnational exchange from one moment to another has long been inspired by Meaghan Morris's more contemporary insistence that 'empirical work is needed to advance how globalizing forces are working, or *not* working, in culture'. For her, 'the term transnational itself is heavily spatialized today, carrying an insistent flow of images about "global" forces roaming around "borderless" worlds. Yet', she notes, 'this was not always the case.' Meaghan Morris, 'Transnational Imagination in Action Cinema: Hong Kong and the Making of a Global Popular Culture', *Inter-Asia Cultural Studies* vol. 5 no. 2 (2004), p. 181.
8 I adopt the term 'imperialisation' here from Chen Kuan-Hsing's *Asia as Method: Toward Deimperialization* (Durham, NC: Duke University Press, 2010).
9 Tezuka, *Japanese Cinema Goes Global*, pp. 52–3.

10. Takahashi Hidekazu, '1962 nendo naigai eiga sōkkessan – gyōkai (seisaku, haikyū, kōgyō)', *Kinema junpō* vol. 332 no. 1147 (1963), pp. 60–8.
11. 'Gassaku eiga būmu', *Sunday Mainichi*, 24 April 1955, pp. 28–9; and 'Gassaku eiga no hirointachi: Doru o kasegu nihon eiga', *Sunday Mainichi*, 15 April 1956, pp. 3–8.
12. 'Gassaku eiga no hirointachi', pp. 3–8.
13. Tezuka, *Japanese Cinema Goes Global*, p. 28.
14. [Editors' note: for more on the development of colour film-making in Japanese cinema, see also Chapter 18 by Fumiaki Itakura in this volume.]
15. For a fuller account of this, including citations to studio annals and other resources, see DeBoer, *Coproducing Asia*, pp. 37–45. See also Zhang Changyan, 'Sengo no Taiwan eigashi to nihon eiga', in Kirosawa Kiyoshi, Yomota Inuhiko and Yoshimi Shun'ya (eds), *Nihon eiga wa ikite iru*, vol. 3, *Miruhito, tsukuruhito, kakeruhito* (Tokyo: Iwanami shoten, 2010), pp. 177–187, 191.
16. Ibid.
17. Iida Shinbi, '*Tai shikō tei* to 70 miri no iryoku', p. 80.
18. Togawa Naoki, 'Kabe ni butsukatta Asia eigasai', *Kinema junpō* no. 340 (1963), p. 47.
19. For an insightful account of the Asian Film Festival and its Cold War contexts, see Sangjoon Lee, 'The Emergence of the Asian Film Festival: Cold War Asia and Japan's Re-entrance to the Regional Film Industry in the 1950s,' in Daisuke Miyao (ed.), *The Oxford Handbook of Japanese Cinema* (Oxford: Oxford University Press, 2014), pp. 232–50. [Editors' note: for more on Nagata Masaichi and film festivals, see also Chapter 11 by Ran Ma and Chapter 39 by Yoshiharu Tezuka in this volume.]
20. Togawa, 'Kabe ni butsukatta Asia eigasai', p. 47.
21. Dong Yi, 'Kan Haiwan fengyun: Tan Zhongwai hezuo paipian', *United Daily News*, 28 August 1963, p. 8.
22. Iida Shinbi, '*Tai shikō tei* to 70 miri no iryoku', p. 80.
23. Tezuka, *Japanese Cinema Goes Global*, p. 58. See also Lee, 'The Emergence of the Asian Film Festival'.
24. James Caldwell, *Production Culture: Industrial Reflexivity and Critical Practice in Film and Television* (Durham, NC: Duke University Press, 2008).
25. *Bai she chuan*, film pamphlet (Singapore: Chinese Pictorial Review, 1962).
26. Tezuka, *Japanese Cinema Goes Global*, p. 55. Also, for a wider account of the development of colour technologies in Japan, Eastman Kodak's strategies for appealing to and maintaining relationships with Japan during the prewar and postwar periods, Daiei's decision to use Eastmancolor for *Gate of Hell*, and a more detailed analysis of *Gate of Hell*'s use of colour, see Sarah Street, 'The Monopack Revolution, Global Cinema and *Jigokumon/Gate of Hell* (Kinugasa Teinosuke, 1953)', *Open Screens* vol. 1 no. 1 (2018), pp. 1–29, <http://doi.org/10.16995/os.2>.
27. Ibid.
28. Peter Lev, *The Euro-American Cinema* (Austin: University of Texas Press, 1993), p. 20.
29. *Bai she chuan*, film pamphlet.
30. Ibid.
31. Kwai-cheung Lo, 'Erasing China in Japan's "Hong Kong Films"', in Miyao, *The Oxford Handbook of Japanese Cinema*, p. 210.
32. *Eiga nenkan* (Tokyo: Kinema Junpo-sha, 1955), p. 63.
33. Tezuka, *Japanese Cinema Goes Global*, pp. 61–2.
34. Harry Harootunian, *History's Disquiet: Modernity, Cultural Practice, and the Question of Everyday Life* (New York: Columbia University Press, 2000), p. 41.
35. Shunya Yoshimi, '"America" as Desire and Violence: Americanization in Postwar Japan and Asia during the Cold War', trans. David Bust, *Inter-Asia Cultural Studies* vol. 4 no. 2 (2003), pp. 433–50.
36. 'Juzi guniang', *Guoji dianying* no. 1 (1955), p. 27.
37. '"Scarlet Doll" Team Sweats It Out on Location under Mount Fuji', *Guoji dianying* no. 24 (1957), p. 15.
38. Elena Gorfinkel and John David Rhodes, 'Introduction: The Matter of Places', in John David Rhodes and Elena Gorfinkel (eds), *Taking Place: Location and the Moving Image* (Minneapolis: University of Minnesota Press, 2009), p. xviii.
39. 'History Making Picture: "Scarlet Doll"', *Guoji dianying* no. 23 (1957), p. 11.
40. Tezuka, *Japanese Cinema Goes Global*, p. 63.
41. Ibid. See also Nishomoto's own memoirs: Nishimoto Tadashi, *Hong Kong e no michi: Nakagawa Nobuo kara Bruce Lee e*, ed. Yamada Kōichi and Yamane Sadao (Tokyo: Chikuma shobō, 2004).
42. Ibid.

37

JAPANESE CINEMA AND HOLLYWOOD
Frontiers of nostalgia: The Japanese Western and the postwar era

Hiroshi Kitamura

On a sunny afternoon, under a pitch-blue sky marbled with cotton-candy clouds, two fierce gunmen arrive at a ranch. Taken aback by the eerie silence, they pick up their guns and guardedly scope the place. Suddenly, the evil boss appears in sight, with the heroine held in hostage. Crack! A shooting breaks out. One by one, the two rugged men gun down the ruthless henchmen until the greedy villain is brought down to his knees. After order is restored, the two men, on horseback, each depart towards the distant plains. The heroine, sadly but gratefully, sees them off from afar.

This might sound like the heroics of a John Wayne Western, but it is not. The film, *The Plateau Man/Kōgenji* (1961), dramatises the travails of a slender Japanese construction worker, who intervenes in a feud between a ranch-owning family and a band of vicious ruffians. The gun-savvy hero, played by the singer and actor Kobayashi Akira, poses as the heroine's in-law in order to rescue her sister's ranch. In so doing, he gallops through the green pastures of Ōita on horseback, brawls in a local saloon, befriends a rival gunslinger clad in black and quietly expresses his feelings for the heroine before leaving her behind.

The Plateau Man belonged to a body of films that came with a look of a Hollywood Western. Known as 'Japanese Westerns' (*wasei uesutan* or *wasei seibugeki*), this popular film genre revolved around the antics of lone wanderers – usually men – who wielded weapons, experience and knowledge to rescue women and innocent citizens from crisis situations. Flaunting lively brawls, showdowns and horseplay, the Japanese Western thrived by blending Hollywood's conventions with local formulas. First emerging in the prewar era, it played a key role in enlivening Japanese cinema throughout the postwar decades.

This chapter will examine the Japanese Western – a prominent genre that has largely eluded systematic study.[1] My aim is not to cover the entire repertoire but to concentrate on a select group of films that emerged between the 1950s and the 1990s – a time when Japan transformed itself from a struggling, war-shattered society to being one of the wealthiest countries in the world. The nation's 'high economic growth' (*kōdo keizai seichō*) prompted the migration of youths to cities, the expansion of corporations and businesses, and the cultivation of vast farmlands into industrial factories, tourist centres and apartment blocks (*danchi*). These dramatic changes helped turn the gaze of many citizens towards the techno-industrial present and future. As scholars have shown, they also triggered the rise of a nostalgic yearning for an imagined 'homeland', or *furusato*, that seemed to exist in the country's pre-industrial past.[2]

The Japanese Western grew and expanded in response to the changing socio-economic conditions of this long 'postwar era' (*sengo*). It garnered appeal, I argue, as a 'nostalgia text' that stimulated a cultural longing for a distant 'Japanese' past. Often showcasing exquisite provincial landscapes, pure and innocent townsfolk, paternal care and rugged manliness, simple lives in the fields and mines, and good-natured individuals surviving through hard work and perseverance, the cinematic genre invoked a sense of *furusato* that seemed to disappear in the face of modernisation. This imaginary was far more than an isolated formulation of regional and provincial space; as Christine R. Yano argues, it helped form a 'national culture' by 'transform[ing] […] the local into the national' while reformulating marginal ('frontier') spaces into an 'internal exotic'.[3]

Yet 'nostalgia texts' about Japan were not always 'national' creations. I argue that the Japanese Western exemplifies the influence of transnational forces in the making of such 'domestic' narratives. In recent years, film and media scholars have usefully asserted the hybridity of Japanese cinema by turning to colonial representation, international coproduction and cross-cultural consumption.[4] My study will build on this literature by underscoring the influence of Hollywood – a global hegemonic force. As existing work on US cinema and culture has shown, Hollywood's worldwide prowess owed a great deal to its efficient film-making, shrewd diplomacy and strategic marketing practices.[5] By contrast, the Japanese Western reveals the hegemonic impact of US cinema from the receiving end, as Japanese studios and film-makers actively invented this cinematic genre by adapting and appropriating Hollywood's formulas and conventions.[6] The Japanese Western was, then, a transnational creation that paradoxically gave rise to a 'national' nostalgia about Japan. This fascinating genre also exemplifies the formation of Japanese cinema and culture in the shadow of US geopolitics.

LONGING FOR AN AMERICAN 'HOMELAND'

The Japanese Western owes its existence to the hybrid cultural terrain of modern Japan. Much of this was triggered by the new political and cultural climate shaped after the Meiji Restoration – a time when the once self-secluded island nation actively pursued the course of international and transnational engagement under the mantra of 'civilisation and enlightenment' (*bunmei kaika*). Cinema, a medium first imported from the West, became an engine of this cross-fertilisation. During the 1900s and early 1910s, European cinemas were a formidable influence on the Japanese, but Hollywood, since Universal founded its distribution branch in Tokyo in 1916, fiercely extended across the field and quickly began to reign as the most dominant 'foreign cinema' (*yōga*) in a booming film market.

The Hollywood Western was a spearhead of this 'Americanisation'. Since its arrival with Edison's Kinetoscope, the US Western – aided by the likes of William S. Hart, Tom Mix and Will Rogers – enthralled scores of fans during the prewar era.[7] One of the biggest hits was *Stagecoach* (1939). A life-changing influence for many Japanese film-makers, this John Ford classic enjoyed countless re-runs following its initial release. During the Occupation era (1945–52), the Wild West film, together with other Hollywood productions, entered the Japanese market through the Central Motion Picture Exchange.[8] After Japan regained its sovereignty, American studios continued to individually devise marketing and promotional campaigns to sell this popular genre. During the first two postwar decades, Japanese fans savoured hit after hit, from *Shane* (1953), *The Searchers* (1956), *The Big Country* (1958), *Rio Bravo* (1959) and *The Magnificent Seven* (1960) to *The Man Who Shot Liberty Valance* (1962). In 1961, *Eiga no tomo* dubbed Japan a 'heaven of [Hollywood] Westerns' (*seibugeki tengoku*).[9]

The widespread popularity of this genre was the result of government and business strategy. It also owed to the fact that Japanese fans passionately consumed US narratives. Evidence suggests that the audience body seems to have revolved around the 'mass' (*taishū*) audiences to which the genre was often marketed. But the fan base is likely to have also extended to 'intellectuals' and 'culture elites' (*bunkajin*) by way of high-cost, top-bill products (which André Bazin dubbed 'superwesterns'[10]) that were showcased in the finest roadshow and first-run theatres in large cities.[11] The primary fan base appears to have been male.[12] Boys in particular were big fans of the genre; as depicted in Kurosawa Akira's *High and Low/Tengoku to jigoku* (1963), they often 'played cowboy' at home and in parks and streets.[13]

What, then, drew these filmgoers to the US Western? For many, the genre's appeal must have existed in the violent spectacle and breathtaking action. For others, the gun-smoking films cultivated a sense of admiration for the US. Impressed fans, for example, often pointed to the representation of the open landscape (e.g. Monument Valley and the Great Plains), which seemed all but absent in the densely populated island nation. Viewers also appear to have looked up to the portrayal of epic events through which the US became an 'advanced' nation. Narratives about Caucasian pioneer settlers, railroads and cattle ranchers 'civilising' the 'savage' wilderness (and Native Americans) – which Richard Slotkin characterised as 'progressive epic' Westerns – often boasted of the process of America's growth and expansion as a 'modern' and 'democratic' nation.[14] One admirer, the director Ōbayashi Nobuhiko, noted that the Westerns he saw right after World War II inspired him because they 'convey[ed] the American Dream and [its] democracy'. The director and others around him were happy to become the 'heaven-sent children [*mōshigo*] of US Occupation policy'.[15]

Another allure of the Hollywood Western was its celebration of manliness and masculinity. Ashihara Shin, a die-hard fan who grew up in the 1950s and 1960s, argues that the boys of the postwar baby-boom era 'learned how to be a man' by 'studying the male aesthetic' of the US genre. He idolised the lone hero who 'never ran away' and 'once saved, would fight for that person by risking his life'. The protagonist 'most seriously respected parental and brotherly ties' and 'always showed up whenever families were facing a crisis'.[16]

To be sure, this 'learning' from the US Western did not come to mean the blind consumption of 'foreign' behaviours. Japanese viewers often associated the social practices of American frontiersmen with values of their own, such as the notion of 'obligation and human feeling' (*giri ninjō*) – a common trope in Japanese period dramas (*jidaigeki*). During the prewar era, this overlap gave rise to Hasegawa Shin's 'story of the wandering yakuza' (*matatabi mono*) – a forerunner of the Japanese Western – which dramatised the adventures of a lone wanderer, usually a gambler or an entertainer, who saved women and children from nasty villains before drifting away to the next destination.[17] When *Shane* was released in 1953, Japanese critics noted its similarity with the *matatabi* narrative, in which the nomadic hero 'departs on a journey once again, leaving behind a wife and child who long to be with him'.[18]

Fans in Japan also identified an imagined *furusato* in the Hollywood Western. When *Stagecoach* appeared in theatres, the film critic Hazumi Tsuneo claimed to have felt the 'colour of the sky' and the 'smell of the dirt' of his 'home town'. It did not matter to him that John Wayne's actions concerned the American 'homeland'. Kurosawa Akira echoed similar thoughts. In 1947, the Tōhō director remarked: 'when I watch films by John Ford and others, I feel as if I [have] returned to my home town'.[19] Although born in Tokyo, Kurosawa often associated Ford's film with his father's place of origin, Akita. For him, Hollywood Westerns seemed to capture what was missing in the restless Japanese metropolis. Paradoxically, the US Western seemed to offer a sense of an idyllic *Japanese* past.

NIKKATSU'S WILD WEST

The widespread popularity of the Hollywood Western generated a passionate and popular following. It also inspired many film-makers to adapt and appropriate those conventions into their screen narratives. An engine of this trend was the Nikkatsu Studio. Founded in 1912, this historic company gained a broad following as a producer of period films during the prewar decades. In the postwar era, Nikkatsu began its film-making in 1954 and churned out a large body of youth-oriented narratives following the surprise hit of Furukawa Takumi's *Season of the Sun/Taiyō no kisetsu* (1956). Many of these studio productions became known as the 'Nikkatsu Action' film for their representation of violence, action and sex.[20]

Many of the young directors and actors who worked at Nikkatsu Studio were avid fans of the Hollywood Western. It is therefore not surprising that Western-esque narratives would quickly become a core ingredient of the Nikkatsu Action meta-genre. The architects of the 'Nikkatsu Western' transplanted the gun-smoking struggle of good versus evil into Japanese contexts. In these renderings, the outlaw protagonists often appeared on horseback, dressed with cowboy hats and tasselled leather jackets, at diverse rural backdrops – from the high planes in

Ōita and the green forests in Aichi to the picturesque lakefronts of Hokkaido.[21] Here, the provincial sites were typically idyllic spaces of purity and innocence, which, to borrow the words of one Nikkatsu actor, invoked a 'nostalgic scenery' or a 'landscape that reminds him of his mother'.[22]

The provincial landscapes also served to construct a binary framework for conflict – a core formula of the Hollywood Western.[23] These local settings usually involved tensions between two social groups. One was the innocent townspeople, a group to which the pure-hearted heroine usually belonged. The other was a group of gangsters or ruffians, who were exploiting the local population to monopolise wealth and power. Treading between the border of the two worlds, the outcast hero strove to save the innocent citizens. Usually, the resolution involved fierce shoot-outs and duels with the villains. In the end, the hero successfully restored peace but had to leave for his next destination. The film usually ended with the hero's departure into a distant horizon.

One might see these traits in a film such as *There Goes the Covered Wagon/Horobasha wa yuku* (1961), directed by Noguchi Hiroshi. The protagonist, Akagi Keiichirō, belongs to a gang of thieves and suffers a serious injury while raiding a train. He is then picked up by a band of nomadic beekeepers who travel on horse-pulled wagons. Led by a compassionate elder and his granddaughter, the migrant group treks from place to place across rural Japan – free from the ills of the big city – and take Akagi under their wings. Feeling that his 'dirty heart is being purified', Akagi – a 'good bad man' of the Hollywood Western – chooses to stay with the beekeepers. Yet as the hero starts to think twice about his criminal lifestyle, his former gang members forcefully join the nomads to hide for cover against the police. Angry with the gang, Akagi confronts and defeats the boss before being taken away by the police. The hero restores order and saves the 'pure' beekeepers before parting from sight.

The Crimson Plains/Akai kōya (1961), another film by Noguchi, addressed changing economic and industrial conditions more specifically. Starring Shishido Joe, who played the main lead in other Nikkatsu Westerns such as *The Fast-Drawing Guy/Hayauchi yarō* (1961) and *Mexico Wanderer/Mexico mushuku* (1962), the film depicts a number of greedy ruffians in the grassy high planes of Shimane prefecture who attempt to seize a pair of cattle farms to build a large canned-food factory. A former hoodlum who turned straight, Shishido single-handedly fends off the henchmen. This forces the appearance of a burly, chain-smoking boss, who arrives from Tokyo. The representation of this villain as a Tokyoite develops a larger dialectic in which the 'evil' metropolis seeks to 'colonise' the 'innocent' provinces.[24] In the end, Shishido, with the help of a ranch owner-friend, defeats the villains and prevents the local farmers from being exploited by the Tokyo-centric structure of capital. He then leaves despite the attentions of a female admirer.

The 'Wanderer' (*wataridori*) series (1959–62) amplified similar themes.[25] Starring Kobayashi Akira, this popular series highlighted a male outsider who protects the weak from villainous ruffians in provincial settings. To be sure, the plot of the Wanderer series was partly based on the *matatabi* formula, but it explicitly showcased the visual tropes of the Hollywood Western. As a result, the nine Wanderer episodes – eight of them directed by Saitō Buichi – foregrounded fistfights, cavalry chases, shoot-outs and showdowns performed in various scenic backdrops in the countryside.

Yet far from ending with a pure imitation of the US Western, the Wanderer films also offered a political critique of industrial capitalism in the Japanese context. In *The Wandering Guitarist/Guitar o motta wataridori* (1959), for example, Kobayashi plays the transient hero who lands in Hakodate (Fig. 37.1). There, he confronts a thug who tries to seize the property of an innocent woman and transform it into a tourist attraction. In *Whistles Blow in the Harbour City/Kuchibue ga nagareru minatomachi* (1960), Kobayashi, this time on horseback, ventures to Miyazaki and encounters a desolate mine. Once prosperous with some thirty workers, the rustic property is now under siege by a local boss, who is plotting to build a hotel to draw tourists into the region. With the help of Shishido Joe, a fellow gunslinger dressed in black from top to bottom (just like Burt Lancaster in *Vera Cruz*), Kobayashi crushes the evil plot with his revolver and restores peace in the barren landscape.

Fig. 37.1 *The Wandering Guitarist/Guitar o motta wataridori* (Saitō Buichi, 1959, Nikkatsu).

Wanderer of the Great Plains/Daisōgen no wataridori (1960) frames the conflict in a 'national' context. In this episode, Kobayashi appears in Kushiro, Hokkaido, to help reunite an abandoned boy with his mother. In the process, the hero encounters an Ainu village that is falling prey to an entrepreneurial villain – a Tokyoite who aims to build an airport for tourists to drop their cash in the area. He says, 'in this way, the number of tourists will grow fivefold; I will also make money; and this whole area will develop'. Drawn to Asaoka Ruriko, a passionate Ainu advocate, Kobayashi decides to stay in town to defend the indigenous community. In the end, Kobayashi thwarts the mission and his rival gunslinger, Shishido Joe, and defeats the villain in the final showdown. As he departs, the hero has thus protected the 'innocence' and 'purity' of Hokkaido from Tokyo's 'colonial' aspirations.

FROM HIGH-SPEED GROWTH TO THE BUBBLE ERA

The Nikkatsu Western basked in glory between the late 1950s and the early 1960s. Its momentum dipped in the years that followed, as the studio's fortunes began to decline in the face of television, recreational travel and other forms of commercial leisure. But the Japanese Western genre stayed alive and well, as other filmmakers took part in shaping it.

One director who led the way was Tōhō's Okamoto Kihachi, who, in the early to mid-1960s, produced *Desperado Outpost/Dokuritsu gurentai* (1959), *Westward Desperado/Dokuritsu gurentai nishi e* (1960), *Operation Brown Rat/Dobunezumi sakusen* (1963) and *Blood and Sand/Chi to suna* (1965) – a string of 'war Westerns' (*sensō seibugeki*) that depicted the antics of rebellious Japanese soldiers in northern China during World War II.[26] Criticised by some for turning an otherwise traumatising subject into gun-heavy entertainment, Okamoto aimed to 'restore' the humanity of rank-and-file soldiers by rewarding them with emotion and character complexity. These war Westerns also responded to the changing postwar climate, which, in Okamoto's mind, unduly 'standardised' the lives of Japanese citizens in the name of industrial and economic development.[27] In this sense, these unique war films were commentaries on the organisational and institutional life of the high-growth era.

Yamada Yōji also drew on the Western genre. This long-time Shōchiku director is best known for the *It's Tough Being a Man/Otoko wa tsuraiyo* series (1969–97), which featured a briefcase-carrying vagabond who experiences emotional, heart-warming (and heart-breaking) encounters as he drifts between his home in low-city Tokyo and diverse provincial locales. Commonly regarded as a 'national' (*kokuminteki*) series, the so-called Tora-san films adapted the prewar *matatabi* formula in postwar settings. In the inaugural film, the vagabond's young sister, who works as a typist in a modern corporate office in Tokyo, meets a co-worker through her company's superiors, but Atsumi, who returns home after being absent for twenty years, inadvertently ruins the arrangement. While her relatives express anger and disappointment, Atsumi helps a small printer propose to her; she joyfully agrees to marry him, and in doing so, abandons the white-collar lifestyle to stay in her low-city (*shitamachi*) neighbourhood, which increasingly became a site of nostalgic longing as the Japanese economy grew over the decades.[28] Satō Tadao points out that the influence of the US Western is evident in Atsumi's tendency towards 'female worship' (*josei sūhai*). Indeed, one of the routines is to see Atsumi meet a female lead (the 'Madonna'), reform his brawly behaviour in an attempt to impress her and end with a broken heart. This, to Satō, is not unlike the 'good bad man' stories of the Wild West.[29]

Yamada's other films, such as *The Yellow Handkerchief/Shiawase no kiiroi hankachi* (1977), also carry a Western theme. The director once explained that the impetus to make this film was 'Tie a Yellow Ribbon around the Ole Oak Tree', a popular song written by Irwin Levine and L. Russell Brown and made popular in 1973 by Tony Orlando and Dawn.[30] In the song, a convict, sitting on a bus heading home, seeks to find out if his sweetheart had affixed a 'yellow ribbon' on a nearby oak tree to affirm that she still has feelings for him; when he gets there, the tree with a hundred yellow ribbons, to his joy, welcomes his return.

The use of the yellow ribbon as a romantic prop predates the 1970s. According to the folklorist Gerald E. Parsons, the song may have been inspired by John Ford's *She Wore a Yellow Ribbon*, which is anchored around the niece of a cavalry officer wearing a yellow ribbon to express her feelings for her lover, a man in uniform.[31] *The Yellow Handkerchief* blends this 'Western motif' into the plot. Just like 'Tie a Yellow Ribbon', Yamada introduces an ex-convict, Takakura Ken, who seeks to reunite with his significant other (Baishō Chieko) after serving his term behind bars. In a postcard penned to her the day he is released, Takakura asks her to hoist a yellow handkerchief on a pole if she still loves him. When he finally arrives on site, dozens of yellow cloths are fluttering in the breeze.

Takakura's quest to find the yellow kerchief dovetails with the romance between Takeda Tetsuya and Momoi Kaori – the other thrust of the narrative. *The Yellow Handkerchief* begins with Takeda, a lowly factory worker just dumped by his girlfriend, purchasing a new car to embark on a road trip across Hokkaido. On the way, he buys a wine-red cowboy hat before picking up Takakura and Momoi – a young woman with a void in her heart. Yamada positions the younger pair within a spatial dialectic common to the Hollywood Western: both are unhappy in Tokyo – an overcivilised metropolis – and they eventually discover 'pure love' in Hokkaido – the 'virgin land' of the island nation. Takakura also operates in this spatial binary, as a Kyushu native who eventually finds fulfilment in a land far removed from the nation's capital.

Yamada's fascination with the northern 'frontier' also appears in *A Distant Cry from the Spring/Harukanaru yama no yobigoe* (1980), another Hokkaido-staged film starring Baishō and Takakura. The influence of the US Western is evident in this 1980 production, whose title is the Japanese translation of 'Call of the Faraway Hills' – the main theme from *Shane*. The setting is equally similar: in *Shane,* a gun-slinging hero enters a sparsely populated town in Wyoming and works for a pioneer family, whereas in *A Distant Cry from the Spring,* a runaway man lives in Baishō's small farm. In both films, a hint of romance develops. Baishō, in particular, falls in love and, in the climax, confesses her feelings to the taciturn hero. After Takakura surrenders himself to the police, Baishō, in an act that invokes *The Yellow Handkerchief,* gives him a yellow handkerchief to convey her affection for him. As Takakura looks away with tears filling his eyes, the narrative closes and their romance is affirmed.

Allusions to *Shane* are also clear in relationship between Takakura and Baishō's son. Living on the farm without a father, who had died two years earlier, the young boy develops a bond with the outcast protagonist. Takakura not only works with him in the fields but also imparts him with life lessons, particularly while Baishō is hospitalised due to a back injury. In the climax, when Takakura turns himself in to the police, the boy, in tears, runs towards him. Although not as vocal as Brandon de Wilde – the blond-haired boy who delivers the 'Shane, come back!' refrain – Baishō's son does become emotionally attached to the manly visitor.

Itami Jūzō brought a different touch to the Japanese Western. His second film, *Tampopo* (1985), follows Yamazaki Tsutomu, an outcast truck-driver who arrives in town to save a failing ramen shop from its competitors (Fig. 37.2). In a way that appears more Yamada-esque than *Shane*-esque, the eatery is run by a single mother (Miyamoto Nobuko) with a child attending elementary school. Determined to turn things around, Yamazaki – not unlike Yul Brynner's character in *The Magnificent Seven* – assembles a quirky posse (his truck-driving sidekick, a chauffeur, an interior decorator and a gourmet pauper) clad with vests and bandanas. Always donning a cowboy hat, the transient saviour mans a milk truck with bullhorns attached to the roof.

A self-proclaimed 'Ramen Western', *Tampopo* diverges from Yamada by collapsing the geographical distinction between core and periphery. In Yamada's films, the protagonists operate within the spatial dialectic of metropolis and region. Even when he presents the city of Tokyo, as in the *It's Tough Being a Man* series, the Shōchiku director polarises the *shitamachi* (i.e. Shibamata) and the 'modern' (i.e. Ginza) zones. Itami's 'Western' eliminates spatial classifications of this kind. Anchoring the story in the Japanese capital, he creates difference with culture (or Culture), not geography. The narrative juxtaposes the rich and the poor, the 'traditional' and the 'modern', the 'Western' and the 'Japanese' by surrounding Miyamoto's modest ramen place with an elegant French bistro, a formal etiquette class peopled with young women, and a gourmet supermarket carrying Camembert cheese and expensive fruit.

Unlike Yamada, Itami also confuses gender boundaries. While using Yamazaki – the outside hero –

Fig. 37.2 *Tampopo* (Itami Jūzō, 1985, Itami Productions).

to structure the narrative, Itami empowers Miyamoto by stressing her Rocky-esque ascendancy from loser to winner (at one moment, Miyamoto undergoes a training regime that alludes to the Sylvester Stallone films). In doing so, Itami de-masculinises the culinary culture of ramen – an enterprise that is led and even dominated by men. One can spot the male-centred clout of the noodle business, for example, in *Ramen Samurai/Rāmen zamurai* (2012), which presents a stoic young man's chivalric attempt to run a ramen stand of his deceased father. By contrast, *Tampopo* playfully feminises the ramen enterprise and ends by transforming Miyamoto from a timid working woman to a confident 'chef' wearing a toque and an apron. By imparting Miyamoto with a 'Westernised' look Itami diffuses the frontiers of both gender and culture.

Yamakawa Naoto takes things further in *The New Dawn of Billy the Kid/Birii za kiddo no atarashii yoake* (1988). Inspired by the works of novelist Takahashi Gen'ichirō, the narrative begins with the famous outlaw's (Mikami Hiroshi) arrival at an eventful saloon – a closed space where the bulk of the film develops. Its location, however, exists in abstraction, as it appears to be within walking distance of Monument Valley even though the dialogue proceeds in Japanese. What develops from here is a mishmash of genre action. At the saloon, Mikami joins a band of bodyguards to defend the saloon from machine-gun carrying gangsters. The team consists of a samurai (period film), a psychic (science fiction), a poet/music artist (literary film), a battlefront soldier (combat film) and an ideologue named Marx-Engels (political film). The narrative also deconstructs the hero's manly authority by curiously establishing Mikami, who brags that he has a faster hand than Alan Ladd, as a young-girl-loving '*lolicon*' who was named 'Billy' because he 'always finished [eating] last' (*biri*) during lunch hours in elementary school. Yamakawa additionally throws in humour, romance and musical performances by an all-female band, Zelda. Funded by Parco – then an engine of urban fashion and style – *The New Dawn of Billy the Kid* captures all the 'conspicuous consumption' of the 'bubble economy' of the 1980s.

SAMURAIS AND GUNFIGHTERS

Meanwhile, the Japanese *jidaigeki* also engaged with the US Western. Peaking in the mid-to-late 1950s, the postwar period film – which included musicals, horror stories, comedies and 'serious' re-enactments of actual events – drew its fans with star power, dynamic sword-fights, and by forging a nostalgic yearning for '"old things" that were disappearing as a result of urbanization and industrialization'.[32] For some *jidaigeki* film-makers, the Hollywood Western was an inspiration. Their '*jidaigeki* Westerns' not only reinvented the prewar *matatabi* genre but also generated a new set of hybrid narratives that recalibrated US formulas in Japanese settings.

At least two groups of *jidaigeki* Westerns emerged in the postwar era. One was what I would call 'latent hybrids', which embedded the traits of the US Western in Japanese historical settings. Kurosawa Akira's *The Seven Samurai/Shichinin no samurai* (1954) is a good example. This landmark film about a group of hired men who save a peasant village from ruthless bandits is often known to have given rise to John Sturges's *The Magnificent Seven* (1960). But *The Seven Samurai* was itself regarded by Kurosawa and his team as a 'Japanese version of a Western'.[33] The film adopted Hollywood traits in part by colouring the seven bodyguards with rich emotional and character traits. In devoting considerable narrative space to 'humanise' these men, the film deviated from much of the *jidaigeki* genre, which, according to the director Sasaki Yasushi, privileged action over 'the effort to build depth in the characters'.[34] *The Seven Samurai* also dramatised physical confrontation. Famously employing multiple cameras to dramatise the famous battle sequence, Kurosawa's team fortified the village with sticky moats and tall fences while mounting the bandits on horseback to generate speed and excitement. This rendered *The Seven Samurai* a noticeably 'Western-like *action film*' (*seibugekiteki na katsugeki*).[35]

Other latent hybrids brought the 'action traits' of the Hollywood Western – horseplay, gunplay and swordplay – to the forefront of the narrative. A number of these films emerged from Tōei studio, a hub of period film production in the postwar era. According to Kasuga Taichi, Tōei, which took pride in mass-producing 'popular entertainment', aimed to manufacture the *jidaigeki* equivalent of the Nikkatsu Action film by integrating Hollywood's formulas.[36] One can detect traces of the US Western in these crossover productions such as the *Black Hooded Man/Kaiketsu kurozukin* series (1953–60), which introduced a masked duel-fighting hero who roams the late Edo era and takes sides with the ordinary populace against corrupt *bakufu* leaders, Caucasian dignitaries and Chinese merchants in 'exotic' port cities such as Nagasaki and Yokohama – places that were 'frontiers' of cultural contact. When the innocent are in trouble, Ōtomo Ryūtarō, who plays the mysterious protagonist, appears to the rescue on a well-tamed white horse, just like the Lone Ranger. The look of the Western is particularly strong in *The Black Hooded Man in Peril/Ayaushi!! Kaiketsu Kurozukin* (1960), the ninth instalment, which begins with the black-hooded avenger galloping to Nagasaki to prevent the government from seizing a boatload of guns held by anti-*bakufu* forces. Blasting his two revolvers across town to draw the attention of the authorities, Ōtomo enables his allies to transport the guns on boat, before they are reloaded on a train of horse-pulled wagons. However, realising the plot, the government dispatches a large cavalry unit, which chases the wagons and encircles them, until Ōtomo comes to the rescue. After successfully protecting the munitions, the masked hero sets off into the mist, leaving the affectionate heroine behind.

Tōei produced other *jidaigeki* Westerns such as *Samurai Knights/Hakkō ryūkitai* (1961) or the pair of *White Horse Rider/Hakuba dōji* (1960) films, a popular children's story that, once again, drew from the Lone Ranger.[37] But in the 1960s and 1970s, the studio also began to transplant period-film tropes into the Meiji, Taishō and Shōwa eras, as in the 'chivalry film' (*ninkyō eiga*) genre, which typically flaunted the sword and knife fights of fierce yakuza clans.[38] Hollywood-like tendencies can be spotted in Ishii Teruo's *Abashiri Prison/Abashiri bangaichi* series (1965–72). Featuring Takakura Ken, this series follows a stoic convict who spends time in and out of the infamous Abashiri Prison in Hokkaido. In the fifth instalment, *Abashiri Prison: Showdown in the Wilderness/Abashiri bangaichi: Kōya no taiketsu* (1966), Takakura befriends a pony that he earns in a marksmanship contest and rushes on horseback to help innocent workers from being exploited by a greedy rancher. A trailer of the film unabashedly touted Takakura for 'attempting [to act in] a Western'.

Takakura also appears in *Brave Red Flower of the North/Nihon jokyō den: Makka na dokyōbana* (1970) as a lone wolf who glides on horseback with a rifle in hand. However, the film centres on Fuji Sumiko (formerly Fuji Junko), who became a top-bill star for Tōei with the success of the *The Valiant Red Peony/Karajishi botan* series (1968–72).[39] An unusual Japanese Western that features a lone female wanderer, *Brave Red Flower of the North* follows Fuji to the Hokkaido plains, where she strives to protect a horse-trading business owned by her deceased father. An independent woman who longs to live in Manchuria – a frontier beyond the Hokkaido frontier – Fuji wields her hands and fists to fend off a yakuza mob. Upset with the way in which Fuji's father had treated his family, Takakura initially resents Fuji's intentions but chooses to team-up with her to defeat the cruel villains. After surviving a dangerous shoot-out, they each depart on their horses. Fuji remarks that she will 'follow the wind'.

Meanwhile, some *jidaigeki* Westerns juxtaposed Japanese samurai with Caucasian gunslingers in settings that resembled the Wild West. These were 'manifest hybrids' that placed Japanese swordsmen in 'alien' (non-Japanese) settings. One example of this was *The Drifting Avenger/Kōya no toseinin* (1970). Shot on location in Australia, the film introduces Takakura, this time a mixed-race Japanese who seeks revenge against a clan of cowboys that killed his parents – a Japanese father and an Australian mother. Dressed in a leather waistcoat and shirt, Takakura learns the 'way of the gun' from an elderly outlaw but retains his 'samurai spirit' by carrying his father's sword at all times. In the climax, Takakura completes his vengeance by slashing and killing the Australian villains with his sword. This narrative keeps Takakura's 'traditional' Japanese roots alive and well.

Okamoto Kihachi, who made war Westerns as well as latent hybrids such as *Warring Clans/Sengoku yarō* (1963) and *Kill!/Kiru* (1968), directed a manifest hybrid entitled *East Meets West* (1995), which was shot in the arid US desert. A reinterpretation of the steamship Kanrin-maru's historic voyage, the narrative begins with a group of American robbers stealing a case of oval gold coins (*koban*) from the Japanese delegates who have just arrived at San Francisco. In response, Japanese officials dispatch Sanada Hiroyuki, an able swordsman who cuts his hair loose, dons a leather jacket and carries a gun to hunt down the villains. In addition to befriending a band of American gunmen, Sanada develops a paternal bond with a blond-haired Caucasian boy, whose father was killed in the bank robbery. Like Alan Ladd in *Shane*, Sanada conveys life lessons to the boy. The hero also teaches the art of swordsmanship – a skill that the child uses to slash his father's murderer in a climactic scene. Described as a 'samurai Western' in its press release, *East Meets West* also adds Takenaka Naoto as a Japanese ninja who marries a Crow woman and ends his life as a Native American.[40] Defying earlier US Westerns that antagonised and belittled the Indian Other, Okamoto advances his signature humanism to bridge racial and cultural barriers.

The era after *East Meets West* was a time of struggle in Japanese society. In the aftermath of the 'burst' Bubble economy, the public seemed to linger in the so-called 'unending everyday' (*owarinaki nichijō*).[41] The desire to imagine a 'disappearing past' seemed to grow in this drab milieu. One can see this in the rise of so-called 'Showa nostalgia', a sanitised reflection of the high-growth decades via such texts as the *Always: Sunset on Third Street/Always: Sanchōme no yūhi* series (2005–12).[42] The 'nostalgia boom' of the new millennium was also an intensely transnational phenomenon. For example, many Japanese viewers found unexpected solace in *Winter Sonata/Fuyu no sonata* (2003), a groundbreaking Korean television drama that presented a 'pure' love story that seemed to represent a 'good old Japan' that had long passed.[43] Another popular text was *The Last Samurai* (2003). According to Jayson Chun, who scrutinised fan postings on online discussion boards, the Tom Cruise film about the dawn of the Meiji era was embraced by the Japanese as it 'offered viewers nostalgia for the pre-Meiji past', an era 'seen as one of comfort and stability' in contrast to the post-Bubble climate in which the gap between the rich and the poor had only widened.[44]

The Japanese Western after the 1990s played an active role in shaping this intensely hybridising cultural sphere. One example was the anime-based film *Cowboy Bebop: The Movie* (2001) – a culturally 'odourless' science fiction that featured a quorum of bounty hunters who roam the galaxy to seek their prey and resolve their problems of their pasts.[45] Miike Takashi's *Sukiyaki Western: Django* (2007) creatively re-dramatised the historic feud between the Genji and Heike clans in a fictional town named 'Yuta' (which puns with 'Utah'). The film inserts Quentin Tarantino in a cameo role and, with the entire dialogue performed in English, poses as a US Western. Yet the hero of the film, a lone gunfighter who plays the warring parties to bring them towards destruction, in fact resembles the main lead in *Yojimbo/Yōjinbō* (1961) or Sergio Leone's *For a Fistful of Dollars* – a Spaghetti Western that openly borrowed from Kurosawa's *jidaigeki* film. Although the interplay between the Italian Western and the Japanese Western was already apparent in earlier films such as Okamoto's *Kill!*, Miike accentuates the influence of the European genre by turning the grandson of Momoi Kaori – a legendary gunfighter who runs a saloon – into an infamous icon: Django. While also drawing from a hodge-podge of cultural texts – from Shakespeare to anime – *Sukiyaki Western: Django* thus reveals a set of triangular links to these American and Italian formulas.

To conclude, the Japanese Western may often showcase stylised showdowns and physical violence, but the genre is ultimately a play with a 'lost past'. Invented and reinvented by a wide array of film-makers, the popular genre blossomed by tapping into viewers' nostalgic craving for a 'disappearing Japan'. This may reveal that the imaginary of the past was an object of fascination to both Japanese film-makers and viewers, but it also illustrates the influence of broader transnational forces in the making of Japanese 'nostalgia texts' or, to put it more specifically, the power of Hollywood on Japanese cinema. The Japanese

Western exemplifies the initiative and audacity of Japanese film-makers, but it also illustrates their existence within a larger global matrix – one that has increasingly revolved around the US. The solitary wanderer of the Japanese Western, then, trekked across two frontiers: one belonging to an imagined Japan, and the other related to popular geopolitics in the wider world.

ACKNOWLEDGMENT

I wish to thank Masato Dogase, Hideaki Fujiki, Woojeong Joo, Daneene Kelley, Ran Ma, Daisuke Miyao and Alastair Phillips for their support and feedback.

Notes

1. I have explored this genre in the following publications: Hiroshi Kitamura, 'Shoot-out in Hokkaido: The "Wanderer" (*Wataridori*) Series and the Politics of Transnationality', in Philippa Gates and Lisa Funnell (eds), *Transnational Asian Identities in Pan-Pacific Cinemas: The Reel Asian Exchange* (New York: Routledge, 2012), pp. 31–45; Hiroshi Kitamura, 'Wild Wild War: Okamoto Kihachi and the Politics of the Desperado Films', in King-fai Tam, Timothy Y. Tsu and Sandra Wilson (eds), *Chinese and Japanese Films on the Second World War* (New York: Routledge, 2015), pp. 107–20.
2. For useful studies on nostalgic production and consumption, see, for example, Hidaka Katsuyuki, *Shōwa nostaliga towa nanika: Kioku to radikaru democracy no mediagaku* (Tokyo: Sekai shisōsha, 2014); Jordan Sand, 'The Ambivalence of the New Breed: Nostalgic Consumerism in the 1980s and 1990s Japan', in Sheldon Garon and Patricia L. Maclachlan (eds), *The Ambivalent Consumer: Questioning Consumption in East Asia and the West* (Ithaca, NY: Cornell University Press, 2006), pp. 85–108; Christine R. Yano, *Tears of Longing: Nostalgia and the Nation in Japanese Popular Song* (Cambridge, MA: Harvard University Asia Center, 2002).
3. Yano, *Tears of Longing*, pp. 18, 16.
4. See, for example, Michael Baskett, *Attractive Empire: Transnational Film Culture in Imperial Japan* (Honolulu: University of Hawai'i Press, 2008); Stephanie DeBoer, *Coproducing Asia: Locating Japanese-Chinese Regional Film and Media* (Minneapolis: University of Minnesota Press, 2014); Hideaki Fujiki, *Making Personas: Transnational Film Stardom in Modern Japan* (Cambridge, MA: Harvard University Asia Center, 2013).
5. See, for example, John Trumpbour, *Selling Hollywood to the World: U.S. and European Struggles for Mastery of the Global Film Industry, 1920–1950* (New York: Cambridge University Press, 2002) and Kristin Thompson, *Exporting Entertainment: America in the World Film Market 1907–1934* (London: British Film Institute, 1985).
6. Due to spatial considerations, this chapter focuses on the connections between the Hollywood Western and Japanese cinema, and will not go in depth on other generic forces, such as the Spaghetti Western. [Editors' note: for more on the Japanese reception of Hollywood cinema, see also Chapter 40 by Ryan Cook in this volume.]
7. Iwamoto Kenji, 'Eiga no tōrai: Edison eiga to Nihon', in Iwamoto Kenji (ed.), *Nihon eiga sōsho*, vol. 15, *Nihon eiga no tanjō* (Tokyo: Shinwasha, 2011), pp. 24–7.
8. Hiroshi Kitamura, *Screening Enlightenment: Hollywood and the Cultural Reconstruction of Defeated Japan* (Ithaca, NY: Cornell University Press, 2010), pp. 22–41, 87–111.
9. 'Seibugeki tengoku Nippon', *Eiga no tomo rinji zōkan: Seibugeki dokuhon* (October 1960), pp. 16–17.
10. André Bazin, *What is Cinema?*, vol. 2, trans. Hugh Gray (Berkeley: University of California Press, 1971), pp. 149–57.
11. See, for example, Mishima Yukio's musings on the genre. Mishima Yukio, 'Seibugeki raisan', *Mishima Yukio zenshū* vol. 27 (Tokyo: Shinchōsha, 1975), pp. 286–8.
12. Ashihara Shin, *Seibugeki o mite otoko o mananda* (Tokyo: Shodensha, 2006).
13. 'Okāsan no nayami ni kotaete', *Nihon jidō bunka*, 28 January 1951, p. 2.
14. Kitamura, *Screening Enlightenment*, pp. 104–8.
15. Ōbayashi Nobuhiko, *Boku no American movie* (Tokyo: Kisō tengaisha, 1980), pp. 145–8.
16. Ashihara, *Seibugeki o mite otoko o mananda*, pp. 3–5.
17. Satō Tadao, *Hasegawa Shin ron* (Tokyo: Chūōkōron-sha, 1975). [Editors' note: for more on the yakuza film, see also Chapter 25 by Jennifer Coates in this volume.]
18. 'Ganman ha gengo no nagare o kumu!', *Eiga no tomo: Zoku seibugeki dokuhon*, special edn, May 1961, p. 158. Also see Kawamoto Saburō, '*Shane*: Nihonjin gonomi no "yasashii seibugeki"', *Tosho*, November 1991, pp. 20–5.

19 Both Hazumi and Kurosawa's remarks are quoted in Suzuki Noriko, 'Seibu frontier to Nihon: Sengo Nihon ni okeru seibu gensetsu no "dochakuka" to Nihon no jiko saisei o meguru bunka seijigaku', *Ōtsuma joshi daigaku kiyō: bunkei* no. 45 (March 2013), pp. 63–8.

20 Mark Schilling, *No Borders, No Limits: Nikkatsu Action Cinema* (Godalming: FAB Press, 2007); Watanabe Takenobu, *Nikkatsu action no karei na sekai*, 3 vols. (Tokyo: Miraisha, 1982).

21 There are some exceptions, however. In *Mexico Wanderer/Mekishiko mushuku*, the gun-slinging bad man fights for the younger brother of a deceased Mexican friend in the Mexican plains. *Wanderer across the Waves/Hatō o koeru wataridori* was staged in Hong Kong and Thailand.

22 Kobayashi Akira, *Sasurai* (Tokyo: Shinchōsha, 2001), p. 58.

23 Jim Kitses, *Horizons West: The Western from John Ford to Clint Eastwood* (London: British Film Institute, 2007).

24 Kainuma Hiroshi, *'Fukushima' ron: Genshiryoku mura wa naze umaretanoka* (Tokyo: Seidosha, 2011), pp. 325–8.

25 For more on this, see Kitamura, 'Shoot-out in Hokkaido'.

26 Kitamura, 'Wild Wild War'; Monma Takashi, 'Okamoto Kihachi to sensō eiga: Kahenteki identity', *Geijutsugaku kenkyū*, March 2008, pp. 41–57.

27 Okamoto Kihachi, *Majime to fumajime no aida* (Tokyo: Chikuma shobō, 2011), p. 103.

28 Sand, 'The Ambivalence of the New Breed', p. 92.

29 Satō Tadao, *Minna no Tora-san: Otoko wa tsuraiyo no sekai* (Tokyo: Asahi shinbunsha, 1988), pp. 44–65.

30 Yamada Yōji, *Eiga o tsukuru* (Tokyo: Ōtsuki shoten, 1978), pp. 121–5.

31 Gerald E. Parsons, 'Yellow Ribbons: Ties with Tradition', <http://www.loc.gov/folklife/ribbons/ribbons_81.html>.

32 Tsutsui Kiyotada, *Jidaigeki eiga no shisō* (Tokyo: Wedge, 2008), pp. 165–73. [Editors' note: for more on the *jidaigeki*, see also Chapter 20 by Philip Kaffen in this volume.]

33 Comment by Tsushima Keiko, quoted in Mifune Toshirō, Shimura Takashi and Tsushima Keiko, 'Ame no hi mo kaze no himo', in Hamano Yasuki (ed.), *Taikei Kurosawa Akira*, vol. 2 (Tokyo: Kōdansha, 2009), p. 154. Also see Horikawa Hiromichi, '*Shichinin no samurai* yowa', in Hamano, *Taikei Kurosawa Akira*, vol. 2, p. 159.

34 Sasaki Yasushi, 'Seibugeki ni omou', *Jidai eiga*, June 1961, quoted in Maruo Toshirō and Yokoyama Yukinori (eds), *Rakuten rakkan: Eiga kantoku Sasaki Yasushi* (Tokyo: Waizu shuppan, 2003), p. 197.

35 Kurosawa Akira, 'Jidaigeki deno jikken', in Hamano, *Taikei Kurosawa Akira*, vol. 2, p. 254, emphasis added.

36 Kasuga Taichi, *Akan yatsura: Tōei Kyoto satsueijo keppūroku* (Tokyo: Bungei shunjū, 2013), p. 154.

37 Kishi Matsuo, 'Nihon eiga to katsugeki no miryoku', *Kinema junpō*, special edn, July 1961, pp. 42–3.

38 Satō Tadao, 'Jidaigeki eiga no suitai', *Kinema junpō 40 nen zen kiroku* (Tokyo: Kinema junpōsha, 1985), pp. 44–6.

39 Ayako Saitō, 'Hibotan Oryū ron', Yomota Inuhiko and Washitani Hana (eds), *Tatakau onna tachi: Nihon eiga no josei action* (Tokyo: Sakuhinsha, 2009), pp. 84–149.

40 Shōchiku, press release for *East Meets West*, 1995.

41 Miyadai Shinji, *Owarinaki nichijō o ikiro* (Tokyo: Chikuma shobo, 1998).

42 Hidaka, *Shōwa nostalgia towa nanika*.

43 Kwon Yongseok, '*Kanryū*' to '*Nichiryū*': *Bunka kara yomitoku Nikkan shinjidai* (Tokyo: NHK shuppan, 2010), pp. 46–53.

44 Jayson Chun, 'Learning *Bushido* from Abroad: Japanese Reactions to *The Last Samurai*', *International Journal of Asia Pacific Studies* vol. 7 no. 3 (September 2011), p. 26.

45 Koichi Iwabuchi, *Recentering Globalization: Popular Culture and Japanese Transnationalism* (Durham, NC: Duke University Press, 2002).

38

PERIPHERIES
Japan and Okinawa and the politics of exchange

Andrew Dorman

Despite its relatively small size, Japan is notable for its geographical and cultural diversity with areas such as Okinawa (Ryūkyū), Hokkaido and Kyushu appearing separate (in terms of culture and natural environment) from what one might refer to as a core or 'mainland' Japan, specifically the central island of Honshu. Several scholars, most notably Tessa Morris-Suzuki, Harumi Befu and Mika Ko, have highlighted the marginalisation of peripheral and ethnically ambiguous communities within Japan, for example Okinawans and Ainu, to interrogate concepts of an ethnically and culturally homogeneous Japanese identity.[1] Due to its history as a contested territory, particularly in the aftermath of World War II, and its cultural status as an exotic locale distant from Japan's central islands, Okinawa warrants particularly close attention when discussing the notion of Japanese peripherality. This chapter examines cinematic responses to the core-periphery dialectic by analysing the representation of Okinawa in two films: *Profound Desires of the Gods/Kamigami no fukaki yokubō* (Imamura Shōhei, 1968) and *Dear Summer Sister/Natsu no imōto* (Ōshima Nagisa, 1972). These works will be discussed in terms of the social, political and cultural exchanges between Japan and Okinawa since World War II and, more specifically, the dominant issues that have characterised their relationship, namely primitivism, shared history and the American Occupation of Okinawa. Unlike other peripheral regions, the remoteness of which tends to be defined geographically rather than politically, Okinawa's status as a Japanese prefecture has been continually mediated between Japanese rule – national government and regional political authority – and the US government's legal right to maintain military installations as a result of the 1960 US–Japan Treaty of Mutual Security and Cooperation and the Self-Defence Forces (SDF) agreement that aligned Japan with the US. Given the ongoing presence of US military bases on the islands, Okinawa remains a far more controversial example of Japanese peripherality. Moreover, Okinawa's importance to US–Japan relations complicates any rudimentary definition of it simply as a peripheral other. Okinawa's peripheral status is underlined by the US military's presence and the US government's role in determining Okinawa's future as a US military outpost. Yet, at the same time, Okinawa continues to be a focal point in negotiating Japanese sovereignty and therefore remains a key geopolitical arena for the Japanese state. Significantly, the US military presence in Okinawa emphasises Japan's own peripheral status as a political and military subject of the US, thus undermining Japan's own central role in Okinawa.

Exchanges between core (Japan) and periphery (Okinawa) cannot be understood simply on the basis of a self-other binary relationship. Although *Profound Desires of the Gods* represents peripheral Japan in terms of primitivism (as associated with sex) and a relative lack of modernity, the film nevertheless offers a more complex consideration of core-periphery exchange. Similarly, *Dear Summer Sister* presents Okinawa as a distinct and highly exotic location, yet does not treat it as a fixed other in relation to Japan. Okinawa is more multifaceted geopolitically than its perceived otherness would suggest with its cultural and political status constantly evolving: from a colonial periphery prior to World War II to a Japanese frontline territory during the conflict, and from a 'stateless' US-occupied zone to a Japanese prefecture following the official US–Japanese handover of 1972. Although a self-other relationship based upon Okinawan stereotypes (primitivism, superstition, sex, exoticism, tourism) clearly manifests itself in *Profound Desires of the Gods* and *Dear Summer Sister*, Okinawa cannot be adequately understood in terms of otherness and peripherality given its cultural-political ambiguity and the fact that, in this case, core and periphery are interlinked through cross-cultural exchanges related to the postwar period.

PERIPHERAL 'JAPANESENESS'

Before investigating Okinawa in depth, it is worth addressing the concept of a Japanese core-periphery dialectic and how this construct has been maintained. There are different ways in which Japanese peripherality can be understood: as a geographical status, a non-conformity to Japanese sociocultural conventions or an ethnic category. In the process, 'mainland Japan' has been maintained as a core identity in direct relation to outlying regions and the marginalised communities that inhabit them. As certain scholars have indicated, namely Morris-Suzuki and Befu, 'Japaneseness' as a homogeneous and clearly defined geographical, cultural and ethnic category clearly excludes regions and peoples contained within the Japanese national sphere. The cultural, political and economic centrality of Honshu, the most densely populated of Japan's four main islands, has been carefully maintained, particularly since the Meiji period (1868–1912), through numerous processes of territorial expansion, political and cultural assimilation and, in some cases, exclusion. In discussing a 'master narrative' of racial and cultural homogeneity that precludes minorities, Michael Weiner views Japan as more heterogeneous than it appears to be, a 'home to diverse populations'.[2] However, it is worth remembering that Japanese peripherality is, first and foremost, a historical construct that has served to maintain a hierarchical relationship between a homogeneous core society and marginalised regions.

Distinctions of core and periphery can be given a substantial physical characteristic, in other words a geographical characteristic. There are many ways of demarcating Japan's 'exterior' from its core 'interior', the most rudimentary being a geographical definition of peripheral Japan. Kyushu, for instance, is situated to the south-west of Honshu, a physical separation underlined by the 1,500 metre Kanmon Bridge and the several underground tunnels that connect the two islands. In stark contrast to the subtropical volcanic landscapes of southern Kyushu, Hokkaido, the most northern of the four main islands, represents a more temperate, rugged and sparsely populated (approximately 5.5 million) periphery. Separated from Honshu by the Tsugaru Strait and in close proximity to the Russian islands of Kuril and Sakhalin, Hokkaido is notable for its natural wilderness (showcased by several national parks) and a subarctic winter climate. Similarly, other northern regions are also distinguished by their remoteness; in northern Honshu, or Tohoku, the prefectures of Aomori, Akita, Iwate and Yamagata have often been characterised in literature and popular culture for their hard-to-access rural landscapes, most famously in the seventeenth-century *haiku* poet Matsuo Bashō's travelogue *The Narrow Road to the Deep North*/*Oku no hosomichi*.

Stretching 425 miles south of Kyushu to within 450 miles of Taiwan, the Okinawan archipelago, also known as Ryūkyū, is the most remote Japanese prefecture or *ken* (subnational state or province) from Honshu, its sixty-five subtropical islands forming a natural barrier between the Pacific Ocean and the East China Sea. Despite territorial assimilation with Japan in 1874, the Okinawan islands remain geographically and culturally distinct within Japan. This distinctiveness is partly attributable to an exotic subtropical environment that has made Okinawa a popular tourist destination for Japanese since the 1960s. This has, in turn, informed recurrent cinematic portrayals of Okinawa as an 'eternally festive place',[3] a tourist-centric setting for films including *Dear Summer Sister*, *Boiling Point*/*3-4 x jugatsū* (Kitano Takeshi, 1990), *Sonatine* (Kitano Takeshi, 1993), *Nabi's Love*/*Nabi no koi* (Nakae Yūji, 1999), *City of Lost Souls*/*Hyōryū-gai* (Miike Takashi, 2001) and *Hotel Hibiscus* (Nakae Yūji,

2002). Taking into account differences in climate and physical landscape, one can start to recognise a series of peripheries related to the imagined construct of mainland Japan. But how are peripheries related to this construct and how have they been maintained historically? In order to conceive of the periphery as a cultural and ethnic category, one should consider mainland Japan as a physical representation of a homogeneous and exclusive collective identity, and one that has clearly engendered a core-periphery dialectic.

As defining regional features, climate and landscape provide some indication of Japan's natural diversity, yet these features have also been implicated in the construction of cultural and regional differences and a dominant narrative of national identity. Many *haiku* and *waka* poems, for example, characterise Japan as a nation of four distinct seasons: spring, summer, autumn and winter. Evocations of Japan as a country of four seasons are biased, Befu argues, in favour of central Japan, a 'region from Kansai (Kyoto-Osaka) to Kantō (Tokyo) – where the power to create such cultural narratives has historically resided'.[4] Befu views cultural imbalances between central and peripheral Japan in terms of climactic differences, suggesting that conventional representations of Japan preclude peripheral 'variations' and fail to account for the experiences of all Japanese people: 'From the peripheries of Japan, these seasonal changes are only partially true at best.'[5] In the narratives of seasonality described by Befu, Okinawa, Hokkaido and Tohoku are rendered not only geographically peripheral but culturally marginal as well: 'They are forever condemned to the peripheries, not only literally at the southern and northern ends of the island chain, but also figuratively in the culturally constructed seasonality of Japan.'[6]

Befu approaches a much wider issue in his discussion of cultural narratives of seasonality, specifically the cultural and political dominance of 'core Japan' and its methods of maintaining cultural hegemony. Following their annexation in the late nineteenth century, Okinawa and Hokkaido were assimilated into the political and administrative body of Japan. Yet, this did not guarantee an inclusive definition of the newly expanding Japanese state: 'The policies of assimilation which were used to turn the people of the frontier into Japanese citizens involved a sharpening of the official definition of what it meant to be Japanese.'[7] Though such a definition was not constant or stable,[8] it nevertheless informed a more exclusive conception of nationality based around the rapid modernisation of central Japan after the Meiji restoration of 1868 and the designation of Tokyo as Japan's new capital. Thus, while new territories were officially incorporated into an expanding Japanese state, narrowly defined concepts of nationality served to create a core identity in contrast to newly acquired and culturally ambiguous peripheries.

Discussing Japanese expansion during the first half of the twentieth century, Befu notes the formulation of a core Japan, with politicians and intellectuals basing national identity on ideas of cultural homogeneity:

'Japanese' in the core area, and their culture, were considered to embody the essence of Japan. Those in other territories were considered second-class Japanese at best, not only because they did not speak Japanese, but also because of their lack of other core Japanese cultural accoutrements, and further, because of their colonial status.[9]

When viewed in relation to dominant cultural narratives and the expansion of the Japanese state in the late nineteenth century, peripheral communities take on a contradictory status. On the one hand, they were contained within a core Japan through the political assimilation of Okinawa in the south and Hokkaido in the north, firstly by the Satsuma and Tokugawa shogunates and then later by the Meiji government. In that sense, both regions assumed a Japanese status. On the other, the people of these new frontiers became minorities within Japan. Peripheral communities could be maintained as culturally and socially marginal, unrelated to the central seat of government, yet nevertheless answerable to it, while the relationship between Japan and the peripheries would gradually adopt elements of a self-other binary model. Integral to this was the exotic ethnic character of peripheral Japanese. This proved particularly true during the Meiji period, a time in which Japan phased out feudal systems in favour of industrial development and territorial expansion.

Following the Meiji government's annexation of the Ryūkyū islands in 1874 and the end of Chinese claims to the islands following Japan's victories in the Sino-Japanese War (1894–5), the exotic character of Okinawa was maintained despite Okinawan claims of cultural and ethnic similarity with Japan. In 1903 the Fifth Industrial Exhibition in Osaka featured a display of Korean, Taiwanese, Ainu and Okinawan cultures and ethnicities. As Alan S. Christy notes, Okinawan newspapers reacted angrily, claiming that the display was a slur against Okinawans who had been lined up with 'primitive' and 'inferior' ethnic groups.[10] Interestingly the Okinawan response claimed Japanese status (rather than maintain a peripheral Okinawan identity), while the Meiji government categorised 'Okinawanness' as culturally foreign alongside other annexed territories:

> Subjected to ethnic discrimination which, in practice, associated them with subjugated peoples, Okinawans tended to insist on their legitimate 'Japaneseness,' using a variety of arguments ranging from common archaic origins to their successful absorption of an emperor-centered moral education (*kōminka*).[11]

The categorisation of Okinawans as ethnic-cultural others who were (nevertheless) contained officially as Japanese citizens, did not account for the ambiguities of Okinawan identities, the fact that those identities could at once be Okinawan *and* Japanese. As a seemingly fixed term of reference, Japaneseness can be discussed as an ethnic category, albeit under the assumption that the majority of Japan's population are ethnically assimilated in relation to the ethnic groups originating in the ancient Yamato province. Monolithic concepts of Japanese nationality and ethnicity invariably exclude minorities (who may or may not consider themselves conventionally Japanese) while not accounting for the fact that 'Japanese' itself is not a fixed ethnic category due to genealogical links to Chinese, Koreans and to some extent Pacific islanders. Such cultural and ethnic essentialism presupposes the otherness of people outside the core Japan, namely Okinawans who, as Christy suggests, viewed themselves as Japanese.

Whether defined geographically, culturally or ethnically, Japanese peripheries are identifiable in particular regions where climate, environment, cultural traditions and ethnic background do not conform to conventions of a core Japanese identity. The distinctions made by dominant cultural narratives and restrictive definitions of Japaneseness, particularly those discussed by Befu, underline a clear self-other binary relationship that has informed a core-periphery dialectic. *Profound Desires of the Gods* and *Dear Summer Sister* depict encounters between Japan and Okinawa that correspond to this dialectic. However, encounters between the two extend beyond a basic self-other relationship. Although both *Profound Desires of the Gods* and *Dear Summer Sister* broadly distinguish core and periphery through stereotypical representations of Okinawa, they also articulate Okinawa's geopolitical ambiguity in the postwar period. Whether through the fundamental links of primitivism and the shared history of war with and occupation by the US, Japan and Okinawa are in fact shown to be interlinked in ways that underline both Okinawa's peripheral status and its deep economic, political and historical connections with Japan.

PRIMITIVISM IN THE PERIPHERY

Geographical peripheries have often been presented cinematically as culturally archaic and economically underdeveloped variations of modern Japan, and in ways that reaffirm distinctions between the mainland and the periphery. In the work of Imamura Shōhei the cultural authenticity of peripheral Japan constitutes a more natural state preferable to the restrictions imposed by Japan's economic and urban transformations during the Meiji period and the decades following World War II. The supposedly primitive periphery therefore serves to articulate ambivalence towards Japanese modernisation and the master narratives of cultural homogeneity that correspond to it.

Imamura's focus on primitivism in several of his films does not simply bring peripheral Japanese communities to the fore; it highlights what the core of Japan seemingly lacks in comparison to these communities. If we think of the periphery as serving a specific purpose in certain films – that of an alternative, primitive world – it could be argued that Okinawa offers a nostalgic space in which to imagine an alternative to an increasingly industrialised Japan, a purer, more traditional rural environment untouched by accelerated social and economic change. Like Imamura, Ōshima is also notable for moving towards a premodern, rural past in his work following the making of *Dear Summer Sister*.[12]

Donald Richie differentiates between 'two Japans' in relation to Imamura's work, one the 'official' version composed of Japanese stereotypes (Noh theatre, tea ceremonies, etc.) and the other a more natural, more authentic Japan, albeit one very much on the periphery of the official core Japan:

> The other Japan might, judging from Imamura's films, be called the 'real' version. His people, it has often been noted, do not behave like 'Japanese' because none of the rules of order and decorum insisted upon by the official version apply. These people, always from the so-called lower classes, do not know the meaning of fidelity and loyalty. They are completely natural and are to that extent 'uncivilized' if civilization means (as it does) a removal from the natural. They are selfish, lusty, amoral, innocent, natural and all of the vitality of Japan comes from their numbers.[13]

Adopting a quasi-anthropological approach to filmmaking, Imamura developed a vented interest in the primitive as a response to the 'artificial', transient lifestyles engendered by industrialised conditions. His preoccupation with the primitive is obvious, as is a tendency to portray characters from the periphery. *The Insect Woman/Nippon konchūki* (1963), otherwise known as 'An Account of Japanese Insects', portrays a young woman from a rural background working as a prostitute in Tokyo, her social status linked to that of 'lower animals'. *Intentions of a Murder/Akai satsui* (1964) features a housewife from the remote northern city of Sendai, while the direct translation of *The Pornographers/Jinruigaku nyūmon* (1966), 'A Primer in Anthropology', further emphasises Imamura's interest in and symbolic use of the primitive.

As depicted in various films – *Profound Desires of the Gods*, *Dear Summer Sister*, *Extreme Private Eros Love Song 1974/Kyokushiteki eros: Renka 1974* (Hara Kazuo, 1974), *Boiling Point*, *Sonatine*, *Nabi's Love* and *Hotel Hibiscus* – Okinawa emerges through a conjugation of specific images: exotic subtropical landscapes, holiday resorts, sex and archaic social customs. The prevailing mode of representation in Japanese-Okinawan cinema is one of exoticism and primitivism, and it is in the remoteness of Okinawa that Imamura presents his most overtly anthropological film. Set on the fictional island of Kurage (filmed on the Okinawan-Yaeyama island of Ishigaki), a place identifiable as a distinctly Okinawan location through segments of Okinawan language and music, *Profound Desires of the Gods* offers a highly exaggerated representation of a community steeped in exoticism, nature, superstition, sex and violence. Despite its agriculture having been based on sugar cane, Kurage is in the process of economic transformation. Kariya (Kitamura Kazuo), a representative from a mainland sugar company, arrives from Tokyo to oversee the establishment of a factory and the construction of a water pipeline that soon encroaches upon the islanders' religious beliefs. At the centre of the film are the Futori family – Yamamori (Arashi Kanjurō), his children Nekichi (Mikuni Rentarō), Uma (Matsui Yasuko) and Toriko (Okiyama Hideko), and grandson Kametarō (Kawarazaki Chōichirō) – a family ostracised from the island's community for various reasons, including incest, poaching and Nekichi's refusal to give up his rice paddy to make way for sugar cane planting.

Central to Kurage's primitivism is its abundance of nature and the fervent sexuality of its inhabitants. Nature is omnipresent, acting as a fundamental essence woven into the working lives of the islanders. As a result, their livelihood is constantly dependent on environmental factors, particularly in the case of the Futoris (Fig. 38.1). A series of opening shots establish the importance of nature in Imamura's film: a glaring orange sun, a striped snake twisting through shallow waters, a sea slug, snails, a flat fish on the sea bed, an intense close-up of a puffer fish out of water and an octopus plucked from the sea. Not dissimilar to other quasi-anthropological films such as *Walkabout* (Nicolas

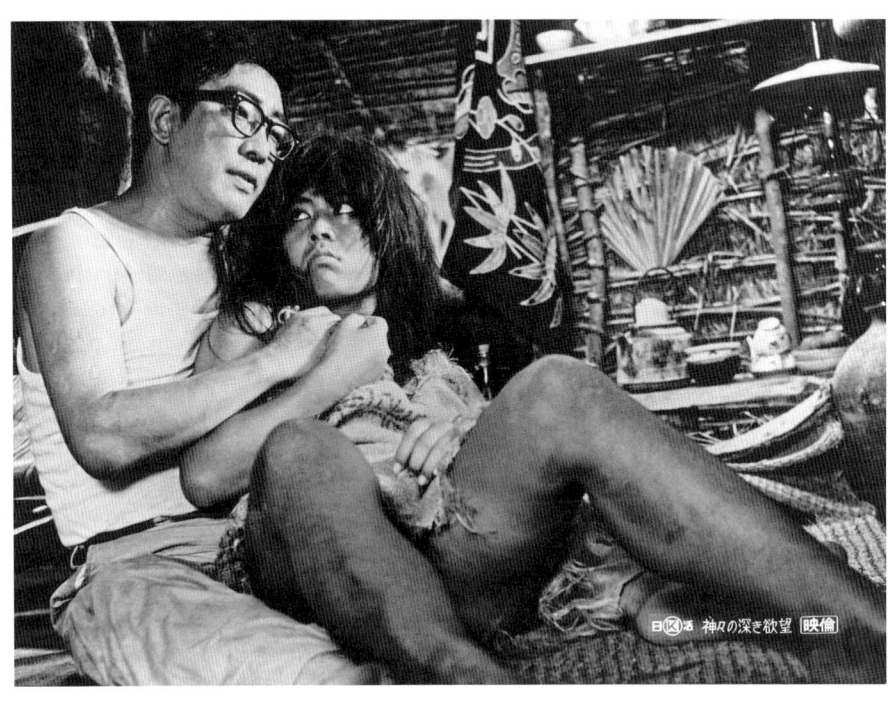

Fig. 38.1 *Profound Desires of the Gods/Kamigami no fukaki yokubō* (Imamura Shōhei, 1968, Imamura Productions).

Roeg, 1971) and *Aguirre, the Wrath of God/Aguirre: der Zorn Gottes* (Werner Herzog, 1973), *Profound Desires of the Gods* is notable for the use of animals as constant reminders of the oppressive natural conditions surrounding its characters, particularly when Imamura uses snakes, lizards and ants in transitional shots.

To underline Kurage's primitive state, Imamura places the natural world in sync with human sexuality. Sex, like nature itself, is ever present, from the incestuous creation myths sung by a local storyteller (a narrative that parallels the Shinto creation myth of Izanagi and Izanami) to the bawdy songs sung by young islanders in preparation for the annual Dongama coming-of-age festival. A dominant presence throughout the film, Toriko Futori embodies the equation of nature and sex, her primitivism not only stemming from a young mental age but also from an animalistic sexuality typical of Imamura's portrayal of women:

> Imamura's female characters [...] represent a 'primitive' image of female sexuality free from the taboos of modern society. [...] Imamura's characters [...] devoid of a modern social sensibility, appear to have an exaggerated sexual energy which spills over into quasi-incestuous relationships.[14]

Toriko forces herself upon Kariya, her primal lust both unsettling and eventually seducing the mainlander. The implication of Toriko's rampant sexuality is that because sex is natural, it is also animalistic. One scene in particular underlines this as Toriko toys with a lizard before letting it run under her clothes while, at the same time, the storyteller sings of man's desire for woman.

Imamura's anthropological treatment of Okinawa reinforces the stereotypical primitivism of the periphery, leading Aaron Gerow to criticise an approach that renders the 'Okinawan self' as more natural, more original than the Japan of the high economic growth era.[15] However, Imamura does not simply reduce the islanders in *Profound Desires of the Gods* to primitives. It should be noted that the Futoris, an oftentimes grotesque and dysfunctional unit, are not indicative of Kurage as a whole and therefore not a microcosm of 'Okinawanness'. They are of course outcasts on the island. Furthermore, though the Futoris, and Nekichi in particular, are opposed to the economic changes on Kurage (as are its religious elders), others accept modernisation, such as the workers employed by the company and Kametarō Futori, who shadows Kariya as an apprentice.

By presenting the Futoris as caricatures of rural, peripheral primitivism, and by juxtaposing them so sharply with the other inhabitants of Kurage, Imamura avoids both an idealisation of primitivism and a wholly negative representation of Okinawa. The social structure of Kurage is far more complex, with the community's need to embrace modernisation clashing with agriculture and religious observance. Therefore, Imamura does not simplify the periphery as entirely primitive, allowing for conflicting ideologies of community, progress and morality to play themselves out. On the one hand, primitivism is evident given the director's emphasis on nature and sexuality, yet, on the other, the peripheral community, with the exception of the Futoris, adapts to the 'civilising' processes of modernity.

As conveyed through the natural world and the pronounced sexuality of its inhabitants, Kurage functions as a space for the Japanese self, a space in which mainland Japan can be reflected in the apparent otherness of a peripheral Okinawan setting. However, as both *Profound Desires of the Gods* and *Dear Summer Sister* demonstrate, the relationship between core and periphery is more complex than the self-other relationship suggested by Imamura's anthropological representation of Kurage's primitivism. The stark contrasts between a 'natural' Okinawan way of life and the 'civilised' mainland belie the fact that Okinawa and Japan are interlinked by a shared history, namely the events of World War II and the resultant periods of US military occupation.

SHARING HISTORY

Prior to World War II Okinawa did not hold the same colonial status as more disputed Japanese territories annexed at China's expense, such as Taiwan (1895), Korea (1910) and Manchuria (1931). Established as a Japanese prefecture in 1879, Okinawa was more effectively absorbed as an official region of Japan, as opposed to the colonial outposts of Korea and Manchuria, which served specific military purposes, particularly during the second Sino-Japanese War (1937–45). However, both Okinawa's peripheral status and its official status as a Japanese territory would come into renewed focus because of the Pacific conflict between Japan and the US during World War II. While representations of primitive Okinawa reveal a relationship of cultural contrasts, the shared history of World War II and American Occupation complicates Okinawa's status as a remote periphery. In short, the inescapable legacies of war and occupation, evoked most vividly in *Dear Summer Sister*, serve as reminders that Okinawa was a Japanese frontline territory during wartime and then a key geopolitical arena for postwar Japan–US relations.

By 1945 US forces had gradually pressed the Japanese to the Okinawan islands, prompting some of the most intense fighting of the campaign. Totalling approximately 250,000 Japanese military and civilian deaths and 13,000 American, the battle for Okinawa left an indelible mark on the islands, particularly as Okinawan non-combatants became embroiled in the conflict. Now major tourist locations on the southern tip of the island of Okinawa, several battle sites – Cape Kyan, Himeyuri no Tō, Konpaku no Tō and Mabuni Hill – focus attention on the civilian and military loses incurred in 1945. Monuments serve to reinforce a shared history between Japanese and Okinawans, and significantly some are featured in *Dear Summer Sister*'s early sequences. Two young women – Sunaoko (Kurita Hiromi) and her future mother-in-law Momoko (Lily) – visit Okinawa in order to trace the whereabouts of a man (Ishibashi Shōji) who may or may not be Sunaoko's brother. During their visit they also find time to experience Okinawa as tourists. Sunaoko, Momoko and war veteran Sakurada (Tonoyama Taiji) take a bus tour to the Tower of the Lilies (Himeyuri no Tō), a memorial dedicated to a group of volunteer nurses killed by American attacks. This early encounter between Japanese visitors to Okinawa and the visible traces of World War II prompts a drunken Sakurada to publically mourn his fellow Japanese and, for the first time, acknowledge the loss of Okinawan life (Fig. 38.2).

Fig. 38.2 *Dear Summer Sister/Natsu no imōto* (Ōshima Nagisa, 1972, Sōzōsha and ATG).

In referencing Okinawan deaths so explicitly, Ōshima takes the step of acknowledging both Japan's use of the Okinawan archipelago as a frontline in Japan's war and the role of Okinawan civilians in the conflict. Although resigned to a subaltern and culturally peripheral status within Japan since the late nineteenth century, the people of Okinawa were expected to fulfil certain duties as 'Japanese' citizens during wartime, thus their sub-Japanese status was reinterpreted according to the strategic imperatives of the Japanese military. As Matthew Allen argues:

> Throughout the early twentieth century, Okinawa remained a Japanese prefecture, albeit the least developed, lagging behind mainland Japanese in standards of living, education, literacy and health. Nominally a prefecture, it was more like a colonial possession. Tragically for Okinawans, it was not until the Battle of Okinawa in May 1945 that they truly understood the nature of their relationship with mainland Japan.[16]

The nature of the relationship between Japan and Okinawa became apparent in that Okinawa was now very much a part of Japan in territorial terms with Okinawans assimilated, willingly or not, into Japanese military efforts. The deaths of Okinawans were thus the deaths of 'imperial subjects', as noted by Mika Ko.[17] At the same time that Okinawan men were recruited into the Imperial Japanese Army, civilians were put to use as strategic subjects. Collective suicide (*shūdan jiketsu*)[18] became a common occurrence, particularly among impoverished Okinawans. In some cases, suicide was voluntary, prompted either by fear or a sense of national-imperial duty. However, it soon became apparent that some civilians were forced into *shūdan jiketsu* by Japanese soldiers. The military were able to exercise Okinawa's subaltern position and with it could not only reposition Okinawa as a vitally important national location but also reinterpret its population as Japanese civilians instilled with certain responsibilities to the war effort.

Following Japan's surrender in August 1945 and with American troops occupying its islands, Okinawa became a US military outpost until it was officially returned to Japan in 1972, the year of *Dear Summer Sister*'s release. However, this did not mark an official end to the US's use of Okinawa for strategic military purposes: 'Over half a century after it began, the American occupation remains a touchstone for a polarized political debate in Japan.'[19] The US military presence has been maintained as a form of mutual security, whereby a demilitarised Japan could be shielded from external risks by US bases. The policy of dependency secured by SDF and the US–Japan Treaty of Mutual Security and Cooperation cannot be divorced, Glen D. Hook has argued, from the 'consequent location of military outposts of the American eagle in Japanese sovereign territorial space'.[20]

The military presence in Okinawa continues in spite of the US Occupation having ended in 1952, a fact that underlines just how convenient Okinawa proved to be as a US military base situated within reasonable distance of Korea and Vietnam. In an explicit reference to this, a military plane is heard passing over Kurage in *Profound Desires of the Gods*, the character Kametarō remarking to his brother Nekichi that its destination is Vietnam. As made abundantly clear in *Dear Summer Sister*, Okinawa's 'usefulness' was not simply of a military nature. Okinawa is firmly sexualised and, furthermore, feminised as a sexual resort in which prostitutes offer a 'playground' for Japanese male tourists and US military personnel based on the island. Unlike sex in *Profound Desires of the Gods*, which is invoked to underline the animalistic vitality of Okinawans in comparison to the Japanese, sex in *Dear Summer Sister* serves a more precise metaphorical purpose. Okinawa's postwar hybridity, its status as a post-Japanese, American strategic territory is expressed by Sunaoko and Momoko's escort as they drive through the streets of Koza: 'As you must know, Koza's 60,000 inhabitants depend for their livelihood entirely on the U.S. base. Koza is more American than Japanese.' To visually confirm the escort's viewpoint, a tracking shot reveals a series of signs advertising Coca-Cola and Pepsi plastered on Koza's bars and shop fronts. The escort continues:

> This area has an English name: centre. It's a playground reserved for GIs back from Vietnam. We've counted 10,000 prostitutes on Okinawa, but the real figure is between 12 and 14,000 for a female population of 50,000, only half of whom are of suitable age.

The utilisation of Okinawa as a sexual 'playground' for visiting GIs is not merely a metaphor for US military interference read as a form of geopolitical 'penetration'; it also relates to Okinawa's political and, to some extent, cultural ambiguity as a Japanese prefecture.

Whereas Okinawa in *Profound Desires of the Gods* is represented within the broad terms of primitivism, in *Dear Summer Sister* Okinawa's cultural distance from Japan is more geopolitical in nature, its postwar hybridity informed not so much by a self-other dialectic but by the US' role in 'othering' it. Allen writes:

> Not only had Okinawans been identified by the Japanese in the war as potentially untrustworthy and, at best, marginal Japanese, in the settlement that followed the mass destruction of Okinawan life and property, Okinawans were once more identified as outside of Japan (by both Japanese and US officials), hence able to be 'sacrificed' by Japan to meet US (and Japan's) regional security needs.[21]

As Allen indicates, 'Okinawaness' becomes paradoxical. With the Japanese constitution of 1947 and the exclusion of Okinawa from its terms and conditions, Okinawa quite literally became stateless.[22] Indeed through core-periphery encounters in *Dear Summer Sister*, the national status of Okinawa is highly ambiguous with the islands drifting in between US Occupation and a post-1972 reversion to a country that had seemingly only considered it a significant region whenever it had served strategic political or military purposes. A shared history clearly blurs the boundaries between Japan and Okinawa, with *Dear Summer Sister* demonstrating the transient nature of Okinawa as a Japanese prefecture. Due to the strategic military priorities of the Pacific War, Okinawa's peripheral status needed reinterpretation, with Okinawans assimilated into the war effort against the US. The final stages of the conflict demonstrate the malleability of this status and thus how Okinawa's perceived cultural remoteness has been manipulated according to changing historical and political contexts. Similarly, Okinawa's peripheral

'Japaneseness' re-emerged after the war as a direct result of the US Occupation and the ensuing influx of US military personnel, another cultural-political alteration that problematises attempts to view Okinawa as either wholly peripheral or firmly Japanese in nature.

As *Profound Desires of the Gods* and *Dear Summer Sister* demonstrate, Okinawa is by no means a fixed periphery. I would contend that Okinawa has often been malleable in its status; Okinawa is Japanese, but arguably only insofar as it suits a US–Japan policy of military dependence. Yet, this in itself underlines Japan's own peripheral status as a political nation, its subaltern status within a US political sphere of power and influence. A continued US military presence in Okinawa remains symptomatic of Japan's relative powerlessness within the prefecture, thus its historical status as the centre of power to which Okinawa is subject is challenged. The political and cultural hegemony of what one may refer to as core Japan is undermined within the periphery, a destabilisation of Japanese power within the Japanese nation state that, in turn, blurs the self-other distinction of Japan as a centre of power vis-à-vis Okinawa.

CONCLUSION

When considering the shared history of World War II, its legacies of occupation and an ambiguous national-political status, exchanges between Okinawa and Japan cannot simply be understood in the broadest terms of self and other. At various stages Okinawa has been a periphery of Japan prior to World War II, a Japanese frontline territory, a 'stateless' zone culturally infiltrated by the US and a focal point for US–Japan geopolitics. These factors involve exchanges that, in one sense, reinforce the peripheral status of Okinawa (primitivism, exoticism, an American presence on the islands) and, in another, blur distinctions between mainland and periphery (shared history, Okinawa's changing political status within the Japanese sphere).

Although both Imamura and Ōshima broadly distinguish between Japan and Okinawa, the cross-cultural exchanges one sees in *Profound Desires of the Gods* and *Dear Summer Sister* allow for a renegotiation of core-periphery distinctions. Furthermore, Okinawa is not a fixed periphery in regards to Japan and therefore cannot be simplified as its cultural other. Multifaceted in its cultural-national status, Okinawa is, depending on changing social, political and economic conditions, a culturally distinctive and geographically remote Japanese prefecture, a key US military outpost, a culturally hybrid space in which Okinawan society meets with American and Japanese influences, and a locus for Japan's postwar relationship with the US. In respect to this latter point, Okinawa is very much a part of the Japanese state rather than merely a periphery of it. By virtue of this, any discussion of the core-periphery dialectic cannot be reduced to self-other distinctions. Although this may help to explain how Okinawa and other peripheries have been historically marginalised from a constructed 'core Japan', it does not account for Okinawa's culturally and politically malleable status as it relates to Japan and the US. In the case of Okinawa, Japan's own peripheral, even subaltern position (in terms of occupation, demilitarisation and the proliferation of US military bases) has been exposed. Whereas Hokkaido, Kyushu and Shikoku were only occupied until 1952, Okinawa has remained effectively occupied since the end of the World War II. Within the Okinawan archipelago, therefore, Japan's own peripherality vis-à-vis US political and military power is underlined and its role as the political 'core' for all its prefectures undermined. As a result, Okinawa has and continues to occupy an ambiguous position within Japan's political orbit. For this reason alone, it is worth considering fluid exchanges between core and periphery, the cultural, social and political constructions of a core-periphery dialectic and the ways in which the core self of Japan has been reassessed cinematically in relation to peripheral Japan.

Notes

1. Tessa Morris-Suzuki, 'The Frontiers of Japanese Identity', in Stein Tonnesson and Hans Antlov (eds), *Asian Forms of the Nation* (Richmond: Curzon Press, 1996); Harumi Befu, 'Concepts of Japan, Japanese Culture and the Japanese', in Yoshio Sugimoto (ed.), *The Cambridge Companion to Modern Japanese Culture* (Cambridge: Cambridge University Press, 2009); Mika Ko, *Japanese Cinema and Otherness:*

Nationalism, Multiculturalism and the Problem of Japaneseness (London: Routledge, 2011).
2. Michael Weiner, 'Editor's Introduction', in Michael Weiner (ed.), *Japan's Minorities: The Illusion of Homogeneity* (New York: Routledge, 2009), p. xvii.
3. Ko, *Japanese Cinema and Otherness*, p. 85.
4. Befu, 'Concepts of Japan, Japanese Culture and the Japanese', p. 22.
5. Ibid.
6. Ibid., pp. 22–3.
7. Morris-Suzuki, 'The Frontiers of Japanese Identity', p. 42.
8. Ibid.
9. Befu, 'Concepts of Japan, Japanese Culture and the Japanese', p. 24.
10. Alan S. Christy, 'The Making of Imperial Subjects in Okinawa', in Tani E. Barlow (ed.), *Formations of Colonial Modernity in East Asia* (Durham, NC: Duke University Press, 1997), p. 141.
11. Ibid.
12. Yuriko Furuhata talks about a trend of 'moving away from actuality' in the early 1970s, with Japanese directors such as Ōshima and Matsumoto Toshio turning their attentions away from journalistic films about modern, urban Japan towards the distant, premodern and rural past. In this regard, Ōshima was 'exemplary': 'Disbanding his production company Sōzōsha after the making of *Dear Summer Sister* (1972), he also turned away from the present and retreated into the distant past.' Yuriko Furuhata, *Cinema of Actuality: Japanese Avant-Garde Filmmaking in the Season of Image Politics* (Durham, NC: Duke University Press, 2013), p. 198.
13. Donald Richie, 'Notes for a Study on Shohei Imamura', in James Quandt (ed.), *Shohei Imamura* (Toronto: Toronto International Film Festival Group, 1999), p. 80.
14. Isolde Standish, *Politics, Porn and Protest: Japanese Avant-Garde Cinema in the 1960s and 1970s* (London: Continuum, 2011), p. 87.
15. Aaron Gerow, 'From the National Gaze to Multiple Gazes: Representations of Okinawa in Recent Japanese Cinema', in Laura Hein and Mark Selden (eds), *Islands of Discontent: Okinawan Responses to Japanese and American Power* (Lanham, MD: Rowman & Littlefield, 2003), p. 277.
16. Matthew Allen, 'Okinawa, Ambivalence, Identity and Japan', in Wiener, *Japan's Minorities*, p. 188.
17. Ko, *Japanese Cinema and Otherness*, p. 66.
18. Ibid.
19. Michael S. Molasky, *The American Occupation of Japan and Okinawa: Literature and Memory* (London: Routledge, 1999), p. 7.
20. Glen D. Hook, 'Intersecting Risks and Governing Okinawa: American Bases and the Unfinished War', *Japan Forum* vol. 22 nos. 1–2 (June 2010), p. 196.
21. Allen, 'Okinawa, Ambivalence, Identity and Japan', p. 191.
22. Ibid., p. 192.

JAPANESE CINEMA AND EUROPE
A constellation of gazes: Europe and the Japanese film industry

Yoshiharu Tezuka

More than any other Asian cinema, Japan has consistently occupied a discursive position of otherness. Japanese cinema has been the object of constant and consistent fascination in Europe and particularly in the United States. […] If Japanese culture and cultural products are part of many people's everyday life, why does Japan still remain distant and unknowable in this era of mass media saturation and local and global formation?[1]

The answer to Gary Needham's question, if one agrees with its premise, can be at least partially found in the ways in which Japanese film industry practitioners, including film-makers, distributors, festival organisers and critics, have historically reacted to the Eurocentric gaze and international reception of Japanese films. As many writers have pointed out, the representation and construction of the Japanese self in terms of an essential otherness against the 'West' has been a core strategy of Japanese cultural and national identity in modern times.[2] Koichi Iwabuchi, someone who has closely studied the spread of Japanese popular culture overseas, has argued, for example, that:

> Japan is represented and represents itself as culturally exclusive, homogeneous and uniquely particularistic through the operation of strategic binary opposition between two imaginary cultural entities, 'Japan' and 'the West'. This is not to say that 'Asia' has no cultural significance in the construction of Japanese national identity. Rather, complicity between Western Orientalism and Japan's self-Orientalism effectively works only when the Japanese cultural power in Asia is subsumed under Japan's cultural subordination to the West, i.e., when Japan's peculiar position as the only modern, non-Western imperial/colonial power tends to be translated with a great skew towards Japan's relation with the West.[3]

Japan's complicity with Western Orientalism and its self-Orientalising representations (as seen, for example, in its films) have both conspired to perpetuate a notion of cultural and historic uniqueness in terms of its national identity. Constructions of national identity (how we come to think of ourselves as a nation) and constructions of national cinema (how we represent ourselves as a nation on film) are profoundly intertwined here. In this chapter, I will tackle just one link in the complex relationship between national identity and its representations by examining how Japanese film industry practitioners re-established and prolonged this notion of Japanese exceptionalism in their films within the geopolitical conditions of the postwar period.

Kurosawa Akira's *Rashomon/Rashōmon* initiated the internationalisation of Japanese cinema in the 1950s by unexpectedly winning the Golden Lion, the highest prize awarded to a film at the Venice Film Festival of 1951. Japanese film practitioners such as the producer Nagata Masaichi (1906–85) quickly became conscious of the cultural values conferred on films at European film festivals and realised that grasping the commercial opportunity of being picked up for US distribution also entailed adopting those values. Their interaction with the European gaze consequently shaped Japanese film from the beginning of its postwar cinematic history.[4]

Japanese cinema soon garnered an international reputation for excellence, but this reputation co-emerged with a Cold War politics that divided the world into Eastern and Western camps. Japan's cultural differences were thus subsumed by the free and democratic capitalist West into a privileged position of 'otherness' that placed Japan above other Asian nations. Popular praise and appreciation for Japanese cinema often came because of its cultural otherness. In the 1970s and 1980s, numerous film scholars drew attention to the formalistic otherness of Japanese cinema.[5] Western critics saw Japanese cinema as a prime alternative to the dominant modes of representation derived from Hollywood. Various prominent film critics and scholars from both sides of the Atlantic discussed and studied the formalist qualities of Japanese films and cinematic practices of directors such as Ozu Yasujirō (1903–63).[6] These perspectives treated Japanese cinema as a sort of modern tribal art comparable to the European 'avant-garde'.[7] The favourable reception of Japanese cinema in Europe and North America thus encouraged a tendency towards self-Orientalism amongst Japanese film people and the Japanese public alike.[8]

This chapter provides a number of case studies of prominent Japanese film industry practitioners who, consciously and unconsciously, manipulated filmic representations of Japan following their interactions with European cinéphiles so as to reach audiences outside Japan in both the US and Asia. Here, I will do my best to distinguish between Europe and the 'West'. Progenitors of postwar Japanese national identity tended to amalgamate the 'West' in opposition to Japan. Most Japanese scholars have followed suit in not differentiating Europe from the US. Treating Europe and the US as a single cultural block fails to reflect the complexity of the interaction between Japan, Europe and the US, and significantly underplays European influence over the development of a certain kind of Japanese film-making.

I will firstly discuss the self-Orientalising strategies of two individuals in the immediate postwar period of the 1950s through to the 1960s: Nagata Masaichi, president of Daiei Film, and Kawakita Nagamasa (1903–81), Japan's leading film importer. I will then move on to the latter part of the twentieth century, a period during which a new constellation of global power was emerging under the American hegemony, by presenting a case study of the career of Horikoshi Kenzō (1945–), the founder of Eurospace, a boutique cinema in Tokyo. Horikoshi is an example of a new generation of independent film distributors who became film producers after the collapse of Japan's large studio production system. Here, I highlight the different ways in which the old and new generation of Japanese film industry practitioners have engaged and interacted with the European gaze.

Since the early twenty-first century, various new waves of Japanese films have been taken up by younger generations of international audiences. These cinéphile and cult film audiences have tended to be more familiar with Kurosawa Kiyoshi (1955–) than Kurosawa Akira (1910–98). Many of the discourses that promote new Japanese films to international audiences remain, however, strongly tinged with Orientalism.[9] The most obvious example of this would the way the British distributor Tartan Films promoted their 'Tartan Asia Extreme' series through the introduction of directors such as Miike Takashi whose films included *Audition/Ōdishon* (1999) and *Ichi the Killer/Koroshiya* (2001). Miike's own ironic representation of the feminised Orient at the 2015 Cannes Film Festival is also significant. Edward Said famously pointed out that the Orient has always been characterised as feminine, weak or infantile within the Western imaginary. Historic representations depicting such qualities have also been used to justify the admiration, protection, domination and colonisation of the Orient by the masculine West. At the end of this chapter, I will therefore interrogate the apparent newness of these films and the ways in which their makers actually complicated the fixed gaze of Orientalism.

NAGATA'S STRATEGIC SELF-ORIENTALISM

Not a single person from Japan attended the Venice Film Festival the year *Rashomon* was awarded the Golden Lion and nobody in the Japanese film industry had the slightest idea of the cultural and commercial ramifications of its success. In fact, it was not a

Japanese person who actually made the submission but a European Japanophile named Giuliana Stramigioli (1914–88). Stramigioli studied Japanese art and religion at Kyoto University from 1934 to 1938, worked at the information bureau of the Italian Embassy in Japan during the war and was then sent to an internment camp in Hakone after the Italian surrender. After the end of war, she established the Tokyo office of Italifilm to import Italian films to Japan.[10] While working in this capacity, she was asked by the Motion Picture Producers Association of Japan to help decide on a film to send to the Venice Film Festival. After viewing a number of possible Japanese films, she chose *Rashomon*.[11]

Daiei Film, the studio that produced *Rashomon*, was not initially keen to submit the film. It only agreed to provide a print and promotional materials, but refused to pay any of the costs of submission and subtitling. In the end, Stramigioli herself translated the script, paid for the subtitling and covered the shipping costs. Without Stramigioli's enthusiastic backing, *Rashomon* would therefore not have made it to the festival and the postwar history of Japanese cinema might have taken a different course.

Nagata Masaichi did not, however, hesitate to take credit for the international success of the film and used this to further his ambitions. Nagata had become the first Japanese film industry practitioner to travel to the US after the war and, according to his autobiography, the trip was a life-changing experience. He became resolved to devote the rest of his life to supporting 'US-Japan friendship'.[12] The trip to Hollywood made him aware of the scale of the film business in the US and consequently the potential size of the international market for Japanese film. An influential businessman, he was outspoken in his belief that an opportunity to export Japanese films had arisen and that Daiei needed to push ahead with more films similar to *Rashomon*.

Nagata pressed the Japanese government to treat the film industry seriously. The postwar government classified industries according to their contributions to the national economy and rationed resources and bureaucratic support accordingly. Since entertainment was regarded as a luxury, rather than a necessity, the film industry had been placed in the third rank of industries least important to the life of the nation. Determined to rebuild the nation after the war, the Japanese government also prioritised earning foreign currency through the development of an export-oriented economy. Nagata therefore advocated support for the film industry by claiming that film was 'an export product par excellence, as ninety-nine per cent of the income is profit. The only cost is film stock and the rest is copyrights'.[13] His argument therefore engaged with the national politics of the time and he became the main proponent of the internationalisation of Japanese cinema. Exporting Japanese films became part of the national project of rebuilding Japan's image abroad along with its national economy, self-confidence and self-identity.

Following *Rashomon*, a slew of Japanese films won awards in European film festivals: *The Tale of Genji/Genji monogatari* (Yoshimura Kōzaburō, 1951) won Best Photography Prize at Cannes in 1952; *The Life of Oharu/Saikaku ichidai onna* (Mizoguchi Kenji, 1952) won the International Director's Award at Venice in 1952; *Ugetsu/Ugetsu monogatari* (Mizoguchi, 1953) won the Silver Lion at Venice in 1953; *Sansho the Bailiff/Sanshō dayū* (Mizoguchi, 1954) and *The Seven Samurai/Shichinin no samurai* (Kurosawa Akira, 1954) shared the Silver Lion at Venice in 1954.

Nagata often publicly commented that 'it would be a mistake to produce films especially for export. *Rashomon* was not made for export. We just have to make films which reflect a genuine Japanese spirit and culture.'[14] In theory, everyone in the film industry seemed to agree with Nagata on this point. In practice, however, Japanese film-makers found it impossible to make films that reflected 'a genuine Japanese spirit and culture' once they had also become aware of the European gaze.

Nagata's *Gate of Hell/Jigoku Mon* (Kinugasa Teinosuke, 1953) won the Grand Prix at Cannes in 1954 and Best Foreign Film and Best Costume Design at the US Academy Awards the following year (Fig. 39.1). Nagata's espousal of making films that were genuinely Japanese coupled with his mostly unconscious self-Orientalising position was mirrored in a two-tier strategy for producing exportable films. Firstly, he retained culturally exotic (i.e. Japanese)

Fig. 39.1 *Gate of Hell/Jigoku Mon* (Kinugasa Teinosuke, 1953, Daiei).

content and demanded simple stories in films made for export. Nagata often said that 'the Japanese feeling of structure is bizarre and too complex for foreigners. So, for foreign audiences, we have to keep the story simple and deal with complexity through the characters'.[15] In taking on the position of a 'colonized subject', Nagata chose to represent Japan in ways that he expected would engage the 'colonizer' (i.e. ex-occupiers) on its own terms.[16]

Secondly, he invested huge sums in new technology in order to modernise the *form* of Japanese cinema. During his first visit to the US in 1949, Nagata saw the latest American film-making technologies used in Hollywood and realised there was a wide technological gap with Japan. He also learned that multilayer colour negative film technology was being developed there. Prior to filming *Gate of Hell*, Nagata sent a team of film-makers to Warner Bros. for five weeks to study colour cinematography.[17] For Nagata, internationalisation and technological innovation were interdependent. Using the latest American technology was considered essential if Japanese films were to successfully penetrate foreign – Euro-American art-house and Asian – markets. In turn, the international reputation derived by competing at European film festivals and the profit acquired by having Japanese films running in foreign cinemas was essential for domestic innovation.[18]

Gate of Hell was the fruit of Nagata's long-term investment in technology along with a deliberate effort to produce 'exotic' films that would appeal to international audiences.[19] By using Hollywood film technology as a medium for representing Euro-American notions of Japanese otherness, Nagata aestheticised and modernised the colourful Japanese Other. This self-Orientalising strategy of technological aestheticisation of Japanese *content* not only made it easier for Euro-American audiences to enjoy Japanese otherness, it placed the Japanese Other above all the other non-Western Others in the world, including Asian countries such as China, South Korea and India. Japan and the US had accepted a European scale of 'civilisation' that ranked European cultures on top, the United States second, and Asian and African cultures in descending order. Despite the striking cultural differences depicted in Japan's films, many American Japanologists saw Japan's ability to adopt and adapt Western technology as proof that Japan could assimilate to the modern civilised 'West'.[20] Meanwhile, praise from European film festivals and critics for Japan's national cinema was seen by many Japanese as endorsing Japan's claim to be on the same level as the US and above its Asian neighbours.

As an individual, Nagata had a complex reaction to European cultural authority. While absolutely dedicated to, and even worshipful of, everything American, his attitude towards Europe was mixed and sometimes antagonistic. As a strongly Americanised subject, maybe he inherited a form of inferiority complex towards European culture. For example, in April 1955, after just having won a second Academy Award for *Gate of Hell*, Nagata displayed a degree of Europhobia to a Japanese journalist by saying such things as: 'I dislike Europe absolutely'; 'I do not like France in particular'; and 'France does not have an industry to speak of. They live on tourism, on the monies foreign tourists throw at them.'[21] This widely circulated and controversial interview eventually reached France, after which Parisian cinemas stopped screening *Gate of Hell*.

The timing of Nagata's diatribe was unfortunate as the scandal erupted just before the opening of the Cannes Film Festival at which Nagata had two films scheduled to be shown: one by Mizoguchi submitted for competition and another outside the competition. The festival organisers announced they would not accept any entries from Japan for the following year, but the film importer Kawakita Nagamasa, who was there to attend the festival, negotiated a settlement on behalf of Nagata and the Japanese film industry. In the end, the festival lifted the ban on Japanese films on condition that Nagata make a substantial donation to a French public fund.[22] Despite Kawakita's intervention, Daiei, which had regularly produced prizewinners up to that point, did not win a single award from European festivals after the Nagata scandal.

Nagata later set aside his Europhobia in an attempt to win more European film festival prizes. He coproduced Alain Resnais's *Hiroshima mon amour* (1959) with the French New Wave producer Anatole Dauman, who then went on to produce Ōshima Nagisa's films *In the Realm of the Senses/Ai no corrida* (1976) and *Empire of Passion/Ai no bōrei* (1978) and Terayama Shūji's film *Fruits of Passion/Shanghai Ijin shōkan: China Doll* (1981). Nagata even attempted to develop a script with Alain Robbe-Grillet, who had written the screenplay for Resnais's *Last Year at Marienbad* (1961). The commissioned script was to be directed by the Japanese director Ichikawa Kon. According to another Daiei producer who was working for Nagata, however, the project went unrealised because Robbe-Grillet's script turned out to be 'beyond the comprehension' of the Japanese team.[23]

KAWAKITA'S SELF-ORIENTALISM: AUTHENTIC JAPAN FOR THE EUROPEAN AUDIENCE

Like Nagata, Kawakita Nagamasa propelled the internationalisation of Japanese cinema. Kawakita was not much like Nagata in other respects, however. Whereas Nagata came from a humble family background, Kawakita's own father was a high-ranking military officer who was stationed in China during the Japanese Occupation. Nagata left school at 17 years of age to work as a runner in the film industry; Kawakita attended high school in Tokyo, then continued his education at universities in China and Germany. Also unlike Nagata, Kawakita was a self-proclaimed cosmopolitan individual on good terms with various European cinéphiles.

Upon returning to Japan from Germany in 1928, Kawakita established the Toa Trading Co. to import films from Europe. The company became the Japanese agent of UFA GmbH. Kawakita also enthusiastically endorsed exporting Japanese films to Europe. He attempted to export Japanese films to Germany in 1929, but was disappointed by their reception amongst German audiences who found Japanese customs strange and laughed at the screen.[24] Kawakita felt European audiences did not have enough knowledge about Japan and its culture to appreciate Japanese cinema. He therefore believed there was a need for greater cross-cultural understanding and that international coproduction of films was the best means of achieving that end.²⁵ His idea was to invite an established European film director and have him shoot a film in Japan with meaningful Japanese cultural elements for European audience.²⁶ He thus went on to coproduce, with Nazi Germany, *The Daughter of the Samurai/Die Tochter des Samurai/Atarashiki Tsuchi* (Arnold Fanck and Itami Mansaku, 1937).

During the war, Kawakita was in charge of the China Film Company in Shanghai. His memorial website makes the claim that he 'resisted the pressures from the Japanese military regime and allowed Chinese filmmakers the freedom to make films'.²⁷ After the war, Kawakita was temporarily expelled from the film industry as a war criminal. After he was reinstated in 1950, he took up an executive position at Tōhō. He and his wife Kashiko became well known on the European film festival circuit, not only because of his status working at one of Japan's biggest importers of European films but in their own right as cultural ambassadors for Japanese cinema.

Kawakita believed that his lifelong dedication to promoting Japanese culture through cinema began when he was a student in Germany.²⁸ At that time, Kawakita attended a production of Puccini's opera *Madam Butterfly*, at the National Opera House in Hamburg. This proved to be a formative moment. *Madam Butterfly* is probably the best-known example of an Orientalist representation of Japan. Kawakita was shocked, shamed and infuriated by how he saw Japanese culture represented in *Madam Butterfly*. He later wrote that 'what was allegedly presented as a Japanese woman on the stage, her costume and make-up, was a hodgepodge of Chinese, Indian and Mongolian, that was something entirely absurd'.²⁹ He considered this a serious national humiliation and from that moment on cherished the dream of producing *Madam Butterfly* with a 'genuine Japanese actress and showing real Japanese costumes and a real Japanese woman' (Fig. 39.2).³⁰

Fig. 39.2 *Madam Butterfly* (Camine Gallone, 1954, Produzione Gallone Rizzoli Film). Kawakita's long-cherished desire was to produce *Madam Butterfly* with a genuine Japanese actress and to show 'real Japanese costumes and a real Japanese woman'.

It is interesting here to consider why Kawakita was so infuriated by the mistaken signifiers – actress, make-up, costume – of Japanese culture rather than the story of *Madam Butterfly* itself. The subjugation of a Japanese woman by a Western man still happens in the opera regardless of any issue concerning the verisimilitude of the signifiers. Kawakita seems to have never questioned this Orientalist relationship and instead accepted the artistic value of *Madam Butterfly* (including its storyline) simply on the basis that it was a 'world famous opera'.[31] He probably did not comment on the violation of the Japanese woman in the story because the subjugation of a woman by a man was considered as natural in his own culture as in European cultures at the time. He also failed to register that the plot of *Madam Butterfly* metaphorically represented the subjugation of the (feminine) Orient by the (masculine) West. Interestingly, while the depiction of that relationship shook Kawakita emotionally, he interpreted his reaction as primarily being one of upset that 'real' Japanese culture was not being presented and was thus being misunderstood in Europe.

In 1954, Kawakita's dream was realised in the Tōhō release of *Madam Butterfly*. The film was coproduced by the Italian producer and director Carmine Gallone and the Japanese producer Mori Iwao. Mori supervised the shooting script and director's plans to make sure all the historic, cultural and artistic details about Japan were as authentic as possible. Filming actually took place at the Cinecitta Studios in Rome, however. Tōhō shipped all the costumes, wigs and props along with thirty Japanese crew and cast members, including the main actress and sixteen dancers, to Italy.[32] Mori and Kawakita closely supervised the entire process of film-making so that no embarrassing errors in Japanese customs would infiltrate the film and that an authentically Japanese version of *Madam Butterfly* would result. According to Mori, the Japanese and Italian people involved in making the film frequently differed in their opinions concerning how the sets, costumes, make-up and performances should be rendered. In each instance of conflict, Gallone adopted the Japanese preference. At first, Mori thought the Italians just wanted to keep their Japanese partners happy. He was later surprised to find that Gallone truly believed Italian audiences were ready for and desired to see 'authentic' Japanese culture on film.

Neither Kawakita nor Mori was fully aware of the complexity of their complicity in perpetuating an Orientalist gaze in terms of their own self-Orientalism. They weren't deliberately intending to naturalise the feminine Orient or its subjugation to the masculine West by providing 'real things' for the lead female character, Madame Butterfly. They probably believed that if 'real' Japanese culture was being properly presented, 'real' Japaneseness would thus command respect and the subjugation of Japan by the West would cease. What Kawakita and Mori failed to realise was that by presenting Japan as a 'real object' for the Orientalist gaze, they continued to endorse the credibility of the gaze rather than subvert it. In this sense, they unwittingly helped essentialise Japanese otherness by providing a 'real' Japanese woman to embody Japanese culture.

In sum, the significance of the internationalisation of Japanese cinema in the 1950s cannot be measured simply in economic terms. From an economic viewpoint, there was only a short-term spike in the number of Japanese films exported to, or coproduced with, Europe. This was the decade when Japanese film-makers and practitioners first reacted positively to the European gaze, but they had yet to escape that gaze completely.

GLOBALISATION AND THE NEW GENERATION

Cinema attendance in Japan peaked around 1960. The film industry then went into a period of long decline. Nagata's Daiei Film went bankrupt in 1971. Other major studios drastically reduced the number of film productions and survived by renting their studios and distributing films made by smaller independent production companies. The major studios stopped recruiting new personnel altogether. By 1980, the studio production system had ceased to function. The Japanese film industry then reorganised itself in response to an economy that demanded greater flexibility. Throughout the 1980s and 1990s, this new economy encouraged small independent production companies to hire freelancers on a film-by-film basis.

Even established film-makers with international reputations such as Kurosawa Akira and Ōshima Nagisa found it impossible to finance their films in Japan under these circumstances. They began looking abroad, to Europe in particular, to obtain funding. The film producer and distributor Hara Masato, of Japan Herald Films, initiated coproduction of Japanese films with such people as the British producer Jeremy Thomas – *Merry Christmas Mr. Lawrence/Senjō no Merry Christmas* (Ōshima Nagisa, 1983) – and the French producer Serge Silberman – *Ran* (Kurosawa Akira, 1985).[33]

In the late 1980s, at which point Japanese economic power was at its peak, the US intensified pressure on the Japanese government to reduce its trade surplus. Japanese hardware companies such as Sony and Panasonic began buying into global software businesses in Hollywood: Sony purchased Columbia Pictures in 1989 and Panasonic purchased MCR-Universal in 1990. These acquisitions and other mergers in the 1990s turned Hollywood into a global institution within which Japanese capital played a substantial part.[34] At the same time, the Japanese film industry increased investment in foreign films. Hara's junior colleagues Yoshizaki Michiyo and Iseki Satoru, for example, formed Nippon Development and Finance (NDF) in 1991. NDF helped finance such foreign films as *Naked Lunch* (David Cronenberg 1991), *The Crying Game* (Neil Jordan, 1992), *Howards End* (James Ivory, 1992), *Smoke* (Wayne Wang, 1995) and *Kama Sutra* (Mira Nair, 1996).

What did the globalisation of film finance mean to Japanese film industry practitioners and how did this phenomenon compare to the internationalisation of Japanese cinema in the 1950s? As discussed above, the internationalisation of Japanese cinema was a production-based national project that purported to promote Japanese culture through the export of Japanese films. Japanese film-makers and practitioners sought recognition of Japan's essential cultural 'uniqueness' within a Euro-centred universalising scheme that placed Japan on the same level as the US and above other Asian countries.

By contrast, economic globalisation, or what was in the late twentieth century called *kokusaika* ('internationalisation') in Japan, was about ending Japanese cultural exceptionalism.[35] Economic globalisation in Japan entailed:

> The switch from export-led to domestic demand-led economic growth, the gradual diminution of Japan's 'uniqueness', and the sharing of the burdens of maintaining free trade and a growing world economy together with the United States and the European Community.[36]

Kokusaika signalled the beginning of an attempt to integrate Japan's particularity with a new constellation of socio-economic power emerging with the global spread of neoliberalism. In the attempt to ease trade conflict with the US, *kokusaika* became a consumption-based project that purported to further open the Japanese market, as well as the hearts and minds of Japanese people, to foreign goods and symbols.

There is a revealing anecdote about a cultural side effect of the Japan–US trade conflict. As part of the media campaign to promote *kokusaika*, the Japanese prime minister Nakasone made an appeal to the public in which he stated that, as a member of the international community, 'every single Japanese person should spend at least 100 US dollars on foreign products in order to reduce Japan's trade surplus'.[37] A television programme covered the prime minister's visit to an imported products fair held in a high-class department store. There, he spent approximately 280 US dollars of his own money on imported goods. When the contents of his shopping bag were revealed, however, it turned out that he had only purchased European products: an Italian tie, French brands of clothing and so on. He had not bought any American items. His purchases made sense given that discerning Japanese consumers during the period of Japan's 'bubble economy' considered that mass-produced American cultural products signified the sameness of a democratised lower-middle-class culture that mainstream Japanese culture had appropriated long ago. 'European designer products […] enjoy[ed] higher consumer esteem' because they signified something new and different.[38]

This trend applied to film imports as much as to any other consumer products. In the 1980s, the number of foreign films imported to Japan, which had remained constant at around 200–250 films per year throughout the postwar era, suddenly jumped to around 500. The founding of the Tokyo International Film Festival in 1985 further supported an interest in imported films. The percentage of box-office proceeds for foreign films in the 1960s was 20–30 per cent and in the 1970s around 50 per cent; the figure then went up to nearly 70 per cent in the 1990s.[39] This increase in the number of imported films in the 1980s and 1990s created an environment where an amazing variety of European films, world cinema and small independent films from the US became available to Japanese cinéphiles for the first time.

The external pressure to change instigated by the government's *kokusaika* policy coincided with an internal drive for renewal and diversification within the Japanese film industry itself. The combination of the end of the Japanese studio tradition and the politico-economic milieu of *kokusaika* opened the way for a new generation of film directors, producers and distributors.[40] Economic globalisation provided opportunities for the new generation to escape the homogeneous national imaginary of the old film industry and carve out niche spaces for cultural production, distribution and exhibition. Small independent cinemas, called 'mini-theatres', began to proliferate in major cities to cater to the increasingly diverse tastes of Japanese audiences.

This new type of cinema experience was distinctive in two ways. Firstly, the mini-theatres did not participate in the Japanese block-booking system thus making individual programming a possibility. Secondly, many of the mini-theatres were equipped with comfortable chairs and tastefully furnished, luxurious lobbies in order to attract a younger female audience.[41] Young, educated, female office workers ironically had more disposable income and leisure time than their male counterparts because of the structural exclusion by Japanese companies of women from any jobs with long-term career prospects.

Eurospace was one of the first two mini-theatres to open in Japan.[42] The founder of Eurospace, Horikoshi Kenzō, had studied German literature at Johannes Gutenberg University Mainz. Upon returning home from Germany, he set up the Japan–Euro Association in 1972, from which he ran a language school and travel agency. He began organising film screenings there and then founded a cinema club in the same location, which he named Eurospace. Horikoshi initially purchased 16mm prints of *Kings of The Road* (Wim Wenders, 1976), *Wrong Move* (Wim Wenders, 1975), *The Enigma of Kasper Hauser* (Werner Herzog, 1974) and *Fox and his Friends* (Rainer W. Fassbinder, 1975), but did not acquire commercial rights to show the films in a conventional cinema. It was only after organising the week-long New German Cinema Festival in 1977, which turned out to be a popular success, that he developed Eurospace into a successful commercial enterprise.

Horikoshi opened a small (85-seat) multi-event hall, also called Eurospace, in Shibuya in central Tokyo in 1982. The space was turned into a specialist cinema in 1985 with the screening of David Cronenberg's *Videodrome* (1983). A second screen was opened in the same building in 1994, due to popular demand. Through Eurospace, Horikoshi went on to distribute not only European art films but also Asian, Japanese and North American independent titles. One legendary success for the mini-theatre was the screening of the controversial Japanese documentary *The Emperor's Naked Army Marches On/Yuki yukite shingun* (Hara Kazuo, 1987). The film ran for twenty-six weeks, sold 53,000 tickets and created a scandal since it touched upon Japan's greatest taboo topic: the emperor's responsibility for the war.

Under the climate of *kokusaika* Horikoshi also became involved in the financing and production of international films. He supported many new and talented film-makers such as Leos Carax, Aki Kaurismaki, Wayne Wang and Abbas Kiarostami. As a producer, he worked with foreign as well as young Japanese directors. To date, Horikoshi has been involved in financing the production of twenty-five films. Looking back on his career as a film practitioner, the 69-year-old stated that the most memorable film he produced was *The Written Face* (1995), directed by Daniel Schmid.[43] This Swiss-born film-maker was associated with the New German Cinema. Although Schmid was little-known internationally at the time, Horikoshi believes he played a crucial role in the formation of Japan's late twentieth-century film culture:

> Japanese film audiences now take the diverse range of films available in Japanese cinemas for granted. But in fact, apart from France [where public subsidies are substantial], there is not a single country in the world like Japan, where over 40 independent cinemas – mini theatres – exist. This is actually a wonder of the world. […] Today, between 600–700 independent Japanese films are released annually […]. This would not be possible without the existence of mini-theatres. […] And it was Daniel Schmid and his films that ignited the mini-theatre boom at the beginning.[44]

In Europe, Schmid was an underrated film-maker, dismissed as a mere Rainer Fassbinder epigone because of his early relationship with the legendary director. According to Horikoshi, it was the Japanese film critic Hasumi Shigehiko who recognised Daniel Schmid as an artist in his own right internationally and helped build his fan base in Japan.[45] Schmid's popularity in Japan and ensuing critical acclaim then went on to change the perception of critics and film industry practitioners in Europe. As Horikoshi points out, this has been one of the very rare occasions when 'a standard of aesthetic judgment by a Japanese film critic has been accepted' and was therefore a moment marking Japan's cultural, as well as economic, presence in the international film world.[46]

The film journalist Ōtaka Hiroo notes that there were a number of discernible common characteristics amongst the films that led to their success in the mini-theatre.[47] He has described these characteristics with two key words – edginess or subversiveness (*abunasa*) and fashionableness (*fashion-sei*) – and points out the consistent success of gay-themed films in the mini-theatre.[48] As Horikoshi has also claimed, it is plausible to argue that the camp, kitsch, operatic aesthetic of Schmid's films contributed to shaping the tastes of Japanese mini-theatre audiences and 'ignited' the explosion of the mini-theatre boom.

The Written Face is a documentary film on the kabuki actor Bandō Tamasaburō (1950–) and the art

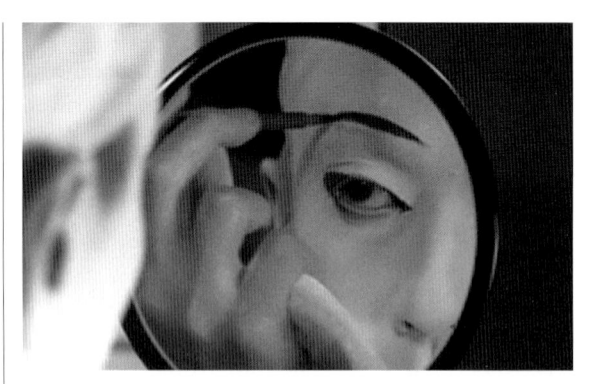

Fig. 39.3 *The Written Face* (Daniel Schmid, 1995, T&C Film and Euro Space). The kabuki actor Bandō Tamasaburō and the art of men performing as women.

of men performing as women (Fig. 39.3). The film also features the avant-garde *butoh* dancer Ōno Kazuo (1915–2010) as well as Sugimura Haruko (1909–97), an actress famous for her roles in numerous Ozu Yasujirō films. Tamasaburō is said to be the most accomplished and beautiful *oyama* or *onnagata* (female impersonator) in recent kabuki history. At the time of filming, Tamasaburō was in his mid-forties and at his peak physically and artistically. In contrast to the previous generation of Japanese film practitioners, who believed their mission was to present 'real' Japanese women as the embodiments of authentic Japanese culture, Horikoshi seems to have been unconcerned about the authenticity of Japanese cultural artefacts presented in the films he produced. Rather, he seems happy to watch a European director dissect the object of his own gaze: the Orient, Japan and portrayals of Japanese femininity and place it in front of mini-theatre audiences. In this film, 'the European gaze' itself emerges as an object of gaze for the Japanese audience.

The Written Face illustrates an ideological structure by which the *oyama* is a sign that constructs a patriarchal perspective and power. The title of the film comes from a chapter in the book *Empire of Signs* (1982), written by the French semiotician and critic, Roland Barthes. In this book, Barthes uses Japanese cultural material as a vehicle for his discussion of 'writing' and pictorial 'signs'. In the chapter 'Written Face', Barthes talks about the Japanese theatrical tradition, noting that 'the theatrical face is not painted (made up), it is written

[…] *to paint* is never anything but *to inscribe*'. He then probes the way in which the *oyama* functions as a 'pure signifier'. Unlike 'Western drag shows', for Barthes the *oyama*:

> Is not a boy made up as a woman, by a thousand nuances, realistic touches, costly simulations, but a pure *signifier* whose *underneath* (the truth) is […] simply *absent*; the actor, in his face, does not play the woman, or copy her, but only *signifies* her; if, as Mallarme says, writing consists of 'gesture of the idea', transvestism here is the gesture of femininity, not its plagiarism.[49]

Barthes observes that the Oyama is a '*pure signifier* whose *underneath* (truth)' is '*simply absent*'. However, Schmid's documentary film, *The Written Face*, takes the issue of what lies within the *underneath* (truth) much further than Barthes's linguistic structuralism by filling in the '*absence*' with a voice from within. It touches on the question of power that constitutes 'the truth' about femininity. In the film, Tamasaburō (during an interview by Schmid) says:

> Because I had played female roles since I was very small, I formerly thought I could act like a woman naturally. But then I recognized that I have never seen the world through the eyes of a woman. Never from her viewpoint. I understand that my vision is that of a man. […] I act a woman with the eyes and the feeling of a man […] like a man painting the portrait of a woman. I try to portray an ideal image of woman, in the same way as a male writer.[50]

Tamasaburō testifies that as an *oyama*, he inscribes the same 'gesture of femininity' perceived as an ideal by the male gaze. These gestures were often transferred over to biologically female actors in modern Japanese theatres. The veteran actress Sugimura Haruko reiterates this point in another interview within the film. Both Bandō Tamasaburō and Sugimura Haruko note that the *underneath of the pure signifier* is *not* 'simply *absent*'. The underneath is a space – the subject position – where the male gaze produces an ideal of femininity with which biological women can identify.

Initiated by Horikoshi and the Japanese producer and distributor Matsumoto Masamichi from Athénée Français Cultural Center, this 1995 Japan–Switzerland coproduction on one level indicated the typical way that European intellectuals mystified – Orientalised – Japan's cultural otherness. Yet, on another level, it also deployed a gay film-maker, Daniel Schmid, in order to analyse and deconstruct the Western myth of Japan's absolute cultural otherness. It is almost a cliché to say that the *oyama* is more feminine than a real woman. Schmid interrogated the seeming 'absence' of the masculine/feminine binary in the Japanese traditional theatrical arts and, in the process, learnt, however, that the matter is not as simple as all that. Tamasaburō, the *oyama*, turned out to be very self-aware and reflexive concerning the construction of her own gestures and explained the way in which the patriarchal male gaze operates to naturalise the masculine/feminine ideology underneath in a way that is more or less compatible with Western semiotic theory.

IRONIC SELF-ORIENTALISM IN THE EARLY TWENTY-FIRST CENTURY

The list of foreign film-makers supported by revenue from Japan's mini-theatres is long; many of them became internationally established names. Despite the success of the mini-theatres, large cinema complexes came to dominate the Japanese market by the early twenty-first century. Mini-theatres now had to struggle to remain viable in the new market. Consequently, in 2006, Horikoshi moved Europace to its present site in Shibuya as part of a new art complex called Kino House. The five-story building houses a café, three screens (Eurospace screens 1 and 2 and Cinemavera Shibuya, which specialises in showing classic and second-run films) and EuroLive, a multi-use theatrical space for talk shows, etc. An office for the Community Cinema Center, an initiative to support the cinema club movement set up by Horikoshi in 2001, is also located there. The Film School of Tokyo, a night school for film-making set up by Horikoshi in 1997, was moved into the basement of Kino House in 2011.[51]

Horikoshi also drove the establishment of a national institution for the training of a new generation of film-makers. He was the force behind the founding of the Graduate School of Film and New Media at the Tokyo University of the Arts in 2005, where he held a professorship until he retired in 2013.[52] The school is the first national institution to train film-makers and media artists. There, he organised and ran two programmes focused on international film coproduction: one with the French film school FEMIS (Fondation Européenne pour les Métiers de l'Image et du Son) and the other with the Korean film school KAFA (Korean Academy of Film Arts). The FEMIS programme requires Japanese students to travel to Paris to make contacts in the French film industry and learn about coproducing films with French producers and Europeans from other countries as well as how to circulate films through European film festivals. In turn, French students are invited to study in Japan, where they are encouraged to develop screenplays with Japanese student film producers.

The Japanese film industry press often asserts that links to Hollywood and access to mainland and diasporic Chinese markets are the two most important avenues in the promotion of globally successful commercial films. After years of ground-level experience as an independent film producer, Horikoshi disagrees. He suggests that this approach is neither realistic nor interesting for Japanese film-makers today. Instead, he sees two ways that Japanese film-makers can make their mark internationally. The first is the conventional route into Europe either through the screening of Japanese films at film festivals or the circulation of films within various cinéphile/cult DVD distribution networks. Almost all of the internationally minded Japanese film-makers of the past have taken this route. When European art-house distribution and DVD circulation proved successful, their films were regularly picked up for North American distribution. Some were remade by Hollywood.[53]

The second approach is to take a more active role in Asian regional cinema. Ethnic Chinese film-makers already work with other Asian nationalities beyond China's national borders under the aegis of 'Pan Asian Cinema'. The popularity of Japanese media content in the urban areas of East and South East Asia during the 1990s has been well documented.[54] The recent international success of the Korean film and television industry has persuaded the Japanese government to review its cultural policies and provide more support for its own media industry and incentives for Japanese and Korean film industry practitioners to build closer creative and business relationships. A closer Japanese–Korean partnership will provide another drive towards the regionalisation of the Asian media industry. Horikoshi's KAFA programme is part of that drive. Korean and Japanese KAFA students actually coproduce short films. They develop ideas and scripts together and shoot the scripts in either country using crew and cast members from both countries. According to Horikoshi, both of the joint programmes with French and Korean film schools are intended to equip students with two realistic options, so that the next generation of Japanese film-makers has greater cinematic opportunities to explore than did previous generations.[55]

It could be argued that taking the European route is likely to sustain the Orientalism of the Euro-American gaze in Japanese films. But perhaps the savvy new generation of independent Japanese film-makers are at least conscious of, and reflexive about, the self-Orientalism of their forebears. For example, director Miike Takashi, who is known as a genre extremist, deliberately played with Orientalist themes in a video message sent to the Cannes Film Festival to accompany his world premiere of the vampire gangster comedy, *Yakuza Apocalypse/Gokudō daisensō* (2015). Miike appeared on screen in full geisha costume, twirling a paper umbrella, to apologise for his absence from the festival. He then declared he was retiring from directing violent films to work at a teahouse in the shadow of Mt Fuji. One of the film reviewers at Cannes wrote that:

> The most amusing part of this juvenile action-horror comedy is not actually part of the film at all. […] Miike appeared via video message in superannuated geisha drag, apologizing for his absence and informing us he was preparing to have breast implants. OK, so transgender gags are tired and insensitive, but it's comical to hear Japanese filmdom's most outré extremist declare he's abandoning violence to make movies about love and friendship.[56]

By attaching this video to his feature film, Miike layered the extreme poles of Japanese stereotypes – geisha and yakuza – over one another as if to say that the cultural otherness he exploits is but a mere simulacrum or bad copy of classic self-Orientalist imagery. His performance in the video message, probably meant as a joke, laughs at both Europe's Orientalist gaze and Japan's self-Orientalism. It also ironically exposes the unsavoury masculinity suppressed under the written face as well as the residue of the unrepresentable desire beneath Japan's castrated masculinity, so long perpetuated in international Japanese cinema.

CONCLUSION

As we have seen in the cases of Nagata and Kawakita, European film people were seen as cultural authorities during the early postwar period. Some Japanese film-makers and practitioners loved to hate them for it. For Nagata, Europe was a pompous gatekeeper for the international film market; he strategically sought European awards for his films while simultaneously reviling the European perspective. For Kawakita, Europe provided a universal aesthetic judgment; he felt a strong urge to seek European recognition and understanding of Japanese culture. Both film-makers returned Europe's Orientalist gaze by representing Japan's cultural otherness as a positive difference. In doing so, they were interpolated into the self-Orientalist subject position that had become available within the sociopolitical structure of the Cold War. At that time, Japanese masculinity was suppressed or dismissed as barbaric by Europeans and North Americans, while women were seen as the embodiment of Japanese culture. This version of self-Orientalism is exemplified in Kawakita's *Madame Butterfly*, which essentialised Japan's apparent cultural uniqueness.

As the Cold War ended, East–West tensions waned and the US–Japan trade conflict mounted. A new generation of Japanese film producers, such as Horikoshi of Eurospace, became active in co-financing and coproducing European, Asian and small independent American films in the late twentieth century. The Tokyo metropolis became hospitable to numerous international art-house directors who sought to finance their pet projects, many of which they found difficult to realise in their own countries.

Numerous European, American and other non-Japanese film-makers worked in Japan and on Japan, with Japanese finances. They – mostly Occidental film-makers - made several films that touched on Japan and its cultural otherness during the 1980s and 1990s. This provided opportunities for Japanese film practitioners to learn and develop a certain gaze:[57] a way of looking at these Occidental film-makers and a way, too, of looking at Japanese otherness through their perspective. This sometimes included the chance to re-present this otherness with irony. In so doing, one may thus conclude, these Japanese gazes further complicated the original gaze of Orientalism.

ACKNOWLEDGMENT

This research was supported by Komazawa University's Special Research Program 2019.

Notes

1. Gary Needham, 'Japanese Cinema and Orientalism', in Dimitris Eleftheriotis and Gary Needham (eds), *Asian Cinema: A Reader and Guide* (Edinburgh: Edinburgh University Press, 2006), pp. 8–10.
2. For example, see Naoki Sakai, 'Modernity and its Critique', in Masao Miyoshi and Harry D. Harootunian (eds), *Postmodernism and Japan* (Durham, NC: Duke University Press, 1989), pp. 93–122; Marilyn Ivy, *Discourse of the Vanishing: Modernity Phantasm Japan* (Chicago: University of Chicago Press, 1995).
3. Koichi Iwabuchi, 'Use of Japanese Popular Culture: Trans/nationalism and Postcolonial Desire for "Asia"', *Emergences* vol. 11 no. 2 (2011), pp. 199–222.
4. For a discussion of the prewar reception of Japanese films in Europe, see Nakayama Nobuko, 'France de hajimete kōkai sareta nihon eiga: Exoticism to kōkishin', and Harald Salomon, 'Deutsch ni okeru nihon eiga no juyō: Sai shoki no kanshō kai kara *Jūjiro, Hawai Maley oki kaisen e*', in Iwamoto Kenji (ed.), *Nihon eiga no kaigai shinsyutsu: Bunka senryaku no rekishi* (Tokyo: Shinwasha, 2015), pp. 39–72. A number of attempts were made to export Japanese

films to Europe before *Rashomon*. For example, the 'Pure Cinema Movement' advocated by Kaeriyama Norimasa (1893–1964) aimed to produce 'exportable' films in order to improve the technical qualities of Japanese cinema. During the Fifteen Years' War, the politician Iwase Ryō proposed a national cinema policy in 1933. The motive behind this proposal was said to be the desire to counteract the derogatory and stereotypical image of Japan in Europe.
5. For instance, Noël Burch, *To the Distant Observer: Form and Meaning in the Japanese Cinema* (London: Scolar Press; Berkeley: University of California Press, 1979); David Bordwell and Kristin Thompson, 'Space and Narrative in the Films of Ozu', *Screen* vol. 17 no. 2 (Summer 1976), pp. 41–73.
6. Wim Wenders made a documentary film on Ozu, *Tokyo-Ga*, in 1985.
7. See Mitsuhiro Yoshimoto, 'The Difficulty of Being Radical: The Discipline of Film Studies and the Postcolonial World Order', in Masao Miyoshi and Harry D. Harootunian (eds), *Japan in the World* (Durham, NC: Duke University Press, 1993), pp. 338–53.
8. See Yoshiharu Tezuka, *Japanese Cinema Goes Global: Filmworkers' Journeys* (Hong Kong: Hong Kong University Press, 2012), pp. 40–60.
9. The most obvious example being the British distributor Tartan films' 'Tartan Asia Extreme' series that introduced the director Miike Takashi – *Audition* (1999), *Ichi the Killer* (2001) – to Western cult audiences. See Oliver Dew, '"Asia Extreme": Japanese Cinema and British Hype', *New Cinemas: Journal of Contemporary Film* vol. 5 no. 1 (2007), pp. 54–73.
10. Yoshimura Shinjirō, 'Tsuisō Italifilm-sha', in 'Japan-Italia Cinematic Exchange', special issue of *Italia tosho* no. 33 (2005), pp. 2–8.
11. Kurosawa Akira, *Gama no abura: Jiden no yōna mono* (Tokyo: Iwanami shoten, 1990), p. 343; Yoshimura, 'Tsuisō Italifilm-sha', pp. 2–8. [Editors' note: for more on Japanese film culture and international film festivals, see also Chapter 11 by Ran Ma in this volume.]
12. Nagata Masaichi, *Eigadō massigura* (Tokyo: Surugadaishobō, 1953) p. 75.
13. Nagata Masaichi, 'Gaika kakutoku shudan toshiteno eiga', *Eiga jihō*, 20 July 1953.
14. Nagata Masaichi, 'Rashōmon o uridasu', *Geijutsu shinchō*, November 1951, p. 89.
15. Nagata Masaichi, *Eiga jiga kyō* (Tokyo: Heibonsha, 1957), pp. 122–3.
16. See Mary Louise Pratt, 'Arts of Contact Zone', *Profession* (1991), pp. 33–40, <http://www.histal.ca/wp-content/uploads/2012/08/PrattM-1991-Arts-of-the-Contact-Zone.pdf>.
17. Suzuki Akinari, *Rappa to yobareta otoko: Eiga producer Nagata Masaichi* (Tokyo: Kinema junpōsha, 1990), p. 113; Midorikawa Michio, 'Cameraman no eigashi: Midorikawa Michio no ayunda michi', in Yamaguchi Takeshi (ed.), *Cameraman no eigashi: Midorikawa Michio no ayunda michi* (Tokyo: Shakai shisōsha 1987), p. 193.
18. Nagata, 'Rashōmon o uridasu', pp. 135–44.
19. Suzuki, *Rappa to yobareta otoko*, pp. 112–15.
20. See Harry D. Harootunian, 'America's Japan/Japan's Japan', in Miyoshi and Harootunian, *Japan in the World*, pp. 186–221.
21. Nagata Masaichi, 'France wa kiraida', *Nikkei News*, evening edition, 17 April 1955.
22. Hamano Yasuki, *Itsuwari no minshu shugi: GHQ/eiga/kabuki nosengo hishi* (Tokyo: Kadokawa shoten, 2008).
23. Author's interview with Fujii Hiroaki, 5 August 2005, in Tokyo. [Editors' note: for more on Nagata Masaichi, see also Chapter 36 by Stephanie DeBoer in this volume.]
24. Kawakita Nagamasa, 'Watashi no rirekisho', *Nikkei News*, 11 April 1980.
25. Kawakita Nagamasa, 'Aru cosmopolitan no chichi to ko', *Bungei shunjū*, July 1960, pp. 306–7.
26. Kawakita Kashiko and Satō Tadao, *Eiga ga sekai o musubu* (Tokyo: Soujusha, 1991), pp. 39–42.
27. Kawakita Memorial Film Institute web page, <http://www.kawakita-film.or.jp/zaidan_3.html>. [Editors' note: for more on Kawakita Nagamasa, see also Chapter 31 by Ni Yan in this volume.]
28. Kawakita Nagamasa, 'Eiga yunyū gyōsha toshite', *Chūōkōron*, April 1957, pp. 172–7.
29. Ibid.
30. Ibid.
31. Ibid.
32. Mori Iwao, 'Gassaku eiga seisaku no jissai', *Kinema junpō* no. 109 (1955), pp. 34–7.
33. See Tezuka, *Japanese Cinema Goes Global*.
34. Robert McChesney, 'The New Global Media', in David Held and Anthony McGrew (eds), *The Global Transformations Reader* (London: Polity, 2000), pp. 260–8.
35. *Kokusai* literally translates to 'internationalisation', but I use the term to indicate a particular Japanese configuration of economic globalisation.

36. Chikara Higashi and Peter Lauther, *The Internationalization of the Japanese Economy* (Norwell, MA: Kluwer Academic Publisher, 1990), p. 6. [Editors' note: for more on globalisation, see also Chapter 35 by Cobus van Staden in this volume.]
37. Quoted in Hara Hiroyuki, *Bubble bunka ron: Post-sengo toshiteno 1980 nendai* (Tokyo: Keiō gijuku daigaku shuppan, 2006), p. 8.
38. Gerard Delanty, 'Consumption, Modernity, and Japanese Cultural Identity: The Limit of Americanization?', in Natan Sznaider, Rainer Winter and Ulrich Beck (eds), *Global America?: Consequences of Globalization* (Liverpool: Liverpool University Press, 2003), pp. 114–33.
39. Motion Picture Producers Association of Japan website, <http://www.eiren.org/toukei/index.html>.
40. See Tony Rayns, *Eiga: 25 years of Japanese Cinema* (Edinburgh: Edinburgh International Film Festival Catalogue, 1984), p. 7; Ōkubo Ken'ichi, 'Subete wa koko kara hajimatta', in Lindy Hop Studio (ed.), *Alternative Movies in Japan: Nihon eiga no punk jidai 1975–1987* (Tokyo: Aiikusha, 2006), pp. 1–96; Inuhiko Yomota, 'Stranger than Tokyo: Space and Race in Postnational Japanese Cinema', trans. Aaron Gerow, in Jenny Kwok Wah Lau (ed.), *Multiple Modernities: Cinema and Popular Media in Transnational East Asia* (Philadelphia, PA: Temple University Press, 2003), p. 76–9.
41. See Hara, *Bubble bunka ron*, pp. 69–70.
42. The other was Cinema Square Tokyo, discussed in Tezuka, *Japanese Cinema Goes Global*, p. 80.
43. Horikoshi Kenzō, 'Bandō Tamasaburō "sagi musume"', 6 August 2014, <http://www.wonderlands.jp/archives/25824/#more-25824>.
44. Horikoshi Kenzō, 'Independent no eikō/Eurospace 9: Documentary "kakareta kao" no genba', interviewed by Takasaki Toshio, *Chikuma* no. 592 (April 2015), pp. 26–7.
45. Ibid. Daniel Schmid Film Festival was organised by the Athénée Français Cultural Center in 1982.
46. Ibid.
47. Ōtaka Hiroo and Inaba Mariko, *Mini Theatre o yoroshiku* (Tokyo: JICC shuppankyoku, 1989), pp. 48–9.
48. See Tezuka, *Japanese Cinema Goes Global*, pp. 80–97, for more discussion on the popularity of gay films among mostly female mini-theatre audiences in the 1980s and 1990s.
49. Roland Barthes, *Empire of Signs*, trans. Richard Howard (New York: Hill and Wang, 1982), p. 89.
50. Interview with Bandō Tamasaburō in Daniel Schmid's film, *The Written Face* (1995).
51. For a discussion on Japan's practice based film education, see Yoshiharu Tezuka, 'Dynamics of the Cultures of Discontent: How is Globalization Transforming the Training of Filmmakers in Japan?', in Mette Hjort (ed.), *The Education of Filmmakers in Europe, Australia, and Asia* (New York: Palgrave Macmillan, 2013).
52. For more details, see ibid.
53. The scriptwriter Takahashi Hiroshi, who wrote the original script of *The Ring* (Nakata Hideo, 1998), teaches at Horikoshi's The Film School of Tokyo. The director Shimizu Takashi, who remade his own Japanese versions in Hollywood, *The Grudge* (2004) and *The Grudge 2* (2006), is a graduate of the same institution.
54. See, for instance, Koichi Iwabuchi, *Recentering Globalization: Popular Culture and Japanese Transnationalism* (Durham, NC: Duke University Press, 2002).
55. Author's interview with Horikoshi Kenzō, 15 May and 20 June 2012, in Tokyo.
56. David Rooney, 'Yakuza Apocalypse (Gokudō daisensō) Cannes Review', *Hollywood Reporter*, 22 May 2015, <https://www.hollywoodreporter.com/review/yakuza-apocalypse-gokudo-daisenso-cannes-797606>.
57. See Horikoshi, 'Independent no eikou/Eurospace 1–15', interviewed by Takasaki Toshio, *Chikuma* nos. 521–35 (August 2014–October 2015).

40

TRANSNATIONAL REMAKES AND ADAPTATIONS
Casablanca karaoke: The program picture as marginal art in 1960s Japan

Ryan Cook

JAPANESE CINEMA AND ADAPTATION: ROMANTICISM, GEO-POSITIONING OR FOLK ART

On some level, the problem of adaptation calls into question whether such a thing as 'Japanese cinema' even exists. Histories of Japanese cinema tend to start with the introduction of 'foreign' motion picture technology to Japan and proceed through struggles of Japanese film-makers to find a place for themselves, and for Japanese cinema, at the margins of the overwhelming influence of Western models. Such narratives of struggle introduce the themes of hybridity and impurity into national film history and can thus be seen to threaten the coherence of the very idea of 'Japanese cinema' itself. But an inverse argument is also possible: that if something does indeed distinguish Japanese cinema as coherent or unique, it may be precisely the ways its films have grappled with the problem of influence. Adaptation would thus not threaten Japanese cinema but become an actual condition of its existence.

Consider three approaches to adaptation that might inform a practical definition of Japanese film. First, there is the 'anxiety of influence' option, in which the struggle for originality among Japanese film-makers would resemble that (in Harold Bloom's reading) of Romantic poets rebelliously misinterpreting the poems of their precursors in order to forge new ground of their own. I will argue that this approach seems off the mark, at least with regard to a very substantial part of Japanese cinema, which is to say, the popular genres that will be the subject of this essay. More than Romantic disavowal, a second kind of adaptation comes to the fore when thinking of Japanese film history: the 'geo-positioning' model of adaptation where the adaptation or citation of Hollywood films, for example, functions as a mapping of coordinates that positions films themselves within film history and Japanese cinema within the world. This is no doubt a sensible approach to films that often stage self-conscious dramas of positioning and hierarchy and, as we will see, others have compellingly carried out such analyses. But this is still not an entirely satisfying explanation of the procedures at play in many Japanese films.

This chapter will instead pursue a third kind of adaptation and analysis and argue that in spite of their perhaps rebellious citation of film historical models, and notwithstanding the maps and diagrams they plot, a large body of Japanese films are on some level all too routine and indifferent to aesthetic originality or to geopolitical manoeuvring to accommodate such readings exclusively. Looking to a 1967 Japanese genre film adapted from the 1942 Warner Bros. classic *Casablanca* – both films in which maps figure centrally – I will argue that adaptation in this context raises global positioning as a motif but ultimately covers it over with a haze of *atmosphere*. On the one hand, this atmosphere spreads a fog across the map, making it less reliable for purposes of navigation, but on the other hand it also helps constitute the environment in which the films circulate (or did so at the time): an everyday life space of aestheticised routine. This argument will therefore take us from Romantic originality through geopolitical mapping to the realm of everyday life practices and 'folk' art, which is where I argue the popular Japanese film seems to end up.

There is undoubtedly room for Romantic narratives of artistic rebellion and renewal in individual cases throughout Japanese film history. These narratives are perhaps most relevant in relation to figures such as Kurosawa Akira and Mizoguchi Kenji who crafted hybrid art films intended for international film festival audiences in the postwar years, or to the young directors who joined a form of global auteur practice from the late 1950s, partially in response to the emergence of niche markets among the fragmented post-studio-system cinema audience in Japan. By 1970, the film critic Iwasaki Akira could observe that Japanese cinema no longer had a 'Japanese' audience, by which he meant a mass public in the form of a unified national community. The circumstances of films and their reception had changed to the extent that the relevant context was arguably an international and intertextual New Wave instead.[1]

Of course, prewar Japanese cinema was certainly rife with dramas and comedies artistically influenced by others: Ozu Yasujirō's early comedies, decorated with references to American films, were also touched by Ernst Lubitsch; Kinugasa Teinosuke's cosmopolitan 1920s modernism bore the imprint of German Expressionism; Mizoguchi similarly channelled the Germans with treatments of *The Cabinet of Dr. Caligari/Das Cabinet des Dr. Caligari* (1920) and F.W. Murnau's American masterpiece *Sunrise* (1927) while Yamanaka Sadao reworked contemporary French cinema of the 1930s into Japanese period films with examples such as René Clair's *Le Million* (1931) and *The Million Ryō Pot/Hyakuman ryō no tsubo* (1935), and Jacques Feyder's *Pension Mimosas* (1935) and *Humanity and Paper Balloons/Ninjō kami fūsen* (1937). But even assuming that such films can be characterised by poetic struggles for originality, it is not clear that this attitude should be taken as representative of Japanese cinema. Any national cinema is arguably best represented not by its exceptional examples but by its more ordinary, everyday routines.

A less Romantic account of the stakes of adaptation is undoubtedly called for in talking about one of the foremost genres in the history of Japanese cinema: the 'program picture', which 'nine-to-fived' alongside the more rarefied toil of art cinema during the postwar years. The program picture is a concept that was itself adopted from the 1930s American studio system. Originally, it referred to low-budget genre productions that were made quickly to fill programmes (usually double bills), in contrast to the more expensive and prestigious major features that enjoyed exclusive marketing and event status. Program pictures were in part tied to the binding distribution arrangements of the block-booking system that existed during the American studio era, which encouraged mass production. A similar industrial structure existed in postwar Japan (outliving the US system that was broken up by the 1948 Supreme Court Paramount Decision).

Like many loan words, the term *puroguramu pikuchā* was applied somewhat differently, and more broadly, in Japanese. It could be linked to release dates, for example, indicating films made to be released out of season in between the customary peak filmgoing periods such as the summer and New Year, but it could also refer to films made in series form such as celebrated institutions including *Tora-san/Otoko wa tsurai yo* (1969–95) and *The Yakuza Papers/Jingi naki tatakai* (1973–6). It is therefore generally associated with an organisational form of production and releasing that tends towards the franchise model and is in this sense an example of what Alex Zahlten calls 'industrial genres', in which aesthetic generic formations are inseparably bound up with industrial practices.[2]

Why single out the program picture as an example of adaptation in the Japanese cinema? First of all, the program picture was a profoundly popular cinematic form, but one that has not always inspired scholarly appreciation. With exceptions, writing on program pictures has tended to be memoiristic, journalistic or nostalgic. To be sure, a thorough academic study of such mass-produced cultural ephemera would be a daunting undertaking as many of the films have not been individually memorialised in film history. But a thorough accounting may not even be what is called for. In fact, the enticement of these films is in part related to the way that many of them now amount to cultural detritus, like the tattered period movie posters peeling off the walls of the Yūraku Concourse in Tokyo, for example, where such program picture remnants today function as nostalgic background décor to beer and grilled chicken. How use and obsolescence relate to adaptation in Japanese cinema is an often-overlooked matter that such films invite us to consider.

The cinéphile memoirist Kashima Shigeru has dramatised this disposable feeling in a homage to the fading films of his youth. Claiming to have seen more than three thousand program pictures during years of truancy and unemployment spent in dingy third-run cinemas during the 1970s, he describes how the individual films blend together in his memory over time, forming a hazy atmosphere. What emerges from this mental fog, he writes, are not individual accomplishments or exceptions such as star performances or directorial signatures (with no offence to program picture auteurs such as Suzuki Seijun), but minor details reinforced by repetition: the *wakiyaku*, or bit parts and supporting players, that became comfortably familiar in unremarkable repeat appearances from film to film.[3] This indicates something about the aesthetic procedures of these films and the way audiences may have related to them: they were characterised by a sense of routineness.

Program pictures are heavily associated with the Shōwa era, properly the period of Japanese history from 1926 to 1989, but also a signifier that in practice often connotes a culture ambivalently bound up with the postwar moment. Shōwa as a postwar atmosphere still hangs over corners of contemporary Japanese society as a now often nostalgic presence, especially in a dwindling number of old cinemas. Shōwa was the golden era for program pictures and in their glory they were the stock-in-trade of studios, at once programme-fillers and the vital organs of Japanese cinema. In fact, the program picture effectively sustained Japanese studios through the 1960s. This is especially true of Nikkatsu. Historically Japan's oldest full-service film studio, Nikkatsu had only resumed production in 1954 after a wartime hiatus. In forging a place for itself within the competitive environment of 1950s Japanese cinema, the studio marketed youthful energy, an identity that was cemented by the 'Sun Tribe' (*taiyōzoku*) boom it precipitated in 1956 with a number of erotically charged films about passionate youthful disaffection. The program picture lines that the studio subsequently established to fulfil booking obligations and supply regular vehicles for its contract talent drew to an extent on the youthful volatility and eroticism of the Sun Tribe films, but they can also be characterised by another pervasive characteristic: their penchant for adaptation and citation.

The fundamental intertextuality of Nikkatsu's program pictures has been frequently noted – an intertextuality even found in the Sun Tribe films, the major example of which (*Crazed Fruit/Kurutta kajitsu* [1956]) was inspired by the 1951 American film *A Place in the Sun* (and was later remade in Hong Kong by the same Japanese director). Nomura Takeshi, a former contract director at Nikkatsu, has remembered the early 1960s as a time when he and his colleagues made a regular practice of modelling program picture scenarios on foreign films, usually poaching source material without attribution. Nomura admits, for example, that his own 1962 film *Man in a Torrent/Gekiryū ni ikiru otoko* was a loose adaptation of the 1953 Alan Ladd Western *Shane*, and moreover that the Nikkatsu action star Akagi Keiichirō, who was also known as Tony because he styled his appearance after Tony Curtis, studiously adapted the persona of Ladd's drifter in that film.[4] Sekikawa Natsuo notes that such unattributed borrowing was practised so regularly in Nikkatsu program pictures that it might be thought of as analogous to the practice of *honkadori*, or 'allusive variation',[5] a poetic technique associated with the early Kamakura-period *Shinkokinshū* poetry anthology. Allusive variation was a highly rule-governed practice of poetic citation that drew on the codes of older model texts in order to create a 'new poetic spirit from old words'.[6]

Sekikawa likely did not intend a rigorous analogy with his passing, even humorous, reference to allusive variation, and the comparison is indeed questionable. Allusive variation was an elite poetic practice that involved displays of literacy in relation to canonical poems and a politics of citation as a means of social positioning and critique. Such serious considerations are not to be dismissed in the program picture context and in what follows, the motif of 'positioning' will be given its due. But if Japanese poetics are to supply an analogy for the open textuality and the semiotic play of such popular culture ephemera as program pictures, we will ultimately need to turn to less privileged poetic practices.

ADAPTATION AS MAPPING AND TRANSLATION

In many cases, program pictures self-consciously mapped their coordinates in geopolitical terms. In the case of Nikkatsu, such consciousness of orientation can be traced to the industrial context of the studio itself. Before resuming production activity in the postwar years, Nikkatsu had operated as a distributor of foreign films in Japan and through affiliation with Fox and Universal, released numerous American Westerns and action films. The so-called 'stateless' (*mukokuseki*) action films that Nikkatsu itself subsequently produced quite recognisably adapted such American genre films. The new Nikkatsu also had the most modern production facilities in Japan at the time and was known as an 'Eastern Hollywood'. But as Yomota Inuhiko has observed, Nikkatsu's relationship to Hollywood was not merely one of imitation. It involved a self-conscious distance, reflected in a poignant sense of 'resignation' that the model itself was always out of reach.[7]

Michael Raine, writing more broadly about Japanese film history through the postwar years, has pursued this point further in arguing strongly that the influence of American films on Japanese cinema far exceeded the other more regionally proximate networks and flows that have often been highlighted in recent Asian cinema scholarship. He suggests that it is best to think of such adaptation in terms of strategies for responding to what he calls a 'geopolitical incline'. Viewed in this way, adaptation becomes a reflection of the experience of living on the periphery of a world system where America and Hollywood formed the centre. Raine's point is that Japanese films did not adapt source material from Hollywood from the vantage point of shame or embarrassment about their relative position in the world; rather, adaptation in this context lent itself to playful (self-) criticism and parody.[8]

Cartographic varieties of adaptation, however playful, also had much to do with the everyday discourse that constructed 'Japanese cinema' (*hōga*) as distinct from the messy category of the 'Western film' (*yōga*). Of course, it was not only the classical Hollywood studio film that constituted the cinematic counterpart reductively named 'Western' but also an array of foreign films that involved various hierarchical relationships among themselves. *Shane* and *Roman Holiday* (1953) supplied inspiration for Nikkatsu films, but so did such continental sources as Fellini's *La Strada* (1954) and *Nights of Cabiria/La Notte di Cabiria* (1957), Wajda's *Ashes and Diamonds/Popiół i diament* (1958) and Godard's *Breathless/À bout de souffle* (1960). Traces of these films can be found in Kurahara Koreyoshi's *Glass Johnny: Like a Beast/Garasu Jonī: Yajū ni miete* (1962) and Masuda Toshio's *Crimson Shooting Star/Kurenai no nagareboshi* (1967), for example.[9]

It goes without saying that these Nikkatsu films were neither systematic nor faithful adaptations. Rather, they sampled from the Western repertoire in selective, and often oblique, ways. Take for example the director Nakahira Kō. Around the time that François Truffaut was watching Japanese films and famously praising Nakahira's aforementioned *Crazed Fruit* in the pages of *Cahiers du cinéma*, Nakahira was looking to French cinema as a source of inspiration – not primarily in terms of its content but its cadence and speech. While making his 1957 film *Street Lights/Gaitō*, he reportedly directed his actors to pronounce their lines in a quick, impassive manner, in mimicry of what he perceived to be the intonation of French cinematic dialogue.[10] Similarly, in later years, the director Morita Yoshimitsu would also direct his actors to speak their lines 'as though post-dubbing a foreign film' in order to create an effect of strangeness or unnaturalness.[11] Such examples show how adaptation could be staged self-consciously as a process of translation, whether in the form of lip-synching (borrowing a foreign voice) or dubbing (putting one's voice into a foreign body). However, rather than making the foreign intelligible, as such cinematic ventriloquism is usually meant to do, its purpose was to render a Japanese film somehow foreign to its intended audience, advertising a faux cosmopolitanism while at the same time calling attention to how Japanese cinema was itself constructed around Western cinema and fundamentally involved translation.

When we consider that Nakahira's *Street Lights* features a 'Japanese *chanson*' set to a Parisian accordion refrain, the lip-synching metaphor expands to encompass musical imitation. In fact, it was de rigueur at Nikkatsu that films feature theme songs (*shudaika*) and such songs routinely reflected pragmatic musical fraudulence like that of the 'faked' *chanson*. At the time, unfavourable exchange rates prohibited securing permissions from rights holders outside Japan, and there was no question of legitimately borrowing the allure of popular foreign tunes. Foreign songs were adapted in-house through a figurative lip-synching that played on the boundaries between foreign musical genres and the familiarity of Japanese lyrics and variations. In this way, Nakahira's Japanese *chanson* and 'foreign'-style cinematic speech reflect a spatial oscillation on the level of language and translation. Such oscillations between orientation and disorientation are also evident in the cartographic dimensions of film adaptations 'resigned' to being neither here nor there. Nonetheless, as I will argue by means of a case study, this sense of spatial displacement was complicated by another effect of the theme song and the voice in the program picture: the *familiarity* of atmosphere, routinely represented through motifs of mood and ambience.

JAPANESE *CASABLANCA*: ADAPTATION AS ATMOSPHERE

One specimen of the Nikkatsu program picture in its maturity directly dramatises the clouding of spatial positioning with environmental atmosphere: a 1967 'remake' of Michael Curtiz's wartime Hollywood classic *Casablanca* (itself an adaptation of a stage play), entitled *A Warm Misty Night/Yogiri yo kon'ya mo arigatō*. The film was a vehicle for Nikkatsu's romantic pair Ishihara Yūjirō and Asaoka Ruriko. It was directed by Ezaki Mio, a program picture specialist who was known for his ability to work fast – *A Warm Misty Night* was one of five films directed by Ezaki that Nikkatsu released in 1967. It is easy to imagine, given the speed of the production process, that the considerations leading film-makers to adapt existing source material were not only aesthetic or political in nature. Adaptation had a pragmatic function and Ezaki's *Casablanca* certainly did not disdain such efficiencies. In fact, by the often artfully oblique standards of poaching and lip-synching at Nikkatsu, the film stands out for the relative directness with which it poaches plot material.

Yūjirō plays a former sailor who has travelled the world and is acquainted with its injustices. He is a stateless person by vocation, like Bogart's expatriate Rick in *Casablanca*, though unlike Rick, he remains planted on his native soil throughout the action of the film; he is a foreigner even at home. As the film begins, he telephones a marriage proposal to his girlfriend (played by Ruriko). After she unexpectedly fails to show up for their engagement rendezvous, Yūjirō begins a desperate search for her that ends in crestfallen resignation at having been snubbed. Little does he know that his fiancée was hit by a car en route to the chapel and sustained injuries that made her incapable of bearing children. This is a variation on Ingrid Bergman's romantic conflict in *Casablanca* – conjugal ties to a Resistance leader returned from the dead – that translates the story logic in accord with Japanese gender norms. Not wanting Yūjirō to forfeit his dreams of raising children for the sake of their relationship, Ruriko has sacrificed her love and entered a barren marriage with the very man who tragically ran her over, disappearing from Yūjirō's life without even a farewell.

Four years later, Ruriko shows up in Yokohama where Yūjirō now runs a nightclub. In his spare time he uses his shipping industry connections to smuggle sympathetic political refugees out of Japan. Ruriko has re-emerged along with her new husband, who is a 'Southeast Asian revolutionary' desperately in need of passage to the transfer point of Singapore in order to rejoin the struggle in his undisclosed home country. The couple have nowhere to turn but to Yūjirō, who is still bitter over having been abandoned. But once he learns of Ruriko's self-sacrificing reasons for breaking their engagement four years earlier, he agrees to help and sacrifices his own happiness in turn to put the couple safely on their way.

The settings and characters, as well as the themes of poignant self-sacrifice and political intrigue, are all familiar from *Casablanca*. The film's final scene also replays the iconic farewell at the Casablanca airstrip in which Bogart sends Bergman off with her Resistance leader husband, but substitutes the Moroccan fog with the 'warm mist' and murky waters at a Yokohama dock. However, in spite of its similarities, *A Warm Misty Night* also differs substantially from its source. It takes place on the other side of the world from Rick's cosmopolitan cafe and is evidently set in the present of 1967. It also does not conspicuously tip its hat in homage as it borrows more from the original film's plot than from its iconic imagery or legendary repartee. In this sense, its relationship to film history is unlike what we find in adaptations such as Woody Allen's 1972 *Casablanca* film *Play It Again, Sam*, where Bogart is resurrected as the castigating superego of a neurotic cinéphile fixated on a monochrome fictional world. In fact, the imagery and dialogue in the Nikkatsu film more recall Nikkatsu formulas than the wartime Hollywood classic.

One Nikkatsu formula is the house genre to which the film belongs: the so-called 'mood action' (*mūdo akushon*) film. *A Warm Misty Night* adapts not only *Casablanca* but also a 'mood song' (*mūdo kayō*), recorded by Yūjirō himself and released as a single in advance of the film. This was not unusual. Since theme songs tied in with record labels had become compulsory in Nikkatsu program pictures by the late 1950s, adapting or expanding a pre-existing song into a scenario was a rational approach and was something on display in other Yūjirō vehicles such as the 1962 *Ginza Love Story/Ginza no koi no monogatari* (which also bears resemblance to the 1951 film *An American in Paris*, a film inspired in turn by a George Gershwin melody). *A Warm Misty Night* adopts the title of its source song as its own ('Yogiri yo kon'ya mo arigatō') and the now-classic song itself is played at multiple points across its duration even though its lyrics bear only a general relationship to the film's plot (they describe furtive lovers who are able to meet only under the cover of the evening fog and long for a day when they will openly enjoy the sunshine together). What *A Warm Misty Night* takes from its source song is the theme of thwarted love, the image of fog and, perhaps most importantly, its mood. In this sense, the atmosphere it adopts from a song, while echoing the fog of Casablanca, clouds over the compass coordinates of the Hollywood film.

Nikkatsu's trademarked branding of 'mood action' poses an interesting paradox: the problem being that mood and action are fundamentally incompatible. Mood is not goal-oriented or vectoral and not conducive to agency (think of the gamut of moody and pessimistic postwar American noir films where the heroic protagonists of classical cinema lose agency and control over their destinies). Instead, moods tend to be introspective and abstract – deterrents to productivity. Being in a mood is better suited for sitting pensively at a piano with a glass of whisky (as Yūjirō does throughout *A Warm Misty Night*) than for taking action (Fig. 40.1). This is a dilemma depicted in

Fig. 40.1 *A Warm Misty Night/Yogiri yo kon'ya mo arigatō* (Ezaki Mio, 1967, Nikkatsu). Yūjirō in a mood.

Nikkatsu films themselves, where action springs into implausible relief against inertia. The situation of action within mood tends to promote a sense of absurdity and the films can thus be seen more as parodies of action than as simply action films in their own right.

But mood also cites the visual texture of a cinematic lineage. As the title *A Warm Misty Night* implies, mist or fog is central to the atmosphere of mood hanging over the film and immersing its field of action. In fact, fog was a recurring motif throughout Nikkatsu mood action films of the period. It became such a motif in the late 1950s and 1960s that the 'fog film' even seems to emerge as a subgenre. Looking to further examples, we can see a specific affinity with the aesthetic world of 1930s French poetic realism and its legacy in film noir. Kawashima Yūzō's celebrated 1957 Nikkatsu comedy *Sun in the Last Days of the Shogunate*/*Bakumatsu taiyōden* was openly an adaptation of Japanese *rakugo* stories and a humorous transposition of Nikkatsu's own Sun Tribe franchise into the period film genre, but the film was also modelled on Marcel Carné's 1938 film *Hôtel du Nord*. Likewise, the film *Red Pier*/*Akai hatoba* was based on the model of Julien Duvivier's 1937 *Pépé le Moko*.[12] In *Call of the Fog Horn*/*Muteki ga ore o yondeiru*, a 1960 adaptation of Carol Reed's *The Third Man*, Nikkatsu even transplanted a narrative of black market intrigue and deception from the misty streets of Vienna to the reliably foggy port of Yokohama, thus further extending film historical atmosphere over the program picture. But whereas France's poetic realism was a cinema of 'atmosphere' and 'mist' in contrast to the 'eventfulness and violence' of American cinema,[13] Nikkatsu put mood and action together in striking dissonance and to near parodic effect, as just described. As an insubstantial medium, fog thus abstracted action from contextual grounding, leaving it to swim.

Casablanca was an apt source for such atmospheric adaptation. In fact, 1967 was not even the first time Nikkatsu had remade *Casablanca*. The 1963 film *Dockside Gambler*/*Hatoba no tobakushi* had already revisited the iconic source material, with Kobayashi Akira playing the Bogart role. But the 1967 version was significant in part because it represented a reworking of Yūjirō's star persona. As a younger lead, Yūjirō had portrayed the smouldering rebellions of passionate young men. By 1967, he was transitioning to middle-age roles and Bogart became a new model for a more inured, astringent variety of disillusioned heroism appropriate to the maturing star. Yūjirō's performance was not only a modelling of middle-aged cinematic masculinity: the striking disconnect between his introspective moods and his decisive agency also underlined the abstraction and fictionality of the whole undertaking. Likewise, in copying *Casablanca*, Nikkatsu borrowed not only its story material but also the particular sense of fictionality that derived from its relationship to history, a relationship symbolised by the fog that hangs over the airstrip connecting the port town to the outside world and effectively erasing the world from view.

The historical context for *Casablanca* in 1942 was of course the flight of refugees from the ongoing war in Europe; colonial Morocco being a cosmopolitan port on the edge of the European continent. Needless to say, the high-growth Japan of 1967 was a far different place, though the fact that Japan was constitutionally restricted from engaging directly in the conflict in Vietnam may have made the port of Yokohama vaguely analogous to 1940s Casablanca as a refugee camp and centre of geopolitical intrigue (in fact, the film may have been inspired by actual cases of American military deserters who sought covert passage through Japanese ports). Moreover, the 'Southeast Asian revolutionary' who replaces *Casablanca*'s Czech Resistance fighter undermines the historical context in the process of establishing it. Guen, as he is called, suggests the Vietnamese name Nguyên in Japanese pronunciation and speaks the French of perhaps colonial Indochina (albeit in a very unconvincing way), but he never mentions his country or even his cause by name. The tease escalates when he is pictured authoring important revolutionary missives beneath not the Vietnamese but the Philippine national flag. The historical context of 1967 Yokohama as a locale is thus replaced with a highly fictional construct that is supported by the idea of South East Asia as an abstract space without a particular history, all the more so because the history of Japanese imperialism is especially missing.

Of course, *Casablanca* itself approached history with a high quotient of fictionality, especially since its story was more or less set in the present of an ongoing conflict. Shot mostly on a sound stage in Burbank, California, the film marshalled stars, fictional archetypes and clichés in the service of what was ultimately more an iconography than a historiography of a crisis. Nikkatsu's turn to this Hollywood classic had much to do with such fictionalisation of history. Take for example two maps: the first a rotating globe that opens the American film and the second a relief map of the world that decorates the wall behind the piano in Yūjirō's Yokohama nightclub (Fig. 40.2). Both diagrams establish cartography as a motif. The globe in *Casablanca* is itself clearly artificial, but the map in Yokohama, which is a more insistent piece of *mise en scène*, goes one step further towards spatial abstraction. Its Roman alphabet lettering identifies a large body of water, perhaps in Esperanto, as the 'Pathific Oceano' and is accompanied by anachronistic, fanciful illustrations of a jumping fish and listing ship; semiotic elements characteristic of less than reliable historical nautical charts. The Japanese archipelago moreover occupies the centre of this map, which is not unusual given that the setting is in Japan, except that the pronounced unreliability of the surrounding geography throws this centrality into relief. It is as if the film's cartography were performing a fictionalisation of the globe itself, purposely (and implausibly) moving Japan from periphery to centre. The port town milieu that emerges is thus not 'stateless' in the sense of Nikkatsu's own playful, and highly suspect, characterisation of its Eastern Westerns. The *state* of Japan is decidedly centre-stage but also decidedly fictional and encircled in the atmosphere and abstraction of a fanciful map.

In recycling *Casablanca*, *A Warm Misty Night* thus plots the coordinates of its own process of adaptation. Tom Conley has described how maps in films present location as an ontological problem: the question 'what is cinema' equals 'where is cinema' and what I am (as a spectator) becomes a matter of where I am and where I'm going.[14] By orienting viewers, films promise to answer such pressing questions. But maps in films also remind us of our dislocation as cinema spectators and that we are absent from the world that seems to be present, and mapped, on screen. A map such as the one found in *A Warm Misty Night*, which is itself more affective and abstract than objective and reliable, seems to symbolise that fundamental cinematic dislocation. Mapping also involves translation, as the Esperanto-esque legible text on the map in *A Warm Misty Night* implies. The phrases of English and French that trip inexpertly here and there off Yūjirō's tongue while he does business at the ports (subtitled in large Japanese

Fig. 40.2 *A Warm Misty Night/Yogiri yo kon'ya mo arigatō* (Ezaki Mio, 1967, Nikkatsu). The world mapped on the wall in Yūjirō's night club.

text on the screen) extend the motif of translation and, in so doing, return us to the theme song as it relates to language, and specifically to the voice.[15]

On the one hand, the motif of 'lip-synching' detaches the voice from the singer and divides presence between two locations in the 'geo-positioning' sense. Arguments to this effect can be made about the aforementioned Japanese *chanson* in Nakahira's *Street Lights*, and even about Yūjirō as he mouths lyrics at the piano to the playback recording of his own voice singing the theme song of *A Warm Misty Night*. But in light of the metaphysical association of the voice with presence, theme songs in program pictures can also be interpreted as protests against the 'ontological' uncertainty of Japanese cinema that sing 'I am here' whereas unreliable maps conjure instead a space that is closer to 'nowhere'. The voice is of course only present for the duration of a song, much as films are limited by their duration, and the 'here' it creates is a floating environment of atmosphere – a fog or mood – that needs continuously to be recreated. In program pictures, atmosphere is not the product of some specialised aesthetic project but of the routine, business-like rehearsal of cinematic and musical numbers. Through them, the films sustain an ongoing aesthetic environment that accompanies both 'Japanese cinema' and, for audiences, everyday life routines carried out around the movies.

ADAPTATION AS ROUTINE: JAPANESE CINEMA AS MARGINAL ART

The atmosphere of program pictures can be productively related to *genkai geijutsu*, or 'marginal art', a concept that the critic and sociologist Tsurumi Shunsuke developed during the 1960s.[16] This did not refer specifically to minority arts, though the spatial metaphor could point in such directions. Marginal art was directed towards the limits or 'margins', away from the centre, whether from the West as global centre or Tokyo as the centre of national culture in Japan. Spreading outward, it also tended towards openness and incompleteness, breeding site-by-site variation and adaptive reuse. This was in contrast to the symmetry and equilibrium of more institutionally anchored aesthetic practices such as the classicism of academic painting. In his case studies, Tsurumi often sought marginal art in the folk traditions of the countryside, or in the household, but more to the point, he located it in everyday life and with ordinary people. In this regard, marginal art was distinct from both fine art and popular art, both of which involved 'professionals' (intellectuals, craftsmen, skilled practitioners) whether as producers, consumers or both. Marginal art referred to practices on the 'margins' of institutions and 'close' to the sensory experiences and work of people.

Specific examples of marginal art cited by Tsurumi included festival dances, *bonsai* cultivation and miniature gardens, decorative pickled vegetables, doll making and tattoos. He was interested in folk ceramics and the aesthetics of useful objects: a tea bowl, for example, was something that grew more beautiful with use. His taxonomy of marginal arts does not include film, likely because he would have considered film a *popular* rather than a marginal art, though he did spend time with individual films as examples of cultural values rooted in *kōdan* oral tradition and vernacular literature.[17] Television was a somewhat different case insofar as it was more integrated into everyday rituals and routines, whereas film for Tsurumi arguably remained associated with novelty and spectacle as a privileged aesthetic practice somewhat more cut off from the flow of everyday life.[18] But do novelty and privilege adequately describe the program picture as it has been defined here? Yomota Inuhiko has since borrowed 'marginal art' from Tsurumi and applied it to film as a way to describe what he sees as a fundamental characteristic of Japanese cinema: forever tainted by its early association with *misemono* fairground attractions and marked as the lowest of the arts, film in Japan has maintained a proximity to ordinary life that situates it in the domain of the marginal.[19]

The importance of adaptation and the theme song to the Nikkatsu program picture helps illustrate how Japanese cinema may in fact fit within such parameters. Among all the folk arts that appeared in Tsurumi's studies, folk songs (*min'yō*), including work songs that accompanied people's labour, received sustained attention. He was interested in their relationship to *kaeuta* – 'modified' or parody songs – that were full of double meanings, repurposed lyrics and nonsense play. The significance of these songs as marginal art can in part be attributed to the intimacy of singing as situated in the voice, something straddling aesthetic and practical everyday experience. Extrapolating from this, and placing the emphasis on sensory environment as much as on aesthetic representation, we can think of the program picture as a form that 'whistled while it worked', creating and sustaining a mood, and an aesthetic sense of place, around its daily endeavours.

Program pictures as disposable cultural ephemera were moreover like marginal art in their openness and their ongoing routines of reuse. 'Popular art' analysis focused on the specialised commercial, industrial and textual dimensions of the films can overlook the ways that such incompleteness opened out into an atmospheric everyday environment, an environment that could be called 'Japanese cinema' or, even more broadly, 'Shōwa'. The subsequent memorialisation of such films as heritage has capitalised on their marginal art dimensions. Hou Hsiao-hsien's 2001 Taiwanese film *Millennium Mambo* captures this when its concluding images visit Yubari, a former coal-mining town in Hokkaido actually reinvented in the 1990s as a film festival destination. Yubari's Road of Cinema, a street lined with old movie poster reproductions, is a heritage museum-like atmospheric homage to Japanese cinema as part of Shōwa history. When Hou's camera drifts across a poster for none other than *A Warm Misty Night* hanging over the empty, snow-covered Road of Cinema, the program picture appears poignantly mummified and also dramatically abstracted from another side of the past: the imperial project in which coal-mining towns such as Yubari played a material role with the help of conscripted Taiwanese and Korean labour.[20] Hou's film is a reminder that memory is part of the aesthetic environment of program pictures.

As a performance and a memory exercise, *A Warm Misty Night* is not like an operatic aria or some virtuoso exercise held up for admiration. It is closer to the familiarity and openness of a popular hit single, a *chanson* or even a folk song. It is important in this respect that the film's theme song became part of the standard repertoire of karaoke, a cultural form that was incipient in 1967 at the time of the film's release.[21] As a karaoke number, the song has invited carousers to 'try on' the mood of Yūjirō's Bogart across the decades. The empty orchestra accompaniment suggests the atmosphere in ways similar to the film itself, which can be thought of as a karaoke construct composed of the most rudimentary parameters of *Casablanca*, just well enough articulated to support the ambience of a routine, soon to be repeated, performance. This is why the anxiety of influence is a foreign concept: the program picture is not concerned with longevity but with the momentary atmosphere of everyday life.

What finally does this mean for a 'poetics' of Japanese cinema, understood through the program picture? In contrast to the aristocratic games of poetic citation that characterised 'allusive variation', a more commonplace model is needed. The film-maker Suzuki Noribumi (of *Truck Guys*/*Torakku yarō* franchise fame) offered such an alternative analogy when he said that his own work in film should be remembered like the *yomibito shirazu* poems, or poems composed by 'nameless' ordinary people collected in the early Heian-period *Man'yōshū* poetry anthology.[22] The nameless poet does not vie for position but uses and repurposes available resources to aestheticise life in the moment. Hasumi Shigehiko perceived this attitude in Suzuki Noribumi's films themselves and, with the hint of a joke, called it 'alarming (*taihen*) for Japanese cinema'. Unlike the directors of Nikkatsu's Roman Porno 'sensual program pictures' of the 1970s, who Hasumi said were giving their all to the cause of Japanese cinema as ambitious artists (even within the incongruously low genre of the erotic film), Suzuki was just going through the motions, not even trying. Recognising that he would never surpass his 1972 'outrageous masterpiece' *The Lusty Shogun and His Twenty-One Dolls*/*Ero shōgun to nijūichi-nin no aishō*, Suzuki had decided, in Hasumi's view, not to waste his energy and was just carrying on without any sense of mission or necessity, or even so much as the 'impatience' of a B film-maker. But oddly, people continued to 'believe in' Suzuki precisely *because* of his lack of seriousness.[23] The discernible irony of Hasumi's alarm over the condition of Japanese cinema points towards the reason why the idea of adaptation as marginal art is significant: the discourse of Japanese cinema depends not only on 'ambitious boys' staking a place on the map of world cinema but at least as much on the routineness, perfunctoriness and half-hearted harmonising of (figuratively) unnamed poets such as Suzuki Noribumi, Ezaki Mio and even Ishihara Yūjirō, all performing one number after the next. Nikkatsu's *Casablanca* karaoke thus followed a poetics of everyday life on the level of sensory experience and contributed, more broadly, to the overall 'theatre of life' called Shōwa.

Notes

1. Iwasaki, Akira, *Gendai eiga geijutsu* (Tokyo: Iwanami shoten, 1971), pp. 192–3.
2. See Alex Zahlten, *The End of Japanese Cinema: Industrial Genres, National Times, and Media* (Durham, NC: Duke University Press, 2017).
3. See Kashima Shigeru, *Yomigaeru Shōwa wakiyaku meigakan* (Tokyo: Kōdansha, 2005).
4. Nozawa Kazuma, *Nikkatsu 1954–71: Eizō o sōzō suru samuraitachi* (Tokyo: Waizu shuppan, 2000), p. 19.
5. Sekikawa Natsuo, *Shōwa ga akarukatta koro* (Tokyo: Bungei shunjū, 2002), p. 107.
6. I thank Tomiko Yoda for guidance about the literary history surrounding *honkadori*.
7. Yomota Inuhiko, *Ajia no naka no Nihon eiga* (Tokyo: Iwanami shoten, 2001), p. 10.
8. See Michael Raine, 'Adaptation as "Transcultural Mimesis"', in Daisuke Miyao (ed.), *The Oxford Handbook of Japanese Cinema* (Oxford: Oxford University Press, 2014), pp. 101–23. [Editors' note: for more on the Japanese reception of Hollywood cinema, see also Chapter 37 by Hiroshi Kitamura in this volume.]
9. As Yomota Inuhiko notes in his reminiscences about discovering traces of European films in Nikkatsu program pictures as a young man. See *Asia no naka no Nihon eiga*, p. 14.
10. Nozawa, *Nikkatsu 1954–71*, p. 84.
11. Kaneko Shūsuke, 'Honkakuteki Nihonsei kayō eiga, moshikuwa misoshiru musical e no tenbō', *Kinema junpō* no. 1257 (January 1999), p. 89.
12. I thank Ayako Saitō and Michael Raine for pointing out the relevance of poetic realism in discussion of an earlier version of this chapter.
13. Dudley Andrew describes the distinction between the two in *Mists of Regret: Culture and Sensibility in Classic French Film* (Princeton, NJ: Princeton University Press, 1995), p. 6.
14. Tom Conley, *Cartographic Cinema* (Minneapolis: University of Minnesota Press, 2006), pp. 3–6.
15. [Editors' note: for more on popular song and Japanese cinema of the period, see also Chapter 24 by Michael Raine in this volume.]
16. This term, glossed with that English, supplied the title of a book published by Tsurumi in 1967, from which the argument presented here derives: *Genkai geijutsu-ron* (Tokyo: Keisō shobō, 1967).
17. See, for example, Tsurumi's essay on the 1952 Daiei period film *Crazed Maiden/Furisode kyōjo*, 'Hitotsu no Nihon eiga-ron', first published in *Eiga hyōron* in 1952, reprinted in *Genkai geijutsu-ron* (Tokyo: Chikuma gakugei shobō, 2015).
18. Tsurumi Shunsuke, *Sengo Nihon no taishū bunkashi: 1945-80-nen* (Tokyo: Iwanami shoten, 1987), pp. 111–15.
19. Yomota Inuhiko, *Nihon eigashi 100-nen* (Tokyo: Shūeisha, 2000), pp. 16–19.
20. Hyon joo Yoo, *Cinema at the Crossroads: Nation and the Subject in East Asian Cinema* (Lanham, MD: Lexington Books, 2012), p. 20.
21. Japanese audio equipment manufacturers began marketing 'singer-less tape recordings' (*kashu nashi rokuon tape*) and microphone systems for playback from at least the early 1970s, though the word karaoke (meaning empty orchestra) appears not to have been popularised until the mid- to late 1970s.
22. 'Tōei Pinku & Violence eiga sai-boom! Suzuki Noribumi kantoku dokusen interview', *livedoor News*, 22 August 2009, <news.livedoor.com/article/detail/4309868>.
23. Hasumi Shigehiko, 'Suzuki Noribumi', in Hasumi Shigehiko, *Shinema no kioku sōchi* (Tokyo: Film art-sha, 1990), pp. 228–31, first published in *Eiga geijutsu* in 1978.

SELECT BIBLIOGRAPHY OF ENGLISH-LANGUAGE BOOKS ON JAPANESE CINEMA

Adachi, Ann, Rebecca Chelamn and Lori Zippay (eds), *Vital Signals: Early Japanese Video Art* (New York: Electronic Arts Intermix, 2010).

Anderer, Paul, *Kurosawa's Rashomon: A Lost Brother, A Vanished City and the Voice inside His Iconic Film* (Cambridge: Pegasus, 2016).

Anderson, Joseph L. and Donald Richie, *The Japanese Film: Art and Industry*, rev. edn (Princeton, NJ: Princeton University Press, 1982).

Andrew, Dudley and Paul Andrew, *Kenji Mizoguchi: A Guide to References and Resources* (Boston, MA: G.K. Hail, 1981).

Andrew, Dudley and Carole Cavanaugh, *Sanshō Dayū* (London: British Film Institute, 2000).

Balmain, Colette, *Introduction to Japanese Horror Cinema* (Edinburgh: Edinburgh University Press, 2008).

Baskett, Michael, *The Attractive Empire: Transnational Film Culture in Imperial Japan* (Honolulu: University of Hawai'i Press, 2008).

Bernardi, Joanne, *Writing in Light: The Silent Scenario and the Japanese Pure Film Movement* (Detroit, MI: Wayne State University Press, 2001).

Bernardi, Joanne and Shōta T. Ogawa (eds), *Routledge Handbook of Japanese Cinema* (Abingdon: Routledge, 2021).

Bingham, Adam, *Contemporary Japanese Cinema since Hana Bi* (Edinburgh: Edinburgh University Press, 2015).

Bock, Audie, *Japanese Film Directors* (Tokyo: Kōdansha International, 1985).

Bolton, Christopher, *Interpreting Anime* (Minneapolis: University of Minnesota Press, 2018).

Bolton, Christopher, Istvan Csicsery-Ronay and Takayuki Tatsumi (eds), *Robot Ghosts and Wired Dreams: Japanese Science Fiction from Origins to Anime* (Minneapolis: University of Minnesota Press, 2009).

Bordwell, David, *Ozu and the Poetics of Cinema* (London: British Film Institute; Princeton, NJ: Princeton University Press, 1988).

Bowyer, Justin (ed.), *The Cinema of Japan and Korea* (London: Wallflower Press, 2004).

Broderick, Mick (ed.), *Hibakusha Cinema: Hiroshima, Nagasaki and the Nuclear Image in Japanese Film* (London: Routledge, 1996).

Brown, Steven T., *Cinema Anime* (Basingstoke: Palgrave Macmillan, 2008).

Brown, Steven T., *Tokyo Cyberpunk: Posthumanism in Japanese Visual Culture* (London: Palgrave Macmillan, 2012).

Buchan, Suzanne (ed.), *Pervasive Animation* (London: Routledge, 2013).

Buckley, Sandra (ed.), *Encyclopaedia of Contemporary Japanese Culture* (New York: Routledge, 2002).

Burch, Noël, *To the Distant Observer: Form and Meaning in the Japanese Cinema* (London: Scolar Press; Berkeley: University of California Press, 1979).

Cather, Kirsten, *The Art of Censorship in Postwar Japan* (Honolulu: University of Hawai'i Press, 2012).

Cazdyn, Eric, *The Flash of Capital: Film and Geopolitics in Japan* (Durham, NC: Duke University Press, 2002).

Chan, Felicia, Angela Karpovich and Xin Zhang (eds), *Genre in Asian Film and Television: New Approaches* (London: Palgrave Macmillan, 2011).

Choi, Jinhee (ed.), *Reorienting Ozu: A Master and His Influence* (Oxford: Oxford University Press, 2018).

Choi, Jinhee and Mitsuyo Wada-Marciano (eds), *Horror to the Extreme: Changing Boundaries in Asian Cinema* (Hong Kong: Hong Kong University Press, 2009).

Clements, Jonathan, *Anime: A History* (London: British Film Institute, 2013).

Clements, Jonathan, *Schoolgirl Milky Crisis: Adventures in the Anime and Manga Trade* (London: Titan Books, 2009).

Coates, Jennifer, *Making Icons: Repetition and the Female Image in Japanese Cinema, 1945–1964* (Hong Kong: University of Hong Kong Press, 2016).

Coleman, Lindsay and David Desser (eds), *Killers, Clients and Kindred Spirits: The Taboo Cinema of Shohei Imamura* (Edinburgh: Edinburgh University Press, 2019).

Condry, Ian, *The Soul of Anime: Collaborative Creativity and Japan's Media Success Story* (Minneapolis: University of Minnesota Press, 2013).

D., Chris, *Gun and Sword: An Encyclopedia of Japanese Gangster Films 1955-1980* (Poison Fang Books, 2013).

Davis, Darrell William, *Picturing Japaneseness: Monumental Style, National Identity, Japanese Film* (New York: Columbia University Press, 1995).

Davis, Darrell William and Emilie Yeuh-yu Yeh, *East Asian Screen Industries* (London: British Film Institute, 2008).

Deamer, David, *Deleuze, Japanese Cinema, and the Atom Bomb: The Spectre of Impossibility* (London: Bloomsbury, 2016).

DeBoer, Stephanie, *Coproducing Asia: Locating Japanese-Chinese Regional Film and Media* (Minneapolis: University of Minnesota Press, 2014).

Denison, Rayna, *Anime* (London: Bloomsbury, 2015).

Dennison, Stephanie and Song Hwee Lim (eds), *Remapping World Cinema: Identity, Culture and Politics in Film* (London: Wallflower, 2006).

Desjardins, Chris, *Outlaw Masters of Japanese Film* (London: I.B.Tauris; New York: Palgrave Macmillan, 2005).

Desser, David, *Eros Plus Massacre: An Introduction to the Japanese New Wave Cinema* (Bloomington: Indiana University Press, 1988).

Desser, David (ed.), *Tokyo Story* (Cambridge: Cambridge University Press, 2010).

Dew, Oliver, *Zainichi Cinema: Korean-in-Japan Film Culture* (London: Palgrave Macmillan, 2016).

Dissanayake, Wimal (ed.), *Melodrama and Asian Cinema* (New York: Cambridge University Press, 1993).

Dorman, Andrew, *Paradoxical Japaneseness: Cultural Representation in 21st Century Japanese Cinema* (Basingstoke: Palgrave Macmillan, 2016).

Dym, Jeffrey, *Benshi, Japanese Silent Film Narrators, and Their Forgotten Narrative Art of Setsumei: A History of Japanese Silent Film Narration* (Lewiston, NY: Edwin Mellen Press, 2003).

Edwards, Matthew (ed.), *The Atomic Bomb in Cinema* (Jefferson, NC: McFarland & Company, 2015).

Eleftheriotis, Dimitris and Gary Needham (eds), *Asian Cinema: A Reader and Guide* (Edinburgh: Edinburgh University Press, 2006).

Field, Simon and Tony Rayns, *Branded to Thrill: The Delirious Cinema of Suzuki Seijun* (London: Institute of Contemporary Arts, 1994).

Freiberg, Freda, *Women in Mizoguchi's Films* (Melbourne: Japanese Studies Centre, Monash University, 1981).

Fujiki, Hideaki, *Making Personas: Transnational Film Stardom in Modern Japan* (Cambridge, MA: Harvard University Asia Center, 2013).

Fujitani, Takashi, *Race for Empire: Koreans as Japanese and Japanese as Americans during World War II* (Berkeley: University of California Press, 2013).

Fukushima, Yukio and Abé Mark Nornes (eds), *The Japan/American Film Wars: World War II Propaganda and Its Cultural Contexts* (Langhorne, PA: Harwood Academic Publishers, 1994).

Furuhata, Yuriko, *Cinema of Actuality: Japanese Avant-Garde Filmmaking in the Season of Image Politics* (Durham, NC: Duke University Press, 2013).

Galbraith, Patrick W. and Jason G. Karlin (eds), *Media Convergence in Japan* (Ann Arbor, MI: Kinema Club, 2016).

Galbraith, Stuart, *The Emperor and the Wolf: The Lives and Films of Akira Kurosawa and Toshiro Mifune* (London: Faber & Faber, 2001).

Galbraith, Stuart, *Japanese Cinema* (Cologne: Taschen, 2009).

Galbraith, Stuart, *The Japanese Filmography: A Complete Reference to 209 Filmmakers and the Over 1250 Films Released in the United States, 1900 through 1994* (Jefferson, NC: McFarland & Co, 1996).

Galloway, Patrick, *Stray Dogs and Lone Wolves: The Samurai Film Handbook* (Albany, CA: Stone Bridge Press, 2005).

Gerow, Aaron, *Kitano Takeshi* (London: British Film Institute, 2007).

Gerow, Aaron, *Page of Madness: Cinema and Modernity in 1920s Japan* (Ann Arbor: Center for Japanese Studies, University of Michigan, 2008).

Gerow, Aaron, *Visions of Japanese Modernity: Articulations of Cinema, Nation, and Spectatorship, 1895–1925* (Berkeley: University of California Press, 2010).

Gerow, Aaron and Abé Mark Nornes (eds), *In Praise of Film Studies: Essays in Honor of Makino Mamoru* (Ann Arbor, MI: Kinema Club, 2001).

Gibbs, Michael H., *Film and Political Culture in Postwar Japan* (New York: Peter Lang, 2012).

González-López, Irene and Michael Smith (eds), *Tanaka Kinuyo: Nation, Stardom and Female Subjectivity* (Edinburgh: Edinburgh University Press, 2018).

Goodwin, James, *Akira Kurosawa and Intertextual Cinema* (Baltimore, MD: Johns Hopkins University Press, 1994).

Grossman, Andrew (ed.), *Queer Asian Cinema* (Binghamton, NY: Harrington Park Press, 2000).

Harper, Jim, *Flowers from Hell: The Modern Japanese Horror Film* (Hereford: Noir Publishing, 2009).

Hashimoto, Shinobu, *Compound Cinematics: Akira Kurosawa and I* (New York: Vertical, 2006).

High, Peter B., *The Imperial Screen: Japanese Film Culture in the Fifteen Years' War, 1931–1945* (Madison: University of Wisconsin Press, 2003).

Hirano, Kyoko, *Mr. Smith Goes to Tokyo: Japanese Cinema under the American Occupation, 1945-1952* (Washington, DC: Smithsonian Institution Press, 1992).

Hori, Hikari, *Promiscuous Media: Film and Visual Culture in Imperial Japan, 1926-45* (Ithaca, NY: Cornell University Press, 2017).

Hunt, Leon and Leung Wing-Fai (eds), *East Asian Cinemas: Exploring Transnational Connections on Film* (London: I.B.Tauris, 2009).

Hutchinson, Rachael (ed.), *Negotiating Censorship in Modern Japan* (Abingdon: Routledge, 2013).

Iwabuchi, Koichi (ed.), *Feeling Asian Modernities: Transnational Consumption of Japanese TV Dramas* (Hong Kong: Hong Kong University Press, 2004).

Iwabuchi, Koichi, *Recentering Globalization: Popular Culture and Japanese Transnationalism* (Durham, NC: Duke University Press, 2002).

Jacoby, Alexander, *A Critical Handbook of Japanese Film Directors* (Albany, CA: Stone Bridge Press, 2008).

Joo, Woojeong, *The Cinema of Ozu Yasujiro: Histories of the Everyday* (Edinburgh: Edinburgh University Press, 2017).

Kazsa, Gregory, *The State and Mass Media in Japan, 1918–1945* (Berkeley: University of California Press, 1998).

Kim, Dong Hoon, *Eclipsed Cinema: The Film Culture of Colonial Korea* (Edinburgh: Edinburgh University Press, 2017).

Kirihara, Donald, *Patterns of Time: Mizoguchi and the 1930s* (Madison: University of Wisconsin Press, 1992).

Kitamura, Hiroshi, *Screening Enlightenment: Hollywood and the Cultural Reconstruction of Defeated Japan* (Ithaca, NY: Cornell University Press, 2010).

Ko, Mika, *Japanese Cinema and Otherness: Nationalism, Multiculturalism and the Problem of Japaneseness* (London: Routledge, 2011).

Kurosawa, Akira, *Something Like an Autobiography*, trans. Audie E. Bock (New York: Vintage Books, 1983).

Lamarre, Thomas, *The Anime Ecology: A Genealogy of Television, Animation and Game Media* (Minneapolis: University of Minnesota Press, 2018).

Lamarre, Thomas, *The Anime Machine: A Media Theory of Animation* (Minneapolis: University of Minnesota Press, 2009).

Lamarre, Thomas, *Shadows on the Screen: Tanizaki Jun'ichirō on Cinema and 'Oriental' Aesthetics* (Ann Arbor: Center for Japanese Studies, University of Michigan, 2005).

Lau, Jenny Kwok Wah (ed.), *Multiple Modernities: Cinemas and Popular Media in Transcultural East Asia* (Philadelphia, PA: Temple University Press, 2003).

Le Blanc, Michelle and Colin Odell, *Akira* (London: British Film Institute, 2014).

Lee, Laura, *Japanese Cinema between Frames* (Basingstoke: Palgrave Macmillan, 2017).

Lippit, Akira Mizuta, *Atomic Light: Shadow Optics* (Minneapolis: University of Minnesota Press, 2005).

Macias, Patrick, *Tokyoscope: The Japanese Cult Film Companion* (San Jose, CA: Cadence Books, 2004).

Magnan-Park, Aaron Han Joon, Gina Marchetti and See Kam Tan (eds), *The Palgrave Handbook of Asian Cinema* (London: Palgrave Macmillan, 2018).

Marran, Christine L., *Ecology without Culture: Aesthetics for a Toxic World* (Minneapolis: University of Minnesota Press, 2017).

Mars-Jones, Adam, *Noriko Smiling* (London: Notting Hill Press, 2011).

McCarthy, Helen, *Hayao Miyazaki: Master of Japanese Animation* (Albany, CA: Stone Bridge Press, 2004).

McCarthy, Helen and Jonathan Clements (eds), *The Anime Encyclopedia*, rev. and exp. edn (Albany, CA: Stone Bridge Press, 2007).

McDonald, Keiko I., *From Book to Screen: Modern Japanese Literature in Film* (New York: M.E. Sharpe, 1999).

McDonald, Keiko I., *Mizoguchi* (Woodbridge, CT: Twayne Publishers, 1985).

McDonald, Keiko I., *Reading a Japanese Film* (Honolulu: University of Hawai'i Press, 2006).

McDonald, Keiko I. (ed.), *Ugetsu* (New Brunswick, NJ: Rutgers University Press, 1993).

McRoy, Jay, *Japanese Horror Cinema* (Edinburgh: Edinburgh University Press, 2005).

McRoy, Jay, *Nightmare Japan: Contemporary Japanese Horror Cinema* (Amsterdam: Rodopi, 2008).

Mellen, Joan, *In the Realm of the Senses* (London: British Film Institute, 2004).

Mellen, Joan, *Seven Samurai* (London: British Film Institute, 2002).

Mellen, Joan, *The Waves at Genji's Door: Japan through Its Cinema* (New York: Pantheon Books, 1976).

Mes, Tom, *Agitator: The Cinema of Takashi Miike* (Goldaming: FAB Press, 2006).

Mes, Tom and Jasper Sharp, *The Midnight Eye Guide to New Japanese Film* (Albany, CA: Stone Bridge Press, 2005).

Miyao, Daisuke, *The Aesthetics of Shadow: Lighting and Japanese Cinema* (Durham, NC: Duke University Press, 2013).

Miyao, Daisuke (ed.), *The Oxford Handbook of Japanese Cinema* (Oxford: Oxford University Press, 2014).

Miyao, Daisuke, *Sessue Hayakawa* (Durham, NC: Duke University Press, 2007).

Nagisa, Ōshima, *Cinema, Censorship, and the State*, ed. Annette Michelson, trans. Dawn Lawson (Cambridge, MA: MIT Press, 1993).

Napier, Susan J., *Anime from Akira to Howl's Moving Castle: Experiencing Contemporary Japanese Animation*, rev. edn (London: Palgrave Macmillan, 2005).

Napier, Susan J., *From Impressionism to Anime: Japan as Fantasy and Fan Cult in the Mind of the West* (New York: Palgrave Macmillan, 2007).

Nogami, Teruyo, *Waiting for the Weather: Making Movies with Akira Kurosawa*, trans. Juliet Winters Carpenter (Albany, CA: Stonebridge Press, 2006).

Nolletti, Arthur Jr., *The Cinema of Gosho Heinosuke: Laughter through Tears* (Bloomington: Indiana University Press, 2005).

Nolletti, Arthur Jr. and David Desser (eds), *Reframing Japanese Cinema* (Bloomington: Indiana University Press, 1992).

Nornes, Abé Mark, *Cinema Babel: Translating Global Cinema* (Minneapolis: University of Minnesota Press, 2007).

Nornes, Abé Mark, *Forest of Pressure: Ogawa Shinsuke and Postwar Japanese Documentary* (Minneapolis: University of Minnesota Press, 2007).

Nornes, Abé Mark, *Japanese Documentary Film: The Meiji Era through Hiroshima* (Minneapolis: University of Minnesota Press, 2003).

Nornes, Abé Mark (ed.), *The Pink Book: The Japanese Eroduction and its Contexts* (Ann Arbor, MI: Kinema Club, 2014).

Nornes, Abé Mark and Aaron Gerow, *Research Guide to Japanese Film Studies* (Ann Arbor: Center for Japanese Studies, University of Michigan, 2009).

Nygren, Scott, *Time Frames: Japanese Cinema and the Unfolding of History* (Minneapolis: University of Minnesota Press, 2007).

Ōshima Nagisa, *Cinema, Censorship, and the State: The Writings of Nagisa Oshima, 1956–1978*, trans. Dawn Lawson (Cambridge, MA: MIT Press, 1993).

Osmond, Andrew, *Spirited Away* (London: British Film Institute, 2008).

Otmazgin, Nissim and Eyal Ben-Ari (eds), *Popular Culture and the State in East and Southeast Asia* (London: Routledge, 2012).

Patten, Fred, *Watching Anime, Reading Manga: 25 Years of Essays and Reviews* (Albany, CA: Stone Bridge Press, 2004).

Phillips, Alastair and Julian Stringer (eds), *Japanese Cinema: Texts and Contexts* (London: Routledge, 2007).

Posadas, Baryon Tensor, *Double Visions, Double Fictions: The Doppelgänger in Japanese Film and Literature* (Minneapolis: University of Minnesota Press, 2018).

Prince, Stephen, *A Dream of Resistance: The Cinema of Kobayashi Masaki* (New Brunswick, NJ: Rutgers University Press, 2017).

Prince, Stephen, *The Warrior's Camera: The Cinema of Akira Kurosawa* (Princeton, NJ: Princeton University Press, 1999).

Prindle, Tamae, *Women in Japanese Cinema: Alternative Perspectives* (Honolulu: University of Hawai'i Press, 2013).

Quandt, James (ed.), *Kon Ichikawa* (Toronto: Toronto International Film Festival Group, 2001).

Quandt, James (ed.), *Shohei Imamura* (Toronto: Toronto International Film Festival Group, 1999).

Rayns, Tony, *Eiga: 25 Years of Japanese Cinema* (Edinburgh: Edinburgh International Film Festival Catalogue, 1984).

Richie, Donald, *The Films of Akira Kurosawa* (Berkeley: University of California Press, 1998).

Richie, Donald (ed.), *Focus on Rashomon* (Englewood Cliffs, NJ: Prentice Hall, 1972).

Richie, Donald, *A Hundred Years of Japanese Film* (Tokyo: Kōdansha, 2005).

Richie, Donald, *Japanese Cinema: Film Style and National Character* (New York: Doubleday, 1971).

Richie, Donald, *Ozu: His Life and Films* (Berkeley: University of California Press, 1992).

Richie, Donald (ed.), *Rashomon: Akira Kurosawa the Director* (New Brunswick, NJ: Rutgers University Press, 1987).

Ridgely, Steven C., *Japanese Counterculture: The Antiestablishment Art of Terayama Shuji* (Minneapolis: University of Minnesota Press, 2011).

Russell, Catherine, *The Cinema of Naruse Mikio: Women and Japanese Modernity* (Durham, NC: Duke University Press, 2008).

Russell, Catherine, *Classical Japanese Cinema Revisited* (London: Continuum, 2011).

Salomon, Harald, *Views of the Dark Valley: Japanese Cinema and the Culture of Nationalism, 1937–1945* (Wiesbaden: Harrassowitz Verlag, 2011).

Sas, Miryam, *Experimental Arts in Postwar Japan: Moments of Encounter, Engagement, and Imagined Return* (Cambridge, MA: Harvard University Asia Center, 2011).

Satō Tadao, *Currents in Japanese Cinema*, trans. Gregory Barrett (New York: Kōdansha, 2000).

Satō Tadao, *Kenji Mizoguchi and the Art of Japanese Cinema*, trans. Aruna Vasudev and Latika Padagaonkar (Oxford: Berg, 2008).

Schilling, Mark, *Contemporary Japanese Film* (New York: Weatherhill, 2004).

Schilling, Mark, *No Borders, No Limits: Nikkatsu Action Cinema* (Goldaming: FAB Press, 2007).

Schilling, Mark, *The Yakuza Movie Book: A Guide to Japanese Gangster Films* (Albany, CA: Stone Bridge Press, 2003).

Schrader, Paul, *Transcendental Style in Film: Ozu, Bresson, and Dreyer* (Berkeley: University of California Press; New York: Da Capo Press, 1972).

Shapiro, Jerome F., *Atomic Bomb Cinema: The Apocalyptic Imagination on Film* (London and New York: Routledge, 2001).

Sharp, Jasper (ed.), *Historical Dictionary of Japanese Cinema* (Lanham, MD: Scarecrow Press, 2011).

Silver, Alain (ed.), *Samurai Film* (New York: The Overlook Press, 2005).

Silverberg, Miriam, *Erotic Grotesque Nonsense: The Mass Culture of Japanese Modern Times* (Berkeley: University of California Press, 2006).

Solgenfrei, Carol Fisher, *Unspeakable Acts: The Avant-Garde Theatre of Terayama Shuji and Postwar Japan* (Honolulu: University of Hawai'i Press, 2006).

Stahl, David C., *Narrative Memory, Trauma and Recovery in Japanese Literature and Film* (London: Routledge, 2019).

Standish, Isolde, *Myth and Masculinity in the Japanese Cinema: Towards a Political Reading of the 'Tragic Hero'* (London: Curzon, 2000).

Standish, Isolde, *A New History of Japanese Cinema: A Century of Narrative Film* (London: Continuum, 2005).

Standish, Isolde, *Politics, Porn and Protest: Japanese Avant-Garde Cinema in the 1960s and 1970s* (London: Continuum, 2011).

Stein, Wayne and Marc DiPaolo (eds), *Ozu International: Essays on the Global Influence of a Japanese Auteur* (London: Bloomsbury, 2016).

Steinberg, Marc, *Anime's Media Mix: Franchising Toys and Characters in Japan* (Minneapolis: University of Minnesota Press, 2012).

Steinberg, Marc and Alexander Zahlten (eds), *Media Theory in Japan* (Durham, NC: Duke University Press, 2017).

Stoll, Diana C. (ed.), *Tokyo 1955–1970: A New Avant-Garde* (New York: Museum of Modern Art, 2012).

Tam, King-fai, Timothy Y. Tsu and Sandra Wilson (eds), *Chinese and Japanese Films on the Second World War* (New York: Routledge, 2015).

Tasogawa, Hiroshi, *All the Emperor's Men: Kurosawa's Pearl Harbor* (Milwaukee, WI: Applause, 2012).

Taylor-Jones, Kate, *Divine Work: Japanese Colonial Cinema and Its Legacy* (London: Bloomsbury Academic, 2017).

Teo, Stephen, *The Asian Film Experience: Styles, Spaces, Theory* (London: Routledge, 2012).

Tezuka, Yoshiharu, *Japanese Cinema Goes Global: Filmworkers' Journeys* (Hong Kong: Hong Kong University Press 2012).

Thornton, Sybil, *The Japanese Period Film: A Critical Analysis* (Jefferson, NC: McFarland & Co., 2008).

Tsutsui, M. William and Michiko Ito (eds), *In Godzilla's Footsteps: Japanese Pop Culture Icons on the Global Stage* (New York: Palgrave Macmillan, 2006)

Turim, Maureen, *The Films of Oshima Nagisa: Images of a Japanese Iconoclast* (Berkeley: University of California Press, 1998).

Usui, Chizuru (ed.), *The Guide to Japanese Film Industry and Co-Production* (Tokyo: UniJapan, 2009).

Vick, Tom, *Time and Place Are Nonsense: The Films of Seijun Suzuki* (Washington, DC: Freer Gallery of Art and Arthur M. Sackler Gallery, 2015).

Wada-Marciano, Mitsuyo, *Japanese Cinema in the Digital Age* (Honolulu: University of Hawai'i Press, 2012).

Wada-Marciano, Mitsuyo, *Nippon Modern: Japanese Cinema of the 1920s and 1930s* (Honolulu: University of Hawai'i Press, 2008).

Washburn, Dennis and Carole Cavanaugh (eds), *Word and Image in Japanese Cinema* (Cambridge: Cambridge University Press, 2001).

Watson, Robert N., *Throne of Blood* (London: British Film Institute, 2014).

Weisser, Thomas, *Japanese Cinema: Essential Handbook* (Miami, FL: Vital Books, 2004).

Weisser, Thomas, *Japanese Cinema Encyclopedia: The Sex Films* (Miami, FL: Vital Books, 2004).

White, Jerry, *The Films of Kiyoshi Kurosawa: Master of Fear* (Albany, CA: Stone Bridge Press, 2009).

Wild, Peter, *Akira Kurosawa* (London: Reaktion Books, 2014).

Yau, Shuk-ting Kinnia, *Japanese and Hong Kong Film Industries: Understanding the Origins of East Asian Film Networks* (London: Routledge, 2010).

Yasui, Yoshio and Noriko Tanaka (eds), *The Legendary Filmmaking Collective NDU and Nunokawa Tetsuro* (Kobe: Cinematrix and Kobe Documentary Film Festival Committee, 2012).

Yoda, Tomiko and Harry Harootunian (eds), *Japan after Japan: Social and Cultural Life from the Recessionary 1990s to the Present* (Durham, NC: Duke University Press, 2006).

Yomota, Inuhiko, *What Is Japanese Cinema? A History*, trans. Philip Kaffen (New York: Columbia University Press, 2019).

Yoo, Hyon Joo, *Cinema at the Crossroads: Nation and the Subject in East Asian Cinema* (Lanham, MD: Lexington Books, 2012).

Yoshida, Kijū, *Ozu's Anti-Cinema*, trans. Daisuke Miyao and Kyoko Hirano (Ann Arbor: Center for Japanese Studies, University of Michigan, 2003).

Yoshimoto, Mitsuhiro, *Kurosawa: Film Studies and Japanese Cinema* (Durham, NC: Duke University Press, 2000).

Yoshimoto, Mitsuhiro (ed.), *Television, Japan, and Globalization*, repr. edn (Ann Arbor: Center for Japanese Studies, University of Michigan, 2016).

Zahlten, Alexander, *The End of Japanese Cinema* (Durham, NC: Duke University Press, 2017).

INDEX

À bout de souffle (1959) 42
A2-B-C (2013) 385
Abashiri bangaichi (1965–8) *351*, 351–2, 354, 359*n*13, 526
Abashiri bangaichi: Kōya no taiketsu (1966) 526
Abashiri Prison, see Abashiri bangaichi (1965–8)
Abe, Akira 455
Abe, Kōbō 364
Abe, Shūya 195
An Account of the Chivalrous Commoners of Japan, see Nihon kyōkaku den (1964–71)
action films 118, 559
'actor-network-theory' 165, 176*n*13
actors
    kabuki 550
    in post-war period 182
    in the studio system 111–12
    (***see also*** stars)
An Actor's Revenge, see Yukinojō henge (1935)
Actress, see Joyū (1947)
actresses 31–2
    birth of 180–2
    decline 182
    social connotations of word 245
    (***see also*** stars)
Adachi 8mm Film Archive 223
Adachi, Kan 140–1
Adachi, Masao 198, 199, 466
Adachi no kioku (2013) 221
adaptations 16, 82, 183, 556–66
    approaches 556–7
    and authorship 40
    early cinema 328
    and geo-politics 559–60
    of horror plays 300
    josei eiga 97
    of Kikuchi's work 98
    literary 41

of literature 85, 296*n*35
of manga 203–13
as 'marginal art' 564–6
television anime 495
of Western works for anime 495
(***see also*** program picture)
adult films, *see* 'pink films'; pornography
The Adventure of Denchu-Kozo, see Denchū kozō no bōken (1987) 170
advertising 1, 3, 11, 120, 344, 538
    and age restrictions 142
    animated 319
    for *kaiki eiga* 299
    for *Sakuran* 208
    under studio system 121
Affron, Charles & Affon, Mirella Jona; *Sets in Motion* 259
Aga ni ikiru (1992) 373
age ratings 142, 146, 264, 497
Agency for Cultural Affairs 223
Aguirre, the Wrath of God (1973) 535
Ahiru to kamo no coin locker (2007) 82
Ai no bōrei (1978) 545
Ai no corrida (1976) 545
Aihwa Ong 491
'Aikoku kōshinkyoku' 338
Ainu 272, 406*n*44, 479, 522, 530
Aizen katsura (1938) 334*n*22
Aka no inbō (1952) 455
AKA Serial Killer, see Ryakushō renzoku shasatsuma (1969)
Akagawa, Kōichi 129
Akagi, Keiichirō 'Tony' 558
Akai hatoba (1958) 562
Akai kōya (1961) 521
Akai satsui (1964) 534
Akanishi Kakita (1936) *290*, 290–1, 296*n*33
Akarui katei seikatsu (1950) 456
Akasaki, Yōko 164, 171
Akasegawa, Genpei 199
Akasen chitai (1956) 273

Akibiyori (1960) 411
Akiyama, Kiyoshi 352, 358
Akiyama, Kuniharu 269, 270
Akutagawa, Ryūnosuke 129
    In a Grove/Yabu no naka 82, 91
    Rashomon/Rashōmon 82
Alberoni, Francesco 180
Alexander Nevsky (1938) 272
All Living Things Are Friends: Lullabies of Birds, Insects and Fish, see Ikimono minna tomodachi: Tori, mushi, sakana no komoriuta (1987)
All Must Live: People, Insects, Birds, see Minna ikinakerebanaranai: Hito, mushi, tori (1984)
All Quiet on the Western Front (1930) 140
Allen, Matthew 537, 538
Allen, Robert 58
Allen, Woody 561
Alps no shōjo Haiji (1974) 495, 495–6
Althusser, Louis 54
Altman, Rick 137*n*44, 325, 335, 336–7, 340, 343, 345*n*3
Altman, Robert 231
Always: Sanchōme no yūhi series (2005–12) 262, 407, 432, 527
Ama no obake yashiki (1959) 306
amateur film
    gauge and stock 217–20
    projecting equipment 227*n*53
    and sound 222, 227*n*56
    in wartime 219
America no bokuchiku (1949) 456
America no joshi daigaku (1948) 456
America no salaryman (1951) 456
American Film Institute (AFI) 238
An American in Paris (1951) 561
American Stock Raising, see America no bokuchiku (1949)
An American Women's College, see America no joshi daigaku (1948)

Index

Anderson, Benedict 31
Anderson, Joseph L. 25, 38, 42
   on *benshi* narration 27
Anderson, Joseph L & Richie, Donald;
   The Japanese Film: Art and Industry 4, 5, 25, 38, 42, 109
Ang, Ien 57
Ani imōto (1936) 40
animation
   advertising 319–20
   Chinese 451
   cinema 315–18
   cut-out 314
   development of techniques 313, 314
   early cinema 311–15
   experimental 194, 198
   full vs limited 318–19
   gender in 105n34
   government initiatives 316
   import of US series 318
   new media 321–2
   original video animation 320
   production costs 314
   short films 313, 315
   stop-motion 196
   wartime 315, 316–17
   (*see also* anime)
Animation for the Stage, **see** *Butai no tameno animation* (1960)
anime 1, 8, 14, 310–24
   adaptations of Western works 495–6
   and art 311
   and cultural diplomacy 498
   digital technology 321–2
   increased popularity 310
   and international perception of Japan 323n2
   loose definition 310–11, 321, 322
   vs manga 312
   and 'media mix' 17
   orientalism 322n1
   origin and definition of term 310–11
   Oshii on 321
   out-sourcing 310
   pre-cinema influences 311, 312
   in South Africa 495–6
   spectatorship in 60
   superflat style 312
   and technological boom 320
   on television 318–21, 324n30
   (*see also* animation)

Annett, Sandra; *Anime Fan Communities* 60
Another Day of a Housewife (1977) 195, 196
ANPO, **see** US-Japan Security Treaty
ANPO jōyaku (1959) 466
Anti-Monopoly Act 109
Anti-prostitution Law 187–8
Aoi ribbon to kinpai (1949) 456
Aoki, Tsuruko 28
Aoyama, Shinji 47, 169
Aoyama, Sugisaku 251
Apartheid 495–6
Applause (1929) 336
Arashi, Kanjūrō 115, 288, 534
archives 10, 13, 214–27
   and amateur film 215–17
   as community projects 223–4
   digital 221
   digitisation 217
   ethics of digitisation 222
   vs film festivals 215
   local 221
   network archives 215
   reformatting 217
   selection criteria 217–20
   (*see also* specific archives)
Arima, Ineko 424
Arima neko (1937) 301, 303
Arima neko (1956) 302
Armageddon: The Great Battle with Genma, **see** *Genma taisen* (1983)
Armed Forces Radio Service (AFRS) 338
Armored Fleet Dairugger XV, **see** *Kikō kantai dairagā fifteen* (1983)
Army Aviation Film Production Committee 115
Arnheim, Rudolf 54, 69, 70
Art Film Association 199–200
Art Theatre Guild (ATG) 43, 120, 131, 167, 190n37, 197
   and protest movements 466
Aru kikan joshi (1963) 473
Aru shōwashi: Jibunshi no kokoromi (1975) 368
Aruitemo aruitemo (2008) 49
Asahi Film Company 129
Ash, Ian Thomas 381, 385
Ashes to Honey: Toward a Sustainable Future, **see** *Mitsubachi no haoto to chikyū no kaiten* (2011)
Asian Film Festival 517n19

'Asianism' 493–4
Assatsu no mori – Takasaki keizai daigaku tōsō no kiroku (1967) 15, 362, 367, 467, 472–4, 474
   critical response 364
   exhibition of 364, 474
Association for Asian Studies (AAS) 10
Association for Cultural Typhoon 10
Association of Documentary Arts 429
Association of Moving Image Archivists (AMIA) 214, 216
Astaire, Fred 254
Astro Boy, **see** *Tetsuwan atom* (TV)
Atarashii rinjin (1952) 456
Atarashiki tsuchi (1937) 130, 272, 405n6, 453, 546
Atman (1975) 195
Atsugi, Taka 105n34
Attack on Titan, **see** *Shingeki no kyojin* (TV 2014–15)
Audition (1999) 299, 307, 554n9
Autant-Lara, Claude 41
auteur cinema 8, 38–52
   and gender 96
   post-war 557
   scholars focus on 11
authorship 8, 11, 38–52, 98, 513
   in early cinema 28
   female 100–1
   French origins of concept 39
   Japanese theories of 39
   modern cinema 47–50
   and modernism 83–4
   and Orientalism 83
   postwar era 40–7
   in postwar era 39
   prewar era 40
   in program pictures 558
   signs and signatures 49
   Western academia on 38
   (*see also* auteur cinema; *sakka*)
Autry, Gene 337
An Autumn Afternoon, **see** *Sanma no aji* (1962)
Avalanche, **see** *Nadare* (1937)
avant-garde 194
Ayaushi!! Kaiketsu Kurozukin (1960) 526
Aznavour, Charles 179
Azuma, Hiroki 8, 319

Babes in Arms (1937) 339
The Baby Carriage, **see** *Ubaguruma* (1956)

Badlands (1979) 87
Bai she chuan, **see** *Byaku fujin no yōren* (1956)
Baimao nü films 451
Baishe chuan (1939) 442
bakumatsu 274, 282n35
Bakumatsu taiyō den (1957) 273, 562
Bakushū (1951) 60, 98, 99
Bakuto (1964) 352
Bal, Mieke 82
Balázs, Béla 54, 69
Ballad of Narayama, **see** *Narayama bushikō*
Banchō sarayashiki (1914) 300, 307
Banderas, Antonio 239
Bandō, Tsumasaburō 115, 288
Bangiku (1954) 422
Banshun (1949) 338, 453
Bara no sōretsu (1969) 120, 187, 195
The Barga Prairie, **see** *Sōgen Barga* (1936)
Barnes, George 233, 235
Barsacq, Léon
  Le Décor de film, 1895–1969 260
Barthes, Roland 186, 190n32
  The Death of the Author 42
  Empire of Signs 6, 27, 550–1
Basic Act for the Promotion of Art and Culture 173
Baskett, Michael 167, 440
The Battle of Dingjunshan, **see** *Dingjunshan* (1903)
The Battle Front for the Liberation of Japan – Summer in Sanrizuka, **see** *Nihon kaihō sensen – Sanrizuka no natsu* (1968)
Battle of Shanghai 440
The Battle of the Honnoji Temple, **see** *Honnōji kassen* (1908)
Battle rowaiaru (2000) 138, 145–8, *147*, 298
  awards 150n62
  ban in US 150n65
  casting 148
Battle Royale, **see** *Battle rowaiaru* (2000)
Battles without Honour or Humanity, **see** *Jingi naki tatakai* (1973)
Battleship Potemkin (1925) 69
Baudry, Jean-Louis 54
Bazin, André 44, 50, 54, 76, 158
Beast King GoLion, **see** *Hyakujū-ō golion* (1981)
Before Dawn, **see** *Reimei izen* (1931)

Behind the Wall, **see** *Kabe no naka no himegoto* (1965)
Being Two Isn't Easy, **see** *Watashi wa nisai* (1962)
Benedict, Ruth; *The Chrysanthemum and the Sword: Patterns of Japanese Culture* 4
Benjamin, Walter 54, 294, 434n32
Bennett, Bruce 152
benshi 3, 6, 25, 26, 40, 126, 134, 160
  Burch on 27
  criticism of 31
  Dym on 27
  female 99, 100
  rules governing 139
  strikes and protests 160
Bentham, Jeremy 72
Berlin: Die Sinfonie der Grosstadt (1927) 194, 201n4, 428, 434n45
Berlin Film Festival 172, 174
Berlin: Symphony of a Great City, **see** *Berlin: Die Sinfonie der Grosstadt* (1927)
Bernardi, Joanne 27–8, 32
Berque, Augustin 419, 421, 432
Best Years of Our Lives (1946) 236
The Betrothed, **see** *Nagasugita haru* (1957)
Beyond the Great Wall, **see** *Wang Zhao Jun* (1964)
Bhabba, Homi 58
Bierce, Ambrose
  The Moonlit Road 91
The Big Country (1958) 519
Birii za kid no atarashii yoake (1988) 525
Biruma no tategoto (1956) 82
Bizet, George 254
Black Cat's Revenge, **see** *Kaidan nobori ryū* (1970)
Black Hooded Man, **see** *Kaiketsu kurozukin* series (1953–60)
The Black Hooded Man in Peril, **see** *Ayaushi!! Kaiketsu Kurozukin* (1960)
Black Lizard, **see** *Kurotokage* (1968)
Black Rose Mansion, **see** *Kurobara no yakata* (1969)
The Blair Witch Project (1999) 298
Blind Woman's Curse, **see** *Kaidan nobori ryū* (1970)
Blood and Sand, **see** *Chi to suna* (1965)
Blood: The Last Vampire (2000) 322

Bloom, Harold 556
The Blue Angel, **see** *Der Blaue Engel*
Blue Ribbon and Gold Cup: CIE Film Sketch No. 8, **see** *Aoi ribbon to kinpai* (1949)
Boai (1942) 440, 446–50
  cast 447
  historians on 446
  as propaganda 447
  structure 446
Bobo, Jacqueline 58
Bolero (1934) 254
Bordwell, David 6, 26, 27, 47, 82, 269, 295n17
  on *Higanbana* 424
  on Mizoguchi Kenji 261
  Making Meaning 55
  Narration in the Fiction Film 55
  on 'Othering' of Japanese cinema 68
  on Ozu 83–4
  Ozu and the Poetics of Cinema 7, 38, 56
  on production design 263
  on *Rashomon* 84–5
Bored Hatamoto, **see** *Hatamoto taikutsu otoko* (1958)
Bōrei kaibyō yashiki (1958) 304, 305
The Boshin War 293, 297n45
Bow, Clara 60
box-office
  attendance figures 124n45
  decline in late 20th century 238
  director as draw 43
  in modern era 131
  for musicals 347n29
  post-war boom 182, 547
  Rashomon 92n2
  Shintōhō performance 116
  in wartime Shanghai 441
  wartime studios 115
  yakuza films 349, 358n5
Boys Over Flowers, **see** *Hana yori dango* (1995)
Boys Over Flowers (TV 1996–7) 209
Boys Over Flowers Final, **see** *Hana yori dango final* (2008)
Boys Over Flowers franchise 209–11
  overseas adaptations 209
Brain Man, **see** *Nō otoko* (2013)
Branigan, Edward 6, 82, 83
Brave Red Flower of the North, **see** *Nihon jokyō den: Makka na dokyōbana* (1970)

Brereton, Patrick 381
Brewer, Theresa 339
Brewster, Ben 249
Brides of the Frontier, see *Kaitaku no hanayome* (1943)
Bridge, see *Qiao* (1949)
Bright Red Flower of Courage, see *Nihon jokyōden: Makkana dokyōbana* (1970)
British Film Journal 10
Brooks, Peter 325
Brother (2000) 50
Brown, L. Russell 523
Browning, Robert; *The Ring and the Book* 91
Brundson, Charlotte 421
Buddha, see *Shaka* (1961)
Buddhism 71, 96, 263, 401
Buell, Lawrence 379
Bungei Konwakai Award 40
bunka eiga 316–17, 361
bunraku 6, 56, 253
Bunraku (2007) 493
Burch, Noël 7, 11, 26, 27, 33, 39, 47, 82
 criticism of 27
 To the Distant Observer: Form and Meaning in the Japanese Cinema 6, 26, 46, 56, 83
 on kabuki acting 246
 Life to Those Shadows 55
 on Pure Film Movement 28, 31
 Theory of Film Practice 54–5
The Burmese Harp, see *Biruma no tategoto* (1956)
The Burning of a Brave Warrior, see *Sōshi shokuten* (1937)
The Burning Sky, see *Moyuru ōzora* (1940)
A Burning Star, see *Gyōsei* (1999)
bushidō 141, 145, 246
Buta to gunkan (1964) 350
Butai no tameno animation (1960) 198
Butler, Judith 99–100
Byaku fujin no yōren (1956) 506, *507*, 512–16

Das Cabinet des Dr. Caligari (1920) 557
Café Lumière, see *Kōhī jikō* (2003)
The Caged Bird, see *Kago no tori* (1924)
Cahiers du cinéma (journal) 39
 on Japanese cinema 41
Cahiers du cinéma Japon 47

Caldwell, James 512
Call of the Fog Horn (1960), see *Muteki ga ore o yondeiru* (1960)
cameras 232
 in animation 314
 digital 240
 and experimental film 193
'camp' 181
Cannes Film Festival 168, 172, 177*n*35, 543
 ban on Japanese films 545
capitalism 3, 5, 26, 96, 456, 490–1
 cold War 514
 criticism of 475
 and culture 285
 and Imperialism 32
 industrial 409
 nature of 72
 in post-war period 325
 social impacts 367, 395, 514
 and Western hegemony 490–1
The Captain's Daughter, see *Taii no musume* (1929)
Carax, Leos 549
Carroll, Noël 309*n*24
Casablanca (1942) 16, 265, 556, 560–4
 historical accuracy 563
 remakes 562
Castle in the Sky, see *Tenkū no shiro Rapyuta* (1985)
Cather, Kirsten 142
Caughie, John 38–9, 42
Cavalcanti, Alberto 194
Cayette, Andre 41
Cazdyn, Eric 42
The Ceiling at Utsunomiya, see *Utsunomiya no tenjō* (1956)
celluloid 314
censorship 13, 138–51
 aims of 138
 of *Battle rowaiaru* 146–7
 and depictions of sexuality 139, 142–3, 264, 265
 extra-marital relationships 245
 in history 138–40
 of ideology 139
 of *kaiki eiga* 302
 of Soviet films 70
 of suicide 246
 under US occupation 116, 140–1, 350, 456
 in wartime 397

Centeno, Marcos 430
Central Motion Picture Company 505
Central Motion Picture Exchange (CMPE) 455, 519
CGI 322
 in *jidaigeki* 262
 and production design 262
chanbara 14, 269–82, 287
 hallmarks 269
 in *Rashomon* 141
 in *Yōjinbō* 143–4
Chatman, Seymour 82
The Cheat (1915) 239
Cheers to the Jazz Girl, see *Jazz musume kanpai* (1955)
Chen Yunshang 449, 450
Chernobyl 392*n*27
Chernobyl Heart (2003) 392*n*27
Chi to suna (1965) 522
Chiang Kai Shek 511
Chiba, 'Sonny' Shin'ichi 497
Chichiariki (1942) 4
Chiisaki koe no canon – Sentaku suru hitobito (2014) 384, 387, 388
Chikamatsu monogatari (1954) 273
Chikemuri takadanobaba (1937) 292
Chikyōdai (1903) 328
Children of the Classroom, see *Kyōshitsu no kodomotachi* (1954)
Children's Council, see *Kodomo gikai* (1947)
chima chogori 480
Chin, Daryl 196
China 96
 animation 451
 box-office successes 441
 film festivals 174
 film-making under Japanese occupation 439–52, 546
 first productions 440
 immigrant workers from 479
 importance as export market 552
 and indoctrination 447
 Japanese co-productions 440, 506
 and Japanese Empire 8
 Japanese film distribution 115, 129
 Japanese perception of 514
 Japanese propaganda about 101
 New Wave cinema 168
 out-sourcing anime to 310
 postwar 450–1
 puppet government of 442, 451*n*8
 as setting for Japanese Westerns 522

Western films in 439
  (*see also* Shanghai; Sino-Japanese War)
China Nights, *see Shina no yoru* (1943)
China United Productions, *see* Zhonglian
Chion, Michel 273
  The Voice in Cinema 185
Chisso chemical plant 381
Chivalrous Geisha, *see Nihon jokyōden: Kyōkaku geisha* (1969)
Chōeki Taro: Mamushi no kyōdai (1971) 483, 484
Chōjikū kidan southern cross (1984) 496
Chōjikū yōsai Maross (1982) 496
Chōjū jimbutsu giga emaki 312
Chōkon (1926) 289
Chow, Rey 7, 11, 58
Christy, Alan S. 533
Chu Minyi 451*n*13
Chūji tabi nikki (1927–8) 289, 296*n*33, 349
Chuji's Travel Diary, *see Chūji tabi nikki*
Chūko, Satoshi 261
Chun, Jayson 527
cinemas
  architecture 133
  art-house 194, 197
  attendance by region 130
  block-booking 111, 116, 118, 549, 557
  block-booking vs free booking 121
  home movie day 217
  introduction of sound technology 152
  mini-theatres 170, 175, 549, 551
  'mini-theatres' 131
  multiplexes 131
  opening of 109
  postwar boom 129
  projecting small-guage film 227*n*53
  in Shanghai 439
  studio control of 114
  vs theatres 133
  Tōei-exclusive 117–18
  Tōhō owned 114, 116
Cinématographe 126
cinematography 14, 231–42
  definition of 232
  in documentaries 469–70
  in Hollywood 232–3
  Hollywood vs Japan 233, 235, 237
  lack of academic work on 240*n*1
  shadow 235–6

technological breakthroughs 235–6
  (*see also* 'director of photography')
Citizen Kane (1941) 76, 233
  lighting and cinematography 236
City of Lost Souls, *see Hyōryū-gai* (2001)
City of Purity, *see Junjō no miyako* (1933)
Civil Censorship Detachment (CCD) 140, 245
Civil Information Education Section (CIE) 16, 245, 291, 454, 468
  formation 116
  productions 454–7
Clarke, Charles G. 233
class
  after Meiji restoration 294*n*1
  and fandom 344
  and inequality 4
  and religion 401
  in Westerns 524
  in *Yoru no kawa* 267
  (*see also minshūshi* movement)
Coates, Jennifer 432
Cold War 5, 16, 453, 542, 553
  Asian co-productions 507–11, 512–16
  cultural diplomacy 164–5, 169
  film festivals 169
  technology and location 507–11
Cole, Nat King 342
colonialism 3, 16
  discrimination against natives 62
  and film exhibition 128
  Japanese 96
  in Manchuria 100
  in *Nihon shunka-kō* 484
  Ozu's use of 424
colour 260, 505, 509, 517*n*26
  early Japanese films 260
  expense 263
  film stock 268*n*19
  history in Japanese cinema 263
  impact of technology 512
  in *Yoru no kawa* 263–4
comedy 118
'comfort women' 480
Committee on Children's Film Viewing 142
communism 440, 450, 454
  (*see also* Japanese Communist Party; Marxism)
The Communist Conspiracy, *see Aka no inbō*

composers
  early 271
  training 272
Conde, David 116
Confessions, *see Kokuhaku* (2010)
Conley, Tom 563
Conrich, Ian 337
Cook, Ryan 46
Coppola, Francis Ford 493
cosplay 498, 501*n*48
Cowboy Bebop: The Movie (2001) 527
Crayon Shin-chan (1990–) 321, 322, 492
Crazed Fruit, *see Kurutta kajitsu* (1956)
Crenshaw, Kimberlé Wiliams 479
Crimson Peacock, *see Shinshokoku monogatari benikujaku* (1954–5)
The Crimson Plains, *see Akai kōya* (1961)
Crosby, Bing 337
Cross Talk Intermedia 199
Cruise, Tom 527
The Crying Game (1992) 548
The Cuckoo, *see Hototogisu* (1898–9)
cultural diversity 530
cultural isolation 489
culture films, *see bunka eiga*; *Kulturfilm*
Curtin, Michael 59
Cybersix (TV 1999) 310

Daibō, Masaki 270, 272
Daiei 259
  affiliated cinemas 116
  bankruptcy 121, 238, 547
  box-office performance 115
  colour techonology 509
  as distributor for other studios 117
  film festivals 164
  formation of 114
  horror films 299
  kaiki films 303
  overseas focus 167
  post-war period 116
  visual style 240
  during wartime 114–15
  yakuza films 353
Daisōgen no wataridori (1960) 522
Daito Films 114
The Dance of Geisha, *see Geisha no teodori* (1899)
danchi 412, 414
  lay-out 417*n*25
  rent 417*n*28
  sociological context 413

Dancing Dragon Palace Castle, see Odoru ryūgūjō (1949)
Daniels, Inge 412
D'Annuzio, Gabriele; *The Dream of a Morning in Spring/Sogno d'un mattino di primavera* 252–3
Danryū (1939) 262
Danryū (1957) 179
Dare mo shiranai (2004) 407
Daughter of Romance, see Romance musume (1956)
The Daughter of the Samurai, see Atarashiki tsuchi (1937)
Daughters, Wives and a Mother, see Musume tsuma haha (1960)
Dauman, Anatole 545
Davis, Bette 104n10
Dawn, see Reimei (1927)
The Dawn of Japanese Documentaries (1989) 361
Day, Doris 339
De Forest, Lee 152, 336
Dear Summer Sister, see Natsu no imōto (1972)
Death by Hanging, see Kōshikei
deep focus shot 76
Dekigokoro (1933) 409
Deleuze, Gilles 11
Delsarte, François 249
DeMille, Cecil B. 234, 239
Denchū kozō no bōken (1988) 170
Denkikan 127, *133*
Deorbit (2013) 201
depleted uranium 383
Der Blaue Engel (1930) 156
Desjardin, Chris; *Outlaw Masters of Japanese Film* 353, 358n4
Desperado Outpost, see Dokuritsu gurentai (1959)
Desser, David; *Eros Plus Massacre: An Introduction to the Japanese New Wave Cinema* 7
Devotion (2000) 406n47
Diao Chan (1938) 441
Diary of a Shinjuku Thief 187
Diary of Chuji's Travels, see Chūji tabi nikki (1927)
Die Tochter des Samurai, see Atarasiki tsuchi (1937)
Dietrich, Marlene 40, 339
digital
    animation 311, 321–2
    archives 221
    cameras 240
Dingjunshan (1903) 439
Director Disqualification 132
'director of photography' 231, 232–9
    definition 233
    emergence in Japan 235–8
    in Hollywood 232–3
The Dish Mansion at Bancho, see Banchō sarayashiki (1914)
Disney, Walt 315, 316
A Distant Cry from the Spring, see Harukanaru yama no yobigoe (1980)
distribution
    in China 129
    of foreign films in Japan 112, 519
    identity based 494
    overseas 491
    Shōchiku 116
Doane, Mary Ann 483
Dobunezumi sakusen (1963) 522
Dockside Gambler, see Hatoba no tobakushi (1963)
Document kōsei: Nippon zero nen (1969) 467, 472–3, 475–7
    influences 475
documentaries 10, 14, 15, 361–75
    avant-garde theories 364
    dialogic style 468–71, 473, 476, 477n6
    ecological 381
    exhibition of 131
    festivals 172–3, 174, 198
    on Fukushima 384
    on kabuki 550
    and *minshūshi* movement 365–8
    on nuclear disasters 383
    post-war history 361–4, 468–72
    pre-war 361–2
    as propaganda 100–1
    rise of 398
    and social protest 466, 467
    and subjectivity 362
    techniques 367–8
    television 471
    use of narrative 389
dōga, see animation; anime
Dogtanian and the Three Muskehounds, see Wanwan sanjūshi (1981)
Dokkoi! ningenbushi: Kotobukichō: Jiyūrōdōsha no machi (1975) 368, 369
Dokkoi! Songs from the Bottom, see Dokkoi! ningenbushi: Kotobukichō: Jiyūrōdōsha no machi (1975)
Dokuritsu gurentai (1959) 522
Dokuritsu gurentai nishi e (1960) 522
Dogase, Masato 28
Donelly, K.J. 270
Doraemon (TV 1969–) 321, 492
double features 117, 118, 124n49
    vanishing of 119
Dower, John 244, 464
The Downfall of Osen, see Orizuru Osen (1935)
Downtown, see Shitamachi (1957)
Dracula (1931) 298, 301
Dragnet Girl, see Hijōsen no onna (1933)
Dreams (1990) 493
The Drifting Avenger, see Kōya no toseinin (1970)
Drunken Angel, see Yoidore tenshi (1948)
Duel at Takadanobaba, see Chikemuri takadanobaba (1937)
Durbin, Deanna 346n19
Dutchman's Photograph, see Orandajin no shashin (1974)
DVDs 17, 122, 498, 552
    and globalisation 491
    and spread of Japanese culture 494
Dyer, Richard 58, 181
    Heavenly Bodies 180
    Stars 180
Dym, Jeffrey 27

early cinema 2, 7, 25–37
    animations 311–15
    authorship in 28
    Chinese 439
    colour 260
    difference from modern cinema 25–8
    difficulty researching 34
    and editing 26
    exhibition of 29
    exhibition sites 132–3
    film festivals 164
    gender swapping performers 181
    historical context 28–31
    hybrid nature 30
    importance 33
    intermediality 158, 202n19
    intertextuality in 27
    Japanese vs Western 26–7
    kaiki films 300–2
    in Kyoto 286
    melodramas 328

morality and censorship 138–9
multi-viewpoint narratives 82
musicals 336
pre-cinematic techniques 28–9
stars 28
studios 109, 110–11
theatrical influence 25–6, 138
use of *benshi* 111
in the West 26
Early Summer, see *Bakushū* (1951)
Earth, see *Tsuchi* (1939)
The Easily Burning Ears 199
'East Asian Race' 54, 61–4, *62*, 448
contradictions 62–3, 64
and Imperial colonies 61–2
Japanese supremacy 63
paternalism 63
East Meets West (1995) 527
Eat (1972), 195
Echigo okumiomote: Yama ni ikasareta hibi (1984) 372
ecology 12, 379–93
depictions in Hollywood 381
documentaries 365, 372
interdependency 382
landscape 380–1
and Marxism 395
as opposed to environment 379
economy 119, 344, 527, 547–8
depression 201*n*5
and globalisation 548
during Meiji period 533
(*see also kokusaika* policy)
Edinburgh International Film Festival 168
Edison, Thomas 2
editing 470
conflict theory 74–5
and early cinema 26
in early cinema 27
and montage 69
Edo period 312, 349, 401
ghost stories 299, 307
theatre in 327
(*see also bakumatsu*)
Edogawa, Ranpo 179, 183
education 8, 139, 361
in *Battle rowaiaru* 148
and 'East Asian Race' 62
film festivals 169
for film-makers 551–2
in occupied Shanghai 442–3
propaganda films 468
under US occupation 16, 454

Educational Film Festival 169
Eguchi, Matakichi 40
Ehrlich, Linda 254–5
eiga bijyutsu 260
Eiga hyōron 39
Eiga nenkan 39
eigasai 164, 169–71
genealogy of 169
(*see also* film festivals)
8mm Memories, see *8mm no kioku* (2010)
8mm no kioku (2010) 221
Eihai 114
dissolution 116
Eirin 138, 141, 142, 144, 147–8, 259, 260, 264
Eisenstein, Sergei 54, 69, 72, 83, 194, 272
Beyond the Shot 70
and dialectical montage 74–5
The Dramaturgy of Film Form 70
The Fourth Dimension in Cinema 70
Eizō jikken-shi Fs: Experimental Image Movement 219
Eizō no eizō – mirukoto (1973) 195
Elegant Beast, see *Shitoyaka na kedamono* (1962)
Elsaesser, Thomas 154, 176*n*13, 325, 332
The Emperor's Naked Army Marches On, see *Yuki yukite shingun* (1987)
empire 3, 5, 15, 16, 439–52
and Chinese cinema 8
influence on East Asian cinema 16, 31
Empire of Passion, see *Ai no bōrei* (1978)
The Empress Wu Ze Tian (1963) 516
Enami, Kyōko 182, 355, 356
Ending Note (2007) 131–2
An Engineer's Assistant, see *Aru kikan joshi* (1963)
English, Lawrence 201
The Enigma of Kasper Hauser (1974) 549
Enoken no seishun suikoden (1934) 336
Enoken's Tale of Youth's Folly, see *Enoken no seishun suikoden* (1934)
Entotsu no mieru basho (1953) 409
Epstein, Jean 69
Equinox Flower, see *Higanbana* (1958)
Eri, Chiemi 338–40
Ero shōgun to nijūichi-nin no aishō (1972) 565

Eros plus gyakusatsu (1970) 44, *45*
Eros Plus Massacre, see *Eros plus gyakusatsu* (1970)
erotic-grotesque films 116, 119
ethnicity 7
and gender 104*n*16
and identity 531
and inequality 4
and national identity 530
ethnography 165, 187, 477
documentaries 370–1
in Tsuchimoto's work 382
Etō, Fumio 342
Europe 18*n*5, 541–55
colonial attitude 545
exporting cinema to Japan 545
influence on Japanese cinema 2–3, 260
Japanese co-productions 548
Orientalism 168
popularity of Ozu Yasujirō 42
prewar Japanese films 553*n*4
reception of Japanese films 166, 542–3, 543–4
trade with Japan 548
Eurospace 549, 551
Evil Spirit, see *Jaganrei* (1988)
Excessive Economic Power Deconcentration Law 109
exhibition 13, 126–37
benshi 132
of documentary films 131, 364, 366, 474
of early cinema 60
early days 109
early film programmes 126–7
of early films 29
of experimental films 197–8
of exports 130–1, 166–8
for home and amateur movies 223
independent and alternative cinema 131, 169
of Japanese films overseas 491–2
in Manchuria 129
mobile 128–9
in modern era 131–2
newsreels 127
of 'pink films' 131
politics of 128–9
post-war 129–31
previous studies 126
prewar vs postwar 130
regulations 56

research on 36*n*28, 135*n*2
in rural areas 130
and talkies 133–4
of widescreen films 118
(*see also* cinemas)
The Exorcist (1973) 298
experimental film 13, 190*n*37, 192–202, 429
    amateur film-makers 193–4
    animations 194, 198
    exhibition of 197–8
    feature length 197
    feminism in 195
    festivals 198, 201*n*10
    global audience 200
    intermediality 199
    internationalism 200–1
    Japan vs other asian nations 192
    magazines 198, 201*n*11
    networks 198–201
    re-emergence post occupation 194
    vs studio films 192
    terminology and history 192–3
    and theatre 200, 202*n*19
    in the US 200
    video vs film 195–6
    Western hegemony 201
    (*see also* independent cinema)
EXPRMNTL 3 194
Extreme Private Eros Love Song 1974, *see Kyokushiteki eros: Renka 1974* (1974)
Ezaki, Mio 16

Faire, lucy 58
Fallen Blossoms, see Hanachirinu
family, *see* homelife
The Family Game, see Kazoku game (1983)
fandom 498–9
    and class 344–5
    of Misora Hibari 339–40
    magazines 343–4
Far East Network (FEN) 338
Fassbinder, Rainer 550
The Fast-Drawing Guy, see Hayauchi yarō (1961)
Federation Internationale des Associations de Producteurs de Films (FIAPF) 165, 172, 175, 176
female body 31–2
    and ecological approach 406*n*49
    and male performers 184

    in *panpan eiga* 98
    in performance 252–3
    in postwar period 246
    in *Red Peony* series 356
    of *zainichi* 481
female directors 100, 105*n*30
    biographies of 103*n*6
    discrimination against 95
Female Prisoner no. 701: Scorpion, see Joshū 701 gō: Sasori (1972)
feminism 12, 26
    development in Japan 94–5
    in experimental film 195
    film scholarships 94–106
    Japanese vs Anglophone 94
    in the Third World 479
FEMIS (Fondation Européenne pour les Métiers de l'Image et du Son) 552
Feuillade, Louis 292
Fighting Soldiers, see Tatakau heitai (1939)
Film als Kunst (1932) 70
film criticism 4, 13, 68–80
    Anglophone 1–2
    gender discrimination 95
    Japanese tradition 69
    Japanese language 6, 8
    Marxist 5, 6, 69
    Methodological shift 68
    nationalism 68–9
    'outsider critics' 71–4
film festivals 10, 13, 164–78
    amateur 194
    vs archives 215
    during Cold War 517*n*19
    development in Japan 169–71
    documentaries 172–3, 174, 198
    early cinema 164
    educational 169
    engaging with cinema 169
    European recognition of Japanese cinema 543
    experimental 198, 201*n*10
    feminist 95, 100
    as gateway to international exhibition 173, 552
    and geo-politics 171
    government support 172
    home movies 220–2
    independent cinema 164, 173–4
    international vs local 174–5
    Japanese cinema in Europe 166
    Japanese vs international 166

    'J-horror' 169
    LGBT 181, 188*n*1
    mini-theatre 175
    as mode of globalisation 491–2
    New Wave cinema 167–8, 549
    Orientalism in Europe 168
    'pink films' 167–8
    planning 165
    terminology 164
    (*see also eigasai*; specific festivals)
Film Independents 198
Film Law 3–4, 62, 114, 219, 405*n*9, 452*n*19
    and censorship 139, 302
Film Preservation Society 214, 216, 221
film stock 114
    and cinematography 232, 236–7
    colour 268*n*19
    'heritage' status 221–2
    for home movies 214, 217–18
    wartime shortages 236, 451*n*12
film studies 8, 22*n*38
    focus on urban settings 394, 404*n*1
    and musicals 345
    neglect of cinematography 240*n*1
Final Fantasy 492
Fisher, Eddie 339
Fishman, Marvin 200
Fiske, John 57
A Fistful of Dollars (1964) 144, 492
Five Company Agreement 118
Five Scouts, see Gonin no sekkōhei (1938)
Flaherty, Robert J. 456
Fleeting Life, see Ukiyo (1916)
Fleischer Brothers 315, 316
Flinn, Caryl 483
The Flower of Carnage/Shura no hana 359*n*13
The Flower-Selling Girl, see Mai hua nü (1942)
Flowing, see Nagareru (1956)
'focalisation' 85–7
    in *Rashomon* 89
    and unreliable narration 85
The Fog (1980) 185
For a Bright Home Life, see Akarui katei seikatsu (1950)
For a Fistful of Dollars (1964) 527
Ford, John 519
The Foreign Duck, Native Duck, and God in a Coin Locker, see Ahiru to kamo no coin locker (2007)

foreign films
    distribution under studio system 112
    Japanese financing of 548
    liberalisation of import rules 124n55
    (*see also* Europe; German cinema; Hollywood)
Forest of Oppression – A Record of Struggle at Takasaki City University of Economics, *see Assatsu no mori – Takasaki keizai daigaku tōsō no kiroku* (1967)
The Forgotten Army, *see Wasurerareta kōgun* (1963)
Forrest, Jennifer 209
The 47 Ronin, *see Genroku Chūshingura* (1941–42)
Foucault, Michel 28, 215
Fox and his Friends (1975) 549
Frankenstein (1931) 299, 301
Frankfurt School cultural theory 26, 72
    and globalisation 490
Freeze Me, *see Furīzu mī* (2000)
Freiburg, Freda 47
    on gender and imperialism 104n16
    on Mellen 104n9
    Women in Mizoguchi's Films 38
Freud, Sigmund 187, 262–3, 304, 309n25, 364
Friday the 13th Part VI (1986) 298
Friends of Minamata Victims, *see Minamata o kokuhatsu suru kai – Tent mura Video nikki* (1972)
Fu, Poshek 440
Fūfu (1953) 409
Fuji, Junko 182, 350, 351, 353, 354–6, 359n11, 359n13
    body 356
    popularity 357
Fuji no chishitsu (1943) 402
Fuji, Sumiko, *see* Fuji, Junko
Fuji Television 122, 204
Fujicolour 509
Fujii, Hidetada 335
Fujiki, Hideaki 28, 249–50
    on early studio system 110
    Making Personas 181
Fujimoto, Masazumi 345n1
Fujimoto, Sanezumi 345
Fujita, Shigeya 15, 467
Fujitani, Takashi 440
Fujiwara, Toshi 380–1, 385, 392n42
    vs Kubata 388
Fujiwara, Yoshie 157

Fukai, Shirō 273
Fukasaku, Kinji 138, 145–8, 180, 183, 497
    anti-Americanism 145
    critical reputation 145
    experience of atomic bombs 150n54
    use of violence 146
Fukasaku, Mitsusada 187
Fukuda, Katsuhiko 365
Fukuhōdō 110
Fukui International Video Biennale 195
Fukuoka City Public Library Film Archive 216
Fukuro, Ippei 78n12
    A Voyage to Soviet/Russian Cinema 73
Fukurō no shiro (1999) 262
Fukushima 12, 174, 379–93
    criticism of filmic descriptions 380
    documentaries 383–7, 391n3
    fiction films 381, 387–9, 389–90, 391n11
    government criticism 384, 385
    government response 390
    vs Minamata 383
Fukushima ni ikiru: Josen to fukkō no monogatari (2013) 385
Fukushū suru wa ware ni ari (1979) 406n45
Funakoshi, Eiji 413
The Funeral of Commander Hirose, Admiral Itō and Other Visitors, *see Hirose chūsa no sōgi Itō taishō ika kaisō* (1904)
Funeral Parade of Roses, *see Bara no sōretsu* (1969)
Furīzu mī (2000) 298
Furstenau, Marc 152
Furuhata, Yuriko 199, 364, 469, 540
Furusato (1930) 281n11, 336
Furuta, Hisateru 124n55
Fushimizu, Osamu 338
Futaba kara tōku hanarete (2012) 385
Futurism 160
Fuwa no niji (1998) 196
Fuwa, Suketoshi 4
Fuyu no sonata (2003) 527

Gabin, Jean 40
Gaines, Jane 467
Gaitō (1957) 559, 560
Galaxy Express, *see Ginga tetsudō 999* (TV 1978–81)
Galbraith, Stuart 143
Gambler, *see Bakuto* (1964)

Gangster Women, *see Gokudō no onnatachi* (1986–95)
Garden/ing (2007) 196
Gate of Hell, *see Jigoku mon* (1953)
Geisha no teodori (1899) 127
Gekiryū ni ikiru otoko (1962) 558
Gekitotsu! satsujin ken (1974) 497
Gendai no josei (1923) 328
Gendai yakuza: Hito kiri yota (1972) 359n5
gendaigeki 285, 287, 328
    censorship of 139
gender 3, 7, 8, 12, 38, 393n50, 479–88, 551
    in animation 105n34
    and authorship 100–1
    in early cinema 181
    and ethnicity 104n16
    and imperialism 104n16
    inequality 4
    and Korean minority 12
    and Miwa Akirhiro 179
    in *Nishi Ginza ekimae* 427
    and Orientalism 553
    and performance 180–2
    in postwar Japan 355
    in pre-war period 96
    in Pure Film Movement 31–2
    in *Sakuran* 208
    and spectatorship 98
    stereotypes 94
    in Sun Tribe films 182
    and transnationalism 101–3
    and voice 185–6
    in *Wanshi liufang* 448, 449
    in Westerns 524–5
    and yakuza films 348, 353
    in yakuza films 183
    in *zainichi* community 480
    (*see also josei eiga*; sexuality)
General Headquarters, Supreme Command for the Allied Powers (GHQ/SCAP) 60, 115–16, 140, 291, 453–4, 470
Genesis Climber MOSPEADA, *see Kikō sōseiki Mospeada* (1983)
Genette, Gérard 82, 85–6
Genji monogatari (1951) 543
Genma taisen (1983) 186
Gennin hōkokusho: Haneda tōsō no kiroku (1967) 473
genre 7, 14
    cyclical nature 353

early studio system 110
Fujimoto on 345*n*1
studio specialities 118–19
theatrical influence 327
(*see also* specific genres)
Genroku Chūshingura (1941–42) 261
Gentle Breeze, *see Soyokaze* (1945)
gentō (magic lantern) 28
geography, *see* landscape
Geology of Fuji, *see Fuji no chishitsu* (1943)
German cinema 332
   importing 545, 549
   influence on Japan 557
   new wave 550
Gerow, Aaron 9, 39, 111, 295*n*10
   on authorship 40
   on criticism 68
   on development of Japanese cinema 313
   on Eirin 146
   Kitano Takeshi 353
   on musicals 336, 346*n*8
   on representation of Okinawa 535
   Visions of Japanese Modernity 56
Gerow, Aaron & Nornes, Abé Mark; *In the Praise of Film Studies: Essays in Honor of Makno Mamoru* 10
The Ghost Cat and the Mysterious Shamisen, *see Kaibyō nazo no shamisen* (1938)
Ghost Cat of Otama Pond (1960) 305
The Ghost Cat of Otama Pond, *see Kaibyō otama ga ike* (1960)
Ghost of Yotsuya, *see Shinshaku Yotsuya Kaidan*
The Ghost Story of the Mandarin Duck Curtain, *see Kaidan oshidori-chō* (1938)
The Ghost Story of Yotsuya (1912) 300
Giants and Toys, *see Kyojin to gangu* (1959)
gidayu 133
Ginga tetsudō 999 (TV 1978–81) 312
Gingakei (1967) 197
Ginoza Naomi 96, 102
Ginza Love Story, *see Ginza no koi no monogatari* (1962)
Ginza no koi no monogatari (1962) 561
Gitā o motta wataridori (1959) 522
globalisation 10, 16, 176, 489–501, 547–51
   and anime 498

and authorship 50
and children's television 493
cinema as tool of 519
definitions 490
and education 551–2
and film financing 548
foundational theories 490–1
Frankfurt School on 490
and independent cinema 549
models of 489
modes of 491–5
of montage theory 71
and national identity 491
in South Africa 494–9
through film festivals 491–2
(*see also* transnational)
Glotfelty, Cheryll 379
Gluck, Carol 368
Gō (2001) 480
Gōda Mariko 218
Godard, Jean-Luc 7, 41
Godzilla, *see Gojira* (film series)
Gohatto (1999) 231, 233, *239*
Gojira (film series) 1, 299, 308*n*6, 493
Gokudō daisensō (2015) 552
Gokudō no onnatachi (1986–95) 352
Goldberg, Michael 195
The Golden Demon, *see Konjiki yash*a (1897–1903)
Gonda Yasunosuke 33, 63
   Katsudōshashin no genre oyobi ōyō 18*n*5
   Principles and Application of the Motion Picture 54
Gonda, Yasunosuke 4
Gonin no sekkōhei (1938) 9
Good Morning, *see Ohayō* (1959)
Gosho, Heinosuke 40, 153, 407, 409
Gōtō, Shinpei 129
Grand shō 1946-nen (1946) 338
Grand Show 1946, *see Grand shō 1946-nen* (1946)
Great Depression 232
Great East Japan Earthquake 2011 373, 385, 386
Great Kantō Earthquake 1923 19*n*23, 32, 201*n*5, 286, 331, 409, 419
   impact on studios 112
The Great Wall, *see Shin shikōtei* (1962)
Greater East Asian Co-Prosperity Sphere 62, 64, 448
Gregory, Carl 235
Grieveson, Lee 28

Griffith, D.W. 235, 249
Grimault, Paul 312
The Grudge (2004) 554*n*53
The Grudge 2 (2006) 554*n*53
Gunbuster, *see Top o nerae* (1988)
'Gunkan kōshinkyoku' 338
Gunning, Tom 26
Guohua 441
Gutai Bijutsu Kyōkai (Gutai Art Association) 423, 434*n*33
Gyōsei (1999) 201

H Story (2001) 50
Habuto, Eiji 189*n*6
Hadaka no machi (1937) 421
Hadaka no shima (1960) 261–2
haiku 6, 56, 532
   and montage theory 72, 401–3
   and nature 394, 402–3
Haiwan fengyun, *see Kinmontō ni kakeru hashi* (1962)
Hake, Sabine 28
Hakkō ryūkitai (1961) 526
Hakoiri musume (1935) 417*n*15
Hakuba dōji (1960) 526
Hakujaden (1958) *316*
Hall, Hal 232
Hall, Stuart; *Encoding/Decoding* 57
Hamada, Tatsuo 261
Hamano, Sachi 103*n*6
Hamasaki, Ryōta 195
Hammett, Dashiell; *Red Harvest* 492
Hana yori dango (1995) 208
Hana yori dango final (2008) 210
Hana-Bi (1997) 168
Hanachirinu (1938) 6
Hanada, Kiyoteru 364
Hanayagi, Shōtarō 253
Haneda, Sumiko 95
Hanford Nuclear Reservation 383
Hani, Gorō 365
Hani, Susumu 76, 131, 167, 429, 431, 467, 468–9
   Camera and Microphone/Camera to mic: Gendai geijutsu no hōhō 469
   editing style 470
Hansen, Miriam 11, 33, 58–9, 96, 102, 326, 332
   Babel and Babylon 55
   transnationalism 101
Hara, Kazuo 362, 373, 467
Hara, Keiichi 321–2
Hara, Masato 548

Hara, Setsuko 60, 99, 100, 116, 453, 459
Hara, Tadashi 369
Hara, Takeshi 413, 414
Harakiri, see Seppuku (1962)
Harootunian, Harry 19*n*17, 96, 514
Harry Potter franchise 492
Hart, Willilam S. 519
Harukanaru yama no yobigoe (1980) 523
Harumi, Befu 530, 532
Hase, Masato 30
Hasebe, Hideo 485
Hasegawa, Kazuo 116
Hasegawa, Nyozekan 4
Hasegawa, Ryūsei' 347*n*45
Hashiguchi, Ryōsuke 105*n*30
Hashimoto, Osamu 285
Hashimoto, Shinobu 297*n*38
Hashimoto, Yoshio 368
Hasumi, Eiichirō 203
Hasumi, Shigehiko 6, 19*n*21, 39, 43, 44, 47, 550, 565
　career as educator 7
　Eiga no kioku sōchi 6
　Foucault, Deleuze and Derrida 7
　Kantoku Ozu Yasujirō 7
　on Ozu 46
Hatakeyama, Chōko 324*n*30
Hatamoto taikutsu otoko (1958) 273
The Hate Remaining at the End of the Ming Dynasty, see Ming mo yihen (1939)
Hatoba no tobakushi (1963) 562
Hattori, Tadashi 272
The Haunted Castle, see Le Manoir du diable (1896)
The Haunting (1963) 307
Hawaii Malay oki kaisen (1942) 5, 115, 233, 235, 237
Hawks, Howard 46
Hayakawa, Sessue 28
Hayama, Rei 201
Hayasaka, Fumio 269, 272, 273
Hayashi, Takeji 365
　Tanaka Shōzō: Sono sei to tatakai no 'konpongi' 366
Hayauchi yarō (1961) 521
Hazumi, Tsuneo 520
Hearn, Lafcadio 274
Heath, Stephen 6, 26, 54, 82
Heian era 27
Heibon (magazine) 335, 339, 342–4
　circulation 342
　supplements 342

Heidi, A Girl of the Alps, see Alps no shōjo Haiji (1974)
Heinosuke, Gosho 38
Heisei tanuki gassen ponpoko (1994) 312
Heitai Gokudō (1968) 351
Held, Michael 491
A Hen in the Wind, see Kaze no naka no mendori (1948)
Henderson, Brian 85
henshū eiga 70
Hepburn, Katherine 60, 98, 99, 104*n*10
Her Brother, see Otōto (1960)
Hi no ataru sakamichi (1958) 415, 421
Hibakusha: Sekai no owarini (2005) 383
Hibari no mori no Ishimatsu (1960) 359*n*13
Hibotan bakuto (1968–72) 12, 145, 182, 349, 354–6
　social context 354
　theme song 359*n*13
Hibotan bakuto Oryū sanjō (1970) 356
Hidden Fortress, see Kakushi toride no san akunin (1959)
Higanbana (1958) 411, 412, 420, 424–6, 425, 427
　set design 424–5
　use of colour 424
High and Low, see Tengoku to jigoku (1963)
High, Peter B. 402, 440
　The Imperial Screen: Japanese Film Culture in the Fifteenth Years' War, 1931–1945 8
Higo, Hiroshi 194
Higson, Andrew 102
Higuchi, Naofumi 353
Hijōsen no onna (1933) 260
Hikari to kage (1940) 421
Hikyō nekka (1936) 129
Hills, Matt; *Fan Cultures* 57
Himizu (2012) 391*n*11
Hinson, Hal 189*n*12
Hirano, Kyoko 245
　Mr. Smith Goes to Tokyo: Japanese Cinema Under the American Occupation, 1945–1952 8
Hirano, Yoshimi 235
Hirohito 461
Hirose chūsa no sōgi Itō taishō ika kaisō (1904) 127
Hiroshima 379, 391*n*4
Hiroshima mon amour (1959) 545
Hisaishi, Joe 282*n*47

A History of the Showa Era: An Attempt to Document a Personal History, see Aru shōwashi: Jibunshi no kokoromi (1975)
Hitori musuko (1936) 255, 421
Hobsbawm, Eric 31
Hōjō, Nobuhiko 352, 357
Hokkaido 130, 134, 406*n*44, 440, 479, 522–3
　landscape 531
Hōkoku bakushin (1937) 129
Hollywood 518–29
　distribution in Japan 519
　and ecology 381
　gender in 97
　global power 519
　and great depression 232
　importance as expot market 552
　influence on Japanese cinema 16, 31, 307, 455
　vs Japanese cinema 6
　Japanese co-productions 526
　Japanese criticism of 63
　and *jidaigeki* 289–90, 296*n*32
　melodramas 328
　popularity in Japan 60
　studio system vs Japanese studios 43
Hollywood Zen (1992, unreleased) 239
Holmberg, Ryan 392*n*48
home 407, 408
Home Movie Day 214, 225*n*11
　genres and modes 220
　Tokyo vs other cities 222
　venues 217
home movies 214–27
　definition 215
　festivals 220–2
　film stock 217–18
　and sound 222
　(*see also kojin eiga; shō-eiga*)
Homeland, see Ieji (2014)
homelife 12, 407–19
　intergenerational conflict 414–15
　in Meiji period 408
Hong Kong
　influence on Japanese action movies 497
　Japanese co-productions 510, 513
　martial arts movies 496
　new wave 168
Honk Kong no hoshi (1962) 507
Honnōji kassen (1908) 128
Honshu 531

Hontō ni atta kowai hanashi (1991) 298
Hook, Glen D. 538
Hori, Kyōko 427
Horikoshi, Kenzō 549–50, 551
Hōrō Zanmai (1927) 296n33
Horobasha wa yuku (1961) 521
Horoyoi jinsei (1933) 270
horror 1, 14, 298–309
    broad definition 298
    direct to video 298
    global appreciation 47
    Japanese vs Western 300
    vs kaiki 299
    (***see also*** 'J-Horror')
The Horse, ***see*** *Uma* (1941)
Hotel du Nord (1938) 562
Hotel Hibiscus (2002) 531–2
Hototogisu (1898–9) 328
Hou Hsiao-Hsien 49
houses 412
    (***see also*** home, danchi)
Howards End (1992) 548
Howl no ugoku shiro (2004) 186
Howl's Moving Castle, ***see*** *Howl no ugoku shiro* (2004)
Huabei Dianying 440, 442
Hudie furen (1942) 445
Hugo, Victor; *Les Miserables* 296n35
Humanity and Paper Balloons, ***see*** *Ninjō kami fūsen* (1937)
Hunter, Stephen 189n12
Husband and Wife, ***see*** *Fūfu* (1953)
Hyakujū-ō golion (1981) 496
Hyōryū-gai (2001) 531

I Flunked, But ..., ***see*** *Rakudai wa shitakeredo* (1930)
Ibsen, Henrik; *A Doll House* 244, 251
Ichi the Killer, ***see*** *Koroshiya Ichi* (2001)
Ichiban utsukushiku (1944) 104n10, 140
Ichii, Saburō 365
Ichikawa, Danjūrō IX 248
Ichikawa, Kon 40, 44, 545
    criticism of 44
Ichikawa, Miyabi 199
Ichikawa, Sadanji 250
Ichikawa, Sai
    The Creation and Construction of Asian Cinema 62
Ichikawa, Utaemon 115
Idemitsu, Mako 195
Ieda, Shōko

Gangster Wives/Gokudō no tsumatachi 352
Ieji (2014) 380, 387–9, *388*
    vs *Rokkasho Rhapsody* 389
Ifukube, Akira 269, 272
Ihōjin no kawa (1975) 480
Iida, Tōkichi 216
Iijima, Tadashi 20n28, 25, 54, 63, 74, 154
    translation of European authors 70
Iimura, Takahiko 194, 197, 198, 200
Ikegami, Kaneo 274
Ikegawa, Reiko 100
Ikegaya, Hōmei 475
Ikemiya, Shōichirō, ***see*** Ikegami, Kaneo
Ikimono minna tomodachi: Tori, mushi, sakana no komoriuta (1987) 404
Ikiru (1952) 44, 82
Image Forum Film Festival 170
Image Modulator (1969) 195
Image of Image-Seeing, ***see*** *Eizō no eizō – mirukoto* (1973)
Imai, Norio 199–200
Imai, Tadashi 9, 40, 41, 403–4
Imaizumi, Kōichi 105n30
Imamura, Shōhei 9, 44, 167, 426, 533
Imamura, Taihei 4, 9, 54, 74, 323n24, 397
    On the Cartoon Film/Manga eiga ron 315, 316
    on Imperialism 296n32
    on influence of montage theory 77
Immigrant workers 479
Imperial Japan at the Movies (1997) 361
imperialism 3, 31, 174
    and cinema 451
    and gender 104n16
    Japanese supremacy 63
    propaganda and identity 62
    in Shanghai 439–52
    of the United States 515
    use of propaganda 115
In Spring (1929) 73
In the Realm of the Senses, ***see*** *Ai no corrida* (1976)
Inagaki, Hiroshi 291, 359n12
Inazuma (1952) 409
Ince, Thomas H. 234
Income Doubling Plan 119
independent cinema 43, 164
    exhibition of 131–2, 169, 549
    film festivals 164
    production design 261–2
    programming festivals 173–4

    rise of 121, 170
    and social protest movements 466
    (***see also*** experimental film)
Indian cinema 489
Indonesia 511
The Informer (1935) 281n13
An Inn in Tokyo, ***see*** *Tokyo no yado* (1935)
An Innocent Maid, ***see*** *Hakoiri musume* (1935)
The Innocents (1961) 307
The Insect Woman, ***see*** *Nippon konchūki* (1963)
Institute for the Association of Japanese Animations 204
Intentions of a Murder, ***see*** *Akai satsui* (1964)
Inter-Asia Cultural Studies Society (IACS) 10
Intermedia Art Festival 199
intermediality 14, 58, 203–13
    and anime 61
    early examples 22n45
    'expanded cinema' 199, 200
    in experimental film 199
    in *Joyū Sumako no koi* 246–53, 253–6
    in *kouta eiga* 155
    montage theory 72–4
    and sound 151–63
    and stardom 343
    studios use of 122
    and theatrical tradition 156
International Alliance of Theatrical Stage Employees (IATSE) 232, 235
International Congress of Independent Film 194
International Federation of Film Archives (FIAF) 216, 224n2
internationalisation 171–2
    and independent cinema 173
intersectionality 479
Intertextuality 17
    in early cinema 27
    and globalisation 492–3
    and manga adaptations 203
    of program pictures 558
Iraq 383
Irie, Takako 302, 306
Irigaray, Luce 184
Irokawa, Daikichi 365, 366, 375n20
    Meiji seishinshi 367
Isao, Nakauchi 434n33

Isayama, Saburō 233
Iseki, Satoru 548
Ishibashi, Shōji 536
Ishihara, Yūjirō 105n28, 182, 560, 562, 563
Ishii, Yasuharu 209
Ishikawa, Toshishige 452n20
Ishikawa, Yoshihiro 305
Ishikkoro (1961) 194
Ishimatsu the One-Eyed Avenger, **see** *Hibari no mori no Ishimatsu* (1960)
Ishimure, Michiko 365
Ishizaka, Kenji 9
Itakura, Fumiaki 60, 296n27
Italian neo-realism 43
Itami, Jūzō 524
Itami, Mansaku 40, 74, 290, 291, 293–4
Itō, Akio 40
Itō, Daisuke 27, 71, 262, 288–9, 296n27
  early work 289
  visual style 289
Ito, Mizuko 205, 206
Itō, Ryūsuke 196
Itō, Tari 105n30
It's Tough Being a Man, **see** *Otoko wa tsuraiyo* series (1969–97)
Ivan the Terrible Part One (1944) 272
Ivy, Marilyn 411, 417n19
Iwabuchi, Koichi 209, 493, 541
Iwamoto, Kenji 8, 9
  on export of Japanese cinema 166
  on Japanese vs Western early cinema 27
  on pre-cinematic practices 28–9
Iwanami Film Company 238, 467, 468–9
Iwasak, Yatarō 465n27
Iwasaki, Akira 9, 20n28, 33, 77, 157, 189n6, 332, 449, 557
  on authorship theory 41
  on talkies 160
  translations of Soviet works 69
Iwashigumo (1959) 424
Iwata-Weickgenannt, Kristina 381
Izo (2004) 294
Izumi Kyōka 328
Izumi, Toshiyuki 309n24

J Movie Wars (TV 1993–7): 169
Jacobs, Lea 234, 249
Jaganrei (1988) 298
Jancovich, Mark 58
Janken Girls, **see** *Janken musume* (1955)

Janken musume (1955) 335, 340–2, *341*, 343
Japan Academy Awards 81
Japan Community Cinema Center 174
Japan Fair Trade Commission 109
Japan Housing Corporation 413
Japan International Video Television Festival 195
Japan Society for Studies in Journalism and Mass Communication 10
Japan Society of Image Arts and Sciences 10
Japan Underground Centre (JUC) 198
Japan, Year Zero, **see** *Document kōsei: Nippon zero nen* (1969)
Japanese Communist Party 362
  and antiwar protests 476
Japanese Constitution 463
  exclusion of Okinawa 538
Japanese Documentaries of the 1960s (1993) 361
Japanese Documentaries of the 1970s (1995) 361
Japanese gardens 6
Japanese independence, **see** Treaty of San Francisco
A Japanese Village: Furuyashikimura (1982) 371, 372, 374n6
Japan-Taiwan Peace Treaty 1952 509
Jazz musume kanpai (1955) 339
jazz 159, 273, 338
Jenkins, Henry 58, 205, 206
Jesty, Justin 381
'J-horror' 47, 146, 307–9
  at film festivals 169
  international popularity 298
  traditional influences 307
  violence 307
  Western influence 307
jidaigeki 14, 74, 285–97, 294n2, 328
  ambiguity of term 285–6, 296n31
  and birth of Japanese cinema 286
  duplicity 288–93
  in early studio system 112
  and Hollywood 289–90, 296n32
  and horror 299–300
  lighting 238–9
  and manga adaptations 208
  meaning of term 14, 285
  in modern era 297n43
  modern examples 293
  origin of term 287
  post-war decline 292–3

  realism 289–91
  on television 292
  in Tokyo 419
  under US occupation 117, 140
  and use of CGI 262
  violence in 141–2, 143
  in wartime 289–91
  wartime productions 115
  Westerns 525–8
  and yakuza films 350, 352, 357
Jigoku mon (1953) 131, 167, 263, 268n28, 512, 543–5, *544*
jikken eiga, **see** experimental film
Jikken Kōbō Experimental Workshop 200
Jingi naki tatakai (1973) 146, 359n5, 557
Jingi naki tatakai: Dairi sensō (1973) 359n5
Jingi naki tatakai: Hiroshima shitō hen (1973) 359n5
Jinmen wan fengyun, **see** *Kinmontō ni kakeru hashi* (1962)
Jinruigaku nyūmon (1966) 534
Jinsei gekijō: Seishun, aiyoku, zankyō hen (1972) 359n5
Jirochō sangokushi series (1952–4) 292, 297n41
Jirocho's Tale of Three Provinces, **see** *Jirochō sangokushi* series (1952–4)
Jirokichi the Rat, **see** *Oatsurae Jirokichi kōshi* (1931)
jishu (seisaku) eiga, **see** Independent cinema
jishu jōei 169–71
  diversification 170
  political activism 170
J.O. Studios 112
Johnson, Derek 206
Jokyū (1930) 328
Jōnouchi, Motoharu 199
Joo, Woojeong 422
josei eiga 97–8
  ambiguity of term 97
Joshi ni eiga 209
Joshū 701 gō: Sasori (1972) 359n5
Jost, François 85
Joyū (1947) 245
Joyū Sumako no koi (1947) 12, 243–58, *244, 247, 255*
  censorship 245, 246
  contemporary critics 243
  death scene 255

gender issues 245–6
historical context 244–6
vs Mizoguchi other work 253
Jūjiro (1928) 130
Jun'eiga geki undō 2, 27–8, 31–3, 111
criticism of 18n5, 31
gender in 99
screenwriting 32
use of sound 157
Jung Yeonghae 480
Junjō no miyako (1933) 270
Ju-on films 298
Jūsannin no shikaku (1963) *277*, 355
music 270, 273–5
Jūsannin no shikaku (2010) *275*, *277*
music 270, 275–9
Juzi guniang (1955) 515

Kabe no naka no himegoto (1965) 167
Das Kabinett des Doktor Caligari (1920) 91
kabuki 6, 25, 27, 83, 262
documentaries on 550
early cinema 111
emergence 327
and film genre 327
influence on cinema 56, 138
morality 138
movie ban 128
performance style 248–9
Kadokawa Shoten 121, 122
Kaeriyama Norimasa 32, 39, 157
Katsudō shashin geki no sōsaku to satsueihō 18n5
on sound 158–9
Kaeriyama, Norimasa 25
KAFA (Korean Academy of Film Arts) 552
Kagi (1959) 413–14
Kago no tori (1924) 155
Kaguya hime no monogatari (2013) 312
Kaibyō nazo no shamisen (1938) 301
Kaibyō okazaki sōdō (1954) 302
Kaibyō otama ga ike (1960) 300
Kaidan kasane ga fuchi (1957) 303, 309n25
Kaidan nobori ryū (1970) 357
Kaidan oshidori-chō (1938) 301
kaijū films 308n6
kaiki eiga 15, 298–309
advertising 299–300
decline of genre 307

definition 299
in early cinema 300–2
vs horror 299
influence on J-Horror 307, 308
modern day 306–7
origin of term 300–1, 308n7
postwar 304–6
status 299
Kairo (2001) 308
Kaitaku no hanayome (1943) 101
Kaizoku to onna (1923) 287
Kaji, Meiko 350
Kakeshita, Keikichi 157
Kakushi toride no san akunin (1959) 424
Kalinak, Kathryn 274
Kama Sutra (1996) 548
Kamanaka, Hitomi 379, 381, 383–4, 392n30
film-making strategies 384
on *Rokkasho Rhapsody* 383
vs Tsuchimoto 383
Kamei, Fumio 71, 361, 362, 401–3
on landscape 394
use of montage theory 402
Kami, Kyōsuke 270
Kamigami no fukaki yokubō (1968) 12–13, 530, 533, *535*, 538
sexuality in 535–6
Kamikaze 246
Kamio, Yōko 210
Kamiyama, Akira 252
Kanada, Yoshinori 312
Kanashiki kuchibue (1949) 339
Kanaya Koume (1929) 154
Kanba, Michiko 199
Kanbara, Tai; *What Should We Give Voice To?* 160
Kanesaka, Kenji 198
Kanno, Yuka 60, 97, 105n25
on spectatorship 98
Kano, Ayako
Acting Like a Woman in Modern Japan 181
Kano, Masanao 367
Shihonshugi keiseiki no chitsujo ishiki 365–6
Kant, Immanuel 491
Kantoku shikkaku (2007) 132
'Kappa boogie-woogie' 338–9
Kara, Jūrō 187, 190n35
Karajishi botan series (1968–72) 526
Karasawa, Hiromitsu 289
Karatani, Kōjin 248

Karloff, Boris 301
Kasagi, Shizuko 338, 339
Kashima, Shigeru 558
kasutori 246
Kasza, Gregory 139
Kataoka, Chiezō 115, 288, 290, 338
Katō, Atsuko 440
Katō, Hidetoshi 132–3
Katō, Mikirō 8, 9
Katō, Shū 134
Katsu, Shintarō 292, 505
Katsudō shashin tenrankai (The Exhibition of Moving Pictures) 164
Katsura hime (1937) *314*
'Katyusha no uta' 257n29
Kaufman, Mikhail 73
Kaurismaki, Aki 549
Kawabe, Kazuo 15, 467
Kawaguchi, Tatsuo 195, 199–200
Kawai, Masayuki 195
Kawajiri, Yoshiaki 320
Kawakita, Kashiko 197, 342
Kawakita Memorial Film Institute 10
Kawakita, Nagamasa 440, 442, 443, 444, 545–7
Kawanaka, Nobuhiro 198
Kawarazaki, Chōichirō 534
Kawase, Naomi 168, 169
Kawatō, Yoshio 131
Kawazu, Yoshirō 429
kayō eiga 335, 345
Kazakura, Shō 199
Kaze no naka no mendori (1948) 45
Kazoku game (1983) 407
Keaton, Buster 99
keikō eiga 70, 288, 296n23, 466
Kelly, William 423
kengeki 287
Kenkoku no haru (1932) 129
Kessen no ōzora e (1943) 453
Khanjian, Arsinée 385
Kiarostami, Abbas 549
Kibō no kuni (2012) 380
The Kid From Spain (1932) 336
Kido, Shirō 4, 43, 112, 118, 260
Kigeki: Ekimae danchi (1961) 412
kihachimono 409, 417n15
Kikō kantai dairagā fifteen (1983) 496
Kikō sōseiki Mospeada (1983) 496
Kikuchi, Kan 98, 328
Kikuchi, Yūhō 328
Kill!, **see** *Kiru* (1968)

Kill Bill (2003) 352, 359*n*13
Kim, Dong Hoon 440
Kim Ki-duk 494
Kim Puja 486
Kimura, Sato 369
Kimura, Shōhachi 423
Kimura, Sotoji 270, 336
Kindaiteki na dōro (1950) 456
Kinema Club 10
Kinema junpō 2–3, 39, 69, 209, 358*n*5, 396
kineorama 29
King, Barry 180
King Kong (1933) 281*n*13
Kings of The Road (1976) 549
Kinmontō ni kakeru hashi (1962) 507
Kino Drama (1937) 200
Kinō kieta otoko (1941) 296*n*33
Kinoshita, Chika 69, 78*n*9, 346*n*16, 422, 434*n*45
   definition of 'J Horror' 298
   on intermediality 158–9
   on introduction of sound 152
Kinoshita, Keisuke 407
Kinugasa, Teinosuke 33, 40, 200, 291, 557
   use of montage 71
Kirihara, Donald; *Patterns of Time: Mizoguchi and the 1930s* 7
Kirishima, bukatsu yamerutteyo (2012) 82
The Kirishima Thing, see Kirishima, bukatsu yamerutteyo (2012)
Kiru (1968) 527
Kisu, Takashi 260
Kitagawa, Fuyuhiko 74
Kitakōji, Takashi 368, 477
Kitamura, Hiroshi 245, 463
   Screening Enlightenment 60
Kitamura, Kazuo 534
Kitamura, Ryūhei 50
Kitano, Takeshi 47, 122, 147, 168, 173, 352
Kitayama, Seitarō 313, 315, 316
Kitt, Eartha 339, 341, 342
Klaffki, Roy Henry 232
Klinger, Barbara 57
Knights of Sidonia, see Sidonia no kishi (TV 2014–15)
Ko, Mika 530, 537
Kobayashi, Akira 518, 521
Kobayashi, Atsushi 269, 273–4

Kobayashi, Hakudō 195
Kobayashi, Hideo 286
Kobayashi, Ichizō 114
Kobayashi, Issa 401
Kobayashi, Masaki 41, 262
Kobayashi, Masaru 142
Kobayashi, Nobuhiko 92*n*2
Kobayashi, Sadahiro 31
Kobe Documentary Film Festival 174
Kobe Planet Film Archive 216, 225*n*11
Kobori, Akio 292
Kōchiyama Sōshun (1936) 296*n*33
Kodomo gikai (1947) 468
Kogata eiga (journal) 219
Kōgenji (1961) 518
Kōhī jikō (2003) 49
Koike, Teruo 194
kojin eiga 215
Kokkatsu 111
Kokuhaku (2010) 81, 87–91, 89
   awards 81
   characters and plot 81
   vs novel 91
   vs *Rashomon* 81, 87–8
kokumin eiga (national cinema) 3–4, 15
   musicals as 338
Kokuren to nihon (1956) 453, 454, 457, 458, *459*, 460, 461
Kokuren to sekai no funsō (1950) 459
Kokurenki no shitani (1950) 459
kokusaika policy 548–9, 554*n*35
Kokushi musō (1932) 296*n*33
Komatsu, Hiroshi 9, 28, 33, 39, 328
   on development of Japanese cinema 30
Kome (1957) 403
Konishiroku 219
*Konjiki yash*a (1897–1903) 328
Kono kubi ichiman goku (1963) 262
kontentsu 204, 209
Koos, Leonard R. 209
Korea 5, 135*n*3
   annexation 536
   early cinema 36*n*43
   Film Ordinance 62
   (*see also* South Korea; *zainichi*)
Korean resident(s) in Japan, *see zainichi*
Korean War 291, 454, 459, 538
Kore-eda, Hirokazu 1, 203
   as author 50
   international reputation 47
Korega Russia da!, see Man with a Movie Camera (1929)

Koroshiya Ichi (2001) 499, 554*n*9
Koschman, Victor J. 362, 373
Kōshikei (1968) 84, 92*n*17, *120*, 131, 187, 480
Kosugi, Takehisa 199
Kotani, Sōichi 'Henry' 25, 32, 111, 154, 231–2, 233–5
   influence on Japanese industry 234
   at Shōchiku 234
   work in the US 234
kouta eiga 155–6, 162*n*29, 338
Kōya no toseinin (1970) 526
Koyama, Eizō 63
Kracauer, Siegfried 54
Kubata, Nao 387–9, 392*n*47
   vs Fujiwara 388
Kubo, Yutaka 220
Kuchibue ga nagareru minatomachi (1960) 521
Kuchinskaya, Olga 392*n*27
Kujira (1927) 314
Kūki ningyō (2009) *204*
Kuki, Shūzō 72
Kuleshov, Lev
   Art of the Cinema 70
   The Practice of Film Direction 70
Kulturfilm 317
Kumonosu jō (1956) 291, 340
Kunisada Chūji (1924) 359*n*12
Kunisada Chūji (1935) 359*n*12
Kunisada Chūji (1960) 359*n*12
Kunisada, Chūji 350
Kunisada Chuji: Flight to Ōshū/Kunisada Chūji ochiyuki Ōshūji (1926) 359*n*12
Kunisada Chuji trilogy (1933) 359*n*12
Kuno, Osamu 295*n*21
Kurahara, Korehito 69
Kurata, Fumindo; *A Theory of Screenwriting* 74–5
Kuri, Yōji 198
Kurihara, Thomas 25, 32
Kurita, Hiromi 536
Kurita, Toyomichi 231–2, 233, 238–9
   training in the US 238
Kurobara no yakata (1969) 182, 183–5, *184*, *185*
Kurosaka, Keita 194
Kurosawa, Akira 1, 38, 40, 50, 138, 557
   auteur theory analysis 44
   awards 117
   books on 5
   Burch on 83

European influence 91
funding difficulties 548
influence on Hollywood 527
international recognition 182
production design 261
use of music 272–3, 274–5
wartime work 140, 281*n*21
on Westerns 520
Kurosawa, Haruyasu 303
Kurosawa, Kiyoshi 9, 47, 168, 173, 300, 307, 322
   on definition of horror 299
   on Nakagawa 309*n*27
Kurotokage (1968) 179, *183*, 183–5
Kurutta ichipēji (1926) 33, *33*, 200
Kurutta kajitsu (1956) 142, 182, 558
Kusakabe, Kyūshirō 429
Kushner, Barak 139
Kuzui, Kinshirō 197
Kwaidan (1965) 273
Kyō, Machiko 513
Kyojin to gangu (1959) 424
Kyojinden (1938) 296*n*35
Kyojyū meikyū (2008) 196
kyōkaku 350
Kyokushiteki eros: Renka 1974 (1974) 534
Kyōren no onna shishō (1926) 130
Kyōshitsu no kodomotachi (1954) 468, 469
Kyoto 3, 31
   as centre of film production 238, 287
   and early cinema 286
   early movie houses in 109
   experimental film in 199–200
   film museums 217, 225*n*11
   and *jidaigeki* 127
   studios in 110, 112, 119–20
   theatre districts 127, 131
   vs Tokyo 286
Kyōwakai 128–9
kyūgeki 110
kyūha 327–8
Kyushu 531

La Coquille et le clergyman (1928) 194
La Sacrifice (2003) 392*n*27
A Labyrinth of Residence, see Kyojyū meikyū (2008)
Ladd, Alan 525
Lady Meng Jiang, see Meng jiang nu (1939)
Lady Snowblood, see Shirayuki hime (1973)

Lamarre, Thomas 9, 60, 206
Lampert, Andrew 221
Land of Hope, see Kibō no kuni (2012)
landscape
   Cold War co-productions 507–11
   diversity of 491
   and ecological cinema 380–1
   in Fukushima documentaries 385
   in Japanese Westerns 520–1, 524
   and national/regional identity 403, 532
   regional differences 531
   rural 394–406
   in Westerns 519–20
L'assassinat du grand-duc Serge (1905) 127
The Last Emperor (1987) 58
The Last Samurai (2003) 527
Last Year at Marienbad (1961) 545
Lastra, James 151
Late Autumn, see Akibiyori (1960)
Late Chrysanthemums, see Bangiku (1954)
Late Spring, see Banshun (1949)
Latour, Bruno 165
Lauretis, Teresa de 100
Lawrence of Arabia (1962) 274
Le Cinéma Eiga (1975) 196
Lee, Bruce 496
Lee, Peggy 339
Lee, Sangjoon 511
Lefebvre, Martin 380, 381, 393*n*54
Legend of the Ghost Cat of Saga, see Saga kaibyō den (1937)
Legend of the White Snake, see Baishe chuan (1939)
Les Diaboliques (1955) 299
lesbianism 96–7, 184
L'Etoile de mer (1928) 194
'Let's Meet in Yurakucho'/'Yūrakuchō de aimashō' 426
Lev, Peter 513
Levine, Irwin 523
Li Daoxin 440
   Zhongguo dianying shi 1937–1945 446
Li Xianglan, *see* Ri, Kōran
Liberal Democratic Party (LDP) 453
The Life of Oharu, see Saikaku ichidai onna (1952)
Light and Shadow, see Hikari to kage (1940)
lighting 32, 233, 332

kabuki theatre 234
Lightning, see Inazuma (1952)
Lim, Desiree 105*n*30
Lin Baisheng 445
Lin Dai 515
Lin Zexu 448
Lingbo xianzi (1943) 445
Lingering Memories, see Suguruhino yamaneko (2014)
literature
   adaptations of 85
   and film 75
   and montage theory 71
Little Voices from Fukushima, see Chiisaki koe no canon – Sentaku suru hitobito (2014)
Liu Naou 444, 451*n*17
Living, see Ikiru (1952)
Living in Fukushima: A Story of Decontamination and Reconstruction, see Fukushima ni ikiru: Josen to fukkō no monogatari (2013)
Living on Earth, see Tsuchi ni ikiru (1941)
Living on the River Agano, see Aga ni ikiru (1992)
Lo, Kwai-cheung 514
'the long take' 75, 261, 387
   in early cinema 132
   in Japanese New Wave 76
Louisiana Story (1948) 456
Love Canal 379
Love Live!, see Love live! (2013)
Love live! (2013) 322
Love Me Tonight (1932) 336
The Love of Sumako the Actress, see Joyū Sumako no koi (1947)
Lowenhaupt Tsing, Anna 60
Lubitsch, Ernst 557
Lugosi, Bela 301, 306
Lumière brothers (Auguste & Louis) 28
The Lusty Shogun and His Twenty-One Dolls, see Ero shōgun to nijūichi-nin no aishō (1972)
The Lytton Investigation Team in Manchuria, see Manshū ni okeru ritton chōsadan (1932)

M. Pathe Company 110
The Machinist (2004) 91
Mackenzie, Adrian 152
Madam Butterfly (1954) 546, 546–7

Madame Butterfly, **see** *Hudie furen* (1942)
Madame White Snake, **see** *Byaku fujin no yōren* (1956)
Madame to nyōbō (1931) 112, *113*, 260, 270, 336
Maeda, Tamon 465*n*33
Magami Gitarō 78*n*12
Magino monogatari – Yōsanhen (1977) 15, 363, *369*, 369–72, *370*, *372*
  background 369
  vs other Ogawa Productions 371
  as part of a larger work 370
The Magino Village Story – Raising Silkworms, **see** *Magino monogatari – Yōsanhen* (1977)
Magnetic Scramble (1968) 195
The Magnificent Seven (1960) 519, 524
Mai hua nü (1942) 445
Makabe, Jin 365
Maki, Morinage 181
Makino, Mamoru 10
Makino, Masahiro 44, 297*n*39, 338
  jidaigeki 292
Makino, Mitsuo 115
Makino, Shōzō 110, 286, 300
Makino, Takashi 201
Malaysia 511
Maltby, Richard 265
The Mamushi Brothers, **see** *Chōeki Tarō: Mamushi no kyōdai* (1971)
Man in a Torrent, **see** *Gekiryū ni ikiru otoko* (1962)
Man of the West (1958) 339
The Man Who Shot Liberty Valance (1962) 519
Man with a Movie Camera (1929) 73, 194
  Japanese release 201*n*4
The Man Worth 10,000 Bushels, **see** *Kono kubi ichiman goku* (1963)
Manabe, Hiroshi 197–8
Manchukuo 128, 439
  League of Nations decree 465*n*25
Manchukuo Film Association 446
Manchuria 5, 100, 101
  annexation 536
  film exhibition in 128, 129
  prostitutes 482, 483
  as setting for Westerns 526
Manchurian Film Association 100, 101
Man'ei 115, 129, 440, 447
manga 17, 122, 203–13, 317, 392*n*48
  vs anime 312

'art' cinema 206–11
film adaptation trends 204
homosexuality in 102, 106*n*43
self-publishing 501*n*51
wartime 318
manga jissha eiga 203
Le Manoir du diable (1896) 300
Manovich, Lev 321
Manshū ni okeru ritton chōsadan (1932) 129
Mansion of the Ghost Cat, **see** *Bōrei kaibyō yashiki* (1958)
Man-Slashing, Horse-Piercing Sword, **see** *Zanjin zanbaken* (1929)
Mantetsu 129, 482
'Mantetsu kouta' 481–4
Marcantonio, Carla; *Global Melodrama: Nation, Body and History* 326
Marco Polo Bridge Incident 114
Marine Snow (1960) 198
Marran, Christine 380
Martenot, Maurice 282*n*37
Martial Arts films 231, 496–8
Maruo, Sadamu 429
Maruyama, Masao 295*n*21
Marxism 5, 26, 69, 296*n*32
  and authorship theory 40
  and documentary theory 367
  and early cinema 26
  and ecology 395
  and *shutaisei* 362
Masaoka, Kenzō 315, 318
'mass culture theory' 7, 9
Matatabi sannin yakuza (1965) 355
The Matrix (1999) 205
Matson, Yuri 429
Matsuda, Masao 474
  on *Assatsu no mori* 364
Matsui, Shōyō 250
Matsui, Sumako 12, 243–58, *244*
Matsui, Yasuko 534
Matsumoto, Jun 210
Matsumoto, Shōji 199–200
Matsumoto, Toshio 77, 195, 429, 466, 540
  on Ogawa's work 364
  on subjectivity 362
Matsuo, Bashō 531
Matsuyama, Masako 324*n*30
Matsuyama, Takashi 261
Matsuyama, Zenzō 131, 429
Maurice (1988) 102
Mayer, Moe 181

Mayne, Judith 97, 100, 189*n*24
  Cinema and Spectatorship 57
Mayuzumi, Toshirō 273, 338
McDonald, Keiko 353
  From Book to Screen 85
McDonnell, Carrie 337
Mechademia 10
'media mix' 8, 17, 204–6, 317, 320
  in *Boys Over Flowers* franchise 210
  definitions 205
  influence on Western media 206
  and *Magino monogatari* 369–70
  and stardom 210
  theme songs 210
Meet Me in St. Louis (1944) 337
Meeting of the World, **see** *Sekai no tsudoi* (1952)
Meiji Restoration 14, 110, 166, 285, 294*n*1, 327, 349, 396, 519
  censorship 138
  family life 408
  and national identity 531, 532
  as setting for *jidaigeki* 357
  Tokyo 420
'Meke meke (meque meque)' 179
Méliès, Georges 300
Mellen, Joan 95–6
  Freiburg on 104*n*9
  The Waves at Genji's Door 95
melodrama 14, 266, 325–35
  components of genre 328
  historicisation 326–9
  modernity 331–3
  nature of genre 325
  sensationalism 325
  shinpa theatre influence 325
  theatrical influence 327
  Western influence 328
Memento (2000) 91
Memories of Adachi, **see** *Adachi no kioku* (2013)
memory 91
  cultural 395, 433*n*10
  and performance 251
Men Who Fish, **see** *Sun in the Last Days of the Shogunate*
The Men Who Tread on the Tiger's Tail, **see** *Tora no o o fumu otoko tachi* (1945/52)
Meng jiang nu (1939) 442
mercury poisoning 381
Merry Christmas Mr. Lawrence, **see** *Senjō no Merry Christmas*

Messmer, Otto 315
Metz, Christian 54, 75
Mexico mushuku (1962) 521
Mexico Wanderer, **see** *Mexico mushuku* (1962)
The Midnight Meat Train (2008) 50
Mifune, Toshirō 143, 291, 529n33
Mighty Morphin' Power Rangers, **see** *Super sentai*
Mihara, Yōko 353
Miike, Takashi 47, 274, 307, 322, 493, 554n9
Mikami, Hiroshi 525
Miki, Shigeru 395, 399
Mikuni, Rentarō 534
Mill, John Stuart 72
Millennium Mambo (2001) 565
Le Million (1931) 557
The Million Ryo Pot, **see** *Tange sazen yowa: Hyakuman ryō no tsubo* (1935)
Milne, Tom 42
Mimasu, Aiko 116
Mimura, Akira 'Harry' 231–2, 233, 235–7, 336
 work for Tōhō 235
 work in Hollywood 235
Mimura, Shintarō 114
Mina Talkie 153–4
Minagawa, Yoshizō 153
Minakata, Kumagusu 371
Minamata disease 381–3, 473
 compared to Fukushima victims 383
Minamata: Kanjasan to sono sekai (1971) 381, *382*, 472
Minamata o kokuhatsu suru kai – Tent mura Video nikki (1972) 195
Minamata: The Victims and Their World, **see** *Minamata: Kanjasan to sono sekai* (1971)
Minami, Hiroshi 54
Minawa, Ichirō 281n28
Ming mo yihen (1939) 441–2
Minna ikinakerebanaranai: Hito, mushi, tori (1984) 372, 404
Minnelli, Vincente 263
minshūshi movement 363, 365–8
 origin of term 374n16
 social context 367
Misaki, Tomeko 455
Misawa, Mamie 63, 440
mise en scène 249
misemono 29

Mishima, Yukio 179, 180, 183, 197
Misora, Hibari 335, 338–40, 350, 353, 355, 359n13
 acid attack 344–5, 347n46
 popularity 343
Miss Kukiko, **see** *Juzi guniang* (1955)
Miss Okichi, **see** *Ojō Okichi* (1935)
Mitchell, Richard 139
Mitsubachi no haoto to chikyū no kaiten (2011) 380, 384, 387
Mitsuhashi, Junko 423
Miura, Mitsuo 235
Miwa, Akihiro 12, 179–91
 international vs domestic fame 179
 queerness 181–2
 stage roles 185, 187
 star quality 185
 star vehicles 183–5
 and theatrical tradition 181
 voice 185–6, 190n32
 in *Woman Gambler* series 182–3
Mix, Tom 519
Miyamoto, Nobuko 524, 525
Miyao, Daisuke 28, 32, 331
 on Shōchiku productions 123n16
Miyazaki, Hayao 1, 186, 310, 312
Miyoshi, Daisuke 221, 222
Mizoguchi, Akiko 99
 Theorizing BL As a Transformative Genre: Boys' Love Moves the World Forward 102
Mizoguchi, Kenji 27, 40, 71, 75, 100, 167, 243, 254, 269, 291, 422, 513
 awards 117
 Burch on 83
 feminist perspective on 95
 influences 557
 international recognition 182
 reputation in Europe 41–2
 visual style 261
Mizutani, Hiroshi 261
Mobiles and Vitrines (1954) 200
Mochinaga, Tadahito 451
Modern Highway, **see** *Kindaiteki na dōro* (1950)
Modern Woman, **see** *Gendai no josei* (1923)
Modern Yakuza: Outlaw Killer, **see** *Gendai yakuza: Hito kiri yota*
modernism
 in documentary theory 367
 in melodrama 326
 and *Rashomon* 81
 scholars 84

modernity 2, 249, 333n9, 426
 and authorship 47–50
 and melodrama 331–3
 and the melodrama 15
 and narrative 83
 and national identity 326
 and representation of women 96
 (**see also** vernacular modernism)
Moe no suzaku (1997) 168
Moeyasui mimi (1967) 199
moga 96
Mokuren jūgun (1939) 441, *441*, 443, 447, 449, 450
Momotarō umi to shinpei (1945) 315, 318
Momotaro's Divine Sea Warriors, **see** *Momotarō umi to shinpei* (1945)
monomane 347n32
Mononoke hime (1997) 168, 186
Monroe, Marilyn 342
monster movies 118–19, 308n6
montage 69–80, 427, 434n45, 470
 anti-montage discourse 74
 arrival in Japan 69–71
 critical response 69
 decline in Japan 74
 in early cinema 30
 global spread of 71
 goal 74
 Hikaru on 70
 in horror 306–7
 impact on non-cinema media 71, 73
 Japanese theories of 72
 Nakai Masakazu on 73
 and philosophy 72
 and reality 75
 and sound 74–6, 272
 Soviet writing on 69–70
 translation into Japanese 69
Moonlight and Pretzels (1933) 336
Mori, Iwao 157–8
 Regarding the Global Popularity of the Sound Film 158
 on sound technology 159–60
Mori, Kakuko 253
Mori, Kazuo 44
Mori, Masayuki 513
Mori, Mineko 290
Mori, Ōgai 296n36
Mori, Tatsuya 386–7
Mori to mizuumi no matsuri (1958) 406n44

Morin, Edgar 185, 190n26
  Les Stars 180
Morita, Yoshimitsu 559
Morley, David 57
Morocco (1930) 158, 339
Morris-Suzuki, Tessa 530
The Most Beautiful, *see* Ichiban utsukushiku (1944)
Mother, *see* Okāsan (1952)
Mother (1926) 70
Motion Picture Code of Ethics Committee, *see* Eirin
Motion Picture Exhibition Regulations 56
Motion Picture Film Inspection Regulations 1925 139
Moussinac, Léon; *Le Cinema sovietique* 70, 73
Movie (magazine) 41
Moyuru ōzora (1940) 115
Mudan hua xia (1942) 445
Mujin chitai (2012) 380–1, 384–7, 386
  vs *311* 386
Mukōjima 111
Mulan cong jun, *see* Mokuren jūgun (1939)
Mulan Joins the Army, *see* Mokuren jūgun (1939)
Mulvey, Laura 54
  Visual Pleasure and Narrative of Cinema 55, 95
Muncel, Albert 268n24
Münsterberg, Hugo 69
  The Photoplay: A Psychological Study 54
Mura, Haruo 399
Mura no fujin gakkyū (1957) 468
Murakami, Tadahisa 296n26
Murakami, Takashi 312, 313
Muraki, Yoshirō 261
Murao, Kaoru 400
Muraoka, Saburō 195
Murayama, Kyōichirō 9
Murayama, Tomoyoshi 32
Murnau, F.W. 557
Murō, Saisei 40
Mushanokōji, Kanzaburō 429
music 14, 133, 157–8, 269–82
  choice of instruments 273
  classical vs jazz 159
  early development 270–3
  and experimental film 201
  at P.C.L. 157
  postwar period 280
  sheet music excerpts 271, 276, 278
  'talkie music' 159
  traditional 276
  Western vs Japanese 269–70
  (*see also* gidayu; song; sound)
musicals 14, 335–47
  early cinema 270
  genre theory 336–7
  Hollywood vs Japanese 335
  in Shanghai 445–6
  yakuza 350
Musser, Charles 26, 126
Musume tsuma haha (1960) 415
Muteki ga ore o yondeiru (1960) 562
'My Blue Heaven' 336
My Neighbours the Yamadas, *see* Tonari no Yamada-kun (1999)
Myriad of Colours 445

Nabi no koi (1999) 531
Nabi's Love, *see* Nabi no koi (1999)
Nada, Hisashi 218
Nadare (1937) 334n22
Nagae, Michitarō 74
Nagai, Frank 426
Nagareru (1956) 422
Nagasaki 379, 384, 391n4
Nagasugita haru (1957) 179
Nagata, Hideo
  Carmen Has Passed Away/Carmen ikinu 245
Nagata, Masaichi 116, 130, 164, 166, 302, 511, 541, 542–5
  on France 545
  on Western audiences 544
Nagato, Yōhei 253, 269, 273
Nagatsuka, Takashi; *Tsuchi* 396
Nagaya shinshiroku (1947) 409
Nagib, Lúcia 11
Nagoya 31
Naibu hibaku o ikinuku (2012) 384
Naitō, Akira 260, 374n13
Naitō, Masatoshi 365, 366
Naitō, Rune 341
Nakagawa, Nobuo 299, 303–6, 309n21
  influence on J-horror 307
  influence on later directors 307
  use of montage theory 306–7
  visual style 303
Nakai, Masakazu 72, 73, 286, 294n6
  on montage theory 73–4
  theory of film 74

Nakamura, Hideyuki 455, 472
Nakane, Hiroshi 157, 158
Nakanishi Binji 463
Nakano, Minoru 343
Nakasone, Yasuhiro 171, 548
Nakata, Hideo 47, 50
Nakaya, Fujiko 195
Nakayama Shichiri (1930) 154
Naked Island, *see* Hadaka no shima (1960)
Naked Lunch (1991) 548
The Naked Town, *see* Hadaka no machi (1937)
Namiko (1931) 334n22
Nani ga kanojo o sō sasetaka (1930) 70
Naniwa, Chieko 425
Naniwa onna (1940) 253
Nanook of the North (1922), 456
Napier, Susan J. 203
Narayama bushikō (1959) 424
The Narcissus Fairy, *see* Lingbo xianzi (1943)
Naremore, James 249
Narita International Airport 404, 467, 473
Narita, Ryūichi 367
narrative 17, 81–93, 389
  Burch on 83
  in early cinema 111
  and landscape 380
  and montage 75
  multi-viewpoint 82, 91, 92n1
  and spectatorship 55
  trends 82–3
  types 55
  and unreliable narration 85
Naruse, Mikio 38, 40, 261, 407, 409, 422
  representation of women 96
Naruto (1997–) 321
national cinema 557, *see* kokumin eiga
National Cinema Circle Association 170
National Film Archive of Japan 10, 135, 215
  early amateur film project 201n3
  kogata eiga 218
National Film Center, *see* National Film Archive of Japan
national identity 31, 96, 169, 557
  and cinematography 232
  and diversity 530
  exclusion of minorities 531
  and globalism 491
  and jidaigeki 285

and landscape 403
and modernity 326
and Okinawa 531–3
postwar period 464, 542
National Spiritual Mobilization Movement 3
Natori, Yōnosuke 431
Natsu no imōto (1972) 13, 530, 533, 534, 536–7, *537*, 538
naturalism 398–9
Needham, Gary 541
Negishi, Kan'ichi 115
The Neighbour's Wife and Mine, see Madame to nyōbō (1931)
Nemuri Kyōshiro series 116
neoliberalism 176
Never a Foot Too Far, Even (2012) 196–7
New Art School 71
The New Dawn of Billy the Kid, see Billy za kid no atarashii yoake (1988)
The New Earth, see Atarashiki tsuchi (1937)
New Film System 444, 452n19
New German Cinema Festival 549
New Neighbors, see Atarashii rinjin (1952)
the New Wave 43, 44, 557
at film festivals 167–8
use of montage 76
New York 199, 200, 458–9
New York Motion Picture Company 234
newsreels 127, 439
Newton, Esther
Mother Camp 181
NHK 318, 471
Nichidō 318
Nichols, Bill 477, 477n8
Nigerian cinema 489
Night of the Living Dead (1968) 298
Nihon Amateur Cinema League 218
Nihon bōryoku rettō (1975) 482–3, 484
Nihon jokyōden: Kyōkaku geisha (1969) 350
Nihon jokyōden: Makkana dokyōbana (1970) 350, 526
Nihon kaihō sensen – Sanrizuka no natsu (1968) 364–5
Nihon kaihō sensen – Sanrizuka (1970) 365, 467
Nihon kyōka den (1973) 359n5
Nihon kyōkaku den (1964–71) 350
Nihon no sugao (TV 1957–64) 471, 472

Nihon Shōmei Kyōkai (Japanese Association of Film Lighting) 233
Nihon shunka-kō (1967) 16, 479–88, *482*, 484, 487
differences from novel 488n10
plot 481
use of female body 481
use of song 481–2
Nihon University College of Art 8
Nihonjin to Jirochō (TV 1958) 471
Nikkatsu 128, 313, 396, 426
action movies 118
bankruptcy 121
collapse 113
films for distribution in China 129
formation of 29, 109, 520
house genres 561
importing foreign films 559
kaiki films 300
melodramas 328
'pink films' 121, 131, 238
program pictures 558, 559
restarted production 118
studio destruction 286
television productions 120
Westerns 520–2
Nils no fushigi na tabi (1980) 495
Ninagawa, Mika 206
Ninjō kami fūsen (1937) 76, 114, 557
Ninkyō nakasendō (1960) 358n5
Nippon Development and Finance (NDF) 548
Nippon Documentarist Union (NDU) 362
Nippon konchūki (1963) 534
Nishi Ginza ekimae (1958) 420, 426–9, *427*
gender politics 427
song 427–8
Nishi, Gorō 271
Nishida, Kitarō 72
Nishikawa, Etsuji 236
Nishikawa, Tomonari 197
Nishioka, Tatsuhiko 222
Nishiyama, Uzō 413
Nixon, Rob 381
No Man's Zone, see Mujin chitai (2012)
Nō otoko (2013) 239–40
No Regrets for Our Youth, see Waga seishun ni kui nashi (1946)
Nobody Knows, see Dare mo shiranai (2004)

Noda, Shinkichi 362
Nodo jiman-kyō jidai (1949) 338
Noguchi, Hiroshi 521
Noh 6, 245
Nolletti, Arthur Jr. 409
Nolletti, Arthur Jr. & Desser, David;
Reframing Japanese Cinema 7
Nomura, Takeshi 558
Nomura, Yoshitarō 41
Nongue, Lucien 127
Nornes, Markus 9, 15, 59, 370–1, 467, 476
on *Assatsu no mori* 474
Forest of Pressure: Ogawa Shinsuke and Postwar Japanese Documentary 362
Japanese Documentary Film: The Meiji Era through Hiroshima 361–2
nostalgia 387–9, 528n2
boom in the 21st century 527
in music 271
post-economic bubble 527
and 'the Shōwa 30s' 407
and Westerns 519–20
in yakuza genre 348–9
Notes on the Shinano Climate: Kobayashi Issa, see Shinano fūdoki: Kobayashi Issa (1941)
Nowell-Smith, Geoffrey 262–3
NTV 318
nuclear bombs 145–6, 379, 391n4, 476
survivors 475
nuclear disasters 383, 384
(*see also* Chernobyl; Fukushima)
Nuclear Nation, see Futaba kara tōku hanarete (2012)
Nykvist, Sven 238

Ōatari sanshoku musume (1957) 335, 340
Oatsurae Jirokichi kōshi (1931) 296n33
obake eiga 301
Ōbayashi, Nobuhiko 121–2, 194, 198, 219, 520
Obitani, Yuri 194
O'Brien, Charles 151
Odawara Daizō 463
Odayaka na nichijō (2012) 389–90
Odd Obsession, see Kagi (1959)
Odoru ryūgūjō (1949) 339
Ōe, Masanori 200

Ōfuji, Nobuo 314, *314*
Ogawa Productions 15, 172, 361–75, 365–7
  camera technology 367
  change of location 368, 369
  exhibition of films 366–7
  legacy 372–3
  limitations 373
Ogawa, Shinsuke 15, 172, 361, 366
  on *Assatsu no mori* 364
  depression 369
  early recognition 363, 364
  essays 375*n*32
  and Iwanami Films 472
  spectatorship theory 59
Ogi, Masahiro 131, 429
Ogino, Shigeji 193, 215, 226*n*22
Oguma, Eiji 473
Ohayō (1959) 408, 409–10, *410*, 414
Ōizumi Film Company 117, 456
Ojō Okichi (1935) 296*n*33
Okada, Susumu 76, 470
Okada, Tokiko 329
Okamoto, Kihachi 522, 527
Okāsan (1952) 409
Ōkawa, Hiroshi 120, 316
Okayama Orphanage 128
Okazaki, Kōzō 456
Oki, Hiroyuki 105*n*30
Okinawa 12–13, 15, 530–40
  assimilation by mainland Japan 532–3
  discrimination against natives 533
  documentaries on 361
  handover 531
  in Japanese cinema 534
  vs other Japanese colonies 536
  pre-war 530–1
  prostitution on 538
  regional identity 533
  US military bases on 515, 530, 537–9
  in wartime 536–7
Okiyama, Hideko 534
Ōkōchi, Denjirō 116, 289
Ōkubo, Ryō 28–9
Ōkuma, Nobuyuki 72
Ōkura, Mitsugi 116, 303
Old and New (1929) 71
Older Brother, Younger Sister, *see* Ani imōto (1936)
Olympic games 432
Ōmori, Seitarō 269

On Wings of Love, *see* Ōatari sanshoku musume (1957)
One Piece, *see* One piece (TV 1997–)
One piece (TV 1997–) 321
Onibaba (1964) 273, 298
Ōnishi, Keiji 201
The Only Son, *see* Hitori musuko (1936)
Only Women at Night, *see* Onna bakari no yoru (1961)
Onna bakari no yoru (1961) 97
Onna dearu koto (1958) 179
Onna kyūketsuki (1959) 306
Onna tobakushi (1967–71) 182, 351
Onna tobakushi tsubokurabe (1970) 182–3
onnagata 3, 6, 25–6, 111, 179, 180–2, 185, 550
  defence of 33
  disappearance of 31
  origin of practice 181
  phasing out 111
Ōno, Kazuo 550
Ono, Yoko 197, 199
Onoe, Kikugorō VII 359*n*11
Onoe, Matsunosuke 3, 28, 110, 286, 295*n*9, 300, 328
Operation Brown Rat, *see* Dobunezumi sakusen (1963)
Opium War 439, 447, 449
Opium War (1943) 447
Orandajin no shashin (1974) *196*
Orientalism 5, 7, 27, 68, 294*n*4, 541
  and anime 322*n*1
  and authorship 83
  in European festivals 168
  and European film festivals 168
  ironic use 551–3
  of Kawakita Nagamasa 545–7
  in *Madame Butterfly* 546
  of Masaichi Nagata 542–5
  and narrative 83
Orizuru Osen (1935) 334*n*22
Orochi (1925) 287, 290, 295*n*17, 295*n*22
O'Rourke, Jim 201
Osaka 31
Osanai, Kaoru 111, 250
Oshidori utagassen (1939) 292, 296*n*33, 338
Oshii, Mamoru 321
Ōshima, Keitarō 197
Ōshima, Nagisa 1, 6, 16, 43, 50, 167, 261, 285, 294*n*3, 364, 479, 548

financial backing 466
  primitivism 534
  subjectivity 362
  urban vs rural films 540*n*12
Ōtaka, Hiroo 550
otaku 60–1, 494, 498–9
Otoko wa tsuraiyo series (1969–97) 409, 522–3, 557
Otome gokoro sannin shimai (1935) 157
Ōtomo, Ryūtarō 526
Otōto (1960) 413–14
Ōtsu, Kōshirō 364, 474
Ōtsuka, Eiji 8, 317, 323*n*25
Our Neighbour, Miss Yae, *see* Tonari no Yae-chan (1934)
The Outsiders, *see* Mori to mizuumi no matsuri (1958)
OVA 320–1
overseas distribution
  arthouse 491
  film festivals and 173, 491
  mainstream 492
Owl's Castle, *see* Fukurō no shiro (1999)
Ōya, Sōichi 420
Ozaki, Kōyō 328
  The Golden Demon/Konjiki Yasha 155
Ozawa, Eitarō 245
Ozu, Yasujirō 1, 6, 15, 27, 38, 40, 71, 218, 289, 329, 338, 407, 422, 542, 554*n*6
  books on 5
  Burch on 83
  focalisation 87
  on his own work 42, 417*n*16
  influences 557
  production design 261
  recognition in Europe 42
  rejection of widescreen 262
  spectatorship approach 56
  use of colour 424
  visual style 410
  Yoshida on 45

Pacchigi! (2005) 480, *481*
A Page of Madness, *see* Kurutta ichipēji (1926)
Pagel, Caren 147
Paik, Nam June 195
'Pan Asian Cinema' 552
Panasonic 548
panpan eiga 98
Paramount Studios 109

Park, Chan-wook 494
Parsons, Gerald E. 523
Partisan zenshi (1969) 476, 478n39
Passing Fancy, see Dekigokoro (1933)
The Passion of a Woman Teacher, see Kyōren no onna shishō (1926)
P.C.L., *see* Photo Chemical Laboratory
Peace Preservation Law 139
Pearl Harbour 76, 114, 233, 317
Pearson, Roberta E. 249
Peerless Patriot, see Kokushi musō (1932)
Pension Mimosas (1935) 557
The Peony Lantern (1914) 300
'people's history' movement, *see minshūshi* movement
People's Rights Movement 294n1, 367
Pépé le Moko (1937) 562
performance 243–58
    exteriority vs interiority 246–53
    naturalism 249
    pantomime traditions 249
    physicality 252–3
    psychological style 249
    styles and approaches 246–7
    Western methods 250
period films, *see jidaigeki*
Perry, Tyler 231
'petit bourgeois film,' *see shōshimin eiga*
Philippines 463, 511
    immigrant workers from 479
    US military bases 515
Phillipe, Gérard 41
philosophy 292
    of globalisation 490–1
    and montage theory 72
Photo Chemical Laboratory (P.C.L.) 112
    founding 112–13
    music 157
    musicals 270, 336
    sound 154
Pia Film Festival 169, 170, 171
    scholarships 174
    selection process 173–4, 177n42
Piaf, Edith 185, 342
picture scrolls 6
Pigs and Battleships, see Buta to gunkan (1964)
'pink films' 121
    exhibition of 131
    in film festivals 167–8
    production design 262
    and social protest 466

    and violence 145
    and yakuza genre 352, 360n24
The Pirate and the Woman, see Kaizoku to onna (1923)
A Place in the Sun (1951) 558
The Plateau Man, see Kōgenji (1961)
Play It Again, Sam (1972) 561
playhouses 127
Pokémon 492
Pollock, Sheldon 491
Pom Poko, see Heisei tanuki gassen ponpoko (1994)
Popular Front movement 72
pornography 105n30, 238, 357, 489
    exhibition of 131
    Nikkatsu 121
    (*see also* 'pink films')
The Pornopgraphers, see Jinruigaku nyūmon (1966)
postwar era 259
    and authorship theory 40–7
    cinema funding 543
    decline of family 417n30
    film exhibition 129–31
    and gender roles 355
    Japanese national identity 542
    and Japanese Western 518–19
    male stardom 182–3
    melodramas 334n21
    music 280
    rise of yakuza films 349
    romance 184
    in Shanghai 450
    use of long takes 76
The Postwar Flourishing of Japanese Documentary and *Media Wars: Then & Now* (1991) 361
poverty 140, 396–7, 401, 444
The Power of Plants (1934) 73
Prehistory of Partisans, see Partisan zenshi (1969)
presentationalism 6
prewar era
    authorship theory 40
    documentaries 361–2
    gender in 96
    Japanese films in Europe 553n4
Price, Vincent 299
primitivism 533–6
    sexuality 534–5
Prince, Stephen 83
Princess Katsura, see Katsura hime (1937)

Princess Mononoke, see Mononoke hime (1997)
Princess Yang Kweifei, see Yōhiki
production design 259
    and widescreen technology 262
Profound Desires of the Gods, see Kamigami no fukaki yokubō (1968)
program picture 16
    auteurs 558
    definition 557
    as 'marginal art' 564–6
    and Shōwa era 558
    US vs Japanese meaning 557
Prokino 70, 201n6, 361, 466
    film formats 194
proletarian film movement 70
propaganda 3, 361
    about the UN 458–9
    animation 315, 316–17
    anti-Soviet 461
    and censorship of war films 140
    Hollywood Westerns as 520
    in Manchuria 100, 101
    in Shanghai 442–5, 446
    under US occupation 16, 245, 455–6, 468
    wartime 115, 362
'Proud of My Voice'-Crazy Age, *see Nodo jiman-kyō jidai* (1949)
Provisional Government of the Republic of China 442
Psycho (1960) 298
Puccini, Giacomo; *Madame Butterfly* 546–7
Pudovkin, Vsevolod 70, 75, 272
    Film Acting 69
    The Film Director and Film Material 69
    Film Technique 69
Pulse, see Kairo (2001)
Punishment Room, see Shokei no heya (1956)
'Pure Film Movement,' *see Jun'eiga geki undō*
Purokino 70
The Pursuit of Japanese Documentary: The 1980s and Beyond (1997) 361
'puzzle film' 91

Qiao (1949) 451
Qinshi huangdi, see Shin shikōtei (1962)
Les Quatre cents coups (1959) 42

queerness 12, 179–91
    in *Black Lizard* 184
    film boom 102–3
    film festivals 95, 181
    indentity 100
    manga 106*n*43
    and politics 188
    pornography 105*n*30
    spectatorship 98–100
    (*see also* lesbianism; sexuality)

radiation 381, 384, 390
Radiation: A Slow Death, see Hibakusha: Sekai no owarini (2005)
radio 14, 155, 156, 338
The Rainbow of Odds, see Fuwa no niji (1998)
Raine, Michael 78*n*13, 151, 559
    on stardom 105*n*28
Raised as Sisters, see Chikyōdai (1903)
Rakudai wa shitakeredo (1930) 260
Rāmen zamurai (2012) 525
Ran (1985) 274, 548
Rashōmon (1950) 47, *84*, 90
    awards 41, 117, 166, 492, 541, 542–3
    censorship 141
    contemporary critical response 92*n*2
    critical status 81
    export of 131, 166–8
    and focalisation 85
    and genre conventions 141
    impact on industry 167, 291, 491, 509, 541
    vs *Kokuhaku* 86
    poster *166*
    as prototype 81
    structure and plot 84
    use of music 272
Rayns, Tony 168
realism 44, 362, 397, 398
    and censorship 140
    and *jidaigeki* 289–91
    vs montage theory 75
    and violence 141
Rebecca (1940) 233
Record of a Tenement Gentleman, see Nagaya shinshiroku (1947)
Record of Blood: Sunagawa, see Ryūketsu no kiroku: Sunagawa (1956)
The Red Peony Gambler, see Hibotan bakuto (1968–72)
Red Peony Gambler – Three Yakuza, see Matatabi sannin yakuza (1965)

Red Pier, see Akai hatoba (1958)
Reformed Government of the Republic of China 442, 451*n*8
Reimei (1927) 152
    music 270
Reimei izen (1931) 71
Rēkan! (2015) 322
rekishi eiga (historical film) 289
remakes 16, 556–66
    of *13 Assassins* 275–9
    of Asian films in Hollywood 231
    of Japanese films as Westerns 492
    of J-Horror films 298
    of US films in Japan 493
Rengō tsūshin 130
Renoir, Jean 76
Report from Haneda, see Gennin hōkokusho: Haneda tōsō no kiroku (1967)
Retribution, see Sakebi (2006)
The Return of the Swallow, see Yan guilai (1942)
Rhodes, Eric 42
Rhythm (1934) 193
Ri, Kōran 104*n*16, 115, 338, 448, 449
Ribbon o musubu fujin (1939) 272
Richie, Donald 5, 83, 194, 198, 200, 421, 427, 491
    on censorship 140
    on Japanese identity 534
    on Tokyo 419
    in *Tokyo 1958* 430
Richter, Hans 194
Ring, see Ringu (1999)
Ringu (1999) 50, 298, 307, 308, 554*n*53
Rio Bravo (1959) 339, 519
River (1933) 193
The River of the Strangers 480
Road for the East Peace, see Tōyō wahei no michi (1938)
Road of Chivalry, see Ninkyō nakasendō (1960)
The Road to Peace in the Orient, see Tōyō heiwa no michi (1938)
Robbe-Grillet, Alain 545
Roberts, Mark Downing 43
Robotech (1985) 496
Roden, Ronald 180
Rodowick, David 54
Rogers, Ginger 254
Rogers, Will 519
Rohmer, Eric 41
Rojō no reikon (1921) 82

Rokkasho Rhapsody, see Rokkashomura rhapsody (2006)
Rokkashomura rhapsody (2006) 380, 384
    vs *Ieji* 389
Roman Holiday (1953) 559
Roman Porno 131, 565
A Romance of Kanaya-Koume, see Kanaya Koume (1929)
Romance musume (1956) 335, 340, 359*n*13
Ronald, Richard 412
Rosolato, Guy 483
Ross, Andrew 181
Rotha, Paul 39
    on directors as authors 50*n*9
Rudolph, Alan 231
A Rush for the Patriotism, see Hōkoku bakushin (1937)
Russell, Catherine 38, 96, 326, 409, 414, 421–2
    The Cinema of Naruse Mikio 59
Russo-Japanese War (1904–5) 29, 60, 127, 439
Ruttman, Walter 194, 434*n*45
Ryakushō renzoku shasatsuma (1969) 406*n*45
Ryū, Chishū 411
Ryūketsu no kiroku: Sunagawa (1956) 466, 467, 472
Ryūkyū 531
Ryūtanji, Yū 71

Saburi, Shin 424
The Sad Whistle, see Kanashiki kuchibue (1949)
Sada, Keiji 424
Sadoul, Georges 41
Saga kaibyō den (1937) 301
Said, Edward 294*n*4
Saikaku ichidai onna (1952) 117, 543
Saito, Ayako 9, 95, 182
    on Kinoshita Keisuke 104*n*17
Saitō, Buichi 521
Saïto, Daïchi 196–7, 200
Sakamato, Hirofumi 192, 201
Sakamato, Ryūichi 239
Sakamoto, Kazue 411–12
Sakane, Tazuko 85, 100, *100*
    post-war career 101
    sexuality 101
    wartime career 100
Sakebi (2006) 308
Sakisaka, Ryuichirō 429

sakka 40
Sakuhin (1958) 196
Sakuran (2007) 206–8, *207*, 209
samurai films 1, 139–40
   and Westerns 525–8
Samurai Knights, **see** *Hakkō ryūkitai* (1961)
San Francisco Peace Treaty 459, 462
San xiao (1940) 442
Sanada, Hiroyuki 293
Sanjuro, **see** *Tsubaki Sanjurō* (1962)
Sanma no aji (1962) 411
Sanrizuka – Heta Village, **see** *Sanrizuka: Heta buraku* (1973)
Sanrizuka – Heta buraku (1973) 15, 363, 368
Sanrizuka – Peasants of The Second Fortress (1971) 365
Sanrizuka series (1968–77) 362, 363, 366
Sanshō dayū (1954) 117, 543
   export of 131
Sansho the Bailiff, **see** *Sanshō dayū* (1954)
Sas, Miryam 180, 199
Sasagawa, Keiko 31, 156
Sasayama, Keisuke 248, 249
Satō, Chiyako 156
Satō, Jyūshin 198
Satō, Makoto 373
Satō, Naotake 461
Satō, Tadao 9, 25, 47, 170, 421, 440, 484, 523
   Japanese Film History 109
   on montage theory 77
   Nihon eiga shi 8
   in *Nippon zero nen* 475
   on *Nippon zero nen* 477
Satomi hakkenden (1954) 117
Satsuma shogunate 532
Sawada, Renzō 461
Sawamura, Tsutomu 74, 75
Sawato, Midori 99
Scary True Stories, **see** *Hontō ni atta kowai hanashi* (1991)
Scenario bungaku undō 74, 75
Scenario Literature Movement, **see** Scenario bungaku undō
The Scent of Quilts on a Warm Spring Day, **see** *Xiang qin chunnuan* (1942)
Schickel, Richard 180
Schilling, Mark; *The Yakuza Movie Book* 353

Schisgall, Oscar; *Nine to Nine* 329
Schmid, Daniel 549–50, 551
School for Village Women, **see** *Mura no fujin gakkyū* (1957)
Schrader, Paul 5, 83, 352, 353
Science and Technology Film/Video Festival 169
Scorpio Rising (1963) 197
screenwriting
   and auteur theory 74
   pure film movement 32
   theories of 74–5
Scrolls of Frolicking Animals and Humans, **see** *Chōjū jimbutsu giga emaki*
Sea of Youth – Four Correspondence Course Students, **see** *Seinen no umi – Yonin no tsūshin kyōikuseitachi* (1966)
The Searchers (1956) 519
The Seashell and the Clergyman, **see** *La Coquille et le clergyman* (1928)
Season of the Sun, **see** *Taiyō no kisetsu* (1956)
Secret Window (2004) 91
Security Treaty, **see** *ANPO jōyaku* (1959)
Seinen no umi – Yonin no tsūshin kyōikuseitachi (1966) 364
Sekai Meisaku Gekijō (World Masterpiece Theatre) 495, 496
Sekai no tsudoi (1952) 459
Sekikawa, Natsuo 558
Sekitome, Michiru 430
Selznick, Barbara 505
Selznick School of Film Preservation 214
Sen to chihiro no kamikakushi (2001) 492
Senda, Koreya 244, 250
   Modern Acting Method/Kindai haiyūjutsu 250
Sengoku yarō (1963) 527
Senjō no Merry Christmas (1983) 1, *2*, 548
Sen'nen kizami no hidokei – Magino mura monogatari (1986) 363, 404
Sentō, Takenori 169
Seo, Mitsuyo 315, 316
seppuku 246, 276
Seppuku (1962) 273
The Serpent, **see** *Orochi* (1925)
set design 259–68
   European influence on Japan 260
   in *Higanbana* 424
   history of 260–2
   independent vs studio 261–2
Setoguchi, Tōkichi 338

Setsudan sareta film (1972) 196
setsumei 27 (**see also** benshi)
Seven Miles to Nakayama, **see** *Nakayama Shichiri* (1930)
Seven Samurai, **see** *Shichinin no samurai* (1954)
Severed Film 196
sexuality 8, 12, 96–7, 185
   censorship of 139, 142–3
   metaphorical depiction of 265
   postwar period 246
   and primitivism 534–5
   in *Red Peony* series 355–6
   and transnationalism 101–3
   in *Undercurrent* 260
   in *Yoru no kawa* 265
Shadows of the Yoshiwara, **see** *Jūjiro* (1928)
Shaka (1961) 116
Shane (1953) 519, 520, 523–4, 527, 558
Shanghai 16, 439–52
   civil war 450
   European ownership of 439, 447
   Japanese backed studios 441–5
   post-war reprisals 450
   Western films in 443
   (**see also** China)
Shanghai, **see** *Shina jihen kōhō kiroku: Shanghai* (1938)
Shelter Plan (1964) 199
Shiawase no kiiroi hankachi (1977) 523–4
Shiba, Shizuko 455
Shibukawa Bangorō (1922) 328
Shibuya, Minoru 40
Shichinin no samurai (1954) 141, 272–3, 525, 543
Shiga, Shigetaka
   Theory of Japanese Landscape 394
Shiganhei (1941) 63
Shimamoto, Shōzō 196
Shimamura, Hōgetsu 244–5, 248, 250
Shimazaki, Kiyohiko 237
Shimizaki, Tōson; *Hakai* 406n34
Shimizu, Chiyota 39
Shimizu, Hikaru 70
Shimizu, Hiroshi 40
Shimizu, Takashi 554n53
Shimokawa, Ōten 313
Shimura, Miyoko 98
Shimura, Takashi 529n33
Shin shikōtei (1962) 16, 505, 508, *510*
   reviews 511
   target audience 510

Shina jihen kōhō kiroku: Shanghai (1938) 395
Shina no yoru (1943) 449
Shinano fudoki: Kobayashi Issa (1941) 12, 395, 401–3
   depiction of nature 403
Shindō, Kaneto 167, 273
shinematekku 29
shingeki 111, 243, 246
   Western influence 252
Shingeki no kyojin (TV 2014–15) 322
Shingler, Martin 180
Shinjuku Bunka Cinema 131, 187, 188, 197
Shinjuku district 179–80, 186–8, 190*n*41, 191*n*43
   gay bars 187–8
Shinjuku dorobō nikki (1968) 187, 190*n*35
Shinkankakuha (new impressionists) 32
Shinkō eiga 70
Shinkō Kinema 114, 301, 303
Shinkū chitai (1952) 466
Shinoda, Masahiro 262
Shinohara, Ushio 197
Shinozaki, Makoto 47
shinpa 25, 30–1, 110, 128
   definition 34*n*1
   and melodramas 325
shinpa-higeki 325, 326–7
Shinshaku Yotsuya Kaidan (1949) 82
Shinshaku Yotsuya Kaidan (1956) 303
Shinshaku Yotsuya Kaidan (1959) 306
Shinshokoku monogatari benikujaku (1954–5) 117
Shintōhō 118, 259
   bankruptcy 116
   break from Tōhō 116
   collapse 119, 307
   formation of 116
   horror movies 303–6
Shinryaku ni kotaeru kokuren (1950) 459
Shirai, Shintarō 111
Shiraishi, Yōko 369, 371–2
Shiranui Sea 379, 381
The Shiranui Sea, see Shiranuikai (1975)
Shiranuikai (1975) 381
Shirayuki hime (1973) 352
Shirayuki hime satsujin jiken (2014) 82
Shishido, Joe 521
shitamachi 40, 409
Shitamachi (1957) 421
shitamachi ninjōgeki 409

Shitoyaka na kedamono (1962) 412
Shōchiku 32, 43, 96, 128, 133, 184
   decline of 119–20
   double features 118
   introduction of sound 153
   kabuki origins 111, 234
   'nouvelle vague' films 415–16
   postwar distribution 116
   rivalry with Tōhō 235
   studios in Kyoto 112
   visual style 123*n*19
   wartime struggles 115
   'woman's films' 97
Shōchiku Kinema School 250
Shōchiku's Ōtani Library 245
shō-eiga 218
Shokei no heya (1956) 142, 260
Shōnen club 317
Shore, Dinah 339
shōshimin eiga 112
Shōwa era 407 558
   'the Shōwa 30s' 407–19
   depression 201*n*5
   Nostalgia 407
Shuling Huang 494
Shundō, Junko, *see* Fuji, Junko
shutaisei 362
Sidonia no kishi (TV 2014–15) 322
Sight and Sound (magazine) 42
Silverberg, Miriam 30, 96, 428
   Erotic Grotesque Nonsense 71–2
Silverman, Kaja 186, 483
Simmel, Georg; *On Social Differentiation* 72
Sing a Song of Sex, see Nihon shunka-kō (1967)
Sing! Sun, see Utae! taiyō (1945)
Sing! Youth: Hard-Working Girl, see Utae! seishun: Harikiri musume (1955)
Singapore 511
Singing Lovebirds, see Oshidori utagassen (1939)
Siniawer, Eiko Maruko 349
Sino-Japanese War (1894–5) 394, 439, 533
Sino-Japanese War (1937–45) 61, 114, 394, 536
   impact on filmmaking 397
Sirk, Douglas 263
Sisters of the Gion (1936) 104*n*9
The Sleepy Eyes of Death, see Nemuri Kyoshiro series

A Slope in the Sun, see Hi no ataru sakamichi (1958)
Slotkin, Richard 520
Smith, Henry D. 419, 420
Smoke (1995) 548
The Snow White Murder Case, see Shirayuki hime satsujin jiken (2014)
social protests 15, 198, 201*n*6, 364, 466–78
   against Anpo 186
   anti-war 466, 476
   farmers 365
   during Meiji era 367
   miners 466
   pre-war 466
   student 472–7, 474, 476, 477
Society for Cinema and Media Studies (SCMS) 10
Sōgen Barga (1936) 129
Sōgetsu Art Centre (SAC) 170, 197, 198
   opening of 423
Sōgetsu Experimental Film Festival 170, 198
Soldier Gokudo, see Heitai Gokudō (1968)
'Somebody Bad Stole De Wedding Bell' 339
Sonatine (1993) 352, 531
song
   co-ordination of release 338
   early 'hits' 257*n*29
   early sound films 156
   folk 481
   intermediality 156
   and 'media mix' approach 210
   in *Nishi Ginza ekimae* 428
   parodies 564–5
   television anime 319
   use in *Nihon shunka-kō* 481
   in Westerns 523
   in yakuza films 357, 359*n*13
   (*see also* music; sound)
Sonoyo no tsuma (1930) 15, 326, *327*, *329*
   as melodrama 329–31
   scene analysis 330–1
   social context 331
Sontag, Susan 181
Sony 548
Sorcerer's Orb, see Satomi hakkenden (1954)
Sōshi shokuten (1937) 129

Souls on the Road, **see** *Rojō no reikon* (1921)
sound 8
    and amateur film 222, 227*n*56
    classification 280*n*5
    diagetic 14
    and film exhibition 133–5
    in Hani's documentaries 471
    impact on studio system 112–14
    and intermediality 151–63
    Iwasaki on 160
    and long takes 75
    and montage theory 74–6
    and musicals 335
    national differences 151
    vs picture 158
    prevalent sound systems 153, 161*n*19, 336
    record company collaboration 157
    slowness of transition 152–3
    in Soviet cinema 272
    spread of technology 152
    transitional period 157–60
    (**see also** 'talkies')
South Africa 16, 490, 494–9
    anime popularity 495–6
    Martial Arts films in 496–8
South East Asia 15
    film festivals 168
    Japanese colonialism in 96
    Japanese colonialist legacy 509
    Japanese leadership 512
    modern authorship 49
    out-sourcing of anime to 310
    regional cinema 552
    and transnationalism 10
South Korea 168
    film festivals 174
    iimmigrant workers from 479
    Japanese co-productions 552
    television 494, 527, 552
    US military bases 515
    (**see also** Korea)
Soviet montage theory, **see** montage
Soviet–Japanese Joint Declaration 462
Soyokaze (1945) 338
Spacy (1981) 196
special effects 311
    in *Hawaii Malay oki kaisen* 237
spectatorship 11, 53–67
    as agent 56–61
    ambiguity of term 53
    approaches to 53–4

    vs 'audience' 54, 64*n*3
    in early cinema 27
    and gender 98, 102
    and identity 55
    'implicational' 98, 105*n*25
    queering 98–100
    as subject 54–6
Spielberg, Steven 493
Spirited Away, **see** *Sen to chihiro no kamikakushi* (2001)
Spivak, Gayatri Chakravorty 479
Spriggan 322
Spring of the Founding 129
Spyri, Johanna 495
Stacey, Jackie 57
Stagecoach (1939) 519, 520
Staiger, Janet; *Interpreting Films* 57
Standish, Isolde 38, 104*n*17, 145, 182, 189*n*17, 354
Stanislavsky, Konstantin 244, 246, 249
    An Actor Prepares 251
    The Lower Depths 250
    system vs method 257*n*49
Star of Hong Kong, **see** *Honkon no hoshi* (1962)
Star Wars 492–3
stardom 179–91
    academic studies on 180
    Heibon 343
    intermediality and 343
    male 105*n*28
    male dominance 182–3
    and musicals 335
    prewar vs postwar 343
    television 210
    and Tōei studio 183
The Starfish, **see** *L'Etoile de mer*
stars 28
    in *jidaigeki* 288
    in musicals 338–40
    Nikkatsu 560
    in Shanghai 449
    swordsmen 115
    Yakuza films 182
    (**see also** actors)
Steinberg, Marc 9, 61, 205, 319, 344
Steiner, Max 281*n*13
Stella Dallas (1925) 328
Stella Dallas (1937) 116
stereotypes
    of gender 94
    of Japanese women 95
Sternberg, Josef von 295*n*22

Still Walking, **see** *Aruitemo aruitemo* (2008)
Storaro, Vittorio 238
Storm Over Kinmen Bay, **see** *Kinmontō ni kakeru hashi* (1962)
A Story of Floating Weeds, **see** *Ukigusa monogatari* (1934)
The Story of the Last Chrysanthemum, **see** *Zangiku monogatari* (1939)
A Straightforward Boy, **see** *Tokkan kozō* (1929)
Stramigioli, Giulliana 543
A Stranger of Mine, **see** *Unmei ja nai hito* (2005)
Strasberg, Lee 251
Street Lights, **see** *Gaitō* (1957)
Street of Shame, **see** *Akasen chitai* (1956)
Street, Sarah 268*n*28
The Streetfighter, **see** *Gekitotsu! satsujin ken* (1974)
Stroheim, Erich von 232
Studio Ghibli 168, 310, 312, 315–16, 321
    overseas success 492
studio system 13, 109–25, 259
    collapse of 121–2
    consolidation of production 112
    decline of 119–21, 185, 547
    different production models 113
    directors vs producers 42–3
    distribution of foreign films 112
    early developments 109, 110–11
    economic fragility 153
    establishment of 111–12
    genealogy of *110*, 123*n*3
    Hollywood vs Japan 43, 111
    intermediality 122
    lighting and electricity 233–4
    in moderrn era 121–2
    production committee formula 122
    talkies 112–14
    during US occupation 115–16
    use of advertising 120
    in wartime 114–15
studios
    investment in television 119
    lack of support for experimental film 198
    reluctance to transition to sound 153
    in the US 109
    yakuza films 351
Su, Chongmin 129

subjectivity 362, 372–3
suffrage 62
Sugata Sanshirō I and *II* (1943) 140
Sugie, Toshio 340
Sugimura, Haruko 410, 550
Sugisaku, J-tarō 353
Sugiyama, Heiichi 75
    criticism of montage theory 76
    Essays on Film 75
Sugiyama, Kōhei 236
Suguruhino yamaneko (2014) 174
suicide 246
Sukiyaki Western: Django (2007) 493, 527
Summer Clouds, see *Iwashigumo* (*The Sundial* 1959)
Sun in the Last Days of the Shogunate, see *Bakumatsu taiyō den* (1957)
'Sun Tribe' films 182, 350, 415, 562
    sexuality and censorship 142–3
Suna no onna (1964) 96–7
Sunadoru hitobito (1950) 456
The Sundial Carved with a Thousand Years of Notches – The Magino Village Story, see *Sen'nen kizami no hidokei – Magino mura monogatari* (1986)
Sunrise (1927) 557
Super Dimension Cavalry Southern Cross, see *Chōjikū kidan southern cross*
Super Dimension Fortress Macross, see *Chōjikū yōsai Macross* (1982)
Super sentai (1975) 493
Surviving Internal Exposure, see *Naibu hibaku o ikinuku* (2012)
Susukita, Rokuhei 287
Suzaku, see *Moe no suzaku* (1997)
Suzuki, Hiroshi 235
Suzuki, Noribumi 565
Suzuki, Sumiko 301, 302, 306
Suzuki, Tatsuo 238
Swanson, Gloria 235
Switchback (1976) 196
sword-fights, see *chanbara*
Symphony of Six Million (1932) 281*n*13

Taboo, see *Gohatto* (1999)
Tachibana, Teijirō 3, 111, 248
    on *onnagata* 33
Tagawa, Suihō; *Norakuro* 317
Taii no musume (1929) 154
Taikatsu 32

Taishō era 420
    mass culture 248
Taiwan 5
    annexation 536
    export of Japanese cinema to 509
    film festivals 174
    foreign television in 494
    New Wave 168
Taiyō no kisetsu (1956) 142, 143, 182, 260, 415, 520
Takahashi, Gen'ichirō 525
Takahashi, Hiroshi 307, 554*n*53
Takahashi, Tetsu 190*n*35
Takahata, Isao 312
Takakura, Ken 182, 348, 350, 359*n*13, 526
Takamatsu, Jirō 199
Takami, Koushun 147
Takechi, Tetsuji 466
Takemitsu, Tōru 197, 269
Takenaka, Naoto 527
Takenaka, Rō 288–9
Takeuchi, Kayo 184
The Tale of Chikamatsu, see *Chikamatsu monogatari* (1954)
The Tale of Genji, see *Genji monogatari* (1951)
The Tale of Princess Kaguya, see *Kaguya hime no monogatari* (2013)
The Tale of the White Serpent, see *Hakujaden*
'talkies' 112–14
    classification of 153
    exhibition of 133–4
    first releases 152
    high production costs 159
    Iwasaki on 160
    music 270
    use of music 159
    (see also sound)
Tamaki, Shinkan 201
Tampopo (1985) 524, 524–5
Tanaami, Keiichi 198
Tanabe, Hajime 72
Tanabe, Moich 190*n*35
Tanaka, Eizō 32, 189*n*6
Tanaka, Jun'ichirō
    The History of the Developments of Japanese Film/Nihon eiga hattatsu shi 4, 5, 109
Tanaka, Kinuyo 95, 97, 243–58, *244*, *247*, *255*
    awards 243

    physicality of performance 252–3
Tanaka, Min 293
Tanaka, Satoshi 172
Tanaka, Shōzō 366
Tange, Kenzō 423
Tange Sazen and the Pot Worth a Million Ryo, see *Tange Sazen to hyakuman ryō no tsubo* (1935)
Tange Sazen to hyakuman ryō no tsubo (1935) *270*, 270–2, 296*n*33
    later influence 272
Tanikawa, Takeshi 245, 455
Tanishima, Masayuki 206
Tanizaki, Jun'ichurō; *Naomi/Chijin no ai* 96
Tarantino, Quentin 352, 527
Tartan Asia Extreme 494, 554*n*9
Tashiro, C.S.; *Pretty Pictures* 259
Tasogare no Tokyo Tower (1959) 423
Tasogare seibei (2002) 293
Tatakau heitai (1939) 361, 395
Tatsumi, Shirō 365
Taylor, Gordon 233
Taylor-Jones, Kate 440
technology 14, 151–63
    and animation 320
    and cinematography 232, 235–6
    during Cold War 507–11
    emergence and destabilisation 155
    and experimental film 192, 193
    investment in 544
    and location shooting 394
    and 'media mix' 17
    OgawaPro documentaries 367
    sound 336
    Tōhōs use of 115
    video 194–5
    (see also CGI; colour; sound; widescreen)
Teikine 128
Telcosystems 201
television 1, 17, 192, 351
    animation 318–21
    vs cinema 500*n*4
    and globalisation 493
    impact on film-makers 470
    impact on studio system 119–21, 292
    jidaigeki on 292
    Korean 527
    movie studio investment in 119
    rise of 119, 424
    in 'Shōwa 30s' films 411
    stars 122, 210

Television Decollage (1963) 201*n*7
tendency film, *see keikō eiga*
Tengoku to jigoku (1963) 407, 412, 519
Tenkatsu 111
Tenkū no shiro Rapyuta (1985) 320
Terada, Torahiko 72
Terayama, Shūji 187, 197, 466
    The Hunchback of Aomori/Aomori-ken no semushi otoko 187
    Marie La Vison/Kegawa no Mari 187
Teshigahara, Hiroshi 131, 167, 197, 423, 429
Tetsuwan Atom (TV 1963–6) 17, 61, 318, 319
Tezuka, Osamu 145, 344, 512
Tezuka, Yoshiharu 173, 506, 511
Thailand 511
That Night's Wife, see Sonoyo no tsuma (1930)
theatre 18*n*5
    influence on early cinema 180, 234
    intermediality and experimental film 200, 202*n*19
    in *Joyū Sumako no koi* 246–56
    in Meiji era 327
    scene in Shinjuku district 187
Theatre of Life: Story of Youth, Passion and Spirit, see Jinsei gekijō: Seishun, aiyoku, zankyō hen (1972)
There Goes the Covered Wagon, see Horobasha wa yuku (1961)
There was a Father, see Chichiariki
There's No Business Like Show Business (1954) 342
The Third Man (1949) 562
13 Assassins, see Jūsannin no shikaku
Thomas, Jeremy 239
Thompson, Kristin 6, 82, 83, 269
Thon, Jan-Noël 82
311 (2011) 386–7, 387
    vs *Mujin chitai* 386
'three girl' series 340–2, 347*n*29
Three Sisters with Maiden Hearts, see Otome gokoro sannin shimai (1935)
Three Smart Girls (1936) 340
'3/11,' *see* Fukushima
3-4 x jugatsū (1990) 531
Throne of Blood, see Kumonosu jō (1956)
'Tie a Yellow Ribbon around the Ole Oak Tree' 523
Timoshenko, Semyon 72

The Art of the Cinema: The Montage of Films 69
Tincknell, Estella 337
Tipsy Life, see Horoyoi jinsei (1933)
To Be a Woman, see Onna bakari no yoru (1961)
'Toba pictures' (*Toba-e*) 312
Toba, Sōjō 312
Tochigi, Akira 153
Tōdō, Satoshi 40
Todorov, Tsvetan 249
Tōei 115, 117–19
    animated films 310, 312, 316
    cinemas 117–18, 130
    formation of 117
    genre specialities 118–19
    horror films 299
    Japanese westerns 525–6
    jidaigeki 295*n*20
    period films 269–70
    revenues 130
    yakuza films 182, 353
Tōei Dōga 318
Tōhō 43, 112, 245
    break-up of 116, 121
    cinemas 114
    depictions of violence 115
    documentaries 399
    founding of 112, 137*n*46
    genre specialities 118–19
    lighting style 235
    vs other studios 114
    'producer system' 113
    rivalry with Shōchiku 235
    use of composers 272
    in wartime 114–15
Tohoku 532
Tokieda, Toshie 95
Tokizane, Shōhei 5
Tokkan kozō (1929) 218
Tokugawa period 285, 419–20, 532
    eroticism 145
Tokyo 3, 12, 419–35
    bombing of 419
    as cinematic city 421–2
    as collection of neighourhoods 227*n*60
    as cultural centre 112
    domestic tourism 423
    early movie houses in 109
    film festivals 170
    gay district 179–80, 187, 190*n*41, 191*n*43, 423

    and *gendaigeki* 127
    home movie day 215, 222–3
    vs Kyoto 286
    in medieval period 420
    in Meiji period 420
    in post-war period 422–4
    post-war reconstruction 423
    real estate market 417*n*28
    recreation with CGI 262
    Richie on 227*n*60
    as setting for *jidaigeki* 419
    studios in 110, 113
    theatre districts 127
Tokyo 1958 (1958) 420, 429–32, *431*
Tokyo Broadcasting System (TBS) 122, 211
Tokyo Holiday, see Tokyo no kyūjitsu (1958)
Tokyo International Film Festival 13, 171–3, 549
    classics vs new cinema 178*n*58
    competitions 172
    domestic vs international programming 173, 176
    government support 172
    vs other Asian festivals 172
Tokyo International Lesbian and Gay Film Festival 95
Tokyo International Women's Film Festival 95
Tokyo kōshinkyoku (1929) 78*n*9, 156
Tokyo March 422, *see Tokyo kōshinkyoku* (1929)
Tokyo monogatari (1953) 453
Tokyo Moving Picture Regulations 1917 138–9
Tokyo no bus girl (1958) 423
Tokyo no kyūjitsu (1958) 423
Tokyo no yado (1935) 417*n*15
Tokyo Story, see Tokyo monogatari (1953)
Tokyo Theatre Association 128
Tokyo Tower 423–4, 430
Tokyo Tower at Twilight, see Tasogare no Tokyo Tower (1959)
Tokyo University 7
    student protests 475
Tokyo University of the Arts 552
Tokyo-Ga (1985) 554*n*6
Toland, Gregg 76, 235–6, 336
Tolstoy, Leo; *Resurrection* 247, 248
Tomita, Mika 31
Tomita, Tetsunosuke 365

Tōnan Asia Eigasai (the South East Asian Film Festival, AFF) 164
Tonari no Yae-chan (1934) 334n22
Tonari no Yamada-kun (1999) 312
Tone, Yasunao 199
Tōno, Eijirō 244, 252
Tōno, Yoshiaki 194
Tonoyama, Taiji 536
Top o nerae (1988) 320
Tora no o o fumu otokotachi (1945) 140, 272
Torrance, Richard 145
'total war' 3, 100, 253
Toward Eternity, see Wanshi liufang
Toward the Decisive Battle in the Sky 453
Town Meeting of the World, see Sekai no tsudoi (1952)
Town of Yun, see Yun no machi (1989)
Tōyō heiwa no michi (1938) 130, 440
Toyoda, Shirō 40
Tōyoko Films 117
The Tranquil Everyday, see Odayaka na nichijō (2012)
trans-medial relations, *see* intermediality
transnational 2, 556–66
    co-productions 505–17
    and gender 101–3
    importance to Japanese cinema 10
    and nostalgia 519
    possible concerns 516n7
    and remakes 16
    (*see also* globalisation)
Treaty of Nanking 439, 447
Treaty of Portsmouth 439
Treaty of San Francisco 117
    and resurgence of experimental film 187
Treaty of Shimonoseki 439
The Tree of Love, see Aizen katsura (1938)
Trespasser (1928) 235
Trinh T. Minh-ha 486
The True Face of Japan, see Nihon no sugao (TV 1957–64)
Truffaut, François 44, 45, 559
Tsing, Anna 13, 165, 175
Tsubaki Sanjurō (1962) 138, 143–5
Tsuchi (1939) 12, 395–8, *396, 398*
    awards 396
    documentary style 397
    post-war editions 403–4
Tsuchi ni ikiru (1941) 12, 395, 398–401

Tsuchimoto, Noriaki 361, 379, 380, 381–3, 467, 472
    vs Kamanaka 383
    use of narrative 382
Tsuchiya, Anna 208
Tsuchiya, Moichiō 194
Tsuchiya Shōtō 132
Tsugata, Nobuyuki 318
Tsuji, Hisaichi 444
Tsuji, Hisakazu 440
Tsuji, Nobuo 312
Tsukamoto, Shin'ya 47, 170
Tsuma (1953) 409
Tsumura, Hideo 63, 296n29
    Film and Critique 40
Tsunoda, Takuya 429
Tsuruhachi Tsurujirō (1938) 253
Tsurumi, Shunsuke 9, 564
Tsushima, Keiko 529n33
Turim, Maureen 43
Twilight Samurai, see Tasogare seibei (2002)
Tyler, Parker 84
Tzvetan, Todorov 304

Ubaguruma (1956) 415
Uchida, Nobuteru 389–90
Uchida, Tomu 40, 75, 395
Uchino, Tadashi 252
Uchiyama Iwatarō 463
Udden, James 49
Uechi, Takeshi 353
Ueda, Manabu 29, 31
    Exhibition and Audiences in Early Japanese History 60
Uematsu, Keiji 195
Ueno, Chizuko 486
Ueno, Eishin 365
Ueno, Toshiya 8, 9
Ugetsu monogatari (1953) 41, 117, *130*, 167, 239, 255, 298, 543
    export of 131
Ukigusa monogatari (1934) 417n15
Ukiyo (1916) 132, 133
ukiyo-e 6
Uma (1941) 236–7, *237*
Umemoto, Yōichi 47
Umizaru films 203
UN Association of Japan 459, 461
Under the Flag of the United Nations, see Kokurenki no shitani (1950)
Under the Peony, see Mudan hua xia (1942)

Undercurrent, see Yoru no kawa (1956)
Underground Film Festival 170
UNESCO and Japan, see UNESCO to watashitachi (1952)
UNESCO to watashitachi (1952) 461–2
Unexplored Region, Rehe, see Hikyō nekka (1936)
An Unforgettable Grudge, see Chōkon (1926)
United Nations 16, 453–65
    films about 457–62
    Japanese desire for membership 462–3
The United Nations and Japan, see Kokuren to nihon (1956)
The United Nations and World Disputes, see Kokuren to sekai no funsō (1950)
The United Nations Answers Aggression, see Shinyraku ni kotaeru kokuren (1950)
Universal Brotherhood, see Boai (1942)
Universal Film Studios 519
    horror movies 301
Universum-Film Aktiengesellschaft's (UFA) 73, 545
Unmei ja nai hito (2005) 82
Uno, Akira 198
Urashima Tarō (1918) 313–14
An Urban Affair, see Kigeki: Ekimae danchi (1961)
US Academy Awards 543
US Information Agency (USIA) 454
US Information Service (USIS) 16, 453
    list of UN films 457–8
the US occupation 4, 16, 453–65, 539
    censorship under 116, 350
    impact on Japanese cinema 31
    impact on Japanese culture 60
    import of US Westerns 519
    Japanese cinema during 454–7
    Japanese literature on 464n1
    kaiki eiga under 302
    of Okinawa 537–8
    propaganda 245
    protests against 466
    sexual liberalisation 246
    studio system under 115–16
    yakuza films 350
US-Japan Security Treaty 463, 530
    protests against 186
US-Japan trade conflict 548, 553
The Usual Suspects (1995) 91

Utae! seishun: Harikiri musume (1955) 339–40
Utae! taiyō (1945) 338
Utsunomiya no tenjō (1956) 309n21
utsushie (magic lantern) 29

Valck, Marijke de 165, 176n13
The Valiant Red Peony, **see** *Karajishi botan* series (1968–72)
VAN Film Science Research Centre 199
Vantage Point (2008) 91, 92n1
VCR 320, 497
Vengeance is Mine, **see** *Fukushū suru wa ware ni ari* (1979)
Venice Film Festival 117, 166, 172, 492, 509, 542–3
verisimilitude 249
vernaculuar modernism 11, 38, 56, 58–9, 96, 104n12, 326
Verstraten, Peter 82
Vertov, Dziga 72–3, 194
　From Kino-eye to Radio-eye 70
video 122
　animation 319–20
　artists 195
　and experimental film 194–5
　and home movies 215
　low-budget horror releases 298
video game consoles 320
video games 492
Video Hiroba 195
Videodrome (1983) 549
Vietnam War 475, 485, 538
Vimeo 221
violence 13, 138–50, 497
　under allied occupation 140
　classification of 142, 143
　in early cinema 139
　hyperrealism 145–6
　in J Horror 307
　justifications for 142
　in Kurosawa Akira's work 141–2
　against nature 381
　in 'pink films' 145, 352, 360n24
　in *Rashomon* 141
　Tōhō's depiction of 115
　in war films 140
　in Westerns 519, 527
Violent Islands Japan, **see** *Nihon bōryoku rettō* (1975)
Viva Villa! (1934) 232
Voltron, Defender of the Universe (1984) 496
Volunteer, **see** *Shiganhei* (1941)

Wada, Den 397
Wada, Sanzō 268n28
Wada-Marciano, Mitsuyo 48–9, 96, 118, 168, 326, 354, 422
　on horror 298
　Nippon Modern 56
Waga seishun ni kui nashi (1946) 9, 149n26, 453, 466
Waitress, **see** *Jokyū* (1930)
Wakaki hi no Chūji: Midagahara no satsujin (1925) 359n12
Wakamatsu, Kōji 167, 466
Wakayama, Tomisaburō 351
Wakimizu, Tetsugorō; *Notes on a Japanese Landscape* 402
Wakita, Yoneichi 260
Walkabout (1971) 534–5
Wall Street crash 331
Wallerstein, Immanuel 190n34
Wanderer of the Great Plains, **see** *Daisōgen no wataridori* (1960)
The Wanderer series (1959–62) 521
　political messages 521–2
'wandering gambler' 349
The Wandering Guitarist, **see** *Guitar o motta wataridori* (1959)
Wanderlust, **see** *Hōrō Zanmai* (1927)
Wang Jingwei 443, 445
Wang, Wayne 549
Wang Zhao Jun (1964) 516
Wanshi liufang (1943) 440, 446, 446–50, 448, 449
　critical reception in Japan 448
　historians on 446
Wanwan sanjūshi (1981) 495
Wanzi qianhong (1943) 445
War at Sea from Hawaii to Malaya, **see** *Hawaii Malay oki kaisen*
Warm Current, **see** *Danryū* (1939); *Danryū* (1957)
A Warm Misty Night, **see** *Yogiri yo kon'ya mo arigatō*
Warring Clans, **see** *Sengoku yarō* (1963)
wartime 3, 8
　animation 316–17
　and depiction of landscape 394–406
　impact on amateur film 219
　propaganda films 115, 362
　as setting for Westerns 522
　studio system during 114–15
　theatre 258n64
　yakuza films 350
Wartime Emergency Film System 444, 452n19

Waseda University 8, 365
Washitani, Hana 353
Wasurerareta kōgun (1963) 481
Watanabe, Daisuke 173, 174
Watanabe, Shin 338
Watashi wa nisai (1962) 12, 408, *415*
Watsuji, Tetsurō 406n41, 408
Wayne, John 518
Weber, Louis 232
Weiner, Michael 531
Welles, Orson 236
Wenders, Wim 554n6
Westerns 16, 518–29
　class 524
　emergence 518
　gender 524–5
　golden era 522
　Japanese vs Italian 527
　as *jidaigeki* 525–8
　Nikkatsu studios 520–2
　and nostalgia 527
　popularity in Japan 519–20
　post-war vs pre-war 523
　remakes of Japanese films 492
　and the US occupation 519
　US-Japan co-productions 526, 527
　values and morals 520
Westward Desperado, **see** *Dokuritsu gurentai nishi e* (1960)
Whale, **see** *Kujira* (1927)
What Made Her Do It?, **see** *Nani ga kanojo o sō sasetaka* (1930)
Where Chimneys Are Seen, **see** *Entotsu no mieru basho* (1953)
Whistles Blow in the Harbour City, **see** *Kuchibue ga nagareru minatomachi* (1960)
White Collar Worker, **see** *America no salaryman* (1951)
The White Haired Girl films, **see** *Baimao nü* films
White Horse Rider, **see** *Hakuba dōji* (1960)
White, Patricia 105n33
Wicked City, **see** *Yōjū toshi* (1987)
widescreen 267n11, 304, 306, 413
　Asian co-productions 507–8, 510
　exhibition 117–18
　impact on industry 267n10
　kaiki eiga 304
　and production design 262
　in *Watashi wa nisai* 414
Wife, **see** *Tsuma* (1953)
Wilk, Richard 512

Williams, Linda 325, 329, 332, 357
Williams, Tony 494
Winter in Sanrizuka, *see Nihon kaihō sensen – Sanrizuka* (1970)
Winter Sonata, *see Fuyu no sonata* (2003)
The Wizard of Oz (1939) 196, 305
The Wolf Man (1941) 298
Woman Gambler, *see Onna tobakushi* (1967–71)
Woman in the Dunes, *see Suna no onna* (1964)
The Woman of Osaka, *see Naniwa onna* (1940)
The Woman Who Knots the Ribbons, *see Ribbon o musubu fujin* (1939)
'woman's films,' *see josei eiga*
The Wonderful Adventures of Nils, *see Nils no fushigi na tabi* (1980)
Wong, Howe James (Wond Tung Jim) 232
Work, *see Sakuhin* (1958)
World Experimental Film Competition 429
World War II 61
    bombing of Tokyo 419
    and Imperialism 394
    and Japanese national identity 15
    legacy 539
    modern Japanese attitude to 174
    Okinawa 536–7
    as setting for Japanese Westerns 522
WOWOW 169
The Written Face (1995) 549–51, *550*
Wrong Move (1975) 549
Wurtzler, Steve 155
Wyckoff, Alvin 234, 235

Xiang qin chunnuan (1942) 445
Xianggang zhi xing, *see Honkon no hoshi* (1962)
Xinhua 441
Xu, Gongmei 442, 443, 451*n*10

Yagi, Yasutarō 41
Yagumo, Emiko 329
yakuza 12, 14, 119, 145, 348–60
    academic approaches to 353–4
    under allied occupation 140, 350
    definition of genre 352–3
    depictions of masculinity 354
    emotion in 356–8
    and gender 354–5
    as 'genre of excess' 357
    history of genre 349–52

    musicals 350
    neglect by modern scholars 350
    and 'pink films' 352
    postwar period 349, 351
    repetitive nature 357
    stars 182
    translation 349
    in wartime 350
Yakuza Apocalypse, *see Gokudō daisensō* (2015)
Yakuza Graveyard, *see Yakuza no hakaba: Kuchinashi no hana* (1976)
Yakuza no hakaba: Kuchinashi no hana (1976) 352
The Yakuza Papers vol. 1: Battles without Honour and Humanity, *see Jingi naki tataki* (1973)
The Yakuza Papers vol. 2: Deadly Fight in Hiroshima, *see Jingi naki tatakai: Hiroshima shitō hen* (1973)
The Yakuza Papers vol. 3: Proxy War, *see Jingi naki tatakai: Dairi sensō* (1973)
Yakuza Tale, *see Nihon kyōka den* (1973)
Yamada, Isuzu 116, 245
Yamada, Kazuo 5, 8–9, 44
    on Makino 44
Yamada, Kōichi 39, 44
Yamada, Kōsaku 270
Yamada, Yōji 9, 407, 522
Yamagami, Chieko 105*n*30
Yamagata International Documentary Film Festival 10, 13, 172–3, 198, 216, 385
    city refurbishment plans 176
    importance 174
    influence and impact 174
    launch 361
Yamaguchi, Katsuhiro 195
Yamaguchi, Yoshiko 513, *see* Ri, Kōran
Yamamoto, Fujiko 413
Yamamoto, Kajirō 270
Yamamoto, Rokuba 154
Yamamoto, Satsuo 9
Yamamura, Sō 244
Yamanaka, Sadao 40, 71, 76, 293
Yamaoka, Hisano 427
Yamazaki, Takashi 407
Yan guilai (1942) 445
Yanagi, Shun'yō 328
Yanagihara, Ryōhei 198
Yanagisawa, Shin'ichi 427
Yanagita, Kunio 398–9

Yang Guifei, *see Yōhiki*
Yang In-Sil 480
Yano, Christine R. 519
Yasuda, Yojūrō; *Landscape and History* 402
Yasumaru, Yoshio 365, 367
Yasumi, Toshio 514
Yau, Kinnia 506
Yebisu International Festival of Art and Alternative Visions 198
The Yellow Handkerchief, *see Shiawase no kiiroi hankachi* (1977)
Yi, Young Jae 440
Yodogawa, Nagaharu 9
Yogiri yo kon'ya mo arigatō (1967) 16, 560–4, *563*
    vs *Casablanca* 561
    historical accuracy 563
    mood 561–2
    plot summary 560–1
    popular appeal 565
Yōhiki (1955) 506, *508*, 513, 514
Yoidore tenshi (1948) 350
Yojimbo, *see Yōjinbō*
Yōjinbō (1961) 138, 143–5, *144*, 492, 527
    humour 144
Yōjū toshi (1987) 320
Yokoo, Tadanori 190*n*35, 198
Yokota Company 109
Yomiuri Independent 199
Yomota, Inuhiko 8, 292, 353, 566*n*9
    on Nikkatsu and Hollywood 559
    One Hundred and Ten Years of Japanese Film History 109
    Where Japanese Cinema is Heading 168
Yoneyama, Keizō 63
Yōrō, Takeshi 282*n*47
Yoru no kawa (1956) 14, 259–68, *264*, *265*, *266*
    politics in 266–7, 268*n*27
    sexuality 260
    use of colour 260, 263, 264–7, 268*n*24
    Western influence 263
Yoshida, Kijū 39, 43, 44, 466
    on authorship 44–5
    on Ozu 45
Yoshida, Naoya 471
Yoshimi, Shun'ya 60
Yoshimoto, Mitsuhiro 7, 10, 11, 25, 85, 287, 328, 493–4
Yoshimura, Fuyuhiko, *see* Terada, Torahiko

Yoshimura, Kōzaburō 14, 259–60
   production design 261, 262–7
Yoshizaki, Michiyo 548
Yoshizawa Company 109
Young Chuji: Murder at Midagahara, **see** *Wakaki hi no Chūji: Midagahara no satsujin* (1925)
YouTube 221
Yubari 565
Yue Fei jinzhong baoguo (1940) 442
Yue Fei Serves the Country Loyally, **see** *Yue Fei jinzhong baoguo* (1940)
Yufuin Film Festival 171
Yuki et Nina, **see** *Yuki to Nina* (2009)
Yuki to Nina (2009) 50

Yuki yukite shingun (1987) 549
Yukimura, Izumi 338–40, 339, 343
Yukinojō Henge (1935) 296n33
Yukitomo Rifū; *Kunisada Chūji* 359n12
Yun no machi (1989) 480
Yunhua 441

Za-Koenji Documentary Film Festival 174
Zahlten, Alex 557
zainichi 12, 16, 174, 479–88
   documentaries on 361
   gender issues 481
   intersectionality 480
   in Japanese cinema 480, 488n5
Zangiku monogatari (1939) 253, 261

Zanjin zanbaken (1929) 289
Zatōichi (2003) 169
Zatōichi series 116, 292
Zen'ei eigasha (Avant-Garde Film Company) 194
Zero Dimension 187
Zhang, Shankun 441, 444
Zhonghua Dianying 440–3
   foundation of 440
   goal of project 442
Zhonglian 440, 443–5
   formation of 444–5
Zigomar (1911) 22n45, 29, 29, 61
Zone of Emptiness, **see** *Shinkū chitai* (1952)